W9-AWY-963

WARMAN'S
ANTIQUES
AND THEIR PRICES
18th Edition

---

*The Standard Price Reference for antiques
and collectibles, for collectors, dealers
and professionals in the trade.*

Edited by
Harry L. Rinker

**Completely illustrated
and authenticated**

Warman Publishing Co., Inc.
Elkins Park, PA 19117

ISBN: 0-911594-05-1
ISSN: 0196-2272
Library of Congress Catalog Card No. 82-643542
Printed in the United States of America

Additional copies of this book may be obtained from your
bookstore or directly from the publisher, Warman Publishing
Co., P.O. Box 26742, Dept. 18, Elkins Park, PA 19117. Enclose $10.95 plus $1.50 for postage and handling. Pennsylvania
residents please add 66¢ state sales tax.

EDITORIAL STAFF, 18TH EDITION

Caroline E. Edleman
653 S. Fifth Ave.
Royersford, PA 19468
(215) 948-9128
Nodders

Doug Flynn and
Al Bolton
Holloway House
126 East Main St.
Lititz, PA 17543
(717) 627-4567
*British Royal
Commeratives*

Dan Golden
1030 Robin Hill Dr.
San Marcos, CA 92069
Telephones

David and Betty Hallam
P.O. Box 175
Monmouth, IL 61462
(309) 734-4933
Old Sleepy Eye

David and Sue Irons
Irons Antiques
R.D. #4, Box 101
Northampton, PA 18067
(215) 262-9335
Irons

Ron Lieberman
The Family Album
R.D. #1
Glen Rock, PA 17327
(717) 235-2134
Bibles, Books Americana

Robert A. Limons
R.D. #1, Box 162
Hellertown, PA 18055
(215) 838-8931
Firearms, Pewter

Pamela A. Luttig
Blue Boar Ltd
215 West Main St.
Grand Ledge, MI 48837
(517) 627-5291
Tiles

Clarence and Betty Maier
The Burmese Cruet
P.O. Box 432
Montgomeryville, PA
18936
(215) 855-5388
*Burmese Glass, Crown
Milano, Royal Flemish*

James S. Maxwell, Jr.
Box 5039
Neffsville, PA 17601
(717) 569-7717 or
569-0719
Mechanical Banks

Bea Morgan
Lakeview Terrace
Sandy Hook, CT 06482
(203) 426-5425
Salt and Pepper Shakers

Scott H. Nelson
270 Spanglers Mill Rd.
New Cumberland, PA
17070
Van Briggle

Joan Oates
5912 Kingsfield Dr.
W. Bloomfield, MI 48033
(313) 661-2335
Phoenix Bird Pattern

Arlene Rabin
Valley View 509
15th and Elm
Allentown, PA 18102
(215) 433-3099
Art Pewter, Fry Glass

Dave Rago
P.O. Box 3592, Station E
Trenton, NJ 08629
(609) 585-2546
*Fulper, Grueby, Mar-
blehead, Newcomb Col-
lege, Ohr Pottery*

Richard and Joan
Randles
From The Cutter's Wheel
P.O. Box 285
Webster, NY 14580
(716) 671-3760
Cut Glass

Wayne Reed, Ltd.
P.O. Box 69401
Los Angeles, CA 90069
(213) 934-6356
*Aurene, Cameo Glass,
Steuben*

Roy C. Repsher
256 N. Chestnut St.
Bath, PA 18014
(215) 837-0138
Pocket Knives

INTRODUCTION

Warman's is designed to be a helpful tool for both collector and dealer. As such, the following suggestions on organization, pricing, use, buying and selling will prove valuable.

ORGANIZATION

Warman's is organized into two major units—the American Pattern Glass section and the General Collections section. The General Collections section lists categories alphabetically.

The American Pattern Glass section is divided into three groups—clear, colored and opalescent. We have devoted considerable attention to clarifying pattern names, enhancing the quality of the identification drawings, and listing those patterns most in market demand. Patterns often have many names. You will find these names carefully cross-referenced in our index.

Every collector should know something about the history of his object. We have presented a capsule background for each category. In many cases the backgrounds contain references to museum collections, buying hints, current market trends or directions to reference texts. We hope you find this feature useful.

In assigning prices we assume the object is in very good condition. If otherwise, we note this in our description. It would be ideal to suggest that mint, or unused, examples of all objects do exist. The reality is that objects from the past were used, whether they be glass, china, dolls or toys. Because of this use, some normal wear must be expected. In fact, if an object such as furniture does not show wear, its origins may be more suspect than if it does show wear.

PRICE GUIDE

Our book is a price *guide*. It is not absolute. Whenever possible, we have tried to provide a broad listing of prices within a category so you have a "feel" for the market. We emphasize the middle range of prices within a category, while also listing some objects of high and low value to show the market spread.

We do not use ranges because they tend to confuse rather than help a person. How do you determine if your object is at the high or low end of the range? There is a high degree of flexibility in pricing in the antiques field. If you want to set ranges, add or subtract 10% from our prices.

One of the hardest variants with which to deal is the regional fluctuation of prices. Victorian furniture brings widely differing prices in New York, Chicago, New Orleans or San Francisco. We have tried to strike a balance. Know your region and subject before investing heavily. If the best prices for cameo glass are in Montreal or Toronto, then be prepared to go there if you want to save money or add choice pieces to your collection. Research and patience are key factors to building a collection of merit.

Another factor that affects prices is a sale by a leading dealer or private collector. We have tempered both dealer and auction house figures.

USER'S GUIDE

A great deal of effort has been expended to make our index useful. Always try to find the most specific reference. For example, if you have a piece of china, look first for the maker's name and second for the type. The key is to ask the right questions of yourself.

You may encounter a piece you cannot identify well enough to use the index. Consult the photographs and marks. If you own the last several editions of **Warman's**, you have assembled a valuable photo reference to the antiques field.

We have continued to place emphasis on the quality of the descriptions in our listings. More detail has been included to allow the reader to identify a specific piece. A listing of a 'vase, 10″, red matte glaze' is so general that it could apply to a hundred different items; however, a listing of a "vase, bulbous body, rim foot, flared neck, beaded rim, raised floral motif of yellow roses, red matte glaze, 10″ h," defines the object specifically. We think you'll notice a significant difference when you compare the 18th Edition with other general antique price guides.

In comparing your object to our listing, be conscious of all aspects of the listing — size, description, color and condition. Variations in size and color can greatly influence price. Further, variations in size or material can help you spot originals from reproductions. [Reproduced items in the listings are indicated by an asterisk (*).]

It is not possible for us to list everything. Make your own notes in the margins as you encounter objects in your search. **Warman's** is not designed to sit on your shelf, but to withstand heavy use. Thumb wear is our gauge to success.

Warman's is concerned about market trends. For this reason we occasionally repeat an object so its increase or decrease can be traced in the marketplace.

Where categories also are covered in *Warman's Americana & Collectibles* we make a notation in the category introduction. We recommend *Warman's Americana & Collectibles* for those wanting a detailed guide to the collectibles field.

PRICES

Everyone asks — where do we get our prices? They come from many sources.

First, we rely on auctions. Auction houses and auctioneers do not always command the highest prices. If they did, why would so many dealers buy from them? The key to understanding auction prices is to know when a price is high in range, or low. We think we do this and do it well.

Second, we work closely with dealers. We screen our contacts to make certain they have a full knowledge of the market. Dealers make their living or significant side income from selling antiques. They cannot afford to have a price guide which is not in touch with the market.

Over thirty antique magazines, newspapers and journals come into our office regularly. We read them thoroughly and extract price information from them. They are excellent barometers of what is moving and what is not. We don't hesitate to call an advertiser to ask if their listed merchandise sold.

When the editorial staff is doing field work, we identify ourselves. Our conversations with dealers and collectors around the country have enhanced this book. Teams from **Warman's** are in the field at antique shows, flea markets and auctions recording prices and taking photographs.

Collectors work closely with us. They are specialists whose devotion to research and accurate information is inspiring. Generally, they are not dealers. Whenever we have asked for help from them, they have responded willingly and admirably.

BOARD OF ADVISORS

Our Board of Advisors are specialists, both dealers and collectors, who feel a commitment to accurate information. You'll find their names listed in the front of the book. Several have authored a major reference work on their subject.

Members of the Board of Advisors file lists of prices in the categories for which they are responsible. They help select and often supply the photographs used. If you wish to buy or sell an object in their field of expertise, drop them a note. If time or interest permits, they will respond.

BUYER'S GUIDE

Warman's is designed to be a buyer's guide, a guide to what you would have to pay to purchase an object on the open market from a dealer or collector. **It is not a seller's guide to prices**. People frequently make this mistake; in doing so, they deceive themselves. If you have an object listed in this book and wish to sell it to a dealer, you should expect to receive approximately fifty percent (50%) of the listed value. If the object is not expected to be resold quickly, expect to receive even less.

A private collector may pay more, perhaps seventy to eighty percent of our list price. Your object will have to be something needed for his or her collection. If you have an extremely rare object or an object of exceptionally high value, these guidelines do not apply.

Examine your piece as objectively as possible. As an antique appraiser, I spend a great deal of time telling people their treasures are not 'gold' at all, but items readily available in the marketplace.

In respect to buying and selling, a simple philosophy is that a good purchase occurs when both the buyer and seller are happy with the price. Don't look back. Hindsight has little value in the antiques field. Given time, things tend to balance out.

ACKNOWLEDGEMENTS

1983 was a year of accomplishments. Besides preparing this 18th Edition, we also developed and edited the first edition of *Warman's Americana & Collectibles* as a companion volume to this book.

Connie A. Moore, my wife, had her tolerance tested on many occasions and more than proved equal to the task. She proofread copy, assisted our field photographers, and entertained collectors and dealers at our home.

Doris Ford and Ellen Schroy continued their fine efforts. They spent long hours to ensure that the quality of the 18th Edition surpassed earlier efforts.

In 1983 I traveled to England, Florida, Illinois, New England, and other states along the east coast. Everywhere I went dealers, show managers, collectors and others involved with antiques welcomed me openly. I want to extend my thanks to these people as a whole.

V.I.P. Color Labs of Bethlehem, Pennsylvania, maintained their high professional level in the preparation of our photographs.

Finally, I can not emphasize enough the continued support my staff and I receive from Stanley and Katherine Greene. 1984 promises to be a banner year for **Warman's** largely because of their commitment.

Editorial Office   HARRY L. RINKER
Warman Publishing Co., Inc.
P. O. Box 265
Zionsville, PA 18092
February, 1984

STATE OF THE MARKET

1983 was a year of market recovery. The entire antique and collectibles market showed new vitality and a renewed optimism. Leading the recovery were the auction houses. The reorganizations of the early 1980s at Sotheby's, Christie's, Phillips, and others achieved acceptable profit levels; and, sales again attracted pieces which set record prices.

The general economic recovery in the United States also deserves part of the credit. Inflation was checked; a rising stock market channeled money out of the long term money market accounts. Individuals again were looking for alternate investment opportunities. There is no denying that the antique and collectibles market is directly linked to the general economy.

1983 showed that the cost of collecting antiques is rising and that fine antiques may be limited to those with large pocketbooks. Sotheby's in London sold the 12th century illuminated German manuscript known as "The Gospels of Henry The Lion" for 11.7 million dollars. The $100,000 level in furniture was passed not once, but more than half a dozen times. Objects priced in the $10,000-plus range were not uncommon. We have more objects in this range than ever in this 18th Edition. To restrict an antique price list to objects costing less than $9,999 is no longer realistic.

1983 also demonstrated the power of the strong market existing among collectors themselves. Record prices are not always set at auctions or by dealers. Private sales probably are responsible for over 30% of record prices. While difficult to document, our Advisors report that the private sale market was extremely active in 1983 and that several records were set, especially in the area of "prestige" collectibles.

The potential buyer in 1984 is not the same person who dominated the market in the 1970s. The era of speculative buying linked to decorating trends or publication fads is over. The collector of the 1980s is more conservative and selective. Blue chip antiques, e.g., art glass, furniture, fine English porcelains, etc., are doing well. Buyers want quality and they are willing to wait until they find it.

To achieve full recovery the market needs the low range ($25 to $100) and middle range ($250 to $1,000) buyers back in full force. This has not happened. Buyers of items in these price ranges are perhaps now the most cautious of all. They are checking around, not buying on impulse.

Established collectors have slowed the pace at which they are building their collections. New collectors are emerging, but not with the same frequency or with the same collecting urgency as in the 1970s. Dealers used to be able to count on a given number of new collectors in a category each year. That number in 1983 was half of what it was in the mid-1970s.

In 1983 many dealers worked on smaller profit margins to help stimulate the market. One result was a reduction in price bargaining. Also, more dealers handled material on consignment. Although consignment allows for new merchandise presentation, it further restricts price flexibility.

The operating costs for dealers rose dramatically in 1983. Many promoters raised booth rents. Travel, food and accomodation costs increased as dealers sought new markets. Many found that profits failed to cover costs. The number of "show" oriented dealers has surpassed dealers with a fixed shop.

Dealers that set up in Florida in January were seen in Chicago in March, Pennsylvania in April, and Massachusetts in July. They struggled to present new merchandise at each location. In fact, buyers complained about the "staleness" of some material. A prominent Washington dealer exhibited at a prestige Philadelphia show with the same merchandise two years in a row. This fact was not lost on collectors.

In 1983 we called attention to the breakdown of regional pricing. This trend continues. A recent study trip to England indicates that a breakdown of international price differences may occur shortly. One sign is that over one-half of the books on antiques and collectibles being sold in English bookstores were from American publishers. *Warman's* was being sold at flea markets and shows in the London area. English dealers told us that they were following American prices carefully. It will take several years before this trend fully develops; but the days of profitable buying trips abroad may soon end.

The 1983 market was strong. Merchandise was selling in all categories, although slower in some areas than in others. Those categories which showed unusual strength or weakness at the end of 1983 were:

Gaining	*Declining*
Art Glass	Advertising Materials
Autographs	Bottles
Clothing Accessories	Coin Operated Items
Cut Glass	Firearms
Dolls	Folk Art
Early American Furniture	Spongeware
English Furniture	Stock and Bond Certificates
Mechanical Banks	Wicker
Prints	
Silver	

The establishment of antique cooperatives and indoor flea markets continues. The movement is no longer confined to the west coast and large cities. Several have developed in the Pennsylvania countryside within the past year. Many of the newer flea markets are bringing back the fringe dealers - those with questionable merchandise, lack of knowledge and, most importantly, taste.

We are seeing the elevation of "junk" to the level of antiques and collectibles. Buyers should remain aware of what categories are part of the established antique and collectibles market and stick to them. A second-hand shop is not an antique shop, and should not be confused with one. The fringe dealer is one of the principal sources for bringing the reproductions and outright fakes into the market. In an attempt to secure merchandise they go to large warehouses and "load-up." These suppliers advertise openly in trade papers and journals. Publications throughout the field are reporting on this trend and attempting to rally support for legal action. They deserve our active support.

In summary, we are in a quiet, conservative market. The advantage in early 1984 rests neither with the dealer or buyer. It is a time of reflection and quality buying. It is a time when dealers are building new, strong client relationships, the type which gave strength to the market of the 1950s and 60s.

Buy quality, first and foremost. Buy your antiques because you plan to live with them. Over an extended period of time, you will gain both from the pleasure you receive and their rise in value.

AUCTION HOUSES

The following auction houses cooperated with Warman Publishing Co., Inc., by providing catalogues of their auctions and price lists. In addition, Bourne, Butterfield's, Oliver, Rinsland, Roan and Theriault's provided photographs for use in the General Section. This effort is most appreciated.

Richard A. Bourne, Co. Inc.
Corporation St. (P.O. Box 141)
Hyannis, MA 02647
(617) 775-0797

Butterfield's
1244 Sutter St.
San Francisco, CA 94109
(415) 673-1362

Christie's
502 Park Ave.
New York, NY 10002
(212) 546-1000

William Doyle Galleries, Inc.
175 E. 87th St.
New York, NY 10028
(212) 427-2730

Early Auction Co.
123 Main St.
Milford, OH 45150
(513) 831-4833

Ron Fox
416 Throop St.
N. Babylon, NY 11704
(516) 669-7232

Garth's Auction, Inc.
2690 Stratford Rd.
P.O. Box 369
Delaware, OH 43015
(614) 362-4771 or 369-5085

Hake's Americana and Collectibles
P.O. Box 1444
York, PA 17405
(717) 848-1333

Morton's Auction Exchange, Inc.
643 Magazine St.
P.O. Box 30380
New Orleans, LA 70190
(504) 561-1196 or (800) 535-7801

Phillips
867 Madison Ave.
New York, NY 10021
(212) 570-4830

Lloyd Ralston Toys
447 Stratfield Rd.
Fairfield, CT 06432
(203) 366-3399 or 335-4054

Rinsland's Americana Mail Auction
P.O. Box 265
Zionsville, PA 18092
(215) 966-3939

Roan Bros. Auction Gallery
R. E. 3, Box 118
Cogan Station, PA 17728
(717) 494-0170

Sotheby's
1334 York Ave.
New York, NY 10021
(212) 472-8424

Theriault's
P.O. Box 151
Annapolis, MD 21404
(301) 269-0680

Verlon Webb Auction
311 N. Spruce
Centerville, IN 47330
(317) 855-5542

Woody Auction
Douglass, KS 67039
(316) 746-2694

The following categories, formerly found in this guide, are now treated extensively in our new companion—*Warman's Americana & Collectibles,* First Edition, 1984.

Cowboy Heroes

Degenhart Glass

Dolls, Paper

Fans

Fraternal Items

Fruit Crate Labels

Goofus Glass

Insulators

Marbles

Nutcrackers

Padlocks

Pens and Pencils

Playing Cards

Postcards

Rose O'Neill

Shaving Mugs

Sheet Music

Stereo Viewers and Cards

Sunbonnet Babies

Watch Fobs

World War II Collectibles

AMERICAN PATTERN GLASS

Introduction

HISTORY

Two events chronicled the initial production of pattern glass for the mass market. In 1825 Deming Jarvis founded the Boston and Sandwich Glass Company. In 1829 the technique of pressing glass into hinged molds was patented. Housewives now had inexpensive table glass in unlimited quantities.

From the 1860's through the first decade of the 20th century, hundreds of companies produced thousands of intricate patterns that pictured in glass the elements of everyday life as it was in the late 1800's—flowers, animals, portraits, famous actresses, historical figures, Victorian frills, and whimsies. Production of pattern glass was not without its tribulations. There were rapid changes in public taste, strikes and fires at factories, and involvement in our nation's first energy crisis— the absence of enough natural gas to maintain production.

FLINT GLASS

Until 1865 many patterns, e.g., Ashburton, Bigler, Excelsior and Eureka, were made of lead glass, or bell-tone glass. When struck lightly, the object emitted a clear, bell tone. After 1865, glass of high lead content was slowly replaced by glass made with a soda lime formula. Soda lime glass has no ring. The change was gradual, extending over twenty years.

As a result, some patterns can be found in two or three glass types—flint, semi-flint and non-flint. The flint pieces are most desirable. We have indicated those patterns which fit into a dual or triple classification.

RESEARCHERS

Ruth Webb Lee, Dr. S. T. Millard, and Minnie Watson Kamm were pioneer researchers in pattern glass. They attempted to standardize the names of patterns by adopting those names used by manufacturers in their catalogues. Confusion began because two manufacturers would use a different name for the same pattern. Further, manufacturers' catalogues circulated primarily among the wholesale trade, rarely being seen by the average retail buyer.

The number of manufacturers' catalogues available to the pioneer researchers was limited. If the catalogue name did not seem to suit the pattern a totally new name was created. Not only did the researchers create names at random, but dealers and collectors quickly joined the naming craze. Alice Hulett Metz, a later glass researcher, summed up the problem by noting the "endless confusion" which collectors now face.

Today, William Heacock leads a movement to study the catalogues of manufacturers and bring standardization to pattern glass names. Mollie Helen McCain has helped by more accurately illustrating patterns than has been done in the past. In December 1983 a new semi-annual journal, *Collecting Glass: Research, Reprints & Reviews,* was issued by Peacock Publications, P.O. Box 655, Marietta, Ohio 45750. Annual subscription is $20.00. No serious collector should be without it.

PATTERN NAMES

Being the nation's leading authority on the prices of pattern glass, *Warman's* lends its support to this standardization. For example, authors, collectors, and manufacturers have given the name "Virginia" to five different patterns. Each of these patterns has also been classified under other designations. We have chosen simply to number the "Virginia" pattern 1 through 5. The results are as follows:

No.	Old Pattern Name	Manufacturer
1	*Banded Portland*	U. S. Glass Company
2	*Galloway*	U. S. Glass Company
3	*Henrietta* or *Big Block*	Findlay Glass Company
4	*McKee's Virginia*	McKee Glass Company
5	*Tarentum's Virginia* or *Many Diamonds*	Tarentum Glass Company

A similar catalogue change has been made for the two "Pennsylvania" patterns.

COLLECTING TIPS

The current market in pattern glass is steady. The older, flint glass patterns remain the most collectible, expensive and hard to find. Because of their scarcity, many patterns are not found among our list.

Many non-flint patterns are gaining popularity. One factor is lower prices. Another is that as researchers identify makers and scope of production, collectors of forms want to add a piece to their collections.

Although availability is a key element in pricing, some scarcer patterns may cost less than more numerous patterns. When a pattern is "fashionable," its price rises in value. Patterns in the "States" series occupy this favored position at the moment.

Another trend is the discovery that many patterns come in a variety of colors and with accent highlights such as gilding or ruby staining. The variety within a given pattern seems to be always increasing as more and more collectors visit more and more flea markets, shops, homes, etc.

Collecting a form, rather than a pattern is most popular. Goblets are the most commonly collected form. Within the past years, toothpicks, tumblers, and salt and pepper shakers have gained popularity due in part to the ability to display a large collection in a small space.

REPRODUCTIONS

The pattern glass field has been plagued by reproductions, some made from the original molds. The collector is advised to do three things: (a) read and study as much pattern glass literature as possible, (b) deal with a reputable dealer [found by asking other collectors], and (c) handle and examine as many good examples as you can find.

We have marked items for which reproductions are known to exist with an asterisk (*). We encourage collectors to inform us of any we may have missed so they can be added to future editions.

Using Warman's Listing

The Pattern Glass section is divided into three catagories—Clear, Colored and Opalescent. The Clear Pattern Glass section contains patterns made primarily in clear glass and one additional color (generally emerald green or ruby stained.) Other colors may be available, but are scarce and noted in the introductions.

The Colored Glass section contains patterns found in a variety of pieces in two or more colors. The clear pattern may be one of these colors. Therefore, if you have a piece of clear pattern glass, **check both sections.**

Opalescent glass has a cloudy or opal look. It is found in both clear and colored patterns. Because of its increased collectibilty, we have devoted a special section to it. Two patterns remain in the general section-Holly Amber because it is collected as an art glass and slag because it is so heavily reproduced and collected more for color rather than design.

We have returned to the word "vaseline" in the Colored section. The present manufacturers of vaseline petroleum jelly have changed the color of their product. The current milky white, transparent material is no longer descriptive of anything. But collectors know what vaseline looks like. It is not yellow, it is not canary—it is vaseline. Let's keep it that way!

We have crossed-indexed pattern names. When a pattern has several names, we have retained only those currently in use. We have no desire to perpetuate names losing favor among collectors.

Many illustrations in this edition are new. We are committed to giving you the best representation of each pattern. Line drawings, rather than photographs, allow the details of a pattern to show clearly.

YOU, THE COLLECTOR

Pattern glass collectors represent our most important source for prices, market trends and research. Sharing your information with us will enable other collectors to benefit. We welcome what data you can send.

CLEAR PATTERN GLASS

ACORN VARIANTS
(Acorn, Acorn Band, Acorn Band with Loops, Paneled Acorn Band, and Beaded Acorn).

Flint and non-flint, c1860s and 70s. Flint adds 20%. The Acorn goblet is reported to be reproduced in blue. Originally it was only made in clear. There are additional Acorn patterns, but they were not made in sets.

	Flint	Non-Flint
Bowls		
Covered	—	50.00
Open	—	75.00
Butter, covered	65.00	—
Celery	50.00	—
Compotes		
Covered	185.00	75.00
Open	60.00	60.00
Creamer	45.00	—
Egg Cup	18.00	15.00
*Goblet	27.50	20.00
Pitcher, water	100.00	50.00
Sauce, flat	—	7.50
Spooner	40.00	30.00
Sugars		
Covered	75.00	50.00
Open, buttermilk type	35.00	—

ACTRESS
(Theatrical)

Made by LaBelle Glass Co., Bridgeport, Ohio, and Crystal Glass Co., c1870s. Prices listed are for clear and frosted.

Bowl, 6", footed	25.00
Butter, covered	100.00
Cake Stand, 10"	125.00
Celeries	
Footed, H.M.S. Pinafore	165.00
Plain, Actress head, not Pinafore	82.50
Cheese dish, covered, "The Lone Fisherman" on cover, base 2 Drominos	200.00
Candlesticks, pr.	250.00
Compotes	
Covered, 8", high standard	75.00
Open, 7", low standard	65.00
Open, 10", high standard	80.00
Open, 12", high standard	110.00
Creamer	55.00
*Goblet	65.00
Marmalade Jar with cover	125.00
Mug, Pinafore	50.00
*Pickle Dish, "Love's Request is Pickles," various sizes	37.50–45.00
Pitchers	
Milk, oval, "Pinafore"	210.00
Water, "Miss Neilson"	200.00
Sauce, footed	15.00
Salt, master	68.00
Salt and Pepper, pair, original pewter top	75.00
Spooner	70.00
Sugar, covered	75.00
Tray, Bread	
"Give Us This Day Our Daily Bread," "Pinafore"	65.00
"Maggie Mitchell"	65.00
Tray, Dresser	60.00

ALABAMA
(Beaded Bull's Eye and Drape)

Circa 1898. U. S. Glass Company (One of the States' patterns). Also found in ruby stained and green (rare).

	Clear	Ruby Stained
Butter, covered	50.00	—
Celery	30.00	—
Compote, open, 5"	50.00	—
Creamer	32.50	55.00
Cruet, with stopper	55.00	—
Honey Dish, cov, high sta	65.00	—

	Clear	Ruby Stained
Nappy	22.50	—
Pitcher, water	60.00	—
Relish, oblong, 3 sizes	18–25.00	—
Salt Shakers, single	27.00	—
Spooner	25.00	—
Sugar, covered	45.00	—
Syrup	60.00	—
Toothpick	65.00	—

Syrup, metal top	52.00
Tumbler	13.00
Tray, water or wine	30.00
Wine	20.00

ALMOND THUMBPRINT
(Pointed Thumbprint, Finger Print)

An early flint glass pattern with variants in flint and non-flint.

ALL-OVER DIAMOND
(Diamond Splendor, Diamond Block #3)

Made by George Duncan and Sons, Pittsburgh, Pa., 1891, and continued by U. S. Glass Co. Was made only in clear, occasionally trimmed with gold, in at least 65 pieces.

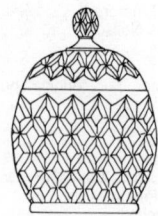

		Flint	Non-Flint
Butter, covered		80.00	47.50
Celery Vase		62.50	—
Champagne		60.00	32.50
Compotes, covered			
4¾", jelly, high std		60.00	35.00
4¾", low standard		55.00	25.00
7", low standard		45.00	20.00
10", high standard		75.00	40.00
Cordial		35.00	18.00
Creamer		62.50	37.50
Cruet, footed		50.00	—
Decanter		70.00	—
Egg Cup		42.50	20.00
Goblet		28.00	15.00
Punch Bowl		100.00 +	—
Salts			
Footed, covered		42.50	—
Large, flat		22.50	—
Sugar, covered		60.00	37.50
Sweetmeat Jar, covered		75.00	—
Tumbler		40.00	—
Wine		20.00	15.00

Biscuit or cracker jar, covered, 3 sizes	35–50.00
Bowl, Berry	16.00
Candelabrum very ornate, 3 and 4-arm with lustres	150.00+
Cakestand	35.00
Celery	22.00
Claret jug	50.00
Compote, covered	40.00
Condensed Milk Jar (can goes into jar)	25.00
Cruets	
4 oz.	42.50
6 oz.	25.00
Decanter	42.50
Dishes, Condiment, various sizes	10–25.00
Egg cup	18.50
Goblet	22.00
Ice tub, handles	35.00
Lamp, Banquet, tall stem	125.00+
Nappy, various shapes, handled	15.00
Pickle dish, long, flat	15.00
Pitcher, water, bulbous type (6 sizes)	42–60.00
Spooner	18.00
Sugars	
Covered	35.00
Open	18.00

AMAZON
(Sawtooth Band)

Non-flint. Made by Bryce Brothers, Pittsburgh, Pa., late 1870s–1880; also made by the U. S. Glass Co., c1890. Mostly found in clear, either etched or plain. Heacock notes pieces in blue and amber. Over 65 pieces made in this pattern. Add 200% for color.

	Etched	Plain
Banana Stand	95.00	75.00
Bowls		
Open, flared, frilled edge	—	45.00
Open, silver frame	—	60.00
Waste	25.00	—
Butter, covered	65.00	55.00
Cake Plate, 9¼″, flat	—	35.00
Cake Stands		
Large	—	50.00
Small	—	37.50
Celery	35.00	—
Champagne	—	35.00
Claret	35.00	25.00
Compotes		
Jelly, 5½″,	45.00	35.00
Open, 9½″, high standard, sawtooth edge	—	50.00
Cordial, etched "Jacksonville, Fla."	45.00	—
Creamer	37.50	32.50
Creamer, child's	—	18.00
Cruet, orig stopper	55.00	40.00
Egg Cup	—	10.50
Goblet	37.50	25.00
Nappy, round with handle	—	18.00
Nappy, lion handles, oval (sometimes with lid, lion finial)	—	45.00
Pitcher, water	65.00	47.50
Salts		
Flat	—	18.00
Footed	—	20.00
Sauces, footed	—	10.00
Shakers, pr	50.00	40.00
Spooner	35.00	25.00
Spooner, child's	—	19.00
Sugar, covered	52.50	35.00
Sugar, covered, child's	—	20.00
Syrup	45.00	40.00
Toothpick	30.00	25.00
Tumbler	—	21.00
Vase, double holder on stand	50.00	—
Wine	32.00	—

ANTHEMION

Non-flint made by Model Flint Glass Co., Findlay, Ohio, c1890–1900. Clear only.

Item	Price
Bowl, 7″, square, turned-in edge, maple leaf in base	20.00
Butter, covered	65.00
Cake Plate, 9½″	35.00
Cake Stand	40.00
Celery	20.00
Creamer	30.00
Marmalade Jar, covered	22.50
Pitcher, water	55.00
Plates	
10″	15.00
10″ with curled rim, triangular shape	30.00
Sauce, square flat	10.00
Spooner	25.00
Sugar, covered	40.00
Tumbler	32.50

APOLLO

Non-flint first made by Adams and Co., Pittsburgh, Pa., c1870s. Later by U. S. Glass Co., c1891, and McKee Glass Co. Clear and frosted. Frosted increases price 10%.

	Clear	Ruby Stained
Bowl, 9″	25.00	30.00
Butter, covered	45.00	55.00
Cake Stand	37.50	40.00
Celery Dish, rectangular	15.00	—
Celery Vase	22.50	30.00
Cheese Dish, covered	—	52.50
Compotes		
Covered, high standard	50.00	62.50
Open, high standard	35.00	40.00
Creamer	27.50	35.00
Egg Cup	18.00	—

	Clear	Ruby Stained
Goblet	32.00	35.00
Lamp, 10"	55.00	—
Pickle Dish	15.00	18.50
Pitcher, water	45.00	55.00
Sauce, footed	10.00	10.00
Spooner	22.50	25.00
Sugar, covered	40.00	45.00
Sugar Shaker	40.00	—
Syrup	—	45.00
Tumbler	—	27.50
Water Tray	35.00	45.00
Wine	—	24.00

ARABESQUE

Non-flint produced by Bakewell, Pears and Co., Pittsburgh, Pa., c1870s. Clear only. Made in limited number of pieces and is becoming scarce.

Butter, covered	50.00
Celery	40.00
Compotes	
Covered, 8", high standard	55.00
Covered, 8", low standard	42.50
Creamer, applied handle	55.00
Goblet	32.50
Pitcher, water, applied handle	75.00
Spooner	25.00
Sugars	
Covered	45.00
Open, buttermilk	30.00

ARCHED FLEUR DE LIS
(Late Fleur De Lis)

Made by Higbee, Bryce and Co., in 1897–1898. Was a good seller when introduced; dropped at a later date. Known in ruby stained but mostly found in clear.

	Clear	Ruby Stained
Banana Stand	30.00	45.00
Butter, covered	40.00	60.00

	Clear	Ruby Stained
Creamer	22.50	35.00
Dish, shallow, 7"	12.50	25.00
Mug, 3¼"	—	19.00
Plate, flat, square, 7"	15.00	27.50
Salt and Pepper Shakers, singles	9.00	38.00
Spooner, double handled	18.00	38.00
Sugar, covered, double handled	35.00	48.00
Toothpick	20.00	45.00
Tumbler	15.00	22.00
Vase, 10"	46.00	50.00
Wine	19.00	27.50

ARCHED GRAPE

Flint and non-flint of the 1870s–late 80s made by Boston and Sandwich Glass Co.

	Flint	Non-Flint
Butter, cov	42.50	37.50
Celery	32.50	—
Compote, cov, high std	50.00	40.00
Cordial	25.00	18.00
Creamer	60.00	40.00
Goblet	30.00	25.00
Pitcher, water, applied handle	60.00	—
Spooner	35.00	25.00
Sugar, cov	45.00	—
Wine	22.50	18.00

ARGUS

Bakewell Pears & Co. made this thumbprint type pattern in flint glass in Pittsburgh, Pa., in the early 1870s.

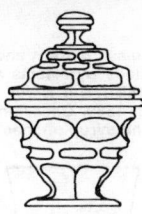

	Clear	Ruby Stained
Celery	32.50	47.50
Compotes		
Covered, ftd, 7"	70.00	—
Open		
8", flared	45.00	55.00
10"	55.00	—
Creamer		
"Hotel," large round shape	45.00	—
Regular	50.00	—
Cruet	65.00	—
Goblet	25.00	—
Mug	25.00	—
Pitcher, water		
2½ qt, squat	55.00	—
Milk	145.00	—
Plate, 10"	35.00	—
Relish	22.50	—
Sauce		
Footed	8.00	—
Pointed at one end	12.50	—
Spooner	27.50	—
Sugar, cov	45.00	38.00
Tumbler	25.00	—
Vinegar Jug, 3 pts	50.00	—
Wine	30.00	—

Ale Glass	77.50
Bitters Bottle	60.00
Bowl, 5½"	50.00
Butter, covered	90.00
Celery, cut	85.00
Champagne	40.00
Creamer, applied handle	70.00
Decanter, quart	70.00
Egg Cup	22.50
Goblet	38.00
Lamp, footed	75.00
Mug, applied handle	75.00
Pitcher, water, applied handle	175.00
Salt, open	30.00
Spooner	45.00
Sugar, covered	40.00
Tumblers	
Bar	65.00
Handled Whiskey	50.00
Wine	35.00

ART
(Job's Tears.)

Non-flint produced by Adams and Co., Pittsburgh, Pa., in the 1870s. Reissued by U. S. Glass Co. in the early 1890s.

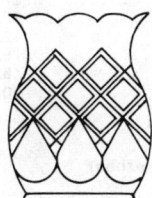

ASHBURTON

A popular pattern produced by Boston and Sandwich Glass Co. and McKee Brothers from the 1850s to the late 1870s with many variations. Originally made in flint by New England Glass Co. and others. Later produced in non-flint. Prices are for flint.

    Note: Wine has been reported in emerald green and is *not* a reproduction. Scarce and valued at $75.00.

	Clear	Ruby Stained
Banana Stand	100.00	150.00
Basket, fruit	75.00	—
Biscuit or Cracker Jar	65.00	75.00
Bowls		
7", low collar base	35.00	—
8", berry, one end pointed	45.00	55.00
Butter, cov	55.00	75.00
Cake Stand, 10"	55.00	—

Ale Glass, 5"	55.00
Bitters Bottle	55.00
Carafe	175.00
Celery, scalloped top	60.00
Champagne, cut	75.00
Compote, open, low	65.00
Creamer, applied handle	175.00

Decanter, quart, bar lip	50.00
Egg Cup, single	22.50
Egg Cup, double	95.00
Flip Glass, handled	90.00
*Goblet	65.00
Honey Dish	7.50
*Jug, pint, quart and three pint . . .	80–100.00
Lamp	75.00
*Lemonade Glass	55.00
Mug, 7″	125.00
Pitcher, water	400.00
Sauce	10.00
Spooner	30.00
*Sugar, covered	55.00
Tumblers	
Water, footed	85.00
Whiskey, handled, applied handle	75.00
Wine bottle with tumble up	65.00
*Wine	
Cut pattern	65.00
Plain	40.00

ASHMAN

Non-flint c1880s. Pieces are square in shape. There are frequent variations within pieces.

	Amber	Clear
Bread Tray, motto	—	55.00
Bowls, many sizes	—	18–26.00
Butter, covered		
Conventional finial	50.00	38.00
Large ball-type finial, some-times with flowers within the ball	—	50.00
Cake Stand, 9″	—	55.00
Compotes		
Covered, 12″	—	65.00
Open	—	37.50
Creamer	45.00	35.00
Goblet	—	38.00
Pitcher, water	—	60.00
Relish	—	15.00
Spooner	—	35.00
Sugar, cov	—	45.00
Tray, water	50.00	40.00
Tumbler	—	25.00
Wine	—	18.00

ATLAS

Non-flint clear glass pattern and occasionally ruby-stained, made by Adams and Co., U. S. Glass Co., in 1891, and Bryce Brothers, Mt. Pleasant, Pa., in 1889. Occasionally etched— celery $30.00 and syrup pitcher $65.00.

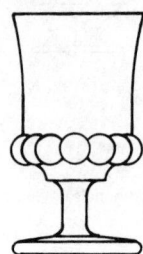

	Clear	Ruby Stained
Bowl, 7″, finger	20.00	—
Butter, cov	45.00	45.00
Cake Stand, 10″	25.00	—
Celery	27.00	35.00
Champagne	25.00	—
Claret	20.00	—
Compotes		
Covered, 5″, jelly	45.00	60.00
Covered, 8″, high standard	65.00	—
Open, 7″, low standard . . .	35.00	—
Creamer	15.00	35.00
Goblet	18.00	—
Marmalade Jar, cov	45.00	—
Pitcher, water	50.00	—
Salt, dip	10.00	—
Spooner	27.50	—
Sugar, cov	37.50	—
Toothpick	12.50	—
Tray, water	75.00	—
Tumbler	18.00	—
Wine	20.00	—

AURORA
(Diamond Horseshoe)

Made in 1888 by the Brilliant Glass Works, which only existed for a short time. Taken over by the Greensburg Glass Co.; and pattern continued by them. Made in clear, plain and with etching, and with ruby stain.

	Plain	Ruby Stained
Bowl, waste or finger	27.50	55.00
Butter, cov	45.00	90.00
Cake Stand	40.00	80.00

	Plain	Ruby Stained
Celery Vase	18.00	36.00
Compote, cov, high std.	65.00	95.00
Creamer	28.00	48.00
Goblet	25.00	42.00
Pitcher, water	40.00	75.00
Platter, round, 10″, Bread Tray, large star in center	18.00	35.00
Relish		
Fish shape, handle	12.00	22.00
Oval, scalloped base	17.00	35.00
Salt and Pepper Shakers, single	22.50	40.00
Sauce		
Flat	8.00	18.00
Footed	10.00	—
Spooner	25.00	48.00
Sugar, cov	45.00	65.00
Tray, water or wine	45.00	65.00
Tumblers		
Lemonade, handled	35.00	62.00
Scalloped base	30.00	60.00
Wine	24.00	40.00

AUSTRIAN
(Finecut Medallion)

Made by Indiana Tumbler and Goblet Co., Greentown, Indiana, c1897–1898. Made in clear, milk white, chocolate, and canary. A few experimental pieces in green, amber, blue, and opaque Nile green. Rare in color. Prices given are for clear glass; color 20% more; caramel or chocolate, 100% more.

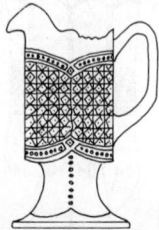

Butter, covered	85.00
Creamer	30.00
Compote, covered	50.00
Goblet	45.00
Nappy, covered	55.00
Pitcher, water	52.50
Plate, 10″	32.50
Punch cup, gold trim	20.00
Salt Shaker, single	12.00
Sugar, covered	40.00
Spooner	30.00
Tumbler	30.00
Wine	20.00

AZTEC

Made by McKee Glass Co., 1900 to 1910. Late imitation cut pattern, often marked "PRES-CUT" in circle base. Made in about 75 items.

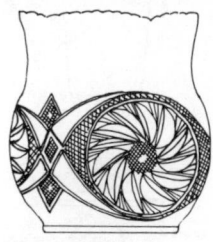

Biscuit or Cracker Jar, cov	35.00
Bowl	
Berry	15.00
Finger bowl with underplate	18.50
Nut, 7″, rolled edge	11.50
Rose	14.50
Butter, covered, 2 types,	42.50
Cake Plate	20.00
Cake Stand	28.00
Carafe, water	28.00
Celery tray or vase	15.00
Champagne	11.50
Compote, open	27.50
Cordial	20.00
Creamer, 2 types	18.50
Cruet	48.00
Cup, custard or punch	7.50
Decanter, wine	32.50
Goblet	32.50
Jars	
Condensed milk can	15.00
Marmalade, footed	42.50
Pitcher, water, tankard, jug shaped	35.00
Punch Bowl, stand, 12 handled cups and ladle	110.00
Salt and Pepper Shakers, single	15.00
Sauce	
Straight edge	5.00
Rolled edge	10.00

Soda fountain accessories
Crushed Fruit Jar	**35.00**
Straw holder, metal lid	**65.00**
Spooner, 2 types	**15.00**
Sugar, covered	**25.00**
Syrup Jug	**47.50**
Toothpick	**18.00**
Tumbler	
Regular water	**15.00**
Tall iced tea or lemonade	**18.50**
Tray, condiment	**25.00**
Whiskey	**12.00**

BABY FACE

Non-flint made by George Duncan & sons, c1870.

Butter, covered	**165.00**
Cake Stand	**125.00**
Celery Vase	**75.00**
Compote, covered, 5¼", high standard	**125.00**
Creamer	**125.00**
*Goblet	**95.00**
Knife Rest	**45.00**
Lamp	**200.00**
Pitcher, water	**225.00**
Salt	**35.00**
Spooner	**72.50**
*Sugar, covered	**150.00**
*Wine	**60.00**

BALTIMORE PEAR

Non-flint, originally made by Adams and Company, Pittsburgh, Pa., in 1874. Also made by U. S. Glass Company in 1890s. It was given as premiums by different manufacturers and organizations. Heavily reproduced. There are 18 different size compotes.

Bowl, Berry, 9"	**30.00**
*Butter, covered	**45.00**
*Cake Stand, 9"	**38.00**
*Celery	**47.50**
Compotes	
Covered, 8½", low standard	**45.00**

Open, large	**35.00**
*Creamer	**27.50**
*Goblet....................	**35.00**
Pickle	**18.50**
*Pitcher, water	
Small size	**75.00**
Large size	**90.00**
Plates	
8½"	**20.00**
10"	**27.50**
*Sauce, footed	**10.00**
Spooner	**45.00**
*Sugars,	
Covered	**55.00**
Open	**20.00**
Tray, 10½"	**35.00**

BANDED PORTLAND
(Virginia #1)

States' pattern c1901. Made by U. S. Glass Company and named by them as one of the States patterns, "Virginia." This state has been given five different pattern names. The reason for these names has become rather obscure, and since Banded Portland seems to be recognized most readily by collectors and dealers as "Virginia," it seemed wise to leave it as such. See further explanation in Introduction. Also found in green flashed, rose-flashed, and ruby stained. *Note* — Metz calls this pattern "Maiden's Blush," referring to the rose-flashed or cranberry color. Many other patterns are found in this color, hence, "Maiden's Blush" is a *color*, not a pattern.

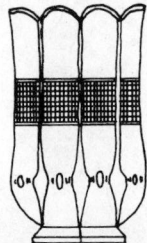

	Clear	Color Flashed
Bowls, various sizes, av. price	40.00	—
Boxes		
Powder or puff	18.00	35.00
Sardine, rectangular	20.00	—
Bureau Bottle, silver top	60.00	—
Butter, covered	50.00	75.00
Butter Pats	15.00	—
Cake Stand	55.00	—
Candlesticks	95.00	—
Celery		
Tray, boat shaped	30.00	—
Vase	25.00	—
Compotes		
Covered	75.00	—
Jelly, covered, 6″	40.00	65.00
Creamers		
Large, regular	38.00	—
Individual, boat shaped	27.00	—
Cruet	55.00	87.50
Cup, Punch	25.00	—
Decanter, handled	50.00	—
Goblet	38.00	—
Lamp		
Flat	45.00	—
Tall	50.00	—
Marmalade Jar, with cover	45.00	—
Pin Tray, souvenir	16.00	—
Pitcher, water, tankard	50.00	87.00
Pitcher, tankard, child's	35.00	—
Pomade Jar, covered	35.00	—
Punch Bowl, on standard	110.00	—
Relish, boat shaped	25.00	—
Long tray	30.00	—
Round, handled, nappy	15.00	—
Ring holder, gold rim and post	75.00	—
Salt and Pepper, single	16.00	—
Sauces		
Boat shaped	12.00	55.00
Round	10.00	—
Spooner	27.00	—
Sugars		
Individual, boat shaped, open	17.00	—
Large, covered	38.00	—
Sugar shaker, orig top	45.00	—
Syrup	45.00	—
Toothpick	22.00	37.00
Tray, for bureau set	50.00	—
Tumbler	27.00	—
Water Carafe	85.00	—
Wine	40.00	—

	Clear Plain	Ruby Stained
Bowl, finger	25.00	35.00
Celery Vase	14.00	45.00
Compotes		
Covered, low standard	25.00	48.00
Open, 8″	14.00	—
Open, 7″	28.00	—
Condiment Set, oblong dish containing salt, pepper and cruet with stopper	68.00	100.00
Creamer	32.00	60.00
Cruet, tankard shape	19.00	—
Decanter	35.00	70.00
Dish, flat, 4¼ x 7″	11.00	—
Goblet	24.00	37.00
Hand Lamp	50.00	100.00
Nappies, flat, many sizes, av.	8.50	20.00
Pitcher, water		
Round shape	57.50	—
Tankard	60.00	—
Platter or bread tray	27.00	43.00
Salt and Pepper in holder	45.00	—
Salt Shaker, single	11.00	—
Sauce, flat	18.00	39.00
Sugar, covered	38.00	48.00
Sugar Shaker	40.00	80.00
Tray, water	47.00	85.00
Wine	26.00	35.00

BARBERRY

Non-flint made by McKee Glass Co. and the Boston and Sandwich Glass Co. in the 1860s and 1880s.

BAR AND DIAMOND
(R and H Swirl Band, Kokomo)

Made in clear glass by Richards and Hartley, Tarentum, Pa., in late 1880 to 1891. No colors mentioned, but sometimes found in ruby stained and etched. About 54 pieces manufactured.

Butter, covered	65.00
Cake Stand	42.00
Celery	30.00
Compote, covered, 8″, low standard	40.00
Creamer	45.00
**Cup Plate	17.50
Egg Cup	18.00
Goblet	20.00
Pitcher, water, applied handle	85.00
Plate, 6″	24.00
Relish	15.00
Salt, footed	20.00
Spooner	40.00
Sugar	
Covered	55.00
Open, buttermilk type	25.00
Syrup	65.00
Wine	17.50

**These small plates were designed as individual butter dishes, or butter pats. (RWLee)

BARLEY

Non-flint, originally made by Campbell, Jones and Co., c1882 in clear. Possibly by others in varied quality. Add 100% for color, which is hard to find.

Bowl, Berry	15.00
Butter, covered	45.00
Cake Stand, 10″	30.00
Celery	15.00
Compotes	
6″, Jelly	20.00
8½″, covered	47.50
Creamer	30.00
Goblet	25.50
Honey Dish	7.50
Marmalade Jar	50.00
Pitcher, water	55.00
Pickle castor, silver frame and tongs	50.00
Plate, 6″	35.00
Platter	28.00
Relish	
Flat	18.00
8″, wheelbarrow, pewter wheels, bottom of dish resembles boards	55.00

Salt, Master. Wheelbarrow, pewter wheels	45.00
Salt and Pepper Shakers, single . . .	22.00
Spooner	20.00
Sugar, covered	35.00
Tray, bread, oval	30.00
Vegetable Dish, oval	12.00
Wine	20.00

BEADED BAND

Maker unknown, c1884. Limited production and scarce pattern.

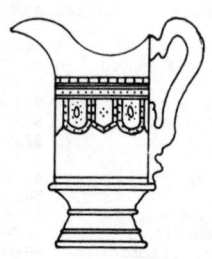

Butter, covered	45.00
Cake Stand	30.00
Compote, covered	55.00
Creamer	32.00
Goblet	25.00
Pickle, covered	45.00
Pitcher, water	60.00
Relish	
Double	35.00
Single	15.00
Sauce, footed	10.00
Spooner	25.00
Sugar, covered	40.00
Syrup	55.00
Wine	18.00

BEADED GRAPE
(California)

Non-flint made by U. S. Glass Co., Pittsburgh, Pa., late 1880s.

	Clear	Emerald Green
Bowl, 8″	26.00	38.00
Butter, cov	50.00	78.00
Cake Stand, 9″	50.00	78.00
Celeries		
Tray	30.00	44.00
Vase	42.50	65.00
Compotes, covered		
3½″, high standard	55.00	—
6½″, high standard	75.00	—
Compotes, open		
4¾″, rare with lid, made for		—
jelly	50.00	
7″, high standard	37.00	75.00
Cordial	42.50	—
Creamer	65.00	70.00
Cruet, stoppered	75.00	95.00
Dish		
Olive dish with handle	20.00	—
Square, 7¼ x 8¼″	20.00	—
Egg Cup	18.00	
*Goblet	23.00	39.00
Pickle	22.00	—
Pitchers, water		
Round	65.00	78.00
Square	70.00	105.00
*Plate, 8¼″, square	22.50	45.00
Platter, 7 x 10″ (originally		
termed bread tray)	20.00	45.00
*Sauces		
4″	10.00	16.00
4½″, handled	12.00	45.00
Shakers, single	22.00	45.00
Spooner	30.00	45.00
Sugar, cov	35.00	55.00
Sugar Shaker	55.00	—
Toothpick	35.00	50.00
*Tumbler	30.00	35.00
Vase, 6″	20.00	48.00
*Wine	35.00	55.00

BEADED GRAPE MEDALLION

Non-flint made by Boston Silver Glass Co., Cambridge, Mass., c1869. Also found in flint; add 100%.

Bowl, 7″	35.00
Butter, covered (Acorn finial)	50.00
Celery	35.00
Castor Set, complete	110.00
Compotes, covered on high and low	
foot, various sizes	75.00
Covered, on a collared base	60.00
Cordial	27.50
Creamer, applied handle	55.00
Goblet, various sizes	25–30.00
Egg Cup	19.00
Honey Dish, 3½″	10.00
Pitcher, water, applied handle	95.00
Plate, 6″	22.50
Relish, marked "Mould Pat'd May	
11, 1869." Originally had a lid.	40.00
Salts	
Footed, master	20.00
Oval, flat	13.50
Spooner	40.00
Sugar Bowl, acorn finial, covered	60.00

BEADED SWAG
(Beaded Yoke)

Made by Heisey Glass Company, c1895. Comes in red stained, custard glass and opalescent glass. See opalescent pattern glass section.

	Clear	Ruby Stained
Bowl, Berry	18.00	25.00
Butter, cov	45.00	60.00
Compote, open	37.00	—
Creamer	35.00	55.00
Mug, souvenir type	37.50	55.00
Spooner	20.00	40.00
Sugar, cov	35.00	60.00
Toothpick	25.00	40.00

BEADED TULIP
(Andes)

Non-flint made by McKee Brothers, Pittsburgh, Pa., c1894. Very rare piece may be found in emerald green.

	Clear	Emerald Green
Butter, cov	45.00	125.00
Cake Stand	50.00	—
Compote, cov, high standard	55.00	—
Creamer	35.00	75.00
Goblet	35.00	—
Marmalade Jar	40.00	—
Pickle, oval	18.00	—
Pitcher, water	65.00	—
Plate, 6″	25.00	—
Sauces		
Flat, irregular leaf-shaped edges	10.00	—
Footed	12.00	—
Spooner	27.50	—
Sugar, cov	48.00	—
Tray, water	50.00	—
Wine	18.00	—

BEAUTIFUL LADY

Made by Bryce, Highbee and Co., in 1905. Clear only, not known to have been made in color.

Bowl, Berry	
8″, on low collared base	15.00
9″, flat	16.00
Cake Stand	
High standard	25.00
Small, (for children's toy set)	30.00
Compote	
Covered, small, high standard	35.00
Open, high standard	22.50

Creamer	18.00
Dish, high stand, bent in sides	14.00
Dishes, Condiment, various shapes and sizes	8–14.00
Pitcher, water	45.00
Salt and Pepper Shakers, single	18.00
Spooner	15.00
Sugar, covered	25.00
Tumbler	12.00

BELLFLOWER

A fine flint glass pattern first made in the 1830s and attributed to Boston and Sandwich. Later produced by McKee Glass Co. and other firms for many years. There are many variations of this pattern — single vine and double vine, fine and coarse, rib, knob and plain stems, rayed and plain bases. Type and quality must be considered when evaluating. Prices are for high quality flint.

Abbreviations:
DV — double vine
SV — single vine
FR — fine rib
CR — course rib

Bowls, 8″, all types	65.00
Butter, covered. SV-FR	77.50
Caster Set, 5-bottle pewter stand	225.00
Celery. SV-FR	165.00
Champagnes	
DV-FR with cut bellflowers	250.00
SV-FR knobbed stem, rayed base, barrel shaped.	50.00
Compotes, open	
7″ d SV-FR. Scalloped top, low standard	90.00
8″ d SV-CR. High standard	100.00
8″ d SV-CR. Low standard	55.00
Cordial. SV-FR. Knob stem, rayed base, barrel shaped	100.00
Creamer. SV-FR	150.00
Dish, SV-FR, 8″, round, flat, scalloped edge	50.00
Egg Cups	
DV, with cut bellflowers	200.00
SV-FR	35.00

Decanter, pint. SV-FR. Bar lip	130.00
Goblets	
DV-FR with cut bellflowers	250.00
SV-CR. Barrel shaped	40.00
SV-CR. Straight sides	35.00
SV-FR. Knob stem, barrel shaped	50.00
*SV-FR. Plain stem, rayed base, barrel shaped	30.00
Hat. SV-FR (made from tumbler mold). Rare	350.00
Honey Dish. SV-FR, 3″, scarce ...	22.00
Lamp, Whale Oil. SV-FR. Brass stem, marble base	150.00
Mug. SV-FR	100.00
Pitchers	
Milk. DV-FR	400.00+
*Milk, quart. SV-CR	125.00
Syrup, with lid. SV-FR applied handle, (scarce)	350.00
*Water. SV-FR	275.00
Plate, 6″. SV-FR	75.00
Salt, Master. SV-FR. Footed	40.00
*Sauce, flat. SV-FR	6.50
Spooner. SV-FR	40.00
Sugars	
Covered. SV-CR	100.00
Open. SV-FR	35.00
Tumblers	
DV-CR	75.00
SV-FR. Footed	125.00
SV-FR with cut bellflowers	250.00
Whiskey, 3½″. SV-FR	95.00
Wines	
DV-FR with cut bellflowers, Barrel shaped	250.00
SV-FR. Knob stem, rayed base, barrel shaped	75.00
SV-FR. Straight sides, plain stem, rayed base	60.00

BELMONT'S ROYAL #1
(Royal, Royal Lady)

Made by Belmont Glass, Co., Bellaire, Ohio, about 1881. All pieces have ball feet. More pieces seem to be coming to light. Has not been reproduced.

	Clear	Light Amber
Butter, cov, 6-sided skirted base	140.00	—
Celery Vase	80.00	—
Cheese Dish, cov, base has portrait center, large dome lid is sometimes engraved	150.00	—
Compote, cov, high standard, 9″, mkd "Fox" in lid design	150.00	—
Compote, cov, plain band, 7″ ..	75.00	—
Creamer	95.00	—
Dish, covered, oval shape	110.00	—
Goblet	60.00	115.00
Platter or Bread Plate, crying child in center	55.00	75.00
Salt, master, 6-sided skirted base	20.00	—
Spooner	90.00	—
Sugar, cov	95.00	—
Tray, Ice Cream	120.00	—

BERKLEY
(Blocked Arches)

Made by U. S. Glass Co. in 1893. Available in clear and some frosted.

	Clear	Frosted
Biscuit Jar, cov	55.00	60.00
Bowl		
Berry	20.00	25.00
Finger	22.00	27.00
Butter, cov	45.00	50.00
Creamer	27.00	32.00
Cruet, orig stopper	60.00	68.00
Cup and Saucer	50.00	60.00
Goblet	35.00	37.00
Shaker, single		
Large	23.00	—
Small	20.00	—
Syrup	32.00	37.00
Tumbler	30.00	35.00
Wine	38.00	40.00

BIGLER

Flint, made by Boston and Sandwich Glass Co., and by other early factories. A scarce pattern with goblets and cordials most common.

		Clear	Color
Bar Bottle		80.00	
Bowls		60–70.00	
Celery		115.00	
Champagne		85.00	
Cordial		60.00	
Creamer		75.00	
Egg cup, double		50.00	
Goblet			
Regular		35.00	
Short stem		45.00	
Lamp, whale oil, monument base		145.00	
Mug, applied handle		45.00	
Plate, Toddy		30.00	
Salt, master		18.00	
Tumblers			
Water		50.00	
Whiskey, handled		75.00	
Wine		42.00	

BIRD AND STRAWBERRY
(Bluebird)

Non-flint, c1890s. Made by Beatty and Indiana Glass Co., Dunkirk, Ind. Pieces occasionally flashed with color.

	Clear	Color
Bowls		
5″	22.50	—
9½″, ftd, oval	42.00	75.00
10½″, ftd	47.00	57.50
Butter, cov	60.00	85.00
Cake Stand, 10″	45.00	52.00
Candy, heart shaped	35.00	—
Celery Tray	35.00	—
Celery Vase	42.00	—

	Clear	Color
Compotes, cov		
High standard, 6½″	85.00	—
Low standard, 6″, ruffled top, open	50.00	75.00
Creamer	37.00	47.50
Goblet	30.00	40.00
Pitcher, water	200.00	—
Plate, 12″	75.00	—
Punch Cup	17.00	—
Spooner	25.00	40.00
Sugar, cov	40.00	65.00
Tumbler	37.50	—
Wine	32.00	—

BLEEDING HEART

Non-flint, originally made by King & Son, Pittsburgh, Pa., c1870s, and by U. S. Glass Co., c1898. Also found in milk glass. Note: A goblet with a tin lid, containing a condiment (mustard, jelly, or baking powder), was made. It is of inferior quality than the one in this pattern.

Bowl, Waste	30.00
Butter, covered	55.00
Cake Stand, 10″	75.00
Compotes	
Covered, high standard, 8½″	65.00
Covered, low standard, oval	40.00
Creamer, applied handle	50.00
Egg Cup	37.50
Goblets	
Knob stem	30.00
Plain stem, round bowl, jelly type	25.00
Mug 3¼″	45.00
Pitcher, water, applied handle	125.00
Plate	35.00
Platter, oval	65.00
Relish, oval	35.00
Spooner	40.00
Sugar, covered	50.00
Tumbler, footed	32.50

BLOCK AND FAN

Non-flint made by Richard and Hartley Glass Co., Tarentum, Pa., late 1880s. Continued by U. S. Glass Co. after 1891.

	Clear	Ruby Stained
Biscuit Jar	55.00	92.00
Bowls		
8", flat	32.00	—
Finger	21.00	—
Rose	22.50	—
Butter, cov	45.00	55.00
Cake Stand, 10"	37.00	—
Carafe	39.00	—
Celery Tray	15.00	—
Celery Vase	25.00	—
Creamer	20.00	35.00
Creamer, individual	—	35.00
Cruets with stoppers		
Large	32.00	55.00
Small	24.00	—
Condiment set with salt, pepper and cruet on tray	75.00	—
Dish, oblong, large	25.00	—
Goblet	55.00	—
Ice Tub	36.00	—
Pitchers		
Milk	35.00	—
Water	46.00	—
Plate, various sizes	28.00	—
Relish, oblong	25.00	—
Salt and Pepper Shaker, single	22.00	—
Spooner	25.00	—
Sugar Shaker	37.50	—
Sugar, cov	45.00	—
Syrup	57.00	87.00
Tray, Ice Cream, rectangular, sauces to match	85.00	—
Tumbler	30.00	—
Wine	40.00	—

BOSWORTH
(Star Band)

Non-flint, c1895–1905. Maker unknown.

Butter, covered	18.50
Bowl, Berry	12.00
Cake Plate	14.50
Creamer	15.00

Goblet	15.00
Pitcher, water	32.00
Spooner	15.00
Sugar, covered	27.50
Wine	15.00
Tumbler	12.00

BOUQUET
(Narcissus Spray)

Made by Indiana Glass Co., c1918. Clear glass with flowers and leaves flashed with cranberry or amethyst color.

	Clear	Color
Bowl, Berry		
6"	14.00	—
9"	18.00	—
Butter, cov	45.00	57.00
Cake Plate	25.00	—
Celery, flat	15.00	27.00
Creamer	22.50	35.00
Goblet	22.00	30.00
Nappy, handled	12.50	—
Pitcher, water	45.00	60.00
Spooner	18.00	—
Sugar, cov	30.00	—
Tumbler	13.00	18.00
Tray, water	40.00	—

BOW TIE

Non-flint made by Thompson Glass Co., Uniontown, Pa., c1888–1890.

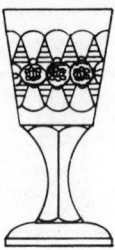

Bowls
8″	20.00
10″ deep	30.00
Punch bowl	100.00
Butter, covered	65.00
Cake Stand, large, 9″ d	45.00

Compotes, open
High standard, 10″, Orange bowl on high stand.	60.00
Low standard, 6½″	45.00
Creamer	45.00
Goblet	40.00
Honey, covered	55.00
Marmalade Jar	85.00
Pitchers, water	70.00
Relish, rectangular	25.00

Salt
Individual	12.00
Master	35.00
Sauce, flat	15.00
Spooner	30.00
Sugar, covered	65.00
Tumbler	35.00

BRITTANIC

Non-flint, c1898. A few pieces can be found in cobalt; add 200%.

	Clear	Color Stained
Banana Stand	75.00	110.00
Bowl, Berry	20.00	—
Butter, cov	40.00	55.00

	Clear	Color Stained
Cake Stand	45.00	—
Compote, cov	55.00	75.00
Creamer	35.00	50.00
Goblet	30.00	45.00
Pitcher, water	50.00	—
Salt and Pepper Shakers, single	22.00	25.00
Spooner	25.00	—
Sugar, cov	40.00	—
Tumbler	20.00	—
Wine	22.50	35.00

BROKEN COLUMN
(Irish Column, Rattan, and Notched Rib)

Made in Findlay, Ohio, about 1891–1892 by Columbia Glass Co. Later made by U.S. Glass Co. Notches can be red stained; few rare pieces found in cobalt blue.

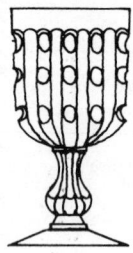

	Clear	Red Stained
Banana Stand	110.00	—
Basket, applied handle, 12 x 15″	95.00	—
Biscuit Jar, cov	85.00	110.00
Bowls		
6″, cov	40.00	—
10 x 5″, oblong	45.00	—
Butter, cov	55.00	—
Cake Stand		
9″	45.00	—
10″	55.00	—
Carafe, water	100.00	—
Celery, oval, flat	25.00	—
Celery Vase	35.00	—
Compotes		
Covered, 10″, high standard	75.00	—
Jelly, covered, high standard	55.00	—
Open, flared rim	50.00	—
Creamer	37.50	—
Cruet	55.00	75.00
*Goblet	45.00	—
Marmalade Jar, cov	55.00	—
Pickle Castor and Tongs	75.00	—

	Clear	Red Stained
Pitchers		
Syrup	80.00	—
Water	75.00	—
Plate, 9"	30.00	—
Punch Cup	20.00	—
Salt and Pepper Shakers,		
singles	30.00	—
Spooner	50.00	—
Sugar, cov	62.50	—
Sugar Shaker	60.00	90.00
Tumbler	35.00	—
Wine	32.00	—

BRYCE
(Ribbon Candy)

Non-flint, made by Bryce Brothers, Pittsburgh, Pa., 1880s. Reissued by U.S. Glass Co. in 1890s. Bowls come in a variety of sizes, open or with lids, and flat or with a low colored foot. Child's toy cake stand reported in emerald green; may be other pieces.

Butter, covered	45.00
Goblet	35.00
Cake Stands	
8"	30.00
10½"	45.00
Claret	22.50
Cordial	22.50
Creamer	25.00
Cruet, stoppered	55.00
Cup and Saucer	35.00
Honey, covered	30.00
Oil Lamp	75.00
Pitcher, water	65.00
Plates	18.00
Relish	11.00
Salt and Pepper Shakers, single	20.00
Sauce, 3 and 4", footed	10.00
Spillholder	32.00
Spooner	18.00
Sugars	
Covered	35.00
Open	20.00
Syrup	65.00
Tumbler	18.00
Wine	25.00

BUCKLE

A flint and non-flint made by Gillinder and Sons in Philadelphia, Pa., in the 1870s. Possibly made earlier by Sandwich Glass Co. in Massachusetts.

	Flint	Non-Flint
Bowl, Berry, large, originally had wire basket frame	60.00	50.00
Butter, cov	65.00	55.00
Compotes, cov		
High standard, open, 8½"	47.00	42.00
Low standard	40.00	35.00
Creamer, applied handle	45.00	37.00
Egg Cup	38.00	30.00
Goblets, various styles	35.00	28.00
Pickle	—	11.00
Pitcher, water, applied handle	—	75.00
Salts, flat, oval shape	25.00	20.00
Spooner	35.00	18.00
Sugars		
Covered	55.00	45.00
Open, buttermilk type	—	25.00
Tumbler	—	30.00
Wine	—	18.50

BUCKLE WITH STAR

Non-flint made by Bryce, Walker and Co. in 1875, U. S. Glass Co. in 1891 and others.

Bowls
6", covered	25.00
10", oval	17.50
Butter, covered	40.00
Cake Stand	30.00
Celery	20.00

Compotes
Covered, 7", high standard	50.00
Open, 9½", high standard	30.00
Creamer	25.00
Goblet	25.00

Pitchers
Syrup (Buckle with Star), handle applied, with pewter or Brittania lid, with head of man as finial	85.00
Water	80.00
Relish	11.50
Salt, master, footed	25.00
Sauces, footed	9.00
Spooner	20.00
Sugar covered	35.00
Tumbler, handle applied	30.00
Wine	22.00

BULL'S EYE

Flint made by the New England Glass Co. in the 1850s. Prices are for flint.

Butter, covered	175.00
Castor Bottle	30.00
Celery	65.00
Champagne	85.00
Cologne Bottle	70.00
Creamer	125.00
Decanter, quart, bar lip	125.00

Egg Cups
Covered but very rare	165.00
Open	45.00
Goblet	45.00
Pitcher, water	85.00
Lamp	85.00

Mugs
Large size whiskey tumbler	75.00
Small size with applied handle, 3⅜"	55.00
Relish, oval	22.50

Salt Dip	25.00
Salt, master, footed, also made with covers but rare.	100.00
Spooner	35.00
Sugar, covered	110.00
Tumbler	65.00
Whiskey	60.00
Water Bottle with tumble up	100.00
Wine	55.00

BULL'S EYE WITH DIAMOND POINT #1

Flint, c1850. Prices are for flint.

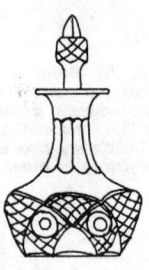

Butter, covered	200.00
Celery	100.00
Champagne	125.00
Cologne Bottle	125.00
Cordial	100.00
Creamer	175.00
Decanter, with stopper, quart	200.00
Egg Cup	50.00
Goblet	95.00
Honey Dish	17.50
Pitcher, 10¼" tankard	225.00
Sauce	8.00
Spooner	65.00
Sugar, covered	125.00
Tumbler	55.00
Tumble-up	150.00

BULL'S EYE WITH FLEUR DE LYS

Flint, c1850.

Bowl, Fruit	85.00
Butter, covered	175.00
Celery	87.50
Creamer	250.00
Decanter, quart, bar lip	100.00
Goblet	75.00
Lamp, with marble base	275.00
Mug, handled	100.00

Pitcher, water	175.00
Sugar, covered	115.00
Wine	35.00

BUTTON ARCHES

Clear and clear with ruby stained tops, non-flint, made by Duncan and Miller Glass Co. in 1885, U.S. Glass Co. in 1897, and Oriental Glass in 1906. Some pieces, known as "Koral," usually sourvenir type, are also seen in clambroth, trimmed in gold. There were other patterns made in "Koral" but Button Arches seems most prevalent.

	Clear	Ruby Stained
Bowl, 8"	20.00	—
Butter, cov	45.00	96.00
Cake Stand, 9"	32.50	—
Compote, Jelly	25.00	45.00
Creamer	20.00	28.00
Cruet, orig stopper	55.00	162.00
Custard Cup or Punch	15.00	20.00
Goblet	25.00	36.00
Mug, small	22.00	27.00
Pitchers, water, tankard	130.00	100.00
Plate	7.00	25.00
Spooner	20.00	47.00
Sugar, cov	40.00	95.00
Toothpick	18.00	33.00
Tumbler	20.00	27.00
Whiskey, shotglass	18.00	30.00
Wine	7.00	22.00

BUTTON BAND
(Umbilicated Hobnail, Wyandotte)

Non-flint, made by Ripley and Co. in 1880s and U. S. Glass Co. in 1870s. Can often be found engraved, priced the same.

Bottle, single	30.00
Butter, covered	45.00
Cake Stand, 10"	65.00
Castor Set, 5 bottles in glass, stand	95.00
Compote, open, small	45.00
Creamer	27.50
Goblet	30.00
Pitcher, water, tankard	50.00
Spooner	20.00
Sugar, covered	30.00
Tray, water	40.00
Tumbler	20.00
Wine	38.00

CABBAGE ROSE

Non-flint made in Wheeling, W. Va., c1870–1881.

Basket, handled, 12" x 14"	75.00
Bowl, Berry, 8½", oval	35.00
Butter, covered	45.00
Cake Stand, 11"	62.50
Celery Vase	45.00
Champagnes	27.50
Compotes, rose finials on lids, covered, high standard	
8" or 9"	65.00
7½"	55.00
Creamer, applied handle	57.50
Custard Cup	75.00
Egg Cup	22.00
*Goblet	48.00

Pitcher, water	92.50
Punch Cup	17.50
Relish Dish, in center horn of plenty design , filled with roses, 5 x 8½"	50.00
Salt, master, footed	25.00
Spooner	35.00
Sugars	
Covered	57.50
Open, buttermilk type	27.50
Tumbler	40.00
Wine	42.00

CABLE

Flint, c1850s. Rare in opaque colors.

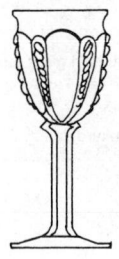

Bowl	25.00
Butter, covered	65.00
Celery	60.00
Champagne	125.00
Compote, open, low standard, 8¼"	62.50
Creamer	350.00+
Decanters, quart, ground stopper	175.00
Egg Cups	
Covered	225.00
Open	75.00
Goblet	65.00
Lamps	
Hand lamp	100.00
Marble base	85.00
Pitchers	
Syrup	125.00
Water, (rare)	300.00+
Plate, 6"	75.00
Salt, footed	25.00
Sauce, flat	10.00
Spooner	65.00
Sugar, covered	85.00
Tumbler, footed	150.00+
Wine	40.00

CANADIAN

Non-flint, made by Burlington Glass Works, c1870s.

Bread Tray	43.00
Butter, covered	60.00
Celery	40.00
Compote	
Covered, 7", high standard	60.00
Open, 8"	32.50
Creamer	50.00
Goblet	45.00
Marmalade Jar	35.00
Pickle Dish, silver frame	50.00
Pitchers	
Milk	67.50
Water	90.00
Plates	
6"	30.00
10", handled	40.00
Spooner	45.00
Sugar, covered	55.00
Wine	45.00

CANE AND ROSETTE
(Flowered Panelled Cane)

Non-flint, made by Duncan Glass, c. mid-1880s.

Bowl, covered, octagonal	45.00
Butter, covered, footed	40.00
Cake Stand, large	30.00
Champagne	20.00
Compote, covered, 8", high standard	40.00
Creamer	30.00
Goblet	25.00
Pickle Jar, covered	45.00

Pitcher, water	48.00
Spooner	20.00
Sugar, covered	37.50

CAPE COD

Non-flint, made by Boston and Sandwich Glass Co., c1870s. Note: The goblet is not the same quality of manufacture as the other pieces.

Bowl, 6″, handled	35.00
Butter, covered	50.00
Celery	30.00
Compotes	
Covered, 12″, high standard	75.00
Open, 7″, high standard	40.00
Cordial	32.50
Creamer	30.00
Cup and Saucer	45.00
Goblet	35.00
Marmalade Jar	40.00
Pitcher, water, two size	60–75.00
Plates	
5″	25.00
8″	30.00
10″	35.00
Platter, open handles	40.00
Spooner	27.50
Sugar, covered	50.00
Wine	28.00

CARDINAL BIRD

Non-flint, c1875, attributed to Ohio Flint Glass Co., Lancaster, Ohio. There has been discussion as to whether this is a cardinal or blue jay. It definitely is a cardinal. There were two butter dishes made: one in the regular pattern and one with three birds in the base–a cardinal, pewit, and titmouse. The later is rare and valued at twice the regular price.

Butters, covered	
Regular	50.00
Three Birds in base	110.00
Cake Stand	45.00

Celery Vase	50.00
Creamer	40.00
*Goblet	32.00
Honey Dish, covered, 3½″	35.00
Pitcher, water	95.00
Sauces	
Flat, 4″	10.00
Footed, 5½″	14.00
Spooner	35.00
Sugars	
Covered	65.00
Open	35.00

CHAIN AND SHIELD

Non-flint, c1875.

Butter, covered	45.00
Cordial	20.00
Creamer	22.00
Goblet	25.00
Pitcher, water	50.00
Platter, oval, Bread Tray, handled	28.00
Spoon Holder	18.00
Sugar Bowl, covered	37.50

CHAIN WITH STAR

Non-flint, made by U. S. Glass Co., c1890s.

Butter, covered	40.00
Cake Stand, 10½″	35.00
Compotes	
Covered, high standard	45.00
Open, low standard	27.50
Cordial	18.00

Creamer	25.00
Goblet	22.00
Pickle, oval	10.50
Pitcher, water	45.00
Plates	
7"	14.50
13½", handled, round bread plate	30.00
Relish	10.50
Sauce, footed	12.50
Spooner	18.00
Sugar, covered	35.00
Wine	20.00

CHANDELIER
(Crown Jewels)

Non-flint. O'Hara Glass Co., Pittsburgh, Pa., c1880 continued by U.S. Glass Co.

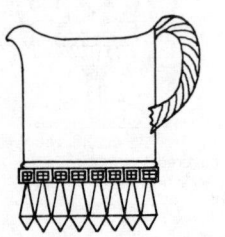

Bowls	
Berry	20.00
Finger	16.50
Butter, covered	75.00
Cake Stand, 10"	85.00
Celery	35.00
Compote	
Covered, high standard	60.00
Open, 9½	67.50
Creamer	35.00
Goblet	35.00
Inkwell	45.00
Pitcher, water	50.00
Salt, individual	18.00

Salt and Pepper Shakers, single	25.00
Spooner	30.00
Sugar, covered	45.00
Sugar Shaker, original top	55.00
Tray, water	50.00
Tumbler	22.50
Wine	40.00

CHERRY & CABLE
(Paneled Cherry)

Non-flint made by Northwood Glass Co. in late 1880s. Reproduced by Westmoreland Glass Co. Old pieces marked  Fruit almost always in color.

Butter, covered	80.00
Condiment set, 4 pcs	235.00
Creamer	50.00
Goblet	30.00
Pitcher, water	85.00
Spooner	35.00
Sugar, covered	48.00
Syrup	62.50
Toothpick	50.00
Tumbler	45.00

CLASSIC

Clear and frosted non-flint produced by Gillinder and Sons, Philadelphia, Pa., in the late 1870s–1880s. If pieces carry the log feet instead of a flat or collared base, they are worth more.

Bowl	190.00
Butter, covered on stippled log feet	195.00
Celery Vase	135.00
Compotes, covered. Can be on log feet or collared base.	275.00
Creamer	180.00
Goblet	150.00
Jar, Sweetmeat	175.00
Pitcher, water	285.00
Plates	
Jas. G. Blaine	165.00
President Cleveland	180.00
Thomas H. Hendricks	165.00
John A. Logan	165.00
Warrior	120.00
Sauce, flat or log feet	35.00
Spooner	115.00
Sugar, covered	175.00

CLASSIC MEDALLION
(Cameo # 1)

A pattern of 1870-1880, maker unknown. This should not be confused with Classic or Three-Face Medallion, which are entirely different patterns.

Bowl, 8", straight sides	25.00
Butter, covered	50.00
Celery	30.00
Compote, covered, high standard	50.00
Creamer	25.00
Goblet	50.00
Pitcher, water	125.00
Spooner	25.00
Sugar, covered	37.50

CLEAR DIAGONAL BAND

Non-flint, c1880s. Also has been found in light amber.

Butter, covered	37.50
Celery	25.00
Compotes	
Covered, high standard	38.50
Covered, low standard	30.00
Creamer	25.00

Dish, oval	10.00
Goblet	20.00
Marmalade Jar	25.00
Pitcher, water	37.50
Plate	16.50
Platter. Originally meant to be bread tray. Carries the word "Eureka" across it. Commemorative of Gold Rush.	55.00
Relish, oval	8.00
Spooner	20.00
Sugar Bowl	37.50
Wine	23.00

CLEAR RIBBON

Made by George Duncan & Sons, c1880s.

Bread Tray. "Give us This Day our Daily Bread", ftd	40.00
Butter, covered	47.50
Cake Stand, 9"	35.00
Celery Vase	18.00
Compote	
Covered, large	40.00
Open	22.50
Creamer	28.00
Dish, oblong, covered	
6"	25.00
8"	28.50
Goblet	32.00
Pickle	10.00
Pitcher, water	47.50

	Clear	
Sauce, footed	6.50	
Spooner	20.00	
Sugar, covered	30.00	

COIN–U. S.

Non-flint frosted and clear pattern made by U. S. Glass Co. in 1891 for three or four months. Production was stopped by U. S. Treasury because real coins were used in the molds.

	Clear	Frosted
Bowls		
6″	300.00	—
9″	500.00	—
Waste	238.00	—
Cake Stand, 10″	395.00	436.00
Celery		
Tray	200.00	—
Vase	135.00	325.00
Champagne	—	300.00
Butter, cov, dollars and halves	275.00	—
Compotes		
Covered, 7″, high standard	400.00	550.00
Open, 7″, high standard, quarters and dimes	195.00	520.00
Open, 7″, high standard, quarters and halves	225.00	520.00
Creamer	375.00	—
Cruet, stoppered	525.00	—
Epergne	500.00	1,200.00
Goblet, regular	230.00	395.00
Lamps		
Round font	300.00	485.00
Square font	350.00	—
Mug, handled	350.00	360.00
Pickle	205.00	—
Pitchers		
Syrup, dated pewter lid	—	480.00
Water	425.00	—
Sauce, footed	100.00	145.00
Shakers, orig tops, pr	150.00	—
Spooner	262.00	345.00
Sugar, cov	300.00	375.00
*Toothpick	180.00	—

	Clear	Frosted
Trays		
Bread, 7 x 10″	290.00	—
Water, 8″, rectangular	300.00	—
Tumbler, dollars	135.00	235.00
Wine	250.00	395.00

CONNECTICUT

Non-flint. One of the States' patterns made by U. S. Glass Co., c1898. Found in plain and engraved.

Bowls	
4″	10.00
8″	15.00
Butter, covered	30.00
Cake Stand	30.00
Celery Tray	15.00
Celery Vase	15.00
Compote	
High standard, covered	37.50
High standard, open, 7″	22.50
Cracker Jar	22.50
Creamer	18.00
Dish, 8″, oblong	16.50
Pitcher, half gallon water	30.00
Relish	10.00
Salt and Pepper Shakers	35.00
Tumblers	
Lemonade, handled	18.50
Water	15.00
Wine	20.00

CORD AND TASSEL

Non-flint, made by La Belle Glass Co., Bridgeport, Ohio, and patented by Andrew Baggs in 1872. Also made by other companies, e.g., Central Glass Co.

Butter, covered	50.00
Cake Stand, 8½″	30.00
Celery	25.00
Compotes	
Covered, 10″ high standard	50.00
Open, low standard	35.00
Creamer	35.00
Egg Cup	18.00
Dish, oval	12.50

	Clear	Emerald Green
Pitcher, water	40.00	—
Punch bowl	87.50	—
Punch cup	8.00	12.00
Nappy, handled, 6"d	12.00	—
Salt and Pepper Shakers, single	10.00	—
Spooner	18.00	40.00
Sugar, cov	55.00	80.00
Toothpick	15.00	—
Tumbler	13.00	—

Goblet	32.50
Lamp, handled	60.00
Mug	40.00
Pitcher, water, applied handle	60.00
Salt and Pepper Shakers, single	22.00
Spooner	20.00
Sugar, covered	40.00
Syrup	60.00
Tumblers	
Whiskey, applied handle	50.00
Water	50.00
Wine	32.00

COTTAGE
(Dinner Bell)

Non-flint made by Adams and Co., Pittsburgh, Pa., and U. S. Glass Co. in the 1890s. Known to have been made in emerald green, amber, light blue, amethyst, and ruby stained.

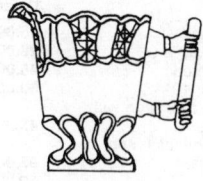

	Clear	Ruby Stained
Banana Stand	55.00	—
Bowls		
9½" oval	22.50	—
Waste or Finger	16.00	—
Butter, cov	40.00	—
Cake Stand, 9"	35.00	—
Celery Vase	22.00	—
Champagne	—	49.00
Compotes		
Covered, low standard	32.00	—
Jelly	22.00	45.00
Open, high standard	25.00	—
Creamer	32.00	50.00
Cruet, orig stopper	47.00	—
Cup and Saucer	40.00	—
Dish, oval, deep	22.00	—
Goblet	20.00	—
Pitcher, water	47.00	—
Plates, 6—10"	18.00	—
Relish	10.00	—
Salt and Pepper Shakers, single	20.00	—
Saucer	22.00	37.00
Spooner	18.00	—
Sugar, cov	27.50	—
Syrup	55.00	—
Tray, water	25.00	—
Tumbler	16.00	—
Wine	22.00	—

CORDOVA

Non-flint made by the O'Hara Glass Co., Pittsburgh, Pa. It was exhibited for the first time at the Pittsburgh Glass Show, December 16, 1890.

	Clear	Emerald Green
Bowls		
Berry, cov	30.00	—
Finger	16.00	—
Bottle, cologne	20.00	—
Butter, cov, handled	42.00	—
Compotes		
Covered, high standard	37.00	—
Open, high standard	25.00	—
Creamers		
Regular	20.00	—
3½" high, green	—	40.00
Cruet	65.00	—
Inkwell, metal lid	85.00	—
Mug, handled	15.00	30.00

CRYSTAL WEDDING

Non-flint made by Adams Glass Co., Pittsburgh, Pa., in the late 1880s and U. S. Glass Co. in 1891. Also found frosted, ruby stained, and cobalt blue (rare). Heavily reproduced in clear, milk and enamel trim.

	Clear	Ruby Stained
Banana Stand	85.00	—
Bowl, Berry, 8"	28.00	—
Butter, covered	45.00	—
Cake Stand, 10"	60.00	—
Cake Plate, flat, large with wide edge	45.00	—
Compote, cov, high and low standard	95.00	—
Creamer	50.00	—
Goblet	40.00	—
Plates		
8"	18.00	35.00
10"	25.00	40.00
Pitcher, water, sq	155.00	—
Salts, individual	22.50	—
Spooner	40.00	65.00
Sugar, covered	50.00	—
Toothpick	50.00	—
Tumbler	45.00	—
Wine	42.00	—

CRYSTALINA

Made by Hobbs Glass Co., Pittsburgh, Pa., in 1880; later carried on by U. S. Glass Co. Made in clear with ruby stained edge on all pieces.

Bowl, Berry, 8", square	17.50
Butter, covered	50.00
Butter, pats, leaf shaped	12.50
Celery, flat, oblong, shaped like leaf	40.00
Creamer	
Individual, small	15.00
Regular	18.50
Cup, short handle, 4" underplate, set, (rare)	50.00
Pickle or Relish, leaf shaped	15.00
Plates	
7", shape of leaf	20.00
10", round	25.00
Platter, or Bread Tray, 19"	30.00
Sauces	
Leaf shaped with handles	7.50
Square	8.25
Spooner	15.00
Sugar	
Covered	22.50
Open, called "Berry sugar"	17.00

CUPID AND VENUS

Non-flint made by Hartley Glass Co., Tarentum, Pa., in the late 1870s.

	Amber	Clear
Bowls		
8" cov, footed	—	124.00
9", oval	—	32.00
10", ftd, scalloped rim	—	124.00
Butter, covered	—	65.00
Cake Plate	—	40.00
Celery Vase	—	40.00
Champagne	—	115.00
Compotes		
Covered, 8", high standard	—	100.00
Open, 9¼", high standard	—	50.00
Cordial	—	50.00
Creamer	—	35.00
Cruet, stoppered	—	75.00
Goblet	—	54.50
Marmalade Jar, orig, glass lid	—	50.00
Milk Pitcher	145.00	60.00

	Amber	Clear
Mugs		
2½″	—	35.00
3½″	—	40.00
Pitcher, water	190.00	62.50
Plate, 10″, round	115.00	25.00
Sauces		
Flat	—	6.00
Footed, 3½″, 4″and		
4½″, av.	—	9.50
Spooner	—	35.00
Sugar, covered	—	65.00
Tray, Bread	69.00	42.00
Wine	—	100.00

CURRANT

Non-Flint, made by Campbell, Jones and Co., and patented in 1871.

Butter, covered	55.00
Cake Stand, 9½″	70.00
Celery Vase	60.00
Compotes	
8″, high standard, covered	55.00
8″, low standard	45.00
Cordial	32.50
Creamer, applied handle	52.00
Egg Cup	22.50
Goblet, regular, large	27.50
Pitcher, water, applied handle	75.00
Plates, oval, 5″ x 7″ and 6″ x 9″	25.–30.00
Salt, footed	20.00
Sauce, footed, 4″and 5″	10.–11.00
Spooner	30.00
Sugar	
Covered	45.00
Open, buttermilk type	35.00
Tumbler, footed	27.50
Wine	30.00

CURRIER AND IVES

Non-flint made by Bellaire Glass Co. in Findlay, Ohio in 1890. Known to have been made in colors, but rarely found.

Bowl, oval 10″ canoe shaped	30.00
Butter, covered	50.00

Compotes	
Covered	55.00
Open	48.00
Cordial	18.50
Creamer	27.50
Cup and saucer	45.00
Dish, oval, boat shaped, 8″	27.50
Egg Cup	15.00
Goblet, plain and knob stem	26.00
Lamp, 9½″, high standard	75.00
Pitcher, water	40–60.00
Plate, 10″, round with handles	20.00
Relish	8.50
Sauce, oval	10.00
Salt and Pepper Shakers, single	12.50
Spooner	20.00
Sugar, covered	35.00
Syrup	45.00
Tray, water, "Balky Mule"	50.00
Water Bottle or Wine Bottle, about	
12″ tall, original stopper	47.50
Wine	16.50

CUT LOG
(Cat's Eye and Block)

Non-flint, made by Greensburg Glass Co., 1888. Also reported in camphor glass, but rare.

Biscuit Jar	50.00
Bowl, 10″, deep, footed and scalloped	40.00
Butter, covered	70.00
Cake Stand, large	57.50
Celery Tray	15.00
Celery Vase	37.50
Compotes	
Covered, 7¼ to 8″	85.00
Covered, 12½″	95.00
Open, 8″, high standard	35.00

Open, 10″, high standard	85.00
Creamer, 5″	25.00
Cruet, orig patterned, stopper	50.00
Dish, candy	25.00
Dish, olive	18.00
Goblet	45.00
Honey Dish, square	40.00
Mug	16.00
Mustard Jar	22.50
Nappy, handled	18.50
Pitcher, water, applied handle	85.00
Relish, boat shaped	47.50
Sauce, flat	7.50
Spooner	30.00
Sugar, covered	47.50
Tumbler	30.00
Wine	25.00

DAISY AND BUTTON WITH NARCISSUS
(Daisy and Button with Clear Lily)

Sometimes found with flowers flashed with cranberry flashing and pieces trimmed in gold. Non-flint made in late 1890s. Later made by Indiana Glass Co., Dunkirk, Ind., into 1920s.

	Clear	With Color
Bowl, 6 x 9¼″, oval, ftd	35.00	—
Butter, covered	40.00	—
Celery, flat	25.00	—
Compote, open	35.00	—
Creamer	25.00	—
Cup, sherbert or punch	9.00	12.00
Decanter, stoppered	45.00	53.00
Goblet	20.00	—
Pitcher, water	50.00	62.00
Sauce, footed, 4″	8.50	—
Salt and Pepper Shakers, single	15.00	—
Spooner	30.00	—
Sugar, covered	25.00	36.00
Tray, water or wine, 10″	25.00	38.00
Tumbler	18.00	—
Water Set, 9 pcs.	—	185.00
Wine	15.00	18.00

DAKOTA
(Baby Thumbprint; Thumbprint Band)

Non-flint made by Ripley and Co., Pittsburgh, Pa., in the late 1880s and early 1890s. Later reissued by U. S. Glass Co. as one of the States' patterns. Prices listed are for etched fern and berry pattern; also found with oak leaf etching. Sometimes comes with ruby stain on pieces. Some very rare pieces were made in cobalt blue.

	Clear Etched	Clear Plain
Basket	165.00	—
Bowl, Berry, or Finger	45.00	30.00
Butter, covered	78.00	70.00
Cake Stand, 10½″	55.00	45.00
Castor Set, wire frame and handle,		
2 oil bottles and salt and pepper	165.00	—
Compotes, covered		
5″and 6″, Jelly compotes	65.00	50.00
12″, used in bakery trade	110.00	—
Creamer	55.00	30.00
Cruet	55.00	30.00
Egg Cup	—	16.00
Goblet	39.00	25.00
Pitcher, water	95.00	75.00
Sauce, footed	13.50	8.00
Salt Shakers, single	—	27.00
Spooner	49.00	38.00
Sugar, covered	65.00	55.00
Tumbler	38.00	32.00
Tray, water	77.00	—
Wine	30.00	23.00

DEER AND PINE TREE
(Deer and Doe)

Non-flint pattern, made by Belmont Glass Co., and McKee Glass Co. c1883. Although this pattern has been reported to have been made in colors, it is seldom encountered except in the platters.

	Clear	Color
Bowl, waste	40.00	—
Bread Tray	32.00	45.00

	Clear	Color
Butter, covered	50.00	75.00
Cake Stand	60.00	—
Celery Vase	45.00	—
Compotes, open, high standard		
7″	40.00	—
9″	55.00	—
Creamer	35.00	45.00
*Goblet	30.00	—
Marmalade Jar, cov	45.00	—
Mug, large	22.00	30.00
Pickle	22.50	—
Pitcher, water	60.00	90.00
*Platter, 8 x 13″	55.00	—
Sauce, footed	27.00	—
Spooner	40.00	—
Sugars		
Covered	50.00	—
Open	35.00	—
Tray, water, 9 x 15″	60.00	75.00

DEW AND RAINDROP

Non-flint, made in the 1880s and continued by the Jenkins Glass Co. in 1900. In the 1890s and until 1903, it was reissued by the Kokomo Glass Co., Kokomo, Ind., of lesser quality without tiny dew drops on stem. Prices listed for the earlier 1880 pattern.

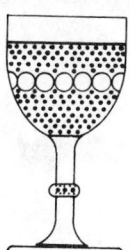

Bowl, Berry	25.00
Butter, covered	50.00
Cake Stand, 9″	40.00
Compote, covered, small	45.00
Cordial	35.00

Creamer	35.00
*Goblet	32.50
Pitcher, water	60.00
Salt and Pepper Shakers, single	15.00
Spooner	27.50
Sugar, covered	45.00
Tumbler	15.00
Vase, scalloped top	20.00

DEWDROP WITH STAR

Non-flint made by Campbell, Jones and Co., Pittsburgh, Pa., in 1877. There was no goblet made originally with this pattern.

Bowls, on collared bases, 7″	20.00
Butter, covered, dome lid	75.00
Cake Stand, very large	60.00
Compotes, covered with large domed lids	
High standard	75.00
Low standard	65.00
Open, high standard	42.50
Cheese Dish, covered, large domed	105.00
Creamer, applied handle	40.00
Honey Dish, plate with large domed cover	65.00
Lamp, patented, 1876	100.00
Pitcher, water, applied handle	100.00 +
*Plate, 9″	25.00
Relish	12.50
*Salts, footed	20.00
Sauces	
Flat	7.50
Footed	8.50
Spooner	32.50
Sugar, covered, domed lid as on compotes and butter	55.00
*Tray, Bread, sheaf of wheat in center	35.00

DIAGONAL BAND WITH FAN

Non-flint, made by Ripley & Co. of Pittsburgh and continued by U. S. Glass after 1891.

Butter, covered	40.00
Celery, scalloped top	22.00

	Flint	Non-Flint
Cake Stand, 14"	185.00	—
Candlesticks	145.00 +	—
Celery, K-S	65.00	30.00
Champagne	69.00	—
Claret, K-S	60.00	—
Compotes		
Covered, 8", high standard	75.00	—
Open, 7½", low standard	48.00	—
Creamer, applied handle	138.00	—
Decanter, stoppered, qt	95.00	—
Egg Cup	35.00	18.00
Goblet	45.00	39.00
Honey	25.00	—
Mustard, with Brittania cover	25.00	—
Pitchers		
Pint	60.00	—
Quart	100.00	—
Plates		
6"	30.00	—
8"	50.00	—
Pepper, with cut neck, Brittania		
screw cap	20.00	—
Salt, master, cov	50.00	—
Spooner	45.00	25.00
Syrup	75.00	—
Sugar		
Covered	65.00	—
Open, buttermilk type	22.50	18.00
Tumblers		
Bar	65.00	35.00
Whiskey, handled	85.00	—
Wine	78.00	30.00

Champagne, 5¼"	25.00
Compotes	
Covered, high standard, 6", 7¼",	
9"	35–45.00
Open, low standard, 6¾" and 9" .	30–35.00
Creamer	27.50
Goblet, 6", 6¼", 6½	25.00
Marmalade Jar, covered	35.00
Pickle	18.00
Pitcher, water	45.00
Plates	
6"	12.00
8"	18.00
Sauce, footed	5.50
Salt and Pepper Shakers, single . .	20.00
Spooner	20.00
Sugar, covered	35.00
Wine	18.00

DIAMOND POINT

Flint originally made by Boston and Sandwich Glass Co., in the 1830–1840 period, and by the New England Glass Co. Many other companies manufactured this pattern throughout the 19th century.

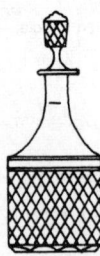

DIAMOND PYRAMIDS

Non-flint made by Fostoria Glass Co., Moundsville, W. Va., c1902.

	Flint	Non-Flint
Bowls		
7", covered	60.00	20.00
8", covered	60.00	20.00
8", open	42.50	15.00
Butter, covered	95.00	50.00

Bowl, Berry	12.50
Butter, covered	35.00
Creamer	17.50
Cruet, with facetted stopper	30.00
Pitcher, water	45.00
Salt and Pepper Shakers, single . .	12.50
Spooner	12.00
Sugar, covered	22.00
Toothpick	20.00
Tumbler	12.50

DIAMOND THUMBPRINT

Flint attributed to Boston and Sandwich Glass Co. and other factories from 1840 to the 1850s.

Bowl, waste	85.00
Butter, covered	165.00
Celery, scalloped top	185.00
Champagne	225.00
Compotes	
Plain, open, 8″, low standard	55.00
Scalloped, open 8″, low standard	65.00
Cordial	150.00
Creamer	165.00
Decanters	
Pint, no stopper	75.00
Quart, original stopper	100.00
*Goblet	350.00+
Honey Dish	15.00
Pitcher, water	400.00+
Spooner	75.00
Sugar, covered	135.00
Tumblers	
Water	95.00
Whiskey, 3″	125.00
Whiskey, handled	300.00
Wine	225.00

DICKINSON

Made by the Boston and Sandwich Glass Co. sometime during the 1860s. It is always bell-toned flint and has been found only in clear glass.

Butter, covered	58.00
Creamer, applied handle	55.00
Compote, open, 5½″	65.00
Goblet	45.00
Pitcher, water, heavy applied ear-shaped handle	130.00

Sauce	10.00
Spooner	38.00
Sugar, covered	62.00

DOYLE'S SHELL
(Shell #2, Cube and Fan #2, Knight)

Made by Doyle and Co., Pittsburgh, Pa., in 1866 and continued by U. S. Glass Co., to about 1892.

	Clear	Emerald Green
Bowls		
Berry	15.00	—
Waste	18.50	27.00
Butter, covered	45.00	52.00
Cake stand	30.00	—
Celery Tray, long, flat	18.00	25.00
Celery Vase	22.00	—
Creamer	20.00	30.00
Goblet	15.00	28.00
Mug	18.00	23.00
Nappies, handled	16.00	—
Pitcher, water	45.00	—
Pickle dish	15.00	—
Salt and Pepper Shakers, single	12.00	—
Spooner	18.00	22.00
Sugar, covered	27.00	35.00
Tray, water	35.00	—
Tumbler	9.00	15.00
Wine	16.00	—

DRAPERY
(Lace)

Non-flint made by Doyle and Co., Pittsburgh, Pa. in the 1870s. Reportedly made by Sandwich Glass Co. at an earlier period.

Butter, covered	45.00
Creamer, applied handle	35.00
Egg Cup	19.00
Goblet	28.00
Pitcher, water, applied handle	60.00
Plate, 6″	30.00
Spooner	30.00
Sugar, covered	25.00

EGG IN SAND

Non-flint, c1880s. Has been reported in colors, but rare.

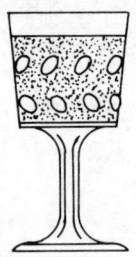

Butter, covered	45.00
Cake Stand	35.00
Compote, covered	45.00
Creamer	27.50
Goblet	28.50
Jam Jar	32.50
Pitcher, water	37.50
Punch Cup	18.00
Relish	12.50
Salt and Pepper Shakers, single	14.00
Spooner	30.00
Sugar, covered	37.50
Tray	
Bread	27.50
Water	32.50
Tumbler	36.50
Wine	18.00

EGYPTIAN

Non-flint, made by Boston and Sandwich Glass Co., c1870s.

Butter, covered	75.00
Celery Vase	60.00
Compote, covered, 7″, high standard	75.00
Creamer	27.50
Goblet	40.00
Honey	14.50
Pickle, oval	20.00
Pitcher, water	80.00
Plate, 12″, handled, Pyramids	45.00

Relish	20.00
Sauce, footed, 4½″	15.00
Spooner	27.50
Sugar, covered	75.00
Trays, Bread	
9″ x 12″, "Cleopatra"	47.50
"Salt Lake Temple"	175.00

ELECTRIC

Made by U. S. Glass Co about 1891. Colors would be 20% more than the price given. It was made in about 40 pieces.

Biscuit Jar, covered	50.00
Bowl, Berry	12.00
Butter, covered	45.00
Cake Stand, various sizes	30–40.00
Compote	
Covered	45.00
Jelly, open	15.00
Creamer, tankard shape	32.00
Goblet	26.00
Jam Jar	40.00
Mug	15.00
Pitcher, water	55.00
Relish	14.50
Salt Shaker, single	29.50
Spooner	25.00
Sugar, covered	40.00
Syrup Jug	52.00
Toothpick	42.00
Tray, water	45.00
Tumbler	12.00

EMPRESS
(Double Arch #2)

Made by Riverside Glass Works, Wellsburg, W. Va., c1898.

	Clear	Emerald Green
Breakfast Set, individual creamer and sugar	55.00	—
Butter, covered	50.00	100.00
Celery Vase	55.00	—
Creamer	32.00	62.00
Cruet	65.00	108.00
Mustard	68.00	—
Oil Lamp	60.00	—
Pitcher, water	85.00	175.00
Salt and Pepper Shakers, pr	125.00	—
Spooner	37.50	45.00
Sugar Shaker	47.50	110.00
Tumbler	30.00	55.00

ESTHER #2
(Tooth and Claw)

Non-flint made by Riverside Glass Works of Wellsburgh, W. Va., c1896.

	Clear	Green
Bowl, 8″	135.00	—
Butter, cov	65.00	80.00
Cake Stand, 10½″	45.00	55.00
Celery Vase	50.00	62.00
Compote, cov, 5″, low standard (Jelly)	47.50	—

	Clear	Green
Creamer	62.00	85.00
Cruet, stoppered	45.00	65.00
Goblet	30.00	—
Pitcher, water	80.00	110.00
Salt and Pepper Shakers, single	22.00	—
Spooner	35.00	—
Sugar, cov	55.00	—
Toothpick	47.50	—
Tumbler	18.00	35.00
Wine	25.00	—

EXCELSIOR

Flint made by several firms from 1850s–1860s. Quality and design vary. Prices are for high quality flint.

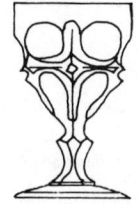

Bar Bottle	50.00
Bowl, 10″, open	125.00
Bitters Bottle	25.00
Butter, covered	100.00
Candlestick	125.00
Celery Vase, scalloped top	50.00
Claret	45.00
Compotes	
Covered, low standard	125.00
Open, high standard	85.00
Cordial	40.00
Covered Pickle Jar	45.00
Creamer	70.00
Egg Cups	
Double	35.00
Single	40.00
Goblet, with Maltese Cross	52.50
Lamp, hand	95.00
Pitcher, water	275.00+
Salt, master	22.00
Spooner	75.00
Sugar, covered	90.00
Tumblers	
Bar	35.00
Whiskey with Maltese Cross	65.00
Wine	40.00

EYEWINKER

Non-flint made in Findlay, Ohio, in 1889. This pattern reportedly made by Dalzell, Gilmore

and Leighton Glass Co., who were organized in 1883 in West Virginia, moved to Findlay in 1888. It was made originally only in clear glass; colors have been reproduced. A goblet and toothpick were not made originally in this pattern.

Banana Dish	85.00
Bowl, 9″	45.00
Butter, covered	67.50
Cake Stand, two sizes	75–85.00
Celery	55.00
Compotes	
Open, 7¼″, with fluted edge	65.00
Jelly, open, 4½″	32.50
Compote with turned up side	35.00
Creamer	35.00
Cruet	65.00
Lamp, Kerosene	92.50
Nappies, bent sides, 7¼″	22.50
Pitcher, water	60.00
Plate	
10″, turned up sides	65.00
Square, with upturned rims	30.00
Syrup, with pewter top	110.00
*Salt and Pepper Shakers, single . .	22.50
*Spooner	32.50
Sugar, covered	50.00
*Tumbler	20.00

FAN WITH DIAMOND

Non-flint, made by McKee Glass Co.

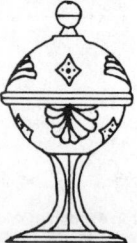

Bowl, flat, oval	12.50
Butter, covered	35.00
Compote, covered, high standard . .	45.00
Cordial	15.00
Creamer, applied handle	45.00
Egg Cup	20.00
Goblet	22.50
Pitcher, water	45.00
Spooner	25.00
Sugars	
Covered	35.00
Open, buttermilk type	21.00
Wine	25.00

FEATHER
(Doric)

Non-flint made in Indiana in 1896 and by McKee Glass. Later the pattern was reissued with variations and quality. A pattern rapidly gaining in popularity.

	Clear	Emerald Green
Banana Dish	65.00	75.00
Bowl, 8″, square	15.00	—
Butter, covered	50.00	—
Cake Plate, 18″	34.00	—
Cake Stand, 9½	35.00	—
Celery Vase	18.50	—
Claret	40.00	—
Compotes		
Covered, 8¼″, low standard	35.00	—
Jelly, 4¼″, cov	25.00	—
Creamer	45.00	—
Cruet, stoppered	46.50	85.00
Dishes, nest of 3, 7″, 8″, and 9″	40.00	—
Goblet	55.00	60.00
Marmalade Jar	45.00	—
Molasses Container	90.00	—
Pitchers		
Milk	42.00	—
Water	50.00	—
Plates, 10″	18.00	—
Salt and Pepper Shakers, single	15.00	—
Spooner	27.00	—
Sugar, covered	35.00	—
Toothpick	50.00	—
Tumbler	58.00	—
Wine, straight and scalloped		
border	35.00	—

FEATHER DUSTER
(Rosette Medallion, Huckel)

Made by United States Glass Co. in 1898, and probably by another company around 1895.

	Clear	Emerald Green
Bowls, Berry		
9″	22.00	—
Waste	20.00	—
Butter, covered	45.00	—
Cake Stand	35.00	—
Celery	22.00	—
Compote		
Covered, high standard	42.50	—
Open, low standard	22.50	—
Creamer	15.00	—
Goblet	30.00	—
Pitcher, water	45.00	55.00
Plate, 9″	22.00	—
Relish or Pickle	18.00	—
Spooner	24.00	—
Sugar, covered	35.00	—
Tray, "McKinley Gold Standard Tray," full length portrait of McKinley, Feather Duster background, 1896	75.00	—
Tumbler	12.00	—

FESTOON

Non-flint, 1890–1894. This pattern contains over 100 pieces. No goblet was made originally in this pattern.

Bowls	
4¼″, Waste	10.00
8″, Berry	20.00
9″, rectangular, flat	18.50
Butter, covered	50.00
Cake Stand, 10″	35.00
Compotes	
Covered, high standard	50.00
Open, high standard	30.00
Creamer	24.00
Mug	15.00
Pickle Jar, covered	40.00
Pitcher, water	50.00
Plate, 8¼″	25.00
Spooner	18.00
Sugar, covered	35.00
Tray, water, 10″	30.00
Tumbler, two sizes	25.00
Wine	17.50

FINE RIB

Flint made by New England Glass Co. in the 1860s. Later made in non-flint.

	Flint	Non-Flint
Bitters Bottle	50.00	—
Bowl, 7″, cov	85.00	—
Butter, cov	75.00	—
Castor Bottle	25.00	—
Celery	50.00	39.00
Champagne	68.00	—
Compotes		
Covered, 7″, 8″, high standard	30.00	—
Open, 9″, 10″, low standard	60.00	35.00
Cordial	45.00	—
Creamer, applied handle	85.00	—
Decanters		
Bar lip, quart	65.00	—
Stopper, quart	85.00	—
Egg Cup	37.00	19.00
Goblet	45.00	40.00
Lamp	150.00	—
Mug	45.00	—
Pitcher, water, applied handle	95.00	—
Plates, 6″ and 7″	20.00	—

	Flint	Non-Flint
Salts		
Covered, footed	85.00	—
Individual	37.50	—
Spooner	65.00	35.00
Sugar, cov	65.00	35.00
Tumbler, Bar	45.00	—
Tumble-up	125.00	—
Whiskey, handled	65.00	14.00
Wine	38.00	22.00

FISH SCALE
(Coral)

Non-flint made by Bryce Brothers, Pittsburgh, Pa., in the mid-1880s and by U. S. Glass Co. in 1891.

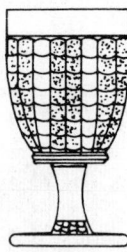

Bowls	
Covered	22.50
Open, 8″	12.50
Waste	15.00
Butter, covered	50.00
Cake Plate	55.00
Cake Stand, 9″ and 10½″	25–32.50
Celery	24.00
Compote, Jelly	25.00
Creamer	30.00
Goblet	28.00
Lamp, Finger	75.00
Mug, large	25.00
Pitchers	
Milk	30.00
Water	55.00
Plates	
7″, round	15.00
9″, square	27.50
Salt and Pepper Shakers, single	30.00
Spooner	20.00
Sugar, covered	40.00
Tray, condiment, rectangular	35.00
Tumbler	22.50

FLEUR DE LYS AND DRAPE
(Fleur de Lys and Tassel)

Non-flint made by U. S. Glass Co., c1892.

Comes in clear and emerald green, with occasional gold trim. Also made in milk glass but rare. Made in many pieces and forms.

	Clear	Emerald Green
Bowls	15.00	30.00
Butter, covered	45.00	55.00
Cake Stand	35.00	—
Compote, covered	35.00	—
Creamer	25.00	42.00
Cruet, stoppered, various sizes	45.00	85.00
Goblet	32.50	—
Mustard Jar, covered	27.00	48.00
Pitcher, water	49.00	—
Plates, 8″	20.00	35.00
Spooner	21.00	35.00
Sugar, covered	30.00	55.00
Syrup, metal top	50.00	85.00
Tumbler	20.00	32.00
Water Tray, 11½″	24.00	50.00
Wine	18.00	23.00

FLOWER POT
(Potted Plant)

Non-flint, c1880s. No goblet has been found.

Bowl, Berry, 8″	18.00
Butter, covered	47.50
Creamer	30.00
Pitcher, water	40.00
Salt and Pepper Shakers, single	20.00
Spooner	22.50
Sugar, covered	37.50
Tray, Bread	47.50

FROSTED CIRCLE

Produced by Bryce Bros., Pittsburgh, Pa., from 1876 to c1885. Later by U. S. Glass Co. in the late 1890s.

	Flint	Non-Flint
Pitcher, water	250.00 +	—
Sauce, flat, 2 sizes	25.00	—
Spooner	35.00	25.00
Sugar, covered	70.00	48.00
Tumbler		
Footed	85.00	—
Regular	90.00	—
Wine	35.00	—

	Clear Circle	Frosted Circle
Bowl, covered		
7"	—	25.00
8"	—	30.00
Butter, covered	45.00	55.00
Cake Stand, 8"	—	35.00
Compotes		
Covered, high standard		
7"	25.00	35.00
8"	40.00	40.00
Open, 10", high standard	39.00	45.00
Creamer	—	38.00
Cruet, stoppered	—	65.00
*Goblet	32.00	35.00
Pitcher, water	—	50.00
Plates		
4"	10.00	22.00
9"	12.00	17.00
Sauce, footed	8.00	10.00
Salt and Pepper Shakers, single	—	28.00
Spooner	—	35.00
Sugar, covered	42.00	50.00
Sugar Shaker	—	60.00
Tumbler	20.00	30.00

FROSTED RIBBON

Non-flint made by George Duncan and Sons, Pittsburgh, Pa., in 1870s. Comes in several variations, e.g., frosted and alternating clear panels or etched. Over 26 different style compotes documented.

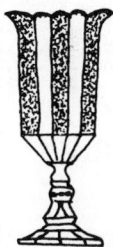

FROSTED LEAF

Flint, c1850s. Listed as being produced by Portland Glass Co. between 1863 and 1874. Later made in non-flint.

	Flint	Non-Flint
Butter, covered	110.00	50.00
Celery Vase	52.00	40.00
Champagne	95.00	—
Compote, covered	100.00	—
Creamer	60.00	35.00
Decanter, stoppered, qt	125.00	—
*Goblet, two sizes, av.	47.50	—

Bitters Bottle	45.00
Bowl, waste	40.00
Butter, covered	47.50
Celery	32.50
Creamer	37.50
Egg Cup	18.00
*Goblet	32.50
Pitcher, water	60.00
Salt, footed	16.50
Spooner	30.00
Sugar, covered	55.00
Tumbler	28.00
Wine	20.00

GALLOWAY
(Virginia #2)

Non-flint made by United States Glass Co., 1904. Clear glass with gold trim, sometimes with cranberry flashing. See Introduction for more about this pattern.

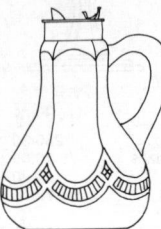

	Clear w/ gold	Cranberry Flashed
Bowls		
Berry, 2 types	26.00	50.00
Punch, 15¼″	95.00	—
Butter, cov, large and small	45.00	85.00
Cake Plate	27.00	—
Carafe, water	48.00	75.00
Celery	28.00	—
Creamer		
Child's	27.50	—
Regular	30.00	48.00
Cruet	45.00	—
Goblet	65.00	—
Lemonade, handled	35.00	—
Nappy, handled	18.00	—
Punch Cup	6.50	15.00
Plate, round	22.00	—
Pitcher, water, ice lip	55.00	—
Salt and Pepper Shakers, single	25.00	—
Sugar, covered	35.00	—
Syrup	35.00	—
Toy Water Pitcher	22.00	—
Toy Water Set, 7 pcs	55.00	—
Tumbler, handled	35.00	52.00
Wine	55.00	—

Creamer	38.00
Cup	18.50
Dish, oval	12.00
Goblet	60.00
Mug	48.00
Pickle, oval	18.00
Pitcher, water	65.00
Plate, 6½″, handled	18.00
Salt, Master	30.00
Spooner	25.00
Sugar, covered	50.00
Toothpick	45.00
Tray, Bread, with motto	30.00

GARDEN OF EDEN
(Lotus and Serpent)

Non-flint, c1870s.

Bowl, 4½″ x 7″, oval	17.50
Butter, covered	75.00
Cake Stand, 11½″	50.00
Celery	25.00
Compote, covered, 10″, high standard	60.00

GARFIELD DRAPE

Non-flint pattern issued in 1881 by Adams and Co., Pittsburgh, Pa., after the assassination of President Garfield.

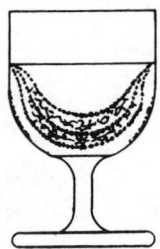

Bowl, 6″	17.50
Butter, covered	55.00
Cake Stand, 9½″	60.00
Celery	35.00
Compote, covered, 8″, high standard	75.00
Creamer	35.00
Goblet	25.00
Pitcher, water	55.00
Plates	
"Memorial," portrait of Garfield	65.00
"We Mourn Our Nation's Loss," portrait of Garfield	75.00
Relish, oval	18.00

Sauce, footed	6.50
Spooner	28.00
Sugars	
Covered	45.00
Open, buttermilk type	20.00
Tumblers	
Garfield likeness in base	35.00
Regular pattern	22.50

Butter, covered	95.00
Creamer	85.00
Pitcher, water	235.00
Plate, 10"	75.00
Salt Shaker, single	50.00
Spooner	50.00
Sugar, covered	75.00
Tumbler	65.00

GIANT BULL'S EYE
(Bull's Eye Variation, Findlay's)

Made by Bellaire Glass Co., Findlay, Ohio and continued by U. S. Glass Co. after 1891. Made in many pieces; known only in clear.

Bottle, Brandy tall, narrow, ground stopper	55.00
Claret Jug, tankard shape	60.00
Compote, covered	50.00
Cruet, orig stopper	60.00
Decanter, orig stopper	48.00
Goblet	35.00
Lamp, night light, handled	75.00
Pitcher, water	65.00
Tumbler	30.00
Vases, 3 sizes	25–40.00
Wine	22.00
Wine Tray, 7¼"	25.00

GIBSON GIRL

Non-flint, early 1904. Made by Kokomo Glass Co.

GOOSEBERRY

Non-flint of the 1880s. Made at Boston & Sandwich Glass Co. and others in clear and milk glass. Reproduced in milk glass.

	Clear	Milk
Butter, covered	50.00	—
Compote, cov, 8", high standard	50.00	—
Creamer	27.00	50.00
Goblet	27.00	45.00
Mug	25.00	35.00
Pitcher, water, applied handle	65.00	—
Spooner	24.00	—
Sugars		
Covered	45.00	—
Open, buttermilk type	35.00	—
Syrup, applied handle	57.50	87.00
Tumbler	29.50	—

GOTHIC

Flint made by McKee & Bros. in the 1860s. Possibly reissued in the 1870s.

Bowl, fruit	75.00
Butter, covered	85.00

Castor Bottle	20.00
Celery Vase	115.00
Champagne	95.00
Compote	
Covered, 8″	110.00
Open, 7″	50.00
Cordial	55.00
Creamer	75.00
Egg Cup	27.50
Goblet	35.00
Sauce, flat	18.00
Spooner	40.00
Sugars	
Covered	70.00
Open	40.00
Tumbler	85.00
Wine	60.00

GRAND
(Diamond Medallion)

Non-flint, made by Bryce, Higbee and Co., 1885.

Bowls	
Covered, 6″	27.50
Waste, collared	16.00
Butter, covered	
Flat	35.00
Footed	40.00
Cake Stand	
8″	27.50
10″	35.00
Celery Vase	18.00
Compote, 9″, high standard, open	35.00
Creamer	17.50
Goblet	25.00
Pitcher, water	50.00
Plate, bread, 10″	20.00
Relish, 7½″, oval	8.00
Salt and Pepper Shakers, single	20.00
Spooner	22.50
Sugar, covered	35.00
Syrup, metal top	55.00
Wine	35.00

GRAPE AND FESTOON WITH CLEAR AND STIPPLED LEAF

Non-flint made by Doyle & Co., Pittsburgh, Pa., in the early 1870s. The variations are: background-clear, leaves-stippled and background-stippled, leaves-clear. Prices apply to both types. Covers have acorn and pine cone finials. A rare variation, Grape and Festoon with shield, has been documented.

Bowl, berry, 7″and 9″	35–45.00
Butter, covered, acorn finial	50.00
Celery Vase	37.50
Compote, open, low standard	75.00
Creamer, applied handle	57.50
Egg Cup	22.50
Goblet	27.50
Mug	18.00
Pitchers	
Milk	65.00
Water, applied handle	85.00
Relish	12.50
Salt, footed	15.00
Sauce, flat, 4″	8.00
Spooner	40.00
Sugar, covered	45.00
Wine	20.00

GRAPE BAND

Issued in flint by Bryce, Walker and Co. in the late 1850s; non-flint in 1869.

	Flint	Non-Flint
Butter, covered	75.00	50.00
Compotes, covered		
High standard	—	49.00
Low, open, high standard	—	20.00
Creamer, applied handle	—	47.00
Egg Cup	—	18.00
Goblet	37.00	24.00
Pickle	—	12.50
Pitcher, water	—	60.00
Plate, 6"	—	15.00
Spooner	—	30.00
Sugars		
Covered	—	45.00
Open, buttermilk type	—	35.00
Tumbler, whiskey, grape band variant-top, Ashburton-type base	—	45.00
Wine	32.00	25.00

GRASSHOPPER
(Long Spear)

Maker unknown; over 40 pieces documented. Pieces without the grasshopper bring 20% less.

	Amber	Clear
Bowls		
Covered	—	27.00
Footed, open	—	20.00
Butter, covered	—	50.00
Celery	85.00	75.00
Compote, cov, 8½", high standard	—	55.00
Creamer	—	29.00
Marmalade Jar, cov, with insert	—	115.00
Pickle	—	16.00
Pitcher, water	110.00	—
Salt, master, footed	—	16.00
Spooner	40.00	37.00
Sugars, covered	—	65.00

GREEN HERRINGBONE
(Panelled Herringbone, Florida States' pattern.)

Non-flint made by U. S. Glass Co., c. late 1880s–1890s. Found in emerald green, clear and milk glass. Should always be called Green Herringbone.

	Clear	Emerald Green
Bowl, 9"	18.00	20.00
Butter, covered	40.00	50.00
Cake Stand	27.00	38.00
Celery	18.00	28.00
Compote, open, 6½", sq, high standard	—	40.00
Cordial	—	22.50
Creamer	15.00	25.00
Cruet	32.00	45.00
Goblets		
Buttermilk	18.00	25.00
Regular	20.00	27.00
Mustard Pot, notched lid, underplate	25.00	35.00
Pitcher, water	48.00	55.00
Plates		
7½", square	10.00	18.00
9¼"	15.00	21.00
Relishes		
6", square	10.00	12.00
8½", square	10.00	14.00
Salt and Pepper Shakers, single	—	20.00
Spillholder	—	22.50
Spooner	20.00	28.00
Sugars		
Covered	32.00	40.00
Open	18.00	25.00
Syrup	40.00	55.00
Tumbler	20.00	27.00
Wine	—	25.00

HAMILTON AND HAMILTON WITH LEAF

Flint, c1869. Both have same values. Some attribute pattern to Boston and Sandwich Glass Co.; other companies also may have made it.

Butter, covered	65.00
Celery	60.00

Compotes
Covered, high standard	75.00
Open, 6″, scallop rim	77.50
Creamer, applied handle	75.00
Egg Cup, frosted leaf	25.00
Goblet	40.00
Lamp, hand	85.00
Pitcher, water	150.00
Plate, 6″	45.00
Salt, footed	30.00
Spooner	37.50
Sweatmeat Dish, high standard, covered	75.00
Sugar, covered	75.00
Tumblers	
Water or Bar	65.00
Whiskey, handled	95.00
Wine	75.00

HAND
(Pennsylvania #2)

Made by O'Hara Glass Co., Pittsburgh, Pa., c1880s. Covered pieces have a hand holding bar finial, hence the name. Pieces with original lids are rare.

Bowl, 10″	22.50
Butter, covered	85.00
Cake Stand	38.00
Celery	42.50
Compotes	
Covered, high standard	90.00
Open, high standard	45.00
Creamer	37.50

Goblet	47.50
Marmalade Jar, covered	50.00
Pickle	17.50
Pitcher, water	50.00
Platter, 8″ x 10½″, or Bread Tray .	32.50
Sauce, footed	12.50
Spooner	27.50
Sugar, covered	45.00
Wine	38.00

HANOVER
(Block with Stars #2, Blockhouse)

Originally made by Richards and Hartley, of Tarentum, Pa., in 1888 and possible earlier. Made in many pieces.

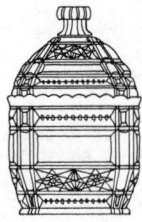

	Clear	Dark Amber
Bowl, Berry, 10″	20.00	40.00
Butter, cov	40.00	80.00
Cake Stand, 10″	42.00	62.00
Celery	27.00	38.00
Cheese Dish, cov 10″	50.00	95.00
Compotes		
Covered, high standard	45.00	90.00
Open, low standard	37.00	45.00
Creamer	30.00	45.00
Goblet	25.00	55.00
Ketchup bottle, pr	50.00	75.00
Mugs		
Large	22.00	47.50
Small	18.00	40.00
Pitcher, water, 2 types	47.50	82.50
Plates		
Small, 4–6″	25.00	40.00
Large, bread, 10″	18.00	30.00
Sauce, footed	10.00	15.00
Spooner	25.00	37.00
Sugar, covered	45.00	55.00
Tumbler	25.00	28.00

HARTFORD

Made by Fostoria Glass Co., Moundsville, W. Va., until about 1930.

	Clear	Emerald Green
Basket, for spoons, flat, handle, turned up sides	18.00	28.00
Bowls, Berry		
6", sq with collared base	8.50	12.00
7"	9.00	11.00
8"	9.00	11.00
Finger bowl, circular, bent up sides	10.00	15.00
Butter, cov, sq	40.00	55.00
Celery	32.50	40.00
Creamer	22.00	28.00
Dish		
5½"sq, olive flat, turned up sides	15.00	25.00
6"sq, sauce, with handle	14.50	18.00
9"rectangular, long	14.50	21.00
Relish, oval, squared	15.00	22.00
Salt Dip, open	6.50	10.00
Salt and Pepper Shakers, pr	45.00	65.00
Sauces, 4½", flat and footed	4.50	8.00
Sugar, covered, 2 shapes		
Regular	35.00	45.00
Tall, covered	40.00	50.00
Syrup, metal top, 2 type tops-flat metal & domed shaped	45.00	75.00
Tumbler	15.00	20.00

HAWAIIAN LEI

Made by Higbee Bryce and Co. during 1900s, in clear; colors not reported. Older pieces are marked with company trade mark — a small bee embossed in glass, with HIG/ and bee.

	Clear
Basket, small, applied handle	37.50
Berry Bowl	
7"	18.50

	Clear	Emerald Green
9"		18.00
Butter, covered		50.00
Cake Stand, 7½"		35.00
Celery vase or tray		15.00
Child's Toy, 4-pc. Table set-complete (signed pcs.)		100.00
Compote, open, 8"		32.50
Creamer		22.00
Dishes, various sizes		12–18.00
Goblet		18.00
Pitcher, water		40.00
Pickle Castor, silver lid		27.50
Rose Bowl		18.00
Salt and Pepper Shakers, single		12.00
Toy Tumbler, children's play set		18.50
Tumbler, regular		13.50
Vase, tall, very flared rim		18.00
Wine		25.00

HEART WITH THUMBPRINT
(Bull's Eye in Heart)

Non-flint, made by Tarentum Glass Co., 1898. Found in clear and emerald green. Made experimentally in custard, opaque nile green and cobalt.

	Clear	Emerald Green
Banana Boat	75.00	—
Bowl, 9"	28.00	—
Barber Bottle	60.00	—
Butter, covered	60.00	110.00
Carafe, water	50.00	—
Card Tray	20.00	—
Celery	39.00	—
Compote, 8½", high standard, open	48.00	—
Creamer, regular	32.50	—
Cruet	75.00	—
Goblet	49.00	55.00
Hair Receiver, metal lid	28.50	—
Ice Bucket	60.00	—
Lamps		
8"	45.00	—
Finger	65.00	—
Nappy, turned up edges	29.00	—
Pitcher, water	58.00	—

Plates	Clear	Emerald Green
6″	24.00	—
10″	45.00	—
Punch Cup	20.00	—
Rose Bowl	30.00	—
Sugar, regular, cov	55.00	—
Syrup	57.00	—
Toothpick	45.00	—
Tumbler	49.00	—
Vase, 10″	42.00	—
Wine	45.00	—

HEAVY PANELLED FINECUT

Made by Geo. Duncan & Sons, Pittsburgh, Pa., c1880s and by U. S. Glass Co., 1891. This pattern is same as "Sequoia"; identified as "Bag Ware" by Heacock. Some handled pieces, such as platter or bread tray, carry small leaves on handles. Also found in amber, blue, and vaseline.

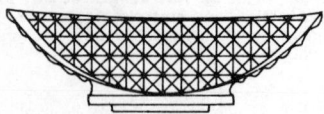

Bowls, Berry, 10″	12.50
Butter, covered	40.00
Cake Stand, three sizes	25-35.00
Castor Set, 5-bottle	75.00
Celery Boat, 11″	30.00
Compote, covered, 8″, high standard	55.00
Creamer	35.00
Goblet	20.00
Pitcher, water	50.00
Platter, handled, or Bread Tray	27.50
Spooner	18.00
Sugar, covered	35.00
Tumbler, Bar	17.50
Tray, small, shaped like large platter, with leaves on handles, 6½″ x 4⅜″	11.50

HICKMAN
(La Clede)

Non-flint pattern made by McKee Glass Co., Pittsburgh, Pa., c1897.

	Clear	Emerald Green
Bowl, Berry	20.00	35.00
Butter, covered	35.00	58.00
Cake Stand, 9½″	30.00	—
Child's Toy condiment set, salt and pepper shakers, 2 cruets on clover shaped tray, complete	—	150.00

	Clear	Emerald Green
Cologne Bottle, facetted stopper	30.00	—
Compote, Jelly, 4½″, open	27.00	32.00
Creamer	25.00	38.00
Dishes		
Bon-Bon, 9″, square	11.00	—
Olive, 4″, long, with handle	10.00	20.00
Square, 4″	16.00	—
Goblet		
Regular	35.00	41.00
Shorter stem (called a Punch Glass)	30.00	—
Jar, mustard, cover and underplate, complete	40.00	—
Pitcher, water	55.00	—
Plate, 9¼″	10.00	—
Punch Cup	10.00	15.00
Rose Bowl	22.00	—
Sauce, 4″, scalloped edge	27.00	—
Salt, individual, flat, sloping sides	8.00	—
Salt and Pepper Shakers		
Round, squat, single		—
Round, with long, cut neck, single	16.00 25.00	—
Spooner	27.00	—
Sugar, covered	26.00	35.00
Sugar Shaker	45.00	—
Tumbler	25.00	—
Vase, 10½″, amethyst	47.50	12.00

HIDALGO
(Frosted Waffle)

Non-flint made by Adams and Co., Pittsburgh, Pa., in the early 1880s. This pattern comes etched and clear, and also with part of pattern frosted. Add 20% for frosted.

	Clear	Amber Stained
Bowls		
10″, square	20.00	—
Waste	18.00	—
Bread Boat, large	58.00	—
Butter, covered	50.00	—
Celery Vase	15.00	32.00

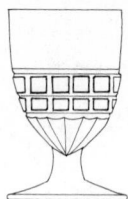

	Clear	Stained
Compote, cov, high standard	37.00	—
Cruets, 2 sizes	40–55.00	—
Cup and Saucer	40.00	—
Goblet	18.00	38.00
Nappy, handled, sq	18.00	—
Pickle or Olive Dish	9.50	16.00
Boat shaped	12.00	—
Pitcher, water	45.00	—
Plate, 10"	25.00	—
Salt, master, sq	12.50	—
Salt and Pepper Shakers, single	16.00	—
Sauces, handled	10.00	—
Spooner	20.00	—
Sugar, covered	35.00	—
Sugar Shaker	45.00	—
Syrup	50.00	—
Tray, water	55.00	—
Tumbler	22.00	—

HOBNAIL BAND

Non-flint, c1900s. Sometimes hobnails are ruby stained.

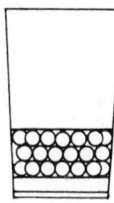

	Clear	Ruby Stained
Bowl, 9¼"	15.00	—
Butter, covered	40.00	58.00
Candlesticks, ball top, pr	35.00	—
Celery Tray	18.00	—
Champagne	12.00	—
Coaster	7.50	—
Creamer	25.00	—
Cup and Saucer	30.00	—
Custard Cup	10.00	—
Goblet	15.00	—
Pitcher, water	35.00	75.00

	Clear	Ruby Stained
Plates		
8", handled	11.00	—
11"	15.00	—
Relish, divided	12.50	—
Salt and Pepper Shakers, matching holder	40.00	—
Sauce, flat	8.50	—
Spooner	20.00	—
Sugar, covered	30.00	—
Tumbler, water	10.00	25.00

HOLLY

Non-flint made by Boston & Sandwich Glass Co., late 1860s, early 1870s.

Butter, covered	135.00
Cake Stand, 11"	85.00
Celery Vase	55.00
Compote, covered, high standard	100.00
Creamer, applied handle	55.00
Egg Cup	27.50
Goblet	80.00
Pitcher, water, applied handle	100.00
Salt, footed	35.00
Spooner	30.00
Sugar, covered	50.00
Tumbler	90.00
Wine	45.00

HONEYCOMB

A popular pattern made in flint and non-flint glass by numerous firms, c1860–1900, resulting in many minor pattern variations.

	Flint	Non-Flint
Ale Glass	60.00	—
Bottles		
Barber	—	22.50
Castor	25.00	15.00
Bowls		
7¼", oval, base marked "Mould patented May 11, 1869," acorn finial on cover	—	35.00
10"	—	40.00
Butter, covered	—	60.00
Celery Vase	35.00	18.00
Champagne	40.00	—
Compotes		
Covered, high standard	55.00	45.00
Open, high standard	40.00	25.00
Creamer, applied handle	39.00	32.50
Decanter		
Pint	—	18.50
Quart, stoppered	—	55.00
Egg Cup	—	15.00
Goblet	25.00	18.00
Honey, covered	—	25.00
Lamps		
All Glass	—	45.00
Marble base	—	38.00
Mug, half pint	—	15.00
Pitcher, water, applied handle	95.00	50.00
Plate, 6"	—	12.50
Pomade Jar	—	15.00
Salt, cov, ftd	—	40.00
Salt and Pepper Shakers, single	—	18.00
Sauce	—	7.50
Spooner	—	20.00
Sugar, covered	—	45.00
Tumblers		
Flat	—	12.50
Footed	—	15.00
Lemonade	40.00	20.00
Wine	25.00	10.00

HONEYCOMB WITH STAR
(Starred Honeycomb)

Non-flint made by Fostoria Glass Co., c1905. Clear and gold trimmed.

Butter, covered	40.00
Cake Stand	30.00
Celery	15.00
Compote, covered, high std	35.00
Creamer	27.50
Cruet	50.00
Nappy, handled	12.50
Spooner	15.00
Sugar, covered	30.00
Tumbler	15.00

HORN OF PLENTY

A fine flint glass pattern reputed to have been first made by Boston & Sandwich Co. in the 1850s. Later made in flint and non-flint by other firms. Prices are for flint.

Bowl, 8½", flat	100.00
Butters, covered	
Conventional, finial	125.00
Head of Washington	400.00
Shape of Acorn	130.00
Cake Stand	350.00+
Celery	165.00
Compotes, open	
7", scalloped rim	125.00
8", high standard	100.00
10½", high standard	135.00
Cordial	95.00
Creamer, regular, applied handle	235.00
Decanters	
Pint	100.00
Quart, stoppered	125.00
Egg Cup	40.00
*Goblet	70.00
Honey, covered, rectangular	500.00
*Lamp, all glass	195.00
Mug, small, handled	155.00
Pitcher, water	300.00+
Plate, 6"	67.50
Relish, 5" x 7"	30.00
Salt, master, oval, flat	75.00
Sauce, 5¼"	22.00
Sauce, bottles, pewter tops	125.00
Spillholder	38.00
Spooner	42.50

Sugar, covered	100.00
Tumblers	
*Water	75.00
Whiskey, 3″	95.00
Whiskey, handled	135.00
Wine	130.00

HORSESHOE
(Good Luck, Prayer Rug)

Non-flint made by Adams & Co. and others in the 1880s.

Bowls	
Covered, 7″ and 8″ x 5″, oval, horseshoe finial,	165.00
Finger	20.00
Waste	40.00
Butter, covered	60.00
Cake Stands	
9″	75.00
10″	95.00
Celery, knob stem	35.00
Cheese, covered, scenic base	275.00
Compotes	
Covered, 7″, horseshoe finial, high standard	50.00
Open, 8″, high standard	67.50
Cordial	150.00
Creamer, Hotel type, 6½″	95.00
Goblet, knob stem, Masonic emblem	35.00
Marmalade Jar, covered	35.00
Pitcher, water	55.00
Plates	
7″	27.50
10″	35.00
Relish, 5″ x 7″	8.00
Salts	
Individual, shape of horseshoe	17.50
Master, shape of horseshoe	50.00
Sherbert, footed	25.00
Spooner	30.00
Sugars	
Covered	55.00
Open	20.00
Trays, Bread	
Double, 10″ x 14″, horseshoe handles	55.00

Single, horseshoe handles	28.50
Vegetable Dish, oval	28.00
Wine	150.00

ILLINOIS

Non-flint. One of the States' Patterns made by U. S. Glass Co. in 1907.

	Clear	Emerald Green
Basket, applied handle, 11½ x 7″	65.00	—
Bowl, 8″	35.00	—
Butter, covered	45.00	—
Celery Tray, 11″	22.00	—
Cheese, covered	50.00	—
Creamers		
Large	34.00	—
Small	18.00	—
Cruet	55.00	—
Lamp, matching shade	—	110.00
Olive	12.00	—
Pitchers, water		
Square	60.00	—
Tankard, silver rim	58.00	93.00
Plate, 7″, sq	21.00	—
Salt and Pepper Shakers, single	15.00	—
Spooner	22.00	—
Straw Holder, metal top	180.00	300.00
Sugar, covered	45.00	—
Sugar Shaker	55.00	—
Syrup, pewter top	95.00	—
Toothpick	30.00	—
Tumbler	15.00	28.00
Vase, 6″ sq	32.00	42.00

INVERTED FERN

Flint, c1860.

Butter, covered	50.00
Compotes	
Open, 8″	55.00
Open, 8¼″	55.00
Cordial	50.00
Creamer, applied handle	85.00
Egg Cup	27.50
Goblet, rayed base	40.00
Plate, 6″	100.00

Pitcher, Water	200.00
Salt, master, footed	27.50
Spooner	30.00
Sugar, covered	75.00
Tumbler	60.00

INVERTED STRAWBERRY

Non-flint, made by Cambridge Glass Co., c1908. Found in ruby stained and souvenir types. No original toothpick made.

	Clear	Ruby Stained
Bowl, 9"	25.00	—
Celery Tray, handled	27.50	—
Compote, open, 5", high std	38.00	—
Cruet	45.00	
Goblet	23.00	—
Mug	18.50	28.00
Nappy	15.00	—
*Pitcher, water	45.00	—
Plate, 10"	22.00	37.00
Punch Cup	11.00	17.00
Relish, 4½ x 7"	11.00	—
Rose Bowl	30.00	—
Salt Dip	20.00	—
Sauce, flat, 4"	18.00	—
Sugars		
Individual	15.00	—
Regular, covered	45.00	—
*Toothpick	25.00	—
Tumbler, Souvenir type	—	45.00

IOWA
(Paneled Zipper)

Non-flint made by United States Glass Co., c1902. Part of the States' Pattern series. Clear glass with gold trim, often found with cranberry flashing. Also in colors, amber, green, and blue, but rare. Add 20% for color. Popular as soda fountain item.

	Clear	Ruby Stained
Bowl, Berry	12.00	—
Butter, covered	45.00	—
Cake Stand	35.00	—
Compote, covered, 8"	40.00	—
Creamer, regular	27.50	—
Goblet	27.00	—
Pitcher, water	50.00	—
Spooner	22.00	—
Table Set, 4 pcs.	—	235.00
Tumbler	12.00	35.00
Wine	24.00	—

IVANHOE

Originally made by Dalzell, Gilmore and Leighton Co., of Findlay, Ohio, in 1897 in a large number of clear pieces. May not have been a good seller.

Butter, covered	40.00
Compote, open, 7"	35.00
Creamer	27.00
Cruet, orig stopper	65.00

Pitcher, water	60.00
Spooner	18.00
Sugar, covered	35.00
Syrup Jug, metal top	75.00
Tumbler	30.00

JACOB'S COAT

Non-flint, c1880. Colors are rare; add 50%.

Bowl, 8″	20.00
Butter, covered	45.00
Celery	26.00
Creamer	22.50
Goblet	30.00

JACOB'S LADDER
(Maltese)

Non-flint made by Bryce Bros., Pittsburgh, Pa., in the 1876 and U. S. Glass Co. in 1891. Reissued in 1890 but of inferior quality.

Bottle, Castor	12.50
Bowls	
7¼″, footed	25.00
Berry, ornate silver holder, ftd	85.00
Butter, covered, Maltese Cross finial	75.00
Cake Stand, 9½″	32.50
Celery	20.00
Compotes, open	
8″, high standard, open	32.50
Dolphin standard	250.00
Creamer	40.00

Goblet	50.00
Honey, covered	65.00
Marmalade Jar	75.00
Pickle	20.00
Pitchers	
Syrup, Knight's head finial	85.00
Syrup, plain top	65.00
Water, applied handles	155.00
Plate, 6½″	30.00
Platters	
8″	20.00
9¾″	28.00
Relish, plain handles	15.00
Salt, master	30.00
Sauces	
Flat, 3½″	8.00
Footed, 4″	20.00
Spooner	35.00
Sugar, covered	40.00
Tumbler, Bar	50.00
Wine	37.50

JEWEL WITH DEWDROP
(Kansas)

Non-flint originally produced by Cooperative Flint Glass Co., Beaver Falls, Pa. Later produced as part of the States' Pattern series by U. S. Glass Co. in 1901. Comes clear, with jewels stained with color.

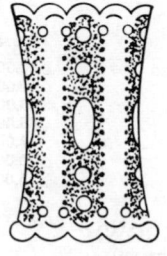

Banana Stand	65.00
Bowl, 7¼″	20.00
Butter, covered	50.00
Cake Stands	
9″	40.00
10″	52.50
Celery	27.50
Compotes, open	
6½″, low standard	40.00
9½″, high standard	50.00
Cordial	28.50
Creamer	25.00
*Goblet	45.00
*Mug, or handled whiskey	10.00
Pitcher, water	50.00

Relish, 8½″	12.50
Salt and Pepper Shakers, single . .	22.50
Sauce, flat	10.00
Spooner	40.00
Sugar, covered	45.00
Syrup	60.00
Toothpick	47.50
Tumbler	35.00
Vegetable Dish, 8½″, ½″ deep . . .	37.50
Wine	40.00

KENTUCKY

Non-flint made by U. S. Glass Co., c1897 as part of the States' Pattern series. The goblet is found in ruby stained and is valued at $50.00.

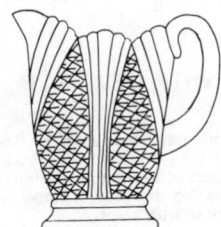

	Clear	Emerald Green
Butter, covered	47.00	—
Cruet	42.00	—
Goblet	20.00	—
Pitcher, water	45.00	—
Punch Cup	7.00	13.00
Toothpick	28.00	48.00
Wine	16.00	40.00

KING'S CROWN
(Ruby Thumbprint)

Known as "Ruby Thumbprint" when pieces are ruby-stained. A non-flint pattern made by Adams and Co., Pittsburgh, Pa., in the 1890s and later. Made in clear, with the thumbprints stained amethyst, green, and sometimes yellow; and clear, with etching and trimmed in gold. It became very popular after 1891 as souvenir ware, often ruby stained and etched with names and places. There have been reported some very rare pieces in cobalt blue. Approximately 87 pieces documented.

NOTE: Pattern has been copiously reproduced for the gift trade market. New pieces are very easily distinguished. In the case of Ruby Thumbprint, the color is a very pale pinkish red; collectors are not apt to mistake it. Also new pieces are in a very off-color green and blue. Pieces with amethyst, green, and yellow stain and gold thumbprints are very likely old ones.

	Clear	Ruby Stained
Banana Dish, flat	92.00	—
Banana Stand	100.00	135.00
Berry Set, bowl and sauces .	—	195.00
Bowl, 9″	30.00	89.00
Bowl, 10″ scalloped edge . . .	45.00	—
Butter, covered	45.00	90.00
Cake Plate, 10″	27.50	—
Cake Stand		
9″	35.00	50.00
12½″	90.00	110.00
Castor Set, all glass, stand, 4		
bottles	400.00	—
Castor Bottle, single	42.50	68.00
Celery Vase	55.00	—
Champagne	35.00	45.00
Claret	47.50	—
Cheese, covered	150.00	—
Dish, round, handled	18.00	—
Compote, covered, open		
6″	55.00	95.00
12″	87.50	230.00
Cordial	21.00	—
Creamer		
Individual	24.00	37.50
Regular	65.00	75.00
Cup and Saucer	68.00	—
Goblet	12.50	37.50
Mug	—	36.00
Mustard, covered	36.00	—
Pitcher, water		
Bulbous		282.00
Tankard	140.00	195.00
Plates		
5″	20.00	—
9″	40.00	—
Relishs		
Oval, regular	12.00	—
Serpentine shape	18.00	—
Salt Shaker, single	18.00	31.00
Saucer	13.00	—

	Clear	Ruby Stained
Spooner	40.00	57.50
Sugar, covered	22.00	45.00
Toothpick	13.00	23.00
Tumbler	18.00	36.00
Wine	10.00	30.00

KING'S #500

Made by King Glass Co., of Pittsburgh, Pa., in 1899. It was made in clear and a beautiful cobalt blue (known as "Dewey Blue"), trimmed in gold. Continued by U. S. Glass Co., in 1891, and made in a great number of pieces.

	Clear w/ gold	Cobalt & gold
Bowl, Berry		
7"	10.00	30.00
8"	12.00	40.00
9"	14.00	50.00
Butter, covered	50.00	125.00
Cake Stand	37.50	60.00
Celery	18.00	—
Compotes		
Covered	45.00	—
Open	30.00	—
Creamer	25.00	48.00
Cruet	75.00	—
Pitcher, water		
Round shape	55.00	100.00
Tankard	50.00	95.00
Relish	20.00	—
Rose Bowl	18.00	40.00
Salt Shaker, single	15.00	—
Spooner	20.00	—
Sugar, covered	45.00	—
Syrup	55.00	130.00
Tumbler	20.00	—

LATTICE
(Diamond Bar)

Non-flint made by King, Son and Co., Pittsburgh, Pa., c1880 and U. S. Glass Co. in 1891.

Bowl, 9½"	20.00
Butter, covered	50.00
Cake Stand, 12½"	45.00
Celery	18.50
Compote, covered, 7½", high std	50.00
Creamer	30.00
Egg Cup	18.50
Goblet	25.00
Pitcher, water	50.00
Plate 6"	8.00
Platter or Bread Tr handled, "Waste Not, Want Not"	50.00
Relish	12.50
Sauce, footed	6.00
Spooner	25.00
Sugar, covered	40.00
Syrup, top dated	55.00
Wine	18.50

LEAF AND STAR
(Tobin)

Made by New Martinsville Glass Co. between 1910–1915. Often decorated with gold. A toothpick, valued at $45.00, has been found in amber stained.

	Clear	Ruby Stained
Bowl, Berry	18.00	25.00
Butter, covered	40.00	55.00
Creamer	28.00	35.00
Goblet	22.00	30.00
Pitcher, water	50.00	65.00
Sauces, flat	7.50	10.00
Sugar, covered	35.00	45.00
Spooner	27.00	35.00
Tumblers	20.00	27.00

LENS AND STAR
(Star and Oval)

Made by O'Hara Glass Co., Pittsburgh, Pa., in 1880; in 1891 and after by U. S. Glass Co. It comes in clear, plain and etched panels, also panels frosted. No colors are known.

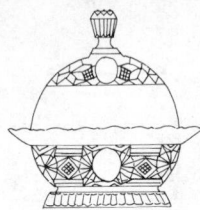

	Clear	Frosted
Bowl, waste	16.00	—
Butter, covered	45.00	55.00
Cake Stand	32.50	—
Compotes		
Covered	47.00	—
Open	35.00	—
Pitcher, water, barrel shape	50.00	65.00
Relish, boat shape	12.00	—
Spooner	18.00	—
Sugar, covered	35.00	—
Tumbler	16.00	—
Tray, handles	45.00	—

LIBERTY
(Cornucopia #2)

Made by McKee Glass Co., in 1892, in clear glass; sometimes found with cranberry flashing.

	Clear	Cranberry Flashed
Bowls, at least 9 sizes, av.	16.50	25.00
Butter, covered	45.00	55.00
Cordial	27.00	30.00
Creamer	29.00	35.00
Champagne	20.00	35.00
Goblet	40.00	42.00
Pitcher, water		
Regular gallon	50.00	60.00
Tall tankard	57.00	67.00
Sauces, flat	10.00	12.00
Sugar, covered	45.00	55.00
Spooner	25.00	30.00
Tumbler	30.00	32.00
Tray, water	45.00	55.00
Wine	16.50	20.00

LIBERTY BELL
(Centennial)

Made by Gillinder and Co., Philadelphia, Pa., for the Centennial Exposition, 1876.

Bowls, footed, 8″	70.00
Butter, covered	
Regular	135.00
Toy	130.00
Compote, open, 8″	90.00
Condiment Set, 4 pieces	585.00
Creamer, applied handle	100.00
Goblet	60.00
Mug, snake handle	195.00
Nappy, 4″	47.50
Pitcher, water, applied handle	500.00+
Platters, Bread	
Clear, 9½″ x 13⅜″, no signatures	75.00
"John Hancock"	200.00
Salt, individual	26.50
Salt and Pepper Shakers, single	65.00
Salt and Pepper Shakers, pr, dated 1876	150.00
Spooner	90.00
Sugar, covered	94.00
Sugar Shaker	75.00
Syrup	90.00

LINCOLN DRAPE

LINCOLN DRAPE WITH TASSEL

Flint pattern made originally by Boston & Sandwich Glass Co., probably continued by

other companies, c1860. Commemmorative of Lincoln's death. Clear flint, and some very rare pieces in cobalt blue, are 200% more. Any piece is becoming rare.

LINCOLN DRAPE   **LINCOLN DRAPE, WITH TASSEL**

Butter, covered	100.00
Compotes, open, 6″, low standard	85.00
Covered, 8½″, high standard	150.00
Creamer, applied handle	125.00
Egg Cup	40.00
Goblet	57.50
Honey	20.00
Lamp	
Marble base	125.00
Miniature	45.00
Pitchers, water, applied handle	350.00
Salt, footed	35.00
Spillholder	50.00
Spooner	50.00
Sugar, covered	125.00
Syrup, applied handle	95.00
Wine	50.00

LION

Clear and frosted pattern made by Gillinder & Sons, Philadelphia, Pa., in 1876. Many reproductions.

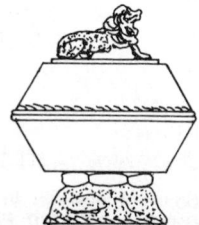

	Clear	Frosted
Butters, covered		
Lion's head finial	75.00	—
Rampant finial	100.00	—
Celery	75.00	—
Champagne	100.00	—
Cheese, cov, rampant lion finial	295.00	—
Compotes, covered		
7″, rampant finial, high standard	150.00	—
9″, rampant finial, oval, collared base	190.00	—
Open, 8″, low standard	65.00	—
Creamer	60.00	—
Egg Cup	45.00	—
Goblet	65.00	—
Marmalade Jar, rampant finial, 2 sizes	85.00	—
Paperweight	135.00	—
Pitchers		
Milk	350.00+	—
Water	200.00	—
Plate, Bread, 10″, Lion handles	62.50	85.00
Relish, Lion handles	28.00	30.00
Salt, master, rectangular ftd	250.00	—
Sauces, ftd, 4″	15.00	22.00
Spooner	48.00	85.00
Sugars, covered		
Lion head finial	65.00	—
Rampant finial	85.00	—
Wine	82.00	150.00

LOG CABIN

Non-flint made by Central Glass Co., Wheeling, W. Va., c1875.

Butter, covered	275.00
Creamer	130.00
Honey Dish	190.00
Marmalade Jar	275.00
Pitcher, water	290.00
Sugar, covered	300.00

LONE STAR
(Squat Pineapple)

Made by McKee Brothers, in 1898; available in many pieces.

	Clear	Emerald Green
Butter, covered	45.00	55.00
Cake Stand	32.00	47.00
Celery Tray	22.00	30.00
Compotes		
Covered	60.00	75.00
Open	35.00	55.00
Creamer	27.00	35.00
Cruet, orig stopper	55.00	65.00
Dishes, various sizes and shapes, av.	20.00	24.00
Goblet	30.00	37.00
Pickle	15.00	22.00
Pitcher, water	47.00	55.00
Relish, handled	18.00	24.00
Salt and Pepper Shakers, 2 types, pr	45.00	55.00
Spooner	22.00	27.00
Sugar, covered	37.00	45.00
Syrup, metal top	55.00	65.00
Tray, water	50.00	65.00
Tumbler	25.00	28.00
Wine	16.00	20.00

LOOP
(Seneca Loop)

Flint, of the 1850s–1860s. Made by several firms, including a rare fiery opalescent by Sandwich. Later produced in non-flint. Yuma Loop is a contemporary with comparable values.

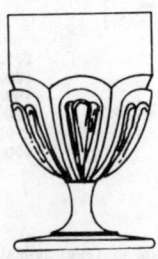

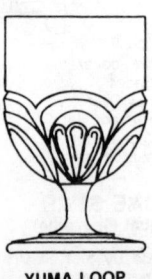

SENECA LOOP   YUMA LOOP

	Flint	Non-Flint
Bowl, 9"	50.00	—
Butter, covered	75.00	50.00
Cake Stand	75.00	—
Celery	50.00	20.00
Compotes		
9½" scalloped rim, fiery opal	235.00	—
Open, high standard, very flaring rim	200.00	—
Creamer	70.00	32.00
Egg Cup	28.00	—
Goblet	29.00	18.00
Pitcher, water	110.00	—
Salt, master	18.00	—
Spooner	22.00	20.00
Sugar, covered	60.00	—
Tumbler, footed	18.00	—
Wine	30.00	—

LOOP AND DART

Non-flint clear and stippled pattern of the 1860s with many variants: Loop and Dart with Diamond Ornaments, Loop and Dart with Round Ornaments, Double Loop and Dart. Leaf and Dart and others. Leaf and Dart made by Richards and Hartley, Tarentum, Pa., in 1888. Prices for all are comparable.

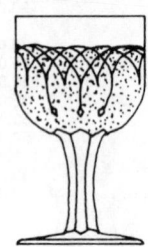

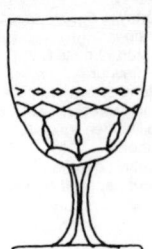

LOOP AND DART   LOOP AND DART WITH DIAMOND ORNAMENTS

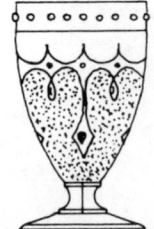

DOUBLE LOOP AND DART   LOOP AND DART WITH ROUND ORNAMENTS

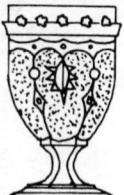

LEAF AND DART

Bowl, 6" x 9", oval	20.00
Butter	
Covered	45.00
Pats	15.00
Cake Stand, 10"	40.00
Celery	32.00
Compote, covered, 8"	65.00
Creamer, applied handle	45.00
Cruet	75.00
Egg Cup	22.50
Goblet	30.00
Pitcher, water, applied handle	85.00
Plate, 6"	25.00
Relish	15.00
Salt, covered	65.00
Spooner	32.50
Sugar, covered	47.50
Tumbler, footed	35.00
Wine	37.50

LOOP AND JEWEL
(Jewel and Festoon)

Non-flint made by Beatty Glass and National Glass Co., then continued by Indiana Glass Co. Made until 1915. About forty pieces known. Clear, with few rare pieces in milk white.

Bowls, 6", 7" and 8"	12.00
Butter, covered	40.00
Compote, 6½"	20.00
Creamer	25.00
Pitcher, water	45.00

Plate, square	15.00
Relish, rectangular, 8"	10.00
Salt, footed	17.00
Sherry, flared	30.00
Sugar, covered	47.50
Syrup	55.00

LOOP WITH DEWDROPS

Early maker unknown. Reissued by U. S. Glass Co. in 1892 and later in 1898.

Bowl, 8"	12.50
Butter, covered	40.00
Cake Stand, 10"	42.00
Celery	25.00
Compote, covered, 8", high standard	55.00
Condiment Set, tray	85.00
Creamer	30.00
Cruet	55.00
Cup and Saucer	25.00
Goblet	27.50
Pitcher, water	40.00
Salt and Pepper Shakers	50.00
Spooner	20.00
Sugar, covered	32.00
Tray, double handles	45.00
Tumbler	16.50
Wine	25.00

LOUISIANA
(Sharp Oval and Diamond, Granby)

Made by Bryce Bros., Pittsburgh, Pa., in 1870s; continued later (about 1892) by U. S. Glass Co. as one of the States' patterns.

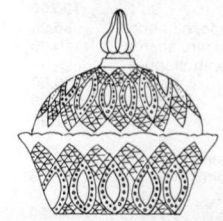

Bowl, Berry, 9″	15.00
Butter, covered	45.00
Celery	15.00
Creamer	25.00
Compote	
Jelly, 5″	42.50
Large, covered, 8″	50.00
Dish, oval, with lid	50.00
Goblet	27.50
Matchholder, attached saucer	30.00
Mug, handled, gold top	18.00
Pitcher, water	45.00
Relish	10.00
Spooner	18.00
Sugar, covered	35.00
Tumbler	14.50
Wine	32.50

MAGNET AND GRAPE

Flint, and non-flint c1860. Also Magnet and Grape with Stippled Leaf, non-flint. Reproductions reported. First in flint by Boston and Sandwich Glass Co. Later made of regular glass with the grape leaf stippled instead of frosted, as in the flint pattern by the same company.

	Flint Frosted Leaf	Non-Flint Stippled leaf
Butter, covered	185.00	40.00
Celery	175.00	25.00
Champagne	125.00	18.00
Cordial	100.00	22.00
Creamer, applied handle . .	85.00	40.00
Compote, open, scarce . . .	110.00	45.00
Decanter, with stopper		
Pint	150.00	75.00
Quart	200.00	85.00
Egg Cup	82.50	22.00
*Goblet		
With American Shield . . .	300.00	22.00
Knob stem	67.50	30.00
Low stem	52.50	40.00
b,6.5 Mug	75.00	22.50

	Flint Frosted Leaf	Non-Flint Stippled leaf
Pitcher, water, applied handle	350.00+	70.00
Relish, Oval	35.00	15.00
Salt, footed	37.50	15.00
Spooner	55.00	22.50
Sugar, covered	275.00	50.00
Syrup Jug	125.00	55.00
Tumbler		
Water	95.00	19.50
Whiskey	100.00	25.00
Wine	85.00	22.50

MAINE
(Paneled Stippled Flower)

Non-flint made by U. S. Glass Co., Pittsburgh, Pa., c1890s. Goblets were not made originally. Found in clear and green, sometimes with enamel trim.

	Clear	Emerald Green
Bowl, 8″	27.50	40.00
Butter, covered	48.00	—
Cake Stands		
8½″	40.00	—
9½″	50.00	—
Creamer	22.00	—
Pitchers		
Milk	—	83.00
Water	—	75.00
Sugar, covered	45.00	—
Syrup	60.00	210.00
Wine	39.00	52.00

MANHATTAN

Non-flint made by U. S. Glass Co., c1902. It has been reproduced in clear and color.

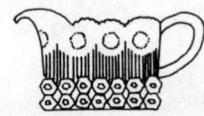

	Clear	Ruby Stained
Butter, covered	37.00	—
Bowls		
10"	20.00	—
12½"	12.00	—
Cake Stand, 10"	40.00	—
Celery	12.50	—
Compote, cov, 9½", high standard	45.00	—
Creamer, regular	16.00	60.00
Cruet		
Large	65.00	—
Small	50.00	—
Goblet	20.00	—
Lamp	80.00	—
Pitcher, water, tankard	60.00	—
Plate, 8"	18.00	—
Punch Cup	5.00	—
Punch Set, 14 pcs	95.00	—
Strawholder, lid, for drug store trade	65.00	—
Sugar, covered	30.00	65.00
Syrup	47.00	—
Tumbler	11.00	—
Wine	18.00	—

	Clear	Ruby Stained
Compotes		
Covered, high standard	45.00	—
Jelly, 4½", covered	30.00	55.00
Cordial	34.00	—
Creamer		
Individual	17.00	—
Regular	32.00	48.00
Goblet	27.90	—
Pitcher		
Milk	50.00	—
Water, silver plated spout	130.00	—
Punch Cup	9.50	—
Relish	12.50	—
Shade for gas light	48.00	—
Spooner	18.00	—
Sugar, cov, large	35.00	—
Syrup, metal lid	55.00	—
Tumbler, bar or regular	25.00	—
Vase, trumpet shape	47.00	—

MARDI GRAS
(Duncan and Miller #42, Paneled English Hobnail with Prisms)

Made by Duncan and Miller Glass Co. c1898. Made in clear only, sometimes with band of color around top. Rare pieces with ruby stain, often trimmed with gold.

	Clear	Ruby Stained
Bowls		
Berry, 8"	18.00	—
Finger	14.00	—
Butter, covered	45.00	—
Cake Stand, 10"	65.00	—
Celery Dish, oblong, folded edges	15.00	—
Champagne, saucer shape	45.00	—
Cocktail, flared, sherry	18.00	—

MARQUISETTE

Non-flint made by Cooperative Glass Co., Beaver Falls, Pa., c1880.

Butter, covered	40.00
Celery	42.50
Compotes	
Covered, high standard	60.00
Open, low standard	35.00
Creamer, applied handle	55.00
Goblet	30.00
Spooner	20.00
Sugar, covered	55.00

MARSH PINK
(Square Fuschia)

Maker unknown. It is of the 1870-1880 period. Originally made in clear glass; some amber has been reported. Some of the pieces are square shaped.

Bowl, 6" x 9"	18.50
Butter, covered, double handled	45.00

Cake Stand	45.00
Compote	
Covered, 7½″	47.00
Jelly, covered, 5½″	25.00
Creamer	32.50
Dish, 5″, covered	30.00
Goblet	35.00
Honey Dish, footed, covered, complete	50.00
Marmalade Jar, covered	50.00
Pitcher, water	60.00
Pickle Castor, silver frame	48.00
Plates, large, square shaped	25.00
Salt and Pepper Shakers, old tops, single	25.00
Sauces, flat, sometimes with lids	
Handled	10.00
Footed	12.00
Spooner	25.00
Sugar, covered	35.00
Wine	18.00

	Clear	Ruby Stained
Compotes		
Covered	65.00	—
Open	45.00	—
Creamer	27.50	55.00
Dishes		
Candy	18.00	—
Jelly	12.00	—
Olive, handled	12.00	—
Goblet	32.00	48.00
Pitcher, water	62.00	85.00
Relish, oval	11.50	—
Salt and Pepper Shakers		
Pair	65.00	—
Single	30.00	—
Sauce, flat	6.50	—
Spooner	22.00	—
Sugar, covered	45.00	—
Tumbler	25.00	—
Toothpick	45.00	65.00
Tray, listed as "Preserve or Olive Tray"	45.00	—
Wine	40.00	60.00

MASCOTTE

Non-flint made by Ripley and Co., Pittsburgh, Pa., in the 1870s. Reissued by U. S. Glass Co. in 1898.

	Clear	Etched
Bowl, 9″	25.00	34.00
Butter, covered		
Regular	48.00	—
Special (See Note)	100.00	—
Butter Pats	7.00	18.00
Cake Basket, handle	80.00	—
Cheese, covered	50.00	65.00
Compotes		
Covered, 8″, high standard	60.00	—
Open, 8″, low standard	40.00	—
Creamer	27.00	35.00
Dishes or Bowls, 7″–8″d, one fits into other and forms tall jar-type containers, three sizes with lids, called "Pyramid Jar"	40.00	—

MARYLAND
(Inverted Loop and Fan; Loop and Diamond)

Made originally by Bryce Brothers, Pittsburgh. Continued by U.S. Glass Co., as one of their States' patterns. Clear with gold and sometimes ruby stained.

	Clear	Ruby Stained
Bowl, Berry	15.00	—
Butter, covered	40.00	82.00
Celery		
Tray	15.00	—
Vase	20.00	—

	Clear	Etched
Goblet	24.00	30.00
Marmalade Jar, cov, Pat'd May 20, 1873	35.00	—
Pitcher, water	47.00	69.00
Plate, turned in sides	38.00	—
Salt and Pepper Shakers, single	10.00	—
Sauce, footed	8.00	—
Spooner	21.00	28.00
Sugar, covered	45.00	—
Tray, water	—	55.00
Tumbler	18.00	34.00
Wine	25.00	—

Note: The butter dish shown on Plate 77 of Ruth Webb Lee's "Victorian Glass" is said to go with the Mascotte pattern. It has a horseshoe finial, and was named for the famous "Maude S.," "Queen of the Turf" trotting horse during the 1880s. Made by Ripley Bros. The pattern was named "Mascotte" in honor of this event.

MASONIC
(Inverted Prism)

Non-flint made by McKee Glass Co., Jeannette, Pa., c1894. Pattern continued into 1920s. Rare pieces found in emerald green.

Bowl, Salad, 9", silver frame	45.00
Butter	
Covered	45.00
Flat, open butter dish	37.50
Cake Stand, 9" and 10"	35–42.50
Celery	20.00
Creamer	25.00
Handle, for a salad fork	20.00
Honey Dish, flat, square, covered	40.00
Nappy, heart shaped, handled	27.50
Pitcher, water, tankard	60.00
Relish, serpentine shape	15.00
Sardine Box, flat, rectangular	22.50
Spooner	22.00
Sugar, covered	37.50
Tumbler	14.00

MASSACHUSETTS
(Geneva #2, M2-131)

Made in 1880s, maker unknown, and continued in 1898 by U. S. Glass Co. as one of the States series. Made in clear glass, some reported in emerald green.

	Clear	Emerald Green
Bottle, Bar	70.00	—
Bowls, Berry, sq shaped, 9"	16.00	—
Butter, covered	55.00	—
Celery, flat, oblong	22.00	—
Compote, open	35.00	—
Creamers, several sizes, av.	30.00	—
Cruet, miniature, with stopper 5"	68.00	—
Cruet, regular, facetted stopper	39.00	—
Decanter or Water Bottle	49.00	—
Goblet	45.00	—
Lamp, tall, banquet style with matching globe	150.00	—
Pitcher, water	68.00	—
Plate, 8"	24.00	—
Relish, various sizes, sq and round, folded sides	25.00	—
Rum Jug, resembles a teapot, short spout, made for Xmas trade, lid is not removeable	82.50	—
Shot Glass	15.00	—
Spooner	22.00	—
Sugar, covered	40.00	—
Tumbler	18.00	—
Vase, tall, 7"	12.00	34.00
Wine	—	45.00

MICHIGAN
(Paneled Jewel)

Non-flint made by U. S. Glass Co., c1893, one of the States' Pattern series. The 10¼"bowl ($42.00) and Punch Cup ($12.00) found in yellow or blue stain. Also reported in ruby stained.

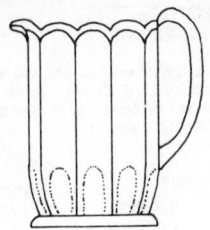

	Clear	Cranberry Stained
Bowl, 10¼"	25.00	50.00
Butter, covered	62.00	—
Celery	30.00	—
Creamers		
Individual	20.00	40.00
Regular	30.00	—
Cruet, stoppered	55.00	75.00
Goblet	32.00	50.00
Pitcher, water	45.00	—
Punch Cup	7.00	—
Salt and Pepper Shakers,		
single	20.00	—
Spooner	35.00	—
Sugar, covered	48.00	50.00
Syrup, lid	55.00	—
Toothpick	40.00	55.00
Tumbler	28.00	40.00
Vase, tall, trumpet shaped	21.00	—
Wine	22.00	—

MINERVA

Non-flint made by Boston and Sandwich Glass Co. and other companies in 1880s.

Butter, covered	65.00
Cake Stand, 10½"	97.50
Compote, covered, 7", high standard	85.00
Creamer	45.00
Goblet	85.00
Marmalade Jar, covered	110.00

Pickle, inscribed "Love's Request is Pickles"	27.50
Pitcher, water	165.00
Plates	
8"	55.00
10", Mars	60.00
Platter, or Bread Tray 9"x 13"	60.00
Sauce, footed	15.00
Spooner	35.00
Sugar, covered	70.00

MINNESOTA

Non-flint made by U. S. Glass Co., c. late 1890s. One of the States' Patterns. A two piece flower frog ($46.00) has been found in emerald green.

	Clear	Ruby Stained
Biscuit Jar, covered	55.00	115.00
Bowl, 8½", round flared edge	30.00	—
Butter, covered	50.00	—
Celery Tray, 13"	18.00	—
Compotes, open		
9", square, low standard	37.00	—
10", flared edge, high standard	60.00	—
Creamer	30.00	—
Cruet	32.00	—
Goblet	22.50	50.00
Pitcher, water, tankard	47.00	200.00
Spooner	22.50	—
Sugar, covered	37.50	—
Syrup	55.00	—
Toothpick, 3-handled	22.50	—
Tumbler	12.00	—
Wine	25.00	—

MISSOURI
(Palm and Scroll)

Non-flint made by U. S. Glass Co., c1899, in the States' Pattern series. Clear and emerald green. Add 20% for green.

Bowl, Berry	18.00
Butter, covered	50.00

Cake Stands, 9"–10"	47.50
Creamer	27.50
Cruet	52.50
Goblet	35.00
Mug	35.00
Pitcher, water	45.00
Salt and Pepper Shakers, single . .	25.00
Syrup	50.00
Relish	18.00
Sugar, covered	45.00
Wine	25.00

MOON AND STAR
(Palace)

Non-flint; first made by Adams & Co., Pittsburgh, in 1874 and later by several manufacturers, including Pioneer Glass, over a long period of time. Six different type compotes documented. Heavily reproduced in clear and color.

Bowls	
8", Berry, pointed end	25.00
12½", round end	42.50
Butter, covered	50.00
Cake Stand, 9"	45.00
Celery	35.00
Champagne	37.50
Cheese, covered	60.00
Compotes	
Covered, 10", high standard	50.00
Open, 9", high standard	30.00
Creamer	42.50
Cruet	65.00
Egg Cup	22.00

Goblet	37.50
Lamp, tall	90.00
Pickle, oval	12.50
Pitcher, water	95.00
Salt Dip	7.50
Salt and Pepper Shakers, single . .	22.00
Spooner	35.00
Sugar, covered	45.00
Tray, water	45.00
Tumbler, footed	42.50

NAILHEAD
(Gem)

Non-flint, made by Bryce, Higbee, and Co., in 1880s. Also found in decorated aquamarine and ruby stained. No tumbler reported.

	Clear	Ruby Stained
Butter, covered	45.00	—
Cake Stand, 9½"	37.00	—
Celery	45.00	—
Compotes		
Covered, 8", high standard	48.00	—
Open, 9½", high standard	45.00	—
Creamer	23.00	—
Goblet	21.00	30.00
Pitcher, water	50.00	—
Plate, square, 7"	25.00	—
Sugar, covered	32.00	—
Spooner	21.00	—
Wine	16.00	18.00

NEVADA

Non-flint made by U. S. Glass Co. as a States' Pattern. Pieces are sometimes partly frosted and have enamel decoration. Add 20% for frosted.

Biscuit Jar	35.00
Butter, covered	42.00
Cake Stand, 10"	25.00
Celery	17.50
Compote, covered, 8", high standard	45.00

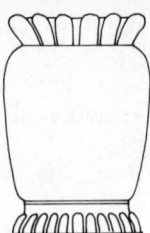

	Flint	Non-Flint
Pitcher, water	295.00	—
Plate, 6″	85.00	—
Salt, master	39.00	—
Sauce, flat	15.00	10.00
Spooner	32.00	27.00
Sugar, covered	85.00	35.00
Tumblers		
Bar	95.00	—
Water	75.00	—
Whiskey, handled	100.00	—
*Wine	135.00	—

NEW HAMPSHIRE
(Bent Buckle, Modiste)

Non-flint made by U. S. Glass Co. in the States' Pattern series. Pieces found in clear with gold trim and some with cranberry flashing.

Creamer	20.00
Cruet	35.00
Pickle, oval	10.00
Pitcher, water, tankard	40.00
Salts	
Individual	5.00
Master	8.50
Salt and Pepper Shakers, single	12.50
Sugar, covered	35.00
Toothpick	25.00
Tumbler	9.00

NEW ENGLAND PINEAPPLE

Flint made by Boston and Sandwich Glass Co. in early 1860s. Continued by other companies in non-flint.

	Clear	Cranberry Stained
Bowls		
Flared, 8½″	15.00	25.00
Round, 8½″	17.50	—
Square, 8½″	25.00	—
Butter, covered	45.00	70.00
Celery	25.00	—
Compote, open	37.00	42.00
Creamers		
Individual	10.00	—
Regular	25.00	35.00
Cruet	55.00	75.00
Goblet	25.00	—
Mug, large	15.00	—
Pitcher, water, tankard	50.00	—
Salt Shaker, single	15.00	—
Sugars		
Covered	45.00	—
Individual	20.00	—
Toothpick	25.00	38.00
Tumbler	23.00	—
Wine	18.00	—

	Flint	Non-Flint
Bottle, Castor	28.50	—
Castor Set, 4 bottles, complete	300.00	—
Champagne	165.00	—
Compote, open, 8½″, high standard	125.00	80.00
Cordial	70.00	—
Creamer, applied handle	150.00	70.00
Decanter, qt, stoppered	100.00	—
Egg Cup	37.50	—
*Goblet, either size	75.00	22.00
Mug	95.00	—

NEW JERSEY
(Loops and Drops)

Non-flint made by U. S. Glass Co. in States' Pattern Series. Sometimes flashed in red; mostly clear with gold trim.

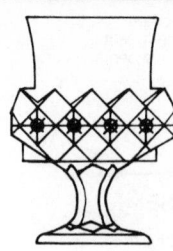

	Clear	Ruby Stained
Bowls		
8", flared	25.00	—
10", oval	25.00	—
Butter, covered	50.00	75.00
Cake Stand, 8"	35.00	—
Celery Tray	25.00	—
Compotes		
Jelly, covered, 5"	45.00	57.00
Open, 8", high standard	40.00	—
Creamer	32.50	42.00
Cruet	55.00	—
Goblet	32.00	—
Pickle	8.50	—
Pitcher, water, gallon, applied handle	57.50	—
Plates		
8"	12.00	—
10½", footed	22.00	—
12"	22.00	—
Relish	10.00	—
Salt and Pepper Shakers, single	21.00	—
Sherry, flared	45.00	—
Spooner	27.00	—
Sugar, covered	40.00	—
Toothpick	45.00	—
Tumbler	22.00	38.00
Wine	30.00	—

	Clear	Ruby Stained
Creamer	20.00	—
Cruet	55.00	—
Cup and Saucer	52.00	—
Goblet	25.00	42.00
Lamp Oil	47.00	—
Plates		
7"	20.00	—
8"	30.00	—
10"	40.00	—
Salt, master	12.00	—
Spooner	20.00	—
Sugar, covered	35.00	—
Sugar Sifter	55.00	—
Syrup	55.00	—
Tumbler	30.00	48.00

ONE HUNDRED ONE

Non-flint made by the Bellaire Goblet Co., Findlay, Ohio, in the late 1870s.

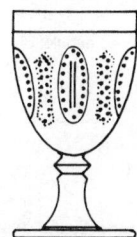

O'HARA'S DIAMOND
(Sawtooth and Star)

Non-flint, made by O'Hara Glass Co. in 1885 and by U. S. Glass Co. in 1890s.

	Clear	Ruby Stained
Butter, covered	45.00	—
Banana Stand	38.00	110.00
Claret	32.00	—
Compotes		
4 sizes, high standard	25-40.00	—
Jelly	46.00	—

Butter, covered	60.00
Cake Stand, 9"	50.00
Celery	50.00
Compote, covered, low standard	60.00
Creamer	37.50
Goblet	40.00
Lamp, Hand, oil, 10"	80.00
Pitcher, water	115.00
Plates	
8"	20.00
11"	22.50

Platters, 101 border
Farm implement center	75.00
Frosted beehive center, scarce .	95.00
Relish	15.00
Spooner	25.00

Sugars
Covered	45.00
Open	15.00

OPEN ROSE

Non-flint, c1870s.

Bowls
Berry, scalloped, handled	35.00
Oval, 6″ x 9″	22.50
Butter, covered	55.00

Compotes
Covered, 9″, high standard	60.00
Open, 7½″, low standard	35.00
Creamer	36.00
Egg Cup	24.00

Goblet
Ladies' small	30.00
Regular	18.00
Pitcher, water, applied handle	150.00
Relish	12.00
Spooner	22.50
Sugar, covered	48.50
Tumbler	27.50

OREGON #1
Beaded Loop

Non-flint. First made in the 1880s. Reissued in 1907 as one of the States' series. Loops may have cranberry flashing. A cruet ($75.00) is known in cranberry stained; and, a goblet ($38.00) in ruby stained.

Bowls
7″	15.00
8″	18.50
Berry, covered	25.00
Butter, cov, flat and ftd	50.00
Cake Stand	28.00
Carafe, water	35.00

Celery	27.00
Compote, open, 9″	22.00
Creamer, flat and ftd	27.00
Cruet	50.00
Goblet	32.00
Honey Dish	10.00
Lamp, miniature	50.00
Mug	21.00
Pickle Dish, boat shape	15.00

Pitchers
Milk	35.00
Water	55.00
Salt and Pepper Shakers, single . .	22.00

Spooner
Flat	20.00
Footed	22.00

Sugar bowl, cov, flat and ftd
Flat	25.00
Footed	30.00
Syrup, orig top	55.00
Tumbler	24.00
Wine	38.00

PALMETTE

Non-flint, late 1870s.

Bowl, 8″	20.00
Butter, covered	55.00
Cake Stand	38.50
Castor Bottle	20.00
Celery Vase	25.00
Compote, covered, 8½″, high standard	60.00

Cordial	25.00	
Creamer, applied handle	47.50	
Egg Cup	27.50	
Goblet	40.00	
Lamp, Oil	75.00	
Pitcher, water, applied handle	65.00	
Relish, scoop shape	12.50	
Salt, master, footed	22.50	
Sauce, 6″	14.00	
Spooner	40.00	
Sugar, covered	45.00	
Syrup, applied handle	57.50	
Tumbler, footed	32.50	
Wine	25.00	

PANAMA
(Finecut Bar, Viking #2)

Made by U.S. Glass Co., in 1890s, in clear; but
there could be other colors. A 1907 trade catalog shows at least 56 pieces.

Bowl, Berry, about 5 sizes	25.00	
Butter, covered	40.00	
Celery Tray	18.00	
Creamer		
Individual	18.00	
Regular	25.00	
Compote		
High stand	45.00	
Low stand, various sizes	20–30.00	
Cake Stand	25.00	
Dish, flaring edges, called a "Sweet		
Pea" bowl	18.00	
Goblet	27.00	
Pickle	15.00	
Pitcher		
Milk	32.00	
Water	42.00	
Sugar, covered	35.00	
Spooner	18.00	
Tumbler	20.00	
Wine	18.00	

PANELED DAISY
(Brazil)

Non-flint made by Bryce Bros., Pittsburgh,
Pa., in the late 1870s and by U. S. Glass Co.
in 1891. Also found in blue and milk glass.

	Clear	Milk
Bowls		
5 x 7″, oval	11.50	—
9″, square	18.00	—
Waste	15.00	—
Butter, covered	50.00	—
Cake Stands		
10¼″	45.00	
11″	50.00	—
Celery Vase	27.00	—
Compotes		
Covered, 5″, 6″, high		
standard, Jelly	45.00	—
Covered, 10″, 11″, high		
standard	60.00	—
Open, 11″, high standard	42.00	—
Creamer	25.00	—
*Goblet	25.00	—
Mug	30.00	—
Pickle, handled	17.50	—
Pitcher, water	60.00	—
Plates		
Round, 7″	22.00	37.00
Square, 9″	30.00	45.00
Relish, 5 x 7″, fish shaped,		
wider at one end	15.00	—
Salt and Pepper Shakers,		
single	20.00	—
Sauce, flat, square	6.00	—
Spooner	17.00	—
Sugar, covered	40.00	—
Sugar Shaker	55.00	80.00
Tray, water	45.00	—
*Tumbler	26.00	—

PANELED DIAMOND BLOCK
(Duncan and Miller #24, Diamond Point and
Quartered Block)

Made by Duncan and Miller Co. in 1894, in
clear only. Comes occasionally with top
flashed in gold or color. One of many patterns of this type which can easily be mistak-
en for each other.

	Clear	Color Stained Top
Bowl, Berry	18.00	—
Butter, covered	45.00	—
Cake Stand	49.00	—
Carafe, water	35.00	—
Compote, open, high standard	40.00	—
Creamer	18.00	32.00
Goblet	25.00	35.00
Pitcher, water	48.00	—
Spooner	20.00	—
Sugar Shaker	25.00	—
Tumbler	20.00	45.00

PANELED "44"
(Reverse "44")

Non-flint made by U. S. Glass Co., c1912. Some pieces bear intertwined U. S. Glass Co. mark in base. Also comes trimmed in gold and in untarnishable platinum. Has been seen with cranberry and green flashing.

	Clear w/Gold	Cranberry or Green Staining
Bowls		
8", round, trimmed in platinum	50.00	—
Finger	20.00	—
Butter, covered	55.00	92.00
Candlestick, 7"	25.00	—

	Clear w/Gold	Cranberry or Green Staining
Creamer	35.00	—
Cruet	65.00	—
Dish		
Bon Bon, ftd with cover	35.00	—
Olive	15.00	—
Goblet	30.00	45.00
Lemonade Set, Pitcher and 6 tumblers	155.00	—
Pitcher, water		
Flat, bulbous	65.00	—
Tall tankard on foot	70.00	—
Salt and Pepper Shakers, single	25.00	—
Sugar, powdered sugar, cov, no handles	30.00	—
Toothpick	45.00	—
Tumbler, regular	25.00	—
Wine	40.00	—

PANELED GRAPE, LATE

Non-flint made by D. C. Jenkins Glass Co., Arcadia and Kokomo, Ind.. c1913 to 1932.

Bowl, 12", covered	29.50
Butter, covered	45.00
Creamer	18.50
Goblet	22.50
Pitchers	
Milk	30.00
Water	40.00
Spooner	16.00
Sugar, covered	40.00
Syrup	35.00
Tumbler	10.00
Wine	15.00

PANELED THISTLE

Non-flint made by J. P. Higbee Glass Co., Bridgeville, Pa., in the early 1900s. This pattern has been heavily reproduced. The Higbee Glass Co. often used a bee as a trade mark.

PAVONIA
(Pineapple Stem)

Non-flint made by Ripley and Co. in 1885 and by U. S. Glass Co. in 1891. This pattern comes both plain and with etching; also with ruby flashing on pieces.

	Clear	Emerald Green
Banana Stand	50.00	—
Basket	40.00	—
Bowl, 8", with Bee	18.00	—
Butter, covered	55.00	75.00
Cake Stand, 9"	35.00	—
Celery		
Tray	18.50	—
Vase	22.00	—
Compotes, open		
5", low standard	18.00	—
8", high standard	27.00	37.00
Cordial	25.00	—
Creamer, with Bee	32.00	37.00
Cruet, stoppered	55.00	—
Egg Cup	30.00	—
Goblet	35.00	—
Honey, cov, sq, with Bee	50.00	—
Pitcher, water	50.00	—
Plates		
7"	18.00	—
10", with Bee	22.00	—
Punch Cup, with Bee	14.00	—
Relish, with Bee	15.00	—
Rose Bowl, large	42.50	58.00
Salts		
Dip	9.00	—
Master, with Bee	12.50	—
Sauces		
Flared, with Bee	14.00	—
Footed	12.00	—
Salt and Pepper Shakers,		
singles	23.00	—
Spooner	25.00	—
Sugar, covered	45.00	—
Toothpick, with Bee	50.00	—
Tumbler, water	20.00	—
Vases		
5"	15.00	—
9", trumpet shaped	20.00	—
Wine	25.00	—
Wine, with Bee	40.00	—

	Clear	Ruby Stained
Bowls		
9"	20.00	—
Finger Bowl, underplate	48.00	114.00
Waste	32.00	—
Butter, covered	70.00	110.00
Cake Stand, large, etched	40.00	—
Celery Vase, etched	28.00	—
Compotes		
Covered, 6", high standard	45.00	—
Jelly, open, etched	38.00	—
Creamer, etched	47.00	—
Goblets, etched	28.00	—
Pitcher, water	65.00	—
Spooner	20.00	49.00
Sugar, covered	50.00	—
Tumblers, etched	30.00	45.00
Wines, etched	34.00	42.00

PEACOCK FEATHER
(Georgia)

Probably Richards and Hartley, but reissued by several glass companies, including U. S. Glass Co. in 1902 as part of their States' series. Rare in blue. No goblet known in pattern.

Bowl, 8"	27.50
Butter, covered	42.50
Cake Stand, 11"	40.00
Compotes	
Covered, 8", high standard	50.00
Jelly	20.00
Condiment Set, tray, oil cruet, salt and pepper	75.00
Creamer	32.50
Cruet, stoppered	55.00
Lamps	
7", oil, hand	65.00
Chamber style, pedestal, blue	275.00
Pitcher, water	55.00
Plate, 5¼"	18.00
Salt and Pepper Shakers, single	27.00
Spooner	27.50
Sugar, covered	40.00
Syrup, metal lid	55.00
Tumbler	25.00

Goblet	
Angular sided	22.50
Rounded bowl	22.50
Pickle	
Flat pointed shape	15.00
Round	12.00
Pickle Jar, covered	40.00
Pitcher, water, ½ gallon	45.00
Platter, or Bread Tray, oval, handled	20.00
Salt	
Covered	25.00
Open, individual	22.00
Sauces	
4"	5.50
5½"	8.50
Spooner	23.50
Sugar, covered	40.00
Tumbler	18.00
Wines	25.00

PEERLESS #1
(Lady Hamilton)

Made by Richards and Hartley Co., Pittsburgh in 1875 and continued for a number of years. Made in a great number of pieces—many size bowls, 22 compotes, 5 cakestands, and two types of goblet and creamer. Only in clear.

Bowls, various sizes, av.	15.00
Butter, covered	40.00
Cake Stands	
Large, 3 sizes, av.	27.50
Small, 2 sizes, av.	24.00
Castor Set	75.00
Celery	27.00
Champagne	18.00
Compotes	
Covered	40.00
Open, av.	26.00
Creamer	
Low foot, rounded bowl	22.50
On stem, angular bowl	25.00
Dishes, Condiment or Preserve	
7"	10.00
8"	15.00
9"	20.00
Egg Cup, with saucer base	18.00

PENNSYLVANIA
(Balder)

Non-flint issued by U. S. Glass Co., 1898. This pattern comes in clear with gold trim and in emerald green.

	Clear	Emerald Green
Biscuit Jar, or tobacco, covered	55.00	98.00
Bowls		
Berry, 8"	29.00	35.00
Punch, 12", all one piece	75.00	—
Square, 8"	20.00	82.00
Butter, covered	55.00	82.00
Carafe	35.00	—
Celery Vase	45.00	—
Cheese, covered	65.00	—
Claret	25.00	—
Creamer, av.	32.00	48.00
Cruet, stoppered	47.00	—
Decanter, handled, stopper	85.00	—
Goblet	17–20.00	—
Molasses Can	49.00	—
Pitchers, water, tankard	50.00	—
Salt, master	15.00	—
Salt and Pepper Shakers, single	12.00	—
Spooner	24.00	32.00
Sugar, regular, covered	40.00	—
Tumbler, water	24.00	40.00
Wine	165.00	—

PICKET

Non-flint made by the King Glass Co., Pittsburgh, Pa., in the 1870s. Pattern has five different size compotes.

Bread Tray	50.00
Butter, covered	50.00
Celery	37.50
Compotes	
Covered, 8″, high standard	55.00
Open, 8″, high standard	35.00
Creamer	32.50
Goblet	40.00
Pitcher, water	50.00
Salts	
Individual	10.00
Master	14.00
Sauce, footed	10.00
Spooner	27.50
Sugar, covered	45.00
Toothpick	35.00
Tray, water	50.00
Waste Bowl	30.00

PINEAPPLE AND FAN #1
(Heisey's #1255)

Made by A. H. Heisey and Co., Newark, Ohio, c1897, before the Heisey trademark was used. Came in about 70 pieces. Made in clear, often trimmed with gold and emerald green with gold. Made also in canary, blue and amber, but only clear and emerald are seen.

	Clear	Emerald Green
Biscuit Jar, covered, 4 sizes, av.	57.50	75.00
Bowls, various sizes	30.00	45.00
Butter, covered	50.00	65.00
Cake Stand	42.50	60.00
Celery Tray, flat, oblong	25.00	—
Compote, open		
7″, 8″, and 9″, av.	27.50	—
Jelly, 4-5″	32.00	—
Creamer, regular	35.00	52.00
Custard, cup	12.00	17.00

	Clear	Emerald Green
Pitcher, water, round, bulbous, 8 sizes	60.00	87.00
Rose Bowl, 6 sizes, av.	18.50	45.00
Spooner	27.00	—
Sugar, covered	45.00	—
Syrup Jug	68.00	92.00
Toothpick	75.00	85.00
Tumbler	45.00	—
Vase, 4 sizes, av.	36.50	—

PINEAPPLE AND FAN #2
(Cube with Fan, Holbrook)

Non-flint made by Adams & Co., Pittsburgh, Pa., later made by U. S. Glass Co. in 1891. Also found in emerald green and milk white trimmed in gold.

	Clear	Emerald Green
Bowls		
8″	25.00	—
Punch, 12″	60.00	—
Waste	15.00	27.00
Butter, covered	40.00	65.00
Cake Stand, 9″	35.00	—
Creamer, regular	25.00	—
Cruet, stoppered	55.00	—
Decanter	38.00	—
Dish, Jelly, handled	18.00	—
Goblet	22.50	—
Pitcher, water, tankard	45.00	—
Plate, 6½″	14.50	—
Rose Bowl, three sizes	12–18.00	—
Spooner	20.00	—
Sugar, regular, covered	30.00	—
Syrup Jug	50.00	—

	Clear	Emerald Green
Tumblers		
Water	11.00	—
Whiskey	14.50	—
Wine	16.00	—

PLEAT AND PANEL
(Derby)

Non-flint made by Bryce Bros., Pittsburgh, Pa., c1870–1880 and by U. S. Glass Co. in 1891. Rare in blue, canary and amethyst.

	Clear	Ruby Stained
Bowls		
5 x 8″, covered	35.00	—
Waste	25.00	40.00
Butter, covered	48.00	—
Butter Pat	25.00	—
Cake Stand, 10″	50.00	—
Celery Vase	32.00	56.00
Compotes		
Covered, 8″, high standard	48.00	—
Open, 8″, high standard	35.00	—
Creamer	—	58.00
*Goblet	—	45.00
Lamp	65.00	—
Marmalade Jar, covered	50.00	—
Pitcher, water	60.00	—
Plates		
6″	19.00	50.00
8″	22.50	50.00
Relish, 5 x 8½″	17.00	—
Salt, master	20.00	—
Shakers, single	22.00	—
Spooner	35.00	—
Sugar, covered	40.00	—
Trays		
Bread, closed, handled	30.00	—
Bread, open, handled	35.00	—
Water	60.00	—
Wine	50.00	—

PLUME

Non-flint made by Adams Glass Co., Pittsburgh, Pa., c1874 and by U. S. Glass Co. in 1891. Also found etched and in ruby-stained. Pattern contained 46 pieces.

Bowls	
8″, square	20.00
8″, shallow scalloped rim	25.00
Butter, covered	50.00
Cake Stand, 10″	40.00
Celery	27.50
Compotes, open	
8½″, low standard, scalloped top	22.50
9″, high standard, crimped edge	38.00
Creamer	35.00
*Goblet	30.00
Lemonade Set, pitcher, tumblers, tray	95.00
Pitcher, water, applied handles	50.00
Spooner	20.00
Sugar, covered	45.00
Syrup	57.50
Tumbler	17.50

POINTED JEWEL
(Spear point)

Made by Columbia Glass Co., Findley, Ohio, in 1888, and by U. S. Glass Co., from 1892 until 1898. A standard creamer ($32.50) is known in ruby stained.

Bowl, Berry	20.00
Butter	
Covered	50.00
Toy, covered	65.00
Cake Stand	35.00
Celery	18.00
Cologne Bottles, pair	52.50
Compote, covered	
Jelly	25.00
High standard	45.00
Open, low standard	32.50
Creamer	
Standard	35.00
Toy size, 3½″	20.00

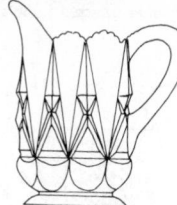

Cup and Saucer	45.00
Dish, flat, oblong, 7½"	18.00
Goblet	20.00
Honey Dish, rectangular, covered	48.00
Pitcher, water	55.00
Sauce	7.50
Spooner	
Standard	25.00
Toy spooner	20.00
Sugar	
Covered	37.50
Toy sugar	30.00
Tray, square shape	45.00
Tumbler	27.50
Wine	18.00
Toy child's set, 4 pcs	100.00

POGO STICK
(Crown)

Made by Lancaster Glass Co., Lancaster, Ohio, in 1910. Originally called "Crown" by the manufacturer but better known by its present name.

Bowl, Berry	15.00
Butter, covered	42.00
Cake Stand	35.00
Celery vase	18.00
Compote, open	18.50
Creamer	25.00
Cruet	22.00
Pitcher, water	35.00
Plate, 7"	8.00
Relish	13.50
Sauce, flat	6.50
Spooner	18.00
Syrup Jug, metal top	45.00
Sugar, covered	37.50
Tumbler	15.00

POPCORN

Non-flint, attributed to Boston and Sandwich Glass Co., late 1860s. Pieces were made with a large outstanding ornament, somewhat like an ear of corn, on bowl of pieces. It was probably continued by another company. The "popcorn ears" were made by a flat oval, filled with lines. Pieces with an outstanding ear should read "With ear" and the others "Lined ear."

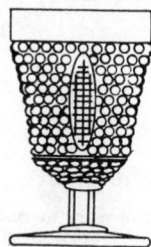

Butter, covered	65.00
Creamer	55.00
Goblets	
Lined ear	30.00
With ear	50.00
Pitcher, water, applied handle	95.00
Sauce	12.00
Spooner	30.00
Sugar, covered	45.00
Wine, with ear	65.00

PORTLAND

Non-flint pattern made by several companies and also by U. S. Glass Co. in the early 1900s. Clear with gold trim. The covered butter ($75.00), cruet ($90.00) and goblet ($40.00) are found with cranberry flashing.

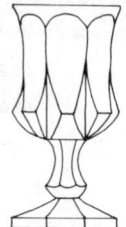

Bowl	
Berry	20.00
Small, flat, covered	20.00
Bureau Jar, silver plate top	27.50

Butter, covered	50.00
Basket, with handle of glass	85.00
Cake Stand, 10½"	45.00
Cafare, water	45.00
Compote, covered, 6"	55.00
Creamer, regular	27.50
Cruet, stoppered	55.00
Goblet	35.00
Lamp Base, 9"	62.50
Pickle or Relish, boat shaped	20.00
Pitcher, toy, water, set	20.00
Pitcher, water, straight sides,	55.00
Puff Box	18.00
Spooner	35.00
Sugar, covered	42.50
Sugar Shaker	40.00
Syrup	50.00
Tumbler	17.50
Wine	25.00

POWDER AND SHOT

Flint and non-flint made by Boston & Sandwich Glass Co., c1870s. Finial of covered pieces is flattened upright fan.

	Flint	Non-Flint
Bowls, 5", ftd and handled	—	45.00
Butter, covered	95.00	75.00
Castor Bottle	—	35.00
Celery	—	35.00
Compotes		
Covered, high standard	—	85.00
Open, low standard	—	45.00
Creamer, applied handle	95.00	55.00
Egg Cup	—	45.00
Goblet	65.00	45.00
Salt, master, ftd	—	39.00
Spooner	65.00	35.00
Sugars		
Covered	—	65.00
Open	—	35.00

PRINCESS FEATHER
(Rochelle)

Non-flint made by Bakewell, Pears, & Co. in the late 70s, later by U. S. Glass Co. in the

1890s. A rare blue opaque tumbler has been reported.

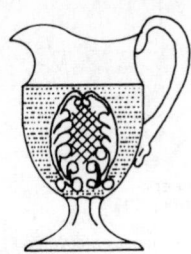

Bowl, 7¼", covered	35.00
Butter, covered	50.00
Cake Stand, 8"	35.00
Celery Vase	30.00
Compotes	
Covered, 8", high standard	50.00
Open, 8", low standard	35.00
Creamer, applied handle	55.00
Dish, oval	20.00
Goblet	27.50
Plate, 9"	30.00
Pitcher, water	65.00
Salt, master	25.00
Spooner	30.00
Sugars, covered	40.00

PRISCILLA #1
(Findlay's)

Non-flint made by Dalzell, Gillmore & Leighton, Findlay, Ohio, in the late 1890s and continued by National Glass Co. Heavily reproduced in clear, colors, and opalescent.

Biscuit Jar, covered	60.00
Bowl, 10¼", straight sides	50.00
Butter, covered	70.00
Cake Stand, 9½" x 5½"	50.00
Celery	55.00
Compotes	
Jelly, covered	45.00
9", high standard	55.00
Open, 9", high standard	45.00
Creamer	25.00
Cruet, stoppered	45.00

Goblet	25.00
Mug	15.00
Pitcher, water, tankard	75.00
Plates	
Regular	22.50
10½″, turned up edge	18.50
Spooner	20.00
Salt Shaker, single	30.00
Sugar, open	20.00
Syrup	45.00
Toothpick	50.00
Tumbler	21.00
Wine	26.00

PRISCILLA #2
(Fostoria's 1898)

Made by Fostoria Glass Co., Moundsville, W. Va., in 1898. Made in clear. An emerald green marmalade jar ($13.00) is known; other colors are white milk and custard with green and gold trim.

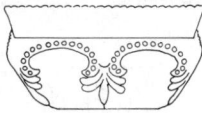

Bowl	
Berry, 8½″	15.00
Finger or Waste Bowl	12.00
Butter covered	65.00
Cake Stand	35.00
Carafe	40.00
Compote	
Covered	55.00
Open	40.00
Creamer	35.00
Cruet, original stopper	65.00
Cup, Sherbet	6.50
Egg Cup	20.00
Marmalade Jar, covered	45.00
Pitcher, water	30.00
Relish or Pickle, oblong	15.00
Salt, individual, 2 sizes	9.50–12.00
Salt Shakers, single	
Large, egg shaped	12.50
Small, wide base, long neck	10.00
Spooner	27.50
Sugar, covered	45.00
Syrup, nickel top	55.00
Toothpick, 4½″	35.00
Tumbler	27.50

PRISM WITH DIAMOND POINTS

Flint made by Bryce Brothers and later U. S. Glass Co.

Butter, covered	75.00
Compote, covered, 6″, high standard	125.00

Creamer	75.00
Egg Cups	
Double	45.00
Single	35.00
Goblet	45.00
Pitcher, water	95.00
Salt, master	17.50
Sugar, covered	50.00
Tumbler	40.00

PSYCHE AND CUPID

Non-flint, c1880s.

Butter, covered	60.00
Celery	40.00
Creamer	52.00
Goblet	57.50
Pitcher, water, applied handle	85.00
Sauce, footed, 4½″	12.50
Spooner	52.00
Sugar, covered	45.00
Wine	25.00

QUEENE ANNE
(Bearded Man)

Non-flint made by LaBelle Glass Co., Bridgeport, Ohio, c1879. Finials of covered pieces are Maltese Cross.

Butter, covered	45.00
Celery	27.00
Compote, covered	45.00

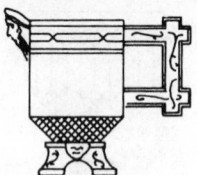

Creamer	35.00
Egg Cup	32.50
Pitcher	
Milk	45.00
Water	50.00
Spooner	25.00
Sugar, covered	40.00

RED BLOCK
(Late Block)

Non-flint with red stain made by Doyle and Co.; later made by five companies plus U. S. Glass Co. in 1892.

Bowl, 8"	60.00
Butter, covered	65.00
Celery	50.00
Creamer, regular	70.00
Decanter, 12", stoppered	115.00
*Goblet	37.50
*Mug	35.00
Pitcher, water	115.00
Rose Bowl	45.00
Sauce, flat, 4½"	22.50
Salt and Pepper Shakers, single	30.00
Spooner	38.00
Sugar, covered	50.00
Tumbler	32.50
*Wine	35.00

REVERSE TORPEDO
(Bull's Eye Band, Bull's Eye and Diamond Point #2.)

Made by Dalzeli, Gillmore & Leighton Glass Co., Findlay, Ohio, c1888–1890.

Banana Stand	105.00
Bisquit Jar, covered	165.00

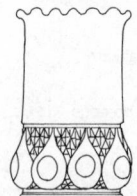

Butter, covered	75.00
Compotes	
Jelly, covered	55.00
Open, 6", high standard	80.00
Open, 9¼", ruffled edge	145.00
Goblet	50.00
Pitcher, water, tankard	110.00
Sugar, covered	77.50
Syrup	165.00
Tumbler	25.00

RIBBED GRAPE

Flint, early 1860s.

Butter, covered	110.00
Celery	50.00
Compotes	
Covered, 6"	125.00
Open, 8", low standard	85.00
Creamer, applied handle	110.00
Goblet	40.00
Pitcher, water, applied handle	165.00
Plate, 6"	37.50
Sugar, covered	85.00
Wine	35.00

RIBBED IVY

Flint, late 1850s.

Butter, covered	110.00
Castor Bottle	35.00
Celery	300.00+
Compotes	
6" Jelly, covered	125.00
9", open, high standard, scalloped edge	85.00

Creamer	125.00
Decanter, quart, stoppered	150.00
Egg Cup	30.00
Goblet	40.00
Hat	350.00
Salts	
Master, covered	115.00
Open, scalloped rim	40.00
Sauce	10.00
Spooner	40.00
Sugar, covered	85.00
Sweetmeat, covered, on stand	165.00
Tumbler, water	75.00
Whiskey	
Handled, bar	75.00
Plain	65.00
Wine	85.00

RIBBED PALM

Flint made by McKee Glass Co., Pittsburgh, Pa., c1868.

Bowl, 8″	40.00
Butter, covered	85.00
Castor Set, pewter base, complete	100.00
Compotes	
Covered, 6″	125.00
Open, 7″, low standard	67.50
Creamer, applied handle	177.50
Egg Cup	27.50
Goblet	45.00
Lamp, all glass	85.00
Pitcher, water, applied handle	150.00
Plate, 6″	35.00
Salt, footed	24.00
Spillholder	40.00
Spooner	45.00

Sugar, covered	75.00
Tumbler	75.00
Wine	40.00

RIBBON

Non-flint made by Bakewell, Pears, Pittsburgh, Pa., in the late 1860s. Other Ribbon patterns are Clear Ribbon, Frosted Ribbon, Double Ribbon, Fluted Ribbon, Grated Ribbon. It seems logical to use "Ribbon" to denote this one, the oldest and best known. (Lee: EAPG, pl. 67) It has been erroneously called "Frosted Ribbon" at times, which can be confusing.

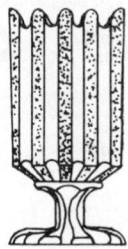

Butter, covered	75.00
Cake Stand, 8½″	45.00
Celery	30.00
Cologne Bottle, stopper, large	65.00
Compotes, covered	
7″, low standard	45.00
8″, high standard	55.00
Compotes, open	
7″, low standard	40.00
10½″, silverplated, Dolphin stand	100.00
Oblong Dolphin stand, large	300.00 +
Creamer	30.00
*Goblet	37.50
Pitcher, water	75.00
Platter, 9″ x 13″, oblong, cut corners	62.50
Sauces	
Footed	18.50
Handled	17.50
Spooner	28.00
Sugar, covered	65.00
Tray, water, 15″ x 16¼″	100.00
Waste Bowl	35.00
Wine	85.00

RISING SUN
(Sunrise)

Made by Ripley and Co., then continued by U. S. Glass Co. in 1908 at Glassport, Pa. Made in clear glass with gold trim; sometimes sun is flashed cranberry or green.

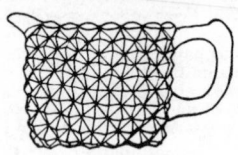

	Clear	Cranberry or Green Flashed
Bowls, Berry	12.00	—
Butter, covered	32.50	47.00
Cake Plate, 10½"	22.50	—
Cake Stand	35.00	—
Celery	25.00	—
Compote		
Covered, high standard	45.00	—
Open, high standard	30.00	—
Creamer		
Regular, Hotel	25.00	—
Tall on foot	22.50	—
Cruet, orig stopper	40.00	—
Dish, with ruffled edge	15.00	—
Goblet	20.00	27.00
Pitcher, water	35.00	—
Relish	15.00	—
Sauce, Flat	6.50	—
Spooner	18.00	—
Sugar, covered, 2 sides		
Regular or Hotel, three handled	40.00	—
Tall on foot	35.00	—
Sugar, open, double handled	25.00	—
Toothpick, handled	18.00	—
Tumbler	15.00	25.00
Wine	25.00	30.00

	Clear	Ruby Stained
Relish Tray	45.00	—
Rose Bowl, 6½", on chain	25.00	—
Sauce, flat	—	19.00
Spooner	20.00	—
Sugar, covered	40.00	—
Tumbler	15.00	—
Wine	30.00	—

ROBIN HOOD

This pattern was made by Fostoria Glass Co., in 1898, in Moundsville, W. Va. Pieces have been reported in clear and emerald green. A creamer ($50.00), molasses can ($65.00) and pickle ($30.00) can be found in milk white. Some of the larger items have two rows of the large eyes of the pattern.

ROANOKE

Made by Ripley and Co., Pittsburg, Pa. Also made by Gillinder and Son, Greensburg, Pa., and continued by U. S. Glass Co., 1891 to 1898. Made in clear, emerald green (creamer at $45.00 and tumbler at $38.00 are known), amber and yellow. Sometimes highlighted with red stain.

	Clear	Ruby Stained
Bowls		
Berry	10.00	25.00
Waste	—	33.00
Butter, covered	45.00	—
Cake Stand, large, sometimes etched	50.00	—
Creamer	30.00	—
Goblet	25.00	30.00
Pitcher, water	50.00	—

	Clear	Emerald Green
Bowls, Berry, 3 sizes, av.	22.50	35.00
Butter, covered	50.00	48.00
Cake Stand	35.00	48.00
Celery	22.00	30.00
Compotes, high standard		
Covered	38.00	65.00
Open	30.00	50.00
Creamer	25.00	35.00
Cruet, orig stopper	45.00	60.00
Mug	18.00	25.00
Molasses can, Brittania lid	38.00	50.00
Nappy, 4½"	12.00	—
Pitcher, water	42.00	65.00
Pickle	15.00	22.00
Salt Shaker, single	18.00	25.00
Spooner	20.00	—
Sugar, covered	27.00	35.00
Tumbler	25.00	35.00

ROMAN KEY

Flint glass pattern of the 1860s made in several variants by Union Glass Co. and others. Sometimes erroneously called "Greek Key" because of the typical Greek band. Prices recorded are for flint glass.

	Clear	Frosted
Bowl, 8″	45.00	—
Butter, covered	50.00	—
Cake Stand, 12″	50.00	—
Celery Vase, footed	—	65.00
Champagne	45.00	77.00
Compote, open, 7″, low standard	95.00	—
Creamer, applied handle	68.00	—
Decanter, stoppered	90.00	—
Egg Cup	35.00	40.00
Goblet	37.00	50.00
Pitcher, water	200.00+	—
Spooner	25.00	35.00
Sugar, covered	60.00	—
Tumbler, bar	25.00	77.00
Wine	50.00	52.00

ROMAN ROSETTE

Non-flint made by Bryce, Walker and Co. 1875–1885. Reissued by U. S. Glass Co. in 1892 and 1898.

	Clear	Ruby Stained
Bowl, 8½″	22.00	—
Butter, covered	45.00	—
Cake Stand, 9″	45.00	—
Celery	18.00	—

	Clear	Ruby Stained
Compotes		
Covered, 6″, high standard	62.00	—
Jelly, covered, 4½″	55.00	—
Creamer	28.00	—
*Goblet	33.00	—
Pickle	15.00	—
Pitchers		
Milk	46.00	—
Water	62.00	—
Plate, 7½″	18.00	—
Salt and Pepper shakers, silver frame, pr	55.00	90.00
Spooner	25.00	—
Sugar, covered	43.00	—
Tray, bread or platter	30.00	—
Wine	30.00	—

ROPE BAND
(Clear Panels with Cord Band)

Made by Bryce Bros., Pittsburgh, Pa.; later made by U. S. Glass Co., in 1870s. Made in clear glass; colors possible, but not reported.

Bowl	15.00
Butter, covered	37.50
Cake Stand, large	27.50
Celery vase	12.00
Compote	
Covered	35.00
Open	22.50
Creamer	18.00
Goblet	27.50
Pitcher, water	37.50
Platter, handled	30.00
Relish	8.50
Sauce, footed	7.50
Spooner	14.00
Sugar, covered	35.00
Tumbler	12.00
Wine	18.50

ROSE POINT BAND
(Water Lily #2)

Made about 1900 by Indiana Glass Co., Dunkirk, Ind., in clear glass only. Sometimes found with floral decorations in color with gold trim.

	Clear	Color Flashed
Bowl, Berry	15.00	22.00
Butter, covered	40.00	60.00
Cake Plate, flat in silver holder, 10″	45.00	—
Compote		
Jelly	25.00	—
7½″ open, ruffled edge	35.00	—
Creamer		
Regular	15.00	22.00
Small size, on legs	18.00	25.00
Goblet	20.00	—
Pitcher, water	40.00	—
Plate, flat, serving	20.00	—
Punch Cup	8.00	—
Sauce, footed	9.00	—
Spooner	15.00	—
Sugar		
Regular	22.00	—
Small size footed, open	18.00	—
Wine	20.00	32.00
Water Tray	30.00	50.00

ROSETTE

Non-flint made by Bryce Bros., Pittsburgh, Pa., in the late 1870s. Continued by the U. S. Glass Co. Later made in Ohio in 1898.

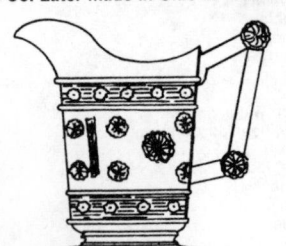

Bowl, 7½″, covered	30.00
Butter, covered	40.00
Cake Stand, 11″	35.00
Compotes	
Jelly	22.50
Covered, 6″, high standard	40.00
Open, 7″, high standard	35.00
Creamer	20.00

Goblet	22.50
Pitcher, water	40.00
Plates	
7″	12.00
9″, handled	14.00
Relish (fish shaped) wider at one end	13.50
Sauce, flat, handled	6.50
Shakers, single	17.50
Spooner	20.00
Sugar, covered	35.00
Wine	18.50

ROSETTE AND PALMS

Non-flint, made by J. B. Higbee Co., c1910.

Banana Stand	52.50
Biscuit Jar, covered	42.00
Butter, covered	45.00
Cake Stand, 9½″	28.00
Goblet	20.00
Plate, 18″	15.00
Spooner	22.00
Sugar, covered	35.00
Wine	18.00

SAWTOOTH

An early flint glass pattern made in the late 1850s by the New England Glass Co. Later made in non-flint.

	Flint	Non-Flint
Butter, covered	85.00	—
Cake Stand, 18″	85.00	55.00
Celery	56.00	—
Celery Vase, 10″	52.00	17.00
Champagne	56.00	—
Compotes		
Covered, 9½″, high standard	85.00	—
High standard, ruffled edge, 12″	95.00	—
Open, 8″, low standard, sawtooth edge	35.00	—
Creamer	75.00	27.00
Cruet, acorn finial	100.00 +	—
Egg Cup	45.00	—
Goblet	40.00	—
Pitcher, water, applied handle	125.00	—
Plate, 6½″	45.00	—
Pomade Jar, covered	50.00	—
Salts		
Covered, footed	47.00	—
Open, smooth edge	25.00	—
Spillholder	50.00	—
Spooner	65.00	14.00
Sugar, covered	65.00	—
Tumbler, flat	35.00	—

SAWTOOTHED HONEYCOMB
(Serrated Block and Loop)

Non-flint pattern made by Steiner Glass Co., Buckhannon, W. Va., 1904–1908. Molds sold to Morgantown Glass Co. about 1921. Clear, sometimes with red stain.

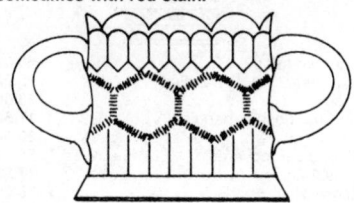

	Clear	Ruby Stained
Bowl, Berry, 9″	12.00	—
Butter, covered	40.00	—
Compotes		
9½″, high standard	45.00	—
Creamer	22.00	35.00
Cruet	50.00	—
Goblet	20.00	—
Pitcher, water, 10″, bulbous, applied handle	50.00	—
Punch Bowl, serpentine base, 14″h	95.00	—
Sugar, covered	35.00	—
Toothpick	24.00	—
Tumbler	15.00	28.00

SCALLOPED DIAMOND POINT
(Late Diamond Point Band, Diamond Point with Flute)

Non-flint pattern. Not to be confused with the old Diamond Point which is flint; this is an entirely different pattern. Made by Central Glass Co., Wheeling, W. Va. Also made by U.S. Glass Co. after 1891. A few rare pieces in cobalt blue, but usually only seen in clear glass.

	Clear	Cobalt Blue
Bowls, many sizes, both round and oval, av.	20.00	—
Butter Dish, covered	45.00	—
Cake Stand, five sizes		
8″	25.00	—
12″	55.00	—
Cheese Dish, covered, 8″	50.00	—
Creamer	35.00	75.00
Goblet	30.00	—
Mustard Jar, covered	20.00	—
Pickle dish, oval	18.00	35.00
Plates, various sizes, all have star centers		
5″	10.00	—
9″	25.00	—
Sauce, footed, 4″	10.00	—
Sugar, covered	35.00	—

SCALLOPED SWIRL
(York Herringbone)

Made by U.S. Glass Co. in 1891. May have been made much earlier. Sometimes found with ruby stain; very rare in emerald green.

	Clear	Ruby Stained
Bowl, Berry	22.00	—
Butter, covered	47.00	—
Cake Plate, 10″	30.00	—
Celery	20.00	—
Compote, covered, 7″	45.00	—
Creamer	25.00	55.00
Goblet	28.00	40.00
Pitcher, water	52.00	—
Spooner	20.00	—
Sugar, covered	35.00	—
Toothpick	—	45.00
Tumbler	20.00	37.50

SCALLOPED TAPE
(Jewel Band)

Non-flint, c1870–1880s. Maker unknown. Occasionally found in amber, blue, canary, and light green. Prices are for clear.

Butter, covered	45.00
Cake Stand	35.00
Compotes	
Covered, 8″	55.00
Open	40.00
Creamer	30.00
Dish, rectangular, covered	45.00
Egg Cup	15.00
Goblet	20.00
Pitcher, water	55.00
Plate, 6″	15.00
Salt	12.00
Spooner	20.00
Sugar, covered	40.00
Tray, Bread	38.50
Wine	20.00

SCROLL

Non-flint, made by Duncan Glass Co., c1880s.

Butter, covered	40.00
Celery	17.50
Compotes	
Covered, high standard	45.00

Open, high standard	35.00
Creamer	25.00
Egg Cup	17.50
Goblet	25.00
Pitcher, water	45.00
Salt, footed	12.00
Spooner	22.50
Sugar, covered	40.00
Tumbler, footed	17.50
Wine	15.00

SCROLL WITH FLOWERS

Non-flint made by Central Glass Co. in the 1870s; then later by Northwood. Occasionally found in color.

Butter, covered	40.00
Cake Plate, 10½″, handled	25.00
Creamer	30.00
Egg Cup, double, handled	17.50
Goblet	30.00
Mustard Jar, covered	35.00
Pickle, handled	17.50
Pitcher, water	75.00
Plate, double handled, 10½″	30.00
Sauce, double-handled	10.00
Spooner	25.00
Sugar, covered	40.00
Wine	25.00

SHELL AND TASSEL
(Shell and Spike)

Non-flint made by George A. Duncan & Sons, Pittsburgh, Pa., in the 1880s. It was patented by Augustus Heisey on July 26, 1881. Two forms were issued, square with shell shaped finials, and later, round with frosted dog finials. Also made in azure blue, amber, and canary, but extremely rare.

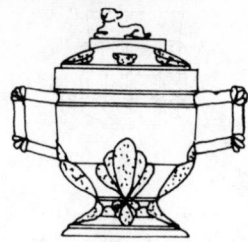

Round

Bowl, 12″, oval, deep	110.00
Butters	
Covered	45.00
Pat, shell shape	15.00
Creamer	32.50
*Goblet	35.00
Ice Cream Tray	45.00
Pitcher, water	65.00
Platter, portraits of Lincoln and Garfield in center, Shell & Tassel border	200.00+
Sauce, footed	16.00
Shakers, single	32.50
Spooner	25.00
Sugar, covered, Dog finial	110.00
Tray, 9″ x 13″	50.00
Vase, scalloped rim, 7½″	135.00

Square

Butter, covered	75.00
Cake Stands	
8″	55.00
12″	90.00
Celery Vase	35.00
Compotes	
4½″, jelly	50.00
10″, open	65.00
Creamer	55.00
*Goblet	Rare
Oyster Plate, large	110.00
Pitcher, water	55.00
Platter, 9″ x 13″	65.00
Salt, shell shaped	18.00
Sauce, flat, shell shaped	10.00
Spooner	35 .00
Sugar, covered	85.00

SHOSHONE
(Floral Diamond)

Made by the U. S. Glass Co. in 1898, perhaps earlier by another company. Made in clear and emerald green, sometimes partly stained in color. Berry Bowl ($35.00) and Water Pitcher ($90.00) reported in emerald green. Fifty or more pieces were produced. Prices given for clear.

Bowl, Berry	18.50
Butter, covered	40.00
Cake Stand	35.00
Celery Vase	18.00
Celery tray, flat	20.00
Compote	
Covered	55.00
Open	35.00
Condiment Set, tray	60.00
Creamer	30.00
Cruet	75.00
Custard cup and saucer	35.00
Goblet	30.00
Horseradish Jar, covered	17.50
Ice Tub	40.00
Jam Jar	18.00
Jelly dish, handled	18.00
Molasses Can, metal top	45.00
Mustard Jar, covered	18.00
Pitcher, water, 2 sizes	45.00–55.00
Salt Shaker, single	12.00
Spooner	25.00
Sugar, covered	40.00
Syrup Jug, metal top	45.00
Toothpick	30.00
Tumbler	22.00
Tray, water	55.00
Wine	45.00

SHRINE
(Jewel with Moon and Star)

Non-flint made by Beatty & Indiana Glass Co., Dunkirk, Ind., c. late 1880s. Design is clear glass with cranberry and yellow flashed moon and stars.

Bowls, many sizes, 9½"	30.00
Butter, covered	45.00
Cake Stand, 8½"	30.00
Champagne	60.00
Creamer	30.00
Goblet	35.00
Pitcher, water	50.00
Spooner	45.00
Sugar Bowl, covered	40.00
Tumbler, regular	25.00

SHUTTLE
(Hearts of Loch Laven)

Made by Indiana Tumbler and Goblet Co., Greentown, Ind., between 1894 and 1903. Made in caramel and clear with gold trim.

	Clear	Caramel
Bowl, Berry	25.00	—
Butter, covered	50.00	150.00
Creamer	30.00	—
Cruet with orig stopper	75.00	—
Mug	22.00	95.00
Pitcher, water	50.00	—
Spooner	18.00	—
Sugar, covered	37.00	—
Tumbler	25.00	80.00
Wine	8.00	38.00

SKILTON
(Oregon #2)

Made by Richards and Hartley of Tarentum, Pa. This is not one of the U.S. Glass "States" pattern series and should not be confused with Beaded Loop, which is Oregon #1, named by U.S. Glass Co. It is better known as "Skilton" and was named by Millard to avoid confusion with Beaded Loop. Known to be stained with ruby, but is mostly seen in clear.

	Clear	Ruby Stained
Bowls, low, shallow, various sizes, 7¾-13", av.	20.00	—
Butter, covered	45.00	—
Cake Stand	35.00	—

	Clear	Ruby Stained
Celery	18.00	—
Compotes		
Low, open	30.00	—
High stand, covered, 7–8"	45.00	—
Creamer	30.00	42.00
Dishes		
Oblong and square	18–25.00	—
Olive, handled	15.00	—
Goblet	48.00	—
Pickle	18.00	—
Pitchers		
Milk	45.00	—
Water	50.00	—
Salt and Pepper Shaker		
Pair	40.00	—
Single	22.00	—
Sauces, footed	10.00	—
Spooner	25.00	—
Sugar, covered	35.00	—
Tray, water	47.00	—
Tumbler	30.00	37.50
Wines	33.00	—

SNAIL
(Compact, Idaho)

Non-flint made by George Duncan & Sons, Pittsburgh, Pa., c1880, and by U. S. Glass Co. in the States' Pattern series. Ruby flashed pieces date after 1891.

	Clear	Ruby Stained
Banana Stand	165.00	—
Bowls		
Berry, 8", oval	28.00	35.00
Finger	25.00	—
Open, 6 x 9"	28.00	—
Butter, covered	85.00	—
Cake Stand	75.00	—
Celery Vase	39.00	65.00
Cheese, covered	65.00	—
Compotes, high standard		
Covered, 10"	50.00	—
Open, 8"	35.00	—
Creamer, regular	30.00	—
Cruet, stoppered	57.00	175.00
Goblet	45.00	—

war. Two pitchers were made by the Beatty-Brady Glass Co., Dunkirk, Ind. The only known matching pieces are listed below.

	Clear	Ruby Stained
Pitchers		
Syrup	70.00	225.00
Water, tankard	150.00	—
Plate, 7″	23.00	—
Relish, 7″, oval	25.00	—
Salt, master	18.00	—
Shakers, Salt and Pepper,		
single	25.00	—
Spooner	32.00	—
Sugars		
Individual, covered	35.00	—
Regular, covered	45.00	—
Tumbler	40.00	—
Wine	30.00	—

Water pitcher, Admiral Dewey, Flag-ship Olympia, flags, cannon, balls around base	70.00
Tumbler, portrait of Dewey, matches pitcher	35.00
Water pitcher, Captain Gridley, "You may fire when ready," bullets around base	85.00
Tumbler to match	80.00

SOUTHERN IVY

Non-flint, c1880s.

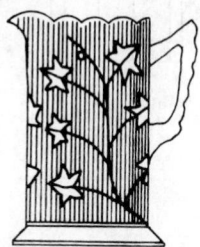

Bowl, 8″	18.50
Butter, covered	25.00
Creamer	25.00
Cruet, stoppered	25.00
Pitcher, water	30.00
Sauce, flat	17.00
Spooner	17.00
Sugars	
Covered	25.00
Open	15.00

SPANISH-AMERICAN

Made in the late 1890s in commemoration of Admiral Dewey and the Spanish American

SPRIG

Non-flint made by Bryce, Higbee & Co., Pittsburgh, Pa., mid-1880s, and by McKee and Bros.

Bowls	
6″, covered	30.00
10″, footed, scalloped	35.00
Butter, covered	45.00
Cake Stand, 10″	35.00
Celery	35.00
Compotes	
Covered, high standard	48.00
Open, high standard	30.00
Creamer	25.00
Goblet	32.50
Pitcher, water	45.00
Platter or Bread Plate	37.50
Spooner	22.00
Sugar, covered	47.50
Tumbler	17.50
Wine	40.00

SQUARE LION
(Atlanta, Clear Lion Head)

Produced by Fostoria Glass Co., Moundsville, West Virginia, c1895. Clear and frosted. Pieces are square in shape.

	Clear	Frosted
Bowls		
5 x 8", low collar base	55.00	—
7", scallop rim, serving bowl	60.00	
Butter, covered	60.00	110.00
Cake Stand, large, 10"	85.00	—
Celery	40.00	75.00
Compotes		
Covered, 7"	75.00	—
Open, 5", jelly	50.00	—
Creamer	45.00	—
Goblet	45.00	60.00
Marmalade Jar	65.00	85.00
Pitcher, water	110.00	—
Relish, oval	35.00	—
Salts		
Individual	30.00	—
Master	48.00	68.00
Salt Shaker, single	45.00	—
Spooner	42.50	—
Sugar, covered	48.50	—
Tumbler	35.00	—
Toothpick	40.00	60.00

STAR ROSETTED

Non-flint made by McKee Bros., Pittsburgh, Pa., c1880.

Butter, covered	47.50
Compotes	
Covered, 8½"	40.00
Open, 8½", scalloped edge	35.00
Creamer	30.00
Goblet	25.00
Pickle	8.00
Pitcher, water	50.00
Plates	
7"	15.00
10", bread plate, "A Good Mother Makes a Happy Home"	40.00
Relish, 9"	10.00
Sauce, footed	10.00
Spooner	25.00
Sugar, covered	45.00

[THE] STATES
(Cane and Star Medallion)

Non-flint made by the U. S. Glass Co. in 1905. Clear with gold trim, found also in emerald green. Add 50% for green.

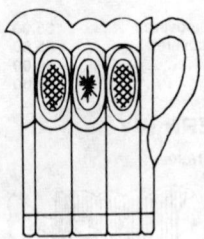

Butter, covered	40.00
Celery Dish, flat	15.00
Compote, open, 7", high standard ..	30.00
Creamer	
Individual	15.00
Regular	25.00
Goblet	35.00
Pitcher, water	45.00
Plate, 10"	35.00
Punch Bowl set, eight cups	110.00
Sauces, 4", flat, shaped like little tubs with handles	8.00
Spooner	25.00
Sugar, covered	37.50
Syrup	65.00
Tumbler	25.00
Toothpick, handled	35.00
Wine	26.00

STIPPLED FORGET-ME-NOT

Non-flint made by Findlay Glass Co. in the 1880s, and after 1891 by the Model Flint Glass Co., Findlay, Ohio.

Butter, covered, acorn finial, complete	50.00
Cake Stand, 12″	45.00
Celery	30.00
Compotes, covered	
6″, low standard	37.50
8″, high standard	50.00
Creamer	30.00
Goblet	32.50
Mug	12.50
Pitcher, water	50.00
Plates	
7″, Baby in Tub reaching for ball	55.00
7″, Star center	30.00
9″, Kitten center	30.00
Relish, oval	13.50
Salt, Master	25.00
Sauce, footed	22.00
Spooner	25.00
Sugar, covered	35.00
Toothpick, hat shaped	75.00
Trays	
Bread	35.00
Water, Aquatic center	47.50
Tumbler	22.00
Wine	32.50

STIPPLED PEPPERS

Non-flint made by Boston & Sandwich Glass Co. in the 1870s.

Creamer, applied handle	32.50
Egg Cup	20.00
Goblet	27.50

Pitcher, water, applied handle	45.00
Salt, footed, scarce	15.00
Sauce	6.50
Spooner	25.00
Sugar, covered	35.00
Tumbler, footed	20.00

STIPPLED STAR

Non-flint made by Gillinder & Sons in the 1870s.

Butter, covered	40.00
Celery	32.00
Compotes, high standard	
Covered, 12″	65.00
Open, 8″	45.00
*Creamer	45.00
Egg Cup	25.00
*Goblet	30.00
Pitcher, water	75.00
Sauce, footed	12.00
Spooner	25.00
*Sugar, covered	45.00
Tumbler, scarce	20.00
*Wine	25.00

STRAWBERRY
(Fairfax)

Non-flint pattern first made in 1870 and patented by John Bryce. Later made by Walker Co. Also found in milk.

	Clear	Milk
Bowl, oval	30.00	—
Butter, covered	55.00	—
Compotes, covered		
8″, high standard	75.00	—
8″, low standard	65.00	—
Creamer, applied handle	55.00	105.00
*Egg Cup	22.00	—
*Goblet	38.00	56.00
Pitchers, applied handle		
Syrup	55.00	—
Water	65.00	—
Spooner	23.00	40.00
Sugar, covered	40.00	50.00
Tumbler, Bar	46.00	—

STRAWBERRY AND CURRANT

One of a non-flint series of fruit patterns which has become known as Multiple Fruits, (Cherry and Fig, Loganberry and Grape, Raspberry and Grape, and Cornucopia and Sprig of Cherries). They were made in Findlay, Ohio. There is also a variation in the goblets in this series, made without the interlocking design, and they are of inferior quality. They were originally made to contain jelly and had a tin lid. The goblets to the set are of better glass, and carry the design which identifies them.

There are matching pieces in all forms, although whether or not all forms were made in all four patterns is not known. Reproduction goblets found in colors.

Butter, covered	50.00
Celery	35.00
Cheese, covered	50.00
Creamer	40.00
*Goblet	18.00
Pitchers	
Milk	37.50
Water	50.00
Sauce, footed	12.00
Spooner	30.00
Sugar, covered	40.00
Syrup	77.50
Tumblers	22.50

TENNESSEE
(Jewel and Crescent; Jewelled Rosettes)

Made by King Glass Co., Pittsburgh, Pa., and continued by U. S. Glass Co., in 1899, as part of the States series. Made in clear, but may come with colored jewels.

	Clear	Color Stained
Bowls, Berry	20.00	45.00
Butter, covered	55.00	—
Cake Stand		
9½″	35.00	—
10½	45.00	—
Celery	25.00	—
Compote, open		
7″	38.00	—
10½″	45.00	—
Jelly, covered, 5″	42.00	52.00
Creamer	22.50	—
Goblet	30.00	—
Pitcher water, ¼ gal.	55.00	—
Platter or Bread Plate	50.00	75.00
Relish	20.00	—
Spooner	20.00	—
Sugar, covered	40.00	—
Toothpick	42.00	50.00
Tumbler	22.00	—
Wine	35.00	—

TEXAS
(Loop with Stippled Panels)

Non-flint made by U. S. Glass Co., c1900 in the States' Pattern series. Pieces are clear, trimmed in gold, sometimes cranberry flashed.

	Clear	Cranberry Flashed
Bowls		
Flat, 7¼″, 8½″, 9½″	25.00	37.50
Scalloped 6″, 7″, 8″	25.00	50.00
Butter, covered	55.00	—
Cake Stand, 10″	45.00	
Celery		
Tray	22.00	—
Vase	25.00	—

	Clear	Cranberry Flashed
Compotes		
5", open, high standard	37.00	—
8", covered, high standard	65.00	—
*Creamers, individual and regular	27.00	15.00
Cruet, stoppered	55.00	95.00
Goblet	45.00	60.00
Pitcher, water	50.00	—
Plate, 9"	18.00	—
Relish	20.00	—
Salt, master	22.50	—
Spooner	30.00	—
*Sugars		
Individual	20.00	—
Regular, covered	35.00	—
Toothpick	45.00	57.00
Tumbler	25.00	—
Wine	35.00	—

TEXAS BULL'S EYE
(Filley, Bull's Eye Variant)

Originated by Bryce Bros., Pittsburgh, Pa., and continued by Findlay Glass, Findlay, Ohio. Originally made in semi-flint, (not bell tone, but some lead content), c1850–1870 and later.

Butter, covered	45.00
Creamer	35.00
Goblet	27.50
Pitcher, water	55.00
Spooner	20.00

Sugar, covered	30.00
Tumblers, regular	57.50
Wine	16.00

TEXAS STAR
(Swirl and Star, Snowflake Base)

Non-flint pattern made by Steiner Glass Co., Buckhannon, W. Va., c1903–1908. Body of pieces are paneled. Pattern appears on the base, which is frosted around the design.

Butter Dish	55.00
Bowl, 9½"	45.00
Cake Plate, 11"	40.00
Celery Tray	16.00
Cruet	47.50
Pitcher, water, tankard, applied handle	60.00
Punch Bowl	125.00
Punch Cup	12.00
Salt and Pepper Shakers	55.00
Syrup	50.00
Sugar Shaker	40.00
Tumbler	18.00

THISTLE

Non-flint, made by Bryce, Walker & Co. in 1872.

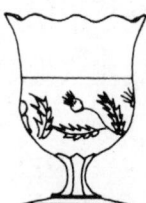

Bowl, 8"	30.00
Butter, covered	50.00
Cake Stand	45.00
Compotes	
High, covered	50.00
Low, covered	40.00

Cordial	40.00
Creamer, applied handle	55.00
Egg Cup	30.00
*Goblet	40.00
Pitcher, water	50.00
Relish	20.00
Salt, footed	18.50
Spooner	35.00
Sugars	
Covered	45.00
Open, buttermilk type	35.00
Tumbler	30.00
Wine	35.00

THREE-FACE

Non-flint made by George E. Duncan & Son, Pittsburgh, Pa., c1872. Designed by John E. Miller, a designer with Duncan, who later became a member of the firm. Companies in the Pittsburgh area produced many patterns in expectation of the 1876 Philadelphia Centennial Exposition. It has been heavily reproduced.

Biscuit Jar	500.00+
Butter, covered	150.00
Cake Stands	
8", 9"	110.00
10", 11"	150.00
Celery	95.00
Champagnes	
Hollow stem	250.00+
Saucer type	150.00
Claret	85.00
Compotes	
Covered, 4"	115.00
Covered, 10"	140.00
Open, 6"–9"	45–90.00
Creamer, with face	100.00
Goblet	80.00
Lamp, Oil	140.00
Marmalade Jar	200.00
Pitcher, water	295.00
Salt Dip	35.00
Sauce, footed	25.00
Shakers, pair	75.00
Spooner	75.00
Sugar, covered	110.00
Tumbler	55.00
Wine	45.00

THUMBPRINT, EARLY
(Giant Baby Thumbprint)

Flint originally produced by Bakewell, Pears, & Co., Pittsburgh, Pa., c1850–1860s. Made by several factories in various forms. The bar tumbler ($45.00) was produced in non-flint.

Ale glass	32.00
Banana Bowl, boat shape	145.00
Berry Set, round, 7 pcs	195.00
Bitters Bottle	135.00
Champagne	95.00
Claret	60.00
Compotes	
4", covered	75.00
8", open, flared and scalloped top base patterned	95.00
12 ¼", extremely large, spherical shape, with cover, (very rare, only two known)	220.00+
Creamer	58.00
Egg Cup	40.00
Goblet, barrel shaped, baluster stem	50.00
Spooner	48.00
Sugar, covered	60.00
Tumbler, Bar	42.00
Tumble-Up	450.00
Wine, barrel shape, baluster stem	75.00

TORPEDO
(Pygmy)

Non-flint made by Thompson Glass Co., Uniontown, Pa., c1889. Clear; goblet ($82.00) documented in ruby stained.

Banana Stand	75.00
Bowls	
8″, covered	40.00
9½″, flared rim, open	35.00
Waist, scalloped rim	40.00
Butter, covered	75.00
Cake Stand, 10″	55.00
Celery, scalloped top	35.00
Compotes	
4″, covered Jelly	50.00
5″, open, flared rim	35.00
9″, open, flared rim, high standard	50.00
Creamer	55.00
Cruet, stoppered	55.00
Cup and Saucer	55.00
Decanter, stoppered	65.00
Goblet	45.00
Lamps	
3⅜″, handled	75.00
8″, plain base, pattern on bowl	85.00
Marmalade Jar, covered	55.00
Pitchers	
Milk, 8½″	65.00
Water, 10½″	95.00
Rose Bowl	60.00
Salts, master	15.00
Salt and Pepper Shakers, single	27.50
Sauce, 4½″, collared base	11.00
Spooner, scalloped top	32.50
Sugar, open	47.50
Syrup	67.50
Trays, water	
10″, round	115.00
11¾″, clover shaped	75.00
Tumbler	30.00
Waste Bowl	40.00
Wine	28.50

Champagne	32.00
Compote 10″	
High standard, open, signed (Davis)	125.00
Open, low standard	45.00
Creamer	
Regular	35.00
In silver holder	75.00
Dish, Fruit, large, silver frame	90.00
Epergne signed, P.G. Co. Pat'd	125.00
Goblet	
Regular, marked P. g. flint	65.00
With clear shield on side	37.50
Plain	32.00
Ice Cream Tray	47.50
Pitcher, water	75.00
Plate	
6″	25.00
12½″, Three footed, shell shape, shallow	55.00
Sauce	
4″	12.00
Leaf shaped	15.00
Spooner, flint	35.00
Sugar, covered	
Silver plated holder	75.00
Without holder	45.00
Toothpick holder	30.00
Tray, water	90.00

TREE OF LIFE WITH HAND

Non-flint made by Duncan & Sons, Pittsburgh, Pa., c1884.

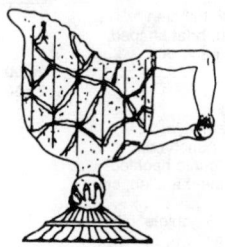

TREE OF LIFE
(Portland's)

Made by Portland Glass Co., 1864–1874. Originally made in green, purple, blue, yellow, light and dark blue, but color is rare today.

Bowls		
Berry, oval shape	30.00	
Finger bowl, underplate	50.00	
Butter, covered	55.00	
Celery vase, silver frame	55.00	
Cologne bottle, facetted stopper	48.00	

	Clear	Milk
Biscuit Jar	—	58.00
Bowls, oval		
8″	25.00	—
10″	35.00	—
Butter, covered	75.00	—
Cake Stand, 10″	100.00	—
Celery	40.00	—
Compote, cov, 6″, high standard	65.00	—
Compotes, open		
5″, low standard	65.00	—
10½″, high standard	80.00	—

	Clear	Milk
Creamer, signed	65.00	80.00
Goblet, signed	40.00	—
Ice Cream Tray	40.00	—
Pitcher, water	75.00	—
Plate, 7″	20.00	—
Punch Cup	15.00	—
Sauce, footed	15.00	—
Sauces, flat, shaped like shells	15.00	—
Spooner	35.00	—
Sugar, covered	65.00	—
Tumbler	29.00	—
Wine	30.00	—

TRIPLE TRIANGLE

Made by Doyle and Co. of Pittsburgh, Pa., in 1890, in clear and with ruby stain. Continued by U.S. Glass Co. after 1891. Pieces with ruby stain are most often found.

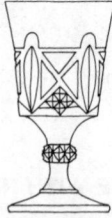

	Clear	Ruby Stained
Butter, cov, handled	—	125.00
Celery dish, boat shaped, high on each end	—	52.00
Creamer	20.00	43.00
Goblet	25.00	39.00
Mug, handled	—	30.00
Pitcher, water	—	100.00
Sherbet or punch cup	—	22.00
Spooner, double handled	—	26.00
Sugar, double handled, cov	—	43.00
Tumbler	—	38.00
Water Set, 6 goblets, pitcher on metal tray	—	225.00
Wine	—	39.00

TRUNCATED CUBE
(Thompson's #77)

Non-flint made by Thompson Glass Co., Uniontown, Pa., c1892. Clear and sometimes stained with ruby.

	Clear	Ruby Stained
Bowl, waste	30.00	—
Butter, covered	50.00	—

	Clear	Ruby Stained
Celery	38.00	—
Creamer, regular	35.00	45.00
Pitcher, water, tankard	45.00	—
Spooner	25.00	—
Sugar, regular, open	27.50	—
Syrup	40.00	62.50
Toothpick	30.00	47.50
Tumbler	28.50	—
Wine	17.50	25.00

TULIP WITH SAWTOOTH

Originally made in flint glass by Bryce Bros., Pittsburgh, Pa., c1860s. Later made in non-flint.

	Flint	Non-Flint
Bottle, Bar	69.00	—
Butter, covered	125.00	82.00
Celery	60.00	23.00
Champagne	—	33.00
Compotes		
Covered, 6″, high standard	90.00	—
Open, 9″, low standard	55.00	—
Creamer	100.00	—
Cruet	60.00	—
Decanters, handled, qt, stoppered	150.00	—
Egg Cup	40.00	—
Goblet	65.00	27.00
Mug	80.00	—
Oil Bottle, stoppered	75.00	—
Pitcher, water	150.00	—
Plate, 6″	60.00	—
Pomade Jar	45.00	—

	Flint	Non-Flint
Salt, master, plain edge	25.00	15.00
Spooner	35.00	—
Sugars		
Covered	95.00	—
Open	45.00	—
Tumblers		
Bar	85.00	28.00
Footed	50.00	—
Footed, semi-flint	35.00	—
*Wine	55.00	19.00

U. S. REGAL

Made by U. S. Glass Co. about 1906; one of the many imitation-cut patterns which were so popular. The bowls are slightly squared in shape. Made in clear only.

Basket, wide handle	35.00
Butter, covered	35.00
Creamer	27.00
Goblet	18.00
Sugar, covered	30.00
Spooner	25.00
Tumbler	18.00

U. S. SHERATON

Made by U. S. Glass Co. in 1912. This pattern was made only in clear but can be found trimmed with gold or platinum. Some pieces bear the interwined U. S. Glass trade mark.

Bowls, Berry

6", footed, square, known as "Almond Bowl"	10.00
8", flat	12.00
8", salad, square, footed, 4 feet	14.00
Finger bowl and under plate, 5" .	20.00
Butter, covered	42.50

Celery Tray, 10", 3 feet	30.00
Compote	
4½", Jelly, open	18.00
6", open, low standard	15.00
Creamers	
After dinner, tall, square foot ...	10.00
Berry, square foot, bulbous	12.00
Cruet	35.00
Dishes	
6", footed, bon-bon	10.00
9", squarish, oval shape	9.50
Goblet	17.50
Lamp, Oil, footed, with handle	65.00
Marmalade Jar, covered	27.50
Mustard Jar, covered	27.50
Mug, or sherbet cup, tall, handled, square foot	12.00
Pickle dish, 8", oblong, footed	14.00
Pitcher, water	
Tankard	35.00
Squat shape, medium	30.00
½ gal.	25.00
Plates,	
4½", square, called coaster or custard plate	8.50
9", square, footed, sandwich plate	12.50
Punch Bowl and cover, 14"	87.50
Salt and Pepper Shakers,	
Regular	40.00
Squat, single	22.00
Tall, on square base, single	22.00
Salt, individual, footed, called celery dip	12.00
Sardine Box, sardine can fits inside	30.00
Spooner, double handled	15.00
Sugars	
After dinner sugar, double handled, square base	14.50
Cafe, oval, sugar with lid	12.00
Sundae Dish on foot	8.50
Syrup Jug, matching cover	40.00
Toothpick, flat, called "Sanitary toothpick" (rare)	45.00
Trays,	
Bureau	55.00
Puff box	12.50
Pomade Jar	12.50
Ring stand	25.00
Pin tray, 3½", rectangular	8.50
Complete set	125.00
Tumbler	
Iced Tea Size	18.00
Regular	15.00

UTAH
(Frost Flower, Twinkle Star)

Non-flint made by U. S. Glass Co. in 1901 in the States' Pattern series.

Bowls

Covered, 6", 7", 8"	20.00

	Clear	Green
Creamer	30.00	40.00
Pitcher, water	40.00	—
Spooner	25.00	—
Sugar, covered	35.00	—
Tumbler	20.00	—

VICTORIA

Flint made by Bakewell, Pears, & Co., early 1870s.

Butter, covered	100.00
Cake Stands	
9"	75.00
15"	120.00
Compotes	
Covered, 8", high standard	95.00
Covered, 8", low standard	70.00
Open, 10", high standard	72.00
Creamer	80.00
Spooner	50.00
Sugar, covered	95.00

Open, 6", 7", 8"	18.00
Butter, covered	37.50
Cake Plates	
9"	20.00
11"	25.00
Cake Stands	
8"	20.00
10"	27.50
Celery	17.50
Compotes	
Covered, 6", Jelly	25.00
Open, 6", Jelly	20.00
Goblet	27.50
Pickle	12.00
Pitcher, water	48.00
Sauce, 4"	7.50
Salt and Pepper Shakers	40.00
Salt and Pepper Shakers, in holder	37.50
Spooner	15.00
Sugar, covered	38.00
Tumbler	15.00

VERMONT
(Honeycomb with Flower Rim)

Non-flint made by U. S. Glass Co., 1899-1903. Made in clear with gold, blue, green with gold, custard, chocolate, caramel, and novelty items in slag.
    Note: Toothpick has been reproduced in colored glasses, especially custard.

VIKING
(Bearded Head)

Non-flint, made by Hobbs, Brockunier, and Co. in 1876. No tumbler or goblet originally made.

Bowl, 8", oblong	22.50
Butter, covered	55.00
Cake Plate, 10", footed	35.00
Celery Vase	40.00
Compotes	
Covered, 8", high standard	70.00

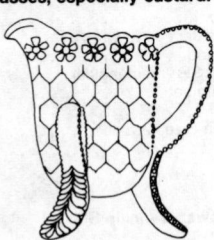

	Clear	Green
Bowl, Berry	25.00	46.00
Butter, covered	37.50	—
Celery Tray	16.00	—

Covered, 8", oval, low standard	55.00
Open, high standard	62.50
Creamer	35.00
Custard Cup	9.00
Egg Cup	35.00
Marmalade Jar	35.00
Mug	45.00
Pitcher, water	80.00
Salt, master	45.00
Spooner	32.00
Sugars	
Covered	37.50
Open	27.50
Tray, Bread	45.00

WAFFLE AND THUMBPRINT

Flint made by the New England Glass Co. and Boston & Sandwich Glass Co., c1850–1860. Later by Bryce Walker & Co., Pittsburgh, Pa.

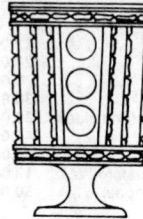

Bowl, 9 x 7"	27.50
Butter, covered	95.00
Celery	110.00
Champagne	70.00
Compote, covered, high standard	100.00
Creamer	125.00
Decanter, quart, stoppered	100.00
Egg Cup	35.00
Goblet, knob stem	70.00
Lamp, 9½"	115.00
Lamp, whale oil, 11"	175.00
Pitcher, water	250.00+
Spooner	45.00
Sugar, covered	95.00
Sweetmeat, 6", covered, high standard	150.00
Tumblers	
Flip Glass, large	135.00
Water, footed	75.00
Whiskey	100.00
Wine	60.00

WASHINGTON (EARLY)

Flint made by New England Glass Co., c1869.

Bowl, 6¼" x 9¼", oval	45.00
Bottle, Bitters	75.00

Butter, covered	175.00
Celery	95.00
Claret	125.00
Compotes	
Covered, 6", high standard	95.00
Covered, 10", high standard	175.00
Cordial	150.00
Creamer	200.00
Decanter, stoppered	150.00
Egg Cup	67.50
Goblet	75.00
Pitcher, water	250.00+
Salt, master	55.00
Spooner	65.00
Sugar, covered	100.00
Tumbler	85.00
Wine	65.00

WASHINGTON (LATE)

Non-flint made by U. S. Glass Co., c1900 in the States' Pattern series. This pattern is often found with ruby stain as a souvenir of a place or event.

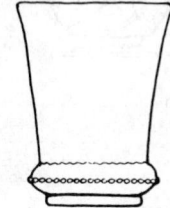

	Clear	Ruby Stained
Bowls		
Finger Bowl	15.00	—
Open, 8"	18.00	—
Butter, covered	50.00	110.00
Cake Stands		
8"	22.50	—
11"	27.50	—
Celery Tray	22.00	
Champagne	20.00	48.00
Claret	20.00	

	Clear	Ruby Stained
Compotes		
Covered, 6"	40.00	—
Open, 8"	35.00	—
Cordial	20.00	
Creamer	27.00	39.00
Cruet, stoppered	50.00	—
Goblet	32.00	38.00
Pickle	12.00	—
Pitchers		
Water	42.00	—
Water, ½ gallon	32.50	—
Plates		
6"	10.00	—
10"	15.00	—
Spooner	18.00	—
Sugar, open	37.00	—
Toothpick	25.00	40.00
Tumbler	20.00	38.00
Wine	20.00	35.00

WASHINGTON CENTENNIAL
(Chain with Diamonds)

Non-flint made by Gillinder & Co., Philadelphia, Pa.

Butter, covered	80.00
Cake Stands	
8½"	45.00
10"	65.00
Celery	62.50
Champagne	65.00
Compote, covered, 9"	60.00
Creamer, applied handle	87.50
Egg Cup	47.50
Goblet	48.00
Pitcher, water	95.00
Platters	
"Carpenter's Hall"	100.00
"George Washington"	110.00
Relish, Bear Paw handled, dated	32.00
Salt, master	25.00
Spooner	45.00
Sugar, covered	70.00
Syrup, metal lid	80.00
Wine	45.00

WEDDING BELLS

Made by Fostoria Glass Co., during 1900 in Moundsville, W. Va. Reported in clear with gold trim; sometimes cranberry flashed. A few pieces have been reported in ruby stained — berry bowl ($35.00), cruet ($72.50), and Pitcher, tankard type ($82.50).

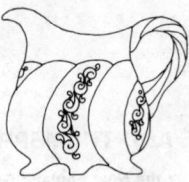

	Clear	Cranberry Flashed
Bowls		
Berry, 10"	22.00	—
Finger	28.00	—
Butter, covered	70.00	87.00
Celery, tall	30.00	—
Celery Tray, upturned sides	35.00	—
Creamer	45.00	58.00
Cruet	55.00	80.00
Cup, punch or custard	12.00	18.00
Decanter and stopper	50.00	—
Pitcher, water		
Regular, 1 gallon	75.00	—
Tankard, ½gallon h36	39.00	55.00
Punch Bowl, 2 pcs	125.00	—
Salt Shakers, 2 shapes, pr	35.00	—
Spooner	30.00	60.00
Sugar, covered	40.00	70.00
Syrup Jug	60.00	—
Tumbler	28.00	45.00

WESTWARD HO

Non-flint made by Gillinder & Sons, Philadelphia, Pa., late 1870s. Has been reproduced in clear and colors.

Butter, covered	165.00
Celery Vase	105.00
Champagne	250.00
Compotes, covered	
5", high standard	250.00
5", low standard	175.00
9", high standard	300.00
8", open	100.00
Cordial	150.00
Creamer	90.00
Goblet	70.00
Marmalade Jar, covered	175.00
Pitcher, water	200.00
Platter, Bread, oval	150.00
Sauce, footed, 4⅛"	35.00
Spooner	85.00
Sugar, covered	125.00
Wine	135.00

WHITTON
(Heavy Gothic)

Made by Columbia Glass Co. in the early 1880s until 1892; then continued by U.S. Glass Co.

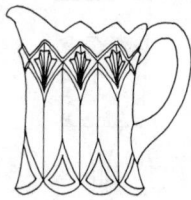

	Clear	Ruby Stained
Butter, covered	40.00	50.00
Cake Stand	47.00	52.00
Celery	27.00	—
Compote, covered, small jelly	45.00	
Creamer	35.00	45.00
Goblet	28.00	—
Pitcher, water	50.00	—
Sauces, footed	10.00	—
Spooner	18.00	25.00
Sugar, covered, 3 sizes, av.	32.50	46.00
Tumbler	30.00	—
Wine	27.00	—

WIGWAM
(Teepee #1, Alhambra)

Made by Iowa City Glass Co. in the late 1880s and also by the La Belle Glass Co., Bridgeport, Ohio. Made in clear only. According to old catalogues, made in limited number of pieces.

Butter, covered	45.00
Creamer	32.00
Goblet	38.00
Spooner	22.00
Sugar, covered	35.00

WINDFLOWER

Non-flint, late 1870s.

Butter, covered	50.00
Celery	32.50
Compotes	
Covered, high standard	65.00
Open, 7", low standard	45.00
Cordial	38.00
Creamer	25.00
Egg Cup	22.50
Goblet	37.50
Pitcher, water	38.00
Salt, master, footed	25.00
Spooner	20.00
Sugar, open	35.00
Tumblers	
Bar	35.00
Regular	25.00
Wine	30.00

WISCONSIN
(Beaded Dewdrop)

Non-flint made in Pittsburgh, Pa., in the 1880s. Later made by U. S. Glass Co. in Indiana, 1903. One of States' patterns. Toothpick Holder has been reported in emerald green ($60.00).

	Clear	Emerald Green
Banana Stand, low standard, turned up sides, 7½"d	75.00	—
Bowls		
7½"	30.00	50.00
7" or 8", round, covered	35.00	57.00
Butter, cov, handled		
Large	50.00	—
Small	35.00	—
Cake Stand, 10"	45.00	65.00
Bottles, oil and vinegar	20.00	—
Celery, vase and flat dish	35.00	—
Condiment Set, 4 pcs in holder	65.00	100.00
Compotes		
Covered, 7"	45.00	—
Open, 10½	35.00	—
Creamer, large	47.50	—
Cruet	55.00	—
Cup and Saucer	50.00	—
Goblet	35.00	68.00
Marmalade Jar, covered	125.00	—
Mug, large	35.00	—
Pitchers		
Milk	52.50	—
Water	57.50	—
Plate, 7", square	12.00	—
Salt, master	25.00	—
Salt and Pepper Shakers, 2 types, single	17.00	—
Spooner	27.00	—
Sugar, large covered	55.00	—
Sugar Shaker	60.00	—
Syrup, lid	48.00	—
Toothpick Holder	55.00	—
Tumbler	30.00	—
Wine	55.00	—

WYOMING
(Enigma)

Made by U. S. Glass Co., in the States' Pattern series, 1903.

Butter, covered	50.00
Cake Stand	70.00
Goblet	30.00

Creamer, 2 shapes	28.00
Sugars	
Covered	35.00
Open	30.00
Spooner	20.00
Wine	45.00

YALE
(Crow Feet, Turkey Track)

Non-flint made by McKee and Brothers Glass Co., 1894.

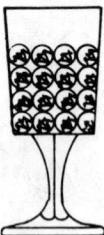

Butter, covered	27.50
Cake Stand	48.00
Celery	25.00
Compotes	
Covered	32.00
Open	25.00
Cordial	15.00
Creamers	
Regular	22.50
Individual	16.00
Goblet	25.00
Pitcher, water	35.00
Syrup	22.50
Salt and Pepper Shakers	40.00
Spooner	25.00
Sugar, covered	35.00
Tumbler	20.00

ZIPPER
(Cobb)

Non-flint made by Richards & Hartley, Tarentum, Pa., c1880s.

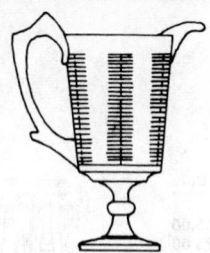

Banana Stand	**50.00**
Bowl, 7″	**15.00**
Butter, covered	**40.00**
Celery	**18.50**
Compote, covered, 8″, low standard	**45.00**

Creamer	**18.50**
Cruet, stoppered	**42.00**
Egg Cup	**18.50**
Goblet	**17.50**
Lamp, Oil	**35.00**
Marmalade Jar, covered	**28.00**
Pitcher, water	**40.00**
Relish	**12.50**
Sauces, flat and footed	**6–10.00**
Spooner	**24.00**
Sugars	
Covered	**30.00**
Open	**15.00**
Salt and Pepper Shakers, single . .	**15.00**
Sugar Shaker	**26.00**
Toothpick	**15.00**
Toy, child's banana stand	**22.50**
Wine	**15.00**

COLORED PATTERN GLASS

ADONIS
(Washboard: Pleat and Tuck)

Pattern made by McKee Bros, of Pittsburgh, Pa., in 1897. It was made in clear, canary and deep blue.

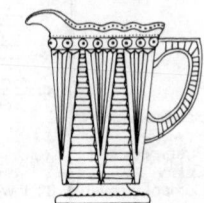

	Clear	Canary	Blue
Bowls, berry (round and oval)			
5"to 8"	12.00	13.50	15.00
Butter, covered	47.50	65.00	75.00
Cake Plate, 10"	18.00	20.00	22.00
Cake Stand, large, 10½"	40.00	45.00	50.00
Celery	30.00	35.00	37.50
Compote, covered	30.00	34.00	36.00
Jelly, open, 4½"	35.00	40.00	42.50
Open 8"	25.00	27.50	30.00
Creamer	22.50	28.00	32.50
Pitcher, Water	50.00	54.00	58.00
Relish	15.00	17.00	20.00
Sauce, flat, 4"	8.50	10.00	12.00
Salt and Pepper, pair	35.00	40.00	45.00
Salt shaker, single, large	20.00	22.00	24.00
Spooner	30.00	35.00	37.50
Sugar, covered	37.50	40.00	45.00
Syrup	40.00	50.00	52.00
Tumbler	20.00	22.00	24.00

ARCHED OVALS

Made by U. S. Glass Co., c1908. Cobalt is very rare.

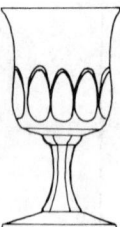

	Clear	Green	Ruby Stained	Cobalt
Bowl, Berry	12.50	17.50	35.00	—
Butter, covered	45.00	50.00	50.00	—
Celery, flat tray	22.50	27.50	35.00	—
Cruet	35.00	45.00	65.00	—
Goblet	25.00	35.00	37.50	—
Matchholder	18.50	20.00	22.00	—
Mugs	15.00	18.00	22.50	36.00
Pitcher, water	30.00	40.00	45.00	—
Plate, cake, 10"	18.00	25.00	35.00	—
Salt and Pepper Shakers, single	20.00	25.00	28.50	—
Spooner	20.00	20.00	20.00	—
Sugar, covered	35.00	40.00	42.50	—
Toothpick	15.00	25.00	35.00	50.00
Tumbler	10.00	15.00	30.00	55.00
Vase	15.00	18.00	25.00	36.00
Wine	7.50	15.00	20.00	—

BARRED FORGET-ME-NOT

Made by Canton Glass Co., Canton, Ohio, c1883.

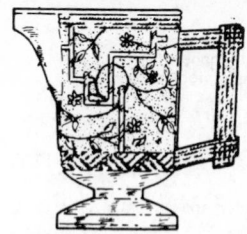

	Clear	Amber	Blue	Milk	Vaseline	Apple Green
Butter, covered	40.00	45.00	48.00	45.00	45.00	60.00
Cake Stand, large	45.00	55.00	58.00	55.00	55.00	75.00
Celery	30.00	50.00	53.00	50.00	50.00	60.00
Compotes						
Covered, high standard	45.00	50.00	53.00	50.00	50.00	60.00
Open, low standard	25.00	45.00	48.00	45.00	45.00	42.50
Creamer	27.50	40.00	43.00	40.00	40.00	48.00
Goblet	30.00	40.00	40.00	52.00	52.00	60.00
Pitcher						
Milk	37.00	55.00	55.00	55.00	55.00	60.00
Water	40.00	60.00	63.00	60.00	60.00	80.00
Plate, 9", handles	28.50	45.00	48.00	45.00	45.00	40.00
Relish, handles	12.00	23.00	26.00	23.00	23.00	25.00
Sauce, flat	8.00	19.00	22.00	19.00	19.00	20.00
Spooner	20.00	28.00	30.00	28.00	28.00	40.00
Sugar, covered	30.00	40.00	43.00	40.00	40.00	60.00
Wine	22.00	30.00	32.00	30.00	30.00	40.00

BASKETWEAVE

Non-flint c1880s. Some covered pieces have a strippled cat's head finial.

	Clear	Canary	Amber	Blue	Vaseline	Apple Green
Bowl, waste, covered	18.00	21.00	21.00	23.00	25.00	36.00
Butter, covered	32.00	35.00	35.00	37.50	39.00	60.00
Cordial	22.00	25.00	25.00	27.50	29.00	38.00
Creamer	27.50	30.00	30.00	32.50	36.00	47.50
Cup and Saucer	30.00	33.00	33.00	35.00	37.00	60.00
Dish, oval	9.50	12.00	12.00	14.00	16.00	20.00
Egg Cup, double and single	15.00	18.00	18.00	20.00	25.00	30.00
*Goblet	25.00	26.00	28.00	30.00	32.50	50.00
Mug	14.00	23.00	23.00	25.00	27.50	40.00
Pickle	14.00	17.00	17.00	19.00	21.00	30.00
Pitcher						
Milk	40.00	43.00	43.00	45.00	47.00	65.00
Water	45.00	48.00	48.00	42.50	32.00	75.00

	Clear	Canary	Amber	Blue	Vaseline	Apple Green
Plate, 11″, handled	20.00	23.00	23.00	25.00	27.50	38.00
Salt, master, footed, rope edge	7.50	10.00	10.00	12.00	12.00	10.00
Sauces	7.50	10.00	10.00	12.00	12.00	14.00
Shakers, pair	25.00	28.00	28.00	32.50	30.00	35.00
Spooner	18.50	21.00	21.00	23.00	25.00	35.00
Sugar, covered	30.00	33.00	33.00	35.00	37.50	60.00
Syrup	45.00	48.00	48.00	50.00	52.00	70.00
Tumbler	15.00	18.00	18.00	20.00	20.00	30.00
Tray, water, scenic center	28.50	35.00	90.00	45.00	48.00	48.00
Wine	25.00	28.00	28.00	30.00	30.00	50.00

BEADED SWIRL
(Swirled Column)

Made by George Duncan & Sons, c1890. The dual names are for the two forms of the pattern. Beaded Swirl stands on flat bases and is solid in shape. Swirled Column stands on scrolled, sometimes gilded, feet, and the shape tapered towards the base. Both forms in clear and emerald green, trimmed in gold.

Some also in milk white. Flat type pieces produced in greater quantity than footed. Footed pieces in Berry bowl, compote, creamer, cruet, sauces, spooner, covered sugar and water pitcher. Prices for both forms are equal. Also found in ruby stained; add 50%.

	Clear	Emerald Green	Milk
Bowls			
Berry, 7″	12.00	20.00	20.00
Flat	18.00	23.00	23.00
Footed, round	18.00	23.00	23.00
Footed, oval	18.00	23.00	23.00
Butter, covered	35.00	45.00	45.00
Cake Stand	35.00	45.00	45.00
Celery	27.50	55.00	40.00
Compotes			
Covered	42.00	52.00	52.00
Open	37.00	45.00	45.00
Creamer			
Flat	30.00	40.00	40.00
Footed	30.00	40.00	40.00
Dish, oval flat	12.00	18.00	18.00
Egg Cup	12.50	15.00	16.00
Goblet	35.00	40.00	45.00
Mug, handled	10.00	12.00	18.00
Pitcher, water	40.00	85.00	50.00
Sauces			
Flat	8.00	12.00	14.00
Footed	10.00	14.00	16.00
Spooner			
Flat	30.00	45.00	45.00
Footed	30.00	45.00	45.00
Sugar, covered			
Flat	35.00	45.00	45.00
Footed	35.00	45.00	45.00
Tumbler	20.00	30.00	30.00
Wine	30.00	35.00	35.00

CANE

Non-flint made by Gillinder Glass Co. and
McKee Glass Co., c1875–1885.

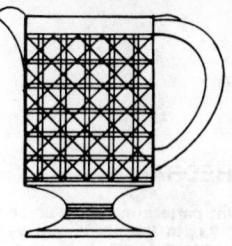

	Clear	Apple Green	Amber	Vaseline	Blue
Bowl, 7½", waste	18.00	28.00	30.00	30.00	30.00
Butter, covered	40.00	55.00	45.00	47.00	50.00
Celery	32.00	—	23.00	—	—
Compote, open, 5¾"	—	—	27.50	—	—
Creamer	20.00	24.00	25.00	30.00	35.00
Cruet, with original stopper	30.00	—	—	—	—
Finger Bowl	15.00	17.00	20.00	22.50	25.00
Goblet	18.00	57.50	30.00	27.00	30.00
Honey Dish	15.00	—	—	—	—
Kettle, Matchholder	31.00	—	15.00	35.00	40.00
Mustard Jar	—	—	37.50	—	—
Pickle	12.50	14.00	23.00	19.00	22.50
Pitcher, water	40.00	50.00	57.50	37.50	65.00
Plate, Toddy, 4½"	12.00	14.00	16.00	17.00	20.00
Salt Dip	7.50	10.00	10.00	12.00	16.00
Shakers, single	15.00	20.00	30.00	34.00	37.50
Spooner	18.50	21.00	25.00	25.00	27.50
Sugar, covered	47.50	50.00	50.00	52.50	55.00
Toothpicks	20.00	22.00	23.00	27.00	30.00
Tray, water	30.00	32.00	33.00	37.00	45.00
Tumbler	18.50	21.00	20.00	25.00	22.00
Wine	20.00	22.00	22.50	27.00	30.00

CANDLEWICK
(Cole, Banded Raindrop)

Non-flint, c1880s.

	Clear	Amber	Milk
Bowls	15.00	18.00	18.00
Butter, covered	35.00	42.00	42.00
Cake Stand	35.00	40.00	42.50
Celery	22.50	24.00	24.00
Compote			
Covered	38.00	54.00	54.00
Open	20.00	35.00	35.00
Creamer	22.50	27.50	27.50
Cup and Saucer	25.00	30.00	30.00
Goblet	20.00	24.00	24.00
Plate, some with turned up edges	10.00	12.50	12.50
Relish, square	20.00	24.00	24.00
Salt and Pepper Shakers	28.50	34.00	34.00
Sauce,			
Flat	4.75	6.00	6.00
Footed	7.50	8.00	8.00

	Clear	Amber	Milk
Sugar			
Covered	35.00	42.00	42.00
Open	20.00	24.00	24.00
Spooner	18.50	21.00	21.00
Wine	19.50	22.50	22.50

CATHEDRAL

Non-flint pattern made by Bryce Bros., Pittsburgh, Pa., in the 1880s and by U. S. Glass Co., in 1891. Found in ruby stained; add 50%.

	Clear	Amber	Canary	Vaseline	Blue	Amythyst
Bowl, Berry, 7″, 8″	25.00	32.50	28.00	45.00	40.00	50.00
Butter, covered	45.00	58.00	58.00	60.00	62.00	110.00
Cake Stand	38.50	41.00	41.00	43.00	45.00	75.00
Celery	30.00	33.00	33.00	35.00	37.00	60.00
Compote						
Covered, 8″, high standard	65.00	53.00	42.00	55.00	57.00	85.00
Open, 7″, low standard	25.00	39.00	39.00	30.00	32.00	75.00
Creamer						
Tall	32.50	42.50	43.00	45.00	47.00	80.00
Square, flat	45.00	45.00	47.50	48.00	—	82.00
Cruet, stoppered	—	90.00	90.00	—	—	—
Egg Cup	25.00	28.00	28.00	30.00	32.00	50.00
Goblet	30.00	40.00	38.00	45.00	42.00	70.00
Pitcher, water	55.00	58.00	58.00	60.00	62.00	110.00
Relish, fish shaped	—	—	30.00	—	55.00	33.00
Salt, boat shaped	10.00	14.00	17.50	17.50	—	20.00
Sauce						
Turned in-ruffled edge with ruby stained	25.00	—	—	—	—	—
Footed	15.00	18.00	15.00	20.00	22.00	35.00
Spooner	27.50	28.00	28.00	40.00	32.00	50.00
Sugar, covered	42.50	35.00	35.00	37.00	39.00	65.00
Tumbler	24.00	32.00	32.00	34.00	22.00	30.00
Wine	29.50	44.50	29.00	55.00	31.00	47.50

CHAMPION
(Greentown #11)

Made by McKee Bros., and Indiana Tumbler and Goblet Co., in 1894–1917. The clear and emerald green pieces were often trimmed in gold.

	Amber Stained	Clear	Emerald Green	Ruby Stained
Bowl, Berry	—	16.00	—	—
Butter, covered	—	45.00	—	—
Cake Stand	—	32.50	—	90.00
Compote, covered	—	55.00	—	—
Compote, open, fluted top	80.00	40.00	—	—
Creamer	—	25.00	—	—
Cruet	—	—	85.00	—
Goblet	—	25.00	—	—
Ice Bucket	—	38.00	—	—
Marmalade Jar	—	25.00	—	—
Pitcher, water	—	69.50	—	—
Rose Bowl	—	20.00	45.00	—
Spooner	—	20.00	—	45.00
Sugar, covered	—	37.00	—	82.00
Syrup, metal top	—	75.00	—	—
Toothpick	50.00	18.00	40.00	28.00
Tumbler	—	15.00	—	—
Tray, water	—	45.00	—	—
Wine set, tray, wine decanter	—	150.00	—	—

COLORADO
(Lacy Medallion)

Non-flint made by U. S. Glass Co. in 1897 for States' pattern. Made in clear, green, blue and amethyst. A ruby stained creamer ($57.50) and tumbler ($30.00) have been documented. Also found in opaque white with enamel floral trim. The State pieces (Colorado) may have ornate silver frames or feet. Lacy Medallion is flat on base.

	Clear	Green	Blue	Amethyst
Banana Stand	25.00	37.00	40.00	58.00
Bowl, 6″	12.50	28.00	28.00	46.00
Bowl				
7½″, footed	20.00	32.00	35.00	53.00
8½″, footed	45.00	57.00	60.00	69.50
10″, footed, flared	55.00	67.00	70.00	88.00
Butter, covered	50.00	115.00	65.00	83.00
Cake Stand	55.00	67.00	70.00	88.00
Candy, 6″	15.00	27.00	30.00	48.00
Celery	35.00	45.00	48.00	66.00
Compote				
Open, 6″, low standard	27.50	45.00	42.00	60.00
Open, 9½″, low standard	35.00	47.00	50.00	68.00
Creamer				
Individual	20.00	27.00	35.00	53.00
Regular	32.50	30.00	48.00	35.00
Mug	18.50	30.00	33.00	50.00
Nappy, footed	20.00	22.00	35.00	53.00
Plate, 6″, square	22.50	45.00	48.00	66.00
Punch Cup	16.00	26.00	30.00	48.00
Salt Shaker, single	10.00	22.00	25.00	43.00
Sauce, footed, flat, ruffled	15.00	20.00	30.00	48.00
Spooner	22.00	35.00	38.00	56.00
Sugar, regular, covered	45.00	57.50	60.00	78.00

	Clear	Green	Blue	Amethyst
Toothpick	22.00	40.00	38.00	56.00
Tray, Card	25.00	28.00	31.00	48.00
Tumbler				
Handled	20.00	25.00	27.50	35.00
Regular	18.00	27.50	33.00	51.00
Vase				
12″	35.00	47.50	50.00	68.00
14″	40.00	52.00	55.00	73.00
Wine	35.00	45.00	—	—

CORD DRAPERY

Made by National Glass Co., at Greentown, Ind., from 1899 to 1903; later by Indiana Glass at Dunkirk, Ind., after 1907. Made in clear, amber, blue and green.

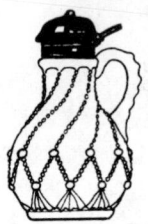

	Clear	Amber	Blue	Green
Bowl Berry	22.50	24.00	25.00	27.50
Butter, covered	65.00	72.00	75.00	78.00
Cake Stand	45.00	50.00	55.00	60.00
Compote, covered				
6″	40.00	43.00	45.00	47.50
7″	70.00	75.00	75.00	75.00
Creamer	42.50	45.00	50.00	52.00
Cruet	70.00	72.00	75.00	78.00
Cup, Punch or Sherbet	15.00	17.50	17.50	17.50
Dishes, various sizes	20.00	22.50	25.00	30.00
Goblet	45.00	47.50	50.00	52.00
Plates, turned up edges	20.00	35.00	37.50	39.00
Pitcher, water	45.00	47.50	50.00	55.00
Relish, 9½″, oval	15.00	22.00	24.00	26.00
Sauces	10.00	10.00	12.00	12.00
Spooner	27.50	30.00	32.00	34.00
Sugar, covered	50.00	54.00	56.00	58.00
Tumbler, (rare)	25.00	27.50	30.00	35.00
Wine	40.00	42.00	46.00	48.00

CROESUS

Made in clear by Riverside Glass Works, Wheeling, W. Va., in 1897. Produced in color by McKee in 1899.

	Clear	Green	Amethyst
Bowl,			
6¼″, footed	75.00	125.00	225.00
10″, footed	—	—	110.00
*Butter, covered	100.00	175.00	300.00
Celery Vase	65.00	135.00	195.00
Compote, Jelly	25.00	140.00	170.00
Condiment Tray	—	17.00	—

	Clear	Green	Amethyst
Creamer, regular	65.00	120.00	160.00
Cruet, stoppered	75.00	155.00	230.00
Cruet, Salt and Pepper Shakers, on small tray as set	195.00	200.00	225.00
Pitcher, water	90.00	185.00	200.00
Relish	35.00	60.00	70.00
Sauce	20.00	35.00	40.00
Salt and Pepper Shakers, single . . .	25.00	65.00	70.00
Spooner	40.00	75.00	85.00
Sugar, covered	85.00	175.00	190.00
*Toothpick	40.00	75.00	85.00
*Tumbler	30.00	65.00	75.00

DAHLIA

Non-flint, made by Canton Class Co., c1880s.

	Clear	Blue	Apple Green	Amber	Vaseline
Bowl, 5″ x 7″, oval	15.00	22.50	22.50	28.50	28.50
Butter, covered	32.50	68.00	68.00	80.00	80.00
Cake Stand, 10″	27.50	46.50	46.50	75.00	75.00
Champagne	80.00	65.00	65.00	80.00	80.00
Compote					
Covered, 7″, high standard	55.00	85.00	85.00	100.00	100.00
Open, 8″, high standard	30.00	45.00	45.00	57.00	57.00
Cordial	30.00	46.50	46.50	55.00	55.00
Creamer	18.00	32.50	32.50	40.00	40.00
Egg Cup					
Double	45.00	65.00	65.00	80.00	80.00
Single	16.50	36.00	36.00	52.00	52.00
Goblet	35.00	55.00	55.00	65.00	65.00
Mug					
Large	35.00	55.00	55.00	65.00	65.00
Small	30.00	42.50	42.50	50.00	55.00
Pickle	18.00	27.50	27.50	32.50	32.50
Pitcher					
Milk, applied handle	45.00	55.00	55.00	66.00	66.00
*Water, applied handle	35.00	95.00	95.00	110.00	110.00
Plate, 7″	22.00	37.50	37.50	45.00	45.00
Plate, Cake, 9″, closed handles	24.00	45.00	45.00	60.00	60.00
Platter 8″ x 12″	28.00	42.00	42.00	50.00	50.00
Salt, footed	5.00	30.00	30.00	35.00	35.00
Sauce, footed	10.00	15.00	15.00	18.50	18.50
Spooner	37.50	40.00	40.00	50.00	50.00
Sugar, covered	40.00	58.00	58.00	72.00	72.00
Syrup	55.00	—	—	—	—
Wine	35.00	52.00	52.00	62.50	62.50

DAISY AND BUTTON

Non-flint pattern made in the 1870s by several companies in many different forms. Practically every piece in this pattern has been reproduced in a variety of colors.

	Clear	Amber	Yellow	Blue	Vaseline	Apple Green
Bowl						
Finger	18.00	25.00	25.00	35.00	42.00	48.00
Triangular	30.00	30.00	28.00	37.50	30.00	45.00
Butter Chip	6.50	8.50	8.50	13.50	21.50	21.50
Butter, covered						
Round	65.00	68.00	68.00	73.00	80.00	80.00
Square	100.00	105.00	105.00	110.00	117.00	117.00
Butter Pat	25.00	27.00	27.00	35.00	35.00	37.50
Canoe						
4″	7.50	10.00	10.00	15.00	22.00	22.00
8½″	15.00	18.00	18.00	23.00	30.00	30.00
12″	20.00	23.00	23.00	28.00	35.00	35.00
14″	25.00	28.00	28.00	33.00	40.00	40.00
Castor Set						
Glass holder, 4-bottle	80.00	85.00	85.00	92.50	75.00	77.50
Metal holder, 5-bottle	100.00	103.00	103.00	108.00	95.00	95.00
Celery, square	25.00	28.00	28.00	33.00	41.00	41.00
Compote						
Covered, 6″, high standard	25.00	55.00	35.00	45.00	47.50	47.50
Open, 8″, high standard	42.50	53.00	53.00	58.00	65.00	65.00
Creamer	14.00	33.00	33.00	37.50	37.50	40.00
Cruet, stoppered	40.00	45.00	45.00	50.00	50.00	52.00
Egg Cup	15.00	18.00	18.00	23.00	30.00	30.00
Goblet	32.00	40.00	40.00	45.00	45.00	47.50
Hat, various sizes	10–13.00	14–35.00	14–35.00	36–50.00	51–57.00	51–57.00
Ice Tub	—	—	—	—	75.00	
Inkwell	30.00	40.00	40.00	45.00	45.00	47.50
Parfait	20.00	23.00	23.00	28.00	35.00	35.00
Pickle Castor, complete	75.00	78.00	78.00	83.00	90.00	90.00
Syrup	30.00	33.00	43.00	38.00	45.00	50.00
Pitcher, water						
Bulbous, reed handle	85.00	87.50	87.50	90.00	90.00	95.00
Tankard	40.00	43.00	43.00	55.00	60.00	65.00
Plate						
5″, leaf shaped	17.50	20.00	20.00	16.00	23.00	23.00
6″, round	6.50	10.00	10.00	15.00	22.00	22.00
7″, square	10.00	20.00	20.00	18.00	35.00	35.00
10½″, 2″ deep	20.00	28.00	28.00	35.00	40.00	45.00
Platter, handled, 9″ x 13″, oval	15.00	25.00	25.00	38.00	40.00	40.00
Punch Bowl, with stand	85.00	88.00	88.00	93.00	100.00	100.00
Sauces, various sizes and shapes	7.50–15.00	10–18.00	10–18.00	19–27.00	25–35.00	28–35.00
Shakers, pair	20.00	30.00	30.00	35.00	35.00	37.50
Slipper						
5″	18.50	21.00	21.00	26.00	33.00	33.00
Scuff type, 11½″	35.00	40.00	40.00	45.00	47.00	50.00
Spooner	15.00	18.00	18.00	25.00	30.00	35.00

	Clear	Amber	Yellow	Blue	Vaseline	Apple Green
Sugar covered	35.00	40.00	42.00	45.00	50.00	50.00
Toothpick						
Urn shape	10.00	13.00	13.00	18.00	25.00	25.00
Round, silver rim and base	40.00	43.00	43.00	48.00	55.00	55.00
Trays, various sizes and shapes	20–35.00	36–50.00	36–50.00	51–65.00	66–80.00	66–80.00
Tumbler	12.00	15.00	15.00	20.00	27.00	27.00
Vase, wall pocket	—	125.00	—	—	—	—
Wine	10.00	13.00	13.00	18.00	25.00	25.00

DAISY AND BUTTON WITH CROSSBARS

Non-flint pattern made by Richards and Hartley, Tarentum, Pa., c1888.

	Clear	Yellow	Amber	Vaseline	Blue
Bowl					
6″, open	18.50	26.00	26.00	26.00	30.00
9″, open	22.50	32.50	38.50	32.50	38.50
Butter, covered					
Flat	45.00	52.00	55.00	52.00	55.00
Footed	50.00	60.00	—	60.00	75.00
Celery	25.00	35.00	32.50	40.00	37.50
Compote					
Covered, 8″, high standard	45.00	55.00	55.00	55.00	65.00
Open, 8″, high standard	30.00	45.00	45.00	45.00	50.00
Creamer					
Individual	20.00	28.00	28.00	28.00	35.00
Regular	28.50	40.00	35.00	40.00	48.00
Cruet, stoppered	32.50	45.00	75.00	45.00	55.00
Goblet	30.00	40.00	35.00	35.00	42.50
Pitcher					
Milk	35.00	52.50	45.00	52.50	50.00
Water	42.50	60.00	65.00	70.00	70.00
Sauce					
Flat	10.00	15.00	15.00	15.00	20.00
Footed	15.00	22.50	22.50	22.50	25.00
Salt and Pepper Shakers, pr	30.00	38.50	38.50	38.50	42.50
Spooner	22.50	32.50	32.50	32.50	35.00
Sugar, covered	40.00	55.00	55.00	55.00	65.00
Syrup	35.00	50.00	50.00	50.00	58.00
Toothpick	15.00	25.00	40.00	32.50	40.00
Tray, bread	20.00	27.50	27.50	35.00	45.00
Tumbler	15.00	22.50	25.00	25.00	28.50
Wine	20.00	28.50	28.50	28.50	35.00

DAISY AND BUTTON WITH "V" ORNAMENT

Made by A. J. Beatty & Company, 1886–1887.

	Clear	Amber	Yellow	Blue	Vaseline
Bowl					
9"	22.50	35.00	35.00	42.50	55.00
10"	25.00	38.50	38.50	45.00	45.00
Butter, covered	65.00	85.00	85.00	90.00	90.00
Celery	30.00	42.00	42.00	50.00	50.00
Creamer	26.50	40.00	40.00	48.00	50.00
Goblet	25.00	36.50	36.50	45.00	50.00
Mug	15.00	22.50	22.50	27.50	35.00
Pickle Castor, complete	85.00	110.00	110.00	120.00	90.00
Pitcher, water	40.00	55.00	55.00	68.50	60.00
Punch Cup	7.50	12.50	12.50	18.00	27.50
Sauce, 5"	10.00	15.00	15.00	18.50	30.00
Spooner	22.50	32.50	32.50	40.00	45.00
Sugar, covered	40.00	60.00	60.00	75.00	75.00
Toothpick	12.50	18.50	18.50	45.00	48.00
Tray, water	35.00	50.00	50.00	65.00	55.00
Tumbler	15.00	24.50	24.50	28.00	35.00

DELAWARE
(Four-Petal Flower)

Non-flint pattern made by U. S. Glass Company circa 1899. Made in amethyst (scarce) and about 1900 in ruby with gold trim.

	Clear	Green with Gold	Rose with Gold
Bride's Basket, silver plated frame	—	110.00	—
Bowl, Finger	21.00	48.00	45.00
Bowl, Banana	60.00	65.00	55.00
Butter, covered	70.00	125.00	135.00
Celery	40.00	80.00	68.00
Creamer	20.00	44.00	70.00
Cruet, stoppered	100.00	200.00	60.00
Cup and Saucer	35.00	45.00	50.00
Pin Tray	17.50	—	—
Pitcher, water	110.00	195.00	125.00
Puff Box	—	—	110.00
Punch Cup	15.00	37.50	18.00
Spooner	30.00	40.00	75.00
Sugar, covered	65.00	125.00	135.00
Tray, water	18.00	22.00	—
Tumbler	18.00	65.00	35.00

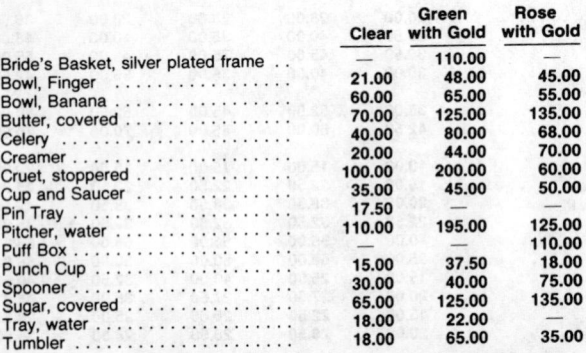

DEWEY
(Flower Flange)

Made by Indiana Tumbler & Goblet Co., Greentown, Ind., 1894. Later by U. S. Glass Co. until 1904. Some experimental colors were made; a nile green opaque mug ($46.00) has been documented.

	Clear	Green	Amber	Caramel	Vaseline
Bowl, footed, 8″	—	—	35.00	—	—
Butter, covered	30.00	61.00	61.00	150.00	90.00
Creamer, cover	45.00	56.00	42.50	146.00	60.00
Cruet, stoppered	70.00	130.00	135.00	148.50	120.00
Mug	32.50	63.50	63.50	153.50	55.00
Parfait	—	—	35.00	—	—
Pitcher, water	65.00	135.00	80.00	162.50	135.00
Plate, 7½″, footed	35.00	37.50	35.00	130.00	65.00
Relish dish, serpentine shape	25.00	48.00	42.50	145.00	40.00
Spooner	20.00	35.00	40.00	130.00	45.00
Sugar, covered	30.00	50.00	50.00	140.00	55.00
Tumbler	25.00	45.00	56.00	146.00	50.00

DIAGONAL BAND

Made in 1875–1885 period; maker unknown. A popular pattern with pieces seen frequently. Do not be confused with pattern known as Clear Diagonal Band; they are entirely different.

	Clear	Amber	Apple Green
Butter, covered	42.00	61.00	80.00
Cake Stand	27.00	40.00	55.00
Compote, covered	40.00	60.00	80.00
Creamer	25.00	38.00	50.00
Dish, oval	8.75	12.00	18.00
Goblet	20.00	30.00	45.00
Pickle dish, oval	12.00	22.00	30.00
Pitcher, water	45.00	67.00	92.00
Platter, or bread plate, oblong	21.00	30.00	45.00
Spooner	18.00	24.00	36.00
Sugar, Covered	29.00	37.00	50.00
Wine	22.00	33.00	45.00

DIAMOND QUILTED

Non-flint, c1880.

	Clear	Vaseline	Amber	Blue	Amethyst
Bowl, flat	—	22.50	17.50	—	—
Butter, Covered	40.00	80.00	50.00	125.00	125.00
Celery	40.00	47.50	45.00	42.50	75.00
Compote, covered, high standard	45.00	87.50	75.00	120.00	120.00
Creamer	25.00	55.00	45.00	55.00	55.00
*Goblet	27.50	35.00	42.50	37.50	42.00
Mug	—	—	—	40.00	—
Pitcher, water	50.00	72.50	60.00	85.00	85.00
Salt Shaker	—	—	—	35.00	—
Sauce, footed	12.00	18.00	16.00	14.00	18.00
Spooner	25.00	55.00	35.00	38.00	38.00
Sugar, covered	30.00	62.50	50.00	55.00	75.00
Tray	30.00	65.00	55.00	80.00	80.00
*Tumbler	35.00	30.00	25.00	40.00	40.00
Wine	12.00	30.00	25.00	42.00	42.00

FINECUT

Non-flint made by Bryce Bros., Pittsburgh, Pa., c1879, and by U. S. Glass Co. in 1891.

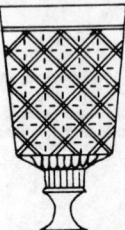

	Clear	Amber	Vaseline	Blue
Bowls				
Berry	12.00	15.00	15.00	18.00
Waste	30.00	35.00	50.00	72.50
Butter, covered	40.00	55.00	60.00	68.50
Celery, boat shape	20.00	—	35.00	40.00
Creamer	26.50	32.50	37.50	45.00
Goblet	17.50	25.00	34.00	42.50
Pitcher, water	40.00	45.00	52.00	85.00
Plate				
7"	18.00	22.50	30.00	38.00
10"	22.50	25.00	42.00	50.00
Relish, boat shape, long	25.00	32.00	35.00	40.00
Sauce	8.50	12.50	12.50	14.50
Spooner	17.50	22.50	28.50	35.00

	Clear	Amber	Vaseline	Blue
Sugar				
Covered	32.50	45.00	45.00	55.00
Open	25.00	38.00	38.00	45.00
Toothpick, hat shaped	—	—	—	17.50
Tray				
Bread	25.00	35.00	35.00	42.00
Water	35.00	48.00	48.00	55.00

FINECUT AND BLOCK

**Made by King Glass Co., Crystal Glass Co. in
1888, and McKee Glass Co., c1892 and for
several years after. Made in clear, amber, yellow and blue and in clear with blocks of amber, blue, yellow and pink stain.**

	Clear	Colored Pieces	Color-Stained Blocks
Bowl, listed as "Orange Bowl", 2 handles	75.00	—	—
Butter, covered			
Flat	40.00	—	—
Footed	50.00	165.00	—
Cake Stand			
Large	40.00	—	—
Small	35.00	—	—
Celery Vase	20.00	—	60.00
Cordial	—	—	85.00
Cologne Bottle	30.00	—	—
Compote			
Jelly, open	—	50.00	75.00
Open, 7"	45.00	—	72.00
Creamer	32.00	—	51.00
Egg Cup	22.00	—	—
Goblet			
Regular	37.00	—	64.00
Very large bowl, often called "true buttermill"	—	—	72.50
Lamp, flat	60.00	—	—
Pitcher, water	45.00	85.00	90.00
Plate			
Round, plain	12.00	—	—
Shaped like a star	25.00	—	—
Relish, rectangular	12.00	—	55.00
Salts			
Individual	12.00	—	—
Shaker, single	12.00	—	—
Sauce, handled, tub shape	17.00	—	—
Spooner	—	18.00	62.00
Sugar, covered	40.00	—	—
Tumbler	22.00	50.00	42.00
Tray			
Cracker, folded sides	85.00	75.00	—
Ice Cream	55.00	—	—
Water	60.00	—	
Wine	31.00	—	45.00

FINECUT AND PANEL

Non-flint pattern made by many Pittsburgh factories in the 1880s. Reissued in the early 1890s by U. S. Glass Co.

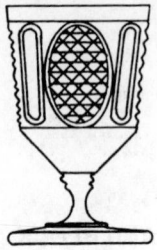

	Clear	Amber	Vaseline	Blue
Bowl, 7"	15.00	26.50	26.50	35.00
Butter, covered, square	40.00	60.00	60.00	75.00
Cake Stand, 10"	30.00	48.00	48.00	55.00
Compote				
Covered, high standard	50.00	125.00	130.00	135.00
Open, high standard	35.00	60.00	55.00	60.00
Creamer	25.00	37.50	37.50	45.00
Dish, candy, footed	—	—	18.00	—
Goblet	17.50	50.00	35.00	50.00
Pitchers				
Milk	—	—	50.00	—
Water	47.50	85.00	42.50	65.00
Plate, 7¼"	17.50	22.50	22.50	30.00
Platter	25.00	30.00	30.00	50.00
Relish	17.50	18.00	18.00	27.50
Sauce, footed, square	8.00	14.00	15.00	22.00
Spooner	25.00	32.00	32.00	45.00
Sugar, open	30.00	20.00	30.00	40.00
Tray				
Bread	25.00	—	—	—
Water, 12"	45.00	60.00	60.00	55.00
Tumbler	18.00	22.00	35.00	27.50
Wine	18.00	30.00	25.00	34.00

FRANCESWARE

Made by Hobbs, Brocunier & Co., Wheeling, W. Va., c1880s. A clear frosted hobnail or swirl pattern glass with amber stained top rims. A finger bowl ($50.00) and sauce ($32.00) are documented in amber stained. It may be pressed or mold blown. (Swirl pieces are noted, otherwise they are hobnails.)

	Clear	Frosted
Bowl		
4", finger	28.50	45.00
7½"	50.00	75.00
Box, 5¼", round, covered	45.00	65.00
Butter, covered	80.00	110.00
Creamer	50.00	70.00
Pitcher		
8½"	90.00	150.00
11"	150.00	200.00
Sauce, 4", square	12.50	22.50
Shakers, pair	50.00	65.00
Shakers, pair, swirl	60.00	75.00
Spooner	45.00	52.00

	Clear	Frosted
Sugar		
Covered	60.00	75.00
Open	40.00	60.00
Sugar Shaker, swirl	65.00	78.00
Syrup, swirl	65.00	80.00
Tumbler	35.00	42.00
Toothpick	40.00	50.00
Tray, leaf shaped, 12"	75.00	100.00

HARTLEY
(Paneled Diamond Cut with Fan)

Made by Richards and Hartley in 1880s, later by U. S. Glass Co. in clear, amber, blue, and perhaps vaseline. Comes plain and with engraving in panel; twenty-three pieces documented.

	Clear	Amber	Blue
Bowls, Berry			
7", footed	15.00	35.00	40.00
9"	18.00	37.50	42.00
Butter, covered	40.00	42.00	45.00
Cakestand	38.00	45.00	50.00
Celery	22.00	24.00	26.00
Compotes			
Low, 7¾", footed	—	40–80.00	—
Open, 2 sizes	15–18.00	20–30.00	30–40.00
Creamer	22.50	18.00	25.00
Dish, centerpiece	18.00	37.50	42.00
Goblet	18.00	22.00	35.00
Pitchers			
Milk	22.00	30.00	40.00
Water	30.00	35.00	40.00
Plate, Large Bread	20.00	27.50	37.50
Plate, Clover-shaped	40.00	45.00	50.00
Relish	15.00	18.00	20.00
Spooner	12.00	15.00	18.00
Sugar, covered	25.00	35.00	45.00
Tumbler	20.00	27.50	35.00
Wine	32.00	28.00	32.00

HOBNAIL, WITH FAN

Non-flint, made by Adams and Co., c1880.

	Clear	Amber	Blue
Bowl, Berry	25.00	35.00	40.00
Butter, covered	40.00	55.00	60.00
Celery	27.50	35.00	40.00
Creamer	25.00	40.00	45.00
Dish, oblong	22.50	—	—
Goblet	20.00	35.00	40.00
Salt, individual	8.50	10.00	15.00
Sugar, covered	30.00	45.00	50.00
Tray, 8" x 12"	20.00	30.00	35.00

HOBNAIL, POINTED

Non-flint c1880. Also found in apple green, dark green and vaseline, besides colors listed.

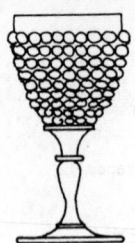

	Clear	Amber	Blue
Bone Dish	18.00	23.00	28.00
*Bowl	20.00	25.00	30.00
Butter, covered	40.00	45.00	47.00
Cake Stand, 10″	35.00	40.00	45.00
Celery Vase	18.00	27.50	35.00
Compote, open, 8″, high standard	35.00	40.00	45.00
Cordial	20.00	25.00	27.50
Creamer	25.00	30.00	35.00
Goblet	25.00	30.00	35.00
Inkwell	25.00	30.00	35.00
Pickle	12.00	15.00	20.00
*Pitcher, water	35.00	40.00	45.00
Plate, 7″	12.00	14.00	16.00
Salt			
Individual	5.00	10.00	15.00
*Shakers, pair	16.00	20.00	25.00
*Sauce, flat	8.50	10.00	12.00
Spooner	18.00	23.00	28.00
*Sugar, open	15.00	20.00	25.00
Toy Mug, child's	9.00	—	14.00
Tray			
Pen	15.00	20.00	25.00
Water, 11½″	30.00	35.00	40.00
*Wine	12.00	20.00	25.00

HUMMING BIRD
(Flying Robin)

Non-flint, c1880s.

	Clear	Canary	Vaseline	Amber	Blue
Butter, covered	45.00	65.00	67.50	70.00	75.00
Celery	45.00	48.00	50.00	55.00	60.00
Compote, high standard	48.00	51.00	55.00	62.50	65.00
Creamer	32.00	48.00	50.00	57.50	60.00
Goblet	30.00	40.00	42.50	45.00	50.00
Pitchers					
Milk	50.00	—	—	—	—
Water	85.00	87.50	87.50	95.00	110.00
Sauce, footed	12.00	15.00	20.00	26.50	28.00
Spooner	30.00	32.50	35.00	37.50	40.00
Sugar, covered	40.00	55.00	62.50	65.00	67.50
Tray, water	50.00	55.00	60.00	110.00	120.00
Tumbler, bar	27.50	30.00	32.00	45.00	47.50
Water Set, 7 pieces	—	—	—	360.00	—
Wine	40.00	42.50	45.00	45.00	47.50

JERSEY SWIRL
(Swirl)

Non-flint pattern made by Windsor Glass Co.,
Pittsburgh, Pa., c1887. Heavily reproduced in
color.

	Clear	Canary	Vaseline	Amber	Blue
Bowl, centerpiece, 9¼″	35.00	45.00	45.00	49.00	52.00
Butter, covered	40.00	50.00	50.00	55.00	55.00
Cake Stand, 9″	45.00	55.00	55.00	60.00	60.00
Celery	26.50	36.00	36.00	41.00	41.00
Compote	35.00	45.00	45.00	45.00	50.00
Creamer	30.00	40.00	40.00	45.00	45.00
*Goblet					
Small	25.00	35.00	35.00	40.00	40.00
Pitcher, water	35.00	45.00	45.00	50.00	50.00
Plates, fan shape					
6″	22.50	15.00	15.00	18.00	18.00
8″	27.50	17.00	17.00	17.50	20.00
10″	16.00	19.00	19.00	22.00	22.00
Salt,					
Individual	8.50	12.00	12.00	15.00	15.00
Master	12.00	14.00	14.00	16.00	16.00
Sauce	10.00	15.00	15.00	20.00	20.00
Spooner	20.00	25.00	25.00	28.00	28.00
Sugar, covered	27.50	32.50	32.50	37.50	37.50
Tumbler	16.50	22.50	22.50	26.00	26.00
Wine	45.00	50.00	50.00	52.50	52.50

KLONDIKE
(English Hobnail Cross)

This pattern reported to have been made
originally by A. J. Beatty And Co., c1885. It
was also made by Hobbs, Brocunier Co., and
Dalzell, Gilmore and Leighton Co. Made in
colors other than the clear and amber
stained, which are the original colors.
    Said to have been made to commem-
morate the Alaskan Gold Rush. The frosted
panels depict snow; the amber bands, gold.
Found clear and frosted, with or without
scrolls, depending on the maker. Prices are
listed for frosted; clear panels, approximately
30% less.

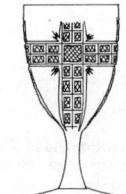

	Frosted		Frosted
Bowl, Berry, 8″	175.00	Creamer	175.00
Butter, covered	300.00	Cruet, stoppered	550.00
Cake Stand, 8″, square	500.00	Goblet	250.00
Celery	200.00	Pitcher, water	200.00

	Frosted
Punch Cup	85.00
Sauce, flat	75.00
Shakers, pair original tops	200.00
Sugars	
Covered	285.00
Open	225.00
Syrup, pewter lid	650.00

	Frosted
Toothpick	250.00
Tray, 5½", square	200.00
Tumbler	135.00
Vase, trumpet shape	
8"	275.00
10"	265.00

LEAF AND FLOWER

Made by Hobbs, Brocunier and Co., Wheeling, West Va., in 1890. It was made in clear, with color in combination, usually amber, although there could have been other colors. Also frosted in combination with color. Prices are for the usual clear with amber.

	Clear with Amber
Bowls	
9"	82.50
8", 2 types, deep and shallow	75–80.00
7"	65.00
Finger or Waste	60.00
Butter, covered, shaped like a bowl, with lid.	90.00
Castor Set — Salt and pepper, mustard, oil bottle, on handled tray shaped like leaf. Bottles have been found with ruby stain with no design on sides (usual). Some price as amber	175.00
Celery	
Vase	60.00

	Clear with Amber
Tray, turned up sides with handle, termed "Basket Celery"	75.00
Creamer	42.50
Pitcher, water, tankard shape	95.50
Sauce, flat	
4½"	30.50
5"	32.50
Salt and Pepper Shakers, pair	52.50
Spooner	40.00
Sugar, covered	47.50
Syrup Jug	90.00
Tumbler	30.00
Water Set — tankard pitcher, 6-tumblers, metal tray	220.00
Water Set — tankard pitcher, 2 tumblers and waste bowl	185.00

LEAF MEDALLION

Made by Northwood Glass Co., c1904. With gold trim, beading and medallions. Cobalt and amethyst are hard to find.

	Clear	Green	Cobalt	Amethyst
Bowl, Berry, footed	12.00	24.00	48.00	48.00
Butter, covered	45.00	75.00	120.00	120.00
Cake Stand, 10"	35.00	70.00	140.00	140.00
Compote, open, Jelly, 5", 6"	27.50	55.00	67.50	75.00

	Clear	Green	Cobalt	Amethyst
Condiment Set, Salt and Pepper, cruet, tray	—	200.00	225.00+	—
Creamer	30.00	60.00	85.00	90.00
Pitcher, water	50.00	100.00	225.00	225.00
Spooner	25.00	50.00	95.00	95.00
Sugar, covered	35.00	70.00	140.00	150.00
Tumbler	25.00	50.00	65.00	95.00

MEDALLION

Non-flint, c1880s.

	Clear	Amber	Canary	Vaseline	Blue	Green
Butter, covered	35.00	40.00	40.00	45.00	50.00	50.00
Cake stand, 9¼″	22.50	—	—	—	—	—
Celery	20.00	25.00	25.00	30.00	40.00	40.00
Compote, covered, high standard	40.00	45.00	45.00	50.00	60.00	60.00
Creamer	25.00	30.00	30.00	35.00	45.00	45.00
Egg Cup	18.00	23.00	23.00	28.00	38.00	38.00
Goblet	25.00	27.50	30.00	35.00	45.00	45.00
Pickle	15.00	18.00	18.00	20.00	30.00	30.00
Pitcher, water	45.00	50.00	50.00	70.00	87.50	65.00
Sauce						
Flat	7.50	9.50	9.50	12.00	17.50	24.00
Footed	10.00	12.00	12.00	14.00	25.00	25.00
Spooner	18.00	20.00	20.00	22.00	30.00	37.50
Sugar, covered	25.00	30.00	30.00	30.00	40.00	40.00
Tumbler	18.50	22.50	22.50	25.00	35.00	35.00
Wine	20.00	25.00	25.00	25.00	35.00	35.00

MITRED DIAMOND
(Pyramid, Sunken Buttons)

Maker not known but believed to be of Ohio origin. Made between 1880 and 1890.

	Clear	Amber	Blue	Vaseline	Apple Green
Bowl square, 8″	—	22.00	—	—	—
Butter, covered	55.00	60.00	67.00	65.00	69.00
Celery	18.00	22.00	25.00	27.00	30.00
Compote					
Low collared base	55.00	58.00	60.00	62.00	65.00
Same, open	40.00	42.00	45.00	47.00	50.00

	Clear	Amber	Blue	Vaseline	Apple Green
Creamer	30.00	32.00	35.00	37.00	40.00
Goblet	27.00	30.00	35.00	37.00	40.00
Pickle or Relish	15.00	18.00	22.00	20.00	22.00
Pitcher, water	50.00	55.00	58.00	58.00	60.00
Platter, or bread tray	32.00	35.00	35.00	35.00	37.00
Salt Shaker, single	18.00	22.00	25.00	25.00	28.00
Sauce, flat, square	10.00	15.00	10.00	15.00	10.00
Sugar, covered	45.00	48.00	50.00	50.00	52.00
Spooner	27.00	30.00	30.00	30.00	30.00
Tumbler	—	—	22.00	—	—
Wine	30.00	45.00	35.00	35.00	35.00

NESTOR

Non-flint pattern made by Northwood, Indiana, Pa., 1903. Decorated with enamel.

	Clear	Green	Blue	Amethyst
Bowl, Berry	25.00	30.00	45.00	45.00
Butter, covered	35.00	40.00	55.00	55.00
Cake Plate	35.00	40.00	55.00	55.00
Compote, open, Jelly, 5″, 6″	40.00	45.00	60.00	60.00
Creamer	35.00	60.00	45.00	55.00
Cruet, with stopper	40.00	45.00	60.00	60.00
Pitcher, water	50.00	55.00	70.00	70.00
Salt Shakers, pair	50.00	55.00	70.00	70.00
Spooner	30.00	35.00	35.00	50.00
Sugar, covered	35.00	75.00	45.00	55.00
Toothpick	30.00	35.00	50.00	50.00
Tumbler	40.00	45.00	60.00	60.00

PANELED FORGET-ME-NOT

Non-flint pattern made by Bryce Bros., Pittsburgh, Pa., c1870s. Amethyst and green are rare.

	Clear	Amber	Vaseline	Blue
Butter, covered	40.00	45.00	50.00	60.00
Cake Stand, 10 ″	50.00	25.00	35.00	45.00
Celery	30.00	50.00	60.00	70.00
Compotes				
Covered, 8″ high standard	52.50	55.00	65.00	75.00
Open, 7″, shallow	30.00	—	—	—
Creamer	25.00	30.00	40.00	50.00
Goblet	35.00	40.00	50.00	60.00
Marmalade Jar, covered	40.00	45.00	50.00	60.00
Pickle, boat shape	16.50	17.00	18.00	35.00
Pitcher, water	57.50	60.00	62.50	65.00
Sauce, footed	12.00	12.00	14.00	17.50

	Clear	Amber	Vaseline	Blue
Spooner	20.00	25.00	30.00	40.00
Sugar, covered	30.00	35.00	45.00	50.00
Wine	30.00	35.00	45.00	50.00

PRESSED DIAMOND
(Zephyr)

Made by Central Glass Co., Wheeling, West Va., in 1880s. Comes in clear, amber, blue and light straw colored (yellow, not vaseline). Blue and amber, scarce.

	Clear	Amber	Blue	Yellow
Bowl, Berry	12.00	15.00	20.00	16.00
Bowl, Finger	14.00	16.00	22.00	18.00
Butter, covered	40.00	56.00	60.00	90.00
Cake Stand	—	30.00	—	—
Celery	22.00	25.00	45.00	40.00
Creamer	30.00	45.00	50.00	52.00
Cup, custard or sherbet, (rare)	12.00	15.00	22.00	20.00
Goblet, (clear goblet will sometimes have a purple or gold top)	30.00	35.00	45.00	40.00
Pitcher, water	50.00	55.00	65.00	62.50
Salt Shakers, single	12.50	20.00	35.00	42.00
Spooner	25.00	45.00	60.00	45.00
Sugars				
Covered	35.00	56.00	75.00	65.00
Open	30.00	50.00	70.00	60.00
Wine	20.00	25.00	35.00	40.00

PRIMROSE

Non-flint pattern made by the Canton Glass Co., Canton, Ohio, c1880s. Apple Green is very rare.

	Clear	Amber	Vaseline	Canary	Blue
Bowl, 8″	22.50	26.50	26.50	26.50	32.50
Butter, covered	40.00	50.00	50.00	50.00	68.50
Cake Stand, 10″	45.00	50.00	50.00	50.00	65.00
Celery	25.00	30.00	30.00	30.00	40.00
Compote, covered, 6″ low standard	30.00	32.50	32.50	32.50	45.00
Creamer	30.00	35.00	35.00	35.00	47.00
Egg Cup	20.00	25.00	25.00	25.00	32.50
Goblet					
Plain stem	22.00	35.00	35.00	35.00	37.50
Knob stem	26.50	36.00	36.00	36.00	45.00
Pickle	12.50	16.50	16.50	16.50	20.00
Pitcher					
Milk	35.00	45.00	45.00	45.00	55.00
Water	40.00	42.00	42.00	42.00	50.00

	Clear	Amber	Vaseline	Canary	Blue
Plate					
4½"	14.50	16.00	16.00	16.00	19.00
9" handled	18.50	20.00	22.50	22.50	25.00
Platter, 12 x 8"	22.00	—	—	—	—
Sauce, footed	12.00	15.00	15.00	15.00	18.50
Spooner	18.00	22.00	22.00	22.00	30.00
Sugar, covered	30.00	40.00	40.00	40.00	55.00
Tray, water	35.00	50.00	50.00	50.00	60.00
Waste Bowl	20.00	30.00	30.00	30.00	32.50
Wine	28.00	32.00	32.00	32.00	32.00

PRISM ARC
(Cross Log)

Unknown maker.

	Clear	Amber	Milk White
Bowl, Berry, 8"	18.00	—	—
Butter, covered	37.00	42.00	—
Cake Stand	32.00	—	—
Celery	24.00	—	—
Creamer	25.00	—	—
Cruet with orig stopper	48.00	—	55.00
Goblet	22.00	—	—
Mug	18.00	—	—
Pitcher, water, 3 sizes, av.	44.00	—	—
Plate	10.00	—	—
Sauce	7.50	—	—
Spooner	25.00	—	—
Sugar, covered	30.00	—	—
Tumbler	30.00	—	—
Wine	20.00	27.00	—

PUFFED BANDS
(Snow Band)

Unknown maker, c1885.

	Clear	Amber	Blue
Bowl	18.00	22.00	25.00
Butter, covered	40.00	45.00	50.00
Cake Stand	22.00	27.00	30.00
Creamer	25.00	30.00	35.00
Goblet	20.00	27.00	45.00
Pickle	15.00	18.00	27.00
Pitcher, water	47.00	52.00	55.00
Sugar, covered	37.00	40.00	42.00
Spooner	22.00	25.00	27.00
Tumbler	25.00	30.00	37.00
Wine	18.00	20.00	25.00

RAINDROP

Non-flint, c1880s. Scarce in apple green.

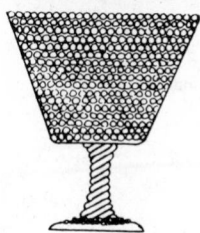

	Clear	Amber	Vaseline	Blue
Compote, open, 8″, low standard . . .	20.00	35.00	35.00	45.00
Creamer	20.00	35.00	35.00	45.00
Cup and Saucer	25.00	40.00	40.00	50.00
Egg Cup, double	25.00	35.00	35.00	45.00
Finger Bowl	15.00	25.00	25.00	35.00
Lamp, miniature	—	95.00	95.00	—
Pickle	16.00	22.50	22.50	32.50
Pitcher, water	35.00	45.00	45.00	55.00
Plate, Cake	26.00	40.00	40.00	50.00
Sauce				
Flat	8.00	12.00	12.00	14.00
Footed	10.00	15.00	15.00	18.00
Syrup	35.00	50.00	50.00	60.00
Tray, Water	35.00	45.00	45.00	55.00

ROSE-IN-SNOW

Non-flint pattern made by Bryce Bros., Pittsburgh, Pa., in the square form, c1880. Also made in the round form by Ohio Flint Glass Co. and after 1891 by U.S. Glass Co.

	Clear	Amber	Canary	Vaseline	Blue
Bowl, 4″	10.00	13.00	13.00	13.00	20.00
Butter, covered					
Round	40.00	50.00	50.00	50.00	65.00
Square	50.00	60.00	60.00	60.00	75.00
Cake Stand, 9″	57.50	65.00	65.00	65.00	75.00
Compote, Covered					
8″ high standard	45.00	75.00	75.00	75.00	90.00
7″ low standard	50.00	60.00	60.00	60.00	75.00
Open, 5¾″ low standard	25.00	35.00	55.00	55.00	60.00
Creamer					
Round	37.50	45.00	45.00	45.00	55.00
Square	28.00	38.00	38.00	38.00	60.00
*Goblet	25.00	35.00	35.00	35.00	50.00
Marmalade Jar, covered	50.00	60.00	60.00	60.00	75.00
*Mug, "In Fond Remembrance"	50.00	45.00	45.00	45.00	55.00
Pickle					
*8½″ x 7″, double, (scarce)	40.00	45.00	45.00	45.00	55.00
Oval, handles at ends	18.50	25.00	25.00	25.00	32.50

	Clear	Amber	Canary	Vaseline	Blue
Pitcher, water, applied handle	95.00	105.00	175.00	105.00	150.00
Plate, 6½"	18.00	22.50	22.50	22.50	38.50
*10" handled	35.00	40.00	40.00	40.00	55.00
Powder Jar	30.00	—	—	—	—
Sauce					
Flat	15.00	16.00	16.00	16.00	20.00
Footed	8.00	10.00	10.00	10.00	22.50
Spooner					
Round	25.00	35.00	35.00	35.00	40.00
Square	32.50	42.50	42.50	42.50	48.00
Sugar, covered					
Round	40.00	50.00	50.00	50.00	60.00
Square	45.00	55.00	55.00	55.00	70.00
Tumbler, bar	45.00	—	—	—	55.00
Vegetable, 7" x 10"	65.00	70.00	70.00	70.00	105.00
Wine	28.00	35.00	35.00	35.00	42.50

ROSE SPRIG

Non-flint pattern made by Campbell, Jones & Co., Pittsburgh, Pa., 1886.

	Clear	Amber	Canary	Vaseline	Blue
Biscuit Jar, dome lid	97.50	—	—	—	—
Cake Stand, 9"	50.00	52.50	52.50	52.50	55.00
Celery	35.00	45.00	38.50	38.50	47.50
Compotes					
7"	—	32.50	—	—	—
8", oval	—	35.00	—	—	—
Creamer	32.50	32.50	30.00	32.50	50.00
Goblet	30.00	32.50	35.00	37.50	45.00
Lemonade Glass	35.00	40.00	40.00	42.50	50.00
Pitcher, water	47.50	55.00	50.00	55.00	65.00
Plate, 10"	27.50	30.00	30.00	37.50	45.00
Relish, boat shaped	25.00	40.00	40.00	42.50	45.00
*Salt, Sleigh	22.50	30.00	30.00	30.00	40.00
Spooner	22.50	25.00	25.00	27.50	32.50
Sugar, covered	42.50	50.00	50.00	50.00	60.00
Tray, water	45.00	55.00	55.00	55.00	68.50
Tumbler	25.00	30.00	30.00	30.00	37.50
Wine	25.00	30.00	30.00	32.50	45.00

ROYAL IVY

Non-flint made by Northwood Glass Co. in 1889 and 1890. Made clear and frosted, with cranberry flashing. Also made in cased spatter, cracquelle (clear and frosted), amber stained and clambroth. These last mentioned were experimental pieces, and not made in collectible sets.

	Clear	Frosted	Rubina Clear	Rubina Frosted
Bowls				
Finger	120.00	120.00	—	—
Rose	85.00	85.00	70.00	86.00
Butter, covered	170.00	195.00	250.00	250.00
Creamer, applied handle	50.00	60.00	150.00	
Cruet	—	90.00	—	375.00
Jam or Marmalade Jar, silver cover	115.00	125.00	—	—
Pitcher, water, applied handle	90.00	100.00	350.00	250.00
Spooner	43.00	43.00	83.00	45.00
Sugar, covered	110.00	150.00	—	150.00
Sugar Shaker	—	—	—	150.00
Syrup, silver cover	110.00	125.00	—	—
Tumbler	28.00	28.00	—	60.00

ROYAL OAK
(Acorn)

Non-flint made by Northwood Glass Co., Martins Ferry, Ohio, c1899. Made in clear and frosted with cranberry flashing. In early 1900 it was made in opaque, white with colored tops, and colored acorns and leaves. Milk white pieces are rarer, and are more expensive.

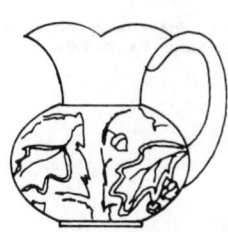

	Clear	Frosted	Milk Glass	Clear Rubina	Frosted Rubina
Butter, covered	115.00	195.00	250.00	—	185.00
Creamer	100.00	150.00	—	—	—
Cruet, stopper	200.00	215.00	225.00	425.00	480.00
Mustard Jar, covered	85.00	90.00	95.00	—	—
Pickle Castor Insert	—	—	—	—	237.00
Pitcher, water	85.00	100.00	125.00	46.00	325.00
Salt and Pepper Shakers, single	75.00	—	—	—	—
Spooner	55.00	120.00	87.50	—	102.00
Sugar, covered, acorn finial	150.00	65.00	175.00	—	—
Sugar Shaker, metal top	78.00	65.00	100.00	—	—
Syrup, metal top	125.00	135.00	150.00	—	—
Tumbler	85.00	65.00	95.00	—	80.00

SHELL AND JEWEL
(Victor)

Non-flint made by Westmoreland Glass Co., C1893. Clear and rare in blue and green.

	Amber	Blue	Clear	Cobalt Blue	Green
Banana Stand	—	—	65.00	—	—
Bowl, 8″	35.00	—	25.00	—	—

	Amber	Blue	Clear	Cobalt Blue	Green
Butter, covered	—	—	60.00	—	—
Cake Stand, 10″	—	—	48.00	—	—
Compote, open, 7″, high standard	—	—	35.00	—	—
Creamer	—	—	40.00	—	72.00
Pitcher, water	50.00	—	35.00	98.00	—
Spooner	—	—	20.00	—	—
Sugar, covered	—	—	35.00	—	—
Tumbler	35.00	33.00	16.00	—	45.00
Water Set					
5 pcs.	—	—	111.00	—	—
7 pcs.	249.00	275.00	—	—	—

SHERATON

Non-flint pattern mady by Bryce, Higbee & Co., Pittsburgh, Pa., c1880s.

	Clear	Amber	Blue
Bowl, 8″ x 10″	13.50	35.00	40.00
Butter, covered	25.00	40.00	50.00
Celery Vase	20.00	30.00	35.00
Compote, open, 7″, low standard	20.00	25.00	30.00
Creamer	30.00	32.50	35.00
Goblet	35.00	37.50	40.00
Pitcher			
Milk	20.00	27.50	35.00
Water	28.00	35.00	40.00
Relish, handled	16.00	23.00	28.00
Sauce, flat	10.00	15.00	18.00
Spooner	16.00	22.00	25.00
Sugar, covered	27.50	35.00	45.00
Tray, Bread	15.00	42.50	50.00
Wine	25.00	25.00	30.00

SPIREA BAND

Non-flint pattern mady by Bryce, Higbee & Co., Pittsburgh, Pa., c1885.

	Clear	Vaseline	Amber	Blue
Bowl, 8″	22.50	27.00	27.00	37.00
Butter, covered	32.00	44.00	44.00	54.00
Cake Stand, 11″	47.50	42.00	42.00	55.00
Celery	25.00	37.00	37.00	47.00
Compote, covered, 7″, high standard	40.00	44.00	44.00	54.00
Cordial	20.00	32.00	32.00	42.00
Creamer	17.50	34.00	34.00	44.00
Goblet	20.00	20.00	34.00	44.00
Pitcher, water	35.00	47.00	47.00	57.00
Platter, 10½″	17.50	32.00	32.00	42.00
Relish	16.00	27.00	27.00	39.00

	Clear	Vaseline	Amber	Blue
Sauce, footed	8.00	14.00	14.00	18.00
Spooner	15.00	24.00	24.00	30.00
Sugar, open	18.00	30.00	30.00	37.00
Tumbler	—	—	22.50	35.00
Wine	18.00	28.00	28.00	32.00

TEARDROP AND TASSEL
(Sampson)

Non-flint pattern made by the Indiana Tumbler & Goblet Co., Greentown, Ind., c1890, to celebrate Admiral Sampson's victory in the Spanish American War.

	Clear	Green	Cobalt	Green opaque
Bowl, 7½"	40.00	45.00	55.00	75.00
Butter, covered	42.50	46.00	65.00	76.00
Celery	30.00	—	—	—
Compote,				
Covered, 7", high standard	75.00	80.00	90.00	110.00
Open, 8", low standard	28.00	33.00	43.00	63.00
Creamer	18.00	25.00	45.00	53.00
Goblet	60.00	65.00	75.00	95.00
Pickle	15.00	20.00	30.00	55.00
Pitcher, water	70.00	75.00	90.00	110.00
Shakers, pair	75.00	80.00	90.00	110.00
Spooner	30.00	35.00	45.00	65.00
Sugar, covered	50.00	55.00	65.00	85.00
Tumbler	40.00	35.00	50.00	65.00
Wine	65.00	70.00	80.00	95.00

TEUTONIC
(I. H. C., Pittsburgh Fan)

Made by McKee Glass Co. in 1897. Originally made in clear; reported in emerald green and with the blocks stained in colors of pink, blue, amber, and ruby.

	Clear	Blocks Color Stained	Emerald Green	Ruby Stained
Bowls, various sizes, av.	18.00	—	—	—
Bowl, finger, underplate	35.00	45.00	—	—
Butter, covered	45.00	—	—	—
Cake Stand	25.00	—	—	—
Celery vase	18.00	—	—	—
Creamer	27.00	—	35.00	—
Cup, custard or punch	9.00	—	15.00	—
Goblet	22.00	—	—	35.00

	Clear	Blocks Color Stained	Emerald Green	Ruby Stained
Pickle, handled	18.00	—	23.00	—
Plates, 7″, 8″, 10″, av.	10.50	—	18.00	—
Salt Shaker, 2 sizes, single	12.00	—	—	—
Spooner	18.00	—	22.00	—
Sugar				
Individual, open	15.00	—	—	—
Regular, open	20.00	—	—	—
Tumbler	15.00	—	—	30.00
Water Bottle	42.00	—	—	—

THOUSAND EYE

Non-flint pattern made by Adams Glass Co., Tarentum, Pa., 1875, and by Richards & Hartley, c1888, and New Brighton Glass Co., New Brighton, Pa., at about the same time. It was made in two forms, with the plain stem, and with a three-knob stem. Covered pieces of this type have three-knob finials. Three knob should be 50% more than plain.

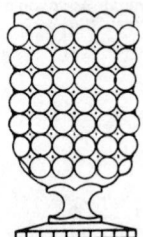

	Clear	Amber	Vaseline	Blue	Apple Green
Butter, covered	50.00	65.00	65.00	70.00	90.00
Celery, hat shaped	40.00	48.50	48.50	53.00	73.00
Cologne Bottle	25.00	32.50	32.50	37.50	57.00
Compote, covered, 6″, high standard	65.00	50.00	50.00	65.00	97.00
Cordial	25.00	32.00	32.00	37.50	57.00
Creamer	40.00	47.00	47.00	52.00	72.00
*Cruet	40.00	37.00	37.00	42.00	62.00
Egg Cup	50.00	60.00	60.00	70.00	90.00
*Goblet	30.00	37.00	37.00	42.00	62.00
Inkwell	35.00	45.00	45.00	75.00	—
*Hat	15.00	22.00	22.00	27.00	47.00
Lamp					
Handled, low	55.00	62.00	62.00	67.00	87.00
High standard	85.00	92.00	92.00	97.00	117.00
*Mug	15.00	22.00	22.00	27.00	47.00
Pitcher, water	75.00	72.00	72.00	79.00	99.00
*Plate					
6″	15.00	22.00	22.00	27.00	47.00
*8″	20.00	27.00	27.00	34.00	54.00
*10″	25.00	32.00	32.00	39.00	59.00
Platter, 11″, oblong	35.00	42.00	42.00	49.00	69.00
Sauce, footed	10.00	14.00	14.00	17.00	37.00
Shakers, single	30.00	32.00	42.00	49.00	69.00
Spooner	22.50	27.00	27.00	34.00	54.00
Sugar, covered	45.00	47.00	47.00	54.00	74.00
Syrup, pewter top	55.00	87.50	62.00	69.00	90.00
Toothpick	16.00	23.00	23.00	30.00	50.00
Tray, water					
14″, oval	55.00	62.00	62.00	64.00	87.00
12½″	50.00	57.00	57.00	64.00	84.00
*Tumbler, water	22.00	27.00	27.00	34.00	54.00
*Twine holder	25.00	32.00	32.00	37.00	57.00
*Wine	20.00	35.00	27.00	30.00	50.00

THREE PANEL

Non-flint pattern made by Richards & Hartley Co., Tarentum, Pa., c1888, and U. S. Glass Co. in 1891.

	Clear	Amber	Vaseline	Blue	Apple Green
Bowl					
8½"	20.00	27.50	40.00	40.00	50.00
10"	35.00	35.00	47.50	55.00	60.00
Butter, covered	35.00	45.00	50.00	52.50	70.00
Compote					
7", open, low standard	25.00	40.00	45.00	40.00	55.00
10", open, low standard	32.50	42.00	57.00	62.00	67.00
Creamer	22.50	40.00	30.00	40.00	57.00
Goblet	25.00	30.00	40.00	52.00	57.00
Lamp, Kerosene	—	135.00	—	—	—
Mug	17.50	25.00	35.00	45.00	50.00
Pitcher, water	45.00	95.00	63.00	68.00	73.00
Spooner	30.00	27.50	32.50	37.50	55.00
Sugar, covered	30.00	45.00	67.50	65.00	70.00
Tumbler	18.00	35.00	32.50	40.00	45.00

TWO PANEL

Non-flint pattern made by Richards & Hartley Glass Co., Tarentum, PA., early 1880s, and by U.S. Glass Co. in 1891.

	Clear	Vaseline	Apple Green	Amber	Blue
Bowl					
5½" x 7"	15.00	25.00	30.00	35.00	35.00
8" x 10"	25.00	35.00	32.50	37.50	37.50
Butter, covered	30.00	40.00	45.00	50.00	50.00
Celery	25.00	35.00	40.00	45.00	45.00
Compote, 6½", oval	—	—	—	37.50	—
Creamer	22.50	32.50	37.50	42.50	42.50
*Goblet	30.00	42.50	37.50	32.50	32.50
Lamp	45.00	55.00	60.00	65.00	65.00
Mug, large	20.00	30.00	35.00	40.00	40.00
Pitcher, water	40.00	50.00	60.00	57.50	65.00
Platter	—	—	—	27.50	—
Salts					
Individual	5.50	18.50	12.00	16.00	18.50
Master	12.00	14.00	16.00	18.00	18.00

	Clear	Vaseline	Apple Green	Amber	Blue
Sauces					
Flat, oval	8.50	10.00	12.00	10.00	10.00
Footed	10.00	12.00	14.00	12.50	16.00
Shakers, pair	25.00	30.00	35.00	40.00	40.00
Spooner	25.00	35.00	40.00	45.00	45.00
Sugar, covered	30.00	40.00	45.00	50.00	50.00
Tray, water	35.00	45.00	50.00	47.50	55.00
Tumbler	15.00	25.00	30.00	35.00	35.00
Waste Bowl	22.50	32.50	37.50	42.50	42.50
*Wine	20.00	30.00	32.50	40.00	37.50

U.S. RIB

Made by U.S. Glass Co., c1900-09. Comes in square shaped pieces in clear and emerald green with lavish gold trim.

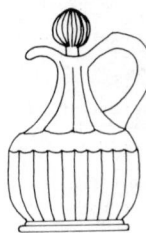

	Clear	Emerald Green
Bowl, Berry, 9½″	15.00	30.00
Butter, covered	25.00	50.00
Creamer		
Breakfast size	22.50	45.00
Regular	25.00	50.00
Cup, Punch or Sherbet	22.50	45.00
Pitcher, water	40.00	75.00
Spooner	20.00	40.00
Sauce, square	12.50	18.00
Sugar		
Breakfast size	28.00	40.00
Covered	35.00	48.00
Toothpick	20.00	38.00

WHEAT AND BARLEY

Non-flint pattern made by Bryce Bros., Pittsburgh, Pa., in the late 1870s. Later by U.S. Glass Co.

	Clear	Amber	Vaseline	Blue
Bowl, covered, 8″	22.00	34.00	34.00	44.00
Butter, covered	35.00	47.00	47.00	65.00
Cake Stand				
8″	18.50	30.00	30.00	45.00
10″	30.00	42.00	42.00	52.00
Compote, covered				
7″ high standard	32.50	45.00	45.00	55.00
8″ high standard	32.50	45.00	45.00	57.00
Open, Jelly, high standard	35.00	47.00	47.00	32.50
Creamer	30.00	30.00	30.00	47.50
Goblet	25.00	37.50	30.00	40.00
Mug, 3¾″	18.50	32.50	30.00	40.00

	Clear	Amber	Vaseline	Blue
Pitcher				
Milk	27.50	40.00	40.00	50.00
Water	45.00	65.00	65.00	65.00
Plate				
7″	18.00	23.00	23.00	33.00
9″, closed, handled	25.00	27.00	27.00	37.00
Sauce				
Flat, handled	9.00	17.50	12.00	15.00
Footed	10.00	17.50	14.00	16.00
Shakers, pair	30.00	42.00	42.00	52.00
Spooner	20.00	30.00	30.00	40.00
Sugar, covered	32.00	40.00	40.00	50.00
Toothpick	12.00	20.00	20.00	30.00
Tumbler				
Regular	18.00	32.50	25.00	35.00
Footed	15.00	20.00	20.00	30.00

WILDFLOWER

Non-flint pattern made by Adams & Co., Pittsburgh, Pa., c1874, and by U.S. Glass Co., c1898. This pattern has been heavily reproduced.

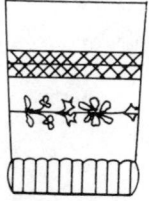

	Clear	Amber	Vaseline	Blue	Green
Bowl, 8″ square	18.00	25.00	25.00	35.00	35.00
Butter, covered					
Collared Base	40.00	42.00	45.00	52.00	52.00
Flat	35.00	37.00	37.00	47.00	47.00
Cake Stand 10½″	47.50	52.00	52.00	62.00	75.00
Champagne	35.00	—	—	—	—
Celery Vase	35.00	55.00	55.00	57.50	60.00
Compotes					
8″, high standard, oblong	50.00	—	67.50	—	—
8″, square	60.00	—	—	—	—
Open	—	—	—	37.50	—
Cordial	25.00	32.00	32.00	42.00	42.00
Creamer	22.50	27.00	45.00	37.00	37.00
Dish, square	20.00	—	—	—	—
*Goblet	27.50	32.00	40.00	30.00	42.00
Lamp, hand	50.00	55.00	55.00	57.50	60.00
Pitcher, water	50.00	52.00	67.50	45.00	75.00
Plate, 10″, square cut corners	25.00	28.00	28.00	45.00	30.00
Platter, 10″, oblong	30.00	37.50	32.50	42.50	47.00
*Salt, Turtle	37.50	42.50	42.50	52.50	52.50
Sauce, footed, 4″, round	12.00	14.00	14.00	18.00	18.00
Shakers, single	40.00	25.00	47.00	35.00	57.00
Spooner	17.00	35.00	30.00	27.50	34.00
Sugar, covered	30.00	45.00	40.00	47.00	47.00
Syrup	—	180.00	—	—	185.00
Tray, water, oval	40.00	47.00	55.00	57.00	57.00
Tumbler, regular	25.00	27.50	27.50	29.00	32.00
Wine	28.50	35.00	35.00	45.00	45.00

WILLOW OAK

Non-flint pattern made by Bryce Bros., Pittsburgh, Pa., c1880s, and by U.S. Glass Company in 1891.

	Clear	Amber	Blue
Bowl, 8″	25.00	28.00	40.00
Butter, covered	48.00	60.00	55.00
Cake Stand, 8½″	45.00	40.00	57.50
Celery Vase	60.00	52.50	45.00
Compotes			
Covered 7½″, high standard	45.00	48.00	52.00
Open, 7″	25.00	—	60.00
Creamer	30.00	35.00	45.00
Goblet	34.00	40.00	50.00
Pitcher			
Milk	50.00	62.50	55.00
Water	57.50	85.00	55.00
Plate,			
7″	25.00	28.00	40.00
9″, closed handled	22.50	32.00	35.00
11″, bread	22.50	—	—
Sauce,			
Flat, square, handled	8.50	14.00	20.00
Footed, 4″	20.00	22.00	27.00
Shakers, single	20.00	25.00	40.00
Spooner	27.50	37.50	42.50
Sugar, covered	35.00	45.00	50.00
Tray, water, 10½″, round	25.00	35.00	40.00
Tumbler	30.00	32.00	33.00
Waste Bowl	32.00	35.00	40.00

VALENCIA WAFFLE
(Block and Star #1)

Made by Adams & Co. about 1885–1895; continued by U.S. Glass Co. after 1891.

	Clear	Apple Green	Amber	Vaseline	Blue
Bowl, Berry	12.00	24.00	15.00	15.00	20.00
Butter, covered	40.00	65.00	42.00	42.00	45.00
Cake Stand, 10″	35.00	40.00	40.00	40.00	45.00
Celery	18.00	30.00	20.00	20.00	25.00
Castor Set, complete	50.00	—	60.00	60.00	65.00
Compote, covered					
High standard	45.00	46.00	50.00	50.00	55.00
Low standard	35.00	—	35.00	35.00	65.00
Creamer	27.50	—	30.00	30.00	45.00
Dish, various sizes, av.	10.00	—	18.50	18.50	24.00
Goblet, 2 types, sq and round base	20.00	—	37.00	30.00	35.00

	Clear	Apple Green	Amber	Vaseline	Blue
Pitchers					
Milk	35.00	—	37.50	37.50	42.00
Water	40.00	—	65.00	45.00	50.00
Platter, bread	28.00	—	20.00	20.00	25.00
Relish or Pickle	13.50	20.00	15.00	15.00	18.00
Sauce, footed, 4"sq	13.00	—	15.00	15.00	16.00
Spooner	18.00	—	22.00	22.00	25.00
Sugar, covered	37.50	—	40.00	42.00	45.00
Tumbler	14.00	—	16.00	16.00	18.00

X-RAY

Non-flint made by Riverside Glass Works, Wellsburg, W. Va., 1896 to 1898. Found with gold trim.

	Clear	Emerald Green	Canary
Bowl, Berry, 8", with beaded edge	25.00	50.00	60.00
Butter, covered	30.00	55.00	65.00
Celery	—	45.00	—
Compote, covered, high standard	35.00	60.00	70.00
Creamer	25.00	50.00	65.00
Pitcher, water	50.00	75.00	85.00
Plate, Bread	45.00	70.00	80.00
Salt Shakers, pair	20.00	35.00	45.00
Spooner	20.00	45.00	55.00
Sugar, covered	25.00	50.00	60.00
Toothpick holder	35.00	60.00	65.00
Tumbler	10.00	14.00	24.00
Water Bottle	—	50.00	—

OPALESCENT PATTERN GLASS

ALASKA
(Lion's Leg)

Non-flint opalescent made by Northwood Glass Company, from 1897 to 1910. Sauces can be found in clear ($27.50); and, the creamer ($110.00) and spooner ($90.00) are known in clear blue.

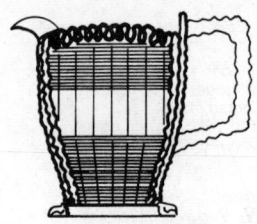

	White Opal.	Vaseline Opal.	Blue Opal.	Clear Crystal Green
Banana Boat	65.00	140.00	290.00	100.00
Bowl, Berry, footed	65.00	70.00	75.00	—
Butter, covered	290.00	295.00	235.00	—
Compote, square on 4 feet	—	—	250.00	—
Celery Vase, enameling	100.00	110.00	125.00	—
Creamer	35.00	75.00	75.00	37.00
Cruet, facetted stopper	165.00	295.00	215.00	255.00
Pitcher, water	290.00	345.00	420.00	60.00
Salt and Pepper Shakers, single	75.00	50.00	60.00	—
Spooner	35.00	50.00	60.00	32.00
Sugar, covered	100.00	135.00	140.00	

ARGONAUT SHELL
(Nautilus)

Non-flint opalescent made by Northwood Glass Co., c1897. Card tray (30.00) is reported in white opalescent.

	Vaseline opal.	Blue opal.	Custard
Bowl, Berry	125.00	150.00	325.00
Butter, covered	225.00	250.00	280.00
Compote, Jelly	250.00	275.00	120.00
Creamer	175.00	200.00	125.00
Cruet	225.00	250.00	475.00
Pitcher, water	325.00	350.00	260.00
Salt and Pepper Shakers	95.00	100.00	350.00
Spooner	—	75.00	—
Sugar, covered	225.00	250.00	225.00
*Toothpick	—	—	275.00
Tumbler	250.00	275.00	125.00

BEADED SWAG
(Beaded Yoke)

Made by Heisey Glass Co., 1895. Limited
number of pieces made in opalescent glass.
(See also Clear Pattern Glass Section).

	Clear opal.	Vaseline opal.	Clear Green	Clear and Ruby	Custard
Bowl, Berry	18.00	20.00	22.00	25.00	40.00
Butter, covered	50.00	55.00	60.00	65.00	85.00
Creamer	40.00	45.00	55.00	45.00	65.00
Goblet	27.50	30.00	32.50	35.00	75.00
Pitcher, water	35.00	40.00	37.50	65.00	85.00
Salt and Pepper Shakers	175.00	45.00	40.00	60.00	75.00
Sauces	12.00	15.00	18.00	20.00	35.00
Spooner	20.00	25.00	22.50	25.00	40.00
Sugar	30.00	40.00	55.00	35.00	75.00
Toothpick	30.00	37.50	55.00	45.00	80.00
Tumbler	30.00	30.00	30.00	35.00	50.00

BEATTY'S HONEYCOMB

Non-flint made by Beatty Glass Co., Tiffin,
Ohio, c1888. Made in white, blue, and vaseline opalescent.

	White opal.	Vaseline opal.	Blue opal.
Bowl, Berry	50.00	75.00	100.00
Butter, covered	90.00	105.00	115.00
Celery	75.00	75.00	95.00
Creamer			
Individual	20.00	25.00	35.00
Regular	25.00	25.00	30.00
Cruet	85.00	90.00	100.00
Mug	25.00	30.00	35.00
Pitcher, water	150.00	—	—
Spooner	25.00	35.00	40.00
Sugar, covered			
Individual	55.00	60.00	65.00
Regular	65.00	70.00	70.00
Toothpick	35.00	30.00	48.00
Tumbler	40.00	42.50	50.00

BEATTY'S RIBBED OPALESCENT
(Ribbed Opal)

Made by Beatty and Sons Glass Co., Tiffin, Ohio, c1888–1889. Rare in vaseline opalescent.

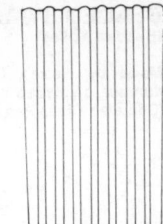

	Clear opal.	Blue opal.	Vaseline opal.
Biscuit Jar	125.00	300.00	350.00+
Bowls			
Berry, rectangular	55.00	60.00	65.00
Berry, round	50.00	55.00	60.00
Finger	40.00	40.00	50.00
Celery	27.50	30.00	35.00
Creamer			
Regular	30.00	40.00	45.00
Small	25.00	35.00	35.00
Dish, covered, round	80.00	95.00	100.00
Salt Dip	22.50	25.00	30.00
Salt and Pepper Shakers, pair	60.00	85.00	95.00
Sauces			
Rectangular	15.00	25.00	27.50
Round	15.00	25.00	27.50
Spooner	32.50	35.00	37.50
Sugar, covered	50.00	60.00	75.00
Toothpick	30.00	35.00	37.50
Tumblers			
Lemonade	—	—	65.00
Regular	32.50	40.00	65.00
Whiskey, taster, 1½"	30.00	40.00	45.00

BEATTY'S SWIRLED OPALESCENT
(Swirled Opal)

Made by Beatty and Sons Glass Co., Tiffin, Ohio, c1889.

	White opal.	Blue opal.	Vaseline opal.
Bowl, Berry	70.00	80.00	90.00
Butter, covered	100.00	115.00	120.00
Celery	55.00	57.50	65.00
Creamer	30.00	40.00	50.00
Mug	27.50	32.50	40.00
Pitcher, water	125.00	155.00	165.00
Sauces	30.00	35.00	35.00
Spooner	40.00	50.00	55.00
Sugar, covered	50.00	55.00	85.00
Syrup	115.00	125.00	150.00
Toothpick	50.00	40.00	50.00
Tray, water	105.00	125.00	130.00
Tumbler	35.00	50.00	55.00

COIN SPOT

Made by various companies over a period of time, c1870s–1890s. The water pitcher is also found in green opalescent ($100.00).

	Clear opal.	Blue opal.	Cranberry opal.
Bowl, Berry, 9½", cranberry	60.00	65.00	75.00
Cruet, with stopper	60.00	65.00	75.00
Pitcher, water, ruffled rim	115.00	145.00	250.00
Sauces	25.00	25.00	28.00
Syrup Pitcher, dated pewter top	90.00	100.00	85.00
Sugar Shaker	30.00	30.00	35.00
Tumbler	35.00	30.00	45.00

DOLLY MADISON
(Jefferson's #271)

Made by Jefferson Glass Co., Follansbee, W. Va., c1907.

	Clear	Blue	Green	Clear opal.	Blue opal.	Green opal.
Bowl, Berry, 9¼"	25.00	30.00	35.00	32.50	50.00	45.00
Butter, covered	20.00	45.00	40.00	65.00	110.00	120.00
Creamer	25.00	25.00	35.00	80.00	75.00	90.00
Pitcher, water	35.00	40.00	45.00	125.00	150.00	140.00
Sauces	12.00	22.00	20.00	40.00	45.00	48.00
Spooner	20.00	35.00	30.00	75.00	75.00	85.00
Sugar, covered	55.00	35.00	75.00	85.00	90.00	100.00
Tumbler	30.00	30.00	30.00	35.00	40.00	55.00

DIAMOND SPEARHEAD

Made by Northwood-Dungan Glass Co., Indiana, Pa., around 1900. No cruet reported. A cake stand has been found, but it was not listed in early catalogues.

	Clear Crystal	Cobalt Blue Opal	Green Opal	Vaseline Opal	Lt. Blue Opal	White Opal
Bowls, Berry	20.00	—	40.00	40.00	35.00	32.00
Butter, covered	40.00	150.00	82.00	82.00	75.00	—
Carafe, water	—	—	—	180.00	—	—
Celery	18.00	—	40.00	40.00	35.00	32.00

OPALESCENT PATTERN GLASS

	Clear Crystal	Cobalt Blue Opal	Green Opal	Vaseline Opal	Lt. Blue Opal	White Opal
Compotes						
Covered, high stand	—	—	72.00	72.00	67.00	—
Jelly, covered	—	—	60.00	60.00	50.00	—
Creamers						
Regular	20.00	70.00	35.00	35.00	30.00	32.00
Small	—	—	—	—	38.00	—
Cup and Saucer	—	—	60.00	60.00	57.50	—
Goblet	—	—	40.00	40.00	35.00	—
Mug	20.00	—	37.50	37.50	32.50	—
Pitcher, water	50.00	200.00+	85.00	85.00	75.00	—
Plate, 10″	—	—	—	78.00	—	—
Relish	—	—	22.50	22.50	18.00	—
Sauce	—	—	15.00	15.00	10.00	—
Salt Shaker, single	—	—	35.00	35.00	30.00	—
Spooner	20.00	—	28.00	28.00	25.00	—
Sugar, covered	27.00	—	50.00	50.00	45.00	—
Syrup Jug, metal top	—	130.00	68.00	68.00	60.00	—
Toothpick	—	—	80.00	80.00	75.00	—

EVERGLADES

Made by Harry Northwood Co., Wheeling, W. Va., c1903. Rare occasional custard piece. Add 200% for green opalescent.

	White opal.	Canary opal.	Blue opal.
Banana Dish, boat shaped	165.00	170.00	175.00
Bowl, Berry	90.00	95.00	100.00
Butter, covered	140.00	145.00	150.00
Compote, Jelly	85.00	90.00	95.00
Creamer	48.00	52.00	58.00
Cruet.......................	165.00	170.00	325.00
Pitcher, water	225.00	230.00	250.00
Salt and Pepper Shakers	55.00	55.00	65.00
Sauces	30.00	30.00	35.00
Spooner	65.00	70.00	75.00
Sugar, covered	85.00	90.00	95.00
Tumbler.....................	22.50	24.00	24.00

FLUTED SCROLLS

Made by Harry Northwood & Co., Indiana, Pa., c1898–1900. Sometimes with burnished gold trim. A covered butter has been reported in clear ($60.00).

	Vaseline opal.	Sapphire blue opal.	White opal.
Bowl, Berry	55.00	100.00	—
Butter, covered	225.00	125.00	125.00
Creamer	30.00	70.00	50.00
Cruet.......................	90.00	90.00	—

	Vaseline opal.	Sapphire blue opal.	White opal.
Epergne, tiny, 2-piece	100.00	125.00	—
Pitcher, water	155.00	210.00	—
Puff Jar	40.00	75.00	—
Salt and Pepper Shakers	95.00	95.00	—
Sauces, 4½"	18.00	25.00	—
Spooner	50.00	50.00	42.00
Sugar, covered	75.00	75.00	75.00
Tumbler	45.00	55.00	—

HOBNAIL OPALESCENT

Made by several companies with avriations in forms of pieces, c1880–1900. Pieces are found round in shape, with frilled tops, pieces on three feet, pieces on four feet, square in shape, octagonal in shape.

	White opal.	Blue opal.	Vaseline opal.	Cranberry opal.
Butter, covered				
Flat	82.00	100.00	105.00	110.00
Four-footed	85.00	102.00	107.00	112.00
Celery	85.00	85.00	100.00	115.00
Creamer				
Flat	85.00	95.00	110.00	115.00
Four footed	95.00	97.50	112.00	120.00
Cruet	25.00	—	125.00	—
Mug	30.00	35.00	50.00	55.00
Pitcher, water	95.00	100.00	120.00	125.00
Sauces	18.00	20.00	30.00	35.00
Spooner				
Flat	15.00	22.50	30.00	37.50
Four footed	22.00	22.50	30.00	37.50
Sugar, covered				
Flat	30.00	40.00	55.00	60.00
Four footed	35.00	42.50	57.50	62.00
Toothpick	20.00	25.00	48.00	50.00
Tumbler	28.50	35.00	50.00	55.00

IDYLL
(Jefferson's #251)

Made by Jefferson glass Co., Follansbee, W. Va., c1907. Often decorated with gold. Made in clear, green, blue crystal, and white, blue and green opalescent. Prices are for blue opal, white and green about 20% more; blue most often seen.

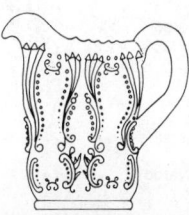

	Blue opal.		Blue opal.
Bowl, Berry 8″	35.00	Sauces, 2 sizes, 4½″ and 6″	12.50-24.00
Butter, covered	50.00	Salt and Pepper Shakers, pair	55.00
Condiment Set, cruet, salt shakers on		Spooner	35.00
tray, (complete)	125.00	Sugar, covered	47.50
Cruet	55.00	Toothpick	35.00
Pitcher, water	50.00	Tumbler	20.00

INTAGLIO
(Flower Spray with Scroll)

Made by Northwood Co., Indiana, Pa., c1899. Also reported in custard trimmed in green and gold. Creamers in blue opalescent were used as premiums in 1901 by Arbuckle Coffee.

	White opal.	Blue opal.	Vaseline opal.
Bowl, Berry, on stands like compotes	100.00	150.00	175.00
Butter, covered	150.00	200.00	210.00
Compote, Jelly	40.00	50.00	75.00
Creamer	50.00	70.00	90.00
Cruet	95.00	130.00	110.00
Pitcher, water	129.00	200.00	275.00
Sauce	25.00	30.00	40.00
Spooner	70.00	150.00	200.00
Sugar, covered	90.00	150.00	200.00
Tumbler	40.00	50.00	55.00

INVERTED FAN AND FEATHER

Made by Northwood Co., Wheeling, W. Va., c1900. (Reproduced in custard glass.)

	Clear opal.	Clear Green with gold	Blue opal.	Custard
Bowl, Berry	100.00	110.00	125.00	225.00
Butter, covered	195.00	195.00	275.00	—
Compote	195.00	195.00	200.00	425.00
Creamer	65.00	65.00	85.00	175.00
Cruet	195.00	195.00	200.00	—
Pitcher, water	200.00	200.00	325.00	500.00+
Rose Bowl	—	—	150.00	—
Salt Shaker, single	—	—	—	95.00
Spooner	75.00	75.00	95.00	100.00
*Sugar, covered	100.00	100.00	145.00	125.00
*Toothpick	100.00	100.00	125.00	545.00
*Tumbler	25.00	35.00	50.00	95.00

IRIS WITH MEANDER

Made by Jefferson Glass Co., Steubenville, Ohio, c1903. This pattern also comes in clear, blue, apple green, amethyst with gold trim. An amethyst toothpick is valued at $45.00.

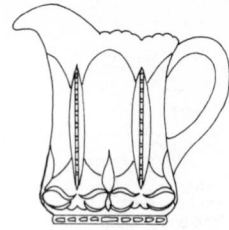

	White opal.	Vaseline opal.	Blue opal.
Bowl, Berry	80.00	90.00	95.00
Butter, covered	95.00	100.00	200.00
Compote, Jelly, 5–6"	75.00	80.00	85.00
Creamer	80.00	80.00	85.00
Cruet, with stopper	100.00	100.00	125.00
Pickle	20.00	22.50	25.00
Pitcher, water	200.00	175.00	225.00
Plate, 7"	35.00	90.00	50.00
Salt Shakers, pair	90.00	100.00	100.00
Sauces, 2 sizes	27.50	27.50	20.00
Spooner	85.00	80.00	55.00
Sugar, covered	80.00	90.00	95.00
Toothpick	50.00	50.00	85.00
Tumbler	27.00	28.00	32.00
Vase, tall, 11"	22.00	32.50	60.00

JEWEL AND FLOWER
(Beaded Oval and Leaf)

Made by Northwood Glass Co., c1908.

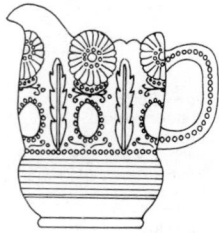

	Clear opal.	Blue opal.	Vaseline opal.
Bowl, Berry	55.00	75.00	85.00
Butter, covered	75.00	95.00	250.00
Creamer	60.00	55.00	100.00
Cruet	75.00	95.00	100.00
Pitcher, water	125.00	140.00	150.00
Sauce, gold trim	25.00	—	—
Spooner	50.00	80.00	80.00
Sugar, covered	75.00	90.00	100.00
Tumbler	45.00	50.00	75.00

JEWELLED HEART

Made by Northwood Glass Co., Indiana, Pa., and others, 1897–1900. Made in blue and apple green opalescent; might occasionally be found in clear. A clear creamer is valued at $18.00 and a clear green toothpick at $45.00.

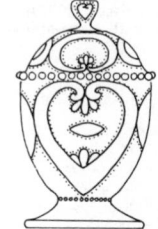

	Clear opal.	Green opal.	Sapphire Blue opal.
Bowl, Berry, ruffled edges	95.00	110.00	125.00
Butter, covered	100.00	125.00	135.00
Cake Stand	110.00	120.00	120.00

	Clear opal.	Green opal.	Sapphire Blue opal.
Compote			
Covered	120.00	130.00	130.00
Open	110.00	110.00	110.00
Creamer	90.00	50.00	100.00
Cruet	85.00	195.50	128.00
Lamp	95.00	95.00	100.00
Pitcher, water	100.00	110.00	120.00
Salt and Pepper Shakers	85.00	85.00	85.00
Sauces	25.00	25.00	28.00
Spooner	50.00	50.00	50.00
Sugar, covered	55.00	75.00	85.00
Syrup	125.00	130.00	135.00
Toothpick	30.00	35.00	35.00
Tumbler	18.00	25.00	25.00

NORTHWOOD'S DRAPERY

Made by Harry Northwood Co., Wheeling, W. Va., c1905. Usually signed "N" in circle.

	White opal.	Blue opal.
Bowl, Berry	80.00	100.00
Butter, covered	145.00	165.00
Creamer	55.00	75.00
Pitcher, water	185.00	175.00
Sauces	20.00	28.00
Spooner	45.00	55.00
Sugar, covered	75.00	85.00
Tumbler	50.00	25.00

PALM BEACH

Reportedly made by U.S. Glass Co., Pittsburgh, Pa., c1905. A wine ($35.00) is known in clear with color staining.

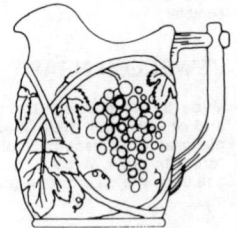

	Blue opal.	Canary opal.
Bowls		
Berry	100.00	110.00
Finger	45.00	45.00
Butter, covered	140.00	265.00
Compote, Jelly	150.00	175.00
Creamer	50.00	50.00
Pitcher, water	200.00	225.00
Spooner	65.00	65.00
Sugar, covered	70.00	75.00
Tumbler	48.50	45.00

PANELED HOLLY

Made by Northwood Glass Co. Wheeling, W.
Va., c1905. It was made in white and blue
opalescent with gold trimmed holly leaves
and enamelling.

	White Opal	Blue Opal
Bowls, Berry, novelty cov bowls, various sizes	12–25.00	15–30.00
Butter, covered	40.00	50.00
Creamer	25.00	30.00
Cruet	—	100.00+
Pitcher, water	—	95.00
Relish	15.00	18.00
Sauces	8.00	10.00
Spooner	18.00	22.00
Sugar, covered	40.00	55.00
Tumbler	30.00	35.00

SCROLL WITH ACANTHUS

Made by Central Glass Co., Wheeling, W. Va.,
in mid 1880s. Comes clear, sapphire blue and
purple marble glass. Later made by
Northwood Glass Co., after 1903, at Wheeling, in clear, blue and canary opalescent.
Novelties were made in green opalescent but
tableware to the set in this color are rare. On
the transparent pieces there is sometimes
enameled decoration. Transparent colors are
20% less, purple marble 50% more, but it is
rare.

	White opal	Blue opal	Canary opal
Bowl, Berry, flat and footed, ruffled edges	35.00	60.00	65.00
Butter, covered, footed	50.00	65.00	75.00
Compote, covered, Jelly, 4" and 5"	25.00	35.00	27.50
Creamer	27.00	30.00	32.50
Dishes, various sizes	15–25.00	25–30.00	30–32.00
Goblet, (rare)	40.00	45.00	47.50
Pitcher, water, (rare)	150.00	250.00	255.00
Relish	18.00	25.00	30.00
Sauces			
Flat	10.00	12.00	14.00
Flooted	12.00	14.00	16.00
Spooner	30.00	45.00	47.50
Sugar, covered	45.00	55.00	60.00
Tumbler	20.00	22.00	25.00

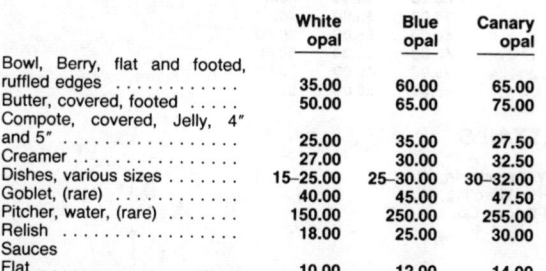

SWAG WITH BRACKETS

Made by Jefferson Glass Co., Steubenville, Ohio., c1904.

	Blue opal.	Green opal.	White opal.
Butter, covered	145.00	150.00	—
Compote, Jelly	25.00	72.50	20.00
Creamer	40.00	50.00	—
Cruet, with original stopper	85.00	255.00	—
Pitcher, water	275.00	200.00	275.00
Salt and Pepper Shakers	80.00	90.00	—
Spooner	40.00	65.00	40.00
Sugar, covered	50.00	90.00	50.00
Tumbler	35.00	50.00	35.00

TOKYO

Made by Jefferson Glass Co., Steubenville, Ohio., c1905.

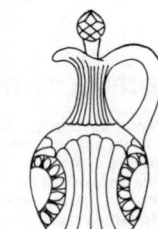

	White opal.	Blue opal.	Green opal.
Bowl, Berry	85.00	60.00	60.00
Butter, covered	90.00	100.00	100.00
Compote, Jelly	35.00	40.00	45.00
Creamer	75.00	85.00	90.00
Cruet	90.00	100.00	110.00
Dish, 6½″	40.00	50.00	75.00
Pitcher, water	195.00	200.00	165.00
Salt and Pepper Shakers	40.00	50.00	50.00
Spooner	30.00	35.00	40.00
Sugar, covered	60.00	85.00	90.00
Toothpick	40.00	50.00	50.00
Tumbler	35.00	45.00	50.00
Vase	45.00	60.00	60.00

WATER LILY AND CATTAILS

Mady by Fenton Glass Co., Williamstown, W. Va., and Northwood Glass Co., Wheeling, W. Va., c1900-1905, and Diamond-Dugan Co.

	Clear opal.	Blue opal.	Green opal.	Amethyst opal.
Bowl, Berry, 8″, ruffled	35.00	45.00	55.00	60.00
Butter, covered	65.00	75.00	90.00	100.00
Creamer				
Individual	25.00	30.00	35.00	40.00
Regular	45.00	40.00	65.00	75.00
Dish, bon bon, tri-cornered	35.00	45.00	50.00	55.00
Pitcher, water	65.00	125.00	175.00	200.00+
Plates	25.00	28.00	30.00	32.00
Relish, handled	30.00	32.00	35.00	40.00
Sauces	8.00	20.00	25.00	35.00
Spooner	35.00	45.00	40.00	40.00
Sugar, covered, regular	30.00	35.00	37.50	40.00
Tumbler	30.00	25.00	35.00	35.00
Water Tray	18.00	—	—	—

WILD BOUQUET

Made by Northwood Glass Co., Wheeling, W. Va., c1900-1905, and other companies.

	White opal.	Green opal.	Blue opal.
Bowl, Berry	50.00	80.00	—
Butter, covered	90.00	190.00	—
Creamer	40.00	50.00	—
Cruet	175.00	195.00	195.00
Cruet Set on tray	300.00+	300.00+	300.00+
Pitcher, water	180.00	245.00	245.00
Salt and Pepper Shakers	100.00	100.00	100.00
Sauces	25.00	25.00	30.00
Spooner	80.00	90.00	90.00
Sugar, covered	120.00	125.00	130.00
Toothpick	100.00	120.00	125.00
Tumbler	38.00	38.00	40.00

GENERAL COLLECTIONS

ABC PLATES

These plates were made for children and meant to help with their education. The rim usually contains the alphabet and/or numbers. Animals, great men, maxims or nursery rhymes are in the center. Most were imported from England and made of glass, pewter, porcelain, pottery or tin. They can range in size from 4 to slightly over 9 inches. Several patterns, especially in tin, have been reproduced.

Reference: Mildred and Joseph P. Chalala's *A Collector's Guide to ABC Plates, Mugs and Things.*

See *Warman's Americana & Collectibles* for an expanded listing of ABC Plates.

Tin, ABC Plate, "Who Killed Cock Robin," 7⅞" d, $50.00.

GLASS

Baby In Tub, forget-me-not pattern, clear	55.00
Carnival Glass, 7½"	55.00
Child's Head, 8", vaseline, Clay Crystal Works	20.00
Christmas Eve, 6", clear, Santa on chimney	65.00
Clock in center, 7"	36.00
Daisy, 6", clear	32.00
Ducks, 6", amber	35.00
Eagle, Centennial Exhibition, 1776–1876, clear	25.00
Flower Bouquet, clear	42.00
Garfield, 6", bust, clear	60.00
Hobnail, pointed	15.00
Jumbo, 6", boy on elephant	48.00
Milk Glass, white, blue beaded edge	30.00
Mother Cat and Kittens, clear	55.00

PORCELAIN OR POTTERY

Baby and Dog	35.00
Baseball, caught on fly	90.00
Behold Him Rising from the Grave	85.00
Cat Driving, 6¾", cat, paws on wheel, W. A. Adams & Sons, Tunstall, England	45.00
Chaffinch & Goldfinch	75.00
Children Play with Puppies, 8½"	40.00
Crusoe Rescues Friday, 8⅛", B. P. Co., Tunstall, England	60.00
Donkey & Foal	65.00
Fox and Goose, 7"	22.00
Gathering Cotton, 5½", black transfer, Staffordshire	48.00
Horse Racing, 7"	35.00
Ice Cream, 7½"	42.00
Man & Dog Sliding, 7"	40.00
Month of October, 7¼", transfer of family in woods and Oct. verse, Staffordshire	68.00
New Pony	65.00
Organ Grinder, children, 7½", stippled border, Staffordshire, c1845	72.00
Parrot, children, God, verse, alphabet border, Elsmore/Foster	39.50
Poor Richard's Way to Wealth, c1830	65.00
Silks & Satins	80.00
Sioux Indian Chief on Horseback, 8¼", c1860	100.00
The Drive	65.00
Tiger Hunt, 7½"	25.00
Tired of Play	75.00
Village Blacksmith	65.00

TIN

Alphabet emb border, 6½", plain center	45.00
Children & Bears, 8"	35.00
Children Rolling Hoops	55.00
Girl on Swing, 3½", litho	35.00
Hey Diddle, Diddle, 9"	35.00
Jumbo the Elephant, 6"	50.00
Kitten, 5"	32.00
Mary Had a Little Lamb, 7"	45.00
Numerals, 6½"	50.00
Tom Thumb, 3"	28.00

ADAMS ROSE

This ware is decorated with brilliant red roses, green leaves on a white background. It was made by Adams and Son, c1820–1840, in the Staffordshire district of England. A variant of the pattern was made later by G. Jones and Son, England, until 1908. The colors are not as brilliant, and the background is a "dirty" white. This type is known as Late Adams Rose and commands less than the price of the early pattern.

Plate, 7½", late, $35.00.

Bowl, 8¾", early	600.00
Creamer, late	95.00
Cups and Saucers	
5¾", plain edge, late	65.00
Scalloped edge, early	225.00
Milk Pitchers	
4⅞", c1840	75.00
6¾", bulbous, emb	130.00
Plates	
7¼", early	145.00
7½", late	35.00
8½", early	185.00
8½", late	45.00
9¼", early	175.00
9½", late	70.00
10½", soup, early	225.00
10½", soup, late	125.00
Platter, 15⅛", oval, early	300.00
Suger, covered, impressed "Wood"	500.00
Teapots	
Early	600.00
Late	210.00
Vegetable Dish, covered, 12⅝", c1850	500.00
Wash Bowl and Pitcher, early	1,000.00

ADVERTISING ITEMS, MISCELLANEOUS

In the days before television put a manufacturer's product before the public instantly, merchants used many different methods of advertisement. The first and most effective were advertising cards. People collected them avidly and carefully pasted them in scrapbooks and albums. There were also give-aways; calendars were very popular, as were plates, kitchen utensils and spoons, which were collected in sets. There is hardly an object which was useful to a householder which was not utilized in this way. Today it is still a popular method of advertising and will, no doubt, produce many of tomorrow's antiques and collectibles.

See *Warman's Americana & Collectibles* for a more detailed listing of Advertising Items.

Pot holder, 5½ x 6", cotton front, felt back, $20.00.

Apothecary Jar, 14", swirl top, emb, Geo. E. Sawyer, Portland, ME	65.00
Ashtray, "France," glass, cobalt, gilt ship	15.00
Bean Pot, Sheffield 111, Muscode, WI, brown and white	35.00
Bill Hook, Carolina Life Insurance Co., celluloid, 3½", blue and white, c1920	25.00
Billfold, leather, gold stamped inside "Van Vleet Mansfield Drug Co., Memphis, Aug. 1900, Plantation Chill Cure," etc.	25.00
Bowls	
Groth Bros., St. Ansgar, IA	45.00
Quaker Rolled White Oats, 7¾", white china	20.00
Broom Holder, "De Laval Cream Separators Save $10 to $15 per cow yearly," 3½"	60.00
Cake Knife, Argee Family Flour, Hubbard Milling Co.	8.75
Charm Bracelet, miniature packages of Shredded Ralston, Old Dutch Cleanser, Hi Ho Crackers, Crisco, Snider's Catsup, Sears, brass, c1940	25.00
Chest, "Ferris Woolen Co.," display, hinged, cov in simulated alligator, 1935–1936	75.00
Clothes Brush, Bell Roasted Coffee, litho	20.00

Cordial, Morrison Hotel 12.50
Creamers
    Brunskill Dairy, Cedar Falls, Iowa   6.50
    Nestle's Hot Fudge, glass 15.00
    Walnut Dairy Farms 6.50
Cup, Majestic Range, measuring
    with sifter 12.50
Door Push, Toastmaster Brand ... 10.00
Egg Lifter, Rumford Baking Powder 10.00
Flour Sifter, Bromwell's, tin, green
    wood handle 5.00
Fly Swatter, "Williams Ice Cream"
    on handle, other side "Every fly is
    the potential ancestor of millions
    of other files. Kill this cycle," swat-
    ter 4½ x 6", 11" handle 12.00
Fur Brush, Jones Fur Service, Fair-
    mont, WV, wood handle 30.00
Glass, Bromo-Seltzer, 5", blue, white
    lettering, c1930 .... 18.00
Jars
    Bordens Malted Milk, aluminum . 18.00
    Ramon's Pills, counter display, tin
    lid 45.00
Jug. 4", Fuller Music Store, Iowa
    Fall, IA 75.00

Juice Glass, Kellogg's Grape Juice,
    etched grapes and lettering 20.00
Memo Booklet, Fleischmann's
    Yeast, celluloid cover, 1911 .... 12.00
Paint Book, Dutch Boy Paints, 4 x 6",
    1921 .... 15.00
Pencil Clip, Morton's Salt 8.00
Pitcher, Andrew Westin & Co., Merry
    Christmas, blue and gray, cherry
    band 65.00
Plate, Heinz "57" Varieties, 5", oval,
    camphor 5.00
Rolling Pin, Kelsey & Wagner, Adair,
    Iowa, crockery 120.00
Ruler, Upon Nut Co., brass & wood
    folding 15.00
Shoestore Foot Measurer, Ritz,
    wood 15.00
Spoon, Baker's Chocolate 30.00
Storybook, Colgate's Jungle Pow
    Wow, 1911 .... 20.00
Toy, wooden, swinging man, "Drink
    Hawel's Root Beer" 20.00
Tureen, Miner's Beef Malt, 9" l, 6¼
    h, porcelain, sheafs of wheat in
    relief, wheat finial, 1907 .... 135.00
Wall Clock, E. C. Simmons Keen
    Kutter, c1930 .... 175.00
Watch Fob, "Consign Your Live-
    stock To Doud & Co., Chicago,"
    emb boy and girl with cow and pig
    pull toys 35.00

ADVERTISING SIGNS

The decorators of America have discovered the advertising sign as a colorful and inexpensive decorative form. Many restaurants and bars use local signs or theme-related signs to establish a decor from the late 19th century through the 1950s. The early signs are indicators of the high quality achieved in the American lithograph and printing industry. Condition is a critical factor; bent edges or color loss lower price by 20 to 40%.

See *Warman's Americana & Collectibles* for an expanded listing of Advertising Signs.

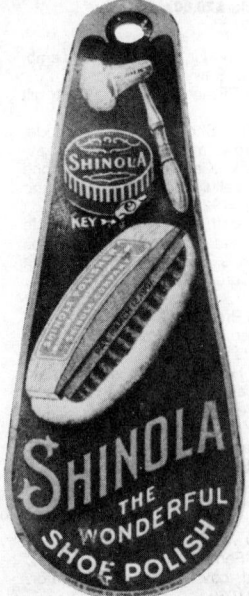

Shoehorn, made by Chas. W. Shonk Co., Litho., Chicago, $25.00.

Burger Beer, 8 x 14¼", litho tin, $75.00.

American Railway Express, 12 x 72", wood 325.00

Ashland Whiskey, 24 x 20", tin, self framed, hunter in lodge drinking, 1900 . . . . 750.00

Atlantic & Pacific Tea Co., logo, reverse on glass, c1935 . . . . 115.00

Blue Jay Corn Plasters, 13½ x 7", old man in rocking chair, whittling 125.00

Blue Ribbon Bourbon, 38 x 28", litho on stretched canvas, wagon pulled by oxen 350.00

Buckshoe & Tiger Stripe Tobacco, 28 x 14", 1895 . . . . 275.00

Chi-Namel Varnish, 20 x 13", metal, die-cut, chinaman with paint brush, 1920 . . . . 195.00

Clark's O. N. T., 20 x 15½", girl, doll, cats, 1880s 250.00

Cupples Cord, 20 x 28", emb tin rhino inside auto tire, 1920 . . . . 250.00

Dalley's Pain Extractor, 32 x 16½", elk, 1889 . . . . 350.00

Drink Sun Spot/Bottled Sunshine, 15¼", metal 300.00

Duke's Mixture, 32 x 22" paperboard, wood frame, 1899 . . . . . . 395.00

Duluth Imperial Flour, 18 x 25", tin, black lady cook making bread . . 750.00

El Bart Gin, 9 x 13", tin, bulldog chained to door, 1910 . . . . 175.00

Elgin Watches, 15 x 23", litho on wood, Tom Sawyer type boy holding watch, 1900 . . . . 375.00

Gold Dust Twins, litho, twins scrubbing dishes, kitchen sink 225.00

Grape Nuts, tin, girl and St. Bernard, 1905 . . . . 620.00

Harvard Rye, 29 x 22", tin, wood frame, cap and gown graduates, drinking 450.00

I. W. Harper, 33 x 44", litho on stretched canvas, auto, "Just Got Married," 1915 . . . . 650.00

Indian Gasoline, Montana, 6', porcelain, round, 2 sided 395.00

Ithaca Featherlight Ammo 60.00

Jeweler's Wedding Ring, nickel on brass hand, large facetted glass diamond, lights up 465.00

Kayo Root Beer, tin 75.00

Kist Beverages, 14 x 15", tin, c1930 25.00

Krueger Root Beer, 10 x 27", tin . . 16.00

Lash Bitters, 14 x 21", litho on wood, Victorian lady, horse 395.00

London Life Cigarettes, 34 x 18", paperboard, man in tux, wood frame, 1905 . . . . 225.00

Munsingwear, 24 x 36", cardboard, woman 85.00

Nat'l Fire Ins., Hartford, 16 x 2", brass 275.00

National Phonograph Co., 32 x 24",

paperboard, wood frame, old man and woman listening to Edison phonograph 375.00

OFC Bourbon, 31 x 22", paperboard, wood frame, 2 hunters on log drinking, elk behind them, 1900 . . . . 495.00

Old Dutch Cleanser, 22 x 32", porcelain 130.00

Old English, 31 x 24", paper, framed, 1900 . . . . 220.00

Oliver Plow, frame, 34½ x 25½", sgr. 395.00

Optometrist, Eyes Tested, glass sign, eyeball at top, eye glasses . 165.00

Overland Motors, 24 x 36", porcelain, whippet 175.00

Paul Jones Co., 21 x 14", litho on wood, negro woman, child and man with bottle, 1890 . . . . 650.00

Red Cross Cotton, 33 x 24", paperboard, wood frame, negroes picking cotton, 1894 . . . . 375.00

Royal Ins., reverse on glass, 27 x 21" 350.00

Vernor's, convex porcelain, 11 x 17" 35.00

ADVERTISING TRADE CARDS

These cards are small, thin cardboard, extolling the merits of a product and bearing the name and address of a merchant.

With the invention of lithography, colorful trade cards became a popular advertising media in the late 19th and early 20th century. They were made to appeal especially to children. Young and old alike collected and treasured them in albums and scrapbooks. Very few are dated; 1880 to 1893 were the prime years for trade cards; 1810 to 1850 can be found, but rarely. Most range in price from $1.00 to $7.50. A few command higher prices because of subject matter, artist or scarcity.

Many were made in sets, and collectors still seek a complete them today. Cards taken from old albums should be handled with care, as there is often valuable information on the reverse side.

CLOTHING

Koch Bros., Allentown's Leading Clothing Makers, girl, large umbrella, holding handled fan, boy in sailor suit, Maud Humphrey, 1902 10.00

Mandel Bros., advertising for new leatherware department, shape of handbag, with pink, blue flowers, foliage, brown background, blue, white handkerchief extending from opening, reverse describes wares to be sold 3.00

Food, Armour's Extract of Beef, multi-color, Edwards, Deutsch & Heitmann, Chicago, $4.00.

F. Mayer Boot & Shoe Co., Milwaukee, 3 boys playing hopscotch, garden, fence in background, Milwaukee custom made shoe emblem on front with poem "Jimmy's First Boots" by Ella Wheeler Wilcox, reverse side advertisement for shoes 2.00

Quakermaid Stockings, Young, Knight, Field & Co., Phila., PA, distributor's New Year's card, c1930 . . 2.00

FOOD

B. F. Clark, Ice Cream, Fruit, Confectionery, Phila., Mother Goose flying thru sky 50

Calumet Baking Powder, Co., 1918, young boy in soldier suit saluting photograph of soldier, mother in pink gown, infant in white wicker basket 3.50

Daniels & Smith, groceries, canned, dried and green fruits, vegetables, La Crosse, WI open pink rose, buds, foliage 2.00

Excelsior Starch Co., folding card, cover plus 4 scenes, advertising starch, paper pail 5.00

Jell-O Ice Cream Powder, blonde girl serving older lady, molded ice cream with strawberries, reverse has directions for use 2.50

Maiden Blush Vinegar, children playing 3.00

Mellin's Baby Food, hold to light, baby sleeping and awake, 1888 . 15.00

Sanford's Ginger, black girl rocking baby 7.00

Troy Branch of the Bennett Tea House of Vesey St. Troy, NY, blonde girl lying in grass daydreaming, red umbrella, colorful basket of flowers 3.00

COFFEE

Flint's Ground Golden Rio Coffee, white vase, open pink rose, foliage, pink rose bud, grapes 1.50

Grandma's Coffee, 3 x 5″, cat and dogs 2.50

Lion Coffee Co., girl in picture hat, basket of cherries 4.50

McLaughlin's XXXX Coffee, jungle scene, brown bear fighting lion, marked one of 16 cards 5.00

FARM MACHINERY

Columbus Buggy Co., horse and buggy, mechanical, wheels turn . . 15.00

Moline Wagon Co., Moline, IL, "A Mobile Bridal Trip," couple in Moline wagon 3.00

Oliner Chilled Plow Works, South Bend, IN, "Casaday Sulky Plow," plow and plant 10.00

GUM & CANDY

Adams 'Tutti Fruitti' Chewing Gum, man's hands holding playing cards 12.00

E. H. Kelly, Dealer In Fine Confectionery, girl holding horse 10.00

MEDICINE

Dr. J. C. Ayer & Co., Lowell, MA, Ayer's Cherry Pectoral for the cure of coughs, colds, asthma, croup, bronchitis, whooping-cough, and consumption, girl gazing at robins in cherry tree 3.00

Chesebrough Manufacturing Co., Vaseline, girl in apron playing with cat & 2 puppies 2.50

Chinkalyptus, 36 pills, 25¢, cures chills and fever, silhouette of 4 girls, washing doll clothes, playing, boy bringing water, garden background 3.00

Conkey's Poultry Remedies, "Don't Worry! Conkey Will Cure Me," copyright 1908 by G. E. Conkey Co., rooster on one leg with bandaged head, reverse describes remedies, prices 4.00

Medicine, Ayer's Cathartic Pills, multi-color, copyright 1880, $5.00.

Dalley's Magical Pain Extractor, the great family ointment, 3 horses, riders, running steeple-chase 3.00

Lydia E. Pinkham, portrait sgd "Yours for Health, Lydia E. Pinkham," reverse side explains virtues of Lydia E. Pinkham's vegetable compound 2.50

Morse's Pills, girl in orchid dress feeding 2 kittens, 1890 .... 3.00

Mrs. Winslow's Soothing Syrup for Children Teething, mother in bed, 2 children, calendar, 1886 on reverse side 6.00

MISCELLANEOUS

Audubon County Fair, 4 cats, 1 female, large bonnet, holding umbrella, 3 men in top hats and coats 4.00

Buckeye Force Pumps, Mast, Fous & Co., Springfield, OH, boy pumping water in front lawn of burning house, Krebs Lithograph Co., Cincinnati 8.00

Howe Scales, Page, Fargo & Co., Pittsburgh - Philadelphia, black man seated on scale hiding behind cotton bale 6.00

Mayer, Merkel & Ottman, NYC, advertising Mexican Hammock with braided edge, girl lying in hammock, man standing at tree, man

sitting, group in background playing badminton 5.00

Wanamaker's Ladies' and Gents' Dining Rooms, Phila., cream pink rose buds, green foliage 4.00

MUSICAL

Needham Piano & Organ Co., NYC, die-cut of envelope, holding orchestra seat tickets 8.00

Sohmer Piano, agents Messrs. D. S. Andrus & Co., Elmira, NY, oval card, blue forget-me-not border, blue background, girl with long blond hair in blue dress, pink flowers in hair 4.00

Weaver Organ Factory, York, PA, cat, c1880 .... 8.00

Wheelock Piano, lady playing piano 7.00

SOAP & CLEANERS

Bixby Boot Black, shoeshine boy .. 2.00

Enoch Morgan & Sons, "Sapolio," small boy, fancy clothes 2.00

Colgate & Co., Cashmere Bouquet Toilet Soap 3.00

Pear's Soap, mother and child, "A specialty for infants" 3.00

Pearline Soap Co., Pyle's Pearline, court jester in pain 2.00

Tobacco, West Virginia Mail Pouch, 5 x 3½", $8.00

THREAD & SEWING

"Domestic" Sewing Machine Co., NYC, 2 ladies, girl, black coachman in open carriage driven by 2 brown horses, stopping to read road sign advertising sewing machine 3.50
Golden Eagle Knitting Wools, Willey & Pearson, Ltd., Trafalgar Works, Halifax, woman in green dress in front of mirror 2.00
Merrick Thread Co., woman and child at the beach 2.00
Willimantic Thread, cupid flying around world tying it with thread .   3.00

TOBACCO

W. S. Kimball, cigarette card, Jack Dempsey 8.00
Smoke La Pastora, kittens in top hat, Currier & Ives 20.00
Owl Cigars, die-cut, bird cage, owl inside 10.00

TRANSPORTATION

Flexible Flyer Sleds, mechanical, steering movement of sled moves, c1910 . . . .   14.00
State Line, for Europe, ship anchored in foreign harbor 9.00
Wise's Axel Grease, 2 negros talking in house 20.00

ADVERTISING TRAYS

It was the custom, in the 1880s to 1900, for businesses, bars, country hotels and general stores to issue colorful trays advertising their place of business or product. Beer companies gave these trays to hotels and bars, and general stores issued them, especially at Christmas. They have become very collectible today.

See *Warman's Americana & Collectibles* for an expanded listing of Advertising Trays.

Anheuser Busch Brewing Ass'n., St. Louis, 12", round, large "A" and eagle 175.00
Bartels Beer, painted for The Greater New York Brewery, Inc. by Herbert Bohnert, 1936, scene of men in tavern 45.00
Beer Driver's Union, German submarine and captain 250.00
Bergdoll Brewing Co., 12 x 15", brass engraved, floral, 1917 . . . .   50.00
Carstair's White Seal, 4", change . .   13.00

Stegmaier Brewing Co., Wilkes-Barre, PA, 12" d, $17.00.

Cutter Whiskey, 16½", oval, ship, sunset 250.00
Diamond Wedding Rye, woman, large hat, drinking, 1900 . . . .   195.00
"Dr. Pepper," rectangular, woman holding 2 bottles 115.00
Erie Brewing Co., Erie, PA, 4", round, change, trademark in center 35.00
Excelsior Bottling Co., beer and soft drinks 175.00
Falls City Brewing Co., 12", round, waitress, 1915 . . . .   140.00
Heptol Splits, 4", round, change, cowboy on bucking horse, 1904 .   65.00
Heck's Capudine, medicine tray . . .   195.00
Hires Root Beer, 13", round, boy holding early barrel mug, yellow rim 225.00
King's Pure Malt, 4½ x 6" oval, change, waitress 48.00
Merrigans, boy and girl eating ice cream at beach 160.00
Moxie, 6", round, change, green . .   42.00
New Lebanon Brewing, Lebanon, PA, 4", round, change, trademark in center 45.00
O.F.C. Bourbon, 12", round, stag . .   85.00
Old Pepper Whiskey, oval, 1910, Revolutionary War soldiers drinking 175.00
Pabst Tonic, 12 x 17", girl drinking glass of tonic 80.00
Pepsi Cola, 4 x 6", oval, change, c1920 . . . .   105.00
Red Raven Splits, giant bird with bottle 225.00
Ryan's Pure Beer, 4", change, girl with long hair, 1907 . . . .   45.00
Robert Smith Ale, 24"oval, tin, self framed tiger head, 1900 . . . .   850.00
Wright & Taylor Whiskey 175.00

Yuengling's Beer, 4", round, change, girl in wide brimmed hat 55.00

AGATA GLASS

Joseph Locke of the New England Glass Co., Cambridge, Mass., is credited with producing this art glass in the 1880s. Agata is usually an opaque pink shading to dark rose. The surface was left glossy and coated with a metallic stain which was spattered with alcohol and fired. Gloss finish predominates. It is rarely found in satin finish.

Bowls
  5" d, tricornered 1,400.00
  6½", ruffled top 1,800.00
Creamer 1,200.00
Cruet, stopper matches handle . . .   600.00
Finger bowl, ruffled edge, orig paper
  label 800.00
Pitcher, milk, 4" sq mouth 1,050.00
Sauce Dish 300.00
Toothpicks
  Ruffled mouth, exceptional mottling 750.00
  Square mouth, excellent mottling   700.00
Tumbler 950.00
Vases
  Lily shape 1,200.00
  Morgan shape, amber griffin holder 1,500.00
Whiskey glass, gold mottling 400.00

Juice Glass, 3¾" h, $825.00.

AKRO AGATE GLASS

The Akro Agate Co. was formed in 1911, first as jobbers, selling marbles made by the Navarre Glass Marble Specialty Co. to chain stores and wholesalers.

In 1914 the owners moved from near Akron, Ohio, to Clarksburg, W. Va., where cheap labor and a plentiful supply of natural gas were available. They opened a factory, known as the Akro Agate Co., for production of marbles which continued in profitable operation until 1929.

In 1932 the company was diversified and started making bowls, ashtrays, flower pots, etc., in green, red and blue onyx. Operations continued successfully until 1948. Finally, because of the lack of profits, the firm was dissolved and the factory was sold in 1951 to the Clarksburg Glass Co.

See *Warman's Americana & Collectibles* for an expanded listing of Akro Agate Glass.

Sugar, Concentric Ring, children's dish, yellow, $7.50.

Apothecary Jar, black, gold trim,
  Jean Vivaudou Co. 20.00
Ashtrays
  Ellipsoid, green, white 11.00
  Goodrich tire 12.50
Basket, 1 handle, white, light green
  marbelized 165.00
Bells, 5¼" h
  Cream 50.00
  Green 65.00
  Pumpkin 48.00
Children's Toy Dishes
  Bowl, Interior Marbelized, large,
    red, white 24.50
  Creamer and sugar, Plain Jane,
    baked on blue 15.00
  Cup, Raised Daisy, green 19.50
  Plate, Concentric Ring, large
    transp., cobalt 40.00

Teapot, cov, Concentric Ring, large transp., cobalt	55.00
Tumbler, Interior Panel & Stippled, green	5.75
Cigarette Jar, Mexicalli, blue, white .	35.00

Flower Pots

2¼", Ribbed Top, cream, caramel	3.50
3½", Ribs & Flutes, pumpkin . . .	4.50
4½", Ribs & Flutes, pumpkin . . .	12.00

Jardinieres

4¾", bell shaped, rectangular top, yellow marbelized	20.00
5", ribs & flutes, sq top, pumpkin	18.25

Lamps

Hanging wall, white shade	65.00
Table, Akro shade, white, caramel marbelized	75.00

Marbles

Set of 25, Cardinal Red, orig box	35.00
Boxed set of 100, orig box	26.50
Match Holder, blue, white	12.00
Mortar & Pestle, Jean Vivaudou Co., jar and lid, white, pink, green floral, orig paper labels	16.00

Powder Boxes

Colonial Lady

Lime Green	130.00
Transp. Amber	100.00
Concentric Ring, amethyst, transp. lid, yellow opaque	16.00

Scotty Dog

Dark Green	115.00
White	45.00

AMBERINA GLASS

The New England Glass Co. of Cambridge, Mass., introduced Amberina Glass in 1883 under a patent granted to Joseph Locke. Amberina is a transparent glass shading from deep ruby to amber in color. The colors were produced by adding small amounts of gold to an amber glass batch and reheating portions of the piece (generally the top) to bring out the deep red. The Mt. Washington Glass Co. called their similar ware Rose Amber. Most early Amberina is of flint quality glass, blown or pattern molded in the familiar diamond quilted pattern. Some pieces are found in the pressed Daisy and Button pattern and have been attributed to Sandwich.

Amberina Glass was made by several Midwestern factories, c1890. The shading from cranberry to amber was produced by giving the amber glass a thin flashing of cranberry on upper portions of the piece. This gave the piece a sharp line of demarkation between the two colors. This less expensive version caused the death knell for the New England variety.

In the 1920s Amberina Glass was revived for a short time by Edward D. Libbey at his factory which was then situated in Toledo, Ohio. These pieces are signed and are included under the New England listing since they were of that quality.

Amberina Glass has been widely reproduced.

DQ = Diamond Quilted; IVT = Inverted Thumbprint.

Vase, 7¼" h, inverted thumbprint, $285.00.

NEW ENGLAND

Bowls

7½" d, DQ, roll over scalloped edge	180.00
8½", cradle shaped, Daisy & Button	250.00
Cologne Bottle, 5", DQ, MOP, emb silver top, blistered	225.00
Compote, 8¾" d, thumbprint	325.00
Creamer, 4", bulbous, sq mouth, IVT, amber reeded handle	365.00

Finger Bowls

2⅛ x 4¼" d, tricorn top	195.00
2¾ x 4⅜" d, round, swirl	145.00
2¾ x 5¼" d, fluted edge, deep fuchsia	275.00
Hat, elongated diamond mold	195.00
Goblet, wine, Sandwich	90.00
Juice Glass, 4¼", waisted ribbed fuchsia top	135.00
Lemonade Glass, 5" h, paneled, handle	150.00
Muffineer, inverted coin spot	235.00

Pitchers
5", IVT	375.00
7 x 4⅛" d, milk, tankard, DQ, round mouth, amber applied handle	325.00
8", sq mouth, hobnail, cranberry to red, amber handle	475.00
8½", water, DQ panels on sides, straight ribbing in front of spout, roped handle extending around neck	475.00

Punch Cups
2¾ x 2½" d, DQ, amber reeded applied handle	125.00
2¾ x 2½" d, DQ, orig New England Glass Co. label	300.00
Salt, baby thumbprint dimple side ..	110.00
Sauce Dish, sq, Daisy & Button, fuchsia	110.00
Sugar Shaker, 5¼", DQ, MOP, pewter top	650.00

Toothpick Holders
2¼" sq top, deep red, fuchsia ..	195.00
New England, DQ, tricorn top ...	225.00

Tumblers
3⅝", elongated diamond pattern, deep red top, slight fuchsia tinge	140.00
3¾", Moire pattern, cranberry ..	145.00
3¾", DQ, New England	80.00
4⅛", sq top, baby thumbprint, deep red	195.00
4½", cranberry to fuchsia	175.00

Vases
10½", Libbey, No. 3006, sgd ...	500.00
11", long stemmed lily, Form #3002, sgd Libbey	450.00
11", Libbey, slender neck, Form #3004	400.00

Whiskey Tasters
2½", baby DQ, deep red	200.00
2¾ x 2⅛" d, tiny DQ, deep red to golden amber	165.00

MIDWESTERN

Bowl, fold over top, gold floral decor, swirl design	150.00
Celery Vase, 6½", thumbprint	135.00
Juice Glass, thumbprint	30.00

Muffineers
Baby thumbprint	155.00
Baby thumbprint, enamel decoration	70.00

Mugs
Cut flanged bottom, fuchsia	175.00
Swirled, gold floral decoration, rope handle	130.00

Pitchers
6½", water, reverse swirled	190.00
8", water, paneled, ground pontil, ribbed handle	175.00
8½", tricorn top	155.00

8½", water, IVT, sq top	100.00
Salt and Pepper Shakers, inverted coin spot, pewter tops	105.00
Toothpick Holder, DQ, drum shape .	70.00

Vases
3", miniature, DQ, rigaree decoration	150.00
5½ x 4⅛" d, IVT, amber applied feet	150.00
6¾", ribbed lily	150.00
9¾ x 4¾" d, emb basketweave pattern, amber applied ruffled top, ground pontil	145.00
Whiskey Bottle, 11", double pouring spout, matching stopper	120.00

AMBERINA GLASS—PLATED

Plated Amberina glass was patented by Edward Libbey in 1889 for the New England Glass Co., Cambridge, Mass. Its characteristic coloring of deep amber shading to deep ruby is enhanced by vertical ribbing and a fiery opalescent lining. A cased Wheeling glass of similar appearance has an opaque white lining, but is not opalescent and the body is not ribbed. Plated Amberina was made in a limited quantity, was susceptible to breakage, and is consequently rare.

Vase, bulbous base, ribbed motif, $2,200.00.

Bowl, 8", 3½" h, squatty, bulbous, crimped top	6,150.00
Celery	2,250.00
Lamp shade, 14", hanging, swirled, ribbed	4,750.00
Lemonade mug, handle	2,500.00

Pitchers
7½", water, bulbous	3,750.00
8¾", water	5,750.00
Sugar, handles	1,800.00
Syrup pitcher	5,200.00
Toothpick, ribbed	2,250.00
Tumbler	1,985.00
Vase, 7¼", lily shape	2,500.00

AMPHORA

The dictionary defines amphora as a two-handled vessel with a narrow neck used by the ancient Greeks to hold wine, water or oil. The Amphora wares found on today's market were made in Austria in the late 1880s. They are usually marked "Amphora" with a crown. Occasionally a piece is cross-indexed with "Teplitz" and signed twice.

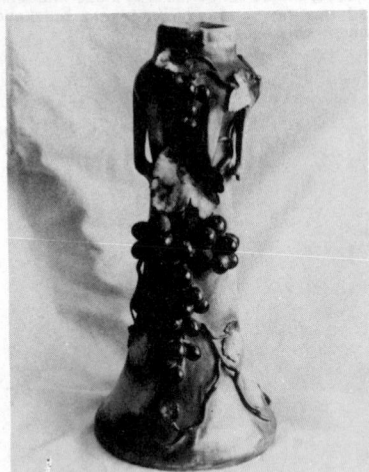

Vase, 16¾" h, triangle mark, "EDDA," impressed "Amphora/8675/56, $275.00.

Baskets
6 x 7", incised floral decor, blue	70.00
10" l, 8½" h, figural peasant girl kneeling, artist signed, imp Amphora, Austria	255.00

Bowls
4 x 3½", handles, raised enamel poppies	275.00
6" h x 10¾" l x 6" w, blown, with mauve, orange, white and green, enameling and jewels, imp crown mark	235.00
Bust, woman, pastels, sgr Amphora	190.00
Compote, black berries, leaves	200.00
Ewer, green, gilt leaves, stem rises to form handle, mottled blue, green ground, imp mark, 3853/42	425.00
Figurine, hen, egg, sculpted	180.00
Jug, 5¾ x 5¾", sgr.	110.00
Mug, 3" h, Arab on horseback, Stellmacher	40.00
Pitcher, Art Deco, made by Resner, Shellmacker & Kessel, blue, red, yellow, and orange on green mottles ground, c1900	215.00
Rose Bowl, 4¾", enamel poppies decor, pebble finish	90.00
Urn, 12 x 14", green glaze, purple highlights, gold flowers, sgr Amphora with crown	285.00

Vases
2", handpainted multicolor floral design, Amphora Holland, 1921	26.00
5" h, Grecian lady, Stellmacher	35.00
6½", basket weave, delicate molded and applied pink roses, 4 gold twig handles, Imperial mark	65.00
7", beige, purple, red gooseberries, sgr.	170.00
8" h, bizarre face at top, imp beehive, Austria	48.00
8¼", bud, blue, vivid floral decor	400.00
9⅛" h, 6⅜" d, matte gray ground, shadow flowers, cobalt blue gloss top band, trim, large stylized glossy raised colored flowers in band at center, base	185.00

ANIMAL DISHES, COVERED

Covered animal dishes became popular in the late 1800s and continue their popularity today.

Among the leading American manufacturers were McKee Glass Co., Pittsburgh, Pa., and Atterbury Glass Co., also of Pittsburgh, which made the famous Atterbury duck covered dish, which was patented on March 15, 1887. The most popular collectible in this category is the hen on nest, as collectors concentrated on size, color and type of glass.

Reproductions are found in almost every form. Collectors must use caution and discretion in purchasing these articles.

Also see MILK GLASS and VALLERYSTAHL for added listings.

Cat, reclining, ribbed base, white milk glass, imp 3 on inside of base, 5⅜" w at base, Westmoreland, $45.00.

Bear, 3⅜" h, black milk glass 135.00
Canary, white milk glass, McKee .. 100.00
Cats
  4¾" h, white glass, hamper base,
    Greentown 225.00
  6⅜", White milk glass, Atterbury,
    lacy base 120.00
Chick on sleigh, white milk glass .. 55.00
Chicken and eggs on nest, white
  milk glass, Atterbury 135.00
Cows
  5½", white milk glass, McKee .. 150.00
  6", amber glass, ribbed base,
    frosted 95.00
Dogs
  5", amber on wide ribbed base .. 90.00
  5", Chow, white milk glass,
    McKee 15.00
  6⅝" l, standing, setter on grassy
    field, E. C. Flaccus 150.00
Dolphin, 7½", fish, finial, chocolate
  glass 150.00
Dove, 4 x 4½", white milk glass,
  basketweave base, McKee 150.00
Ducks
  5", clear aqua 75.00
  7⅝", blue, purple sponge on emb
    surface, Russian procelain ... 90.00
  8½"l x 5¼"h, wavy base, milk
    glass, glass eyes 135.00
  Blue milk glass, without eyes,
    Atterbury, (rare) 450.00
  *White milk glass, amethyst head,
    Atterbury 225.00
Eagles
  6⅛", ovoid, white milk glass, "The
    American Hen," Puerto Rico,
    Cuba, Phillipines 145.00
  7⅛", white milk glass outstret-
    ched wings of mother, gathering
    three chicks, Challinor, Taylor &
    Co. 400.00
Elephant, clear 45.00

Fish
  White milk glass, Atterbury 175.00
  White milk glass, flat, finely de-
    tailed, ribbed base 125.00
Fox, 6⅜" l, white milk glass, ribbed
  base 135.00
Hens
  6½", custard 100.00
  6½", dark amber 65.00
  7", lavender, flat eye sockets,
    braided edge basket base 235.00
Hens, Staffordshire
  6½", painted 125.00
  7½" h x 6½" w x 8½" l, colored
    bisque, gold basketweave base 495.00
Horse, white milk glass, McKee ... 150.00
Lions
  5½", white milk glass, picket base 80.00
  5¾", white milk glass, scroll base 45.00
Lobster, milk glass 100.00
Owls
  White milk glass, red eyes,
    Atterbury 150.00
  Jar, opaque blue 200.00
Rabbits
  White milk glass, Atterbury, 9",
    red eyes 110.00
  White milk glass, blue ribbed base 175.00
  White milk glass, wheat base,
    drooping ears, E.C. Flaccus .. 115.00
Ram, 7" l, teal blue, white coat, gild-
  ed horns, black transfer mark,
  Russian porcelain 95.00
Robin, white milk glass, twig nest,
  Indiana Tumbler Co. 95.00
Roosters
  8½"h x 6¾", l, frosted 40.00
  White milk glass, blue head 75.00
  *White milk glass, ribbed base .. 75.00
Squirrel on acorn, white milk glass . 95.00
Swans
  5", blue milk glass, closed neck . 65.00
  *5", white milk glass 125.00
  6½", clear glass, frosted head
    and neck, Sandwich 150.00
  7", white milk glass, open neck,
    Atterbury 125.00
Turkeys
  5" blue gray cast, milk glass split
    rib base, McKee 100.00
  8", white with brown nest, Staf-
    fordshire 200.00
Turtle, 6", clear 25.00

APOTHECARY ITEMS

Yesteryear's apothecary shop was quite removed from today's version of the modern
drug store which sells everything from gift
items to prescriptions from corporate manufacturers. Early pharmacists concocted shot-

gun prescriptions in a mortar and pestle, rolled pills by hand, percolated cough syrup, sold over-the-counter remedies and acted as the country doctor, neighborhood psychiatrist and checker partner. Bygone apothecary items are being collected for nostalgia, especially by those in the medical field.

Glass, 4¼", acid etched, $25.00.

Bleeder & folding lancet, silver colored tooled case, 2¼" l	75.00
Bleeding Bowl, 8¾" d, 2¼" h, pewter, ring hanger, crown touch mark, P.I.W., inscription "C1760, J/M/50, 1839"	300.00
Bottles	
6½" h, emerald, ribbed, recessed panel for label, glass stopper	40.00
8" h, glass labels, P. Digetal, Chloroform, Oi Absenth, Oi Gaulth, Ac Acetic, each	125.00
8½", white porcelain, floral decor, Azahar label	32.50
14", bulbous, IVT pedestal, base	70.00
Chest, 49 x 13 x 59", pine, 24 nailed drawers, bracket feet, refinished	850.00
Cupboard, 56 x 18¼ x 89", one pc. walnut, paneled doors, scalloped apron, 43 drawers, dovetailed	4,200.00
"The Calkins Disinfector," cast iron wall dispenser, emb, bottle, c1901, Rochester Germicide Co.	145.00
Drawers, 28 x 9¾ x 16¾", hanging, 3 tiers of 15 drawers, red and black paint	175.00
Funnels, 24½" h, 6½" d top, 9" sq wooden base, clear glass, pr	110.00

Graduate, 5" d base, 24" h, cylindrical, 2000cc size	55.00
Jars	
8½", amber, ground stopper	35.00
10", acidized inside stopper, swirl top, emb "Geo. E. Sawyer, Portland, Me."	65.00
16", blown glass, beautiful electric blue pedestal footing	60.00
Statue of Liberty	55.00
Label Dispensers, 3 x 6 x 6", brass, hinged top, McCourt Label Cabinet Co. Bradford, PA, Pat. June 11, 1912, dispenses roll 2½" w, emb	56.00
Literature	
American Druggists Journals, 1936	2.00
The Pharmaceutical Era, 85 pgs., pocketsize, complete list of drugs, preps, U.S.P. 1905, FE	18.00
Mortars and Pestles	
4½" h, brass, early	75.00
4½", burl wood	75.00
5¾" h, cast iron, worn green paint	30.00
6" d, 5" h, carved stone	25.00
6¼" h, ash burl, hand carved	105.00
6¾" h, cast iron	55.00
9" h, turned ash burl, wide turned foot, plain birch pestle	115.00
Pill Roller, 7 x 14", walnut, brass, makes 24 pills, 2 pcs	90.00
Scale, counter top, marble top, wooden base, 2 brass pans, weights	170.00
Spatula, advertising, Antiphlogestine	5.00
Thermometer, advertising, 15", wooden, Ex-Lax, Constipation & Liver Complaints	50.00

ART DECO

The Art Deco period was named for an exhibition held in Paris in 1927, "L'Exposition Internationale des Arts Decoratifs." It is a later period than Art Nouveau but sometimes crosses since they were relatively close in time and are often confused with the flowing and sensuous female forms of the earlier era.

The designs of Art Deco are angular and of simple lines. This was the period of skyscrapers, movie idols and the cubist work of Picasso and Legras. It was used for every conceivable object being produced in the 1920s–1930s, including ceramics, furniture, glass and metals, not only in Europe, but in America as well.

This is a special market for the "new" collector and the best of this style is now commanding prices comparable to earlier periods.

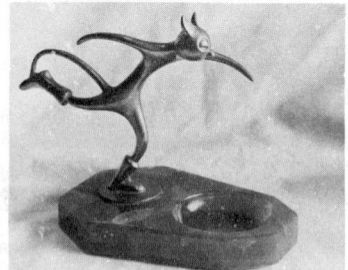

Ashtray, 5¾ x 4 x 5⅞", Puss & Boots, metal with gold wash (Vienna bronze), alabaster base, marked Austria, $375.00.

Ashtray, 5½ x 3½", metal, blown out comic figures, both sides . . .	32.00
Basket, brass, lacquered zinc white latticework sides, 4 brass feet . . .	1,100.00
Bookends, 7", bronze, figural nudes, Austria, pr	120.00
Box, cov, 9¾" d, octagonal, pottery, Victorian couple bidding farewell to train, trains and flowers in reserves, mkd La Belle Adventure, France	290.00
Bracelet, designs in relief, SS	125.00
Brooch, woman in light rose hat and scarf	20.00
Brush, 5", woman with flowing hair, SS	60.00
Cigar Case, 8¼" l, silver, blue enamel cabochon clasp, L. Schuch & Nache, Vienna	470.00
Cigarette Holder with case, dog carved on it	35.00

Box, 6"h, pyramid, MOP, abalone, jet, terra cotta, $475.00.

Clock, Golden Girl, Sessions, mahogany base	150.00
Coaster Set, lacquerware	22.00
Cocktail Shaker, oval tray and 6 goblets, hammered chrome, red celluloid handle, set	75.00
Compote, 2½" h, SS, circular bowl, floral stem, ribbed and beaded foot, imp Georg Jensen, Sterling, 181, Denmark	200.00
Desk Sets	
2 pcs, metal, ink stand and stamp box, sgr Aronson, 1924	45.00
3 pcs, bronze, perpetual calendar, inkwell with cobalt blue glass liner, roller blotter, sgr JB	175.00
Figures	
11½ x 17", chalk, flesh pink, draped nude, kneeling, goat butting her from behind	70.00
13¾", bronze, bather, green onyx base, sgd Bruno Zach	900.00
14", bronze, sorceress, kneeling, cold painted, black marble base, F. H. Hofenrichter, 1926	340.00
Lamps	
12", lighthouse, blue and white frosted glass shade, stepped base	75.00
14½", iron, nude, standing, arms elevated, fixture behind her holds frosted Lalique-type globe in molded flame shape	135.00
20¼", bronzed metal, lady with elevated legs, green molded ball shade, wired	150.00
Boudoir, blue bullet shades geometric, chrome bases, pr	42.00
Magazine Rack, 16", bronze, figural, Diana, The Huntress, with hound, green patina	300.00
Perfume, with stopper and atomizer, tall, opaque orchid, black designs, brass fittings, mkd De Vilbiss . . .	40.00
Picture, Parrish Daybreak, 10 x 18", orig frame	90.00
Pipe Stand, aluminum, stylized monkeys, ruby glass insert	42.00
Plate, 9¾" cobalt blue rim, green eyes in center separated by yellows & reds, Clarice Cliff, Newport Pottery, Bizarre Series	165.00
Purse, beaded bag, lg, "France" . . .	65.00
Rug, 29½ x 52", rectangular, geometric design in blue and dusty rose, Eric Bagge	500.00
Russian Wolfhounds, 12", bronze, green patina, oval green onyx base, Austrian, pr	500.00
Stationary Box, copper, large lady's head stenciled on top	45.00
Table, 31", bentwood, circular top, hourglass base	65.00

Tobacco Humidor, 13¾" l, rectangular, bevelled glass cover, SP, 4 ball feet 500.00

Tray, 16" l, silver, round, cast pea in pod handles, Woodside Silver Co. 400.00

Vases

6", green, geometric design, Germany 35.00

10", green, black bamboo, large dragonfly 65.00

18", glass, clear, thick walled foot with trapped bubble, shading into pink & white trumpet with flared brim, Schneider, mkd . . .   250.00

18", glass, clear, footed, trumpet, Steuben 250.00

Wall Mirror, 10¼ x 3½", Phillips 66 pin-up girl 18.00

Wall Pocket, 6⅜" w x 9⅜" h, pottery, lady masque, light gray, mkd Clarice Cliff 165.00

Water Pitcher, 12¾", SP, pat. May 1924 . . . .   27.00

ART NOUVEAU

The French term for the new art, "Art Nouveau," had its beginning in the 1890s and swept the continent and America for almost 40 years. Some of its more recognized artists were Galle, Lalique and Tiffany. But there were other artists of the period, not as proficient or promoted, and knowledgeable collectors are now searching out their works. Art Nouveau can be identified by its flowing, sensuous lines, floral forms, insects and the feminine form. These designs were incorporated on almost everything produced at that time, from art glass to furniture, to silver, to personal objects.

Ashtray or soap dish, bronze, 5½" h x 6½" w, unsigned, $375.00.

Bowl, 5" l, oval, pewter, 4 feet, Kayserzinn 85.00

Box, cov, 7½", sq, glass, molded tree of life on cover, mkd #2146   195.00

Bread Tray, 14" oval, SS, chased repousse decor of poppies, Unger Bros, Newark, NJ 250.00

Brush, 6", poppy decor 35.00

Brush Set, man's, 2 brushes, hand mirror, silver, German 60.00

Buckle, SS, Floral, 2 leaves, 2 pc . .   125.00

Bust, 6", Roman Princess, bronze, cast, green marble base, inscribed E. Villanais 185.00

Button Hook, SS, Liberty & Co 40.00

Carving Set, 15" knife, swirling leaves on SP, 2 pc 55.00

Centerpiece Bowl, 12¼", SS, round, hexagonal lobed design, chased, scrolls and hibiscus blossoms, Whiting Mfg Co. 500.00

Chamberstick, brass, 6½", heart shaped footed base, leaf handle .   40.00

Cigar Box, 12" l, rectangular, silver, cover insert under glass with gouache coaching scene, cedar lined, sgr G. Wright, Goldsmiths and Silversmiths Company, London, 1900 . . . .   1,100.00

Cigarette Case, 3⅜", silver, parcel gilt, female holding cabochon ruby fruits, foliate grapevines, ruby thumbpiece, Tiffany & Co., NY, c1890 . . . .   465.00

Coffee Pot, tankard shape, copper and brass, trophy, 1905, engraved on back 125.00

Compote, bronze nude holding green glass dish 55.00

Cuff Links, SS, lady with flowing hair   40.00

Demitasse Service, pot, creamer, sugar bowl, 10⅜" round tray, silver, monogrammed, applied borders of mistletoe, Gorham Co., Providence, RI, c1900 . . . .   990.00

Dish, 9⅝", oval, silver, wide border with chased, random flower sprays and berries, hammered surface, gilt interior, Gorham Co., Providence, RI, retailed by Spaulding & Co., Chicago, c1913   825.00

Figures

16", bronze, polychromed, slave woman, seated on granite speckled bronze base, red skirt, red turban, gold earrings, in chains, inscribed E. Villanais . .   990.00

20", pottery, lady dressed in scant jade green bodice, skirt held by outstretched arm, face framed by matching hat, Hertwig & Co., Germany 450.00

Firescreen, 22", brass, rectangular

ftd panel mounted with Tudric style martele insert, English **80.00**

Hand Mirrors

Christmas, angel, holly, star, quadruple plate, 10¼″ l x 6″ w ... **90.00**

SP, girl with flowers in her hair, monogram **25.00**

Hatpin, brass, floral swirls **22.00**

Inkstands

6¾″ d, circular, pewter, swirled design with flower heads, marked CB#31 .... **135.00**

9″ d, bronze, Dore, figural, octopus well with tentacles encircling mirrored center joining mermaid, seaweed with lower pen tray, marked Geschutzt **200.00**

Jewel Casket, pewter, woman with flowing hair **100.00**

Knife Sharpener, bronzed, stylized bird **35.00**

Lamps

12″, Boudoir, gilt, cupid figure, red silk covered beaded shade, electrified **185.00**

22″ h base, 15½″ d shade, leaded glass shade, apple green geometric, pink, yellow dogwood border, sgd Handel .. **900.00**

23″ h base, 16″ d shade, green patina, melon shaped base, shade of ice chipped, reverse painted Indian brave sipping water, painted tassels, Pittsburgh . **1,100.00**

25″, bronze base with molded iris, 3 green oil spotted jack-in-the-pulpit shades **1,300.00**

26″, copper, 4 sided base, 8 panel textured slag glass dome **200.00**

27″, 5 light, lily bronze base, gold irid bell shades with blue feather pull design **750.00**

Letter Holder, 2 sections, bronze, 4 ladies, flowing hair, floral decor .. **60.00**

Necklace, SS, Danecraft **150.00**

Ring, figural, orange jade stone, 14K **175.00**

Shaving Mug, raised crocus, dated 1904, Derby Silverplate mark **55.00**

Teapot, cov, 6¼″, silver, short rectangular spout, arched wood handle, Mappin & Webb, English, c1900 .... **357.00**

Tray, 20″ l, rectangular, silver, raised bar border, Reed & Barton, Tauton, MA **475.00**

Toothpick Holder, 4 x 4¾″, bisque, lady on horn of plenty type seashell, swan, pastel colors **48.00**

Vases

8″, enamel, painted figure of maiden, flowers, landscape ground, c1900 .... **550.00**

8 x 3″, SS daffodils on bronze,

Vase, 9½″ h, Royal Bonn, 4 handles, multicolored floral, Old Dutch/ 147/1997/12/Germany, $285.00.

dated 1913, sgd Heintz **85.00**

8½″, mottled art glass, Austria .. **55.00**

11″, SS, paneled, hammered surface, chased flowers, leaves, wavy rim and base, monogrammed **880.00**

12½″, green, molded iris, figural surmount at shoulder of nude kissing cherub, by Gerbruder Heubach **250.00**

17″, silver, round on spreading base, chased, iris leaves, openwork rim with iris flowers in relief, Theodore B. Starr, NY, c1900 .... **800.00**

21″, silver, tapering cylinderical form, monogrammed, Tiffany & Co., NY, c1915 .... **1,000.00**

Watch Holder, brass **65.00**

Water Pitcher, 8½″, silver, hammered surface, N.G. Wood & Sons, Boston **425.00**

ART POTTERY (GENERAL)

The period of Art Pottery reached its zenith in the late 19th and early 20th century. Over a hundred companies produced individually designed and often decorated wares which served a utilitarian as well as an aesthetic

purpose. Artists moved about from company to company, some forming their own firms.

Quality of design, beauty in glazes, and condition are the keys in buying art pottery. This category covers some companies not found elsewhere in the guide.

See also: Cambridge, Clewell, Clifton, Cowan, Dedham, Fulper, Grueby, Jugtown, Marblehead, Moorcroft, Newcomb, Ohr, Owens, Paul Revere, Peters and Reed, Rookwood, Roseville, Van Briggle, and Weller.

Arequpa Pottery (1913-18), Fairfax, CA

Plate, 7", white, gray, and blue border, initials in center not legible, dated 1912	80.00
Vase, 9", reddish brown matte glaze surface, molded aqua band of geometric design at waist, marked	200.00

California Faience Co. (1916-30), Berkeley, CA

Vase, 4½", inverted bell body, outward flaring base, extended flat circular neck, blue and green high glaze	80.00

Cincinnati Art Pottery (1880-91), Cincinnati, OH

Ewer, 12", bowl base, extended concave body, shaped edge on top, free form handle, blue and orange flowers on white ground, bowl base area in blue, heavy gold decoration	90.00

Denver China and Pottery Co. (1901-05), Denver, CO

Vase, 3", gray, green high glaze inside, sgn "Denver, 1904" . . .	75.00

Kenton Hills (1939-42), Erlanger, KY

Vase, 7", blue matte, Deco design, lines and beads motif, sgn "W. Hentschel"	110.00
Vase, 7¼", cup form, ring foot, incised leaf decoration, blue high glaze, sgn "W. Hentschel/May 1, '40/Gone War"	250.00
Vase, 8¼", tapered cylinderical shape, extended straight neck, large red, 4 petal flower design, white ground with blue	275.00

Markham (c1885-1913; 1913-21), Ann Arbor, MI and National City, CA

Vase, 5½", tapered cylinder, slightly extended circular neck, leaf and vine design, rust and cream color	325.00

Merrimac Ceramic Company (1897-1908), Newburyport, MA

Bowl, 6½", circular, undulating rim, metallic black glaze, im-

Norse, bowl, 4½" d, 2½" h, bronze finish, incised decoration in green, tripod feet, marked "NSS", $110.00.

pressed "MERRIMAC" and a sturgeon	90.00
Vase, 8½", ovoid, circular cover, matte green glaze, both impressed with a sturgeon and "MERRIMAC"	250.00

Norse (1903-04;1904-13), Edgerton, WI and Rockford, IL

Vase, 7" d, 4" h, flattened urn with straight neck, 2 serpent handles, 3 feet, incised decoration, marked "#70"	110.00

Overbeck Pottery (1911-55), Cambridge City, IN

Vase, 4¼" h, red matte, 3 panels of figures and trees, initials "E.F." on bottom	450.00

Pewabic Pottery (1903-61), Detroit, MI

Vase, 3½" d, 2" h, bulbous, lavender iridescent lava glaze, sgn, paper label	200.00
Vase, 5½" d, 3¾" h, bowl base, inward rounded flared neck, metallic glaze, bottom marked "AA/1923"	180.00
Vase, 10", urn shape, inward flaring and extended shoulders to extended and slightly outward flaring neck, hand thrown, metallic blue lustre glaze	375.00
Vase, 11½", baluster form, turquoise iridescent, orig paper label, inscribed	475.00

Pisgah Forest (1913 - Present), Mt. Pisgah, NC

Bowl, white cameo of wagon train, mountains, cabin and people, forest green ground, sgn "STEPHEN," 1951	275.00
Pitcher, 8", cameo of covered wagon, oxen, 4 people, dog, tree & mountains, brown ground at top, high glaze turquoise glaze on bottom, sgn "STEPHEN," 1943	475.00

Teapot, 5¾″ h, white cameo of wagon train, green color with flecks of brown **200.00**

Vases

6¾″, bulbous base, long inward tapering and extended neck, ring collar, high glaze of cream, blue, and white with blue and green crystalline glaze **100.00**

7½″, crystalline high glaze vase, white to green, pink inside, marked "1950, Pisgah Forest" **85.00**

Robertson (1935-50), Hollywood, CA

Vase, 3½″, bulbous body, straight extended neck, Chinese blue high glaze **50.00**

Vase, 3½″, yellow crackle glaze, sgn with "R" **60.00**

School of Mines, University of North Dakota (1892 - Present)

Vase, 3″, Art Deco multicolored floral design, high dark blue glaze **195.00**

Vase, 3¾″, oviform, molded with a band of flowers at the shoulder in a blue and raspberry glaze, inscribed "PERSON H 193," and stamped "UNIVERSITY OF NORTH DAKOTA GRAND FORKS, N.D. MADE AT THE SCHOOL OF MINES N.D. CLAY" **225.00**

Swastika Keramos

Vase, 5⅞″, cylindrical, flat shoulders, narrow mouth, gold, red, and green shiny glaze, drip design **65.00**

Vase, 7⅞″, conical extended body, bulbous bowl neck, 2 handles, shiny woodland scene with bright purple like clouds **80.00**

Teco (1886-1930), Terra Cotta, IL

Vase, 9″, cylindrical, molded with leaves and narcissi in a mint green matte glaze, impressed twice "TECO" **150.00**

Vase, 13½″, broad cylindrical shape, 4 handles, cucumber green with dark green streaks, impressed twice "TECO", paper label **625.00**

Vance/Avon Pottery (1892-1908), Tiltonville, OH and Wheeling, WV

Jardiniere, 18″ d, four handled, waisted below the shoulder, painted with stylized lotus blossoms, shoulder with heart motifs in tones of green blue, and yellow, inscribed factory mark **675.00**

Vase, 10¾″, tapered four sided form, strong flat shoulder, openings at each corner of shoulder with relief rococo designs beneath each, extended outward flaring neck, high glaze of green and brown with orange, marked "Vance JF Co, #117" **100.00**

Volkmar, Charles (1882-88;1888-1903), Tremont, NY and numerous other NY and NJ locations

Mug, 1909, 5″, delftware blue and white design of three-masted schooner headed by dolphin, titled "Hudson-Fulton," marked and dated **85.00**

Vases

6½″, balustered body, painted with navy arches on a textured blue and green ground, inscribed "Volkmar. J-R," attributed to Jean Rice **200.00**

7″, blue-green volcanic type glaze, geometric decoration under glaze, sgn **300.00**

12″, extended urn shape, "L" handles, limoges style hand painted decoration of draped nude on front underglaze, red clay body with different shades of browns and white ground, clay body showing through, artist inst., impressed "CV" on bottom, handle repaired **775.00**

Walrath Pottery, candleholder, 7¼″ h, light green, impressed "Walrath Pottery/1914", $450.00.

Walrath, Frederick E., Pottery, Rochester, NY

Bowl 7½" d, 6" h, nude centerpiece, bowl in green matte, nude in flesh tones and green . . **225.00**

Paperweights

3¾", scarab, green matte **90.00**

4½", nude curled in fetal position, green/flesh color glaze . **160.00**

Sculpture, 7" h, nude female seated on a short column rising from a low bowl in a blue glaze, inscribed "Walrath - E Pithard" **325.00**

AURENE GLASS AURENE

This type of art glass was invented by Frederick Carder for the Steuben Glass Works of Corning, New York. The name Aurene was given to the glass by the originator from the Latin "Aureus," a Roman gold coin. Aurene glass has a smooth, uniform, iridescent surface in gold, blue or silvery blue. It was made by the Steuben Glass Works from 1904 to 1933. Some items were marked with "Steuben" or "Aurene" or both scratched in the base, others have the name and the factory number. Many pieces were unmarked and had only a paper label. Unmarked pieces are difficult to distinguish from Tiffany's "Favrile."

Atomizer, 7½", blue, irid	350.00
Baskets, 12"	
Blue	2,400.00
Gold	1,800.00
Bottles, Perfume	
4¼", gold, #6234, sgd	285.00
6", blue, #1414, sgd	325.00
Bowls	
2½ x 5", blue, #2687, sgd	290.00
8" d, blue, low circular on 3 pad feet, mkd, orig paper label	275.00
9½" d, circular, mkd #2852 . . .	200.00
11" d x 4¾" h, ftd, gold with blue irid	350.00
12" d, gold, #5019, sgd	385.00
Box, cov, 6" w x 4½" h, gold, pagoda shaped cover	500.00
Candlesticks	
8", blue, #504, sgd	325.00
10¼", blue, twisted stem, sgd, pr	1,250.00
Chandeliers	
5½" h, three gold bell shades mounted on hammered brass fixture with three curved arms attached to spherical body . . .	365.00
12" h, gold glass globe, brass tassel drip, mkd	450.00
Compote, 6" h, gold, richly colored	

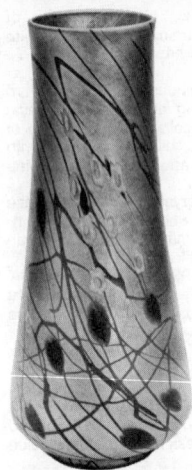

Aurene vase, 9½" h, gold, irid, decorated with leaves and vines, twenty-two Millefiori, sgd Aurene/580, $2,950.00.

red hues on inside, sgd Aurene, #2064	900.00
Finger Bowl, underplate, gold, calcite interior, #2889 sgd	175.00
Flower Frog, 2 x 3¼", gold	90.00
Goblet, 8", blue, #6279, sgd	140.00
Salt, 2½", gold, #2653, sgd	135.00
Vases	
3½", gold, baluster, mkd Aurene #210	165.00
4", green, tapering cylindrical, mushroom brim, purple irid, inscribed Frederick Carter	250.00
6", blue, rustic 1 prong, #2471, sgd	275.00
6", gold, #674, sgd	325.00
8½", blue, stick, sgd Aurene, #2546	595.00
10", blue, flower form, #184, sgd	900.00
10½", red, decorated, #533, sgd	8,000.00
12", blue circular foot supporting tall vase, ruffled brim, #312, sgd	450.00

AUSTRIAN WARE

During the late 19th and early 20th centuries, much fine porcelain and pottery were produced in Austria. Although Carisbad, known as Karisbad after World War I when Austria became part of Czechoslovakia, was the center of the industry, other factories existed. These factories were either owned or supported by Americans, thus, their wares were produced mainly for export to the United States. The U. S. firm of Lazarus and Rosenfeldt imported large amounts of porcelain from Czechoslovakia after World War I marked "Victoria." For additional listings, see specific manufacturers listed alphabetically in this book.

Cup and Saucer, orange florals, green leaves, cream ground, gold trim, marked MZ Austria, $45.00.

Banks
4¼ x 2¼", pig, dark brown, rust blue, white ground	90.00
4¼ x 2¼", pig, light brown, blue, beige ground	75.00
Bone dishes, decor, 8 pcs.	15.00
Bowl, berry, large green, pink flowers, white ground, scalloped lavender edge, M. Z. Austria	165.00
Box, cov, 4½"d, hand painted scene of cupids, maidens, cobalt blue ground	140.00
Cake Set, Master, 4 serving plates, violets, gold enamel beading, 5 pcs.	85.00
Celery, white, pink, yellow delicate florals, gilt edged	40.00
Centerpiece, stylized duck, 8¼ x 11" l, Amphora potter, beige, green, purple, etc.	600.00
Chocolate Pot, violets, white ground, gold enamel trim	135.00
Creamer, 3", floral decor, lattice handle, marked M. Z. Austria . . .	20.00

Demitasse Cups and Saucers
Cobalt blue, gilt decor, blue, green marks	25.00
Cobalt blue, gold, panel of couple in garden, blue beehive mark . .	30.00
Lavender lusterware, gilt interior scrolling foliate decor, panel of young women in garden, sgd F. Measauer, blue beehive mark .	30.00

Dresser Set, bluebird decor, marked Victoria, 4 pcs	80.00
Fairy Lamp, 5¼ x 4½", cream bisque shade, green Christmas Tree on both sides, studded with jewels, wood ring base with maroon plush covering, clear cup inside mk Clarke, registry number & "Made in Austria" inside shade . .	325.00

Figures
7" h, Art Deco Dance Girl, lavender dress, florals, gray base . .	400.00
13" h, Goldscheider, gypsy woman, plum, jonquil peasant dress, flower garlands, imp, Lindner, Austria	850.00
Hair Receiver, floral decor, marked M. Z.	25.00
Humidor, pine cone decor, artist sgd Vienna	110.00
Nautilus Cup, 19½", ruby glass, ormolu, stag's head on hinged lid, strapwork mounts, griffon support, leaf cast circular base	490.00
Oyster Plate	30.00

Plates
8", cupid, light blue, heart pierced border, Victoria	35.00
8½", mulberries, leaves on cream ground, border, imperial	60.00
9", autumn leaves, gold decor, scalloped rim	40.00
10", pink roses, blue, gold border, HP, imperial	45.00
Sardine Dish, sgd Victoria, Austria .	35.00

Vases
6", high shouldered & waisted body, enameled in relief, gold, iris & prunus blossoms	225.00
12", pink, yellow floral decor, ivory ground, gold trim, footed, handles, bisque finish	125.00

AUTOGRAPHS

Autographs occur in a wide variety of formats—letters, documents, photographs, autograph books and cards, etc. Most collectors focus on a particular person, country, or category, e.g., opera singers.

The condition and content of letters and documents bears significantly on value. Collectors should know their source since forgeries abound and copy machines compound the problem. Further, some signatures of recent presidents and movie stars are done by machine rather than by the person themselves. A good dealer or advanced collector can help one spot the differences.

See *Warman's Americana & Collectibles* for an expanded listing of Autographs.

The following abbreviations denote type of autograph material and their sizes.

ADS	Autograph Document Signed
ALS	Autograph Letter Signed
AQS	Autograph Quotation Signed
CS	Card Signed
DS	Document Signed
LS	Letter Signed
PS	Photograph Signed
TLS	Typed Letter Signed

Sizes (approximate):

Folio	12 x 16 inches
4to	8 x 10 inches
8vo	5 x 7 inches
12mo	3 x 5 inches

COLONIAL AMERICA

Contract for Provisions for Continental Army, ADS of Theodore Sedwick, 1 p, 8vo, Kinderhook, May 15, 1777, allowing Henry Van Schaack to transport milled wheat safely **50.00**

Dudley, Sir Joseph, Gov. of MA, ALS, 1 p, 8vo, Boston, June 11, 1711, letter to New Hampshire asking for representatives to meeting of Congress of Governors of Her Majesty's Provinces, address leaf bearing Governor's free frank **450.00**

Hancock, John, ALS, 1 p, folio, Council Chamber, Boston, July 18, 1782, franking signature on verso, orders Gen. Goodwin of MA militia to raise men for guards **1,000.00**

Johnson, Sir William, ALS, 1 p, 8vo, n.p., March 26, 1742, Johnson, Col. Com. for the affairs of the Six Nations, writes to instruct a Mr. Collins to begin legal proceedings against a Mr. Cony **175.00**

Morris, Robert, signer of Declaration, endorsement sgd "Robert Morris S. J. Finance" on verso of 8vo, 30 day sight draft drawn on May 7, 1784 on Nelson Herron Co. **100.00**

Paca, William, signer of Declaration, DS, 1 p, oblong 8vo, April 27, 1795, payment receipt **650.00**

Revere, Paul, ALS, 1 p, 4to, Boston, March 25, 1810, writes to son about business matters **5,000.00**

Sherman, Roger, signer of Declaration, DS, 1 p, 4to, Feb. 21, 1759, as justice of peace, ordering sheriff of Litchfield Co. to arrest men . **120.00**

EUROPEAN

Albert, Prince Consort to Queen Victoria, three words and his signature in his hand, probably from letter or document **60.00**

Anne, Queen of England, DS, 2 pgs, folio, March 27, 1702, to treasurer of Jewel House ordering medallions and chains, sgd on top of first page **850.00**

Astor, Nancy, first woman in British Parliament, ALS, 2 pgs, 12mo, n.d., extends invitation to Mrs. Suffern **15.00**

Edward VII, King of England, ANS, initials, 1 p, 8vo, (London), Thursday, n.d., regrets, Buckingham Palace letterhead **60.00**

Erhard, Ludwig, German statesman, PS, 4 x 5¾" **15.00**

Philip III, King of Spain, sgd "Yo El Principe," DS, Madrid, March 20, 1598, to Don Diego de Guierra concerning men and supplies to Brittany **225.00**

Russell, Bertrand, English philosopher, TLS, 1 p, 8vo, Petersfield, March 11, 1932, to Mr. Warman thanking him for first number of *David* **85.00**

Victoria, Queen of England, DS, 3 pgs, folio, Feb. 3, 1858, appointing Edward St. James Neale as the British Consul at Patras **175.00**

Wellington, Duke of, third person, ALS, 1 p, 4to, London, Feb 27, 1828, respects to Mr. Patman ... **85.00**

GENERAL

Bell, Alexander Graham, 3½" sq. magazine picture of Bell in old age, sgd on lower white margin .. **275.00**

Bradley, Omar N., folded 8vo card, front insignia of 12th Army Corps and fine signature of Bradley, inside short story of 12th, with letter from assistant sending autograph, Sept. 13, 1945 .... **45.00**

Eastman, George, CS, 1922 ...... **50.00**

Ericsson, John, engineer and inventor, ALS, 1 p, to 4to, integral address leaf, New York, Dec. 27, 1837, writes to Ashbell Welch asking his assistance **140.00**

Keller, Helen, ALS, 1 p, long folio, n.p., n.d., Keller writes to *St. Nicolas* magazine describing the way the blind write **800.00**

Lewis, Meriweather, promissory note, "No. 6," drawn by Lewis in his hand, as Gov. of Louisiana Territory, on Bank of U.S., payable to Thomas Prather, 1 p, 8vo, Louisville, Feb. 15, 1808 .... **1,100.00**

Morse, Samuel F. B., account, 1 p,

folio, Washington, D.C., March 20, 1845, abstract of salaries for Electromagnetic Telegraph for month ending Feb. 10, 1845, Morse's retained copy in his own hand 375.00

Morton, William T. G., discoverer of ether anaesthesia, ALS, 1 p, 4to, integral blank, Washington, D.C., April 19, n.y. (1847?), writes to Mr. Carlisle about his book on anaesthesia 1,600.00

North, Luther, Indian fighter and friend of Buffalo Bill, ALS, 2 pgs, 4to, Columbus, NE, March 22, 1931, to Agnes Urbank giving his ancestry and mentioning Winnebago Indians 235.00

Penn, William, DS, 12¼ x 15″, vellum, August 12, 1705, wax seal in orig case, grant of land in Philadelphia (Plymouth Twp.) to Francis and Elizabeth Fox 800.00

Rockefeller, John D., TLS, 1 p, 4to, Pocantico Hills, NY, May 26, 1910, to Dr. Buttrick of NYC thanking him for material sent 475.00

Warhohl, Andy, black and white glossy postcard, boldly sgd in felt tip 30.00

LITERATURE

Burroughs, Edgar Rice, TLS, 1 p, 4to, Tarzana, Dec. 27, 1937, to Billy Elliott thanking him for holiday wishes, orig envelope 45.00

Doyle, Arthur Conan, ALS, Haslemere, May 5, 1904, to Mackenzie Bell about Charles Martineau, framed with envelope 175.00

Fitzgerald, F. Scott, CS, to Paul Clute about his poems 250.00

Guiterman, Arthur, Am. poet, personal bookplate, sgd, bookplate shows old fashioned library scene, imprinted with names of he and his wife 15.00

O'Neill, Eugene book *Dynamo,* 1929, limited edition of 775, No. 331, bound in blue-green vellum with gilt lettering, purple board box 175.00

Sinclair, Upton, TLS, 1 p, 4to, Gulfport, Miss., June 28, 1915, to poet Edwin Markham offering to send anthology *The Cry For Justice* . . . 125.00

Twain, Mark, CS, framed with photograph 200.00

PRESIDENTIAL, AMERICAN

Adams, John, ALS, 1 p, 4to, Quincy MA, March 14, 1813, Adams writes to President James Madi-

Davis, Jefferson, ALS, 4to, letter of introduction, $225.00.

son recommending the brother of Rev. Henry Coleman for a commission 1,500.00

Adams, John Quincy, ALS, 1 p, 4to, Washington, D.C., Oct. 11, 1822, cover letter by Adams who sends one of his pamphlets to Jefferson at Monticello 1,200.00

Fillmore, Millard, printed check, dated June 26, 1849, drawn on New York State Bank, payable to William Beeke & Co., NYC, made out and sgd by Fillmore, mounted with a portrait 2,600.00

Ford, Gerald, TLS, "Jerry," 1 p, 4to, Congressional letterhead, Dec. 14, 1964, to constituent complimenting him on patriotic sentiment . . . 110.00

Garfield, James A., autographed note, 1 p, 8vo, Mentor, OH, July 2, 1880, thanks to Thomas Donaldson for recent letter 225.00

Grant, Ulysses S., ALS, 2 p, 8vo, Headquarters Of The Armies Of The United States, Washington, D.C., Nov. 24, 1865, thanks to Mrs. Fisher for afghan 180.00

Grant, Ulysses S., printed check, Washington, D.C., March 23, 1868, drawn on Jay Cooke & Co., payable to "slf," made out and sgd by Grant, mounted with portrait 1,100.00

Harrison, William Henry, LS, 1 p, 4to, Headquarters, Franklintown, Oct. 24, 1812, writes to Col. Thomas Bufford of Kentucky about food and provisions for army 650.00

Hoover, Herbert, PS, half length portrait of Hoover and dog, image 9⅛ x 7¼″, inscribed and sgd on lower margin "kind regards of Herbert Hoover" 160.00

Jefferson, Thomas, ALS, 1 p, 4to, Washington, D.C., Feb. 25, 1804, writes to Mr. Payton about mill on property ajoining his at Monticello 3,000.00

Johnson, Andrew, DS, 1 p, 4to, Washington, D.C., June 2, 1865, direction to Sec. of State to seal warrent for pardon 225.00

Lincoln, Abraham, DS, 1 p, folio, vellum, Washington, D.C., March 29, 1864, commission appointing Henry Payne, Captain and Aide-de-Camp, sgd by Lincoln and Stanton 1,000.00

Taft, William Howard, TLS, 1 p, 8vo, War Dept., Washington, D.C., March 23, 1904, writes Col. Harvy, ed. of *North Am. Review,* introducing L. R. Wilfley 90.00

Washington, George, ALS, 3 pgs, folio, Mount Vernon, August 22, 1785, address on verso of second leaf in Washington's hand, writes to Mr. Muse about market variations in price and quality of wheat 3,250.00

Wilson, Woodrow, TLS, 1 p, 8vo, President's Room, Princeton Univ., June 17, 1909, writes to Taft recommending Russell Moore, a Princeton graduate, for next vacancy in office of General Appraiser 275.00

RELIGION

Alexander VI, Pope, Document, Sept. 19, 1496, Papal brief issued in his name, sgd "Picherier" 200.00

Gregory XV, Pope, DS, July 7, 1621, Bull of indulgence to the priory of St. Jean at Bere 110.00

Mather, Rev. Cotton, autograph note, n.p., n.d., mounted on letterhead of Henry Jacobs 275.00

Muhammad, Elijah, leader of Black Muslim sect, TLS, 1 p, large 4to, Chicago, 1957, to Brother Roy C. X. of Jersey City, NJ, concerning financial reports of C. X.'s temple 275.00

Potter, Alonzo, Episcopal Bishop, educator and author, ALS, 1½ pgs, 8vo, Feb. 26, 1841, to N. S. Benton introducing Francis Lieber 25.00

SHOW BUSINESS

Barrymore, John, autographed drawing, Feb. 29, 1940, to Albert Miller concerning radio spots for Vitalis . 60.00

Bolger, Ray, ANS, 1 p, 12mo, personal memo pad, n.d., autobiographical notes 65.00

Brando, Marlon, postcard photograph, Brando as young man, facsimile signature genuinely inscribed and sgd 30.00

Chevalier, Maurice, ALS, 1 p, 4to, New York on Waldorf-Astoria letterhead, Oct. 12, 1955, rejecting appeal for time 100.00

Crosby, Bing, TLS, "Bing," 2 separate pages, 4to, Nov. 21, 1960, to Charles Graves in London, personal and mentions golf 35.00

Gish, Lillian, ANS, personalized calling card sending Christmas wishes, 1941 .... 15.00

Petrova, Olga, silent screen and stage star, series of 11 ALS, 18 pgs, 4to and 3 pgs 8vo, all sgd "Olga," "Nady," or "Bunny," 1940 –41, to Louise, personal content . 50.00

Robinson, Edward G., program for "Darkness at Noon," given at Princeton, NJ, in 1951, sgd on front cover 20.00

STATESMEN, AMERICAN

Acheson, Dean, TLS, 1 p, 4to, Jan. 23, 1954, to Ellis of Four Freedoms Foundation thanking him for photographs 25.00

Bryan, William Jennings, TLS, 1 p, 8vo, letterhead of the Commoner, Lincoln, NE, June 15, 1922, to Prof. Russell sending his autograph 50.00

Davis, Jefferson, ALS, 1 p, 4to, Senate Chamber, Washington, D.C., Feb. 3, 1848, to Sec. of War W. L. Marcy recommending appointment of Mr. Taylor 335.00

Gallatin, Albert, LS, 1 p, 4to, "Treasury Department," March 6, 1809, to Joseph Wilson, Collector, Marblehead, withdraws authorization to hire vessel to enforce embargo 150.00

Hamilton, Alexander, ADS, 2 p, 4to, integral leaf, Treasury Dept., Philadelphia, July 20, 1792, letter to Custom Officers informing them to lay down uniform rules of interpretation of U. S. Revenue Laws . 300.00

Jay, John, autographed message, 1 p, 4to, New York, Nov. 7, 1796, Jay replies to NY State Senate address of congratulations on his election as Gov. 750.00

Stevenson, Adlai E., ALS, Chicago, Sept. 21, 1960, to Albert Miller about assistance in preparing Ste-

venson's speeches 40.00
Sumner, Charles, ALS, 1 p, 12mo,
"Senate Chamber, Aug. 25th,"
n.y., stating he has not received
letters from Webster on specific
subject 25.00
Webster, Daniel, free frank, enve-
lope addressed in his hand to S.
A. Appleton for Miss Cordelia
Fletcher, Boston, MA 90.00

AUTOMOBILE ITEMS

**The amount of items related to the automo-
bile is endless. Collectors seem to fit into
three groups—those collecting parts to re-
store a car, those collecting information
about a company or certain model for research purposes, and those trying to use automobile items for decorative purposes. Most
material changes hands at the hundreds of
swap meets and auto shows around the
country. The leading publication is *Hemmings
Motor News,* Box 100, Bennington VT 05201.**

Advertising Signs
"Marine the Gasoline Supreme,"
cloth banner 100.00
Olizum Oil, 60 x 36", tin and wood 175.00
Wolfs Head Motor Oil, 30 x 22" 90.00
Bank, Chrysler, 1951 . . . . 40.00
Bumpers, rear
Cadillac, 1953 . . . . 100.00
Chrysler, 1948 . . . . 75.00
Oldsmobile, 1963 . . . . 110.00
Carburetor, Hudson, 1929–31 . . . . 75.00
Coins, brass
Chrysler, Chicago World's Fair,
shows 1924 touring and 1934
Airflow, "A Century of Progress
In A Decade" 25.00
General Motors, 1955 . . . . 5.00
Oldsmobile, Futuramic 88 . . . . . 12.50
Cuff Links and Tie Bar, Thunderbird,
1958–60, factory promo 50.00
Emblems 15–25.00
Employee Badge, Reo Motor Works,
metal 22.50
Engines
Cadillac, 1929 . . . . 750.00
Chevrolet, 1929–30 . . . . 450.00
Packard, 1940, 120 Straight 8 . . . 250.00
Rutenber, 1909–12, 4 cy. 1,500.00
Gearshift Knobs
Fiat, wooden, enameled center . . 20.00
Red Dice 20.00
Grilles
1937, Lincoln, Zephyr 350.00
1941, Cadillac 245.00
1954, Buick 175.00
1964–66, Mustang 40.00

Horns
Champion siren, 6 volt Darley
#657763, chrome 75.00
Dodge, 1934, trumpet 85.00
Olympic 40.00
Schwarze #5 . . . . 50.00
Sterner Warner #136A 50.00
Hubcaps
Buick, 1934–35, 6½", each 40.00
Buick, 1963, Skylark, set of 4 . . . 60.00
Chevrolet, 1949, each 25.00
Jack, Ford, 1947–48, hydraulic bum-
per jack 100.00
Lamps, brass
Caste #240 bail sidelamp 75.00
Corcoran, large size, pr 250.00
Dietz Regal bail sidelamp with
bull's-eye lens 100.00
Packard, 1912–14, CM Hall fender
mount bail tail lamp 75.00
Rambler, 1910–11, script, pr 150.00
Letterhead, Jackson, 1917, parts or-
der 5.00
License Plates
Enameled, each 10–25.00
Porcelain, each 25–60.00
Literature
Cadillac, 1937 Prestige, color cat-
alog, series 60/65, 12 x 9", 12
pgs 60.00
Chrysler, 1941–42, shop manual . 35.00
Hudson, 1934, non-color catalog,
11 x 16", 8 pgs, Terr & Hudson 20.00

Literature, Pontiac, owner's manual,
1950, 64 pgs., $12.00.

Lincoln, 1955, dealer's manual . .	75.00
Oldsmobile, 1960, press kit, 9 photos, 15 sheets, no folder . .	35.00
Reo Flying Cloud, 1929, color brochure, 16 pgs	50.00
Stutz, 1929, color brochure, 24 pgs	150.00
Willys, 1930, part color catalog, 8 x 9", 8 pgs, Whippet	25.00
Mileage Tester, Gauther, 1930s . . .	65.00

Ornaments

Hood

Ford, 1949–51, Bullnose type .	25.00
Ford, 1950	125.00
Lincoln, 1949–50	30.00
Pontiac, Chief	25.00

Radiator

Chevrolet, enamel, oval and cross shape, blue and white .	20.00
Dodge, 2¼", 1918, enamel, black, blue, and white	35.00
Model T, airplane	60.00

Postcards

Cadillac, 1955, color, Eldo Biarritz (Eisenhower)	8.00
Lincoln, 1962, large, color, convertible	9.00
Pontiac, 1940, four door sedan . .	4.00

Promotional Models

Cadillac, 1955, coupe	35.00
Chevrolet, 1964, Impala SS convertible	80.00
Chevrolet, 1967, Camaro pace car, white with blue	225.00
Oldsmobile, 1963, Starfire, maroon	50.00
Studebaker, 1960, Lark, 2 door, hardtop, white	65.00

Radios

Chevrolet, 1941	50.00
Edsel, 1958, Garland	80.00
Hudson, 1950	30.00
Oldsmobile, 1962, Starfire	80.00
Scrapbook–Robinson, Pope-Robinson, and Charles J. Glidden, photos, clippings, and letters from 1901–06, includes 24 postcards sent to John Robinson by Glidden while on European tour in a Napier in 1902	500.00

Steam Gauges

Boyce Motor Meter, DeLuxe, 3½"	10.00
Unknown, 2¼"	15.00

Tire Gauge

Schrader Truck Tire Gauge, 1923	8.00
Unknown, dated 1909	10.00
Tire Lock, Miller Chapman Co., 1914	125.00
Trophy, Readville Race Track, early 1900s, "Third Place To 40hp Stearns"	250.00

Vases

Pierce Arrow, pewter	45.00
Unknown, pressed glass, pr	45.00

Watch, Pocket, Studebaker, 21 jewel, gold case	75.00

AUTOMOBILES

Automobiles can be classified into several categories. In 1947 the Antique Automobile Club of America (AACA) devised a system whereby any motor vehicle (car, bus, motorcycle, etc.) made prior to 1930 is an "antique" car. The Classic Car Club of America (CCCA) expanded the list focusing on luxury models from 1925 to 1948. The Mile Stone Car Club (MSC) developed a list for cars in the 1948 to 1964 period.

Some states, such as Pennsylvania, have devised a dual registration system for older cars—antique and classic. Models from the 1960s and 1970s, especially convertibles and limited production models, fall into the "classic" designation depending on how they are used.

The cost to own cars made prior to 1940 has risen dramatically. New collectors are focusing on those makes and models which have the potential to become tomorrow's antiques. The list reflects the wide variety of the market place.

The prices here are based upon a car in running condition, with a high percentage of original parts, and somewhere between 60 and 80% restored. *Prices can vary by as much as 30% in either direction.*

Many older cars, especially if restored; now exceed $15,000.00. Their limited availability makes them difficult to price. Auctions, more than any other source, are the true determinant of value at this level.

Before buying, new collectors are advised to attend several antique car shows, seek out specialized collector clubs in the makes and models they find appealing, and secure the advise of a mechanic and body restorer familiar with old cars. Especially helpful are the catalogues and sale bills of Kruse Auctioneers, Inc., Auburn, Indiana, 46706.

AUTOMOBILES

Abbott-Detroit, 1912, Touring	12,500.00
Adams-Farewell, 1911, Model 40/45, Touring, 5 cyl	10,000.00
Alfa Romeo, 1962, 2000 Spyder, Convertible	7,000.00
Alvis, 1932, Speed Twenty, 6 cyl . .	37,500.00
Auburn, 1929, Model 8-120, Phaeton	75,000.00
Bentley, 1939, Sedanca Coupe, 4¼ litre	50,000.00
Biddle, 1916, Speed Touring, outside exhausts, wire wheels	16,000.00
Bricklin, 1975, Model SV-1, Gullwing Coupe	9,500.00

Bentley, 1954, "Countryman," 4 door Sedan, $7,000.00.

Buick, 1929, Model 29-47, Sedan, 6 cyl	9,500.00
Buick, 1937, Series 40, Convertible	20,000.00
Buick, 1959, Invicta, 4 door Hardtop, 445 wildcat engine	5,000.00
Cadillac, 1935, Model 355E, Convertible Coupe, V8	47,500.00
Cadillac, 1941, Model 61, Fastback Coupe, V8	6,000.00
Cadillac, 1947, Model 62, Sedan, V8	10,000.00
Cadillac, 1955, Eldorado Convertible, V8	13,500.00
Cadillac, 1956, Fleetwood 60-S, Sedan, V8	5,500.00
Cadillac, 1968, Coupe de Ville, 2 door, V8	2,000.00
Case, 1920, Model V, Touring, 7 passenger	20,000.00
Chevrolet, 1925, Superior K, Touring, 4 cyl	13,000.00
Chevrolet, 1932, BA Deluxe, Special Sedan, 6 cyl	12,000.00
Chevrolet, 1940, Special Coupe, 8 cyl	6,000.00
Chevrolet, 1949, Styleline Deluxe, Convertible, 6 cyl	12,000.00
Chevrolet, 1955, Corvette, Roadster, V8, 3 speed manual model	27,500.00
Chevrolet, 1956, Bel Air, 4 door Hardtop, V8	5,000.00
Chevrolet, 1957, Nomad, 2 door Wagon, V8	7,000.00
Chevrolet, 1963, Nova SS, Convertible, 6 cyl	4,250.00
Chevrolet, 1969, Corvair Monza,	

Chevrolet, 1931, Model AE, two door Sedan, 6 cyl, $7,500.00.

Convertible, 6 cyl	4,500.00
Chevrolet, 1971, Corvette, Coupe T-Top, V8, 350	12,000.00
Chrysler, 1928, Imperial LaBaron, Town Coupe, 6 cyl	27,500.00
Chrysler, 1936, Imperial Airflow, Model C-10, 4 door Sedan, 8 cyl .	9,500.00
Chrysler, 1953, Crown Imperial, 2 door Hardtop, V8	8,000.00
Cole, 1910, Model 30, Roadster . . .	13,500.00
Cord, 1937, Winchester, Model 812, V8	25,000.00
Daimler, 1959, Model SP250, V8 . .	7,000.00
Delage, 1914, Roadster, 4 cyl	14,000.00
DeLorean, 1981½, twin turbo charged 5 speed, factory stripe package	17,000.00
DeSoto, 1930, Model CF, 3 window Coupe, 8 cyl	9,000.00
DeSoto, 1954, 4 door Sedan, V8 . .	3,000.00
Dodge, 1919, Model 19-Four, Touring, 4 cyl	8,500.00
Dodge, 1925, Model 25, 4 door Sedan, 4 cyl	5,000.00
Dodge, 1933, Saloon Brougham, 4 door	9,000.00
Dodge, 1949, Wayfarer, Roadster, 6 cyl	7,500.00
Dodge, 1956, Suburban Wagon, 8 cyl	4,250.00
Durant, 1929, Model 63, rumble seat Coupe, 6 cyl	6,750.00
Edsel, 1960, Ranger, 4 door Hardtop, V8	3,500.00
Elcar, 1931, Princess Coupe, 8 cyl .	8,500.00
Essex, 1929, 4 door Sedan, 6 cyl . .	4,000.00
Fiat, 1967, Siata Spring Roadster . .	3,500.00
Ford, 1914, Model T, Touring, 4 cyl .	12,500.00
Ford, 1922, Model T, Roadster, 4 cyl	6,750.00
Ford, 1930–31, Model A, Deluxe Coupe, rumble seat, 4 cyl	10,000.00
Ford, 1931, Model A, Station Wagon, 4 cyl	12,000.00
Ford, 1933, Model 40, Cabriolet, V8	12,500.00
Ford, 1935, Model 48, Phaeton, V8 .	18,000.00
Ford, 1941, Deluxe, Station Wagon, V8	11,500.00
Ford, 1950, Custom, Convertible, V8	9,600.00
Ford, 1955, Fairlane, Crown Victoria, V8	7,000.00
Ford, 1964, Thunderbird, Convertible, V8	5,750.00
Ford, 1965, Mustang GT, Convertible, V8	14,000.00
Ford, 1968, Galaxie XL, V8	3,000.00
Franklin, 1925, Model 11A, 4 door Sedan, 6 cyl	15,000.00
Franklin, 1933, Model 18B Olympic, Cabriolet, 4 door, 6 cyl	9,000.00
Graham, 1940, Hollywood Sedan, 6 cyl	4,500.00
Grant, 1914, Model M, Roadster, 4 cyl	5,750.00

Hillman, 1952, Minx Mark V, Convertible, 1.25 litre 2,600.00

Holsman, 1902, High Wheel, Buggy, 2 cyl 20,000.00

Hudson, 1948, Super 6, Sedan, 6 cyl 6,000.00

Hudson, 1953, Hornet, 4 door, Hydro 2,000.00

Hupmobile, 1936, Aerodynamic Model 618, Touring Sedan 6,000.00

Jackson, 1916, Touring, V8 (Ferro) . 10,000.00

Jaquar, 1960, Model XE150 Coupe, 3.8 litre 9,000.00

Jensen, 1974½, Interceptor III, Coupe, 440 V8 . . . . 10,000.00

Kaiser, 1954, Darrin, Roadster, 6 cyl 14,500.00

Lagonda, 1937, Model LG45, 4 place open Tourer, Sanction III engine 42,500.00

LaSalle, 1939, Model 50, Convertible Coupe, V8 . . . . 18,000.00

Lincoln, 1925, Model L, Doctor Coupe, V8 . . . . 13,500.00

Lincoln, 1937, Model K, Convertible Roadster, V12, rumble seat, only 15 built 85,000.00

Lincoln, 1948, Continental, Cabriolet, V12 . . . . 24,000.00

Lincoln, 1959, Mark IV, Convertible, V8 . . . . 7,000.00

Locomobile, 1922, Model 648, Sportif 25,000.00

Maxwell, 1909, Roadster 12,500.00

Mercedes-Benz, 1937, Model 540K, Cabriolet, 8 cyl 250,000.00

Mercedes-Benz, 1965, Model 220EB, classic Coupe 13,500.00

Mercury, 1940, Series 09A, Convertible, V8 . . . . 16,000.00

Mercury, 1954, Monterey, Hardtop, V8 . . . . 4,000.00

Mercury, 1970, Marquis, Convertible 2,750.00

Metz, 1914, Sport Roadster 7,000.00

MG, 1949, Model TC, Roadster, 4 cyl 9,000.00

Nash, 1934, Model 1280, 4 door, 8 cyl 4,250.00

Nash, 1958, Metropolitan, Convertible 4,000.00

Oakland, 1927, Landau Coupe 3,500.00

Oldsmobile, 1941, Model 98, Club Coupe, 8 cyl 5,000.00

Oldsmobile, 1950, Rocket 88, Station Wagon, V8 . . . . 3,750.00

Oldsmobile, 1958, Model S-88, 4 door Sedan, V8 . . . . 3,000.00

Oldsmobile, 1964, Starfire, Convertible, V8 . . . . 7,000.00

Packard, 1926, Model 343, Touring, 7 passenger 25,000.00

Packard, 1934, Model 1103, Super Eight Sedan, 8 cyl 14,000.00

Packard, 1940, Model 1803, Sedan, Super Eight 10,000.00

Packard, 1951, Ultramatic 300, 4 door 3,750.00

Paige, 1919, Larchmont, Touring, 6 cyl 12,000.00

Plymouth, 1934, Model PE, Coupe, 6 cyl 6,000.00

Plymouth, 1950, Special Deluxe Woody, Station Wagon 12,500.00

Plymouth, 1953, Cranbrook, Sedan, 6 cyl 2,500.00

Pontiac, 1949, Chieftan, Convertible, 8 cyl 13,500.00

Pontiac, 1959, Bonneville, Sedan, V8 4,000.00

Pontiac, 1968, Firebird, Convertible, 400 V8 . . . . 5,750.00

Porsche, 1965, Model 356, Cabriolet 10,500.00

Rambler American, 1964, Ambassador, Model 990, 4 door, 8 cyl 2,500.00

Rickenbacker, 1925, Landau Sedan 7,500.00

Riley, 1954, Sports Saloon, 1.25 litre 5,000.00

Reo, 1917, Touring, 7 passenger, 6 cyl 11,000.00

Rolls Royce, 1948, Silver Wraith, 2 door Saloon Coupe, 6 cyl 20,000.00

Rolls Royce, 1959, Silver Cloud I, Drop Head Coupe, 6 cyl 29,000.00

Stanley, 1917–18, Touring, 5 passenger, 6 cyl 20,000.00

Star, 1925, Roadster, 4 cyl 11,000.00

Stearns-Knight, 1918, Touring, 5 passenger, 6 cyl 18,000.00

Studebaker, 1915, Roadster, 6 cyl . 8,000.00

Studebaker, 1928, Commander, Sedan, 8 cyl 6,000.00

Studebaker, 1950, Champion, 4 door Sedan 3,000.00

Stutz, 1929, 4 door Sedan, 8 cyl . . . 14,000.00

Sunbeam, 1928, Saloon, 6 cyl 16,000.00

Triumph, 1956, Model TR2, Roadster 5,500.00

Volkswagon, 1959, Sedan, model 1192cc engine 3,500.00

Volvo, 1961, Model 544, 2 door Sedan, 4 cyl 1,200.00

Wolseley, 1932, Hornet Special, 6 cyl 8,000.00

MISCELLANEOUS

Fire Engines

Ahrens Fox, 1922, KS-4 piston Pumper 13,250.00

American LaFrance, 1920, fire truck 20,000.00

American LaFrance, 1951, 700 Series, 700 gpm Pumper 3,500.00

Ford, 1929, Pumper 12,000.00

Peter Pirsch, 1945, 65′, wood aerial ladder 7,000.00

Seagrave, 1949, Model J, 1000 gpm cab Pumper, V12 . . . . 4,000.00

Seagrave, 1952, Model 400B, open cab, 750 gpm, V12 . . . . . 2,000.00

USA, 1940, Pumper, Continental engine, Hale pump, water tank .	10,000.00

Motorcycles

Harley-Davidson, 1917, twin, ex-WWI Army bike	5,000.00
Harley, 1942, Model EL, sidecar .	6,000.00
Indian, 1930, Scout, Model 101 . .	4,400.00
Indian, 1948, Chief	5,500.00
Scott, 1939, Flying Squirrel, 600cc twin	2,500.00
Triumph, 1970, Model TR6	800.00
Vincent, 1951, Series C, Black Shadow	4,500.00

Trucks

Chevrolet, 1923, Huckster Wagon on truck chassis	6,500.00
Diamond T, 1938, 1½ ton rack truck	4,500.00
Ford, 1928, Model A, Pickup	7,500.00
Ford, 1939, 1½ ton, Stake, 95 hp V8	8,500.00
Ford, 1962, Econoline, Pickup . . .	2,750.00
International, 1953, Pickup	2,500.00
Maxwell, 1920, 1½ ton, roadster top	3,500.00
Studebaker, 1948, ½ ton Pickup, 6 cyl	5,000.00
Studebaker, 1953, 1½ ton	2,500.00
White, 1915, "C" cab panel	3,500.00

Willys

Jeepster, 1949	2,800.00
Wagon, 1952	3,750.00

AUTUMN LEAF PATTERN

The only exclusive premium line pattern produced by Hall China, East Liverpool, Ohio. The "Autumn Leaf" pattern was designed for the Jewel Tea Company in 1933 by Arden Richards. At first this Hall-Jewel design had no name and in the early years was called "Hall-Jewel" or "Autumnal." Then in April, 1942, it was designated "Autumn." Finally in 1960 it was called "Autumn Leaf."

It is still a Jewel property. However, the Jewel catalogue has not listed any "Autumn Leaf" since 1978. The pattern has not been officially discontinued. Hall China Co. still makes replacement pieces in this pattern and stamps these with the date on the back.

The pattern is especially strong in the Midwest and South. Prices in that region are 20 to 35% higher than those listed.

Baking Dish, 3 pint	12.00

Bowls

7½"	12.00
9", mixing	9.00
Cream soup, 2 handles	17.00
Bean Pot, 2¼ qt, 2 handles	58.00
Bread box	135.00
Butter dish, 1 pound	135.00

Coffee Pot, 9", silver gilding, marked "Hall's Superior", $35.00.

Candy dish, base	130.00
Canisters, round, coppertone lids, set of 4	125.00
Casserole, cov, tab handles	21.00
Cleanser Can, sq, 6"	82.50
Clock, wall, electric, Hall, 1940s . . .	300.00
Coffee service, 9-cup server, cov, metal dropper, creamer, sugar, cov, metal tray	125.00
Cookie Jar, 2 handles	60.00
Condiment Jar, cover	115.00
Cup and Saucer, St. Denis	17.00
Custard, 6 pcs	20.00
Fairy lamp, hand painted	69.00
Granulator	95.00
Mayonnaise, lid, underplate	35.00
Pitcher, ice lip	18.00

Plates

6", bread & butter	2.75
10" dinner	10.00
Platter, 11½"	13.50
Salt and Pepper set, pr	12.00
Saucer, St. Denis	5.00
Souffle, ind, 2" h, 4" d	12.00
Teapot, Newport	75.00
Tumbler, 9 oz, frosted, 3¾"	18.00
Vegetable dish, divided	30.00

BACCARAT GLASS

Baccarat glass was established by royal decree from Louis XV in 1764. The factory was located in Alsace-Lorraine, France. From its very beginning, Baccarat glass has always been of the finest quality and highly regarded by all connoisseurs of crystal.

During the Classic Era of Paperweights (1845-1860), Baccarat was one of the major producers of exquisite weights. In 1953 Baccarat again re-entered the paper weight market with an assortment of limited editions. Also see PAPERWEIGHTS.

Bottle, water, 7"h, light red shading to amber, $70.00

Bobeches, signed, pair	50.00
Bottles, Cologne	
6½" h, amberina swirl, orig stoppers, pr	150.00
7 x 2¾" d, swirl pattern, orig stoppers, pr	75.00
Bottles, Perfume	
4", crystal, "Guerlain"	48.00
Rose Teint swirl, orig stopper . . .	75.00
Bowls	
3¼", rose cut, enamel floral decor	145.00
7", lacy with underplate	65.00
11¾", clear, 6-pointed starfish shape	90.00
Box, 4 x 4", crystal, covered, angular designs	125.00
Breakfast Set, gold grape-pattern, 43 pcs	1,800.00
Candelabrum, 3-light	
Frosted glass dolphin shape standard, cut glass prisms, acid etched, molded factory mark, 23" h, mid 19th C	220.00
Pink opaline, hanging crystal prisms, 27" h, mid 19th C	400.00
Candlesticks, 8", serpents coiling . .	150.00
Champagne, 7", engraved	30.00
Compote, etched, oak leaves and grapes, gold trim	130.00
Cordial, set of 6	150.00

Creamer and Sugar, handled tray, crystal	90.00
Cruet, Amberina Swirl	100.00
Crystal Ball, 5½" on stand	85.00
Cup and Saucer	75.00
Decanter	
7½", opaque and clear swirled, red and white latticino ring at shoulder and lip	100.00
8½", lacy	90.00
Fairy Lamp, base mkd Clarke's Cricklete, Patent	175.00
Hurricane Lamps, 13" h, baluster shape base, brass candle holders, urn shaped cut glass shades, flared rim, pr	120.00
Inkwell, crystal bowl with green leaves, brass top	150.00
Liqueur Set, gilt bronze mounted, elephant, howdah opens to reveal 4 decor decanters, 12 matching liqueurs hanging from trappings . .	21,000.00
Mayonnaise, underplate, 4¾" bowl, 6¼" d, plate, ruby red, gold decor	325.00
Pelicans, 6½" h, sgd, pr	275.00
Pin Tray, Rose Teint swirl	35.00
Pitcher, 9", shouldered cylindrical shape, mitre cut base, stenciled Baccarat, France on base	125.00
Ring Tree, 3 x 3¾" sq, Rose Teint, ribbed swirl design	55.00
Toothpick, crystal	35.00
Tumblers	
Panels of clear cut to light amber	40.00
Rose Teint, emb swirl, 3⅝"	40.00
Tumble-Up with plate	175.00
Vases	
5", fan shaped, butterfly decor . .	45.00
5½", enamel decor, ormolu base	55.00
7", teardrop shape, sgd	50.00
9¼", crystal, elongated thumb cut sides	225.00

BANKS, MECHANICAL

Banks which display some form of action while utilizing a coin are considered mechanical banks. Although mechanical banks are known which date back to ancient Greece and Rome, the majority of collectors center their interests in those made between 1867 and 1928 in Germany, England and the United States. Recently there has been an upsurge of interest in later types, some of which date into the 1970s.

Initial research suggested that approximately 250 to 300 different or variant designs of banks were made in the early period. Today that number has been revised to 2,000–3,000 types and varieties. The field remains ripe for discovery and research.

Over 80% of all cast iron mechanical banks produced between 1869 and 1928 were made by J.E. Stevens Co., Cromwell, CT. Tin banks tend to be German in origin.

Reproductions, fakes, and forgeries exist of many banks. Forgeries of some mechanical banks were made as early as 1937, so age alone is not a guarantee of authenticity. In our listing two "**" indicate banks for which serious forgeries exist and one "*" banks for which casual reproductions have been made.

While rarity is a factor in value, appeal of design, action, quality of manufacture, country of origin, and history of collector interest also are important. Radical price fluctuations may occur with an imbalance of these factors. Rare banks may sell for a few hundred dollars while one of more common design with greater appeal will sell in the thousands.

While a few mechanical banks have dropped in value, far more have risen dramatically this past year. The most important event ever to take place in mechanical bank collecting circles, the dispersal of the Edwin Mosler Collection at an individually priced outright sale, occurred in 1983. The Mosler collection was the most comprehensive of all known mechanical bank collections. On Mosler's death, rumors swept the field of a possible upcoming collapse in mechanical bank prices due to the large number of banks that would appear in the market. In reality, several million dollars' worth of banks were absorbed readily within a few days; and, there was an upward surge in the market stimulated by the supply.

The prices on our list represent fairly what a bank sells for in the specialized collectors market. Some banks are hard to find and establishing a price outside auction is difficult.

The prices listed are for original old mechanical banks with no repaired, missing, or replaced parts, in sound operating condition, and with the vast majority of the original paint intact.

Frog on Rock, iron, $200.00.

**Acrobats, iron	875.00
African Bank	1,250.00
Alligator, grabs coin in mouth, tin	1,000.00
**American Sewing Machine, iron	3,500.00
*Artillery, four-sided block house	450.00
Atlas, lead & wood	575.00
Australian William Tell, brass, wood & tin	3,500.00
Automatic Coin Savings, tin, strong man in leopard skin holding man by hair	900.00
*Bad Accident, iron	750.00
Bank of Education & Economy	950.00
Barking Dog, wood & steel	850.00
**Bear, iron, sulky bruin	200.00
**Bear Standing, iron	350.00
**Billy Goat, iron	1,000.00
**Bismark, iron	2,000.00
Bonzo, tin	750.00
Bowing Man in Cupola, iron	3,000.00
**Boy & Bull Dog, iron	450.00
**Boy on Trapeze, iron	875.00
*Boy Scout Camp, iron	850.00
**Boys Stealing Watermelons, iron	675.00
British Lion, tin	700.00
**Bull & Bear, iron	3,000.00
*Bull Dog, iron, coin on nose	250.00
Bull Dog Savings, iron, key wind	1,000.00
Bull Tosses Boy in Well, brass	1,150.00
Bureau, Freedman's, wood	400.00
Bureau, tin, Ideal	200.00
Bureau, wood, Serrill Pat. Appld. For	250.00
Bureau, wood, stenciling on front	200.00
**Butting Buffalo, iron	700.00
Butting Ram, man thumbs nose	1,250.00
**Calamity, iron	2,000.00
**Called Out, original unpainted iron	3,000.00
Called Out, lead master pattern	3,700.00
Calumet with Calumet Kid, tin can	100.00
Calumet with Soldier, tin can	350.00
Calumet with Sailor, tin can	350.00
**Cannon, U.S. & Spain	1,500.00
Cat & Mouse, iron & brass, cat standing upright	1,750.00
Cat Chasing Mouse in Building, tin	450.00
Chandlers, iron	75.00
Child's Bank, Clark Thread	250.00
**Chimpanzee, iron & tin	650.00
Chinaman, iron, reclining	1,200.00
Chocolat Menier, tin	75.00
**Circus Ticket Collector, man at barrel	600.00
Clown & Dog, tin	750.00
Clown, tin, black face	350.00
**Clown, Harlequin, Columbine, iron	12,000.00
**Clown on Globe, iron	575.00
Coin Registering, iron, domed building	350.00
Confectionery, iron	3,250.00
Crescent Cash Register, iron	225.00
Crowing Rooster, tin	400.00
Dapper Dan, tin	250.00
Darky Bust, tin	450.00

**Dentist, iron	1,750.00
Dinah, aluminum	90.00
Dog Goes Into House, lead & brass	500.00
Dog, pot metal, spring jawed	200.00
**Dog With Tray, iron, oval base	650.00
Ducks, lead, two	500.00
Electric Safe, steel	50.00
Elephant Baby, lead, with clown at table	3,200.00
**Elephant With Howdah, iron, man pops out	175.00
**Elephant With Locked Howdah, iron, oval base	600.00
**Elephant, iron, "Light of Asia" on wheels	800.00
Elephant, tin, Royal Trick	675.00
**Elephant On Wheels, iron, trunk moves	700.00
**Elephant, iron, trunk moves, raised coin slot	50.00
Face, wood	75.00
**Feed the Kitty, iron	200.00
**Ferris Wheel, iron & tin, marked "Bowen's Pat."	500.00
Fire Alarm, tin	750.00
Flip The Frog, tin	700.00
Football, iron, black man & watermelon	10,500.00
Fortune Teller Safe, iron	350.00
Freedman (man at desk)	22,000.00
**Forty-Niner, iron	200.00
Frog On Arched Track, iron	1,500.00
Frog On Round Base, iron	155.00
Fun Producing Savings, tin	275.00
Germania Exchange, iron, tin & lead	3,500.00
**Giant Standing, iron	5,500.00
**Girl in Victorian Chair, iron	2,350.00
Give Me A Penny, wood	900.00
**Glutton, brass, lifts turkey	425.00
Golden Gate Key, aluminum	125.00
Grasshopper, tin, wind-up	5,000.00
Guessing, lead & iron, man's figure	850.00
Hall's Excelsior, iron & wood, no figure	75.00
Hall's Excelsior, iron & wood, policeman figure	350.00
Hall's Lilliput, Type II	150.00
Hall's Yankee Notion, brass	350.00
Harold Lloyd, tin	1,250.00
Hillman Coin Bank, wood, iron, & glass	2,500.00
**Hold The Fort, iron, five holes	750.00
Home, iron	125.00
Home With Dormer Windows, iron	200.00
**Horse Race, iron with tin horses, flanged base	1,150.00
**Humpty Dumpty, iron	425.00
**I Always Did 'Spize a Mule, black sitting on bench in front	375.00
Huntley And Palmers Readings	450.00
*Indian And Bear, iron, white bear	750.00
**Initiating First Degree, iron	3,700.00
Jack on Roof, tin	200.00

Joe Socko, tin	175.00
John R. Jennings Money Box, wood	550.00
Jolly Joe Clown, tin	700.00
**Jolly Nigger, aluminum	90.00
**Jolly Nigger, aluminum, moves ears	150.00
**Jolly Nigger, aluminum, string tie	100.00
**Jolly Nigger, iron	100.00
**Jolly Nigger, iron, high hat	125.00
Jonah And Whale, iron, footed base	18,500.00
Key, iron, World's Fair	300.00
Kick Inn, paper on wood	275.00
**Leap Frog, iron	850.00
**Lighthouse, iron	600.00
Lion Hunter, iron	2,200.00
Little High Hat, iron	500.00
Little Jocko Musical, tin	800.00
Little Moe, iron, tip hat	450.00
Long May It Wave, iron & wood	200.00
Lucky Wheel Money Box, tin	325.00
**Magic Safe, iron	175.00
**Magician, iron	575.00
**Mama Katzenjammer, iron, 1930's	550.00
Mama Katzenjammer, iron, 1905 08, low cut dress with white fringe	1,500.00
Man on Chimney	200.00
**Mason, iron	1,275.00
Merry-Go-Round, mechanical	4,500.00

Owl, turns head, iron, $225.00.

Metropolitan, iron	150.00
Mikado, iron	5,500.00
Minstrel, tin	150.00
Model Railroad Stamp Dispenser, tin	1,500.00
Model Railroad Sweet Dispenser	1,750.00
Model Savings, tin	800.00
*Monkey & Coconut, iron	650.00
Monkey & Parrot, tin	175.00
Monkey With Tray, tin	275.00
Moonface, iron	15,000.00
Mosque, iron	250.00
*Mule Entering Barn, iron	400.00
Musical Church, wood, rotating tower	475.00
Musical Savings, tin	800.00
Musical Savings, wood house	1,200.00
New, iron, lever in center	350.00
New Creedmoor Bank, iron	175.00
**Novelty, iron	175.00
Octagonal Fort, iron	750.00
Old Woman In The Shoe	60,000.00
*Organ, iron, cat & dog	250.00
**Organ, iron, miniature	350.00
**Organ Grinder With Performing Bear, iron	1,250.00
Owl, iron, slot in head	250.00
*Paddy & Pig, iron	660.00
Pascal Savings, tin	250.00
**Peg Leg Begger, iron	600.00
**Pelican With Mammy, iron	300.00
**Pelican With Rabbit, iron	450.00
**Piano, iron, old conversion to musical	1,500.00
Pig In High Chair, iron	450.00
Pistol, stamped metal	275.00
Postman, tin, English	100.00
Presto, iron, penny changes to quarter	2,500.00
Presto, paper on wood, mouse on roof	2,500.00
Pump & Bucket, iron	475.00
*Punch & Judy, iron	400.00
Punch & Judy, tin	800.00
Queen Victoria Bust, iron	3,000.00
**Rabbit, iron, large	175.00
Rabbit In Cabbage	200.00
**Red Riding Hood, iron	4,000.00
Rival, iron	3,500.00
Rollerskating, iron	3,000.00
Safety Locomotive, iron	1,000.00
Saluting Sailor, tin	500.00
Sam Segal's Aim To Save Target, iron	1,500.00
Savo, tin, round drum	125.00
Savo, tin, rectangular with children	200.00
Savo, tin, round with children	125.00
Scotchman, tin	175.00
Sentry, tin, raises rifle	575.00
Sentry, wood, c. 1910	300.00
Shoot The Hat, brass	1,500.00
Signal Cabin, iron	275.00
Snake & Frog In Pond, tin	1,000.00
Sportsman, iron, fowler	1,200.00

*Speaking Dog, iron, $450.00.

**Squirrel & Tree Stump, iron	600.00
Stollwerk, tin, Victoria	250.00
Sweet Thrift, tin	150.00
*Tammany, iron	145.00
*Tank & Cannon, aluminum	200.00
Target, iron, fort and cannon	2,750.00
Ten Cent Adding Bank, iron	400.00
Thrifty Tom's Jigger, tin	300.00
Tiger, tin	1,200.00
Time Lock Savings, iron	1,500.00
Toboggan, silver plated Britannia metal	325.00
Treasure Chest Music, pot metal	750.00
**Trick Dog, iron, solid base	100.00
*Trick Pony, iron	275.00
Trick Savings, wood, front drawer	125.00
Try Your Weight Scale, tin	250.00
**U.S. & Spain (see Cannon)	
**Uncle Remus, iron	1,750.00
**Uncle Sam Bust, iron	425.00
Uncle Tom, iron, star base	100.00
United States Bank, iron, picture pops up	675.00
Viennese Soldier, lead	1,500.00
Volunteer, iron	200.00
Watch Dog Safe, iron	175.00
Weeden's Plantation, tin, wind-up	375.00
Wimbledon, iron	1,750.00
Wireless, iron & tin	150.00
Wishbone, brass	3,700.00
Woodpecker, tin, 1920's	1,500.00
World's Banker, tin	850.00
**Zoo, iron	675.00

BANKS, STILL

Banks with no mechanical action are known as Still Banks. They are usually made of cast iron, with tin as the second most prominent metal.

GLASS STILL BANKS

Atlas Mason Jar	15.00
Barrel, emb	8.00
Baseball, camphor glass	15.00
Bear, milk glass	25.00
Clown	8.00
Elephant	10.00
House, 3", c1887	25.00
Liberty Bell, 3⅝", marigold carnival	18.00
Log Cabin, milk glass	48.00
Lucky Joe, 4⅜", contained Nash's Prepared Mustard	10.50
Milk Bottle, Elsie the cow, 4½"	22.50
Monkey, Jocko	20.00
Rabbit, amber	20.00
Safe, 4"	20.00
Schoolhouse, milk glass	50.00

METAL STILL BANKS

Animals

Bear with staff, 6", brass	90.00
Buffalo, 3", cast iron	58.00
Camel, mother and baby on rockers, 5", gray, green rockers, gold trim, emb "Oriental" on rocker	555.00
Cat, seated, 5", cast iron, black and gold, c1905	52.00
Cow, 3", cast iron	185.00
Deer, 9½", antlers, cast iron	55.00

Metal, Pig, 7", marked "Bann on Republic," $100.00.

Dogs

Boston Bulldog, standing, black and white, cast iron	65.00
Boxer, cast iron	68.00
Fido, on a pillow, 5½", black and white, cast iron	170.00
German Shepard, 9", cast iron	75.00
Spaniel Begging, 4½", white, black ears	50.00
Eagle, 4", cast iron	75.00
Elephant with howdah, 3"	40.00
Horse, "Beauty," 4¼"	55.00
Lion, 4", gold, cast iron	40.00
Mule, cast iron	62.00
Owl, 4¼", cast iron	90.00
Ox, 5¼", black, cast iron	55.00
Panda Bear, black and white	35.00
Oscar, billy goat, 7¾", black, cast iron	55.00
Pig, Thrifty the Wise Pig, iron, gold paint	60.00
Rabbit, sitting	115.00
Rooster, 5", red comb, cast iron	85.00
Turkey, cast iron	70.00

Other

Black Sharecropper, cast iron	60.00
Beehive, cast iron	60.00
Ben Franklin, bust, cast iron	45.00
Billiken, seated, 4½"	45.00
Boot, 5¼", copper	22.00
Boy Scout, cast iron	75.00
Buildings	
Bank with cupola, 3¼", pale green and orange, cast iron	38.00
Blackpool Tower, silver finish	90.00
City Bank, bronze finish, English	75.00
Skyscraper, 6½", gold and silver, cast iron	75.00
Captain Kidd, 5⅝", cast iron, c1901	225.00
Casey Jones, steam engine and coal car, 5⅜" l, bronze finish, white metal	30.00
Commonwealth Three Coin, 1905	55.00
Crown, 4¼", brass coronation, 1952, made in England	40.00
Dot Stove, "Cook With Cash," door opens, high back, cast iron	85.00
FDR, bust 5", metal, bronzed, die-cast	150.00
Fireman, cast iron	92.00
General Pershing, bust, 7¾", bronze, cast iron, Pat. July 10, 1918	90.00
General Sherman	475.00
Globe, on stand, 5¼", red, cast iron	80.00
Graf Zeppelin, 6¾", silver	120.00
Horseshoe and Horsehead, 3¾", gold, cast iron	48.00
Houses	
3", gold, cast iron	35.00

4½", paneled windows, doors, brown and yellow paint 65.00
Independence Hall — Tower Bank, bell 220.00
Indian Head, 5", gold 20.00
Liberty Bell, Sesquicentennial, cast iron, 1926 . . . . 75.00
Mail Box on legs, 4", green, cast iron 25.00
Mutt & Jeff, 5⅛", gold, cast iron . 110.00
Pirate sitting on chest, parrot on shoulder, pegleg, cast iron 300.00
Safe, Stevens Key lock, maltese cross on door, nickel plated . . . 45.00
Santa Claus, pack, 1910 . . . . 295.00
Sharecropper, 5⅜", cast iron . . . 75.00
Shoe, high button, 5", tan 80.00
Statue of Liberty, 9½" 265.00
Stump with elf, 2⅝", white metal, hinged lid with small brass padlock 105.00
Sunbonnet Baby, 7½" 145.00
Tank, 4⅜", gold, cast iron, Tank Bank U.S.A., 1918 . . . . 95.00
Two Face Black Boy, 3⅛", black and gold, cast iron 50.00
Uncle Sam 3 coin cash register . . 25.00
Water Tank, cast aluminum 35.00
Windmill, 3⅜", brass, silvered . . . 58.00

POTTERY STILL BANKS

Acorn, 3½", Rockingham glaze . . . 38.00
Apples
  2½", red, redware 80.00
  Red and White, chalkware 25.00
Bear, 12", ceramic, black and white, Hamm's 30.00
Cat Head, 4", emb features, amber glaze, brown and tan sponging . . 110.00
Dog, poodle head, ¾ x 4½", Staffordshire 75.00
Donkey, white, Staffordshire 38.00
Frog, 4", amber and green glaze . . 70.00
Gourd, 4" 45.00
House, 3¾", emb detail, Rockingham 140.00
Incense Burner 25.00
Kewpie, black, chalkware 50.00
Keystone Cop, 3½", head and hat, brown 30.00
Peach, 2⅝", pale yellow and peach 50.00
Pigs
  3⅝", 2 tone white and amber, running brown and rust, white clay 40.00
  6" l, blue and brown sponge spatter 100.00
  Bisque 48.00
Monkey Head, 3¾", green glaze . . 60.00
Sphere on Pedestal Base, small dog finial, 4⅞", dark albany slip glaze 130.00

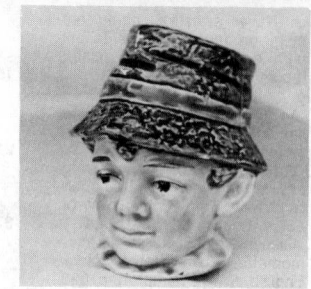

Pottery, Majolica, 3½" h, green hat, blue collar, violet band, $35.00.

BAROMETERS

A barometer is an instrument for measuring atmospheric pressure which, in turn, aids in the forecasting of weather. For example, low pressure indicates the coming of rain, snow, or a storm, while high pressure indicates fair weather. They were popular home accessories in Victorian England and later in America.

Banjo, A&V Cattania, hygrometer, thermometer, barometer with balancing level, mahogany case, York, England, 38½" l, $400.00.

Aneroid Type
  Boston Brand, 7¼" highly polished brass case 195.00
  Holosteric, brass 5½", ring hanging mount, marked France, USLH Establishment, from New London Lighthouse, not working 160.00

Nazi Navy, swastika, eagle emblem on face, millibars, aluminum case, 6½" silver painted mount 150.00

Banjo Type
C. A. Wheeler, mahogany on pine, line inlay, engraved dials, ivory adjusting knob, 36" 210.00
C. Barkham, Seven Oaks, mahogany veneer, line inlay, brass, ebony, ivory trim, convex mirror, 43" h, English 375.00
P. Giusani, balancing level, thermometer, hygrometer clock, English, Wolverhampton, c1835, 42½" l 100.00
Short and Mason, #2404, London, 26½" l 265.00

Pocket Type
Barometer/altimeter, leather lined case, green velvet, 2½", case marked "Compensated," outer bezel rotates for altitude 150.00
Short and Mason L.T.D. London, 2", brass case, worn leatherized cardboard case 95.00

Stick Type
A. Chevallier, wood panel, floral decor, thermometer, Paris, orig label, French, 19th C 130.00
British Naval Cadet's, uncased brass tube mercury unit, mahogany plaque, 38½" l, thermometer, ivory label of H. F. Angusa Co., 83 Wigmore St., London, NW 500.00
E. C. Spooner, Boston, mahogany, ebonized moldings, 42" l 285.00
R. N. Destero, Lisbon, gimballed brass, double ring mount, sgnd JJBLH 16.22, 37½" l 495.00
Simmons Portable, mahogany case, thermometer, New York . 450.00
Timby's Pat. Nov. 3, 1857, gold painted plaster border on wood, New York 400.00
Wall, Louis XV style, gilt bronze, rococo cast case, scrolls, foliage, 19th C, 41" 4,250.00

Wheel Type
J. Davis, mahogany, mirror, London, 4' 1,600.00
Short and Mason, inlaid mahogany, Fahrenheit, centigrade, London, 12" 1,400.00
Watkins & Hill, inlaid, 4' 1,700.00

BASALT

This type of black vitreous pottery was originally made in ancient times and rediscovered in the latter part of the 18th century by Josiah Wedgwood. It was later produced by other English potters.

Plaque, Venus and Cupid, 6¾", $750.00.

Beaker, 5⅜", figures in relief, gilt decor, imp Wedgwood and Z, 19th C 130.00
Bowl, 9½", acorn border in relief .. 235.00
Busts
Aristotle, 12⅜", bronzed, gazing to right, circular socle, imp Aristotle, Wedgwood, 1877 ...... 790.00
Bunyan, John, 13½", long hair, lace collared jacket, circular socle, imp Bunyan, E. W. Wyon. F, Wedgwood, late 19th C 470.00
Rousseau, 21¼", head turned to right, circular socle, imp Wedgwood, late 19th C 670.00
Shakespeare, 4", head turned to right, circular socle, imp Wedgwood, late 19th C 300.00
Candlesticks
7", allegorical figures and foliage in high relief 230.00
7⅝", enameled oriental floral sprays with iron red line borders, imp Wedgwood and V, mid 19th C 330.00
Child's Teapot, 3½", engine turned flutes, sybil knop, imp Wedgwood and S, late 18th C 95.00

Condiment Set, mustard pot, castor with pierced top, salt and salt shovel, berried laurel in relief, rope twist borders above floral festoons suspended from rams heads, imp Wedgwood, 19th C 390.00

Creamer, 4⅝", neck decor in rosso antico relief with flowers, fruit and foliage, imp Wedgwood, 19th C . 320.00

Cup and Saucer, 3⅛ and 5", Bacchanalian Boys in relief above band of engine turned flutes, imp Wedgwood, c1780 .... 350.00

Figures
Bird, 4½", glass eyes, Wedgwood only 575.00
Sphinx, 9", seated on rectangular base, imp Wedgwood, 19th C . 450.00
Tiger and Buck, 7½ x 12½" l, artist sgd J. Skeaping, imp Wedgwood 575.00

Inkwell, cov, 3⅝", drum shape, acanthus leaves and bellflowers in relief, imp Wedgwood, late 18th C 165.00

Lamp Base, 12¼", young faun running beside a tree trunk, circular molded base with grapes and pan pipes, imp Wedgwood 680.00

Pitcher, 5¼", florals, fruit and foliage in relief, imp Wedgwood, c1880 . 290.00

Plaques
Augustus and Nero, 5¾", oval, c1780, pr 285.00
Benjamin Franklin, portrait, 3½", oval, Wedgwood and Bentley, c1760 .... 300.00
Hercules and The Lion, 7¼", c1780 .... 260.00

Plate, 7", orange and white rim, berried laurel border within orange band, imp Wedgwood, late 18th C 400.00

Sugar, cov, 3⅞", enameled florals, imp Wedgwood, incised X, c1850 .... 120.00

Teapot, 4⅛", cov, enameled florals, imp Wedgwood and M, 1869 ... 125.00

Tea Set, 3 pcs., beaded oval medallion of a Muse in relief, imp Wedgwood and O, 19th C 390.00

Vases
5¼ x 3⅝", handled, enameled flowers, green leaves, raised masques at base of handles .. 372.00
6", raised polychrome enameled floral motif, late 19th C 110.00
9", cov, relief, border of acanthus leaves, loop handles ending in Satyr's masks, ball knop, imp Wedgwood, incised No. 275 .. 475.00
12¾", ovoid shape, incised wide border of scrollwork, imp Wedgwood Made in England, c1935 350.00

BASKETS

Baskets were invented when man first required containers to gather, store, and transport goods. Thus, basketry is probably one of the earliest indigenous crafts of all cultures. There are baskets for every use — egg baskets, cheese baskets, market baskets and even bed baskets for infants.

Baskets were made in a variety of shapes and sizes to fulfill specific needs. Methods and techniques used in construction — coiling, plaiting, wicker type, rib cage, etc. — mainly depended on the raw materials available or intended usage. Enthusiastic collectors of baskets prefer to view basketry more of an art form than a craft.

Storage, 18½", ryestraw, $170.00.

Buttocks Shaped
3¾ x 4¼", miniature, finely woven, split, wide handle 125.00
7 x 12", white oak, split handle .. 82.00
10" h x 14 x 17", woven, split, worn brown varnish, wood handle ....: 170.00

Cheese, woven, split
1½", miniature 75.00
10" 155.00
18" 250.00
20" 245.00

Church Collection, 4½ x 12", oak, c1850 .... 32.00

Cotton, 30 x 31", woven, split, hand holds in sides 110.00

Egg, 12", round, willow, Pennsylvania 70.00

Field
10½ x 18 x 24", oval, woven, split, rim handles 62.00
12 x 17½", woven, split, double wood swivel handles 85.00

Garden, 13 x 20", wooden handle, woven, split 65.00

Gathering
　13 x 23", woven, split, Kentucky . **300.00**
　14 x 23½", woven, split, wooden
　　handle **125.00**
Kitchen, 5 x 11", carrying handles,
　woven, split, bleached finish . . . **95.00**
Lunch, double handles, 5 x 8" **40.00**
Maine, 12 x 13", well shaped han-
　dle, Woodland Indian, woven,
　split, natural and dark blue **95.00**
Market
　2½ x 4½", miniature, woven split,
　　curlicues, handle **55.00**
　11" plus handle, oak splint **120.00**
Melon, 8 x 14", ash, woven, split,
　c1890 . . . . **95.00**
Nantucket, 8 x 15", round, woven,
　split, wooden swivel handle, dark
　varnish finish **85.00**
Oriental Export, 3 x 5½", miniature,
　polychrome painted floral decor . **80.00**
Pantry, 9½ x 14", oak, woven,
　Pennsylvania, c1880 . . . . **85.00**
Picket Fence, 30 x 19¾", red and
　green paint **170.00**
Pie Carrier, 2½ x 13", oak, woven,
　split, double handle, c1900 . . . . **110.00**
Ryestraw, 8½ x 19", 2 woven han-
　dles, Pennsylvania **245.00**
Sewing, 12", willow **32.00**
Shaker, 10 x 15½", woven and bent
　sapling frame, woven split panels,
　sgd H. Scheffler **165.00**
Storage
　11½" h x 20 x 25", woven, split,
　　bentwood rim handles **60.00**
　12 x 15", woven, split, cov, red
　　and black painted detail **70.00**
Wall, 8" h x 6 x 5", oak, c1900 . . . **62.00**

BATTERSEA ENAMELS

**Battersea enamel is a generic name for
painted enamels on metal.**

　**Stephen T. Janssen first demonstrated this
method of transferring prints from engraved
copper plates onto enamelled surfaces in the
early 1750s at the York House, in Battersea,
London. In 1756, financial difficulties forced
the enterprise to be discontinued. All materials, including the copper plates were sold
and subsequently used by other firms, mainly
in the Staffordshire district.**

　**Small gift boxes of Battersea-type enamels
are currently being produced in France and
available in fine retail outlets at a fraction of
the cost of the earlier examples.**

Boxes, Patch
　Laurel leaf wreath, crown, eagle,
　　crossed standards, white ground

top, mottled green base, 1 x
　1⅝" **145.00**
Woman in bonnet, deep pink,
　white lid, round, 1½" **140.00**
Boxes, Snuff
　Inscriptions
　　Have Communication with few
　　　. . . , white, red, blue floral
　　　rim, black verse, blue mir-
　　　rored interior, 1¾" l **195.00**
　　Love The Giver, oval, 2¼" . . . **195.00**
　　Maybe Friendship & Love Be
　　　Eve United, c1750 . . . . **110.00**
　　The Gift of A Friend, green,
　　　white lid, black script inscrip-
　　　tion, 1¼" **155.00**

**Box, Snuff, inscription, "Friendship
shall ever be sacred between my
worthy friend and me", blue base,
black letters, 1¾" oval, $275.00.**

　Scenic
　　Aberystwith Castle, oval, mirror
　　　interior, 2½" **215.00**
　　Blockly, England, oval, 1¾" . . **185.00**
　　Margate, England, oval, 1⅜" . . **195.00**
　　Oxford, black and white land-
　　　scape, mirror interior **225.00**
　　Sunderland Bridge, England,
　　　oval, 1⅝" **210.00**
　　Truro, England, round, 2" **200.00**
　　Windsor Castle, oval, 2⅛" . . . **200.00**

BAVARIAN CHINA

**Bavaria was an important porcelain produc-
tion center in Germany, similar to the Staffordshire districts in England. However, very
little of the production from this area was
imported into the United States before 1870.
The term covers the products of several
companies operating there.**

Basket, 7 x 7", blue, floral decor, gilt
　handle, trim **70.00**

Bowls
7", pink roses, green, gold trim, reticulated sides 35.00
9", pink, yellow, red roses, white ground 28.00
Cake Plates
10" d, pierced handles, gold acorns, leaves, red border 28.50
11" d, pink, yellow roses 20.00
Celery Tray, 10 x 4½", poppies & leaves decor, gold trim 40.00
Chocolate Pot, cov, violets, leaves, white ground, lavender borders, gold trim 70.00
Cookie Jar, cov, handles, Roman key border 45.00
Creamer and Sugar, cov, peony decor, leaves, gold trim, hp, pr 55.00
Demitasse Cup and Saucer, white scrolls, florals, burgundy ground, gold trim 22.00
Dinner Set, Empress pattern, white, colored flowers surrounded by scattered blossoms, shaped and molded, gilt rim borders, lion within a shield surmounted on crown, Schuman, Bavaria, Germany, U.S. Zone, 173 pcs. 650.00
Fish Set, platter and 12 plates, fish picture with gold trim 315.00
Hair Receiver, lavender, yellow florals 20.00
Pitcher, Alpine pattern, matching beer mugs, 5 pcs 350.00
Plates
6", salad, gold, white 5.00
7¼", fruit, gold rose decor, black ground, gold trim 15.00
8", violets, leaves, white ground, hp 18.00
8¼", classical scene, gold band, dark blue inner band, scalloped edge, marked Z/S & C/R 25.00

9½", red berries, green leaves, white ground, scalloped border 20.00
Powder Jar, daisy decor, gold finial, trim 20.00
Ramekin, underplate, red berries, green leaves, scalloped border, gold edges 10.00
Relish, 6¾ x 4¾", pink, white roses, hp, gold edge, handles 18.00
Salt & Pepper Shakers, 3", pink, white daisies, green leaves, gold tops 20.00
Sugar Castor, 4¼ x 3⅛", pastel, hp pink roses, gold feet & top, artist sgd 40.00
Tea Set, teapot, creamer, cov sugar, 4 - 7½" plates, lustre band, flowers in panels, gold band and trim, c1915 . . . . 65.00
Toothpick, barrel shape, pink roses 25.00
Tray, center floral medallions, gold pierced border, Schumann 20.00
Vase, 4¾", gold, hp florals, sgd . . . 14.00

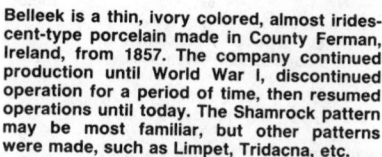

BELLEEK

Belleek is a thin, ivory colored, almost iridescent-type porcelain made in County Ferman, Ireland, from 1857. The company continued production until World War I, discontinued operation for a period of time, then resumed operations until today. The Shamrock pattern may be most familiar, but other patterns were made, such as Limpet, Tridacna, etc.

Several different identifying marks were used including the Harp and Hound (1865–1880) and Harp, Hound and Castle (1863–1891). Some items are marked "Belleek Co., Fermanagh." After 1891 the word Ireland, or Eire was added.

A Belleek-type porcelain was made in America by several firms. The first was Ott and Brewer Co., Trenton, New Jersey, in 1884. Another early manufacturer was Willets. Other American firms were the Ceramic Art Co. (1889), American Art China Works (1892), Columbian Art Co. (1893) and Lenox, Inc., (1904).

There is an Irish saying . . . if a newly married couple receive a gift of Belleek, their marriage will be blessed with lasting happiness.

Abbreviations: 1BM—1st Black Mark; 2BM—2nd Black Mark; 3BM—3rd Black Mark. See also LENOX.

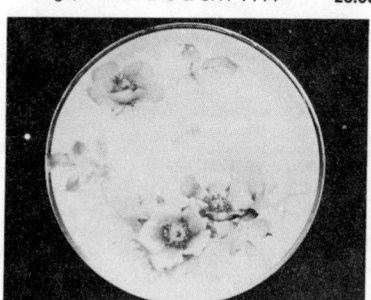

Plate, 8¾", pink flowers, green leaves, gold rim, mkd "Bavarian China," $10.00.

Sugar, open clover, basketweave, mkd "Fermanagh, Ireland," $22.50.

Baskets
2½ x 5¼", 4 strand, applied pink roses and green leaves, blue trim 2BM, Irish 365.00
Heart shaped, 4 strand, rose bud border 295.00

Bowls
2 x 3½", Shamrock, 2BM 55.00
7½", ruffled top, pink roses decor, pale pink inside, gold handles, Willets 150.00
9", pink shaded to green with hp white dogwood blossoms, 2 gold handles, ruffled rim, Willets 125.00

Boxes
2¼ x 6½" l, mask, 3BM 450.00
3½ x 2½", trinket, covered, 2BM Irish 290.00

Cake Server, 10½", round, 3 strand, Irish 890.00
Chalice, 11", grape decor, Willets . 175.00
Coffee Pot, Limpet, 3BM 184.00
Compote, lilac luster with dolphins, shallow shell bowl, 1BM 1,250.00
Condiment Dish, Shell, gilded, 1BM 290.00

Creamers
3¼", pansies, enameled, Ott and Brewer 165.00
3½ x 2½", Celtic, 1BM, Irish . . . 75.00
4½", Shamrock, green mark . . . 60.00
Shell and Coral, 2BM 65.00

Creamers and Sugars
Limpet, 3BM 100.00
Neptune, 2BM 150.00
Thistle, gilded, 2BM, Irish 350.00

Cups and Saucers
Grasses, 1BM, Irish 165.00
Institute ware, 2BM, Irish 190.00
Shamrock, harp handle, 1BM . . . 69.00
Tridacna, pink trim, 2BM, Irish . . . 55.00

Dish, Shamrock, basketweave, brownish twig handle, 2BM 38.00
Egg Cup, basketweave, pink trim, 1BM, Irish 150.00

Figures
3⅛ x 4⅜", swan, 1BM, Irish 165.00
9¾", "Kneeling Angel Font," Parian biscuit, glazed, 1BM 1,900.00
14½", "Affection," woman, draped, Belleek Parian, 1BM, Irish 1,800.00

Flower Pot, 3⅝ x 4¼", scalloped top, lustred applied rose, buds, and leaves, shamrocks on back side, 3BM 195.00
Hat Pin Holder, 5", swirled floral, silver overlay, Willets 100.00
Jam Jar, 3⅝ x 2¾", green shamrocks, 3BM, Irish 75.00

Jugs
6", Lily shape, pink trim, 2BM, Irish 365.00
7½", pearl, harp handle, 1BM, Irish 475.00

Juice Set, pitcher, 4 matching tumblers, raised enameled fruit, flowers, Willets 350.00

Mugs
5", corn decor, Ceramic Art Co. . . 50.00
Tankard shape, hp, "Gambling Ladies," signed "M. Hunter," Ceramic Art Co. 150.00

Mustache Cup, basketweave, green clover, twisted handle, 2BM, Irish 425.00
Nut Dish, oval, pearlized ivory, multicolored flowers, gold handles and rim, Lenox palette and L mk 55.00

Pitchers
8 x 5", silver overlay, Willets, c1879 . . . . 89.00
14", grape cluster decor, ornate handle, artist sgd, dated 1906 . 175.00
Cider, ocean scene, artist sgd, 1910 . . . . 175.00
Raised gold leaves, blossoms, solid gold embellishments on body, American Art China Works 450.00

Plates
8", Shamrock, basketweave, 3BM 55.00
9", bread 95.00
10", Bacchus 110.00
11½", Grasses, 1BM, Irish 185.00
Cone, green trim, 2BM 65.00
Echinus, green trim, 1BM 62.00
Hexagon, bread plate, 2BM 75.00

Platters
Hawthorne 195.00
Shamrock, basketweave, 3BM . . . 75.00
Twig handles, 2BM 85.00

Root Center, 2¾ x 3¼ x 4¼", brown and green branch with pink water lily bud, large open water lily in pink with yellow lustre inside . . 325.00

Salts

1¼ x 2 x 3⅛″, oval, green seaweed and rim, emb shells, 2BM, Irish 65.00

Floral decor, cream ground, gold rim and ball feet, Willets, pr ... 35.00

Master, Shell and Coral, 2BM ... 40.00

Sherbert, 3½″, egg shell, ftd, fluted edge, gold paste 150.00

Spoon Rest, 4½″ l, oval shape, 1BM, Irish 295.00

Sugars

Etruria, blue and white, late 35.00

Neptune, 2BM 85.00

Teakettle, 5 x 8¾″, head and arms of chinaman on lid, winged dragon on each side, 2 gold rings for handle, gold trim, 1BM, Irish 695.00

Teapots

8½″, Bamboo, 1BM 500.00

Grass, 1BM 500.00

Hexagon, green trim, 2BM 250.00

Neptune, green trim, 2BM 250.00

Roses, hp, pink, cream, jewelled scrollwork, gold handle and finial, Lenox 175.00

Tea Set, Hexagon, green, gilded, teapot, sugar, creamer, 2 cups and saucers, 2 cake plates, 2BM, Irish 790.00

Tray, 15″ d, round, Hexagon, green trim, 2BM 950.00

Vases

3″, open water lily, Willets 100.00

6″, pink, yellow, blue florals, green leaves, Lenox 125.00

6½″, pearl, 3BM 125.00

6½ x 4½″ d, trunk stump, Shamrock, 3BM, Irish 110.00

7″, gold handles, crimped rim, salmon pink, yellow rose decor, Willets 160.00

8½″, Shamrock, panel, green petals, 2BM 235.00

9½ x 5″ d, Aberdeen, lustred applied rose, buds, daisy, carnation and small flowers and leaves, 2BM, Irish 525.00

13″, Nile, pearl lustre, yellow leaves, 3BM 350.00

13 x 6″ d, white, raised vine, 2BM, Irish 550.00

BELLS

Bells have been used for centuries for many different purposes, and have been traced as far back as 2697 B.C., though at that time they did not have any true tone. One of the oldest bells is the "crotal," a tiny sphere with small holes and a ball of stone or metal in-side. This type now appears as the sleigh bell, the Christmas bell or the bells on Indian dancers.

True bell making began when bronze, the mixing of tin and copper, was discovered. There are now many types of materials of which bells are made—almost as many materials as there are uses for them. In the last twenty years bells have become a very popular collectible item.

See specific categories, such as GLASS, etc.

See *Warman's Antiques & Collectibles* for additional Bell listings.

Desk Bell, side tap, bronze, white marble base, c1875, $40.00.

Animal Bells

Camel, second bell as clapper .. 90.00

Cows

Bronze, cast tassel clapper, 5″ 15.00

Handmade, riveted seam, folded iron clapper, 7″ 25.00

Horse, brass, triple, saddle, parade 55.00

Sheep, sheet iron, cast iron clapper, 2 x 2½ x 3″ 16.00

Church steeple bell, sgd "Vanduzen and Tift, Cincinnati" 575.00

Door Bell, brass, "Connell's Pat 1873" 60.00

Farm yard bell, cast iron with yoke, #2 .... 150.00

Figurals

French lady, jug, brass, 6″ 110.00

Ladies

Fan, hat, full skirt, brass, 6″ .. 110.00

Hat, emb flowers on full layered skirt, carrying basket, brass, 6 x 2¾ x 4¼″ 65.00

Hat, full skirted dress, arm extended in air, heavy brass, 5 x 3¼″ 95.00

Hoopskirt, powdered wig, holding fan, brass, 5½ x 3¼″ .. 65.00

Medieval woman's head finial, cherubs around bell, brass, 7 x 4⅝"	225.00
Nesting storks on sides, 2 fish handles, small raised fish in water brass, 4¾ x 3⅞"	75.00
Shakespeare, brass, 5¾"	110.00

Hand Bells

Animals, emb below "Ovi Me Tangit Vocem Meam Avdit", brass, 7 x 4½" d	100.00
Art Nouveau, SS handle, pansies	22.00
Assyrian Warriors carrying masks, emb, brass, 7¼ x 5" d	110.00
Fish handle, brass, 5"	45.00
R.A.F. Victory Bell, aluminum, painted, made from German aircraft shot down over Britain, name of foundry inside, emb heads of Stalin, Roosevelt & Churchill, 5½ x 4½"	60.00
Horse Hames, set of four	350.00
Locomotive, bronze, clapper, stationary yoke, 13" d	310.00
Mechanical, figural turtle, cast iron, bronze finish	95.00
Plantation, cast iron, rocker arm, 13 x 10"	385.00
Ship, 2 feet, brass	1,100.00

Sleigh

8 brass crotal-type bells on leather strap, dated 3/14/78	85.00
18 brass, 1¼" ring	145.00
27 brass crotal-type bells riveted to leather strap, c1870	110.00
Tap Bell, brass, twist ring	65.00
Trolley Car, double action, Starr Bros. Bell Co.	95.00

BELLS, GLASS

Although bells made of metal are more practical, glass bells were produced in England and the United States in the early 1800s. They can be found in clear or colored glass, large or small. Some were made for use on the tea tray or dining table, while others were purely decorative, an example of the glass blower's talent and the glass manufacturer's product.

Glass bells are still being manufactured. Be careful of the reproductions which are coming in from Europe.

Amethyst, Pairpoint	130.00
Bohemian, 4½", ruby, Deer & Castle, clear handle and clapper on chain	85.00
Bristol, 13¼", wedding bell, red barrel in swirl pattern, clear swirl handle, 4 ball finial, clapper	130.00

Fenton, 7", Rosaline, $29.00.

Candlewick, Imperial	39.00
Carnival, figural, Southern Belle, white Imperial	35.00
Cranberry, 11¼" h, 4¾" d base, bride's, art glass handle, Thomas Webb	225.00
Crystal, 4½" clear, acid etched decor, band of fernery & shells	25.00
Custard, Wide Band	145.00
Heisey, frosted Victorian Belle	135.00
Milk Glass, blue rim	40.00
Ruby stained, Button Arches, glass clapper	45.00
Vaseline, yellow and white ribbon ..	15.00

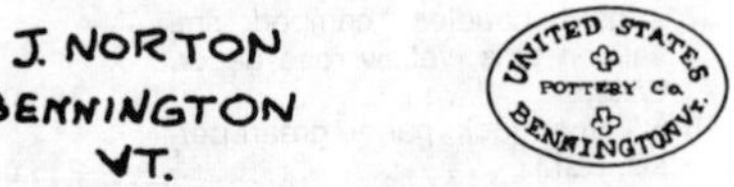

J. NORTON
BENNINGTON
VT.

UNITED STATES POTTERY Co. BENNINGTON VT.

BENNINGTON POTTERY

The two potteries located in Bennington, Vt., were Norton Pottery and Fenton Pottery, owned and operated independently. When Capt. John Norton began making pottery in 1793, he offered only crocks and jugs. Later, stoneware, colored porcelains, Parian, stoneware, colored porcelains, and much more were produced. They were marked with several different names: J. and E. Norton, E. and L. P. Norton, L. Norton Co., and others. The pottery existed as a family business until 1894.

In 1845, Christopher Fenton entered the business. He introduced additional lines, including the "Rockingham Glaze," which had been produced originally in England. The American "Rockingham Glaze" as known to-

day was developed by the Jersey City Pottery in 1829. It was peddled door to door throughout the country and was common tableware for two generations, being made between 1830 and 1900 by some 150 potteries in 11 states, most of them in the Middle West. The hound-handled pitcher was also made by some 30 other potteries in the United States, and there are approximately 55 variations of it.

Bennington also produced a beautiful line of Parian ware, sometimes called "Statuary Ware." First made by Copeland in England in 1842, it is translucent and vitreous, and Parian proper is unglazed. It is usually molded and uncolored, but Bennington added color to the slip, and this is known as Parian on a colored background. American ware included pitchers, vases, boxes, animal and human figures (which are seldom marked). Bennington Parian is considered to be the earliest and finest made in America.

Bennington also made a ware known as "Scroddled Ware," which was different colored clay, mixed with cream colored clay, put into a mold, turned on a potter's wheel and coated with feldspar and flint glaze. It was a slow and costly process, therefore very little was made at Fenton. When marked, it has the United States Pottery oval mark "H," or Fenton "E."

NORTON

Norton, Crock, 1½ gal, cobalt blue stylized floral decor, imp E.&L.P. Norton, Bennington, Vt, $165.00.

Butter Crock, gray stoneware, cobalt blue, stylized leaf decor, imp "E. & L. P. Norton, Bennington, Vt." . .   **185.00**
Chamber Pot, gray stoneware, Julius Norton **100.00**
Crocks
  2 gal, 9" h, stylized floral cobalt design, imp E. & L. P. Norton, Bennington **200.00**
  6 gal, 13" h, stylized floral cobalt slip, imp E. B. Norton & Co. . .   **150.00**
Inkstand, 6", J. Norton & Co. **160.00**
Jars
  2 gal, 11¼" h, cobalt blurred bird, imp J. & F. Norton, Bennington, Vt.   **195.00**
  2 gal, 11¾" h, stoneware, cobalt blue floral design slip, imp E. & L. P. Norton, Bennington, Vt. . .   **135.00**
Jug, 2 gal, 13½" h, ovoid, cobalt blue simple floral design, imp Julius Norton, Bennington **225.00**
Pitcher, 11", hexagonal, brown birds and flowers, Norton & Fenton . . .   **250.00**

FENTON

Bowl, 15" d, Rockingham glaze, 1849 mark **425.00**

Candleholder, 3¼" h, ring handle, olive flint enamel glaze, yellow-brown, brown, base impressed "J" **875.00**
Candlesticks
  6½" h, columnar, large water flint enamel **450.00**
  6⅝" h, columnar, flint enamel, base underside chipped **225.00**
  6¾" h, columnar, blue flint enamel glaze, yellow-brown **325.00**
  7¾" h, columnar, flint enamel glass **400.00**
  9¼", columnar, Rockingham glaze, pr **950.00**
Chamber Bowl, Pitcher, 15" d bowl, 12¾" h pitcher, olive green, blue, brown flint enamel glaze, imp 1849 mark **700.00**
Creamers
  4¼" h, Parian, pond lily pattern . .   **75.00**
  5⅜" h, cow, Rockingham glaze, long glaze crack **175.00**
  6" h, tulip & heart pattern, blue-green flint enamel glaze, brown, handle repaired **300.00**
Cuspidor, 8¾" d, scroddled ware, diamond pattern, c1853 . . . . . .   **125.00**
Dog, 5½" h, finely detailed, foliage emb base, free standing front legs, emb chain, flint enamel glaze **550.00**

Flasks, Book

- 5½", Battle of Bennington, yellow, brown, blue flint enamel glaze, prof. repairs to glaze 300.00
- 5½", Departed Spirits, yellow, brown flint enamel glaze 575.00
- 6", Life of Kossath, blue flint enamel glaze, brown, yellow .. 670.00
- 10⅝", brown, yellow flint enamel glaze 500.00

Flower Pot, 7" h, acanthus leaves, Rockingham glaze 150.00

Frame, 10¾ x 2", oval, Rockingham glaze 475.00

Inhalator, 6½", inset spout, Rockingham glaze 600.00

Paperweight, 2¾" h, spaniel reclining on cushion, yellow, brown Rockingham glaze, imp 1849 .... 650.00

Pipkin, cov, 6¼" h, alternate rib pattern, yellow-brown, brown glaze .. 475.00

Pitchers

- 5⅝" h, scroddle ware, clear, greenish glaze, lid missing ... 175.00
- 8½" h, hound handle, emb stag, doe scenes, flint enamel glaze . 350.00
- 9" h, scallop rib pattern, dark brown flint enamel glaze, 1849 mark 450.00
- 9¾" h, swirled alternate rib, imp 1849 .... 500.00

Fenton Vase, 9⅝" h, Tulip, flint enamel glaze, $550.00.

- 10¼" h, alternate rib pattern, dark brown, yellow-brown, blue flecked flint enamel glaze 425.00

Soap Dish, 4⅝ x 5⅞ x 4", cov, insert, Rockingham glaze, 1849 mark 375.00

Sugar Bowls, covered

- 6¾" h, green, brown, ochre flint enamel glaze, 1849 mark 900.00
- 8" h, octagonal panel shape, blue, yellow-brown, brown flint enamel glaze, green touches on base, dark brown, yellow-brown, blue touches on lid 600.00

Toby Bottles

- 8½", coachman, Rockingham glaze brimmed hat 625.00
- 10½" h, coachman, mustache, goatee, brimmed hat, Rockingham glaze, 1849 mark 475.00

Trinket Boxes

- 4¼" l, blue, white Parian, babe on cover 125.00
- 5" l, Parian, high relief floral 85.00

Vases

- 9¾" h, tulip, flint enamel glaze, prof. repair 200.00
- 10¾", mantle, Parian, shepherd, shepherdess standing by wheatsheaf spill holders 550.00

BENNINGTON-TYPE

Bank, 3¼" h, ewe, oval base, Rockingham glaze 85.00

Bowl, 13½ x 4" h, octagonal, Rockingham glaze 125.00

Cuspidor, 8¼ x 9¾ x 4¾", octagonal, emb floral designs, 4 eagles, shields, chipped 100.00

Pitcher, 9¼" h, cov, emb gentleman beside lecturn 300.00

Platter, 10" l, Rockingham glaze ... 115.00

Soap Dish, 6" d x 2⅜" h, Rockingham glaze 95.00

Turk's head mold, 6⅝" d, Rockingham glaze 85.00

BIBLES

The Bible, in its many early editions, versions, languages, and translations, is the most popular and most diversely collected book in the world. Recently Bible collecting has gained wider appreciation with a corresponding increase in prices.

King James version English Bibles printed after 1800 are common, not eagerly sought, and command little value. Other versions and languages often are of substantial interest if in very good condition.

A fine leather binding or handsome illustrations add to a Bible's value. Check for owner-ship information, family records, and other ephemera concealed within the pages of a Bible. These items may produce value above the book itself.

Sizes (approximate)

Folio	=	12 x 16 inches
4to	=	8 x 10 inches
8vo	=	5 x 7 inches
12mo	=	3 x 3 inches

Arabic, 1811, Newcastle (England), *Old and New Testament*, 4to, 19th C gilt morocco leather armorial binding . . . . — **180.00**

Choctaw, 1848, New York, *New Testament . . . translated into the Choctaw Language*, 12mo . . . . . — **100.00**

English

1611, London, *Bible*, Robert Bark-er, 1st Edition of the King James Bible, reads "He" in Ruth III:15, 2 vols in 1, folio, calf over wooden boards, brass clasps . . . . — **5,000.00 +**

1683–80, Cambridge (England), *Bible*, John Hayes, 4to, contem-porary calf gilt, bound with *Book of common Prayer* & the *Whole Book of Psalms*, both 1679 . . . — **80.00**

1716–17, Oxford (England), *Bible* ("Vinegar Bible"), John Baskett, 2 vols, folio, contemporary mo-rocco gilt, arms of George I . . . — **1,600.00**

1722, Edinburgh (Scotland), *Bible*, 8vo, old calf . . . . — **50.00**

1743, Dublin, *Bible*, cloth covered spine, Cresson Family record . — **50.00**

1763, Cambridge (England), *Bible*, John Baskerville, folio, contem-porary calf gilt . . . . — **525.00**

1782–81, Philadelphia, *Bible*, Rob-ert Aitken, 1st Edition of Bible in English printed in America, 12 mo, contemporary sheep leath-er binding . . . . — **4,500.00**

1791, Trenton, NJ, *Bible*, Isaac Collins, 4to, contemporary calf — **150.00**

1791, Wilmington, DE, *New Testa-ment*, Jane Adams, full leather, 408 pgs . . . . — **140.00**

1791, Worcester, MA, *Bible*, Isaiah Thomas, 2 vols in 1, folio, 50 plates, contemporary calf . . . . — **175.00**

1798, Philadelphia, *Bible*, Thomp-son & Small, 2 vols in 1, folio, contemporary calf . . . . — **60.00**

1801, Philadelphia, *Bible*, Carey, full leather binding, color book-plate of Christian Hoober . . . . — **90.00**

1808, Philadelphia, *Bible*, Jane Aitken, 4 vols, 8vo . . . . — **250.00**

1811, Philadelphia, *Bible*, Carey . — **30.00**

1822, Philadelphia, *New Testa-ment*, Mentz, 12mo, 336 pgs, ownership inscription of J. Krawne, 1828 . . . . — **30.00**

1824, Philadelphia, *New Testa-ment*, Phila. Bible Society, 352 pgs . . . . — **14.00**

1828, Philadelphia, *Bible*, Bruce, full leather . . . . — **18.00**

1838–39, London, *The Pictorial Bi-ble*, Charles Knight, 4 vols, 4to, contemporary morocco . . . . . . — **100.00**

1846, New York, *The illuminated Bible*, 4to, morocco gilt, 2 en-graved titles, 1,600 plates . . . . — **225.00**

1850, Philadelphia, *Bible*, woodcut illus., English medical recipe [Pow-Wow] broadside on rear paste down, Petre family record — **25.00**

1866, Philadelphia, *Bible*, 4to, en-graved plates, full embossed morocco binding . . . . — **32.00**

1870, Pittsburgh, *Bible with Bag-ster's References*, gilt tooled full morocco leather . . . . — **20.00**

Eskimo-Labrador, 1813, London, *The Gospels according to St. Mat-thew, St. Mark, St. Luke and St. John*, W. M'Dowell, 12mo . . . . . . — **300.00**

German

1743, Germantown, PA, *Bible* (Lu-ther's version), Christoph Saur, 4to, contemporary calf binding . — **800.00**

1763, Germantown, PA, *Bible*, Christoph Saur, 2nd Edition, 4to, morocco binding, clasps . . . . . — **600.00**

1776, Germantown, PA, *Bible* ("Gun Wad Bible"), Christoph Saur, 4to, orig calf over wooden boards, ties . . . . — **400.00**

1787, Germantown, PA, *Das Neue Testament . . . Erste Auflage*, Michael Billmeyer, pgs 537 and 5, homemade backed leather binding . . . . — **40.00**

1805, Reading, *Biblia, Das Ist: Die Ganze Gottliche Heilige Schrift . . . Erste Auflage*, Gottlob Jungmann, thick 4to, 1,235 pgs, contemporary polished calf binding . . . . — **100.00**

1813, Somerset, PA, *Biblia, Das Ist . . . Die Erste Auflage*, Friederich Goeb, folio, pgs 527, 66, and 169, orig full leather binding, first Bible printed west of Allegheny Mountains . . . . . . — **225.00**

1825, Carlisle, PA, *Das Neue Tes-tament . . .*, Moser & Peters, 516 pgs, illus, full leather . . . . . — **30.00**

1835, New York, *Das Neue Testa-ment . . .*, American Bible Soci-ety, 12mo, 288 pgs, full leather — **10.00**

1839, Philadelphia, *Das Neue Testament* . . . , Mentz, 504 pgs, illus, full leather, clasps	16.00

Latin

1582, London, *New Testament*, Thomas Vautrollerus, 16mo, contemporary calf	75.00
1618, Rome, *Bible*, A. Phaei, 4to, later calf	100.00
1967, New York, *The Lorsch Gospels*, folio, limited edition, half vellum	90.00
Mohawk, 1839, New York, *Ne kaghyadonghsera ne royadadokenghdy ne Isaiah*, 16mo, cloth	100.00
Polyglot, 1657, *Leipzig Folio*, contemporary pigskin over boards . . .	120.00

BIG LITTLE BOOKS AND BETTER LITTLE BOOKS

The Whitman Publishing Co. of Racine, WI, began its Big Little Book series in the early 1930s. Several of the early printings were used as premiums by Cocomalt. All books have a code number.

In the late 1930s the size was expanded to create Better Little Books. The same heroes of the earlier series were continued. As movie and radio personalities developed, they were added to the series.

The books are printed on pulp paper and have weak bindings. They should be handled with care. The quality of the cover art often is a key factor in pricing, as is condition. Big Little Books generally range from $10.00 to $25.00. Better Little Books range from $6.00 to $15.00.

   hc = hard cover
   sc = soft cover
   ss = standard size, 3⅝ x 4½ x 1½″

See *Warman's Americana and Collectibles* for an expanded listing of Big Little Books and Better Little Books.

BIG LITTLE BOOKS

Big Chief Wahoo, 1443, 1938, Elmer Woggon artist, Allen Saunders, ss, hc, 432 pgs	12.50
Black Silver And The Pirate Crew With Tom Trojan, 1414, 1937, ss, hc, 300 pgs	18.00
Chester Gump At Silver Creek Ranch, 1933, Sidney Smith artist and author, 5⅝ x 4⅛ x ³/₁₆″, sc, stapled, 48 pgs	18.50
Clyde Beatty, Lions And Tigers, 632, 1934, Universal Pictures, 4⅝ x 5¼ x 1″, hc, 160 pgs	24.00
Dan Dunn, Secret Operative 48 And	

Coach Bernie Bierman's, Brick Barton And The Winning Eleven, #1480, 1938, R.W. Williamson, artist, Coach Bernie Bierman author, ss, hc, 300 pgs, $14.00.

The Border Smugglers, 1481, 1938, Norman Marsh artist and author, ss, hc, 432 pgs	15.00
Doctor Doom And The Ghost Submarine, 1460, 1939, Al McWilliams, artist, Conrad Vane author, ss, hc, 432 pgs	15.00
G-Man And The Radio Bank Robbers, 1434, 1937, Herbert Anderson, artist, Allen Dale, author, ss, hc, 432 pgs	20.00
Gangsters In Action, 1451, 1938, Henry E. Vallely, artist, Issac McAnally, author, ss, hc, 432 pgs	20.00
Gene Autry And Raiders Of The Range, 1409, 1947, Till Goodman, author, ss, hc, 352 pgs	25.00
Little Big Shot Starring Sybil Jason, 1149, 1935, Warner Brothers Pictures, ss, hc, 240 pgs	7.00
Lone Ranger And The Black Shirt Highwayman, 1450, 1939, adapted from Fran Striker, ss, hc, 432 pgs	22.00
Lost Patrol Starring Victor McLaglan, 753, 1934, RKO Pictures, 4⅝ x 5¼ x ⅞″, hc, 160 pgs	18.00
Mac Of The Marines In China, 1400, 1938, Frank J. Hoban, artist, Mark Smith, author, ss, hc, 432 pgs . .	22.00
Mickey Mouse Runs His Own Newspaper, 1409, 1937, Floyd Gottfredson, artist and author, ss, hc, 432 pgs	28.00
Punch Davis Of The Aircraft Carrier, 1440, 1945, J. R. White, artist, Roy J. Snell, author, ss, hc, 352 pgs	7.00

Secret Agent X-9 And The Mad Assassin, 1472, 1938, Alex Raymond, artist, Robert Storm, author, ss, hc, 432 pgs 25.00

Smokey Stover The Foo Fighter, 1421, 1938, Bill Holman artist and author, ss, hc, 432 pgs 18.00

S.O.S. Coastguard, 1191, 1936, Henry E. Vallely, artist, William Engle, author, ss, hc, 432 pgs . . 12.00

This Is The Life, Jane Withers, 1179, 1935, 20th Century Fox, artist, Eleanor Packer, author, ss, hc, 240 pgs 21.00

Tom Beatty, Ace Of The Service And The Big Brain Gang, 1420, 1939, William Mark Young, artist, Rex Loomis, author, ss, hc, 432 pgs 13.00

BETTER LITTLE BOOKS

Andy Panda And The Pirate Ghosts, 1459, 1949, Walter Lantz Productions, ss, hc, 288 pgs 17.50

Blondie, No Dull Moments, 1450, 1948, Chic Young artist and author, ss, hc, 288 pgs 22.00

Bugs Bunny And The Giant Brothers, 706–10, 1949, Warner Brothers Productions, 3⅛ x 5½ x ⅝", hc, 200 pgs 18.00

Dick Tracy And The Bicycle Gang, 1445, 1948, Chester Gould, artist, Helen Berke, author, ss, hc, 288 pgs 19.00

Donald Duck And Ghost Morgan's Treasure, 1411, 1946, Carl Barks, artist and author, ss, hc, 352 pgs . 40.00

Gangster's Boy, Starring Jackie Cooper, 1402, 1939, Monogram Pictures, artist Karl Brown, Robert Andrews, author, ss, hc, 288 pgs . 17.50

Gun Law, Starring George O'Brien, 1418, 1938, RKO Pictures, artist, Eleanor Packer, author, ss, hc, 240 pgs 16.00

Little Orphan Annie And The Ancient Treasure Of AM, 1414, 1939, Harold Gray, artist and author, ss, hc, 432 pgs 19.00

Men With Wings Starring Fred MacMurray, 1475, 1938, Paramount Pictures, artist, Eleanor Parker, author, ss, hc, 240 pgs . . 12.00

Nancy And Sluggo, 1400, 1946, Ernie Bushmiller, artist and author, ss, hc, 352 pgs 35.00

Peggy Brown And The Secret Treasure, 1423, 1947, Henry E. Vallely, artist, Kathryn Heisenfelt, author, ss, hc, 288 pgs 15.00

Popeye And The Deep Sea Mystery, 1499, 1939, Elzie C. Seyar, artist and author, ss, hc, 432 pgs 32.00

Skyroads With Clipper Williams Of The Flying Legion, 1439, 1938, Russell Keaton, artist, Lt. Dick Calkins, author, ss, hc, 432 pgs . . 12.00

Smilin' Jack And The Jungle Pipe Line, 1419, 1947, Zack Mosley, artist, Helen Berke, author, ss, hc, 352 pgs 15.00

Uncle Wiggily's Adventures, 1405, 1946, Howard Garis author, ss, hc, 352 pgs 18.00

Woody Woodpecker, Big Game Hunter, 710-10, 1950, Walter Lantz Productions, 3⅛ x 5½ x ⅝", hc, 200 pgs 15.00

BISCUIT JARS

The biscuit or cracker jar was the forerunner of the cookie jar. They were made of various materials by many major glass makers and potteries. All items listed have silver plated mountings unless otherwise noted.
See also individual categories.

Wavecrest, 7¾" h to top of finial, floral transfer with pink, blue flowers, unsigned, $295.00.

Cranberry, 9 x 6¼", clear feet, 2 clear ring applied handles, clear flower prunt underneath, clear ribbed finial knob with prunt 165.00

Crown Milano, 7 x 5¼", satin finish, Burmese, flower and leaves outlined in heavy gold decor, white lining, mkd M.W., orig Mt. Washington paper label **695.00**

English

6⅛ x 5⅜", sq, green, lady in garden scene, pastel colors **88.00**

Creamy beige, hp, lavender, rose, maise florals, W. Wood & Co. Burslem **95.00**

Peach colored molded base shading to cream, Locke & Co. Shrubhill Works, Worcester, England **75.00**

Etched Glass, 5", round, cylindrical, 4 etched branches **110.00**

Florentine Cameo, white floral decor **225.00**

Jasperware, 5 x 5", round, blue, white biblical figures, Wedgwood/Made in England **225.00**

Lenox, 5½ x 4", narrow gold trim, wreath mark **75.00**

Majolica, bright green basketweave, red apples, leaves and twigs in relief, knob handles, wicker bale . . **58.00**

Moriage, melon shape, cream, pink roses and green leaves **130.00**

Satin Glass, green, Beaded Drape pattern **150.00**

Warwick, brown, Beech Nut pattern, logo mark **85.00**

Wavecrest

8½", creamy white to light yellow, hp florals, lid mk C.F.M. **375.00**

10", white, pink wild rose decor . **140.00**

BISQUE

Bisque or biscuit china is the name given to wares that have been fired once and are not glazed. Some were decorated with colors, and the body is soft and porous. Bisque figurines and busts were popular during the Victorian era. They were made by numerous potteries in the United States and abroad. Bisque wares are being produced today in Japan.

Box, egg shape, footed, windmill scene in relief **45.00**

Busts

15¾", Louis XVI and Marie Antoinette, blue porcelain pedestal base, late 19th C, pr **125.00**

23", young lady, blonde hair pulled back with ribbon, decollete striped bodice, pink rose between breasts, c1880 . . . . **550.00**

Dishes, condiment, 9½" l, painted, figural, reclining lady and gentleman, each supporting a boat shaped dish on shaped molded and gilded base, pr **200.00**

Fairy Lamp, castle **300.00**

Figures

9¾ x 4½" d, newsboy, light green cap and jacket, white shirt, tan pants, Heubach **155.00**

11 x 12" w, boy and girl seated on dark wood bench, girl holds metal cream parasol, cream dress and suit, pink flowers, green leaves **750.00**

11½ x 6½", girl dancing, blonde, blue sanded dress with white ruffles, gold trim, pastel base, imp Heubach mk **245.00**

17½", man and lady in 18th C costume under glass dome, on circular wood base, late 19th C **400.00**

23½", country girl going to market, baskets on yoke, ochre scarf, blue bodice, pink shawl, floral dress and apron, c1890 . **390.00**

Hatpin Holder, clown, 5½", figural, one leg forward **60.00**

Match Holder with striker, Dutch Girl, figural, copper and gold trim **32.00**

Figures, 9", peasant girl, green dress, pink purse, marked 959, $45.00.

Night Lights

3¼ x 3", cat head, brown glass
eyes, gray and white, pink collar 145.00

3⅝ x 3", lady head with hat,
brown glass eyes, pink hat, tan
leaves 190.00

3¾ x 3⅜", dog head, brown glass
eyes, tan and brown, black collar 165.00

Nodders, Sultan & Sultaness, 3¾ x
2½", soft green, pink robes, rust
hats, gold trim, pr 175.00

Piano Babies

4½", seated, holding apple, white
gown, yellow-green trim 65.00

5", lying on stomach, mkd
Heubach 225.00

Pin Cushion Half Doll, 8", gray hair,
arms extended, lavender pin cushion 195.00

Plaques, 10¼", scalloped and
waved edges, light green, white
figures, lady in 18th C dress, large
hat, holding basket, man playing
mandolin, pr 200.00

Salt With Matching Spoon, 2⅜ x 3"
d, walnut, figural, cream with
branch base 68.00

Shoe, blue flower, yellow center, lavender frill 50.00

Sugar Shaker, floral decor 60.00

Tobacco Jar, figural, shape of little
boy, hair forms cover, Heubach . 145.00

BLOWN THREE MOLD

The Jamestown colony in Virginia introduced glass making into America. The method used by the artisans was "free blown."

Blowing molten glass into molds was not introduced into America until the early 1800s. Blown Three Mold glass used a pre-designed mold that consisted of two, three, or more hinged parts. The glass maker placed a quantity of molten glass on the tip of a rod or tube, inserted it into the mold, blew air into the tube, waited until the glass cooled, and removed the finished product. The three part mold is the most common and lends its name to this entire category.

The impressed decorations on blown mold glass usually are reversed, i.e., what is raised or convex on the outside will be concave on the inside. This is a useful tool to identify the blown form.

The most detailed reference book remains George L. and Helen McKearn's *American Glass*. It still is available, being reprinted by Crown in 1975. The numbers used refer to the McKearn classification system.

By 1850 American made glassware was in relatively common usage. The increased de-

mand led to large factories and the creation of a technology which eliminated the smaller companies. Two leaders in production in the mid-nineteenth century were Boston and Sandwich Glass Co. and the New England Glass Co.

Pitcher, 7", quart, G-I-29, $600.00.

Celery Vase, Pittsburgh, G-V-21 ... 650.00

Condiment or Castor Bottles

3½", Mustard, clear, cylindrical
body with sloping shoulder,
rayed base — type VIIB, no cover, G-I-23 .... 55.00

4", Shaker, clear, sides spreading
to long rounded shoulder, plain
base, solid loop and turned
back end handle, pewter cover,
G-II-17 .... 60.00

4½", Cruet, clear, cylindrical body
with sloping shoulder, rayed
base — type I, small circular
stopper, G-V-5 .... 60.00

Cordial, clear, 2", drawn conical
body and hollow steam, heavy circular foot, ringed base — type III,
Sandwich, G-II-16 .... 250.00

Creamers

2½", miniature, cobalt blue, sunburst motif — pattern 7, ovoid
body, rayed and ring base —
type III, solid loop and crimped
end handle, G-III-21 .... 750.00

3", clear, semi-barrel body, sloping shoulder, rayed and ring base—type III, solid semi-ear shaped handle with crimped end and without heavy medial rib, G-III-21 .... **225.00**

3⅞", clear, ovoid body, diamond base—type XII with 15 diamonds, small solid loop handle with crimped end, G-II-18 .. **200.00**

Decanters, Pints

Blue, cylindrical body with sloping shoulder, plain base, pattern molded and expanded in ribbing, molded collar rib at base of neck, stopper, G-V-8 ...... **950.00**

Green, medium, flattened ovoid irregular body, plain base, G-II-7 **2,400.00**

Decanters, Quarts

"GIN," slender barrel body, no collar, ringed base—type I, stopper, G-I-8 .... **250.00**

Plain, barrel body, plain base, molded collar rib at base of neck, stopper, G-V-13 .... **150.00**

Dishes

6", clear, variety of body shapes and base markings, G-II-18 ... **50.00**

7", clear, sunburst motif, ringed base—type III, G-III-25 ...... **125.00**

7", sapphire blue, sunburst motif, ringed base—type III, G-III-25 . **1,000.00**

7⅞", yellow-green, circular sides rising vertically about 1" then flaring to folded rim, plain base, G-II-6 .... **5,500.00**

Flips

5⅛", clear, three body shapes and variety of bases, mahogany paddle, G-II-18 .... **100.00**

8½", clear, G-II-18 .... **650.00**

Goblet, clear, three bowl variations, applied stem and foot, rayed base —type VIA, G-II-19 .... **500.00**

Hats, Beaver

Clear, tapering crown, rayed base —type VI, G-II-18 .... **125.00**

Olive Green, tapering crown, diamond base—type X with 16 diamonds, G-II-18 .... **900.00**

Purple Blue, cylindrical crown with heavy band instead of brim, diamond base—type XI with 16 diamonds **550.00**

Inkwells

Gray Blue, drum, flat top, flat collar around small round mouth, plain base, G-II-15 .... **2,100.00**

Olive Amber, conical and drum, flat top, flat collar around small round mouth, plain base, G-II-16 **125.00**

Olive Amber, cylindrical and conical, rounded shoulder with flat top, flat collar around small round mouth, plain base, G-II-2 **125.00**

Olive Green, drum body, flat top, flat collar around small rounded mouth, plain base, G-II-18 .... **130.00**

Pitcher, 4⅛", sapphire blue, G-III-6, MUTZER FAKE **200.00**

Salts

Clear, geometric motif, rayed base —type IV, G-III-24, small chip . **180.00**

Clear, sunburst motif—pattern 4, plain base, G-III-13 .... **220.00**

Purple Blue, sunburst motif—pattern 11, ringed base—type III, G-II-25 .... **475.00**

Sapphire Blue, geometric motif, diamond base—type XII with 15 diamonds, G-II-18 .... **350.00**

Sugar Bowls, clear

Geometric motif, hemispherical bowl with galleried rim, diamond base, cover of swirled ribs with daimonds, G-III-18 .... **800.00**

Sunburst motif—pattern 9, hemispherical bowl with galleried rim, applied high pedestal foot, molded and expanded in ribbing, folded edge, rayed base, cover, G-III-20 .... **1,300.00**

Toilet Bottle, purple blue, tapering ovoid body, ringed base—type III, solid tam o'shanter type stopper, G-I-3 .... **125.00**

Tumblers

3", olive amber, geometric motif, diamond base, G-II-18 .... **650.00**

3¼", clear, geometric motif, diamond base, G-II-18 .... **200.00**

3¼", clear, geometric motif, rayed base—type VIA, G-II-19 ..... **175.00**

3¼", clear, shell and ribbing motif, plain base, G-V-8 .... **250.00**

Wine, clear, hemispherical bowl, applied solid knop stem with triangular knop, flat circular foot, G-II-18 . **300.00**

BOHEMIAN GLASS

The once independent country of Bohemia, now a part of Czechoslovakia, produced a variety of fine glassware—etched, cut, overlay and colored. Their glasswares were first imported into America in the early 1820s and continue today. Perhaps Bohemia is known for their "flashed" glass that was not only produced in the familiar ruby color, but also in amber, green, blue and black. Common patterns include "Deer and Pine Tree," "Deer and Castle" and "Vintage." Most of the Bohemian glass encountered in today's market is of the 1875-1900 period. A Bohemian type

glass was also made in England, Switzerland and Germany.

Basket, 5¼", pale red, cut to clear, fans, stars and thumb cutting, clear molded cut handle	68.00
Bell, 5", green, white overlay, cut, floral design	50.00
Bowls	
9", Deer & Pine Tree, ruby	75.00
Finger, Vintage, colbalt blue	30.00
Bread Plate, Deer & Pine Tree, ruby, etched, frosted and clear	50.00
Candlestick, 8½", ruby, brass base and socket	45.00
Candy Dish, cov, Deer & Castle, ruby	78.00
Celery Dish, Deer & Castle, ruby, c1875	75.00
Cologne Bottle, matching stopper, ruby, enameled yellow decor . . .	92.00
Compotes	
6½ x 6½", crystal, cobalt blue and white overlay pedestal, geometric designs	180.00
8½", 2 part, ruby overlay, cut to clear, alternating panels of bull's eye and stars at scrolling rim, 19th C, pr	330.00
Cordial Set, 6 glasses, ruby, cut to clear	125.00
Creamer, 3½", ruby, gold trim	85.00
Cruet, 6", ruby cut to clear, orig faceted stopper, applied clear notched handle	85.00
Decanters	
9", ruby, engraved, dimpled sides, high shoulders, pr	175.00
11⅛", clear, ruby glass overlay, thumb cut faceted sides swirling to base	50.00
15", red, cut glass, hand blown .	60.00
19", rose/beige, gold bands at neck, gold cartouche beneath, enamel blossoms, fluted tapered stopper with gilt scroll, pr	120.00
Epergne, 22", 3 pcs, red, cut to frosted, forest scene with deer, grape leaves border, faceted baluster base	450.00
Fairy Lamp, 4¾ x 3½", red, cut, diamond, matching base	150.00
Flask, 6", enameled lovebirds and florals, pewter mounts, 19th C . .	275.00
Girandoles, 14½", red glass, enamel with flowers, gilt borders, baluster bases suspending clear faceted lustres, pr	300.00
Goblets	
7½", cranberry, gold and enamel decor, artist sgd	125.00
7½", deep pink, hp gold decor on top, c1895	60.00

Tumbler, 3¹¹/₁₆" h, ruby, grapes, vines, leaves, $35.00.

Jar, 6", cov, ruby, etched leaf and bird, gold trim	55.00
Lamps, ruby, etched base with brass and marble, pr	150.00
Mantel Lustre, 12¾", ruby, engraved with deer, building and latticework cartouches, suspending triangular prisms, pr	225.00
Muffineers	
Blue, cut	100.00
Ruby, cut	160.00
Perfume Bottle, 5¼", ruby, paneled sides, cut stopper	110.00
Pitcher, 7¾", Deer & Castle, ruby, clear applied handle	100.00
Plate, 8½", Deer & Castle, ruby . . .	80.00
Powder Box, 4¼" d, round, straight sides, flat top, cover etched to clear with leaping stag in a forest setting, sides have landscape and birds, clear glass bottom	50.00
Rose Bowl, 8½" d, Deer & Castle, ruby	200.00
Salt, Vintage, ruby, gold trim, scroll feet	25.00
Sherbert Glass, short stem, ruby to clear, etched	40.00
Steins	
3½", ruby and clear, etched	75.00
6", Deer & Pine Tree, ruby, pewter fittings	275.00
Sugar, cov, amber, etched hunting scene	150.00
Tumble-Up, 8¼", cobalt blue to clear, etched, floral and leaf decor	85.00
Tumblers	
5", Deer and Pine Tree, ruby	44.00
Footed, blood red, hp, heavy gold and white floral overall	65.00

Urn, 20", cov, ruby, white overlay, cut floral decor	275.00

Vases

7", Wildlife, amber, etched and frosted	110.00
8½", ruby, 2 gilt rimmed enamel panels, one a seated man writing, other a spray of forget-me-nots, gilt scrollwork	185.00
10", bulbous base, ruby, clear and engraved, cut, circles, scrolls, thumbcut and diaper	150.00
10", ruby, etched butterflies, pr . .	150.00
10¼", urn shape, round stepped base, ruby overlay, cut and etched, birds, thumb cut, diamond .	100.00
11½", Birds and Palm Trees, ruby	125.00
12½", ruby, overlaid, faceted flaring neck, arcaded panel sides, pr	175.00
13 x 4", ruby, frosted, dog retreiving bird, gold trim, pr . . .	75.00
Water Set, pitcher, 6 glasses, Deer & Castle, etched	175.00
Wine Glasses, cut to clear, hobstars, fans and flowers, clear fluted stems, set of 12	300.00

BONE

Items carved from dried animal bones are desirable collector's items. Some bone items are being misrepresented as ivory on today's market and buyers should use caution.

Napkin Ring, ⅞" h, 1½" d, $20.00.

Bookmark, 2½", floral top	18.00
Butter Paddle, 16", made entirely of panbone	225.00
Dominoes, bone & ebony, boxed . .	80.00
Figure, bear, 2¼", in relief	72.00
Glove Stretcher, 6½"	28.00

Jogging Wheel, 6½" l, inlaid with abalone shell squares and diamonds	300.00
Lance Head, fitted with whalebone handle, 9½", used as flensing tool	120.00
Lantern for candle, 8¼", whalebone, sq, sits on round base	1,500.00
Needlecase, ornate carvings, Niagara Falls pictured	75.00
Netsuke, bat on leaf	125.00
Pin Cushion, carved, painted design	45.00
Ship, model of American ship of war *North Carolina*, 20 x 23½", guns run out on 3 decks, elaborate detail, sits on teakwood base with inlays of MOP	3,000.00

BOOKENDS

Bookends have been, and are made of every conceivable shape, size, form and material imaginable. Very popular in the early 1900s, those of Art Nouveau and Art Deco designs are highly collectible and command high prices.

Cast metal, Sailing Ships, 5" h, 5" w, *Constitution,* three masted, $35.00.

Brass

Elephants, sgnd, pr	50.00
Horse with saddle, grazing, pr . . .	45.00
Horsehead, 6¾ x 7½", horseshoe shaped base, mkd PMC and numbered, pr	80.00
Indian, 8 x 5", full headdress, pr .	100.00

Bronze

German Shepherd, 4 x 5", reclining	80.00
Nude, 6¼", Art Nouveau	100.00
Woman Buddha, 5½ x 6", figural, sgnd Tiffany, pr	350.00

Cast Iron

Columned building entrance, bronzed, Bradley & Hubbard, pr	22.00
Pirate Ship, 6", painted, pr	50.00

Cast Metal

Birds, black with celluloid beaks, pr	65.00

Bowlers, ready to throw ball, 5¾ x 3¾ x 2¼", rectangular base, mkd W B in shield, pr	55.00
Elephant, bronzed, Art Deco, pr	30.00
Golfer swinging club, 5 x 4", figural, Art Deco	350.00
Lindbergh, 6", pr	65.00
Nudes, kneeling, Art Deco, pr	38.00
Teddy Roosevelt, 6", pr	45.00
Chalkware, Raggedy Ann and Andy, 5½", P.F. Vollard, c1931, pr	35.00
Chrome, Terrier dogs, 4¼", stand on round base, c1920 pr	95.00
Copper, parrot, 5½ x 6¼", figural, pr	60.00
Glass, molded	
Eagle, Cambridge, pr	140.00
Elephants, pr	45.00
Ivory, Southern Belles, seated, figural, sgnd Rockwood, 1935, pr	95.00
Pottery	
Owls, 5", turquoise, Van Briggle, pr	145.00
Peacocks, dark rose, Van Briggle, pr	95.00
Soapstone	
Chinese, pr	45.00
Dragons, pr	50.00
Teakwood, elephant head, 10", ivory trim, pr	100.00

BOOKS, AMERICANA

America's fascination with local, regional, state and national history owes its origin to the nation's centennial in 1876. The next thirty years witnessed a proliferation of histories, atlases, genealogies and photographic studies. Historical groups organized and published pamphlets or annual studies. A renewal of interest in local history occurred with the historic preservation movement of the 1950s forward. As communities and states celebrated the 50th, 75th, 100th, 150th, 200th, and more anniversary of their establishment, committees organized celebrations, one byproduct of which was a local history publication.

The number of books and pamphlets ranges in the hundreds of thousands. Pennsylvania has been chosen as a typical example. Readers are asked to compare what they have to the items cited. The prices are approximately the same nationally for the identical type of material. More recent publications within the last twenty-five years, rarely are valued above their initial selling price.

An exception to this rule is Western Americana where recent editions and texts are eagerly sought after. Books about the opening of the West, cowboys, Indians, and outlaws have been popular with collectors for nearly a century. They are adventurous historical tales full of vitality and spirit. Especially valuable are the early (pre-1860) travel accounts and first editions with illustrations of famous western artists, e.g., Frederic Remington and Charles Russell.

Please remember that condition is perhaps the greatest factor in properly pricing a book. Also, local and region books will bring slightly higher prices in the areas to which their subjects relate.

See *Warman's Americana and Collectibles* for additional listings in Miniature Books, Paperback Books, and Western Americana.

PENNSYLVANIANA

American Philosophical Society. *Calender of Correspondence In The America Philosophical Society Library Relating To The American Revolution:* Generals George Weedon, Nathaniel Green, Arthur Lee, and Richard Henry Lee. Philadelphia, 1900. 255 pgs, wraps	8.00
Ashburton Coal Company. *Prospectus & Reports On The Company's Estate In Schuylkill And Luzerne Counties, Pennsylvania.* New York, 1864. 16 pgs, map, plain paper wraps	22.00
Atlases	
Forest County, Pennsylvania. Smith, Philadelphia, 1877	30.00
Luzerne County Atlas. Beers, Pomeroy & Co., Philadelphia, 1873. 183 pgs.	150.00
York Atlas Of The City Of York, Pennsylvania. Roe, Philadelphia, 1903. 22 double page colored property maps	80.00
Barber, Edwin Atlee. *Tulip Ware Of The Pennsylvania-German Potters.* Philadelphia, 1903. 233 pgs, color frontis, illus, printed wraps	42.50
Brodhead, L. W. *The Delaware Water Gap: Its Scenery, Its Legends And Early History.* 2nd ed, Philadelphia, 1870. 276 pgs, color chromolithograph frontis.	50.00
Carmer, Carl. *The Susquehanna.* New York, 1955. 493 pgs, illus, dj. Volume in Rivers of America series.	22.50
Condit, Uzal W. *The History Of Easton, Pennsylvania 1739–1885.* Easton, 1889. 500 pgs, illus.	100.00
Day, Sherman. *Historical Collections Of The State Of Pennsylvania.* Philadelphia, 1846. 708 pgs, 165 wood engravings	55.00

Egle, Dr. William H. *An Illustrated History Of The Commonwealth Of Pennsylvania. . . . Harrisburg, 1876.* 1,186 pgs, illus, orig ½ morocco, thick 4to 44.00

Ferguson, Russell J. *Early Western Pennsylvania Politics.* Pittsburgh, 1838. 300 pgs, illus. 20.00

Frackenthal, Dr. B. F., Jr. *The Durham Iron Works.* Buckingham Friends Meeting, Holicong, PA, 1932. 34 pgs. 12.00

Gibson, John. *History Of York County, Pennsylvania.* Chicago, 1886. 979 pgs, litho plates, ½ morocco, thick 4to 160.00

Hain, Harry H. *History Of Perry County, Pennsylvania.* Harrisburg, 1922. 1,088 pgs. 150.00

Hoenstine, Floyd G. *Soldiers Of Blair County, Pennsylvania.* Holidaysburg, 1940. 426 pgs. 24.00

Hudson Coal Co. *The Story Of Anthracite.* New York, 1932. 425 pgs. 18.00

Illick, Joseph S. *Pennsylvania Trees.* Harrisburg, 1914. 232 pgs, 100 plates 12.00

Jenkins, Howard M. *Historical Collections Relating To Gwynedd, A Township Of Montgomery County, Pennsylvania.* Philadelphia, 1884. 400 pgs, illus, rebound 70.00

Johnson, W. Fletcher. *History Of The Johnstown Flood: With Full Account Of The Destruction Of The Susquehanna And Juniata Rivers.* Philadelphia, 1889. 459 pgs, illus. 12.50

Keith, Charles P. *Provincial Councillors Of Pennsylvania 1733–76.* Philadelphia, 1883. 476 pgs, uncut 85.00

Lambert, James H. *Pennsylvania At The Jamestown Exposition, 1907.* Philadelphia, 1908. 360 pgs, illus. 14.00

Lambert, M. B. *A Dictionary Of The Non-English Words Of The Pennsylvania German Dialect.* Pennsylvania German Society, Lancaster, 1924. 187 pgs. 36.00

Lytle, Milton S. *History Of Huntingdon County, Pennsylvania.* Lancaster, 1876. 361 pgs. 75.00

McKinney, Wm. W. *Early Pittsburgh Presbyterianism . . . 1758–1839.* Pittsburgh, 1938. 345 pgs, map . . 14.00

Meginness, John F. *Biographical Annuals Of Lancaster County: Biographical And Genealogical Sketches Of Prominent Citizens & Early Settlers.* Chicago, 1906. 1,524 pgs, illus, ½ morocco 100.00

Myers, Elizabeth L. *The Story Of*

The Gemein Haus. Bethlehem, 1924. 12 pgs, printed wraps 8.00

Nicklin, Phillip. *A Pleasant Pereginátion Through The Prettiest Parts Of Pennsylvania Performed By Peregrine Prolix.* Philadelphia, 1836. 148 pgs, orig publisher's cloth 75.00

Norristown, Pennsylvania — 100th Anniversary Souvenir. Norristown, 1912. 42 pgs, illus, wraps 6.00

Pennypacker, Samuel W. *The Autobiography Of A Pennsylvanian.* Philadelphia, 1918. 564 pgs, illus. 16.00

Rahn, Claude J. *Genealogical Information Regarding The Families Of Brubaker, Bomberger & Fogelsanger.* Vero Beach, FL, 1952. 105 pgs, printed wraps 25.00

Rogers, Henry D. *The Geology Of Pennsylvania.* Vol. I (of 2), Philadelphia, 1858. 586 pgs, litho plates, large 4to 80.00

Rupp, I. D. *History Of Northampton, Lehigh, Monroe, Carbon, And Schuylkill Counties . . .* Harrisburg, 1845. 582 + 69 pgs, 5 Sinclair lithographs 70.00

Shoemaker, Henry Wharton. *North Mountain Mementoes: Legends And Traditions Gathered In Northern Pennsylvania.* Altoona, 1920. 383 pgs, illus, clothbound 34.00

Warren, B. H. *Report On The Birds Of Pennsylvania.* 2nd ed, Harrisburg, 1890. 434 pgs, 100 color chromolithograph plates 80.00

WESTERN AMERICANA

Andrist, Ralph K. *The Long Death: The Last Days Of The Plains Indians.* 1st ed, New York, 1964. 382 pgs, maps by Rafel D. Palacios, illus, dj 25.00

Brininstool, E. A. (ed.). *Crazy Horse, The Invincible Oglalla Sioux Chief . . .* Los Angeles, 1949. 88 pgs, illus, 12mo, autographed by author 60.00

Bronson, Edgar B. *Cowboy Life On The Western Plains: Reminiscences Of A Ranchman.* 1st ed, New York, 1910. 370 pgs, illus. . . 28.00

Burns, Walter N. *The Saga Of Billy The Kid.* Garden City, 1926. 322 pgs, Edward Borein illus. on end papers 8.50

Coe, U. C. *Frontier Doctor.* Macmillan Co., 1939. 264 pgs. 9.00

Clum, Woodworth. *Apache Agent: The Story of John P. Clum.* Houghton Mifflin, 1936. 297 pgs, illus. 55.00

Dobie, J. Frank. *Apache Gold And Yaqui Silver.* New York, 1939. 384 pgs, illus. by Tom Lea **18.50**

Eagle, Chief D. *Winter Count.* Boulder, 1967. dj. **10.00**

Fellows, Muriel H. *The Land Of Little Rain: A Story Of Hopi Indian Children.* 1st ed, New York, 1936. 122 pgs, color illus. by author **12.00**

Fletcher, Sydney E. *The Cowboy And His Horse.* New York, 1951. 160 pgs. intro by Joseph Henry Jackson, drawings by author **17.50**

Griffith, A. Kenney *Free (Mickey) Manhunter.* 1st ed, Caldwell, Idaho, 1969. 240 pgs, photos **15.00**

Hardin, John W. *Life Of John Wesley Hardin . . . By Himself.* 1st ed, Seguin, TX, 1896. 144 pgs, illus, 12 mo, wraps **125.00**

Harris, Burton. *John Colter: His Years In The Rockies.* 1st ed, Scribners, 1952 . . . . **13.00**

Hodge, Frederick W. *Handbook Of American Indians North Of Mexico.* 1st ed, 2 vols, Washington, D.C., 1907 and 1910. . . . . **80.00**

Hyde, George E. *Pawnee Indians.* 1st ed, Denver, 1951. 318 pgs, illus, fldg maps **47.50**

Iliff, Flora Gregg. *People Of The Blue Water: My Adventures Among The Walapi And Havasupai Indians.* New York, 1954. 284 pgs, illus, map **22.50**

James, Wharton Geo. *The Wonders Of The Colorado Desert.* 2 vols, Little Brown, 1906. 300 + pen and ink sketches of nature **75.00**

Lathrop, Amy. *Tales Of Western Kansas.* Larue Printing Co., Kansas City, MO, 1948. Sgd by author **18.00**

Lyford, Carrie A. *Iroquois Crafts.* Lawrence, 1945. 98 pgs, map, illus, wraps **10.00**

Marcy, Randolph B. *Paraire Traveler: A Handbook For Overland Expeditions: With Maps, Illustrations, And Itineraries Of The Principal Routes Between The Mississippi And The Pacific.* New York, 1859. 340 pgs, 12 mo. **225.00**

Materson, V. V. *The Katy Railroad And Last Frontier.* 1st ed, Univ. Of Oklahoma Press, 1952 . . . . **15.00**

Monaghan, Jay. *The Overland Trail.* 1st ed, Indianapolis, 1947. 432, pgs, plates, maps **35.00**

Penrose, Charles B. *The Rustler Business.* 1st ed, Douglas, Wyoming, 1959. 56 pgs, edition limited to 500 copes **60.00**

Post, C. C. *Ten Years A Cowboy.*

Rhodes & McClure, 1895. . . . . . . **24.00**

Paxson, Fred L. *History Of American Frontier, 1763–1893.* 1st ed, Houghton Mifflin, 1924. . . . . **22.50**

Rascoe, Burton. *Belle Star: The Bandit Queen.* 1st ed, Random House, 1941 . . . . **17.50**

Remington, Frederic. *Crooked Trails.* 1st ed, New York, 1898. 49 plates, pictorial tan cloth **125.00**

———. *Drawings.* 1st ed, New York, 1897. 61 plates, oblong folio, pictorial boards and cloth . . . **250.00** +

——— *John Ermie Of The Yellowstone.* 1st ed, New York, 1902. Brown cloth. (Note: First edition copies, as well as reprints, misspell the author's name "Reminigton" on spine.) **75.00**

Rollins, Philip Ashton. *The Cowboy: His Characteristics, His Equipment, And His Part In The Development Of The West.* New York, 1922. 368 pgs. **22.00**

Russell, Charles M. *Good Medicine.* 1st ed, New York, 1930. Intro. by Will Rogers, cloth, dj. **150.00**

———. *Pen Sketches.* 1st ed, Great Falls, 1898. 12 plates, oblong, leatherette **800.00**

Sabin, Edwin L. *Gold! A Tale of Great And Romantic Adventurings By Argonauts Upon Sea And Land, etc.* 1st ed, Philadelphia, 1929. 336 pgs, illus. **15.50**

Shipp, Richard E. *Intermountain Folk Songs Of Their Days And Ways.* 1st ed, Casper Stationary Co., Wyoming, 1922. Illus. in color **30.00**

Shirley, Glenn. *Six-Gun And Silver Star.* 1st ed, Albuquerque, 1955. 236 pgs, maps **21.00**

Talbot, Ethelbert. *My People Of The Plains.* 1st ed, Illustrated Harper, Nov. 1906 . . . . **15.00**

Vestal, Stanley. *New Sources of Indian History, 1850–1891.* Univ. Of Oklahoma Press, 1934 . . . . . . **55.00**

Wells, Edmund. *Argonaut Tales.* Grafton Press, Published by Fredr. Hitchcock, 1927. Illus. by Evan T. Wilson **25.00**

BOOT JACKS

Various types of Boot Jacks were made to facilitate the removal of boots. Some were constructed of wood while others were made of metals such as brass or iron. Two of the popular designs were the "Beetle" and "Naughty Nellie."

Wood, metal, spring mechanism, 15″ l, $50.00.

Brass
Beetle, 10″ 85.00
Naughty Nellie 85.00
Cast Iron
American Bull Dog, pistol shape, 8⅜″ l 90.00
Bowed type, "C. Hull, Birmingham" and "Regd. Boot Jack" on back, 7″ 25.00
Beetle, hand forged, c1890, 12½″ 40.00
Center design, Downs and Co., 13″ 30.00
Double Strength, beetle type . . . 10.00
Horse, stylized 105.00
Horseshoe 25.00
Mechanical, carpet cov, movable jaws to grip boot, Pat 1850 . . . 50.00
Naughty Nellie, 9¾″ 45.00
"Try It" 25.00
Portable
Primitive, 16″ 25.00
Walnut, cast iron frame, carpeted top 45.00
Wooden
Folk art monkey, painted suit, c1900, 15″ l 30.00
Mahogany, George III, early 19th C, 16″ l 225.00
Maple
Hand hewn, 13″ l 12.00
Leather cuff in cut out, 12″ l . . 18.00
Pine, oval ends with square nails, 25″ 25.00

BOTTLES

APOTHECARY—See Apothecary Items

AVON BOTTLES

David H. McConnell founded the California Perfume Co. in 1886. He hired saleswomen, a radical concept for that time. These women used a door-to-door technique to sell their first product, "Little Dot," a set of five perfumes; thus was born the "Avon Lady." In 1979 there were more than one million. In 1929, the California Perfume Co. became the Avon Company. In the 1960s Avon began to attract collector interest. Prices are for full containers, in mint and boxed condition.

See *Warman's Americana & Collectibles* for an expanded listing of Avon Bottles.

Early Items

Eau de Quinine, glass bottle, cork stopper, metal cup, front label of Eureka California Perfume trade mark, 1908 . . . . 125.00
Face Lotion, 6 oz glass bottle, cork stopper, green front, neck label, small sponge tied to neck, 1918 . 85.00
Massage Cream, glass jar, glass stopper, Art Nouveau label, 1896 135.00
Perfumes
Atomizer, green opaque, gold plated top, 1928 . . . . 85.00
Cut glass, 2 oz, crab apple blossom, white leatherette box, 1918 . . . . 215.00
Violet Perfume, Eureka trade mark, 1900 . . . . 175.00
Rose Pomade, white glass jar, script label, 1914 . . . . 60.00
Rose Water, Glycerine & Benzoin, 6 oz waisted, cork stopper, 1924 . . 90.00
Tooth Wash, glass bottle, cork stopper, metal crown top, Eureka trade mark on neck label, 1908 . 135.00

Figurals

Alaskan Moose, 1974 . . . . 7.50
Candlestick Cologne, 3 oz, 1966 . . 10.00
Fairy Tale Frog, 1976 . . . . 2.50
Jaquar Car, jade green glass, green plastic trunk, 1974 . . . . 5.00

Figural Avon Bottle, Country Style Coffee Pot, 10 oz, hand lotion, $11.75.

MG 1936, red painted glass, red plastic cap, white plastic top, 1975 .... 5.00

Parlor Lamp, white milk glass base, amber glass shade, 1971 ...... 8.00

Rainbow Trout, green glass, green plastic head, 1973 .... 5.00

Snowmobile, blue, yellow plastic front, 1974 .... 6.50

Studebaker '51, blue glass, 1975 .. 2.00

Town Pump, black glass, gold cap, plastic handle, 1968 .... 5.00

Uncle Sam Pipe, white opal glass, blue band, blue plastic stem, 1975 .... 6.00

Western Boot After Shave, dark amber glass, 1974 .... 4.00

BARBER BOTTLES

Barber bottles are disappearing from the American scene, as the old time barber shop has been replaced by its modern counterpart. The barber, in days gone by, was a very important person in town, and he often took the part of doctor and dentist. His "bench bottles," as they were called, were cared for and replenished by him when his supplies ran low; and, he knew what each bottle contained by its color and form. The older barber bottles were usually imported from Europe, and American bottles were made from the 1860s through 1900. The earliest American bottles were Hobnail, the rarest of which were crystal or clear Hobnail, opalescent hobnail, swirl, and striped, and amberina. These bottles are being reproduced, especially in the opalescent colors.

Amber, hobnail 75.00
Amethyst 50.00
   Enameled decor, IVT, blown 50.00
   Enameled floral decor, ribbed ... 195.00
   Paneled, applied lip, 7¼" h 95.00
Blown
   Amber, DQ 75.00
   Canary 30.00
   Clear, paneled 50.00
   Green, DQ 75.00
   Green, olive, enamel decor 65.00
Blue
   Sapphire, paneled, applied lip, 7½" 90.00
   White enamel flowers, orange, gilt 60.00
Bohemian, 8½", ruby, enamel floral decor 75.00
Bristol, 9½", black enamel decor ... 50.00
Clambroth, enameled pinwheel decor, orig pewter stopper 80.00
Cranberry
   Enameled floral decor, 8¾" h .. 95.00
   IVT, no stopper 80.00
   Opal, hobnail, polished pontil, c1900 .... 110.00

Milk Glass; (Left) Bay Rum, 9½" h, pink banding, lighthouse scene; (Right) Tonic, 9½" h, bright gray banding, cabin scene, both personalized for Frank Lambert, marked W.T. & Co. #52, pr, $2,000.00.

Cut Glass
   Pewter top, 5" 45.00
   Sterling top 135.00
Green
   Enamel floral decor, pewter stopper 115.00
   Irid, orig. stopper 135.00
*Hobnail
   Cobalt 100.00
   Vaseline 95.00
Mary Gregory-type
   Amethyst, girl 185.00
   Cobalt, white enamel boy chasing butterfly 195.00
Milk Glass
   "Bay Rum," name in tall letters, painted flowers 50.00
   "Witch Hazel," tall tapering, fluted base, space for label 50.00
Opalescent
   *Hobnail, white 75.00
   *Swirl 85.00
Satin Glass
   10½", cranberry with white looping, pewter stopper 225.00
   10½", DQ, MOP, one pink, one blue, original pewter stoppers, pair 800.00
   *Spanish Lace, 8½", cranberry ... 85.00
   Spatter glass, orig stopper 320.00
Wedgwood, tri-color, four cameos of classical scenes 750.00

BEER BOTTLES

Beer was bottled in the United States as early as 1860. Perhaps the earliest beer containers were hand thrown pottery, later blown glass and eventually mass produced machine made.

See *Warman's Americana & Collectibles* for an expanded listing of Beer Bottles.

Ashland Brewing Co, blob top, amber	12.00
Born & Co, Columbus, OH, amber, qt	8.00
Consumers Ice Co, porcelain spring, stopper	9.00
Falstaff Lemp, amber	5.00
Gutsch Brew Co, 8½" h, red	14.00
Haefner's Brewing, amber	24.75
Massachusetts Breweries Co, Boston, amber, crown top, 9½"	4.00
Pabst Brewing Co. of Milwaukee, amber, 12"	8.00
Ruff's Quincy Beer, amber	8.00
Southern Brewing Co, green	3.50
Wisconsin Select Beer, aqua	6.00

Pilser's Maltcrest Brew, Pilser Brewing Co. Inc, Bronx, NY, 12 oz., $7.00.

BITTERS BOTTLES

Our forebearers did not have the medical treatment that we are lucky enough to have today, so they leaned very heavily on patent medicines. Bitters, a "remedy" made from natural herbs and other mixtures, had an alcoholic base, and was said to cure anything. It was made by hundreds of different makers, put in most intriguingly-shaped and colored bottles, and highly advertised by almanacs, advertising cards, and other methods used in those days. Their names were imaginative, (though they seldom did what their makers

claimed for them), but people had faith in them. Alcohol was never mentioned. In 1907 when the Pure Foods Regulations went into effect, "an honest statement of content on every label" put most of these manufacturers out of business.

References: *Bitters Bottles*, Richard Watson, 1965, (RW); *Bitters Bottles*, J. H. Thompson, (JHT)

Rohrer's Bitters Expectoral Wild Cherry Tonic, Lancaster, PA, ¾qt, square tapering sides, rope side edging, emb 4 sides in beehive design, name, $75.00

Abbott's Bitters, amber, 8"	7.00
Acorn Bitters, amber, 5-star, JHT	200.00
African Stomach Bitters, amber, 9½"	40.00
Alther's, Dr., lady's leg shape, clear	45.00
Amazon Bitters, amber, 5-star, JHT	200.00
American Life Bitters, cabin shape, lt amber, P. Eiler Mfg.	175.00
Appetine Bitters, Geo. Benz & Sons, St. Paul, MN, orig label, 7½"	20.00
Argyle Bitters, dark amber, 5-star, JHT	200.00
Atherton's, Dr., Dewdrop Bitters, lt. honeyamber	125.00
Ayala Mexican Bitters, amber, 9½"	75.00
Baker's High Life Bitters, pint	24.00
Ball's, Dr., Vegetable Stomach Bitters, aqua	100.00
Barber's Indian Veg. Jaundice Bitters, 12-sided, aqua	80.00

Bavarian Bitters, amber	75.00
Belle of Anderson, amber	60.00
Bell's, Dr., Blood Purifying Bitters, amber	125.00
Belmont Tonic Herb Bitters, amber .	75.00
Bender's Bitters, aqua	50.00
Bennet's Wild Cherry Bitters	45.00
Berliner Magen Bitters, green	85.00
Berry's Vegetable Bitters, sq, amber, iron pontil	35.00
Bird Bitters, Phila. Pa, clear	75.00
Blake's, Dr., Aromatic Bitters, aqua	75.00
Boerhane's, Dr., Stomach Bitters, lt. olive green	75.00
Boneset Bitters	35.00
Boston Malt Bitters, round, green . .	45.00
Botanic Bitters amber	45.00
Bourbon Whiskey Bitters, barrel shape, yellow olive, 9″	200.00
Brady's Family Bitters, olive amber .	50.00
Brown's Celebrated Indian Herb, figural Indian head, amber	295.00
Bull, John, Cedron Bitters, sq, clear	70.00
Bull's Genuine Wild Cherry Bitters, embossed, clear, extremely rare, (one to five specimens known), c. 1890, JHT, P.21, #54	350.00
Burgundy Bitters, amber	100.00
Burton's Stomach Bitters, amber . .	100.00
Calabash Bitters, aqua	75.00
Caldwell's Herb Bitters, amber, 12⅝″	195.00
California Wine Bitters, olive green .	75.00
Capital Bitters, Fredonia, NY, aqua .	45.00
Carpathian Herb Bitters, amber . . .	40.00
Carter's Liver Bitters, amber	75.00
Castilian Bitters, lt. honey amber . .	100.00
Catawba Wine Bitters, emb grape cluster, green	85.00
Celebrated Crown Bitters, (Chevalier), amber	125.00
Celebrated Parkers Bitters-Stomach, tapered top, amber	100.00
Celery Tonic Bitters, paper label, clear	15.00
Clarke's Vegetable Sherry Wine Bitters, rect, aqua	45.00
Columbo Peptic Bitters, amber	28.00
Damiana Bitters, aqua	25.00
Doyle's Hop, 1872, amber	20.00
Drake's Plantation, cabin shape, 6 logs, olive amber	140.00
Eagle Aromatic Bitters, amber	25.00
Excelsior Aromatic Bitters, smoky amber	100.00
Fowler's Stomach Bitters, lt. amber .	100.00
Gilbert's, Dr., Rock and Rye Bitters, bluish-green	100.00
Hanlon's Tuna Bitters, clear amethystine	50.00
Hentz's Curative Bitters, pale green	100.00
Johnson's Indian Dyspeptic Bitters, aqua	75.00
Kaufmann's Celebrated Anti-Cholera Bitters, puce	125.00
Kickapoo Bitters, Indian Sagwa, (part of label still on), aqua	150.00
Niagara Star Bitters, sq, amber . . .	90.00
Night Cap Bitters, 3-sided, clear . . .	80.00
Old Homestead Wild Cherry Bitters, amber, shape of tall log cabin . . .	200.00
Old Jamaica Stomach Bitters, handled jug	175.00
Poor Man's Family, rect, aqua	35.00
Radium Bitters, rect, clear	20.00
Reed's Bitters, round, amber	145.00
Richardson, Dr. S.O., green	35.00
Seaworth Bitters, lighthouse shape .	275.00
Stanley's, Dr., South American Indian Bitters, amber	85.00
Star Kidney & Liver Bitters, sq.	55.00
Turkish Bitters, amber	75.00
Uncle Tom's Bitters, lt. amber	75.00
Von Humboldt's Stomach Bitters, sq, amber	80.00
Whitwell's Temperance Bitters, aqua or clear green, very early, 1847, 5-star, one of top ten	350.00

FIGURAL BOTTLES

Bottles which are shaped in any recognizable form, such as animals, objects, people, are known as figural bottles. Such bottles, in the past, could have held anything from perfume to vinegar. Many new ones are coming on the market, which in time, will become collectible.

See *Warman's Americana & Collectibles* for an expanded listing of Figural Bottles.

Bear, black, Kummel type	65.00
Bulldog, sitting up, blue	20.00
Bullfrog, seated	85.00
Carrie Nation, with satchel, clear . .	110.00
Cat, porcelain	45.00
Cigar, amber	32.00
Clock, clear glass, paper dial under glass, metal cap, US in relief on back, 5 x 4½″	90.00
Crying Baby, Pat 1874	49.00
Cucumber, 6″, pottery, green	40.00
Ear of Corn, 6½″, good old paint, metal screw top	25.00
Elk's tooth, milk glass	55.00
Fox Trot, couple dancing, bisque front, tree trunk back made in Germany	120.00
Hand, clear, 5″	232.00
Henry Ward Beecher, Pat. 1874 . . .	59.00
Klondyke flask, milk glass, orig cap	125.00
Leprechaun	25.00
Monkey, wrapped around green bottle	30.00
Nineteenth Hole, golfer in yellow suit, 3⅝″ h x 3¾″ w	85.00

6½" h, Sailor, cartoon, high gloss front, white pants, blue blouse, hat, image back, made in Germany, $95.00.

Nude, frosted, French, 13½", standing in foliage	50.00
Owl, orange clear glass, painted face, feet, 8" h	55.00
Pickwick, coat, and spectacles, vinegar	50.00
Poodle, sitting on a hassock	45.00
Potato, 5", emb, "World's Fair, 1893"	35.00
Slipper, clear glass, 5¼"	33.00
Your Health, flask shape, bisque front, tree bark back, jolly man toasting 4½ x 4" w	68.00

FOOD BOTTLES

Ketchup, Heinz, urn shaped, blob top, 7"	12.50

Milk

Abbots Dairy, Conway, NH, round, emb, qt	8.00
Badger Farm Creameries, Portsmouth, NH, round, emb, qt	8.00
Bay State Creamery, Salem, tin top, ½ pint	20.00
Cherry Hill Farm, Beverly, MA, round, emb, ½ pint	5.00
Chestnut Farms, Chevy Chase Dairy, Wash., DC, round, emb, qt	15.00
Dairylee Milk, Our New Baby, sq, quart, double baby face, red, orange letters	25.00
Dominick Bava, Pittsfield, MA, round, emb, qt	8.50
Frates Bros. Dairy, MA seal, round, emb, qt	5.00
Hillmans Dairy, Sunnydale Farms, ME seal, round, pyro, qt	4.00
New Jersey Milk Products Co. Inc., Penns Grove, NJ	8.00
Pratt, W. M., Farmington, ME, round, emb, pint	5.00
Oakhurst Dairy Store, emb in script, ME seal, round pint	3.00
Shady Hill Dairy, William L. Turner, Tubercular Tested, round, emb, qt	10.00
Universal Store Bottle, 5¢, round, emb, pint	4.00
Waterville Dairy, Waterville, ME, R. J. Gagnon, round, pyro, qt	5.00

Milk Bottle, R. M. Deger, Phoenixville, PA, Pure Milk, 9½ x 3¾", $2.50.

Peanut Butter, Jumbo, emb elephant, writing, 1 lb jar	2.00
Pepper Sauce, E. R. D. & Co., Pat. Feb. '77, green, 8"	30.00
Pickles, Cathedral Arches, sq, aqua, 7½"	65.00
Vinegar, White House, light green, round, emb bottom, 9" h, cork top	1.50

INK BOTTLES

Early ink bottles were made of ceramics and glass, designed to be "tip-proof." Most were imported. They were first used in America in the early 1800s.

See *Warman's Americana & Collectibles* for an expanded listing of Ink Bottles.

Umbrella style, octagonal base, open pontil, light teal, 2½", $35.00.

Antoine Et Fils, 8¾ x 3", pottery, glazed brown pouring lip	10.00
Aqua, 3", round, applied lip and collar, c1880	8.50
Boss Brothers, 2⅛", conical stoneware, imp Vitreous Bottles, Middlebury, OH	135.00
Carter's	
Cathedral, cobalt, quart	45.00
"Ma and Pa," 3⅝", pair	75.00
Emerald green, 2⅛" h 8-cut panels, flat cut top, star, side spout, copper fittings	200.00
Hover, Phila., umbrella shape, 2⅛ x 2¼", 8 panels, aqua	200.00
Illinois Glass Co, cone, double collared, c1880	12.50
Improved Process Blue Company	
Cone, aqua 2½"	6.50
Pyramid, 2¼" h pontil, aqua, . . .	5.00
Sanford's, 2 x 2", machine made . .	7.50
Stafford's Ink, 9¾" h, deep aquamarine, applied pouring spout	50.00
Superior Black Ink, 2⅝" h, pyramid, aqua, orig paper label	7.50
Travel, Umbrella, blue, no pontil . . .	25.00
Turtle, 2 x 4", travel, aqua	75.00
Underwood, 9¾", pinch spout, cobalt	40.00

MEDICINE BOTTLES

Not all medicines were patented in early America. During the 1880s, the "medicine show," which introduced American's first traveling salesmen, was very popular. For one dollar small town residents could see a traveling show and buy a bottle of medicine which was said to cure anything. Luckily for today's collectors, some of the bottles still exist. The 1907 Pure Food and Drug Act ended this era, but remedies of the 1890s and early 1900s are still interesting to collectors. Some of these early bottles were made in the South Jersey glass manufacturing area and are good specimens of early bottle manufacture. It is said that "Turlington's Balsam" had been carried by soldiers in the Revolution.

See *Warman's Americana & Collectibles* for an expanded listing of Medicine Bottles.

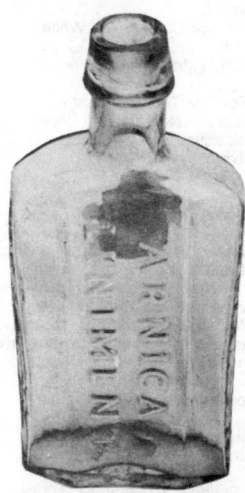

Burdsell's, J.R., Arnica Liniment, NY, aqua, open pontil, 5⅜", $20.00.

Abilena Natural Cathartic Water, round, amber, 9¾ "h	4.00
Angier Petroleum Emulsion	12.00
Bateman's Drops	7.50
Bear Oil, pontil, aqua	12.50
Bell's Pine Tar Honey For Coughs and Colds, rect, aqua, 5⅝"	3.00
Carter's Spanish Mixture	7.50
Cole's Cough Balsam	15.00
Chamberlain's Cough Remedy	7.50
Clickmer's Purgative Pills	15.00

Crab Orchard Water Co., clear	1.75
Dalley's Magic Pain Extract	20.00
D.D.D., sq, clear, 3½"	3.00
Ely's Cream Balm, Owego, NY, amber	4.00
Fellow's Syrup of Hypophos, aqua .	7.50
Frank Tea & Spice Co, Castor Oil .	5.00
Hick's Capudine Cure, applied lip, reverse painted label, amber . . .	70.00
Johnson's Chill and Fever Tonic . .	4.00
Kalo Compound For Dyspepsia . . .	20.00
Madame M. Yale Fruitcura Womans Tonic, Chicago, aqua	9.00
McMinn's Elixir of Opium	30.00
Nyal's Emulsion of Cod Liver Oil . .	5.00
Omega Oil, cylindrical, aqua	4.75
Opodeldoc, (bottle made in South Jersey)	50.00
Porter's Pain King, aqua	6.00
Radam's Ready Relief, rect, aqua .	18.00
Schenk's Pulmonic Syrup, cylindrical, aqua	7.50
Shaker Digestive Cordial, A.J. White, NY, 5¾" h	15.00
Shaker Fluid, Extract Valerin, aqua, 3⅝"	25.00
Teaberry For The Teeth & Breath .	9.00
Uncle Sam's Nerve & Bone Linament, aqua	10.00
Wood's Elixir	25.00

MINERAL WATER BOTTLES

Mineral water is the natural spring water found beneath the earth's surface. In the 1850s to 1900s, health conscious people favored this water for drinking. Many resorts were built around a natural spring. Several establishments had special bottles produced to ship and store their mineral water.

Adams Spring Mineral Water, Lake County, CA, Dr. W.R. Prather, Prop, light blue, c1895, 11½" h .	16.00
Buffalo Lithia, paper label, aqua, ½ gal.	10.00
Congress Spring Co., Saratoga, NY, dark green, quart, tapered top, ring	40.00
Empire Spring Co., E. Saratoga, NY, dark green, quart	30.00
Hathorn Spring, Saratoga, NY, blue-green, pint	28.50
Lytton Spring, emb pelican, Sweet Drinks, San Francisco, aqua, 6½"	20.00
Mills Seltzer Spring, blob top, aqua	20.00
Oak Orchard Acid Springs, H. W. Bostwick, teal green, quart	45.00
Saratoga Red Spring, dark green, quart	40.00
Thompson's Premium Mineral Water, ten pin shape, Union Soda	

Works, San Francisco, blob top, aqua	25.00
Watchung Spring, NY, green, quart	20.00

NURSING BOTTLES

Early nursing bottles were of the blown-type. They were first used in the mid-19th century. Increased popularity and demand necessitated improved design and production—machine made, embossed, graduated and disposable.

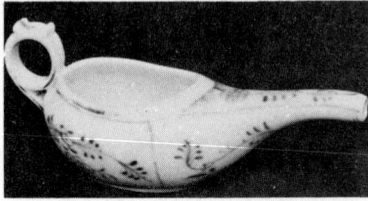

Delft, blue lines, decor, gold trim, 6" l, marked WI in diamond, $45.00.

"Acme Nursing Bottle," 6½", with monogram and star, W.T. & Co., (Whitall, Tatum Co., Millville, NJ) .	100.00
Blown, glass nipple, 8¾"	250.00
"Empire Nursing Bottle," 5½"	45.00
"Normandie Nursing Bottle," clear, flat oval, raised neck, early nurser	50.00
"Sunny Babe," 4 oz., full length figure of baby on his tummy, embossed	10.00
Teddy's Pet, emb, turtle shape, clear	60.00
"Three Star Nurser," 6½", (Pat. June 19, 1894)	45.00

PERFUME BOTTLES

Cologne and perfume bottles were made in various shapes and sizes to hold highly prized perfumes and scented oils. A perfume bottle has a stopper that is often elongated to be used as a applicator. An atomizer has a spray mechanism.

Also see specific categories in regards to materials, manufacturers.

Atomizers

Art Deco
Clear, raised swirl design, triangle brass top, 3½" tube, orig bulb, 4" h	20.00
Square, yellow painted panels, stylized flowers, stars on glass top, 3¾" h	25.00

Atomizer, DeVilbiss, hexagonal extended base, green frosted with gold lattice work middle band, 4¼" h, $155.00.

Baccarat, Rose Teinte, swirl pattern, 7" 50.00

D'Argental, double overlay cameo, pear shape, amber translucent ground, overlay red flowers, brown grape leaf trellis, sgd, Marney, France, 9" h 300.00

DeVilbiss

   Cranberry, gold decor, 10" 225.00

   Egyptian motif, gold leafing, orig label DeVilbiss/Toledo, 8" h .. 225.00

Franck, Marcel, cut crystal 90.00

Lalique, opalescent glass, tapered cylindrical bottle, row of vertical bubbles, 6" h, molded R. Lalique, France 210.00

Limoges, hp reclining nude, blue ground 115.00

Moser, amethyst to clear, frosted rings 165.00

Cologne

Apple green, 5¼", hexagonal, bulleyes and punty, cut, ground stopper 510.00

Aurene, blue irid, 3 lug feet, stopper, unsigned Steuben 800.00

Blown, thumbprint, 6 sides 75.00

Canary, hexagonal, cut stopper, lip, top of stopper ground, 5" h 185.00

Cranberry, floral decor, gold trim, clear stopper 250.00

Malachite, 6½", sgd Moser 235.00

Perfume

Amber, applied grapes, gold insect on bottle 330.00

Amberina, yellow stopper, stamped Libbey, c1920 .... 275.00

Art Deco

   Amber, triangular motif, intaglio stopper, brass collar, 3¾" h .. 75.00

   Green crystal, half sphere base, green leaf stopper, 6¾" h 65.00

   Enamel on copper, Germany ... 35.00

Baccarat

   Rose Teinte, pinwheel pattern, ball stopper, sgd 130.00

   Shield shaped, ftd, light blue, shell stopper, Guerlain, Paris 70.00

Black glass, bell shape, cork stopper, mkd Made in France, 1¾ x 1½" 22.00

Blown, stopper, Debrook's Perfumers, Detroit 10.00

Bohemian, clear base, painted pink center, gold borders, all over white, royal blue flowers, teardrop shaped stopper, 9½" h 65.00

Cameo glass, white blossoms, foliage, red ground, clear glass stopper, silver mounts, orig case, Thomas Webb & Sons, c1900 .. 1,250.00

Cased, lemon yellow, heavy gold leaves, red, green jewels, white interior, orig gold ball stopper 100.00

China

   Pillow shape, turquoise body, rose cartouche, white ground, matching ground stopper, Vienna, 2½ x 3" 135.00

Perfume Bottle, Art Deco, conical style, Chinese red and black, 2⅜" h, $65.00.

Shocking pink ground, white flowers, green leaves, gold trim, orig pink stopper, 5⅛ x 2⅝" **125.00**

Cranberry glass

Lavender, gold flowers, 4", 2" d . **170.00**

Melon rib, emb in 3 section shape, lacy gold enamel fern leaves, clear cut faceted stopper, 4¾", 2¾" d **135.00**

Opalescent swirl, clear pressed swirl stopper **135.00**

Cut glass, heart shape, Sterling top . **130.00**

Lalique, Je Reviens Eau de Cologne, globe shape, stars, coin shape stopper, base sgd Made In France by Lalique, 2½ x 4½" ... **85.00**

Latticino, pink striping, flattened bulbous shape **90.00**

Lithyalin, shade of dark brown to terra cotta, orig stopper, 5" h, c1830 **1,250.00**

Marinot, inside painted charcoal gray, white streaks, inscribed Marinot, 4¾" h **1,850.00**

Old Landers Co., orig paper label, cobalt, 6½ x 6 x 4½" **8.50**

Opalescent, Oriental Jade, green-white, unsigned Steuben, c1915 . **1,250.00**

Paperweight base, clear, round, multicolored paperweight, long oval stopper, 5 x 2½" **28.00**

Pink, long neck, gold trim, oval pink stopper, 10½" h **40.00**

Quezal, flattened teardrop form, multicolored irid, monogrammed foliate mounts, bulbous stopper, 5" h, c1915 .... **625.00**

Silver, adv. Lydia Pinkham's Pills For Constipation, 2½" **37.50**

Shoe, high button **20.00**

Stevens & Williams, moss rose cased glass, silver mounted, cap monogrammed, 5" h, unsigned, c1895 .... **725.00**

Webb, white cameo ferns, blue ground, gilt sterling hinged top, crystal stopper, hallmarked, England, c1900, 2½" h **675.00**

POISON BOTTLES

Poison bottles were designed to warn and prevent accidental intake or misuse of their poisonous substances, especially in the dark of the night. Poison bottles were generally made of colored glass, embossed with the word "POISON," a skull and crossbones, ribbed, ghastly-shaped, anything to call attention to their deadly contents.

Browns Rat Killer, C. Wakefield Co, applied lip, aqua, 3" **12.00**

Poison, emb, ¾ panel side, blown, stopper missing, aqua, 12¾", $20.00.

Durfee Embalming Fluid Co, amethyst, 8¾" **25.00**

Ikey Einstein, Poison, rect, ring top, clear, 3¾" **24.00**

Norwick coffin shape, poison emb vertically down front, diamond emb, amber **20.00**

Skull and crossbones, Poison Tinq Iodine, sq, amber, machine made, 3³/₁₆" **6.00**

Whitall Tatum Co, deep blue, sharp diamond points, emb poison, c1896 .... **45.00**

Wyeth Poison, vertical letters, round ring base, top, cobalt **18.00**

SARSAPARILLA AND SODA BOTTLES

Sarsaparilla was a soft, sweet drink, made from natural roots of plants for flavoring. It often was sold for medicinal purposes. Early bottles for carbonated drinks dated from approximately 1840; the first were, no doubt, stoneware. Glass bottles date from about 1850. A group of them may all look the same, but all are different, being made by many companies. Closures were of different types, some had glass marbles in sliding grooves as stoppers. Others had pull-out sealers with hooks that were pushed in to open. They must be studied closely to mark their differences.

Sarsaparilla

Allen's Sarsaparilla, vertical lettering, oval shape, aqua, 8⅛"	20.00
Baker's, Dr. Ira, Honduras Sarsaparilla, clear, 10½"	18.00
Belding's, Dr., Wild Cherry Sarsaparilla, emb letters, aqua, 10"	12.00
Bristol's, sunken front panel for label, thick, aqua	8.00
Foley's Sarsaparilla	15.00
Guysott's Yellow Dock & Sarsaparilla	35.00
Hall's Sarsaparilla, vertical letters on sunken panel, J. R. Gates & Co., Prop. on side, rectangular, aqua .	28.00
Higgin's, Dr. H. R., back reads Romney, Va., other side Sarsaparilla Pure Extract, aqua, pontil	60.00
Riker's Compound Sarsaparilla, rectangular, beveled corners, aqua . .	30.00
Skoda's Sarsaparilla, amber	20.00
Wynkcop's, Dr., Kathatismic Honduras, Sarsaparilla, NY, 10½"	22.00

Soda, Stollo Co, Troy, NY, The Temperance Beverage, 12 oz, $6.50.

Soda

American Soda Works, trade mark, Portland, OR, green, 7¾"	8.50
Blackhawk Ginger Ale, dark green .	7.00
California Soda Works, emb eagle, green	20.00

Canada Dry, Ginger Ale, carnival glass, machine made, crown top, 10½"	18.00
Cincinnati, horseshoe letters reads Soda Water & Ginger Ale Co., aqua	9.00
Dinets, J, Superior Soda Water, Chicago, 6 panels, graphite pontil, blue, 8"	65.00
Eagle, W, Canal St, NY, squat type, blob top, dark green, 6¾"	60.00
Fleming Bros., Meadville, PA, aqua	10.00
Globe Bottling Works, Savannah, GA	6.00
Hawaiian Soda Works, Honolulu, aqua	12.00
Hutchinson Soda Bottling Works, Hutchinson, MN, aqua	8.00
Imperial Bottling Works, Portland, OR, aqua	15.00
James Bottling Co., aqua, 6¾" . . .	10.00
Krueger, H. O., Grand Forks, ND, aqua, 7½"	12.00
Los Angeles Soda Co., Mineral Water Factory, H. W. Stoll, blob top, aqua, 6¾"	15.00
Martin, C. H. & Co., Soda Works, Avon, WA, aqua	9.00
Mission Orange Dry Rey, black . . .	7.50
Newton Bottling Works, aqua	5.00
Ozark Fruit Co., Memphis, TN, aqua	12.00
Pepsi-Cola	
Amber, Albany Bottling Co. Inc. .	35.00
Aqua, Newberry, SC	8.00
Rocky Mountain Bottling Co., Butte, MT	15.00
Southern Phosphate Co., clear	8.00
Try-Me Beverage Co., machine made, clear	2.00
Union Bottling Work, Victor, CO, aqua	20.00
Union Soda Water Co., W & C on bottom, "This Bottle Never Sold Please Return" on back, aqua . .	7.50
Vicksburg Steam Bottling Works . .	8.00
Virginia Fruit Juice Co., amethyst . .	6.00
Wheaton, Hiram & Sons	8.00
Yetter & Moore, amethyst	8.00
Zimmerman, Mrs., B. Z., New Brunswick, NJ, letters in circle, T.B.N.T.B.S. under circle, amethyst	12.00

SCENT AND VINAIGRETTE BOTTLES

A small glass bottle used to hold a scent or smelling salts is a scent bottle. These bottles were used by fashionable ladies in the 18th and 19th centuries. They were carried in purses in case of a sudden fainting spell or if the "vapors" overcame them.

A vinaigrette is an ornamental box or bottle with a perforated lid used to hold aromatic vinegars or smelling salts and used for the same purpose as a scent bottle.

Scent Bottle, glass, 2½″ h, light yellow ground, painted abstract floral design, red, orange, blue, shaped triangular motif, silver cap, $140.00.

Scents

Amethyst, pewter cap, emb roses .	60.00
Blue glass, flattened pear shape, faceted, rococo overlay ornament, inscribed Amour Sans Fin, 2½″ .	500.00
Frosted, clear, sienna patina, circular, molded with flower-heads, by R. Lalique for Jay Thorpe Co., NY, 2¾″ h	300.00
Opalescent, pewter cap, 2½″ h . . .	45.00
Opaque opalescent, rosetted molding around lower edge, emb eagle on top, Boston and Sandwich, orig pewter screw top, 2⅝″	165.00
Opaque white, Gothic paneled shape, pewter cap, 2⅜″ h	85.00

Vinaigrettes

Gold
  Flattened cartouche shape, putto playing lute, another playing with hound, base of carnelian intaglio of 2 lovebirds below a

chaplet, inscribed Vivons Fidelle, 2½″, English mid-18th C	650.00
Rectangular, hinged cover, base, floral, engraved grill, scrolling foliage, A. J. Strachan, London, 1800, 1⅛″ l	1,320.00
Silver	
Purse-shaped, florals at clasp, engraved basketwork body, John Lawrence & Co., Birmingham, England, 1819, 1″	425.00
Victorian, rectangular, emb view of Windsor Castle on cover, leaf tip emb sides, mkd Gervaise Wheeler, 1839, 1¾″ l	715.00

SNUFF BOTTLES

Tobacco usage spread from America to Europe to China during the 17th century. Europeans and Chinese preferred to grind the dried leaves into a powder and sniff it into their nostrils. The elegant Europeans carried their snuff in boxes and took a pinch with their finger tips. The Chinese upperclass, because of their lengthy fingernails, found this inconvenient and devised a bottle with a fitted stopper and attached spoon.

In the Chinese manner, these utilitarian objects soon became objects d'art. Snuff bottles were fashioned from precious and semiprecious stones, glass, porcelain and pottery, wood, metals, and ivory. Glass and transparent stone bottles often were enhanced further with delicate hand paintings, some done in the interior of the bottle.

Collecting snuff bottles has enabled collectors to explore the varieties of Chinese art without large capital expenditures or consuming a large amount of space.

Snuff bottles of superior quality still are being made today and command relatively high prices

Agate, banded, 2⅜″ h, turquoise stopper, late 19th C	110.00
Agate, mottled, 2⅝″ h, collared carnelian stopper, late 19th C	75.00
Amber	
2⅝″, carved in form of Budda's hand, citron fruit, turquoise stopper	300.00
3⅛″, chrysanthemum and bamboo carving, high relief carving of rock, bird, green jade stopper, mid-19th C	250.00
Amethyst, 2¼″ l, pear shape, carving, carved stopper, flat foot . . .	175.00
Aquamarine, 1¾″, carved leaves, butterfly, rose tourmaline stopper, wood stand, 20th C	1,700.00

Bamboo, 2⅝" h, carving, coral stopper, 19th C **250.00**

Chalcedony, 3", butterscotch, medium high relief, Shou symbol, early 19th C **80.00**

Cinnabar

2½", double gourd design, leaves, flowers, matching carved stopper, seal of Chien Lung under foot, 20th C **50.00**

2¾", deep blood red, carving of figures, scenic design, matching stopper, apocryphal seal of Chien Lung, 20th C **100.00**

Cloisonne, 2⅞", 20th C **90.00**

Coral, 2⅜", carving, turquoise stopper, late 19th C **350.00**

Enamel on Metal

2¼", Maiden reading book, sgd, mid-20th C **80.00**

2⅜", prunus blossoms, flowers, mid-20th C **90.00**

Inside Painted Glass

2⅜", three fantail fish, jade stopper, unsigned **300.00**

2½", large cabbage, insect, coral stopper with emerald jadeite knop, sgd Kuan Yu-t'ien, (1895–1918) **125.00**

3¼", 4 children playing under a tree, sgd. Yung Shao-t'ien, c1898 . . . . **175.00**

Ivory, Hornbill, 2¾", dragon carving, matching stopper, 20th C **150.00**

Jade

Apple green, 2¼", floral carving in yellow skin **275.00**

Brown, 2", peacock carved in white coloration of stone, 20th C **225.00**

White, 3½" h, low relief carving, Tourmaline stopper **200.00**

Lapis Lazuli, 2", carved foo dog holding coral ball stopper in mouth, 20th C **350.00**

Malachite, 2½", high relief carved snake coiled around oval bottle, light green specks in very dark green stone, jade stopper, late 19th C **250.00**

Mother of Pearl Inlay, 2½", 20th C . **120.00**

Peking Glass

2⅝", stylized trees, birds, waves, mid 19th C **60.00**

3⅛", five color overlay of fish, aquatic plants, early 19th C . . . **350.00**

Porcelain

2⅜", Famille rose enamels, silver mounted jade stopper, late 18th C **140.00**

3" h, small deer in white enamel, overglaze enamel, underglaze red, late 19th C **50.00**

3¼", cylindrical, blue underglaze on creamy crackle ground, shows Governor, servants leaving city gate, mid - 19th C **30.00**

Puddingstone, 2½" h, black collared carnelian stopper **75.00**

Quartz, Rose, 3" h, relief carving of 2 birds, blossoms, carved foot, matching carved stopper, late 18th C **325.00**

Rock Crystal

2⅜", black collared carnelian stopper **60.00**

3½" h, elongated flattened form tapering down to foot, carved in low relief of bats, clouds, green Peking glass stopper, mid-18th C **160.00**

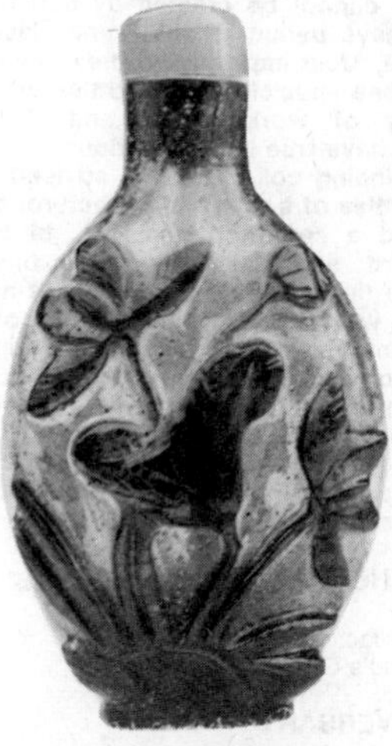

Peking Glass Snuff Bottle, 2½", floral motif, red on amber, $110.00.

Tourmaline, Rose, 2⅝" h, Kuan Yin carving, matching stopper, 20th C **350.00**

Sea Pine, 3" h, mottled brown, 2 large pomegranates, poor hollowing, 20th C **25.00**

Turquoise, 2⅞" h, highly polished, 20th C **120.00**

Turquoise Matrix, 2⅞" h, silver base, matching stopper, mid-19th C **130.00**

Wood, 2½", ocher color, natural markings, late 19th C **25.00**

BOTTLES, WHISKEY

COLLECTORS' SPECIAL EDITIONS

The Jim Bean Distillery began the practice of issuing novelty (collectors' special edition) bottles for the 1953 Christmas trade. By the late 1960s over one hundred other distillers and wine manufacturers followed suit.

The "Golden Age" of the special edition bottle was the early 1970s. Interest waned in the late 1970s and early 80s as the market was saturated by companies trying to join the craze. Prices fell from record highs. Many manufacturers dropped special edition bottle production.

A number of serious collectors, clubs, and dealers have brought stability to the market in the past year. Realizing that instant antiques cannot be created by demand alone, they have begun to study and classify their bottles. Most importantly, they have focused on those special edition bottles which show quality of workmanship and design and which have true limited editions.

Beginning collectors are advised to focus on bottles of a single manufacturer or collect around a central theme, e.g., birds, trains, western, etc. Make certain to buy bottles whose finish is very good (almost no sign of wear), with no chips, and with the original labels intact. A major collection still can be built for a modest investment, although some bottles such the Beam Red Coat Fox now command over $2,000.

See *Warman's Americana & Collectibles* for an expanded listing of Whiskey Bottles, Collectors' Special Editions.

AESTHETIC SPECIALTIES INC.

Cadillac, 1903, white	35.00
World's Greatest Hunter, 1979 . .	40.00

ANNIVERSARY

Baltimore, 1979	18.00
Happy Anniversary	22.00
Massachusetts, 1972	20.00

JIM BEAM

Centennial Series, First Issue, 1960

Chicago Fire, 1971	15.00
Lombard Lilac, 1969	4.00
New Mexico, 1976	10.00
Statue of Liberty, 1975	9.00
Santa Fe, 1960	200.00

Executive Series

1961, Golden Chalice	62.50
1965, Marbled Fantasy	67.50
1971, Fantasia	10.00
1973, Phoenician	8.00
1977, Golden Jubilee	9.00
1979, Mother of Pearl	22.50
1981, Executive	27.50

Glass Series

Cleopatra Yellow, 1962	14.00
Coffee Warmer, clear, black handle, stand, 1956	6.00
Crystal Pressed	
1967, Ruby	10.00
1968, Propietors Own	9.00
Crystal Sunburst	
Blue, 1974	5.00
Trave Chocolomi, 1975	4.00
Dancing, short bottle, 1963	85.00
Ducks & Geese, 1955	7.00
Olympic, 1971	4.00
Royal Opal, 1957	7.00

Miscellaneous

Beam Clubs

Beaver Valley Club, 1977	20.00
California Mission Club, 1970 .	24.00
Fox, Surfer, 1975	24.00
Republic of Texas Club, 1980 .	37.50
Rocky Mountain Club, 1970 . . .	12.00

Casino Series

Golden Gate, 1969	45.00
Harold's Club	
Pinwheel, 1965	60.00
Slot Machine, blue, 1967 . . .	12.00
VIP, 1971	65.00
VIP, 1975	25.00
VIP, 1979	35.00
Harvey Hotel, glass, 1969	5.00
Prima Donna Club, 1969	6.75

Clubs and Organizations

Cedars of Lebanon, 1971	4.50
Ducks Unlimited, #4, 1978 . . .	17.00
Homebuilder's Association, 1979	22.50
101st Airborne, 1977	10.00
Shriner, El Kahir Temple, 1975	17.50
Trout Unlimited, 1977	14.00

Collector's Editions, Volumes 1 to 5, each 2.00

Conventions

#9, Houston, rocket ship, 1979	77.50
#10, Norfolk, Waterman, silver, 1980	200.00

Customer Specialties

ABC Florida, 1973	15.00
Bohemian Girl, 1974	16.00
Katz Cat, Black, 1968	11.00
Marina City, 1962	32.50
Richard's New Mexico, 1967 . .	5.00
Zimmerman, Bell, light blue, 1967	12.50

Foreign Countries

Australia, Hobo, 1979	20.00
Boystown of Italy, 1973	6.00
Germany, Pied Piper, 1974 . . .	5.50

People Series

Hongi Hika, 1980	125.00
John Henry, 1972	60.00

Beam customer specialties, Broadmoor Hotel, 1968, $5.00.

Petroleum Man, 1971	6.00
Viking, 1973	9.00
Political Series	
1956, Ashtray Donkey	15.00
1964, Boxer Elephant	27.00
1976, Kansas City Convention Elephant	10.00
Sports Series	
Baseball, 1969	7.50
Bing Crosby, 30th National Pro-Am, 1971	8.00
Clint Eastwood, 1973	10.00
Hawaiian Open, Golf Ball, 1973	11.00
Louisiana Superdome, 1975 . .	8.50
Preakness, 1975	7.00
Seafair, 1972	12.00
Regal China Series, First Issue, 1955	
Bellringer, #1, Plaid, 1970	7.00
Coffee Grinder, 1980	20.00
Grand Canyon, 1969	10.00
Hawaii "Aloha," 1971	7.50
Las Vegas, 1969	6.00
Musicians on Cask, 1964	5.50
Pony Express, 1968	5.00
Stone Mountain, 1974	7.00
Treasurer Chest, 1980	20.00
State Series	
Arizona, 1968	6.00
Delaware, 1972	7.00
Illinois, 1968	6.00
Montana, 1963	77.50
New Hampshire, 1968	7.00
North Dakota, 1964	85.00
South Carolina, 1970	6.00

Trophy Series, First Issue, 1967

Birds	
Blue Jay, 1969	8.50
Pheasant, 1966–68	15.00
Cat, Burmese, 1967	12.50
Dog, Poodle, gray or white, 1970	10.00
Fish	
Bluegill, 1974	10.00
Crappie, 1979	15.00
Pretty Perch, 1980	17.50
Panda, 1980	22.50

BENEAGLE

Barrel with Thistle, miniature	6.00
Golf Ball, miniature	7.50
Loch Ness Monster, miniature, 1960s	9.00

BOLS

Crock, each	8.00
Elephant	7.50
Pitcher, Delft	10.00
Radio	12.50

Bols, Dutch Boy, 10½″, $20.00.

EZRA BOOKS

Animal Series

Brahama, 1971	12.00
Fox, Redtail, 1979	40.00
Mule, Missouri	12.50
Tiger, Bengal, 1979	42.50

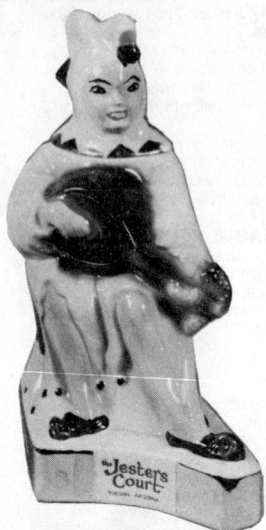

Ezra Brooks, People Series, Jester-Court, 1971, $8.00.

Automobile/Transportation Series

Corvette, 1957, blue or yellow, 1976	40.00
Deadwagon, 1970	10.00
Ford Mustang, Indy Pace Car, 1979	25.00
Lincoln Continental, 1941, 1979	27.50
Stagecoach, Dakota Express, 1977	27.50
Train, Iron Horse, 1969	10.00

Bird Series

Goose, 1974	16.00
Macaw, 1980	42.50
Owl #2, Eagle, 1978	37.50
Rooster, Fighting Gamecock, 1970	12.00

Fish Series

Sturgeon, 1975	24.00
White Shark, 1977	12.50

Heritage China Series

Bell, Liberty, 1969	7.00
Dollar, Silver, black or white bottom, 1969	5.00
Dueling Pistol, Japanese, 1968	27.50
Pot Belly Stove, 1968	10.00

Institutional Series

Amvet, Dolphin, 1974	12.00
American Legion, Texas, 1971	50.00
Buffalo Hunt, 1971	8.00
Club Bottle, #3, USA Map, 1972	15.00
Foremost, Dancing Man, 1969	10.00

Horseshoe Club, Horseshoe, 1970	8.00
Iowa Farmers Elevator, 1978	28.00
Kachina #6, Buffalo Dancer, 1977	30.00
Liquor Square Jug, 1972	7.00
New Hampshire, Man on Mountain, 1969	10.00
Saddle, Silver, 1972	26.00
Shrine, Sphinx, 1980	30.00
Wichita Centennial, 1970	7.00

People Series

Betsy Ross, 1975	15.00
Goldpanner, 1969	7.00
Iowa Farmer, 1977	65.00
Keystone Cops, 1971	15.00
Max "The Hat" Zimmerman, 1976	30.00
Pirate, 1971	6.25
Stonewall Jackson, 1974	27.50

Sports Series

Basketball Players, 1974	8.00
Bluejay, Creighton, 1975	15.00
Bulldog, Georgia, 1971	17.50
Go Big Red, #3, rooter, 1972	12.00
Greater Greensboro Open, Golfer, 1973	22.50
Hunter and Dog, 1973	10.00
Trojan, USC, 1973	15.00

Cabin Still, Quails Rising, $8.00.

CABIN STILL

Bourbon, 1963	5.00
Diamond, 1970	4.50

Ducks Unlimited, 1973	36.00
Hillbilly, pint	32.00
Pheasant, 1956	7.00

CLEM HARVEY

Alaska Pipeline	14.00
Seattle Stadium, 1974	10.00

COLLECTORS ART

Blue Jay, miniature	25.00
Brahma, 1973, fifth	37.50
Chipmunks, miniature	25.00
Mexican Fighting Bull, miniature	22.50
Robin, miniature	17.50
Shepherd, brown, miniature	24.00
Skunks, miniature	28.00

CYRUS NOBLE

Animal Series

Beaver & Kit, 1st Edition, 1978	100.00
Buffalo Cow & Calf, Nevada Edition, 1977	80.00
Deer, White Tailed Buck, 1979	75.00
Mountain Lion & Cubs, 2nd Edition, 1977	110.00

Mine Series

Blacksmith, miniature, 1976	17.50
Gold Miner, 1970	475.00
Landlady, 1977	34.00
Music Man, miniature, 1978	15.00
Snowshoe Thompson, 1972	175.00

Miscellaneous

Carousel Series, 1979, each	42.50
Dancers, South of the Border, 1978	40.00

J. W. DANT

Alamo, 1969	4.50
Boston Tea Party, eagle right, 1968	10.00
Constitution & Cuerrier, 1969	5.00
Indy 500, 1969	6.00

DAVIESS COUNTY

American Legion, Boston, 1980	25.00
American Legion, New Orleans, 1978	30.00
Eighteen Wheeler, I.M.L., 1979	25.00
Porsche 935, No. 90, Dick Barbour, 1979	25.00

DOUBLE SPRINGS

Bicentennial Series, Washington Monument issued with a state motif

Colorado	15.00
Florida	16.00
Maryland	12.75

J.W. Dant, Washington At Delaware, $6.00.

Rhode Island	18.00
Wisconsin	10.00

Car Series

Bentley, Touring, 1972	25.00
Duesenberg, Phaeton, 1978	22.00

Miscellaneous

Coyote, gold, 1971	10.00
Matador, 1969	15.00
Peasant, boy or girl, 1968, each	6.00

DUG'S NEVADA BROTHERS

No. 7, La Belle, miniature	18.00
No. 13, Doll House, miniature	24.00

EARLY TIMES, 1976

Cannon Fire, California	12.50
Continental Congress, New Mexico	27.50
Drum and Fife	
Hawaii	27.50
Texas	17.50
Minuteman, Oklahoma	24.00
Paul Revere, Kentucky	18.00
Washington Crossing the Delaware, Missouri	21.00

FAMOUS FIRSTS

Airplanes
P-51 Mustang, 1974 . . . . 60.00
Spirit of St. Louis, midi, 1972 . . . 80.00
Bell, Liberty, miniature, 1976 . . . . 9.00
Car—Transportation Series
Corvette, 1953, convertible, minia-
ture, 1978 . . . . 20.00
Dino Ferrai, 1975, white 21.00
Honda   Motorcycle,   miniature,
1979 . . . . 19.00
National Racer, #8, 1972 . . . . . 60.00
Renault Racer, #3, 1969 . . . . . . 60.00
Sea Witch, 1976 . . . . 67.50
Golfer, He, pint, 1973 . . . . 32.50
Phonograph, miniature, 1973 . . . . . 16.00
Rooster, Richardo, 1970 . . . . 18.00
Sewing Machine, 1970 . . . . 30.00
Skier, Jack, pint, 1975 . . . . 27.50
Telephones
Floral, 1973 . . . . 25.00
Yankee Doodle, 1973 . . . . 26.00
Warrior Series
Centurian, 1969 . . . . 17.00

Napoleon, 1969 . . . . 18.00

GARNIER

Cardinal 17.50
Coach, Antique 30.00
Ford, 1913 . . . . 24.00
Goldfinch 11.00
King of Clubs, miniature 11.00
Monuments 22.00
Policeman, Canada 22.00
Pony, n. 185 . . . . 30.00
Spaniel 15.00

GRENADIER

American Revolution Series, 18th
Continental, 1970 . . . . 20.00
British   Army   Series,   Grenadier
Guards, Officer, miniature 13.50
Civil War Series
Captain, Union Army, miniature . . 14.00
General George Custer, 1971 . . . 20.00
Miscellaneous
Appaloosa, 1973 . . . . 30.00
Fireman Statue, 1974 . . . . 60.00
General Billy Mitchell, 1975 . . . . 25.00
General Ulysses S. Grant, Club
Bottle series, 1975 . . . . 25.00

**(left), Double Springs, Bicentennial Series, Iowa, $60.00; (right), Grenadier, British
Army Series, Kings African Rifle Corps, Fifth, $22.50.**

Joan of Arc, 1972	85.00
Moonlight Ranch, miniature, 1977	60.00
Santa Clara De Asis, Mission series, 1978	27.50
Santa Claus, green sack, 1978 ..	29.00
Tennessee Walking Horse, 1978 .	30.00

Napoleonic Series

Dragoon 17th Regiment, 1970 ..	20.00
Napoleon, 1969	55.00

I. W. HARPER

Grand Prize, 1960	8.50
Harper Man, green, 1968	22.50

HOFFMAN

Hoffman, Street Swingers #1 Series, Fiddler, miniature, music, 1978, $15.00.

Bird Series

Baby Titmice, blue or red, 1979 .	27.00
Eagle, Open Wing, miniature, 1979	20.00
Geese, Canada, pr, 1980, 200 ml	34.00
Born Free Series, each	50.00

Car Series

Foyte #2, 1973	95.00
Johncock #20, 1974	35.00
Johncock Commemorative, 1973	20.00
Duck Decoy Series, 1978, each ..	25.00

Miscellaneous

Alaska Pipeline, 1975	27.50
Lady Godiva, 1974	40.00
Womans Lib, miniatures, pr, 1976	18.00

Mr. Lucky Series, #1 to #5, music

Electrian	35.00
Harpist	25.00
Harpist, miniature	12.00
Mailman, miniature	13.00
Photographer	38.00
Policeman	30.00

Mr. Lucky, miscellaneous

Caroliers, miniature	14.00
Organ Player	45.00
School Series, each	45.00

INCA PISCO

#2, Head, fifth	7.50
#3, Figure, silver, miniature	11.00
#7, black, miniature	9.00
Llama, 1977	10.00

JAPANESE FIRMS

House of Koshu

Children, 7 oz.	5.00
Geisha Violet, 1969	22.50
Mask, Okame, 1961	37.00
Princess, 1970	15.00

Kamotsuru

God #5, Hotei, God of Wealth and Wisdom, 1965	15.00
Joan & Darby, 1967	30.00

Kikukawa

Doll	6.00
Harunobu	8.00
Roosevelt, Teddy, 1970	16.50

JON-SOL, MINIATURES

Cardinal	30.00
Totem Pole	5.00

KONTINENTAL

Editor, miniature	18.00
Innkeeper, 1978	35.00
Lennon, John, gold, 1981	65.00
Medicine Man, 1977	37.50

W. A. LACEY

Faro Bank, Bisbee, 8 oz, 1975	15.00
Log Animals, Raccoon, 1978	32.50
Tennis, Women, 8 oz, 1976	16.00
Tun Tavern, 8 oz, 1975	12.00

LEWIS AND CLARK

Charonneau, 1972	52.50
Montana State, 1976	42.00
Troll Family, Mrs. Troll, 1978	28.00
Trooper, 1975	53.00

LIONSTONE

Bicentennial Series, Mecklenburg, 1975	28.00

Bird Series

Canadian Goose, 1980	85.00
Cardinal, 1972	27.50
Mallard	70.00

From left: Lionstone, Fire Fighter #2, 1974, $100.00; Old Commonwealth, Volunteer Fireman #3, The Valient Volunteer, 1980, $45.00: Poncho Villa, 1975, $32.50; Ski Country, Leadville Lady, Blue Dress, 1973, $25.00.

Roadrunner, miniature	12.00
Car—Transportation Series	
Olsonite Eagle #6, 1973	30.00
Stutz Bearcat, miniature, 1978	15.00
Miscellaneous	
Buccaneer, 1973	32.50
Lionstone Lion, 1.6 oz.	6.50
Primadonna Club, 1978, set of 5 units	250.00
Old West Series	
Barber, 1976	40.00
Calamity Jane, 1973	32.50
Camp Follower, 1969	21.00
Gold Panner, miniature, 1975	12.00
Indian, Casual	11.00
Lonely Luke, 1974	32.00
Professor, miniature, 1973	12.00
Renegade Trader, 1969	26.00
Trapper, 1976	30.00
Sports Series, Fisherman, 1980	45.00

LUXARDO

Ampulla	22.50
Babylon	10.00
Buddha Goddess	20.00
Curva Vaso	32.00
Diana	17.00
Euganean Bronze	30.00
Gambia	20.00
Sir Lancelot	22.50
Tower of Flowers	16.00

MCCORMICK

Barrel, stand, plain hoops, 1968	15.00

Bicentennial Series	
Patrick Henry, miniature, 1976	14.00
George Washington, 1975	35.00
Entertainer Series	
Elvis No. 1, miniature	30.00
Elvis, silver	150.00
Hank Williams, Jr., 1980	45.00
Great Americans Series	
George Washington Carver, 1977	20.00
Meriwether Lewis, 1978	26.00
Mark Twain, 1977	27.50
Football Mascots	
Arizona Sun Devils	32.50
Georgia Tech Yellowjackets	15.00
Louisiana State Tigers, 1974	15.00
Texas A & M Aggies, 1972	24.00
Tennessee Volunteers, 1974	12.00

McCormick, Train Series, Wood Tender, 1969, $32.50.

Miscellaneous

Buffalo Bill, 1979	42.50
French Telephone, 1969	27.50
Julia Bulette, 1974	225.00
Pony Express, 1978	30.00
Tom Sawyer, 1980	35.00
Warrior Series, each	19.00

MICHTER'S

Bell, Liberty, brown, 1969	40.00
Christmas Tree, 1978	57.50
Football, Pennsylvania, 1979	35.00
Jug, 1978	
Quart	12.00
Pint	8.00
Pagoda, Reading, PA, 1977	50.00
Policeman, New York, 1980	30.00

MIKE WAYNE

Christmas Tree, white, 1980	65.00
Masonic, 1981	39.00
Pope John Paul	55.00
John Wayne, Statue	64.00

OBR

Bus, 5th Avenue, 1971	15.00
River Queen, 1967	10.00
W. C. Fields, Bank Dick, 1976	15.00

OLD BARDSTOWN

Christmas Card, 1977	8.00
Foster Brooks, 1978, signed	120.00
Stanley Steamer, 1978	40.00
Wildcat #3, 1980	125.00

OLD COMMONWEALTH

Apothecary Series

Houston University, 1977	25.00
Maryland Terps, 1977	25.00
Tiger, Auburn, 1979	40.00
Waterfowler No. 3, 1981	50.00

OLD FITZGERALD

Crown, 1957	8.00
Eagle, 1973	4.50
Florentine, 1961	7.50
Four Seasons, 1965	5.00
Illinois, 1972	15.00
Lexington, 1968	6.00
Old Monterrey, 1970	13.00
Sons of Erin, 1969	12.00
Venetian	4.00

OLD MR. BOSTON

Berkeley, West Virginia	20.00
Clown Head, 1973	22.50

Cog Railway, 1978	16.00
Eagles Convention, 1976	14.00
Molly Pitcher, 1975	12.00
Mooseheart, 1972	12.00
Prestige Bookend, 1970	8.00
Tennessee Centennial	12.00

PACESETTER

Corvette, moving wheels, 1975	40.00
Corvette, 1980, white	60.00
Vokovich #2, 1974	26.00

PANCHO VILLA

Pancho Villa & Obrecon, 1976	25.00
Pancho Villa, Standing, 1972	27.50

POTTERS

Geese, Canada, 1978	45.00
Polar Bear, miniature	17.50

SKI COUNTRY

Bicentennial Series

Birth of Freedom, gallon, 1976	2,300.00
Eagle on Drum, 1976	45.00

Circus Series

P. T. Barnum, miniature, 1976	27.00
Elephant on Drum	40.00
Tom Thumb, miniature, 1974	19.00

Customer Specialties

Bull Rider, 1980	55.00
Phoenix Bird, miniature	45.00
Skier, blue suit, 1975	32.50
Submarine, miniature, 1976	20.00

Indian Series

Arizona Wolf Dancer, miniature, 1981	30.00
Warrior #2, with lance, miniature, 1979	17.00

Waterfowl Series

Ducks	
Blue Winged Teal, miniature	45.00
Pintail, 1979	62.50
Red Headed, 1974	65.00
Penquin Family, 1978	45.00

Wildlife Series

Deer, White Tail, 1982	70.00
Condor, California, 1973	37.50
Eagles	37.50
Hawk Ornate, miniature	45.00
Mountain, 1973	140.00
Ferret, Black Footed, miniature, 1976	32.00
Grouse, Sage, 1974	60.00
Koala, 1973	35.00
Otter, River, miniature	22.00
Owls	
Horned, gallon, 1974	1,050.00
Screech Family, 1977	65.00
Raccoon, 1974	40.00

Raccoon, Wall Plaque, 1982	100.00
Swallow, Barn, miniature, 1977 ..	29.00
Woodpecker, Ivory Billed, miniature, 1974	27.00

WILD TURKEY

Series #1

No. 1, Female, 1971	360.00
No. 7, Taking Off, 1977	27.50
Turkey Lore, No. 3, 1981	45.00

EARLY WHISKEY BOTTLES

The earliest whiskey bottles made in America were blown by pioneer glass makers in the 18th century. The Biningers (1820–1880s) were the first bottles specifically designed for whiskey. After the 1860s, distillers favored the cylindrical 'fifth' form.

The first embossed brand name bottle was the amber E. G. Booz Old Cabin Whiskey bottle which was issued in 1860. Many stories have been told about this classic bottle; unfortunately, most are not true. Research has proved that "booze" was a corruption of the words "bouse" and "boozy" from the 16th and 17th centuries. It was only a coincidence that the Philadelphia distributor also was named Booz. This bottle has been reproduced extensively.

Prohibition (1920–1933) brought the legal whiskey industry to a stand still. Whiskey was marked "medicinal purposes only" and distributed by private distillers in unmarked or paper label bottles.

The size and shape of whiskey bottles is standard. Colors are limited to amber, amethyst, clear, green, and cobalt blue (rare). Corks were the common closure in the early period, with the inside screw top being used in the 1880–1910 period.

Bottles made prior to 1880 are the most desirable. In purchasing a bottle with a label, condition is a critical factor. In the 1950s, distillers began to issue collectors' bottles to help increase sales.

Absolutely Pure, Albany	125.00
Belle of Anderson, milk glass	80.00
Crigler, Merry Christmas, ½ pt	20.00
Cutter, Old Bourbon, A No. 2, tooled top, amber, fifth	15.00
Eagle Liqueur Distilleries, olive	50.00
Gagle Glen Whiskey, San Francisco	65.00
Groe & Co., Old Governor, Sour Mash, St. Louis	35.00
Hoffman House Pure Rye, Cincinnati	35.00
Imperial, aqua, ½ pint	20.00
Jack Daniel's Gold Medal Old No. 7, clear	25.00
Lambe & Denmarke Fine Whiskey, Arkansas City, AK	30.00

11½″, Spruance Stanley & Co, San Francisco, CA/1869, amber, $23.00.

Macy & Jenkins, NY, handled, amber	18.00
O'Reilly & Sons, Queenstown, 3 pc. mold, deep gold	18.00
Peacock, Honolulu, monogram, cylinder, light amber	65.00
Preacher Whiskey, curved, amethyst	30.00
Queen Mary Scotch Whiskey, amber, quart	24.00
Richardson, Brunsing Co., San Francisco, amber	28.50
Silver Leaf Rye, Carolina Grocery Co., Richmond, VA, amethyst ...	15.00
U. S. Mail, clear	75.00
Van Buren, Kummel Whiskey, Chicago, amber, quart	25.00
Waldorf & Tavern, Reno, NV, amethyst	30.00
Winedale Co., Oakland, CA, monogram, amber	15.00

BOTTLES, WINE

Wine Bottles are collected primarily for decorative purposes with concentration placed on shape, color, and applied basketry. The majority of these bottles are imported from Italy. Bottles are made in both glass and china with several styles being covered in leather.

Prices range from a few dollars to $25.00. Interest has fallen in the last several years as collectors withdrew from this area. Most selling now takes place at collectors' club meetings and through specialized publications and dealers.

Alligator, seated, top hat	12.50
Bacchus Jug, 1963, Bacchus seated on cask	7.50
Church Steeple	10.00
Drum Major, Scottish	27.50
Elk Head, BPOE, 1969	35.00
Fish, qt, clear glass, rests on fin and tail	10.00
Friar John Holding a Wine Glass	12.50
Gondola, ash tray, 1969	14.00
Heidi, peasant girl holds jug resting on hip	42.50
Horsehead, Roman style, 1969	20.00
Owl, seated on limb	20.00
Peacock, tail feathers spread	17.50
Pitcher, Murano, rose motif	16.00
Queen Nefertiti, miniature, standing pose	12.50
Totem Pole	10.00
Wagon Barrel, 1969, frame, glass barrel	17.50

BRASS

Brass is a durable, malleable and ductile metal alloy consisting mainly of copper and zinc. It was and continues to be used by many cultures to make a variety of utilitarian and decorative objects.

See also specific categories, e.g., BELLS, CANDLESTICKS, FIREPLACE EQUIPMENT, etc.

Pastry cutter, 5½″ l, $25.00.

Altar Stick, 37″ fluted column, triangular base, paw feet, late 19th C, pr	225.00
Andirons	
Bell shaped	32.00
Brass and iron, topped by birds amidst foliage	75.00
Ashtray, hunter's scene	40.00
Baby's Bed, ornate, c1900	300.00
Bed Knobs, 3¾ x 2½″ d, pr	22.00
Bed Warmers	
43½″ l, turned wooden handle, bird on tulip tree engraved on lid	235.00
44″ l, 11¾″ floral engraved lid, turned wooden handle, flame painted red, yellow, black, brown decor	540.00
Bell, hand, Chinese, animal head handle	22.00
Bellows, emb with brass	22.00
Bird Cages	
15″ h	70.00
Wire, wooden frame, worn layers of green, white paint, 11½ x 16½ x 20″ h	75.00
Bowls	
12″ etched dragon design, teakwood base and stand	85.00
14″, hand hammered, early	150.00
Boxes	
1¼ x 4⅞″, hinged, incised flowers, mahogany lined, China	40.00
3 x 3″, stamp, mkd China	25.00
Buckets	
10″, dated 1866	100.00
11½ x 7¾″ h, spun, stamped label on bottom "Hayden's Patent 1851, Manuf. by Waterbury Brass Co."	45.00
13½″, iron bail, "E. Miller and Co., Meriden, Conn."	125.00
Candle Snuffer, 15¾″ l, figural, arrow, pilgrim's hat, Chase mkd	22.00
Candelabra, 11″, three branch	125.00
Candleholder, 7″, regency c1820, pr	75.00
Candlesticks	
4″ h, Victorian, miniatures, pr	55.00
4½″ h, baluster stem, saucer base	250.00
5½″ h, gimbol	55.00
6⅛″ h, octagonal base, screw in stem, octagonal baluster	175.00
8¼″, 3 cups, incised with facing dragons, China	48.00
Chafing Dish and tray, 2 qt	125.00
Chamber Stick, 4¼″ h, pushup	135.00
Champagne Bucket, large, with lion's heads	95.00
Chestnut Roaster, 20″, English, 19th C	145.00
Clock Jack, 13″ l, sgd Salter's Economical Warrented	50.00

Coffee Pot, 7¼", tankard shape ..	125.00
Compote, 7 x 10¾", round base with molded rim, baluster pedestal cast with foliage, bowl cast with flowers and gilt butterfly in varying shades of brass	150.00
Cuspidor, 12"	90.00
Door Latch, 7½" l, iron bar, keeper	35.00
Easel, floor, 62", triangular shape, c1880	150.00
Ferner, 3 ball feet	70.00
Firescreen, 18 x 54", early 19th C .	160.00
Foot Warmer, oval shape	95.00
Ginger Jar, 6", mkd China	50.00
Hand Warmer, French	25.00
Hearth Scoop, round	20.00
Ice Tongs	42.00
Jardiniere, 8", three ball feet, polished	75.00
Kettle, ftd 17", ball and claw feet, globular body, loop handles	415.00
Lamps	
6¼" h, whale oil	45.00
Aladdin, Model 8, spring mounted wall bracket, chimney, 9¾" d, milk glass shade	65.00
Lantern Clock, 18", Victorian, double fuse movement, J.W. Benson, 62 + 64 Ludgate Hill, c1840	1,000.00
Letter Holders	
Fish in relief, both sides	35.00
Jester in relief, both sides	40.00
Letter Opener, Art Nouveau, nude, swirling hair	35.00
Microscope, 13", fitted in mahogany case, Victorian, c1880	130.00
Mustache Curling Iron, alcohol burner, repousse decor on handle and stand	55.00
Night Light, ftd, handle, top plate, burner, 3 ruby glass panes, clear cut rosette, 4th pane clear for thumbscrew	65.00
Pail, 10½" d, bale handle	40.00
Pastry Cutter, 6¼" l, pinch fluter wheel, ornate handle	45.00
Salver, 7" d, 5½" handle, turned wood handle, brass ferrule	175.00
Samovar, 20"	150.00
Sander, 1¼" h	50.00
Scale, 6½ x 6½", cupid, stands with arms raised over head, scale resting on head	35.00
Scissor wick trimmers, 5½" l, stamped C.F.M.	60.00
Sconce, 7" h, candle, early 20th C .	20.00
Scoop, candy	25.00
Skater's Lamp, kerosene, tin bail handle	45.00
Skimmers	
20½" l, handle, blade, decorative pierced	105.00
20¾" l, pierced heart design on	

blade	115.00
21¼" l, pierced blade, simple tooled edge, polished	65.00
Steam Whistle, 16", round top, Lunkenheimer	125.00
Teakettle, dovetailed, early, American	250.00
Tray, 12½", hammered, 1885	28.00
Umbrella Stands	
21", iron base	140.00
24", lion's heads handles	125.00

BREAD PLATES

From the mid 1880s, special serving plates were made for serving bread and rolls, and many were made in the different table sets in pattern glass. There were also special large plates made by certain glass companies to expand their lines. These honored heroes, special events, and historical events. There are 10" plates in some patterns, designated as bread plates, but bear no mottoes which mark them as such. Plates were also made in porcelain, milk glass and silver, and were very popular on the Victorian dining table.

References: Alice Hulett Metz, "Much More Early American Pattern Glass," Bk.II.

See also Pattern Glass Section for various patterns.

Lord's Supper, frosted grape leaf border, 10⅞ x 7", $55.00.

American Eagle, 8½", Centennial, sheaf of wheat handles	35.00
Bible	50.00
Clear Diagonal Band, says "Eureka" in commemmoration of Gold Rush	40.00
Clear panels cord band	25.00
Cleveland	175.00
Cupid and Venus, 10" round	35.00
Continental platter, clear	45.00
Dahlia, grape handles	40.00
Daisy and Button	
Oval, amber	25.00
Scalloped, vaseline	35.00

Dewdrops, wheat sheaf, amber ...	48.00
Elaine	65.00
Faith, Hope and Charity	65.00
Frosted Lion's head, "Give Us This Day," 12", handled	78.00
Frosted Stork, frosted center, clear border, Iowa City	55.00
Give Us Our Daily Bread, wheat, farm implements center, border .	45.00
Gladstone	32.00
Good Luck, Horseshoe	48.00
Heavy Paneled Finecut	18.00
Jefferson Davis	80.00
Jewel Band (Scalloped Tape), "Bread is the Staff of Life" ...	40.00
Jewel and Dewdrop, colored jewels	50.00
Lion with mate	85.00
Maltese Cross	17.00
McCormick Reaper	80.00
Medallion with Open Rim	25.00
Minerva, gold decor	45.00
Mulberry with Railroad Track Border	35.00
Nellie Bly	185.00
Niagara Falls, frosted and clear ...	125.00
Old Statehouse, Phila., PA	80.00
Oregon	35.00
Pope Leo XIII	30.00
Prescott, Stark, Warren, Putman, 1776–1876	55.00
Railroad, Transcontinental	90.00
Rock of Ages, milk glass center ...	130.00
Royal Crying Baby	35.00
Scroll with flowers	16.00
Star Rosetted, motto	27.00
Teddy Roosevelt with dancing bears	95.00
Three Graces, motto	45.00
U. S. Thumbprint (Carolina), double handled, beaded edge	35.00
Virginia Dare	38.00
Warrior	150.00
Washington Centennial, Independence Hall	95.00
"Waste Not, Want Not" (Lattice pattern)	50.00
Wheat & Barley, motto	25.00
Willow Oak	26.00

9⅜" d, cased, white exterior, pink interior, gold floral decoration, base marked "Stand—Superior Silver Co., Quad Plate," $100.00.

BRIDE'S BASKETS

The bride's basket derived its name because it was a popular wedding gift of the 1880–1910 era. The glass bowls, usually with a ruffled edge, were made by many American and European glass makers . . . from the finest art glass to the style of the day glass. The metal holders, most often silver plated, were fitted with a bail handle, thus, resembling a basket. Reproductions exist, especially the glass bowls.

Prices listed include accompanying silver plated holder unless otherwise noted.

Amber, ribbon edge, floral decor .. Cased	130.00
9" d, shaded white to blue, green pontil, Pairpoint holder	275.00
10¼ x 10½", pink, fluted and crimped, figural squirrel set inside ring	145.00
10¾ x 9¼", red maroon to pink, scalloped edge, white underside, frame mkd Roman Silver Plating Co.	195.00
11 x 11¼", shaded pink, white exterior, quadruple plate stand, Middletown	145.00
11¾ x 9½" d, shaded pink, sanded gold leaves, white veining ..	295.00
Cranberry to rose, outside citron green, white enameled leaves and flowers, quadruple silver-plated stand with repousse Indian heads, Thomas Webb ..	695.00
Pink, black edges, emb rose, trimmed bail, Van Berg holder .	125.00
White to pink, glossy Peach Blow, holder mkd Van Bugh	325.00
White to rose, glossy, geometric ruffles, ground pontil	235.00
Coralene, 9 x 10½" d, stain glass, MOP, pale yellow inside, white satin outside, deep coral coralene frosted edge, blackberries and leaves holder, mkd Pairpoint	750.00
Cranberry to pink, 8½", Victorian, scalloped, raised enamel flower at center	225.00
Egg Shell, irid, enamel decor	250.00
Mt. Washington Cameo Glass, 4¼ x 8¼" sq, white inside, deep rose cut to white dragons, flowers and leaves, rose bands, bowl only ...	695.00
Peach Blow	
9½ x 7", cased, pink shading to	

white, satin finish, enameled white frilly hearts against pink at top 795.00

New Martinsville, large, fluted, gold trim, hallmkd Homan Bros 497.00

Pressed Glass, Daisy & Button, clear, bowl only 95.00

Rubina Verde, 10″, ruffled bowl, Pairpoint 345.00

Satin Glass

6⅞ x 9½″, pink overlay, white underside, frosted edging, maroon flowers, green and blue leaves, gold trim, auroba base 295.00

Pink over caramel, ruffled rim, gold decor, 6½″ medallions of ladies' heads, brass frame, ball and claw feet, sgr Thomas Webb & Sons 750.00

Spangled, blue, silver mica flecks, twisted thorn handle, Vasa Murrhina Glass Co. 220.00

Spatter, 12″, pink and white, pleated and ruffled rim 125.00

BRISTOL GLASS

Bristol glass was made in several glass-houses in Bristol, England, and in the U.S. in the 18th and 19th centuries. The name has become generic and to collectors it means glass of semi-opaque nature, usually decorated with enameling.

Bottles, Perfume, Bristol Glass, blue neck, teardrop stopper, gilt, hp blue bird in center medallion, pr, $200.00.

Biscuit Jar, pastel blue, hp, lilacs, leaves and tendrils, pagoda shape lid and handle 135.00

Box, large, hinged lid, tan opaque with enamel floral decor 90.00

Bottles

Claret, 15″, pale amber, sterling top, English, c1845 .... 195.00

Dresser, 10″, pink, Petticoat stopper 45.00

Perfume, 3¼ x 1¾″, turquoise blue, white enameled flowers, green leaves, gold trim 95.00

Perfume, 7⅝ x 3″ d, matching teardrop stopper, gold band trim 95.00

Epergne, blue, decorated bowl in base, vase at top, frame decorated with two birds 220.00

Fairy Lamp, white, enamel floral decor, matching base 170.00

Honey Pot, 4″, blue, enameled florals and bees, metal rim, lid and bail 60.00

Lamp, dresser, 15½″, blue, orig silk pleated shades, wired at top, pr . 115.00

Mantel Lustres, 14″, custard color, portrait of young girl, enamel shasta daisies and gold leaves .. 850.00

Mug, 4½″, opaline, enameled flowers, applied handle, "Remember Me" 25.00

Plate, 11″, hp, pansies 52.00

Salt Dip, 1¾ x 2″, bucket shape, gray, enameled pink, blue and yellow florals, green leaves, SP top rim and bail handle 58.00

Sweetheart Jar, 5¼ x 3″, pink overlay, duck in flight, enameled blue and white florals, green foliage, SP rim, cover and bail 100.00

Urn, 14″, cov, aqua, overall enameled bird decor 135.00

Vases

6½″, Jack-in-the-pulpit, white, enameled blueberries, pink throat, pontil, pr 95.00

7½″, bulbous, slender neck, white, hp, pink flowers, brown and gold leaves, lake scene with tree and flying birds 22.00

9″, baluster shape, pale pink, painted reserve of birds in a landscape, mounted as a table lamp, 19th C 95.00

10¼″, pale blue, flowers, pr 75.00

11″, soft green, hp, ruffled top .. 65.00

12″, heart shape, cylindrical neck, circular foot, jet glass, hp birds, flowers, c1880, pr 400.00

12″, urn shape, short pedestal, round base, opaque pink, white fret band above white enamel rose branch, pr 90.00

Wine Glass, 4½″, green 25.00

BRITISH ROYALTY COMMEMORATIVES

Souvenirs to commemorate coronations and other royal events were made as early as the 1600s. Few predating Queen Victoria's reign are found today at popular prices. The Royal Wedding of Prince Charles to Lady Diana Spencer and the subsequent birth of their son Prince William Arthur Philip Louis, heir to the British throne, heralded a new wave of commemoratives. Serious collectors still turn to the past for choice china, glass, and silver pieces, as well as other rare and unusual commemoratives.

See *Warman's Americana & Collectibles* for an expanded listing of British Royalty Commemoratives.

Silk, woven, Victorian, 1897 Jubilee, 15 x 17¾", black on white, $125.00.

Beakers
    Elizabeth II, Jubilee, 3¾", enamel
        on copper, Halcyon Days .... | 75.00
    Charles/Diana - Wedding, 3¾",
        sepia portraits, Royal Doulton . | 42.50
    William, birth, 4½", gold lion head
        handles, Caverswall, limited edi-
        tion of 1,000 .... | 47.50
    Edward VIII, Investiture as Prince
        of Wales, 1911, 3½", color por-
        trait, Royal Wintonia .... | 135.00
    George V/Mary, Coronation, 4⅜",
        their color portraits along with

that of Prince of Wales (later
    Edward VIII), no mark .... | 80.00
Edward   VII/Alexandra,   Corona-
    tion, 3¾", sepia portraits, Royal
    Doulton .... | 72.50
Victoria, 1897 Jubilee, 3¾", 1837/
    1897 portraits, enamel on tin .. | 65.00
Bowls
    Elizabeth II, Coronation, 8" d,
        4¼" w at bottom, crown shape,
        pressed glass .... | 40.00
    Edward VIII, Coronation, 6½" d,
        blue portrait and decoration,
        Copeland Spode .... | 60.00
    George V/Mary, 1935 Jubilee, 10"
        d, pressed glass .... | 40.00
    Edward VII/Alexandra, 25th Wed-
        ding   Anniversary,   8½"   d,
        pressed glass .... | 80.00
    Charlotte Memorial, 5" d, three
        black transfers, pink lustre trim | 125.00
Box, enamel, William, birth, 1½"
    square, 1" h, Crummles .... | 100.00
Cups and Saucers
    Elizabeth II, Coronation, Clarice
        Cliff design .... | 35.00
    Charles/Diana,   Wedding,   color
        portrait in wedding attire ..... | 35.00
    William,   birth,   color   portrait
        Charles/Diana, Crown Stafford-
        shire .... | 30.00
    George VI/Elizabeth, Coronation,
        brown lion handle, Paragon ... | 95.00
    Edward VIII, Coronation, Shelley . | 65.00
    George   V/Mary,   Jubilee,   1935,
        Royal Albert .... | 67.50
    Edward   VII/Alexandra,   Corona-
        tion, Royal Doulton .... | 95.00
    Victoria, 1897 Jubilee, Foley .... | 70.00
    Princess Royal, Prince of Prussia,
        pink lustre .... | 125.00
    Charlotte Memorial, black trans-
        fers, pink lustre .... | 185.00
Figurine,   Charles/Diana,   Wedding,
    study in wedding attire, 7" h, 9" w,
    John Bromley, Coalport, limited
    edition of 500 .... | 700.00
Jugs, character, pair, George/Mary,
    6", colorfully decorated .... | 250.00
Lithophanes
    Alexandra In Mourning Veil and
        Crown, miniature three handled
        Loving Cup, Arms of Bristol on
        cup, 2¼" .... | 125.00
    Edward VII Mug ("1902" on mug),
        crown and cypher, 2¾" ..... | 82.50
    George V Mug ("George V - Mary
        - 1911" on mug), Coats of Arms
        and name, 2¾" .... | 115.00
    George V Mug ("1911" on mug),
        crown and cypher, 2¾" ..... | 95.00
    Mary and Prince of Wales Feath-
        ers, Cup, 2¾" .... | 135.00

Loving Cups (measured handle to handle)

Elizabeth II, Silver Jubilee, 7", Drury Lane Theater on reverse, Coalport, limited edition of 1,000	115.00
Charles/Diana, Wedding, 5½", gold lion handles, Paragon . . .	80.00
William, birth, 5½", color christening portrait, Caverswall	75.00
George VI/Elizabeth, Coronation, 6¼", brown lion handles, Paragon	145.00
Edward VIII, Coronation, 5¼", brown lion handles, Paragon	120.00
George V/Mary, 1935 Jubilee, 6", colored flower handles, Paragon . .	175.00
Mask, Edward VIII, Abdication, 6½ x 4"	75.00

Mugs

Elizabeth II, Coronation, 3½", sepia portrait, gold "E" handle, Royal Doulton	95.00
Elizabeth II, Jubilee, 3¼", Kings/Queens of England on reverse, Aynsley	40.00
Charles, Investiture 1969, 4", R. Guyatt design, Wedgewood . . .	95.00
Charles/Diana, Wedding, 4½", color portraits, footed, Crown Staffordshire	42.50
William, birth, 4", Snowdon triple portrait, Coronet	25.00
George VI/Elizabeth, Coronation, 3⅞", Elizabeth/Margaret portrait on reverse, Shelley	65.00
Queen Mother Elizabeth, 80th Birthday, 3½", lavender toned portrait, Coronet	40.00
Edward VIII, Coronation, 4", color portrait, Royal Doulton	72.50
George V/Mary, 1935 Jubilee, 2⅞", color portraits, Shelly . . .	65.00
Edward VII/Alexandra, Coronation, 3", Foley	52.50
Victoria, 1897 Jubilee, 3½", charcoal portrait, Doulton Burselm	110.00

Plates

Elizabeth II, 1975 Tokyo Visit, 10½", portraits of Queen and Emperor Hirohito, Mercian	95.00
Charles/Diana, Wedding, 8½", large color portrait, Royal Grafton	30.00
William, birth, 10¾", Caverswall .	72.50
George VI/Elizabeth, Coronation, 8½", Marcus Adams sepia portrait with Elizabeth and Margaret, Alfred Meakin	75.00
Edward VII, 7", ribbon plate, Edward as young Prince of Wales, color portrait, no mark	95.00
Edward VIII Memorial, 10", dates	

Plate, 10", Edward VIII Memorial, dark blue, $120.00.

and quotes on reverse, Panorama	70.00
George V/Mary, Coronation, 7", Hammersley	50.00
Edward VII/Alexandra, Coronation, 9", color portraits plus future King George/Mary and young Edward VIII, no mark . . .	125.00
Victoria/Albert, 9", pink lustre, no mark	125.00
Princess Royal/Prince of Prussia, 9", pink lustre, no mark	145.00

Playing Cards

Elizabeth II, Coronation, unused .	25.00
Elizabeth II, Jubilee, unused	20.00
George V/Mary, Coronation, double deck, red and blue, used . .	50.00
Victoria, 1897 Jubilee, used	100.00
Shaving Mug, George VI/Elizabeth, Coronation, 3 x 5½", Empire	47.50

Spoons, Sterling

Elizabeth II, Accession, annointing spoon, 3⅞", gold wash bowl . .	35.00
George VI/Elizabeth, Coronation, 4¾", profiles atop handle	32.00
George V/Mary, 4½", profiles, crown atop handle	40.00
Edward VII, Coronation, annointing spoon, 6¾", gold wash bowl . .	70.00
Victoria, 1897 Jubilee, 3½", head atop handle	45.00
Monarchs - Victoria through George VI/Elizabeth, set of 8, 4¾", made for coronation of George VI	300.00
Tea Set, Elizabeth II, Coronation, consists of teapot, creamer and sugar, light blue on white Wedgwood Queensware	275.00

Tins

"The Royal Princesses" (Elizabeth/Margaret as young girls), 5" d, round, Marcus Adams portrait 37.50

Charles/Diana, Wedding, tray, 12", large color portrait 10.00

George/Mary, 4 x 3 x ⅜", color portraits on hinged lid 32.50

Victoria, "South Africa 1900," 6 x 3 x ¾", profile on hinged lid ... 42.50

Vase, Edward VII, Memorial (birth, accession, death dates), 3¼", Goss 115.00

BRONZE

Bronze is an alloy of copper, tin and traces of other metals. It has been used since Biblical times not only for art objects but also for utilitarian purposes.

After a slump in the Middle Ages, bronze was revived in the 17th, 18th, and 19th centuries. Today bronzes have become a highly sophisticated collectible in the antique trade. Prices have reached new heights.

Do not confuse a "bronzed" object with a true bronze. A bronzed object is usually made of white metal and then coated with a reddish-brown material to give it a bronze appearance. A signed bronze commands a higher price than an unsigned object. There are also "signed" reproductions on the market. It is terribly important to know your dealer, the history of the mold and the background of the foundry.

Andirons, winged dragon holding coiled snake in mouth, gilt, late 19th C, 24¼" 700.00

Animals

Bear, Russian sculptor, 9¾" h .. 400.00

Bull, brown patina, titled J. Clesinger Rome 1857 F. Barbedienne, imp seal Reduction Mecanique/A Collas/Brevete, black basalt plinth, 18" l 1,800.00

Bulldog, watchdog chained to post, brown patina, inscribed CH. Valton, ovoid black stone plinth, 31½" h 3,000.00

Camel, 9 x 10" 310.00

Dogs

Cocker Spaniel, Hamilton Foundry 145.00

Greyhound, 8 x 11", Mene ... 550.00

Pointer, 8 x 11½" 715.00

Scottie, 5 x 7", E. B. Parsons . 565.00

Elephant, standing, head raised, 6 ½ x 8", Valton 710.00

Fawn, dancing, dark patina, late 19th C 475.00

Horses

Circus, brown patina, inscribed Walter Winas, 20th C, 25" l . 3,100.00

Race, jockey, red-brown patina, inscribed I. Bonheur, late 19th C, 29" l 7,200.00

Hummingbirds, perched on swaying cattail, green patina, black marble base inscribed Editions Reveyrolis, Paris, 14" l 225.00

Lions

Stalking, rocky base, dark green patina, inscribed I. Bonheur, c1900, 20" l 400.00

Standing, green patina, inscribed Rosa B (Bonheur) late 19th C, 22" l 900.00

Lioness, stalking, rocky base, dark green patina, inscribed I. Bonheur, c1900, 18" l 410.00

Parrot, yellow, gray enamel plummage, perched on green swing, gilt bronze frame of coiling vines, white florets, 32¼" h 550.00

Rabbit, crouching, green patina, inscribed Swiss foundry mark, 2 ½" h 250.00

Squirrel, small 110.00

Tiger, walking, dark brown patina, inscribed Barye, F. Barbedienne Fondeur, 17" l 625.00

Bowls

Art Deco, stepped cov, green patina, Carl Sorinsen, 8½" d 60.00

Figural, mermaid frolicing in seaweeds, 6" d 145.00

Busts

Diana, upswept hair, horn strap across right shoulder, c1900, 24 ½" h 550.00

Napoleon, brown patina, inscribed R. Colombo 1885, circular foundry mark of Bronze Garant: Au Titre, late 19th C, 22¾" h . 1,650.00

St. George, brown patina, wood socle, late 19th C, 13½" h ... 4,500.00

Bookends

Figural nudes, Haugenauer, Austria, 7" h 125.00

Scottish Terriers, playful, inscribed Gorham, cast from model by Edith Baretto Parsons, 7" l ... 275.00

Box, cov, rectangular, green glass grape leaf, green patina, Tiffany, mkd #58, 9½ x 7" 480.00

Calendar Frame, green glass grape leaf, green patina, sgd Tiffany, 8½ x 7¼" 180.00

Candelabras

7 light, classical figure supporting

scrolling foliate branches, parcelgilt, shaped black stone plinth, inscribed L.V.E. Robert, late 19th C, 35″ h, pr **965.00**

7 light, Louis XV style, gilt, French, 19th C, 30″ h, pr **1,500.00**

9 light, gilt, Sevres floral plaques on base, late 19th C, 33″ h ... **1,000.00**

Centerpiece, oval, gilt, Napoleon III, flower molded rim, 8 scrolling foliate candleholders, dolphin-form feet, 17½″ l **495.00**

Chandelier, 12 lights, French gilt, crystal drops **200.00**

Clock, mantel, barrel shaped clock supported by 2 coiling dragons, surmounted by eagle, stepped marble base, mkd Tiffany, 19½″ h **675.00**

Desk Ends, graduate pattern, Tiffany, mkd #1796, 19″ l, pr **140.00**

Desk Set, gilt, abalone, inkstand, pen tray, letter rack, Tiffany, mkd #1157, #1159, #1156 .... **300.00**

Dish, pierced cov, swirling lily pads, flowers, frog, Japanese Art Nouveau, 18″ l **550.00**

Figures

Buddha, seated on lotus blossom, swastika on chest, 14¼″ h ... **150.00**

Dancing Lutenist, youth, floral hat, loosely gathered breeches, brown patina, inscribed A. Carrier, 16¾″ h **825.00**

Dante, light brown patina,

Figure, Equestrian by Emmanuel Fremiet, French, 1824–1910, 14″ h, $400.00.

inscribed carrier scpt, basalt base, 20″ h **550.00**

Joan of Arc, spindle at foot, golden brown patina, inscribed E. Drouot, late 19th C, 28½″ h ... **900.00**

Moslem Soldier, brown patina, inscribed Angles, late 19th C, 34¼″ h **1,870.00**

Napoleon, 8½″, marble base ... **450.00**

Neptune, dark brown patina, inscribed I. DE Rudder, late 19th C, 18¾″ h **1,200.00**

North African Soldier, pale puce, black garb, white, silver and gold highlights, marble base, cold painted, Austrian, late 19th C, 23″ h **2,475.00**

Pan, dark brown patina, inscribed Marius Montagne, late 19th C, 27½″ h **1,300.00**

Tambourine Player, headdress laden with grapes, brown patina, inscribed A. Carrier, 17¼″ h ... **1,000.00**

Venus, brown patina, gray marble base, gilt bronze beaded border, 19″ h **715.00**

Woman, dark brown patina, French, inscribed 1872, 32″ h . **2,100.00**

WWI Doughboy, standing throwing grenade, reddish brown patina, inscribed Albert Jeagers, stamped Gorham Co. Founders QBZY G.A.C., American, 20th C, 8¾″ h **300.00**

Finial, lamp, Tiffany, 5½″ h **145.00**

Firescreen, gilt, fan shaped, pierced reticulated opening, 26″ h **60.00**

Flower Frog, seated nude, rocky plinth, inscribed © Berge, #20, R.B.W., 6½″ h **125.00**

Frames

Gilt, cream slag glass spider web design, sgd Tiffany, 13 x 10½″ **800.00**

Oval opening, gilt, amber glass spider web, Tiffany, mkd #949, 7¼ x 6½″ **250.00**

Jewelry Caskets

Gothic style cathedral, reliefs of saints, silver colored patina, 21 ½ x 27″ **610.00**

Nude courtesan sleeping on chaise lounge on lid, divided wooden compartment interior, green marble base, 16″ l **2,900.00**

Jug, cast, scrolling foliate handle ending in satyr mask, Naples, c1870, 8″ h **80.00**

Lamp, table, baluster form, ring handles, Chinese style enamel flower blossoms, scrolling tendrils, leaves, 18½″ **350.00**

Medal, 2 11/16″ d, Napoleon Empereur et Roi, La Banque de

France, J.P. Droz, Fecit An 1809 marker's mark	70.00
Note Pad Holder, cream glass spider web, mounted on later oak base, sgd Tiffany, 7½" l	135.00
Table, 31 x 18", multi-figural scene of Orpheus, tripod pedestal base of griffins on vulture legs	725.00

Urns

Baluster shape, stem foot, frieze of dancing nymphs cast on body, brown patina, inscribed © Mabel Conkling, Kunst-Foundry, NY, 26⅜" h, pr	7,000.00
Birds, grapes, foliage, fluted white marble base, pr	100.00
Continental, ribbed body, 2 panel gilt scrolling handles, swags, pedestal foot, circular stepped marble base, 13" h, pr	695.00

Vases

Child rising from sunburst holding floral pocket, parcel gilt, 6" . . .	250.00
Flat-sided oval, hammered base decor by Celtic freize, Gustar Gurschner, parcel gilt, 6"	260.00

BUFFALO POTTERY 1907

19

MADE AT YE BUFFALO POTTERY

DELDARE WARE UNDERGLAZE

BUFFALO POTTERY

Buffalo Pottery Co., Buffalo, New York, was chartered in 190?. The first kiln was fired in October 1903. Larkin Soap Company conceived Buffalo Pottery to produce premiums for its extensive mail order business. Wares also were sold to the public by better department and jewelry stores. Elbert Hubbard and Frank L. Wright, who designed the Larkin Administration Building in Buffalo in 1904, were two prominent names associated with the Larkin Company.

Early production consisted mainly of dinner sets of semi-vitreous china. Buffalo was the first pottery in the United States to produce successfully the Blue Willow pattern, marked "First Old Willow Ware Mfg. in America." Buffalo also made a line of hand decorated, multicolored Willow ware, Gaudy Willow, that is scarce and much in demand. Other early items include a series of game, fowl, and fish sets, pitchers, jugs, and a line
of commemorative, historical, and advertising plates and mugs.

In 1908–09 and 1921–23, Buffalo Pottery produced the line for which it is most famous, Deldare Ware. The earliest of this olive green, semi-vitreous china depicts hand decorated scenes from the English artist Cecil Aldin's *Fallowfield Hunt.* Hunt scenes only were done in 1908–09. English village scenes also were characteristic and found throughout the series. Most are artist signed.

In 1911 Buffalo Pottery produced another type of Deldare, called Emerald Deldare, with scenes from Goldsmith's *The Three Tours of Dr. Syntax* and characterized by an Art Nouveau type border. Completely decorated Art Nouveau pieces also were made.

In 1912 Abino was born. Abino was done on Deldare bodies and showed sailing, windmill, and seascape scenes. The main color was rust; and, all pieces are artist signed and numbered.

In 1915 the pottery was modernized, giving it the ability to produce vitrified china. Consequently, hotel and institutional ware became their main production, with hand decorated ware de-emphasized. Buffalo china became a leader in producing and designing the most famous railroad, hotel, and restaurant patterns. These wares, especially railroad items, are eagerly sought by collectors.

In the early 1920s fine china was made for home use, e.g., the Bluebird pattern. In 1950 Buffalo made their first Christmas plate. They were given away to customers and employees from 1950–60. Hample Equipment Co. ordered some in 1962. The Christmas plates are very scarce.

The name Buffalo Pottery and Buffalo China are synonomous. The difference being one is sem-vitreous ware and the other vitrified. In 1956 the company was reorganized and Buffalo China became the corporate name. Today Buffalo China is owned by Oneida Silver Company. The Larkin family no longer is involved.

All the plate numbers refer to Vi and Si Altman's *The Book Of Buffalo Pottery* (Crown, 1969).

ABINO WARE

Candlestick, 9", sailing ships, 1913 (251)	475.00
Matchbox Holder and Ash Tray combination (252)	675.00
Pitcher, 7", Portland Head Light (256)	695.00
Plates	
8½", Portland Head Light (246) .	550.00
10", Windmill Scene (240)	575.00
Tankard, 10½", sailing scene (255)	900.00
Tea Tile, 6", nautical scene (259) . .	650.00

BLUE AND GAUDY WILLOW

Blue Willow
Cup and Saucer (26)	25.00
Pitcher, 7" (27)	150.00
Platter, 13 x 16" (24)	40.00
Relish (27)	45.00

Gaudy Willow
Pitcher, 8" (C8)	350.00
Plate, 10½" (28)	125.00

CHRISTMAS PLATES

1950 (260)	50.00
1953 (263)	50.00
1962 (271)	225.00

COMMERCIAL SERVICES

B & O Railroad, Harpers Ferry, Plate, 9½" (282)	300.00
Roycroft Inn, Cake Plate, 10" (288)	150.00
Skier Plate, 10½" (305)	65.00
George Washington Service, Platter (275)	600.00
World's Fair Plate, 1939, 10¼" (286)	100.00

DELDARE WARE

Bowls
Fern, 8", insert, Ye Village Street (153)	450.00
Fruit, 9", Ye Village Tavern (152)	450.00
Calling Card Tray, 7¾", Fallowfield Hunt (129)	300.00
Candlestick, shield back, Colonial Days, 1909 (157)	675.00
Candlesticks, 9½", pr (156)	600.00
Creamer, village scenes, 1924 (138)	175.00
Cup and Saucer, Ye Olden Days, 1909 (150)	190.00
Dresser Tray, 9 x 12", Dancing Ye Minuet, 1909 (144)	550.00

Mugs, Fallowfield Hunt, 1909
2½", (122)	265.00
3½", (122)	235.00

Pitchers
7", To Spare An Old Soldier (166)	450.00
9", With A Cane Superior Air (167)	525.00

Plates
6½", Fallowfield Hunt, 1909 (132)	120.00
7½", salesman's sample plate, 1908 (116)	500.00
9¼", Fallowfield Hunt, 1908 (124)	200.00
9½", Ye Olden Times, 1908 (145)	160.00
10", Cake, Ye Village Gossips, 1908 (142)	325.00
10", Fallowfield Hunt, Breaking Cover (124)	250.00
Relish Dish, Fallowfield Hunt, The Dash (135)	350.00

Sugar, covered, village scenes, 1925 (138)	190.00
Tankard, 12½", Fallowfield Hunt, 1909 (118)	750.00
Tea Tray, 10½ x 12", Heirlooms, 1908 (141)	600.00
Teapot, 3¼", village life, 1909 (138)	250.00

DELDARE WARE, MISC.

Humidor, 8", There Was An Old Sailor (227)	750.00
Salt and Pepper Shakers, Art Nouveau	500.00

EMERALD DELDARE

Cup and Saucer, Dr. Syntax At Liverpool (181)	275.00
Humidor, 7", Dr. Syntax Returned Home	850.00
Mug, 4¼", Dr. Syntax Again Filled Up His Glass	350.00
Pitcher, 6", Dr. Syntax Stopped By Highway Men (207)	500.00
Plaque, 13½", Penn's Treaty With The Indians, 1911 (217)	1,500.00
Plate, 9¼", Syntax Star Gazing (213A)	475.00
Tea Tray, 10¼ x 13¾", Dr. Syntax Mistakes A Gentleman's House For An Inn (180)	875.00

GAME SETS

Buffalo Hunt, oval platter, 1907 (62)	175.00
Champion-Bromley Crib Dog, plate, 9½" (73)	500.00
Deer, platter, sgd R. K. Beck, 1909 (66)	125.00
Dusky Grouse, plate, 9", 1908 (64)	60.00
Elk, plate, 9" (68)	50.00

Fish
Plate, 9" (59)	50.00
Platter, 1909 (58)	125.00

HISTORICAL, COMMEMORATIVE AND ADVERTISING WARE

Calumet Club, mug, 4½" (111)	75.00
Faneuil Hall, Boston, MA, plate, 10" (84)	50.00
Fraternity Hall, mug, 4½" (109)	75.00
Gate Circle, Buffalo, NY, plate, 7½" (97)	90.00
Improved Order Of Red Men, plate, 7½" (90)	75.00
Trinity Church, New York City, plate, 7½" (94)	75.00
U. S. Capitol, Washington, D.C., plate, 10" (79)	50.00
George Washington, plate, 7½" (101)	200.00

Buffalo Pottery, Calumet Club Mug, 1915, 4⅜″ h, green, $75.00.

Women's Christian Temperence Union, plate, 9″, 1908 (86B)	150.00

MISCELLANEOUS

Automobiling, plate, 9½″ (369)	300.00
Baby Bunting Tea Set, 22 pieces, 1904 (327)	200.00
Beverly Dinner Set, 1920, 100 pieces (316)	400.00
Blue Bird Tea Set, 56 pieces, 1919 (320)	350.00
Campbell Kids Feeding Dish, 7¾″, 1913 (329)	65.00
Canister Set, covers, 1906, each (353)	40.00
Chocolate Pot, 11″, 1908 (335) . . .	85.00
Dr. Syntax	
Plate, 9″, blue (363)	195.00
Platter, 14 x 11″, blue, 1909 (362)	250.00
Forget-Me-Not Dinner Set, 1909–17, 100 pieces (317)	400.00
Geranium Rose Bowl, 3¾″, 1907 (358)	75.00
Portland Vase, 8″, 1925 (341)	3,000.00
Roosevelt Bears, pitcher, 5″ (330) .	125.00
Tankard, 4 mugs, green, 1905 (337) .	350.00
Toilet Set, Chrysanthemum, 11 pieces (326)	400.00
Tom and Jerry Punch Set (352) . . .	150.00

BURMESE GLASS

Burmese glass is a translucent art glass originated by Frederick Shirley and manufactured by the Mt. Washington Glass Co., New Bedford, Mass., from 1885 to approximately 1891. Burmese glass shades from a soft lemon to a salmon pink. Uranium was used to attain the yellow color and gold was added to the batch so that upon reheating one end turned pink. Upon reheating again, the edges would revert to the yellow coloring. The blending of the colors was so gradual that it was difficult to determine where one color ended and the other began.

Although some of the glass has a surface that is glossy, most of it is acid finished. The majority of items were free blown but some were blown molded in a ribbed, hobnail or diamond quilted design. American-made Burmese is quite thin, fragile and brittle.

The only other factory licensed to make it was Thos. Webb & Sons in England. Out of deference to Queen Victoria, they named their wares "Queen's Burmese."

Reproductions abound in almost every form. Since uranium can no longer be used, some of the reproduction is easy to spot. In the 1950's Gunderson produced many pieces in imitation of Burmese.

MW = Mount Washington
Wb = Webb
a.f. = acid finish
s.f. = shiny finish

Toothpick, 2½″ h, MW, s.f., sq top, optic diamond quilt, $285.00.

Biscuit Jar, 5½″, MW, a.f., jewel starfish decor, butterfly on SP lid	1,250.00
Bon Bon, 2″, MW, a.f., tricorner, 5″ long on each side, undecorated .	285.00
Bowls	
2½″, Wb, a.f., prunus blossoms decor	400.00
4¾″ d rose bowl, MW, a.f., heavy enamel blossoms decor	885.00
5½″, 7″ d, MW, a.f., berry pontil, 4 applied feet, Queens Design decor, rare	1,500.00
Undecorated	950.00

5¾" d, MW, a.f., ruffled edge
fingerbowl, undecor **345.00**

6", MW, s.f., scalloped top, berry
pontil, 4 applied feet, enamel
daisy decor **1,050.00**

Brides Basket, 4½ x 8" d, MW, a.f.,
in SP holder, enamel chrysanthemums decor on bowl **1,300.00**

Cologne, 4½", Wb, a.f., sterling
monogramed top, gold foliage,
enamel butterfly decor **885.00**

Condiment, 3¼" h, MW, a.f., cruet,
faceted stopper, ribbed body,
same size, shape as salt & pepper
shakers, SP holder **585.00**

Cream and Sugar, 2⅛" sugar, 3¾"
creamer, MW, a.f., undecor **585.00**

Cruets
4", MW, a.f., salt shaker-shaped,
faceted stopper, undecor **245.00**

7", MW, a.f., melon ribbed, mush-
room stopper
Forget-me-not decor **1,750.00**
Undecorated **950.00**

7", MW, a.f., melon ribbed, shot
glass stopper **985.00**

Demi-tasse, 1¾" h, MW, s.f., undecor **485.00**

Jam Set, 2¼ x 4⅞" d bowls (2),
MW, s.f., rigaree collar, SP holder **985.00**

Lamps
7", sgnd W., a.f., minature, base,
shade undecor, unsignd burner **950.00**

19", MW, a.f., brass base, Guba
ducks decor on shade **2,500.00**

Muffineer, 4", Wb, a.f., SP top, floral
decor **685.00**

Pitchers
3½", MW, a.f., dainty undecorated
creamer **465.00**

6", MW paper label, a.f., owl decor, verse by Shakespeare ... **2,950.00**

7¾", MW, a.f., rare decor of Royal Flemish coins, swags of
raised gold, enamel blossoms . **2,950.00**

9", MW, s.f., tankard, applied handle, undecor **850.00**

Plate, 9", MW, a.f., flying Ibis decor,
Queen Anne's lace in raised gold **1,500.00**

Salt Dip, 1¼ x 2¼" d, Wb, a.f.,
prunus blossoms decor, very rare **485.00**

Salt Shakers, 3¼", MW, a.f.
Ribbed enamel decor **335.00**
Ribbed, undecor **185.00**

Shades
5½", MW, a.f., gas shade, 2¼"
fitter, enamel birds, butterflies
decor **350.00**

5½", MW, s.f., gas shade, 2¼"
fitter, fluted edge, very fine color **345.00**

Toothpick Holders, 2½", MW, a.f.,
ruffled top
Optic diamond quilt **385.00**

Rigaree collar **485.00**

Tumblers, MW, a.f
Two fish and a net of raised gold
decor **1,000.00**
Undecorated **285.00**

Vases
2¾", Wb, a.f., leaves, berries decor **300.00**

3¼", MW, a.f., enameled snails
decor **650.00**

4" sgnd W., a.f., gold leaves, berries decor **435.00**

9½", MW, a.f., bulbous, enamel
decor of 2 fish swimming behind
a raised gold net, rare **3,000.00**

10¾", MW, a.f., bulbous, verse by
James Montgomery, daisies and
butterfly decor **2,250.00**

12", MW, a.f., jack-in-the-pulpit,
pie-crust crimped edge
Profuse, heavy enamel floral decor **1,150.00**
Undecorated **850.00**

13", MW, a.f., raised gold decor of
stylized floral, geometric design **1,150.00**

BUSTS

**The portrait bust originated from pagan and
Christian traditions. The first were mainly of
Roman heroes. Later, images of Christian
saints were made for reliquaries. It was not
until the Renaissance that is was deemed
proper that 'ordinary' man should be represented. Busts of notable persons were popular adornments in 18th and 19th century
home libraries. Considering the number of library pieces produced, a collector can still
find excellent examples at reasonable prices
based on artist, subject and material.**

**By the very nature of their simplicity, busts
can add a very spectacular image to the
most modern setting. Also see "Bronzes"
and "Parian."**

Bacchante, 15½", bronze, green-
brown patina, separate green marble plinth, cast from model by Jef
Lambeaux, sgd **490.00**

Buddha, 20¼", bronze, green mottled brown patina, traces of gilding
and red pigment, solid cast, sheer
sanghati draped over one shoulder with tassels, tightly curled hair,
wood plinth, Northern Thai,
Chiengsen type, c15th C **6,050.00**

Child, 8½", bronze, "4 months,"
inscribed © Beach, stepped red
marble base **80.00**

Circi, 11½", patinated metal, gazing
over right shoulder, hair in chignon

Young lady, 13½" h, marble, marble base, unmarked, $195.00.

tal, sq base	140.00
Slave Girl, 20½", zinc, arab head-dress, self socle	110.00
Woman, 28" l, bronze, brown patina, inscribed W/1909	900.00
Wright, Frank Lloyd, wood, carved from life sketches by John K. Daniels	125.00

BUTTER PRINTS

Butter prints are made up of two categories —butter molds and butter stamps. Butter stamps are of one piece construction, sometimes two piece if the handle is from a separate piece of wood. Butter molds are generally of three piece construction: the design, the screw-in handle, and the case. Stamps decorate the top of butter after it is molded; molds both mold and stamp the butter at the same time.

The earliest prints were one piece and hand carved, often thick and deeply carved. Later prints were factory made with the design forced into the wood by a metal die.

Some of the most common designs are sheaves of wheat, leaves, flowers, and pineapples. Animal designs and Germanic tulips are difficult to find. Rare prints include unusual shapes, such as half-rounded and lollipop, and those with designs on both sides.

Heart and Flower, stamp, 5½ x 3½", crimped stylized edges, $400.00.

with band of round medallions at the front, rect. base, Circi in gilt	120.00
Cupid, marble, carved pedestal	250.00
Dante, 4½", white marble, carved, mounted on black painted frame	68.00
Diane, 8½", bronze, green onyx base, cast from model by E. Villanis, French, inscribed Paris foundry mark	190.00
Franklin, Benjamin, 34 x 21", 12½" d, wood, pine, carved, painted, neck scarf, cloaked shoulders, rect. plinth, molded rims	4,200.00
Franklin, Benjamin, parian	185.00
Jesus Christ, 9", parian, unmarked	115.00
Madame Du Barry, 11½", porcelain, polychrome, socle base	130.00
Maiden, 22½", marble, hair crowned with fruiting vines	260.00
Man and Woman, Victorian, bisque, pr	175.00
Miranda, 6", parian, Bell, c1872	62.00
Princess Alexandra, 12", parian, commissioned by Crystal Art Palace Association, registered 2/23/1863, Copeland	275.00
Queen Victoria, 7⅜", parian, memento, 1887 Jubilee	145.00
Renaissance Lady, 10½", Italian pottery, sgd Minghatti	85.00
Roman, 11", bronze, sculptured, gazing over left shoulder, pedes-	

Acorn, mold, 4⅞" d, minor age cracks, refinished	65.00
Chestnut and Leaf, stamp, 4" d, block and reed edge	70.00
Christian Lamb with cross and banner, stamp, 3¼" d, turned, minor age cracks and edge damage	225.00
Cows and Leaves, stamp, 4⅜"	200.00
Eagle, stamp, 4" d, crimped edge	160.00
Floral, stamp, almond shape, 4⅜ x 9", stylized design of circular center with 2 daisy like plants, "v" leaf motifs on side, carved handle,	

some edge damage and filled in worm holes 275.00

Four Part, mold, 5½ x 6″, scored into quarters, acorn and sheaf of wheat motif 75.00

Heart and Leaves, stamp, half round, 7 x 3½″ 220.00

Leaf, stamp, 3⅞″ d, strongly leafed plant, crimped edges, turned handle 55.00

Pineapple, mold, 4¾″ d, age cracks and wear 60.00

Sheaf of Wheat
Mold, double, 4¾″ l 60.00
Stamp, 4¼″ d, crimped edge ... 67.50

Star, geometric, stamp, 4¾″ d, sq carved handle with Matese cross 125.00

Star Flower, stamp, 5¼″ d, 5½″ h, 12 petal flower with dot separating each petal 90.00

Tulip, stamp, 4¼″ d, 4½″ h, deeply stylized carving, carved handle .. 225.00

Tulip and Star Flower, stamp, 5⅜″ d, 5⅝″ h, carved handle, some worm holes 175.00

BUTTONS

The collecting of buttons is one of the most fascinating of hobbies, as there is a wealth of historical material in their development. Caspar Wister was making brass buttons in Philadelphia as early as 1750 and the Shaker colony at New Lebanon, N. Y. was making them in 1789. The most popular of the Victorian period were the story buttons. They were usually brass or gilt, and the subjects were from well-known stories, fairy tales, heroes, nursary rhymes, nature subjects and literary characters.

Also collectible are tole or painted tin buttons, which were done by the Pennsylvania Dutch. Most buttons found today are of the later two-piece variety of late 19th century.

The term "pearl," refers to the inside of fresh-water shells. In small towns along the Mississippi River, small industries turned out the fresh water pearl shell which was used in button manufacture.

Museums: Cooper Union Museum for the Art of Decoration, New York, N. Y.

See *Warman's Americana & Collectibles* for an expanded listing of Buttons.

Bandmaster or musician's uniform button, embossed lyre, 2 pc brass, set of eight 3.00

Castle towers, 2″, brass 15.00

"Chateau" center, heart and fleur de lis border, 2 pc brass, 1¼″ 2.50

Confederate uniform
C 10.00

CSA 15.00
F 12.00

"Cupid at Rest," wide steel rim, brass, 1½″ 8.00

Ethan Allen's coat, brass, attached to card from 1895 Mass. Colonial Exhibit 50.00

Eureka, nickel plated, ⅞″, crossed nozzle, trumpet in center 10.00

"Garden of Eden," or "Thehion and the Snake," from fable by La Fontaine, 2 pc. brass, 1⅜″ 15.00

"Gardens at Karnak, Egypt," 2 pc brass, 1″ 5.00

"Grapes and Leaves," black glass, brass shank, Pat 1899 .... 1.50

"Hector," pewter head, Roman gladiator, brass rim 5.50

Inaugrals
George Washington, brass, eagle, star, 1 pc 325.00
George Washington, copper, "GW" in center oval, "Long Live The President" imp above, 1 pc 225.00

Irid purple, brass filigree, 2pc 5.00

Jet, black, faceted, round, 1 pc ... 8.00

New Haven F.D., gilded, 1″, horse drawn engine in center 6.00

Painted porcelain, orange, strawberries, and apple, "Goofies" set of three 2.50

Paperweight, blue flower, green leaves, brass shank 10.00

Pearl in brass filigree frame, 2 pc. brass, ¾″ 2.00

Porcelain, hand painted, rose garlands, artist signed, 1¼″ 6.00

Strawberries, filigree design, 2 pc. brass, 1″ 2.00

Success to the Plough, plated copper filled with lead, ⅞″, 1 pc ... 45.00

Vermont Militia 30.00

Vigilant Fire Co., brass, 1¼″, wooden hydrant and All Seeing Eye in center 18.00

CALENDAR PLATES

Calendar plates were first made in England in the late 1880s. They became popular in the United States after 1900, their peak years being between 1909 and 1915. The majority of the advertising type were made of porcelain or pottery with a calendar, the name of a store or business, a scene, portrait, animal or flowers featured. Occasionally, some were made of glass or tin.

See *Warman's Americana & Collectibles* for an expanded listing of Calendar Plates.

Calendar Plate, 1911, 7″, two horse-heads inside horseshoe, calendar on horseshoe, Compliments of H.B. Schanely, Jewelers, Quakertown, PA, $25.00.

1906, 9″, flowers, York, Pennsylvania	37.50
1908, 9″, fruit	25.00
1909, 8½″, holly spray	28.00
1909, 8½″, spray of small tea roses	28.00
1909, 9″, lady & man in patio garden	25.00
1909, 9¼″, flowers, New Jersey	18.00
1909, 9½″, dog's head, New York City	30.00
1910, 8″, flowers, New Hampshire	15.00
1910, 8″, flowers, Ohio	15.00
1910, 8¼″, Gibson Girl	28.00
1910, 8½″, roses, Minnesota	15.00
1910, 8½″, 2 angels, Sonora, California	15.00
1910, 9″, Washington's Old Home	28.00
1910, Astoria, South Dakota	26.00
1910, Betsy Ross, Dresden	30.00
1911, 7½″, pink flowers, Byers, Hagerstown, Maryland	27.00
1911, 7⅝″, man & woman, celluloids, Should Auld Acquaintance Be Forgotten	25.00
1911, 8″, hunt scene, Markell Drug Co., Chelsea	25.00
1912, 7½″, bowl of pink roses	28.00
1913, 8″, aircraft over coastal town	42.00
1913, 9″, roses and holly	25.00
1914, Grouse, sgd Beck	40.00
1915, 7″, Panama Canal	25.00
1915, 7½″, compliments of Hobbs, Rawlins, Wyoming	25.00
1916, 7½″, man in canoe, Iowa	25.00
1916, 9½″, bluebirds	40.00
1920, "The Great World War," Abercrombri, North Dakota	45.00
1920, 9¼″, Peace, Illinois	25.00
1924, 9″, Happy New Year	25.00
1929, 6¼″, flowers, Sylva, North Carolina	25.00
1929, 7½″, boy with dog	28.00
1981, 9¼″, Land of Liberty	15.00

CALLING CARD CASES

During the Victorian era, leaving a personal calling card was the social custom. The engraved cards were carried in a proper case. Card cases were made of various materials—silver, gold, ivory, mother of pearl, etc.; many were handsomely monogrammed. This gracious custom passed into oblivion after World War I.

Calling Card Case, silver, SS shaped edges, engine turned design, monogram, hallmarked, 3½ x 2½″, $95.00.

Abalone, pearl, diamond design, 3 x 4″	35.00
Gold, 14K, ribbed motif, sapphire initials	900.00
Ivory, carved flowers and vines, 2½ x 2½″	75.00
Pearl, carved profile of classical woman, floral engraving	35.00
Silver	
Chinese, applied dragon, sgd	100.00
Coin, shaped edges, engine turning, 3½ x 2½″	65.00
English, emb scroll work, 2¾ x 4″	145.00

Plated, floral engraving	35.00
Sterling	
Art Deco, blue enamel, 3⅛ x	
3⅞"	230.00
Embosed, chain handle	75.00
Tortoise Shell	
19th C, 4" 1	70.00
Oriental carving	65.00

CAMBRIDGE GLASS

Cambridge Glass Co., Cambridge, Ohio, was incorporated in 1901. In the beginning their main line was clear tableware. Later they expanded into colored, etched and engraved glass. Over 40 different hues were produced in their fine blown and pressed glass. Five different marks were employed during the production years, but not every piece was signed.

The plant closed in 1954. Some of the molds were later sold to the Imperial Glass Co., Bellaire, Ohio.

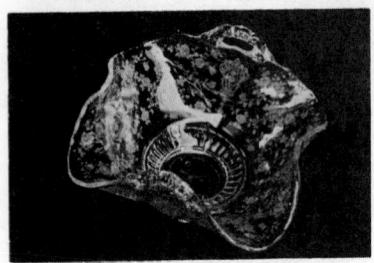

Bowl, 5½", Rosepoint, handled, $26.00.

Ashtrays	
Bowling Ball, 11"	65.00
Minerva etch, crystal	11.00
Bon Bons	
6", Caprice, blue	30.00
6¼", Cleo etch	25.00
7", Mt. Vernon	45.00
Bowls	
6", sq, Caprice, blue	22.50
6", Decagon, light emerald green,	
2 handled	8.50
11", Caprice, blue	35.00
11", Seashell	50.00
12", Cleo	30.00
12", Decagon, black	35.00
12½", Crown Tuscan	35.00

Ramshead, Eleanor, blue, ftd . . .	250.00
Candlesticks	
4", Star, crystal, pr	14.00
5", Heatherbloom, Martha etch, pr	98.00
5", Rosepoint, pr	60.00
5½", Everglades, crystal, pr	72.00
7¼", amethyst with twist stems,	
pr	35.00
9", Doric Column, ivory, single . .	72.00
9½", dolphins, green, pr	145.00
Celery, 11½", Rosepoint	22.50
Champagnes	
Apple Blossom, Mandarin yellow .	24.00
Apple Blossom, topaz	17.00
Cigarette Holder, Diane, crystal . . .	65.00
Cocktails	
Achilles	25.00
Crown Tuscan, nude stem, yellow	
bowl	135.00
Farberware, amber insert, ribbed	
stem	12.50
Cocktail Shaker, 48 oz, Pristine . . .	35.00
Compotes	
6½", Talisman Rose, crystal . . .	25.00
7", Farberware, cobalt insert . . .	40.00
7", Farberware, amethyst insert .	20.00
8", Crown Tuscan, nude stem . .	135.00
Condiment Set, 2 oz oil and vinegar,	
tray, SP	55.00
Console Sets, 3 piece	
Cleo, pink, gold decor	90.00
Decagon	125.00
Cordial, Regency, yellow	25.00
Creamers and Sugars	
Chantilly	20.00
Rosepoint, small	45.00
Tally Ho, amber, ftd	25.00
Wildflower	38.00
Cups and Saucers	
Decagon, green	7.50
Tally Ho, amber, ftd	10.00
Decanters	
Amber with 4 glasses	90.00
Nautilis, amethyst	45.00
Flower Figures (Frogs)	
8½", Draped Lady, amber	150.00
8½", Draped Lady, crystal	55.00
8½", Draped Lady, mocha	250.00
8½", Draped Lady, pink	95.00
9", Heron	65.00
Goblets	
Caprice, blue	40.00
Caprice, pink	35.00
Carmen	32.50
Cascade	14.00
Chantilly	20.00
Mt. Vernon, crystal	6.00
Roselyn	27.50
Rosepoint	28.00
Ice Buckets	
Gloria etch, with tongs, pink, sgr .	90.00
Tally Ho, cobalt, Farberware hold-	
er	95.00

Iced Teas

Chantilly	20.00
Cleo, light blue	22.00
Portia	23.00
Rosepoint, ftd	25.00
Wildflower, ftd	22.00

Ivy Balls

Amethyst	40.00
Crown Tuscan, nude stem	135.00

Jar with lid, Yardly, Crown Tuscan	15.00
Lamp, 12", Seashell Vase	275.00
Marmalade, open, Diane	40.00

Mayonnaise Sets, 3 pieces

Portia	40.00
Rosepoint	40.00

Mustard, Farberware, 4½" amber insert	8.00

Plates

8", Apple Blossom, topaz	8.00
8", Laurel Wreath	8.50
8", Tally Ho, cobalt	12.50
8½", Cascade	8.00
8½", Lorna, pink, sgr	6.00
8⅜", Decagon, green	5.00
Lunch, Everglades, blue	15.00

Platters

10½", Decagon, pink	29.50
14", Gloria, pink	75.00

Powder Jar and Hair Receiver, amber, celluloid lids, pr	45.00

Relish Dishes

2 part, Tally Ho, amber	9.00
3 part, Chantilly	18.00
3 part, Diane	16.00
4 part, Ebony	25.00
5 part, Elaine	35.00

Rose Bowl, 8", amethyst	32.00
Salt and Pepper, Diane, pr	38.00

Sherbets

Cleo, green, ftd	13.00
Portia, flared rim, tall stem	18.50
Rosepoint, low	25.00
Wildflower	15.00

Shot Glass, Caprice, blue	40.00

Swans

3", pink	28.00
3¼", green	29.50
6½", black	90.00
8½", forest green	160.00
8½", topaz	145.00
10½", crystal, frosted	110.00

Tumblers

Apple Blossom, 2½ oz, dark green, ftd	18.00
Decagon, 10 oz, light emerald green, ftd	14.00
Mt. Vernon, 5 oz, crystal, flat	5.00
Nautilus, 4", royal blue	8.50
Tally Ho, 9 oz	20.00

Vases

8", Portia, gold encrused	45.00
8½", Crown Tuscan, candlelight, pedestal, gold decor	70.00

9", keyhole	45.00
10", bud, Rosepoint, crystal	55.00

Vegetable Dishes

9½", Decagon, pink	35.00
9½", Decagon, blue	45.00

Wines

Apple Blossom, yellow	25.00
Chantilly	30.00
Farberware, amethyst flared insert	17.50
Nude, 6½", ebony stem	85.00
Portia	22.50
Pristine, 3 oz	15.00

CAMBRIDGE

CAMBRIDGE POTTERY

The Cambridge Art Pottery was incorporated in Ohio in 1900. Between 1901 and 1909, the firm produced the usual line of jarinieres, tankards, and vases with underglazed slip decorations and glazes similar to other Ohio potteries. Their line names included "Terrhea," "Oakwood," "Otoe" and others. In 1904, the company introduced Guernsey kitchenwares. It was so well received that it became the plant's primary product and in 1909 the name was changed to Guernsey Earthenware Company. All wares were marked.

Bowls

8", berry motif, glozzy brown glaze	75.00
9½", floral slip decor, glossy brown glaze	80.00

Candlesticks, 4" Terrhea, standard glaze, pr	45.00
Cookie Jar, 14", brown glaze	65.00
Plate, 8", royal blue	20.00
Tankard, 12", Oakwood	125.00

Vases

3½", bulbous, floral decor, standard glaze	75.00
5", Oakwood, brown glaze	110.00
5½", ovoid, decor grapes, leaves, artist sgd	110.00
6", floral decor, artist sgd M.W.	145.00
6½", green, acorn mark	65.00
8", berry motif, two-handled, artist sgd	175.00
10¾", cherry spray, high brown glaze	125.00
13", bulbous base, slender neck, artist sgd	250.00

Cambridge Pottery, Vase, 8″, Oakwood, high glaze, mold 235, tones of yellow, green, brown, $130.00.

CAMEO GLASS

Cameo glass is a form of cased glass. A shell of glass was prepared; then another layer or more of glass of a different color(s) was faced to the first. A design was then cut through the outer layer(s) leving the inner layer(s) exposed.

This type of art glass originated in Alexandria, Egypt, 100–200 A.D. The oldest and most famous example of Cameo glass is the Barberini or Portland vase which was found near Rome in 1582. It contained the ashes of Emperor Alexander Serverus who was assassinated by his own soldiers in 235 A.D.

Emile Gallé, son of a French glassmaker, is probably one of the best known artists of Cameo glass. He established his factory at Nancy, France in 1884. Although much of the glass bears his signature, some he only designed while his many assistants did the actual work, even to signing his name. Glass made after his death in 1904 has a star before the name Gallé. Other makers of Cameo glass located in France included D'Argental, Daum Nancy, LeGras and Delatte.

English Cameo is made in the same manner as French Cameo; however, the English Cameo does not have as many layers of glass (colors) and the number of cuttings. The outer layer is usually white and the cuttings are usually very fine and delicate. Most pieces are not signed. The best known makers are Thomas Webb & Sons, Stevens and Williams and, of course, George Woodall.

The majority of Cameo glass found on the market today was made in 1884–1900 period. It is being reproduced in limited quantities in France but is inferior in quality.

ENGLISH

Bottles, Perfume and Scent
  Lay Down Type
    Citron ground, white water lilies, 8½″ 600.00
    Red ground, carved long stemmed leaves, orig SS hinged cap 575.00
  Stand Up Type
    Blue ground, white apple blossoms, 3″ 325.00
    Deep amber ground, overlaid in white flowers, SS top with Chester hallmark, 1884 .... 300.00
    Pink ground, white leaves, 3½″ 350.00
    Sapphire blue ground, carved with plants, bee in opaque white, hinged SS top, Birmingham, c1880 .... 750.00
    Turquoise ground, white flowers and leaves, SS hinged lid .. 695.00
Chalice, 2¼″, miniature, brown ground, floral work, gilding, Webb 395.00
Lamp, 8″, yellow ground, red fucshia and leaves, sgd Stevens & Williams 2,500.00
Rose Bowl, 3″, brown ground, white morning glories 350.00
Salt, red Florentine, matching spoon, sgd Thomas Webb in cameo ... 250.00
Vases
  4½″, citron ground, baluster shape, carved white lilac sprays, lotus trim at neck 380.00
  5½″, green ground, white tulips . 350.00
  5½″, yellow ground, round, raised neck, carved overlay with white roses, unsigned 175.00
  8″, brown ground, white florals, brass ormolu stand, sgd Thomas Webb 750.00
  9″, blue ground, white florals and butterflies 1,400.00
  9″, citron translucent ground, carved white leaves, lotus trim at neck, sgd Webb 600.00
  9″, royal blue ground, white roses overlay, sgd Thomas Webb & Sons 3,500.00
  10½″, bright blue ground, overlaid in white leaves, flowers, script sgd Stevens & Williams, dated 1885 above sgr 8,500.00

12", rose ground, pear shape, white overlay carved with morning glories, unsigned **475.00**

Vase, 6⅜", reddish amber frosted ground, dark red design, Japanese Ginko leaves, sgd Galle, $750.00.

FRENCH

Biscuit Jar, frosted ground, pink flowers, SP lid, handle, sgd Val St. Lambert **350.00**
Bowls
2½" h x 5¼" d, crimped top, mottled yellow orange ground, serene lake scene in reds, browns, acid etched, sgd Daum Nancy **700.00**
10 x 5", oval, green satin ground, brown chestnuts, leaves, Loetz **1,000.00**
12 x 11", Deco, acid cut tiers, Daum Nancy **350.00**
Boxes, covered
3½" h, circular, green ground, 3 amber butterflies, sides carved with amber dogwoods, Galle . . **500.00**
4¾ x 2¾", tan ground, green grapes and leaves, Daum Nancy **450.00**
6 x 3", 8 sided, blue ground, white swans, Galle **950.00**
6¾", mottled orange brown and yellow ground, carved ivy leaves in allover design, applied lady bugs, jewels, inscribed Daum . . **615.00**
Candlestick, 17½" h, peach ground carved with overlay purple lilacs, Galle **900.00**
Chandelier, 13½", inverted dome, blue translucent glass overlay with

green, brown scene of bird perched in grape laden bower, grape leaf border, orig silk tassels, sgd DiPede **215.00**
Cup and Saucer, Clair De Lune, sgd Daum Nancy **350.00**
Compote, 9 x 4", lime green ground, maroon swirl, wheel cutting, Burgun & Schverer, rare **1,000.00**
Decanter, 9½", frosted ground, purple violets, leaves, clear cut stopper, sgd Val St. Lambert **610.00**
Dish, 5½" h, canoe shape, scenic landscape, amber tinted gray glass overlaid with deep blue, cameo mark Galle **1,100.00**
Ewer, mottled green ground, blue, gray-white decor, clear serpentine handles, Daum Nancy **420.00**
Flask, 6", yellow frosted ground, lavender flowers, Daum Nancy **500.00**
Lamps, Table
17½" h, 8¼" d shade, domical shade and base overlaid in shades of deep blue, green, peach on off-white ground depicting mountain and lake scene, cameo sgr of Muller Fres Lundeville **3,500.00**
19", Chinese Junk scenic dome shade, matching base, sgd Daum Nancy **2,200.00**
21", gold frost ground, red blossoms, Galle **5,000.00**
24", trumpet shaped base, conical shade of translucent yellow glass overlaid in sapphire, lavender, brown, etched with azalea, cameo sgr Galle **7,200.00**
31", trumpet base, conical shade of translucent yellow glass overlaid in yellow-orange, lime-green and brown etched with leaves, branches and oranges, cameo sgr Galle **24,200.00**
Plate, 13¾", kaleidoscope, clear to opaque to red in center, spreading pattern of four arms in red, sgd Charder, La Verre Francais **1,175.00**
Punch Bowl, 20 x 12", yellow ground, large orange and blue morning glories, La Verre Francais **550.00**
Salt, 1¾", rain scenic, Daum Nancy **175.00**
Rose Bowl, 3¼", dark blue ground, lake scenic, De Vez **300.00**
Tumblers
2¾", gold fleur-dy-lys, frost ground, Daum Nancy **150.00**
3", frosted ground, topaz thistles, Galle **300.00**
Vases
3", frosted ground, yellow, gray flowers, Galle **250.00**

3″, green ground, scenic, De Vez **250.00**

3½″ h, frosted ground, yellow, green, apricot foliage, Galle ... **350.00**

3½″, rain scene, Daum Nancy .. **325.00**

3½″, oval, spring scene, Daum Nancy **300.00**

4″, cream ground, brown berries, leaves, candlestick shape, Galle **750.00**

4″, flattened oval, red-brown ground, forest scene, fall colors, Daum Nancy **575.00**

4″, yellow ground, orange floral, La Verre Francais **225.00**

4½″, yellow ground, Freesia, Delatte **250.00**

5¼ x 4″ d, pastel blue ground, green and blue cut scene of mountains, lake, three acid cuttings, sgd DeVez **650.00**

5½″, blue ground, 6 blue ships, 6 fisherman, sgd Galle, rare ... **2,200.00**

5¾″, gray ground overlaid in purple, iris blossoms, leaves, fire polished, sgd Galle **795.00**

5¾″, red ground, dark blue berries, Richard **325.00**

6½″, frosted ground, pink flowers, Val St. Lambert **300.00**

6½″ x 12″, geese scenic, LaVerre Francais **500.00**

7″, cream ground, green and gold thistles, rectangular shape on metal base, Daum Nancy **475.00**

7″, white ground, light blue graceful lacy flowers, sgd Galle ... **875.00**

8″, blue ground, red parrots, Muller Freres **975.00**

8½″, oval, cylindrical, lake mountain scene, sgd Le Gras **775.00**

8½″, ball with stem and base, mottled brown to orange to yellow ground, flowers and foliage, geometric, sgd LaVerre Francais **425.00**

8″, frosted ground, Fox and Raven, green, black, Daum Nancy **1,275.00**

9″, barrel shape, late summer scene, Daum Nancy **1,950.00**

9″, clear ground, blue grape and vine, fan shape, Galle **1,150.00**

9″, yellow ground, overlay of sienna carved umbels, D'Argental . **240.00**

9″, yellow, white, brown acid ground, amber pine cones and needles, flared base, Galle ... **650.00**

10″, opaque pink ground, green branches, peach fleurettes overlay, marked Arsall **385.00**

10⅛ x 5¾″ d, yellow satin ground, lighthouse scene, boat, sgd Michel, Paris **995.00**

11″, waterlilies in two shades of lavendar, yellow, Galle **995.00**

12″, cut black to purple to green, sgd Galle **1,400.00**

12″, translucent yellow ground overlay with carved purple iris at neck, flowerhead borders, sgd St. Louis **500.00**

12¼″, three sided, milky beige ground, acid cut back chrysanthemums painted in amber tones, blue-green leaves, sgd S. D. LeGras **535.00**

12½″, pale yellows and lavenders, stick shape on donut shape base, Daum Nancy **950.00**

13½″, cream ground, scenic, brown stepped circular foot supporting flat sided heart shaped reserve of river landscape in greens, brown, tapering to brown neck, Galle **1,540.00**

13¾″, oviform, translucent sky-blue ground overlaid with white, lavender and plum etched with gentians, cameo sgr Galle **4,000.00**

14″, frosted ground, orange chrysanthemums, Galle **1,250.00**

14″, gold ground, blue geometric, La Verre Francais **475.00**

14″, pink to cream ground, lilac wisteria, green leaves, candlestick shape, Galle **880.00**

14¾″ x 4″ d, satin, lavender to green, scenic lake and trees, sgd Le Gras **895.00**

18″, orange frosted ground, light green floral, stick shape, Galle . **1,500.00**

CAMERAS

Photographica, the collecting of cameras and related items, is still in its infancy. The current market in photographs as an art form has brought attention to the instruments and equipment used to make them.

Any camera older than twenty years is considered collectible. Among the makers, the most desirable are Leica and Zeiss. The two key elements are good exterior condition and good working condition. The original box does not add greatly to the value.

See *Warman's Americana & Collectibles* for additional listings of Cameras.

Agfa Isolette, Super, folding 6 x 6 cm on 120 film, f3.5/75mm Solinar, Agfa Kamerawerke (Munich, Germany) **90.00**

Ansco (Binghamton, NY; merged with Agfa in 1928)

Korona V, folding, 5 x 7 plate, Gundlock Optical Co., Rochester, NY, $65.00.

Ansco Automatic Reflex, Twin Lens Reflex, 120 film, f3.5/83-mm Anastigmat lens, 1947–49 . 135.00
Buster Brown Folding Camera, Model 3A, postcard size, Actus shutter 20.00
Folding Camera, Model 7, post-card size rollfilm, red bellows, brass Wollensak lens 27.50
Anthony, E. & H. T. (Binghamton, NY; merged with Scovill in 1902)
Buckeye Box Camera, 12 exp. on daylight loading rollfilm, c1896 . 70.00
View Camera, 11 x 14, studio type 250.00
Bell & Howell, Fonton, spring motor driven, 35mm, f2/50mm, case, c1948, Bell & Howell (Chicago, IL) 550.00
Blair Camera Co. (Boston, MA; merged with Eastman Kodak in 1907)
Detective Hawkeye, wooden box, 4 x 5 plates, 1890s 175.00
No. 4, Folding Weno Hawkeye, 4 x 5, box, single shutter speed, two finders 60.00
Bosley Model B2, compact 35mm, f3.2/44mm, double exposure pre-vention and sync. shutter, c1949-56, manufactured for U.S. Air Force, Bosley Corp. of America (New York, NY) 25.00
Candid Camera, Perfex Forty-Four, 35mm, couple rangefinder, f3.5/-

50mm Anastigmat, exp. meter, 1939–40, Candid Camera Corp. of America 37.50
Contessa-Nettal, folding plate cam-era, 9 x 12 cm, f4.5/150mm Zeiss Tessar, ground glass back, black leather cov body, Contessa-Nettal (Stuttgart, Germany; merged with Zeiss in 1926) 160.00
Dossert Detective Camera, box, 4 x 5 plate, reflex viewing, leather cover designed to look like satch-el, c1885, Dossert Detective Cam-era Co. (New York, NY) 675.00
Eastman Kodak (Rochester, NY)
Autographic No. 3, 3¼ x 4¼, 118 film, f7.7/130mm, BB shutter, 1914–26 . . . . 18.00
Boy Scout Camera, 1⅝ x 2½, 127 rollfilm, green vest pocket, em-blem on bed, 1930–34 . . . . . . 40.00
Brownie No. 2, box, 2¼ x 3¼, 120 film, maroon bellows, Me-niscus lens, 1901–24 . . . . 14.00
Brownie Stereo, No. 2, 3¼ x 2½, rollfilm, red bellows, 1905–10 . 200.00
Eureka No. 4, 4 x 5″, 109 car-tridge film in roll holder, 1899 . 82.00
Kodak No. 3, string set box cam-era, Bausch & Lomb Universal Lens, 3¼ x 4¼ 60 or 100 expo-sures, factory loaded 400.00
Medalist II, 2¼ x 3¼, 620 film, f3.5/100mm Ektar, flash super-matic shutter, 1946–52 . . . . . . 145.00
Retina, Model 1B, 35mm, f3.5/50 Xenar 60.00
Zenith, box 3¼ x 4¼ plate, similar to Eureka cameras, late 1890s 135.00
Ernemann, Ermanox, collapsible bel-lows model, 6.5 x 9 cm, f1.8 Ernostar, Heinrich Ernemann Werke Aktien Gesellschaft (Dres-den, Germany) 800.00
Expo Watch Camera, shaped like railroad pocket watch, winding knob serves as lens cap for pic-ture taken through winding stem, special film cartridge, 1905–36 . . 145.00
Franke & Heidecke, Rolleiflex, Twin Lens Relfex, 4 x 4 cm, 127 film, f2.8/60 mm Tesar, 1957 gray body type, Franke & Heidecke (Braunschweig, Germany) 100.00
Goerz, Tenax, folding camera, 6 x 9 cm, f6.3/100mm Tenastigmat, Compur shutter, C. P. Goerz (Ber-lin, Germany; merged with Zeiss in 1926) 22.00
Graflex, Inc. (Rochester, NY) Auto-Graflex, 4 x 5, focal plane shutter 85.00
Press Graflex, 5 x 7, c1907–23 . . 175.00
Guthe & Thorsch, KW Patent Etui,

folding plate, 6 x 9 cm, f4.5/100-mm Tessar, Ibsor shutter, Guthe & Thorsch Kamera Werkstatten (Dresden, Germany) 50.00

Houghton, Midget, folding, 3.5 x 4.5 cm, 127 film, Meniscus lens, c1912, George Houghton & Son Ltd (London, England, merged with Butcher in 1925) 42.50

ICA, Cupido, folding camera, 6 x 9 cm plates, F4.5/12cm, Compur dial set shutter, A. G. ICA (Dresden, Germany; merged with Zeiss in 1926) 40.00

Konishiroku Kogaku (Japan), Pearlette, folding camera, 127 film, f6.3/75mm Rokuohsha Optar, 1920s 35.00

Krauss, Photo Revolver, 18 x 35 mm on 48 plates in magazine or rollfilm in special back, 1920s, G. A. Krauss (Stuttgart, Germany, and Paris, France) 2,000.00

Manhatten, Night-Hawk Detective Camera, 4 x 5 plates, Rapid Achromatic lens, leather cov. wood case, string set shutter, Manhatten Optical Company (New York, NY) 400.00

Minolta, 35, rangefinder (Leica copies), f2.8/45mm Kokkor, late 1940s, Chiyoda Kogaku Seiko Co., Ltd (Osaka, Japan) 75.00

Nagel, 18, folding camera, 6 x 9 cm plates, f6.3 Nagel Anastigmat, c1928, Dr. August Nagel Camerawerk (Stuttgart, Germany) 65.00

Polaroid, Model 95, c1950 . . . . 22.50

Reflex, Junior, box, 3¼ x 4¼ plate, simple lens, 4 speed shutter coupled to mirror, c1904, Reflex Camera Co. (Yonkers, NY) 155.00

Rochester Optical Co. (Rochester, NY; merged with Kodak in 1907)
  Favorite, box, 8 x 10 plates, Emile No. 5 lens with waterproof stops, 1890s 210.00
  Premo Long Focus, folding, triple extension red bellows, 5 x 7 . . . 95.00

Scovill Triad Detective, box 4 x 5 plates or rollfilm, variable speed string set shutter, leather cov., c1892, Scovill Manufacturing Co. (New York, NY; merged with Anthony in 1902) 950.00

Universal, Buccaneer, rangefinder, 35mm, f3.5/50mm Tricor, 1940s, Universal Camera Corp. (New York, NY) 14.00

Voigtlander Superb, Twin Lens Reflex, 120 film, f3.5/75mm Skopar, 1930s, Voigtlander & Sons (Braunschweig, Germany) 125.00

CAMPAIGN ITEMS

Since 1800 the American presidency always has been a contest between two or more candidates. Initially, souvenirs were issued to celebrate victories. Items issued during a campaign to show support for a candidate were actively being distributed in the William Henry Harrison election of 1840.

Campaign items cover a wide variety of materials—badges, bandannas, buttons, tokens, etc. The only limiting factor seems to be a promoter's imagination.

Items selling below $100.00 move frequently enough to establish firm prices. Items above that price fluctuate according to supply and demand. Many individuals now recognize the value of political items, acquiring them and holding them for future sale. As a result, modern material has a relatively low market value.

Two recent books have greatly assisted identification and cataloguing of campaign material: Herbert R. Collins's *Threads of History* and Edmund B. Sullivan's *American Political Badges and Medalets 1789-1892.* These expand the identification work done by Theodore L. Hake.

The abbreviation "h/s" is used to identify a head and shoulder photo or etching of a person.

See *Warman's Americana & Collectibles* for an expanded listing of Political and Campaign Items.

Badge, 1934, Roosevelt, $30.00.

Badges

1896, Bryan, 1½" oval base with celluloid h/s photo in ornate wreath like frame, flag ribbon, eagle pin top, 2¾" h 37.50

1904, T. Roosevelt, 1¾" celluloid sepia h/s portrait button, 2 x 5" blue ribbon, gold letters "Roosevelt Committee" 60.00

1912, Taft, 1¾" celluloid sepia jugate of Taft-Sherman at top which reads "Republican Candidate/1912/Taft & Sherman," 2 x 4" blue ribbon with gold letters "Prosperity/And/The Whole/Republican/Ticket/We Are/Prosperous/Under/Taft/'Why Change?' " 175.00

1928, Hoover, 1¾" celluloid red, white and blue button, h/s photo of Hoover, border in block letters reads "Regular Republican Candidates," 2 x 7" white ribbon, blue letters, "HOOVER" vertically, "Election Day/Nov. 6, 1928/7:00 AM to 7:00 PM" . . .   150.00

Ballots, Sample

1868, Grant, 3¼ x 7", Ohio Republican Ticket, text only . .   15.00

1880, Weaver & Chambers, Greenback Labor Party, 3½ x 7¼", jugate among flag motif . .   50.00

1888, Harrison-Morton, blacksmith hand and hammer, Maryland Republican ticket 10.00

Belt Buckle, 2½ x 3½", Cleveland-Thurman, initials "C & T" in center rectangular cartouche, star border   30.00

Bandannas

1892, Cleveland-Stevenson, jugate, 19 x 22", engraved portraits in shields, crossed flags and flag shield above, banner beneath, star border, "OUR CHOICE," red, white, and black   150.00

1912, Wilson, 17" sq, multicolored, center h/s photo of Wilson surrounded by state seals, eagles in corners 90.00

Buttons

1884, Blaine, slogan, block letters "Blaine and Logan," silvered brass shell pinback, 36mm . . .   40.00

1896, McKinley-Hobart jugate, 1¼", celluloid, McKinley looks to left, text above and below, red, white, and blue 35.00

1904, Parker-Davis jugate, 1¼", Am. eagle motif at top, elongated flag ribbon separates h/s portraits, scrollwork design at bottom, multicolored 50.00

1908, Taft, 1¼", h/s in suitcase,

Button, 1900, McKinley and Roosevelt, 1¼" (30mm), blue and gold, $75.00.

block letters "Commercial Travelers//For/Taft" 250.00

1908, Taft, 1¼", h/s on star ground enclosed by wishbone, white outer border, black, yellow, and natural 27.50

1912, T. Roosevelt, Progressive, 1¼", hand holds deck of cards, four suites plus picture card of TR, "Stand Pat," red, white, blue, and black 67.50

1912, Wilson, ⅞", open figure 8 with "Woodrow Wilson" inside, red, white, and blue 10.00

1916, Hughes, ⅞", center h/s photo, red and white stripes on side, blue banner at top with "For President" in block letters, "Chas. E. Hughes" in block letters on bottom, red, white, blue, and black 15.00

1920, Cox, 1¼", silhouette center h/s photo, block letter border "Peace/Progress/Prosperity/For President," black and white . . .   300.00

1920, Harding, ⅞", center h/s photo, block letters on white border "For President/Warren G. Harding," black, blue, and white 6.00

1924, Coolidge, ⅞", slogan, white block letters on green, "Keep Coolidge" 17.00

1928, Hoover, 1¼", litho slogan, "Hoover-Howey," red, white, and blue, Florida coattail 20.00

1928, Smith, 1¼", silhouette center h/s photo, block letter border "For President" (top) and

"Alfred E. Smith" (bottom), black and white . . . . — 60.00

1932–36, F. Roosevelt, 1¾", silhouette photo, block letter border "Roosevelt/Labor's Choice," red, white, and blue . . — 60.00

1936, Landon, ⅞", slogan, yellow letters on brown ground, "Business Women's League" surrounds sunflower ring with "LANDON" in center . . . . — 15.00

1940, F. Roosevelt, ⅞", slogan, "Roosevelt/Wallace" in block letters surround ear of corn, green, white, and yellow . . . . . — 5.00

1940, Willkie, 1¼", slogan, brown derby with white block letters "East Side/West Side/Wants Willkie" . . . . — 8.00

1944, Dewey-Bricker jugate, 1", silhouette h/s portraits, names above in sweeping arch, black and white . . . . — 50.00

1948, Truman, 1¾", photo, graytone, block letters at bottom "For President/Harry S. Truman" . . . . — 15.00

1952, Eisenhower, 1⅛", silhouette h/s photo in center, white and black hands shake beneath, Ike flanked by "My Friend/IKE" . . . — 8.00

1952, Stevenson-Kefauver, jugate, 1¾", litho square framed h/s photos (Stevenson to right) surround block letters "Dollars/ For//Democrats," red, white, and blue . . . . — 20.00

1952, Taft, 1¾", silhouette portrait, block letters around bottom "Robert A. Taft," brown and white . . . . — 4.00

1960, Kennedy-Johnson, jugate, 1⅜", litho, silhouette h/s portraits in football shaped opening, above "New Leadership," below "Kennedy/Johnson," red, white, blue, and black . . . . — 6.00

Cigar Boxes and Labels

1924, LaFollette, multicolored h/s portrait flanked at top by capitol and scale of justice, picture on both sides of lid . . . . — 50.00

1930s, F. Roosevelt, square black and white photo plus "Roosevelt For President" in block letters, 8½" . . . . — 25.00

Costume, Jackie Kennedy, child's Halloween costume, gold sequins on black dress, mask, orig box . . — 25.00

Cup Plates

Clay, 3½", small center portrait, two concentric floral border rings, no name . . . . — 37.50

Harrison, 3½", "Fort Megis," log cabin center, meandering floral vine border in which is "Tippecanoe/W. H. Harrison" . — 45.00

Fans

1912, Wilson, 8" heart shape, stick, red, white, and blue star border, portraits of Washington, Lincoln, and Wilson, multicolored . . . . — 25.00

1964, Goldwater, 6", shield shape, silhouette h/s photo of Goldwater and block letters "Goldwater Fan Club," rev. has Rep. elephant sitting on donkey . . . . . . — 10.00

Fobs

1912, Taft, black enamel on brass, cut in side facial profile, h/s, name on bottom . . . . — 27.50

1920, Cox, brass, shield center with head of Cox in relief, rococo side wings, banners at top read "For Pres. James M. Cox 1920" . . . . — 85.00

1920, Harding-Coolidge, jugate, gold color, hollow, eagle at top, names under picture, "Our Choice" on bottom . . . . — 45.00

1932, Democratic National Convention, brass, hexagonal shape, picture of Jefferson in center . . . . — 15.00

Glasses

1896, McKinley, 3¾", portrait in wreath, shield at top with initials "McK," facsimile signature below . . . . — 35.00

1896, McKinley-Bryan, 2¾", measuring shot glass, ad for "Parry Buggies, Indianapolis" . . . . . . — 60.00

1952, Barkley (VP) and Lauche, 5¼", Gov. Jackson Day, Middleton, OH, blue and white transfers . . . . — 15.00

Inaugural Items

Police Badges

1949, Truman-Barkley, Metropolitan Police, silver finish . . . — 200.00

1953, Eisenhower-Nixon, Metropolitan Police, silver finish . . . — 125.00

Programs, Official Souvenir

1909, Taft, fine engravings inside . . . . — 30.00

1961, Kennedy, eagle and flag on cover, 66 pgs . . . . — 17.50

Tickets

1949, Truman-Barkley, 5 x 2½", multicolor, jugates, elaborate — 15.00

1969, Nixon-Agnew, 7¼ x 2¾", red, white, blue, and black . . — 5.00

License Plates

1928, Hoover, 11½ x 3¾", red, white, and blue, block letters

"Hoover For President" 22.50

1936, Landon, 8¾ x 6″, white block letters on green ground, "Landon/Barrows/White" 27.50

1948, Truman, 9¾ x 2″, red, white, and blue, dome top, center banner with TRUMAN AND BARKLEY flanked by donkeys, above "Look At The Record/ Vote For" 30.00

1968, Nixon, 12 x 5¼″, red, white, and blue, Nixon/Agnew in block letters 10.00

Matchcovers

1928, Hoover, Hoover-Curtis jugate in keystone motif, red, white, blue, and black 10.00

1952, Eisenhower-Nixon, silhouette of Ike on front, Nixon on back, red, white, and blue 3.50

Mugs

1908, Taft, toby, 5½″, three quarter portrait, pastel tones, made in Germany 75.00

1930s, F. Roosevelt, barrel shape, 4″, "The New Deal" with FDR profile, gold color 12.00

1952, Eisenhower, facial toby, 5″, cream color 25.00

Paperweights

1896, Bryan, sepia tone h/s portrait, name on shoulder 25.00

1900, McKinley-T. Roosevelt, jugate, sepia h/s portraits 40.00

1908, Taft-Sherman, jugate, octagon, multicolor, flags above portraits, banner below 65.00

Pencils

1940, Willkie, red and blue, white ground upper two-thirds, "Elect Wendell L. Willkie for President," flag 7.00

1972, McGovern, red and blue on white ground, "McGovern-Eagleton" in block letters, h/s portait of McGovern in circle . . 3.00

Pennants

1909, Taft, inaugural, "Taft in White House, March 4, 1909," green, gold, and white, 11½″ . . 15.00

1948, Truman, blue and white, h/s on left, "35th Division Reunion," on rest, orange and green trim, 26 x 10″ 24.00

1960, Kennedy-Johnson, names in banner across center, diagonals of names, red, white, and blue, 30 x 12″ 10.00

Pens, Ball Point

1956, Eisenhower, red, white, blue, and black, picture of Ike, "We Want Ike in '56" 12.50

1964, Goldwater, red, white, and

blue, "Goldwater in '64" 6.00

Pins

1888, Cleveland, wisk broom, cardboard picture on brass shell 55.00

1920, Smith, donkey, white enamel, "Al and Joe" 35.00

1930s, F. Roosevelt, donkey's face holding banner with Roosevelt in block letters, white enamel on silver, ¾″ 12.00

1944, Willkie, key with "WILL" in dome over shaft, 1⅝″, metal . . 15.00

1964, Goldwater, "64" on back of elephant over banner with "GOLDWATER", 1″, metal . . . 4.00

Plates

1888, Garfield, 8¼″ d, silhouette portrait, facsimile signature, gold border, black and white 27.50

1908, Taft-Sherman, jugate, 9¾″, blue and white, 7 scenes of Washington, D.C. around border, made by Rowland & Marsellus 60.00

1948, Truman, 9¼″, natural color oval portrait, facsimile signature 15.00

Pocket Knives

1908, Taft-Sherman, jugate, rectangular h/s of Taft on top, Sherman on bottom, capitol and white house on reverse 75.00

1912, Roosevelt-Johnson, jugate, rectangular h/s of Roosevelt on top, Johnson on bottom 150.00

1920, Harding, picture of Harding on top, U. S. Shield below, silver and gray 60.00

Postcards

1900, McKinley, ¾ portrait in costume, "Sir Knight Wm McKinley," black and white 20.00

1912, Wilson, red and blue pennant reading "Wilson" to right, h/s portrait to left, black and white 10.00

1920, Cox, Gov. Cox in Dayton, OH, during great flood of March 1913, surrounded by three men, black, white, and red 27.50

1952, Eisenhower, multicolor photo to of Ike in open Cadillac convertible in front of Margaret Truman Launderette 15.00

Posters

1920, Harding-Coolidge, jugate, 16 x 11″, multicolored, flag and eagle motif, facsimile signatures at base 65.00

1936, Landon, 11 x 16″, rectangular brown h/s photo on white, "Landon for President//Alf M. Landon/ Republican candidate for President" 20.00

1964, Miller, 13½ x 22″, rectangular h/s portrait, bottom "MILLER/for VICE PRESIDENT," yellow, black, and white **10.00**

Ribbons

1845, Jackson Memorial, 3 x 7¾″, seated portrait of Jackson, poem below, black and white .. **75.00**

1860, Bell rebus, 2⅜ x 7½″, picture of bell "And/Everett/Union" **450.00**

1896, McKinley, 2¼ x 7″, engraved h/s portrait of McKinley in center, "Aide/Lockport(NY)/October 30, 1896," black and blue **25.00**

1920, Smith Press Ribbon, 2¼ x 7⅜″, black and white, oval photo, "Notification/Ceremonies/for/ Alfred E. Smith/ . . . /State Capitol/Albany, NY/August 22, 1920/Press" **50.00**

Sheet Music

1840, Harrison, "National Whig Song," engraved h/s portrait of Harrison in center **50.00**

1876, Tilden-Hendricks, "Tilden-Hendricks Grand March," Wm. H. Adams, composer, jugate h/s portraits on cover, pub. by Major & Knap **75.00**

1924, Coolidge, Coolidge-Dawes jugate, official campaign song, brown and white **35.00**

1944, Dewey, "Dewey-We Do!," Uncle same in "V" with drum, red, white, and blue **30.00**

1968, Wallace, "Stand Up For Wallace," red, white, and blue, square h/s portrait on cover, biog. on reverse **10.00**

Soaps

1896, Bryan, soap baby, Bryan's picture and slogans **65.00**

1952, Ike, bath size, "Clean Up With Ike," h/s portrait in oval, white ground **9.00**

Soda Can, Eisenhower, cartoon of Rep. elephant waving flag with banner "I LIKE IKE," red, white, and blue **12.00**

Studs

1888, Harrison, vertical Am. flag, Harrison in block letters across center, ⅞″ sq, red, white, blue, and black **25.00**

1896 or 1900, McKinley, ⅞″ d, h/s portrait in center, stars and stripes border, red, white, blue, and black **10.00**

Tabs

1920, Coolidge, 1¾″, black block letters on white, litho **8.00**

1944, Willkie, ⅞″ d, flag shield, block letters of "Willkie" (top) and "McNary" (bottom), red, white, and blue **6.00**

1952, Eisenhower, "Back Ike/Vote Duff," red, white, and blue **3.00**

Ties

1948, Dewey, red and white, "Dewey 1948" under picture of capitol **14.00**

1964, Goldwater, H_2O symbol on gold ground **8.00**

Tokens

1840, W. H. Harrison, obv. bust and name, rev. log cabin, cider barrel, etc., "The Peoples Choice/The Hero of Tippecanoe," white metal, orig lustre, 38mm **100.00**

1852, W. S. Scott, obv. h/s, rev. eagle, brass, 30mm **25.00**

1876, S. Tilden, h/s/Manhatten Club Reception, white metal, 31mm **40.00**

T-Shirt, Carter, 1976, blue letters on white ground, "I'm voting for (standing Mr. Peanut symbol) in 76," large size **6.50**

Umbrellas

1964, Rockefeller, convention item, red, white, and blue, utilizing button picture on every white panel **30.00**

1968, Humphrey, black and white, name in white on purple on every other panel **40.00**

CAMPHOR GLASS

Camphor glass derives its name from its color. It has a cloudy, white appearance, similar to gum camphor. This was accomplished by treating the glass with hydrofluroic acid vapors.

Basket, hp decor **35.00**
Bookends, 7″, horses heads, pr ... **80.00**
Bottles
4″, stopper **15.00**
6½″, stopper **30.00**
8½″, perfume, pinch type, mushroom stopper **35.00**
Bowl, 15½″ d, ftd, hp flying birds decor **70.00**
Boxes
3″, oval, scroll design **40.00**
5″, hinged, holly spray **75.00**
6 x 4″, powder, cov, owl figural .. **42.50**
Candlesticks, 7″
Centennial Expo. Phila., 1876, pr **150.00**
Roses, hp, pr **65.00**

Creamer, 2½″ h, Souvenir of Youngstown, Ohio, $35.00.

Compote, 8″ w x 5½″ h, pink, wide lattice rim	15.00
Console Set, compote, candlesticks, stems are seated cherubs, 3 pcs	150.00
Creamer, Wild Rose and Bowknot, pink highlights	25.00
Ewer, clear handles, gold design . .	55.00
Hair Receiver, scroll design	50.00
Owl, standing, green glass eyes . . .	35.00
Pitchers	
7¾″, lemonade, enamel decor . .	45.00
8″, water, hobnail, applied handle, ground pontil	125.00
Plates	
6½″, Easter Greeting	25.00
7¼″, Fleur-de-lis decor	25.00
8″, holly border	20.00
Playing Card Holder, ftd, 3¾″	16.00
Rose Bowl, hp violets, green leaves	45.00
Shoes	
2½″, Boot	22.50
5″, Lady's, Libbey Glass Co., Toledo, OH, for 1893 World's Fair	40.00
6″, Lady's, with bow, from Centennial Expos., mkd "Gillinder" . . .	45.00
Sugar, Wild Rose and Bowknot, 2 handles	25.00
Toothpick holder, swirled, ruffled top	27.50
Tray, 8 x 10½″, Wild Rose and Bowknot	28.50
Vase, 10½″, Grecian shape, double handled, clear base	100.00

CANDLE MOLDS

Candles were a necessity of life in the past and candle making a major household chore. First, a supply of animal fat had to be collected. The fat was then purified by boiling with water. The resulting tallow rose to the top and was then skimmed off.

There were two methods used to make the final product, dipping and molding. Dipped candles were made by repeatedly dipping the wick in and out of the tallow until the desired size was formed. Molded candles were made in a tubular mold. The wick was threaded through the center of the tube and securely fastened. Then, the tallow was poured into the mold and allowed to harden. Candle molds were usually made of tin in various sizes, from a single candle mold to a grouping that made dozens of candles at a single time.

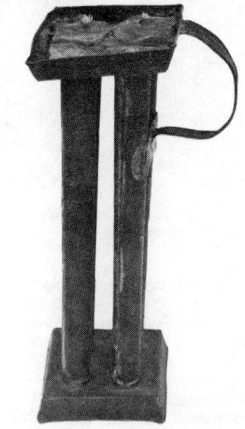

4 candle, tin, 10″ h x 3¾″ w, $50.00.

1-Candle, 9¾″	50.00
1-Candle, 15″	100.00
4-Candle	60.00
6-Candle, 11″ h tin, handle	50.00
8-Candle, 10¼″ h, tin	45.00
12-Candle, 11″ h, tin, 2 side handles	70.00
16-Candle, pewter with wood frame	900.00
18-Candle	225.00
18-Candle, pewter with wood frame	1,000.00
24-Candle	200.00
48-Candle	350.00
50-Candle	450.00
64-Candle, 17 x 8½ x 29″, tin, pine frame	400.00

CANDLESTICKS

A candlestick or candleholder is a portable holder with a hollow cup or spike to support a single candle. These very necessary implements have developed over the centuries into a myriad of shapes, sizes and types of materials. Candelabra, or candelabrum, is a large candlestick which has more than one branch or arms. These decorations have become very collectible and may be made of various materials. See specific categories for different types.

Soapstone, 5⅛", red tones, flowers and vases, pr, $85.00.

Bennington, 8¼", Rockingham glaze	320.00
Brass	
3¾", sq base, stems thread into base, c1850, pr	95.00
4½", chamber stick, pushup	100.00
6½", pushups, sq base, multi-knopped stems, c1835, pr . .	168.00
8", cylindrical candlecup with stump, removable hole and baluster above circular drip pan on domed circular foot, English, c1600, pr	770.00
8¾", cylindrical shaft, mid-molding on circular domed foot, serpentine footrim, late 18th C, pr . . .	290.00
Glass	
Amber, 10", pressed, pr	120.00
Blown, 9½", clear, applied foot, pillar mold stem, hollow candlesocket, Pittsburgh	625.00
Canary Flint, 7", petal and loop, Sandwich	160.00
Clambroth, 8¾", reeded, scalloped bases, pr	150.00
Cut, 7⅜", clear with prisms, strawberry and diamond point, fans on prism band socket, Pittsburgh, pr	575.00
Cut, 10", Harvard & Variant, teardrop	395.00
Iron, 8⅛", hog scraper, brass ring, pushup, lip hanger	150.00
Pewter	
4", chamber sticks, pushups, pr .	185.00
6½", pushups, weighted bases, pr	160.00

Sconces	
6¼" h extends to 9½", brass, bird on arm, polished and lacquered	195.00
10½", pewter, open work crest with 2 rampant lions, pair of removable "S" curve candle arms with drip pans, touch mkd with crown and sawtooth cross, simple hallmk in quandrant	300.00
Silver, 11⅛", octagonal base with reeded border and engraved formal decor, engraved and initialed fluted tapering stem, fluted vase shape socket, detachable wax pan with reeded border, Bigelow, Kennard & Co., Boston, 1920, pr	350.00
Tin, 3¼ x 6¼", chamber stick, white porcelain insert, wide drip pan . .	80.00
Wood, 7½", candleholder, turned base with 4 turned columns, tin collar and socket, adjustable by turning thumb screw on bottom . .	160.00
Wrought Iron	
7", spiral, wooden base, lip hanger, pushup	100.00
12¼", elaborate detail, 3 ftd., Alpine, c1890	175.00

CANDY CONTAINERS

Candy containers were small glass toys, holding tiny pellets of sugar candy when purchased, in the shape of boats, cars, trains, dogs, etc.; when the child had eaten the candy, he still had a toy to remember. Some had small metal cap, and the earlier ones had corks for stoppers. They were very popular for gifts and stocking stuffers at Christmas time. Today they are very popular for collectors, and ones made in commemoration of movie stars and well known characters are quite expensive.

See *Warman's Americana & Collectibles* for an expanded listing of candy containers.

Automobiles	
Pierce Arrow	40.00
Sedan, 4¼", light clambroth	60.00
Baseball Player, 3¼" h, bat	450.00
Bear beside tree trunk, honey, papier mache	95.00
Bulldog, sitting, metal screw lid . . .	55.00
Cane, 9⅜" l, clear, gilt band, tip . .	130.00
Cat, 5", stretched neck	600.00
Chevrolet Station Wagon, 1936 . . .	25.00
Clock, 3¼" h, milk glass	90.00
Colorado, S.S., 6½"	325.00
Dirigible, Los Angeles	85.00
Duck, rope top basket, green	50.00
Elephant, 7½" l, pink	20.00

Papier mache rabbit pulling basket, pasteboard wheels, 9″ long, $50.00.

Gas Pump	120.00
Girl In Rabbit costume, 7″ h, wax, composition, paper	50.00
Goblet, pontiled, c1850	285.00
G.O.P. Elephant, 2¾″ h	105.00
Grandpa riding rooster, orig paint, flexible spring legs, papier mache	270.00
Happifats	175.00
Hot Dog, 5¼″	280.00
Indian motorcycle, side car, 3¼ x 5″, orit tin snap on closure, painted wheels	450.00
Kiddy Car	45.00
Mailbox, 3¼″ h	50.00
Opera Glasses, swirl rib, 3⅝″ h	40.00
Piano, 6¼″ l	75.00
Pocket Watch, orig strap, brass eagle fob, tin back	320.00

Rabbits
Crouching, 3¾″l	50.00
Pushing Wheelbarrow	100.00
Sitting on hind legs	25.00
Top hat, 4¾″, painted papier mache, glass eyes	40.00
Rocking Horse, 3″ h	120.00
Rooster, crowing	125.00

Santas
12″ h, crepe paper, cotton, white, gold snowflakes, painted plaster feet, face, German	225.00
Glass, standing by chimney	125.00
Singing Apple, 3¾″ h, painted papier mache	175.00
Skookum Indian, orig tree trunk, 3⅝ x 3½″, slotted tin closure, 1916	370.00
Straw Hat, glass, 3½″ d	35.00
Street Light, glass, japanned finish	325.00
Telephone, glass, wooden hand receiver, patent 1907, orig closure, contents	42.50
Toonerville Trolley, 3½″ h	850.00

Traffic Signs
Don't Park Here, 4½″ h	55.00
Stop & Go, 4¼″ h, mechanical	210.00
Train engine, smokey glass, tin wheels, Jeannette Glass	100.00
Turkey, 4″ h, painted papier mache, plaster, German	20.00
Uncle Sam by barrel, 3¾″ h	210.00

Washer, Midget	25.00
Wolf with book, 4⅝″ h	50.00

CANES

Canes and walking sticks have become highly collectible. Ornamental canes and walking sticks demand a higher price than the functional type of cane. Canes and walking sticks are made of various materials and can be found with intricate handles and decorations.

Walking stick, walnut, ball and trap, 4 twisted pieces, 35″, $75.00.

Glass
38½″, l, aqua, twisted	135.00
49½″, clear, red center stripe, twisted at handle, tip	145.00
51½″, clear, twisted, dark red liquid fills hollow center	125.00
59″ l, aqua glass, twisted handle, straight rib	90.00
76″, aqua, sq, twisted handle, top	95.00

Scrimshaw
31″l, lady's, whalebone, carved walrus ivory, dog's head handle	150.00
33¾″, wood shaft, carved walrus ivory handle in form of knee with laced legging and boot, tassle	200.00
Sword, 35″ l, stag horn handle, silver colored mountings, brass tip	135.00

Wood
34″ l, sapling, gnarled handle, silver plate M. Wilson	20.00
35″ l, carved wood, carved shaft, eagle head handle, flying bird at handle base	65.00
35½″, root cane, silver colored studs, engraved plate "Compliments of Niles Tool Works"	45.00
36″, whimsey cane, 5 open latticed sections, some containing moveable balls, Pa. origin, last quarter 19th C	245.00
42″, commemorating 100 years, Newburgh, NY, Stanhope, shows Washington's headquarters, c1883	75.00

Walking Sticks
Glass, 54½″, clear, gold interior	70.00
Horn, 34″ l, segmented horn	35.00
Scrimshaw, 34″ l, turned whale ivory head, wooden shaft	95.00

Wooden
30¾" l, gnarled wood, stag horn handle, chased colored ferrule 30.00
33¾" l, emb panels of oriental figures, bamboo, calligraphy on silver colored head 36.00
35½" l, primitive carved dog's head handle, old dark finish . 40.00
36" l, pine folk art carved, clenched fist head, cuff, cuff link, V.W. Williams, snake, old varnish finish 95.00
39½", simple chip carved designs 20.00
42", walking, Chinese, silver handle, silver dragon wrapped around, "Peking, China, Great Wall" 600.00
42", walking, wood carving, talons gripping ball 135.00
Handles Only
Faceted rock crystal, alternating bands of gold, scrolling foliage, opaque white, translucent red border, lower border of white enamel, 3⅛" l, fitted leather case, 19th C 1,540.00
Viennese painted enamel of maidens, putti frolicking in clouds, gilt bronze mount, curved, tapering cylindrical, 6" 330.00

CANTON CHINA

Canton china is a type of oriental porcelain made in Canton, China, for export to America from the 1820s to the present. These wares were hand decorated in light to dark blues underglaze on white, with simple scenes of houses, mountains and a bridge in the center panel. Borders on earlier Canton feature a rain and cloud motif while later pieces usually have a straight line border. The Canton pattern has the second greatest variety of forms found in Chinese export porcelain. The markings "Made in China" and "China" indicates wares made after 1891.

Bottles, water
8½" 325.00
9", 19th C 425.00
Bowls
4½", waste 85.00
8", 19 C 220.00
9¾", landscape, 19th C 375.00
10¼", shallow, scalloped rim, 19th C 425.00
15", Punch, polychrome enamel, court ladies 1,150.00
Rice, with saucer 45.00

Plate, 10⅛" d, water edge scene, $100.00.

Butter chip, 3" d, 19th C 50.00
Coffee Pot, 9", dome lid 800.00
Condiment Jars, pr, 3¼", cov, pagoda, late period 160.00
Creamer, 3", Chinese, 19th C 190.00
Cups and Saucers
Cross handle 80.00
Loop handle 45.00
Curry Dish, on high base, 13¾", Chinese, 19th C 850.00
Dishes
Fish shaped, 6", late 85.00
Leaf, 7¼" 185.00
Fruit Bowl, 8¾", undertray, reticulated, 19th C 275.00
Garden Seat, 19", octagonal 1,250.00
Ginger Jars, covered
3" 80.00
9" 360.00
Hot Water Plate, 8¾", octagonal, scenic, 19th C 200.00
Lamp, 6½", ginger jar base, brass fittings 215.00
Mug, pint size, scenic, twined handle, 19th C 230.00
Pitchers
5¾", scenic, 19th C 250.00
9½", landscape scenic, blue rim, 19th C 500.00
Plates
6", scenic, 19th C 60.00
8" 65.00
9⅞", oval, Chinese, 19th C 170.00
10¼", square 255.00
Platters
7¾ x 10", scenic, 19th C 195.00
12⅛", deep, covered, 19th C . . . 575.00
Posset Cup, 3", polychromed 155.00

Pot, 4¼ x 5¾" d, scenic, 19th C . .	165.00
Sauce Boat, 7", scenic intertwined handle, 19th C	185.00
Serving Dish, shell shape, flat handle, landscape	300.00

Sugars, covered

4½", berry finial, strap handles, scenic, 19th C	275.00
Intertwining handles	250.00

Teapots

6", Butterfly, court scene decor around circumference	395.00
6¼", domed lid, scenic, 19th C .	225.00
Tile, 6" square	225.00
Tray, landscape center, reticulated forget-me-not patterned rim	425.00
Tureen, 12", cov, boar's head handles, landscape, 19th C	1,100.00

Vases

15¼", baluster form, Chinese, 19th C	900.00
10⅜", cylindrical, 19th C	500.00

Vegetable Dishes, covered

8½ x 7¼", oblong, landscape, 19th C	275.00
11½", oval, strawberry finial, scalloped rims	475.00

CAPO-DI-MONTI CHINA

The Capo-di-Monti factory in Naples started production in 1736. In 1743, King Charles of Naples established a factory there that made relief decoration. The molds were acquired by the Doccia factory of Florence in 1886, and they have since made reproductions of original Capo-di-Monti pieces, with the "N" mark beneath a crown. Very early pieces are extremely valuable but most of these are in museums. Pieces found today are considerably lower and should be known as "Capo-di-Monti-type."

Ashtray, 6", crown mkd	18.00

Bowls

4", ftd, putti and Pan masks decor, crowned "N" mkd	75.00
4½", cov, green and white, twisted handles, lid with kneeling figure	65.00
4½ x 3½", oblong, cov, mythological scenes, figures molded in relief, gilt beaded rim, fruit knops, pr	225.00

Boxes

2 x 2 x 3", children in relief, brass trim, blue crown, "N" under glaze	95.00
3 x 5½" d, round, angels playing instruments and frolicking in the	

Capo-di-Monti China, figures, 6"h, boy with garland, yellow coat, pink garments, girl reading, blue coat, yellow pants, marked Italy, pr, $495.00.

flowers, enameling, gilt bronze closure, inside also decorated, sgr	139.00
Casket, 12¼", hinged lid, enameled in relief panel on lid depicting Bacchanalian celebration, sides with goats and masks, gilt bronze mounts, c1910	600.00
Compote, 9", cov, oval, relief molded cherubs on sides, cherub finial and handles	225.00
Cup and Saucer, floral, twisted branch handles	65.00
Demitasse Set, large round ftd tray (6 feet), creamer and sugar, cov pot, classical design sgd P. Capo-di-monti, Italy	250.00
Desk Set, 7¾ x 4" casket, rect, curved lid with biblical scenes, pin box, cigarette box, 2 ashtrays, gilt brass trim, 5 pcs	160.00
Ewer, 11", babies, animals and people decor	350.00

Figures

6¾", boy and girl, white, applied florals, c1850	475.00
9", boy with dog, artist sgd, G. Ormanis, modern	150.00
9½", girl carrying flower basket, c1890	325.00
12", cherub standing on pedestal above 3 maidens, flower garlands, oval base	130.00
Jardiniere on wrought iron stand, 15", molded in relief, frieze of dancing putti suspending chains of roses beneath a frieze of putti and vases and applied with 4 ram's head mounts	350.00
Lamp, 13", molded in relief frolicking cherubs, brass fittings, no shade, "N" blue crown mark	75.00

Plaques
10", Marie Antoninette, portrait
bust, molded in relief, gold
ground, gilt and molded border,
blue crowned "N" mark 150.00
22½ x 16½", harvest scene, high
relief, velvet covered molded
frame 290.00
Plate, 11", Napolean & soldiers . . . 140.00
Stein, molded in relief, enameled,
pastel colors 175.00
Trays
13½", rect, central panel of classical dancing figures 150.00
15 x 12", white, gold trim, gambol-
ling figures, crown over "N" . . 75.00
Urn, 28 x 12", cov, 3 cherubs seated at base blowing trumpets,
repeated on finial, heavy relief
work on sides 675.00

CARLSBAD CHINA

**This porcelain was made at Carlsbad, Austria,
by a number of factories. Most of the items
found in shops and collections today were
made after 1891.**

Berry Dish, 5¾", white, pink and yellow roses, green buds and leaves,
shaped gold rim, c1905 . . . . 20.00
Bone Dish, crescent shape, pink
flower, gold trim 15.00
Bowls
8", white, fluted, yellow roses,
green leaves 40.00
8¾", shallow, green border, gold
center with death of King Lear,
artist sgd 65.00
9½", portrait, toasting scene, bur-

gundy, gold tracing, Victoria
Carlsbad 75.00
10", portrait, green border, gold
tracing, sgd Bucher, Victoria
Carlsbad, Austria 58.00
Box, 6½", floral, gold scroll trim . . . 80.00
Butter Pat, 3", round, white, spray of
green rose buds, gold trim, c1900 15.00
Chocolate Pot, 9", violet, blue bach-
elor's buttons, gold trim 120.00
Coffee Pot, 8", classical scenes,
marked 85.00
Creamer and Sugar, Bluebird pat-
tern, marked 55.00
Cup and Saucer, rosebuds, vines
and leaves, marked 35.00
Ewer, 12", cream, orange and green
leaves 55.00
Hair Receiver, 4" d, white, cobalt
blue flowers, gold trim, emb
basketweave at top 30.00
Jam Jar, cov and underplate, white,
violets, lily-of-the-valley and gold
trim, marked 45.00
Match Striker, skull shape, Victoria
Carlsbad 30.00
Muffineer, 5½", egg shape, floral
decor, marked 60.00
Oyster Plate, 8", gold trim 60.00
Pin Tray, 8½", irregular scalloped
shape, white, bunches of small
roses, green leaves, Victoria
Carlsbad, Austria 28.00
Pitchers
8", cream, gold floral decor, ornate handle, marked 60.00
11", pink, cobalt blue band at top
and bottom, gold trim 85.00
Plates
7¼", hp rosebuds, gold trim, A.C.
Carlsbad, Austria 30.00
9", white, floral center, lattice border, Victoria Carlsbad 40.00
9⅝", white, spray of pink and yellow roses, green buds and
leaves, shaped gold rim, c1905 42.00
Platter, 15¼", blue floral decor, gold
trim 35.00
Tea Caddy, pink to white, women
with cupid decor 75.00
Vases
9", handled, white, colonial cou-
ple, Victoria, Austria, pr 70.00
9½", hp orange poppies and
green leaves with gold outline
and rim 65.00
15", violets, butterflies, Carlsbad,
Austria 115.00
Vegetable Dish, cov, 6¼ h x 9½" w,
square, chamfered corners, pink
and yellow roses, green buds and
leaves, gold trim, buckle handles
and finial, c1900 . . . . 70.00

**Vegetable Dish, Carlsbad, cov, 6½ x
8½", blue bachelor buttons and light
brown floral motif, $22.50.**

CARNIVAL GLASS—AMERICAN

Although not known by Carnival Glass originally, it was created to give a moderate-priced glass resembling costly hand-blown glass. Carnival glass was sold in china and glass shops, department stores, and by mail order.

An American invention, Carnival Glass is colored pressed glass with an iridescent finish fired on. Arriving on the market about 1905, it was immensely popular, both in America and abroad. Boat loads were shipped to England and Australia, for example. The closing date of old Carnival is 1925.

Most of this glass was produced by four companies—Northwood, Fenton, Imperial, and Millersburg. Only the Northwood prod-

ucts were trade-marked with some variety of a capital "N."

In Carnival, color is the most important factor. This can easily be determined by holding a piece to the light and looking through it. Prices vary greatly according to color.

For easy pricing, we have here for the first time given the user three columns: marigold, dark (blue, green, or purple) and pastel colors (white, light blue or green and vaseline). Please remember this is a sampling of patterns. There were originally over 1,000 produced.

For serious collectors we recommend the books by Marion T. Hartung, Emporia, KS.

Abbreviations: cov.—covered; compl.—complete; ftd.—footed.

APPLE BLOSSOM TWIGS (DUGAN)	Marigold	Dark	Pastel
Banana Boat, ruffled	35.00	48.00	180.00
Bowls			
6"	18.00	45.00	85.00
8"	25.00	75.00	52.00
9"	25.00	75.00	50.00
Plates			
9"	50.00	155.00	100.00
10½", ruffled	75.00	100.00	125.00
BEADED CABLE (NORTHWOOD)			
Candy dish, ftd.	38.00	45.00	68.00
Rose bowl, ftd.	55.00	45.00	225.00
BLACKBERRY WREATH (MILLERSBURG)			
Bowls			
5½"	50.00	70.00	—
8"	50.00	35.00	350.00
10", ice cream	110.00	150.00	—
Plate, 6"	500.00	625.00	—
BUTTERFLY AND BERRY (FENTON)			
Berry Set			
5½", bowl	19.50	35.00	75.00
9"–10", bowl	55.00	85.00	425.00
Hatpin holder—rare	250.00	310.00	—
Plate, blue	—	1,000.00	—
Table Set			
Butter, cov.	95.00	210.00	—
Creamer or Spooner	38.00	80.00	—
Sugar, cov.	65.00	82.00	—
Vase 7"–10" — scarce	28.50	42.00	—
Water Set			
Pitcher	140.00	310.00	—
Tumbler	25.00	35.00	—
CAPTIVE ROSE (FENTON)			
Bon-Bon	30.00	48.00	—
Bowl, 8½"–10"	38.00	50.00	75.00

Beaded Cable, rose bowl, dark, $45.00.

Butterfly and Berry, berry bowl, 9", $85.00.

Dragon and Lotus, bowl, 9", ftd, dark, $65.00.

Farmyard, bowl, 10", dark, $2,000.00.

Fine Cut and Roses, rosebowl, dark, $90.00.

Good Luck, bowl, 8½", dark, $125.00.

	Marigold	Dark	Pastel
CAPTIVE ROSE (FENTON)			
Compote	35.00	48.00	72.50
Plate 9"–10"	76.00	180.00	295.00
CARNIVAL HOLLY (FENTON)			
Bowl 7¼"–10½"	25.00	45.00	60.00
Compote	18.50	29.00	48.00
Hat shape	18.00	36.00	58.00
Miniature compote	15.00	—	—
Plate, 9"–10"	62.50	98.00	135.00
COIN DOT (FENTON)			
Basket	65.00	80.00	—
Bowls			
6"	40.00	50.00	—
9"	65.00	80.00	—
Plate, 6"	155.00	165.00	—
Rose Bowl	60.00	75.00	—
Water Sets			
Pitcher	300.00	400.00	—
Tumbler	80.00	125.00	—
COSMOS AND CANE, (IMPERIAL)			
Bowls			
5"	35.00	—	65.00
10"	60.00	—	110.00
Butter, cov.	165.00	—	300.00
Compote	50.00	—	100.00
Creamer	105.00	—	245.00
Rose Bowl	90.00	115.00	130.00
Spittoon	500.00	—	200.00
Spooner	90.00	—	95.00
Sugar, cov.	115.00	—	235.00
COUNTRY KITCHEN (MILLERSBURG)			
Berry Set			
5" bowl	145.00	—	—
9", bowl	190.00	—	—
Table Sets			
Butter, cov.	300.00	400.00	—
Creamer	175.00	230.00	—
Spooner	165.00	225.00	—
Sugar	185.00	245.00	400.00
Vase	400.00	435.00	—
CRACKLE (IMPERIAL)			
Bowls			
5"	15.00	20.00	—
10"	20.00	25.00	—
Candy Jar, cov.	30.00	35.00	—
Plate	35.00	45.00	—
Punch Bowl and base	50.00	60.00	—
Punch Cup	12.00	15.00	—
Water Set			
Pitcher, domed, ftd.	90.00	135.00	—
Tumbler	20.00	35.00	—
Window Planter	90.00	—	—

	Marigold	Dark	Pastel
DRAGON AND LOTUS (FENTON)			
Bowl, 8½"	40.00	—	100.00
Bowl, 9", footed	45.00	65.00	110.00
Bowl, 9½", flat	36.50	56.00	110.00
Plate, 9", rare	165.00	320.00	465.00
FARMYARD (DUGAN)			
Bowl 10", rare	—	2,000.00	—
Plate 10", rare	—	8,000.00	—
FINE-CUT AND ROSES (NORTHWOOD)			
Candy dish, footed	40.00	45.00	90.00
Rose bowl, footed	65.00	90.00	200.00
FLORAL AND GRAPE (FENTON)			
Water Set			
Pitcher	75.00	150.00	275.00
Tumbler	18.00	30.00	50.00
GOOD LUCK (FENTON AND NORTHWOOD)			
Bowl, 8½"–9¼"	60.00	125.00	190.00
Plate, 9"	140.00	185.00	230.00
GRAPE (IMPERIAL)			
Berry Set			
5", bowl	10.00	17.00	19.00
10" bowl	16.00	35.00	45.00
Bowl, fruit, 7½"	17.00	36.00	—
Compote	20.00	30.00	—
Cup and Saucer	60.00	—	—
Goblet	40.00	85.00	—
Plates			
6"	30.00	50.00	—
8½", ruffled	35.00	50.00	—
Punch Set			
Bowl and base	90.00	155.00	—
Cup	10.00	20.00	—
Water Set			
Carafe	—	149.00	—
Pitcher	70.00	175.00	—
Tumbler	18.00	35.00	—
Wine Set			
Decanter, stopper	90.00	145.00	—
Wine, stemmed	7.50	35.00	—
GRAPE & CABLE (NORTHWOOD)			
Bowls			
Centerpiece	150.00	250.00	450.00
Footed, Orange, 9½"	100.00	125.00	300.00
Candleholder	65.00	100.00	110.00
Cologne Bottle	135.00	125.00	110.00
Dresser Tray	70.00	150.00	300.00
Hatpin Holder	135.00	160.00	300.00
Nappy, 1 handle	25.00	88.00	150.00
Plates			
7"	40.00	50.00	80.00

GRAPE & CABLE (NORTHWOOD)	**Marigold**	**Dark**	**Pastel**
8″, ftd.	55.00	55.00	85.00
Powder Jar	70.00	190.00	235.00
Punch Sets			
Bowl and Base	240.00	650.00	975.00
Punch Cup	15.00	30.00	75.00
Sweetmeat	700.00	125.00	—
Table Set			
Butter, cov.	150.00	200.00	500.00
Creamer	55.00	60.00	180.00
Sugar, cov.	60.00	95.00	200.00
Water Sets			
Pitcher	150.00	235.00	465.00
Tumbler	30.00	30.00	55.00

HOBNAIL SWIRL (MILLERSBURG)

Cuspidor	—	550.00	—
Rose Bowl	—	265.00	—
Vase, green	—	160.00	—

LUSTRE ROSE (IMPERIAL)

Berry Set			
5″	10.00	18.00	—
9″	20.00	45.00	—
Bowls			
7½″, ftd.	35.00	37.50	—
10″, ftd.	45.00	45.00	—
Fernery, ftd.	32.00	50.00	60.00
Plate, 7″	20.00	42.00	55.00
Table Set			
Butter, cov.	55.00	95.00	—
Creamer	20.00	28.00	—
Spooner	18.50	25.00	—
Sugar, cov.	20.00	28.00	—
Water Set			
Pitcher	55.00	200.00	200.00
Tumbler	15.00	45.00	45.00

MAPLE LEAF (UNCERTAIN)

Ice Cream Set, stemmed			
Large bowl	55.00	135.00	—
Small bowl	16.00	32.50	—
Table Set			
Butter, cov.	90.00	115.00	—
Creamer or Spooner	42.00	58.00	—
Sugar, cov.	48.00	65.00	—
Water Set, 7 pc	—	—	300.00
Pitcher	110.00	200.00	—
Tumbler	25.00	38.50	—

MILLERSBURG DIAMOND

Water Set			
Pitcher	—	485.00	—
Tumbler	—	85.00	—

NORTHWOOD'S DANDELION

Mug	125.00	225.00	400.00
Mug, Knights Templar	—	—	750.00

Maple leaf, tumbler, dark, $38.50.

Millersburg Diamond, tumbler, $85.00.

Northwood's Dandelion, pitcher, dark, $575.00.

Peacock and Urn, bowl, 9″, dark, $85.00.

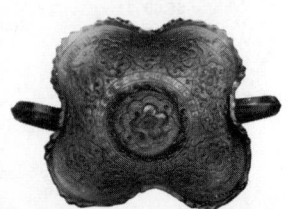

Persian Medallion, nappy, 2 handles, dark, $30.00.

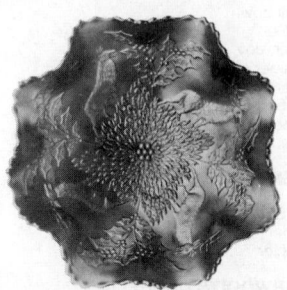

Stag and Holly, bowl, 13″, ftd, dark, 170.00.

NORTHWOOD'S DANDELION	Marigold	Dark	Pastel
Water Set			
Pitcher	250.00	575.00	1,200.00
Tumbler	55.00	65.00	150.00

PEACOCK AND URN (FENTON, N'S, MILLERSBURG)

	Marigold	Dark	Pastel
Bowl			
5", matches 11"	29.50	42.50	65.00
9"	100.00	85.00	135.00
11", ice cream	120.00	235.00	295.00
Chop Plate, 11", rare	1,800.00	4,500.00	—
Compote	90.00	60.00	95.00
Compote, large, green, Millersburg	—	1,100.00	—
Plate	—	140.00	—
Spittoon	—	3,000.00	—

PERSIAN GARDEN (DUGAN)

	Marigold	Dark	Pastel
Ice Cream Bowl			
Large, 11"	85.00	185.00	235.00
Small, 6½"	40.00	58.00	75.00
Chop Plate, 12"–13", rare	—	2,550.00	2,000.00
Plate, 6", rare	55.00	92.50	110.00

PERSIAN MEDALLION (FENTON)

	Marigold	Dark	Pastel
Bon-Bon	26.50	39.50	85.00
Bowl, 8½"–10"	40.00	52.00	—
Compote	40.00	55.00	85.00
Plate, 9", scarce	95.00	135.00	275.00
Rose Bowl, collar base	48.50	40.00	135.00
Nappy	—	30.00	—

ROSE SHOW (UNKNOWN)

	Marigold	Dark	Pastel
Bowl, 8¾"–9¾"	185.00	235.00	360.00
Plate, 8¾"–9¾"	200.00	325.00	379.00

SAILBOATS (FENTON)

	Marigold	Dark	Pastel
Bowl, 5"	20.00	35.00	—
Compote	25.00	—	—
Goblet	250.00	350.00	—
Wine, stemmed	25.00	60.00	—

SINGING BIRDS (NORTHWOOD)

	Marigold	Dark	Pastel
Berry Set			
Bowl, 5"	—	42.00	—
Bowl, 10"	—	95.00	—
Mug, one size	46.00	85.00	600.00
Table Set			
Butter, cov.	150.00	260.00	—
Sugar, cov. Creamer, or Spooner	65.00	85.00	—
Water Set			
Pitcher	220.00	385.00	—
Tumbler	32.00	35.00	—

	Marigold	Dark	Pastel
STAG AND HOLLY (FENTON)			
Bowls			
10½"	65.00	95.00	—
12"	35.00	40.00	—
13", ftd.	95.00	170.00	—
Plates, ftd.			
7"	250.00	—	—
12"	200.00	—	—
STIPPLED RAYS (NORTHWOOD)			
Bon-Bon, handled	20.00	15.00	—
Bowls			
8", ruffled	18.00	30.00	—
11", tight ribbon candy edge	16.00	20.00	—
Compote	—	40.00	—
Table Set			
Creamer, ftd.	20.00	35.00	—
Sugar, ftd.	20.00	35.00	—
Vase, tri-corner	12.50	35.00	—
TREE BARK (IMPERIAL)			
Candy Dish, cov.	12.50	—	—
Vase	10.00	—	—
Water Set			
Pitcher, tankard	70.00	—	—
Tumbler	15.00	—	—
VINTAGE (FENTON)			
Berry Set			
5", bowl	10.00	17.00	—
9", bowl	20.00	30.00	—
Bon-Bon	18.00	45.00	—
Bowls			
7½", collar base	18.00	27.00	—
7½", ftd.	20.00	30.00	—
Compote	35.00	40.00	—
Epergne	80.00	110.00	—
Fernery	—	25.00	—
Plate, 7"	25.00	35.00	—
Powder Jar	25.00	—	—
Rose Bowl, 6 feet	58.00	80.00	—
Wine glass, stemmed	20.00	35.00	—
VINTAGE GRAPE (MILLERSBURG)			
Bowls			
9", hobnail exterior, ruffled	—	450.00	—
10", ice cream, hobnail exterior	200.00	—	—
WISHBONE (NORTHWOOD)			
Bowls			
8", ftd.	50.00	59.00	125.00
10½", flat	40.00	65.00	100.00
Epergne	165.00	200.00	400.00
Plates			
9", footed	—	325.00	—
10"	—	410.00	—

WISHBONE (NORTHWOOD)	Marigold	Dark	Pastel
Water Set			
Pitcher	—	900.00	1,600.00
Tumbler	90.00	135.00	275.00

MISCELLANEOUS AND SPECIAL ITEMS

Acorn, (Millersburg), compote, vaseline	1,800.00
Acorn Burrs (Northwood) punch bowl, base, 5 cups, aqua opal, estate of M. Hartung	12,500.00
Grape Leaves (Millersburg), bowl, radiam finish	400.00
Northwood Dandelion mug, aqua, opalescent, estate of M. Hartung	500.00
Ohio Star (Millersburg) vase, marigold	200.00
Pipe Humidor (Millersburg), green	3,500.00
Wild Rose, syrup, lid, marigold	475.00

CAROUSEL FIGURES

The fun and excitement of riding the merry-go-round or carousel exists today as much as when first invented. Prancing steeds, snarling tigers and graceful swans set to calliope music bring joy regardless of age.

By the late 17th century carousels were found in most of the capital cities of Europe. In 1867 Gustav Dentzel carved this country's first carousel. By 1880 C. W. Parker was the name best known in the amusement park field. His horses were especially beautiful. The animals that go up and down are called "jumpers".

The prices listed only serve as a guide as condition is extremely important.

Horse, 38" l, $1,500.00.

Camel, 47", 2 humps, darkly painted, walking, head raised . . .	1,800.00
Cat, leaping, 51 x 19", wood and gesso, polychrome, probably French, c1880	1,100.00
Donkey, 60 x 66", wood, carved, glass eyes, ornate brass fittings, sgd Vol Angers, France, c1910 . .	3,800.00
Goat, Billy, wood, traces of old colorful paint, mounted on rockers .	1,000.00
Horses	
42 x 38", Raggedy Andy head, carved, painted	1,300.00
46 x 55", prancing, open mouth, brown glass eyes	4,100.00
52 x 59", rearing, carved wood and gesso, polychrome, Friedrich Heyn, German, c1880	3,000.00
72 x 56", flying, carved pine, stripped of paint, attributed to William Geggie, 20th C	1,900.00
Jumping, stationary, carved saddle, Dentzel	2,750.00
Ostrich, running, 66", carved and painted wood, 19th C	4,000.00
Pig, leaping, pink, saddle, French, 19th C	2,000.00
Roosters	
40" h, strutting, wood, carved and painted, red, yellow, green, and brown	2,420.00
47", strutting, carved wood, red with white neck, mounted on slab base, made in St. Johnsburg, VT, 19th C	10,000.00
Stag, leaping, 73" h, carved, painted wood, G. A. Dentzel & Co., Philadelphia, c1900	5,250.00

CASTLEFORD

Castleford is a soft paste porcelain made in Yorkshire, England in the early 1800s for the American trade. The ware has a warm, white ground, scalloped rims, (resembling castle tops) and trimmed in deep blue. Occasionally, pieces were further decorated with a coat-of-arms, eagles, or "Liberty." Few pieces, if any, are marked.

Milk Jug, 4¾" h, oval, relief of American Eagle on one side, Liberty and cap on reverse, acanthus leaf border	145.00
Sugar, cov, relief of classical figure leaning on urn, acanthus leaf pan-	

Castleford Teapot, cov, 9″ l x 5¼″ h, low relief decor, blue enamel bands, $200.00.

el, blue enamel border, scalloped edge, 3 enamel bands on cover . 235.00
Teapot, cov, 5⅞″h, brown ground, oval medallion relief on both sides depicting boy, dog, panels of trophies, foliate borders, heightened in blue enamel, hinged cover ... 240.00
Tea Set, teapot, cov, milk jug, sugar bowl, cov, relief panels of mythological figures, animals, shell, bead borders, fluted bases, dolphin knobs, blue enamel line borders, glazed interiors 400.00

CASTOR SETS

A castor set is a set of matched condiment bottles, held within a frame or holder. Most castor sets consisted of three to five pressed glass bottles in a silverplated frame. Some consisted of cut glass bottles and a sterling silver holder. Occasionally, an all-glass set is encountered. Although castor sets were known as early as the 1700s, most found today are from the Victorian period when they were quite popular.

3-bottle, cranberry, open salt with glass spoon, pepper pot, mustard jar, SP holder, 7¼ x 4″ d 175.00
3-bottle, ribbed, SP holder, English . 50.00
3-bottle, Ribbed Palm, pewter tops, frame 100.00
3-bottle, Rubena, cut panels, salt shaker, mustard pot, spoon, oval open salt, SP holder, 5½″ h x 4″d 165.00
4-bottle, cut crystal, faceted stoppers, SP holder, 8¼″ h x 5¼″ d . 165.00
4-bottle, cut glass, cut green to clear, holder marked W. Briggs & Co., Sheffield, EPNS 285 ...... 165.00
4-bottle, Czech. crystal, pineapple cutting, master salt, ftd Reed & Barton frame, greek key trim, center handle 135.00

6-bottle, cut and etched bottles, SP holder, 14″h, $125.00.

4-bottle, milk glass, plain pattern bottles, metal holder 100.00
4-bottle, minature, revolving tin base 75.00
4-bottle, Rubena cut glass, ftd sq SP holder with center post 195.00
5-bottle, Button Band, pattern glass stand 100.00
5-bottle, clear bottles, blue glass base with center post, 11″ high to top of handle 175.00
5-bottle, clear leaf etched, SP holder, ball feet, 13¾″ h x 6½″ d ... 115.00
5-bottle, crystal, silver holder, Weeke & Co., c1820 .... 185.00
5-bottle, cut and etched, SP Reed & Barton holder 125.00
5-bottle, Gothic, pewter holder, "Israel Trask" 175.00
5-bottle, green glass bottles, Meridan SP holder 225.00
5-bottle, Honeycomb, resilvered holder, Meriden #39 .... 175.00
6-bottle, cut diamond, oval, SP holder 175.00
6-bottle, fluted glass, 3 silver mounted tops, circular revolving vertically fluted SP base, baluster stem, Tiffany & Co., NY 1,200.00
6-bottle, crystal, cut, etched, SP, pierced round holder, ornate center handle, hallmarked 175.00
8-bottle, pressed glass, SP tops, holder, Simpson H. Miller Co. ... 225.00

CATALOGUES AND MAGAZINES

These old publications are of great value to collectors in all fields because they contain valuable information as to prices and items formerly in great demand. Catalogues give vital information as to what products were manufactured, year, date of manufacture, and names of companies who made them.

Magazines, especially older ones, have many ads of items which are today highly collectible, which antique buffs find very useful in their search for their particular item. Magazine covers, taken for granted in the 1920's to 1940's, are valuable today for the art work by their famous originators; lithographs of these artists' work are very much in demand today.

Catalogue, L.S. Starrett Company, Athol, Mass, Catalog #26, copyright 1938, 4⅞ x 7", $20.00.

CATALOGUES

Abbey and Imbrie, fishing catalogue, c1915	30.00
Aisenstein & Gordon Wholesale Jewelers, 1930, 501 pgs	30.00
American Specimen Book of Type Styles, American Type Founders Co., 1912, 1301 pgs, hardbound	50.00
Francis Bannerman & Sons, military goods, 1945	25.00
W. Bingham Co., hardware, 1937, 1372 pgs, hardcover	40.00
Geo. Brodnax Diamond Merchants, Goldsmith, Silversmiths, 1923, 183 pgs	20.00
Brown & Sharpe Small Tools #34, 512 pgs	18.50
Burroughs Welcome, Inc., medical supplies, "Excerpta Therapeutica," hardcover, c1935, 381 pgs	35.00
A. J. Child, Farm, Household, 1920, 72 pgs	25.00
Colie & Son, Parlor Furniture, 1866	25.00
Colt's Revolvers, c1919, 40 pgs	45.00
Dauch Co., stained glass windows, 1900, 60 pgs	45.00
Edison Record catalogue, listing all records to 1907	35.00
Farrel Foundry Machine Co., machines for bicycle spoke headings, spoons burnishing, etc., Waterbury, Conn., 269 pgs, hardcover	65.00
Fostoria Glass, Lamps, 1901, 13 colored pgs	38.00
A. H. Fox Gun Company, "The Finest Gun in the World - Made and Guaranteed," 6 x 9", 1909, 20 pgs	50.00
Fuller Drugstore, 1906-1907, hardcover	44.00
Geyer's Stationers Illus. Cat., 1879, 215 pgs	70.00
J.C. Iverson, furniture, c1870	35.00
Jensen-Byrd Hardware, Spokane, 1951, hardbound	22.50
Johnson and Smith Co., novelties, games, magic, tricks, practical jokes, c1932	28.00
KNY-Scheerer Co., 12th Ed., c1900	25.00
Louden Machinery, #50, 1920, barn, stables, farm equipment	27.50
J.G. & J.F. Low, art tile catalogue, 30 plates, 13½ x 10½", hardcover, c1881-1884	55.00
Charles May Co., jewelers supplies, early, 672 pgs	35.00
Oil Well Supply, 1928, 1388 pgs, hardbound	45.00
Pelton Water Wheels, 1902	22.50
Perry, Dame & Co., New York, ladies fashions, 175 pgs	27.50
Albert Pick Co. Cat. U60 Hotel, Restaurant & Institution World, 1915 387 pgs	40.00
Ranger Bicycles, 1917	20.00
Star Brand, 1907, 283 pgs, hardbound	23.00
J. Stevens Arms and Tool Company, 5¼ x 8", 1908, 160 pgs	30.00
Frank H. Stewart Elec. Co. #22, 667 pgs, hardbound	30.00
Victor, bicycle catalogue, c1894	35.00
Winsor-Newton, NYC, easels, Japanned boxes, China blanks, china color pans, etc., 88 pgs	35.00

MAGAZINES

American Agriculturist, 1852	7.00
American Builder, 1928, 373 pgs	12.00
American Museum, Vol. 3, Phila. 1789	35.00
Antiques, Sept. 1956	4.00
Cosmopolitan, 1935	70.00
Country Gentleman, N.C. Wyeth cover, cowboy on horse with fire-crackers, July 1926	10.00
Delineator, 1892	5.50
Field & Stream, 1920	1.50
Floricultural Magazine, 1836	50.00
Frank Leslie's Monthly, 1877	3.00
Godey's Lady's Book, 1842, bound	42.50
Harper's Bazaar, 1883, bound	50.00
Harper's Monthly, 1884	3.00
Harper's Weekly, March 1883	9.00
Home Needlework, 1906	6.00
The Independent, 1917	3.00
Ladies Home Journal, complete year, 1891	75.00
Life Magazine, 1939, Bette Davis cover	15.00
McCall's, 1875	12.00
Motion Picture Classic, October 1925, Mary Philbin cover	25.00
National Geographic, March 1919	12.00
Naturalist's Library of Birds, 1843	75.00
Peterson's Ladies Magazine, June 1885	9.00
Pharmaceutical Era, 1893-1896, 13 issues	65.00
Photoplay, July 1922, Rudolph Valentino cover	25.00
Photoplay, July 1938, Clark Gable cover	25.00
Photoplay, Dec. 1940, Judy Garland cover	25.00
Saturday Evening Post, "Boy with Teddy Bear" cover, Leyendecker, Dec. 1906	12.00
Saturday Evening Post, Leyendecker cover, June 1904	8.00
Saturday Evening Post, Rockwell, June 1932	10.00
Schribner's, 1879	3.00
Screenland, Oct. 1934, Shirley Temple cover	35.00
St. Nicholas, 1892	5.00
Woman's Home Companion, 1900	7.00
The Young People's Weekly, Jan. 17, 1890	5.00
Youth's Companion, The, cloth, bound, 1931	26.00

CELADON

Celadon is an Oriental porcelain with a characteristic of pale gray-green glaze. The name was taken from the character Celadon in D'Urfe's "L'Astree" of the 17th century. The ware has been made for centuries in China, Japan and Korea.

Nut dish, Mandarin, $500.00.

Bowls

7½" d, molded floral decor, Chinese	750.00
8", octagonal, green glazed interior, birds and flowers outside	100.00

Chargers

14" d, white overlay floral design, Chinese, 19th C	220.00
14¼ x 10¾", octagonal, peacock, flowers	175.00

Dishes

6" cov, shallow, openwork chrysanthemum handles suspending loose rings, carved low relief flowers on flange, openwork ribbon pattern ground, wood stand, Mughal	3,600.00
9½" d, circular, incised floral, foliate motifs, L'ung Ch'uan	175.00
13" d, circular, fluted, lotus motif center, gray-green to olive, Ming	175.00

Figures

Elephant, 6" h x 10" l, Chinese porcelain	200.00
Mandarin Duck, 5½" w, swimming among finely combed breaking waves, lotus pod in beak, folded lotus leaves, buds in waves, wave scroll base, Qianlong	4,000.00

Incense Burner, 6½", jade covered, carved, foo dog finial, foo dog ring handles on tripod base, wood stand, Chinese	300.00
Lamp, 12" h, bottle vase base, scrolling vines, relief decor, gourd handles, crackle glaze, Tao Quan	200.00
Planter, 7 x 10 x 7", rect, scroll feet, blue enamel lozenges, white scroll work	85.00

Plates

7", collared base, scalloped rim, 19th C	185.00

10", peony and daisies, butterflies, Chin Lang mark 265.00
Rose Jar, cov, 3 part, 5¾ x 4¼", bulbous, pink, red and blue flowers in relief, green foliage, gold trim 115.00
Tea Set, teapot, sugar, creamer, pink floral, green leaves, gold trim, wicker handles, 3 pcs 175.00
Vases
   3", lotus blossoms and bees, Lungch-mon 150.00
   19½" h, baluster form, scroll handles 350.00
   22" h, painted birds, flowering branches, blue ground, pr 275.00
   22", painted foo lions, blue, white ground 100.00

CELLULOID ITEMS

Celluloid was developed for J. W. Hyatt in 1869 as a substitute for ivory because whole herds of elephants were being destroyed to supply the market.

It was known as Ivorine or "French Ivory" and was made of nitrocellulose and camphor. Early pieces have a creamy color with stripes and grooves to imitate the texture of ivory or bone and was advertised in Sears catalog as early as 1897. It was widely used until the 1950s when synthetics appeared. Celluloid is now a general term for all early plastic.

Celluloid bookmark, 2 x 2⅝", The Whitehead & Hoag Co., Newark, NJ, $12.00.

Animals
   Bison, 2" h 20.00
   Cat, 12", orig paint 45.00
   Lion, 2½" h 22.00
   Navy Goat 3.00
   Rhino, 2" 20.00
   Swan 8.00
Bank, Red Cross, 2", round, WWI . 25.00
Box, dresser, cov, creamy 22.00
Brush, advertising, 3½" d, Rainier Hardware Co., Seattle, WA, scene of Mt. Rainier 12.00
Cookie Jar, 12", Aunt Jemima 80.00
Cowboy and Tin Horse 85.00
Doll Carriage, 2¾", pink and blue, moveable hood, Acme 20.00
Dresser Sets
   6 pcs., dark ivory, mirror, hair receiver, 2 brushes, nail buffer, powder box with small elephant on top 15.00
   14 pcs., handled round beveled mirror, comb, hair brush, hair receiver, rouge box, nail box, nail buffer, powder box, pin cushion, nail parer, scissors, button hook, tweezers, orig box 200.00
Foam Scraper, Anheuser Busch, c1890 . . . . 18.00
Lamp, pin up 15.00
Mirror, display, 10", round, Bull's Eyes 10.00
Napkin Ring, Buster Brown and Tige 22.50
Pencil Sharpener, 3", figure of Pinocchio 65.00
Purse, oval, emb flower pattern, handle and tassle 45.00
Rattle, 5½", shape of child's head, painted and molded features, yellow molded bonnet with ribbon trim, spiral twist handle, c1920 . . 70.00
Reading glasses, magnifying, black 25.00
Ring, carved 10.00
Roly Poly, gorilla porter holding 2 suitcases 25.00
Santa, pack on back, pulling sleigh, c1930 . . . . 23.00
Sign, Quaker Oats, Toby 18.00
Spinner, red, white and blue 3.00
Syrup Dispenser, Aunt Jemima . . . 15.00
Tape Measure, policeman, figural, pull gun to measure 45.00
Tatting Shuttle 6.00
Travel Set, 20 pcs., leatherette case 37.00

CHALKWARE

Chalkware figurines are made of plaster-of-paris and decorated with water base paints. The animal forms are imitations of the Staffordshire and other European models.

There is a discrepancy concerning the origin of chalkware. Some say that it was developed from the folk art of the Pennsylvania Dutch or Germans; others insist that the figurines were made and sold in America by Italian immigrants during the mid-nineteenth century.

Ewe and lamb, 4″ d x 7¼″ h x 8⅝″ l, $300.00.

Ashtray, black girl, boy eating watermelon, pr 40.00
Banks
  Dog with basket in his mouth, 10″, stylized, brown and yellow paint, red sponging 260.00
  Pig, 8″, yellow, large red spots, black eyes 950.00
Bird on pedestal, 6¼″, white with red, black, brown and yellow paint 225.00
Busts
  Diana, 13″ 80.00
  Girl with turban, 7½″, red, yellow and green paint, eyes highlight in black 150.00
Cats
  7″, seated, carnival type 22.00
  15″, black smoked coat, red, yellow and black paint, ribbon with bell around neck 1,000.00
Deer, 5¼″, brown and red paint . . . 295.00
Dogs
  7″, standing, French poodle 65.00
  10½ x 8″, German Shepherd, painted 20.00
Ewe and Lamb, 6¼ x 9¼″, red, black, yellow and green paint . . . 170.00
Fruit Basket with pair of Love Birds, 7¾″, yellow, red and black paint 325.00
Garnitures, 9¼″, pineapple, yellow paints, red and brown decor on one, red and black on the other, pr 325.00
Horse, 7″, red and black, green base 95.00

Lamb, 5¼″, standing, white with red and yellow face, green base 210.00
Love Birds, 4″, black and ochre, pr 250.00
Parrot, 10″, hollow, polychrome, green, maroon, orange, blue, green, red, c1860 . . . . 450.00
Rooster, 4¾″, gold with black and red paint 210.00
Squirrel with nut, 7″, white with orig yellow, red, black and brown paint 275.00
Toy Snake, 12″, jointed, green, red and yellow paint, c1910 . . . . . . 20.00

CHARACTER AND PERSONALITY ITEMS

Children raised in the age of radio, television, and comic strips looked forward to their favorite programs and the premiums they offered and/or products they promoted. Fictional characters assumed very real personalities.

This area of collectibles is rapidly growing. Collectors are advised to specialize early. Because of the abundance of these items, garage sales have been a fruitful and inexpensive way to add to a collection.

See also COWBOY COLLECTIBLES and DISNEYANA

See *Warman's Americana & Collectibles* for expanding listings in Cartoon Characters, TV Personalities, and Space Adventures.

Andy Gump, Ashtray, 28″h, figural wooden, holding metal ashtray, c1930 . . . . 225.00
Betty Boop, Match Safe, 1¼″ sq, celluloid, c1930 . . . . 150.00
Brownies, Stickpins, c1896
  Black, white, green enamel 18.00
  Sailor 20.00
  With horn 19.00
Buck Rogers
  Atomic Pistol, Daisy Mfg., c1930 . 60.00
  Button, 1¼″, celluloid, Buffalo Evening News, orig paper insert, c1930 . . . . 40.00
  Solar Scouts Manual, secret codes, illus, other info, c1930 . . 200.00
  Watch, pocket, strap, orig box, copyright J. F. Dille Co. 650.00
Buster Brown
  Bank, iron, Buster Brown, Tige, horse, horseshoe shape 125.00
  Book, *Buster Brown Abroad*, Outcalt, 1904 . . . . 35.00
  Doll, 16½″h, composition, decal sleep eyes, red cotton knicker suit, cap, Ideal 100.00
  Stickpin, Buster plays fiddle, c1900 . . . . 22.00

Fanny Brice, doll, 13″, Baby Snooks, composition head, hands, feet, flexible wire body, "Flexy" label, Ideal, $175.00.

Captain Hawks, Badge, Sky Patrol Propeller Members, brass, red enamel ... 18.50

Captain Marvel
Iron-Ons, 8 tissue sheets, 2 colors ... 25.00
Pennant, dark blue felt with maroon picture ... 20.00
Wristwatch, copyright 1948 Fawcett Publications, red strap, not running, orig box ... 125.00

Captain Midnight
Flight Patrol Badge ... 10.00
Glass, Ovaltine ... 17.50
Membership Badge ... 10.00

Charlie Chaplin, lapel pin, 1⅝″, metal figural c1920 ... 25.00

Charlie McCarthy
Button, 1¼″, black, white, red ... 18.00
Ring, green plastic, black and white photo, c1940 ... 30.00

Danny O'Day & Humphrey Higsbye, hand puppets, vinyl heads, cloth bodies, Texaco hat, copyright 1952 Jimmy Nelson Enterprises, Inc., pr ... 45.00

Dick Tracy
Camera, 3 x 5″, Seymore Products, Chicago, black plastic ... 40.00
Card Game, Whitman, 1934, thirty-five cards ... 25.00
Pistol, click, tin, litho "Junior" ... 30.00
Salt and Pepper, plaster, Dick and

Junior ... 32.50

Dionne Quintuplets
Books
The Story of the Dionne Quintuplets, 44 pgs, 1935, Whitman ... 24.00
We're Two Years Old ... 22.00
Calendar, Queens of the Kitchen, 1946 ... 15.00
Fan ... 15.95

Don Winslow
Book, Breaking The Sound Barrier, Magic State Series #1, 1953, Strathmore Co. ... 21.00
Pin, Ensign, high relief metal ... 42.00

Dragnet
Badge 714, gold color, emblem LA Sgt. 714, MIB ... 14.00
Detective Special Repeating Revolver, die cast metal cap gun, pearline handle, badge, Knickerbocker, MIB ... 42.00
Jack Webb Dragnet whistle ... 8.00

Eddie Cantor, New Game ... 35.00

Elsie The Cow, Doll, cloth, stuffed ... 24.00

Felix The Cat
Button, 1¼″, black and white cloth face, cardboard ears, c1924 ... 50.00
Doll, 8½″l, wood, jointed, decals, leather ears, Schoenhut, c1920 ... 200.00

Fibber McGee, Game, The Merry Game of Fibber McGee and the Wistful Vista Mystery, Milton Bradley, c1940, NBC ... 18.00

Flash Gordon, Rocket ship, 12″l, tin, litho, Marx Toy Co. ... 285.00

Frank Buck, Button, 1¾″, black, white, blue, Bring 'Em Back Alive, c1930 ... 30.00

Henry Figure, composition, jointed at shoulders, yellow shorts, copyright 1934, Carl Anderson ... 120.00

Horace Horsecollar, Tumbler, 4¾″, glass, bending down to pick up a coin, Libbey, c1930 ... 32.00

Jack Armstrong, Bullet Flashlight ... 25.00

Jiggs, Match Holder & Striker, 13″h, wooden plaque ... 38.00

Jiminy Cricket, glass, 4¾″, full figure, poem, c1940 ... 18.00

Katzenjammers, Christmas light bulb shades, set of seven, c1930 ... 21.00

Laurel and Hardy, 1925 Roadster Kit, Lesney ... 25.00

Little Orphan Annie
Charm, 1⅛″, celluloid, c1930 ... 20.00
Clicker, Mysto members, red, white, black, 1941 ... 35.00
Decoders
1938 ... 20.00
1939 ... 18.00
Ring, March birthstone ... 80.00
Whistle, signal, three tones, tin ... 30.00

Lum and Abner

Almanac, 1936 . . . . **18.00**

Badge, Walkin Weather Prophet . **26.00**

Mutt & Jeff, Bottle opener, ⅞", black and white celluloid set in metal, c1910 . . . . **25.00**

Popeye

Celluloid, 12¼ x 8¾", Popeye fighting Bluto as Olive Oyl hangs in mid-air, watercolor . . . **600.00**

Charm, celluloid **5.00**

Christmas lights, G.E. Textolite, set of eight, MIB, c1929, King Features **65.00**

Paint Box, 4½ x 5¾", tin litho, American Crayon Co., copyright 1933 King Features, Inc. **25.00**

Pencil Sharpener, celluloid, c1930 . . . . **24.00**

Toy Popeye Pirate Pistol, 9½"l, litho tin, Marx Toy Co., c1935, MIB **125.00**

Toy, Windup, parrot cage **115.00**

Rootie Kazootie Club, Buttons, 1⅛", black and white

Big Todd Russell **20.00**

El Squeko **20.00**

Little Nipper **20.00**

Poison Zoomack **20.00**

Scrappy

Pencil box, 5½ x 8⅝", Dixon, copyright Columbia Pictures, c1930 . . . . **20.00**

Soap, 3 bars, Scrappy, Margy, Yippy, colorful illus box, Columbia Pictures, Kirk Guild c1935 . . **45.00**

Shirley Temple

Button, 1¼", black and white photo, brass pin, c1930 . . . . **50.00**

Breakfast set, 3 pcs, orig, excellent decals **100.00**

Smitty, Cookie Cutters, Comicooky Baking Set by Pillsbury, litho box, copyright 1937, Famous Artists Syndicate **20.00**

Snoopy, Family Car, 6½"l, plastic, battery operated, Snoopy driving, Lucy, Charlie Brown, Patty as passengers, Woodstock as hood ornament, United Features, MIB . . . **15.00**

Space Patrol

Captain Video

Leather belt and holster, decor with silver metal studs **37.50**

Puzzle, 10½ x 14½", two men flying rocketship **40.00**

Supersonic Space Ships, Capt. Video & His Video Rangers, rocketship play set by Lido, punch out figures **50.00**

Diplomatic Pouch, 11½" sq, Top Secret, brown and white cardboard folder **80.00**

Gun, plastic, fires darts, Space Patrol emblem on grip **120.00**

Space Patrol Card, Wheat Chex premium **17.50**

Superman

Hand puppet, 10", cloth body, vinyl head, 1956 . . . . **20.00**

Muscle Building Set, 11½ x 18", Golden, Milton, contains handles, springs, hand grippers, jump rope, etc., orig box **85.00**

Superman

Snorkel, Super, 29", blue plastic, orig box **30.00**

Wallet, leather, zippered on three sides, Pioneer **15.00**

The Shadow, Matches, unused **25.00**

Tom Corbett Space Cadet

Ring, insignia **10.00**

Ring, space suit **16.00**

Toonersville Folks, Salt & Pepper, ceramic Mr. Bang, c1930 . . . . . . **28.00**

Uncle Wiggily, Mug, ceramic, Ovaltine, orig mailing box **48.00**

Willie Whopper, Pencil Box, 6 x 10¾", five scenes on front, back, silver, black, tan on green ground, U.B. Iwerks, copyright 1934 Celebrity Productions **45.00**

Woody Woodpecker, Clock, animated, MIB **375.00**

Yellow Kid, pin cushion, metal figurine, "I'm Weightin For Yer See", 4⅝", $50.00.

Yellow Kid
Button
 Clean Streets **15.00**
 Ireland **15.00**
Figure, goat drawn cart, 7¾"l, wheels painted yellow, silver goat, brown cart, cast iron, c1897 . . . .   **400.00**

CHELSEA

Chelsea is a fine English porcelain which was made to compete with Dresden. The factory began operating in the Chelsea area of London, England, in the 1740s. Chelsea products can be divided into four periods: (1) Early period, 1740s, with incised triangle and raised anchor mark, (2) The 1750s, with red raised anchor mark, (3) The 1760s, the gold anchor period, (4) The Derby period from 1770–1783. In 1924, a large number of the molds and models of figurines were found at the Spode-Copeland Works and many items were brought back into circulation.

Bowl, 6½" d, molded leaves on exterior, floral spray in center, red anchor **1,000.00**
Candlestick Figures, 7½", draped putti holding flower, seated on tree stump, supporting pierced

Figurine, 6½" h, $480.00.

candle nozzle, wax pan, scroll molded base encircled in puce, gilt, pr **825.00**
Cups, coffee, baluster form, figures in purple, iron-red clothes within gilt foliage cartouches, blue ground, gold anchor mark, c1765, pr **500.00**
Dessert Service, beige, leaf decor, 15 pcs, c1840 . . . .   **360.00**
Dishes
 10", peony shape, yellow, blue, puce, 2 molded leaves, black veins, stalk forms handle, iron-red anchor mark, c1755 . . . . .   **565.00**
 10½", leaf shape, oval pierced basketwork, green, puce, painted carnation spray, gilt rim   **500.00**
Figurines
 4⅜" h, Pantaloon, Italian comedy, red anchor **1,500.00**
 7", Tyrolean Dancers, red anchor   **2,500.00**
 8½", Woman with tray, white background with rust, red and blue decor, late **250.00**
 9", Woodsman and Milkmaid, late, pair **500.00**
Jardiniere, 11", cov, hexagonal shape, red anchor **1,275.00**
Plates
 8", bouquets, scattered flowers, shaped chocolate rims, iron red anchor marks, c1755, pr **460.00**
 9⅜", floral decor, red anchor . . .   **875.00**
Sauce Boat, 7½" w, Strawberry leaf mold, hp flowers, leaves, iron red anchor mark **350.00**
Tureen, cov, 3½" l, melon shaped, yellow, green, brown, snail finial on cov, iron red anchor, 45 mark on tureen, 31 on cover, c1755 . .   **1,220.00**

"CHELSEA" GRANDMOTHER'S WARE

Wares decorated with the familiar grape, sprig, or thistle pattern in relief and lustred are erroneously called Chelsea. These wares were not made in Chelsea, but in the Staffordshire district of England in the early 1880s. There is a movement to rename this decorated procelain "Grandmother's Ware."

Bowl, 6", berry, grape **7.50**
Butter Pats, 4" d
 Grape **8.00**
 Sprig **12.00**
Cake Plate, 10", grape **45.00**
Coffee Pot, grape lustre **190.00**
Creamers
 Grape lustre **45.00**

Eggs Cup, grape, marked "Royal Adderley/Blue Chelsea/Ridway Potters Ltd", $25.00.

Sprig lustre	50.00
Cups and Saucers	
Sprig lustre, wishbone handle . . .	25.00
Thistle	25.00
Plates	
8″, Grape lustre	20.00
8¾″, Adderly blue sprig	20.00
9½″, Sprig lustre	27.50
10″, Grape lustre	18.50
Sauce Dish, grape	4.50
Sugar Bowls	
7″, Grape lustre	50.00
7½″, Sprig, cov	110.00
Teapot, 10″, Grape lustre, octagonal	125.00

CHILDREN'S BOOKS

Because there is a bit of the child in all of us, collectors always have been attracted to children's books. In the 19th century books were popular gifts for children with most of the children's classics written and published during this time. These books were treasured and often kept throughout a lifetime. Developments in printing made it possible to include more attractive black and white illustrations and lovely color plates. The work of these artists and illustrators has made some of the books valuable and of great interest to collectors.

See *Warman's Americana & Collectibles* for an expanded listing of Children's Books.
  1st ed — first edition
  dj — dust jacket
  unp — unpaged
  wraps — paper covers

Nast, Thomas, *The Night Before Christmas*. Illustrated by Frances Brundage, $25.00.

Alcott, Louisa May. *Little Men.* Roberts Bros., 1871, 376 pgs, 1st ed.	95.00
Andersen, Hans Christian. *Han's Andersen's Fairy Tales.* Mabel Lucie Attwell, illus. McKay, 1914, 143 pgs, 1st ed.	60.00
Bannerman, Helen. *The Story Of Little Black Sambo.* Grant Richards, 1899, 57 pgs, 1st ed.	775.00
Baum, L. Frank, *Father Goose: His Book.* W. W. Denslow, illus. George M. Hill, 1899, 106 pgs, 1st ed.	850.00
Caldecott, Randolph. *Sing A Song Of Sixpence.* Routledge, n.d., 1880, 1st ed.	40.00
Carroll, Lewis. *Alice's Adventures In Wonderland.* D. Appleton, 1866, 1st ed.	750.00
Child's Book About Whales. Rufus Merrill, 1843, 16 pgs, wraps	55.00
Cinderella or the Glass Slipper. McLoughlin, n. d. (c1860s), 8 pgs, hand colored, wraps	40.00
Cone, Helen Gray. *Bonnie Little*	

People. Maud Humphrey, illus. Stokes, 1890, 12 pgs, 1st ed. . . .	450.00
Cox, Palmer. *The Brownies Through The Union.* Century, 1895, 144 pgs, 1st ed.	100.00
Cradock, Mrs. H. C. *Josephine And Her Dolls.* Honor C. Appleton, illus. Blackie & Son, n.d. (c1920s), 47 pgs	35.00
DeAngeli, Marguerite. *Skippack School.* Doubleday, 1939, unp, 1st ed., dj.	40.00
Doyle, Richard. *Jack The Giant Killer.* Eyre & Spottiswoode, 1888, 48 pgs, 1st ed.	225.00
Duplaix, Georges. *Topsy-turvy Circus.* Tibor Gergely, illus. Harper, 1940, 40 pgs, 1st ed., dj	45.00
Field, Rachel. *Hitty, Her First Hundred Years.* Dorothy Lathrop, illus. Macmillan, 1929, 207 pgs, 1st ed., 1930 Newbery Medal	50.00
Gates, Josephine Scribner. *The Live Dolls' House Party.* Virginia Keep, illus. Bobbs-Merrill, 1906, 103 pgs, 1st ed.	40.00
Goodrich, Samuel G. *Peter Parley's Book of Fables.* Silus Andrus & Son, 1834, 128 pgs, 1st ed.	50.00
Greenaway, Kate. *Under The Window.* Routledge, 1878, 1st ed. . . .	80.00
Gruelle, Johnny. *The Magical Land Of Noom.* Volland, 1922, 157 pgs, 1st ed.	95.00
Hawthorne, Nathaniel. *Tanglewood Tales.* Edmund Dulac, illus. Hodder & Stoughton, 1938, 222 pgs, 1st ed., dj.	100.00
History Of The Children In The Wood. G. S. Peters, n.d. (c1835), 18 pgs, wraps	225.00
Hogan, Inez. *Nicodemus and the Goose.* Dutton, 1945, 54 pgs, 1st ed., dj.	30.00
LeMair, H. Willebeek. *Mother's Little Rhyme Book.* McKay, n.d., unp. .	45.00
Little Pets Panorama Pictures. Nister, n.d. (c1890), 24 pgs, 4 pop-ups	175.00
Milhous, Katherine *The Egg Tree.* Scribner's, 1950, unp, 1st ed., dj., 1951 Caldecott Medal	40.00
Milne, A. A. *A Gallery Of Children.* Saida, illus. (H. Willebeek, LeMair) McKay, 1925, 105 pgs, 1st ed., dj.	85.00
Minarik, Else Holmelund. *Little Bear's Friend.* Maurice Sendak, illus. Harper, 1960, 64 pgs, 1st ed., dj.	25.00
Moore, Clement. *The Night Before Christmas.* Tasha Tudor, illus. Archille J. St. Onge, 1962, unp, 1st ed, dj., miniature	35.00

Newbery, Clare Turlay. *Mittens.* Harper, 1936, 29 pgs, 1st ed., dj. .	40.00
Newell, Peter. *Topsys & Turveys.* Century, 1902, 36 pgs, 1st ed. . . .	85.00
Old Mother Hubbard. McLoughlin, n. d. (c1870), unp, wraps	40.00
Pogany, Elayne. *The Golden Cockerel.* Willy Pogany, illus. Thomas Nelson, 1938, unp, 1st ed., dj. . . .	100.00
Potter, Beatrix. *The Tale Of Two Bad Mice.* Warne, 1904, 85 pgs, 1st ed.	200.00
Pyle, Howard. *Otto Of The Silver Hand.* Scribner's, 1888, 173 pgs, 1st ed.	60.00
Stewart, Mary. *The Way To Wonderland.* Jessie Willcox Smith, illus. Hodder & Stoughton, n.d. (c1917), 147 pgs, 1st ed.	250.00
Thompson, Kay. *Kay Thompson's Eloise In Moscow.* Hilary Knight, illus. Simon & Schuster, 1959, unp, 1st ed., dj.	40.00
Thompson, Ruth Plumly. *Kabumpo In Oz.* John R. Neill, illus. Reilly & Lee, 1922, 297 pgs, 1st ed.	85.00
Upton, Bertha. *The Adventures Of Two Dutch Dolls And A Golliwog.* Florence K. Upton, illus. Longmans Green, n.d. (c1895), unp	130.00
Walker, Dugald Stewart. *Dream Boats.* Doubleday, 1918, 64 pgs, 1st ed, dj.	50.00
With Father Tuck In Playtime. Tuck, n.d. (c1913), 8 pgs, 4 pop-ups . . .	135.00

CHILDREN'S FEEDING DISHES

During the late 19th century and into the 20th, tablewares designed especially for children's personal use were very much in vogue. Even major pottery firms catered to the demand. Today these children's items are very collectible and sometimes command very high prices.
Also see CHILDREN'S TOY DISHES, GLASS, PORCELAIN AND TIN.

Bowls	
Cereal, Royal Doulton Bunnykins	35.00
Tom Tom Piper's Son, rolled edge, Roseville	75.00
Cup and Saucer, boy, girl, bunny, red mark, Germany	10.00
Egg Cup, Bunnykins, Royal Doulton	8.00
Feeding Dishes	
"Baby" bowl, children, dolls, chicks, bunnies, Czechoslovakia	35.00
Bunnykins, Easter Finery	24.00
Clown, take-apart set	12.50

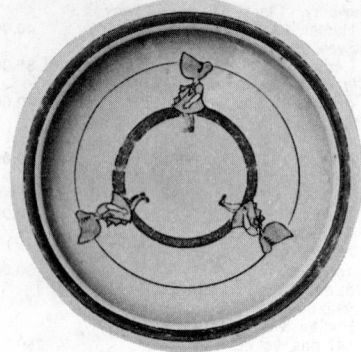

Roseville, 7¾″ d, c1910, $55.00.

English China	38.00
Hankscraft, pink, baby	15.00
Little Bo Peep, divided	13.00
Mexican scenes, 3 compartment china dish, aluminum hot water shell	10.00
Mother Goose, hot water shell, SP, Reed-Barton	65.00
Nursery rhyme figures, 3 compartment, 8″ china bowl, Salem	10.50

Mugs
Bunnykins, Royal Doulton	35.00
Mexican scene, Salem	4.00
Ovaltine, Uncle Wiggily, china	26.00
"The Romper Room" ceramic, jack-in-the-box says "Do Bee a Milk Drinker"	10.00

Plates
7″, Cameo, Harker	9.00
8½″, Uncle Wiggily	50.00

Sets
Bowl and Plate, Little Jack Horner, white ceramic with red border	20.00
Mug and Plate, Mt. Clemens	25.00
Sugar, Royal Doulton Bunnykins	20.00

CHILDREN'S ITEMS—MISCELLANEOUS

Bath Tub, tin	40.00

Beds
Child's, country Sheraton, turned legs, posts, railing of wooden slats, old green paint, 29 x 48 x 30½″ h	215.00
Doll, walnut, turned spindles, 11½ x 15¼ x 15½″ h	125.00
Blocks, 4 nesting, wooden, colorful litho paper covers, Little Bow	

Peeps Alphabet & Picture Blocks, McLoughlin Bros., NY, 1890, 7″ cubes, worn, incomplete set	75.00

Chairs
Corner, Sheraton styling, bamboo turnings, old rush seat, worn gilding over yellow paint, early 20th C, 19″ h	155.00
High, arrowback, primitive, worn black paint, yellow striping, 32″ h	70.00
High, spindle back, scrolled arms, old worn black paint, yellow striping, worn foot rest, 33¾″ h	95.00
Queen Anne, Centenniel, mahogany serpentine frame, violin shaped back splat, green leather seat	825.00
Coffee Grinder, drawer, wood finial, ornate plates	65.00

Costumes
Charlie McCarthy costume by Edgar Bergen, Inc., 2 pcs, black suit, with hat, for small child	35.00
Prairie Ranger Cowboy Suit, complete with mask, gun, and holster, orig box	15.00
Counting Board, ABC, metal and wood, 1917	50.00
Cradle, doll, poplar, 26½″ l, sq nail construction, old dark paint, small heart cut-outs both ends	95.00
Drum, child's, 11″ d, brass colored tin, colorful litho scene of American soldiers	155.00
Horse, wooden, primitive old Appaloosa paint, 13″ l, 12½″ h	200.00
House, toy, wooden, orig red, white,	

Block Puzzle, 5 lithographs, 18 x 13⅛″, German, $285.00.

gray, black paint, green base, 6½ x 9½ x 4¼" h 80.00

Ice skates, wooden, curved wrought iron blades, old worn orange paint, 12" l 105.00

Jumping Jack, wooden, cat, orig brown stain, yellow spots, stripes, 19" l 400.00

Rocking Horses

Laminated wood, bentwood frame, stationary base, glass eyes, horsehair tail, old dappled gray paint, mane, 36" l 275.00

Wooden, orig harness, stirrups, blanket, saddle, brown paint, red striped base, 30" h, American, c1840 . . . . 450.00

Wooden, worn orig brown, yellow graining, green rockers, worn old leather harness, saddle, orig mane, branded label "B.P. Crandell, Griland St., NY," 54" l 725.00

Sewing Machine, red flowers on black casing, MIB 65.00

Sleigh, wooden top, iron runners, wooden tongue, worn orig red, green paint, worn paper label, 20 x 43" 95.00

Sweeper, Bissell Midget, wood 45.00

Toy Stove, cast nickel steel, Pat, 6¼ x 9 x 7¼" h, plates, lifter, skillet, 2 pots 60.00

Wagon, wooden, worn old red paint 145.00

Walker, wooden, horse head, c1875 100.00

Wheelbarrow, wood, old paint, yellow stripes 130.00

CHILDREN'S TOY DISHES

Children's glass dishes evolved in the 1900's by a recycling process. Glass manufacturers had a surplus problem stemming from producing only two new patterns a year. To remedy the waste, the manufacturers began to produce dishes for children. The dishes were used as premiums with grocery items and were also sold to the Sears Roebuck and Montgomery Ward catalog houses.

See *Warman's Americana & Collectibles* for an expanded listing of Children's Toy Dishes.

PORCELAIN

Candlestick, 2¾", Staffordshire . . . 3.00

Chamber Set, pitcher, bowl, soap dish, spongeware 40.00

Casserole, Blue Willow 39.50

Coffee Set, coffee pot, cov, sugar, cov, creamer, handled basket, 2 mugs, 2 bowls, 3 x 5" rect tray, all white ground, rims of molded blue

Porcelain, Tea set, 17 pcs, boy in blue shirt, girl in orange dress, white ground, made in Japan, orig box 8¾ x 10⅜", $35.00.

flowers, Dresden-like flowers, marked Germany, c1875 . . . . . . 150.00

Condiment Sets

Transfer, children and dolls, Germany, 3" h, cannisters, 15 pcs., set 150.00

Four bottles, in pewter stand, flat, not castor set 60.00

Demitasse set, 21 pcs, white porcelain, Germany 165.00

Plate, 4", Staffordshire, red transfer, girl, goat, c1840 . . . . 35.00

Platters, 5 x 3½", black and white fish in center, gold trim, no mark . 18.50

Tea Sets

14 pcs, yellow floral, cinnamon, black leaves, gold trim, teapot, creamer, 4 cups, 4 saucers, 3 plates, made in Japan 22.00

16 pcs, Happy Fats, white ground, German 165.00

18 pcs, lustre, hp, Japan 95.00

21 pcs, flow blue, Mother Hubbard decor, teapot, creamer, sugar, service for 4, c1870 . . . . 160.00

21 pcs, ironstone, teapot, creamer, sugar, service for 4 . . . . . . 55.00

21 pcs, lustre, beige, portrait of woman in bright colors on each piece, teapot, creamer, sugar, service for 4, orig box, German 210.00

22 pcs, blue, white chintz pattern, Stoke-on-Trent, teapot, creamer, sugar, service for 4, tray, c1883 . . . . 195.00

Tureen, soup, cov, ladle, underplate, house, tree, man, woman, horse scene 195.00

Water Set, 4½", pitcher, "Red Riding Hood and Wolf," 6 tumblers . 175.00

TIN

Coffee pot, graniteware **65.00**
Cooking set, Like Mother's, No. 08082 Made in USA, 14 pcs **40.00**
Ice Cream Freezer, 5½" h, hand crank, Baby Jeannette Freezer, Jeannette Toy & Novelty Co. Jeannette, Pa, includes directions for use **80.00**

Tea Sets
  9 pcs, red, blue, cats and dogs decor, Germany **60.00**
  10 pcs, litho, fruits, nuts, gold, soldered handles, Germany, teapot, cov, creamer, open sugar, 3 cups, 3 saucers, c1880 . . **85.00**
  15 pcs, litho, Oriental design, soft colors, tab handles, teapot, cov, creamer, open sugar, 4 plates, 4 cups, 3 saucers **90.00**
  15 pcs, litho, "Happynak Teaset Made in England By Permission of Walt Disney Mickey Mouse, Ltd" on front of all pieces, Mickey, Minnie, Pluto, and Donald Duck having tea, tray, teapot, cov, 3 plates, 3 saucers, 3 spoons **130.00**

CHILDREN'S TOY GLASS DISHES

Children's glass dishes evolved in the 1900's by a recycling process. Glass manufacturers had a surplus problem stemming from producing only two new patterns a year. To remedy the waste, the manufacturers began to produce dishes for children. The dishes were used as premiums with grocery items and were also sold to the Sears Roebuck and Montgomery Ward catalog houses.

See _Warman's Americana & Collectibles_ for an expanded listing of Children's Toy Dishes.

Berry Sets
  Amazon (or Sawtooth Band), 6 pieces **85.00**
  Tappan, 6 pieces **80.00**
Bowls
  Hawiian Lei, (Bee mark) **25.00**
  Little Bo Peep, alphabet border . **15.00**
  Kokomo (Bar and Finecut) **22.50**
Butter, covered
  Dewdrop, clear **135.00**
  Galloway (Virginia #2) **50.00**
  Wabash **75.00**
  Wee Branches **125.00**
Cake Stands
  Beautiful Lady **35.00**
  Strigil **30.00**

Butter dish, cov, creamer, sugar, Sweetheart, $140.00.

Candlestick, amber swirl **30.00**
Carafe, water, 4⅛", Truncated Prisms (Thompson's #77), pair . **100.00**
Castor Sets
  English Hobnail, 3-bottle, tin stand **35.00**
  Milk glass, plain bottles, metal stand **40.00**
Creamers
  Arrowhead **20.00**
  Dewdrop, clear **55.00**
  Inverted Strawberry **45.00**
  Star and Bar, blue **25.00**
Cups and Saucers
  Basketweave, blue **45.00**
  Daisy Band, amber **50.00**
  Dog and Cat **30.00**
  Lion **50.00**
  Stippled Leaf and Grape **32.00**
Mugs
  Butterfly **25.00**
  Hobnail **10.00**
  Humpty Dumpty **22.50**
  Tom Tom, The Piper's Son **25.00**
Pitcher, water, Michigan **25.00**
Punch Bowl Sets
  Inverted Strawberry, bowl and six cups **175.00**
  Red Riding Hood, scenes around bowl, six cups **260.00**
  Tulip and Honeycomb, bowl and six cups **145.00**
  Wheat Sheaf, six cups **70.00**
  Wild Rose, milk glass, bowl and six cups **100.00**
Spooners
  Clear and Diamond Panels **45.00**
  Drum **60.00**
  Menagerie **85.00**
  Pennsylvania #1 . . . . **22.00**
  Wee Branches **70.00**
Sugars, covered
  Beaded Swirl **26.00**
  Ring Around Rosie **30.00**
  Lion, frosted **350.00**
  Sugar, open, Dewdrop, clear . . . **35.00**

Table Sets, (four pieces, creamer, covered sugar, covered butter and spooner.)
Diamond Panel, blue 200.00
Hawaiian Lei 85.00
Sawtooth 115.00
Tappan 85.00
Tray, Flattened Diamond & Sunburst, amber 45.00
Vegetable Dish, lacy Sandwich, oval 55.00

CHRISTMAS ITEMS

There are many reasons why individuals collect Christmas decorations and related items from the past . . . nostalgia, return to the basics, acceptance of traditions. Perhaps they seek assurance that in this contemporary world, an old fashioned Christmas will always be in vogue.

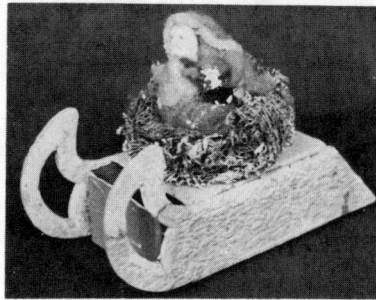

Candy Container, St. Nicholas on Sled, 3⅝″l, $12.00.

Advertising, Whitman's Chocolate, Santa, die cut 45.00
Angel, wax, spunglass wings 65.00
Baby Rattle, Santa, celluloid 4.00
Books
Night Before Christmas, Florence Saral Winship, Whitman, 1943 . 16.00
Old Santa Claus, Conkey, color litho cover, 1901 . . . . 18.00
The Birds Christmas Carol, illus. Wireman, 1912 . . . . 12.00
Candle Holder, 3¼″ h, tin, lantern, red, white glass sides 30.00
Candy Container, papier-mache, Father Christmas 580.00
Cards
9 x 7″, stand-up, fold-out, 4 dogs singing in snowy woods 10.00
Double sided, color litho, children, purple fringed, #204 sgr. Bufford 15.00

Doll, Santa, 12″, felt and vinyl, swivel head, molded features, fur moustache, beard and hair, jointed, felt hands, Steiff, yellow paper label 325.00
Folder, die cut, litho
Raphael Tuck 5.00
Tennyson poem, Germany 10.00
Ink Blotter, celluloid, 3 pcs. 15.00
Lights
3½″, DQ, green 52.50
3¾″, DQ, cobalt blue 52.50
Nativity, 7 pcs., figures, 9″, terra cotta, sculpted, painted, orig costume of colored silk, satin, gilt braid, turbans, Italian, 19th C 900.00
Santa Claus
10″ h, papier-mache 32.00
24″, red suit, face painted on stiff cloth 225.00
47″, wooden, hand painted 150.00
St. Nicholas and Reindeer, 20″, papier-mache, cloth costume, rough-hewn sleigh, 2 plush covered reindeer, metal antlers, heads remove to form hollow candy containers, c1890 . . . . 600.00
Toys
Santa on scooter, battery operated, MIB 35.00
Santa, 12½″, battery, rings bell, eyes light up 45.00
Tree
26″, goose feather, off-white, wooden base 85.00
52″, green fiber branches on twisted wire, turned wood base 125.00
Tree Lights, electric
Blimp, 2½″h, glass, painted white, red, green, American flag 40.00
Bull dog, 2¾″h, glass, red, black 25.00
Clown, milk glass 6.50
Parrot, 3¼″ h, pink, green, glass 8.00
Pouter pigeon, 3″ h, glass, magenta, blue 15.00
Santa Claus, 8½″ h 38.00
Tree Light Set, Walt Disney characters, 7 ind bulbs, 3″ h, electric, orig box 85.00
Tree Ornaments
Baby on ball, 3¼″ h, blown glass, gold, red 65.00
Balloon, 4¾″ h, pink, printed paper Santa, tinsel 90.00
Basket of fruit, 2¾″ w, blown glass, polychrome 25.00
Bird, 4½″ l, blown glass, silver, red, angel hair tail, spring clip . 40.00
Christ child head 65.00
Cloth doll, 4″ h, caroler, felt body, composition face, white, blue boots, salmon muff 40.00
Clown, standing on ball 40.00

Duck, 3" h, blown glass, silver, red, blue **55.00**
Fish, 3¼" h, blown glass, silver, red, blue **50.00**
Revolver, 5¼" l, blown glass, silver, pink grip **140.00**
Santa in airplane **40.00**
Star, 10", punched tin, cut out, curled edge **30.00**
Tree Stand, 5 x 12", cast iron, evergreen trees, stars, metallic green, gold, silver, marked Germany . . . **30.00**
Tree-top Ornaments
10" h, bisque doll head, hooded cape, on stuffed heart shape, trimmed with tinsel **50.00**
12" h, Santa, printed paper, pink angel hair **15.00**
13½" h, finial, silver, red horns, blue Santa, magenta and white **25.00**

CIGAR CUTTERS

Cigar cutters of the pocket and counter-type were used primarily at the end of the 19th and the beginning of the 20th century. They were often an advertising and promotion item. Pocket-type cigar cutters were not only utilitarian to a smoking man but often a fine piece of jewelry that was attached to his watch chain. With the return of the vested suit and watch chain, cigar cutters have regained their popularity. They are again being made and sold in tobacco shops and jewelry stores.

COUNTER TOP

Advertising
Brunholl Co., cast iron, emb ash base, 9 x 6" **150.00**
Charles Denby Cigars, cast iron, reverse painted glass **130.00**
East Rock Cigars, mountain scene on glass top **80.00**
Five Bros. Tobacco Works, John Finzer & Bros., Louisville, KY . . **48.00**
Great Ohio 5¢ cigar, pig shape, cast iron **425.00**
Lorillard's Tomahawk Brand, cast iron, Pat. 1871, 75, 18" l **45.00**
Rose-O-Cuba, Always Good Cigars, J. B. Watkins & Bros Distributor, wood, metal, 6 x 8 x 4½" **200.00**
Schartz & Sons, mechanical **140.00**
Star Tobacco, Griswold Mfg., Erie, PA, cast iron, 19 x 7" **40.00**
Figurals
Brass, Russian wolfhound head . **160.00**
Cast iron, donkey, tail lifts for plunger cutter **200.00**

Counter Cigar Cutter, Arora Cigar, E. Kleiner & Co, NY, $150.00.

POCKET

Advertising
New Bachelor, cigars, brass **15.00**
Swift & Co., on watch chain **12.00**
Figurals
Dog's head, 5¾" l, silver metal . **62.00**
Male soda jerk, arm moves to operate blade **60.00**
Log shape, wood grain, bakelite . **15.00**
Guillotine Types
Silver metal
Blade enclosed on oblong barrel **10.00**
Sliding blade, Gofa patent **15.00**
Sterling, sliding blade, floral pattern **25.00**
Mechanical, finger type, pretty girl

Pocket Cigar Cutter, scissors type, Sterling Silver, 2⅛", $40.00.

does curtsy when squeezed to cut
cigar **35.00**
Scissors Types
Black and white, cigars **12.00**
Sterling, floral **25.00**

CIGAR STORE FIGURES

Cigar store Indians, squaws or turks were familiar sights in front of cigar stores and tobacco shops. These figures are now scarce
and command a good price when offered for
sale. They are being reproduced in various
sizes, styles and materials.

Indian, 72″, $6,500.00.

Hercules, 66″, carved and painted
wood, English, 19th C, restoration
to paint **1,540.00**
Indian, 108″, eagle feather head-
dress, beads, spear in left hand,
tomahawk in right hand, on base **9,500.00**
Indian Chief, 6′, full headdress,
c1900 . . . . **5,200.00**
Indian Chief, 81″, carved, painted
wood, holds rifle, square base,
American, 19th C **5,500.00**
Indian Maiden, 62″, on 3″ base,
wooden, hand carved **5,400.00**
Indian Princess, 90″, on pedestal,
raised hand, headdress, orig paint **3,500.00**
Indian Squaw, life size, wooden,
buckskin and beaded outfit **6,000.00**
Indian Squaw, 55″, cast iron,
painted, circular base **5,800.00**
Indian Warrior, 87″, cast metal,
painted, William Demuth, NY,

c1872, mounted on pedestal with
"Wolf's Choice," restoration to
paint **6,000.00**

CINNABAR

Cinnabar is a ware made of numerous layers
of a heavy mercuric sulphide, often referred
to as vermillion. It was carved into boxes,
buttons, snuff bottles, and vases. The best of
this ware was made in China.

**Snuff Bottle, Cinnabar, 2¾″ h, lapis
lazuli top, late 19th C, $285.00.**

Boxes
Floral carvings on red, black interi-
or, 2 x 3″ **75.00**
Carved bird on lid, marked "Chi-
na" **50.00**
Carved scenic decor, brass bo-
und edges **75.00**
Carved scenic decor, florals, 2 fig-
ures, divided interior, 4 x 3 x 2″ **68.00**
Figurine, horses, 10½″ h, jade with
turquoise inlay **2,500.00**
Plate, 9″, carved scene of people . **250.00**
Snuff Bottles
2¾″, cylindrical, continuous scenic carving, apocryphal seal of
Chien Lung, matching carved
stopper, 20th C **160.00**
3½″, carved scene, minute detail,
matching carved stopper, early
19th C **210.00**
Stand, 15 x 12″, pedestal, rectangu-
lar, scrolling relief decor **160.00**
Tray, 8 x 12″, scenic decor **200.00**
Urns, 17″, cov, carved Chinese
scenes, fitted stands, 19th C, pr . **850.00**

Vases
  6½", baluster form, continuous
    carved garden scene, 4 figures,
    mkd china 175.00
  16", baluster form, carved, wood
    stand, late 19th C, pr 475.00

CLAMBROTH GLASS

Clambroth glass derives its name from the color of the glass. The semi-opaque grayish-white color resembles the broth from clams. This type of glass ware was popular in the Victorian period.

Barber bottle, 7"h, Witch Hazel, M.A. Co., $25.00.

Barber Bottle, 7⅝" h, Bay Rum, thin
  red bands, porcelain stopper . . . 35.00
Candlesticks
  7⅜" h, hexagonal base, petal
    socket 145.00
  8¼" h, hexagonal, opaque blue
    socket, sanded finish 250.00
  11" h, acanthus design, blue
    socket 475.00
Lamps
  11", sq stepped vase, acanthus
    leaf detail on stem and font,
    brass collar 480.00
  13¼"h, Ripley marriage lamp,
    brass connector, match holder
    on stem, medium blue translu-
    cent fonts, brass collars, burn-
    ers, D.C. Ripley, Pat. Pending . 300.00
Mug, birds and wheat, fence post
  handle 40.00
Plate, 8" 35.00
Pomade Jar, 3¾" h, bear shape,
  base marked F.B. Strouse, NY . . 215.00
Spill Holder, 4½", horn of plenty
  pattern 155.00
Toothpick, souvenir 30.00
Tumbler, souvenir, "Atlantic City,
  N.J.," floral enamel decor 40.00
Whiskey Tasters, 2⅜" h, 7 arches, 7
  panels, iron pontil 75.00

CLEWELL POTTERY

Charles Walter Clewell was first a metal worker and second a potter. In the early 1900s he opened a small shop in Canton, Ohio, to produce metal overlay pottery.

Metal on pottery was not a new idea, but Clewell was perhaps the first to completely mask the ceramic body with copper, brass, "silvered" and "bronzed" metals. One result was a product whose patina added to the character of the piece over time.

Most of the wares are marked with a simple incised "CLEWELL" along with a code number. Because Clewell used pottery blanks from other firms, the names "Owens" or "Weller" are sometimes found.

A limited quantity of his art work exists, because he operated on a small scale with little outside assistance. He retired at the age of 79 in 1955, choosing not to reveal his technique to anyone else.

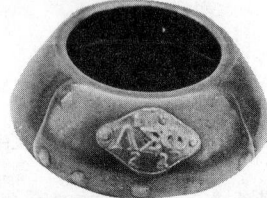

Ashtray, 1¼"h, 3¾"d, copper, 1922 imp mark in circle, Clewell, Canton, Ohio, $148.00.

Bowl, 8 x 2", blue-green patina . . . 125.00
Mug, 5", riveted design, brown pati-
  na 75.00
Punch Bowl and Cups, 12 x 12",
  pedestaled bowl, riveted design,
  matching handled cups, brown pa-
  tina, set 1,200.00

Vases
4 x 4", round, green patina **135.00**
7½", bulbous bottom, small flaired
mouth, blue-green patina **165.00**
12 x 8", peacock blue patina **450.00**
14", two piece oil burner, Arts and
Crafts reticulated base, handled
top, brown patina, also mkd
Vance/Avon **400.00**

Teapot, 5½" h, finial on cover, matte finish, yellow green glaze, stamp mark, imp Clifton Pottery, #272-42, $140.00.

CLIFTON

CLIFTON POTTERY

The Clifton Art Pottery, Newark, N.J., was established by William A. Long, once associated with Lonhuda Pottery, and Fred Tschirner, a chemist.

Production consisted of two major lines: "Crystal Patina," that resembled 'true porcelain' with a subdued crystal-like glaze, and "Indian Ware" or "Western Influence," an adaptation of the American Indians' unglazed and decorated pottery, but with a high glazed black interior. Other lines included "Robin's Egg Blue" and "Tirrube". Robin's Egg Blue is a variation of the crystal patina line but in blue-greens instead of straw colored hues and with a less prominent "crushed crystal" effect in the glaze. Tirrube is on a terra cotta background but features brightly colored, slip decorated flowers and is often artist signed.

Marks were incised or impressed. Early pieces may be dated and shape numbers impressed, and Indian wares were further identified by tribes.

Bowl, 8⅞" d x 4" h, brown stamped
"Clifton Indian Cookingware" . . . **45.00**
Candleholder, 7 x 4", 2 handled . . . **100.00**
Jug, 4½", handles, red clay with
brown Indian design, imp Clifton
mark, incised Indian mark, #230,
Four Mile, Arizona **110.00**
Mug, 4", Arkansas Tribal Design,
signed W. A. Long, c. 1905 . . . . **65.00**
Pitcher, 4½" h, red clay, dark brown
designs **120.00**
Vases
6", cream rust design outlined in
black **100.00**
6¾ x 5" w, flat, handles, cream
and brown, green crystalline
glaze, sgd, 1906 . . . . **120.00**

8 x 5", poppies clustered to form
a jagged opening **150.00**
8½", 1905, marked #164 . . . . . **80.00**
9 x 6", bulbous shape, 2 handled **175.00**

CLOCKS

The sundial was the first man-made device for measuring time. Its basic disadvantage is well expressed in the saying: "Do like the sundial, count only the sunny days."

With the need for greater dependability, man developed the water clock, the oil clock and the sand clock respectively. All these clocks worked on the same principle—time was measured by the amount of material passing from one container to another.

The wheel clock was the next major step toward more accurate time. These clocks can be traced back as far as the 13th century. Many improvements on the basic wheel clock were made and they continued to be the most accurate time piece available until the quartz crystal movement was introduced in 1934.

Recently an atomic clock, that measures time by the frequency of radiation, that only varies one second in a thousand years, has been invented.

Identifying the proper model name for a clock is critical in establishing price. The indispensable source for this is Roy Ehrhardt's *Clock Identification and Price Guide*, Book 1 and Book 2.

Condition of works is a critical factor in collecting clocks. Examine the works to see how many original parts remain and examine the clock in running condition. If repairs are needed, try to include this in your estimate of purchase price. Few clocks are purchased purely for decorative value.

ALARM

Ansonia, Cupid's Cart, 8 day, 4" dial, bell on top sits on gazebo structure in which is statue of cupid, 16" **160.00**

New Haven, Champion, 1 day, 4½" dial, bell on back of nickel case, rococo handle, independent second hand, 6" **45.00**

Russell & Jones, Meteor Time, 1 day, lever, 4" luminous dial, round case **27.50**

Thomas, Seth, Lodge, 1 day, nickel case in shape of house, pitched roof, relief basket of flowers motif in lower front corners **100.00**

Tiffany, travel, 8 day, 2¾" d, orig black leather case **50.00**

Waterbury, Rome, 1 day, 4" dial, nickel case, bell on top **27.50**

Waterbury, Stunner, 8 day, 4½" dial, bronze case, French Provincial style **60.00**

Welch, E. N., Fairy Queen, 1 day, lever, 2½" dial, expanded molding style round nickel case, bell on bottom **40.00**

Howard & Davis, Boston, MA, rosewood grained case, 32", $2,100.00.

BANJO

Cummins, William, Boston, MA, c1810–15, Federal, gilt case, gilt eagle finial, brass fillets, presentation glass in waist, naval engagement with oculus in base, 42" . . . **7,000.00**

Gates, Zacheus, Charlestown, MA, c1820, Federal giltwood and eglomise, cast metal eagle finial, eglomise throat panel with floral motif and maker's name, brass fillets, Boston harbor scene, orig pine packing box, 34½" **19,800.00**

Howard, E., Boston, No. 1 Regulator, banjo shape, 12" d enamel zinc dial, Graham movement, cherry stained rosewood, 50" . . . **4,750.00**

Ingraham, Nile, 8" iveroid dial, 8 day, strike, mahogany case, wood waist, turned tapered column fillets, 39" **300.00**

New Haven, Banjo No. 2, electric, 4⅞" silver dial, light mahogany, eagle finial, brass fillets, Mt. Vernon painted glass, 24½" **120.00**

Sessions, Wellfleet, 8 day, lever, 5" metal dial, green lacquer finished case, eagle finial, brass fillets, Mediterranean scene painted panel, 22½" **175.00**

Thomas, Seth, Brookfield, electric, hour strike, mahogany case, eagle finial, brass fillets, sailing ship glass, 28¾" **150.00**

Unsigned, Federal mahogany giltwood and eglomise, MA, c1820, missing finial, eglomise throat in floral motif, brass fillets, base with naval engagement panel (The *Constitution's* Escape), 30" **1,200.00**

Waltham, No. 1505, Harvard Model, 8 day, weight driven pendulum, mahogany case, cast metal foliate fillets, leaf and fern motif in glass, 42" **1,400.00**

Waterbury, No. 1 Willard, 8 day, weight, Flemish oak case, ball finial, case gilt fillets **1,000.00**

Williard, Simon (attr. to), Federal inlaid mahogany and eglomise
32", works with "T-Bridge" pendulum, cast metal eagle, waisted crossband case, eglomise throat panel with floral and acorn motif, brass fillets, eglomise panel below painted with acorn and bow-knot motifs . . . **4,000.00**

34½", works with "T-bridge" pendulum, cast gilt eagle finial, waisted crossbanded case, eglomise throat panel depicting stellate devices, brass fillets, eglomise panel below with inscription "S. WILLARD'S PATENT" **11,000.00**

BRACKET

English, George III, mahogany, Bonington & Thorpe, London, c1800, anchor escapement movement (converted from orig crown wheel, etc.), silvered chapter ring, gilt metal mahogany case, brass ogee bracket feet, 20″ **2,000.00**

English, 8 day, fusee movement, no strike, inlaid mahogany case, fish scale brass grills below circular dial, brass grills on side, 14″ **225.00**

French, Louis XV ormolu mounted and ebony Boulle, c1745, face with inset enamel roman numerals, bellow an arched top with cupid surmount, four scrollwork legs, spiral fluted pad feet, orig movement backplate inscribed "FELLE'S PARIS," 28″ **4,500.00**

CABINET

Ansonia, Senator, 8 day, half hour strike, cathedral gong, antique oak case, full figured Grecian women flank dial, elaborate brass appointments, 22″ **1,350.00**

Gilbert, Wm. L., Chester, gilt perforated dial, oak case, half round top in leaf motif, 15½″ **190.00**

Ingraham, Cabinet A, 8 day, hour strike, antique oak cabinet, brass trimmings, 19″ h **250.00**

New Haven, Westminister Chime No. 3, 8 day, quarter hour strike, cathedral gongs, 5½″ ornamental dial, oak case, elaborate metal attachments, e.g., Greek side columns, grape cluster finials, etc., 18″ **300.00**

Thomas, Seth, Bee, 15 day, half hour strike, ebony case, marqueterie panel, 14″ **200.00**

Waterbury, Cabinet F, 8 day, half hour slow strike, porcelain dial, cherry case, Eastlake style, 19½″ **200.00**

CALENDAR

Inkwell
Ansonia, Parlor Ink No. 3, solid brass, 1 day, 4″ dial in rococo diamond, two glass bottles, 11″ **320.00**

New Haven, Scribe, 1 day, plated, 14″ **350.00**

Shelf
Davis Clock Co., Column Flat Top, Columbus, MS, 8 day, strike, 7″ dial, 25″ **425.00**

Ingraham, Chicago Combination, 8 day, half hour strike, barometer and thermometer, oak, highly embossed, 23″ **250.00**

Ithaca, No. 8 Shelf Library, 30 day, double spring, lever, walnut case, 25½″ **900.00**

Macomb Company, 8 day, strike, spring, moon phase dial, 30″ . . **3,000.00**

New Haven, Sampson, 8 day, half hour strike, oak case, thermometer and barometer, lion's head top, 25″ **225.00**

Thomas, Seth, Empire, Plymouth Hollow label, 8 day, strike, weight, 30″ **850.00**

Waterbury, Selborne, 8 day, strike, black walnut, 23″ **180.00**

Welch, E. N., Ruddygore, 8 day, perpetual calendar, mahogany case, 24″ **425.00**

Wall
Ansonia, 10″ Drop Octagon, 8 day, strike, rosewood veneer with gilt molding, 24″ **275.00**

Gilbert-McCable, Berkshire, 8 day, walnut case, 38″ **1,250.00**

Gilbert-Wm. L., Columbia, 8 day, cathedral gong, Egyptian motif, 37½″ **600.00**

Ithaca, No. 6, Hanging Library, 8 day, spring, walnut case, 32″ . . **1,050.00**

Jerome & Co., Dneister, 8 day, walnut case, 37½″ **1,100.00**

New Haven, Rutland, 8 day, gong, oak case, 48″ **600.00**

Thomas, Seth, Office Calendar No. 8, 8 day, weight, 14″ d . . . **3,000.00**

Waterbury, Bahia, mosaic figure 8, 8 day, half hour strike, 22″ **340.00**

CARRIAGE

American, porcelain paneled gilt repeating, silvered platform lever escapement with split bimetallic compensation balance, sgd T. Kirkpatrick, New York, river scene on porcelain dial, side panels with allegories of love, back with rural scene, cannelle case, 7″ **1,650.00**

French
Collet of Paris, circular, brass case, 4″ d, orig leather carrying case **125.00**

Drocourt, Paris, miniature lacquered brass *Petite Sonneire*, gilt platform lever escapement with split bimetallic compensa-

tion balance, simulated ivory
dial, gilt mask, gorge case, 4½" **1,210.00**
Russel & Jones, Envoy Plush, 1 day,
lever, alarm, blue color, nickel
trimmings **100.00**
Waterbury, repeater, half hour strike,
4¼" **250.00**
Welch, E. N., Outing, 1 day, nickel,
independent second hand, 5" ... **150.00**
Zenith Watch Co., gold colored,
stripe motif, Swiss movement,
leather case, 2⅛" **125.00**

GALLERY

Ansonia, Corridor, varnished oak finish, 24" **160.00**
Gilbert, Wm. L., Alpine, 8 day, calendar, 12" d, oak case, 24" **275.00**
Gilbert Wm. L., Fulton, 30 day, mahogany, 18¾" **130.00**
Thomas, Seth, Office, strike, old
oak, 16" **150.00**

GARNITURE, FRENCH

Gilt Bronze and Enamel, 3 pc, seven
light candelabra and clock enameled in vivid tones of blue, red,
green, yellow and white upon a
black ground, clock face sgd
"Schneider Campbell & Co./Union
Sq. N.Y.," late 19th C, 29¼" **12,650.00**

Louis Majorelle, rosewood, iron metal work with bronze patina, 8", $1,500.00.

Gilt Bronze, Enamel and Onyx, 3 pc,
clock and pair of footed bases,
each with figural gilt bronze
mounts on onyx ground, enameled
in tones of turquoise, brick and
blue, face inscribed "A. GIROUX
A PARIS," works marked "JAPY
FRERES & CIE/ EXPOSITION/
1855/ GRANDE/ MED./
D'HONNEUR," c1875, 16½" ... **2,100.00**
Porcelain Mounted Gilt Bronze, 3 pc,
clock mounted with porcelain delicately painted with classical figures on gilt ground, pair of six light
candelabra *en suite*, c1880, candelabra 25" h **6,600.00**

Cottage, Seth Thomas, time and strike, miniature, $145.00.

MANTEL

China Cased
Ansonia, Glory, 1 day, 6¼" **125.00**
Ansonia, La Orb, 8 day, hour
strike, porcelain dial, visible escapement, floral motif, 13" **400.00**
Boston Clock Co., No. 560, 8 day,
half hour cathedral strike, wave
shaped sides, rural scene
across bottom, 10" **275.00**
New Haven, Rockland, 8 day, half
hour strike, 10¾" **210.00**
Cottage
Ansonia, Theban, 1 day, strike,
rosewood veneer, octagon top,
18½" **150.00**

Atkins Clock Co., Bristol, CT, octagon top, rosewood veneer, orig label on reverse, miniature, 12⅜" **125.00**

Gilbert, Comet, 30 hour, spring, strike, octagon top, 14¾" **100.00**

Kroeber and Co., peaked roof, brass 8 day movement, strike, 18¼" **125.00**

Terry Clock Co., Tuscan, 8 day, strike, orig label, 17⅞" **250.00**

Thomas, Seth, Victorian walnut case in style of Swiss chalet, time and alarm, orig glass, 10¼" **90.00**

Crystal Regulator

Ansonia, Dutchess, 8 day, hour strike, visible escapement, green onyx top and bottom, 11" **425.00**

Ansonia, Emperor, 8 day, half hour strike, visible escapement, polished brass, gold ornaments, cloisonne inlay, 13" **1,250.00**

Gilbert, Wm. L., Tuscan, 8 day, half hour strike, ivory porcelain dial, visible escapement, Brazilian green onyx columns, ormolu gold finish, urn and wreath finial, 19" **800.00**

Thomas, Seth, Empire No. 2, 8 day gold finish, 11¾" **400.00**

Waterbury, Orne, 8 day, half hour strike, gong, visible escapement, cut glass columns, 13⅛" **1,100.00**

Delft

Church, stepped roof, clock in center of roof, two windows above open arcade, side front pillars, 8 day, strike, open work pendulum, 18½" **700.00**

House, 17½", gable roof, pent roof forms outline over round dial, one level bldg on left side, 8 day, strike, Dutch signature on back, 17½" **800.00**

Marble

Ansonia, Dorothy, 8 day, half hour strike, engraved scroll design, 9½" **175.00**

Boston Clock Co., No. 207, 8 day, half hour cathedral strike, plain tinted dial, inlaid and engraved, 9½" **325.00**

Metal

Bronze or Ormolu finish

Ansonia, Eureka, 8 day, half hour strike, cathedral gong, black enamel, finished in old silver, phoenix brids at end . . **1,200.00**

Ansonia, Modern, 1 day, Art Nouveau case, 4¼" **50.00**

French, gilt and champleve enamel in cream, dark blue, red, light blue, and green, late 19th C, 14¼" **1,250.00**

Gilbert, Wm. L., Fairy, 8 day, half hour strike, Venetian bronze finish, 15½" **150.00**

Jennings Bros., No. 694, 1 day, Art Nouveau, pansy motif, roman gold finish, 8½" **90.00**

New Haven, Flower Girl, 8 day, half hour strike, cathedral gong, visible escapement, bronze finish, marbelized base, 26" **300.00**

New Haven, Heath, 1 day, ormolu, standing infant, 6¾" . . **100.00**

Terry Clock Co., Chapel, 8 day, spring, bronze, 13" **400.00**

Thomas Seth, Huntress, 15 day, hour strike, seated Grecian figure with greyhound seated on clock, hunting motif base, 15" **450.00**

Thomas, Seth, Josephine, woman's head emerges from flowing robes, Art Nouveau bronze finish, 21" **275.00**

Pot Metal or Iron

Ansonia, Timbrel, enamel, half hour strike, lion's head handles on side, 13" **175.00**

New Haven, Montrose, enameled iron, 8 day, half hour strike, cathedral gong, marble columns, gilt ornaments, visible escapement, 10" **150.00**

Waterbury, Louis XV, applied with gilt metal scrollwork, visible escapement, 8 day rack and snail count, 16½" **200.00**

Welch, E. N., Tuba, 8 day, half hour strike, cathedral gong, bronzed columns, white dial, 10½" **125.00**

Onyx

Ansonia, Wagner, 8 day, half hour strike, cathedral gong, Brazilian green onyx, bronze urn trimmings, 11¼" **175.00**

Boston Clock Co., No. 423, 8 day, half hour strike, cathedral gong, Grecian urn gilt ornamentation, 10¾" **300.00**

Bulle, set, Le Roses, elecric, Art Deco dome case, Italian marble, gold relief, 8", garnitures 5" . . . **300.00**

Welch, E. N., No. 488, 8 day, half hour strike, cathedral gong, visible escapement, gilt ornamentation, 12½" **200.00**

Wood

New Haven, Los Santos, Mission style, 8 day, half hour strike, cathedral gong, solid oak, Flemish finish, brass hands and numerals, 13¼" **150.00**

Russell and Jones, Mikado, 8 day, half hour strike, cathedral gong, marble finish, engraved scrolls, 10" **110.00**

Welch, E. N., Camilla Urso, 8 day, half hour strike, bronze feet and side ornaments, moldings and panels marbelized, gilt dial, 11" **135.00**

NOVELTY

Advertising, $1,050.00.

Figure
Ansonia, Good Morning, Dutch peasant maiden carrying clock, 8 day, bronze finish, 11¾" **200.00**
Ansonia, Poodle, 1 day, 6" **110.00**
Gilbert, Wm. L., Father Time, 1 day, ormolu finish, 10¼" **95.00**
New Haven, Atlas, 1 day, bronze finish, 9¼" **100.00**

Inkstand
Ansonia, Office Inkstand, clock supported by infant, 1 day, calendar, 13" **300.00**
Gilbert Wm. L., Parlor Ink, bird on branch separates two bottles, 6½" **120.00**
New Haven, Scribe, 1 day, brass finish, snail reversable inks . . . **350.00**

REGULATOR

Ansonia, Argentina, parlor, 8 day, hour strike, silver dial, walnut case, 33" **450.00**

Ansonia, Regulator A, 8 day, hour strike, black walnut case, 32" . . . **400.00**
Ansonia, Regulator No. 14, 8 day, weight, mahogany case, 84" **4,000.00**
Gilbert, Wm. L., Regulator B, 8 day, oak case **325.00**
Gilbert, Wm. L., Regulator No. 3, 8 day, dead beat escapement, 50" . **1,250.00**
Howard, E., No. 13, Watchmaker's Regulator, beats seconds, dead beat escapement, black walnut, 56" **2,850.00**
Ingraham, Alliance, 8 day, strike, calendar, oak case, 38¼" **500.00**
Ingraham, Regulator No. 2, 8 day, strike, oak case, octagon top, 32" **400.00**
New Haven, Enquirer, 8 day, strike, oak, 50½" **1,250.00**
New Haven, Hebe, 30 day, calendar, oak, 49" **1,000.00**
New Haven, Regulator D. R., 8 day, strike, figure 8, oak leaf dividers, 31" **350.00**
Prentiss, Regulator, 60 day, beats seconds, mahogany case, 62" . . . **950.00**
Sempire, Jeweler's Regulator, No. 65, electric, sweep second, three jar mercury pendulum, mahogany, 78" **2,000.00**
Thomas, Seth, Regulator No. 11, 8 day, weight, beats seconds, Graham dead beat escapement, golden oak, 56" **1,600.00**
Thomas, Seth, Regulator No. 16, 8 day, weight, beats seconds, Graham pallets, walnut, 75" **3,500.00**
Thomas, Seth, Regulator No. 25, 8 day, weight, Flemish oak, 32" . . . **850.00**
Waterbury, Regulator No. 3, 8 day, brass weight, dead beat escapement, cherry case, 46" **1,050.00**
Waterbury, Regulator No. 61, hall model, dead beat escapement, walnut case, 96" **4,500.00**

SCHOOL HOUSE

Ansonia, 12" Drop Octagon, 8 day, strike, oak case, 24" **275.00**
Gilbert, Wm. L., Janeiro, 8 day, strike, calendar, figure 8, rosewood veneer **425.00**
Gilbert, Wm. L., Standard Admiral, 8 day, strike, oak case, 26¾" **300.00**
Ingraham, 10" Drop Octagon, Bristol, 8 day, oak case **240.00**
Imperial, Regulator No. 4T120E, electric, oak finish, 34½" **400.00**
New Haven, 12" Mosaic Drop, 8 day, octagon top, 24" **225.00**
Terry Clock Co., O. G. Octagon Drop, 8 day, strike, 23" **400.00**
Thomas, Seth, Litchfield, 30 day,

spring, Graham dead beat escapement, mahogany finish, 31" . **480.00**

Waterbury, 12" Arion, 8 day, half hour strike, oak finish, 24" **250.00**

Waterbury, English Drop No. 2, calendar, veneered oak case, 27¾" **425.00**

SHELF

Shelf, E.N. Welch, tear-drop, 22½" h, walnut, 8 day movement, $275.00.

Beehive

Ansonia, 8 day, brass movement, strike, rosewood veneer, orig label, 18¾" **350.00**

Brown, J. C., 8 day, walnut case, ripple front **900.00**

Gilbert, Wm. L., Star Round Top Extra, 8 day, spring, strike, 16¾" **150.00**

Ingraham, Venetian No. 2 Mosaic, 8 day strike, 18" **200.00**

Jerome, Chauncy, 8 day, alarm, mahogany veneer, yellow sun rays and floral motif, 18⅞" . . . **450.00**

New Haven, Guide, 1 day, strike, castle scene in glass **120.00**

Welch, E. N., Italian No. 3 V. P, 1 day, strike, spring, rosewood, 14" **125.00**

Connecticut Style

Birge and Fuller, triple decker, strap brass movement, strike, gilded, applied basket of fruit and leaves, 35⅜" **725.00**

Bishop and Bradley, miniature,

Terry Patent, 1 day, wooden movement, orig label, reverse painted glass crest, new stenciling on door, 25½" **800.00**

Marsh, George, Bristol, CT, 8 day, wooden movement, eagle hands, acanthus and rosette carved side columns, carved crest in basket of fruit motif, ball and eagle brass finials, 41½" . . **650.00**

Terry, Eli, Jr., carved and gilded eagle crest, wooden movement, mirrored door, 35⅛" **600.00**

Terry, Henry, 8 day, wooden movement, acanthus carved half columns, flame finials, carved crest in form of bowl of fruit with urn above, carved paw front feet, 41¾" **950.00**

Gingerbread

Ansonia, Chile, 8 day, strike, dark wood, 26" **250.00**

Gilbert, Wm. L., Laurel, 8 day, half hour strike, wire bell, thermometer and barometer, oak, 24" . . . **200.00**

Gilbert, Wm. L., Trenton, 8 day, half hour strike, oak, 22½" . . . **175.00**

Ingraham, Maine, 8 day, half hour strike, oak, 27" **275.00**

New Haven, Nereid, 8 day, strike, oak, 23½" **180.00**

Thomas, Seth, Capitol No. 1, 8 day, half hour strike, cathedral gong, oak, 23" **220.00**

Waterbury, Gibson Calendar, 8 day, strike, barometer and thermometer, walnut, 24" **260.00**

Welch, E. N., Fannie Rice (Prima Donnas series), 8 day, half hour strike, 23" **150.00**

Welch, E. N., No. 12, 8 day, half hour strike, oak **140.00**

Kitchen

Ansonia, Ringgold, 8 day, half hour strike, 24¾" **200.00**

Gilbert, Wm. L., Rocket, 1 day, spring, 15½" **110.00**

May, S. Elwood, Ideal O, 8 day, strike, wire bell **325.00**

New Haven, Electra, 8 day, strike, walnut, brass ornaments, 19½" **190.00**

New Haven, Olga, 8 day, strike, oak, 13¾" **175.00**

Russell and Jones, Lowell, 8 day, spring, strike, walnut, 21" **165.00**

Thomas Seth, Athens, 8 day, spring, strike, black walnut, 17" **120.00**

Waltham, Pallanza, 8 day, strike, 13" **150.00**

Welch, E. N., Lucca, 8 day, spring, strike, 23½" **285.00**

Mirror Side

Ansonia, Triumph, 8 day, silvered

cupids, bronze ornaments, 24½" **325.00**

New Haven, Occidental, 8 day, strike, walnut with gilt ornaments, 24" **360.00**

O. G.

Ansonia, No. 488, 1 day, weight, strike, 26" **250.00**

Canada Clock Co., Hamilton, Ontario, brass 1 day, strike, mahogany case, 26" **150.00**

Forestville Mfr. Co., CT, double door, brass 8 day, strike, 31" .. **350.00**

Gilbert, Wm. L., 1 day, weight, 25⅞" **150.00**

Welch, E. N., 8 day, strike, weight, 29" **220.00**

Pillar and Scroll

Hopkins and Alfred, 1 day, wood movement, painted dial, mahogany case, brass finials **1,000.00**

North, Norris, Wolcottville, CT, swan's neck, three brass urn finials, painted dial with foliate spandrels, cottage in wood scene glass (repainted), 30⅜" . **1,200.00**

Terry, Eli, mahogany, swan's neck, three brass urn finials, painted dial with foliate spandrels, bucolic scene, 28¾" ... **1,800.00**

Thomas, Seth, mahogany, swan's neck, three brass urn finials, painted dial with foliate spandrels, collegiate building, 31" .. **2,250.00**

Pillar & Scroll, Terry type, 29″ h, inlaid mahogany, mahogany veneered case with replacement brass finials, CT, 19th C, $900.00.

Steeple

Ansonia, 1 day, strike, alarm, rosewood veneer case, floral decorated glass, small size **200.00**

Ansonia, Turkey, 8 day, half hour strike, oak case, 15¾" **175.00**

Birge and Fuller, Bristol, CT, double steeple, fusee movement, orig cut and frosted door glass, 27½" **1,500.00**

Birge and Fuller, double steeple, twin candle wagon spring, mahogany veneered case, 26" ... **3,100.00**

Gilbert, Wm. L., Sharp Gothic, 8 day, spring, strike, 19½" **175.00**

Jerome and Co., miniature, 1 day, mahogany **175.00**

Manrose, Elisha, steeple on steeple, 8 day, double fusee movement, 23" **1,750.00**

New Haven, Dolphin, 8 day, strike, urn finials, zibra veneer, stork on glass, 17¾" **165.00**

Pratt, Daniel, and Sons, Reading, MA, 8 day, strike and alarm, walnut and mahogany veneer, mirror front, 19⅝" **450.00**

Waterbury, 8 day, strike and alarm, rosewood (striped) veneer, marsh and bird in tree scene on glass, 19¼" **425.00**

Tambour

Ansonia, Tambour Cabinet, 8 day, mahogany, 6⅝" **60.00**

New Haven, Jacobean No. 55, silver dial, 8 day, lever, 13½" ... **37.50**

New Haven, Tambour No. 15, silver dial, rack and snail movement, half hour strike, 12½" .. **120.00**

Sessions, Dulciana, c1930 ..... **40.00**

Waterbury, Parisian Ivory, 1 day, 4½" **30.00**

TALL CASE (GRANDFATHER)

Brokaw, Isaac, Bridgetown, NJ, Federal inlaid, mahogany, c1810, 8 day, white painted dial with minute and date registers above inscription, bonnet with broken swan's neck cresting ending in stellate inlaid caps, centering one brass finial, shaped bookend inlaid frieze, arched door, and inlaid colonnettes, waisted case with fan inlaid door centering an inlaid shield reserve, spread winged eagle with banner in its beak, inlaid quarter columns, fan and circle inlaid base, bracket feet, 103" **14,750.00**

Burnap, Daniel, East Windsor, CT, Federal, cherrywood and maple, c1780–1800, 8 day, engraved silvered brass dial, inscribed "BURNAP/WINDSOR," painted moon, bonnet with shaped crest surmounted by three turned finials, arched door, and reeded colonnettes, waisted case with thumb molded arched door flanked by reeded quarter columns, covered base on ogee bracket feet, 89¾" 5,000.00

Filber, John, York(town), PA, Chippendale, carved, cherrywood, c1800, 30 hour, white painted dial with bird and butterfly motif, date register, and inscription, bonnet with molded swan's neck pediment ending in carved rosettes, centering a turned finial, arched door, and colonnettes, waisted case with arched door flanked by quarter columns, base has quarter columns and bracket feet, 98½" . 4,125.00

Goddard, Nichols, Rutland, VT, c1800, Federal inlaid, cherrywood and mahogany, 8 day, white painted dial with phases of moon, minute, and date registers, centering inscription, bonnet with swan's neck cresting centering three brass ball finials and arched door, waisted case with arched top door inlaid with vertical oval and shell, line inlaid quarter columns, molded and inlaid base on ogee bracket feet, 92" 2,500.00

Hopf, George, Lancaster, PA, c1760, Queen Anne painted poplar, 30 hour, silvered and red painted dial with cast foliate spandrels centering maker's name and "Lancaster," bonnet with projecting molded cornice and hinged glazed door, waisted case with thumb molded rectangular door with oculus, rattail hinges, rectangular base with top molding, front splayed feet, painted brown and cream, 87" 3,850.00

Owen & Sile, Chester, PA, Chippendale, carved mahogany, c1790–1810, 8 day, white painted dial, sgd "Owen & Sile Chester," painted moon face, bonnet with scrolled pediment with dentil molding and rosettes, centering an urn and leaf finial above trailing leafage, glazed arch door, and fluted colonnettes, waisted case with leaf carved molding over a shaped door flanked by fluted quarter columns, base with shield panel, ogee bracket feet, works may not be orig to case, 97½" .. 16,500.00

Smith, Joseph, Chester (England), George II inlaid, walnut, 8 day, 12" brass dial with cast spandrels, bonnet with molded cornice with blind fretwork beneath, hinged door, and turned colonnettes, waisted case with beveled edge door with oculus, plinth on bracket feet 2,500.00

Tarber, Elnathan, Roxbury, MA, Federal inlaid, mahogany, c1805, 8 day, white painted face with minute register and centering inscription "Warranted by E. Tarber," bonnet with shaped cresting centering three turned wood finials, arched hinge door, and fluted colonnettes, waisted case with hinged door flanked by brass stop fluted quarter columns, string inlaid base on bracket feet, 86" ... 7,150.00

Thomas, Isaac, Willistown, PA, c1780, Chippendale, carved walnut, 8 day, brass dial with minute register and foliate spandrels, name and location in oval in arch area, bonnet with shaped and molded architectural cresting, arched and glazed door, and fluted three quarter columns, waisted case with thumb molded shell and volute carved door flanked by molded pilasters with volute capitals, paneled base flanked by molded pilasters, ogee bracket feet, 90" 14,250.00

Thomas, Joseph, Norristown, PA, Federal inlaid, cherrywood, c1820, white painted dial with phases of moon and minute registers, bonnet with molded swan's neck pediment ending in inlaid rosettes, centering a turned finial, arched door and tapered and fluted colonnettes, waisted case with shaped door, base with double half round top string inlay, bracket feet, 101" 3,850.00

Unknown maker, CT, cherrywood, c1795, 8 day, white painted dial with date and minute registers, bonnet with shaped cresting flanked by brass finials and hinged arched door, waisted case with hinged door flanked by fluted quarter columns, plain base with molded top, ogee bracket feet, 89½" 2,350.00

Unknown maker, PA, Federal, walnut, c1800, 8 day, white painted dial with phases of moon, minute, and date registers, bonnet with molded swan's neck pediment centering three turned wood finials, arched and glazed door, and turned colonnettes, waisted case with shaped hinged door flanked by fluted quarter columns, recessed panel base, bracket feet, 92½" **3,750.00**

Wilder, Joshua, Hingham, MA, c1815, Federal inlaid, mahogany, dwarf, 8 day, white painted dial with shield spandrels, above dial marked "WARRANTED by JOSHUA WILDER, HINGHAM," top with shaped and pierced cresting centering three brass urn finials, arched door opening, and turned colonnettes, waisted case with rectangular molded hinged door, shaped skirt leading to bracket feet, 50½" **12,000.00**

Willard, Aaron, Boston, Federal, inlaid, mahogany, c1825, 8 day, white painted dial with phases of moon, bonnet with pierced cresting centering three brass ball finials, arched door, and fluted colonnettes, waisted case with hinged door flanked by fluted quarter columns with brass capitals, crossband base on bracket feet, 100" **5,500.00**

Willard, Simon, Roxbury, MA, c1785, Federal inlaid, mahogany, 8 day, white painted dial with phases of moon, minute and date registers centering the marker's name, bonnet with pierced cresting centering three brass finials, arched door, and brass stop fluted quarter columns, waisted case with hinged door flanked by brass, stop fluted quarter columns with brass capitals, fan inlaid base on bracket feet, 98" **20,500.00**

Wood, John, Jr., Phila., Chippendale, walnut, 1730–1735, 8 day, brass dial with minute register and foliate spandrels, bonnet with molded cornice over frieze carved with Chinese blind fretwork, glazed door, and cylindrical columns, waisted case with hinged and molded door with oculus in center, bracket feet, 86" **14,250.00**

VIENNA REGULATOR

2 weight, Gustav Becker, walnut case, 42" **800.00**

2 weight, fully carved black forest style case with birds, foxes, and a running stag, stained oak, 47" ... **1,500.00**

WALL, HANGING

Ansonia, Queen Mab, 8 day, strike, dark wood, 36¼" **500.00**

French, Louis XIV style, ormolu mounted mahogany, thermometer, Ch. le Roy a Paris, drum shape case surmounted by flaming urn surrounded by oak leaves, tapered lower section, 60" **6,750.00**

Gilbert, Wm. L., Gladstone, 8 day, spring, strike, oak case, 40" **850.00**

New Haven, Mission style, Minho, 1 day, solid oak case in Flemish finish, 12" **85.00**

Thomas, Seth, Chime Clock No. 102, mahogany case, 31" **300.00**

CLOISONNÉ

Cloisonné is the art of enamelling on metal. The design is drawn on the metal body; wires are then glued or soldered which follow the design. The cells thus created are packed with enamel and fired; this step is repeated several times until the level of enamel is higher than the wires. A buffing and polishing process is done to bring the level of enamels flush to the surface of the wires.

This art form has been practiced in various countries since 1300 B.C. and in the Orient since the early 15th century. Most cloisonné found today is from the Victorian era, 1870-1900, and comes from China and Japan.

Vase, 5", black ground, metallic base, pastel flowers, Japanese, $110.00.

Bowl, 4½x 5", yellow, multicolored florals, imp China mark 85.00

Boxes

2¾ x 4¾", high puffy shape, glossy black, all over lotus flowers and leaves, long life symbol on lid, Japanese 425.00

3½ x 3", hinged, green, white flowers, China 70.00

Brush Pots, blue, flowers and white cartouche front, flowers and leaves on back, sgr, pr 350.00

Chargers

9¾", goldfinch, butterfly, floral and foliage, decorative border, Japanese 335.00

11¾" d, gray-green, white and black long legged birds, pink and white flowers, green leaves, detailed band around edge ... 475.00

12", turquoise, pink flowers, green leaves, 2 birds in flight, one sitting on bush, scalloped edge 450.00

Dish, 12", blue, pair of quail, c1900 180.00

Floor Lamp, 64", translucent green globe, orig oil fixture, Chinese, 19th C 575.00

Hatpin, 8¼" h, domed button top ⅞" d, colorful open work 35.00

Humidor, 6¼ x 4½", yellow, multicolored lotus scroll, brass Foo dog finial 195.00

Jar, 4", cov, 3 ftd, black, flowers, butterflies, goldstone flecks, Japanese, c1890 .... 225.00

Planter, 8¼ x 6⅜", barrel shape, cobalt, high glaze, blue and white top border, multicolored vine and floral on white, separates 2 large blue reserves, dragonfly, beetle, iris 850.00

Plate, 8", green, butterflies and cherry blossoms 150.00

Pot, 2½ x 3½", miniature, rectangular, cloisonne work in relief, holds minature tree of blooming enamel flowers 50.00

Potpourri Jar, 3¾ x 3⅜", pink ground, white, blue and gray flowers, lacy vines 225.00

Snuff Bottle, 2⅜", yellow, floral, 19th C 240.00

Teapot, 4 x 6", melon shape, black with flowers, butterflies, turquoise border 135.00

Tray, 12½" w x 1" deep, footed, geometric center design 350.00

Umbrella Stand, 24¾", cylindrical, irises, peonies and roses 590.00

Urns, 7½", bronze, open work, gold plated Foo dog handles, late 1700s, pr 1,250.00

Vases

3½ x 3", tapers to small opening, mauve reserves on blue, flowers, grapes, cobalt and pink border top and bottom with copper squares, character writing on base 250.00

3¾", green and foil, white herons, silver wires, c1890 .... 125.00

4½", narrow neck, blue, black decor 40.00

5 x 3", bud, squat bulbous base, narrow neck, spring scroll cloisons on white, blue reserves of colored flowers 135.00

6", ice blue foil, blue and purple iris 450.00

7", light green to white fish scale, lavender and red blossoming florals and green blue foliage .. 175.00

10", pod shape, 5-toed Imperial dragons on back 180.00

12 x 7½", red etched enamel floral ground, tiny white floral branches, green leaves with five birds, Japanese 1,200.00

CLOTHING

Clothing worn in past decades has become highly collectible, especially the dramatic styles of the late 1930s and early 1940s. Evening gowns; beaded bags; cloche hats of the "Flapper Age;" beaded dresses, which were so highly fashionable in the age of the "Charleston;" are all very eagerly sought by collectors. Laces, lawn petticoats, camisoles, cambric underthings, are all collectible today. Old furs and other accessories are making a come-back that their creators never dreamed of.

The mesh and beaded handbags, which were in vogue in the 1920s and 1930s, are very much in demand right now. They are quite fashionable with evening clothes and cocktail wear. Sterling silver bags, and those set with precious stones, are valuable; the intricate bead work on beaded bags are very popular with collectors.

See *Warman's Americana & Collectibles* for an expanded listing of Clothing.

Blouses

Cotton, lace, high necked 65.00

White bastiste, lace trimmed and tucked 40.00

Bodices

Flannel, soft, blue-gray, long sleeved, button front, gray trim, c1900 .... 35.00

Nightgown, white cotton, c1848, $35.00.

Satin

Beige, fully lined, 9 satin-lace covered buttons, pleated "Tail-back, fitted waist-line, 9 ½" ruffled self material cuff trim, 22" waist, semi-high neckline, lace overlay **25.00**

Navy blue, purple irid beaded trim, tassels, lace collar, c1890 . . . . **30.00**

Bustle, c1870 . . . . **15.00**

Camisoles

Black, beaded heavily, c1920 . . . **75.00**

White handkerchief linen, embroidered with feather stitch, floral sprays, sewn with pin tucks, lace and ivory ribbon, c1905 . . **80.00**

Capes

Cashmere, light blue, cut work, ivory silk pleated trim **175.00**

Fortuny, stenciled black gauze, printed foliate scrolls, tied at shoulders, hem threaded with striped Venetian glass beads, 36" l **385.00**

Monkey fur, long haired **500.00**

Chemise, neckline, hem lace trimmed, 24" waist **60.00**

Christening Gown, baby's, long, white batiste, openwork embroidery, smocked yoke **48.00**

Cloak, child's, Amish **20.00**

Coats

Cashmere, black, tuxedo front, braid frog closure, silver fox velvet-backed collar, shocking pink lining, "Jacques Ferber, Blum Store, Phila." label, 38" **120.00**

Furs

Broadtail, full length, "Dein Bacher of the Waldorf" label **950.00**

Child's full length mink, matching hat **75.50**

Leopard-spotted lamb **200.00**

Persian lamb, lady's, 40" l **45.00**

Raccoon, gentleman's stadium, double breasted, shawl collar, cuffed sleeves **650.00**

Velvet, black, "Worth" theatre coat, fold back ivory satin collar, dolman sleeves, draped back lacquer side closure, beaded fringes, "C. Worth" label, c1910 **475.00**

Dresses

Daytime

Cotton

Floral embroidery lace insets, 23" waist **145.00**

Plaid, portrait buttons of Jenny Lind, c1860 . . . . **75.00**

Lawn, white, summer, delicate floral embroidery, lace edging **150.00**

Evening

Beaded

Licorice chiffon, crenellated hem, embroidered overall scrolling lines, diamonds of irid coal black beads, 38" waist **90.00**

Marine green chiffon, handkerchief hem skirt, silver sequins, pastes, crystal bugle beads embroidered in goemetric design, faux turquoise, 34" waist **230.00**

Chiffon, cream, printed pink roses, blue tasseled ribbons, cream lace edge on bodice, hem **100.00**

Crepe, salmon pink, bands of net embroidered with pewter sequins, beads, 28" waist . . . **65.00**

Lace, black, sq neckline, puffed sleeves, dropped waistline, full bias cut skirt, 30" waist . . **95.00**

Net, blue, embroidered blue, silver sequins, matching jacket, c1930 . . . . **110.00**

Taffeta, black, sequin flowers, "Jeanne Lanvin, Paris Hiver 1938–1939, Unis France" label **300.00**

Tea

Georgette, chemise style, pink, embroidered large rosettes,

foliage of artificial pearl, rhinestones, crystal beads, beaded fringed hem, c1920 . . . . **150.00**

Lace, chemise style, cream, embroidered floral motifs, c1920 . . . . **185.00**

Pleated silk, Fortuny
Black, dolman sleeves, V neck, black, white, blue Venetian glass beads, 57" l **1,760.00**
Black, short sleeves, 2 belts, 64" l **1,980.00**
Champagne, attached tunic, belt, striped Venetian glass beads, sleeveless, orig box, 60" l **605.00**
Deep rose, sleeveless attached tunic, striped glass beads, gilt metal leaf form belt, MOP clasps, 60" l **2,310.00**
Shell pink, cap sleeves, striped Venetian glass beads, stenciled belt, 55" l, orig box **935.00**

Dressing Gowns
Cotton, handmade, embroidered, with piping **95.00**
Georgette, mint green, lace, purple silk and velvet floret appliques **90.00**

Jackets
Lace, black chantilly, bell sleeves, black lace shawl, c1910 . . . . . . **170.00**
Muskrat fur, excellent lining, size 12 . . . . **90.00**

Kimonos, silk
Gentleman's, cream, pointed circle clusters of pale taupe, silver squares **220.00**
Oriental Ceremonial Wedding, white, extensive design in gold and silver, accented with red, hand embroidered, late 19th c . **1,800.00**

Morning Coat, cotton, white, passamenterie embroidery on cuffs, yoke **90.00**

Nightgowns
Cotton, white, pintucks, insert bonds of Valenciennes lace net embroidered with flowers, V-neckline, pale yellow ribbon decor **250.00**
Silk, chemise, cream, trimmed with Valenciennes lace, French knot garlands of flowers, bedcap, pink silk, c1920 . . . . . **350.00**

Peignoir, cotton Batiste, ruffled collar, handkerchief sleeves, bonds of lace trim, c1895 . . . . **80.00**

Robes, Fortuny
Black, gauze, gilt foliate scrolls, medallions, decor, 44" l **880.00**
Green velvet, gilt foliate design, circular label, 40" l **1,100.00**

Skirt, black Spanish lace, cov with appliqued flowers, petals and leaves, size 7 . . . . **250.00**

Skirt and Blouse, cotton, high necked blouse, 2 pcs, lace insets, 25" waist **150.00**

Suit, walking, women's lavish silver fox trim, lame blouse, c1930 . . . . **95.00**

Suit, woman's, brown wool plush, jacket, shawl collar, dolman sleeves, straight wrap skirt, label "Henry Morgan & Co. Montreal", rusty pink crepe blouse, crystal beads and pearl embroidery, c1930 . . . . **140.00**

Teddy, peach silk, handmade, edged with Alencon lace, peach, pink and white silk drawers, trimmed with Valenciennes lace, c1920, 3 prs **90.00**

Wedding Gowns
Satin
Ivory, heavily embroidered pastes, crystal beads in geometric pattern, sewn at one hip with paste halfmoons, petalled train, silver gilt edge self slip, long train of embroidered ivory satin, 36" waist, c1920 . **150.00**
Victorian, matching shoes, berry bouquet, mitts **175.00**
Velvet, cream, fitted bodice, train, silk bustle, c1880 . . . . **145.00**

CLOTHING ACCESSORIES

See *Warman's Americana & Collectibles* for additional listings in Clothing Accessories.

Man's hat, straw, navy, red stripes, size 7, Cosmopolitan, 1911, $35.00.

Apron, cotton, hand sewn, patchwork design, waist length, ties . . **25.00**
Boa, 70", ostrich feathers **55.00**

Bonnets

Baby, newborn, fine crochet, ribbon insertion 12.00

Velvet, navy and red, lined, streamers, c1880 .... 10.00

Coat Collar, mink, brown, 36 x 4" .. 4.00

Collars

Black net, yoke ruffle, black sequins, beads embroidered in geometric pattern, c1905 .... 150.00

Point de Gaze, mid 19th C 95.00

Gloves, white kid, 3 pearl buttons, elbow length 15.00

Handbags

Alligator, ladies' 80.00

Beaded

Black Star & Frost, 14 K. gold frame, jeweled clasp 375.00

Carnival, cobalt, all over crisscross beaded design, clamp over beaded closure, chain handle 45.00

Carnival, red woven ground, expandable top 65.00

Faille, black, French, embroidered with steel beads, floral pattern, silver mounted black stone thumbpiece, c1920 ... 40.00

Gold tone, frame mkd France, floral design, fringed 75.00

Steel gray beads, 5 rows, black beaded purse, drawstring top 42.00

Evening

Faille, black, mount set with marcasite, green onyx monogram, c1930 .... 60.00

French facetted steel bead, stylized foliate motifs in gold, mint green, pink, silver on lavender ground, gilt metal mount, band of leafy scrolls . 40.00

Pierced gilt-metal mount set with coral beads, bag of black watered silk, embroidered with gilt chainstitch, coral beads, "E. Gauthier", c1920 99.00

Victorian, Metro Bag World Paris, made in France, ornate frame, cov with crewel flowers, metal beads 150.00

Victorian, petty point, roses on silk, brass frame cov with 48 stones, different colors 150.00

Mesh

18 K yellow gold 800.00

Enameled gold, black, white enameled curved frame, cabochon sapphire thumbpiece, foxtail tassel, seed pearls, mesh strap, enamel slide ... 1,000.00

Rectangular, 2 round cabochon cut sapphires on clasp, stamped 14 K, yellow gold, sgd Cartier, NY 1,000.00

Hats

Felt

Black, turned-up brim, burgundy ostrich plume, black quill, Rose Valois-Paris label, c1940 .... 60.00

Flapper, pink, gold braid band, sparkly gold ornament in each side 25.00

Gray, black velvet piping, fuchsia curly ostrich feather plume, Henri Bendel, NY label 55.00

Net, cocktail, pillbox turban, black, black lead pony egret, Mr. Arnold-Made to Order - Bonwit Teller label 50.00

Silk, top hat, black 65.00

Straw, black, pearl ornaments, c1918 .... 30.00

Muff, Persian lamb, black, zippered compartment 20.00

Parasols

Bamboo handle, shade of ivory silk woven with pink, lavender and green flowers, leaves and scrolls, trimmed with ivory patterned silk gauze ruffles, SS tip, mkd Tiffany & Co., orig box, c1905 .... 350.00

Wooden handle, English gold band, monogram, amber tip, pale yellow silk 150.00

Shawls, silk

Cream, multicolored flowering foliage embroidery, knotted fringe 90.00

Ivory, Chinese, self-embroidered in flowering vines, knotted silk fringes 80.00

Spanish, deep magenta, embroidered large flowers, white leaves, knotted silk fringes 110.00

Shoes

Child's, leather, 2 tone, Freed Bros., c1900 .... 65.00

Lady's

Black leather, high button 50.00

Silk, beaded, c1910 .... 45.00

White kid leather, French heels 30.00

Men's, leather

High button 40.00

Suede, black 35.00

Spats, Men's

Brown 15.00

Gray 20.00

White 18.00

Sunglasses, Claire McCardle, black, white and red striped plastic, dark green lenses, stamped "Claire McCardle", c1950 .... 175.00

COALPORT

Coalport porcelain has been made by the Coalport Porcelain Works in England since the late 1700s. It is currently being produced at Stoke-on-Trent. One of their more popular patterns, is "Indian Tree." See "Indian Tree Pattern."

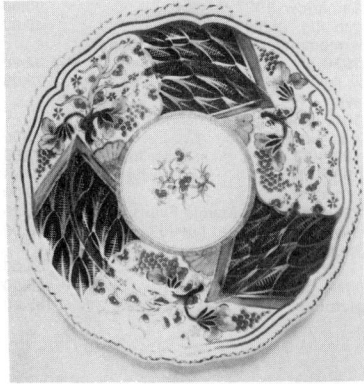

Plate, 10", Crimped edge, shallow well, Indian tobacco leaf design, gold trim, unmarked, $135.00.

Compote, 14", boat shape, pierced sides, end handles, pierced base, gray, floral decor, gilt, c1820	185.00
Creamer, ecru, bell flower bands, shaped handle, gold decor, raised wreath	125.00
Ginger Jar, butterflies	35.00
Plates, dinner, basket of flowers in bittersweet, powder blue and cobalt blue, c1820, set of 12	475.00
Platters	
13¾", oval, salmon marly with gilt key-fret border, the cavetto painted with gilt vermiculation and centered with neoclassical medallion in chocolate brown and grisaille, c1810	130.00
20¾" x 15½", rectangular, big scale pattern in shades of bittersweet, apricot, pink, aqua and cobalt blue, c1825	350.00

Shell Dishes, bittersweet, green and cobalt blue, intricate gilding, c1815 pr	195.00
Soup Tureen and Stand, round, elaborate gadroon border, handles and finial, basket of flowers in bittersweet decor, powder blue and cobalt blue, c1820	570.00
Sugar Bowl, cov, dark blue, multicolored flowers, gilt, No. 3050, c1820	110.00
Teapot, 6½", dark blue, multicolored flowers, gilt, No. 3050, c1820 . . .	175.00
Vases	
6", gold with raised enamel turquoise dots, gold tracery, red enamel jewels, lion head handles	445.00
16¼", 2 scroll handles, apple green, multicolor floral reserves, gilding, c1830	265.00

COCA-COLA ITEMS

The originator of Coca-Cola was John Pemberton, a pharmacist from Atlanta, Ga. In 1886, Dr. Pemberton introduced a patent medicine to relieve headaches, stomach disorders and other minor maladies.

Unfortunately, his failing health and meager finances forced him to sell his interest. In 1888, Asa G. Candler was the sole owner of Coca-Cola. Candler improved the formula, increased the advertising budget and widened the distribution. Accidentally, a 'patient' was given a dose of the syrup mixed with carbonated water instead of the usual still water. The result was a tastier, more refreshing drink. As sales increased in the 1890s, Candler recognized that the product was more suitable for the soft drink market and began advertising as such. From the beginning a myriad of advertising items have been issued to invite all to "Drink Coca-Cola."

Dates of interest: The first unauthorized Coca-Cola tray was issued in 1900. "Coke" was first used in advertising in 1941. The distinctive shaped bottle was registered as a trademark on April 12, 1960.

See *Warman's Americana & Collectibles* for an expanded listing of Coca-Cola Items.

Ashtray, cards, different suites, c1940	40.00
Binoculars, 1910	138.00
Blotter, boy and bottle, 1947	10.00
Booklet, *The Truth About Coca-Cola*, 1912	32.00
Bottle Opener, bottle shape	20.00
Calendar, WWI girl, 1917	220.00
Can, bottle in diamond, c1960	15.00
Carrier, 6 pack, aluminum, c1950 . .	15.00

Blotter, 7¾ x 3½", 1944, $2.50.

Chess Set, c1950	25.00
Cigarette Box, 50 Ann., frosted glass, 1936	100.00
Clocks	
Art Deco type, c1950	110.00
16 x 16", wood frame, square, 1939	95.00
Cooler, floor model	125.00
Fan, wood handle, c1940	20.00
Frisbee	65.00
Glass, 6 oz, acid etched, 1935	15.00
Hat, Soda Jerk, cloth, c1920	10.00
Lapel Pin, 5-year service, 10K gold	60.00
Machine, Coke 10¢	165.00
Magazine Ad, black and white, 1907	22.00
Matchbook, c1930	4.00
Menu Board, wood and masonite, 1939	95.00
Nature Study Cards, Series 1 - 8, orig box	55.00
Paperweight, round, glass	160.00
Playing Cards, WWII airplane spotter	30.00
Ping Pong Set	75.00
Pocket Mirror, Lillian Russel, round, c1904	72.00
Poster, 12 x 16½", Eddie Fisher, "Drink Coca-Cola in Bottles," 1954	75.00
Radios	
8", bottle shaped, plastic case, made in Hong Kong	32.00
Ice chest shape	140.00
Record & Film, 16", merchandising	55.00
Signs	
11", round, mirrored glass	90.00
14 x 30", cardboard, snowman, 1936	60.00
Tin, arrow, 1927	90.00
Syrup Jug, 1920s	45.00
Thermometer, 30", tin, bottle shape, 1958	32.00
Toy Truck, pickup, 1960	70.00
Trays	
1917, Elaine, oval, change, Passaic, NJ Metal Co.	75.00
1922, 10 x 14", girl in sailor hat .	225.00
1930, 10 x 14", girl talking on phone	150.00
1935, 10 x 14", Madge Evans . .	75.00
1943, 10 x 14", red haired girl . .	20.00
1958, TV tray, 13½ x 19", picnic cart	15.00
Wallet, 1928	15.00
Watch Fob, 1908	135.00

Tray, 1939, 13 x 10", Sunblom artist, $50.00.

COFFEE MILLS

Coffee mills or grinders were once used in almost every household. They were made in a variety of shapes and sizes, from large cast iron store models to table top, lap and wall models for the home. The first home sized coffee mill was introduced in the 1890s. With the advent of improved packaging, the coffee grinder has become obsolete. Reproductions are starting to appear.

Child's, Little Gem	50.00
Commercial Types	
Elgin National Coffee Mill, Woodruff and Edwards Co.	300.00
Enterprise Mfg Co.	
66", 2 sheels, cast iron, red, blue paint, stenciling, eagle finial, tin coffee holder, c1873	1,100.00
72", mint condition	1,300.00
Fairbanks Morse	500.00
Lap	
Delmew Coffee Mill, Simons Hardware, St. Louis	65.00
Elma, tin, wood handles	34.00

Enterprise No. 1, painted, black cast iron, mkd. Philadelphia 1876 Exposition, $175.00

Kendrick, cast iron, brass plate with name, porcelain lined cup, iron drawer	75.00
Pride, wood, one drawer, iron handle	48.00
Unmarked Wooden	
2½ x 2½ x 3″, cast iron cup, crank, one drawer	50.00
5 x 5 x 5⅞″, brass fittings, refinished	55.00
6 x 6 x 7″, iron cup, handle	55.00
Side Mount	
Enterprise Mfg, cast iron	48.00
Universal	40.00
Wall Mount	
Lunbrack, Czech.	65.00
National Specialty Co., Phila., PA, cast iron, orig. red scroll, gold decor	75.00
Paneled glass container, cast iron	40.00
Parker, #50, black cast iron, tin emb eagle	45.00
Peugeot Freres, brass top, 8″ h	25.00

COIN OPERATED ITEMS

A wide variety of coin operated machines have been made in the past. Games of skill and chance have always held a fascination for many people; candy and gum machines have a well known fascination for children.

People are collecting the earlier coin operated machines for entertainment as well as investment value.

See *Warman's Americana & Collectibles* for additional listings under Jukeboxes, Pinball Machines, Slot Machines, and Vending Machines.

GAMES

Adam's Ball Game, 1¢, 20″, glazed wood case, drawer	110.00
Baffel Ball, Gottlieb, countertop, pinball, c1931	600.00
Big Broadcast, Gottlieb, c1933	500.00
Chicken Sam, Seeburg	800.00
Home Run, 1¢	60.00
Little Dream Play Baseball, 1¢, c1930	150.00
Poison This Rat, 1¢, 1940, poisons Hitler	600.00
Uncle Sam Grip Test, 1¢, restored	3,300.00

JUKEBOXES

Rockola, 1955	800.00
Wurlitzers	
Model 41, countertop, glazed front, 12 selections, c1940	1,625.00
Model 71, countertop, walnut case, yellow, red, plastic panels, 12 78 rpm selection mechanism, restored, 23″ h, c1940	2,500.00
Model 1015, bubble tubes framing glazed front, veneered wood case, 50″ h, c1947	2,800.00
Model 1100, venerred case, front window reveals 24 selection mechanism, chrome-framed selector buttons, revolving colored lights on sides, 60″, c1948	2,600.00

SLOT MACHINES

Callie, Superior, 5¢, 3 reel, single jackpot, 1926	950.00
Field's, 4 Jacks, 5¢, pocket payout, penny-flip, four jackpots, c1930	600.00
Jennings, Dutch Boy and Girl, 5¢, 3 reel, c1925	900.00
Mills	
Castle Front, twin jackpots, c1933	1,000.00
Extraordinary, 5¢, three reel, double jackpot, c1933, restored	1,350.00
F.O.K., 2 column vendor, twin jackpots, c1931, restored	1,500.00
Poinsetta, 25¢, 3 reel, jackpot, c1929	1,850.00
War Eagle, 5¢, 3 reel, double jackpot, unrestored, c1931	2,000.00
Pace	
Bantam, 1¢, 3 reel, c1935	800.00
Comet Deluxe, 3 reel, twin jackpots, restored c1939	1,500.00

Slot machine, Mills Special Award 7-7-7, c1940, $850.00.

Rockola
Roberts Black Front, 5¢, c1932 ..	1,250.00
Roberts Blue Front, 5¢	1,000.00
Watling, Operator's Bell, cast iron, 5¢, 3 reel, c1915	1,400.00

VENDING

Chicago Mint Co., Puritan Confection, gum, repainted, c1930	400.00
Climax Tab, gum	85.00
Climax 10, peanut, orig paint	550.00

Cash Registers, 20 x 16¾x 23″, National 1912 Model 442, small cranker, $0.00 to $9.99, mahogany base, bronze, $675.00.

Doremus, 5¢ cigar, cast iron, glass .	800.00
Griswald, gum, orig paint, decals ..	375.00
Pulver	
Professor, gum, c1899	1,000.00
Yellow Kid, 1¢ gum, red porcelain finish	200.00
Smilin Sam From Alabam, c1931	600.00
Stuart & Maguire, 1¢ and 5¢, art deco style, restored	185.00
Superior 5¢ gum, wall machine ...	90.00
Try Some, 1¢ peanut, ruby glass top	75.00
Universal Vendors of St. Louis, almondette	50.00
Zeno, 1¢, stick gum, porcelain over steel	300.00

MISCELLANEOUS

Callie Peep Show, restored	900.00
Cash Registers	
McCaskey Account Register, roll top, orig key	450.00
National	
Brass, ornately cast, registers up to $9.99, 17½″	400.00
Model No. 20, #252389, brass, ornately cast, registers up to $4.99, 22″	350.00
No. 944, #1952939, plain brass, nickel plated, registers up to $99.99, side receipt machine, electric, mahogany stand, 61″	600.00
Serial #23335, rosewood, brass, foliate inlay, keys up to $30.00, 18½″ h	1,200.00
Mills Wizard Fortune Teller, 1¢, c1920	600.00
Stamped Envelope and writing paper vendor, 5¢, c1920	350.00

COLLECTORS' PLATES

The first collectors' plates were made by Bing and Grondahl in 1895. Royal Copenhagen issued their first Christmas plate in 1908. In the late 1960s and early 1970s several potteries, glass factories, mints and artists began issuing plates commemorating events, people, animals, etc. Christmas plates were supplemented by Mother's Day plates, Easter plates, etc. A sense of speculation swept the field, fostered in part by flamboyant ad in newspapers and flashy direct mail promotion.

The bubble burst in the late 1970s and early 1980s. Old standbys such as Bing and Grondahl, Rosenthal, and Royal Copenhagen weathered the price drop well. Newer plates still are in a state of price flux. Some plates have held value; many have dropped considerably from the issue price. During 1982 the marketplace began to show signs of stability, resulting from a growing strength of plate collectors' clubs throughout the nation.

Collectors often favor the first plate issued in a series above all others. Condition is a prime factor. Having the original box also influences price.

Collector's plates, more than any other object in this guide, should be collected for design and pleasure and only secondarily for rise in value.

See *Warman's Americana & Collectibles* for an expanded listing of Limited Editions or Collector Items.

ANRI (ITALY)

Christmas Plates, various artists, 12" d

1972 — Pipers At Alberobello . . .	105.00
1974 — Young Man And Girl	100.00
1976 — Alpine Christmas	185.00
1978 — The Klockler Singers . . .	95.00
1980 — Wintry Church-going In Santa Christina	160.00
1981 — Star Singers	165.00

BAREUTHER (GERMANY)

Christmas Plates, Hans Mueller artist, 8"

1968 — Kapplkirche	40.00
1970 — Chapel in Oberndorf	18.00
1972 — Christmas in Munich	50.00
1974 — Church In The Black Forest	28.00
1976 — Chapel in the Hills	32.50
1978 — Mittenwald	32.50
1980 — Miltenberg	40.00

Father's Day Series, Hans Mueller artist, 8" d

1970 — Castle Pfalz	21.50
1972 — Castle Hohenschwangau .	23.50
1974 — Wurzburg Castle	50.00
1976 — Castle Hohenzollern	35.00
1978 — Castle Falkenstein	31.00
1980 — Castle Cochum	40.00
1982 — Castle Zwingenberg	39.50

BERLIN (GERMANY)

Christmas Plates, undisclosed artists, 7¾" d

1971 — Christmas In Rothenburg on Tauber	26.00
1973 — Christmas In Wendelstein	41.00
1975 — Christmas In Dortland . . .	25.00
1977 — Christmas Eve In Hamburg	34.00
1979 — Christmas Eve In Greetsiel	52.00
1981 — Christmas Eve In Hahnenklee	53.00

BING AND GRONDAHL

Christmas Plates

1895 — Behind The Frozen Window	4,000.00

Bing and Grondahl, Christmas, 1936, $75.00.

1896 — New Moon Over Snow-covered Trees	1,975.00
1897 — Christmas Meal Of The Sparrows	1,300.00
1898 — Christmas Roses And Christmas Star	700.00
1899 — The Crows Enjoying Christmas	1,350.00
1900 — Church Bells Chiming In Christmas	780.00
1901 — The Three Wise Men From The East	425.00
1902 — Interior Of A Gothic Church	375.00
1903 — Happy Expectation of Children	275.00
1904 — View of Copenhagen From Frederiksberg Hill	124.00
1905 — Anxiety Of The Coming Christmas Night	127.00
1906 — Sleighing To Church On Christmas Eve	100.00
1907 — The Little Match Girl	125.00
1908 — St. Petri Church of Copenhagen	85.00
1909 — Happiness Over the Yule Tree	106.00
1910 — The Old Organist	89.00
1911 — First It Was Sung By Angels To Shepherds In The Fields	95.00
1912 — Going To Church On Christmas Eve	90.00
1913 — Bringing Home The Yule Tree	96.00
1914 — Royal Castle of Amalienborg, Copenhagen	79.00
1915 — Chained Dog Getting Double Meal On Christmas Eve	115.00

1916 — Christmas Prayer Of The Sparrows	95.00
1917 — Arrival Of The Christmas Boat	75.00
1918 — Fishing Boat Returning Home For Christmas	85.00
1919 — Outside The Lighted Window	82.00
1920 — Hare In The Snow	80.00
1921 — Pigeons In The Castle Court	68.00
1922 — Star Of Bethlehem	72.50
1923 — Royal Hunting Castle, The Ermitage	68.00
1924 — Lighthouse In Danish Waters	72.00
1925 — The Child's Christmas	80.00
1926 — Churchgoers On Christmas Day	75.00
1927 — Skating Couple	109.00
1928 — Eskimo Looking At Village In Greenland	70.00
1929 — Fox Outside Farm On Christmas Eve	78.00
1930 — Yule Tree In Town Hall Square of Copenhagen	115.00
1931 — Arrival Of The Christmas Train	85.00
1933 — The Korsor-Nyborg Ferry	64.00
1935 — Lillebelt Bridge Connecting Funen With Jutland	85.00
1937 — Arrival of Christmas Guests	75.00
1939 — Ole Lock-Eye, The Sandman	150.00
1941 — Horses Enjoying Christmas Meal In Stable	315.00
1943 — The Ribe Cathedral	170.00
1945 — The Old Water Mill	142.00
1947 — Dybbol Mill	85.00
1949 — Landsoldaten, 19th Century Danish Solider	73.00
1951 — Jens Bang, New Passenger Boat Running Between Copenhapen and Aalborg	109.00
1953 — Royal Boat In Greenland Waters	78.00
1955 — Kalundborg Church	112.00
1957 — Christmas Candles	146.00
1959 — Christmas Eve	130.00
1961 — Winter Harmony	115.00
1963 — The Christmas Elf	127.00
1965 — Bringing Home The Christmas Tree	50.00
1967 — Sharing The Joy Of Christmas	40.00
1969 — Arrival Of Christmas Guests	34.00
1971 — Christmas At Home	20.00
1973 — Country Christmas	26.00
1975 — The Old Water Mill	24.00
1977 — Copenhagen Christmas	25.00

1979 — White Christmas	36.00
1981 — Christmas Peace	50.00

Mother's Day Plates, Henry Thelander artist, 6″ d

1969 — Dog And Puppies	440.00
1971 — Cat And Kitten	20.00
1973 — Duck And Ducklings	22.00
1975 — Doe And Fawns	20.00
1977 — Squirrel And Young	24.00
1979 — Fox And Cubs	29.00
1981 — Hare And Young	40.00
1983 — Racoon And Young	39.50

Goebel, 1975, Hummel, Ride Into Christmas, stylized bee, $96.00.

GOEBEL

Christmas Plates

1971 — Heavenly Angel, #264	790.00
1973 — Globe Trotter, #266	200.00
1977 — Apple Tree Boy, #270	108.00
1979 — Singing Lesson, #272	75.00
1981 — Umbrella Boy, #274	100.00
1983 — Postman, #276	108.00

GORHAM (UNITED STATES)

Christmas Plates, Rockwell

1974 — Tiny Tim	75.00
1975 — Good Deeds	65.00
1976 — Christmas Trio	60.00
1977 — Yuletide Reckoning	35.00
1978 — Planning Christmas Visits	25.00
1979 — Santa's Helpers	25.00
1980 — Letter to Santa	28.00
1981 — Santa Plans His Visit	30.00
1982 — The Jolly Coachman	30.00
1983 — Christmas Dancers	30.00

De Grazia, Ted, Children Series
   1976 — Los Niños 850.00
   1977 — The White Dove 160.00

Jansen, Leo, Sugar and Spice Series
   1976 — Dana and Debbie 140.00
   1977 — Becky and Baby 75.00
   1978 — Jeanette and Julie 60.00
   1979 — Ramona and Rachel 90.00

Spencer, Irene, Annual
   1974 — Dear Child 115.00
   1975 — Promises To Keep 40.00

HAVILAND (FRANCE)

The Twelve Days Of Christmas Series, Remy Hetreau, artist, 8⅜" d
   1971 — Two Turtle Doves 55.00
   1973 — Four Colly Birds 34.00
   1975 — Six Geese A'Laying 29.00
   1977 — Eight Maids A'Milking . . .   48.00
   1979 — Ten Lords A'Leaping 55.00
   1981 — Twelve Drummers Drum-
       ming 60.00

Bicentennial Series, Remy Hetreau, artist, 9¾" d
   1973 — Boston Tea Party 40.00
   1975 — Ride of Paul Revere 50.00

HAVILAND & PARLON (FRANCE)

Christmas Series, various artists, 10"
   1972 — Madonna And Child, Ra-
       phael, FE 145.00
   1974 — Cowper Madonna And
       Child, Raphael 80.00
   1976 — Madonna And Child, Botti-
       celli 50.00

Haviland & Parlon, Tapestry Series, The Start of the Hunt, 1972, $75.00.

   1978 — Madonna And Child, Fra
       Filippo Lippi 63.00

Lady And The Unicorn Series, artist un-known, 10"
   1978 — Sight 45.00
   1980 — Touch 102.00
   1982 — Taste 59.00

Tapestry Series, artist unknown, 10"
   1974 — End Of The Hunt 125.00
   1976 — The Unicorn Is Brought To
       The Castle 58.00

LENOX

Boehm Bird Series
   1970 — Wood Thrush 300.00
   1972 — Mountain Bluebird 75.00
   1974 — Rufous Hummingbird 65.00
   1976 — Cardinals 55.00
   1978 — Mockingbird 60.00
   1980 — Black Throated Blue War-
       bler 80.00

Boehm Wildlife Series
   1974 — Red Fox 50.00
   1976 — Chipmunks 60.00
   1978 — White-Tailed Deer 60.00
   1980 — Bobcats 95.00
   1982 — Otters 100.00

Colonial Christmas Wreath
   1981 — Colonial Virginia 65.00
   1982 — Massachusetts 70.00

MISCELLANEOUS

Artists Of The World (United States)
  Children of Aberdeen Series
   1979 — Girl With Little Brother .   60.00
   1980 — Sampan Girl 58.00
   1981 — Girl With Little Sister . .   55.00
   1982 — Girl With Seashells . . .   60.00
   1983 — Girl With Seabirds 60.00

Danbury Mint
  Bicentennial Silver
   1973 — Boston Tea Party 130.00
   1974 — First Continental Con-
       gress 128.00
   1975 — Paul Revere's Ride . . .   125.00
   1976 — Declaration of Indepen-
       dence 125.00
   1977 — Washington At Valley
       Forge 125.00
   1978 — Molly Pitcher 125.00
   1979 — Bon Homme Richard . .   125.00
  Christmas
   1975 — Silent Night 25.00
   1976 — Joy To The World 28.00
   1977 — Away In The Manger . .   28.00
   1978 — The First Noel 30.00

Franklin Mint

Christmas Plates, Norman Rockwell, artist, etched sterling silver, 8"

1971 — Under The Mistletoe ..	170.00
1973 — Trimming The Tree ...	165.00
1975 — Home For Christmas ..	190.00

Mother's Day
Parian

1977, A Mother's Love	70.00
1979, A Mother's Gift	75.00

Silver, Irene Spencer

1973, Mother and Child	145.00
1975, Mother and Child	175.00

Hutschenreuther (Germany)

Christmas, Ole Winther

1978 — Christmas	260.00
1979 — Christmas	300.00
1980 — Christmas	365.00
1981 — Christmas	400.00
1982 — Christmas	410.00

Enchantment Series, Valenza, Dolores

1979 — Princess Snowflake ...	60.00
1979 — Blossom Queen	63.00
1980 — Princess Marina	88.00
1981 — Princess Starbright	85.00
1981 — Harvest Queen	85.00
1982 — Princess Aura	85.00

Lalique (France)

1965 — Deux Oiseaux, FE	1,700.00
1966 — Dreamrose	330.00
1968 — Gazelle Fantasie	130.00
1970 — Peacock	110.00
1972 — Coquillage	75.00
1974 — Silver Pennies	70.00
1976 — Eagle	180.00

Reed & Barton (United States)

Christmas Series, Damascene silver, 11" d through 1978, 8" d 1979 to present

1971 — We Three Kings Of Orient Are	70.00
1973 — Adoration Of The Kings	70.00
1975 — Adoration Of The Kings	65.00
1977 — Decorating The Church	62.00
1979 — Merry Old Santa Clause	63.00
1981 — The Shopkeeper At Christmas	75.00

Royal Devon (United States)

Christmas, Norman Rockwell

1975 — Downhill Daring	75.00
1976 — The Christmas Gift	85.00
1977 — The Big Moment	80.00
1978 — Puppets for Christmas .	35.00
1979 — One Present Too Many	35.00
1980 — Gramps Meets Gramps	33.00

ROCKWELL, SEE ROCKWELL, NORMAN

ROSENTHAL (GERMANY)

Christmas Plates, various artists, 8½" d

1911 — The Three Wise Men	320.00
1913 — Christmas Lights	235.00
1915 — Walking To Church	190.00
1917 — Angel Of Peace	200.00
1919 — St. Christopher With The Christ Child	225.00
1921 — Christmas In The Mountains	195.00
1923 — Children In The Winter Wood	200.00
1925 — The Three Wise Men	215.00
1927 — Station On The Way	200.00
1929 — Christmas In The Alps ...	230.00
1931 — Path Of The Magi	220.00
1933 — Through The Night To Light	190.00
1935 — Christmas By The Sea ...	185.00
1937 — Berchtesgaden	195.00
1939 — Schneekoppe Mountain ..	198.00
1941 — Strassburg Cathedral	245.00
1943 — Winter Idyll	295.00
1945 — Christmas Peace	400.00
1947 — The Dillingen Madonna ..	975.00
1949 — The Holy Family	185.00
1951 — Star Of Bethlehem	450.00
1953 — The Holy Light	185.00
1955 — Christmas In A Village ...	190.00
1957 — Christmas By The Sea ...	195.00
1959 — Midnight Mass	190.00
1961 — Solitary Christmas	225.00
1963 — Silent Night	190.00
1965 — Christmas In Munich	185.00
1967 — Christmas In Regensburg	190.00
1969 — Christmas In Rothenburg .	220.00
1971 — Christmas In Garmisch ..	96.00
1973 — Christmas In Lubeck-Holstein	103.00

Bjorn Wiinblad (artist) Christmas Plates Series

1972 — Caspar	650.00
1974 — Balthazar	572.00
1976 — Angel With Trumpet	240.00
1978 — Angel With Harp	265.00
1980 — Angel With A Glockenspiel	360.00
1982 — Christening of Christ	375.00

ROYAL COPENHAGEN

Christmas Plates

1908 — Madonna And Child	1,800.00
1909 — Danish Landscape	170.00
1910 — The Magi	145.00
1911 — Danish Landscape	130.00
1912 — Elderly Couple By Christmas Tree	150.00
1913 — Spire Of Frederik's Church, Copenhagen	135.00

Royal Copenhagen, Mothers Day Series, 1980, An Outing with Mother, $35.00.

1914—Sparrows In Tree At Church Of The Holy Spirit, Copenhagen	115.00
1915—Danish Landscape	160.00
1916—Shepherd In The Field On Christmas Night	95.00
1917—Tower Of Our Savior's Church, Copenhagen	83.00
1918—Sheep and Shepherds	96.00
1919—In The Park	82.00
1920—Mary With The Child Jesus	75.00
1921—Aabenraa Marketplace	75.00
1922—Three Singing Angels	78.00
1923—Danish Landscape	92.00
1924—Christmas Star Over The Sea And Sailing Ship	105.00
1925—Street Scene From Christianshavn, Copenhagen	85.00
1926—View of Christmas Canal, Copenhagen	88.00
1927—Ship's Boy At The Tiller On Christmas Night	152.00
1928—Vicar's Family On Way To Church	75.00
1929—Grundtvig Church, Copenhagen	85.00
1930—Fishing Boats On The Way To The Harbor	80.00
1931—Mother And Child	90.00
1932—Frederiksberg Gardens With Statue Of Frederik VI	90.00
1933—The Great Belt Ferry	125.00
1934—The Hermitage Castle	122.00
1935—Fishing Boat Off Kronborg Castle	140.00
1936—Roskilde Cathedral	138.00
1937—Christmas Scene In Main Street, Copenhagen	141.00
1938—Round Church In Osterlars On Bornholm	258.00

1939—Expeditionary Ship In Pack-Ice Of Greenland	200.00
1940—The Good Shepherd	325.00
1941—Danish Village Church	320.00
1943—Flight Of Holy Family To Egypt	480.00
1945—A Peaceful Motif	380.00
1947—The Good Shepherd	200.00
1949—Our Lady's Cathedral, Copenhagen	160.00
1951—Christmas Angel	320.00
1953—Frederiksborg Castle	105.00
1955—Fano Girl	210.00
1957—The Good Shepherd	115.00
1959—Christmas Night	145.00
1961—Training Ship Danmark	185.00
1963—Hojsager Mill	95.00
1965—Little Skaters	70.00
1967—The Royal Oak	40.00
1969—The Old Farmyard	32.00
1971—Hare In Winter	23.00
1973—Train Homeward Bound For Christmas	25.00
1975—Queen's Palace	20.00
1977—Immervad Bridge	28.00
1979—Choosing The Christmas Tree	46.00
1981—Admiring The Christmas Tree	53.00
1983—Merry Christmas	54.50

Mother's Day Plates, various artists, 6¼″ d

1971—American Mother	15.00
1973—Danish Mother	16.00
1975—Bird In Nest	18.00
1977—The Twins	28.00
1979—A Loving Mother	28.00

Peanuts, Schmid, Mother's Day, 1972, First Edition, $15.00.

SCHMID (JAPAN)

Walt Disney
Christmas Series, undisclosed
artists, 7½" d
1973 — Sleigh Ride, FE	310.00
1975 — Caroling	20.00
1977 — Down The Chimney . . .	16.00
1979 — Santa's Surprise	18.00
1981 — Happy Holidays	18.00

Mother's Day Series
1974 — Flowers For Mother, FE	60.00
1976 — Minnie Mouse And Friends	23.00
1978 — Flowers For Bambi	19.00
1980 — Minnie's Surprise	18.00
1982 — A Dream Come True . .	18.50

Peanuts
Christmas Series, Charles
Schulz, artist, 7½" d
1972 — Snoopy Guides The Sleigh, FE	68.00
1976 — Woodstock's Christmas	25.00
1978 — Filling The Stocking . . .	18.00
1980 — Waiting For Santa	55.00
1982 — Perfect Performance . .	18.50

Mother's Day Series, Charles Schulz, artist, 7½" d
1972 — Linus, FE	15.00
1974 — Snoopy And Woodstock On Parade	20.00
1976 — Linus And Snoopy	17.00
1978 — Thoughts That Count . .	15.00
1980 — A Tribute To Mom	20.00
1982 — Which Way To Mother? . .	18.50

Valentine's Day Series, Charles Schulz, artist, 7½" d
1978 — Heavenly Bliss	20.00
1980 — From Snoopy, With Love	21.00
1982 — Love Patch	17.50

Raggedy Ann Annual Series, undisclosed artist, 7½" d
1980 — The Sunshine Wagon . . .	60.00
1982 — Flying High	18.50

WEDGWOOD (GREAT BRITAIN)

Christmas Series, jasper stoneware, 8" d
1970 — Christmas In Trafalgar Square	27.00
1972 — St. Paul's Cathedral	41.00
1974 — The Houses Of Parliment	38.00
1976 — Hampton Court	46.00
1978 — The Horse Guards	38.00
1980 — St. James Palace	72.00
1982 — Lambeth Palace	80.00

Mother's Series, jasper stoneware, 6½" d
1972 — The Sewing Lesson	32.00
1974 — Domestic Employment . . .	30.00
1976 — The Spinner	35.00
1978 — Swan And Cygnets	33.00
1980 — Birds	48.00
1982 — Cherubs With Swing	55.00

COMIC BOOKS

Throughout history drawings and cartoons were important visual images for learning, political and social satire and entertainment. The advent of mass circulation newspapers opened the way for Sunday and daily comic features. The first comic Sunday feature appeared in the New York World in February 1896.

Some of these comics were extracted into pulp magazine form in the 1915 to 1930 period. However, these pulps contained reprints of comics from the newspapers and did not appear on a regular basis.

By the late 1930s comic books achieved their own identity. Initially, the characters chosen were those familiar to comic strip readers — Captain Easy, Maggie and Jiggs, Orphan Annie, etc. As the comic book idea caught hold, publishers hired artists to create new characters and special adventure plots. Bulletman, Capt. Marvel, Plastic Man, Spy Smasher, and Superman arrived upon the scene.

Disney and the early cowboy heroes saw the comic book as a way to increase popularity and make a handsome profit. Today the comic book helps promote movies and television programs.

Comic books are collected for a variety of reasons — aesthetic (some artwork is avantguard or classic), social commentary (one professor used comics to study the image of science in popular culture), and rarity. Although the price of most comic books of the 1950 to 1970 period is five to twenty-five dollars, rare and first editions command hundreds of dollars.

Comic books are printed on poor quality paper. Serious collectors must spend substantial sums to protect their investment. Condition is a prime factor in price. Tears, missing pages or corners of pages, signs of heavy use, and dirt lower prices quickly.

The prices below are for books in fine condition, showing some use but still crisp and clean. The numbers represent issue numbers, i.e. #1 is first issue, #2 is second issue, etc.

Comic books have been reissued; and, different publishers published the same title in different years. Check carefully.

See *Warman's Americana & Collectibles* for an expanded listing of Comic Books.

Andy Panda, Feb.–April 1958, Dell Publishing, $.60.

FIRST ISSUES

Abbott and Costello, Vol. 1, Feb. 1948, St. John Publishing Co. . . .	**45.00**
Blondie, No. 1, Spring 1947	**25.00**
Ellery Queen, No. 1, March 1952, Ziff-Davis Publishing Co., Saunders cover	**50.00**
Flash Gordon, No. 1, January 1940, National Periodical Publications .	**925.00**
Justice League Of America, No. 1, Oct.–Nov. 1960, origin of Despero	**150.00**
Popeye, No. 1, Feb.–April 1948, Dell	**45.00**
Straight Arrow, No. 1, Feb.–March 1950, Magazine Enterprises	**40.00**
Uncle Scrooge, Four Color #386 (No. 1), Dell Publishing	**300.00**

OTHER

Amazing Spider-Man, The, No. 101, introduces Morbius, Marvel Comics Group	**5.00**
Archie Comics, No. 85, Archie Publications	**9.00**
Batman, No. 62, origin of Catwoman	**50.00**
Captain Video, No. 6, Dec. 1951, Fawcett Publications	**35.00**
Dennis The Menace, No. 33, Summer 1965, in California	**3.25**
Fantastic Four, No. 62, Marvel Comics	**4.00**

Fightin' Marines, No. 22, St. John .	**1.75**
Four Color, No. 392, Hi-Yo Silver, Dell Publishing Co.	**7.00**
Gabby Hayes Western, No. 17, Fawcett	**8.00**
Huckleberry Hound, No. 2, 1978, Marvel Comics Group	**.35**
Joe Palooka, No. 110, Harvey Publications	**4.00**
Korak, Son of Tarzan, No. 7, Gold Key	**3.00**
Mickey Mouse, No. 68, Dell Publishing Co.	**2.50**
Movie Comics, Fantastic Voyage, No. 10178-702, Feb. 1967, Wood and Atkins artists	**5.00**
Realistic Romances, No. 6, Avon . .	**12.00**
Rudolph, The Red Nosed Reindeer, 1960 issue, not numbered	**6.00**
Superman's Girlfriend Lois Lane, No. 72, National Periodical Publications	**.80**
Tex Ritter Western, No. 40, Charlton	**6.00**
The X-Men, No. 33, Marvel Comics Group	**3.00**

COMMEMORATIVE AND HISTORICAL GLASS

Collectors have always sought commemorative and historical items made of glass, and since the bicentennial celebration in 1976, there has been an increase in demand for them. Consequently, there has been a substantial increase in the price of such things as "Liberty Bell" pattern glass, the commemorative trays and bread plates, as well as many new collectibles which were made expressly for the 1976 event. Collectors should be aware of this and separate new items from the old glass when it is available. There also are many other collectible items which are commemorative, but not especially historical.

See *Warman's Americana & Collectibles* for additional Souvenir and Historical China and Glass listings.

Bank, Independence Hall	**225.00**
Bottles	
6½" h, Henry Ward Beecher, emb, "T. P. Spencer, N. Y." . .	**50.00**
½ pt., General Douglas MacArthur, aqua, 1942	**35.00**
1 qt., "Moses," Poland Water, clear	**30.00**
Charley Ross	**85.00**
Bread Plates	
10", round, "Cleveland Reform" plate, hobnail border	**35.00**

Tumbler, At Last! 1933, 4% beer, etched, red rim, 3⁹⁄₁₆", $30.00.

10½ x 7½", "President Taylor" plate, successor to Brigham Young, also Curtain Tieback pattern 50.00
Butters, covered
Bullet Emblem, covered 100.00
Liberty Bell, clear 135.00
"Maude S" (Mascotte pattern), horseshoe finial 75.00
Compotes
7", "Westward-Ho," oval 165.00
12⅜", "Rebecca at the Well" . . 350.00
Goblets
"Actress," Lotta Crabtree and Kate Claxton, clear 80.00
Centennial, draped roses 40.00
G.A.R., issued 1887, 21st Encampment 95.00
Greeley, Brown, clear, ball stem . 200.00
Liberty Bell 55.00
Jars
7½", "Lafayette," aqua, profile emb 75.00
Statue of Liberty 150.00
Lamps
Fine Rib and Star 150.00
8", Lincoln Drape, cobalt blue, flint 300.00
3⅛ x 2¾", log cabin shaped, side handle, emb "Pat'd, April 18, 1875" 75.00
Mugs
Columbus 45.00
Martyrs 40.00
Tennessee 55.00
Washington-Lafayette 45.00
Paperweights
4⅜ x 6⅛", Memorial Hall, inscribed 1776–1876," Memorial Hall sculptured in glass, all frosted, mirror glass beneath, black opaque glass base, (rare) 150.00
Lincoln 195.00
Plymouth Rock, 3¼" 65.00
Pickle Dish, Liberty Bell 44.00
Pitchers
"Dewey," cannonballs around base, portrait 75.00
Garfield Drape, clear 70.00
Plates
Atlantic Cable 45.00
Columbus milk glass 60.00
Eureka, c1848 California gold rush 50.00
McKinley, Protection and Plenty, 7¼" 20.00
Platters
George Washington 125.00
Independence Hall 100.00
Theodore Roosevelt 125.00
Statuettes
Columbus, frosted 75.00
Pres. Grant, frosted, white opaque, Philadelphia Centennial, sgd Gillinder, 1876 . . . . . 300.00
Trays
11½ x 9½", "Columbia," shield shaped, head of Columbia in center 100.00
"Flag," later made with 48 stars, sometime prior to 1912 . . . . . 50.00
Tumblers
Admiral Dewey, decal transfer, 3¾ x 2¾" 25.00
America 25.00
"Louisiana Purchase," milk glass . 45.00
Wilkie, 4½", etched 35.00

COMMEMORATIVE AND SOUVENIR SPOONS

These spoons were made as mementos of special events, personages or places of interest, reaching their highest peak of popularity in the 1880s–1890s. Commemorative spoons are currently being made and spoon collecting is regaining favor. Spoons listed are sterling silver unless otherwise noted. *American Spoons, Souvenir and Historical* by Rainwater and Felger is a good reference.

See *Warman's Americana & Collectibles* for an expanded listing of Souvenir and Commemorative Spoons.

Admiral Dewey, Flagship Olympia, SP 5.00
Atlantic City, NJ, Steel Pier, chased floral handle, demitasse 25.00
Baltimore 50.00
Battleship Maine, SP 6.00

Louisana Purchase Exposition, Festival Hall, Cascades in bowl, scenes of progress, 1803–1903, demitasse, marked Ball, $25.00.

Benjamin Franklin, high relief handle, Philadelphia, "Mary" engraved in bowl	150.00
Champlain, high relief on handle, oar, rifle entwined with Canadian crest	60.00
Charleston, SC, Fort Sumter, state seal on handle, reverse decor, demitasse	48.00
Chicago, Ft. Dearborn in bowl, Chicago in script on handle, teaspoon	40.00
Chief Oshkosh	40.00
Christ Church, Alexandria, VA	18.00
Commodore Schley, Flagship Brooklyn emb bowl	9.00
Dennis The Menace, SP	6.00
Detroit, MI, bust of Cadillac on handle, teaspoon	45.00
Garfield Memorial	40.00
Hamburg, harbor scene, enameled bowl, ornate handle	130.00
Jacksonville, FL, Indian	17.50
La Belle Chocolatiere, SP	15.00
Lachine Rapids, Montreal, steamship, Canadian enameled crest on handle, teaspoon	38.00
Los Angeles engraved in bowl, emb cupids on handle, teaspoon	50.00
New York, Flat Iron Building, emb view in bowl, state seal, other views on handle, teaspoon	45.00
Ohio state seal, crest handle, teaspoon	30.00
Old Man Of Mountains, demitasse, Durgin	15.00
Oregon Grape	25.00
Paul Revere, Washington Elm emb on handle, 19th C Boston harbor view in bowl, demitasse, reverse also decor	35.00
Quakertown, PA, demitasse, corn stalk handle	12.50
Rhododendron	25.00
Rochester, MN, St. Mary's Hospital, state seal on handle, reverse decor, teaspoon	65.00
Santa Claus	32.00
Schenectady, NY, Indian, demitasse	15.00
Shirley Temple, photo	20.00
Star of David, SP	9.00
Stork, teaspoon	45.00
University of Missouri	18.00

Washington, DC, cherry tree, dated May '96	17.50
Yokohoma, Grand Hotel in bowl, emb flowers, dragon	45.00

COMMEMORATIVE, HISTORICAL, AND SOUVENIR CHINA

Commemorative, historical and souvenir china, celebrating special events, places or people, have always ranked high with collectors. Since the Bicentennial in 1976, interest in these items has increased greatly. Back in the 1880s, collectors were equally zealous, and their interests embraced both new and old objects and places.

In 1910, the firm of Jones, McDuffee and Stratton collaborated with Wedgwood to produce historic dessert-sized plates depicting scenes throughout the United States.

From the Philadelphia Centennial in 1876 to the New York World's Fair in 1939, a series of American scenes on plates were also made by Rowland and Marcellus (R & M), of Staffordshire, England, like "Old Blue," with a wide, rolled edge which differentiates them. All of these plates are marked, and should not be confused with the actual old soft paste plates made by early Staffordshire potters.

Plates were also made by other potters in England and United States, see: COPELAND-SPODE, BUFFALO POTTERY, etc.

See *Warman's Americana & Collectibles* for additional Souvenir and Historical China and Glass Listings.

Mug, Wesleyan College, gilded	22.00
Plates	
Rowland and Marcellus, 10½" d, vignettes border, rolled edges, dark blue	
Allentown, PA, Souvenir of The Pike	30.00
Atlantic City, NJ	35.00
Bathing Hour	30.00
Buffalo Library & Soldiers Monument	35.00
Buffalo, NY	32.00
Capt. John Smith, Admiral of New England, portrait	40.00
Carlisle, PA	32.00
Cleveland, OH	30.00
Garfield Memorial	35.00
Historic Boston Faneuil Hall	32.00
Lafayette Square	32.00
Landing of Henry Hudson	35.00
Longfellow	35.00
New Denny Hall	35.00
Niagara Falls, view of falls	32.00

Plate, Asbury Park, NJ, Rowland and Marsellus, 8½", dark blue, $15.00.

Thos. Jefferson center, Souvenir St. Augustine, FL	50.00
Williamsport, PA, City Hall	35.00
Zion's Union Church, Berks Co., PA	50.00
Wedgwood, 7½" d, blue	
Boston Tea Party	50.00
Fort Ticonderoga, NY	35.00
Library of Congress	30.00
Mt. Vernon	25.00
Old Man of the Mountains, NH	35.00
Priscilla and John Alden	40.00
Wash. DC, Union Station	35.00
Williamsburg	35.00
Miscellaneous Makers	
Johnstown Flood Memorial, 1889, 7"	18.00
Marblehead's Cradle of Liberty, Ye Old Towne House, Erected 1727, Marblehead, Mass, blue and white, W. Adams & Co. Adams Tunstall, England, 10"	25.00
Marine Hospital, Louisville, KY, Wood & Sons, 9¼"	300.00
Pres. Coolidge, home, VT, Adams series for Ruth Aldrich, 10"	16.00
Presidential, Grover Cleveland, ironstone, 8"	30.00
Pitchers	
Derby, library, black transfer, Germany	18.00
Trinity College, blue transfer	18.00
Vases	
Bridgeport, 8¼"	12.00
Middletown, ornate	22.00
St. Vincent's Hospital, Germany	18.00

COPELAND

COPELAND AND SPODE CHINA

Josiah Spode, a pupil of Thomas Whieldon, started the Spode Works in Stoke-on-Trent in 1770, with the help of William Copeland, a banker and tea merchant of London. The original idea was that the new-found beverage of tea would find more patrons if associated with a teapot to enhance its flavor. The firm has been handed down through the two families and W. T. Copeland and Sons have operated the works since 1847.

The company emphasizes the fact that Spode designs are hand engraved on imperishable copper. Every design is recorded in pattern books; no design is ever discontinued or lost; every Spode pattern is always available. This may or may not be entirely true today, but Spode patterns that are available are quite collectible. Most pieces found today carry the late Spode mark, and pieces prior to 1843 should be attributed to Spode.

Tea Set, 6½" h x 9¼" l teapot, 3 x 5" creamer, 4¾" h x 6½" l sugar, brown transfer of farm scene, imp Copeland, $100.00.

Basket, 5", scrolling garden flowers, gilt, loop handle, c1815	250.00
Bottles	
Flowering plants in reserves, dark green ground, gilt rim, gilt stopper, 4", pr	110.00
Mayflower on obverse, Pilgrims on reverse side, brown mark	65.00
Bowls 5", "Armorial," grey, cobalt blue, gold, c1890	50.00
Butter Dish, stoneware, grapevines, acanthus leaves, c1850	155.00

Chocolate Set, pot, 6 cups and saucers, "Indian Tree," set 200.00

Coffee Pot, 18", "Brown Delft," brown borders, yellow floral decor, scenes of ruins of old English castles and abbeys 175.00

Cups and Saucers
  Cobalt blue and floral decor 85.00
  Christmas Holly 75.00
  Demitasse, blue, white transfer, c1890 . . . .   25.00
  Imari-type decor, Orange Blossoms   45.00
  "Tobacco Leaf," Spode's Newstone mark, c1820 . . . . . .   50.00

Dessert Plates, Japon pattern, bowpot with fans in border, bittersweet, cobalt blue, gilt, Newstone, c1876, 9 pc 450.00

Egg Server, 4½ x 6", 4 egg cups and center salt dip, 4 silverplated spoons, salt spoon, "Pink Willow"   275.00

Figurine, 13", unglazed, cherub holding a bellflower 60.00

Jars, oviform, 2 handles, cov, Pattern 3086, oriental birds on flowering peony branches, iron red, pink, gilt, apple green ground, gilt knob finials, Spode mark, c1820, pr 1,320.00

Pitchers
  5¼ x 6¼", squatty, blue, white relief hunters, horses, dogs 75.00
  8", cameo, blue, white, c1885 . .   45.00
  8½", blue tower, mkd England . .   120.00

Plates
  10", "Fairy Dell," swirl-patterned edges, late 25.00
  8", Peacock, hen, peonies, blue transfer, gold trim, c1815 . . . .   90.00
  8", scenic, highland mountain, lake, cobalt border, inner jeweled ring 135.00
  9", white, heavy gold, cobalt border, c1920 . . . .   75.00
  8", "Rosebud Chintz," all-over rosebud design, late 20.00
  9", Willow, transfer for Tiffany and Co. NY, gold trim 25.00

Platter
  13", round, Wicker Lane 35.00
  16", "Gainsborough," floral, blue, crimson, purple, yellow on ivory ground over sepia print, late . .   200.00

Soup Plates, pattern 3067, Famille rose border, center scene of oriental figures, boat, Newstone, pr, c1810 . . . .   150.00

Teapot, 6", blue, white relief hunters, horses, dogs 110.00

Tureens
  Miniature, cov, oval, brown leaf decor, matching 4 x 3" underplate, Imperial crown mark   20.00

Soup, round, stand, pattern 3875, bittersweet, green, medium blue, aqua, cobalt, c1810 . . . . .   650.00

Vases
  5½", ftd, pattern 967, Imari style, flowering plants, loop gilt handles, iron red script Spode mark, c1810, pr 900.00
  7¾" h, Potpourri, pierced cov, 2 handles, ftd, flaring rim, gilt knob finial, pattern 967, floral decor, iron red script Spode mark, c1810 . . . .   575.00

COPPER

Copper has been an important metal throughout the centuries. Buckets, pots and pans were few of the applications. It was also used for jewelry, plaques, lighting fixtures, weather vanes and decorative items.

Georgian Pub measure, 6⅛", 1 qt, marked 1826 N-P on spout, $225.00.

Apple Butter Kettle, 24", dovetailed, iron handle 225.00

Ashtray, individual, 2"d, hammered, sq base, imp windmill mark, Dirk van Erp 10.00

Basin, 17", two handles 135.00

Bookends, Figural horse heads on horseshoe 20.00

Bowl, 10", round, lobed sides, hammered, imp, maker's mark, Dirk van Erp 200.00

Candy Kettle, 17", iron ear handles, 19th C 325.00

Centerpiece, 11¼", round dish sup-

ported by 4 slender curved legs on circular stand, imp windmill mark, Dirk van Erp	200.00
Coal Bucket, 11 x 12¼ x 16″1, base handle stamped "1876"	145.00
Coffee Pot, 10″, handle at right angle, American	125.00
Coffee Server, iron stand, 16½″ overall height	315.00
Crumber, 9″, polished, imp windmill mark, Dirk van Erp	35.00
Dipper, 40″1, strainer cup, wrought iron handle with curved hook . . .	55.00
Dish, chafing, 3 parts, Empress Ware, Pat 1907	65.00
Flour Canister, cylindrical, tin lining, lift out sifting tray	70.00
Hot Water Bottle	85.00
Inkwell, sterling and green enamel overlay "Artcrafts Shop-Buffalo" .	100.00
Letter Opener & Rolling Blotter, van Erp, pr	250.00
Lighter, Cape Cod, brass and copper "Old Mission, Calif."	75.00
Match Box Holder, 3 sided with open ends	10.00
Measures	
½ pt	40.00
1 qt, wrap around pouring lip, strap handle	85.00
Pan Lid, cast iron handle, 19th C . .	28.00
Pitcher, 8½″, baluster shape, cylindrical neck, polished, imp windmill mark, Dirk van Erp	400.00
Pot, 11⅜″, circular, straight sides, brass handles, hammered, smooth lid, brass finish	125.00
Sauce Pan, 7¾″d x 9¼″, wrought copper flat handle, dovetailed . . .	100.00
Skillet, 8¼″d, 8″cast iron handle, mkd B.D. Co. New York	55.00
Still, 20″, 3 gal size, brass spigot, tin inside, A.H. Pierce Mfg. Co.	300.00
Tankard, 14″, copper and brass, pewter lined, Wheat (barley) design, possible English	285.00
Tea Kettles	
8″, gooseneck spout, dovetailed construction, wide handle, stamped John Getz (Lancaster, PA)	470.00
10″, gooseneck spout, dovetailed, acorn finial	185.00
12″, gooseneck spout, cast brass handle and finial, stamped mark on lid and side of pot	120.00
Tray, 21 x 11″w, rectangular, galleried, handled, footed, sloping ends, fitted copper liner with loop lift handles, imp windmill mark, Dirk van Erp	200.00
Wash Boiler, 11½ x 22″, cov, wooden handles, polished	65.00

COPPER LUSTRE

Copper lustre wares were first made in the early 1800s by potters in the Staffordshire district, England. A copper compound added to the glaze resulted in the fine metallic-like surface. Quantities were imported into the United States during the 19th century. Reproductions are on the market, especially creamers and the so-called "Polka Jug." The new wares are heavier in appearance and weight when compared to the earlier.

Pitcher, 5½″ h, blue band, emb hunting scene decor, $135.00.

Beaker, 2¾″, blue band	65.00
Bowls	
4″, blue band, red roses	55.00
4½″, blue band, scroll decor . . .	30.00
Chalice, 4″, relief design, colored enamel	55.00
Compote, 4¾ x 8″d, scalloped edge, floral decor	60.00
Cups and Saucers	
Blue band, c1820-40	55.00
Orange band, floral decor	45.00
Flower Pot and Stand, 4″, wide white band, floral sprays and sprigs, lion's mask and ring handles, c1815	160.00
Goblets	
4½″, wide pink band, flowering vine	55.00
4¾″, white band with floral motif, ridges at base of bowl	60.00
Mugs	
3″, wide blue leaf and berry band	37.00
3″, wide pink band	35.00
3¼″, blue band, floral motif	35.00

Mustard Pot, 2⅝", cov, handle, orange band with blue blossoms .. 80.00

Pitchers
2", raised textured band 25.00
2½", wide tan band 25.00
3", molded feather bands 27.00
4", green and yellow bands 35.00
5", blue band, relief design, serpent handle 70.00
5¼", blue ground, acanthus leaves and flowering plants, grapevine border, c1825 ..... 140.00
5½", blue band, cottage 75.00
6½", yellow pebble band, polychrome flowers 85.00
6¾", melon shape, blue bands, white collar with polychrome flower 85.00
7½", blue band, polychrome cherubs and sheep cart 110.00

Plates
6", Phoenix bird, yellow ground, silver lustre 75.00
8", orange floral decor 25.00
8½", blue floral border 40.00

Quill Holder, 4¼", porcupine shape, 6 rows of small holes down back, c1830 .... 200.00

Salts
2 x 3" d, ftd, cream band, foliage and blue blossoms 48.00
Sanded band, pedestaled 35.00

Sugar Bowl, blue band, raised floral and leaf design 85.00

Tankard, 8⅛", cov, tapering cylindrical shape, Staffordshire, c1840 .. 125.00

Teapots, covered
7½", turquoise enamel decor ... 110.00
9⅝", faceted baluster shape, floral sprays and sprigs, c1820 .. 130.00

Urn, 8½", green band 175.00

Vase, 6½", transfer printed puce clock face on obverse, mother and 2 children inscribed Charity on reverse, scroll handles, Llanelly, c1840 .... 140.00

CORALENE

Coralene is a term used to describe glass or china objects to which the design was painted on the surface of the piece, then tiny glass colorless beads were applied with a fixative. The object was then placed in a muffle to fix the enamel and set the beads.

The glass Coralene was made in the 1880s by several American and English companies. The design most commonly used resembled seaweed or coral. Other designs were "Wheat Sheaf" and "Fleur-de-Lis". Most of the base glass used was satin finished.

The china and pottery Coralene was made from the late 1890s to the post WW II era and referred to as Japanese Coralene. The beading on pottery is opaque and inserted into the soft clay and is therefore only half to three quarters visible.

Reproductions are on the market. Some reproductions have been made using old glass. The beaded decoration on new Coralene has been glued on and can be scraped off.

Lamp Base, 7¼" h to top of font, yellow satin raindrop ground, blue beading, sgd Webb (script), $250.00.

China
Compote, 4¼ x 5", white, pink roses, green leaves, blue, gold leaf 225.00
Ewer, 8", light blue matte, white and tan sailboat, Mt. Fuji, "Pat. Applied for 38257" 460.00
Plates
8½", white lilies, green leaves . 120.00
10½", butterflies and floral decor 395.00
Vase, 4¾", tan, morning glories, cobalt blue trim 130.00

Glass
Bowl, 5½", ruffled, peachblow .. 95.00
Cracker Jar, 6", blue, gold foliage decor under beading, silver bail and handle 400.00

Ewer, 8½" tan to yellow, flowers
of pink, green and white **185.00**
Finger Bowl and Underplate,
Steuben **250.00**
Pitcher, 4½" yellow bottom shading to green top, pink, white and
orange flowers, orange and
green leaves, gold trim, gold
beading **45.00**
Vases
5½", pink DQ and MOP, wheat
decor **275.00**
7¾" rose satin glass, white lining, yellow seaweed pattern . **495.00**
10", two tone green beads,
beaded gold swirls, large medallions front and back, pink
flowers **350.00**

CORKSCREWS

The corkscrew is a utilitarian device used to
draw a cork from a bottle. It continues to be
made in a variety of shapes, styles and materials.

As early as the 17th century, the figural
corkscrew was favored. Mechanical models
were popular in the Victorian era. Elaborate
examples with handles of Mother of Pearl,
ivory and sterling proliferated throughout the
Art Nouveau period for people with champagne tastes.

Advertising
Jack Daniels **8.00**
Listerine **3.00**
Bone, whale, silver cap, 5½ x 5¾" **60.00**
Brass, 5", long key **25.00**
Commemorative, inscribed "Chica-
go's World's Fair, 1893" **12.50**
Figural
Fish, 5½", combination bottle
opener, can piercer, corkscrew,
brass **48.00**
Parrot, corkscrew tail, cast iron .. **17.00**

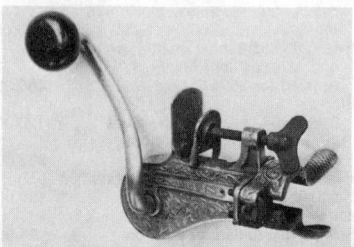

**Yankee #7, corkscrew, table mount-
ed, bar model, 7¼"l, $275.00.**

Horn, 4¼", capped with continental
silver, English **40.00**
Steel
4½", flat ring top, American **25.00**
7" Captain's Key, Germany **35.00**
Wood
4¼", iron hatchet shape, emb,
wooden handle **20.00**
4½", hand turned, black stain,
English **30.00**
5½", hand turned walnut with ring
top, American **30.00**
6", burl **25.00**
6½", Grape, Welch, Westview,
NY **15.00**
6¾", Cooderham & Worts, folding **15.00**

COSMOS GLASS

Cosmos glass is pressed milk glass decorated with cosmos flowers in relief. The flowers
were "stained" or "flashed" with pale shades
of blue, pink and yellow. It is attributed to
Dithridge & Son, New Brighton, Pennsylvania,
c1900.

**Cosmos Glass Butter Dish, covered,
$210.00.**

Basket, ftd **120.00**
Cologne Bottle, orig stopper **195.00**
Condiment Set, salt, pepper, mus-
tard **340.00**
Creamer **125.00**
Lamps
7½", base only **45.00**
Mini base, paneled, chimney **80.00**
16" base, Eagle burner **250.00**
Pickle Castor, no lid, no tongs **175.00**
Pitcher, water **250.00**
Powder Box, cov, pink band decor . **200.00**
Shakers, pair **95.00**
Spooner **100.00**
Sugar, covered **150.00**
Tumbler **85.00**

COWAN POTTERY

R. Guy Cowan founded the Cowan Pottery in 1913 in Cleveland, Ohio. The establishment remained in almost continuous operation until 1931 when financial difficulties forced closure.

Early production was redware pottery. Later a porcelain-like finish was perfected with special emphasis placed on glazes. Lustreware is one of the most common types. Commercial type wares marked "Lakeware" were produced from 1927 to 1931.

Early marks include an incised "Cowan Pottery" on the redware (1913–1917), impressed "Cowan," and impressed "Lakewood." The imprinted stylized semi-circle with or without the initials R.G. was later.

Vase, 5¼ x 8¼" w, green tones, semi-crystaline glaze, $78.00.

12", fan vase, seahorse base . . .	95.00
16", thrown vase, red clay, orange lustre glaze, hand sgd R.G. Cowan	450.00

Bookends, 5", Sunbonnet Girls, white glaze	350.00
Bowls	
9½ x 4", seahorse pedestal, flared top, blue lustre glaze . . .	45.00
11½ x 5½ x 3", molded fruit pedestal base, yellow exterior, pink interior	55.00
Candlesticks	
3½", seahorses, pink lustre glaze, pr	35.00
12½", figural deco nudes, white glaze, pr	450.00
Figurals	
3", elephant on pedestal, black glaze	165.00
6½", female, nude, flower frog, with scarf, white glaze	95.00
7½", Pierot, clown with ruffled collar and pointed hat, matte yellow glaze	250.00
9½", robed Chinese woman, white glaze	250.00
14 x 7", Madonna, terra cotta . . .	850.00
Lamp, 13½", "Aztec Man," Art Deco male figure, metallic black, silver, bronze glaze	600.00
Plate, 10", sports plate, molded design, artist sgd VS in mold	450.00
Vases	
5", bud vase, blue lustre glaze . .	15.00
6 x 5", blue and green glaze, hand decor of mushrooms . . .	350.00
8", pink lustre glaze	45.00

COWBOY HEROES

Warman's Americana & Collectibles, 1st Edition, contains 307 listings in this category; see also page xii.

CRANBERRY GLASS

Cranberry glass is a transparent glass that gets its name from the color which results when gold is added to the molten mixture. It is first amber in color, then reheated at a low temperature which develops the cranberry or ruby color.

It was during the last half of the 17th century that this glass first began to make its appearance, but was not until the last half of the 19th century that it was made by the glass factories in America. It was blown, pressed, molded or blown into molds and often decorated with gold or enamel. The less expensive type was made by substituting copper for the gold, but this gave the glass a bluish-purple tint.

Cranberry glass has been widely reproduced. The newer pieces are heavier and off color; the quality is not the same.

Ashtray, 8", round, cut to clear . . .	125.00
Basket, 7", hanging, rigaree for epergne	50.00
Box, 3" d, hinged, enamel floral decor	125.00
Bowls	
3⅛ x 6¼" d, applied orange crystal ruffles & rigaree, clear pedestal foot, clear berry pontil . . .	195.00
3¾ x 4" d, tricorn top, vaseline applied around top, vaseline scroll feet & berry pontil	175.00

6¼ x 3 x 9″, boat shape, clear ruffled pedestal foot, scalloped, white & multicolored leaves . . . **395.00**
Brandy Snifter, cut to clear **75.00**
Castor Set, 3 bottles, 7¼ x 4″ d, swirl pattern, open salt with glass spoon, pepper pot & mustard jar, SP holder **165.00**
Chimney Lamp, 10 x 3⅞″ d, base diameter 2½″ **95.00**
Compotes, 8¼ x 7″ w, cut to clear, leaf decoration, clear twist stems, pr **250.00**
Cologne Bottles
5 x 3½″ d, crystal cut glass, matching stopper, silver top rim **195.00**
7″, gold scrolls & small flowers, clear bubble matching stopper with same gold decor **125.00**
7 x 3¼″ d, gold scrolls, flowers, clear bubble matching stopper with gold decor **135.00**
Cracker Jar, silver cover, collar bail **295.00**
Creamer, 3⅝ x 2⅝″, clear applied handle, 2 small bands of white enamel dots, white flowers around center **69.00**
Cruets
7½ x 3″ d, clear applied handle & wafer foot, gold scrolls, foliage engraved around cruet & neck, clear bubble stopper, gold trim **165.00**
8 x 3½″ d, clear applied handle, bubble stopper, blue & cream enamel flower with gold leaves decor **165.00**
8⅜ x 3¾″, bulbous, 3-petal lipped top, clear applied handle, clear bubble stopper, paneled, blue enamel orchid, cream center, cream foliage **165.00**
Cups and Saucers
2¾ x 5½″, clear applied handle, gold cov, white enamel flowers, cranberry windows with gold foliage and white florals **135.00**
Clear handle with gold trim, gold bands with gold garlands, fine white enamel lining edges **80.00**
Condiment Set, 5⅛ x 5⅜″, 2 sq bottles with cut polished sides, open salt in center, SP holder . . . **165.00**
Decanters
8¼ x 4⅛″, bulbous, clear applied handle, clear bubble stopper, white enameled lilies of the valley, gold trim **145.00**
9″, flatten oval body, optic rib, clear applied handle, clear blown teardrop stopper **110.00**
Dish, 10¾ x 9″ d, leaf shape, Moser decor in gold **425.00**
Dresser Set, 3 pcs, 4 x 5″ d jar, two,

Fairy Lamp, overshot, matching base, 3⅜″h, $75.00.

2 x 4″ jars, cut and polished panels, SP lids **135.00**
Epergnes
9″, 4 lilies, ruffled **345.00**
15″, 3 lilies, round metal base with mirror **235.00**
Ewer, 4¾ x 3″, clear applied handle, all over tiny white enameled flowers, gold trim **95.00**
Finger Bowls
Diamond pat **65.00**
Grape cut **45.00**
Hat, 2⅝ x 4¼″ d, SP brim **110.00**
Jam Dishes, 8½″ h x 5¼ x 11″, two in SP holder, ruffled clear applied center rigaree trim **145.00**
Jars, covered
5 x 4¼″, bulbous, clear and cranberry knob with enameled & gold decor, jar and lid with light gray leaves and grapes detailed in gold **145.00**
7 x 3½″ d, inverted thumbprint, clear ribbed snail finial **110.00**
Lamps
12 x 6½″, hanging, hall, diamond quilted, sq, brass fixtures, chains & top **250.00**
13½ x 5″ d, peg, brass bases, gold decor, cranberry fonts and fluted shades, clear chimneys, pr **595.00**
Liquor Set, 7 pcs, octagon shaped bottles, gold band filigree, tall clear solid crystal stopper **625.00**
Mantel Set, 3 pcs, 8¾″ pr vases,

11⅜ x 4¾" cov urn, sanded gold leaves, band top & bottom, white enamel outlining, blue dots, white flowers 650.00

Muffineer, cov, white opalescent quilted pattern, ribbed, SP, orig lid 135.00

Perfume Atomizer, 6 x 2⅞", white enameled dot & fan decor, metal mounts 75.00

Perfume Bottles

4¾ x 2" d, clear stopper, gold thistles & leaves, white flowers with aqua centers 115.00

4¾ x 2⅝", white enamel lacy decor, clear ball stopper with lace decor 110.00

5½ x 2" d, gold bands, small blue & white flowers, gold ball stopper 118.00

Pickle Castor, 12 x 4¼", inverted thumbprint, white enamel daisies, yellow centers, green leaves, SP frame, 2 lid & tongs 350.00

Pitchers

3¾", blown, crackle, applied amber handle & rim 35.00

3⅞ x 2½" d, frosted, clear applied handle, round mouth, gold bands, leaves outlined in white, gold trim 85.00

4½ x 3¼", slight ribbing, round mouth, applied vaseline handle 75.00

5¼", melon shape, diamond pat . 50.00

6 x 4½" d, crackle, round mouth, clear applied handle 95.00

6⅝ x 4½", fluted top, white enamel dot floral decor, gold band & trim 135.00

9¼ x 4¾", tankard, overshot, round mouth, clear reeded applied handle 165.00

Plate, 7" 48.00

Punch Set, 11½, tray, bowl, ribbed, cov with green cut fauceted knob, 6 glasses, green stems and bases, matching ladle 295.00

Rose Bowl, 3 x 3½", 8 crimp top, blue & white enameled flowers, green leaves 118.00

Sugar Shaker, 5½", cut panels, SP top 65.00

Tumblers

4", juice, inverted thumbprint 32.00

Royal Ivy, frosted 75.00

Tumble-up, inverted thumbprint 55.00

Urn, 11¼ x 4½", crystal applied handle, thorny knob finial, gold enamel scrolls and small florals .. 265.00

Vases

2", squat, ribbed 58.00

3½", pinched top and bottom, painted bouquet of white flowers on front 35.00

5¼", sanded gold leaves outlined in white, blue dots, sanded gold collar bands, pr 165.00

6", deep etched grapes & leaves . 165.00

8¾ x 4", sanded gold leaves outlined in white enamel, blue dots, lacy white enamel branches, white florals, sanded gold top & bottom bands with white enamel 165.00

10½ x 5⅛", gold enameled scrolls and foliage, blue and white enameled flowers, pr ... 325.00

CROWN MILANO

Crown Milano is an American Art Glass produced by the Mt. Washington Glass Works at New Bedford, Mass. The original patent was issued in 1886 to Frederick Shirley and Albert Steffin.

Normally it is an opaque white satin glass finished with light beige or ivory color background embellished with fancy florals, decorations and elaborate heavy raised gold. When marked, pieces carry an entwined CM with crown in purple enamel on the base. Sometimes paper labels were used. The silver plated mounts often have MW impressed or the Pairpoint mark as they supplied the mountings.

Biscuit Jar, 5½"h, 6¼"d, MW. melon shape, SP top, crab in relief, coral ground, brown ground upper quarter, raised gold blossoms, leaves, foliage, sgd CM/Crown/521, MW on lid, $1,000.00.

Boxes

2½" h x 4" d, orange, red florals on a shiny finish, decor on lid only, sgnd 850.00

3¾" h x 5½" d, unusual decor of
8 storks in flight on the lid, sgnd ... **1,650.00**

Biscuit Jars, 5½" h

Blossomed outlined panel, boy
blowing bubbles, sgnd SP lid,
shiny finish **1,000.00**

Hobnail, jewel starfish decor, emb
SP lid, butterfly, lid marked MW,
slight damage to jewel decor . . **850.00**

Melon shaped body, unusual Royal Flemish-like pale brick-red
background, SP lid, bail, crab on
lid **1,000.00**

Ewers

8", applied dolphin-like handle,
heavy gold water lily, pale green
ground, sgnd **1,950.00**

9¾", applied twisted rope-like
handle, raised gold jewels over
an intricate enamel design on
cream color ground, sgnd **1,950.00**

13", applied twisted handle, raised
enamel geometric design,
enamel jewels, 8 colors,
unsgnd **1,950.00**

Muffineer, 4½" h, melon ribbed, SP
top, handle, colorful florals on a
pristine white background, sgnd . **685.00**

Sugar and Creamer, 3½" sugar
bowl, glass lid, 4" creamer, SP
handle, tiny floral bouquets enam-
el decor, sgnd **685.00**

Syrups, 5¾"

Excellent SP lid, handle, enamel
dots in a design similar to
Queen's Design **985.00**

Fair SP top, handle, raised gold
edged enamel thistles, incised
MW in lid **900.00**

Tray, 9½ x 7", shiny finish, rolled
over, serrated sides, raised gold,
enamel thistle decor, sgnd **1,150.00**

Vases

7", courting couple on obverse, a
country scene on reverse, 2 ap-
plied handles, sgnd **1,200.00**

8", sq sided, 2 applied handles,
oak leaves, acorns in raised
gold on ground of pastel decor,
orig paper label **1,400.00**

10", on shiny, 2 applied handles,
Guba ducks, sgnd with early
Albertibe/Crown Milano wreath,
gold borders are not raised and
decor in general is not as fine
as later items **1,650.00**

11", fancy roll-over top forms a diminutive handle, blooming or-
chids decor **1,350.00**

11", Hershey kiss shape, 6 geese
flying across a rayed sun **1,850.00**

12", slender neck encircled by
snake-like glass decor, pale

gold leaves, enameled, jeweled
blossoms **1,600.00**

13", tableau of 3 cherubs in a
playful encounter, most unusual,
rare **2,750.00**

CRUETS

**Cruets are small bottles used for storing or
serving vinegar and oil. Cruets were very
popular during the Victorian art glass era.
Practically every glass manufacturer produced cruets.**

**Also see specific wares such as Amberina,
Cranberry Glass, Satin Glass, Pattern Glass,
etc.**

**Cruet, 6¼"h, aqua with opal., apple
blossom mold, applied blue handle,
not original stopper.**

Amber

8 x 4", golden, 4 dimpled sides,
sapphire blue bubble stopper
and handle **110.00**

9½ x 3⅛", olive amber, slightly
flattened bulbous shape, 3 petal
top, amber bubble stopper, applied handle, white and rust
enameled flowers, green leaves,
gold trim **85.00**

Amberina, 7 x 3½", IVT, amber applied handle, amber cut faceted
stopper, 3 petal top **175.00**

Cobalt Blue Glass, 4 x 2⅛", gold trim ball stopper and handle, gold panels, lacy gold scrolls **95.00**

Cranberry, 8½ x 3¾", three petal top, bulbous, clear applied handle, blue, white, cream enamel flowers, leaves, clear bubble stopper **165.00**

Custard, Chrysanthemum Sprig . . .   **125.00**

Cut Glass, flashed fan, flairs and modified holstars, cut stopper with teardrop **115.00**

Green
5¾ x 3½", all over yellow florals, gold band, round mouth, applied green handle, green stopper with gold decor **125.00**

10¼ x 4", lime, bulbous, 3 petal top, clear bubble stopper and applied handle, lacy white enameled decor, gold trim **110.00**

10¾ x 3⅞", sq bulbous, lime, IVT, 3 petal top, clear bubble steeple stopper, clear reeded handle . .   **95.00**

Lavender Stained Glass, 8 x 3¼", clear applied handle and ball stopper, white enameled flowers and leaves, gold trim **88.00**

Pigeon Blood, enameled, matching stopper, gold "14" mk **100.00**

Ruby Glass, engraved and cut to clear, Vintage pattern, matching stopper, pontil **65.00**

Satin, Satina Swirl, orig stopper . . .   **135.00**

CUP PLATES

Many early cups and saucers were handleless, with deep saucers. The hot liquid was poured into the saucer and sipped from it. This necessitated another plate for the cup . . the cup plate.

The first cup plates made of pottery were of the Staffordshire variety. In the mid-1830's to 40's, glass cup plates were favored. Boston and Sandwich Glass Co. was one of the main contributors to the lacy glass type.

It is extremely difficult to find glass cup plates in outstanding (mint) condition. Collectors expect some marks of usage, such as slight rim roughness, minor chipping (best if under rim), and in rarer patterns a portion of a scallop missing. Prices are based on plates in "average" condition. The type of rim is given to aid positive identification.

The standard guide to glass cup plates is *American Cut Glass Plates* by Ruth Webb Lee and James H. Rose. All plates are illustrated. The numbers below are from this book. The book is difficult to find, even in libraries. Yet, it continues to be used by dealers and collectors.

Beware of reproductions.

GLASS

LR 1, brown, clear	**120.00**
LR 20, diamond with fans, clear . . .	**24.00**
LR 41A, opal, sheaf of wheat border	**75.00**
LR 46, amethyst, diamonds, early .	**350.00**
LR 55, clear, waffle	**45.00**
LR 61, opal, waffle center	**300.00**
LR 88, bluish opal, ringed center . .	**245.00**
LR 99, clear, acorn center	**45.00**
LR 99, pale green, acorn center . . .	**275.00**
LR 109, opal, octagonal scallops . .	**125.00**
LR 145C, clear, waffle with center device	**30.00**
LR 151, clear, bull's-eye edge	**35.00**
LR 154A, clear, star center	**25.00**
LR 205, clear, midwestern hairpin .	**225.00**
LR 242, blue, quatrafoil center	**325.00**
LR 266, clear, rosebud shoulder . .	**40.00**
LR 269A, peacock blue, rosebud shoulder	**400.00**
LR 277, peacock blue, diamonds . .	**400.00**
LR 299, clear, 40 serrations	**20.00**
LR 301B, clear, ten sided	**40.00**
LR 324, amethyst, starburst	**95.00**
LR 324, clear, starburst	**2.00**
LR 379, clear, daisy like center . . .	**15.00**
LR 455C, electric blue, hearts	**225.00**
LR 459B, opal, hearts	**85.00**
LR 459E, emerald green, hearts . . .	**375.00**
LR 459E, clear, hearts	**5.00**
LR 500, blue, starburst	**95.00**
LR 520A, blue, starburst	**120.00**
LR 524, peacock, starburst	**75.00**
LR 546, deep blue, starburst	**120.00**

GLASS, HISTORICAL

LR 562, clear, Clay	**350.00**
LR 563, clear, Clay	**5.00**

Staffordshire, Historical, Woodlands near Philadelphia, 3⅛", dark blue, Stubbs, $325.00.

LR 566A, clear, Clay	**40.00**
LR 576, sapphire blue, Victoria . . .	**400.00**
LR 585, clear, Ringgold	**750.00**
LR 601A, medium blue, round Consitution	**200.00**
LR 612A, clear, Consitution	**200.00**
LR 665, clear, small eagle	**100.00**
LR 680, sapphire blue, eagle	**300.00**

PORCELAIN OR POTTERY

Copper Lustre, floral decor	**45.00**
Gaudy Dutch, butterfly pattern	**600.00**
Spatterware, floral motif	**45.00**
Staffordshire, Historical	
3½", dark blue, Franklin Tomb (so called), unknown maker	**450.00**
3½", dark blue, Landing of Lafayette, Clews	**450.00**
3¾", medium blue, Boston State House, Wood	**250.00**
3¾", pink, Sandy Hill, Clews . . .	**65.00**
3¾", purple, Texas Campaign, Shaw	**200.00**
Staffordshire, Romantic	
Balantyre, 12 sided, J. Alcock . . .	**52.50**
Damascus, blue and white, Wm. Adams and Sons	**50.00**
Oriental, Ridgway	**50.00**

CUSTARD GLASS

Custard glass, as we know it, was made first in England in the early 1880s. Among the English makers who came to America, Harry Northwood brought custard glass to his factory in Indiana, Pa., in 1898. It has become very popular and collectible, the demand having increased the price, and it is still desirable to collectors today.

Two patterns which have been heavily reproduced are Argonaut Shell (Nautilus) and Grape and Cable (Grape with Thumbprints). This glass gets its "custard" color from uranium salts which were added to the molten glass.

Several patterns of custard glass were decorated with a nutmeg stain to highlight the design. Other patterns were hand decorated and many were highlighted with gold trim.

Banana Boat, oval	
Geneva, 11", ...	**145.00**
Grape & Cable, nutmeg stain . . .	**330.00**
Berry Bowls	
Beaded Circle, enamel florals, gold trim	**225.00**
Fluted Scrolls, ftd, gold decor . . .	**100.00**
Intaglio	**180.00**
Louis XV	**145.00**
Ring Band	**140.00**

Creamer, Argonaut Shell, 4¾", gold decor, $85.00.

Berry Sets	
Cherry and Scale, bowl and 5 sauces, nutmeg stain	**375.00**
Chrysanthemum Sprig, 5 pcs., bowl and 4 sauces	**600.00**
Diamond with Peg, bowl and 6 sauces, roses decor, gold trim .	**500.00**
Fluted Scrolls, bowl and 6 sauces, gold trim	**300.00**
Geneva, bowl and 6 sauces, oval shape, gold trim	**375.00**
Ring Band, 6 sauces, 7 pcs	**365.00**
Bowls	
Chrysanthemum Sprig, 10½" d . .	**245.00**
Grape & Cable, nutmeg stain, sgd. Northwood	**425.00**
Winged Scroll, 8½ d x 3½" h, no gold	**85.00**
Butters, covered	
Argonaut Shell	**260.00**
Cherry & Scale, nutmeg stain . . .	**230.00**
Chrysanthemum Sprig	**250.00**
Everglades	**300.00**
Geneva	**150.00**
Inverted Fan and Feather	**245.00**
Maple Leaf	**225.00**
Wild Bouquet	**350.00**
Cake Stand, Winged Scroll, ftd . . .	**325.00**
Celeries	
Chrysanthemum Sprig	**800.00**
Ring Band, roses, gold trim	**300.00**
Victoria (Tarentum's)	**225.00**
Winged Scroll	**275.00**
Compotes, Jelly	
*Argonaut Shell	**110.00**
Beaded Circle	**350.00**
Chrysanthemum Sprig, gold decor	**85.00**
Everglades, green and gold decor	**350.00**
Geneva	**95.00**
Intaglio, green	**95.00**
Inverted Fan and Feather	**175.00**
Ring Band, roses decor	**110.00**
Winged Scroll	**70.00**

Creamers

Geneva, red, green decor	65.00
Louis XV	70.00
Maple Leaf, gold decor	80.00
Ring Band, roses decor	78.00

Cruets

*Argonaut Shell, orig stopper	300.00
Beaded Circle, enamel florals, gold trim	650.00
Chrysanthemum Sprig, blue, gold trim, orig stopper	625.00
Fluted Scrolls	175.00
Maple Leaf, good decor, orig stopper	900.00
Ring Band, roses decor, gold trim	245.00
Winged Scroll (Ivorina Verde), undecorated	100.00

Goblets

Beaded Swag	65.00
Grape and Gothic Arch, nutmeg stain	60.00

Ice Cream Dish, Master, Peacock and Urn, nutmeg & stain | 195.00

Mugs

Diamond with Peg, souvenir, roses decor	40.00
Star and Punty, souv. Tilton, NH, gold trim, 3⅜"	35.00

Pitchers, water

Chrysanthemum Sprig	380.00
Diamond with Peg, tankard, with roses	150.00
Everglades, good decor	600.00
Fluted Scroll, ftd	190.00

Plates

*Grape and Cable, 7", nutmeg stain	35.00
Prayer Rug, 7½"	22.50

Powder Jars

Georgia Gem, light enamel sprig decor	45.00
*Grape and Cable, nutmeg stain	215.00
Winged Scroll (Ivorina Verde)	80.00

Punch Bowls

*Grape and Cable, nutmeg stain, 2 pieces	950.00
Inverted Fan and Feather	2,500.00

Punch Cups

Diamond with Peg, roses decor	42.50
Ring Band, roses, gold	35.00

Rose Bowl, Beaded Cable, good nutmeg | 75.00

Salt and Pepper Shakers

Beaded Circle, orig top, single	200.00
Chrysanthemum Sprig, good decor, pr	125.00
Everglades, good decor, orig tops, pr	250.00
Fluted Scrolls, orig tops, pr	115.00
Geneva, orig tops, pr	120.00
Intaglio, orig tops, pr	175.00
Inverted Fan and Feather, orig tops, pr	425.00
Louis XV, orig tops, pr	170.00
Maple Leaf, good decor, orig tops, pr	500.00
Ribbed Drape, roses decor, pr	200.00
Winged Scroll, decorated, pr	155.00

Sauces

Beaded Circle, roses decor	55.00
Chrysanthemum Sprig	60.00
Diamond with Peg, roses	53.00
Fan (Northwood's)	57.00
Fluted Scrolls	42.00
Geneva, oval	45.00
Geneva, round	36.00
Georgia Gem, regular	25.00
Inverted Fan and Feather	68.00
Louis XV, oval, 5", ftd	48.00
Maple Leaf, decorated	90.00
Ribbed Drape, decorated, roses	40.00
Ring Band, roses, gold trim	35.00

Shaving Mug, Georgia Gem | 25.00

Spooners

Beaded Circle	115.00
Beaded Swag	80.00
Cherry and Scale, nutmeg stain	90.00
Chrysanthemum Sprig	95.00
Diamond with Peg, roses, decor.	55.00
Everglades, green decor	120.00
Intaglio, gold and blue, decor	110.00
Louis XV	70.00
Ribbed Drape, roses decor	145.00
Ring Band, chrysanthemum decor	95.00

Sugars, covered

Beaded Circle	165.00
Cherry and Scale, nutmeg stain	125.00
Chrysanthemum Sprig, gold decor	165.00
Diamond with Peg, rose decor	145.00
Everglades, decorated	165.00
Fluted Scrolls	115.00
Grapes and Gothic Arch	95.00
Louis XV	100.00
Maple Leaf, gold decor	100.00
Winged Scroll	170.00

Syrups

Geneva, original lid	265.00
Winged Scroll, original lid	350.00

Table Set, cov butter, cov sugar, creamer, spooner

Intaglio, gold, blue decor	590.00
Ring Band, chrysanthemum decor, gold trim	410.00
Winged Scroll	430.00

Toothpicks

Diamond with Peg, roses, decor	50.00
Geneva	140.00
Georgia Gem, gold decor	75.00
Maple Leaf, decor	650.00
Ring Band, roses gold	80.00
Winged Scroll	100.00

Tumblers

Beaded Circle, gold and floral decor	75.00
Chrysanthemum Sprig	45.00
Diamond with Peg	42.50

Everglades, green and gold	110.00
Intaglio, gold, green	55.00
*Inverted Fan and Feather	80.00
Prayer Rug	80.00
Ring Band	60.00
Winged Scroll	90.00
Water Set, pitcher, tumblers	
Intaglio, 7 pc	650.00
Louis XV, 4 pc	285.00
Ring Band, roses decor, 5 pcs . .	425.00
Wine Glasses	
Diamond with Peg, 6 sided, ftd,	
Souv. Straton, ME	32.00
Honeycomb	60.00

CUT GLASS, AMERICAN

Glass is cut by the process of grinding decoration into the glass by means of abrasive-carrying metal wheels or stone cutting wheels. A very ancient craft, it was revived in 1600 by Bohemians and eventually spread through Europe, Great Britain and to America.

American cut glass came of age at the Centennial Exposition in 1876 and the World Columbian Exposition in 1893. The American public recognized American cut glass to be exceptional in quality and workmanship. Our country's most significant output of this high quality glass occurred from 1880–1917, a period which has come to be known as the "Brilliant Period."

Early Brilliant cut glass on blown blanks and wood polished will not be signed. Yet, the quality of the product is excellent; and, these pieces often won awards at exhibitions and fairs.

About the 1890s some companies began adding an acid etched "signature" to their glass. This "signature" may be the actual company name or its logo or chosen symbol. Today, signed pieces can command a premium over an unsigned piece since the signature establishes an origin.

However, caution should be exercised in regard to signature identification. Objects with forged signatures have been in existence for some time. To check for authenticity, run your finger tip or finger nail lightly over the area with the signature. As a general rule, a genuine signature cannot be felt; a forged signature exhibits a raised surface.

Collectors also should be aware that many companies never used the acid etched signature on the glass and may or may not have affixed paper labels to the items originally. For example, Dorflinger made excellent quality products, but never acid stamped their glass. A cut glass object with some silver decoration may have the Dorflinger name on the silver.

Finally, since the quality of cut glass varied from company to company, a signed piece from one company may be much finer quality than a signed piece from another company. In contrast, an unsigned piece might be of exceptional quality, especially if from the Brilliant period, compared to a poorer quality signed piece. All of these factors must be kept in mind and weighed against one another when determining value.

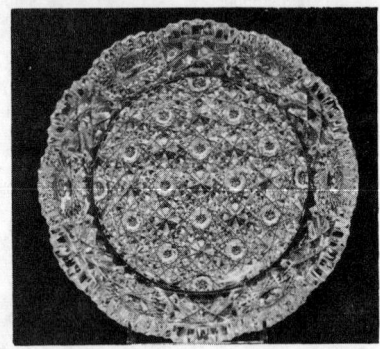

Bowl, 9″, "Royal," Hunt, $275.00.

Baskets	
5″ h x 8″ d, ovals of hobstars, hobnail, and fan, rope twist handle	385.00
13″ h, hobstars, strawberry diamond, and fans, triple notched handle, sgd Libbey	850.00
Bells	
Dinner size, blown blank, Brilliant period cuttings	275.00
4½″ h, "Monarch," Hoare	235.00
Boat, 9½ x 3¾″, geometric and floral, sgd Clark	265.00
Bottles	
Whiskey, Brilliant period cuttings, sgd Hoare	450.00
Worcester, 6¼″ h, "Creswick," Egginton	95.00
Bowls	
7″, "Royal," Hunt	260.00
8″, "Columbia," square shape, Blackmere	500.00
8″, "Iris," sgd Hawkes Gravic	450.00
8″ d, 4″ h, "Harvard," sgd Hoare	295.00
8 x 11½″, oval, "Star and Feather" variation, sgd Libbey	300.00
9″ d, 3¾″ h, "Joan," Straus	200.00
9″, "Wisteria," sgd Libbey	700.00
10″, "Filigree," Egginton	400.00
10″, low bowl, "Gladys," sgd Hawkes	310.00

10", low bowl, "Lansing," Ander-
son 300.00

Boxes

6½ x 6½ x 2", heart shaped, "Silver Threads," sgd Sinclaire . . . 600.00

7 x 4¾ x 4", footed jewelry, "Harvard," rayed base 695.00

8" d, 4" h, round hinged jewelry,
hobstars and fans on top,
hobstars around base 650.00

Butters, covered

Cut all over in hobstars, strawberry diamonds, fans and pyr.
stars, blown blank 385.00

"Electric," small quarter pounder
size with two matching butter
pats, Bergen 495.00

"Shield" pattern, 7½" d under-
plate 250.00

Butter Pats

3" d, diamond and fans, rayed
centers 27.50

Set of 6, sgd Hawkes 150.00

Cake Stands

8" d, "Rosemere," sgd Tuthill . . . 600.00

9" d, 7" h, 6½" d base, hobstars
and fans with cross-hatched ve-
sicas, Dorflinger 1,100.00

10" d, 7" h, "Vintage," sgd
Sinclaire, Gorham Sterling Silver
base 600.00

Candlesticks, pair

8", hobstars, miters, and cane . . . 625.00

10", hobstars, beading, and
flashed fans, hollow 650.00

13½" h, silver thread-type cut-
tings, sgd Hawkes 350.00

Candlesticks, single

8½", flowers and leaves, hollow
stem and base 65.00

12", intaglio "Vintage" on base
and stem 150.00

12", sgd Hawkes 160.00

Green cut to clear, scalloped top
and petticoat base, hobstars
and strawberry diamonds 625.00

Chamberstick, 7" d base, 3" h, 24
point hobstar base 600.00

Carafes

"Berkshire," Bergen, beaded Ster-
ling Silver top 295.00

"Design #17," Elmira, well cut . . 295.00

"Ivy," Bergen 120.00

"Louisville," Empire 95.00

"Nevada," Pairpoint 175.00

"Oval & Split," 32 point star base,
Dorflinger, pair 200.00

"Venetian," Hawkes 210.00

Casserole, covered, intaglio fish design, matching underplate, sgd
Hawkes, rare 975.00

Celeries

"Bakers' Gothic," Clark 350.00

"Florence," Meriden 135.00

Hobstars (large), cane, and hobnail fans, rayed base, vase
shape, 4½" d, 6½" h 185.00

"Royal," 11½ x 5½", sgd Hunt . . 135.00

"Triple Square," 12 x 4¼", sgd
Clark 175.00

Cheeses, covered

8½" d underplate, 7" h, center hobstar with hobstar chain around 625.00

9" d underplate, 7" h, dome, cane
and fans in crossed ovals 450.00

9" d underplate, "Shield" pattern . 300.00

9½" d underplate, 10" h, 8" d
dome, "Strawberry Diamond,"
Mount Washington 850.00

Clocks, 5½" h, 4 x 3" base, boudoir
size

Flowers and leaves 150.00

Flowers, leaves and cane 250.00

Colognes

6¼" h, "Venetian," sgd Hawkes . 395.00

7½" h, 6½" d, heavy braided
twisted stem, sgd Hawkes 175.00

"Russian and Clear Panels," pair,
fine 125.00

Compotes

8" d, 7" w, "Colonna," sgd Libbey 280.00

8" h, "Silver Threads," sgd Sin-
clair, pair 550.00

12" h, 6½" d, pinwheel, beading
and hobstars, teardrop stem,
hobstar base, sgd Clark, pair . . 750.00

Compotes, covered

10½", teardrop stem, star base . . 1,000.00

Hobstar chain and fans, sgd
Hawkes on top and base 2,900.00

Champagne Cooler, 9" d, 9½" h,
peg handles, 12 lbs weight 3,050.00

Cornucopia, 10" h, 24 point hobstar
base, rare 1,700.00

Cruets

Hobstars, strawberry diamonds
and fans, honeycomb handle,
tri-pour spout, 6½"h 125.00

Intaglio floral garlands, trumpet
shape, Sterling Silver stopper,
sgd Hawkes 75.00

"Prism Special," squat oil, Eggin-
ton 55.00

"Russian," matching cut stopper . 375.00

Decanters

"Basketweave," honeycomb neck,
notched handle, 13" h 700.00

"Brazilian," bulbous, gooseneck,
Hawkes 575.00

"Corinthian," handled, Libbey . . . 325.00

"Delft," Hoare, 12½" h 395.00

Hobstars and cane bands, teardrop notched prism stopper, ex-
tra large whiskey, 14½" h 550.00

Snowflakes and fans, citron cut to
clear, pedestal, notched neck,

teardrop stopper pattern cut, 15" h **400.00**

Bulbous shape, sgd Taylor Bros. . **500.00**

Dishes

4½", "Alhambra," Sterling Silver rim, Wilcox **325.00**

5½", heart shaped **60.00**

6¼", shell shaped, hobstars, sgd Hawkes **90.00**

6½", "Russian" with cranberry buttons, Mount Washington ... **275.00**

6½", stickdish, sgd Libbey **450.00**

7½", heart shaped, "Bakers' Gothic," Clark **295.00**

8", "Crossed Bars," sgd Libbey .. **175.00**

9 x 5½ x 2", "Venetian," Hawkes **495.00**

Cavier, stemmed, two handled ... **600.00**

Club shaped, hobstars, fans, and crossed bars of beading **100.00**

Three sections, deep cross cut diamond **175.00**

Epergne, 11" h, single vase, pin-wheel major motif **950.00**

Ferners

Brilliant period cuttings, sgd Straus **175.00**

Hobstars all over **145.00**

Finger Bowls

"Renaissance," underplate, Dorf-linger, set **55.00**

"Renaissance," blue cut to clear . **42.00**

"Russian," clear buttons, 5¼" d, 2¾" h **150.00**

Flasks

"Russian," sharp cuts, extra large, Gorham Sterling Silver base and hinged cap **450.00**

"Wheat" and tiny sharp Russian, Hoare, Sterling Silver cap by Gorham **285.00**

Flower Centers

8" d, 6½" h, "Bengal and En-graved," Sinclaire **695.00**

10" d, body cut in hobstars, straw-berry diamonds, fields and beading, hobstar base **500.00**

10" d, 8½" h, "Russian" with strawberry diamonds, hobstar base **835.00**

Hair Receivers

Harvard variation and notched prisms, Art Nouveau floral silverplate top **95.00**

"Russian" **125.00**

Humidor, 6" d, 9" h, pinwheels, ver-tical notched prisms, fan, and hob-nail, cut cover, rayed base **725.00**

Ice Cream Sets

Fan and strawberry diamonds filled areas bounded by beaded double miters, rectangular shape master plate, 8 individual plates, Dorflinger **1,595.00**

"Jewel," master tray (17¾ x

10¼") and 10 round (6" d) plates, Libbey **1,100.00**

Inkwells

Round, 4" d, clear glass with all over controlled bubbles, Sterling Silver cap by Pairpoint **195.00**

Square, 2", 3" h, notched prims, Sterling Silver hinged top with heavy beading and large mono-gram **115.00**

Jars

Cigar, 5¼" d, 8½" h including matching hollow stopper, hob-stars, fans and double cross cut diamond, sgd Hawkes **975.00**

Cookie, covered, 5½" d, 8½" h, hobstars, sgd Hawkes **725.00**

Dresser, Art Nouveau repousse Sterling Silver cover, dated 1903 **70.00**

Jam, hobstars in checkerboard design, wood polished, Sterling Silver top and long spoon **230.00**

Pill, 4½" h, pinwheel, fluted and notched neck, rayed base, hol-low stopper **125.00**

Powder, hobstars, fans and cross cut diamond, star base, Sterling Silver cover with heavy floral design **115.00**

Juice Glasses

Florence stars, single stars, and checkered diamonds, 3½" h, set of 6 .... **160.00**

"Louis XIV" **45.00**

"Strawberry Diamond and Star," by Clark **35.00**

Jugs

7" h, 6" d, "Glenwood," strawber-ry diamond cut handle, ring cut neck, Bergen **825.00**

7¾" h, handled, flutes, fans, blazing and strawberry diamond, pattern cut teardrop stopper, sgd Hawkes **550.00**

11" h, handled, "Basketweave," Sterling Silver neck, handle and stopper, Hawkes **850.00**

Rum, handled, pulled spout with stopper, sgd Libbey **1,400.00**

Knife Rests

Individual

4" l, red color **95.00**

Floral and threading cut body, ends cut and beveled, pair .. **60.00**

Master

5½" l, notched prism ball ends **85.00**

Hobstars and tiny hobnail, com-pletely cut **110.00**

Ladles

14", "Venetian," shell shaped silverplated bowl by Gorham, teardrop handle, sgd Hawkes .. **595.00**

14½", double spout, large "Har-

vard" and teardrop cut handle,
sgd Bergen 350.00

Lamps

13½", boudoir, mushroom dome,
wheel cut flowers with polished
leaves, matching baluster and
domed base 450.00

18", mushroom shade, strawberry
and hobstar cut base 2,000.00

19", 8" d (inside rim) one light
mushroom shade, intaglio cut
floral & leaf design with hobstar
chain borders 1,600.00

21", 15" d (inside rim) two light
mushroom shade, pinwheel . . . 2,250.00

28", 12" d two light shade, all
hobstars and "Harvard" 3,500.00

29", strawberry dome, geometric
pattern, trumpet shaped base . . 5,000.00

29", strawberry dome, "Harvard"
and intaglio flowers, pair 9,000.00

"Harvard," three arm with trumpet
vase center, Bergen, one shade
damaged 1,800.00

Loving Cups

4¾", three handled, hobstars and
prisms, St. Louis diamond handles, beaded Sterling Silver top 325.00

6¾", three handled, hobstars,
nailhead diamond, fans, and
notched handles, Libbey blank . 650.00

7¾", three handled, "Middlesex,"
cross cut diamond handles, 24
point hobstar base, Hawkes . . . 900.00

Mayonnaise Sets

"Basket," bowl and underplate,
sgd Fry 210.00

Hobstars, all over 180.00

"New Brilliant," pedestal, hobstar
foot, sgd Libbey with sword . . . 320.00

Miniatures

2½", rose bowl, cross cut
diamond fields and bull's-eyes . 115.00

3" h, 3½" w, flower center,
hobstars, strawberry diamond,
and fan, rayed base 175.00

3", loving cup, three handled,
notched prism, repousse Ster-
ling Silver top 325.00

3", spade, hobstars, sgd Hawkes 70.00

4¾" h, 3" d, pitcher, hobstars,
block diamond and notched
prism, notch cut handle, rayed
base 185.00

Ice Tub, 5" d, 3¼" h at handles,
and matching underplate, 7" d,
hobstars, fans, strawberry
diamond and beading 250.00

Muffineer, prisms, notch cut handle,
repousse Sterling Silver lid 265.00

Mustards, covered

"Monarch," round, lid cut in large
hobstars, Hoare 135.00

Notched prism and nailhead
diamond, 4" h 65.00

Napkin Rings

Cut, all over, sgd with maple leaf . 30.00

Cut in hobstars, diamond and fan,
2¼" w 90.00

"Harvard," dinner size 75.00

4½" d, sgd Clark 55.00

Nappies

5", "Alex," sgd Fry 80.00

6", "Argand," handled, Hoare . . . 75.00

6", flashed stars and hobstars,
sgd Fry 70.00

7", "Heart," round, sgd Libbey . . 125.00

11", "Royal," two cut handles,
Hunt 190.00

Hobstars, cane, and beading, four
sections, two handles 175.00

Perfumes

Block Diamond pattern, cranberry
cut to clear, teardrop stopper . . 125.00

Cane, lay down, blue cut to clear,
Gorham Sterling Silver top 285.00

"Chrysanthemum," 14K gold stoppers, sgn Hawkes Gravic,
pair 850.00

Pitchers

Champagne, 11¼" h, 5" d, "Split
Vesica and Bead," sgd Straus . 425.00

Cider, 6½" h, hobstars and cane,
hobstar base, sgd Libbey 500.00

Milk, triple notched handle, 24
point hobstar base 350.00

Syrup, 5" h, hobstars, nailhead,
and fan, silverplated top and
handle 100.00

Tankards

"Heart," 10" h, probably P & B 395.00

"Triple Square," sgd Clark 385.00

"Heart," pedestal 2,000.00

"Lotus," bulbous, Egginton 325.00

15" h, pedestal 1,200.00

Plates

6⅞", "Grecian," Hawkes 375.00

7", tiny "Russian" cut center with
engraved wreath and floral bor-
der, sgd Sinclaire 375.00

10", "Primrose Comet," Tuthill . . 1,000.00

12", "Colonna," sgd Libbey 325.00

Punch Bowls

One Piece

Floral and Swag pattern, 14" d
bowl, 9 matching cups, green
cut and engraved to clear,
Hawkes, c1920 . . . . 2,700.00

"Parisian," 14" d, 7" h, Dorf-
linger 850.00

Two Piece

Hobstars, cane, strawberry diamond and stars, 11" d bowl,
48 point hobstar base 900.00

"Keystone," 12" d bowl, 10
matching cups 1,350.00

"Wheat," 12" d bowl on matching tray, curved in rim, Hoare **3,500.00**

Punch Cups
Set of 2, "Mary," Libbey **50.00**
Set of 6, "Double Lozenge" **120.00**
Set of 7, "Harvard," pedestal ... **280.00**
Set of 8, "Venetian," Hawkes ... **600.00**

Relish, 8" l, pinwheels at ends, cross hatching on base, sgd Clark **80.00**

Ring Tree, 3½ x 4", strawberry diamond design, cranberry cut to clear **115.00**

Rose Bowls
6½" d, 6" h, "Parisian," hobstar base, Dorflinger **475.00**
7" d, "Harvard," Libbey **250.00**
6½" h, "Genoa," Clark **560.00**

Salad Set, Gorham silver, Dorflinger cut glass handles **395.00**

Salts (Salt dips)
2", sgd Fry **25.00**
Master
Paperweight type, 3½" d **95.00**
"Russian," thick blank, scalloped top **85.00**
Pedestal, all over cut, sgd Libbey **110.00**

Salt and Pepper Shaker Sets
Cross cut diamond, 5½" h, pedestal, Sterling Silver tops and bases, sgd Hawkes **145.00**
Cut glass bodies, Sterling Silver Tops **38.00**

Spooners
Hobstars, fans, single stars and cross hatching, star base, two handles **145.00**
Strawberry diamond and fan, 4½" h **75.00**

String Holder, "Brunswick" variation, Gorham Sterling Silver top **195.00**

Stemware
Champagnes
Set of 2, "Encore," teardrop stems with faceted knob, hobstar base, Straus **195.00**
Set of 2, "Russian," starred buttons, each **145.00**
Set of 6, "Diamond and Star," 5" h, hollow stem, hobstar foot, Mount Washington **485.00**
Cordials
Single, "Middlesex," green, cut to clear, Dorflinger **225.00**
Set of 6, hobstars and fans, plain stem, rayed base, sgd Hawkes **300.00**
Set of 7, "Plymouth," Meriden . **295.00**
Goblets
Set of 6, roses and leaves engraved, green cut and engraved to clear, paneled stem, clear base with engraving, tall **475.00**

Set of 6, "Russian," starred buttons, each **165.00**
Set of 10, "Renaissance," Dorflinger, each **45.00**

Parfait, "Cane," 7" h **70.00**

Rhine Wines
7½", "Arcadia," cobalt cut to clear **325.00**
7½", "Arcadia," green cut to clear **325.00**
8½", ruby cut to clear, tulip shaped bowl, double teardrop stem, hobstar cut foot with scalloping **370.00**

Sherberts
Set of 2, "Kalana Lily," Dorflinger, each **75.00**
Set of 6, hobstars and curved mitres, hobstar base, each .. **80.00**

Sherries
Set of 4, "Greek Key and Laurel," 4¼" h **190.00**
Set of 12, "Renaissance," Dorflinger, each **45.00**

Wines
Single, cranberry cut to clear, hobstar base **275.00**
Set of 2, "Russian," starred buttons, each **125.00**
Set of 4, hobstars, strawberry diamond, triple split, and fans, 4¼" h, sgd Maple City **175.00**
Set of 9, "Ithaca," 4½" h, Huntley **540.00**

Sugar and Creamer Sets
Hobstars and fans, knobbed stem with teardrop, 6" h on pedestal **2,500.00**
"Lovebirds," sdg Libbey **375.00**
"Pinwheel," sgd Sinclaire **90.00**
"Rosaceae" with hobstars, ovoid, extra long, sgd Tuthill **375.00**
"Russian" panels, creamer (3½" d; 3¼" h), sugar (4¼" d; 3" h), sgd Egginton **195.00**
Shagbark Flower motif, notched handles, sgd Hoare **130.00**
"Strawberry," 16 point hobstar base, sgd Hawkes Gravic **350.00**
"Wheeler," Mount Washington .. **130.00**

Sugar Shakers
"Alhambra," Sterling Silver top .. **275.00**
Florence stars, single stars, and block and fan, rayed base, 3" d, 3¾" h, Sterling Silver chased top and rim **175.00**

Teapot, copper wheel engraved, sgd Hawkes **850.00**

Toothbrush Holder, 7¼" h, fluted sides, Sterling Silver top **95.00**

Toothpick Holders
"Harvard," pedestal **135.00**
"Lapidary," sgd Egginton **60.00**
Pedestal, engraved, sgd Tuthill .. **200.00**

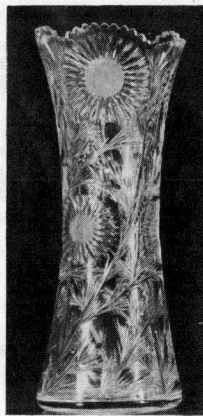

Vase, 12″, Sunflower, $425.00.

Trays
10″ d, "Brunswick," sgd Hawkes .	475.00
10″ d, "Queens," sgd Hawkes . .	1,100.00
10 x 17½″, brilliant cutting, sgd Clark	800.00
11 x 6½″, "Pansy with Russian Border," Tuthill	2,200.00
12″, "Middlesex," extra heavy blank, Dorflinger	550.00
12″, "Senora," sgd Libbey	425.00
14 x 7½″, "Atlantic," sgd Fry . . .	185.00
14¾″, woodland scene with moose wading across a river, acorn border, sgd Sinclaire . . .	1,500.00

Tumblers
Single
"Brunswick," sgd Hawkes	70.00
Feathers, hobstars, and fans, rayed base, sgd Libbey	75.00
"Rosemere," sgd Tuthill	60.00
"Ulysses," sgd Straus	55.00
Signed Libbey	45.00
Set of 2, "Russian," each	92.00

Set of 4
"Drape," sgd Libbey, each	300.00
"Jubilee," whiskey size, sgd Hawkes	80.00
"Middlesex," sgd Hawkes	135.00

Vases
4½″, bud, strawberry diamond . .	80.00
8″, "Panel," Hawkes	1,800.00
10″, "Vintage with Hobstar Chain," square sided, 4″ d, sgd Tuthill	575.00
12″, hobstar, fan, strawberry, and zipper, rayed base, sgd Libbey .	325.00
12″, "Navarre," hobstar base, Hawkes	595.00

14″, trumpet shape	
"Harvard," green cut to clear, Libbey	725.00
"Queens," faceted knob, hobstar base, sgd Hawkes	900.00
"Teutonic," Hawkes	375.00
16″, "Lotus," solid green on standard, Egginton	2,000.00

Water Sets
"Harvard and Floral," pitcher and 6 tumblers	300.00
Zipper and Hobstars, pitcher and 4 tumblers, sgd Libbey	400.00
Whiskey Set, 14″ h pedestal decanter and 4 matching whiskey tumblers, "Double Lozenge," orig teardrop stopper cut in pattern . .	650.00

CUT VELVET

Cut Velvet is a satin finished art glass made with two layers of glass—the outer layer in color with a white liner. The ribbed or diamond shaped designs were cut in high relief, exposing the white interior. The name Cut Velvet is a descriptive name given to this glass because of its velvet like appearance. It was a product of several glass manufacturers in the Victorian era, 1870–1900.

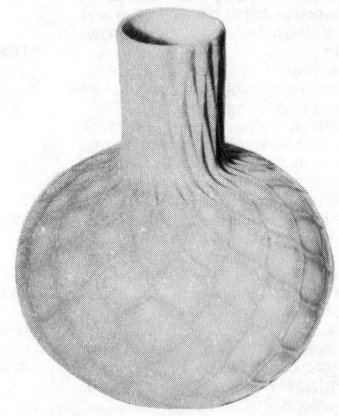

Vase, 6″ h bottle neck, blue, $225.00.

Biscuit Jar, pink, silver plated mountings	230.00
Cruet, blue, DQ	295.00
Ewer, 4⅝″, rose, DQ	200.00
Jar, jam, 4⅛″, rose, DQ	295.00

Rose Bowls
3¼", blue, DQ, 4 crimp top	175.00
4", pink, DQ	180.00

Vases
6", stick, blue	120.00
6¼", bulbous base, blue, DQ ...	100.00
6¾", ruffled, pink, DQ	195.00
7½", pink, ribbed	225.00
9", ruffled, blue, DQ	235.00
10", ruffled, blue, DQ	275.00

CZECHOSLOVAKIAN ITEMS

Objects marked "Made in Czechoslovakia" were produced after 1918, when the country claimed its independence from Austria Hungary. The people became more cosmopolitan, liberating and expanding their scope of life. They approached the arts on the principle "art for art's sake." Their porcelains, pottery and glassware reflect many influences. A specific manufacturer's mark may be identified as being much earlier than 1918 but indicates that the factory existed in the Bohemian or the Austrian-Hungarian Empire period.

Baby Dish, 5", rolled edge, 2 children with animals inside	25.00
Basket, 9 x 8¼", Art Deco, woman on front, building and steeples on reverse, winged handles, blue and red enameled leaves, deep cobalt rim	170.00
Bowl with underplate, 5⅛" bowl, 6½" plate, ruby cut to clear, Vintage pattern, sgnd.	25.00
Bathroom Bottle Set, 14 pcs, black glass, enameled, castle scene, ground stoppers with matching numbers on lids and bottles, pontil on bottoms, mkd, c1920	130.00
Demitasse, scenic cup, gold inside .	19.00
Dinnerware, white, shaped gilt borders with swags of small flowers centering a spray of German flowers, Epiag, 31 pcs	225.00
Figure, Group of Charioteers, 16 x 19½" 1, porcelain, glazed in tones of cream and olive, gilt highlights, c1925	190.00
Fruit Bowls, set of 3, cut glass, diamond, fruit and leaves	250.00
Inkwell, double, 24K gold decor ...	95.00
Lamp, 12", reverse painted, scenic	180.00
Loving Cup, 3 handled, Art Deco, royal blue, portrait of woman in reserves, dark cobalt handles, mkd	155.00
Perfume Bottle, 3¼", sgnd	45.00
Pitcher, 7", light blue, cobalt handle	37.00
Plate, dessert, 7½", cut glass, diamond, fruit and leaves	20.00

Mug, shaving, courting couple, iridescent background, Gloria/Karlovarsky/Kvalitnil/Porculan, $22.50.

Powder Box, cov, 4 x 3½", cut glass, mkd	50.00

Vases
5", lime green, 3 cobalt blue handles	65.00
7", pink, cased yellow, purple and red overlay	85.00
7½", fan shape, mottled red, yellow	85.00
8½", bud, blue, enameled flowers	37.00
11½", bulbous, red cased, sgnd .	95.00

DAGUERREOTYPES

The earliest attempts to project images involved the camera obscura, a device known to the Greeks and Romans. The Scientific Revolution of the 17th Century, especially in chemistry, opened the way to capturing images on plate and film.

In 1839, J. M. Daguerre of France patented a process consisting of covering a copper plate with silver salts, sandwiching the plate between glass for protection and exposing the plate to light and mercury vapors to imprint the image. The process produced Daguerreotypes.

Fox Talbot of Britain patented the method for making paper negatives and prints (calotypes) in 1841. Frederick Scott Archer introduced the wet collodian process in 1851. Dr. Maddox developed dry plates in 1871. When George Eastman produced roll film in 1888, the photographic industry reached maturity.

Ambrotypes and tin types are contemporaries of the daguerreotype. Ambrotypes are photographs made on glass by backing a thin negative with a black surface. Tintypes, or ferreotypes, are positive photographs made on a thin iron plate having a darkened surface.

Daguerreotypes were generally housed in embossed gutta percha cases padded and lined with fabric and ornamented with metal mounts. These cases have some collecting value independent of the prints they house.

The subject matter has the greatest effect on value. Next comes the photographer, if known, followed by condition, size, and finally, style of case. The following prices are guidelines. If a daguerreotype has that extra something, e.g., a pet with the child, value should be increased.

Prices held firm during 1981 and 1982, resisting the decline occurring elsewhere in the market place.

Small = 1⅝ x 2⅛" to 2 x 2½"
Medium = 2⅛ x 3¼" to 3¼ x 4¼"
Large = 4¼ x 6½" to 6½ x 8½"

Photographer Identified—Add 20 to 40%

See *Warman's Americana & Collectibles* for listings of Cartes De Visite and Cabinet Cards.

Ambrotype, gutta percha case, velvet lined, 6¼ x 5¼", Pat. July, 1854, $100.00.

Building or Outdoor Scene
Small	40.00
Medium	50.00
Large	65.00

Boy or Girl
Small	10.00
Medium	15.00
Large	20.00

Coffin or Funerary
Child	35.00
Adult	45.00

Man or Woman
Small	15.00
Medium	25.00
Large	35.00

Soldier, Confederate
Small	45.00
Medium	60.00
Large	75.00

Soldier, Union
Small	30.00
Medium	45.00
Large	60.00

Soldier, other
Small	20.00
Medium	25.00
Large	30.00

Tradesman with tools
Small	50.00
Medium	75.00
Large	100.00

CASES

Angel with trumpet	60.00
Cupid and Wounded Stag, gutta-percha	65.00
Fireman saving child	50.00
Indian chief	55.00
Scrolled, Littlefield and Parsons, gutta-percha	30.00

DAVENPORT CHINA

John Davenport opened a pottery in Longport, Staffordshire, England in 1793. His ware was of high quality, light-weight, cream colored, with a beautiful velvety texture. The firm made soft-paste (Old Blue), lustre trimmed ware, pink lustre with black transfer and there have been pieces of Gaudy Dutch and Spatter ware found with the Davenport mark. Later on he became one of the best makers of ironstone and early flowing blue. His famous "Cyprus" pattern in mulberry became very popular and is highly collectible today. The factory was carried on by his heirs until it was closed in 1886.

Bowls
9¼", fruit, hp roses, gold trim, ftd, c1860	125.00
13", 4½" deep, English scene, floral border, "Old Blue"	150.00
Compote, 8½ x 11" w, scenic, hp	200.00
Cup Plate, light blue, pagoda decor	30.00

Cups and Saucers
Cyprus, mulberry, handleless	50.00
Rose, gold scrolling, c1835	60.00

Platter, 10⅜ x 13⅝″, Flowing blue, marked Amoy, pattern name incised anchor mark, $165.00.

Dessert Set, compote, 8–9″ plates, central gold flower, maroon and gold border, c1840, 9 pcs	365.00
Dish, in plated holder, Imari colors, c1875	85.00
Gravy Boat, blue and white flowers, bird band	95.00
Pitchers	
Squat, gold trim and monogram, c1810	225.00
6″, tan, transfer crack marks, serpent handle	55.00
6¾″, blue, pink floral decor, c1840	95.00
Plates	
8″ octagonal, floral decor, gold rim	40.00
9″, clematis pat., scalloped edge, c1848	58.00
9″ scenic, castle and mountain, hp	60.00
10½″, Cyprus, mulberry	55.00
Platters	
9 x 12½″, Cyprus , mulberry	95.00
9 x 10½″, Blue Willow, c1810 . .	75.00
Sugar, cov, Cyprus, mulberry, shell handles, pagoda shape	150.00
Tazza, 9½″, octagonal, Imari pat, ftd, c1860	110.00
Tea Set, teapot, creamer and ftd sugar, blue and white, mkd Davenport Goddin No 1194, c1880 . .	98.00
Tureen, castle scene, in blue, shell handles, early	125.00
Vase, 6″, enameled flowers and leaves, lion's heads in relief on shoulder, gold feet, c1860	275.00
Vegetable Dish, cov, brown transfer, scenic, c1830	150.00
Wash Bowl, pitcher, toothbrush holder, soap dish with drain, Cyprus, mulberry, set	600.00

DECOYS

Carved wooden decoys, used to lure ducks and geese to the hunter, have in the past several years become widely recognized as an indigenous American folk art form. Demand for them has increased dramatically as have prices.

Many decoys are from the 1880–1930 period when commercial gunners commonly hunted over rigs of several hundred decoys. Many other fine carvers also worked through the 1930s and 1940s.

The value of a decoy is based on several factors: (1) the fame of the carver, (2) the quality of the carving, (3) the species of wild fowl — the most desirable are herons, swans, mergansers, shorebirds, (4) the condition of the original paint (o.p.)

The inexperienced collector should be aware of several facts. The age of a decoy, per se, is usually of no importance in determining value. Since very few decoys were ever signed, it will be quite difficult to attribute most decoys to known carvers. Anyone who has not examined a known carver's work will be hardpressed to determine if the paint on one of his decoys is indeed original.

Repainting severely decreases a decoy's value. In addition, there are many fakes and reproductions on the market and even experienced collectors are occasionally fooled.

Richard A. Bourne Co., Inc., Haynnis, Massachuetts, is one of the leading auctioneers of decoys. At the sale on March 8, 1983, of the Roy Bull Decoy Collection, a hollow carved Brant decoy by Nathan Cobb, Cobb Island, Virginia, brought $28,000.00.

Black Ducks	
Conklin, Hurley, Barnegat Bay, NJ, carved tail and wing tips, branded "H. Conklin" on bottom, o.p., excellent	180.00
Fitzpatrick, Tom, Delanco, NJ, attributed to, hollow carved, excellent scratch feather paint, o.p., minimal wear	325.00
Hancock, Miles, Chincoteague, VA, o.p., very little wear	175.00
Updike, John, Green Bank or Mullica, NJ, hollow carved, o.p., av. wear	160.00
Black-bellied Plover, Cobb Island, unknown carver, letter "A" on bottom, o.p., av. wear, bill replaced .	450.00
Bluebill Drakes	
Ayres, A. Ferman, Brockville, Ontario, o.p., excellent	140.00
Mason's Decoy Factory, Detroit, MI, Standard Grade, glass eyes, o.p., age split in bottom	230.00
Nicholl, David W., Smith's Falls,	

Ontario, carved raised wing tips,
o.p. 350.00

Bluebill Hens

Parker, J., Parkertown, NJ, hollow
carved, o.p., very slight wear .. 175.00

Unknown maker, Canada, carved
feathers and wing tips, o.p., little
wear 100.00

Blue-winged Teal Drake, Kerr, Bob,
Smith Falls, Ontario, carved raised
wing tips, o.p., excellent 225.00

Brants

Conklin, Hurley, Manahawkin, NJ,
hollow carved, o.p., excellent . 400.00

Cranmer, Bill, Beach Haven Terrace, NJ, hollow carved, o.p., little wear 200.00

Indehaven, Wayne, PA, hollow
carved, o.p., av. wear 75.00

Shourds, Harry V., Tuckertown,
NJ, hollow carved, repainted, in-
use wear 650.00

Canadian Geese

Hogg Island, o.p., heavy wear,
some age splitting 450.00

Hudson, Ira, Chincoteague, VA,
head and neck carved into
swimming position, carved
wings on back, in-use repaint,
lightly hit by shot, several age
splits 1,600.00

McLoughlin, John, Bordentown,
NJ, attributed to, hollow carved,
o.p., considerable in-use wear . 350.00

Canvasback Drakes

Elliston, Robert, Bureau, IL, hollow
carved, old combed feather
paint, little wear, "GSO" branded in bottom 280.00

Fulcher, Mitchell, Stacy, NC,
carved "MF" in bottom, o.p., av.
wear, minor age split in body .. 250.00

Mason's Decoy Factory, Detroit,
MI, Premiere Grade, saleman's
sample, solid body, o.p., minor
damage 750.00

Coots

Burton, Willie, London Bridge, VA,
o.p., av. wear 90.00

Murden, Luther, Back Bay, VA,
canvas covered, o.p., av. wear,
c1930 .... 70.00

Curlews

Downes, Hanson, Townsend, VA,
letter "H" carved in bottom,
o.p., heavy in-use wear, small
chip at end of bill 700.00

Hogg Island, running position, o.p.,
av. wear, bill possible replacement 650.00

Goldeneye Drakes

Baker, Gordon, Brockville, Ontario,
o.p., excellent 110.00

Hudson, Ira, Chincoteague, VA,
balsa body, old repaint, much
wear 225.00

Nicholl, Dave, Smith Falls, Ontario, carved wing tips, o.p. 375.00

Green-Winged Teal Drake, Mason's
Decoy Factory, Detroit, MI, Premiere Grade, o.p., lightly hit by
shot, end of bill chewed by dog .. 1,600.00

Hooded Merganser Drake, Barnes,
William, Porksley, VA, head slightly turned to right, carved wings,
o.p., moderately hit by shot 450.00

Mallard Drakes

Mason's Decoy Factory, Detroit,
MI, Premiere Grade, o.p., av.
wear, large chips on back of tail 525.00

Perdew, Charles H., Henry, IL,
feather painting along top, bottom, and sides, orig weight, o.p.,
av. wear, age split in neck 850.00

Merganser Drake, Hancock, Miles,
Chincoteague, VA, o.p., av. wear . 275.00

Mergansers, Drake and Hen

Hendrickson, Eugene, Egg Harbor,
NJ, red-breasted, o.p., little
wear 200.00

Shourds, Harry V., Tuckertown,
NJ, repainted, av. in-use wear . 1,250.00

Merganser Hens

Jester, Doug, Chincoteague, VA,
o.p., some overpaint, several
small age splits 225.00

Verity, Joshua, Long Island, NY,
carved eyes, o.p., heavy in-use
wear 575.00

Pintail Drakes

Hudson, Ira, Chincoteague, VA,
fine scratch feather repaint, av.
wear, age split in bottom 325.00

Mason's Decoy Factory, Detroit,
MI, Standard Grade, glass eyes,
o.p., heavy in-use wear 300.00

Redhead Drake, Mason's Decoy
Factory, Detroit, MI, Challenge
Grade, o.p., av. wear, lightly hit by
shot 600.00

Redhead Hen, Schmidt, Ben, Center
Line, MI, o.p., little in-use wear .. 250.00

**Merganser, Hen and Drake, Hender-
son Harbor, NY, early 1900s, o.p.,
$650.00.**

Ruddy Duck, Bull, Roy, Townsend, VA, carved 1970, o.p., excellent . 150.00
Scoter, Lincoln, Joe, Accord, MA, canvas covered, white winged, o.p., several small tears in canvas, age split in neck 425.00
Swan, Herter's Inc., Waseca, MN, o.p., very good 200.00
Widgeon Drake, Wildfowler, Point Pleasant, NJ, o.p., excellent 130.00
Yellowlegs, Boyd, George, Seabrook, NH, o.p., some dry rot and age splits, bill replaced 275.00

Dedham Pottery, Plate, Bread and Butter, 6⅛″, Horse Chestnut, $95.00.

DEDHAM POTTERY

The business was originally established as Chelsea Pottery in Chelsea, Mass., in 1860 by Alexander W. Robertson. In 1872, it was known as the Chelsea Keramic Art Works.

In 1895, the pottery moved to Dedham, Mass., and the name was changed to Dedham Pottery. The famous Crackleware, or Dedham Pottery, has an unusual spiderweb effect on blue in the glaze. The rabbit pattern was their most popular design. Other patterns include apple, azalea, bird-orange tree, butterfly, chicken, clover, crab, dolphin, duck, elephant, grape, horse chestnut, iris, lion, lobster, magnolia, owl, polar bear, snowtree, swan turtle, and water lily.

The following marks can be used to determine the approximate age of items made by the company: (1) Chelsea Keramic Art Works, name Robertson impressed, 1876–1889. (2) C. P. U. S. impressed in a clover leaf, 1891–1895. (3) Foreshortened rabbit, 1895–1896. (4) Conventional rabbit, with Dedham Pottery stamped in blue, 1897. (5) Word "Registered" added to rabbit mark, 1929–1943.

Ashtray, Polar Bear, 4″ 150.00
Bowls
    Turtle, 7½″ 200.00
    9″ Rabbit, inscribed Dedham Pottery, 1898 . . . . 850.00
    10″, Rabbit 200.00
    10″, Magnolia, oval 200.00
Butter Dish, Rabbit 200.00
Candlesticks
    Azalea, pair 175.00
    Rabbit, pair 200.00
Celery dishes
    Rabbit 180.00
Chocolate Pot, cov, 9″ h, Grape . . 285.00

Creamers
    Azalea, 3″, tankard 180.00
    Elephant, 5″ 575.00
Cups and Saucers
    Elephant 95.00
    Pond Lily 95.00
    Rabbit 95.00
Egg Cup, 4″, double, Rabbit 120.00
Jug, Azalea, 5″ 195.00
Mug, 4½″, fruit band top, Rabbit base 150.00
Plates
    4½″, Rabbit 195.00
    6″, Azalea 68.00
    6″, Grapes 50.00
    6″, Iris 65.00
    6″, Moth 175.00
    6″, Puppy in center 210.00
    6″, Turtle 145.00
    6⅛″, Butterfly 165.00
    6½″, Turkey 125.00
    7½″, Azalea 65.00
    7½″, Elephant 120.00
    7½″, Grape 95.00
    8″, Iris 90.00
    8″, Rabbits 140.00
    8½″, Butterfly 95.00
    8½″, Magnolia 85.00
    8½″, Poppy 125.00
    8½″, Rabbit 75.00
    8½″, Snowtree 110.00
    10″, Azalea 120.00
    10″, Butterfly 285.00
    10″, Iris 125.00
    10″, Pond Lily 135.00
    10″, Rabbit 110.00
    12½″, Crab 260.00
    12½″, Rabbit 175.00

Salt and Pepper Shakers, Rabbit, pair	160.00
Saucer, Swan	175.00
Sugar Bowl, covered Rabbit	135.00

Tiles

Horse Chestnut	100.00
Rabbit	130.00

Vases

8½ x 7″, volcanic dark olive high glaze, marked DP69A, HCR	275.00
9″ h, baluster shape, green ground, dripped speckled green overlay, marked Hugh C. Robertson for Dedham	275.00

DEGENHART GLASS

Warman's Americana & Collectibles, **1st Edition, contains 138 listings in this category; DEGENHART PAPERWEIGHTS contains 13 listings; see also page xii.**

DELFTWARE

Delft ware is a kind of pottery first made in Belgium and Italy as early as the 16th century. Dutch traders made the city of Delft, in Holland, a world trade center, and it became synonymous with the pottery made and exported there.

The body is of soft red clay with a coating of tin glaze. Blue designs on white ground were the first coloring, but polychrome coloring was perfected and used. Most English potteries made this ware. The Delft ware found in the market today will also include other tin-glazed pottery produced in England and on the Continent. Delft, faience, and majolica are all tin-glazed pottery.

Bowl, 12½″, shallow, polychrome, floral decor in blue, green, yellow, red and purple, English, late 18th C	325.00

Chargers

13½″, polychrome, floral group with bird and floral border, blue, olive green, red and ocher, English, mid-18th C	525.00
16″, dark blue and white in red velvet frame, squiggle sgr, 18th C	1,050.00
Cuspidor, 3⅛″, quatrefoil body, blue and white, brown edged rim painted with chinoiserie figures in fenced garden, birds, flowering branches, CK 9 mk in blue, Dutch, c1695	725.00
Dish, polychrome oriental flowering shrub center, rim with border of flutes, tassels, etc., Bristol, England, C 1760	700.00

Delftware Plate, 12¾″, blue, white, wind mill scene, $175.00.

Drug Jars

Dry, 5¼″, cylindrical on flaring foot, blue and white, painted cartouche inscribed E. MART, POM. Dutch, late 18th C	145.00
Wet, 8⅝″, blue and white, painted under spout cartouche inscribed S ALTHAEAE:FERN:, Dutch, c1725	460.00

Figures

Baby in cradle, polychrome, yellow and brown wicker cradle, iron red and green flowered coverlet, Dutch, mid-18th C	825.00
Hound dogs, 5″, seated, white, blue spots, wearing collar with bell, oval base, Dutch, mid-18th C, pr	550.00
Ginger Jar, cov, 7″, three panel, oriental figure	325.00
Jardiniere, 11¼″, sq, tapering, blue and white, peasant figures conversing in landscape, molded mark handles, rope corners and rim, numeral 20 in blue, Dutch, mid-18th C	560.00
Jug, 6¾″, blue and white, polychrome, building, Makkum	150.00
Pilgrim Bottle, 9¼″, ball shape, blue and white, snake edges	600.00
Pitcher, 5½″, shaped sides, sailing ship, relief cartouche, imp 685/2½	122.00
Planter, 6 x 7″ w, white, blue tulips, glazed red clay liner, dtd 1914	50.00
Plaque, 15½″, winter scene, couple riding in one horse sleigh, border pattern, Royal Sphinx by Boch	75.00

Plates
8¼", soup, polychrome, island pavillion center, Bristol, England, c1770 .... 235.00
14", peacock, blue and white, central vase of flowers and feathery leaves, butterfly and floral border, yellow rim, claw mk and 300/2 in blue, Dutch, mid-18th C 275.00
Pot, cov, 7¼", cylindrical, handles, blue and white, panels of stylized oriental flowers, Dutch, mid-18th C 400.00
Slipper, 5" l, polychrome, manganese with iron red, yellow and green flowers, Dutch, c1750 .... 320.00

Stein, 5¼", pewter cover, blue and white, windmill scene, floral decor, mkd 250.00
Teapot, 5¼", cov, blue and white, birds and floral sprigs against dotted field, floral and foliate scroll border, PK monogram mk in blue, Dutch, 1700 .... 825.00
Vases
6⅜", manganese and white, painted, 2 Chinamen near pavilion on hilly landscape, numeral 8 in manganese, Dutch, c1793 . 360.00
6¾", blue and white, wide diagonally striped band reserved with floral cartouche beneath zone of icicle motifs, Dutch, 18th C . 200.00

DEPRESSION GLASS

Depression glass is a general term used to describe the glassware manufactured primarily during the "Depression" years, 1929–1940. It was an inexpensive machine-made glass manufactured by several major glass factories in a wide variety of patterns, and in green, pink, blue, red, yellow, white and crystal. It was sold through variety stores, given as premiums, or packaged with certain products. Movie houses gave it away from 1935 until well into the 1940s.

Interest in collecting Depression glass has risen, including the later hand-made colored glass of the 1950s and 1960s. As with most antiques and collectibles, where demand exceeds the supply, reproductions appear on the market. The majority of the reissued patterns are marked accordingly, but there are some deceivers.

See *Warman's Americana and Collectibles* for additional depression glass pattern listings.

ANNIVERSARY, Jeannette Glass Company, 1947–1949. Made in crystal, iridescent and pink.

	Crystal	Pink	Iridescent
Bowls			
4⅞", berry, small	2.00	3.00	—
6¾"	3.00	—	—
7⅜", soup, flat	4.00	8.00	—
9", fruit	8.00	12.00	—
Butter Dish	22.00	42.50	—
Cake Plate, 12½"	6.00	9.00	—
Candlesticks, 4⅞", pr	13.00	—	—
Candy Dish, lid	18.00	27.00	—
Comports, 3 leg	4.00	8.00	—
Creamer, footed	3.00	5.50	—
Cup	2.25	5.00	—
Cup & Saucer	—	—	3.00
Goblets, 2½ oz., wine	6.00	9.00	—
Plates			
6¼", bread & butter	1.25	2.50	1.50
9"	2.25	5.00	2.75
12½", sandwich server	5.00	7.00	—
Relish, 9"	5.00	8.00	—
Saucer	2.00	2.50	—
Sherbet	3.00	5.00	—
Sugar	5.50	8.00	—
Vases			
6½"	6.00	10.00	—
Wall pin-up	12.00	14.00	—

CIRCLE, Hocking Glass Co., 1930s. Made in green and pink.

	Green	Pink		Green	Pink
Bowls			Plates		
4½″, berry, small ...	3.00	2.50	6″, sherbet	2.25	2.35
8″, berry, master ...	5.50	5.50	8″, luncheon	2.00	2.00
Creamer and Sugar,			9½″, dinner	13.00	10.00
ftd.	12.00	10.00	Sherbet		
Cup	2.00	2.75	3⅛″	3.00	4.00
Decanter, handled ...	17.50	16.50	4¾″	6.00	6.00
Goblets			Tumblers		
4½″, wine	7.00	7.00	4 oz., juice	7.00	6.00
8 oz., water	9.00	9.00	8 oz., water	8.00	7.00
Pitchers, 80 oz.	22.50	20.00	Vase, hat shape	18.00	18.00

COLUMBIA, Federal Glass Company, 1938–1942. Made in crystal and pink.

	Crystal	Pink		Crystal	Pink
Bowls			Plates		
5″, cereal	6.50	—	6″, bread and butter .	1.00	5.00
8″, soup, flat	9.00	—	9½″, luncheon	5.00	10.00
10½″, ruffled	11.00	—	11¾″, chop	4.00	—
Butter Dish	13.95	—	Sandwich	5.00	—
Cup and Saucer	6.00	19.75	Saucer	2.00	3.50

FLORAL (POINSETTA), Jeannette Glass Company, 1931–1935. Made in delphite, green and pink. Experimental pieces in many colors exist.

	Delphite	Green	Pink
Bowls			
4″, berry, small	22.50	10.00	12.00
7½″, salad	—	14.00	10.50
8″, vegetable, covered	45.00	30.00	29.75
9″, covered vegetable, oval	—	12.50	12.00
Fruit, with lid	40.00	—	—
Butter Dish	—	85.00	65.00
Candlesticks, 4″	—	49.75	40.00
Candy Dish and Cover	—	29.75	29.75
Coaster, 3¼″	—	6.50	6.00
Creamer	60.00	12.00	12.00
Cup and Saucer	—	12.00	10.00
Pitchers			
8″, 32 oz., ftd. cone	—	20.00	24.50
10¼″, 48 oz., lemonade	—	225.00	150.00
Plates			
6″, bread and butter	—	3.50	2.75
8″, salad	—	8.75	6.00
9″, dinner	48.00	12.00	9.75
Chop	76.00	—	—
Platter, 10¾″, oval	—	12.00	9.75
Refrigerator Dish, covered,			
5″ sq.	—	45.00	40.00
Relish, 2 parts, oval	—	9.75	9.75
Sherbet	68.50	10.00	9.75
Sugar	48.00	16.00	14.00
Tumblers			
4″, 5 oz., ftd., juice	—	12.00	9.00
4¾″, 7 oz., ftd., water	110.00	12.75	9.50
5¼″, 9 oz., ftd., lemonade	—	32.50	25.00

FLOWER GARDEN WITH BUTTERFLIES (Butterflies And Roses), U. S. Glass Company, late 1920s. Made in pink, green, teal, vaseline, crystal, amber and black.

	Pink	Black	Green	Teal	Amber	Vaseline	Crystal
Ashtray	180.00	120.00	180.00	165.00	230.00	160.00	120.00
Bowl 10″, ftd., console	65.00	140.00	45.00	125.00	50.00	65.00	45.00
Candlesticks							
4″, pr.	55.00	65.00	40.00	140.00	60.00	65.00	40.00
8″	220.00	380.00	120.00	230.00	—	—	—
Candy Dish, 8″, covered	140.00	720.00	140.00	140.00	200.00	—	—
Cheese and Cracker Set, ftd., gold dec.	40.00	42.00	38.00	70.00	45.00	48.00	60.00
Cigarette Box, rect.	—	480.00	—	—	—	—	—
Creamer	125.00	—	125.00	—	—	—	—
Cup and Saucer	115.00	—	150.00	—	—	—	—
Mayonnaise, 3 pcs.	85.00	175.00	80.00	125.00	85.00	80.00	45.00
Perfume	200.00	380.00	120.00	230.00	—	—	—
Plates							
7″	60.00	65.00	40.00	60.00	62.50	60.00	60.00
8″	25.00	28.00	23.00	20.00	20.00	40.00	15.00
10¼″, cup indentation	20.00	—	—	70.00	—	—	—
Sandwich Server, center handle	70.00	75.00	80.00	90.00	90.00	70.00	70.00
Saucer	35.00	—	—	—	—	—	—
Sherbet	—	—	40.00	60.00	35.00	—	15.00
Sugar	85.00	85.00	100.00	80.00	82.00	80.00	80.00
Tray							
5½ x 10″, oval	52.00	60.00	55.00	50.00	60.00	50.00	50.00
11¾ x 7¾″, rect.	70.00	85.00	80.00	90.00	115.00	85.00	85.00
Vase							
6″	120.00	—	120.00	140.00	—	—	—
7¼″	—	325.00	—	—	—	—	—
8½″	—	310.00	—	—	—	—	—
10″	120.00	—	140.00	—	—	—	—
11″	—	230.00	—	—	—	—	—
Wall Vase	—	380.00	—	—	—	—	—

GEORGIAN (Lovebirds), Federal Glass Company, 1931–1936. Made in green and crystal. Prices for both colors are the same.

	Crystal and Green		Crystal and Green
Bowls		Plates	
4½″, berry, small	4.75	6″, sherbet	2.25
5¾″, cereal	14.00	8″, luncheon	6.00
6½″	39.00	9¼″, center design, dinner	12.50
7½″	35.00	Platter, 11½″, closed handles	42.00
Oval vegetable	33.00	Saucer	2.00
Butter Dish	68.00	Sherbet	6.75
Creamer	7.75	Sugar	7.50
Cup and Saucer	9.75	Tumblers	
Nappy, 4½″	4.00	4″, 9 oz.	28.00
		5¼″, 12 oz.	50.00

JUBILEE, Lancaster Glass Company, early 1930s. Made in yellow.

	Yellow		Yellow
Bowl, fruit, 9″, handled	28.00	Cheese and Cracker Set	25.00
Cake Plate, 1 handle	15.00	Creamer and Sugar	21.00

Circle, cup and saucer, green, $4.00.

Columbia, saucer, crystal, $2.00.

Floral, butter dish, cov, pink, $65.00.

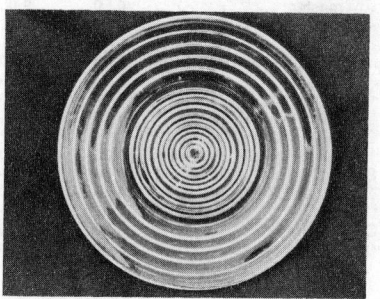

Manhattan, plate, 6″, crystal, $2.00.

Georgian, creamer and sugar, green, $18.00.

Sharon (Cabbage Rose), amber, plate, 9″, $11.00.

	Yellow		Yellow
Cup and Saucer	10.00	8¾", luncheon	6.50
Goblets		13", sandwich	18.00
6", 10 oz.	19.00	Sugar	8.00
6⅛", 12½ oz.	24.00	Tray	
Mayonnaise, plate, ladle	35.00	11", 2 handled	15.00
Plates		Center handled sandwich	20.00
7", salad	4.00		

MANHATTAN (Horizontal Ribbed), Anchor Hocking Glass Company, 1938–1941. Made in pink, crystal; limited production in green and ruby.

	Crystal	Pink		Crystal	Pink
Ashtray	9.75	—	Cup	7.00	—
Bowls			Goblet, wine, ftd., 4"	7.50	—
4½", handled, berry	4.00	5.75	Pitchers		
5⅜", handled, sauce	3.50	4.00	Juice, 42 oz.	9.75	22.00
7½", handled, berry,			Water, 80 oz., tilted	12.00	25.00
master	8.50	9.00	Plates		
8", closed handles	9.00	10.00	6", sherbet	2.00	—
9"			8½", salad	4.00	—
Open handles	12.00	16.00	10¼", dinner	7.25	—
Salad	8.00	10.00	Relish, 14" handle, 5		
9½", fruit	13.00	15.50	red inserts	32.75	40.00
Candlesticks, 4½"	4.00	—	Salt & Pepper Shakers	8.75	16.00
Candy Dish, 3 legs,			Sandwich plate, 14"	10.00	—
covered	18.00	4.50	Sauce Boat	3.00	—
Candy Dish Lid	8.50	—	Saucer	2.00	—
Cheese and Cracker Set	4.75	4.00	Sherbet	5.00	6.00
Coaster, 3½"	4.75	—	Sugar	4.00	5.00
Comports, 5¾"	6.50	7.50	Tumblers, 10 oz.	6.00	7.00
Creamer and Sugar	8.00	9.00	Vase, 8"	6.00	

NEWPORT (Hairpin), Hazel Atlas Glass Company, 1936–1940. Made in cobalt blue, amethyst pink, green and red.

	Amethyst	Cobalt Blue	Green	Ruby
Bowls				
4½", berry, small	6.50	6.00	—	—
4¾", soup, cream	7.00	6.00	—	—
5¼", cereal	9.00	8.75	—	—
8¼", berry, master	22.50	15.00	—	—
Creamer and Sugar	10.00	13.00	—	15.00
Cup and Saucer	5.00	7.00	5.50	8.00
Lunch set, 14 pcs.	—	—	55.00	7.00
Plates				
6", sherbet	2.50	2.50	—	—
8½", luncheon	5.00	5.25	4.50	7.00
Platter, 11¾", oval	18.00	18.00	—	—
Salt and Pepper Shakers, pr.	32.50	37.00	—	—
Sandwich plate, 11½"	17.00	15.00	—	—
Saucer	1.50	1.20	1.50	—
Sherbet	5.50	6.50	—	—
Sugar	9.00	8.50	—	—
Tumblers, 4½", 9 oz.	15.50	15.50	—	—

OLD CAFE, Hocking Glass Company, 1936–1938; 1940. Made in pink, crystal and ruby red.

	Crystal	Pink	Ruby
Bowls			
3¾", berry, small	2.50	2.75	5.00
5", one handle	6.00	6.50	—
5½", cereal	7.00	8.00	10.00
9", closed handles	8.00	7.50	11.00
Candy Dish, 8" low	5.00	5.00	10.00
Cookie Jar	—	50.00	—
Cup	4.50	5.00	5.50
Lamp	9.00	9.00	16.00
Olive Dish, 6" oblong	4.00	5.00	3.50
Pitchers			
6", 36 oz.	46.50	48.00	—
80 oz.	70.00	70.00	—
Plates			
6", sherbet	3.75	5.00	—
10"	14.00	15.00	—
Saucer	5.50	4.00	—
Sherbet, low ftd.	5.00	4.50	—
Tray, 8"	4.50	4.75	6.75
Tumblers			
3", juice	5.00	5.00	—
4", water	6.50	7.00	—
Vase, 7¼"	10.00	10.00	14.00

PRINCESS, Hocking Glass Company, 1931–1935. Made in green, two yellows, pink; some blue.

	Green	Pink	Yellow
Ashtray, 4½"	50.00	60.00	70.00
Bowls			
4½", berry, small	14.00	10.00	24.00
5¼", cereal	16.90	13.00	23.00
9"			
Hat	15.00	12.00	68.00
Octagonal	24.90	24.90	70.00
Oval	15.90	10.00	42.90
Butter Dish	60.00	65.00	400.00
Cake Plate, 3 feet	16.90	12.00	N/A
Candy Dish	32.90	35.00	—
Coasters	18.00	52.00	68.00
Cookie Jar, lid	22.00	20.00	—
Creamer	7.50	8.00	9.75
Cup	6.00	5.00	5.00
Goblets, water	—	15.00	—
Pitchers			
6", 37 oz., juice	22.00	21.00	380.00
8", 60 oz.	30.00	28.00	60.00
Plates			
6", sherbet	4.00	3.75	2.00
8", luncheon	7.90	6.00	6.00
9½", dinner	16.00	9.00	8.00
11½"			
Grill	10.90	5.00	5.25
Handled	14.90	12.00	10.00
Platter, 12"	11.90	9.00	30.00
Relish, 7½", divided	16.90	16.90	48.00
Salt and Pepper Shakers	32.00	28.00	50.00
Saucer	4.00	3.00	4.00

	Green	Pink	Yellow
Sherbet	9.00	8.00	24.00
Sugar, lid	18.75	15.00	18.00
Syrup	—	15.00	—
Tumblers			
3½", ftd., juice	16.00	13.00	17.00
4", 9 oz., flat, water	17.50	14.00	16.00
5¼"			
Flat iced tea	15.00	16.00	16.90
Footed	19.00	14.00	20.00
6½", footed	40.00	25.00	15.90
Vase, 8"	20.00	19.00	—

ROULETTE (Many Windows), Hocking Glass Company, 1935–1939. Made in crystal, pink and green.

	Crystal	Green	Pink
Bowl, 9", fruit	6.00	12.00	9.00
Cup	3.00	4.00	3.50
Pitcher, 8", 64 oz.	20.00	20.00	18.00
Plates			
6", sherbet	1.50	4.50	3.00
8½", luncheon	2.75	3.75	3.50
12", sandwich	9.50	9.75	9.00
Saucer	1.50	1.75	1.65
Sherbet	3.25	3.50	3.00
Tumblers			
3¼"			
5 oz., juice	4.00	4.00	4.25
7½ oz., old fashioned	6.00	6.50	6.00
4⅛", 9 oz., water	8.50	9.00	6.00
5⅛", 12 oz., iced tea	8.50	10.00	9.00
5½", 10 oz., ftd.	10.00	10.75	10.50
Whiskey, 2½", 1½ oz.	8.00	8.00	8.00

SHARON (Cabbage Rose), Federal Glass Company, 1935–1939. Made in pink, green, amber; some crystal.

	Amber	Green	Pink
Bowls			
5"			
Berry, small	6.00	8.00	6.00
Soup, cream	14.00	28.00	25.00
6", cereal	10.00	18.00	6.00
7½", soup, flat	7.00	8.00	26.00
8½", berry, master	4.00	25.00	16.00
9½", oval vegetable	10.00	18.00	12.50
10½", fruit	14.50	18.50	25.00
Butter Dish	38.50	65.00	40.00
Cake Plate, 11½", ftd.	35.00	42.00	20.00
Candy Dish, covered	34.00	175.00	35.00
Cheese Dish and Lid	250.00	—	—
Creamer, ftd.	10.00	12.00	10.00
Cup and Saucer	11.00	12.00	15.00
Cups	8.25	10.00	12.00
Jam Dish, 7½ x 1½"	25.00	39.00	85.00
Pitchers			
80 oz.	97.00	—	100.00
Ice lip	85.00	—	95.00

	Amber	Green	Pink
Plates			
6", bread and butter	3.00	5.00	3.50
7½", salad	12.00	11.50	20.00
9½", dinner	11.00	15.00	11.00
Platter, oval, 12½"	15.00	21.00	12.00
Salt and Pepper Shakers, pr.	27.00	54.00	35.00
Saucer	3.50	4.00	9.50
Sherbet	9.00	9.00	9.00
Sugar	10.00	50.00	9.00
Sugar lid	16.00	18.00	20.00
Tumblers			
4⅛", thin, 9 oz.	17.00	32.25	20.00
6½", ftd. tea, 15 oz.	69.50	—	20.00

SPIRAL, Hocking Glass Company, 1928–1930. Made in pink and green.

	Green	Pink		Green	Pink
Bowls			8"	2.50	2.75
4¾", berry, small ...	5.00	5.00	Sandwich server,		
8", berry, master ...	22.50	10.00	center handle	17.00	15.00
Cereal	9.00	—	Preserve and Cover ..	22.50	20.00
Butter Tub	21.00	18.00	Saucer	1.00	1.50
Creamer and Sugar, ftd.	17.00	15.00	Shaker	18.00	18.50
Cup and Saucer	5.00	5.00	Sherbet	3.50	3.00
Pitchers, 7⅝", 58 oz. .	20.00	18.00	Tumblers		
Plates			3", 5 oz., juice	4.00	4.50
6", sherbet	2.00	2.00	5", 9 oz., water	9.00	8.00

Spiral, sherbert, 4⅛"d, 2⅞"h, green, $2.50.

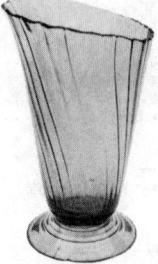

Swirl, vase, 8⅜, ultramarine, $18.00.

SWIRL (Petal Swirl), Jeannette Glass Company, 1937–1938. Made in pink, ultramarine, delphite; limited production in amber and crystal.

	Delphite	Pink	Ultramarine
Ashtray	—	6.25	—
Bowls			
5¼", cereal	7.00	5.00	7.50
8½", berry, master	—	12.75	18.00
9", salad	14.00	10.00	16.00
10", tab handles, ftd.	—	12.00	14.00
10½", console	—	13.00	22.50
Butter Dish	—	100.00	195.00
Candlesticks, double branch, pr ...	—	—	25.00
Candy Dish, covered	—	50.00	32.00

	Delphite	Pink	Ultramarine
Coaster in Goodyear tire	—	12.75	—
Creamer and Sugar	15.00	13.00	16.00
Cup and Saucer	6.50	7.00	9.00
Cups	5.00	4.00	7.00
Plates			
6½", sherbet	3.00	2.50	2.50
7¼"	6.00	5.00	7.00
8", salad	7.00	6.00	7.50
13", sandwich		8.00	10.00
Dinner	6.00	6.50	7.50
Platter, 12", oval	22.00	—	
Salt and Pepper Shaker, 3"		—	32.50
Saucer	3.50	2.00	3.00
Sherbet	—	6.50	9.50
Sugar	8.25	6.00	8.00
Tumblers			
4"	—	5.00	14.50
4⅝", straight	—	6.00	—
Vase, 8½"	—	11.00	18.00

VICTORY, Diamond Glass-ware Company, 1929–1932. Made in amber, green, pink and cobalt blue, limited production in black.

	Amber	Cobalt Blue	Green	Pink
Bowls				
6½", cereal	4.50	5.00	6.25	6.00
8½", soup, flat	10.00	9.50	9.00	8.50
9", vegetable, oval	24.00	24.50	18.00	18.00
12", console	24.00	24.50	18.00	18.00
Candlesticks, 3", pr.	23.00	23.50	15.00	15.00
Cheese and Cracker Set, 12"				
plate	—	—	18.00	18.50
Comports, 6" h, 6¾"	12.50	12.00	10.50	10.00
Creamer	10.00	9.50	6.00	6.50
Cup and Saucer	3.00	5.00	6.00	7.50
Goblets, 5", 7 oz.	12.50	12.50	18.00	18.00
Mayonnaise, 3½" h, 5½" d, 8½"				
plate, ladle	35.00	36.00	25.00	25.00
Plates				
6", bread and butter	3.00	3.50	2.00	3.00
7", salad	6.25	6.00	4.50	5.00
8", luncheon	6.00	6.00	4.00	5.00
9", dinner	7.00	7.50	7.00	7.25
Sandwich server, center				
handle	25.00	26.00	25.00	27.00
Platter, 12"	22.50	23.00	16.00	17.00
Saucer	4.25	4.25	2.25	2.25
Sherbet	8.00	8.00	10.00	10.00
Sugar	10.00	9.50	8.00	8.00

DESIGN SPATTERWARE

Design Spatterware marks the transition period that bridged Spatterware and Spongeware. Early examples are often confused with Spongeware because they are similar to some degree. The earliest patterns were carefully arranged and generally covered the entire piece. In the next period of this ware, various motifs were created such as a decorated border with a tulip in the center.

In the 1850s, Elsmore and Foster in England created the noted Holly Leaf pattern in red and green, and also in purple and green; blue bands divide the primary motif arranged in broader bands. Design Spatterware progressed to more definitive designs and finally was limited to only floral, much of which is attributed to Adams.

Design Spatterware is primarily in blue. Modes of decoration were applied in several ways, including the so-called 'cut-sponge.' Some were hand painted while other pieces were transferred in an endless variety of colors and designs.

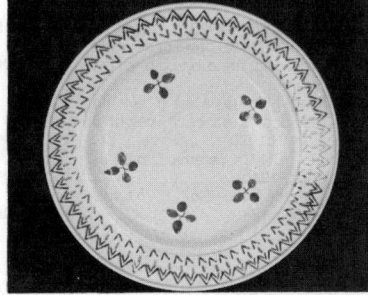

Plate, 8⅝" d, blue lines, red, green borders, green-yellow center decor, $80.00.

Bowls
Foliage, floral, fruit design, 13" d x 4" h 250.00
Green, black, mkd Staffordshire, England, 5⅝" d x 3" h 155.00
Tulip and Pretzels, small, damaged 95.00
Butter, covered, Holly Leaf, lion finial, drain 275.00
Chamber Pot, blue, 9½" d, mkd W.M. Co. 100.00
Charger, 15", elaboration of Adam's Rose 180.00
Cups and Saucers
Adam's Rose, red rosette border 185.00
Blue, green, ochre, red, florals .. 120.00
Holly Leaf, red, green 185.00
Peony, red, green 175.00
Red, blue border 115.00
Jugs
Diamonds and bands, blue, very early form, 5¾" 185.00
Tulip, blue, 3⅞" 165.00
Mugs
Blue and purple, large 125.00
Brown, blue decor, 3⅝" h 95.00
Tree, blue 65.00

Plates, 8½"
Colombine with rose bud and thistle, green, rosette border 165.00
Tulip, blue 225.00
Plate, Soup, six tulips in 6 pointed star, red, blue and purple 155.00
Platters
9", green flowers, red centers .. 60.00
9⅛", red, green, blue, yellow floral 145.00
9¼", blue, green, red, purple flowers 75.00
12", cake, red, blue, green, black, florals 85.00
16" Holly Leaf, red and green, Elsmore and Foster, ... 225.00
Sugars
Large, red and green 85.00
Small, red and green 65.00
Teapot, blue, early form, repaired .. 265.00
Tray, 7½" l, gaudy floral decor, red, blue, green, marked Adams, Titian Ware 180.00

DISNEYANA

Walt Disney and the creations of the famous Disney studio hold a place of fondness and enchantment not only in the hearts of Americans, but people throughout the world. The release of "Steamboat Willie" in 1928 harolded an entertainment empire.

Walt and his brother showed shrewd business acumen. From the beginning they licensed the reproduction of Disney characters in products ranging from wrist watches to clothing. Ceil Munsey's *Disneyana* chronicles this material.

Disneyana collectors are devoted. The products from the 1930s command the most attention. Animated celluloids range in value from $200 to $5,000 depending on subject and complexity of scene. The Disneyana market now is so firmly established that Phillips in New York held a sale devoted exclusively to Disneyana in October, 1981. Sotheby's collector carrousel sales also feature large amounts of Disney material.

See *Warman's Americana & Collectibles* for an expanded listing of Disneyana.

Celluloids
Dumbo, 10¼ x 7½", circus clowns riding a fire engine, applied to airbrushed ground, Courvoisier Galleries label, 1941 165.00
Pinocchio, 9½ x 9½", Pinocchio with donkey ears, under water surrounded by seahorses, applied to airbrushed ground, 1939 660.00

Snow White, 8¾ x 8¾″, Doc holding a lantern followed by Bashful and Sneezy, applied to airbrushed ground, 1937 . . . . . 610.00

Donald Duck

Bowl, cereal, 5½″ d, Beetleware, Post cereal premium, yellow, copyright Walt Disney Enterprises, c1930 . . . . 22.00

Clock, animated, Baynard, MIB . . 110.00

Doll, 16″, leatherette, angry Donald, by Richard G. Krueger c1935 . . . . 750.00

Figure, 3″ bisque, holding bugle in right hand 35.00

Figure, 3″ bisque, long bill, marching pose, c1930 . . . . 22.00

Patch, round, 5″ d, Celebrity Sports Center, Denver, CO, surfboard 65.00

Planter, figural, sitting on top of ABC blocks, 5½″ Leeds, c1940 38.00

Puppet, hand, rubber head, cloth body, Gund, c1940 . . . . 38.00

Dumbo

Bank, 6½″, ceramic, white, gold, black trim, holds coin in trunk, incised Dumbo, Walt Disney USA, c1940 . . . . 35.00

Creamer & sugar, ceramic figural, red, brown, bold, copyright Walt Disney USA, Leeds, c1940 . . . 48.00

Figure, 5½″ h, seated, baby bonnet, incised No. 41 American Pottery, c1940 . . . . 55.00

Pencil Sharpener, celluloid, c1941 23.00

Mickey Mouse

Airplane, rubber, Mickey's Air Mail, 6½″, white rubber tires, rubber propeller, Sun Rubber, c1940 . 65.00

Belt Buckle, c1930 . . . . 24.00

Button, 1¼″ cello, red, black, white, Good Teeth, Mickey brushing Big Bad Wolf's teeth . 68.00

Clock, animated, Ingersoll, 1930s, MIB 600.00

Drinking Glass, 4¼, All Star Parade, orange, yellow, Mickey Mouse, Minnie Mouse, Pluto, Parrot 20.00

Figure, 3½″, bisque, playing saxophone, large ears, c1920 . . . . 150.00

Playing cards, miniature, 1⅝ x 2½″, Walt Disney Enterprises, c1930 . . . . 35.00

Radio, Emerson, simulated wood, 7¼″ w x 7¼″ h, 5¼″ d, Mickey playing bass violin on front, piano on top, flute and tuba on each side, fine condition, c1930 795.00

Toy, tin Movie Jecktor, c1930 . . . 95.00

Umbrella, 2 silk screen poses of Mickey, Minnie on satin-like cloth, 20″ l, Walt Disney Enterprises, c1930 . . . . 150.00

Minnie Mouse

Book, *Story of Minnie*, 1938 . . . . 25.00

Figures

3½″ bisque, playing accordion, orig label, c1930 . . . . 40.00

3½″ bisque, carrying first aid kit, c1930 . . . . 55.00

Pinocchio

Clock, animated, Bayard, MIB . . . 175.00

Doll, 9½″ Conyco, jointed at shoulders, copyright Walt Disney Productions 225.00

Figures

3¼″ bisque, c1930 . . . . 32.00

Geppetto, 5½″ pressed wood, standing, hand on chin, c1940 55.00

Snow White

Drinking glasses, 4½″ h, full figures, poems on each, set of 8, Libbey, c1930 . . . . 125.00

Figure, 6½″, ceramic, pastels, Leeds, 1940 . . . . 25.00

Planter, ceramic 6½″ h, pastels, Leeds, c1940 . . . . 25.00

Snow White, alarm clock, Bayard/ Blanche Niege, Made in France, Par autorisation Walt Disney, $115.00.

Three Little Pigs

Book, *Who's Afraid of the Big Bad Wolf*, McKay, 6½ x 8½″ book copyright 1933 Walt Disney Enterprises 75.00

Match Holder, orange paint 20.00

Soap, MIB, c1930 . . . . 25.00

Miscellaneous

Book, *The Victory March by Walt*

Disney, spiral bound, pull-out, pop-up, 1942, all characters wearing swastikas **50.00**

Bambi, bowl, cereal, 5" d, Bambi on bottom, butterfly on tail, flowers Walt Disney Productions, c1940 .... **18.00**

Fantasia
Planter, ceramic, dancing mushrooms, lt. turq., high relief on both sides, 12" l x 7" w x 2" d, Vernon Kilns, c1940 .... **95.00**

Goofy
Wristwatch, "Backwards," Helbros, 17 jewels, leather band, MIB **275.00**

Mickey Mouse Club, button, 1¼", bw, orange, c1930 .... **80.00**

Pluto
Clock, animated, Bayard, MIB . **110.00**
Mug, ceramic, Pluto on one side, Mickey Mouse on other, Walt Disney Enterprises, Patriot China, c1930 .... **45.00**

Thumper, figure, ceramic, American Pottery
3", looking to left **45.00**
4", looking to right **35.00**

DOLL HOUSES

Although most doll houses were made for the enjoyment of children, some were meant to show the skill and taste of ladies in society. Both types are collected widely.

Antique doll house prices are stable. Rarity greatly effects price, since few truly fine houses come on the market. Condition is the general critical element. Original paper, flooring, and outside paint plus stairs push price higher.

Lithograph on tin, English, rectangular, steeled roof, brightly colored cottage design, Mark: Bicky House, The Lucie Atwell Kiddibisc, William Crawford and Son Display, mfg Great Britain, 4 x 8" **200.00**

Lithograph paper on wood
American, Bliss
2 rooms, 2 story, steeple roof, gable windows, railing, first floor porch with metal grillwork front, paper stained glass windows, Mkd. R. Bliss on doorway, c1900, 18 x 12 x 9" **575.00**
2 rooms, 2 story Victorian, high steeled roof, dormer windows, porch spindled railing, 2 floor balcony, 27 x 18 x 11" **900.00**

Lithograph on board, R. Bliss, 7½ x 11½ x 16¼", hinged, 2 interior rooms, $650.00.

Stable, rectangular, removable steeped roof, 3 arched openings surmounted by second floor storage shed, chimney, hinged doors, c1895, 17 x 15 x 8" **675.00**

European, hinged, 3 stories, balcony facade opening, 12 rooms, paneled Art Nouveau dining room, ormolu decor parlor, chapel, nursery, furnishings, 54" h **20,000.00**

Norwegian, school, 2 rooms, c1930 .... **350.00**

Wooden, American
2 rooms, folk art, wooden, well, bucket in front, orig brown paint, red mullions, open windows, doors backed with brown tissue paper, 20th C, 11¾ x 15¼" .. **140.00**
4 rooms, gabled roof, white, green trim, red shingles, glass windows, opening door, 1" scale, early 20th C, 24¾ x 17¾ x 27" **200.00**
4 rooms, mansard roof, painted brick front, "Rose Cottage" glass windows, 1" scale, 19th C, 23⅝ x 40 x 16¼" **200.00**
5 rooms, Dutch Colonial, yellow, green, red roof, porches, dormer,¾" scale, c1925, 20¼ x 26 ½ x 15" **250.00**

6 rooms, Town House, 2 story, electrified, parquet floors, lap siding, fish scale roof, front porch with columns, bay window 2nd floor, opens from side, built in Philadelphia, 1930 . . . .   **900.00**

16 rooms, Victorian, 2 story colonial, 2 floors, steppled attic rooms, cream wooden exterior, shingled roof, brown shutters, working windows, widow walk, 1st floor circular porch, 3 skylight windows, brick chimney, made by John Bellamy, West Newton, MA, early 1890s, 40 x 77 x 44″ **2,800.00**

DOLLS

Dolls have existed as children's play toys as well as important figurines in the ceremonies of life in all cultures from pre-historic times. The earliest known examples date from the Babylonians, 3000 B.C.

From the 14th through the 18th century, doll making was centered in Europe, namely Germany and France. French dolls were not primarily play toys but were elaborately dressed in the latest couturier designs. All these dolls had one thing in common: they represented adults.

In the mid-19th century the child or baby doll was introduced in England. The famous Jumeau doll with swivel head and sawdust filled kid body had its beginning in France in that era.

The Bye-lo, designed by Grace S. Putnam, was introduced in the 20th century; it was made by firms in Germany and the United States. Doll making in the United States began to flourish in the 1900s with names like Horsman, Effanbee, Alexander, Ideal and others.

See *Warman's Americana and Collectibles* for an expanded listing of Dolls.

Alt, Beck and Gottschalk, 26″, bisque socket head, composition, wooden ball jointed body, gray glass sleep eyes, real lashes, painted features, open mouth, 4 porcelain teeth, brunette human hair, antique dress, c1910. Marks: ABG 1362 Made in Germany 4 . .   **350.00**

American Cloth, 16″, Columbian Doll, muslin, painted facial features, original clothes, bonnet, designed by Emma Adams, Oswego, NY, 1890, for World's Fair Exhibition of 1893 . . . .   **600.00**

Bahr & Proschild, 27″, bisque socket head, composition bent limb baby body, brown glass sleep eyes, real lashes, sculpted, painted features, open mouth, 2 upper teeth, auburn human hair, brown velvet romper suit, tucked, ruffled bib, arms repainted, c1910. Marks: B.P. 585 16 Germany **650.00**

Belton

14″ h, German bisque shoulderhead, cloth body, composition arms, blue eyes, closed mouth, original dress. Marks: incised 3094 . . . .   **600.00**

19″, French bisque socket head, flattened solid dome, composition, wooden ball jointed body, small, almond shaped blue glass paperweight inset eyes spiral threading, painted features, brunette mohair wig, well costumed, c1880. Marks: 11 . .   **850.00**

Casimir Bru, 18″, bisque swivel head, kid lined bisque shoulderplate, French kid body, kid over wooden upper arms, upper legs, repainted wooden lower legs, bisque forearms replacements, almond shaped gray glass paperweight inset eyes, painted features, heavily molded eyelids, wide open mouth, pierced ears, blonde mohair wig over cork pate, antique costume, c1880. Marks: Bru Jne 6 on sides of shoulderplate, incised horizontal crescent on head back **3,000.00**

Bye-Lo

4½″ circ. solid domed bisque swivel head, bisque torso, jointed bent bisque arms, legs, modelled, painted features, well costumed, c1923. Marks: 12 (neck) 4-12 copr. by Grace S. Putnam Germany (torso) **400.00**

10″ circ., baby, bisque solid domed head, flanged neck, orig muslin body, celluloid hands, brown glass sleep eyes, painted baby hair, painted features, original muslin gown, Bye-Lo label ''None Genuine Without Signature'', c1923. Marks: Copr. by Grace S. Putnam/Made in Germany (head) Bye-Lo-Baby, Pat. applied for Grace S. Putnam (purple stamp on torso) **425.00**

16½″ circ., bisque, orig cloth body. Marks: Made in Germany copyright Grace Storey Putnam   **725.00**

Chase, Martha

16½″ , cloth, blonde painted Dutch bob hair, gray-blue eyes,

Left to right: Early Bru bisque head babe, 16″ h, $2,600.00; A.T. bisque head babe, 18″ h, $10,000.00; French bisque head babe, 18″ h, $3,200.00.

orig clothing. Mark: Paper label "The Chase Stockinet Doll Made of Stockinet and cloth/ Stuffed with Cotton/Made by Hand/Painted by Hand/Made by Especially Trained Workers" **775.00**
18½″, cloth, painted features, blue eyes, short blonde hair. Marks: Martha Chase, Pawtucket, Rhode Island **315.00**
Effanbee, 27″, composition socket head, 5 pc. composition body, blue sleep eyes, real lashes, closed mouth, strawberry blonde human hair, orig pink organdy ball gown, gold heart bracelet, c1940. Marked Little Lady **275.00**
Fulper, 30″, bisque socket head, composition and wooden ball jointed body, orig gray tin sleep eyes, painted features, real lashes, open mouth, 4 teeth, dimpled chin, brunette human hair, well costumed, c1917. Marks: CMU in triangle, Fulper, Amberg Dolls, The World Dolls, the World's Standard, Made in USA 70 ..... **400.00**
Gaultier, Ferdinand
12″ fashion lady, bisque swivel head, kid lined bisque shoulderplate, kid fashion body, narrow blue glass paperweight inset eyes, spiral threading, painted features, pierced ears, brunette mohair wig over cork pate, antique rose satin, maroon velvet frock, mauve silk pleated

train, lace trim, matching bonnet, c1875. Mark: O (head) F.G.O. shoulderplate **975.00**
19″, bisque socket head, French composition, wooden ball jointed body, straight wrists almond shaped blue glass paperweight eyes, painted features, beestung lips, pierced ears, blonde human hair, well costumed, c1885. Marks: FG in a scroll/7 .... **1,900.00**
Greiner, Ludwig, Phila., 31″, papier-mache shoulderhead, orig muslin body, brown kid arms, black molded hair, painted features, blue eyes, closed mouth, faded orig body finish. Marks: Greiner's Pat. Head Dolls #12, pat' March 30'58 ext. '72 .... **500.00**
Heinrich Handwerck
22″, bisque socket head, composition, wooden ball jointed body, blue glass sleep eyes, painted features, open mouth, 4 porcelain teeth, pierced ears, blonde mohair wig, c1900. Mark: 99-11 ¾ DEP Germany Handwerck, 3½ **500.00**
22″, bisque socket head, fully jointed composition body, brown glass sleep flirty eyes, open mouth, 4 teeth, pierced ears, blonde wig, old red dress, lace trim overcoat. Mark: Germany/ Heinrich/Handwerck/Simon & Halbig/3 .... **425.00**

23" h, bisque socket head, fully jointed composition body, brown glass sleep eyes, open mouth, 4 exposed teeth, pierced ears. Mark: Germany/Handwerck/4 . **325.00**

28", bisque socket head, composition, wooden ball jointed body, almond shaped grey glass sleep eyes, dark painted features, open mouth, 4 porcelain teeth, pierced ears, brunette mohair wig, well costumed, c1900. Marks: 119-13 Handwerck 5 Germany **400.00**

Heubach, Gebruder

11½", solid domed bisque socket head, composition bent limb baby body, blonde molded hair, gray painted intaglio eyes, sculpted features, c1915. Marks: 4 6970 Germany **600.00**

22½", bisque socket head, fully jointed composition body, brown glass sleep eyes, open mouth, 4 teeth, brown wig, redressed. Mark: Heubach/250-4-/Koppelsdorf/Germany **225.00**

Ideal, 12", Shirley Temple, composition socket head, 5 pc. body, green sleep eyes, real lashes, painted features, open smiling mouth, dimples, blonde mohair curly wig, original white pleated organdy dress, polka dots, red silk ribbon, c1935. Marks: Shirley Temple 11 head, torso, original cloth label, Ideal **425.00**

JDK, 13", Oriental Baby, bisque, oriental coloring, composition body, sleep eyes, open mouth, 2 upper teeth, black wig, orig hat, slippers. Mark: Germany/243/JDK/Made in/Germany **1,700.00**

Jumeau, Emile

15", bisque socket head, composition, wooden ball jointed body, blue glass sleep eyes, painted features, open mouth, 2 porcelain teeth, dimple, blonde human hair, c1915. Marks: D Made in Germany 143 8 . . . . . **500.00**

19", baby, bisque socket head, composition, bent limb baby body, gray glass sleep eyes, painted features, open smiling mouth, 2 porcelain teeth, tongue, blonde mohair wig over plaster pate, blue romper suit, c1915. Marks: K Made in Germany 14 J.D.K. Z 226Z **500.00**

19", French bisque socket head, orig papier mache, wooden body, blue glass sleep eyes,

real lashes, painted features, open mouth, 4 teeth, blonde mohair wig, pierced ears, orig packing box labeled Paris Bebe, Fabrication Jumeau, Paris, orig shoes, black velvet, red satin dress, cap, c1915. Marks: S.F.B.J. 301 Paris 8, Societe Francaise de Bebes Jouets . . . **1,100.00**

22", bisque socket head, French composition, wooden jointed body, deep blue glass paperweight inset eyes, painted features, open mouth, 6 teeth, pierced ears, brunette hair, well costumed, c1890. Marks: 10 incised, Tete Jumeau, red stamp **2,200.00**

30", child, bisque socket head, French composition, wooden ball jointed body, finish worn, almond shaped blue glass paperweight eyes, dimples, blonde human hair, antique blue wool sailor costume, c1880. Mark: Depose Tete Jumeau Bte S.G.D.G. 12 . . . . **2,600.00**

32", child, bisque socket head, French composition, wooden jointed body, almond shaped brown glass paperweight eyes, delicately painted features, open mouth, 6 teeth, dimples, pierced ears, blonde human hair over cork pate, recostumed, c1910. Marks: 1907 14 . . . . . . **2,500.00**

Kammer & Reinhardt

14", Character Baby, solid domed oily bisque socket head, composition bent limb body, painted blonde hair, facial features, intaglio narrow blue eyes, antique baby gown, c1910. Marks: 36 K * R 100 . . . . **525.00**

14", Peter, bisque socket head, composition, wooden ball jointed body, painted features, narrow painted blue eyes, closed mouth, pouty expression, blonde mohair wig, well-costumed, c1915. Marks: K * R 101 34 . . . . **1,900.00**

28", baby, matte bisque socket head, composition, wooden ball jointed body, side hip jointing, gray glass sleep eyes, painted features, open mouth, 2 porcelain upper teeth, porcelain tongue, brunette human hair, well costumed, c1915. Marks: K * R Simon & Halbig 126 Germany 62 . . . . **900.00**

28", soft matte bisque socket head, composition, wooden ball-jointed body, almond shaped blue glass sleep eyes, painted features, real lashes, open mouth, 4 porcelain teeth, pierced ears, auburn human hair, well costumed, c1910. Marks: S&H K * R 70 . . . .   **800.00**

Kestner

11", Hilda, solid domed bisque socket head, composition bent limb baby body, narrow almond shaped gray glass sleep eyes, painted features, open mouth, 2 porcelain teeth, white baby gown, body repainted, c1915. Marks: Hilda c J.D.K. jr. 1070 Ges Gesch Made In Germany .   **750.00**

Kley and Hahn

25", bisque socket head, composition, wooden ball jointed body, brown glass sleep eyes, real lashes, painted features, open mouth, 4 porcelain teeth, dressed in nun's black wool habit, c1910. Marks: 250 KH Walkure 2¼" Germany **350.00**

32", bisque socket head, composition, wooden ball jointed body, almond shaped threaded gray glass sleep eyes, painted features, open mouth, 4 porcelain teeth, pierced ears, blonde mohair wig, c1910. Marks: Walkure Germany **650.00**

Konig & Wernicke, 11", baby, bisque socket head, composition bent limb baby body, gray glass sleep eyes, real lashes, painted features, open mouth, 2 upper teeth, brunette mohair wig, well costumed, c1915. Marks: KW in circle on head, KW Germany red stamp on body **700.00**

Krauss, Gebruder, 5", bisque socket head, 5 pc. papier-mache body, blue glass sleep eyes, painted features, open mouth, tiny teeth, brunette mohair wig, well costumed in old lace, painted black socks, tan shoes, c1910. Marks: G.K.44.12 . . . .   **325.00**

Kruse, Kathe

20", cloth swivel head, pressed mask, 5 pc. muslin body, oil painted facial features, shaded green painted eyes, closed mouth, pouty expression, blonde human hair, new costume, c1940. Marks: Kathe Kruse 2056 on left foot **375.00**

21", celluloid socket head, muslin jointed body, painted facial features, plum colored eyes, closed

(Left) 23", bisque shoulderhead, painted features, molded choker necklace, blue glass threaded in set eyes, molded white camisole, soft rose gown, unmarked, c1870, $1,250.00. (Right) Kathe Kruse, 18", boy, celluloid, socket head, 5 pc pink muslin body, orig costume, post war paper tag, $300.00.

pouty mouth, blonde human hair wig, orig organdy crepe schooldress, post war production. Marks: Original Kathe Kruse Soft Puppe **450.00**

Lenci

11½", painted blue eyes, light brown wig, single braid, blue felt dress, silk bandanna. Mark: Lenci/Turin/Made in Italy **550.00**

28½", Lady, molded felt head, molded, painted brown eyes, brown braided hair, swivel neck, red felt peasant outfit, matching headdress **750.00**

Madame Alexander

13", Dionne Quintuplets, nurse, 7" babies, composition heads, bodies, molded hair, painted features, nurse in uniform, babies in white organdy dresses, bonnets, orig organdy lined wicker basket, c1935. Marks: Alexander, clothes tagged **1,350.00**

14", Snow White, hard plastic socket head, 5 pc. plastic body, green sleep eyes, real lashes, painted features, closed mouth, black saran wig, orig ivory satin gown, gold leaf pattern, gilt brocade vest, c1952. Marks: Alex on head, Walt Disney Snow White Madame Alexander U.S.A. on tag **450.00**

19", Margaret O'Brien, composition swivel head, 5 pc. composition body, green plastic sleep eyes, real lashes, auburn mohair wig in pigtails, pink cotton dress, peplum, puffy sleeves, blue braid, blue suede shoes, straw hat, c1946. Marks: Alexander **425.00**

21", Sonja Henie, composition socket head, straight limbed body, jointed at shoulders, hips, sleep eyes, real lashes, open mouth, 6 upper teeth, blonde human hair, FAO Schwartz special issue, Sonja Henie pin, paper wrist tag, orig white taffeta skating costume, Maribou trim, pink flowers, white skates, c1939. MIB, Marks: Sonja Henie on head **500.00**

22", bisque socket head, French wooden and composition body, brunette mohair wig, silk replica of orig. silk dress, Marks: A. Marque in script on head, "12" in red ink script c1899, $38,000.00.

Marseille, Armand

13", Poupard, bisque shoulderhead, music box torso, blue glass inset eyes, painted features, open mouth, 4 teeth, white mohair wig, orig blue, ivory silk clown outfit, braid trim, c1890. Marks: 3200 AM 10-0 DEP **300.00**

17", Dream Baby, solid domed bisque socket head, composition 5 pc. toddler body, chubby straight legs, molded curls, reddish brown painted hair, blue glass sleep eyes, open mouth, 2 lower teeth, c1923. Marks: AM Germany 351/4.K **250.00**

28½", bisque, jointed composition body, blonde wig. Marks: AM 390 DRGM 246/1 A 12 M **475.00**

Sannier and Caut, 30", bisque socket head, composition, wooden ball jointed body, almond shaped gray glass sleep eyes, spiral threading, painted features, open mouth, 4 teeth, pierced ears, brunette human hair, one hand repainted, c1910. Marks: 14 S & C Germany **850.00**

Schoenhut

15", carved wooden socket head, wooden spring jointed body, carved brown boyish hair, painted features, intaglio brown eyes, closed somber mouth, blue cotton sailor suit, c1911. Marks: Schoenhut Doll Pat. Jan. 17, 1911, USA **1,125.00**

19", carved wooden socket head, spring jointed fully articulated body, blue painted intaglio eyes, closed pouty mouth, blonde mohair wig, 2 pc. linen suit, c1915. Marks: Schoenhut Doll Pat. Jan. 17th 1911 U.S.A. **325.00**

Schmidt, Bruno, 17", Tommy Tucker, bisque solid domed socket head, composition wooden ball jointed body, short brown molded, painted hair, blue glass sleep eyes, painted features, well costumed, c1915. Marks: 2048 4 ... **650.00**

Simon & Halbig

14", oily bisque socket head, composition, wooden ball jointed body, large brown glass paperweight eyes, painted features, open mouth, 2 upper teeth, auburn braided mohair wig, orig white dress, red smocking, c1885. Marks: S & H 949 .... **1,000.00**

16", oily socket head, composition, wooden ball-jointed body, almond shaped brown glass flirty eyes, real lashes, painted features, open mouth, 4 porcelain teeth, pierced ears, blonde mohair wig, well costumed, c1900. Marks: SH 1039 6½ DEP Germany **450.00**

20″, Gibson Girl, matte bisque socket head, composition wooden ball jointed body, adult modeling, oval blue glass sleep eyes, painted features, open mouth, 4 porcelain teeth, pierced ears, brunette upswept mohair wig, soft rose, lace costume, c1895. Marks: 1159 Simon & Halbig S & H 7 . . . . . **950.00**

23″, solid domed bisque socket head, composition, wooden toddler body, side hip joints, painted features, blue eyes, spiral threading, closed mouth, well costumed, c1910. Marks: 1498 10 **2,500.00**

Societe Francaise de Bebes Jouets

18″, child, bisque socket head, French composition, jointed body, blue glass sleep eyes, real lashes, painted features, open mouth, 4 teeth, brunette human wig, orig ethnic costume, green satin dress, embroidered apron, paisley shaw, c1925. Marks: Unis France 71 149 301 E.T. **350.00**

23″, bisque socket head, French composition, wooden body, straight walker legs, almond shaped bright blue glass sleep eyes, painted features, open mouth, 4 teeth, pierced ears, blonde, human hair, well costumed, new hands, cries mama, c1900. Marks: S.F.B.J. 301 Paris 10 . . . . **1,450.00**

Steiner, Jules, 17″, French bisque head, composition body, blue paperweight eyes, pierced ears, closed mouth, orig costume, c1889. Marks: paper label Le Petit Parisien, Bebe Steiner, Medaille d'Or Paris **2,600.00**

Unknown Makers

16″, Frozen Charlotte, one pc molded porcelain figural, arms extended in front of body, painted features, blue eyes, spiral threading, closed mouth, c1880 . . . . **325.00**

18″, French Fashion, bisque swivel head, kid lined shoulderplate, kid over wooden body, dowel jointed at shoulders, hips, knees, bisque arms, plumply

French Fashion, 17″, early but unmarked, bisque head, kid body, articulated arms, orig wig, $1,400.00.

molded, almond shaped blue threaded inset eyes, delicately painted features, pale blonde mohair wig, elaborate costume, c1870 . . . . **2,600.00**

19″, gentleman, papier-mache shoulderhead, French kid body, straight kid arms, legs, black painted pate, scalloped curls outline, black glass inset eyes, open mouth, 2 upper, 2 lower bamboo teeth, antique costume of white periwig, white ruffled shirt, silk vest, blue velvet knickers, jacket, c1850 . . . . **400.00**

21″, American bleached muslin, mask face, water color painted features, curly brown hair at edges of face, blue eyes, orig calico costume, white ruffled apron, 19th C **50.00**

DOLLS, PAPER

Warman's Americana & Collectibles, 1st Edition, contains 63 listings in this category; see also page xii.

DOOR KNOCKERS

Before the advent of the mechanical bell, electric buzzer and chimes, a door knocker

was considered an essential door ornament to announce the arrival of visitors. Metal was used to cast or forge the various forms.

Cast iron, owl, brown, yellow eyes, green ribbon, $75.00.

Brass
Atlantis, head of, dolphin and shell
motif 55.00
Bust of Will Rogers 65.00
Bust of Shakespeare, 4" 65.00
Eagle, figural, large 55.00
Lion's head, 4½" 25.00
Pistol 50.00
Standing bear 55.00
Turtle, marked China 35.00
Bronze
Charles Dickens 85.00
Lion's head, loose ring knocker . 50.00
Cast Iron
Basket of flowers, bow at top of
handle 28.00
Couple kissing 80.00
Parrot on branch, pink, rose body,
4" oval base, 4½" l 35.00
Ram's head, English 65.00
Spur 35.00
Woody Woodpecker, red head,
tree bark base 38.00

Aunt Jemima, 14", painted clothes . 60.00
Bull 40.00
Cat, 10", black, Halloween pose . . 85.00
Conestoga Wagon, 7" 40.00
Deer, full antlered, flatback on base 125.00
Dogs
Airdale, 4¾" 90.00
Boston Bulldog, full figure 50.00
German Shepherd, standing 40.00
Russian Wolfhound 115.00
Dwarf with lantern and keep 135.00
Lady with basket of flowers on head 45.00
Monkey 40.00
Parrot on Perch, 8", c1900 . . . . . . 50.00
Pot of Tulips 65.00
Rhett Butler, brass 50.00
Rooster 50.00
Ships
Mayflower 35.00
Tall Ship, 3 masts, base waves . . 70.00
Shoe, high heeled 75.00
Windmill, 7" 35.00
Wolf 34.00

Fraternal, red base, white bird, gold chain, $80.00.

DOORSTOPS

Door stops became popular in the late 19th-Century. They fall into two types, flat and three dimensional. Although most were made of cast iron and painted, bronze, wood, and other materials were used. Condition is a key factor in price. Repainting lowers the value by 50% or more.

DRESDEN (MEISSEN)

In 1710, Johann Frederick Boettger, an alchemist, accidently discovered a white clay in the area of Dresden, Germany. When he replaced his red stoneware pots with the white kaolin clay product, he produced the first true porcelain in Europe and Meissen Porcelain Works had its beginning.

Meissen porcelain is finely molded, decorated with applied floral motifs, enameled and gilded. In the 19th century, the factory reissued versions of their earlier examples. These debased wares are referred to as Dresden to differentiate them from the original Meissen porcelains.

Many marks were used to identify the porcelain. The first was a pseudo-oriental mark in a square. The famous crossed swords mark was adopted in 1724. The crossed swords mark with a small dot between the hilts was used in the 1763-1774 period. The following years, 1774 to 1814, the dot between the hilts was changed to a star. It has been reported that two new marks are appearing on the modern market—swords with a hammer and sickle and swords with a crown.

Candlestick, 10″, multicolored flowers with gilting, blue crossed swords, $395.00.

Beaker and Saucer, 2⅝″ beaker, 2 handles, 5″ saucer, gold, bird flying above oriental flowing shrubbery, scalloped border, underglaze blue crossed swords, 1725 . . . . .   500.00
Boot, 5¼ x 4⅛″ toe to heel, floral with lacy gold, gold lined interior rim, mkd with lamb and Dresden in blue 45.00
Bowls
   3 x 4½″, white with red, pink, yellow and cobalt blue floral design, gilding, scalloped edge, crossed swords 135.00
   12½″, floral and shell decor, molded and raised foliate, blue crossed swords 250.00
Box, 4″, cobalt, spray of flowers within scroll foliate gilt border, blue crossed swords 85.00
Button, hp, wild rose 65.00
Candlelabras, 20″, Bocage, figural cupids on scroll base, ftd, Dresden, late 19th C, pr 495.00
Candlesticks, 8¼″, 2 holders, hp pastel flowers and fruit, gold trim, sgd, pr 225.00
Charger, 11″, white, gold raised leaf design, blue crossed swords 295.00
Cups and Saucers
   Cabinet, cylindrical, flaring, white with yellow band above floral decor, scroll gilt handle, Dresden 45.00
   Demitasse
     2″ cup, handled, 4¼″ saucer, yellow, lady in portrait 55.00
     White, heavy gold trim, blue crossed swords 65.00

Cutting Board, hanging, 10¾ x 6⅛″, Onion pattern, mkd underglaze Crown with D 135.00
Dish, 8½″, leaf shape, fruit and flowers, molded basketwork border, gilt rim, branch handle, crossed swords and dot, c1765 .   275.00
Dressing Mirror, oval, beveled, 3 cavorting putti, flowers, Dresden, late 19th C 125.00
Figures
   Bacchus, 5¾″, wearing grape wreath and brown goatskin, holding goblet and cluster of grapes, standing by tree trunk and basket of grapes, gilt scroll molded base, underglaze crossed swords and dot, c1765   350.00
   Man and woman, 10″, 18th C costumes, pink, blue and white, woman feeding pigeons, man with dog at his feet, underglaze blue crossed swords, inscribed and imp no. and letters 850.00
   Mouse, 1½ x 2½″, sitting with tail curled over back, crossed swords 185.00
   Nude male, 21″, bisque, wearing fig leaf, Meissen, crossed swords 275.00

Parrots, 6½", sitting on tree stump, flower decor, pr 300.00

Spaniel, 5½", sitting, white with black markings, Meissen, crossed swords 245.00

Winter, cherub, fur draped, skating on icy pond, crossed swords, mid 19th C 375.00

Inkwell, cov, white with floral motif on 2 sides, sq acorn finial, crossed swords underglaze 99.50

Knife and Fork, pistol shaped handles, birds on branches and insects, molded basketwork border, c1750 .... 275.00

Milk Jug, 3⅜", cov, flower sprays and sprigs, red, puce, mauve, yellow and green, gilt edged sprout rim and cover, crossed swords, c1750 .... 195.00

Nodder, 7⅜", pagoda figure, seated, cross-legged, wearing white robe with multicolored flowers, yellow and turquoise trousers, red slippers, gilt edged chamfered sq base, crossed swords, c1750 ... 1,000.00

Parasol Handle, Meissen, sgd., early 19th C 150.00

Pen Tray with 2 Ink Pots, 6½ x 9½", floral decor, irregular yellow-orange border 50.00

Plates
6½", man and woman, courtship scene, "Canoemates," Christy, Dresden 20.00
8¾", Kakiemon, butterflies and flowering shrubs, brown edged rim, underglaze blue crossed swords, c1740 .... 250.00
9¼", Kakiemon, Flying Dragon, flower spray and insect border, shaped rim, blue crossed swords, c1735 .... 495.00

Platter, 19", sgd Collin Meissen ... 150.00

Salt, 3⅛" l, oval, floral sprays and insect, red, yellow, blue, green and gilt, brown rim, crossed swords, c1735 .... 300.00

Scent Bottle and Stopper, miniature, Blanc de Chine porcelain, flower encrusted crossed swords 45.00

Spoon Tray, 6¾", puce monochrome with court figures in garden setting, shaped border with gilt foliage scrolls, blue crossed swords, gilder's mark N, c1745 .. 500.00

Sugar Castor, 2¾", flower sprays and sprigs, red, puce, mauve, yellow and green, crossed swords, c1750 .... 190.00

Teabowl and Saucer, flowering plants, scrolling foliage borders, blue crossed swords, c1740 .... 395.00

Tea Caddy, 5¼ x 3½", sq, lacy gold, flowers on 2 panels, scene of boy and girl courting on 2 panels, crossed swords, letter H and Dresden 130.00

Tea Kettle, 10¾" w, round, floral bouquets, scroll molded spout and handle, peach finial, blue crossed swords, imp 23, c1755 .... 790.00

Teapot, 4½", sprays of flowers, gilt handle, rim and spout, rosebud finial, blue underglaze crossed swords, 19th C 295.00

Tureen, 11⅞" l, cov, Kakiemon, flowering shrubbery and rockwork between molded borders, lady's head handles, crossed swords, imp 26, c1740 .... 860.00

Urn, 24", baluster shape on round stepped pedestal, cobalt blue, white acanthus leaves, S-scroll handles, gilt decor 300.00

Vases
10½", floral bouquets, base drilled and mounted as lamp, crossed swords, c1760 ...... 895.00
10½", serpent handles, late 19th C 135.00

Waste Bowl, 6¼", Bienenmuster, bees, butterflies and Oriental flowers tied with yellow ribbons, blue crossed swords, imp 20, c1740 .. 775.00

DUNCAN AND MILLER GLASS

The firm began in Pittsburgh, Pa., in the late 1860's under the name of George Duncan and Sons. In 1893–94 the glass works moved to Washington, Pa. where they manufactured some of the finest handmade glassware in America for sixty-three years.

George Duncan, the founder, recognized the talents of his designer, John Ernest Miller, encouraged his growth, and made him one of the owners, thus the name Duncan and Miller.

A specialty of the firm was the production of early American Sandwich Glass, but probably the most famous Miller design was "Three Face" and probably the most beautiful is the Duncan and Miller "Swan."

Production ceased in June 1955. The U.S. Glass Co. purchased the molds, equipment and machinery in 1956.

Ashtrays
Dogwood 12.50
Duck, clear, 4½" 19.00
Animals
Dove, 12" l 110.00
Fat Goose 350.00

Plaque, 14″ d, light green, sailing ship, $20.00.

Bonbons
6″, Hobnail, crystal, heart shape .	12.00
7″, Sandwich	15.00

Bowls
5″, Nautical, frosted blue, 2 handles	30.00
8½″, Caribbean, blue	45.00
9″, Canterbury, ruby, crimped . . .	18.00
10″, Canterbury, chartruse	25.00
12″, Ivy, hobnail, pink opalescent	35.00
Butter, covered, Double Snail	125.00

Candelabras
Granada, 3-lite, pair	55.00
Magnolia, 2-lite, pair	60.00

Candlesticks
American Way, pink opal, pr	55.00
Hobnail, pink opalescent, pair . . .	45.00
Sandwich, bobeches, prisms, pr .	70.00
Teardrop, crystal, 4″, pr	24.00
Champagne, Hobnail, crystal, 5 oz .	10.00
Cigarette Box, cov, Mallard duck etching, 2 matching ashtrays . . .	38.00

Coasters
3¼″, Hobnail, green	8.50
5″, Sandwich, crystal	7.50
Cocktail, 4¼″ Hobnail, crystal, 3½ oz	10.00
Cocktail Shaker, Chanticleer, ruby .	110.00

Compotes
5″, Canterbury, vaseline	38.00
5½″, First Love, crystal, etched .	45.00
6″, Spiral Flutes, amber	7.00
Console Set, Caribbean, Cape Cod blue	145.00

Creamers
Amberette	65.00
Whirligig, individual	15.00

Cruet, Caribbean, crystal, cobalt stopper	32.00
Egg Plate, Sandwich, crystal	15.00
Flower Frog, 7½″, Canterbury, ruby, crimped	22.00

Goblets
Canterbury, chartreuse	15.00
Hobnail, crystal, 9 oz	10.00
Teardrop, crystal	8.00
Hat, 4″, Hobnail, blue opalescent . .	20.00
Ice Tub, Spiral Flutes, amber	10.00

Nappies
4½″, Flower Scroll	12.50
6″, Sanibel, Cape Cod, blue opal	26.00

Pitchers
Water, Heavy Panel, fine cut . . .	100.00
Water, Sandwich, crystal	45.00

Plates
6″, Teardrop, crystal, handle . . .	5.00
7½″, Hobnail, crystal	7.00
7½″, Spiral Flutes, green	5.00
8″, Sandwich, crystal	15.00
10½″, Caribbean, blue, 2 handles	24.00
Platter, 12″, Puritan Pink, sterling floral pattern	30.00
Punch Bowl Set, 12 cups, ladle, Hobnail, crystal	125.00
Punch Cups, Ivy, hobnail	6.00

Relishes
Canterbury, divided	12.50
Sanibel, blue, pink	20.00
Rose Bowl, Hobnail, footed, crimped top	20.00

Sherbets
Charmain Rose	16.00
Cretan	16.00
Indian Tree	16.00

Sugars
3″, Canterbury	8.00
8 oz, Teardrop, Crystal	9.00

Swans
4¾″	25.00
7″, ruby, crystal	30.00
11½″, blue opal, open wings	75.00

Toothpicks
Teepee	45.00
Two Ply Swirl	28.00
Tray, 6″, Teardrop, 2 handles	3.00

Tumblers
Arliss, ruby	25.00
Hobnail, pink opalescent	20.00
Sandwich, vaseline	20.00
Tear drop, crystal, 9 oz, flat	9.00

Vases
3½″, Canterbury, pink opal, crimped	16.00
4″, Hobnail, blue opalescent	28.00
5″, pink opal, ruffled top	30.00
8″, Passion Flower, crystal, flared top	22.50
8½″, blue opalescent	40.00
Violet Bowl, 7½″, Hobnail, crystal, ftd	30.00

DURAND

Victor Durand, Sr., reputed to be a descendant of the French family which made Baccarat glass, started a factory in Vineland, N.J., in 1925.

The art glass resembles Tiffany in some respects, especially the iridescent sheen. Much of Durand glass was not marked, some bore a sticker labeled "Durand Art Glass," some had the name Durand scratched in the pontil and a few had the name inside a large V. The factory closed in 1932.

Bowls
8", white, blue lily pad decor . . .	325.00
10½", amber ground, white, blue petal decor	200.00
Box, 3½" d, cov, green lustre glass, gold lustre King Tut decor	950.00
Candlesticks, 10", blue, sgd	375.00
Champagne, 6½", ruby and amber	225.00

Compotes
6", gold, blue, King Tut interior, gold stem, blue highlighted foot	750.00
6½ x 7¾" d, gold blue, signed . .	395.00
Goblet, wine, 7¼" h, ruby red bowl, Spanish yellow stem, ftd	225.00
Ginger Jar, 10½", cov, gold and green, King Tut decor	1,850.00
Lamp, boudoir, 17" h, overall threading on butterscotch ground on base, petal leaves decor on matching shade	1,100.00

Lamp, 9¼", Moorish Crackle, orange, green highlights, $90.00.

Plates
8", pulled white feather, flashed ruby, engraved Bridget Rose by Charles Link	300.00
14", gold scalloped edge, clear green glass trim	245.00

Rose Bowls
3½", blue, ruffled rim, signed . . .	400.00
4", clear, controlled bubbles, sgd	225.00
5½", blue, gold threads, gold foot, sgd	375.00
Sherbet, amber, blue, white petal decor	170.00

Vases
6½", baluster form, blue, gray, gold irid feather design, all over gold horizontal overlay threading, irid gold interior, sgd. V. Durand, 1710-6	300.00
7", gold, deep green, white pulls, ruffled top	425.00
7½", gold, irid, green lustre vine, leaf decor	575.00
8½", beige, pink, green threaded leaves to middle	325.00
10", apple green, gold-platinum King Tut decor, brilliant gold interior, sgd	1,050.00
12½", green ground, King Tut, pink and lavender highlights . .	1,000.00

ENGLISH YELLOW-GLAZED EARTHENWARE

This ware has been called Canary Lustre. It dates back to the early 1800s and is identified with the Staffordshire district of England. The body of the piece is yellow (canary) colored, the transfer picture is usually in black and the decoration in lustre.

Developed at the highest technical moment in English pottery history, English Yellow-Glazed Earthenware embraces the finest quality creamware found toward the end of the century of experimentation and into the nineteenth century. Documented pieces date from the 1780s to 1840, including Wedgwood wares as early as 1785.

While many pieces have silver and, more rarely, copper lustre, some items have none. Examples may be painted in a colorful, freeform manner, or transfer decor in black or brick red, with or without lustre. Pieces without any decoration are uncommon. The yellow overglaze varies in intensity from canary to a very pale yellow.

This category has also been called "Canary Lustre."

Jugs
4½", round medallion encircled in silver lustre depicting Peace as

Bowl, English Yellow Glaze Earthenware 7¼" d, 3¼" h, $395.00.

a young girl, silver luster borders	350.00
5¾", transfer painted in black, inscribed "Accept this trifle from a friend whose love for thee shall never end," George Lawton, 1809 under spout, silver lustre decor	700.00

Mugs
"A Present for a Good Boy," 2¼"	300.00
Child's, 2½" h, bird on branch, silver lustre band borders	450.00
Schoolhouse, 2⅝" h, pink lustre trim, ...	375.00
"Want of care does thee more damage than want of knowledge," Franklin Maxim, 2¼" ..	300.00
Pitcher, 4½", "Faith and Hope" ...	500.00
Plate, 8¼", wide yellow border, white flowers, iron red decor, silver lustre leafy vines, rim	400.00
Vase, potpourri, 7½" h, 6 classical figures by flaming brazier, inscribed "Sacrifice A L' Hymen," figures outlined in black enamel, lion's head handles covered in silver lustre	415.00
Waste bowl, 6¾" d, rose colored flowers on vine, iron red, green enamel on pink lustre leaves, pink lustre rim	375.00

FAIRINGS

Fairings are small decorative china objects which were purchased or given away at fairs. Some were sold as inexpensive souvenirs. The original fairings were made in Germany and Bohemia c. 1870. These were made in molds, highly painted and decorated with gold. They usually consisted of at least two figures and were related to a common domestic scene. They were mass produced and inexpensive enough to be taken home as a remembrance of the fair. Many were given away as prizes. Some fairings also had a utilitarian use such as a match holder or inkwell.

Small trinket boxes with the popular figurines on the lids were also mass produced and are now highly collectible. Most of the fairings have sayings.

Calendar Holders
Gentleman in dressing gown, standing before a wall hung with paintings, slot for calendar cards, orig card, 6½", German	360.00
"Sedan," two military officers seated	300.00
Dresser Box, "Last Into Bed Put Out Lights"	37.50

Figurines
"A Long Pull and a Strong Pull," 3 figures, center having tooth pulled	100.00
"Between Two Stools You Fall to the Ground," 2 men assisting lady to a chair	170.00
"God Save the Queen"	165.00

Figurine, "Ladies of Llangden," 5⅞", $40.00.

"Landlord in Love," man in dressing gown peeking through keyhole	240.00
"Our Best Wishes!" flower decoration	75.00
"Out by Jingo!" three people ...	270.00
"Please Sir, what would you charge to Christen my doll?" 2 girls talking with clergy in top hat	210.00
"The Murderer"	75.00
"The Night Before Christmas," black faced figures, children in bed, woman holding candle ...	220.00

Match holder, "Open your Mouth and Shut your Eyes" **100.00**

Trinket box, "Returning at One in the Morning," woman hitting man on head with shoe, fancy bed . . . **50.00**

FAIRY LAMPS

Fairy Lamps are candle-burning night lights. They were first introduced by the Samuel Clarke Co., England, in 1857, but were made by many other firms in England, Europe and the U.S. from then on.

A wide array were produced, from pressed glass to fine art glass. There are two main classifications: The Fairy Pyramid has a clear glass base and a dome shaped shade that measures approximately 3½" high when assembled. Others are 5" or more high and may have in addition to the clear glass candle insert, a saucer that matches the shade.

Baccarat, wine to clear, swirl, sgd . **235.00**

Brass, rose on ormolu stand **195.00**

Bristol, white, enamel floral decor, matching vase **175.00**

Burmese

5⅜ x 4¾", acid finish, Webb, green leaves and red berries, cream tapestry base with gold trim and large pink flowers, gold leaves, base mkd S. Clarke's Patent Fairy **650.00**

5½ x 4", acorn and brown leaves decor, acid finish, Webb, cream Tunnecliffe pottery base mk Clarke, clear insert cup, gold trim **475.00**

5⅝ x 6¾", acid finish, reheated yellow edges, sgd Thos. Webb, clear Clarke insert cup **595.00**

Cranberry

4¾ x 4", frosted, etched flowers and leaves, clear mkd Clarke base **175.00**

9 x 4½", clear pressed glass base, unmarked, cranberry shade has crystal applied petals **275.00**

Cricklite, 15½ x 5½" d, sq brass candlestick base, clear peg cup mkd Clarke, Cricklite chimney, pink silk shade with beaded fringe, shade has orig box **225.00**

Cut Velvet, 4¼ x 3¾ x 7¼", rose, DQ (Diamond Quilted), white lining, Aladdin lamp shape cream base, gold trim, mkd Tunnecliffe, Clarke **475.00**

Opalescent, 5 x 6", pink and white, sq ruffled base, clear mkd Clarke insert **550.00**

Overlay, 5¼ x 4⅜", pink candy stripe, white lining, matching candle cup, and ruffled base, clear applied feet **365.00**

Peachblow

4¾ x 6" d, satin, Webb, pale to deep rose, cream lining, light tan garlands, flowers and leaves, cream pottery base, pink flowers, green leaves outlined in gold, mkd Tunnecliffe, Clarke **395.00**

5 x 4", satin, cream lining, green, brown and gold leaves and foliage, cream pottery base with gold trim, mkd Tunnecliffe, Clarke **495.00**

6¼ x 7⅞", acid finish, Webb, green and brown leaves, cream lining, cream, fluted pottery base, aqua panels, white flowers, pink trim, green leaves, mkd Tunnecliffe, Clarke **750.00**

Pressed, 3½", green diamond point top, clear sgd Clarke base, orig Cricklite candle **95.00**

Royal Worcester, 19 x 10½", 3 lamps on pedestal base, sgd Made especially for Clarke Cricklite, Royal Worcester **1,500.00**

Satin Glass

3¾ x 4", blue, DQ, MOP, white lining, cream pottery with blue bands, gold trim, pink roses, mkd Tunnecliffe, Clarke **275.00**

Satin glass, rainbow DQ, MOP base, shade, 5" h, $700.00.

4¾ x 3⅝", rainbow striped, DQ, MOP, matching base with frosted wafer foot, white lining, mkd Clarke's Patent Fairy 995.00

5 x 5½", blue, Webb, green flowers and leaves, white lining, cream base with pink and blue tapestry flowers and leaves, gold trim, blue band, mkd Tunnecliffe 450.00

5¼ x 4", butterscotch raindrop MOP, white lining, clear mkd Clarke base 195.00

Spangled Glass, multicolor, gold mica, Cricklite clear base 130.00

Vaseline

3½ x 2⅞", ribbed dome, green pressed base, mkd Clarke 165.00

4⅛ x 3⅛", shellshape, overshot, clear base, mkd Clarke 135.00

Verre Moire (Nailsea)

5¼ x 6¼", frosted cranberry, white loopings, upturned ruffled base, clear mkd Clarke insert cup 450.00

6½ x 7¾", frosted, chartreuse, opaque white loopings on dome shade, matching ruffled base, clear insert cup mkd Clarke . . . 475.00

FAMILLE ROSE

Famille Rose is Chinese export enameled porcelain in which the pink color predominates. It was made primarily in the 18th and early 19th century. Other porcelains in the same family group are Famille Jaune (yellow), Famille Noire (black), and Famille Verte (green).

Decorations include courtyard and home scenes, birds, and insects. Secondary colors are yellow, green, blue, aubergine, and black.

Mid to late 19th century Chinese export wares similar to Famille Rose are identified as Rose Canton, Rose Mandarin, and Rose Medallion.

Basin 16⅛" d rose-robed lady, turquoise robed lady 450.00

Bowls

8" exterior has figural lakeside scene, interior central figural scene, flaring rim, circular foot, 19th C 500.00

10¼", Judgment of Paris, lotus sprays 675.00

Charger

13⅛", octagonal, c. 1740 . . . . . . 380.00

Dish, 9½" lady and man drinking tea with their attendants, wide yellow band with landscape panels and flower sprays, late 18th C 195.00

Dish, 6½" d, ogee shape, heron, peaches, symbols of longevity, immorality, gold rim; central peach medallion, Tongah: seal mark, $175.00.

Garden Seat, 18¾", barrel shape, turquoise, birds, peony blossoms, ornate ruyi and lappet borders, 19th C 3,000.00

Jardinieres, 22" d, wood stands, butterflies and flowers inside and outside, pr 1,650.00

Mug, 5½", floral motif, c1800 . . . . 350.00

Plates

8¼", octagonal, center, lady with fan, bird on perch, aubergine and turquoise border with lotus and daisy heads 375.00

8⅞", bouquet with lappet border 250.00

9", peony spray, multi-colored . . 175.00

10⅛", six sprays of fruit and flowers on rim 425.00

Sauce Boat, 8½" l, women and children flying kites by river, exterior has landscape panels 350.00

Teapot, hexagonal, reticulated, green diaper pattern, panels of branches with blossoms, bracket feet, curved spout, applied handle 570.00

Temple Jar, cov 25", ovoid, white, bird, flower and butterfly decor . . 1,200.00

Tureen, Soup, cover, fishing scene . 1,750.00

Vases

8¾", gourd shape, wide rim neck, white, ladies, boy and court jesters 250.00

18½", sq, yellow, all over scolled foliate and bat decor, 19th C . . 550.00

18¾", faceted quadrangular shape, peafowl, birds, peonies and pine, molded mask and ring handles, late 19th C, pr 1,500.00

Wine Ewer, covered, 5", pear shape, brown scrollground, branch, blossoms, and flower heads, long lavender spout, curved handle, flower head finial, 18th C 580.00

FANS

Warman's Americana & Collectibles, 1st Edition, contains 86 listings in this category; see also page xii.

FENTON GLASS

The Fenton Art Glass Company was founded at Martin Ferry, Ohio, by Frank L. Fenton in 1907. They began production with carnival, chocolate, custard, pressed and mold blown opalescent glass. In the 1920s stretch glass, Fenton dolphins, jade green, ruby and art glass were added to their line.

In the 30s boudoir lamps, "Dancing Ladies," and various slags were produced. The 40s saw crests of different colors being added to each piece by hand. Hobnail, opalescent, and two-color overlay pieces were popular items. Handles were added to different shapes, making the baskets they created as popular today as then.

Through the years, Fenton has added beauty to their glass by decorating it with hand painting, acid etching, color staining and copper wheel cutting. Several different paper labels have been used. However, in 1970 an oval raised trademark was also adopted. Located today in Williamstown, West Virginia, Fenton is recognized as one of the foremost glass companies in the United States.

See also CARNIVAL GLASS.

Cruet, hobnail opal, cranberry, cased neck, tricorn lip, clear applied handle clear hobnail stopper, $60.00.

Atomizer, Hobnail	26.00
Baskets	
10", Hobnail, blue	75.00
10", Hobnail, cranberry	95.00
12", Diamond Optic, green, metal handle	45.00
Bowls	
8", Snowcrest, blue, honeycomb pattern	48.00
9½", Cameo, rolled rim	18.00
10", Hobnail, opal, plum	45.00
10½", Poinsetta etching, 3 ball handles, ball feet	45.00
Candlesticks	
2½", Ming, green, single	12.50
3½", Dolphin, green, pr	35.00
8½", Ruby, cut, pr	220.00
Candy Dish, cov, Dolphin, aquamarine	45.00
Console Set	
Compote, Dolphin stem, shell dish, milk glass	12.00
Console Set, Gold Crest, fluted bowl, cornucopia candlesticks, pr	50.00
Creamer and Sugar, open, 3½" h, Wistaria etching, c1937, pr	65.00
Cruet, Rib Optic, 7" h, cranberry, white opal stripes, black glass stopper, handle	55.00
Decanters	
Dot Optic, cranberry	185.00
Red Flower, 6 shot glasses	85.00
Dresser Set, Daisy & Button, rose, fan shaped tray, cov powder jar, 2 perfumes	165.00
Epergnes	
Single branch, ftd, with swan, ruby, 10½" h	110.00
Three branch, fluted, shaped, blue, opal white to clear, Hobnails in Diamond pattern	175.00
Figure, elephant, transparent green	22.00
Hats	
3¼" d, Dot Optic	37.50
4" d, Peach Crest	35.00
6" d, French opal swirl	75.00
9½", Snow Crest, cranberry	250.00
Jam Set, Hobnail, cranberry, opal, white opal lid, clear spoon, ruffled underplate	35.00
Lamps, glass base, fabric shades	
Cameo, opal, large	100.00
Coin Dot, cranberry opal, solid brass fittings	115.00
Macaroon Jar, 6½" h, Periwinkle blue	120.00
Mayonnaise, ladle, Stretch glass, velva rose	45.00

Nappies
5", Dolphin, green	15.00
7", Stretch, wisteria	60.00
Nut Cup, Stretch, celeste blue 30.00

Paperweight, 3½" h, Bicentennial,
chocolate slag 35.00
Perfume Bottle, Coin Dot, blue, opal 45.00

Pitchers
8", 80 oz, French opal, set of 6 tumblers, 7 pc	95.00
8", Hobnail, cranberry opal	125.00
10", Ming, rose, black handle	125.00

Plates
8", Plymouth, French opal	10.00
9", Rose Pastel, backward C openwork border	42.00

Rose Bowls
Cranberry, opal	49.00
Ivory Crest, 4"	15.00
Slipper, 6" l, topaz, opal 35.00

Tumblers
Georgian, 5", jade green	25.00
Hobnail, 12 oz	20.00

Vases
3½", hand shape, topaz, opal	25.00
4", green opal hobnail, flared	15.00
5", beaded melon, crimped	22.50
6½", Aqua Crest, fan	15.00
6¾", Mosaic, squatty	125.00
7½", Peacock, Mongolian green	95.00
7½", Snow Crest, amber, swirl	27.50
8", Spangled, blue, green	50.00
13", Coin Dot, cranberry, opal	75.00

Casserole, cov, turquoise	45.00
Celery Tray, cobalt	12.50
Compote, 12", ivory	40.00
Cookie Jar, cobalt	100.00
Creamer, red	10.00

Cups and Saucers
Cobalt	17.50
Red	22.50
Yellow	14.00

Egg Cups
Red	30.00
Turquoise	25.00

Gravy
Green	27.00
Red	35.00
Jar, cov, medium red 135.00
Marmalade, cov, green 68.00

Mugs
Cobalt	28.00
Forest Green	28.00
Mustard, cov, red 62.50
Nappy, 4¾", red 12.00

Plates
6", yellow	2.25
9", gray	9.75
10", grill, red	19.00
10", yellow	8.00
Platter, 12", cobalt 13.00
Relish Dish, navy and ivory 65.00
Salt and Pepper Shakers, cobalt .. 12.00
Sauce Boat, dark green 22.00
Soup, cream, red 25.00
Sugar, cov, yellow 12.50
Syrup, lid, red 110.00

FIESTA WARE

Fiesta Ware is a pottery dinnerware made by the Homer Laughlin China Co. in 1936, redesigned in 1969 and discontinued in 1973.

It can be distinguished from other brightly colored dinnerware of the same period by its characteristic band of concentric circles beginning at the rim and the full circle handle on the cups. In 1969, a partial circle handle was used. Most of the wares were incised "Fiesta."

See *Warman's Americana & Collectibles* for an expanded listing of Fiesta Ware.

Ashtray, red	30.00
Bowls	
4¾", gray	10.00
5½", fruit, cobalt	6.00
6", dessert, yellow	18.00
8½", yellow	11.75
Candlesticks, tripod, green, pr	80.00
Carafe, red	110.00

Coffee Pot, green, 10½" h, $36.00.

Teapot, cov, medium turquoise ...	40.00
Tray, yellow	55.00
Tumbler, red	25.00
Vase, bud, cobalt	22.00

FIRE EQUIPMENT

The volunteer fire company has played a central social and functional role in numerous towns and rural areas throughout America. Each company prided itself on its individual uniforms and equipment. Firemen conventions and parades allowed each company to "show off" as well as produced additional memorabilia such as presentation trophies, ribbons, etc.

Fire museums have arisen across America. In addition, many fire houses and local historical societies have a room devoted to old equipment and accouterments. The literature in the field is extensive, enhanced by the collection and publications of the Insurance Company of North America, Philadelphia, Pa.

Helmet, leather, black, gold eagle, red, white, made by Cairns & Brothers, NY, size 7¼", $150.00.

Alarms
Gamewell, cottage style, "Break Glass, Pull Handle Down Once"	65.00
SAFA Register, 1" tape, take up reel	200.00
Axe, Parade, sq edge, red handle .	90.00

Badges
Brooklyn Fire Dept, c1850	185.00
NY, Emergency Crew, nickel plated, NY seal in center, c1900 ..	60.00
Philadelphia, oval, raised letters .	75.00

Bells
7", hose cart	145.00
12", brass, bracket, c1920	230.00

Belts
Augusta, ME, No. 1, Cushnoe, white leather	70.00
Protection, black leather with red and white trim, 40"	110.00
Pumgustu, red, black, white	80.00
Suction Hose, red, black, white ..	75.00

Buckets, leather
Concord, NH, early 19th C., rough condition	500.00
"Phoenix" in scroll, picture of fire chief, rough condition	625.00
Tilley, old black paint insignia of crossed arrows, imp sgr, worn, 12" h	200.00

Extinguishers
Fire Killer Mfg. Co., red, black letters, cardboard, tubular, Syracuse, NY, 10" h	15.00
Nevermyss, black, gold letters, tin tubular, Middletown, NY, 21¾"	25.00

Fire Marks
Fire Assurance Co., Philadelphia, cast iron, oval	165.00
St. Louis Mutual, cast zinc, oval .	120.00
United Fireman's Ins. Co.	140.00

Helmets
Aluminum, lion holder, Hopkins & Wright Mfg.	215.00
Brass, American, eagle finial	225.00

Leather
Chapman Steamer, Cairns & Bro	160.00
Hickory Engine, Wilson	145.00
Jefferson 26, eagle holder, Wilson, NYC stamped on back .	400.00
Phoenix Hose #1, high frontpiece, stitched, black, white letters, red ground ...	50.00
Washington, sea horse holder, Cairns & Bro	165.00

Lithographs, N. Currier, framed, titled The Life Of A Fireman
"The Night Alarm-Start her lively boys!"	875.00
"The Race-Jump her boys, jump her!"	900.00

Nozzles, Hose
20", brass, Eastern Coupling Co., Camden, ME	125.00
36", brass, adjustable by small wheel	300.00

Parade Hat, Hand In Hand, 1741 on front panel, FA, hydrant on back, black felt, gold band, initials on top, gold letters	1,000.00

Speaking Trumpets
Presentation, brass, 16½"	550.00
Presentation, nickel plated, engraved W.V.F.A.	395.00
Presentation, silver plated, floral engraving, emb birds, griffin, classical figures, "Presented to Foreman M.H. Stark by the Members of Spalding Hose No. 3, July 31, 1877," 21½" l, dented	400.00
Presentation, Warren Hose Co. by Bunkerhill Assembly, October 5, 1857, silver plated, ornately decorated	2,600.00

Toys

Firehouse, wood, litho paper, 22 x 12 x 10", 4 stories high, steepled roof, chimney, double doors, 8 panel windows, mkd Gesetzlish Geschutz, late 19th C **750.00**

Hook and Ladder, cast iron, horse drawn, mounted hand axe, wooden ladders, 26" l **145.00**

Steamer, painted tin, motorized, friction drive, 12" l **45.00**

FIREARMS

The value of any particular type of antique firearm will cover a very wide range. For instance, a Colt 1849 pocket model revolver with a 5" barrel could be priced from $100.00 to $700.00 depending on whether or not all the component parts are original, whether some are missing, how much of the original finish (bluing) remains on the barrel and frame, how much silver plating remains on the brass trigger guard and back strap and the condition and finish of the walnut grips. Thus, condition is one of the two variables controlling value.

The other is rarity. A rare type of Colt firearm such as a Paterson belt revolver in just fair condition will command a much higher price than the Colt pocket model in very fine condition because of the rarity.

Values listed below are for firearms in good, complete condition.

FLINTLOCK PISTOLS—SINGLE SHOT

British, 8" half round, half octagon steel barrel, marked "D. EGG" and "LONDON," full walnut stock with steel trigger guard and ramrod pipes, lockplate marked identically to barrel **600.00**

British pocket, 2½" round steel barrel, hammer mounted on top of steel frame, frame marked "H. NOCK" and "LONDON," rosewood grips with silver wire inlay . **300.00**

Kentucky, William Booth, Phila., c1810–20, 8" round all brass barrel, smoothbore, 58 cal., walnut stock **1,500.00**

Kentucky, Joseph Henry, Phila., c1810, 10" round iron barrel, smoothbore, 54 cal., walnut stock **1,200.00**

Kentucky, Daniel Sweitzer & Co., Lancaster, 1807–08, 10½" round barrel, smoothbore, 54 cal., walnut stock, only lock may be by Sweitzer with barrel from Guest . **6,000.00**

U. S. Model 1805, Harper's Ferry, 10" round iron barrel with iron rib underneath holding ramrod pipe, lockplate marked "HARPER'S FERRY" and "1808," with spread eagle and shield over U.S. stamping, 54 cal., walnut half stock with brass butt plate and trigger guard **2,750.00**

U. S. Model 1813, 9-$\frac{1}{16}$" round barrel, smoothbore, 69 cal., lock marked "S. NORTH" over Am eagle, "U/MIDL^n CONN./S," no sights, hickory ramrod **2,000.00**

U. S. Model 1836, 8½" round barrel, 54 cal., lockplate marked "US/R JOHNSON/MIDD^n CONN," and dated 1838, half walnut stock, swivel ramrod attached to barrel, all iron parts **650.00**

PERCUSSION PISTOLS—SINGLE SHOT

Note: Conversion of flintlock pistols to percussion was common practice. Most British and U. S. military flintlock model pistols listed above can be found in percussion. Values for these percussion converted pistols may be from 40 to 60% of the flintlock values given.

Blunt & Syms Side Hammer, c1840s –50s, 5" octagonal barrel, marked "B & S NEW YORK," 36 cal., bag shaped walnut grips **185.00**

Kentucky, 8" octagonal brass barrel, 45 cal., full curly maple stock with brass fore-end cap, brass trigger guard and ramrod pipe, lock marked "GOLCHER" **1,250.00**

U. S. Model 1842, Navy, 6" round barrel, smoothbore, barrel marked "DERINGER/PHILADELA," 54 cal., swivel type ramrod, browned barrel, all mountings brass **700.00**

U. S. Model 1855, pistol-carbine, 12" round barrel, 58 cal., three quarter walnut stock, swivel ramrod attached to barrel, lock marked "U.S. SPRINGFIELD" and "1856," distinguishing feature is walnut carbine stock fitted to rear of pistol **950.00**

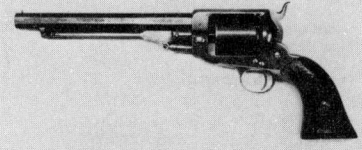

36 Navy Revolver, "E. Whitney/N. Haven," Powder & Ball pattern 6 cyl., $450.00.

PERCUSSION PISTOLS—MULTI SHOT (REVOLVERS)

Colt

1860 Army Model, 8″ round barrel, marked "ADDRESS COL. SAM^L COLT NEW YORK U.S. AMERICA," 6 shot, 44 cal., cylinder engraved with naval battle scene, walnut grips **600.00**

Dragoon, Baby, Model 1848, 5″ barrel, marked "ADDRESS SAM^L COLT/NEW-YORK CITY," 5 shot, 31 cal., octagon barrel, stagecoach holdup cylinder, oval stop slots, varnished walnut one piece grips **1,000.00**

Dragoon, First Model, c1849, 7½″ part round, part octagon barrel, marked "Address Saml Colt, New York City—Colt's Patent," 6 shot, 44 cal. cylinder engraved with Indian fight scene, square backed trigger guard, walnut grips **3,250.00**

Navy, 1851 Model, 7½″ octagon barrel marked "ADDRESS SAM^L COLT NEW YORK U.S. AMERICA, 6 shot, 36 cal., cylinder engraved with naval battle scene, round trigger guard, walnut grips **575.00**

Paterson Revolver No. 5, Holster Model, c1828–40, 9″ octagon barrel, marked "Patent Arms M'g Co. Paterson NJ - Colt's Pt.," 5 shot, 36 cal., cylinder roll scene of stagecoach holdup, hidden trigger, varnished walnut grip **7,000.00**

Pocket Model, Navy, 1862, 1861–1873, 5½″ octagon barrel, marked "ADDRESS COL. SAM^L COLT NEW-YORK U.S. AMERICA," 5 shot, 36 cal., rebate cylinder, one piece walnut grip ... **380.00**

Remington

Army Model, 1861, 8″ octagon barrel marked "PATENTED DEC. 17, 1861 - MANUFACTURED BY REMINGTON'S, ILION, NY," 6 shot, 44 cal., walnut grips **450.00**

New Model Police Revolver, 1863 –73, 5½″ octagon barrel, marked "PATENTED SEPT. 14, 1858, MARCH 17, 1863/E. REMINGTON & SONS, ILION, NEW YORK, U.S.A./NEW MODEL," 5 shot, 36 cal., walnut grips **375.00**

Remington-Beals 1st Model, 3″ octagon barrel marked "F.

BEAL'S PATENT" and date, frame marked "REMINGTONS, ILION, NY," 5 shot, 31 cal., gutta percha grips, round trigger guard **350.00**

Other

Allen & Thurber Sidehammer Target Pistol, part round, part octagon barrel marked "ALLEN & THURBER, WORCESTER," 8″ long, 34, 41, or 45 cal., wood ramrod, trigger guard with spur . **275.00**

Bacon Mfg Co., 5″ octagon barrel marked "BACON MFG CO. - NORWICH, CONN.," 5 shot, round cylinder, 31 cal., round trigger guard, walnut grips **275.00**

Josiah Ells, Pittsburgh, PA, Pocket Model, 3¾″ octagon barrel, spur hammer marked "ELLS/PATENT AUG 1, 1854/APRIL 28/1857," 5 shot, 31 cal. **400.00**

Freeman Army Model, 1863, 7½″ round barrel marked "FREEMANS PAT. DEC. 9, 1862 - HOARDS ARMORY, WATERTOWN, NY," 6 shot, 44 cal., walnut grips, round trigger guard **650.00**

Manhatten Shotgun Style Hammer, single action, c1850s, 6″ half round, half octagon barrel marked "MANHATTEN F. A. MFG. CO. NEW YORK," 36 cal., bag shaped walnut grips . **245.00**

W. W. Marston, Pocket Model, c1858–60s, seventh type, 7½″ round barrel marked "UNION," 6 shot cylinder, 31 cal. **225.00**

Rogers & Spencer Army Model, c1864, 7½″ octagon barrel marked "Rogers & Spencer - Utica, NY," walnut grips, round trigger guard **625.00**

Whitney Pocket Model, c1860s, 2nd Model, 6″ octagon barrel marked "E. WHITNEY/NEW HAVEN," 5 shot, 31 cal., cylinder roll scene of eagle, shield, and lion motif, walnut grips ... **280.00**

DERINGER AND DERINGER TYPE

Percussion

Frank J. Bitterlich, pocket, c1854–60s, octagon barrel marked "FR. J. BITTERLICH/NASHVILLE, TENN.," 41 cal. . **800.00**

Deringer, 1830s–60s, 3½″ barrel marked "DERINGER/PHILADEL^A," identical marking appears on lockplate, 41 cal., checkered walnut stock, German silver trigger guard and butt cap 700.00

Robertson Pocket, Phila., 4½" barrel marked "ROBERTSON/ PHILA.," 41 cal 400.00

Rimfire

Colt, Third Model, c1875–1910, 2½" barrel marked "COLT," pivots to right for loading single shot, 41 cal., varnished walnut grips, plated frame 165.00

Marlin, O. K. Model, c1863–70, 3⅛" barrel, marked on right side "J. M. MARLIN/NEW HAVEN. CT.,", top marked "O.K.," single shot, 32 cal., rosewood grips, brass frame with plated sides 185.00

Stevens Gem Pocket Pistol, c1872–90, 3" part octagon, part round barrel marked "GEM," swings sideways to load, 22 cal., brass frame with nickel plated finish, walnut grips 140.00

PEPPERBOXES

Percussion

Allen & Thuber, Dragoon size, 6" barrel, 36 cal., 6 shot, conventional bar type hammer and trigger, scroll and floral engraving on frame 600.00

William Walker Marston, New York, Bar Hammer Double Action, 5" barrel, ribbed, 6 shot, 31 cal., bag shaped grips 250.00

Robbins & Lawrence, Ring Trigger Concealed Hammer, 4½" ribbed barrel marked "ROBBIN

& LAWRENCE CO./WINDSOR, VT./PATENT. 1849," 31 cal., 5 shot cluster 380.00

Rimfire

Elliot Deringer, 32RF, "Pepperbox," c1863–88, 32 cal., four shot stationary barrel cluster, 3⅜" barrel, ribbed, hand rubber grips 260.00

Sharps, Model 1C, 22 cal, 4 shot, brass frame marked "C. SHARPS & CO. PHILADA, PA" on left, "C. SHARPS PATENT 1859" on right, fluted standing breech, barrel release underside front of frame, wood grips 200.00

FLINTLOCK LONG ARMS

British "Brown Bess" Musket, c1760 –70, 42" round barrel, 80 cal., lockplate marked "TOWER" with British crown stamp, full length walnut stock pinned to barrel, brass trigger guard, butt plate, and ramrod pipes, the major weapon of British infantry troops during the Revolutionary War 900.00

Kentucky Rifle, c1820, 40" octagon barrel, 45 cal., lock marked "LONDON/WARRANTED," curly maple full stock with brass fore-end caps, brass trigger guard, butt plate and ramrod pipes, brass open work patch box on right side of rifle, oval silver inlay on left cheek piece, four silver inlays on each side of stock 3,000.00

U. S. Model 1795, Charleville Pattern, Whitney, 69 cal., single shot, 43¾" round barrel, marked

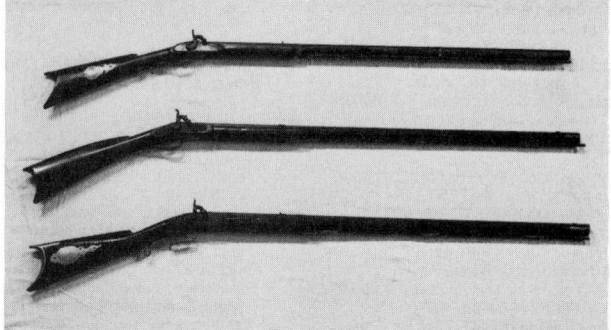

Penna Long Rifles, top: Leman, Lancaster, PA, $375.00 middle: Unknown maker, $275.00 bottom: S. C. Johnston, Allegheny, $400.00.

"ORR," iron mountings, rounded rear of lock, lock marked "U. STATES," walnut stock, steel ramrod with button tip **1,400.00**

U. S. Model 1840 Musket, 42" round barrel, 64 cal., lock marked "U.S." and "SPRINGFIELD," dated 1841, walnut full stock, all fittings iron (Most converted to percussion), orig. flintlock values to **3,250.00**

PERCUSSION LONG ARMS

Note: Conversion of flintlock long arms to percussion was common practice. Most British and U. S. military flintlock model long arms listed in the previous section can be found in percussion. Values for these converted long arms may be from 40 to 60% of the flintlock value noted previously.

Kentucky Rifle, c1845, 39" octagon barrel, 38 cal., full curly maple stock with brass fore-end cap, lock marked "JOSEPH GOLCHER," large brass open work patch box on right side of butt, silver star inlay on left cheek piece, twelve silver inlays on each side of stock, brass trigger guard and ramrod pipes **2,250.00**

Sharps Model 1852, "Slanting Breech," carbine, made by Robbins & Lawrence, Windsor, VT, for Sharps, c1853, 52 cal., 21½" barrel marked "SHARPS RIFLE/ MANUFG CO./ HARTFORD, CONN.," brass butt plate, patchbox, and barrel band, blued frame, breech lock, lock, lever and trigger guard, walnut stock **675.00**

U. S. Model 1855, Maynard Tape Primer, 40" round barrel, 58 cal., full walnut stock, brass fore-end cap, three iron barrel bands, lock marked "U.S./SPRINGFIELD" and "1858," Am. eagle stamped on lid of tape primer compartment **800.00**

RIFLES, LEVER ACTION

Henry Rifle, 1860–66, 24" barrel marked "HENRY'S PATENT. OCT. 16, 1860/MANUFACTUR'D BY THE NEW HAVEN ARMS CO. NEW HAVEN. CT.," 44 cal., rimfire, late brass frame model, oil stained walnut stock **3,500.00**

Marlin, Model 1888, c1888–89, 24" octagon barrel marked "MARLIN FIREARMS CO. NEW HAVEN, CT. U.S.A./PATENTED OCT. 11, 1887," 38–40 cal., buckhorn rear

and blade front sight, plain walnut stock **500.00**

WINCHESTER

Model 1866, rifle, c1866–98, 24" barrel, 44 cal., brass frame, buttplate (crescent), and fore-end cap, oil stained walnut stock, second model **1,650.00**

Model 1886, c1886–1935, rifle, 26" round barrel, various cal., crescent style buttplate, adjustable buckhorn sights, oil stained walnut stock **500.00**

FIREPLACE EQUIPMENT

The fireplace was a gathering point in the colonial home for heat, meals, and social interaction. It maintained its dominate position until the introduction of central heating in the mid-19th century.

Because of the continued popularity of the fireplace, its accessories still are manufactured, usually in an early American motif. Modern blacksmiths are reproducing the old iron implements; examine any item most carefully before purchasing.

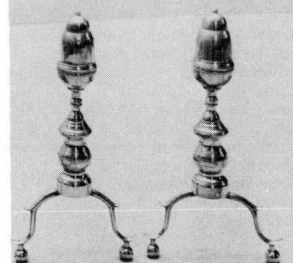

Andirons, brass, 17½" h, Conn, late 18th C, $250.00.

Andirons

Brass

Federal, 17¾", spurred feet, ball arch, sgr Richard Wittingham **1,800.00**

Federal, 18½", ball finial, hexagonal plinth, spurred cabroile legs, ball and claw feet **2,000.00**

Federal, 27⅝", urn shaped finial, swags, columnar supports, plinth base, inscribed N, ball and claw feet **4,500.00**

Queen Anne, 17¼", ball finial, penny feet, rectangular base, RI **1,600.00**

Cast Iron, Hessian Soldiers, 20″ .	500.00
Chrome, Art Deco, 19″, geometric	100.00
Wrought Iron	
17″, Firedogs, 19th C	265.00
18½″, round finial, 2 spit brackets, arched legs, wrought iron billet bar, American	575.00
Bellows, wood	
15½″, turtle back, yellow ground with stencil border	110.00
24¾″, advertising, "Bellows Made and Repaired," iron nozzle, leather trim	175.00
Boxes, Coal	
Brass, slanted lid, ball feet, "Repousse," 12 x 16 x 17″ . . .	250.00
Cast iron, green with floral decoration trimmed in gold, English, 19 x 20″	150.00
Clock Jack, iron, spoked wheel, scrolled front plate, 3 gear movement, arched wall bracket, 14″ h	1,250.00
Fenders	
31″, iron base, brass rail	250.00
34½″, wrought iron, semi-circular, center hinge, double rail for plates	725.00
54″, serpentine, brass, iron, 3 ball finials	1,100.00
55½″, serpentine, brass, iron, kettle stand, kettle	2,225.00
Firebacks	
25″, masonic symbols, one of 3 cast by Paul Revere, 18th C . .	20,000.00
40″, cast iron, two pieces, Gothic Revival, Whitehead and Law . .	1,500.00
Grate, cast iron, 9 x 17½″, mid-19th C	50.00
Hanging hook, wrought iron, swivels, 26″ l	100.00
Hod, brass helmet type, scoop, burnished and lacquered	150.00
Jamb hook, brass, 4½″ rectangular wall plate, hinged c-shaped arm, baluster turned finial, pr	175.00
Roaster, revolving, toaster, broiler, wrought iron, twisted, scrolled uprights, flat oval handle, American, 19th C	400.00
Roasting oven, tinware, half cylindrical, hinged lid, 2 handles, 19″ w .	150.00
Rotisserie, brass, iron, winding, hanging hook, brass plaque emb John Linwood Warranted	500.00
Screens	
George III, painted and gilded, dual screen inset with Chinese wallpaper, early 19th C	200.00
Petitpoint Dutch scene, open handle, walnut frame	200.00
Stained glass insets, marquetry, mahogany, 30½″	400.00
Spatulas, wrought iron, American,	

19th C	
10½″, acorn shape base	95.00
14½″, flared base	75.00
Tongs, wrought iron, engraved, NE, 20¾″, c1780	900.00
Tool set, brass, three pieces, holder, mid-19th C	140.00
Trammels	
27″, wrought iron, sawtooth, candle holder	805.00
46½″, wrought iron, sawtooth pierced hanging hook above pot holder	200.00
37″, hand forged, 10 holes for adjustment	280.00
Trivets, wrought iron	
Primitive, adjustable fork rest, 8½ d x 19″ l x 6½″ h	60.00
Tulip and leaf pattern, round legs, 5½″	55.00
Twisted hanging loop, handle, simple design, 7½″ d x 7″ h . .	55.00

FISCHER J. BUDAPEST.

FISCHER CHINA

Moritz Fischer founded his factory in Herend, Hungary, in 1839. Herend has been a center of porcelain production from the 1790s, but collectors are interested only in porcelain produced after 1839.

There has been much confusion about this porcelain because of its quality and resemblance to the finest wares of Meissen, Chantilly, Sevres, and even Oriental Export wares. Knowingly or unknowingly, it was often bought and sold as the product of these other potteries. It is said that often forged marks of other potteries are found on Herend pieces. The mark "MF," often joined, is the mark of Moritz Fischer's pottery.

Fischer's Herend is very hard paste ware, of lovely luminosity, and exquisite decoration. These pieces are designated by certain pattern names, and the best known of these are Chantilly Fruit, Rothschild Bird, Chinese Bouquet, Victoria Butterfly, and Parsley.

He also made figural birds and animal groups, Magyar figures, individually and in groups, and Herend eagles, poised for flight. It is collectible among advanced collectors, and is not too well known because of its close resemblance to other famous china products.

Cachepot, 5″, handled, Rothchild Bird pattern	150.00

Vase, 12″ h, bulbous with extended neck, ochre ground with multi-colored flowers, gold accents, cobalt blue reticulated handles with deep rose sides, $375.00.

Coffee Pot, domed cov, pear-shaped, landscapes, flower sprays, scroll handle, gilt, fruiting branch finial	195.00
Dish, 5⅞″, covered, on collared base, Parsley pattern	200.00
Ewers	
9½″, relief medallions, blue, beige, gold beads	225.00
16½″, reticulated body, handle, rose, green, blue, gold	295.00
Figurine, 7″ h, music lesson	150.00
Jug, blue butterflies, deer, flowers .	400.00
Plates	
10½″, dinner plate, Chantilly Fruit pattern	110.00
10½″, dinner plate, Parsley pattern	110.00
Sauce Boat, Chantilly Fruit pattern, with underplate and matching china ladle	225.00
Tureen, cov, 8½″, 2 handled, Victoria Butterfly, large molded finial . .	300.00
Urn, 24 x 16″, enameled birds, gilt .	1,600.00
Vases	
7¼″, reticulated, decor with blue florals, green foliage, gold handles	150.00
8¼″, multicolored enameling, reticulated, gold rim	300.00
9″, triangular top and base, polychromed, gold trim	300.00

10″, reticulated, ornate handles, multicolored with heavy gold trim	300.00
11″, reticulated, flowers, 4 cobalt blue handles	200.00
Vegetable dish, open, 9½″, Chantilly Fruit pattern	125.00

FITZHUGH

Fitzhugh is one of the most recognized Chinese Export porcelain patterns. It was named for the Fitzhugh family for which the first dinner service was made. The peak period of production was 1780 to 1850.

Fitzhugh features an oval center medallion or monogram surrounded by four groups of flowers or emblems. The border is similar to that on Nanking china. Occasional border variations are found with butterfly and honeycomb among the rarest.

Blue is the common color. Color is a key factor in pricing with rarity in ascending order of orange, green, sepia, mulberry, yellow, black, and gold. Combinations of colors are scarce.

Spode Porcelain Company, England, currently is producing a copy of the Fitzhugh pattern in several colors.

Platter, 15¾″ l, blue, $435.00.

Basin, blue, 16½″	485.00
Basket, reticulated, blue, 10¼″ . . .	575.00
Basket, reticulated, cov, brown, 10⅜ x 10⅞″	1,800.00
Bowl, green, quarterfoil rim, 9½″, c1820	800.00
Brush Box, blue	525.00
Butter Tub, cover and stand, blue, 5 ¼ x 6⅜″	550.00
Garden Seat, green, 18½″ high, c1850	4,000.00

Plates
  7¼", round, sepia **235.00**
  9⅝", butterflies, honeycomb . . . **400.00**
  9¾", green, white ground **200.00**
  10"
    Blue **215.00**
    Orange **300.00**
    Yellow **510.00**
Platters
  18¾ x 16¼", oval, blue, white,
    c1900 . . . . **450.00**
  21¾ x 18", oval, green, white,
    c1900 . . . . **800.00**
Soup, yellow, peony and breast me-
  dallion, 7⅞" **2,000.00**
Vegetable, cov, blue, 9⅝" long . . . **425.00**

FLASKS

**A flask is a container for liquids, usually hav-
ing a narrow neck. Early American glass
companies frequently formed them in molds
which left a relief design on the front or
back. Historical flasks with a portrait, building, scene or name are the most desired.
When possible, both the front and back design is given in our listing.**

**Scroll flasks are generally fiddle shaped
and have a scroll or geometric design. A
chestnut flask is hand blown and usually is
small with a flattened bulbous body. The
Pitkin type is a blown globular body, associated with the typical "colonial" tavern spirits
bottle.**

**Dimensions can differ for the same flask
because of variations in the molding process.
Color is important with scarcer colors de-
manding more money; aqua and amber are
most common. The key condition effecting
price is "sickness," an opalescent scaling in
the bottle which eliminates clarity. Collectors
are advised to avoid flasks with this as a major problem.**

**The best book remains George L. and
Helen McKearin's _American Glass_. Their identification numbers often substitute for full descriptions of the design.**

Chestnuts
  6½", aqua, 16 swirled ribs **85.00**
  7", amber brown, blown applied
    handle **125.00**
Historical Types
  Cornucopia and vase of fruit, olive
    green, pint, GV-4 . . . . **60.00**
  Double eagle, 7½", olive amber,
    pint, Pittsburgh, Pa. in oval . . . **55.00**
  Eagle, spread-wing, aqua, quart,
    ribbed on all sides, Kentucky
    Glass Works **190.00**
  Grandfathers, 8½", amber, blown,

Historical, 6¾", George Washington,
Father of His Country, General Taylor
Never Surrenders, Dyottville Glass
works, Phila, $67.50.

  24 vertical ribs, swirl slighty at
    neck, Zanesville **950.00**
  Hunter/Fisherman, 7¼", calabash
    shape, aqua, pontiled **65.00**
  Jenny   Lind/Glass   Factory
    (Fislerville   Glass   Works,
    Fislerville, NJ), calabash shape,
    aqua, quart **110.00**
  Railroad, olive amber, pint, Coven-
    try **50.00**
  Soldier on horseback/dog, aqua,
    quart, GY 111-16 . . . . **375.00**
  Success to the Railroad, a horse
    and wagon, green, pint, Keene,
    GV-4 . . . . **175.00**
  Union and clasped hands, 8¾",
    aqua, quart **65.00**
  Union, 13 stars, shield, clasped
    hands, reverse, eagle, banner
    and shield, aquamarine, quart . **175.00**
  Washington/Jackson, amber ½
    pint, Coventry, McKearin G 1-34 **90.00**
Pitkin Type
  7", pale yellow, blown globular
    bottle, applied lip **275.00**
  7½", amber, blown globular bot-
    tle, 24 swirled ribs, Zanesville . **325.00**
  8¾", golden amber, blown globu-
    lar bottle, Zanesville **325.00**
  9¾", amber, quart, plain sides,
    applied lip, small anchor on bot-
    tom **300.00**
Ravenna Glass Co., 6¾", amber,

pint, Ravenna Glass Co., reverse, Traveler's Companion, iron pontil	275.00
Scroll Type	
6¾", aqua, pint	45.00
7", aqua, pint, pontiled	50.00
South Jersey, 6¼", cranberry to clear at neck, white loopings, ½ pint	125.00
Sterling Silver, ladies, red velvet drawstring case	110.00

FLOW BLUE

Flowing Blue or Flow Blue, as it is sometimes called, is a cobalt blue on white earthenware or ironstone, that had been let "flow" in the firing, producing a deep, flowing or smudging effect in the pattern. Its designs were copies of Japanese and Chinese motifs and carried names suggesting Oriental places. It was made from 1825–1850, by various potters in the Staffordshire district — Adams and Co.; Davenport, Podmore and Walker; Alcock (Samuel); Wedgwood; Ridgeway, etc.

About 1880 to 1890 and well into the 1900s flowing blue again was made, this time a little more to the Victorian taste. The "flowing" was not quite so pronounced, ware was lighter than ironstone, but not so fine as porcelain, patterns were daintier and gold trim was added. Henry Alcock, Samuel's son, made "Touraine," one of the later patterns that is most popular among collectors today.

The older ware is becoming quite scarce and expensive. Collectors have been concentrating on the later patterns, although older pieces are still much sought-after, when available. These older patterns were also made in colors other than blue, one of them being a "flowing," deep brown, almost black which is commonly known as "mulberry." Prices would be about the same for older blue and mulberry.

See also MULBERRY CHINA.

See *Warman's Americana & Collectibles* for additional listings of Flow Blue.

EARLY PATTERNS, c1825–1850

Bowls

Amoy, 5¼", Davenport	40.00
Chapoo, 6" oval, Wedgwood	165.00
Kin Shan, 8½", Phillips and Sons, c1840–1850	95.00
Manilla, 8", Podmore and Walker	90.00

Butters, covered

Amoy, Davenport, c1840–1850	125.00
Athens	75.00
Brunswick, Wood and Sons	125.00
Chusan	100.00
Pelew, Challinor, c1840–1850	195.00
Chamber Pot, Kyber, Adams, & Co.	175.00

Early Pattern, Tonquin, Heath, gravy boat, 4⅞ x 7¾", $225.00.

Creamers

Athens	80.00
Corean, Podmore and Walker, c1850	95.00
Ferrarra, Wedgwood	100.00
Formosa	85.00
Hong Kong	75.00
Indian Jar, T. F. & Co., (Thomas Ford) c1840	175.00
Lahore, Thomas Phillips & Son	190.00
Leipsic, Clementson, octagonal	157.50
Lugano, Ridgeway	75.00
Manilla, Podmore and Walker	85.00
Oregon	80.00
Penang, Ridgeway	85.00

Cups and Saucers

Chapoo	85.00
Jeddo, Adams and Co., handleless, c1840	75.00
Chen Si, John Meir	75.00
Pelew, Challinor, handleless, c1740–1850	85.00
Scinde, J. & G. Alcock	95.00
Sobraon, T. W., handleless	125.00

Gravy Boats

Amoy	225.00
Damascus, T. F. and Co.	175.00
Jeddo	145.00
Kyber	115.00
Madras	100.00
Manila, Podmore and Walker	200.00
Mongolia	150.00
Poppy, Wedgwood	215.00
Scinde	195.00

Plates

Amoy, 7½", Davenport	55.00
Birmah, "C", 7¼"	35.00
California, 9½", Podmore Walker & Co.	45.00
Chapoo, 9", J. Wedgwood, Ironstone	55.00
Chusan, 7¼"	35.00
Formosa, Ridgeway, 7¼",	42.50
Indian, 9", F. & R. Pratt	68.00
Manila, 8½" d	65.00

Pelew, 9½", ...	50.00
Scinde, 10"	55.00
Sobraon, 10"	55.00
Temple, 10"	60.00
Wamphoa, 10"	55.00

Platters

Amoy, 14"	175.00
Chapoo, 10"	125.00
Coburg, 18 x 14"	195.00
Scinde, 20"	295.00

Sauces

Amoy	40.00
Atlanta, Wedgwood	25.00
Chapoo	25.00

Soup Plates

Amoy, wide rim	60.00
Athens	50.00
Sugar, cov, 8" h, Chapoo	210.00
Teapot, Ferrara, Wedgwood, ...	225.00
Tureen, cov, Chusan, ...	150.00
Vegetable cov, ...	75.00
Wash Bowl and Pitcher set, Cambridge, Meakin, ...	550.00

MIDDLE PATTERNS, c1850–1870

Bowls

Cashmere, 4½", Francis Morley .	135.00
Rhoda Gardens, Hackwood	125.00

Creamers

Coburg, John Edwards	100.00
Genevese, Edge Malkin	95.00
Simla, Elsmore & Foster	115.00

Cups and Saucers

India, G.L. Ashworth & Bros.	95.00
Vine, Josiah Wedgwood, handleless	100.00

Plates

Cashmere, 8½"	75.00
Morning Glory, 9½"	60.00
Shanghai, 7½", W. & T. Adams . .	45.00
Simla, 8½", Elsmore & Forster . .	48.00
Vegetable Dish, cov, Coburg	125.00

LATER PATTERNS, c1880–1900s

Later Pattern, Manhattan, soup plate, 9", $20.00.

Bone Dishes

Alaska	12.00
Non Pareil, Burgess & Leigh, each	20.00
Touraine	18.00

Bowls

Conway, 9", New Wharf Pottery Co., ...	28.00
Kelvin, 7", Meakin	47.50
Persian Moss, 4⅞", Utzschneider, Germany	12.00
Verona, 9", Meakin	20.00

Butter Pats

Touraine	18.00
Verona, Meakin	18.00

Creamers

Argyle	20.00
Beaufort	28.00
Chiswick, Ridgeway, c1897	35.00
Conway	35.00
Holland, Johnson Bros.	85.00

Creamers,

Irene	28.00
Oxford, Johnson Bros.	75.00
Persian Moss, 4⅛", Utzschneider	45.00

Cups and Saucers

Conway, New Wharf Pottery	45.00
Gironde, W. H. Grindley	35.00

Gravy Boats

Claremont	55.00
Eclipse, Johnson Bros., ...	55.00
Holland, The, Meakin	45.00
Lancaster, New Wharf Pottery Co., ...	65.00
Marie, W. H. Grindley	65.00

Pitchers

Beatrice, 4¾", cobra handle, John Maddock	70.00
Beaufort, 6", Grindley	69.00
Dorothy, 10", Grindley, c1897 . . .	95.00
Touraine, Alcock	150.00

Plates

Andora, 6" Johnson Bros., ...	15.00
Argyle, 7", scalloped, F & Sons . .	20.00
Beaufort, 6", Grindley	10.00
Clarence, 7", Grindley	8.00
Countess, 8", Grindley	30.00
Del Monte, 9½", Johnson Bros., .	20.00
Elsa, 9", W. & E. Corn	42.00
Holland, The, 10", Meakin	30.00
Jewel, 10"	22.50
Lancaster, 10", New Wharf Pottery	25.00
Peach Royal, 10", Johnson Bros.	50.00
Richmond, 10" Grindley	25.00
St. Louis, 10" Johnson Bros.	30.00

Platters

Ayr, 10", W. & E. Corn	40.00
Eclipse, Johnson Bros.	100.00
Lotus, 14", Grindley, gold trim . . .	60.00

Soup Plates

Chatsworth, 8½", Hanley	25.00
Conway, 9"	20.00
Eclipse 9", ...	15.00

Roseville, 8¾", John Maddock ..	35.00
Touraine, 7½", Alcock	20.00
Sugars, covered	
Cecil, Till and Sons	52.50
Touraine, Alcock	125.00
Tureens, covered	
Florida, 12 x 8"	160.00
Lancaster, New Wharf Pottery ...	175.00
Lorne	160.00
Lotus, Grindley, gold trim	150.00
Vegetables Dishes, covered	
Eton, oval, T. Till & Sons	85.00
Holland, The, Meakin	125.00
Lancaster, 12½", New Wharf Pottery	110.00

FOOD MOLDS

Decorative food molds were made for a variety of foods—butter, cakes, candles, puddings, etc. Their main object was to present the food in a pleasing and appetizing manner. Most early food molds are collected today for decorative purposes, but also they are used for their original purpose.

BUTTER MOLDS, SEE BUTTER PRINTS

Acorn, one pound, rectangular	45.00
Cloverleaf, one pound, rectangular .	50.00
Cows	
Cylinder type	95.00
Hexagon barrel, pewter bands ..	130.00
Daisy, 4"	50.00
Ferns	
Rectangular	45.00
Round, 4½"	45.00
Letters	
L., Rectangular	35.00
W., Round	35.00
Maltese Cross, hinged	65.00
Maple Leaves, two, rectangular ...	75.00
*Pineapple	60.00
Plain, glass	35.00
*Sheaf of Wheat	
Rectangular	65.00
Round, two stars	185.00
Star	45.00
Strawberries, two, rectangular	65.00
Swan, one pound	85.00
Thistle, 1½"	30.00

CANDY MOLDS (TIN, TIN AND COPPER, ETC.)

Basket, 3½ x 6"	30.00
Bridge set, heart, spade, diamond .	55.00
Clown, 10", 4 pcs	40.00
Eggs, emb rabbits, 6 mold, 6½", Germany	20.00
Frog, 5"	25.00

Candy, tin, 3 elephants, $70.00.

Groom, 3½"	17.50
Hen on nest, 3¼" l	25.00
Horse, 5¼" l	87.00
Humpty Dumpty, 5½", two side, locks emb	70.00
Jenny Lind, 3 pcs	70.00
Pineapple	25.00
Rabbits	
5¾", tin	27.50
7½"	30.00
10" l, wooden, 2 pcs	80.00
Rose	20.00
Santa Claus, 6½"	55.00
Three Wise Men on Horses, 8 pieces	85.00

ICE CREAM MOLDS (PEWTER, IRON, ETC.)

Airplane	20.00
Artichoke	25.00
Basket, scalloped 5"	40.00
Bell	35.00
Book, imp Pat Ap'd for 1888	35.00
Cabbage, 3½"	35.00
Camel, 2¼ x 6¼"	30.00
Cat, 3½"	70.00
Clover, 5" imp E & Co. NY	50.00
Colonial Lady	30.00
Cow, 4½"	100.00
Dahlia, 4"	40.00
Desk, man, woman, 3¾"	55.00
Eagle, American	70.00
Fire Engine, 4½"	40.00
Football, 3"	22.50
Heart and Cupid	30.00
Hen	20.00
Hobby Horse	35.00
Horseshoe	60.00
Jack-o-Lantern, top hat	55.00
Leaf	25.00
Lincoln	65.00
Man in top hat, 5"	45.00
Pansies, 3 individual flowers on one mold	45.00
Possom, 5" l	65.00
Rooster	25.00
Santa Claus, pewter, 4⅝", imp E & Co.	45.00
Sea Shell	20.00
Shield with Stars and Stripes	50.00

Steamer, 7"	40.00
Tulip, 3"	20.00
Turkey, 4"	30.00
Uncle Sam	40.00
Washington George, bust, S & Co	50.00
Watermelon	25.00
Witch on broom, 5½"	80.00

POTTERY MOLDS (PUDDING, CUSTARDS, ETC.)

Asparagus, 3½ x 6 x 8"	35.00
Flute & Sunburst creamware, dark mustard glaze, 4½" d	30.00
Pea Pods	35.00

MISCELLANEOUS MOLDS

Bear, cookie, wooden	20.00
Cats, lady fingers, tin, 6¼ x 8"	25.00
Grape, 4", glass, c1897	25.00
Melon, graniteware, 5" h, gray	75.00
Melon, tin, 8¾" l, 2 pcs	35.00
Pear, 2 x 7¾", copper	25.00
Rabbit, 4½", copper	25.00

FOSTORIA GLASS   FOSTORIA

Fostoria Glass Co. began operations at Fostoria, Ohio, in 1887. A few years later they moved to Moundsville, W. Va., where they continue to manufacture quality glassware. Many of their discontinued patterns and items are being collected today.

Pitcher, American, straight sides, 8¼" h x 5¾" d, $110.00.

Bonbons	
American, 7", 3 ftd	10.00
June, topaz	20.00
Bowls	
8", American, handled	35.00
9", Fairfax, oval, baker	20.00
13", Holly	20.00
Cake Stand, 10" square, American	32.00
Candlesticks	
2", June, pair	25.00
3", Versailles, Azure blue	35.00
5", Fairfax, pair	25.00
Celery, American, 10" oblong	12.50
Champagnes	
Chintz, etch	18.00
June, topaz	24.00
Trojan, topaz	16.00
Versailles, topaz	30.00
Cheese compote, Meadow Rose	15.00
Compote, Colony	10.00
Console bowl, Versailles, pink	35.00
Creamers and Sugars	
Coin, pr	40.00
Versailles	42.50
Cups and Saucers	
Farifax, green, ftd	9.00
Meadow Rose, crystal, each	15.00
Demitasse, Mayfair, crystal, black	18.50
Goblets	
Buttercup, 10 oz	22.00
Chintz, each	20.00
Colony	7.75
June, topaz	25.00
Versailles, azure	25.00
Jar, dresser, elephant on lid, crystal	15.00
Lemon, Midnight Rose, 5", handle	10.00
Mayonnaise, American, 2 pcs	20.00
Nappy, Chintz, handled, 3 corners	15.00
Plates	
6", Versailles, green	4.50
7", Mayfair, topaz	4.00
9½", American	6.00
9½", Fairfax, pink	10.00
9¾", Pioneer, amber	8.50
10½", Royal, amber	15.00
Relishes	
2 pt, American	10.00
2 pt, Colony, crystal	8.00
2 pt, Midnight Rose	16.00
3 pt, Chintz	35.00
Salt and Peppers	
Fairfax	25.00
June, pink	95.00
Sherbets	
American, 5 oz, flared	9.00
Baroque, yellow	6.00
Spooner, Colony	25.00
Syrup, Priscilla, green with gold	70.00
Toothpicks	
Sylvan, all over diamond	22.00
Brazilian	24.00
Tumblers	
Buttercup, 5 oz, ftd	18.00

Chintz, 13 oz, ftd	**20.00**
June, footed, topaz	**22.00**
Meadow Rose, souvenir, ftd, crystal	**12.00**
Trojan, topaz	**10.00**
Versailles, yellow, 9 oz	**20.00**
Vases	
6½", Colony, crystal, bud	**20.00**
7½", American, flared	**16.00**

FRAKTUR

Fraktur, the calligraphy associated with the Pennsylvania Germans, is named for the elaborate first letter found in many of the handdrawn examples. Throughout its history printed, partially printed-handdrawn, and fully handdrawn works existed side by side. Fraktur often were made by the school teachers or ministers living in the rural areas of Pennsylvania, Maryland and Virginia. Many artists are unknown.

Fraktur exists in several forms—geburts and taufschein (birth and baptismal certificates), vorschrift (writing example, often with alphabet), haus sagen (house blessing), bookplates and marks, rewards of merit, illuminated religious text, valentines, and drawings. Although collected for decoration, the key element in Fraktur is the text.

Fraktur prices rise and fall along with the American Folk Art market. Occasionally a special sale tests the market. The handdrawn pieces listed below were sold by Sotheby's in June 1983 as part of the Fred Wichmann Collection. They represent prices somewhat above those found in the field. The next year will be spent seeing if the market moves up to this new price level.

The key market place is Pennsylvania and the Middle Atlantic states. The major study collection of Fraktur is found in the Rare Book room of the Free Library of Philadelphia.

HANDDRAWN

Brubacher, Hans Jacob, religious text, Lancaster Co., PA, 1800, 14¾ x 12¼", two vertical panels of text separated by central column with heart motif, artist sgd	**4,500.00**
Cross Legged Angel Artist, birth and baptismal, Berks, Co., PA, 1791, 15 x 12⅛", angel at top flanked by parrot in tree, floral side borders, center text block, birth of Catharina Koch	**2,500.00**
Ebbecke, F. T., vorschrift, Berks Co., PA, c1800, 11¾ x 7½", calligraphic text, tulips at top, standing eagle at lower left, Lamb of God	

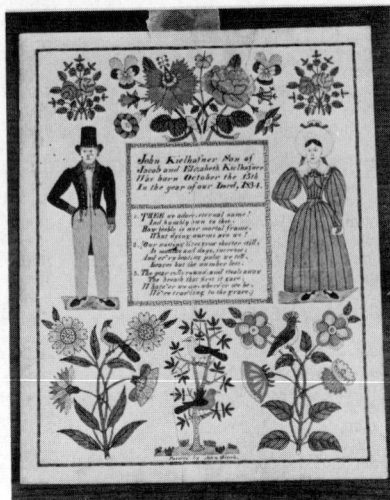

Zinck, John, birth and baptismal, Lancaster Co., 1834, 7⁵⁄₁₆ x 10⅛", artist signed, $3,500.00.

at lower right, for Heinerich Riddel	**450.00**
Engelhard, Heinrich, house blessing, probably Berks Co., PA, 1830, 11¾ x 9½", large strapwork lettering and ornamental German calligraphy	**1,750.00**
Farber, Wilhelmus Antonius, birth and baptismal, Bucks Co., PA, 1791, 14⅞ x 11⅞", central text block, cutwork border of hearts, tulips, and other flowers, birth of George Beringer	**2,250.00**
Leopolt, Valentin, birth and baptismal, Lancaster Co., PA, 1802, 12⅞ x 15⅞", concentric circles, moon in sun motif flanking crown at top, circles in corners, artist sgd, birth of Catarina Lascher	**5,000.00**
Mount Pleasant Artist, birth certificate, Lancaster Co., PA, 1825, 7½ x 9½", English text, clock face motif, birth of John Stoll	**4,650.00**
Otto, Heinrich, drawing, Lancaster Co., PA, late 18th C, 6½ x 7⅞", large parrot on flowering branch above strutting peacock	**6,000.00**
Stony Creek Artist, birth and death certificate, Shenandoah Co., VA, 1814/15, 13 x 16⅛", large text, first letter contains Am. eagle and shield, ruled borders with mean-	

dering floral vines, some paper loss, birth and death of Johannes Lindemuth . . . . — **2,750.00**

Trevits, Conrad, birth and baptismal, Berks Co., PA, 1811, 16¼ x 13¼", central heart motif, birds in upper corners, birth of Thomas Schmith . . . . — **3,000.00**

Unknown artist, birth and baptismal certificate, Maryland, 1793, 15½ x 12¾", central heart at bottom center with three hearts as part of it, five hearts across top, flanking angels, birth of Magdelena Neu . — **1,2500.00**

Unknown artist, vorschrift, Southeastern PA, 1787, 14¼ x 9", text block surrounded by "pattern book" borders, scored with a grid work with letters of alphabet, trees and human figures . . . . — **825.00**

Unknown artist, vorschrift, Southeastern PA, 1815, 12¾ x 7¾", large script letters on first line "Liebes Kind . . . ," alphabet at bottom of text, meandering floral vines in border, probably Mennonite . . . . — **2,000.00**

Young, Rev. Henry, birth and baptismal, Clinton Co., PA, 1849, 7¼ x 9½", couple holds hands over table, English text, star in upper corners, birth of Dianah Krenninger . — **2,400.00**

HANDDRAWN–PRINTED

Krebs, Friedrich, birth and baptismal, Berks Co., PA, 1774, 16 x 13", central heart with two small hearts at bottom, scallop design around outside borders of printed hearts . — **600.00**

Otto, Heinrich, birth and baptismal, Lancaster Co., PA, 1774, 16½ x 13⅜", bird blocks on sides, handdrawn horizontal floral designs between text, birth of John Adam Bassler . . . . — **1,200.00**

Pseudo-Otto Artist, birth and baptismal, Frederick Co., MD, 1807, 16 x 13", reverse border block motif from Otto form, handdrawn floral motif between text, birth of Catherina Konig . . . . — **900.00**

Speyer, Friederich, birth and baptismal, Lancaster Co., PA, 1752, 15¾ x 13", central heart, kings bearing tulips in upper corners, parrots at base of hearts, mermaids in lower corners, birth of Catharina Pfrank . . . . — **2,000.00**

PRINTED

Adam and Eve
Engleman, C. F., Reading . . . . . . — **175.00**

Ville, H. W., Lancaster . . . . — **275.00**
Birth and Baptismal
Bauman, John, Ephrata . . . . — **250.00**
Currier & Ives, New York . . . . — **30.00**
Eagle Book Store, Reading . . . . . — **50.00**
Grater und Blumer, Allentown . . . — **75.00**
Hanzsche, J. T., Baltimore, MD . . — **100.00**
Lange, Dan. Phil., Hanover, vertical form . . . . — **125.00**
Mentz, Georg W., Philadelphia . . . — **85.00**
Peters, G. S., Harrisburg . . . . — **75.00**
Sanno, Friederich, Carlisle . . . . . . — **200.00**
Schnee, Joseph, Lebanon . . . . . . — **250.00**
Sebald, H., Philadelphia . . . . — **30.00**
Siegfried, S., Bath . . . . — **100.00**
Walter, Johann, Reading . . . . — **50.00**
Geistlicher Irrgarten (Spiritual Labyrinth)
Ephrata (probably Bauman), decorated by Krebs . . . . — **125.00**
Rudy, Heinrich, Chambersburg . . — **67.50**

FRANKART

The firm known as Frankart, Inc., was located in New York City during the 1920s and 1930s. This company mass produced decorative items such as ashtrays, lamps and bookends in the Art Deco style. They used animals, birds and nudes as their subjects. The items were made of a white lead composition and then spray painted or given a bronze type finish. Pieces of Frankart are easily identified as they are marked with the patent number, year of production and stamped Frankart.

Ashtray, kneeling female nude holding green custard glass ashtray, green patina, 9¼" h, $225.00.

Ashtrays

Horse, standing, orig paint, label .	95.00
Nude, No. T301	120.00

Bookends, 6½ x 5½″, seated nude
women, painted white metal	285.00

Candlesticks, 12″, nudes, orig paint,
pr	275.00

Figurines

Elk, 6¼″ h, bronze patina finish .	115.00
Irish Setter, gold painted finish . .	45.00
Nude, 12″, bronze patina finish . .	150.00

Lamps

Desk, eagle on side, pen tray . . .	200.00
Table, child reading book, green patina	150.00
Table, 2 inverted nude figures balance 8″ ball of handmade glass of gold irid, decorated with green leaves, Patent Design No. D77202–1928, 18″, bronze finish	850.00

Night Light, 11″, sailor leaning against lamp post, bronze patina, orig shade	250.00
Vase, 12″, seated figure mounted on wrought iron stand, holds removable green Steuben vase, marked No. F603	675.00

FRANKOMA

John N. Frank, an instructor of ceramics at the University of Oklahoma, founded the Frankoma Pottery at Sapulpa, Ok., in 1936. After a fire in 1938, the pottery was inactive until its reactivation in 1943. Modern pieces are marked with "FRANKOMA."

The recent interest in American Art pottery has focused attention on Frankoma pottery. Collectors should concentrate on early examples, many of which still are available at reasonable prices.

See *Warman's Americana & Collectibles* for an expanded listing of Frankoma.

Indian Jar, H-7, designed by John Frank, 27″ circum, $85.00; if marked "Frank Potteries," $250.00.

Bookends, Mountain Girl, 5¾″ h . .	55.00
Bowl, 10″, Carved Cactus	35.00

Candleholders

#307, Ada clay, pair	35.00
Monk, 4½″ h	75.00
Christmas Card, 1960, Gracetone .	65.00
Coin, 1¾″, Elect John Frank	15.00
Decanter, 2 qt., Fingerprint, stopper	25.00

Flower Frog, matching colored
bowl	60.00

Humidor, lid	75.00
Jar, carved, #70	25.00

Jewelry

Ear Clips, Teepees, pr	15.00
Pin, Cacti, 1½″	25.00
Jug, three cup, stopper	45.00

Jugs, miniature, 2¾″ h, 3 on brass
chain	25.00

Lamp Base, 6″, barrel	25.00
Lazy Susan, #2Z, Gracetone	35.00
Match Holder #89A, 1¾″ h	12.00
Paperweight, Norman	85.00
Pipe Rest	50.00

Pitchers

5″, Thunderbird	50.00
17″, Fireside	30.00
Planter, 12″, large swan, #230 . . .	85.00

Plaques

Buffalo Mask, 3½″ h	20.00
Will Rogers, without border	38.00

Salt and Pepper Shakers, mono-
grammed, pr	22.50

Sculptures

Amazon Woman, 6¼″	225.00
Buffalo, 3½″ h	225.00
Cowboy, 7¾″	75.00
Fan Dancer, 8½″, Ada clay	180.00
Gannet, 9″	225.00
Greyhound, 14″ 1, peach glow or woodland moss	125.00
Pekingese Dog, 7¾″	225.00
Rearing Clydesdale, 6¾″	55.00
Terrier Dog, 5¼″	60.00
Walking Ocelot, 7″	175.00
Sign, Pacing Leopard	225.00
Spoon rest, #2y, Gracetone	35.00
Trivet, Lazybones #4TR	28.00

Vases

3″, marked "FRANK POTTER-IES"	150.00
3½″, Hobby Horse flower holder	75.00
7½″, Indian Jar #72, large	75.00
9″, Chinese Bottle, Chinese red glaze	85.00

9¼″, Ram's Head, tall
Pacing leopard logo	70.00
Unmarked	45.00

9½″, Grecian #50c, only handles
glazed	40.00

11½″ 1, Flowerabrum #58	65.00

17″

Fireside	30.00
Lotus	65.00

Wall Pockets
  Leaf, 8½" 35.00
  Ram's Head 50.00
  Reed 35.00
Wreath, back reads "WITH OUR
  LOVE, FRANKOMA" 35.00

FRATERNAL ITEMS

Warman's Americana & Collectibles, 1st Edition, contains 136 listings in this category; see also page xii.

FRUIT CRATE LABELS

Warman's Americana & Collectibles, 1st Edition, contains 120 listings in this category; see also page xii.

FRUIT JARS

Fruit or canning jars for preserving food have become very collectible. Thomas W. Dyott, one of Philadelphia's earliest and most innovative glass makers, was promoting his glass canning jars in 1829. John Landis Mason patented his screw-type canning jar on November 30, 1858. This date refers to the patent date, not age of jar. There are thousands of types of canning jars in many colors, types of closures, and embossings.

Atlas, E-Z seal, blue, qt, $4.00.

ABGA, aqua, glass lid, metal band, 1
  qt 9.00
AGWL, aqua, qt, waxseal, hand-
  made, Pittsburgh, PA 27.50
American Porcelain Lined, blue, qt,
  zinc lid 25.00
ARS, aqua, qt, tapered glass stop-
  per, handmade 65.00
Atlas Good Luck, 4 leaf clover,
  clear, ½ gal, glass lid, wire bail .. 12.00
Atlas Special Mason, aqua, qt, metal
  lid 6.00
Ball
  Aqua, ½ pt, zinc lid 9.00
  Blue, Mason's Patent 1858, qt,
    zinc lid 5.00
  Green, standard, qt, zinc lid 3.50
BB Wilcox, Pat March 26, 1867,
  aqua, qt 50.00
Bee Hive Trademark, aqua, qt 125.00
Burlington BG Co., R'D 1876, clear,
  qt, glass lid, metal band, hand-
  made 55.00
Cassidy, aqua, qt, glass lid, wire bail,
  handmade 180.00
Chef, clear, ½ pint, glass lid, wire
  bail 7.00

Cleveland Fruit Juice Co., clear, qt,
  glass lid, wire bail 8.25
Crown Mason, clear, ½ gal, zinc lid . 3.50
Daisy, F.E. Ward & Co., clear, qt,
  glass lid, wire bail, handmade ... 15.00
Diamond Fruit Jar, clear, qt, glass
  lid, screw band 6.00
Dominion Special Wide Mouth, clear,
  qt, metal lid 2.50
Drey Perfect Mason, amber, qt, zinc
  lid 22.00
Dyson's Pure Food Products, Mal-
  tese cross, clear, qt, glass lid ... 20.00
E.G. Co., amber, qt, zinc lid, hand-
  made 55.00
Everlasting Jar, green, qt, glass lid,
  toggles 18.00
F. W. Fitch Co., clear, pt, metal lid . 2.75
Fruit-Keeper, aqua, qt, zinc lid, hand-
  made 45.00
Gaynor Mason, clear, qt, glass lid,
  wire bail 6.00
Gem, clear, ½ gal, glass lid, zinc
  band 6.75
Genuine Mason, aqua, qt, zinc lid .. 7.50
Haine's 2, Pat March 1, 1870, green,
  qt, glass lid, metal clamp 80.00
Hazard & Co., Shrewsbury, NJ,
  green, qt, glass lid, metal clip ... 15.00
Hazel Atlas Lightning Seal, clear, pt,
  glass lid, wire bail 10.00
Hero Improved, aqua, pt, glass lid,
  screw band 24.00
Ideal Wide Mouth Jar, clear, ½ gal,
  zinc lid 6.00
J & B Fruit Jar, Pat June 14, 1898,
  aqua, pt, zinc lid 65.00

Kerr Economy, clear, ½ pt, metal lid,
clip 2.50
King, clear, qt, glass lid, wire bail . . 11.00
Lindell Glass Co., amber, qt, wax
seal, handmade 80.00
Liquid Carbonic Co., clear, qt, glass
lid, wire bail 3.00
Lynchburg, aqua, pt, zinc lid 15.00
Mason's
Fruit Jar, aqua, pt, zinc lid 5.00
Porcelain Lined, aqua, qt, zinc lid 22.00
Millville Pat June 18, 1861, green, 2
qt, glass lid, yoke, handmade . . . 45.00
Mission, bell, trademark, clear, qt,
zinc lid 12.00
Newmark Special Extra, clear, qt,
zinc lid 9.75
Perfection, clear, pt, glass lid, wire
bail, handmade 35.00
Perfect Seal, amber, square, qt, wire
bail 25.00
Princess, aqua, qt, glass lid, wire bail 15.00
Red Mason, aqua, clear, qt, zinc lid,
handmade 12.00
Reliable Home Canning Mason,
clear, qt, metal lid 2.00
Reliance Brand Wide Mouth Mason,
clear, pt, zinc lid 4.00
Rose, Imperial, clear, qt, zinc lid . . . 15.00
Safe Seal, clear, ½ gal, glass lid,
wire bail 5.00
Sealtite Wide Mouth Mason, green,
qt, metal screw top 9.00
Standard Mason, light green, qt, zinc
lid, handmade 8.00
Sun, green, qt, glass lid, clamp,
handmade 60.00
Sure, aqua, qt, glass lid, spring valve
clip, handmade 215.00
Swayzee's Improved Masion, aqua,
pt, zinc lid 5.00
Texas Mason, clear, qt, zinc lid 12.00
United Drug Co., clear, qt, glass lid,
side clamps 10.00
Universal, aqua, qt, zinc lid, name
emb upside down 7.00
Weir, Pat March 1, 1892, amber
glass lid, pottery base, qt 35.00
Yeoman's Fruit Bottle, aqua, qt, ½
gal, cork stopper, handmade 65.00

FRY GLASS

The H. C. Fry Glass Co. of Rochester, Pennsylvania, began operating in 1901 and ceased production in 1933. Their first products were brilliant period cut glass, then black trimmed depression glass and amber, pink, and blue depression type tablewares. In 1922, they patented heat-resisting ovenware in an opalescent color. This "Pearl Oven Glass" was produced in a variety of oven and table pieces including casseroles, meat trays, custard cups, pie and cake pans, trivets, butter tubs, etc. Most of these pieces are marked "Fry" with model numbers and sizes.

Fry's beautiful art line, called Foval, was produced only in 1926–27. It is pearly opalescent, with jade green or delft blue trim. It is rarely signed, except for occasional silver overlay pieces marked "Rockwell." Foval is always evenly opalescent, never striped like Fenton's opalescent line.

In the 1970s, reproductions of Foval were made in abundance in Murano, Italy. These pieces, including candlesticks, toothpicks, water jugs and jack-in-the-pulpit vases, have a teal blue transparent trim.

Goblet, 5¾", cobalt blue stem, $70.00.

Berry Set, 7 pcs, Foval with blue
foot, silver overlay, sgd Rockwell 375.00
Bowls
7", flat soup, all Foval 35.00
Foval with blue trim 45.00
Bud Vase, 10", all Foval 95.00
Candlesticks
10", Foval with Delft blue spirals,
pr 225.00
12", Foval with jade spirals, pr . . 275.00
Casserole, cov, 8", oval, ovenware
in chrome holder 22.00
Compote, 6" d, blue stem 160.00
Creamer and Sugar, Foval with blue
foot and handles, pr 135.00

Cup and Saucer, Foval with jade
handle 42.00
Custard Cups, ovenware, set of 6 . 18.00
Juice Reamers, ovenware
Round 21.00
Scalloped 32.00
Meat Platter, 15", ovenware in
chrome tray 32.00
Pie Plates, 8", 9", 10", ovenware .. 8.00
Pitcher, lemonade, Foval with jade
handle and finial on lid 195.00
Plates
8", luncheon, blue trim 44.00
10½", divided grill, ovenware ... 12.50
Ramekins, ovenware, set of 6 .... 15.00
Teapots
Full Size
All Foval 155.00
Foval with blue spout and han-
dle 125.00
Individual Size, Foval with jade
spout and handle 145.00

FULPER POTTERY

The American Pottery Company of Flemington, New Jersey, made pottery jugs and housewares from the early 1800s. They made Fulper Art Pottery from approximately 1910 to 1930.

Pieces made between 1910 and 1920 are products of a less production oriented period and subsequently are of a better quality. Almost all pieces are molded.

Bowls
7¾" h, effigy supports, cafe-au-
lait matte glaze, multicolored
flambe accents, marked 130.00
9⅜" d, 2½" h, 12 sided, mustard
color glaze with white overglaze
drippings, stamped backmark in
rect. cartouche 90.00
15" d, 4" h, round edged, black
and silver flambe 125.00
Petal, four rounded lobes, early
"Vasekraft" design in green
matte glaze 75.00
Box, lidded, porcelain, 7 x 5", kneeling Egyptian woman, painted in 6
or 7 colors 175.00
Candleholder, 5" d, 4" h, high back
and handle, red flambe glaze ... 50.00
Lamp, bisque figural, night lamp, 6"
h, form of seated ballerina

accented with green on matching
base, marked, artist sgd "J. Martin
Stangl" 80.00
Perfume Lamp, 8" h, 6" w, hand
painted robin on a porcelain base 175.00
Platter, 13" d, embossed fish swimming around interior rim,
copperdust to green glazes 375.00
Vases
4½" h, 3" w, cabinet, tapering cylinder form, brown flambe glaze
over a mustard matte glaze ... 40.00
5" h, 5" w, squat, bulbous bottom,
collared neck, brown flambe
over a sandy matte glaze 55.00
5" h, 5" w, bulbous, tripod footed,
brown matte finish 75.00
6" h, 6" w, teardrop shade, 2 thin
curving handles, blue flambe
glaze with scattered crystals .. 65.00
7" h, 7" w, squat, bulbous, rolled-
in opening at top, brown to
beige flambe 100.00
7½" h, 4½" w, bulbous, thin collared neck, rich mahogany glaze 75.00
9" h, 6" w, chine shape, bulbous
bottom and midsection, tick collared neck, gentle flare at top,
mirrored black finish 165.00
10" h, 4½" w, thin, Chinese form
with flared opening, Wisteria
matte finish (shades of mauve
and beige) 80.00
13" h, 5" w, cattail, emb cattails
from top to bottom, green matte
glaze, very desirable form 400.00
13" h, 9" w, bulbous form with 4
ringed handles, collared lipped
neck, flowing blue crystalline
and flambe glaze 300.00
"Pilgrim Flask," 2 curly handles
attached to the top shoulder,
flared opening, flambe and
black mirrored glazes, early ... 275.00

Bowl, 7½" h, 10⅝" d, effigy supports, dark blue high glaze drip over gray matte glaze, $200.00.

FURNITURE

Prices vary considerably on furniture. The original quality, style, desirability and condition, i.e., original finish, amount of restoration and the quality of the workmanship in the restoration, are all influencing factors in determining prices.

Region also is critical. Victorian furniture is popular in New Orleans, and unpopular in New England. Oak is in demand in the Northwest, not so much in the Middle Atlantic States. Learn your area before you buy.

Collectors are urged to shop around before buying. Furniture is plentiful unless you are after a truly rare example. Find a piece which fits your needs, is pleasant, and has a price you can afford. An attempt has been made to arrive at an average price on each item listed. This list should only serve as a guide. The above enumerated factors must be taken into consideration in arriving at a final price.

FURNITURE STYLES APPROXIMATE DATES

William and Mary	1688–1710
Queen Anne	1710–1750
Chippendale	1754–1780
Hepplewhite	1786–1800
Sheraton	1790–1810
Empire	1810–1830
Duncan Phyfe	1800–1840
Victorian	
Early	1840–1850
Rococo or Louis XV	1845–1870
Louis XVI	1865–1880
Renaissance	1860–1885
Eastlake	1875–1895

BEDS

Brass
Double, standard tubular styling . **775.00**
Single, standard tubular styling . . **425.00**
Cannon Ball, poplar, double urn turnings, shaped headboard, yellow paint, 51¾ x 80 x 46½" **250.00**
Child's
Oak, 4 sides inset with spindles, head and foot crest rails, headboard with rod to hold shirred fabric, 1½" red Gustav Stickley decal, c1907, 42¾" h x 35½" w x 55½" l **2,200.00**
Solid maple posts, orig dark green paint over red, PA, 18th C, 78" l x 35½" w x 34" h **900.00**
Day
Federal, carved mahogany, reeded, acanthus carved seatrail ending in scrolling acan-

Victorian bed, walnut, arched headboard, all orig. wooden slats, 70" w x 7' l x 7'4" h, $525.00.

thus carved foot and head boards, circular tapering legs, Philadelphia, c1805, 6'11" l . . . **2,200.00**
Mission, Limbert, oak, sloping sides form backrest, head panels pierced with heart form handles, branded label, c1910, 23" h x 6'2½" l **385.00**
Regency, painted **600.00**
Empire, mahogany, 4 poster, shaped headboard, endposts carved in upper portion in leaf and vine motif, pineapple finial, tapered and ball feet, 55 x 73 x 81½" **1,500.00**
Federal, pine, turned posts, shaped headboard **300.00**
French, faux bamboo, maple and bird's eye maple, c1900, 47 x 80 x 46" **650.00**
Georgian, pine, provincial **600.00**
Louis XV, walnut, diamond veneer, shaped headboard and footboard, oval motif in skirt and siderails . . **250.00**
Louis XVI, caned, gilded, wreath motif on footboard, fluted tapered feet **350.00**
Rope Beds
Birch, square tapered posts, simple cut pine headboard, rails lengthened **525.00**
Curly maple turned posts, urn finials, turned blanket bar on poplar shaped headboard, 53 x 77½ x 59" **650.00**

Poplar, dark, natural finish, high
posters, PA, c1800, 80½ x 78 x
59" **2,500.00**
Poster, low, pumpkin color, brown
graining, orig finish, American,
early 19th C, 30½ x 50" **1,000.00**
Shaker, maple, shaped head-
board, square tapered legs,
wooden wheel casters, green,
mid 19th C, 35½ x 74" **1,200.00**
Spruce, shaped headboard carved
with foliate and thistle motifs, circular reserve with pair of painted
love birds, footboard carved with
foliate and bird motifs above a reserve depicting farmyard scene,
painted in red, blue, yellow, green,
brown, gilt highlights, c1840, 5'11"
x 38 x 6'6" **880.00**
Tester Beds
Federal, mahogany, foot posts
reeded, swag and tassle, acanthus carved, ring turned bed
posts, shaped mahogany headboard, square tapering legs,
Philadelphia, c1800, 7'5" x 5'4"
x 6'7½" l **14,850.00**
George III, mahogany, pierced
waved tester, carved with cabochons, scrolled acanthus, wave
pattern, fretwork, fluted circular
tapering posts carved with
acanthus, headboard carved
with wave pattern, scrolled
acanthus, 74 x 90" **12,100.00**
Sheraton, curly maple, fluted foot
posts, tester, plain pencil post
headboard, 4 urn finials, ¾ size,
69½" h **3,250.00**
Sheraton, mahogany, fluted foot
posts, plain headboard, Ameri-
can, c1880, 92 x 69" **800.00**
Stuart, carved oak, fluted canopy,
cornice carved with masks,
paneled headboard, footboard,
6'2" h x 4' w x 6' l **1,750.00**
Trundle, poplar, rope, turned posts,
orig side rails, refinished, 40¾ x
65¾ x 16"h **325.00**

BENCHES

Cabinetmaker's, pine and maple,
mortised construction, 2 wood
screw vices, 2 steel bench stops,
early 20th C, 59 x 25" **450.00**
Cobbler, poplar, tool and nail hold-
ers, 45 x 22½ x 44¼" **250.00**
Hall, ebonized oak, iron, scrolling
antler form sides, carved front,
iron hardware, green stained interior, Charles Rohlfs, c1900, 45½ x
24½ x 35¼" **17,600.00**

**Settle bench, American or English
late 17th C or early 18th, pine, oak,
paneled front, sides, back, lift top
seat, 30" l, 19" d, 27" h, $550.00.**

Kneeling
Pine, cut out feet, mortised, 51" l   **65.00**
Shaker, pine, green paint, Canter-
bury, NH, 7' x 25¾ x 7½" h . .   **115.00**
Mammy, arrowback, turned legs,
plank seat, scrolled arms, old
weathered repaint, rockers, 55" l .   **425.00**
Plank Seats
Four sets of legs, simple scrolled
arms, spindle back, worn brown
finish, 108" l **600.00**
Stencil decor, PA, c1830, 85½ x
21¼" d seat **700.00**
Shaker, carved, cherry, rectangular
top, bootjack feet, c1850, 8' l x
10" w **2,000.00**
Sheraton, country, maple, curl, bird's
eye, 8 turned legs, turned stretchers, corner legs curve outward,
orig rush seat, 17 x 72 x 18" h . .   **1,700.00**
Walnut, cut out feet, mortised
through top, 10 x 78 x 19" h **200.00**
Water
Ash, poplar backboards, scalloped
top, sides, old worn blue-gray
paint, Indiana, 49" w x 12" d x
34¾" h . . . .   **450.00 -**
Pine, old brown paint, cross mem-
ber brace, board top, 10 x 39½
x 26½" h **165.00**
Windsor
Bamboo turned legs, spindles,
plank seat, splayed legs, turned
stretchers, finish stripped to
green stain, 75½" l **1,350.00**

Bamboo, painted, straight crest rail over 9 spindles flanked by stiles, boxed arm rails, D shaped seat, 72½″ l **1,540.00**

Bamboo, 2 chair bases as supports, orig, gray-tan, green and red paneled striping, early 19th C, 96″ l **2,100.00**

Work, heavy maple top, 2 all wooden clamps, end clamp with dovetail frame, well for tools, holes for bench stops, 25 x 80 x 32″ h . . . **375.00**

BENTWOOD

In 1856, Michael Thonet of Vienna perfected the process of bending wood using steam. Shortly after, Bentwood furniture became popular. Other manufacturers of Bentwood furniture were Jacob and Joseph Kohn, Philip Strobel and Son, Sheboygan Chair Co. and Tidoute Chair Co. Bentwood furniture is still being produced today by the Thonet firm and others.

Chairs
Arm, child's, worn red paint **125.00**
Rocker, child's **175.00**
Side, three horizontal turned wood slat back, carved cornice, 5 turned wood vertical rods, solid seat, stencil decor on 4 straight legs, paper label, Joseph Hoffman, 36″ h **145.00**
Side, attr. Samuel Gragg, Boston, c1815, shaped crest above shaped uprights, slat seat on shaped legs ending in hoof feet, turned strechers **1,350.00**
Cradles
22″ high **300.00**
50″ high, on stand with bonnet top, swing-type, all original **1,300.00**
Easel, Artist's **75.00**
Hall tree, 19th C **325.00**
Hat Rack
28 x 32″ long, 7 pegs, glove holder **175.00**
Screen, 3 fold, Thonet, c1904, inset with green glass above laminated panels cut with geometric devices, "Spanish Wand" model **3,000.00**
Settee, flanking swirl centers, side loop decor, cane inset seat, 4 cabriole legs, paper label Model #2001, Thonet 38″ h **880.00**
Shaving Stand and Mirror, designed by J. Hoffman, Thonet, c1906, 54″ h **2,200.00**
Sleep Sofa, adjustable backrest raised on scrolling legs, Model #9752, Thonet, 5′10″ l **950.00**

BLANKET CHESTS

Oak and pine, Pilgrim Century, E. Massachusetts, c1760–90, rectangular hinged lid, facade of 3 molded diamond panels centering black painted split balusters, 4 short molded drawers, stiles form feet, minor restoration, 35½″ h x 4′4″ l x 21″ d **1,980.00**
Pine, Alpine, rosemulled decor on red ground, Ole Zuren, Ano 1823 on front, dovetailed, wrought iron strap hinge, 16½″ h x 27″ w x 13½″ d **425.00**
Pine, orig brown vinegar painting on yellow ground, scalloped base, stiles inset with herringbone reeding in contrasting reddish sponging, 2 dovetailed drawers in base, interior till, 4 pigeonholes beneath, 42″ h x 44″ l x 19″ d **8,000.00**
Pine, Pennsylvania, Dauphin County, c1800, rectangular hinged lid, molded, well with till, 3 short drawers, bracket feet, front painted with stylized tulip and heart motifs in blue, green, white on red ground, 29½″ h x 50″ l x 22″ d . . **5,225.00**
Pine, Pennsylvania, late 18th C, decor of rosettes, swirls, pinwheels, black on red, orig jaw lock, hinges, 25½″ h x 52″ l x 22½″ w **3,500.00**
Poplar, Pennsylvania, Lebanon County, orig paint, brown sponging on ochre wash, harlequin banding in red, black on white, black strippled corners, front and ends have tombstone arched white reserves with thin edge striping, and red, dark gray-blue sponged designs, lid is plain, dovetailed case, bracket feet, till, wrought iron strap hinges, bear trap lock, key, 24″ h x 53″ l x 23¼″ d **4,500.00**
Walnut, Chippendale, Pennsylvania, c1760, rectangular molded top, dovetailed case, 2 thumb molded drawers, molded skirt, shaped bracket feet, 30″ h x 48½″ w x 22″ d **2,650.00**

BOOKCASES

Eastlake, maple and bird's eye maple, bamboo, labeled R. J. Horner, American, c1890, 4′8″ h x 31½″ w **1,045.00**
Empire, mahogany, Gothic beehive arches in glazed upper section, 2 glazed door base, c1850 . . . . **1,400.00**
Federal, mahogany, 4 parts, overhanging rectangular cornice,

beaded molded edges, 2 bookcase units each with Gothic arch glazed doors, adjustable shelves, bottom section of 2 paneled cupboard doors, molded base, c1810, 100½" h x 92¾" l x 20⅝" d **6,600.00**

George III

Library, molded breakfront, rectangular cornice above 3 rectangular glazed cupboard doors over 3 conforming fielded panel doors, 81" w **5,000.00**

Mahogany, molded rectangular cornice over fluted frieze, 2 rectangular glazed doors, lower half secretary drawer over 2 cupboard doors, 36" w **4,000.00**

Mission

Gustav Stickley, red decal mark, paper label, 56" x 48" w, c1910   **1,320.00**

Limberts, rectangular top, caned inset splashboard over 2 door cabinet, glass doors, 4 straight legs, paper label, 60" h x 35" l .   **418.00**

Oak, 3 section, glass fronts lift up, barrister type **400.00**

BOXES

Ballot

8½ x 11 x 16", walnut, wide dovetailing, brass hardware . . .   **125.00**

9½ x 6 x 4½", walnut, scrimshaw, balls, black cubes, whale ivory and wood handle **325.00**

Band

New England, printed paper, rural country scene, yellow, 10½ x 15" **350.00**

Oval, orig decor of polychrome ruse mulling on orange ground,

Bride's Box, oval, Bentwood, 22" l x 14¾" w, $150.00.

decoupage print on lid, laced seams, 11½ x 18" **425.00**

Pennsylvania, white floral pattern on rainbow ground, black beaver hat by C. Nickerson, 8" h . .   **110.00**

Bible,

7 x 15¼ x 21¾" w, walnut, dovetailed, diamond inlays, initials MG Chester County, PA, 18th C, ...   **500.00**

9½ x 14½ x 25½" w, walnut, dovetailed, turned feet, base and lid edge molding, wrought iron strap hinges with rosehead fastening nails **450.00**

Bride's

17¼" l x 10¾" w x 7¾" h, decor of women on top, tulips on sides, laced with rawhide, hard pine box, PA, early 19th C **750.00**

19¼ x 11¾", detailed colorful bride and groom surrounded by tulips, flowers, calligraphy on bottom, Scandinavian, late 18th   **1,150.00**

22" l x 14½" w x 9¾" h, oval, painted pine, orig green band, gold eagle, shield breat, clutching tulips, rawhide laces, early 19th C **800.00**

Candle

4¼ x 14" x 7", pine, sliding cov, orig blue paint **175.00**

5 x 7½ x 15¼", hanging, dovetailed, orig blue paint **265.00**

6 x 9 x 13" l, carved, sliding lid . .   **225.00**

13", pine, hanging, primitive, truncated, circular crest, sq nails . .   **75.00**

15 x 11½ x 7", hanging, carved, lovebirds, step carved molding at sides, front panel, orig red paint, late 18th C **400.00**

Cigar, 5" l, brass, top and bottom covered with letters and numbers, sgd, dated 1787, Dutch **110.00**

Document

Pine, dome top, old alligatered brown graining, iron lock and hasp, iron hinges, 13" l **125.00**

Tole, dome top, orig black paint, yellow striping, 8¼" l **115.00**

Handkerchief, brass, inlaid, 2⅝" w x 7" d, x 6" l **100.00**

Hat

9 x 20, triangular, pine, applied diamond shape decor **150.00**

9¾" h x 14½ x 16½", oval, wood, wallpaper covering, white ground, brown, blue decor **125.00**

Knife

Empire, leaf carved, veneer paneled square top, rectangular case, carved front, 18¼" h x 14½" w, Phila, c1820, pr **2,000.00**

George III, mahogany, serpentine slope front, inlaid chevron pattern, fitted interior, circular brass locks, matching pair with one smaller matching box, 13½" h and 12" h 3,300.00

Regency, late, satinwood, incurved square hooded lifting top, finial, fitted interior, gilt metal paw feet, 29½", pr 1,000.00

Liquor Box, Continental, walnut, relief carving of interlocking flowers, elaborate finial, 4 decanters, 11 glasses 450.00

Netting, 21 x 5½ x 4½" d, bird's eye maple veneer, hinged lid, early 19th C 530.00

Pantry, 14½ x 7" d, splint wood, orig stain 95.00

Puzzle, Tunbridgeward, 2" sq 75.00

Salt, hanging, pine dovetailed, scalloped crest, 2 compartments, sliding lids, 6 x 10 x 9½" 165.00

Seed, wooden, orig paper labels, J. M. Philips Sons, Mercerburg, Pa, interior with unused paper seed packs, 12 x 25½" 205.00

Sewing, rectangular, mahogany, rosewood, inlay of whale ivory, MOP, abalone shell, baleen, hinged, interior consists of center well, 2 drawers, 2 lift top compartments, 8 whalebone spool holders, sewing thread eyelets, Nantucket, c1840, 5¼ h x 12" l x 9" d 5,500.00

Spice

Pine, 8 drawers, hanging, wire nail construction, 9¾ x 5 x 16½" . . 115.00

Pine, 11 drawers, poplar case, crest marked "Compliments of The Golden Eagle, Ohio" 10" w x 25½" h 195.00

Poplar, hanging, 2 drawers, dovetailed, carved crest, slant top lid, scroddleware knob, 12¼" w x 9½" d x 13" h 175.00

Snuff, 4½" d, turned, portraits of Washington & Lafayette, label A. Goodyear & Sons, Manufacturers, Waterbury, Conn. 175.00

Stationery, Victorian, leather covered, 9" 65.00

Straw work, Prisoner of War, elaborate scene of village, ship on cover, 3 cov compartment interior, flowers, floral sprays on covers, chessboard on bottom, 10⅞" l x 7½" w x 3¼" h 350.00

Strong Box, dovetailed, decor wrought iron hardware with strap hinges, handle, lock with large face plate and stylized applied leaves, 7 x 7¼ x 12½" 200.00

Tool, pine, dovetailed, wrought iron bound corners, decor lock hasp, worn dark green paint 165.00

Trinket, Tunbridgeware, hinged, floral decor, 3½" 70.00

Utility, hanging, old red paint, 19" h x 16¾" l x 5½" d 750.00

Writing

Cherry, table top, walnut, orig dark brown paint, yellow striping, stenciled birds, eagle on lid, front panel, interior fitted with pigeon holes, dovetailed drawer, 24½ x 21 x 16¾" h 400.00

Mahogany, military, brass banding, 20", c1810 . . . . 195.00

CABINETS

China

French Provincial, oak, 2 pairs of doors over 2 pairs of cupboard doors, arched glass panels in doors, central shell cartouche at top, recessed and carved cupboard doors, fluted quarter columns on side, 74½ x 14 x 91" . 1,550.00

Mahogany, satinwood banding, 2 doors, shaped apron, carved cabriole legs, paw feet, 3½10" w, mid 18th C 1,500.00

Oak, c1875, arched door, surmounted by carved mask,

Store cabinet, Belding Bros & Co., oak, 6'7" h x 40" w, $1,500.00.

separated from bowed sides by flat reeded and ring turned pilasters, carved paw feet, 53" w ... 800.00

Victorian, bowed, mahogany, satinwood, marquetry decor, drawer above, 2 doors, 7'9" h x 4'7" w 3,375.00

Dye, Diamond, oak, litho tin scene of children playing, 29¾" 300.00

Hardware, bolts, octagonal, revolving base, oak, 4 drawers 400.00

Jewelry, Victorian, mahogany, inlaid, boxwood, string borders, 9¾" w . 275.00

Kitchen, oak with glass inserts in door, porcelain work surface with blue agate edges, flour bin, spice racks, etc., brass McDougall plates, orig factory tags 400.00

Liquor, George IV, mahogany, inlaid, brass banded corners, 18" w, c1830 .... 400.00

Mahogany, oak drawer fronts, inlays of holly, walnut, teak, whalebone inlay sides in hexagonal design, beveled mirrors on 2 front doors, 3 shelves interior, secret compartment, brass knobs, escutcheons, Nantucket, John Baker, c1860, 32" h x 20¼" w x 6¼" d 3,630.00

Music

Art Nouveau, walnut 350.00

Edwardian, mahogany, 6 drawer, squat cabriole legs, 21" w 185.00

Renaissance Revival, rosewood, Gustave Herter, NY, c1865, 47½" h x 35" w x 21⅛" d 1,980.00

Parlor, Renaissance Revival, inlaid, ebonized, gilt decor, 87¾" h x 51" w x 21" d 4,000.00

Side

Louis XV, kingwood, gilt bronze mounted, tulipwood parquetry, marble top, 44" h x 5' w, late 19th C 5,225.00

Louis XVI, ebonized, gilt bronze mounted, central door mounted with bronze plaque, 36" h x 27" w, late 19th C, pr 18,800.00

Smoking, oak, Gustav Stickley, one drawer above cabinet door, compartment interior, copper hardware, c1912, 29" h x 20" w x 15" d 1,430.00

Vitrines

Italian, walnut, parcel gilt, rococo carved pediment, fitted shelves, 2 glazed doors, serpentine stand with marbled bordered top above carved pierced apron, cabriole legs, C scroll stretchers, 19th C, 93½" h x 50" w x 27½" d 3,500.00

Louis XV, kingwood, gilt bronze

mounted, marble top, 45" h x 4' 8" w, c1900 .... 6,000.00

Louis XVI, kingwood, gilt bronze mounted, 6 legs, 4'4" h x 4'3" w, c1900 .... 3,575.00

CANDLE SHIELDS

47", Regency, finely carved base, brass mounts, c1820 .... 1,200.00

54", George III, mahogany, adjustable screen, easel on ratchet, pair of silvered brass candleholders, cabriole legs, c1775 .... 700.00

61", mahogany, inlaid tripod base, woven silk picture, c1820 ...... 400.00

CANDLESTANDS

Birch, Queen Anne, square top, incurved corners, snake feet, 27" x 13" square 400.00

Cherry, Federal, NY, circular top, ring turned and tapering standard, tripod base, snake feet, 28½" x 17½" d 3,250.00

Chinese Export, black, lacquer, hexagon dish top over 3 part joined long C scroll supports, quadruple base, gilt flowerheads, leaf tips, 40½" h 1,430.00

Country, circular tilt top, tripod base, cabriole legs, c1790 25½ x 22" d 175.00

Candlestand, cherry, 8 sided top, 14¾ x 17¾" top x 27½" h, $450.00.

Mahogany
George III, painted white, polychrome decor of grapevines on
pale blue ground, spiral fluted
pedestal, square tripod legs,
15¾″ w, pr 3,300.00
Hepplewhite, birdcage, oval tilting
top, fine string inlay, urn column
tapered shaft, cabriole legs,
platform pad feet, 29 x
16¼″ d 5,250.00

Maple
Hepplewhite, country, curly,
square tilt top, NE, c1790 . . . . 475.00
Queen Anne, circular top, snake
feet, 27 x 14½″ d 650.00
Queen Anne, oval, tilt top, turned
stem, snake feet, 26½″ x 22″ l
x 14½″ w 1,800.00
Standing, screw adjustment, NE,
c1700, 35½″ h 2,900.00
Tiger Maple, Federal, tilt rectangular
top with shaped sides, urn shaped
standard with spiral carved band,
quarter circle top on legs 625.00
Walnut, Queen Anne, tilt top, circular
molded top, bird cage support,
vase and ring turned standard, tripod base, shod snake feet, 27 x
19½″ 4,500.00

CHAIRS

Arrowbacks
Full, plank seat 225.00
Half, plank seat, orig stenciling . . 200.00
Art Deco
Arm, tiger eye maple, brown leather inserts, red lacquered fret-
work 500.00
Club, Ebené de Macassar, barrel
back, straight sides and front,
vertical concave fluting around
sides and back, green cut velvet
upholstering, attri. Louis Süa
and André Mare c1930 . . . . . . 600.00
Balloon back, side, yellow striping,
stenciled foliage, black ground,
eagle on crest 125.00
Banister back, arm, sausage turn-
ings, front posts terminating in
mushroom tops, old worn black
paint over red, NE, early 18th C . . 3,250.00
Belter, side, rosewood, pierced,
carved grapes and roses, upholstered needlepoint set and back . 3,500.00
Carver's, twined seat, American,
17th C, 28½″ h 4,000.00
Children's
Arm, ladderback, 3 splat back,
sausage turnings, mushroom
posts, wicker like seat, orig
black paint 1,500.00

Shaker chair, hardwood, ladderback, rush seat, heavy bulbous turning, $1,050.00.

High Chair, maple, ash, splint
seat, turned legs, oval finials,
NE, 18th C 440.00
High Chair, Queen Anne, NE,
fruitwood, rush seat, bulb and
wheel frontal stretcher, splayed
legs, molded vertical slats, 18th
C 1,600.00
Potty, pine, painted and stenciled 145.00
Windsor, yoke back, flat
outscrolled arms, serpentine
braces, curly maple seat, legs,
oak arms and back 1,600.00
Chippendale Style
Arm, mahogany, pierced slat,
knuckle arms, Philadelphia,
c1770 . . . . 1,750.00
Arm, wing, mahogany, serpentine
crest, scrolled wings and arms,
c1800 . . . . 4,000.00
Chinese, mahogany square mold-
ed legs, H stretcher, fretwork,
high back, needlepoint uphol-
stery 1,500.00
Corner, CT, c1750, cherry, shaped
crest rail, two vase shaped
splats, baluster shaped sup-
ports, square slip seat 1,100.00
Dining, Phila, walnut, claw and ball
feet, gothic form, pierced back
splat, set of 5 . . . . 10,000.00

Side, Phila, mahogany, carved ball
and claw feet, acanthus carved
knees, carved shell on apron,
fluted posts, curly mahogany
pierced splat, crest rail with
carved ears, foliage shell de-
sign, gold damask slip seat ... **14,500.00**

Side, Phila, 18th C, walnut, shell
carved, claw and ball feet, cupid's bow crest rail with fluted
terminals **3,500.00**

Wing, Phila, mahogany, shaped
crest, wings continuing to
scrolled arms, squared leg,
joined by stretchers **3,600.00**

Eastlake, Victorian
Arm, walnut, upholstered back
and seat **300.00**
Side, walnut, small arms, cane
seat **200.00**

Empire Style
Arm, mahogany, square back, upholstered seat, brass castors,
eagle terminals on arms, c1825 **800.00**
Side, mahogany, veneer, fiddle-
back, serpentine seat, saber leg **185.00**

Federal
Arm, NE, c1810, bamboo turned
crest, spindles, arms, splayed
legs, cane seats, painted ochre,
green, red florals, 34" h, pr ... **1,540.00**
Arm, NE, late 18th C, Martha
Washington, mahogany **3,000.00**

George III
Arm, mahogany, serpentine top
rail, neo-Gothic splat, S shaped
arms, padded seat, marlborough
legs, red silk brocade upholstery **1,540.00**
Arm, mahogany, library, earred
rectangular padded back, arms,
seat, circular tapering fluted
legs, upholstered in yellow and
white silk **3,850.00**

Gothic style, arm, walnut, upholstered seat, c1845 .... **880.00**

Hepplewhite Style
Arm, Newburyport, MA, mahogany, square legs, spade feet, line
inlay, curved arm supports, oval
back, gold damask upholstery . **3,800.00**
Arm, NY, c1820, wing, mahogany,
canted back, arched cresting .. **900.00**
Side, mahogany, shield backs of 5
splats, molded tapered legs, H
stretcher, reupholstered seats,
set of 6 .... **7,800.00**
Side, NY, mahogany, tapered
molded legs, H stretcher, well
detailed shield backs, carved
classical detail, seats reupholstered, old finish, pr **6,000.00**

Hitchcock, plank seat, orig paint and
stenciling, c1840 .... **625.00**

Ladderback
Arm, NE, 18th C, 5 splat back,
simple scrolled arms, rush seat,
sausage turnings **400.00**
Side, Delaware Valley, c1740–70,
6 arched graduated slats, rush
seat, turned legs, frontal ring
and baluster stretcher, black .. **2,200.00**

Louis XV Style
Arm, slightly bowed sides, some
relief carving, green velvet upholstery **150.00**
Side, carved base, needlepoint
slip seat **75.00**

Mission
Arm, Gustav Stickley, c1910, oak,
V back, branded mark **445.00**
Arm, L. & J. G. Stickley, c1910,
wing, oak, clamp decal mark .. **900.00**
Side, Gustav Stickley, oak, three
slat back jointed to square padded seat on 4 straight legs, 39"
h **130.00**

Morris
Oak, Limbert, c1910, pierced wide
stretchers, paper label **525.00**
Oak and leather, L. & J. G.
Stickley. c1912, flat open arms,
orig decal **1,320.00**
Office, desk, arm, oak, flat spindles,
revolving seat, tilt back, c1910 .. **250.00**
Potty, wing back, pine, lifting lid, sliding back door, light brown
graining, 19½" w x 17¼" d x
40¾" h **305.00**

Queen Anne Style
Arm, wing, walnut, padded back,
ears, out scrolled padded arms,
cabriole legs, flame stitch velvet, 46½" **1,550.00**
Corner, American, c1760, walnut,
balloon, slip seat, cabriole legs . **1,500.00**
Corner, NE, c1750, maple, dark
finish, orig rush seat, flame
stitch slipcover **2,000.00**
Side, Mass., c1750, spoon back,
Spanish feet, needlepoint covered seat **1,500.00**
Side, Rhode Island, c1750, walnut, shell crest, balloon back,
seat **6,000.00**
Wing, mahogany, banty feet with
high pads, chamfered back
legs, turned H stretcher, old finish, reupholstered **9,500.00**

Sheraton Style
Country, side, curly maple,
Hitchcock type, turned legs,
cane seat, plain splat, crest ... **900.00**
Side, mahogany, tapered carved
legs with spade feet, carved
back, classical urn design, drapery swags, fluted fans, old dark

finish, ivory damask upholstered seats, pr 2,100.00
Transitional, Queen Anne to Chippendale, attributed to Goddard, Newport, RI, side, walnut, detailed cabriole legs, ball and claw feet, carved shells on knees, well shaped vase splat with boldly carved shell on crest, slip seat leather covering under pale green damask 9,000.00
Victorian Style
Arm, NY, c1870, walnut incised crest rail, skirt, upholstered, pr . 7,700.00
Side, walnut, balloon back, upholstered seat 200.00
Wallace Nutting, early 20th C, pilgrim century style, turned oak, arm, spindle back, rush seats, sgd, pr 700.00
William and Mary, NE, c1740, maple, banister back, 44½" h 1,000.00
Windsor
Arm, bowback, comb, 7 spindles, bamboo legs 500.00
Arm, bowback, NE, 18th C, 7 spindles 800.00
Arm, RI, 18th C, continuous, 12 spindles 2,200.00

Windsor chair, bow back, arm, maple, NE, 18th C, $1,400.00.

Arm, hoopback, 7 spindle back, turned legs 300.00
Arm, Phila, c1785, lowback, walnut, broad saddle seat, molded out scrolled arms 3,000.00
Arm, NE, writing, drawer 3,000.00
Side, NE, 18th C, bow back, 9 spindle, chalked D under seat . 700.00
Side, c1780, fan back, ash, pine seat, scroll carved ears 800.00
Side, I. Clark, Hartford CT, 18th C, fan back, deeply shaped pine seat, deep turnings 1,100.00
Side, Samuel Vinson, RI, 18th C, fan back, carved ears, sunburst design 850.00
Side, hoop back, 10 spindles, bamboo turnings, deep saddle seat 450.00

CHESTS OF DRAWERS

Chippendale
Cherry, bracket base, 4 graduated drawers, fluted quarter columns, 18th C, 35½" h x 43" w x 21½" d 3,500.00
Cherry, NE, late 18th C, oxbow front, ogee bracket base, fluted quarter columns, maker's brand LF in square with sawtooth edge on second and fourth drawers, 37⅞" w 18,000.00
Mahogany, Boston or Rhode Island, c1770 serpentine front, 4 graduated drawers, ogee bracket feet, 36½" w 7,500.00
Country, NE, 18th C, curly birch, orig hardware, 37½" w 8,250.00
Eastlake, walnut, 3 long graduated drawers, white marble top, mirror flanked by candle stands, 32" w . 550.00
Empire, country, cherry, turned feet, pilasters, 4 dovetailed drawers, refinished, 43¼" w x 21½" d x 47½" h 375.00
Federal
Painted, shaped splashboard, 4 long graduated drawers, turned legs, painted and grained in shades of red and black crossbanding on yellow and brown grained ground, 42¼ x 20½ x 49" 12,500.00
Tiger Maple, PA or NJ, c1800, 4 drawers, double molding at top, 38¼" h x 32¾" l x 19⅛" d . . . 4,900.00
Hepplewhite
American, late 18th C, mahogany, swell front, French splay bracket base, fine inlaid bands top, bottom, 4 graduated drawers, 41¾" l 1,300.00

Hepplewhite chest, cherry, 4 graduated drawers, bow front, applied bracket feet, thumb molded top, 36½", $4,000.00.

Chester County, PA, walnut, French feet, reeded posts, dovetailed drawers, cock beading, 4 drawers, 36" w x 39½" h	1,050.00
Upper Conn. Valley, late 18th C, cherry, applied pilasters, orig hardware, 36½" l	2,250.00
Mission, Gustav Stickley, c1910, oak, 2 small drawers, 3 long graduated drawers, partial paper label, 43" h	3,250.00
Queen Anne, country, cherry, high cut out bracket feet, dovetailed case, 2 small drawers, 4 long graduated drawers, wide molded cornice, new brasses, 35¼ x 15¾ x 48¾"	3,250.00
Sheraton, country, tiger maple, 4 graduated drawers, simple turned legs, paneled ends, front facings of curly maple and bird's eye maple veneer, c1800, 40½" w x 40" h x 20"	600.00
Victorian, veneer, 3 long graduated drawers, top drawers extend out from body, scored and molded side posts, red Italian marble top, 42⅛ x 17⅞ x 33"	575.00
William and Mary, CT, pine, 2 small drawers, 3 long graduated drawers, ball foot, painted, 37½ x 21 x 39"	6,750.00

CHESTS, OTHER

See also Blanket Chests and Chests of Drawers

Chest-on-Chest
  Chippendale, NE, c1770, mahogany, flat top, bracket base, orig pine tree brasses, 76½" h x 38½" w x 22½" d 7,000.00

George I, inlaid walnut, molded rectangular cornice above 2 short over 3 long crossbanded drawers, lower section with writing slide over 3 graduated drawers, lower drawer with central concave cavity inlaid with a half star, bracket feet, 45½" w x 74½" h	4,400.00

Commode
Biedermeier, walnut, 2 fitted drawers, gray marble slab, tapered legs, 33" h x 34" w	1,000.00
Regency, Provincial, oak, molded rectangular top, 3 drawers, 30¾" h x 36½" w	2,400.00

Highboy
Chippendale, CT River Valley, cherry, bonnet top, fan carvings, 42" w x 89" h	15,000.00
Queen Anne, NE, c1760, curly cherry, cabriole legs, slender ankles, fine slipper feet, upper case of chamfered corners, fluted pilaster strips, graceful scalloped skirt, 2 drop finials, beaded lips, orig hardware, locks, 71⅛" h x 38¾" w	26,000.00
Queen Anne, Phila, c1760, walnut, curl, cabriole legs with shell carved knees, drake feet, upper and lower case with chamfered corners, fluted pilaster strips, 3 small drawers, 4 graduated drawers top, 5 drawer base, orig hardware, 74¼" h x 40" w x 22" d	10,000
William and Mary, inlaid, upper case with molded cornice, 2 small drawers, 3 long graduated drawers, lower case with 3 small drawers, deeply valanced skirt, vase and trumpet turned legs, 39½ x 21¼ x 63"	22,000.00
Mule, pine, 6 board, scalloped base, 2 overlapping dovetailed drawers, orig staple hinges, 38" w x 18" d x 38¾" h	750.00

CRADLES

Austrian, Bois Clair, carved, attr. to Kolman Moser, c1900, each side containing conventialized floral bouquet, 53" l, extension arm to hold cloth or fabric	1,750.00
Birch, pine hood, worn red finish, dovetailed, 21¾" x 39 x 26½" h	275.00
Mahogany, hooded, 40" l, orig finish, late 18th C	800.00

Cradle, mixed woods, 37″ l x 31½″ h, 5 spindle ends, 8 on sides, Pat. 1869, replaced cushion, $285.00.

Maple, open hand holds, trestle rockers, refinished, 38″ **275.00**

Pine
  Hooded, 3-panel, c1840, shaped apron beneath front hood, quarter moon rockers, solid sides, grain painted, nail construction, 41″ l, 25½″ h **375.00**
  Open, c1820, painted and grained, sponge decoration, 42″ l **450.00**

Walnut, shaped sides, heart shaped hand holds, heart design in circular top of end boards, rockers with cut out ends, 41½″ **275.00**

Windsor, country, c1800, arched hood and foot board, shaped rockers, 38″ **750.00**

CUPBOARDS

Apothecary, 9 drawers, primitive, 21″ w x 11½″ d x 16¼″h **110.00**

Corner
  Butternut, poplar, open, 1 pc, primitive fluting on sides, 2 batten doors, 2 full shelves, 2 setback shelves on top, arched top, square cut relief carving, 44″ w x 80″ h **1,150.00**
  Cherry, PA, early 19th C, green painted interior, 2 panel doors on base section, 1 shelf, upper door of 9 panes, 2 shelves, arched panes at top, dentil border, 74½″ h x 46½″ w x 23″ d **1,700.00**
  Cherry, pale blue interior, 2 pc, paneled doors on base, top single 12 pane glazed door, molded cornice, 40½″ w x 83″ h . . .   **1,300.00**
  Curly maple, country, 1 pc, bottom

with paneled doors, 2 round front drawers and scalloped skirt, top with double 4 light doors, scalloped edge shelves, well developed cornice, 44½″ w x 84¾″ h **3,250.00**

Mahogany, Empire, New York, upper case of 2 glazed doors, half columns, base of 2 closed doors, carved paw feet **700.00**

Pine, American, lower panel door, upper door with 12 lights of glass, butterfly hinges, 6 shells inside, poplar backing, 83″ h x 44″ w x 19″ h **1,900.00**

Pine, Chippendale, ogee cornice over 2 cupboard doors, 3 fielded panels, 3 shelves, over 1 cupboard door, straight bracket feet, 78½″ h **2,500.00**

Pine, Federal, c1800, carved molded cornice, open cupboard door on base, 82″ h x 36½″ w x 16″ d, pr **8,000.00**

Pine, paneled sides, doors, applied moldings, glazed top doors, brass thumb latches, porcelain knobs, 52½″ w x 87″ h, refinished **2,150.00**

Poplar, PA, 18th C, dentil molding around top, green painted interior, 12 pane double door top, 2 shelves, ogee bracket base, 90½″ h x 44″ w x 24″ d **4,100.00**

Flat Wall of Side
  Cherrywood, PA, c1800, 2 parts, glazed doors, drawers, 84 x 50¾ x 18¾ **4,250.00**
  Pine, 1 pc, raised panel doors base, open top, 3 shelves,

Flat wall cupboard, walnut, 3 shelves, 3 drawers over 2 doors; 12 glass pane doors, brass hardware, 18½″ deep x 52″ w x 84″ h, $3,500.00.

molded cornice, 53" w x 18½"
d x 86" h **1,150.00**
Pine, 2 board and batten doors,
interior shelves, old red paint,
49¾ x 13¼ x 69" h **325.00**
Poplar, cherry, country, 1 pc, continuous feet, molding at base,
between sections, 2 paneled
doors base, double doors
above, 8 panes each, 91¼" h x
46" w x 16" d **1,200.00**
Victorian, English, c1860, incised
and ebonized rosewood marquetry, gilt bronze mounts, column front, concave sides, 59" w
x 41" h **2,250.00**
Walnut, Eastlake, single panel
glazed doors, 2 drawers over 2
blind doors, machine carvings . **700.00**

Hanging
Cherry, 2 doors with glass panes,
brass and procelain fittings, orig
condition, c1900, 19¾ x 25" .. **145.00**
Mahogany, corner, English, well
molded cornice, single door,
geometric arranged glass,
crossbanding, line of stringing,
interior shelves, 36" w x 47¾"
h **850.00**
Pine, Scandinavian, 18th C, 22½"
h x 19" w x 10¼" d **200.00**
Poplar, painted graining, one shelf,
blind door, 20 x 29" h **485.00**
Walnut, country, raised panel
door, scalloped crest, 1 shelf,
14" w x 9¾" d x 23" h **185.00**

Jelly
Pine, poplar, cut out feet, paneled
doors, worn old dark brown
flame graining, 43" w x 17" d x
51" h **250.00**
Poplar, paneled doors, 2
overhanging drawers, shaped
skirt, red and black graining,
orig hardware, 41¼ x 21½ x
46" **600.00**

Pie Safes
Pine, pierced tin panels, red
painted interior, old natural finish, early 19th C, 62" h x 42½"
w x 18" d **900.00**
Pine, screened panels, old natural
finish, 44½" h x 26⅝" w x 17"
d **550.00**
Walnut, square corner ´posts,
paneled sides, single door, 3
punched tin panels with stars,
circles, old green paint, replaced feet, 30½" w x 21" d x
60" h **225.00**

Schranks
Walnut, corner, 1 pc, bracket feet,
1 dovetailed drawer, single

raised panel door, rattail hinges,
cover molded cornice, 1 shelf, 7
hooks, 43½" w x 48½" d x 77"
h **5,750.00**
Walnut, carved, Chippendale,
Chester County, PA, c1760,
broad deeply molded frieze,
projecting cornice, fielded panel
cupboard doors, interior of
shelves and compartments, two
molded drawers, paneled ends,
ogee bracket feet, 7'1" h, x 6'
11" w x 28½" d **9,900.00**
Walnut, inlaid, Southeastern PA,
1765, molded projecting cornice
above frieze, inlaid inscription
GEO. R. 1765, pr of paneled
hinged doors, center inlaid stellate devices, molded base with
2 drawers, flattened ball feet, 6'
7½" h x 5'11" w x 23" d **12,000.00**

DESKS

Chippendale Style
Block front, MA, c1765, mahoga-
ny, carved fan, 45¼ x 41¾" .. **7,000.00**
Slant front, NE, 18th C, curly maple, 4 drawers, 6 open pigeonholes, 1 enclosed center
compartment, orig hardware,
39¾" l **2,500.00**
Slant front, NE, 18th C, tiger maple, interior of 8 stepped small
drawers, pigeonholes, secret
compartment, 39" w x 29½" h . **6,750.00**
Davenport, walnut and burl walnut,
c1845, carved "S" supports, 21"
w x 36¾" h **1,350.00**
Eastlake, Victorian, c1890, walnut,
drop front, machine carvings, gal-
lery top, fitted interior 35 x 62" .. **650.00**

**Wooton, walnut, burl walnut veneer,
patented, $8,500.00.**

Federal

Butler's, inlaid mahogany, hinged writing surface, 7 small drawers, pigeonholes, 3 graduated drawers, French feet, 48″ w **2,500.00**

New York, c1805, mahogany, writing, top with shaped gallery, hinged leather insert lid opening to well fitted with sliding writing surface, 1 small divided drawer, frieze faced to simulate 1 long drawer, circular reeded tapering legs, 32½″ h x 27″ w x 23¼″ d   **1,320.00**

Hepplewhite, slant front, cherry, French feet, scalloped apron, inlay of banded diamonds, inlaid compass star on lid, figured mahogany veneer interior, 9 dovetailed drawers, 42¾″ w x 21″ d x 45¾″ h . .   **1,150.00**

Lap Desk, Victorian, brass fitted, rosewood **175.00**

Mahogany, Peruvian, folding, c1835 light, dark mahogany inlay, MOP escutcheon, initials EBS, ivory cross hatch corners on bottom, interior compartments, 18¼″ w x 7″ h x 9¼″ d **1,045.00**

Partner's Desk

George III, mahogany, molded rectangular inset leather top, frieze, 3 drawers on either side, 2 pedestals, 70½″ w **11,000.00**

Mission, L. & J. G. Stickley, oak, rectangular top over 2 short drawers, 4 straight legs, stretchers, paper label, 29″ h x 40″ l .   **250.00**

Queen Anne, slant front, Mass., 18th C, cherry, turned feet, slightly stepped interior, 16 drawers, 6 pigeonholes, 39¾″ w **2,000.00**

Roll Tops

Oak, S shaped roll top, 3 drawers on each side, plain interior **1,000.00**

Oak, S shaped roll top, Victorian, wooten type doors on sides, elaborate carving, fancy interior   **2,750.00**

Schoolmaster's, slant top, oak legs, birch top, pigeonhole interior, 26¾ x 21½ x 35″ **200.00**

Sheraton, country, pine, slant front, one deep drawer, gallery back, 32″ w **1,500.00**

Table top, pine, slant lid, gallery with 2 rows of arched top pigeonholes, lift lid, old black paint, 36¾ x 32¼ x 27″ **225.00**

Traveling

Ivory inlays, engraved garlands, reticulated ivory carving, 12¼″ l   **475.00**

Painted, earthworm like graining, 22″ l **550.00**

Victorian, burr walnut, pedestal, rectangular top, molded edge, 3 small drawers, kneehole opening flanked by 6 drawers, molded plinth base, 51″ w **500.00**

Wooton, c1875, walnut and burl walnut, standard grade, pierced and carved ¾ gallery over a double panel lifting frieze, maple veneer fitted interior, trestle feet, 41″ closed, 69½″ h **5,500.00**

DOUGH TROUGHS

Table top dough trough, 32 x 16 x 9½″ h, $60.00.

Cherry, dovetailed corners, turned feet, white porcelain knobs, name "Hardin" scratched on base **200.00**

Chestnut, 18 x 28 x 28″, pine legs .   **400.00**

Mahogany, 19th C **230.00**

Pine

17½ x 32½″, canted sides, arched ends, old worn blue paint, varnished **205.00**

28½ x 48 x 29¼″, chip carved detail, 2 board top, hardwood base, turned splayed legs, H stretcher .   **215.00**

29½ x 41¾″, rectangular top, exposed dovetails, over skirt, turned cylindrical legs **130.00**

Poplar, turned splayed legs, worn finish, 17½ x 29¾″ **110.00**

Poplar and pine, hand carved, decorated overhang, interior rough . . .   **175.00**

DRY SINKS

Butternut, 20 x 35 x 42″, 2 doors, one shelf inside, original stippling and finish **425.00**

Maple, 60½ x 30½″, rectangular top, single drawer, 2 doors painted, Pa. German **750.00**

Oak, 19 x 34 x 44″, zinc lined, 2 doors **500.00**

Pine

32½ x 17¼ x 34″, primitive, c1840, door, interior shelves, bootjack feet **400.00**

44¾ x 42 x 21 ″, grained to resemble oak, 3 drawer top, 2 doors, American, c1850 . . . . . .   **550.00**

51 x 23½", pencil post legs, shaped apron, zinc liner, original blue paint **375.00**
72" w x 21½" d x 27" h, sq nail construction, center pull out bin, doors, narrow shelf **500.00**
Pine and Poplar, 41¾ x 17", cut out feet, paneled doors, 2 drawers, worn black graining **650.00**
Poplar, Amish (Holmes Co., OH), 49 x 20¼", paneled doors, shaped skirt, 2 drawers, yellow paint with black graining over original blue paint **1,900.00**
Poplar, 2 paneled doors, 2 dovetailed drawers, galvanized sheet metal liner, top shelf, 41" w x 17" d x 44½" h **550.00**

FRAMES

Folk art style frame, assorted soft woods, 14 x 17", $125.00.

Brass
6½ x 4½", floral scroll decor **85.00**
8 x 14", Florentine styling, easel back **65.00**
Curly maple, cherry, butternut, 19½ x 15½ x 3" w, pr **250.00**
Empire, mahogany veneer, wide molding, 20 x 26" **50.00**
Folk Art, 5¾ x 7⅜", orig red paint, abstract and floral decor, American **425.00**
Ivory, carved, 3³/₁₆ x 2⁹/₁₆" **50.00**
Mahogany, gold liner, 9 x 16" opening **85.00**
Oak, 10½ x 38½" **60.00**
Pine, 15 x 18", flat, block corners with metal stars **60.00**

Poplar, decor, half turnings with corner blocks, orig red paint, black graining, 12½ x 22¾" **45.00**
Shadow Box, Victorian
Circular, 21½", deep **90.00**
Oval, 19¾ x 22¾", deep **90.00**
Rectangular, 28 x 32", walnut, double liner **115.00**
Silver, Sterling
6¼", Art Nouveau, photograph holder, cast scrolling heart shaped, leafy sprays, poppies, turquoise and violet enameling, maker's mark G. A. D. W. D. Chester, 1905 . . . . **280.00**
12", Art Nouveau, W. N. Chester, 1907, pr **635.00**
Tramp Art, 47 x 40", deeply layered and chip carved geometrics, top panel with heart in center, American, c1930, pr **560.00**

HAT RACKS AND HALL TREES

Bamboo, old dark finish, mirror, 2 shelves **495.00**
Brass, 3 butterfly type hooks, porcelain knobs **135.00**
Cast iron, 10" beveled mirror, 12 hooks, umbrella holders, 4 arched legs, c1880 . . . . **250.00**
Oak, 60" h, 8 brass hooks, c1910 . . **100.00**

Renaissance hall tree, Victorian, walnut, beveled mirror, brown marble insert, 80" h, $600.00.

Mahogany, single carved standard with leaves, twist design in upper half, 4 hooks, tripod legs ending in paw feet, c1870

Victorian, solid brass, large beveled plate glass mirror supported by side posts with hooks, base of mirror supported by rectangular shelf with round legs joined at base by identical shelf, cast paw feet, brass scrolls, sunflower rosettes at mirror corners, foliate crest with cartouche, 81″ h x 38″ l x 12″ d **1,800.00**

Walnut, Reform style, rectangular mirror, 5 brass hooks, 2 short drawers, Herter Bros, c1875, 78″ h x 43½″ w x 18½″ d **1,540.00**

ICE CREAM PARLOR FURNITURE

Chairs
    Heart back, refinished **70.00**
    Spectacle, refinished **80.00**
    Arm, wood seat **125.00**
Stools
    26½″ high, refinished **50.00**
    30″ high, 12″ dia., seat, refinished   **60.00**
Tables
    27″ square, oak top **200.00**
    30″ dia., oak top **250.00**
Table and 2 chairs, child's, table 18″ dia.; chairs, 9½″ dia. seat, set . . .   **200.00**
Table and 4 chairs, table, 30″ dia., wood top; Chairs, 14″ dia. replaced seats, refinished, Set **550.00**

LOVE SEATS

Empire, French, mahogany and parcel gilt, upholstered, carved sphinx heads, tapering supports, claw feet, c1810 . . . .   **800.00**

George III, mahogany, adjustable armrests, square chamfered legs, upholstered, c1779, 4′9½″ l **3,300.00**

Louis XVI, painted white **1,100.00**

Queen Anne, walnut **600.00**

Renaissance, gilt bronze mounted rosewood, American, c1865 . . . .   **990.00**

Rococo, laminated rosewood, bird carving, attributed to Alexander Roux, American, c1855 . . . .   **15,000.00**

Venetian, rococo, gilt carved wood, floral brocade upholstered cushion, carved frieze, cabriole leg, 19th C, 15″ h x 24½″ w x 21½″ d   **700.00**

MAGAZINE RACKS

Canterbury
    George III, mahogany, 3 bays, short turned feet, casters, 23 x

Magazine rack, walnut, 17¼″ deep x 22¾″ w x 23¼″ h, acorn finials, brass castors, American, Canterbury, $600.00.

    17 x 20″ **450.00**
George III, late, mahogany, fieze drawer, 2 bays, short turned legs, casters 18 x 12½ x 20″ . .   **400.00**
New York, c.1810, 4 x-form uprights, single drawer case, turned legs mounted on casters, 19½″ l, 20½″ h **3,750.00**
Gallé, Emile, inlaid mahogany, floral frieze on drawer, 4 open compartments, carved apron, saber legs, side inlays of floral, butterfly, 45¾″ h x 24″ w x 12¾″ d **1,880.00**
Mission
    Roycroft, oak, c1910, carved emblem, 37″ h **450.00**
    Stickley, L. & J. G., oak, c1910, rectangular decal mark, 45″ h .   **475.00**
Victorian, Eastlake, walnut, 13½ x 26″, pierced sides, turned posts, machine carved **125.00**

MANTELS

Marble
    Black, Louis-Phillipe, shaped top, post column leg at 45° angle . .   **375.00**
    Rouge Royale, Napoleon III, carved molding style **1,250.00**
    White, Louis XVI, fluted columns, recessed frieze panels, ormolu mounts **1,000.00**
Pine, Federal
    NE, carved, painted, punch-carved frieze, fluted pillasters, 58¼ x 79″ **1,100.00**
VA, applied turned detail, cut out odd fellow insignia, from lodge, 63″ w x 62″ h **500.00**

Pine, simple pilasters, shelf, 53¼ x 50" h **185.00**

Poplar, molded pilasters, plain top blocks, applied moulding supports curved shelf, 76" w x 57½" h ... **360.00**

MIRRORS

Adam style, veneer frame, ebonized molding, gilt crest in form of urn of flowers, 48" l **250.00**

Chevals

58" h, Dutch marquetry **500.00**

67" h, mahogany oval frame, 4 paw feet **500.00**

75" h, Empire, arch shape mirror frame supported by 2 columns, urn turned finials, double brass candle arms, arched bracket feet **1,000.00**

Chippendale

Mahogany veneer on pine, gilded carved and geossoed trim, broken arch pediment with carved foliage rosettes, removable carved phoenix, orig mirror, 28¾ x 57" **17,000.00**

Mahogany veneer on pine, inlay, gilded shell crest, American, late 18th C, 31¾" h **625.00**

Dresser swing mirror, mixed woods, 7½ x 13½ x 21" h, orig. finish, $350.00.

Dresser

Brass, oval, cupid and floral decor, 15 x 16" **175.00**

Centennial, inlaid mahogany, 5 drawers, large oval mirror, 26¼ x 11 x 26" **135.00**

Cherry, oval mirror on set drawer, lift top lid, 13½ x 33 x 34½" .. **300.00**

Chippendale, walnut and parcel gilt, rectangular, molded supports, late 18th C, 18 x 12" ... **300.00**

Federal, shaving, bow front, mahogany on pine, 3 dovetail drawers, line inlay, cherry turned mirror posts, 19¾" w x 71½" d x 20½" h **240.00**

Hepplewhite, mahogany, inlaid stripes, 2 drawers, glass knobs **650.00**

Federal Style

Architectural, American, ship reverse painted on upper glass, orig label of E. Lothrop, Boston, 1822, 24½" h **700.00**

Architectural, gilt molded cornice hung with gilt spherels, leaf molding, white painted and gilt panel, reeded pilaster, 48¾" h x 25½" w **715.00**

Cherry, string decor, shoe foot, all orig, 12 x 13" **325.00**

Convex, carved spread eagle finial, gilt egg and dart molding and acanthus leaf molding, ebonized reeded molding, acanthus carved pendant, 52" h x 31" d . **1,750.00**

Georgian, convex, English, second period, carved and gilded with griffin, foliage, shell, pr sconces, 29" d x 46" w **700.00**

Hepplewhite, mahogany, scrolled base, ears inlaid, gilded frame, scrolled gilded pediment with inlaid shell, urn finial with flowers, grain, side garlands with bellflower detail, old mirror, reverse painted panel in white, silver with black, gold scene of cabin, 25¼ x 65" . **1,300.00**

Overmantel, Queen Anne, walnut frame, carved, gilt inner border, 3 part glass, scrolled ears holding two brass sconces, 21½" h x 52½" w **1,760.00**

Pier, 42 x 8½" h, gilted, ornate shell type crest, fluted columns, marble shelf **1,000.00**

Plateau

12", silverplate, ornate tine back, beveled mirror **85.00**

14", silverplate, ornate base, beveled mirror **95.00**

Queen Anne

Bronze painted finish, Cape Cod style, late 18th C, 20½" h x 12" w **225.00**

Country, shaped, molded crest centering eglomise polychrome floral panel, floral border, 17″ h x 12″ w 550.00

Heavy mahogany veneer over pine, American, 18th C, shaped crest, 19″ h x 12″ w 425.00

Rococo, gilt, shaped vertical plate, pierced frame, scrolling acanthus, 50½ x 34″ 500.00

Sheraton
Architectural, reverse painting of municipal building flying American flag, c1800, 21⅜″ h 400.00

Shaving, mahogany, serpentine, small cut out ogee feet, 3 conforming drawers, dovetailed, line inlay, mirror frame of cross banded inlay, cut out crest, 18 ¼″ w x 8″ d x 24½″ h 550.00

ROCKERS

Arrowback, bamboo turnings, scrolled arms, 3 slat back, red and black graining, stenciled floral designs on slats 100.00

Bannister back, NE, 18th C, fruitwood, ash, maple, rush seat . 200.00

Boston, sgd Hitchcock, orig paint and decor 400.00

Rocker, mixed woods, 7 spindle, orig paint and stencil, c1900, $195.00.

Country, American, c1830, carved and painted, shaped comb above rectangular back rails, curved seat, turned legs joined by stretchers, trestle rockers, painted with eagles, pears, floral motif, rosewood ground, yellow, black striping 3,850.00

Eastlake, late 19th C, mahogany platform, incised and pierced cresting over square panel back, center, pad arms, seat upholstered in pink velvet, reeded arms, supports 200.00

Ladderbacks
Arm, Shaker #7, Mt. Lebanon label, turned arm supports, turned finials, replaced woven splint seat 625.00

Arm, turned supports, shaped arms, 4 slats, turned finials, woven splint seat 250.00

Child's, arm, 3 slats, turned posts, finials, woven cane seat 75.00

Mission
Gustav Stickley, c1907, mahogany, 9 spindle back, rush seat, 1″ red decal 715.00

L & J. G. Stickley, c1910, arm, vertical slats side, vertical slats back, clamp decal mark 625.00

Roycroft, c1915, oak, rectangular back, sides with vertical slats .. 625.00

Oak
Child's, dog head and gallery, turned spindles, cane seat, 30″ h 195.00

Pressed back, 7 spindle back, 4 arm support spindles 185.00

Windsor Style
Bamboo turnings, old pale yellow paint, floral decor on crest 280.00

Comb back, 7 spindle back, orig black paint, American, 19th C .. 900.00

SECRETARIES

Biedermeir 1,800.00

Chippendale, CT, cherry, top with flaring cornice over pair of paneled cupboard doors, fitted interior, bottom with slant top, fitted interior, 4 graduated drawers, ogee bracket feet, 38 x 19½ x 84″ 8,250.00

Country, cherry, 2 pc, square turned legs, 1 dovetailed drawer, slant top lift lid base, bookcast top with 2 drawers, simple cornice, one pane of glass in door, mullions removed, 27″ w x 21½″ d x 70¾″ h 745.00

Country, accountant's, American, c1800, pine, paneled doors above

Secretary, Chippendale, American, c1760–1780, birchwood, upper part with 3 tiers of filing compartments, cut valance, pair of paneled doors, stepped, molded cornice, slanting full front base, stepped, arched pigeonholes, 36″ w x 19¼ d x 79″ h, $8,500.00.

and below, fold out writing lid, 66½″ h x 41¾″ w x 19″ d 900.00

Federal, mahogany, Kinnan & Mead, NY, upper case with flaring cornice, pair of glazed and mullioned cupboard doors, shelved interior, bottom with pull out writing section, pr of paneled cupboard doors, turned legs with brass caps, 49½ x 25½ x 99″ 7,150.00

Hepplewhite, mahogany, bracket feet, 3 dovetailed drawers, line inlay rectangles with invected corners, 4th drawer with inlaid ovals, pull out desk fitted with 7 dovetailed drawers, 10 pigeonholes, top 2 doors, line inlay, frieze, removable cornice with scrolled pediment, carved rosette, inlaid almond sunburst, dentil molding, gilt eagle finial, geometric arrangement of glass panes in doors, attributed to Wm Appleton, Salem, MA, 43″ w x 23½″ d x 101½″ h 12,000.00

Queen Anne, mahogany, Newport, RI, upper with swan's neck pediment, 3 finials, pair of arched panel cupboard doors with fluted pillasters, fan carved and fitted interior, candleslide, bottom with hinged lid, shell carved interior, 4 molded graduated drawers, bracket feet, 39¾ x 21½ x 97½″ 28,000.00

Sheraton, mahogany, string and band inlays on drawers and 2 cupboard doors, oval inlay on prospect door, turned feet, 38½″ w, 49¾″ h 3,500.00

Victorian, Renaissance, walnut, arched pediment, 2 glazed doors, fitted interior, bureau style base . .   1,750.00

SETTEES

Classical, maple, shaped crest, pierced splats, ring turned legs, brass castors, painted in chinoiserie in yellow and gold on black ground, 6'4″ l 1,430.00

English, country, pine, high back, yew wood seat, curved paneled back, refinished, 81″ 375.00

Federal, mahogany, carved fluted swag and tassel cresting, reeded, carved arm supports, caned seat, back, 6'5″ l, NY, c1805 . . . .   3,200.00

George III, carved pak, molded crestrail, 4 relief carved chair backs, blind fretwork splats, cabriole legs, 43″ h x 73¼″ w x 23″ d   3,000.00

Regency, gilt decor, ebonized dipped backrest, scrolled arm rests, loose cushion seat, scrolled legs, 7'2″ l, c1820 . . . .   1,430.00

Rococo, pickled rosewood, John Henry Belter, NY, triple arched back carved with floral bouquets, scallop shells, upholstered in lavendar damask, 84″ l 4,500.00

SIDEBOARDS

Empire

Curly maple, mahogany veneer around doors and crest panel, 3 drawers divided by leaf carved segments, 71¾ x 23½ x 44″ plus crest 550.00

Mahogany, rope turned molding, carved eagles heads, 3 drawers, brass line inlay, beaded molding, open center flanked by 2 pedestal supports, 2 panelled cupboard doors, 49½″ h x 75″ w x 22½″ d, Boston, c 1820 . .   4,180.00

Federal

Mahogany, NY, oblong top with inlaid edge, one serpentine, 2 bowed, and 2 frieze drawers, base with 2 bottle drawers and 2 pair of cupboard drawers, line inlaid square tapering legs, 79 x 26¾ x 40" **2,500.00**

Mahogany and figured birch, attr. to Judkins & Sentor, Portsmouth, NH, oblong top, 3 frieze drawers over 2 pairs of cupboard doors centering bottle drawers and seeded colonetes, ring and vase tapering legs, 71 x 24½ x 42½" **7,250.00**

Hepplewhite, American, c1800, inlaid mahogany, serpentine, 40" h x 75" l, $4,250.00.

George III, mahogany, serpentine, rectangular satinwood top, drawer, arched kneehole, two short drawers, bottle drawer, sq tapering legs, block feet, 63½" w **1,650.00**

Hepplewhite, mahogany, figured veneer, inlay, sq. tapered legs, satinwood veneer on posts, facade of rectangles, ovals, circles of line onlay, banding, figured veneer, conceals 4 doors, 1 dovetailed drawer, 66½" w x 23¾" d x 40" h **6,750.00**

Victorian, English, inlaid satinwood and mahogany, Wright and Mansfield, c. 1870, 2 parts, upper with convex cupboard doors, painted neoclassical panels, distressed flanking shelves, lower with 3 frieze drawers, above single drawer, arched recess flanked by cupboards and shelves, leaf carved toupic feet, 95" x 65" **5,000.00**

Victorian, Rennaissance 78½ x 102", walnut, elaborately carved backboard with shelf and three stands, marble top, hunting and grape motif on cupboard doors, Mitchell and Rammelsberg, Cincinnati, OH, c. 1860 .... **2,000.00**

120" x 78", Continental, walnut and oak, mirrored backboard, elaborate carvings of figures, scrolls, wreaths and vines, fans, etc., 4 frieze drawers, pedestal supports with fitted interior **2,750.00**

SOFAS

Chippendale, NY, c1770, mahogany, camel back, shaped crest, outward scrolling arm supports and seat, square molded legs, flat stretchers, 80" **10,000.00**

Empire, mahogany, cylindrical crest rail ending in acanthus carved scrolls above back flanked by S scroll arms, upholstered seat, foliate legs, claw feet, attributed to Duncan Phyfe, 34" h x 88" w x 25" d **4,000.00**

Empire, mahogany, scrolled tablet crest rail over elongated oval upholstered back, stylized eagle's heads, upholsted escrolled arms, applied decor, 44" h x 140" w x 22" d **900.00**

Federal, Phila., rectangular and slightly stepped crest, downward sloping arms, reeded vase form supports, bowed seat, square tapered legs, 75½" **4,500.00**

Federal, NY, attr. Duncan Phyfe, rectangular crest, swag carving, reeding in arms, seat rail, and tapered legs, 81¼" **6,500.00**

George III, mahogany, serpentine padded back, arms, seat, moulded marlborough legs, pale green damask upholstery, 106" **1,430.00**

Hepplewhite, mahogany, square moulded legs, spade feet, cabriole back, rosette carved arms, upholstered in gold raw silk damask, NY, 81" w **9,000.00**

Mission, oak, Gustav Stickley, c1905, red decal mark, 72" **1,850.00**

Rococo, laminated rosewood, John Henry Belter, NY, c1855, applied floral cresting, 74" **2,000.00**

Victorian, early, mahogany, shaped back, center medallion with carved leaf motif, bowed side arms with flat shaped front board, scroll, leaf, and sunburst relief carving on front apron, incised winged style feet, 85" **750.00**

SPINNING WHEELS

Flax Wheels (Saxony)
Mahogany, inlaid with enamel bosses and bands, turned ivory finial hung with brass bells, 64" **143.00**

Mixed woods, PA, c1840, turned . **275.00**

Wool Wheels (Walking)

Oak, 44½" d wheel, turned legs, posts, spindles, bobbin reel missing **150.00**

Oak, 45" d wheel, 60" h **225.00**

Walnut, PA, mid 19th C **375.00**

STANDS

Stand, highly carved, marble insert, 10" dia. top x 36" h, $500.00.

Cottage, rustic, natural bark base, worn gold, brown painted top, 13½ x 14½ x 27" h **45.00**

Country

Butternut, turned legs, 1 drawer, thumb molded top, 17½ x 24¼ x 29" **200.00**

Cherry, heavy turned legs, single dovetailed drawer, 15 x 18⅜ x 28¼" h **225.00**

Empire, mahogany, 2 drawer, square top, tapered feet, 28½ x 34½ x 17" **275.00**

Federal, NY, early 19th C, sewing, mahogany, pedestal base, acanthus carving, 2 drawers **900.00**

Folk Art, triangular shelves, wooden cotton spools, dividers, 58" h . . . **55.00**

Hepplewhite

Cherry, square one board top, dovetailed drawer, 20 x 28" h . . **400.00**

Mahogany, corner washstand, 3 drawers, slightly splayed legs . . **550.00**

Walnut, country, square turned legs, one dovetailed drawer, 20½ x 24 x 28¾" h **235.00**

Sheraton

Cherry, poplar, turned, reeded legs, 2 dovetailed drawers with cockbeading, one board top, 20 ¼ x 16¾ x 28¼" h **375.00**

Cherry and tiger maple, 2 drawers, beaded, mushroom pulls, 20 x 28¾" **350.00**

Mahogany, turned legs, posts, one dovetailed drawer, top cut out for bowl, gallery, some veneer damage, 20" w x 16" d x 30½" h **250.00**

Umbrella, cast iron, ring grip, pierced scalloped disk, baluster support, pierced circular umbrella holder, scalloped drip pan, 3 scroll feet, 40" h **286.00**

Victorian, brass, 33" h, marble inserts **300.00**

STEPS

Bed

Federal, inlaid mahogany, 2 steps, top with deep compartment, 21" h x 16½" w, Rhode Island, c1790 . . . . **1,100.00**

Regency, hinged rectangular inset leather top above two steps, circular ring turned legs, 16½" w . **1,210.00**

Library

Georgian, mahogany, embossed green leather insets, top step hinged, compartment beneath second step contains holder for chamber pot, 17⅜ x 25 x 25⅝" **425.00**

Sheraton, satinwood, green leather seat, inlaid banding, 24" h . . **1,800.00**

William IV, c1830, mahogany, hinged, 5 leather inset threads, 32" h x 19" w **2,090.00**

Victorian, oak, 4 steps, arm rail support, 76" h **450.00**

STOOLS

Five board stool, pine, 6¾" x 9" h x 17" l, $45.00.

Foot

Country, NE, rectangular, chamfered sides, peg legs, top painted and grained in shades of red and black, yellow line decor, 7″ h x 12″ l 412.00

Empire, carved mahogany, rectangular half upholstered seat above scrolling side rails, scrolling curule legs, carved lotus petals, turned stretcher, 15½″ h 800.00

French Provincial, 8 legs, carved, walnut, 28″ h 250.00

Inlaid fruitwood, Conn, c1780, rectangular, ebony, ironwood, scalloped skirt, 11″ l 1,760.00

George II, mahogany, rectangular drop seat, cabriole legs, acanthus scrolls with claw and ball feet, white silk upholstery, 24″ w 770.00

Louis XV, carved oak, gilded 300.00

Queen Anne
  Mahogany, cabriole legs with cyma scrolls, slipper feet, upholstered in contemporary crewel, 13½ x 16″ 300.00
  Walnut, NE, c1740, stretcher base, 19″ l x 15¾″ h 2,250.00

Regency, mahogany curule 85.00

Sheraton, English, mahogany, adjustable top, leather and cloth cover, 14 x 18″ 175.00

Victorian, c1880, mahogany, rectangular, needlepoint seat, frieze drawer, short turned legs, casters, 19 x 13 x 11″ 115.00

Windsor, PA, c1825, oval seat, 4 splayed reel turned legs, painted green, 14½″ w x 8½″ h 1,750.00

Milking
  Country, primitive, 3 legs, heart cut out handle, relief carving of cow, old dark finish, 7¼ x 18″ . 275.00
  Country, primitive, 3 legs, burl top, old red paint, 8½ x 10″ 130.00

Monk's, Gustav Stickley, c1909, oak, leather, square oak splayed feet, paper label, 1½″ red decal 480.00

Organ, Victorian, circular, 3 fancy metal legs, ebonized stem, needlepoint top 125.00

Piano, Empire, mahogany, rectangular slip seat, two dolphins with curving tails form handles, fruit carved turned baluster, leaf carved legs, paw feet, 37½″ h .. 1,045.00

Weaver's, Shaker, turned front feet, replaced paper rush seat, 30″ h . 200.00

TABLES

Card
  Chippendale, c1780, cherrywood, rectangular, single drawer, 29¾ x 35¼ x 16⅜″ 3,500.00

Marble top, Renaissance, Victorian, walnut base, white marble, 34″ l x 22 ½″ w x 30½″ h, $450.00.

Federal, NY, c1815, carved mahogany, canted corners, veneered skirt, carved hairy paw feet, 27″ h x 35½″ w x 17½″ d 4,000.00

George III, mahogany, D shape hinged top, frieze inlay, square tapering legs, 36″ w 500.00

Hepplewhite, Baltimore, flame mahogany, tapered legs have stringing, bellflower inlays, almond shaped medallion of oak leaves, acorns on front posts, inlaid flutes on apron, ovolo top with cross banding, green felt playing surface, 36″″ w x 17¾ d x 29¼″ h 6,600.00

Hepplewhite, NE bird's eye maple, inlaid 750.00

Queen Anne, mahogany, 30 x 35 ½″ 1,500.00

Regency, c1815, satinwood and rosewood, inlaid, 29 x 36″ 1,600.00

Sheraton, c1800, mahogany, inlay band around skirt, top 2,300.00

Console, George III, Breccia figured pink marble top, fluted frieze, 6 square tapered legs, paneled block feet, 73¾″ l x 33½″ h 9,350.00

Dining
  Chippendale, Phila, mahogany, drop leaf, claw and ball feet, 28 x 48 x 54″ 4,000.00
  Duncan Phyfe, mahogany, D shaped ends, 3 pedestals with reeded tetrapods, brass paw castors, 9½×4″ 3,500.00
  Empire, mahogany, drop leaf, 1 drawer, paw feet, 28 x 51″ 400.00

Federal, NE, c1800, drop leaf, walnut, 30 x 61 . . . . **700.00**

George I, walnut, gateleg, rounded rectangular twin flap top, circular tapering legs, pad feet, 64″ w **1,600.00**

Hepplewhite, 2 part, inlay mahogany, D shape top, rectangular drop leaves, 42 x 81½ x 30 . . . **1,800.00**

Mission, Limbert, c1910, oak, oval top, branded mark, 44¾″ **775.00**

Queen Anne, drop leaf, mahogany **500.00**

Regency, mahogany, oval, single board top, baluster pedestal on 3 molded sabre legs, castors, 27¼ x 21½ x 20″ **6,500.00**

Sheraton, mahogany, 2 parts, 5 fluted legs on each section, 45¼″ w x 22½″ l **1,250.00**

Dressing, Sheraton, country, pine, gray paint, blue striping, stepped top, whale's tail mirror supports, 60″ h x 35½″ w x 18½″ d **300.00**

Drop Leaf

Empire, mahogany, rectangular top over ogee frieze, square baluster pedestal, concave cut platform base, 57½ x 39½″ . . . **275.00**

Federal, mahogany, canted corners, 1 drawer, ring turned and reeded tapered legs, baluster turned feet, 29¼″ h x 36″ w x 44″ d **550.00**

Queen Anne, cherry, square legs with turning below apron, duck feet, 1 board top, 41⅞ x 13⅜ x 27″ **1,250.00**

Queen Anne, English, 18th C, mahogany, square, duck feet, 29″ sq x 27½″ h **2,500.00**

Sheraton, country, NY or PA, cherry, leaves scalloped near corners, turned spindle legs, 42 x 22¾″ x 29″ **225.00**

Stuart, 17th C, oak, gateleg, oval twin flap top, spool turned legs, 45″ w **1,320.00**

Game, George III, mahogany, divided hinged rectangular top enclosing lifting backgammon tray, drawer, square tapering legs, 25″ h **660.00**

Harvest

Pine, NE, mid 19th C, oblong, X form legs, 28½ x 156″ **2,250.00**

Pine, NE, bread board top, sawbuck, 29 x 57 x 28″ h **250.00**

Sheraton, pine, turned legs, 22 x 72 x 29″ h, 9½″ leaves **600.00**

Library

Regency, c1815, rosewood, frieze with two real and 2 dummy drawers, 4′8″ **900.00**

Victorian, c1840, mahogany, 2 drawers in frieze, 2′5″ x 4′4″ w **1,000.00**

William IV, c1835, rosewood, top of leaf carved molded edges, frieze of 2 bead molded drawers, 2′4½″ h by 4′4″ w . . **11,000.00**

Marble Top

Giltwood, cabriole legs, 3′9″ w . . **1,145.00**

Regency, c1720, console, carved giltwood, mottled top, 3′4″ w . . **11,350.00**

Renaissance Revival, American, c1865, library, walnut, burl veneer, banded top, 45″ **450.00**

Mission, oak, Limberts, rectangular top over 2 short drawers, square copper pulls, 4 legs joined by undershelf, branded mark, 29″ h x 48″ l **264.00**

Papier Mache, Victorian, game, chess board top, shaped apron, inlaid MOP, gilt floral pearl motifs, lyre shaped end supports, scrolled central stretcher, 28″ h x 24″ w x 20½″ d **500.00**

Pembroke

Birch, country, American, late 18th C, dovetail drawer, serpentine shaped leaves, 35¾″ l x 17″ w x 27″ h **625.00**

Cherry, Federal, molded serpentine top, 36″ l x 35½″ w x 28¾″ h **2,000.00**

Pembroke, Chippendale, carved mahogany, American, 18th C, 27½″ h x 38″, $950.00.

Mahogany, Chinese Chippendale, square legs, pierced cross stretcher, fretwork brackets, dovetailed drawer, sgd Ingles, NY, orig finish, 9″ leaves, 19¼ x 28½ x 27¾″ **3,250.00**

Mahogany, George III, oval, cross banded twin flap top, frieze on drawer, square tapering legs, 38½″ **1,870.00**

Poker, oak, swivel iron pedestal
base, 36" d 650.00

Tavern

Maple, Queen Anne, NE, 18th C . 2,700.00

Maple, Buxton, Maine, c1800,
stretcher base, orig dark red
paint, 33" l x 26½" w x 26¼" h 7,500.00

Pine top, NE, 18th C, turned maple base, orig red paint, 33¾ x
25¼ x 22⅝" 3,400.00

Tea

George II, mahogany, marble top,
covered frieze, cabriole legs . . . 8,800.00

Queen Anne, bird's eye maple,
snake feet, molded toes, tilt top,
27½" top x 27½" h 1,600.00

Queen Anne, NE, mid 18th C, ma-
ple, porringer top 3,800.00

Queen Anne, mahogany, tray top,
rectangular, 29 x 20¼ x 25½" h 7,000.00

Regency, rosewood, circular, tilt
top, octagonal swelling pedestal, triangular base, embonized
paws, 49½" d 5,000.00

Work

Biedermeier, 19th C, mahogany, 3
drawers 250.00

Federal, c1800, maple and birch,
painted decor, square tapered
legs, 28½ x 15½" 2,000.00

Hepplewhite, country, square tapered chestnut legs, mortised
maple apron, dovetailed drawer,
pine bread board top, orig drop
leaf, butterfly support, 27½ x
33½ x 28½" h 475.00

Hepplewhite, country, Vermont,
c1800, inlaid birch, one drawer . 600.00

Queen Anne, country, bread board
ends, single drawer, turned legs,
pad feet, 29 x 45" 1,750.00

Sheraton

Cherry, maple and bird's eye
maple, serpentine chased top,
rope and pineapple carved
legs, lacy glass draw pull . . . 650.00

Mahogany, cherry, 2 drawers,
c1800 . . . . 350.00

Tiger maple, Vermont, c1800,
fine reeded legs, split drawer
construction 1,700.00

Victorian, check inlaid octagonal
rising top over fitted interior,
turned and lobed circular base,
3 scroll feet, 19¾" 250.00

TEA WAGONS

Black lacquer finish, raised Chinese
figures in landscape, D drop
leaves, turned legs, support, 2
wheels 200.00

Victorian, brass, glass 700.00

WAGON SEATS

Wagon seats cannot be classified with seats
from a wagon. Early wagon seats were usually constructed with a double frame and a
basketry-type seat. They served a dual purpose: in the house and in the family wagon
for additional seating.

Hickory, spindle back and arms,
leather basketweave seat, 6 legs,
18th century

Ladderback

Two slat back, turned stiles, splint
seat, red paint, 35" 550.00

Three slat back, turned stiles,
worn orig red paint with yellow
striping, polychrome floral decor, painted scenes in ovals on
top slats, replaced paper rush
seat, 34¾" l 355.00

Windsor, pine, spindle back, heart
cut-outs on side 800.00

WICKER

Rattan, reed and willow are all known as
wicker. Wicker items were produced and
imported from the Orient as early as the 18th
century. It was not until the mid 19th century
that wicker furniture was manufactured in the
United States. The elaborate, ornate and
closely woven designs are from this Victorian era. The plainer and coarser reedings are
from the early 1900's.

Ferner, wicker, painted white,
$150.00.

Basket, flower, 20" h, pedestal
shape **100.00**
Bird Cage, painted metal cage, cir-
cular open woven reed wicker
base **200.00**
Carriage, baby, reed scroll work, roll
top siderails, c1895 . . . .   **290.00**
Chairs
Arm, close weave, rattan wrapped,
elaborate scroll and braid, serpentine roll top chestrail, c1900   **340.00**
Arm, child's, scroll work, continuous crestrail braiding, rattan
wrapped legs **200.00**
Corner, solid wood and cane seat,
wrapped arms and legs **135.00**
Library, fancy scroll pattern **225.00**
Rocker, lady's, open, elaborate
scroll and lace pattern, cabriole
legs **350.00**
Chest, 32 x 27 x 18" d, 3 drawer,
rattan wrapped, close weave,
c1900 . . . .   **310.00**
Desk, kneehole, 34 h x 35 w x 24"
d, 1 drawer, 2 ornate compartments on solid wood rectangular
top, wrapped legs, c1900 . . . . .   **390.00**
Etagere, 69", 6 tier, arch crest insert with oval mirror, X stretchers,
cabriole legs, rattan wrapped, fan-
cy scroll **1,000.00**
Ferner, 31", cane and wicker,
wrapped legs **210.00**
Lamp, floor, 69", reed, close weave,
rattan wrapped legs, ornate origi-
nal shade, c1890 . . . .   **350.00**
Settee, 40½ h x 46 w x 15½" d,
scrolled and pierced back in variety of weaves, curved arms, scal-
loped skirt, 6 legs **390.00**
Table, 30 x 30 x 20" d, rectangular,
solid wood molded top, scrolled
legs **400.00**
Tea Wagon, wrapped reed and rat-
tan, close weave, removable glass
top, c1890 . . . .   **450.00**

YARN WINDERS

Floor Type, Primitive, oak, mortised
frame, two reels, one stationery,
one adjustable, 51" h **75.00**
Niddy Noddy, Maple, mortised,
17¼" l **75.00**
Spoke Type
4 spoke table model, chip carved
base, turned standard, geared
counter, one spoke folds back,
old red paint, reel 24" **65.00**
4 spoke, primitive, worn geared
counter, 22½" x 25" h **75.00**
4 spoke, Shaker, Sabbathday
Lake, combination of hard and

soft woods, square nail construction, geared side counter
needle, reel 26", 32" h **375.00**
6 spoke, oak, poplar, and hickory,
turned arms, counting wheel,
reel 30½", 27" h **125.00**
6 spokes, walnut, turned legs, reel
spindles, chip carved details,
geared counter, old worn finish,
worn paper counter dial with
name, 1845, 28½" d x 41¾" h   **165.00**

GAME PLATES

**A general classification of special plates
used to serve game, including fish, is games
plates. They were popular in the late 1800's
and early 1900's. They were decorated with
various species of birds, fish or other game.
A set usually consisted of a service platter,
individual serving plates and sauce boat.
Many sets have been divided and the individual plates used for wall hangings.**

**Platter, 18½" l, dark green border,
gold trim, partridge center, Theodore
Haviland, Limoges, artist signed,
$250.00.**

BIRDS

Plates
9", grouse in winter scene, Imperi-
al Crown China **45.00**
9½", ducks, Limoge **40.00**
10", pheasant, Limoge, sgd Max .   **85.00**
10½", bird and 2 water spaniels,
crimped gold rim, sgd, R. K. Beck   **65.00**
Platters
16", quail chop plate, 2 handles,
hp gold trim, Limoges, T. and V.
France **125.00**
18 x 14¼ x 1½", harvest scene,
large turkey in center, floral border, brown decor, Royal Staf-
fordshire **55.00**

Sets

5 pcs, 12" platter, 8½" plates, pheasants, wild ducks, green to pale blue, emb beaded rims, Victoria, Austria 135.00

8 pcs, 9⅝", different birds, dark brown borders, gold Royal Vienna 225.00

7 pcs, wild game birds, pastoral scene background, molded edges, shell decor, Fazent Mehlem, Bonn, Germany 215.00

9 pcs, 9¼" plates, various birds, gold scalloped edge, hp, Haviland and Co. 350.00

DEER

Sets

5 pcs, artist sgd Beck, Buffalo Pottery 275.00

FISH

Plates

7", picture of muskie jumping out of water, fluted edge, M.Z., Austria 38.50

8½", hanging type, colorful fish swimming on green shaded background, scalloped border, gold trim, signed "Lancy," "Biarritz, W. S. or S. W. Co., Limoges, France" 30.00

9", gold seaweed, cobalt rim, sgd, Haviland, 1899 . . . . 55.00

9", underwater scene of fish, clams, plant life, emb and scalloped rim decor with green and gold seaweed, "T and V Limoge" 45.00

Platters

14", bass, on lure, signed "R. K. Beck 85.00

23", Charonne, hp Haviland . . . 200.00

Sets

7 pcs, 15" platter, 6 — 9" plates, sgd "R. K. Beck," Buffalo Pottery 325.00

7 pcs, Limoges, hp, shells, pink, purple, brown 195.00

8 pcs, 24" platter, 4 plates, cov tureen and sauce boat, attached underplate, Rosenthal . 350.00

10 pcs, 24" platter, 6 — 9" plates, cov casserole, sauce boat, hand painted, Selb, Bavaria 375.00

10 pcs, 20" platter, eight 8" plates, gravy boat, Austria 365.00

12 pcs, 22" platter, white various species of fish in brown, light gold trim, imp "Frieda" 325.00

14 pcs, green border, scalloped edge 250.00

15 pcs, 24" platter, 12 — 9" plates, sauce with attached plate, cov tureen, hp raised gold design on edges, artist sgd, Limoges 750.00

16 pcs, fish caught in net, seaweed, shells, hp Carrie Draper, artist, Limoges 425.00

GAMES

Early versions of old parlor games are collected not only for their quality, but also for the bright, colorful lithography on their covers that reflect so much the history of this country.

Games of the W. & S. B. Ives Company go back to the 1840s. Mass production of games did not take place until after the Civil War, with the firms of Milton Bradley, McLoughlin Brothers, Parker Brothers, and Selchow and Righter leading the way. All these companies, except McLoughlin Brothers, are still in business today. Therefore, the McLoughlin games are rarer and more desirable.

Many common games such as Anagrams, Authors, Jackstraws, Lotto, Tiddledy Winks, and Peter Coddles do not command high prices; nor do the games of Flinch, Pit, and Rook, which still are being published.

See *Warman's Americana & Collectibles* for a listing of Games from the 1950s through the 1980s.

(LEFT) Lindy, Parker Bros, 1927, card game, $20.00; (RIGHT) Touring, Parker Bros, 1926, card game, $15.00.

Advance and Retreat, Milton Bradley, c1910 . . . . 55.00

Air Ship, McLoughlin Bros, 1912, Mother Goose flying a bi-plane . . 65.00

Amateur Golf, Parker Bros, 1928 . . 35.00

Battles, McLoughlin Bros, 1895, many cardboard soldiers, very large 225.00

Broadway, Parker Bros, 1917, board game, box of playing pieces	22.00
Bull In A China Shop, Milton Bradley, early 1920s	25.00
Chivaltry, Parker Bros, 1888	55.00
City Life, McLoughlin Bros, 1889, card game	12.00
Cribbage, inlaid board with ivory pegs	65.00
Crokinole, large octagonal wooden board, playing disks, dated 1880 .	40.00
Dodging Donkey, Parker Bros, early 1920s	35.00
Don'ts, McLoughlin Bros, small card game	15.00
Fox and Geese, round wooden board, clay marbles, c1880	60.00
Grandmama's Geographical Game, McLoughlin Bros, cards	18.00
Halma, Horsman Co., 188, board, box of playing pieces	20.00
How Silas Popped The Question, Parker Bros, card game	14.00
India, McLoughlin Bros, Parcheesi-type board, box of playing pieces	35.00
Jolly Tumblers, Milton Bradley, board game	35.00
Life's Mishaps & Bobbing Around The Circle, McLoughlin Bros, 1891	45.00
Lost Heir, Milton Bradley, card game	15.00
Minoru, 1910, wooden boxed racing game, lead horses	60.00
Motor Cycle, Milton Bradley, 1905 .	25.00
Movie-Land Keeno, Wilder, 1929, Lotto type game with pictures of movie stars	45.00
North Pole By Airship, McLoughlin Bros, 1897	75.00
Old Bachelor, McLoughlin Bros, card game	18.00
Phoebe Snow, Milton Bradley, c1910, girl dressed in white on cover	40.00
Pigs in Clover, Selchow and Righter, maze game, clay marbles	35.00
Pollyanna, Parker Bros, 1915	25.00
Poosh-M-Up Pinball	20.00
Radio Game, Milton Bradley, early 1930s	30.00
Rival Policeman, McLoughlin Bros, 1896, lead police figures	95.00
Robinson Crusoe, Parker Bros, c1910	25.00
Scout, Edgar O. Clark, c1900	30.00
Sherlock Holmes, Parker Bros, card game	18.00
Snap, Milton Bradley, card game . .	10.00
Spider's Web, McLoughlin Bros, 1898	30.00
Telegraph Game, Milton Bradley, early 1920s	55.00
Topsy Turvy, McLoughlin Bros, 1899	40.00
Wonderful Game of Oz, Parker Bros, 1921, pewter playing pieces	65.00

Wyhoo, Milton Bradley, card game .	15.00
Yankee Doodle, Parker Bros, 1895 .	55.00

GAUDY DUTCH

Gaudy Dutch is a hand decorated, opaque soft pasteware made in England's Staffordshire district during the first quarter of the 19th century. Stylistically it is contemporary and similar to the Imari-type wares being made at Derby and Worcester.

The blue decoration was applied to the bisque, glazed, and fired. Other colors were added, glazed, and refired. There is no lustre on any of the standard patterns. Most Gaudy Dutch is unmarked, although occasionally a piece will be found impressed with Wood or Riley.

Reproductions of these patterns have been reported, especially cup plates. These reproductions have a semi-porcelain body and not earthenware; hence, they can be spotted easily.

The known patterns are: Butterfly (two types), Carnation, Dahalia, Double Rose, Dove, Grape, Leaf (scarce), Oyster, Primrose, Single Rose, Strawflower, Sunflower, Urn (two types . . . also known as Vase or Flower Pot), War Bonnet, and Zinnia.

See also KINGS ROSE

Gaudy Dutch, Dove, handleless cup, 2¾ x 3¾″ d, Saucer, 1⅛″ h x 5⅝″ d, $410.00.

Butterfly	
Coffee Pot, 10⅞″	3,500.00
Creamer	450.00
Cup and Saucer	700.00
Plates	
6⅜″	475.00
9¾″	1,250.00
Teapot	2,000.00
Sugar Bowl	650.00
Carnation	
Bowl, 5½″	600.00
Cup and Saucer	500.00
Plates	
7½″	375.00

8¼"	475.00
Teapot	1,000.00
Dahlia	
Creamer	425.00
Cup and Saucer	550.00
Sugar, covered	650.00
Teapot	1,250.00
Double Rose	
Plate	
7½"	475.00
10"	500.00
Dove	
Coffee Pot, 11"	3,000.00
Cup and Saucer	600.00
Plates	
6¾"	350.00
8¼"	500.00
9¾"	700.00
Wash Bowl	650.00
Grape	
Cup and Saucer, handleless	250.00
Plate, 8"	275.00
Toddy, 5¼" d	240.00
Sugar, covered	400.00
Oyster	
Cup and Saucer	525.00
Plate, 8¼"	475.00
Primrose	
Plates	
4¾"	425.00
8⅜", marked Riley	375.00
Single Rose	
Coffee Pot	950.00
Cup and Saucer	275.00
Plate, 8¼"	325.00
Sunflower	
Cup and Saucer	275.00
Creamer, 4⅜" h	250.00
Plate, 8½"	300.00
Sugar, covered	275.00
Urn	
Cup and Saucer	425.00
Plates	
5⅝"	275.00
8¼"	400.00
War Bonnet	
Creamer, 4½"	360.00
Cup and Saucer	500.00
Plate, 9¾"	650.00
Sugar, 5¼"	775.00
Teapot, 6"	1,250.00
Zinnia	
Plates	
8⅜"	550.00
10"	325.00

GAUDY IRONSTONE

Ironstone is an opaque, heavy bodied earthenware containing large proportions of flint and slag. Gaudy Ironstone is decorated with some of the patterns bearing resemblance to

Gaudy Welsh. The shape, texture and registry marks indicates that the ware was made in England in the 1850s. Most items are impressed "Ironstone."

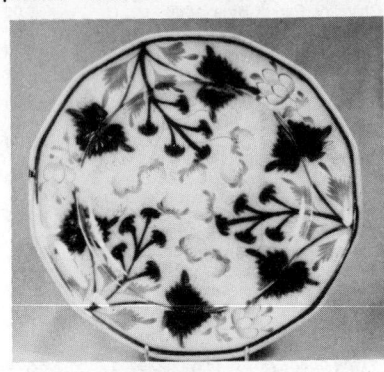

Plate, 9¾" d, strawberry, blue, pink, green, gold highlights, $150.00.

Coffee Pot, 10" high, strawberry	500.00
Compote, 7", Gaudy, green and orange, Amherst Japan pattern	110.00
Cups and Saucers	
Blackberry, demitasse	75.00
Cotton Plant	40.00
Seeing Eye, Niagara-shape	125.00
Pitcher, 8", Imari-type decor	125.00
Plates	
8⅝", Urn	135.00
8¾", blue, green, red, black, J. & G. Meakin	100.00
Seeing Eye,	95.00
9⅝", Urn, design worn	75.00
10½", Amherst Japan, blue, orange	50.00
Platters	
Indiana, 14½", blue, red rim	65.00
Morning Glory, 12¼" l, blue, greens	85.00
Sauce, 6¾", Imari-type decor	35.00
Sugar, covered, 8½" high, Strawberry	395.00
Soup Plate, brown Imar: transfer, polychrome enameling, 10½" d, mkd Real Stone China	35.00
Vegetable, Indiana, blue, red rim, 12"	50.00

GAUDY WELSH

Gaudy Welsh is a translucent porcelain that was originally made in the Swansea area of England from about 1830 to 1845. Although

the designs resemble Gaudy Dutch, the body texture and weight differ. One of the characteristics is the gold lustre on top of the glaze.

In 1890, Allerton made a similar ware. These items are a heavier, opaque porcelain and usually bear the export mark.

Some of the known patterns are: Daisy and Chain, Flower Basket, Grape, Morning Glory, Oyster, Shanghai, Strawberry, Tulip, Urn and Wagon Wheel.

Columbine
Cup and Saucer	60.00
Plate, 5½"	40.00

Daisy and Chain
Creamer	75.00
Sugar, covered	125.00
Teapot	165.00

Feather
Cup and Saucer	40.00
Plate, 5½	25.00

Flower Basket (also known as "Urn" or "Vase")
Bowl, 10½"	175.00
Creamer	85.00
Cup and Saucer, handleless	75.00
Mug, 4"	65.00
Plate, 7½"	60.00
Sugar, covered	95.00

Grape
Creamer	47.50
Cup and Saucer, handleless	85.00

Morning Glory
Compote, 5¾ x 10¼" d	225.00
Cup and Saucer	65.00
Pitcher, 6½", bulbous, Allerton, c1890	85.00
Teapot, 5½" to top of finial	150.00

Oyster
Bowl, 6¼"	60.00
Creamer	75.00
Cup and Saucer	75.00
Jug, 5¾", c1820	195.00

Ring Tree, marked Lion/Unicorn/Shield/Ironstone/Staffordshire/England, $50.00.

Mug, 3"	55.00
Pitcher, 3¼"	95.00

Plates
5½"	55.00
9½"	100.00

Shanghai, Creamer	95.00

Strawberry
Creamer	95.00
Mug, 4⅛" h	125.00
Plate, 8¼"	85.00
Spill holders, 4⅜" h, pr	200.00
Teapot	175.00

Tulip
Creamer, 5¼"	75.00
Cup and Saucer	55.00
Pitcher, Milk	150.00
Plate, 9"	45.00
Sugar, covered, 6¾" h	95.00
Teapot, 7¼", ribbed body	150.00
Waste Bowl, 6⅜" d	75.00

Wagon Wheel
Cup and Saucer	60.00
Mug, 2¾"	55.00

Plates
5½"	35.00
8¼"	65.00

GEISHA GIRL PORCELAIN

Geisha Girl Porcelain is a Japanese export ware produced from the last quarter of the 19th century through the period of Occupation. The colorful wares feature lovely Japanese ladies and children amongst the floral splendor of the Japanese temple gardens.

The most familiar form of Geisha ware is that decorated by hand painting over a stencilled underlying design which is usually red-orange or dark brown in color. There are numerous wholly hand painted examples.

Geisha Girl Porcelain is bordered by one or a combination of over ten colors, the most common being red-orange and cobalt blue. Borders are often further embellished by gold, yellow or white enamels.

Geisha Girl Porcelain was produced in over 125 pattern variations. Commonly found are Parasol, Parasol/Lesson combination, Flower Gathering and Garden Bench patterns. The pieces bear a diverse selection of pre-Nippon, Nippon, and Japan period marks in English and/or kanji.

Geisha ware is being reproduced in the form of tea sets, sake sets, demi-cups, vases, lunch plates, ginger jars, dresser sets, toothbrush holders and tumblers. Most of these have a red-orange border on porcelain which is very white and smooth compared to the coarse gray tones of the earlier wares.

Prices vary according to pattern and border color as well as form and condition. The listing below represents form, pattern, and border color.

See *Warman's Americana & Collectibles* for an expanded listing of Geisha Girl Porcelain.

Cocoa Pot, Butterfly, yellow green with gold, $45.00.

Berry Set, Mother and Son, blue with gold, master marked Torii Nippon, 6 individual bowls marked Kutani 55.00

Bowl, rice, Samurai Dance, red with gold, unmarked 16.00

Cocoa pot, Parasol & Lesson, floral and butterfly ground, blue with gold, unmarked 100.00

Cocoa "set," Butterfly pot, 6 Basket cups and saucers, apple green with gold, unmarked 100.00

Cup and Saucer Sets
   After Dinner, Shi-Shi, red and spring green with gold, marked Dai Nihon Tashiro zo 17.00
   Tea, pedestaled cup, scalloped saucer, Garden Bench, red-or-ange with gold, unmarked 20.00

Dresser Tray, Parasol, pine green with white enamel, unmarked . . . 35.00

Hatpin Holder, Long Stemmed Peony, blue with gold, marked "Made in Japan" 30.00

Jewel Chest, ornate, geisha and daughter, overall red, green, pink, and gold decoration, sgd 47.00

Mayonnaise Ladle, Temple, multicolor, Royal Kaga, Nippon mark . . . 10.00

Napkin Ring, triangular shape, River's Edge, red with gold, un-marked 32.00

Plates
   Cake, scalloped, Circle Dance, red-orange, un marked 5.00

   Lunch, scalloped, Parasol & Les-son, floral and butterfly ground, blue with gold, marked "Japan" 5.00

Dinner, Geisha Presentation, apple green, unmarked 25.00

Powder Jar, Garden Bench, pine green with white, marked "Japan" 21.00

Sake Bottle, Carp, red with gold, repair on neck, sgd 32.00

Salt and Pepper Shakers, Parasol, red, stamped "Nippon" 16.00

Teapot, footed, Butterfly, apple green with gold, unmarked, hair-line on bottom 30.00

Tea Set (pot, sugar, creamer, 6 cups and saucers), River's Edge, gold and brown, Paulownia Nippon mark 45.00

Tea Tile, Feather Fan, gray with gold, Royal Kaga Nippon mark . . 50.00

GIBSON GIRL PLATES

Charles Dana Gibson, an eminent American artist, produced a series of 24 drawings entitled "The Widow and her Friends." Complete book plate titles for each view are given below.

The Royal Doulton Works at Lambeth, England, reproduced the drawings on plates. All the plates are 10½" and have the same wide stylized leaf blue border. Life Publishing Co. copyrighted the plates in 1900 and 1901. Prices for the following range from $85.00 to $95.00 each.

Gibson Girl Plates, "She finds that exercise does not improve her Spirit", $90.00.

She Contemplates the Cloister
She Decides to Die in Spite of Dr. Bottles
Miss Babbles, The Authoress, Calls and Reads Aloud
She Finds Some Consolation in Her Mirror
A Quiet Dinner with Dr. Bottles; After Which He Reads Aloud Miss Babble's Latest Work
Message From the Outside World
Some Think That She has Remained in Retirement Too Long, Others Are Surprised That She Is About So Soon
She Is the Subject of More Hostile Criticism
Mrs. Diggs Is Alarmed at Discovering What She Imagines To Be a Snare That Threatens the Safety of Her Only Child, Mr. Diggs Does Not Share His Wife's Anxiety
She Looks for Relief Among Some Of the Old Ones
She Longs for Seclusion and Decides to Leave Town for a Milder Climate. While Preparing for the Journey, She Comes Across Some Old Things That Recall Other Days
The Day After Arriving at Her Journey's End
She Goes Into Colors
They Go Fishing
Failing to Find Rest, and Quiet in the Country, She Decides to Return Home
Mr. Waddles Arrives Late and Finds Her Card Filled
She Becomes a Trained Nurse
They Take A Morning Run
Miss Babbles Brings a Copy of a Morning Paper, and Expresses Her Indignation and Sympathy Over a Scurrilous Article, Meanwhile, Other Friends Are Calling Upon the Editor
They All Go Skating
She Goes to the Fancy Dress Ball as Juliet
She Is Disturbed by a Vision Which Appears to be Herself
And Here, Winning New Friends and Not Losing the Old Ones, We Leave Her

GIRANDOLES AND MANTEL LUSTRES

Girandole is a highly ornamental candlestick, with marble base and cut glass prisms surrounding the mountings. Mantel lustres are glass vases, with attached cut glass prisms. They are decorative and made of a variety of glass types, enameled or gilded, and were produced in Bohemia and England and various other countries in Europe, and in the United States in the mid-19th century.

Girandoles

11¾", French, 19th C, gilt bronze	630.00
13", tulip shape, Bohemian, cranberry glass, rectangular prisms, gilt decor, circular foot, c1875	300.00

Girandoles, 17" h, 10½" w 8 lustres around each Candle section, 10 lustres, double row across back, pr, $350.00.

15¾", centerpiece of 3 scrolled foliate candlearms, grapevine prism ring hung with cut glass prisms, pierced plinth with beehive, 2 bears, bee swarm in front of Gothic house, 2 matching single light candelabra, stepped white marble bases	350.00
16", 2 branch, cut glass, regency ormolu, bell shaped sockets, bobeches hung with beads, drops, stepped oval base, pr	1,000.00
35½", bronze, glass, seven light, glass drops suspended from pressed glass stars, pr	500.00

Mantel Lustres

9", blue with enameled florals, gold trim, white beading, Waterford crystal prisms, pr	225.00
10", cut glass sunburst base, baluster stem, 9 cut prisms, pr	180.00
10", cobalt blue, small white enamel flowers, prisms, pr	325.00
10½", green, cut to crystal, 10 cut glass prisms, pr	295.00
10⅝", Bristol, pink satin, gold trim, pr	450.00
12", Bristol, lady's portrait, pr	235.00
13", white cut to cranberry, scalloped flaring bowl, facet cut prisms, pr	575.00
14", double cut overlay, white to emerald green, prisms of alternating lengths, pr	265.00

GONDER POTTERY

Lawton Gonder established Gonder Ceramic Arts, Inc., at Zainsville, Ohio, in 1941. He gained his experience at other factories in the area. The corporation remained in existence until 1957.

Among Gonder's glazes where Chinese crackle, gold crackle, and flambe. The overall design of his products is excellent. Lamp bases were manufactured under the name Eglee at a second plant location.

Gonder's pieces are clearly marked. They remain an inexpensive item, although several dealers have begun to purchase them and put them in storage waiting for a market increase.

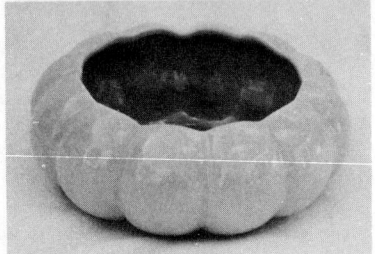

Bowl, 7″ d, melon shape, turquoise exterior, pink interior, imp "E-12/ Gonder/USA," $15.00.

Basket, 8 x 6½″ h, leaf pattern, turq. outside, pink coral interior, marked H-39 Gonder USA	28.00
Bowls	
6½″, ribbed, yellow	8.00
7¾ x 7″, blue and brown glossy glaze, swirl, flower frog	17.50
Cornucopia, 7¼″, brown, gray	12.50
Ewers	
6″, mottled blue, pink interior . . .	20.00
7½″, turquoise	28.00
Planter, green, gray interior	8.50
Vases	
7½″, pink and mottled blue glaze, flower shaped	12.50
8″, beaded, petal and scroll, pink	18.00

GOOFUS GLASS

Warman's Americana & Collectibles, 1st Edition, contains 46 listings in this category; see also page xii.

GOSS CHINA

MARK

W H GOSS

In 1858, William Henry Goss began the production of Parian, ivory-porcelain terracotta, and such at a factory in Stoke-upon-Trent, England. The progress of this company in pure art production was notable. Among it most famous specialties were porcelain, floral jewelry and dress ornaments — brooches, hairpins, scent diffusers, and crosses. Many handpainted scent vases, pomade boxes, rice powder jars, pastil and scented ribbon burners were made, largely for the great Paris and London perfume houses. Goss also produced jewelled porcelain vases, scent bottles, tazzas, and other ornaments, inventing a process for such jeweling.

His ivory-porcelain was soft and mellow in tone and extremely durable; it is of this ware that the little crest souvenir jugs were made.

The Goss China Co. was sold to Washington Potteries (China Craft) Ltd., in 1951. Some Goss pieces are stamped "W. H. Goss." On others, the crest, a falcon rising, ducally gorged, was used either by itself or with the name.

Goss pieces are sometimes grouped with the small colored figures known as "Fairings," because they were sold at fairs and on market-day galas, very cheaply.

CRESTS. All the following pieces have name and Falcon mark.

Beer Barrel, Burton, Kingston-on-Hull	22.00
Beer Bowl, dragon, Worcester	40.00
Bowls, Glastonbury	
Dawlish crest	14.00
Yorkshire crest	19.00
Bust, Shakespeare	50.00
Carafes, Goodwin Sands	
Norwich crest	32.00
Ramgate crest	18.00
Cheese Dish, Greenwich crest . . .	20.00
Coronation Chair, Chichester crest .	25.00
Creamers and Sugars	
Malmesbury Abbey	42.00
Yarmouth	45.00
Cups	
Clacton On The Sea	20.00
Edinburgh Univ., Arms of Scotland, City of Edinburgh, 3 crests, 3 handles	27.00
Lee Crest, 1 handle	24.00
St. George-Devon, Ashburton crest, 3 handles	20.00
Trinity, large	18.00
Egg Cups	
Ancient Arms of Bedford	18.00
Godalming	35.00
Ewers	
Arms of Duke of Devonshire	30.00
Earl of Derby	25.00
Seal of Whitby Abbey	18.00
See of Birmingham	14.00

Mug, 3″ h, Great Yarmouth, marked W.H. Goss, $25.00.

GOUDA POTTERY

Gouda and the surrounding areas of Holland have been one of the centers of the Dutch pottery industry for centuries. Originally the potteries produced a simple utilitarian Delft-type earthenware with a tin glaze and the famous clay smokers' pipes.

When the pipe making portion declined in the early 1900s, the Gouda potteries turned to Art Pottery. Influenced by the Art Nouveau and Art Deco movements, artists expressed themselves with free-form and stylized designs in bold colors.

With the Art Nouveau and Art Deco revival of recent years, modern reproductions of Gouda pottery currently are on the market. They are difficult to distinguish from the originals.

Lamp, Caelon, Cheshire	22.00
Jugs	
City of Bristol	22.00
Hammersmith crest, Scarborough shape	25.00
St. Alban's Abbey crest, Litchfield shape	25.00
Wigan crest, Reading shape	20.00
Milk Cans, Welsh	
Arms of Weymouth Melcombe Regis	18.00
Margate	38.00
St. Helena	20.00
Models	
Egyptian Water Jug, Llandrindor Wells crest	18.00
Gilbraltar, Wallingford Arms crest	20.00
Lanlawren Celtic Sepul church urn, cov, Arundel Castle	50.00
Plate, 6″, Cambridge	15.00
Shaving Mug, Loughborough	25.00
Teapot, Isle of Wight-Sandown	45.00
Tray, 10 x 12¼″, Maidenhead	75.00
Trinket Boxes	
Chicester, large	25.00
Manchester College, round, small	25.00
Vases	
Bud	
Blockgang	24.00
St. Andrew Univ.	24.00
Glastonbury shape	
Arms of Wales	20.00
Gloucester	20.00
Wall Pockets	
Christ Church, large	25.00
Dunster, small	20.00
Sandown	25.00

Vase, Gouda Pottery, 11½″, windmill on obverse/lake on reverse, twig handle, extended bark neck, Springer & Co/Elfagen, Germany, c1890, impressed 1208, $145.00.

Baskets

Art Deco interior, black exterior . . 100.00
Multicolored, handles, floral decor 175.00

Bowls

6", cov, Schoonhaven, stylized
leaves 90.00
8", Teal blue, high matte glaze,
Plazuid, house marks 85.00
8½", multicolored, two handled,
Pelta, floral decor 70.00

Box, carved, black, gold, white, high
glaze, Regina, 4¼" 150.00

Candlesticks

3", chamberstick, green with yellow, blues, and cream, matte
finish, 0139 DAM III, floral motif,
c1885 . . . . 90.00
12", unusual shape, pr 175.00
13", pr, blue, gold, black, c1910 . 150.00

Carafe, 11", sunflower design,
house mark 110.00

Charger, pierced for hanging,
Plazuid, 12" d, 2" deep 175.00

Compotes

3 x 10" d, two handled, multicol-
ored, Sluis 130.00
10", ftd 98.00

Creamer, 2½", sgd. Gratius 55.00

Ewer

4¼", canteen shape, multicolored,
floral motif 60.00
6", Art Deco, multicolored, Arn-
hem 75.00

Figures, 3 chorus girls, pink creamy
crackled glaze, 8" h 45.00

Humidor, cov, floral decor on white
ground, glossy glaze, artist sgr . . 265.00

Inkwell, hexagonal shape, 3", c1920 80.00

Jardinere, Art Nouveau decor of russet, royal blue, mustard yellow,
black ground 80.00

Pitchers

3¼", two handles, multicolor on
black base, floral motif 32.50
5", orange, green, lion design, late 50.00

Plates

8", multicolored, pastel, c1900 . . 80.00
10", Art Deco 110.00

Shoe, multicolored, Lanac, 5" 50.00
Sugar, open, Art Deco, 4" 30.00
Toothpick, sgd Regina 40.00
Trivet, Damascus, 4", c1895 . . . . . 175.00

Vases

4½", rust, cobalt, Art Nouveau,
c1900 . . . . 60.00
6¾", Schoolhouse mark 75.00
7", stick type, multicolored, high
glaze, Arnhem, c1900 . . . . . . 115.00
7", Zuid mark, artist sgr 68.00
9¾", Art Nouveau, 2 handles,
high glaze, multicolored florals,
dark green ground, house mark 235.00
10", multicolored, Art Deco, Isolde 160.00

GRANITEWARE

**Graniteware is the name usually given to iron
kitchenware covered with enamel coating. It
was featured at the 1876 Centennial Exposition, and became popular because it was
light weight and attractive. It is still made, but
the earlier pieces are in great demand by collectors. It was made primarily in mottled
gray, marbleized green and blue. The green
is the earliest color made. It is also made in
pure white with red and dark blue and black
trim.**

**See *Warman's Americana & Collectibles* for
additional listings in Graniteware.**

**Graniteware, Coffee Pot, 8½" h, gray,
$35.00.**

Angel Food cake pan, cobalt blue,
white swirls 30.00
Bowl, 6 cup, mixing, blue, white . . . 10.50
Bread Box, round, hinged, 15" d,
white, blue 45.00

Buckets

Batter, lid, gray 125.00
Berry, child's, blue spatter, tin lid 50.00
Berry, Thistle ware 22.00

Chamberstick, sky blue 35.00

Coffee Boiler, wooden handle, white,
turquoise swirl, 11" 50.00

Coffee Pot, bulbous, blue speckled,
ornate pewter lid, collar, spout,
mkd Manning-Bowman 195.00

Colander, pedestal, green, beige interior, handles 10.00

Cookstove, 3 burner wood stove, tri-angle shaped, tan, red tulips	300.00
Creamer, gray, Manning & Bowman	40.00
Custard Cup, white, blue	4.00
Dipper, blue, white	9.00
Dutch Oven, cov, gray mottled	10.00
Flask, gray, tin screw cap, 2 x 4 x 6"	95.00
Funnels	
Gray, 3¾", canning	14.00
Yellow, black rim, 3⅜"	9.00
Grocer's Scoop, large, gray	65.00
Kettle, stew, gray, bail, side handle, cov, 9" d	11.00
Ladle, red, black hood handle	9.00
Mug, 26 oz, red, black trim, white in-terior	10.00
Pails	
Milk, 2¼ quart, gray	40.00
Water, blue swirl	45.00
Pie Plate, blue swirl	20.00
Potty, blue swirl, matching lid	58.00
Pitcher, Water, blue spatter	70.00
Platter, white, blue swirls	18.00
Pressing Iron, Coleman gasoline, blue speckled	85.00
Soap Dish, blue swirl	55.00
Spoon, white, long black handle . . .	5.00
Teapot, bulbous, blue speckled, or-nate pewter lid, collar, spout, mkd Manning-Bowman	175.00
Tea Set, miniature, medium and light blue spatter on white	150.00
Wash Basin, cobalt swirl	38.00

GREENAWAY, KATE   K. G.

Kate Greenaway, or K.G. as she initialed her famous drawings, was born in 1846 in London. She was naturally talented as an artist. Her father was a prominent wood engraver. She went to art classes at age 12, had her first public exhibition in 1868. She did card illustrations for Marcus Ward, which were all unsigned and would be a good source for collectors today. China companies and potteries in England used her children in all manner of items which were extremely popular at that time, and afford many opportunities for collectors today. Some Greenaway buttons have been reproduced in Europe and sold in the United States and collectors should be aware of this fact.

Books	
Alphabet, 1885, London	90.00
Book of Games	125.00
Language of Flowers	95.00
Toyland	98.00
Box, children on seesaw, Sarre-guemines	72.00

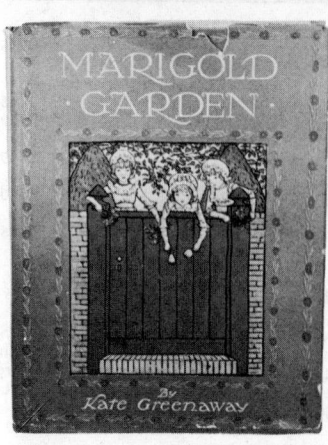

Book, Frederick Warne & Co., Ltd., $85.00.

Butter Pat, boy and girl	32.00
Buttons	
Pussy Cat Where Have You Been	18.50
Ring-A-Rosie	18.50
Coffee Pot, Kate Greenaway figures	165.00
Cup and Saucer, boy and girl	55.00
Decanter, olive green, Kate Greena-way figures	195.00
Dishes	
4¼", dogs and children	65.00
6½", Little Bo Peep	60.00
Figures	
6", boy, top hat, boots and um-brella, white and gold, Stafford-shire	65.00
6½", girl with doll and muff	70.00
Hat, bisque, 3 girls sitting on brim, flowers	90.00
Match Holders	
5½", girl with green basket	45.00
6", girl with muff	65.00
Mugs	
2½", pink, children playing	60.00
Child gardening	60.00
Picture, 10 x 12", sepia, little girl, doll in cradle, title "Shhh," sgd, orig frame	90.00
Pin Tray, Ten O'clock Scholar	65.99
Plates	
7½", 3 children hand in hand . . .	30.00
8½", children dancing and play-ing, scalloped border	65.00
8½", skipping rope	62.00
Salt and Pepper Shaker, 4½", 2 lit-tle girls, old fashioned clothes, SP	75.00
Stickpin, children playing ring around rosie, bronze, figural, c1900	20.00

Tapestry, 14½ x 56″, children play-
ing outdoors 265.00
Toothpick Holders
  Boy holding scythe next to sheath
    of wheat 48.00
  Girl, seated, emb holder 142.00
Tray, girls playing, boy with hoop, sil-
ver frame 135.00
Vases
  6″, 3 girls, ivory bisque 80.00
  6″, green, children playing, Smith
    Bros. Co. 95.00

GREENTOWN GLASS

**Greentown glass was first made by the Indi-
ana Tumbler and Goblet Co., Greentown, Ind.,
in 1894. In 1899, the company was reorganized as the National Glass Co., the second
largest glass manufacturer in the U.S. A factory fire in June, 1903, brought an end to
Greentown glass.**

**The concern produced a variety of pressed
glass wares in clear and colored, including
the limited "Holly Amber." Their "Cactus"
pattern has been heavily reproduced in colors not originally made. Also, see Pattern
Glass Section for additional patterns.**

Animal Dishes, covered
  Cat on hamper, amber 165.00
  Robin on pedestal nest, milk white 210.00
*Berry Set, Cactus, chocolate, 7 pcs 250.00

**Mug, Outdoor Drinking Scene, choco-
late, 4½″ h, $150.00.**

Bowls, Berry
  *Cactus, chocolate 200.00
  Cord Drapery, amber 52.50
  Dewey, green 45.00
  Leaf Bracket, chocolate 225.00
  Herringbone Buttress, chocolate . 250.00
Butter, Covered
  Cord Drapery, amber 61.00
  Daisy, chocolate 175.00
*Cakestand, Cactus, chocolate,
  (rare) 950.00
*Celery, Cactus, chocolate 150.00
Compotes
  Cactus, 5¼″, chocolate 150.00
  Pleat Band, clear 25.00
Cookie Jar, cov. cactus, chocolate . 225.00
Creamers
  Austrian, clear 35.00
  Cord Drapery, clear 40.00
  Dewey, amber 50.00
  Fleur de Lys, chocolate 100.00
  Shuttle, (Hearts of Loch Laven),
    chocolate 90.00
Cruets, orig stoppers,
  Dewey green 160.00
  Wild Rose and Bow knot, choco-
    late 395.00
Goblets
  Cord Drapery, chocolate 75.00
  Diamond Prisms 95.00
Lamp, Wild Rose and Bow Knot,
  chocolate base, clear font 350.00
Mugs
  Cactus, chocolate 75.00
  Dewey, (Flower Flange), green .. 63.50
  Elf, green 65.00
  Herringbone Buttress 50.00
  Serenade, milk white 45.00
  Troubadour 95.00
Nappies
  Leaf Bracket, chocolate 75.00
  Masonic, chocolate 175.00
Picture frame, match holder, amber,
  sgr R & M 170.00
Pitchers, water
  Cord Drapery, chocolate 200.00
  Deer with Oak Tree 145.00
  Dog Hunting 150.00
  Heron 465.00
  Ruffled Eye, green 150.00
  Troubadour, 8¼″ h 200.00
Plates
  8″, serenade, chocolate red agate 150.00
  *Cactus, chocolate, 7½″ 90.00
Relish, cut glass, chocolate 150.00
Sauces
  Dewey 50.00
  Leaf Bracket, chocolate 35.00
Salt and Pepper shakers, Herring-
bone Buttress, emerald green, pair 200.00
Spooners
  Cactus, chocolate 90.00
  Leaf Bracket, chocolate 85.00

Smoking Set, Wild Rose with Bow-
knot, chocolate 850.00
Stein, lidded, Elves, milk white 50.00
Sugars
  *Cactus, chocolate 150.00
  Dewey, (Flower Flange), choco-
  late 141.00
Syrups
  Cactus, chocolate 125.00
  Indian Feather, green 165.00
Toothpicks
  Boot, chocolate 85.00
  *Cactus, chocolate 125.00
  Cord Drapery 65.00
  Wild Rose with Bowknot, choco-
  late 150.00
Tumblers
  *Cactus, iced tea, chocolate 95.00
  Geneva, chocolate 125.00
  Leaf Bracket, chocolate 125.00
  Shuttle 65.00
Vase, Herringbone Buttress, emerald
green, 8½" 90.00
Wheelbarrow, chocolate 375.00

GRUEBY POTTERY

**William Grueby was active in the ceramic in-
dustry for several years before he developed
his own method of producing matte glazed
pottery and founded the Grueby Faience
Company in Boston, Massachusetts, in 1897.**

**The art pottery was hand thrown in natural
shapes, hand molded and hand tooled. A variety of colored glazes, singly or in combinations, were produced with green being the
most prominent. In 1908, the firm was divided into the Grueby Pottery Company and
Grueby Faience & Title Co.; the latter making
art pottery until bankruptcy forced closure
shortly thereafter.**

Bowls
  7" d, low with flat sides, throwing
  swirls evident in center, curdled
  green matte glaze 100.00
  8" d, 5" h, closed bowl with
  carved water lily design 1,500.00
Paperweight, 4½ x 3½", traditional
scarab, yellow 175.00
Tiles
  6" sq, grape decoration 85.00
  12" sq, scenic, oak tree against a
  rolling hillside, multicolored . . .   750.00

Tile, 6" sq, turtle, painted with a
brown, coffee, and pale yellow, green
leaves, mustard ground, unsigned,
$250.00.

Vases
  4½", tapered round urn, ring
  neck, yellow glaze 280.00
  5" h, 4" w, squat, alternating rows
  of leaves and buds, matte green   200.00
  7" h, 7" w, bulbous, closed and
  flared rim, leaves stretching
  from top to bottom and ending
  in points, green matte glaze . .   350.00
  9" h, 4½" w, cylindrical, rows of
  overlapping leaves in a yellow
  matte glaze 400.00
  10" h, 11" w, hand tooled leaves
  and buds on a thrown base, two
  colors, trefoils in yellow against
  a green ground 2,500.00
  18" h, 6½" w, incised leaves
  reaching from top to bottom,
  closed flared top 2,000.00

HAIR ORNAMENTS

**Hair ornaments consist of barrettes, combs
and elaborate hair pins to hold or adorn
women's hair of all cultures, from the past to
the present. They can be in any material,
from simple bone or celluloid set with "Bril-
liants" to precious metals.**

Barrette, 4", bar type, tortoise shell
type with rhinestones 10.00
Bodkins, (Hair Pins)
  Celluloid, imitation tortoiseshell,
  sinuated contours, pique, rhine-
  stone decor, Art Nouveau 5.00

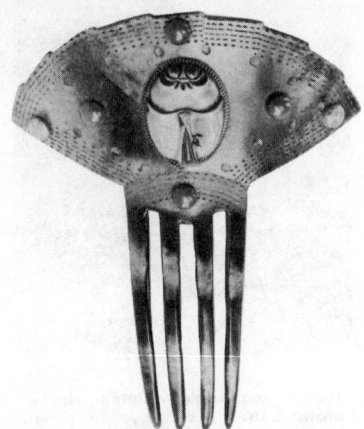

Comb, bakelite, 5 x 4¼", fan shaped, olive, black stripes, applied blue, red plastic ovals, center scarab beetle punched line work edge of fan, $35.00.

Cut Steel, leaves, floral design, c1915	4.50
Sword, cast pewter grip hilt, brass plated mount, 2 edged sinuated blade	25.00
Tortoise shell, 6¼", claw, free moving ball, carved as single pc	95.00
Bun Cover, expandable type, metal with beads, c. 1940	10.00
Chigon Combs	
Sterling silver	55.00
Tortoise shell pins	60.00
Combs	
Silver, coin, 3½", wedge shaped	65.00
Sterling serpent, 4", 2-prong	35.00
Tortoise Shell, 7", 4-pronged, set with beads	45.00
Tortoise Shell, heavy Art Nouveau frame	35.00

HALL CHINA COMPANY

The Hall China Company was founded in 1903 by Robert Hall and son Robert T. Hall. They made many patterns of china, including the popular Jewel T premium line, Autumn Leaf. They also produced types of kitchenware including refrigerator sets and fireproof cooking china.

See *Warman's Americana & Collectibles* for an expanded listing of Hall China.

Also see AUTUMN LEAF.

Ashtray, black	3.50
Baker, flute, 7¾"	18.00
Beanpot, lid, Blue Bouquet	45.00
Bowls	
5", Cameo Rose	3.00
8", flat soup, Cameo Rose	8.00
9", Blue Bouquet	7.00
9", salad, Wildfire	15.00
Mixing, set of 3, blue outside, Wildfire	22.00
Butter, Delphinium pattern	8.00
Cake safe, metal, Red Poppy	24.00
Cannister Set, Orange Poppy, tin, 3 pc.	12.00
Casserole, individual, handle, Blue Blossom	30.00
Casserole & lid, Red Poppy	28.00
Coffee dispenser, Crocus	15.00
Coffee Pots	
Flamingo	21.00
Red Poppy	30.00
Creamer & Sugar, Morning, Chinese Red	30.00
Creamers	
Cameo Rose	9.00
Red Poppy	8.00
Cups & Saucers	
Cameo Rose	8.00
Springtime	5.00
Drip jar, lid, Orange Poppy	23.00
Jugs	
Ball, Crocus	25.00
Daffodil	8.00
Leftover, Delphinium	6.00
Mustard, lid, underplate, Orange Poppy	35.00
Pitcher, Poppy and Wheat	30.00
Plates	
6", Springtime	1.50
7", Bittersweet	2.75

Pretzel Jar, Orange Poppy, $45.00.

9¼", breakfast, Cameo Rose . . .	**5.00**
10", dinner, Wildfire	**6.50**
Salt & pepper, pr, Rose Parade, sani grid	**12.00**
Teapots	
Aladdin, cobalt	**20.00**
Lipton, black	**16.00**
Melody, Orange Poppy	**58.00**

HAMPSHIRE POTTERY

James S. Taft founded the Hampshire Pottery Company, Keene, N.H., in 1871. In the beginning redwares and stonewares were produced. Majolica wares decorated with colors entered in 1879. A semi-porcelain ware with the Royal Worcester glaze was introduced in 1883. Also in 1883, the recognizable matte glazes were developed.

The factory made an extensive line of utilitarian and art wares including souvenir items until World War I when the limited demand for such items forced closure. After the war, the firm resumed operation, but only made hotel dinnerware and tiles. The company was dissolved in 1923.

Pitcher, Hampshire Pottery, 7¾", decal, Long Rock, Apostle Islands, Ashland, WI, red decal mark, $115.00.

Bowls

2¾ x 4½" d, green, rose petals .	**45.00**
4 x 5", artichoke, green	**35.00**
6 x 2½", blue, molded cattails . .	**30.00**
Mug, East Hampton Library, scenic	**48.00**

Nappy, 9", violet on ivory, artist signed	**65.00**
Pitchers	
6", Roman Key	**35.00**
8", Moravian College, scenic . . .	**50.00**
Planter, 4 x 6½", cattails in relief, green	**50.00**
Plate, 7½", Longfellow's Early Home, transfer	**85.00**
Platter, scenic	**45.00**
Urn, 10", mottled blue	**30.00**
Vases	
6½", green, blue	**65.00**
7", brown leaf molded, green streaks	**45.00**
7½", acanthus leaves in relief, green	**85.00**
12¼", cylindrical green, stylized molded leaves	**30.00**

HAND PAINTED CHINA

Hand painting on china was a very popular pastime for ladies in the Victorian era. It is currently being revived. It was done in England and the Continent much earlier than in the United States, where it did not become a popular pastime until after the Civil War.

Many china factories in America made china blanks for the amateur painters, as did the big porcelain factories in Europe; among the American factories that supplied these blanks were A. H. Hews Co., Cambridge, Mass.; Willetts Mfg. Co., Trenton, N.J.; Knowles, Taylor and Knowles, East Liverpool, Ohio.

Prices vary according to origin and type of porcelain blank, and the talent of the artist using it. See also, BAVARIAN, LIMOGES, HAVILAND, GAME PLATES, etc.

Blotter, violets, Haviland	**28.00**
Bread Tray, 12", oval, open handles, roses, sgr	**50.00**
Bowl, 8", yellow roses, Haviland . .	**35.00**
Cake Plate, 10", open handles, pink roses, gold border	**40.00**
Center Bowl, handled, ftd, wild roses, green leaves, gold trim . . .	**60.00**
Cup and Saucer, pink roses, Haviland	**20.00**
Dishes, 5½", candy, handled, pink clover, wide gold rim, sgr, Limoges	**60.00**
Hair Receiver, violets, blue and white, Limoges	**48.00**
Mustache Cup and Underplate, pale pink roses, green leaves, Limoges	**45.00**
Plates	
8", violets, wide gold band, Germany	**55.00**
12", red poppies	**80.00**

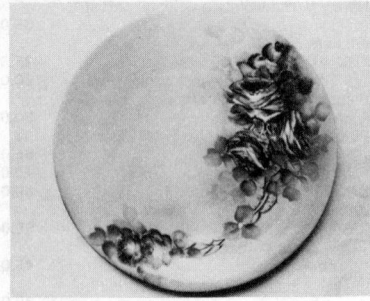

Plate, 8¼″, red roses, sgr Georgianna Frances, $9.00.

Tankard, 14½″, green and purple grapes, green leaves, Lenox	160.00
Urn, 10″, handled, grape decor, sgr	125.00
Vases	
5″, black, white orchids, sgr., Rosenthal	90.00
14″, gold handles, green, pink and red roses, Bellek	175.00

HAT PINS AND HAT PIN HOLDERS

Hat pins became popular in the closing decades of the 1800s when the vogue developed for oversize hats. Designers used various materials to decorate the pin shaft: china, crystal, shells, enamel, gem stones, precious metals and coins. Decorative subjects range from commemorative designs to insects.

Porcelain containers, designed to hold a collection of these pins, could be found on most dressing tables in the Victorian period. Familiar names such as Wedgwood, Meissen, Limoge and Satsuma are associated with the production of hatpin holders.

See *Warman's Americana & Collectibles* for additional hatpin listings.

HAT PINS

Art Nouveau	
Calla Lily, transluscent white, green enamel, c1910	115.00
Lady, flowing hair, SS	30.00
Steel, emerald green oval center	35.00
Ball cut out, swirl design, 14K gold top, c1896	65.00
Butterfly, carnival glass, green-blue irid, 10″ 1	45.00

Filigree, round diamond in center, 14K gold, c1920	110.00
Fleur-de-lys, white enamel, beaded edge	55.00
Floral design, circular, beaded border, pale blue stone	32.50
Four leaf clover, enameled green on gold	50.00
Garnet, Etruscean granulation, round, c1860	85.00
Loop, scrolling foliage, SS, c1890 .	45.00
Loveknot, seed pearl, 14K gold . . .	70.00
Oriental Pearl	50.00
Seed Pearls, cabochon, turquoise center, 14K gold, c1896	75.00
Tear shaped pink quartz	30.00
Thistle shape, SS, amber colored stone	45.00
Tortoise shell, shell shaped mount on SS shaft	50.00
Turtle, enameled green with red eyes	25.00
Violets, hp on china mount	18.00
Wreath and star, 14K gold	60.00
Zig-Zag pattern, carnival glass, purple	50.00

Hat Pins, Left: bronze metal, red stone surrounding imitation diamond center, $8.00; Right: pear shape, amber glass, brass filigree base, $7.50.

HAT PIN HOLDERS

Bavarian, blue flowers, swirled, scalloped, 5″	45.00
Limoge, grapes, pink roses, matte finish, artist sgr	60.00
Nippon	
Cobalt bands, beading, green leaf mark	40.00
Hexagon shape, flower border . .	25.00
Lavender flowers, green leaves, gold beaded edges	32.00
Royal Bayreuth	
MOP, gold top	80.00
Penguin, figural, blue mark	300.00
R. S. Germany, shoe shaped, rose decor	80.00

Hatpin Holder, 4″ h, white china, red roses, green leaves, gilt circles, unmarked, $35.00.

R. S. Prussia, floral bouquet, daisies, roses, red mark	**70.00**
Teplitz, cameo, ram handles	**80.00**

H & Cº
L
FRANCE

HAVILAND CHINA

Treasured from generation to generation, Haviland china remains a favorite of those who deman the finest in porcelain. Four generations of the Haviland family have maintained the high quality and artistic achievement that is evident in the hundreds of patterns and thousands of pattern variations produced by Haviland.

In 1842 David Haviland, an American china importer, established a factory at Limoges, France, under the name Haviland & Co. Daniel, his brother, was a silent partner and headed their importing firm, D. G. & D. Haviland. Other relatives entered the firms. The Alluand works in France was obtained through marriage. A multiplicity of firms using the Haviland name organized, reorganized, and dissolved during the 1863 to 1941 period.

The peak period of production during which the dainty all-over flowered patterns typical of Haviland china were made covers only a short period, roughly 1890 to 1910. Earlier, larger flowers, many in darker colors, were produced. Later the conventional border patterns became more prevalent.

Theodore Haviland contracted with the Shenango pottery to make Haviland wares in the United States beginning in 1936. The wares produced by Shenango for Haviland gained great popularity as a choice of brides for their wedding china. As a result, many of these patterns are being sought as replacements or for extensions of sets already in existence.

In 1941 W. David Haviland, representing the Theodore Haviland Co., bought the assets of Haviland and Co. from the French heirs of Charles Edward Miller Haviland. In 1946 the Limoges plant was furnished with electrically controlled kilns. A gift line was introduced in America in 1963; and, the first Christmas plate was issued in 1970.

See *Warman's Americana & Collectibles* for an expanded listing of Haviland China.

Bone Dishes	
6½″, Autumn Leaf, large leaves in autumn colors, smaller green leaves, Haviland & Co	**15.00**
6½″, Princess, pink flowers, blue scroll, green leaves, Haviland & Co	**18.00**
Bouillon Cup and Saucer, pink and yellow pom poms, gray-green leaves and stems, H & Co	**20.00**
Bowls	
9 x 3″, Silver pattern	**45.00**
11¼″, scenic, flying chimney swifts, blue mottled sky, H & Co/L	**85.00**
Butter Dish, cov, 8″, round, white, green flowers and leaves, gold decor and twisted handle, Theodore Haviland, Limoges	**45.00**
Butter Pat, blue bachelor buttons, pink centers, pale green leaves	**10.00**
Candlesticks, 6½″, Ranson blank with pink flower sprays, pr	**155.00**
Chamberstick, 6″, gold ring handle on saucer base, small florals	**65.00**
Chocolate Pot, Taranto pattern	**125.00**
Coffee Pot, 8½″, small pink floral sprays, gold on handle and spout, Ch Haviland, Limoges	**175.00**
Cream and Sugar, Autumn Leaf, large leaves in autumn colors, smaller green leaves, Haviland & Co	**75.00**
Cups and Saucers	
Demitasse, sprays of delicate pink and yellow roses inside and out, Theodore Haviland, Limoges	**16.00**
Drop Rose, large red roses, green leaves, H & Co	**75.00**
Shaded blue roses, pale green leaves and stems, gray shadow flowers and leaves	**15.00**
Decanter with Stopper, 8½″, 4 floral sprays, deep wine and pink, scattering of small pink and white flowers, green leaves, H & Co	**65.00**

Dinner Set, Princess pattern, white
scalloped molded borders with
scrolling sprays of small pink flowers, green leaves and intertwined
with pale blue scrolling foliate
forms, gold handles, Haviland &
Co, 82 pcs 650.00
Gravy Boat with attached undertray,
yellow flowers and gray-green
leaves, Haviland & Co 65.00
Nappy, Princess pattern 25.00
Oyster Plates
  Ranson pattern, Haviland & Co .. 35.00
  Seaweed, raised, gold, green and
  gold band, Theodore Haviland . 48.00

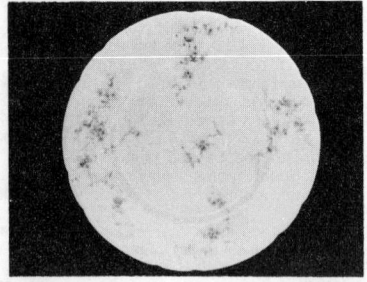

Plate, 8", sprays of pink morning
glories, red mark Porcelaine Theo
Haviland, Limoges, France #8, underglaze, $8.00.

Plates
  6¼", bread and butter, Winchester, shaded pink rose sprays,
  green leaves, H & Co 18.00
  9½", Oriental, gold band border
  with dark blue scrolls and yellow
  flowers, yellow medallion with
  pink and gray center, leaves
  and flowers on each side,
  Haviland & Co 20.00
  9½", Ranson pattern, gold trim .. 20.00
  11", cake, Princess pattern 45.00
Platter, 11½ x 8", Clover Leaf,
green leaves, red blossoms, gold
trim, Haviland & Co 50.00
Relish Dish, blue bachelor buttons
with pink centers, pale green
leaves, Haviland & Co 25.00
Ring Tree, 3½", pink florals, blue-
gray shading, green leaves 32.00
Soup Tureen, cov, 10 x 9½", round,
blue and yellow flowers, shaded
green leaves gold trim, Haviland &
Co 175.00
Sugar, cov, 7¼", pale pink bands,
black outlined, H & Co 32.00

Tea Set, apple blossoms, wishbone
handles, 3 pcs 135.00
Teapot, 5⅝", floral spray, tied with
bow, violet flowers, shaded green
leaves, gold trim, Theodore
Haviland 75.00
Vegetable Dishes
  6½ x 10", scalloped edge, pale
  blue flower sprays, shaded
  green leaves, H & Co 35.00
  7", cov, handled, white, gold
  band, gold acorn finial 45.00

HEISEY GLASS

**The A. H. Heisey Glass Co. began producing
glasswares in April, 1896 in Newark, Ohio. Mr.
Heisey was not a newcomer to the field, having been associated with the craft since his
youth. Many crystal patterns for table set-
tings were produced. Heisey also employed
colored, milk (opalescent) and Ivorina Verde
(custard) glass. Glass figurines were introduced in 1933 and continued until 1957 when
the factory ceased production.**

**Some Heisey molds were sold to Imperial
Glass of Bellaire, Ohio, and certain items
were reissued. These pieces may be mistak-
en for the original Heisey as they are of the
same quality. Some of the reproductions
were produced in colors which were never
made by Heisey. Not all Heisey glassware is
marked with the familiar "H" within a
diamond.**

**The Heisey Glass Museum is located in
Newark, Ohio.**

Animals
  *Donkey 170.00
  Elephant, small 175.00
  *Goose, wings ½ up 65.00
  *Ringneck Pheasant 95.00
  Scottie 200.00
Ashtray, Grape Leaf, moongleam .. 85.00
Baskets
  7", Daisy cutting, crystal, sgr ... 185.00
  8", Recessed Panel, crystal, sgr . 110.00
*Bottles, Puritan, vinegar and oil,
stoppered, pr 32.00
Bowls
  5", Lodestar, dawn, sgr 42.50
  5", Plantation, divided, ftd 42.50
  10", Sunburst, sgr 65.00
  12", Columbia 22.50
  12", Fern, oval, ftd 35.00
  Berry, Panelled Cane, sgr 28.50
  Berry, Peerless, sgr 11.00
  Gardenia, Waverly, Orchid etch . 60.00
Butter, covered, Locket on Chain . 165.00
Button Dish, covered, Waverly, Orchid etch 125.00

Stopper, figural horsehead, crystal, orig label, $25.00.

Candleblocks
Plantation	45.00
Whirlpool, round	12.50

Candlesticks
6", Warwick, cornucopia, sgr, single	25.00
7", Old Colony etch, Sahara, pr .	120.00
10", Ipswich, crystal, pr	110.00
Columbia, crystal, single	35.00
Crystolite, pr	17.50
Wampum, pr	50.00

Candy Boxes
Crystolite, cov	46.00
Lariat, paper label	38.00

Champagnes
Banded Flute	17.00
Creole, Sahara bowl	35.00
Delaware, flamingo	20.00
Duquesne, Chintz etch	28.00
Fairacre, Cleopatra etch	22.00

Cigarette Holder, Crystolite, round . | 10.00 |

Cocktail Shakers
Horsehead	135.00
Orchid, SS base and top	235.00
Rooster head, paper label	75.00

Compotes
6", Lariat	28.00
8¼", Punty and Diamond Point .	85.00

Console Sets, 3-piece
Old Sandwich, flamingo, sgr	380.00
Thumbprint and Panel, Sahara . .	165.00

Cordials
Kohinoor, Coronation etch	100.00
*Oxford, sgr	35.00
Puritan	22.50

Cracker Jar, Pillows, cov, crystal, sgr | 195.00 |

Creamer and Sugars
Empress, ind, sgr	42.50
Lariat, ind, crystal	15.00
Octagon, Sahara, sgr	48.00
Ridgeleigh, ind, sgr	20.00
Saturn, sgr	32.50

Cruets
Plain Panel, cut	65.00
Twist, flamingo	38.00
Victorian, sgr	47.00
Whirlpool	45.00

Cup and Saucers
Empress, Sahara, sgr	27.50
Stanhope	14.00
Yeoman, moongleam, sgr	32.00

Egg Cups
Plain Panel, sgr	18.00
Prince of Wales Plumes, sgr	57.50

Goblets
Creole, Sahara bowl	75.00
Minuet etch	27.00
Oxford, sgr	12.00
Pied Piper, sgr	20.00
Plantation	25.00
Trojan	35.00
Tyrolean, Orchid etch	35.00
Victorian, high ftd	20.00

Iced Tea, Plantation Ivy, crystal . . . | 35.00 |

Jugs, ½ gallon
Greek Key, crystal	150.00
Old Sandwich, crystal	55.00

Juice Glasses
Gascony, tangerine	195.00
Oxford, Westminster cut, sgr	30.00

Knife Rest, Flat Panel . . . . | 35.00 |
Match Holder, fish . . . . | 75.00 |
Mint Dish, Octagon, hawthorne, handled . . . . | 19.00 |
Mug, 18 oz, Old Sandwich, moongleam, handled, sgr . . . . | 350.00 |

Mustards, covered
Banded Flute	55.00
Narrow Flute, sgr	29.00

Nappie, 7" Narrow Flute, sgr . . . . . | 10.00 |

Nut Dishes, Ind
Empress, flamingo, sgr	22.50
Octagon, marigold, sgr	35.00

Parfait, Creole, alexandrite bowl, crystal stem and foot . . . . | 140.00 |
Perfume, Punty and Diamond Point . | 75.00 |
Pitcher, Old Sandwich, Sahara, water, sgr . . . . | 145.00 |

Plates
6", Ridgeleigh, sgr	4.00
6½", Old Sandwich, Sahara, sgr .	9.00
7", Coarse Rib	7.00
8", Ipswich, Sahara	17.50
8", Plantation	15.00
*8", Revere, cobalt	22.50
8½", Plantation Ivy	13.00
9", Fancy Loop	35.00
*13", Whirlpool	22.00

Punch Bowl, 14", ftd, Punty and
Diamond Point, 10 cups, sgr **295.00**
Punch Cups
Continental, sgr **11.00**
Greek Key, sgr **22.00**
Lariat **9.00**
Pillows, crystal **18.00**
Prince of Wales Plumes, sgr **23.00**
Relish Dishes
Plantation, oval, crystal **45.00**
Twist, 3 part, flamingo, floral cut,
sgr **25.00**
Salt, ind, Ridgeleigh, 8 in orig box .. **65.00**
Salt and Pepper, Waverly **35.00**
Sherbets
Creole, alexandrite **75.00**
Ipswich, tall **15.00**
Rose, Rose etch **35.00**
Sodas
Carcassone, wide optic, Sahara .. **18.00**
Narrow Flute, handled, sgr **25.00**
Spooners
Kalonyal, sgr **65.00**
Locket on Chain **65.00**
Sugar, Fandango **22.50**
Syrups
Plantation **50.00**
Sanitary, sgr **35.00**
Toothpicks
Banded Flute, sgr **45.00**
Fandango **70.00**
Priscilla, silver overlay **50.00**
Tumblers
Coleport, dawn, sgr **33.00**
Greek Key, straight, sgr **25.00**
Twentieth Century, cobalt **85.00**
Vases
5", Warwick, sgr, pr **47.50**
8½", Thumbprint and Panel, fla-
mingo, sgr **350.00**
9", Plantation **150.00**
9", Pleat and Panel, sgr **26.00**
10", Fairacre, diamond optic, sgr . **52.50**
Cathedral, cobalt **185.00**
Wines
Beaded Swag **75.00**
Kohinoor, Coronation etch **30.00**

HOLLY AMBER

Holly Amber, a molded glass, was produced
by the Indiana Tumbler and Goblet Co. for
only six months from Jan. 1, 1903 to June 11,
1903. The original name for the glass ware
was Golden Agate Ware. Holly Amber pieces
have shadings that range from brownish amber to opalescent, a holly pattern and a
glossy finish. Due to the short production period pieces of Holly Amber are scarce.

Bowls
4¼", berry, footed **275.00**
8" **450.00**

Tumbler, Holly Amber, 3⅞" h,
$540.00.

Butter, covered **1,000.00**
Compote, 6¾" h, 7⅜" w **900.00**
Creamer, 4½" **500.00**
Cruet, stoppered **1,300.00**
Parfait, 6" **600.00**
Sauce Dish, 4¼" **200.00**
Spooner **450.00**
Sugar Bowl, open, handled **495.00**
Toothpick, flat **300.00**

HORN

Horns from animals have been used for centuries to make items such as powder horns,
drinking cups, small dishes and snuff boxes.
The older pieces of horn are bringing substantial prices today.

Arm chair, **$1,650.00.**

Chairs
  Arm, decoratively carved legs,
    arms, back cut and carved horn,
    19th C Victorian design **550.00**
  Side, Southwest U.S., 19th C . . . **275.00**
Coat and hat rack, hanging **20.00**
Letter Opener, crocodile head **15.00**
Scoop, pressed, 12″ l, c1800 . . . . **30.00**
Snuff Box, American, c1850 . . . . . **40.00**
Sofa and side chair, steer horn . . . **2,650.00**
Stand, Victorian, 4 horns form legs,
    19th C American Southwest **258.00**
Tumbler, 4″ **18.00**

HULL POTTERY

**In 1905 Addis E. Hull purchased The Acme
Pottery Company, Crooksville, Ohio. In 1917
A. E. Hull Pottery Company began making a
line of art pottery for florists and gift shops.
Also made were novelties, kitchenwares and
stoneware.**

**From 1921 to 1929 the firm also imported
European pottery to be sold through their
outlets. In 1950 the factory was destroyed by
fire and re-established in 1952 as Hull Pottery
Company by J. Brandon Hull. The company is
currently in operation but the artline has
been discontinued.**

**The pottery is marked "Hull U.S.A.," "Hull
Art U.S." paper labeled, and pieces made after 1952 "hull".**

**See *Warman's Americana & Collectibles* for
an expanded listing of Hull Pottery.**

**Vase, 9½″, green to pink, marked Hull
Art/USA/W-12, $20.00.**

Ashtrays
  Modern, dark green, boat shaped **10.00**
  Serenade, 13″ w, blue **22.00**
Bank, Little Red Riding Hood,
  6¾″ h **275.00**
Baskets
  Butterfly, blue lining **65.00**
  Camelia, 8″ **65.00**
  Dogwood, 7½″ **65.00**
  Serenade, yellow **25.00**
  Woodland, 10½ **55.00**
Bowls
  Butterfly, rectangular **20.00**
  Parchment & Pine, 5½″ h, oval,
    brown **25.00**
Butter Dish, cov, Little Red Riding
  Hood **250.00**
Candlesticks
  Bird shape, Open Rose, pink,
    blue, single **25.00**
  Dogwood, light blue, peach, pr . . **25.00**
  Water Lily, 4¼″ h, brown, cream,
    pr **35.00**
Cannisters, Little Red Riding Hood,
  coffee, flour, sugar, each **250.00**
Compote, 6½″, Strawberries, pink,
  green **18.00**

Cookie Jar, Duck **50.00**
Cornucopias
  Jack In Pulpit, blue, brown **50.00**
  Modern, black, pink **15.00**
  Open Rose, small **20.00**
Creamers and Sugars
  Bowknot **25.00**
  Little Red Riding Hood, tab han-
    dles **150.00**
  Water Lily, blue-green, pink **50.00**
Ewers
  Dogwood, 13½″, pink, blue **60.00**
  Magnolia, 5″, brown, yellow **28.00**
  Poppy, 13½″, pink, blue **145.00**
Flower Pot, Water Lilly, brown, tan,
  attached saucer **45.00**
Hanging Planters
  Narcissus, 4″, pink, blue **30.00**
  Open Rose, pink, blue **35.00**
Jardineres
  Iris, 5½″, pink, blue **35.00**
  Tulip, 6″, pink, blue **100.00**
Mug, Serenade, 5½″, blue **35.00**
Pitchers
  Butterfly, 5″ **10.00**
  Rosella, 6½″, white, pink, green . **30.00**
  Woodland, 5¼″ **25.00**
Planters
  Giraffe, 8¼″, pink, green, glazed **15.00**
  Madonna, large, white **45.00**
  Poodle, 8″, pink, green, glazed . . **15.00**
  Unicorn, 13″ **35.00**
Rose Bowl, Tulip, 4″, blue, yellow . **15.00**
Tea Set, Ebbtide, gold trim, 3 pc,
  orig box **125.00**

Vases
Camelia, 7", white	35.00
Iris, 4½", cream, brown	20.00
Orchid, 8", pink, blue, orig label	45.00
Parchment & Pine, 5", green	15.00
Thistle, 6½", pink	30.00

Wall Pockets
Cup and Saucer, Open Rose, pink, blue	40.00
Iron, Sunglow, pink	30.00
Whiskbroom, Bowknot, blue	40.00
Window Box, Dogwood, 10½", pink, blue	55.00

1935

1950

1957

©by W. Goebel W Germany 1964

Goebel
1972

Goebel
1979

HUMMEL ITEMS

Hummel items are the original creations of the German artist, Berta Hummel. Born in 1909 in Massing, Bavaria, into a family where the arts were a part of everyday living, her talents were encouraged by her parents and formal educators from early childhood. At the age of 18, she was enrolled in the Academy of Fine Arts in Munich to further her mastery of drawing and the palette.

She entered the Convent of Siessen and became Sister Maria Innocentia in 1934. In this Franciscan cloister, she continued drawing and painting images of her childhood friends.

In 1935, W. Goebel Co. in Rodental, Germany, conceived the idea of reproducing Sister Berta's sketches into 3-dimensional bisque figurines. John Schmid discovered the German made figurines. The Schmid Brothers of Randolph, Mass., introduced the figurines to America and became Goebel's U.S. distributor.

In 1967, Goebel began distributing Hummel items in the U.S. and a controversy developed between the two companies involving the Hummel family and the convent. Law suits and countersuits ensued. The German courts finally effected a compromise. The convent held legal rights to all works produced by Sister Berta from 1934 until her death in 1946 and licensed Goebel to repro-

duce these works. Schmid was to deal directly with the Hummel family for permission to reproduce any pre-convent art work.

All authentic Hummels bear both the signature , M.I. Hummel, and a Goebel trademark. Various trademarks were used to identify the year of production.

Recently, certain early Hummel figurines have been 're-instated' by Goebel from the original molds. The Crown Mark (CM) was used in 1935, Full Bee (FB) 1940–1959; Small Stylized Bee (SSB); 1960–1972; Large Stylized Bee (LSB) 1960–1963; Three Line Mark (3L) 1964–1972; Last Bee Mark (LB) 1972–1980, Missing Bee Mark (MB) 1979–Present.

Buyers should be aware that Hummel's are frequently on sale and may be found for lower prices.

See *Warman's Americana & Collectibles* for an expanded listing of Hummel items.

Ashtrays
Happy Pastime, #62	80.00
Singing Lesson, #34	80.00

Bookends
Apple Tree Boy & Girl, # 252/A/B, 3L	300.00
Good Friends, She Loves Me, She Loves Me Not, #251/A/B, FB	390.00

Candleholders
Angel With Lute, 111/38/0, MB	23.00
Angelic Sleep, #25/1, FB	215.00
Lullaby, #24/111, LB	350.00

Dolls
Chimney Sweep, #1908, 11½"	60.00
Merry Wanderer, #1925, 11½"	55.00
On Secret Path, #1928, 11½"	62.00

Figurines
Adventure Bound, #347, 8¼ x 7"	1,800.00
Apple Tree Boy, #142/V, 10", CM	550.00
Apple Tree Girl, #141/11, CM	450.00
Be Patient, #197/1, 6¼"	110.00
Bookworn, 3/111, 9"	685.00
Celestial Musician, #188, 7"	120.00
Easter Time, #384, 4"	125.00

Figurine, Chicken Licken, #385/1971, LB, $99.00.

Festival Harmony, mandolin, # 172/11, 10¼"	224.00
Follow the Leader, #369, 7"	450.00
Going to Grandma's, #52/1, 6", LB	250.00
Hear Ye! Hear Ye!, #15/11, 7"	185.00
Heavenly Lullaby, #262, 5 x 3½"	85.00
Littlest Cellist, #89/11, 8", CM	535.00
Knitting Lesson, #256, 7½"	220.00
Mail's Here, #226, 6 x 4½"	265.00
Mother's Darling, #175, 5½"	90.00
On Secret Path, #386, 5¼"	118.00
Photographer, #178, 5¼"	110.00
Playmates, #58/0, SB	70.00
Prayer Before Battle, #20, 4¼", 3L	75.00
Ring Around The Rose, #348, 6¾"	1,315.00
Run-A-Way, #327, 5¼"	120.00
School Boys, #170/1, 7½"	530.00
School Girls, #177/1, 7½"	530.00
Shepherd's Boy, #64, 5½, LB	90.00
Shining Light, #358, 2¾"	45.00
Signs of Spring, #203/2/0, 4"	75.00
Smart Little Sister, #346, 4¾"	96.00
Soldier Boy, #332, 6"	75.00
Star Gazer, #132, 4¾", SB	78.00
Street Singer, #131, 5", FB	85.00
Sweet Music, #186, 5"	85.00
Timid Little Sister, #394, 6¾"	200.00
To Market, #49/3/0, 4", FB	88.00
Umbrella Boy, #152/A/O, 4¾"	275.00
Umbrella Girl, #152/B/O, 4¾"	275.00
Village Boy, #51/1, 7¼", FB	115.00
Visiting An Invalid, #382, 5"	100.00
Volunteers, #50/1, 6½", LB	250.00
Wayside Devotion, #28/111, 8¾"	235.00
We Congratulate, #220, 4"	75.00
Whitsuntide, #163, 7"	130.00
Worship, #84V, 12¾", LB	650.00

Fonts

Angel Cloud, #206, FB	85.00
Heavenly Angel, #207, 3L	35.00
Worship, #164, FB	115.00

Lamp Bases

Culprits, #M/44/A, CM	350.00
To Market, #M/223, MB	240.00

Plates, See COLLECTOR PLATES

Wall Plaques

Boy, standing, #168, FB	450.00
Flitting Butterfly, #139, FB	150.00
Mail Is Here, #140, 3L	170.00
Quartet, #134, CM	525.00
Vacation Time, #123, 3L	140.00

IMARI

Imari derives its name from a Japanese port city. Although Imari ware was manufactured in the 17th century, the wares manufactured between 1770 and 1900 are those most commonly encountered.

Early Imari was decorated simply, quite unlike the later heavily decorated brocade pattern commonly associated with Imari. Most of the decorative patterns are an underglaze blue and overglaze "seal wax" red supported by turquoise and yellow.

The Chinese copied Imari ware. Important differences of the Japanese type include grayer clay, thicker glaze, runny and darker blue, and deep red opaque hues.

The pattern and colors of Imari inspired many English and European potteries, such as Derby, Meissen, and others, to adopt a similar style of decoration for their wares. Reproductions of Imari patterns exist.

See also ROYAL CROWN DERBY.

Platter, 12⅜", iron red and cobalt border, c1875, $115.00.

Bowls

7", border of birds and flowers, riverscape center, c1900	90.00
7½", central medallion of phoenix and paulownia, alternating panels of cranes and mouse gnawing at rice bale	350.00
9¾", phoenix within band of lotus meander, cartouches of flowers and pomegranate, blue, red and gilt, c1900	375.00
10", marina motif, orange and yellow, c1860	375.00

Chargers

10", scalloped border, panels depicting birds and garden scenes	170.00
18", alternating reserves of landscapes and birds	225.00
18", figures and symbols	110.00
19½", blue, 4 alternating panels of shiski and phoenix design, central floral medallion, band of foliate scroll exterior, late 19th C	575.00
Cracker Jar, 5¼", cylindrical, stylized flowers	120.00

Cup and Saucer, handled, panels and medallion decor, c1850	65.00
Fish Dish, 14", blue and iron red, gold trim	432.00
Garden Seat, 19", cylindrical, blue and white	1,250.00
Ginger Jar, 14", floral decor	295.00
Jar, cov, 22", globular, phoenix birds flanking ruyi planels with lotus, gilt shishi finial	1,300.00

Plates

8½", blue, green and iron red, scalloped border	95.00
9", blue and white, c1880	120.00
10", iron red, panels of sake bottles, flowers, gold borders	150.00
Platter, 20", fish shape, flowering peony with gilt and red clouds, blue fish	528.00
Teapot, cov, 10¾", fluted sides, floral design, c1740	265.00
Urn, 18 x 12", rust, blue and gold, sgd, c1852	1,950.00
Umbrella Stand, 24½", bird and floral decor, c1875	425.00

Vases

7½", bittersweet and blue, floral spray, gold trim, c1830, pr	750.00
9½", blue and orange	225.00
12½", double gourd shape, fluted, phoenix and flower cluster, panels of birds and flowers, c1900, pr	1,325.00

NUCUT

NUART

IMTPE
RITAL

IMPERIAL GLASS

The Imperial Glass Co., organized in 1901 in Bellaire, Ohio, at first produced mainly clear, pressed glass for the "mass market." In 1910 they began making the popular, inexpensive lustre ware known as Carnival Glass. Then came NUART, an iridescent ware, followed by pressed glass imitations of hand cut glass under the tradename of NUCUT.

In 1916, the company introduced a Lustred Art Glass line, "Free-Hand" and "Imperial Jewels," an iridescent stretch glass that carried the Imperial-cross trademark. Reorganized as Imperial Glass Corporation, in the 1930s the company continued to produce a great variety of wares.

In recent years Imperial has acquired the molds and equipment of several other glass companies—Central, Cambridge and Heisey. Many of the "retired" molds of these companies are once again in use. The resulting reissues are acceptable as such because they are marked to distinguish them from the originals.

For Imperial Carnival see CARNIVAL GLASS.

See *Warman's Americana & Collectibles* for an expanded listing of Candlewick pattern.

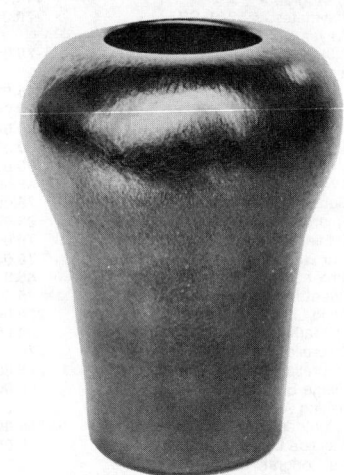

Jewels, Vase, 6½", $125.00.

CUT GLASS (ETCHED OR ENGRAVED)

Basket, 10" h, rose cutting	25.00
Bon Bon, 2 handles, 6 petal flower .	18.00

Bowls

5½", floral spray, rayed bottom .	25.00
9", berry, daisy cutting, cross mark	20.00
Console Set, "Susie" green, 11" bowl, 8¼" candlesticks, etched .	75.00
Pitcher, qt, design No. 110, butterfly florals	50.00
Plate, 8", grape etching	5.00
Tumbler, 4", buzz star	14.00

JEWELS

Bowls

8½" d, amethyst, sgd	60.00
10" d, lemon yellow irid	40.00
Candlesticks, 7", blue, pr	30.00

Compote ftd 6½", marigold 50.00
Rosebowl, amethyst, green irid . . . 65.00
Sandwich Server, 10", blue, center
  handle 25.00
Vases
  6", pear shape, amethyst, green
    irid 95.00
  7", gold irid, webbing and jewels,
    3 handled, Imperial crown mark 275.00

LUSTRED (FREE HAND)

Bowl, 11" d, green loop on clear,
  green wafer base 250.00
Candlesticks, 11" h, orange lustre,
  multicolored cups, bases, orig paper label, pr 280.00
Rose Bowl, 8", irid blue 75.00
Vases
  8", bud, gray irid, hand cut florals 80.00
  8", cobalt and light blue
    marbelized, irid orange interior . 125.00
  9¼", turned down collar, veined
    orange, green leaves, vine on
    irid white ground 295.00
  10", green irid, white hearts and
    vine decor, orange interior 175.00
  10", yellow orange lustre, green
    drag loop 100.00
  10¾", cobalt, white vine and leaf
    decor, pr 300.00

NUART

Ashtray 15.00
Vases
  7", cylindrical, flaring rim, irid
    green, sgd. 50.00
  7½", green over green transpar-
    ent 125.00

NUCUT

Bowls
  5½" 15.00
  8½" 20.00
Celery tray, 11" 12.00
Compote, 4½" 19.00
Nappy, 6" 10.00
Mayonnaise, underplate 18.00
Pitcher, ½ gallon 25.00
Spooner 18.00
Sugar, open, 2 handles 10.00
Vases
  6" 18.00
  10" 25.00

PRESSED

Basket, 6" h, applied handle, Candlewick 22.00
Bowls
  5½", Mount Vernon, 2 handles,
    crystal and ruby 3.00

8½", 3 toes 15.00
9", Old English, ruby 27.00
Butter, cov, rectangular, Candlewick 14.50
Cake Plate, ftd, 12", Pillar Flute, pink 16.00
Candleholder, 4½", 2 light, crystal,
  bell shape 5.00
Cheese Stand, cobalt, Molly 14.00
Compotes
  Candlewick, 5½", low stem 15.00
  Crochet pattern 17.50
Console Set, rolled edge bowl, can-
  dlesticks, pink, Diamond Quilted
  pattern 50.00
Dresset Set, Colonial Hobnail, clear,
  puff box, cov, two colognes, stop-
  pers 28.00
Cups
  Candlewick, coffee 5.00
  Cape Cod 4.50
  Molly, ruby 5.00
Ivy Ball, ftd, 6", white milk glass . . . 9.00
Mayonnaise, underplate, ladle, Cape
  Cod 18.00
Mug, Chesterfield, vaseline 22.50
Pitchers
  60 oz, Cape Cod 62.50
  80 oz, Candlewick 35.00
Plates
  7½", Molly, ruby 5.00
  8", Twisted Optic, irid 2.00
  8¼", Tradition, pink 6.00
  10", Candlewick 10.00
Relish, 8", 2 part, Molly-Munsell,
  pink 8.50
Salt and Pepper Shakers, Victorian,
  crystal 45.00
Stemware
  Champagne, Cape Cod 6.50
  Cocktail, Cape Cod 6.00
  Wine, bell top, four beads in stem,
    Candlewick 12.50
Whiskey Decanter, 24 oz, Cape Cod 30.00

MISCELLANEOUS

Animals-Heisey molds
  Duck, carmel slag 25.00
  Pony, blue, standing 75.00
Hen on Nest 18.50
Purple Slag
  Candlestick, 8" h 40.00
  Owl 12.00
Swan, cov, 4½" 15.00

INDIAN ARTIFACTS, AMERICAN

**American Indian artifacts for the purpose of
this listing, are the objects made on the
North American continent during the pre-historic and historic periods. During the historic
period there were approximately 350 tribes**

which are grouped into the following regions: Eskimo, Northeast and Woodland, Northwest Coast, Plains, and West and Southwest. We have followed this listing since most collectors seek material by region.

American Indian Art is quite popular. The current high prices reflect this. Material from the Eskimo and Northwest Coast are down slightly from the high prices they enjoyed a few years ago.

ESKIMO

Carvings, Ivory, Okvik Culture (100 B.C.–200 A.D.)	
Bear, 6″	1,500.00
Figure, 2¼″	700.00
Harpoon box, wood whale effigy, 18th C	1,200.00
Harpoon rest, whaling, ivory, carved in shape of polar bears, 19th C . .	5,250.00
Hat, hunting, wood, 13½″ long, feathers, 19th C	6,500.00
Net Sinker, ivory, 7″, whale shape, c1200–1700 A.D.	400.00
Work Box, wood, 11″, decorated with engraved ivory plaques, 19th C	2,000.00

GENERAL

Dance Shield, Plains, 18″ d, hide, painted	3,000.00
Doll, Hopi, 7″, Kachina	475.00
Headdress, dance, Apache, 30″ h .	1,000.00
Playing Cards, Apache, hide, painted, 28 pieces	1,000.00
War Club, Sioux, 26″, catlanite	200.00

NORTHEAST & WOODLANDS

Burden Strap, Iroquois, 25″ l, moosehair embroidered, 18th C .	9,500.00
Box, Micmac, 9½″, birchbark, quillwork dec	1,200.00
Mask, face, Iroquois, wood, 20th C .	2,750.00
Moccasins, beaded hide	600.00
Pipe, Micmac, black soapstone, 3″, carved with 2 figures, 18th C ...	1,900.00
Skin Pouch, tanned, Huron, 7″ h, moosehair and quill dec, 18th C .	3,000.00

NORTHWEST COAST

Box, wood storage, 24″ h, painted black and red with totemic faces, 20th C	1,400.00
Dish, grease, Haida, 4″ l, wood, carved totemic symbols, c1900 ..	2,000.00
Hat, twined, Haida, 13″ d, spruce root, painted black and red	1,000.00
Headdress, wood raven, Kwakiutl, 26″, painted black, red, and green	4,000.00

Knife, steel fighting, Tlingit, 20th C .	2,200.00
Rattle, wood, Tlingit, 13″ l, carved raven, dec in red, black, and green, c1900	7,500.00
Totem Pole, 10″ h, Haida, argilite ..	550.00

PLAINS

Plains, moccasins, Cheyenne, tan hard sole, blue, green, white, and yellow beads, c1930s–40s, $175.00.

Bag, "Possible," Cheyenne, beaded hide, 10 x 8″	700.00
Bonnet, feather war, Sioux	1,800.00
Boots, child's, Cheyenne, beaded hide, thunderbird design	750.00
Breastplate, man's, Sioux, 21″ l, bone hairpipe beads strung horiz.	600.00
Doll, 8″ l, hide	200.00
Dress, bead and fringed hide	2,200.00
Pipe, Sioux, 27″ l, wood stem, catlinite bowl, 19th C	800.00
Pouch, "Strike-a-light," Sioux, 5 x 2½″, beaded	300.00
Rifle Scabbard, Blackfoot, 40″ l, beaded hide	1,800.00
Saddle Throw, Sioux, beaded hide .	2,500.00
Shirt, beaded and fringed hide	1,500.00

STONE ARTIFACTS

Axe Head, PA	
8″	75.00
12″	150.00
Banner Stone, Lancaster Co., PA, 7½″ d	365.00
Spearhead, 5″, jasper	55.00

WEST AND SOUTHWEST

Baskets	
Apache, storage, Ola, 9½″ h	400.00
Hupa, twined, 7½″ d	150.00
Makah, twined, finely woven, lid, 5″ d	150.00

Pomo, coiled, feathers, 3″ d	190.00
Washo, coiled, bird motif, 5″ d . . .	275.00

Jewelry

Haida (Northwest Coast), bracelet, gold, totemic beaver design, sgd, contemporary . . . . — 7,500.00

Navajo

Bracelet, silver & turquoise, 6 oval and rectangular bezels, set with green turquoise stones, 3″ w . . . . — 400.00

Necklace, squash blossom, silver, 16 blossoms interspersed with squat globular beads, Naja set with 3 oval green turquoise stones, 15″ . . . . . . — 500.00

Necklace, squash blossom, silver, fleur-de-lis, interspersed with ovoid beads, Naja with stamped details, 15″ . . . . . . — 750.00

Pueblo, necklace, shell & turquoise, graduated blue-green ovoid turquoise pendant . . . . . — 825.00

Zuni, box, silver, 3½″ d, oval, hinged scalloped lid dec with a knife winged god inlaid in mosaic technique using black jet, blue turquoise, and orange and white shells

Pottery — Prehistoric

Casas Grabdas, jar, 9″ h, polychrome . . . . — 400.00

Kayenta, seed jar, 8″ d, black on red . . . . — 575.00

Mimbres, bowl, 10″ d, geometric, black on white . . . . — 880.00

Rio Grande, jar, 13½″ d, polychrome glazeware . . . . — 2,000.00

Sikyatki, jar, polychrome . . . . — 2,100.00

Tularosa, mug, 4½″ d, geometric, black on white . . . . — 450.00

Pottery — Historic

Acoma, jar, bottle form, 13″ d, geometric design . . . . — 350.00

Polacca, bowl, 7″ d, black on cream, Kachina face design inside . . . . — 770.00

San Ildefonso, jar, 8½″ d, blackware, sgd "Marie & Julian" — 850.00

San Ildefonso, jar, 10″ d, polychrome . . . . — 660.00

Santo Domingo, jar, 11″ d, geometric design, polychrome . . . . — 715.00

Zia, jar, 10½″ h, polychrome, two running bird motif . . . . — 880.00

Zuni, dough bowl, 15″ d, polychrome, elaborate design . . . . . — 1,100.00

Zuni, jar, 14″ d, polychrome, stylized bird design . . . . — 1,400.00

Textiles

Hopi

Dance Costume, 44 x 23″, handwoven, cotton embroidered . . . . — 1,750.00

Shawl, woman's 42 x 37″, handwoven, cotton . . . . — 1,200.00

Navajo

Blanket, "Germantown," "Eye dazzler" motif, 54 x 34″ . . . . — 935.00

Blanket, "Germantown," "Eye dazzler" motif, 67 x 46″ . . . . — 3,500.00

Rug, "Teec Nos Pos," 102 x 54″ . . . . — 4,000.00

Rug, "Yei," 107 x 50″ . . . . — 2,100.00

Saddle Blanket, "Germantown," "Sunday Saddle" motif, 34 x 27″ . . . . — 950.00

Saltillo Serape, classic motif, 94 x 48″, c1750–1800 . . . . — 7,700.00

INDIAN TREE PATTERN

The Indian Tree pattern, derived from the Oriental-type shrub or tree that predominates the design, is a popular pattern for porcelain dinnerware from the last half of the 19th century till the present. The pattern was used by several English potteries including Burgess and Leigh, Coalport, Maddox and others.

Bowl, Cereal, Johnson Bros.	9.00
Butter, cov, Coalport	95.00
Chocolate Set, pot, 6 cups and saucers, 14 pcs	225.00
Creamer and Sugar, open, Coalport	50.00

Cups and Saucers

Coffee, Coalport	10.00
Coffee, Maddox	20.00
Demitasse, Coalport	25.00
Demitasse, Minton	35.00

Southwest, tray, White Mountain Apache, 13⅛″ d, coiled, design in black, $900.00.

Indian Tree Pattern, Cup and Saucer, Maddock England, $20.00.

Gravy, Boat, 8″, underplate, Coalport	95.00
Pitchers	
5″, Burgess and Leigh	30.00
6″, Maddox and Sons	40.00
Plates	
6″, Coalport	10.00
6½″, Myott, red shield mark, 1930	9.00
7½″, gold etching, Lion Shield mark, artist sgr	70.00
8″, Coalport	15.00
9″, fluted	20.00
9½″, brown rim, earthenware, John Maddock	18.00
10″, Johnson Bros.	25.00
10″, blue, pink, green, gold trim, Spode	25.00
10½″, square, handled	40.00
Platters	
11½″, S Hancock & Sons	36.00
15½″, Burgess and Leigh	60.00
19½″, Minton	95.00
Sauce, 5″, Johnson Bros.	7.00
Tea Set, pot, creamer and sugar, 6 cups and saucers, 6-7″ plates, Coalport, 23 pcs	295.00
Tureen, soup, 10″ with ladle, Maddox and Sons	125.00
Vegetables, covered	
9″, Maddox	40.00
10″, Davison	32.00
Waste Bowl, Coalport	20.00

INKWELLS

Commercial ink bottles in America date from the early 1800s; inkwells were made much earlier. Ever since man began recording his thoughts and experiences with pen and ink, a suitable container was needed for the ink.

With the advent of the self contained ink pen, inkwells disappeared from the scene. The majority of inkwells found in the collector's field today are ornate examples with Victorian or early 20th century styling.

Also see specific categories in regard to material or manufacturer, e.g., CUT GLASS, LIMOGES, TIFFANY, etc.

See *Warman's Americana & Collectibles* for an expanded listing of Inkwells.

Brass	
4½″, sq marble base, brass globe opens to reveal inkwell, c1850	100.00
6″, emb base, lid, molded, ribbed glass globe well, c1850	125.00
Bronze	
4½″, mountain goat head with long black horns, white metal insert, German	75.00
7¾″, double, bronze base, gold Favrille inkwells, sgd Louis Comfort Tiffany	600.00
10 x 5″, reclining camel, well in saddle	145.00
13″, polished, 2 serpants form border, entwine double inkwells, c1900	230.00
21″, gilt, bronze, Louis XV style, central cartouche monogrammed SB, Quand Meme, 5 scrolling feet, inscribed F. Linke, late 19th C	1,540.00
Glass	
2¼″, white opaque satin glass, petticoat swirl, matching hinged lid, painted floral decor	265.00
4½″, blue pressed chair, daisy and button pattern, cat seated on cushioned lid	365.00
Malachite, 17″ l, gilt bronze stand, porcelain mounted, double, cast dragonfly feet, surmounted by bust of Napoleon, French, late 19th C	1,500.00
Porcelain	
2½ x 2½″, figural, Napoleonic man's head, black cocked hat, holes in top to hold quill pens	85.00

Ceramic, porcelain, white with pink edge and gold floral decor, German, $45.00.

3½", Staffordshire, head of Charles Ridgway, wife, c1830, pr 350.00

3¾ x 5¾", pink, blue shaded ground, bird in flight, gold leaves, vines, hinged lid, attached tray 95.00

4½", Meissen, Louis XV ormolu, sq sander, inkpot, ormolu handle, scenic decor, c1750 . . . . . 2,250.00

6", Continental Faience, blue, white, front trough, high back, painted with ferns, pierced to hold inkwell and pounce pot . . 200.00

7", Minton, basket shape, dahlia flowerheads over inkwells, c1835 . . . . 950.00

7", Scottish Wemyss, heart shaped, rooster decor, double, c1900 . . . . 300.00

15", Coalport, double, scrolling foliate border, handles, c1840 . . 350.00

Pottery, Moorcroft, 3", sq, holes for pen, pears and grapes decor in mauve 90.00

Silver

3", English, ivory insert, enamelled top, R.M.S. Auronia, 1902 . . . . 125.00

7¾", Japanese, double, rectangular tray, hinged top, chased with American Presidential Seal, inscription translated to "Kyoto, token of great esteem", floral sprays on hammered ground, lated 19th C 550.00

11¼" l, English, rectangular, reeded borders, ball and claw feet, central seal box flanked by octagonal cov inkwells, wells for pens both sides, marker's mark J. G. & Sons, London, 1905 . . 650.00

13½", Spanish, rectangular centered by Gothic cupola above figure of scribe, 4 detachable covered urns, partial pierced gallery, border of interlaced strapwork enclosing flowers, winged paw feet, F. Samper, Madrid, c1846 . . . . 3,600.00

Tortoiseshell, 13", MOP inlay, rectangular, bronze serpent form handle, pr of cut glass bottles, silver lids, lidded compartment, frieze on drawer, flared bracket feet, Regency, early 19th C 1,000.00

INSULATORS

***Warman's Americana & Collectibles*, 1st Edition, contains 94 listings in this category; see also page xii.**

IRONS

Old smoothing irons or hand pressing irons were probably one of the least popular domestic objects in a woman's life. The flat iron is sometimes called a 'sad iron.' It derived this name from the obsolete terminology for solid—sad.

There were four methods for heating these irons: (1) The slug was heated and attached to the iron; (2) The iron was heated directly on the fire; (3) Hot charcoal was contained within the iron; (4) The self-heating gas iron.

Irons can be found in various shapes and sizes, many of which were designed to be used on the current fashions of the day—ruffles, stiff collars, mutton sleeves, etc.

See *Warman's Americana & Collectibles* for an expanded listing of Irons.

Box, wrought iron, $90.00.

Charcoal

Chinese, open dish type, pan 5" d, 3" h, inscriptions and designs on sides, bronze construction, carved jade or ivory handle, pre-1700s 250.00

European, dragon, 7" l, 9½" h, dragon head forms raised spout for smoke exhaust, normal charcoal iron base, c1850 . . . . 350.00

Combination, Fluter and Sad, 6½" l, 4½" h, hinged at point, M. H. Knapp, Bay City, MI 90.00

Egg (Standing), egg 2½", cast iron handle, European 125.00

Fluter, Scissor, wrought iron, fluter head 2¾ x 1½", 6 ribs 100.00

Goffering
Double barrel, brass tubes 5½"
with 4½" insert heaters, marble
base, European **350.00**
Single barrel, all brass, 4½" barrel
with insert heater, Queen Anne
feet, English **250.00**
Miniatures
Fluter, hand, New Geneva style, 1
¾" l, 1½" h, two pieces, cast
iron, USA **150.00**
Slug, brass, 2¾" l, 2½" h, with
slug, English **150.00**
*Swan, 3" l, orig paint, trivet, USA **100.00**
Sad, soapstone, 6" l, 5" h, 1¼" h
soapstone insulator, standard triangle shape base, Hood's Patent
Jan. 15, 1867, USA **75.00**
Slug, brass, 6" l, 5" h, engraved on
top surface, ornate brass posts,
pre-1800s, Scandinavia **200.00**

IRONWARE

**Iron, a metallic element that occurs abun-
dantly in combined forms, has been known
for centuries. Items made from iron range
from the utilitarian to the decorative. Early
hand-forged ironwares are of considerable
interest to collectors of Americana.**

**Also see KITCHEN COLLECTIBLES,
LAMPS, TOOLS.**

**Raisin Seeder, 5" h, Ezy Raisin Seed-
er, patent. May 21, 1895, removable
cup, clamp grip, $225.00.**

Andirons, 18" h, faceted finials, adjustable spit rests, pr **175.00**
Ashtray, 4½" d, child with sun
bonnet **10.00**
Bill holder, spindle, ornate, wall hung **20.00**

Blacksmith tongs, 11", hand forged **100.00**
Book Ends, "Constitution **20.00**
Boot Scrapers
Dachshund, 21½" **65.00**
Sling shot type, early **50.00**
Branding Iron, "P," twisted handle . **25.00**
Broiler, 19" handle, 12 x 13", sta-
tionary **55.00**
Bullet Mold, Winchester 32, 1874 . . **35.00**
Candle Snuffer, scissors type **35.00**
Candlesticks
Hog Scraper, with pushup, 7⅛" . **65.00**
Spiral pushup, turned wooden
base **135.00**
Cauldron, 7¼" d, 7½" h, 3 feet,
wrought iron bail handle **55.00**
Cigarette Roller, hinged lid, elephant **180.00**
Door Latches, butterfly **75.00**
Door Lock, 4 x 6", turn handle with
key, c1840 . . . . **100.00**
Fire Dogs, 10" h, brass finials, pr. . **50.00**
Flag Holder, claw feet, c1885 . . . . **25.00**
Hair Curling Iron, 10" **20.00**
Hayfork, 34" long **50.00**
Hinges
18", pair **40.00**
36", pair **85.00**
Hitching Posts
Black Boy, 46", painted **950.00**
Horse head, 53½" h stylized, sim-
ple detail in mane, head, white
paint traces **345.00**
Jockey, 38", painted **350.00**
Hooks, Shutter, 7", "S" **10.00**
Horse Collar **60.00**
Ice Skates, clamp-ons, pair **35.00**
Kettle, 11 x 20½"d. 3 legs, bail han-
dle **150.00**
Key, skeleton, 5½" **18.00**
Lighting Fork, scrolled crest, 10½" l
back spike **70.00**
Lightning Rod, cow design, arrow . . **135.00**
Lizard, 8", long curled tail **65.00**
Mailbox, 11 x 6", eagle, flag **60.00**
Peal, 20¾" l, short handle, twisted
detail **70.00**
Porringer, 4" d **60.00**
Quilt Clamps, pair **30.00**
Rake, oyster, 19 x 10", barred cage **88.00**
Scissors, wick trimmers, 9½" l tole
tray **45.00**
Sheep Shears **5.00**
Skillet, cast, 20" d, 45" l, wrought
handle, pierced end **98.00**
Stove, 23" l x 17½" h, ship reliefs,
Tyson Furnace, Plymouth, VT,
1839 . . . . **175.00**
Sugar Devil, corkscrew type, Pat
1878 . . . . **165.00**
Sugar Nippers, 9" long, hand
wrought **65.00**
Toaster, 22½" w x 29" l, twisted
handle, rack bars, long pan **150.00**

Tongs
Pipe, 18¾", tamp built into handles	**395.00**
Ice, long handled	**15.00**
Tractor Seat, c. 1910–20	**65.00**

Traps
Bear, hand forged	**170.00**
Fox, hand forged	**125.00**
Umbrella Stand, 40", Victorian, ring grip above pierced scalloped dish, sliding locks on baluster support over pierced holder, baluster supported drip pan, 3 scroll feet, Pat 1860	**295.00**
Utensil Rack, 13½ x 32¾", 7 hooks, Scrolled, twisted crest decor	**105.00**
Whip holder, c1900	**750.00**
Wind Mill Weight, 18¼" h, bob tail horse, base set in concrete	**165.00**

IVORY

True ivory, a yellowish white organic material, comes from the teeth or tusks of animals. Ivory lends itself well to carving because of its basic structure and has been used for centuries, by many cultures, for artistic and utilitarian items. The Endangered Species Act of 1973 that prohibited the importation and sale of antique ivory and tortoise shell was amended in 1978, with limitations. If you deal or collect ivory, familiarize yourself with this law.

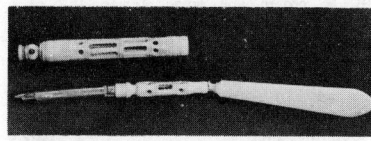

Letter Opener and Pen, 9½", Stanhope with map of Atlantic City, $75.00.

Beads, 24", creamy, graduating, ivory clasp, American made	**40.00**
Bottle with screw stopper, flattened compressed tapering body, carved, low relief, 3 Immortals in conversation, rocks, leafy plantain, 4 characters incised Qianlong mark on base	**500.00**
Box, 1¾ x 1¾", dyed green, swimming gold fish decor, sgd, late 19th C	**140.00**
Brush Pot, 4½", low relief, carved as bamboo, leafy sprays, band of dots around base, wood stand	**470.00**
Candlesticks, 12¼", carved, foliate and strapwork standard, triangular section cut base with Jupiter, Diana and another deity, late 19th C, pr	**650.00**
Cane, 35", black inlaid design	**375.00**
Cane Handle, 4½", skull, snake with inlaid eyes, 19th C	**90.00**
Card Case, 4¼ x 2⅝", carved, intricate and detailed overall	**135.00**
Card Holder, 4½", carved and undercut flowers, leaves around central medallion with scene of figures beside temple	**160.00**
Cigar Holder, carved	**30.00**
Cigarette Holder, 4", engraved crouching leopard encircles	**35.00**
Cordial Glasses, 2", whale ivory, set of 6	**275.00**
Crochet Hook, 6½"	**15.00**

Doctor's Lady
fully carved figure of lying woman with movable ivory bracelet	
4"	**70.00**
6"	**150.00**

Figures - animal
Caribou, Eskimo, carved, pr	**360.00**
Elephant, 1½", Japanese, c1890	**135.00**
Foo dog, 6", Chinese, c1890	**500.00**
Seals, 3, Eskimo, carved, c1890	**150.00**

Figures - people
Boy, 1½", riding boar, sgnd	**250.00**
Cupid, 17", perched on sphere, left arm held aloft, standard and circular base carved with geometric devices	**825.00**
Diana, 8", nude, standing on one foot, looking over left shoulder, marble socle, late 19th C	**650.00**
Goddess of Medicine, 7½", on turtle's back, carved, sgnd	**650.00**
Saint George and the Dragon, carved, armor clad saint upon rearing horse, slaying beast, octagonal wood socle	**1,250.00**
Woman and Putto, 12¾", winged female, windswept drapery, cylindrical socle	**1,100.00**
Glove Stretcher	**20.00**
Knife Rest, 4½", carved beads	**55.00**
Libation Cup, 4½", miniature, calligraphy seal, late 18th C	**35.00**
Napkin Ring, carved, lion stalking prey, Chinese	**52.00**
Needle Case, 4⅜" l, model of parasol	**125.00**
Netsuke, rooster with chick, inlaid eyes	**375.00**
Painting, miniature, Jupiter visiting Danae, 3½ x 5½", after the painting by Titian, inscribed Tiziano, late 19th C	**425.00**

Pendant, 2½", carved, Siamese, dancing figure amid florals, c1800 ... 30.00
Pickle Fork, carved 5.00
Pineapple, 3¾", interior hollowed out and carved with village scene ... 175.00
Plate, 4", carved 125.00
Puzzle, Ball, carved 80.00
Spoon, 3", carved handle 75.00
Tankard, 12½", carved, med and low relief, lion hunt, seated gladiator finial 3,960.00
Tatting Shuttle, 2¾" 80.00
Whistle, 4½", carved 80.00

JACKFIELD POTTERY

Jackfield pottery originated in England in the early 17th century. It is a red clay pottery with a high black glaze, found both plain and decorated with enamels, or designs in relief. It was made at the Jackfield Pottery in Stropshire, England, and most that is encountered today is from the 19th century. It differs from Basalt, which is black throughout the body.

Teapot, Jackfield Pottery, cov, 4½" h, brown glaze, gilding, white, orange, green, pink enamel spots, flowers, marked, $125.00.

Creamers
  Cow, figural, on stand, black glaze with gold highlights 90.00
  7", fluted gold enameling 100.00
Figurines
  7¼", cats, black and white, red and green bases, pair 100.00
  8½", spaniel, c1850 .... 100.00
  9½", poodles, pair 120.00
  Jug, 7⅛", worn red, yellow, blue paint, Chinaman, large blossoms, insects, worn gilding, c1760 .... 185.00
  Pitchers, 7½", floral panels, gold trim 75.00
  Syrup, 7", white enamel decor, pewter lid 65.00

Sugar Bowl, handleless, enameled birds 85.00
Teapots, covered
  4⅝", basket molded spout, crabstock handle, three paw feet, spherical body painted in gold, silver, gilded birdform finial, c1760 .... 175.00
  5½", body cold painted in brown, gold, Scotsman carrying shield, standing beside large thistle plant, three paw feet, bird finial, worn gilding, c1760 .... 150.00
  Miniature, round body, short cylindrical neck, three paw feet, curved spout, loop handle, vase finial on cover, c1770 ...... 200.00

JACK-IN-THE-PULPIT VASES

Vases in the form of a "Jack-in-the-Pulpit" flower were in vogue during the late Victorian period and early 20th century. These vases were made in a wide variety of glass, color and size. See specific categories for additional listings.

Amberina, 12 x 5¼", herringbone pattern, cranberry shaded to golden amber, amber applied edging, ground pontil 175.00
Art Glass, Mount Washington, 10½", Lusterless White 285.00
Bristol, 7", purple ruffle on white .. 58.00
Cased Glass
  6 x 6", cream, white lining, applied pink flowers and amber leaves, amber edge on ruffled top 165.00
  6½ x 6½", maroon shading to lighter, white outside, ruffled .. 135.00
Cranberry, 10 x 4½", clear applied rigaree around center, clear glass foot, ruffled top 125.00
Opalescent
  6 x 3⅜", vaseline, ruffled top ... 59.00
  7", pale blue top to vaseline 50.00
  11⅜ x 5", pink shaded to vaseline, fluted top 125.00
Quezal, 9", gold, decorated, sgr ... 1,200.00
Spangled
  8 x 4¾", green with maroon and white, silver mica flakes 110.00
  8⅛ x 5", green with opaque white and ox blood mottling, mica flakes, frilly top edge 110.00
Spatter, 8¼ x 5¼", pink and white, applied vaseline flower petal top . 95.00
Transparent
  6¼ x 6", blue shaded to vaseline, deep gold enameled leaves and sprays, applied vaseline feet, flower shaped scalloped top .. 150.00

Spatter Glass, 7″, predominately yellow, strips of white, orange, green and blue, $50.00.

7⅛ x 4½″, vaseline, diamond quilted, deep mahogany red opaque edge	95.00
8⅞ x 4⅝″, amber, pink stripes, vaseline branch and leaf, applied pink and white flower with amber center, fluted top	100.00

JADE

Jade is the generic name for two distinct minerals, nephrite and jadite.

Nephrite, an amphibole mineral from Central Asia, has a waxy surface and ranges in hues from white to almost a black-green. All jade carvings before the 18th century were of nephrite.

Jadite, a pyroxene mineral found in Burma, has a glassy appearance and comes in various shades of white, green, yellow-brown and violet. Most jade carvings from the 18th century to the present are jadite.

Jade is held in high esteem as a gemstone and lends itself well to carving.

Altar Cup, 7 x 4¾″, phoenix bird shape, green	158.00
Belt Buckle, 10¼″, 3 pc, pale celadon, domed central section	
hooked onto by 2 animal head plaques, fret and c-scrolls	500.00
Belt Hook, 4″, arched, carved archaistic scrolls below dragon head hook	120.00
Bottle with stopper, tapering baluster body, gray-white with apple green inclusions, carved symmetrical cash medallions between Greek scroll bands	1,100.00
Box, covered, 3 x 1½″, round, white, carved, bird and lotus blossom	250.00
Bracelet, mottled green with blood red inclusions	128.00
Brush Bowl, 4″, round, celadon, carved in relief, bat amongst branches of large hollowed out peach, wide ivory rockwork stand	2,200.00
Dishes	
5¾″, pale celadon, short footring, incised 4 character marks for Imperial use	400.00
8¾″, spinach nephtite with faint brown inclusions, archaistic seal mark	250.00
Ewer, 6″, bulbous with arched spout, light green, dragon head handle with loose ring, Chinese	420.00
Figures	
6½ x 4¾″, Foo lion, urn on it's back with Foo dog finial and 2 loose rings	600.00
6¾″, Quan-Yin, lavender green, ornate flowing robe, bird in her hair	350.00

Snuff Bottle, 3″, mottled brown jade, incised design of animal with body raised vertically, hand carved, green jade stopper, $385.00.

Incense Burners

    3½ x 4¼ x 3½", alter, square, celadon **160.00**

    5¼", carved, Foo dog finial mark ring handles, tripod base with wood stand, Chinese **500.00**

Letter Opener, 6", dark green **95.00**

Mirror, 7½", mottled green-brown, 4 dragons around palmette medallion **220.00**

Netsuke, woman diver after pearls .   **160.00**

Ring, lavender, 14K gold **350.00**

Sake Cups, orig case, set of 12 . . .   **225.00**

Saucer, 5½", pale celadon, ridge on rim, stepped foot **200.00**

Seal, 1½", white, Foo dog design, Chinese **100.00**

Snuff Bottle with stopper, rectangular, rounded corners, white **420.00**

Spoon, 4", white, flute handle, bowl carved with archaistic cicada . . .   **340.00**

Teapot, cov, 6 x 3¼", cream and mottled brown **395.00**

Urn, cov, 7", nephite, Tao-Tieh mask on body, Foo dog handles and finial   **375.00**

Vase, 7¼", flattened oval shape, pale celadon, low relief, bands of lotus petals, seeded bands, masked handles, 18th C **1,800.00**

Wine Cup, 2¼ x 3½", mogul jade, eggshell thin, lined with SS, SS and semi-precious stone base . .   **175.00**

Wine Pourer, cover, 5¾ x 5½", green and white, carved, low relief, bird, bird shape finial **170.00**

Wine Set, wine pourer, tray, 5 cups and saucers, carved, translucent green, loose ring decor **375.00**

JAPANESE CERAMICS

Like the Chinese, the Japanese spent centuries developing their ceramic arts. Each region established its own forms, designs and glazes. Individual artists added to the uniqueness.

Japanese ceramics began to be exported to the west in the mid-19th century. Their beauty quickly made them a favorite of the patrician class.

The ceramic tradition continues into the 20th C. Modern artists enjoy equal fame with older counterparts.

    See also IMARI, KUTANI, AND SATSUMA

Airta

    Bottle, 10" h, blue and white stylized floral motif, globular, elongated neck, thick ring foot, 18th C **130.00**

    Dish, 8" d, shallow, blue and white, landscape, thick ring foot, late 17th C **1,250.00**

Banko, teapot, 6" h, 7½" w, polycolor, glazed and unglazed clay, $350.00.

Banko, Teapot, 5" h, 5½" w, polycolor seven gods of wisdom, glazed and unglazed clay (garyware) **400.00**

Bizen

    Steamer and Cover, 7½" h, deep cylindrical container, applied handle and lug, creamy heavily crackled and underglaze blue, one side with stylized crab, other with calligraphy, lid en suite, late 18th C, cover sgd "kitai," fitted box **740.00**

    Water Bowl, 7½" d, irregular oval bowl, brown glaze with pale brown splashed glaze above, Edo period **260.00**

Hirado (Mikawachi)

    Incense burner, 5½", Shishi form, seated male with paw resting on ball, underglazed blue on white ground, 19th C **350.00**

    Vase, 37" h, baluster form with short flaring neck decorated in underglaze blue, geese taking off from a pond beside flowering shrubbery, neck and foot with lappet designs, mid-19th C **1,700.00**

Horaku, Chawan, deep, 5" d, raised ring foot, creamy glaze and underglaze blue, depicts two kyogen players, early 19th C, sealed "Toyosuke," fitted wooden box . . **600.00**

Kakiemon, bowl, shallow, 8½" d, short raised foot, dec. in colored enamels with ho-oo bird flying over sprays of flowering autumnal plants, 18th C, fitted wooden box **2,750.00**

Kyoyaki, Chawan, deep, 4¾" d, ring foot, flaring rim, dec in gilt and colored enamels, Shochikuba in a irregular cartouche, flowering wisterias in background **325.00**

Oribe, Incense burner, 3½" h, Shishi form, green glaze **360.00**

Raku, Chawan, winter, deep, 4" h, ring foot, glossy black glaze with reddish running at rim, late 18th C, fitted wooden box **650.00**

Seto
Chaire (container), 2½" h, oviform, glaze in brilliant green, three lug handles on the shoulder, sgd below "Toshiro," 18th C, ivory lid, wooden box **675.00**

Chawan, summer, shallow, 6" d, dec with dusty ochre and splashed gray glaze, sgd below "Shuntai," inscribed wooden box **425.00**

Shigaraki, Vase, Sansho, 12" h, heavily potted hexagonal form with short flaring neck, creamy ash glaze with green flashes, late 18th C **480.00**

Sumida Guma
Creamer, 4½" h, seated figure, extended mouth forms spout, hair braid forms handle, black robe, blue garment, unglazed face **150.00**

Vase, 7" h, two monkeys separated by dragon costume, red ground, crackled glaze top, sgd in cartouche **320.00**

Tamba, Storage Jar, 18½", baluster form, wide mouth, flat foot, ash glazed, c1700 . . . . **1,000.00**

JASPERWARE

Jasperware is a hard, unglazed porcelain with a background that varies in colors, from the most common blues and greens to lavender, yellow, red or black. The white designs are applied in relief and often reflect classical tradition. Josiah Wedgwood described Jasperware as "a fine Terra Cotta of great beauty and delicacy proper for cameos."

This ware was first produced at Wedgwood Etruria Works in 1775. While Wedgwood was probably the most prolific and recognized maker, other English potteries produced Jas-

perware. **Jasperware continues to be made today. See also WEDGWOOD.**

Biscuit Jars
6¼ x 5", three color, gold top and bottom bands, center black band with raised white classical ladies and cupids, marked Wedgwood only **695.00**

7½ x 5⅜", greenish-cream, medallions of Franklin, Washington and Lafayette against dark green, acorns and leaves, acorn finial, Wedgwood England **325.00**

Bottle, cov, 10½", light blue, white classical figures **575.00**

Bowls
7", light green, white classical figures, Wedgwood only **160.00**

10", dark blue, white figure, "Dancing Hours," band of acanthus and laurel leaves, laurel rim, imp Wedgwood, Made in England, c1881 . . . . **225.00**

Candlesticks, 5½", black, white classical figures, Wedgwood, pr . **275.00**

Candy Jar, 6", dark blue, white classical figures, oak leaves and acorns on cover, acorn knob, imp Wedgwood/England, c1910 . . . . **80.00**

Cheese Dish, 11", dark blue, white angels, grapevine border, Staffordshire, c1890 . . . . **150.00**

Clock, Jasperware, 6", blue, clock marked "Swiss Made", $550.00.

Chess Piece, Bishop, 3 x 2"d, deep blue base with white band, white figure, marked Wedgwood only, c1850 . . . .   **395.00**

Clock, 12¼ x 3½"d, deep green, white classical women and cupid around center, floral bands around clock, porcelain dial, marked Wedgwood England **595.00**

Creamer and Sugar, 2⅜", blue, white "Poor Maria" and figures from "Domestic Employment," engine-turned fluted, imp Wedgwood, late 18th C **800.00**

Cups and Saucers
  1" cup, 2⅝" saucer, miniature, deep blue, white classical figures around edges, marked Wedgwood Made in England . .   **175.00**
  Dark blue, white classical figures, white glazed interior, Wedgwood England **85.00**

Drum, 4⅝ x 3⅞", black, white classical ladies, cherubs and cupids .   **145.00**

Flower Holder, 7¼ x 4"d, urn with pierced dome lid, finial, deep blue, white Psyche and Cupid, bow around sides, looped handles, Wedgwood only **295.00**

Fumigating Jar, 4 x 3¾", light blue, white cherub and lady masques, lift off lid, slot for fumigating wick, Wedgwood, imp Piesse & Lubins Ribbon Fumigating **298.00**

Jardiniere, 3¾ x 4¼", deep blue, white grapes and leaves, garlands, classical figures, Wedgwood England **125.00**

Matchbox, 3¾", rectangular, dark blue, white "Poor Maria" on cover, classical figures on sides, imp Wedgwood, late 19th C **95.00**

Muffineer, 7", black, white classical figures, vine border, SP pierced cover, imp Wedgwood, c1840 . . .   **135.00**

Mustard Pot, 1⅞", round, SP hinged cover and handle, dark blue, white cupids, imp Wedgwood, 19th C . .   **125.00**

Pitchers
  4", blue, white classical figures, grape and leaf border, rope twist handle, Wedgwood **85.00**
  5½ x 4¼", deep blue, white ornate borders, classical figures .   **145.00**
  6½", green, white classical figures, grapevine border, imp Wedgwood **80.00**

Pomade Pot, 2⅛", circular, dark blue, white classical figures, imp Wedgwood, late 19th C **85.00**

Salt, 3¼", blue, white putti, floral guilloche borders, imp Wedgwood, S, No 3, c1785 . . . .   **350.00**

Scent Bottle, 2½", flattened oval, blue, 2 white classical figures on both sides within stiff leaf border, silver cover and stopper, unmarked **200.00**

Spill Vase, 3¾ x 2⅛", gold, white bands, raised blue figures and leaves **495.00**

Sugar Bowl, cov, 3⅛ x 3⅞"d, red, white classsical figure, Wedgwood   **395.00**

Syrup, 5½", green, white classical figures, imp Wedgwood/England, c1900 . . . .   **80.00**

Tea Bowl and Saucer, 3⅛" bowl, 5⅛" saucer, blue, white cupids, doves, flowers and insects, engine-turned flutes, acanthus and leaves on saucer, imp Wedgwood, late 18th C **225.00**

Teapot, cov, 4¾", dark blue, white classical figures, imp Wedgwood/England, c1900 . . . .   **100.00**

Toothpick Holder, light blue, medallion with angel head **55.00**

Tray, 7⅞", oval, scalloped rim, white alternating acanthus leaves and palmettes, imp Wedgwood, late 18th C **500.00**

Urns, 6⅝", light blue, white nymphs, horses, foliate borders, white rams head and loop handles, white square bases on circular pedestal with swags, imp Wedgwood, dated 1867, pr **475.00**

Vases
  7 x 3½", bulbous with elongated neck, deep blue, white classical figures **125.00**
  7½ x 5"d, handled, pedestal foot, light blue, white classical figures, Wedgwood only **395.00**
  19 x 17"d, handled, bolted base, light blue, white Pan, Bacchus and classical woman, cupids and garland around top, Wedgwood, c1840 . . . .   **1,395.00**

JEWEL BOXES

The jewel boxes listed here are mainly from the late Victorian period. The common variety was made of pot metal, cast in an irregular shape, with scrolls, flowers, etc., in relief and gilded. The interior was lined with satin or velvet.

Bisque, 5 x 4" figural, child's head, bust **48.00**

Bronze, 3 x 4¼ w x 6½" l, gilded, hinged, 4 feet, green velvet lined, overall leaf, flower in relief, 5 classical ladies on lid, Jenning Bros. .   **60.00**

Gilted, 5 x 6″, rose decor, padded, lined in blue silk, $45.00.

Indian, 6″ inlaid, ebony, turq, ivory and silver, c1910	95.00
Leather and Gilt Metal, 18″, rectangular, red leather, foliage, thistles and a cypher, velvet lined, early 20th C	675.00
Porcelain, French, 8½″, lozenge shape, floral decoration, blue and gold	325.00
Silverplate	
6″ ftd, repousse flowers on lid, lined, Wilcox Silverplate Co. . .	35.00
8″ oval, ftd, raised cupids, garlands, roses on lid, lined	50.00
Wood	
6 x 6¾ x 8″, English, burned surface resembles tortoise shell, 2 interior drawers, hinged doors, lift lid, orig brass hardware . .	300.00
11 h x 7½ w x 5¼″ d, gilded, decoupage coverage of colorful fabric, paper, figure of Renaissance lady, gentleman on doors, back is city roof top, spire scene, carved ivory ornaments, turned feet, rope carved pilasters, top compartment, 6 interior drawers	400.00
8 x 5½ x 5″, oak, intricate silverplate filigree, lock, key, tray, lined, "JEWES" written across top	135.00

JEWELRY

Jewelry has been a part of every culture. It was a way of displaying wealth, power, or love of beauty. The metals, stones, and gems used in jewelry have proven endurable over time. Therefore, many examples from the past exist today.

Jewelry items were treasured and handed down as heirlooms from generation to generation. This is still a common practice. Jewelry frequently is given to mark important occasions such as births, weddings, anniversaries, etc. Style and fashions change, but jewelry craftsmen have a knack of redesigning their product to fit any fashion trend.

Jewelry can be reset to modern fashion or treasured for its "antique" value. The choice is sometimes most difficult to make. In examining jewelry from the 19th and 20th centuries, the current value of silver and gold must be taken into consideration.

See *Warman's Americana & Collectibles* for additional jewelry listings.

Beads	
Cherry amber, ovals, 19¾″ l	125.00
Coral, double strand, graduated, gold filled clasp	300.00
Emerald like green, seed pearls, gold pierced discs, 18K, Castellani mark, 16″	750.00
Gold, 14K brushed beads, 50 beads	225.00
Jade, graduated	200.00
Pearls	
Double strand, 6.5 mm pearls .	750.00
Single strand, 46 matched 8mm pearls, 14K white gold clasp with 4 smaller pearls, 6 full cut diamonds, 15″ l	600.00
Triple strand, 7 mm	1,700.00
Bracelets	
Bamboo link, double row of 11 Florentine finished segments of 14K gold	300.00

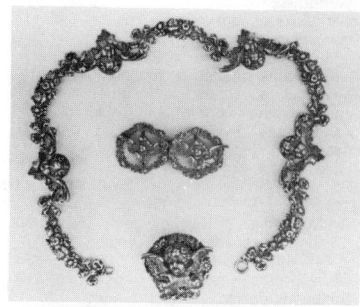

Necklace, clasp, belt buckle, Art Nouveau, putt: motif, SS, Kerr, $950.00.

Charm, 14 charms depicting Hawaiian heritage, surfing 100.00
Heart, circle design, 9 cultured pearls, 9 tiny blue stones, 14K gold 325.00
Link, flexible, heart, leaf pattern, 7½" l 400.00

Brooches
Bar, sq terminals with granulation, wire twist decor, ram's head with jeweled eyes in center . . . 375.00
Cameo, profile, 10K yellow gold setting 200.00
Fish, full cut ⅛ carat diamond set eye, 18K yellow gold, enamel . 240.00
Geometric, rectangular, chased, green enamel motif, inscribed ED (E. Davis), 1½" l 400.00
Insect in flight, 5 small opals, 14 tiny pearls, larger pearl drop, 14K yellow gold 70.00
Scrolled, gold, diamond, 3 carats, in center 550.00
Victorian, 6 small pearls, 18K yellow gold 175.00

Chains
Box link, gold, yellow, 14K gold . 40.00
Cable weave, 15½" l, 14K yellow gold 250.00
Rope, 14K gold and white links . 60.00
Semi-precious stones set in 29" l, 14K yellow gold chain, stones each cut differently, diamonds, sapphires, emeralds, topaz . . . 850.00

Chatelaines
Gold, pearls, bow, foliage swag . 275.00
SS, griffin and snake pin plaque, sliding mirror, scissors case, scent bottle, chased and repousse, c1890 . . . . 365.00
Choker, garnets, triple strand of faceted garnets, 6 scrolled cartouches centering on a diamond shape garnet 350.00
Collar, Lalique, gently arched rectangular plaque of pale green plique-a-jour enamel pine needles on blue enamel branches supporting rose cut diamonds, dark green enamel pine cones, 18K gold frame, black velvet ribbon, sgd . . 7,700.00

Crosses
Gold, yellow, filigree, 2⅛" h 60.00
SS, engraved, florals 45.00

Cuff Links
Art Deco, oval, 14K yellow gold . . 90.00
Cable like shape, semi-circular, 14K yellow gold 130.00
Coral form, 14K gold 110.00
Sunburst design, single opaque star sapphire, 14K yellow gold 100.00

Earrings
Amethyst, emerald cut, accented by various small diamonds, platinum clipbacks 750.00
Cameo, encircled by seed pearls, yellow gold screwback mountings 200.00
Leaf form, gold, each set with 2 blue full cut sapphires, screw backs, 18K yellow gold 60.00
Opal, oval opal in ornate gold mount set with small diamonds, rubys, 14K backings 440.00

Lavaliers
Diamonds, 7 European cut, platinum mounting 1,500.00
Sapphire, one oval faceted, 15 small pearls, one tumbled sapphire suspended in a 14K yellow and rose gold mount 1,300.00

Lockets
Baby, oval, engraved, one round diamond, 14K gold, c1895 . . . . 95.00
Diamond, European cut center, surrounded by field of seed pearls framed by border of small turquoise cabochons, yellow gold swivel locket 400.00
Round, floral motif border, 14K gold 100.00

Necklaces
Love knots, 7 graduated citrines, gold, 19th C 450.00
Sapphires, 4 yellow, 5 blue, 18K yellow gold chain, c1900 . . . . . 1,600.00

Pendants
Geometric, rectangular, enamelled in black, umber, yellow, brown, inscribed ED (E. Davis), c1930, 2" h 800.00
Heart, engraved, chain of hammered links, 14K gold 50.00
Peacocks, pr, enamel foliage, cluster of small pearls, pearl drops, tiny emerald, 9 garnets . 130.00

Pin, Art Nouveau, 1½", SS, woman with flowing hair, $85.00.

Sunburst design, crescent moon
looking towards 3 diamond
stars, made for Tiffany & Co,
1³/₁₆" round 90.00

Woman in turquoise enamelled
dress, playing harp on enamelled gold jetty, gold chain necklace with 2 green plique-a-jour
links of enamelled gold flowers,
c1900 . . . . 1,980.00

Pins

Art Nouveau, poppy, enamelled,
pearl with vine, gold 250.00

Bar, 5 prong set peridots, 50
diamonds, pierced gallery . . . 575.00

Bar, sapphire and pearls, alternating, pierced 14K gallery 160.00

Figure 8 on side, 14K yellow gold
set with 6 matching full cut
white diamonds, large oval cat's
eye drop 125.00

Florets in cannetille work, centered by semi-precious stones,
collet set emerald 325.00

Leaf form, 18K gold, pr 160.00

Jabot, Art Deco, blood coral,
diamond set caps, gold bar . . . 475.00

Rings

Butterfly, 5 small emeralds, small
opal center 150.00

Diamond, ³/₈ carat, 18K white gold
filigree, c1920 . . . . 125.00

Dome, red, white enamel swirls,
18K yellow gold shank 250.00

Gold, pivoting green glass cabochon, molded with concentric
waves, 18K gold band, inscribed
R. Lalique 1,650.00

Opals, three small ovals, 14K yel-
low gold 70.00

Pearl, enamel, mythological female on pink ground, framed by
half pearls on black enamel,
18K gold shank 250.00

Rose zircon, emerald cut, 18K
gold shank 65.00

Wedding, 7 small full cut white
diamonds, wide, 14K yellow gold 100.00

Slides

Diamond shape, diamond center,
reeded edges, engraved SAF,
14K gold 125.00

Engraved florals, gold, rose gold
decor 95.00

Stickpins

Bird, 14K, rose and yellow gold,
c1895 . . . . 95.00

Lobster, one seed pearl, 14K gold 115.00

Rapier capped by natural pearl inset, rose cut, European cut
diamonds in handle, yellow gold
and silver mounts 750.00

Wreath, 6 seed pearls, 14K gold . 85.00

JUDAICA

As members of the Jewish faith spread
throughout the world, artifacts used in their
temples and religious celebrations in the
home assumed the artistic attributes of each
individual region. Thus each basic form,
whether Hanukah Lamp or Torah breastplate,
comes in a wide variety of styles.

Silver is a favored medium for many objects. Hence, objects have value both by
weight as well as artistic content. Signed
items are the most desired. Sotheby's and
Christies both hold at least one special auction of Judaica each year.

Esther Scrolls

Bezalel silver filigree cased, early
20th C, cylindrical case decorated in foliate pattern, flanked by
roundels, embossed with bold
bosses, surmounted by a crown,
interior with handwritten parchment scroll, thumbpiece
inscribed in Hebrew "Bezalel
Jerusalem," case 7¼", scroll
width 2⅜" 550.00

Turkish, ivory, miniature, mid-19th
C, simple cylindrical handle with
minaret form top of three tiers,
holding a *hamelech* scroll well
written on the translucent
parchment, case 8½", scroll
width 2⅝" 1,000.00

Etrog Container, silver, Bagdad,
Iraqui, c1800, form of a pear with
pull off lid, 4½" h, Arabic silversmith stamp for Jewish silversmiths Chaim Meir and Eliahu . . . 1,000.00

Hanukah Lamps

Continental, silver, apparently
unmarked, German, mid-19th C,
form of tree trunk, roots forming
base, branches terminating in
blossom form candle sockets,
center with detachable servant
light, applied birds and beasts,
84 oz, 25" h 9,250.00

Dutch, sheet brass, 18th C, cartouche form backplate, punched
with flower and grape motifs,
beaded border, set with row of
eight oil pans and a servant
light, all under a rectangular drip
pan, 9" h 875.00

North African, brass, Morocco,
c1700, cast backplate, chased
and pierced with scrolls and
mirhabs above line of Hebrew
inscription, fronted by four double oil pans above, a servant
light and hanging ring with four
fleurs-de-lis, 8¾" h 675.00

Polish, brass, 18th C, cast backplate, pierced in a foliate scroll pattern terminating in two birds heads, fronted by eight candle sockets, sides fitted with two replacement servant lights, four pad supports, 8¼" h . . . **1,650.00**

Polish, silver, A. Reidel, Warsaw, late 19th C, backplate of cartouche form, applied with grapevine, crown, lions, palmtrees and birds, fronted by eight oil cups, galleried border, panel feet, later servant light and parrot hanging, 23 oz, 8 dwts, 11" h **2,500.00**

Kiddush Cups

German silver, c1900, hexagonal bowl engraved with a Hebrew inscription, chased with floral bouquets above fluting, set on a knopped stem over a domed base with further floral clusters, 4 oz, 8 dwts, 5" h **400.00**

Polish, silver, c1825–50, tulip form cup, hammered knop stem, square base, lip engraved with Hebrew inscription, 5 oz, 5⅛" h **750.00**

Marriage Belt, silver, Austrian, late 19th C, 38", plaques cast with various Biblical personages and vignettes, connected by spacers and curb links, crowned lion fasteners, two plaques engraved on reverse with Hebrew inscriptions relating to marriage, 5 oz, 10 dwts **1,350.00**

Sabbath Lamps, Hanging

Continental, brass, c1800, typical form with bulbous baluster stem applied with reflectors and knops, engraved with scrolling foliage, eight oil pans, drip pan, all pans similarly engraved, 18½" **700.00**

Italian, brass, c1700, turned suspension bracket hung with a seven light oil pan, drip cup with acorn knop, 18½" **1,400.00**

Sabbath Stew Pot, copper, North Africa, probably Bagdad, 18th C, 8" h, bulbous spherical pot, flat base, applied handle, engraved with Hebrew inscription *Cook everything you can cook*, pull off lid with stylized bird knop **1,400.00**

Spice Containers

Austro-Hungarian, tower form, silver and filigree, c1900, typical form surmounted by pennants, set on a wirework base on hemispherical supports, 3 oz, 8 dwts, 8¼" h **275.00**

Continental, silver, fruit form, miniature, 18th C, pendant representing two acorns hung from vines, engine turned decoration, two screw closures opening to reveal hidden spice containers, larger bearing Hebrew inscription for "spices," 16 dwts, 2½" **1,200.00**

Dutch, silver, windmill form, 1913, movable spokes, base applied with a small figure, 5" h **550.00**

Polish, silver and filigree, tower form, Frenk, Warsaw, 1889, cubic central section composed of filigree, hung with bells and surmounted by pennants, spire with further pennant on a skirted stem and square base, 5 oz, 4 dwts, 9½" h **825.00**

Russian, silver filigree, M.O., Moscow, 1880s, vase form, set on plain stem over a circular base, detachable lid with pennant knop, 4½" h **500.00**

Succah Basket, Persian, pierced brass and enamel, c1800, 8" l, bean form, embossed with beasts and pierced in a geometric design, painted with floral borders, Hebrew and Arabic inscriptions in tones of gilt, red, green, and orange **1,600.00**

Torah Breastplates

Dutch (Amsterdam), silver, 11" h, 1925, pierced cartouche form, decorated with lions supporting the Decalogue crowned, lower section with opening for Torah portion, surmounting scrollwork flanking an oval cartouche with dedicatory inscription, suspension chain, 17 oz, 4 dwts **1,850.00**

Italian (Venice), silver, 4½" h, mid-18th C, crown, embossed and chased with rococo scrollwork and flowers, centering a cartouche with a hand holding a ewer and basin, the lower section embossed in Hebrew *The Third Book*, marked with a winged lion and letter G, 3 oz, 16 dwts **5,500.00**

Torah Finials

Austrian (Vienna), silver, 14½", late 19th C, bulbous form, pierced and chased with floral clusters and foliage, hung with bells, surmounted by a crown . . **2,600.00**

North Africa (Moroccan or Algerian), 17½" h, c1850, pierced and faceted pear form, decorated with scrolling foliage, series of arches hung with bells, fruit form finial, set on faceted, cylindrical stem engraved with Hebrew inscriptions, 58 oz, 16 dwts, including central brass supporting rod 1,350.00

Torah Pointers

German, silver, 9¾″ l, 18th C, spiral stem with spherical knop, other end terminating in hand, maker "VM" or WM" in monogram, struck with a three tower mark, possibly Hamburg 825.00

Polish, silver, 7½″ l, 18th C, circular stem chased with spiral scrolls and foliage, one end terminating in a pierced spherical knop, the other in a cuffed hand, engraved decoration, silver of low alloy 550.00

JUGTOWN POTTERY

Pottery making in North Carolina commenced in the mid-18th century and continued through the 19th and 20th centuries. The Jugtown Pottery encountered today began its colorful and somewhat off-beat operation in 1920. Jacques and Juliana Busbee decided to leave their cosmopolitan world and return to North Carolina to revive the dying craft of pottery making in their native state.

They located in Moore County, miles away from any large city and accessible only "if mud permits." They employed a talented young potter, Ben Owen, to turn all the wares. Jacques Busbee did most of the designing and glazing. Juliana busied herself in promoting.

From 1922 until 1958, with only a few years exception, "Jugtown Ware" was made by Ben Owen under the operation of the founders, Jacques and Juliana Busbee. Utilitarian and decorative items were produced. Although many colorful glazes were used, orange predominated. A Chinese blue glaze that ranged from light blue to deep turquoise was a prized glaze reserved for the very finest pieces.

Jacques Busbee died in 1947. His widow, Juliana, ran the pottery with the help of Ben Owens until 1958 when the pottery was closed. After long legal battles, the pottery was reopened in 1960 and is now owned by

Country Roads, Inc., a non-profit organization. The pottery is still operating and using the old marks.

Bean pot, cov, 8″, yellow-orange . . 20.00

Bowls

2½ x 6″, frogskin 25.00
3 x 7″, Chinese white 60.00

Bowl, Jugtown, 6½″ d, 4″ h, pedestal, turquoise, maroon, oriental style, $150.00.

Candlesticks, 7″, orange, pr 65.00
Jar, 6″, cov, salt glaze 45.00

Pitchers

7″, incised design, frogskin 55.00
8″, Chinese white 100.00

Teapot, 7″, frogskin 55.00

Vases

4″, Chinese white 55.00
6 x 5″, pear shaped, Chinese blue, much red 135.00
7″, four small handles, salt glaze 85.00
10 x 12″, bulbous bottom, Chinese blue 200.00

KPM CHINA

This mark, KPM, had been used by Meissen, but was adopted in 1830 by the Royal Factory, Konigliche Porzellanmanufaktur, in Berlin. This was the factory that worked under the patronage of Frederick the Great in latter part of the 18th century. Other German factories have used this mark also.

Butter Pat, floral decor 20.00
Creamer and Sugar, pink, florals . . 52.00
Dish, divided with handle, 9½ x 12″, lilac mums, green decor, gold trim, blue KPM underglaze 125.00

Figures

4½ x 5″, Diane sitting beside recumbent deer 225.00

Plate, 8¼", blue band, apple and plum, foliage in center, gold trim, $35.00.

KAUFFMANN, ANGELICA

Marie Angelique Catherine Kauffmann was a Swiss artist who lived from 1741 until 1807. Paintings copied from her original work often embellished porcelain and those signed with her name have attracted collectors.

Biscuit Jar, classical scene, 3 figures in center medallion, framed in gold beading, deep greens, burgandy, gold, sgnd A. Kauffman, Prov. Saxe, E. Germany **150.00**

Bowl, 9" square, classical scene center, green border with gold edge, (Vienna Austria, and Beehive mark) **70.00**

Box, 3½"h, egg shaped, porcelain, 3 feet, metal hinged lid, classical ladies, pink roses, sgd. **35.00**

Coffee Set, 9½"h coffee pot, cov, creamer, sugar, cov, oval reserves of maiden, cupids, emb flowers, MOP rainbow lustre, marked B, Germany **145.00**

Cups and Saucers
   Classical ladies **40.00**
   Ornate handle, claw foot, pastoral scene, cerise with gold **69.00**

Jam Jar, cov 5¼", pastoral scene, ladies dancing, pale green with gold trim, Beehive mark, sgd. . . . **100.00**

Pitcher, 6", center medallion, gold borders with roses **80.00**

8 x 3½", classical lady with peacock by her side, seated, holds sceptre, coral and lavender robe, jewels in blond hair **395.00**

8½", man and woman, Empire style clothing, white with lacy black and gold decor, blue KPM underglaze **495.00**

Plaques
   5 x 7", oval, Madonna, sceptre mark, unframed **225.00**
   6", round, biblical figures, gold florentine frame **400.00**
   8½ x 6", child wearing lace collar over pale blue shirt **650.00**
   10 x 7½", female figures, cupids, children, cloud background, gilt wood frame, KPM mark **1,100.00**
   12¾ x 11", Apotheosis of Columbia at end of war between states, imp sgr **195.00**

Plates
   10", cake, portrait, Queen Louise, spray of violets, burgundy, gold rim, marked KPM **85.00**
   Black children, sgd, c1880 . . . . . **150.00**

Platter, 12½ x 17¾", hp, center scene, man with horn, lady with bird in cage, med green border, raised gold decor, gold handles with pink ribbons, blue sceptre underglaze **495.00**

Sweetmeat Dish, double leaf shape, c1890 . . . . **125.00**

Tureen, covered, 16¼", oval, butterfly and floral decor **400.00**

Urn, 16¼", gold swans with ruffled wings forming handles, white with gold highlights **225.00**

Vase, 6½", white, multicolored floral design, pr **65.00**

Plate, 8½" d, scalloped rim, cranberry border, gold decor, portrait center of 3 classical ladies, sgd, beehive mark, Austria, $60.00.

Plates

6", classical maidens, deep green scalloped border with gold scrolls, "Victoria Carlsbad" ... **65.00**

8½", 3 maidens serving seated gentlemen, gold scallops around center, Austria Beehive mark .. **60.00**

9", classic scene, gold tracery center, cobalt blue, triple cut-out border **60.00**

10½", 3 classical figures center, gold border, raised dots **70.00**

Tobacco Jar, 7½", dark green muted with orange, yellow, classical scene, SP rim, lid **300.00**

Tray, 14" cream ground, gold flowers, burgundy scallops **80.00**

Urn, 5¼"h, 2 handles, classical portrait reserved on turquoise, fuchsia ground, gilt decor, bands **55.00**

Vases

8¼", 2 handles, classical figures, deep red ground, gold tracery. Victoria, Carlsbad, Austria blank **60.00**

9½", handles, women, child, green ground, gilt, sgd. **85.00**

KEW BLAS

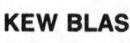

Kew Blas is an iridescent art glass made by the Union Glass Works, Somerville, Mass. Items, when signed, were signed with the name in the center of the base. The ware was a contemporary of Tiffany at the turn of the century.

Bowls, 10", green pulled feather on opaque off-white irid ground, flared edge **1,250.00**

Candlesticks, 8½", irid gold, twisted stems, pair **695.00**

Compote, 3½ x 4½", baluster pedestal, sgr **400.00**

Cordial, irid gold **165.00**

Creamer, 5", pulled feather on iridescent off-white ground, fancy irid handle, (very rare) **1,250.00**

Finger bowl, irid gold, fluted edge .. **295.00**

Goblet, 6", irid gold, knob stem ... **350.00**

Rose Bowl, 4", green feather on irid off-white and gold ground **895.00**

Salt, open, irid gold, ruffled **195.00**

Tumbler, 3½", round foot, irid **195.00**

Vases

4½", butterscotch, green, gold zipper pattern, sgr **575.00**

6", gold decorated lustre over green feathers on opaque body, fluted top **1,250.00**

Tumbler, 3¾" h, gold interior, ribbed, Union Glass Co. 1890-1924, $225.00.

6", irid gold, slightly bulbous with gold handles **695.00**

7", irid rich blue **800.00**

7¾", opaque with gold and green irid rippled designs **1,250.00**

9½", bulbous bottom, trumpet top, silver lustre ground, pulled amber feathers **875.00**

KING'S ROSE

King's Rose is a hand decorated earthenware made in the Staffordshire district, England, in the period 1820–1840. It was heavily exported to the Middle Atlantic states.

The central feature is a large, cabbage type rose in red, pale red, or pink. The pink rose often is called "Queen's Rose." Secondary colors are pastels of yellow, pink, and occasionally green. The borders are varied—a solid band, vined, lined, or sectional. Occasionally, the King's Rose pattern is found with an oyster motif.

Because of the soft paste, the enameled colors do not hold well. It is not unusual to see portions of the decoration flaked off. Further, the ware is subject to cracking and chipping.

Coffee Pot, 11½", dome lid, vine border **750.00**

Creamer, brick red rose, helmet shape, $225.00.

Cups and Saucers, handleless
Line border, interior of cup decorated, exterior plain 68.00
Oyster pattern, pink border 125.00
Scalloped rim 145.00
Plates
6½", vine border, yellow puff balls 135.00
9", red rose, red line border, yellow, green, leaves outlined in black 145.00
9¼", line border, imp, "Wood" . . 125.00
9¾", vine border 130.00
9⅞", sectional border 110.00
10", pink border, brick red swags, polychrome floral design with oyster 145.00
Platter, 13" 285.00
Sauce Boat, 6", red rose 145.00
Soup Plate, 9¼", broken band border, puff balls 135.00
Sugar, cov, pink rose 160.00
Teapot, 5⅞", shell molded, oval, brick red rose, russet ribs, pink trellis border with panels 400.00
Toddy, 5¾", vine border 75.00
Waste Bowl, 5⅝" 100.00

KITCHEN COLLECTIBLES

Kitchenwares and allied primitives of any period are very collectible today. From the days when cooking was done on any open hearth, when cooking pots were made of iron, copper or brass, cast iron, and to the days when they were replaced by lighter and easier-to-clean materials, till well into the 1920s, kitchenwares are part of our past history. Wooden ware dishes, and implements are very much sought after today, as are the patented implements used to make the housewifes' duties easier and more efficiently performed.

See various other categories such as, Graniteware, Woodenware, Copper, Brass, Ironware, etc.

See *Warman's Americana & Collectibles* for an expanded listing of kitchen collectibles.

Apple Peeler, 9½", wooden crank, spikes, moveable peeler, attaches to table 95.00
Bean Slicer, iron, Germany 38.00
Bread Pan, folding tin, Pat. 1872 . . 10.00
Cabbage Cutter, 7¾ x 20", walnut, cut out top and bottom with heart in crest 135.00
Can Opener, tin, c1876 . . . . 12.00
Carpet Beater, steel spring wire, covered with coils, stained handle 20.00
Chestnut Roaster, tin and wire, pat 1879 . . . . 40.00
Coffee Grinder, 9½", Turkish brass, incised designs, c1800 . . . . 40.00
Cutlery Tray, Bentwood, felt lining, c1890 . . . . 25.00
Dipper, 20½" l, wrought iron, brass hammered bowl, polished 65.00
Dish Drainer, 15", wire, flatware basket suspended in center, c1900 . 12.00
Egg Beater, 12½", iron, Dover, dated 1898 . . . . 12.00
Egg Stand, wire, center handle, holds 6 eggs, folds up to fit in drawer when empty, Dover Stamping Co., c1870 . . . . 25.00
Egg Timer, 7", wood frame, c1870 . 50.00
Ferkin, covered, old paint 60.00
Flatware Tray, 2 section, tin 60.00
Food Chopper, 10 x 2", wooden handle, crescent shaped steel blade 10.00

Tea Strainer and base, porcelain, 4" h, marked "Germany," $125.00.

Food Mill, tin and steel, Foley	6.00
Ice Water Cooler, tin, sets on table, c1870	30.00
Measuring Cup, 5″, tin, deep lip, c1890	18.00
Meat Juice Press, Londers, Frary and Clark, c1800	35.00
Mitten Dryer, 11 x 14 x 21″, tin, oval with pierced holes, 2 curved tubular stacks, sat on stove	120.00
Nutmeg Grater, mechanical, tin and wood, c1868	115.00
Pastry Blender, marked Androck . .	6.00
Pie Crimper, wooden and wire, c1860	30.00
Plate Warmer, Japanned tin, with 4 cast iron legs, c1870s	150.00
Pot Scraper, wire rings, wire handle	23.00
Potato Baking Rack, 15¼″, tin and wire, c1900	12.00
Pressure Cooker, heavy tin, clamp on lid, bail handle, c1870	35.00
Raisin Seeder, 10″, upright, c1870 .	45.00
Roaster, game bird, tin, reflector oven for hearthside use, c1870 . .	75.00
Rolling Pins	
Crockery, blue striped, Callender's Dept. Store, Stapleton, NE . . .	145.00
Glass, 14″, black, one piece, handmade, c1860	80.00
Maple, tiger striped, 22″ l, 1870 .	150.00
Sausage Stuffer, 20″, tin with copper bands and wooden plunger, c1850	65.00
Scoop, 15 x 6 x 2″, wood, hand carved, red stain, c1860	50.00
Soap Saver, wire mesh, long handle	12.00
Spice Chest, 6¾″, 10 small overlapping drawers, porcelain pulls, nailed construction, c1880,	125.00
Spice Mill, attaches to table, Enterprise Mfg. Co., c1898	25.00
Spice Set, 14 pcs., porcelain, with names of spices	150.00
Stove Lid Lifters, wrought iron, early 1800	25.00
Toaster, General Electric Model D12, Pat. 1908	57.00
Vegetable Slicer, 16″, Enterprise Mfg. Co. #49	65.00
Waffle Iron, twin, sets vertically on 11″ round stand between 2 long curved bakelite handles	75.00

KUTANI

Kutani, in Kaga province, Japan, is where this ware was made in the mid-1600s. The earliest ware is quite heavy, like stoneware; the next group of collectible ware is somewhat lighter, and is decorated with many colors, such as green, yellow, and purple, with black outlining. The Kutani made since 1875, for Western export, is what is found most often today, and is what most collectors look for. The earlier ware is the most expensive, and is harder to find.

Kutani Vase, 9½, $225.00.

Bottle, 14¾″, bulbous, sageon horse back, boy attendant, pine branches, 18th C	850.00
Bowls	
5″, polychrome, One Thousand Butterflies, red orange border .	175.00
7″, white ground, One Thousand Faces, red designs	90.00
9¾″, brocade with 3 figures beneath pine tree and 4 flower spray panels, exterior has scrolling flower pattern, short raised foot, 19th C	280.00
18½″, panels of figures, flowers and butterflies, 19th C.	565.00
Covered, (sang de boeuf) on carved wooden base	175.00
Box, cosmetic, 2″ h, molded cover, recumbent ox	125.00
Charger	
18″, scene showing attack and defense of royal palace, orange, gold, green, pink and black . . .	695.00
Coffee Set, pagoda scene on front, gold and cobalt blue ornamentation, 3 demitasse cups and saucers, coffee pot, covered sugar, creamer, signed in red circle on each piece	400.00

Dishes
6", petal shape, enameled, fish in sq reserve, intricate wave pattern, round medallions, raised ring feet, C 1700 . . . . 600.00

14", pavilions in mountain landscape, wide rim with black and green geometric patterns and prunes panels 450.00

14¾", sq. panels of pavilions, landscapes, boys around boiling cauldron and flowers, underside green with black floral sprays, 19th C 550.00

Ginger Jar, 5", blue, green and carmine enamel decor, Foo dog finial 85.00

Incense Burner, 7" square, phoenix bird, flowering trees, elephant head decor, loose ring handles 450.00

Plate, 10", thatched roof huts, fish leaping, cranes flying black and gold scrolled border, sgd 350.00

Saki Pot, covered, 10", 2 dragons chasing a pearl, wave and scale motifs, late 65.00

Tea Caddy, white ground, red decor 150.00

Vases
4", polychrome and gilt, courtesans, Mt. Fuji in the background 285.00

15 x 7¾", war lords on front, grouse, flying birds, enameled mums, geometric pattern, red & gold decor on back 375.00

31½", baluster shape, peacocks, prunus tree, trumpet neck with stylized leaves, pr 1,760.00

Wine Ewer, 7", double gourd shape, yellow glaze with green splashes 350.00

LALIQUE

A.LALIQUE

LALIQUE

Lalique is a quality glass designed in the manner of the Art Nouveau and Art Deco style. It is a combination of blown, molded or pressed and/or engraved glass.

Rene Lalique produced this glass in France from the 1890s until his death in 1945. Pieces from this era are signed "R. Lalique." Items made after 1945 are marked "Lalique." Script and block letters were used alternately.

Forgeries of the signature on Lalique-type glass are not uncommon. In some instances the "R" has been added to "Lalique" to misrepresent the circa.

Blotter, 6¼", Mures, handle frosted with mulberry design, sgd R. Lalique France, c1929 . . . . 870.00

Bottles
Cologne
4¾", Jaytho, overall tulips in relief, sgd R. Lalique 169.00

Crystal, frosted, emb flower with black enamel center, sgd R. Lalique 135.00

Perfume
3½", Carre Hirondelles, flying swallows, sgd R. Lalique France, c1928 . . . . 675.00

3½", rings of concentric black dots, sgd R. Lalique 825.00

5½", Dahlia, satin finish, black enameled stamen, sgd R. Lalique 120.00

Bowls
5½", Coquilles, opal, sgd R. Lalique, N3204 . . . . 195.00

8", mistletoe, berry feet, sgd R. Lalique 375.00

8⅝", Vernon pat, emb opal sunflowers, imp signature in raised letters 325.00

10½", opal, 6 sirenes bathing in spray, molded and etched, sgd R. Lalique, c1920 . . . . 495.00

Boxes
6¼", round, Premeveres, opal with flowers in relief, sgd R. Lalique France, c1929 . . . . . . 1,295.00

Powder
1½ x 3¾", three dancing nudes, D'Orsay, sgd R. Lalique 225.00

4", round, Three Graces, molded, mold sgd R. Lalique 245.00

6½", round, Mesanges, 6 small birds on cover, opal mold top and base, sgd R. Lalique, c1930 . . . . 575.00

Car Mascots
Chysis, 5¼", nude, kneeling, arms stretched out back of head, frosted, R. Lalique France, c1929 . . . . 2,225.00

Faucon, 6", falcon jutting forward, molded, frosted highlights, R. Lalique molded block letters, c1930 . . . . 1,550.00

Victorie, 10", frosted, sgd R. Lalique 2,550.00

Carafe, 12¼", pyramid shape, clear, frosted stopper with flower motif, R. Lalique No 3152, c1922 . . . . . 385.00

Decanter Set, 13¾" decanter, six 4" glasses, frosted with brown wash, figures in 6 panels, sgd R. Lalique, c1929 . . . . 2,055.00

Dresser Set, perfume flacon with tall

stopper, cov box and atomizer, clear, diamond shape, marked .. **475.00**

Inkwells

3⅓ ", round, Nenuphar, water lilies, frosted, sgd R. Lalique France, c1930 .... **540.00**

5⅞", Biches, black glass, Art Deco, foliage and deer in relief, R. Lalique, c1926 .... **4,495.00**

Mirror, hand, 11",silver back, frosted leaf, vine and figures, sgd Lalique, c1917 .... **2,450.00**

Panel, 13½", glass, Virgin and Child, clear with intaglio cut frosted figures, rectangular base, sgd in block letters, R. Lalique France . **950.00**

Pendant, 1½", triangular, frosted, molded, dancing nymph **180.00**

Plate, 10½", opal, 6 sirenes bathing in spray, molded and etched, sgd R. Lalique, c1920 .... **695.00**

Seals

3", Tete d'Aigle, bust, eagle, cylindrical, clear, sgd R. Lalique, C1929 .... **695.00**

3½", Aigle, eagle with hunched wings, clear, R. Lalique, c1939 . **1,675.00**

Statuettes

Mermaid, 3⅞", Sirene, opal, R. Lalique France, c1927 .... **885.00**

Nude with arms framing her upturned head, frosted and clear, acid stamped Lalique, France **374.00**

Tumblers

4", clear with frosted swirling leaves, sgd **125.00**

Vase, 8¼", Thistle and leaves. Sgd in acid etched script, R. Lalique France, $850.00.

4½", cherries in relief, sgd R. Lalique **200.00**

Vases

6", round, short neck, Lievres, opal, ferns and band of running hares in relief, sgd R. Lalique France, c1929 .... **915.00**

6 x 3½", straight sides, roosters standing in thicket of tall grass, acid finish, sgd, R. Lalique **450.00**

6½", Gui, lime green, molded, stylized leaves, sgd R. Lalique, c1930 .... **1,075.00**

7", amber, molded, grazing deer, stylized foliage, stenciled Lalique France, c1928 .... **795.00**

7", bust nude, Caryatides, Art Deco, sgd R. Lalique **875.00**

7½", gourd shape, Dentile, frosted with beaded vertical stripes, sgd R. Lalique France, c1939 .. **925.00**

10", babies, frosted, cherries with brown enamel patination decor, molded sig **2,420.00**

Water Set, pitcher, tray, 6 glasses, Bahia pat, yellow, molded leaf motif, R. Lalique, c1929 .... **2,235.00**

Wine Glasses

4½", long molded overlapping ribbed petals all around, thin stem, sgd R. Lalique **58.00**

6", flat stem, silhouettes of 2 dancing nudes, Art Deco **75.00**

LAMP SHADES

Art Nouveau art glass shades created by Durand, Quezal, Steuben and other glass makers of the early 20th century have become highly prized. These glass shades will probably never be used as they were originally intended, since most collectors consider them shelf or cabinet pieces.

Burmese, 4½ x 2¼" fitter, Mount Washington, shiny finish, fluted edge **400.00**

Carnival Glass

Diamond Pattern, 2" **40.00**

Forest Scene, 2" **55.00**

Soda Gold, 2" **25.00**

Custard Glass, nutmeg stain, 2" ... **35.00**

Duncan and Miller, 9½ x 3" fitter, Mardi Gras, teardrop shape **35.00**

Durand

7", green decor on gold ground, feather edge **150.00**

12", heart and cling vine, orange irid **300.00**

Egyptian Crackle for floor lamp .. **275.00**

Quezal, 4¼ x 2½″ collar, gold irid, 10 ribbed sides, sgr, $100.00.

Fostoria
Charteuse, green, gold pulls, gold lining, ruffled edge 125.00
King Tut type, dark green, platinum decor, gold interior 375.00
Wave pattern, dark brown, gold zipper decor, brilliant gold interior 450.00
Handel, mica, sgr 425.00
Imperial-Nuart
Cameo satin, floral border 35.00
Marigold 50.00
Lalique, 13″, crystal, molded ivy, sgr R. Lalique 585.00
Leaded, hanging dome type
11¾″ d, apple blossoms, green ground, rippled band top, bottom, sgd Tiffany Studios, New York 5,500.00
16″, Dogwood band, sgd Handel 1,000.00
23″, twelve green slag panels, brickwork beading, yellow, white Greek Key design 1,000.00
26″, six panels, small pcs of glass, each panel covered by bronze leaf clusters 2,000.00
Lundberg
7″ dome, blue green 200.00
10″ dome, blue, green for Handel floor lamp 275.00
Lustre Art
Blue hooked feather, opal ground, gold interior 230.00
Gold feathers, 5¼ x 2½″, opal ground, gold interior, bell shaped, sgr 165.00
Lily, gold, irid, c1920 . . . . 250.00
Muller Fres-Luneville, 8″, hanging mottled glass dome 125.00
New England, 7¾″ d x 4¾″ h, amberina, swirl ribbing, c1880 . . . 250.00
Quezal
Aurene, 4″, grown, applied border 350.00
Aurene, 9″, gold, bronze overlay, hall fixtures, pr 1,200.00
Calcite-type, gas fixtures, gold liner, sgr 125.00

Ivory, 6″ painted green leaves, all-over spider webbing 165.00
Optic Rib, 7 x 2¼″ fitter 250.00
Reverse painted, boudoir fixture, 10″ d, landscape, yellow, orange ground 175.00
Satin
Rainbow DQ, MOP, ruffled top, 5″ d 575.00
Rainbow DQ, MOP, ruffled top, marked PATENT 600.00
Steuben
Aurene, brown, gold leaf, vine, creamy ivory ground, gold interior, sgr, pr 1,375.00
Calcite, alcite etching 100.00
Dark green pulled feather on white, 6¼ d 150.00
DQ, short green feather 165.00
Ivorine, gold hearts, all over spider webbing, 4½″ h 145.00
Tiffany
Green satin finish, linen fold, 5⅜″ d 265.00
King Tut, 5″ h, green, opal, sgr . . 575.00
Stalactite, Faville, conical, transparent yellow glass, irid gold leaf, vine design, 14″ h 675.00

LAMPS AND LIGHTING

Lighting devices have evolved from simple stone age oil lamps to the popular electrified models of today. Aime' Argand patented the first oil lamp in 1784. Around 1850, kerosene became a popular lamp burning fluid, replacing whale oil and other fluids. In 1879, Thomas A. Edison invented the electric light bulb causing fluid lamps to become out of style. Many older fluid lamps have been electrified. A good source to study kerosene lamps is the Winchester Center Kerosene Lamp Museum in Winchester Center, Connecticut.

Also see specific makers and Pattern Glass Section.

AMERICAN, EARLY

Betty Lamps
3⅝″, wrought iron, hinged lid, sgd Montagne 165.00
4″, plus hanger, wrought iron, iron wick pick, small bird silhouette on font lid 300.00
4¼″, brass, tooled decor 85.00
7¾″, tin, lamp stand, deep dish base, crimped pan 135.00
9½″, tin, stand, wire pick, hanger 125.00
Chandeliers
3 lights, 23″ h, pierced tin, American, 18th C 950.00

6 lights, 17" h x 24" d, punched tin, 6 "S" curved arms with crimped drip pans, punched double conical center, riveted construction, late 19th C **3,400.00**

6 lights, 22½" h x 17" d, wrought iron, 6 arms with pricket sockets, primitive, late 19th C **200.00**

Crusies

6¼", wrought iron, double lamps, rams horn detail **65.00**

6⅜" 1 x 6" h, 5¾" 1 hook, wrought iron, single **120.00**

Fat, 3¾" w x 5" 1 x 2" h, PA pottery, boat shaped, wick holes in end and center **250.00**

Hanging

9½", torch, tin, 6 spouts around cylindrical font **175.00**

15", aqua, blown bell shaped globe, flared rim, applied knobs in tin crown frame, tooling, cut scallops, punching, traces of red paint **675.00**

Kettle

8⅜", tin, saucer base, tapered weight stem, cylindrical gimbal font, center wick support **185.00**

9½", wrought iron, round base, tubular wick support **310.00**

10½", wrought iron, brass feet, spherical font, whale oil burner, twisted stem and pick on chain   **180.00**

Lacemaker's, 16" h, cranberry overshot shade, polished brass base .   **375.00**

Miner's, 9" h, iron, brass chicken finial   **75.00**

Peg

5½" h, brass, acorn shaped wooden base **100.00**

14½" h, opal, matching Corinthian capital candlestick, brass collar, kerosene burner **165.00**

17" h x 6" d, yellow swirl overlay satin, emb, in holders, pr **1,250.00**

Redware, 5¾", saucer base, single spout font **265.00**

Rushlight Holders

8", wrought iron, soapstone base   **350.00**

11", wrought iron, primitive **215.00**

15¼", wrought iron, holder, candle socket, counter balance, ring base, primitive, European .   **150.00**

Skater's, 9" h, brass, PA, 1867 . . .   **185.00**

Sparking, 4", miniature lacy cup plate base, wine glass form, globular font **225.00**

Tin

5½" h, hand, acorn font, whale oil burner **160.00**

8½" l, pig, horizontal font, 3 burners, worn brown japanning . . .   **155.00**

Tole

4¾" h, child's, police type, turns to red or green shutters, orig finish **70.00**

7" h, saucer base, conical font, single spout burner, orig blue japanning **95.00**

7¾" 1 x 4" h, yellow, black striping, fat burner, French, 19th C .   **140.00**

Whale Oil

6¼", tin, saucer base, burner, dark brown japanning **150.00**

7", brass, ftd, lemon shaped font, double drop burner **200.00**

7⅜", pewter, double drop burner, Boston, c1840 . . . .   **225.00**

11⅛", clear, pressed base, blown pear shaped font, brass collar, burner **145.00**

CHANDELIERS

6 lights, 17" h x 17½" d, gilt bronze, 3 scrolling candle branches, 3 floriform lights above 3 putti busts, short chain, ceiling cap, French, c1900 . . . .   **1,500.00**

6 lights, 19" h, brass, baluster form standard above scrolled support, molded drip plates, candlecups, faceted pendant, 18th C **2,400.00**

8 lights, 26 x 34" d, gilt bronze, scrolling branches, 4 rams heads above, pendant from ceiling cap, short chain, French, late 19th C . .   **2,500.00**

8 lights, 45 x 28" d, ormolu, cut glass, Continental, late 19th C . . .   **1,400.00**

15 lights, 5'3" l, Louis XV style, gilt bronze, pear shaped cage cast with acanthus foliage, candle sockets, large facted drop, shaped cut glass prisms, electrified **6,100.00**

DESK

6½" d, leaded glass green shade, bronze base, overhanging style, sgd Handel **2,000.00**

15", oval dome, 2 purple-green irid turtleback medallions, 16 purple irid semiprecious stones imbedded in circular bronze base, imp Tiffany Studios, NY **4,500.00**

FLOOR

57¼" h, 12" d shade, bridge-type, leaded glass shade, Dore bronze base, sgd Tiffany Studios, c1900 .   **3,800.00**

60" h, 18" d shade, Aladdin, No. 1250 . . . .   **325.00**

61" h, 20" d shade, leaded glass, double standard base, sgd Handel   **3,600.00**

62" h, 20" d shade, Favrile glass shade, gilt base, Tiffany **8,500.00**

63" h, 21" d shade, green shaded leaded glass, bronze mounts, wrought iron stand **800.00**

71" h, 31" d shade, rose leaded glass dome, large crimson, red, white roses, white streaked green ground, green patinated metal base, 5 ball feet **8,500.00**

FLUID

4¾" d, brass, tin, wide flat saucer base, shallow font, kerosene burner, mkd Good Night, Pat June 1, 1869 . . . . **40.00**

7½", flint, Bull's Eye and Diamond, rope ring handle, base **100.00**

8", Blackberry pattern, Boston & Sandwich Glass Co **200.00**

8", Eugenie, figural base, Greek Key font **70.00**

8¼", swirled cranberry font with opposite swirls in opaque white, brass stem, marble base **225.00**

9¼", cobalt blue glass, brass collar **90.00**

9½", Acorn & Drapery, stepped pressed base, 3 ring knop, free blown font, cut and frosted pattern, pewter collar, New England Glass Co **200.00**

10", clear, circular foot, stem, brilliant gold amber molded oblong font fitted with later brass collar, camphene burner **725.00**

11", opaque blue and white, Acanthus Leaf, whale oil burner, sandy finish, Sandwich **700.00**

13", opaque white, Onion pattern, Sandwich, c1840 . . . . **650.00**

14¼", opaque, white cut to cranberry, milk glass double step pedestal base, gilt decor, 19th C **550.00**

14½", marriage, opaque white and blue, double fonts, Ripley & Co . . **475.00**

15½", Apollo, amber hobnail open top, scalloped edge shade **165.00**

HALL

7 x 7", Bradley & Hubbard, beveled glass, brass **250.00**

7½", tan slag panels in reticulated frame, Handel **800.00**

14", tin shade, emb brass font **350.00**

Pink satin glass shade, emb florals, swag decor, ceiling cap **500.00**

HANGING

14" d, plated amberina shade, swirled, ribbed, prisms, brass fittings **5,500.00**

15", Mount Washington peachblow hobnail shade, prisms, brass font, fittings **1,000.00**

16½", domical, pattern of small radial marbled medallions in ochre, 3 suspension hooks, imp Tiffany Studios, NY **4,000.00**

PERFUME

4¾", Galle, red acorns and leaves on gold ground, three cuttings, fire polished, bronze ftd base, finial . . **1,500.00**

7½" h, Steuben, gold drag loop on ivorene, gilt bronze base, sgd Devilbiss **650.00**

STUDENT

11¾", brass, miniature, green enameled ribbed shade, orig burner, emb Tiny Miller **120.00**

20", brass, double, peachblow shades, rope twist brass wire coil decor, electrified **500.00**

20¼", brass, peacock blue reservoir marked Perfection Student Lamp Pat Nov. 22, '81, dark green cased shade, folded top rim, electrified **225.00**

24", emb brass base, opaque white shade, electrified **450.00**

24", tin plated brass, milk glass shade **400.00**

40" l 10" d shades, double, hanging, cased green shades, burnished brass, electrified **1,250.00**

TABLE

Argand

13", brass, cast detail, orig finish, gilt, dark patina, shades missing, pr **160.00**

31½", brass, stepped scalloped base, reeded column and flat spherical font, clear cut and frosted shade, prisms **265.00**

Art Deco, girl sitting over green art glass globe **160.00**

Art Nouveau, 19" h, 10" square shade, 4 large angled mottled green and opaque white glass panels, 4 panel collar, pewter colored stem, bronze finish base . . . **135.00**

Astral, gold ormolu stem, cut glass globe, marble base, dated 1870 . . **415.00**

Banquet, 25" h, sq marble base, classical fluted column, Corinthian capital, font labeled Cornelius and Co., Phila, Pat April 1, 1845, prism band, 7 large cut prisms, cut frosted shade with copper wheel engraved foliage, burner missing ... **275.00**

Boudoir

13″ h, Pairpoint, reverse decor floral mottled shade, marked # C3093 .... **475.00**

14″ h, 7″ d shade, Venetian scenic shade sgd Handel #592S, ornate sgd base **600.00**

Bradley & Hubbard

22½″ h, 18″ shade, eight reverse painted panels, bronze base .. **300.00**

23½″ h, 18″ shade, leaded shade, lily decor, ftd base decor in lily pads, flowers **380.00**

Bronze

16½″ h, gun carrying Arab, seated on oriental rug under draped canopy, cold painted, inscribed cast from model by Franz Bergmann **1,000.00**

22″ h, 17½″ shade, bronze base marked Classique, reverse painted shade decor with lovebirds, butterflies **2,500.00**

Cameo Glass, 21½″, trumpet shaped base, dome shade of transluscent yellow glass etched in stylized leaves, Daum Nancy France etched on shade, base .. **3,600.00**

Fulper, inlaid slag glass on green pottery shade, base of green, brown streaked glazed pottery, c1900 .... **625.00**

Galle

5½″ h, wrought iron on marble base, red butterflies **1,650.00**

24″ h, triple overlay, trumpet shaped base, conical shade of transluscent yellow glass overlaid in sapphire, lavendar, brown, etched with azalea, cameo sgr Galle **7,250.00**

Gone With The Wind, shade, base decor with young Indian warrior returning from hunting with game . **1,100.00**

24″, red satin, spelter base, brass burner, fittings **800.00**

29″, DQ, orange satin **750.00**

Pillar & chain, red satin **500.00**

Handel

20″ h, 14½″ d shade, leaded, shade of smoky amber, ruby diamonds around rim, gold, bronze finished metal base, sgr on shade **600.00**

22½″ h, 14″ d shade, frosted, reverse painted sunset landscape umbrella shade, bronzed white metal base, sgr **400.00**

24¼″ h, 17½″ d shade, reverse painted, frosted shade, bronze base, sgr **1,000.00**

Table, Galle, 31″ h, conical shade, trumpet shaped base of translucent yellow glass overlaid in yellow-orange, lime green, and brown, etched with oranges, branches, leaves, cameo sgr., $24,200.00.

Jefferson

21″ h, 16⅛″ d shade, painted in foliage, florals on interior of shade, apricot ground, black finished metal base, sgr **625.00**

22½″ h, 13¾″ d shade, reverse painted, electrified, sgr **600.00**

Leaded Glass

17″ h, octagonal shade, spray of daffodils on purple ground, blue ribbon border, gilt, 2 light boudoir base **1,150.00**

20″, red ribbons, green roping, white panels, bronze base, sgd Duffner & Kimberly **2,800.00**

Muller Les Lundeville, 17¾″, triple overlay, dome shade, base overlaid in deep blue, green, peach, off-white depicting mounting, lake scene, cameo sgr **3,600.00**

Pairpoint

12″ h, 4 panel shade, bronze finish base mkd Pairpoint B3071 . **350.00**

15″ h, puffy, shade decor in pink roses, green leaves, shade, base sgd #C3024 .... **2,400.00**

18″ h, 10″ d shade, floral, puffy reverse painted shade, molded, painted yellow centered fuchsia flowers, green leaves, stamped Pairpoint Corp., red painted metal flower pot base imp

Pairpoint Mf'g Co. P3069, Pat Apl'd For	**2,900.00**
22½" h, 18" d shade, reverse painted, flared cylindrical shade of violet brown trees on blue ground, painted C. Durand sgr, silvered metal base of ornate 4 section column, sgd D3084 P Pairpoint	**1,450.00**
Reverse Painted Shade 21½" h, 17" d shade, snow scene, frosted black metal base with gold, red, green highlights	**325.00**
Tiffany	
17" h, green and gold Damascus stretched shade, gold reactive chimney, gold base, green feather reactive riser, kerosene burner, sgd	**2,500.00**
20" h, 4 gold lustre morning glory type shapes, all sgd L.C.T. Favrille, bronze base, 3 inverted stems, 1 upright, base imp Tiffany Studios	**5,000.00**
24" h, candle, DQ reactive glass, gold feather shade, Queen Anne's Lace bronze base, sgd .	**2,000.00**

529-I, cased, pink, white candy stripe, 7¾" h, $715.00.

LAMPS, MINIATURE

Miniature oil and kerosene lamps, often called "night lamps," are diminutive replicas of larger lamps; they may measure as high as 12" or as small as 2½". Simple and utilitarian in design, these lamps were used primarily as "night lamps" and also in the parlor as "courting lamps" and in sickrooms.

During the Victorian period, beautiful fine art glass shades were introduced in miniatures.

Though elaborate in decor, small glass lamps were simply constructed of several separate parts—base, collar, burner, chimney and shade. A careful study of these individual parts can help determine the age of the lamp, country or origin and also if the miniature is all original or had certain parts replaced.

Note: **Figure numbers refer to illustration figure number in the following books: #I, "Miniature Lamps" by Frank R. and Ruth E. Smith; #II, "Miniature Lamps-II" by Ruth E. Smith. Both of these books are excellent reference books on this subject.**

Caution: **Many reproductions exist.**

7-I, Santa Claus, 9½", scarlet, black milk glass	**1,700.00**
16-II, Jeweler's, cobalt blue	**45.00**
20-I, Improved Banner, milk glass .	**85.00**
26-II, Herringbone ribbed, blue glass	**130.00**
29-I, Nutmeg, green crystal	**170.00**
32-I, Little Duchess, blue crystal . . .	**145.00**
36-I, green	**170.00**
63-II, pink opaline, milk glass, applied handle	**245.00**
81-II, melon ribbed milk glass	**135.00**
88-II, blue glass pedestal base	**65.00**
97-I, jeweled shade, brass	**100.00**
106-I, amber, Octavia	**125.00**
121-I, acron opal	**130.00**
128-I, milk glass, pewter base	**150.00**
156-I, Flowers and Scrolls	**125.00**
169-I, Grecian Key, clear	**85.00**
179-I, milk glass	**135.00**
188-I, milk glass, Torquay pattern . .	**245.00**
191-I, Block & Dot	**115.00**
196-I, Embossed Rims	**200.00**
199-II, emb trademark, finger lamp .	**100.00**
208-I, emb flowers, milk glass	**175.00**
214-I, Maltese Cross	**160.00**
219-I, by Dithridge	**195.00**
224-II, Countess by Cambridge Glass	**130.00**
241-I, blue milk glass	**325.00**
257-I, custard glass	**300.00**
286-I, yellow band, milk glass	**295.00**
301-II, double brass student lamp .	**625.00**
329-II, porcelain elephant	**865.00**
338-I, milk glass, porcelain	**150.00**
387-II, white metal, boudoir lamp . .	**140.00**
432-I, true green	**285.00**
439-I, cranberry	**425.00**
482-I, clear	**200.00**
497-II, Nellie Bly, amber glass	**175.00**

545-II, goofus stem	145.00
550-II, cased end of day glass	775.00
549-I, millefiore	775.00
625-I, glow lamp, milk glass	85.00

LANTERNS

A lantern is an enclosed, portable light source, hand carried or attached to a bracket or pole to illuminate an area. It allegedly derived its name from early times when candles were placed in thin animal horns and were called "Lantern Horns." They were developed into portable lighting devices with glass sides or chimneys as we know them today.

Barn, Dietz No. 2, Blizzard, clear
globe, bail 45.00
Buggy, Rayo No. 80, unmarked
globe, Pat April 10, 1906, brass
burner cone 60.00
Campaign
  35" h, tin, cast iron base made to
    accomodate a 2¾" pole, glass
    damaged 135.00
  66" l, wooden pole in long rifle
    form, cast iron and tin fittings,
    tin font 325.00
Candle
  9", wooden, reeded posts, remov-
    able tin socket 170.00
  11½", tin, hinged door, shaped
    top 75.00

Dietz, No. 30, $50.00.

11½", tin, 7 glass panels, pierced
air holes in base, hinged top .. 125.00
11¾", tin semi-cylindrical, sliding
glass front, hinged door in back 90.00
Coach, 7" h, tin, brass mounting
bracket, red front lens, clear side
lens, marked Duntafil Patent 35.00
Carriage, 34½", painted metal, ornate trim, eagle finial, 6 beveled
glass panes 365.00
Kerosene
  10¼", tin, 4 glass sides, 1 sliding
    panel, removable font, burner,
    pierced top 95.00
  12", tin, clear blown spherical
    globe, applied crimped orna-
    mentation, traces of orig blue ja-
    panning, ring handle, burner
    missing 180.00
  18", tin, reflector, tubular base for
    mounting on top of pole, orig
    globe marked HAM, font
    marked C.I. HAM Mfg Co., No.
    2, worn black paint 40.00
  21", tin, Dietz Tubular Square
    Lamp No. 2, one orig glass, an-
    other cracked, third missing,
    mercury glass reflector 200.00
Ship
  14", brass, round, 5 glass panels,
    hinged top, removable kerosene
    burner 65.00
  22", brass, mast flat back, 3 sides
    bull's eye lens, clear front, red
    on right, green on left, hinged
    door in back 135.00
Skater's
  Red globe, marked Dietz Sport .. 45.00
  Small, tin 35.00
Wagon, tin, square red lens, orig oil
burner 35.00
Watchman's, 6", tin, whale oil burn-
er, c1850 .... 48.00

LEEDS CHINA

The Leeds Pottery in Yorkshire, England, began production about 1758. It made among other things, creamware that was competitive with Wedgwoods. The factory there closed in 1820, but continued under various owners until about 1880. They made exceptional cream colored ware, either plain or salt-glazed, or painted with colored enamels, and glazed and unglazed redware.

Early wares are unmarked, but later pieces bear marks of "Leeds Pottery" sometimes followed by "Hartley-Green and Co." or the

letters "LP." Reproductions may also bear these marks. It is beautiful ware and eagerly sought in the antique market today.

Platter, lady, sheep, Faith in border, $500.00.

Basket, bulbous, scalloped rim, open
work, twig handles **175.00**
Bowls
  Oval, reticulated, footed **150.00**
  11½ x 8¾", vegetable, oval, cut
    corners, blue feathered edge . .   **195.00**
  13", creamware, plain **200.00**
Chestnut Bowl, creamware, 1790–
1800 . . . .   **750.00**
Creamer, 5¼", flowers, leaves,
swags, blue, orange yellow **165.00**
Cup Plate, 4½" d, blue feather edge   **60.00**
Cups and Saucers
  Handleless, enameled 3 color flo-
    ral, miniature **115.00**
  Three color decor, miniature size   **105.00**
Jugs
  8", 3 Masonic panels, fluted base
    band, threaded band on neck .   **400.00**
  11¼", orange rope handle and
    rim, green and orange floral
    band decor, c1820 . . . .   **500.00**
Pitchers
  7½", jug shape, 6 sides, variegat-
    ed tans polychrome, flower
    buds of yellow, orange, black,
    gold, open flower in center,
    buds on reverse, gold base rim,
    sgd. Leeds, Wilton, England . .   **475.00**
  8½" Stoneware, creamy beige
    with incised bamboo leaves, ter-
    ra cotta borders, original pewter
    cover, Leed Burmantofts, c1182   **500.00**
Plates
  5", strawberry center, orange,
    green, brown, blue border **90.00**
  7⅛", green molded feather edge,
    4-color gaudy decor **295.00**
  8", American Eagle and Shield,
    blue feather edge, blue, brown,
    orange, green decor **395.00**

  8¼", blue feather edge, with ea-
    gle and 13 stars, 4-color **475.00**
  9¾", blue feather edge, ochre flo-
    ral design **155.00**
  10", tassel, shell, floral border,
    green feather edge **180.00**
Platters
  5 x 4", blue, brown, orange, green
    floral **280.00**
  15", blue feather edge **100.00**
  16½", blue feather edge **150.00**
Sauce Boat, creamware, silver
shape, with entwined strap han-
dle, and floral terminals, c1785 . .   **275.00**
Soup Plate, blue feather edge **95.00**
Sugar bowl, cov, 7" Gaudy decor,
blues, green decor **100.00**
Teapots
  4¾" h, Pearlware, painted blue
    Chinese scenes **425.00**
  5", octagon shape, white with
    embossed feathers, c1780 . . .   **400.00**
Tea Set, pearlware, silver resist,
trailing flowers, borders of foliage,
berries, molded arches, finials,
oval teapot, cov, sugar, cov, milk
jug, slop bowl, plate, 10 teabowls,
10 saucers, some pcs damaged . .   **1,500.00**
Tea Strainer, Blue Willow pattern,
c1800 . . . .   **100.00**
Tray, 8¾", oval, reticulated loop rim,
brown feather edge **145.00**

LENOX CHINA

Jonathan Cox and Walter Scott Lenox established The Ceramic Art Company, Trenton, N.
J., in 1889. The factory was best known for
its American Belleek. In 1906, the factory became the Lenox Co., and they made quality
American porcelain.

Two marks appear on Lenox China, the
'pallette' mark, and a 'green wreath.' The 'pallette' mark appears on many pieces of hand
painted china, which was supplied in great
quantity when it was the vogue for amateur
hand painting of china, as a hobby. The company is still in existance today and the current mark is stamped in gold.

Bouillon cup, SS holder, 2 handles .   **60.00**
Bowl, 12½" l, flower, oval, molded
as curled leaf, stem, bud form
handle, ivory **55.00**
Box, 6¾" h, coral pink cover, bird
finial, white base **175.00**
Candlestick, 8" **75.00**

Creamer Lenox, 2¾" h and sugar, 4" h, sterling lily of the valley decor on tobacco brown ground, monogram, $95.00.

Candy dish, 3", silver overlay	35.00
Cups and Saucers	
Peachtree pattern, 1948	35.00
Rose Pattern	35.00
Flower holder, 8½", 4 branch extensions attached to bulbous round base	95.00
Honey Pot, bee finial, gold bees on white background, marked	60.00
Lamp base, 10½", brown stylized flowers, light blue ground	120.00
Mug, Monk decor, blue ground	70.00
Plates	
8½", square, Ming pattern	12.00
9¼", Peachtree pattern	18.00
Ramekin, underplate, ivory, gold trim, sterling holder, green wreath mark	28.00
Salt, shape of swan, white, with matching spoon, green wreath mark	40.00
Tea Set, Architects', teapot, cov, creamer, sugar, wastebowl, 12 cups, 12 saucers, 12 dessert plates, all trimmed in copper lustre, dove finials, Great Seal of US on sides of creamer, bowl, rest decor in Colonial scenes, commissioned in 1933	750.00
Urns, 9½", ivory, pedestal base, sgd., pr	75.00
Vases	
4½", Horn of Plenty, coral, gold rim, green wreath mark	32.00
6", bud, fluted base, top gilt, Rotary seal, green wreath mark . . .	24.00

LIBBEY GLASS

In 1888, the New England Glass Works, W. L. Libbey and Son, Proprietors, E. Cambridge, Mass, closed and Edward Libbey established

the Libbey Glass Company in Toledo, Ohio. The firm produced quality cut glass for the "Brilliant Period." In 1930, Libbey's interest in art glass production was renewed. A. Douglas Nash was employed as a designer. Perhaps his "Animal Fair" stemware is best known. The factory continues production today as Libbey Glass Co.

See also: CUT GLASS, AMBERINA GLASS and MAIZE (Colored Pattern Glass).

Fruit Bowl Libbey Glass, 4½" h x 14" d, Hardy & Hayes, sterling silver rim, signed Libbey in circle, $350.00.

Bowls	
7½", shallow, cut, sgr	100.00
9", 2" h, Glenda pattern, sgr . . .	325.00
Butter Dish, Gloria pattern	525.00
Candlestick, 10" h, 4" d, foot intaglio cut floral on stem teardrop stem tapers to ⅜" at bottom . . .	105.00
Champagne glasses, opalescent, squirrel stems, 4 pcs	250.00
Celery tray, 11", brilliant cut glass, sgr	75.00
Creamer and Sugar, brilliant cut, Venetian pattern, pr	155.00
Ice cream Dish, 8" d, scalloped edge, hobnail, sgr	160.00
Sugar Castor, Maize, amber and gold leaf decor	85.00
Wine glass, Kangaroo, opalescent, sgr	60.00

LIMOGES

Limoges porcelain has been produced in Limoges, France, for over a century by numerous factories other than the famed Haviland. One of the most frequently encountered marks is "T. & V. Limoges" which is the ware made by Tressman and Vought. Other identifiable Limoges marks are A.L. (A. Lanternier),

J.P.L. (J. Pouyat, Limoges), M.R. (M. Reddon), Elite and Coronet.
See also HAVILAND CHINA.

Limoges leaf dish, 11⅞″ w, light blue flowers, gold decor, green mark stamped D&C/France, $45.00.

Basket, 8 l x 5″ w, gold emb design and beading, floral design, gold handle, "W" in wreath mark, J.P.L. France 145.00
Bowl and underplate, 9½″ and 11½″, emb gilt, irregular rims; pink, lavender, yellow and orange carnations, white background, T. & V. Limoges 290.00
Cachepot, 7 x 5½″ d, applied handles, knob feet, hp birds, blue ground, W G & Co, Limoges, France 115.00
Candlesticks, 9″, hp berries, flowers, foliage, gold trim, artist sgd, pr . . 75.00
Charger, 13¼″, portrait, girl, lavender and blue, gold trim, shaped rim, artist sgd R. Comby 225.00
Chocolate Set, flared pot, 6 straight cups, 6 saucers, white with small border of green, rose and gold trim 135.00
Cider Set, pitcher, underplate, 3 tumblers, roses decor, T. & V. 120.00
Coffee Set, 12″ pitcher, 6 cups and saucers, pearlized, cobalt blue and gold, light blue bands, gold handles, sgd 479.00
Cream and Sugar, cov, hp violets, gold handles, set 45.00
Cups and Saucers
  Coffee, 8 oz., hp flowers, leaves; gold trim, sgd A. Taylor 65.00
  Demitasse, white, pink and white-trailing flowers, gold edges, gold twig handles 25.00
Dinner Set, floral, pink roses, gray-green leaves and vines, emb irreg-

ular edges; service for 12, 3-size platters, 4 covered turreens, butter pats, bone dishes, open vegetables, (no cups & saucers) A. Lanternier 2,500.00
Diptych, 12¼ x 19″, bishops within architectural setting, 19th C 1,250.00
Dresser Sets
  3 pcs, hp violets, gold trim 100.00
  6 pcs, white, gold and cobalt flowers, gold trim 175.00
Fernery, hp, autumn leaves 65.00
Fish Set, 24″ platter, 6 plates, lemon yellow, gold trim, scalloped, each with different sea shells and marine life 380.00
Game Plate, 13½″, snipes center, gold border, artist sgd 165.00
Gravy Boat with attached underplate, 8½″, oval, white, gold rims and handle, marked 35.00
Hatpin Holder, purple violets decor . 75.00
Inkwell, floral decor, gold trim 25.00
Mug, 6″, hp grapes, gold serpent handle, J.P.L. 60.00
Oyster Plate, 9″, sea shells, oysters, star fish, etc 95.00
Pitchers
  7¾″, bulbous, hp berry decor, gold trim 150.00
  12″, tankard, hp currants, gold trim, J.P.L. 200.00
  13½″, tankard, monk pouring wine, artist signed 275.00
Plaque, 7½ x 5½″, maiden holding dagger and shield, framed, sgd Dorval, late 19th C 1,100.00
Plates
  10″, asparagus, molded asparagus separate well, irregular gold rims. D & C; set of 6 . . . . 225.00
  10″, hp portrait, sgd Dubois 135.00
  10″, kitten, playing, butterfly decor, artist sgd, coronet 55.00
  12″, scalloped, pierced for hanging, pastel colors, man and lady, gold border, marked Limoges . . 225.00
Punch Bowl, 14″, 9″ high; grape decor interior, portrait medallions on exterior, heavy rococo gold trim, T.V., 2 pcs 500.00
Punch Cup, hp grape motif, set of 6 180.00
Ring Tree, 3 x 3½″, pink flowers, sgd Limoges, France 28.00
Tankard, 13½″, white, hp, 5 birds, black & gold, heavy gold handle, sgd J.P. Limoges 235.00
Tea Set, hp pink roses, gold trim, T & V, 3 pcs 125.00
Tray, 14″, narcissus decor, heavy gold trim, artist sgd, c1900–1920 . 120.00
Tureen, cov, 8 x 16″ oval, rose decor, gold and green bands 175.00

Urn, cov, 29½", green and gilt, bronze mounts, center portrait reserve of Marie Antoinette, late 19th C 800.00

Vases

7", hp floral decor, gold handles and trim, J.P.L. France 130.00

12", straight sided, applied gold handles, hp roses, green leaves, Old Abbey Limoges . . . 220.00

LITHOPHANES

Lithophanes are highly translucent porcelain panels with impressed designs. The design is formed by the difference in thickness of the plaque. Thin parts transmit an abundance of light while thicker parts represent shadows. They were first made by the Royal Berlin Porcelain Works in 1828. Other factories in Germany, France and England later produced the items. The majority on the market today were probably made between 1850 and 1900. Be careful of reproductions!

Plaque, unmarked, 5¼ x 4¼", impressed 1308/52, c1860, $125.00.

Candle Shield, brass, frame with alternating circles and spear points, octagonal shaped leaf motif base, panel of 2 children playing in woods 400.00

Dish, 7" d, scallop shell shape, cathedral scene center 60.00

Fairy Lamp, 4 panels, one pc top . . 375.00

Lamps

Hanging Type, 4 panels, 4 x 6", brass frame 875.00

Table, metal, 19", sq plinth base, rococo urn on standard, 6 panels, rural scenes, KPM 1,000.00

Lamp Shade, 4", 4 panels, children's scene 300.00

Matchbox, girl watching boats 100.00

Mug, 4½", butterfly, floral, family scene 85.00

Night Light, 1 pc cylindrical panel in holder, cast metal legs 350.00

Plaques

KPM

2½ x 3¼", view from West Point 165.00

3 x 4", Couple and dog, woodland scene 200.00

3¼ x 4¼", dog flushing bird . . 250.00

4⅝" x 6¼", Rheinstein, colored 310.00

6 x 7½", girl with rose 265.00

PPM

3⅞ x 6⅜", sailboat, barge beside windmill 165.00

5¼ x 4¼", biblical scene of young shepherd bowing to elderly gentleman accompanied by lovely daughter 130.00

P. R. Sickle, 4⅛ x 5¹/₁₀"

Cupid and girl fishing 165.00

Monk and girl 150.00

Woman gazing at sea 175.00

Woman in flowing robe 165.00

Unmarked

4½ x 5¼", two girls visiting across fence, sheep, trees, mountains in background . . . 145.00

5⅛ x 6½", majestic cathedral, all white 185.00

6 x 6¾", Scheherazade, framed 385.00

Steins

Floral front, soldier bidding farewell on back, ½ liter 135.00

Military, train on cover 120.00

Tea Warmer, 5½" h, 4 panels of children and animals, pressed glass base 475.00

Toddy Warmer, 4 colored panels, tin frame 235.00

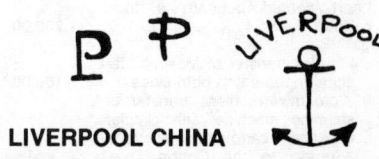

LIVERPOOL CHINA

Liverpool is the name given to products made at several potteries in Liverpool, En-

gland, from 1750 to 1840. Among the early producers were Seth and James Pennington and Richard Chaffers who made tin-enamelled earthenwares. By the 1780s, the tin glazed earthenwares gave way to cream colored wares decorated with cobalt, enamel colors, or blue or black transfers. These are the Liverpool pieces one is most likely to encounter on the market today.

The Liverpool glaze is characterized by bubbles and most often there is clouding under the foot rims. Although the late 18th century black transfer bowls and pitchers (many of historic interest) are eagerly collected, they are only a small part of the total Liverpool production. By the turn of the century, about 80 potteries were working in the town producing not only cream ware, but soft paste, soapstone and bone procelain.

Liverpool China, Jug, 6⅝" h, Commodore Prebler Squadron Attacking the City of Tripoli, Aug. 3, 1804, $100.00.

Bowl, 8¼", blue underglaze, overglaze of iron red, green, gilding, scene of houses on wooded river islands, c1770 . . . . 400.00
Charger, 13⅜", shades of blue, manganese, green, yellow, gentleman doffing his hat to his sweetheart seated beneath a tree, c1760 . . . . 1,200.00
Jugs
5¼", pink transfer of Masonic designs repeated on both sides . 100.00
9", creamware, black transfer of spinning machine with circular crowned cartouche inscribed "Sucess to the Cotton Tree, Sucess to the Friendly Association of Cotton Spinners and

Sucess to Commerce," (sic.) ribbons, wreaths of oak branches, roses, palm branches 600.00
10", polychrome decor of Masonic arms symbols, "John & Ellen Hutchinson/1823" 300.00
Mug, 4⅝", Black transfer of ship's arms, "Success to the Ship's Trade, Industry Procureth Wealth," polychrome enameling . 105.00
Plates
8⅜", blue, white, figure seated beneath flowering tree, 4 leaf-shaped floral panels, orange edge rim 150.00
10¾", polychrome, 3 figures on terrace by a pagoda, russet edge, shaped floral panels, c1760 . . . . 500.00
Pitcher, 11", colored marine scenes 275.00

LOETZ GLASS

Loetz is a type of iridescent art glass made in Austria by J. Loetz Witwe in the late 1890s. Loetz was a contemporary of L. C. Tiffany and worked in the Tiffany factory before establishing his own operation. Therefore, much of the wares are similar in appearance to Tiffany's. Some pieces are signed "Loetz," "Loetz, Austria," or "Austria." The Loetz factory also produced ware with fine cameo effects on cased glass.

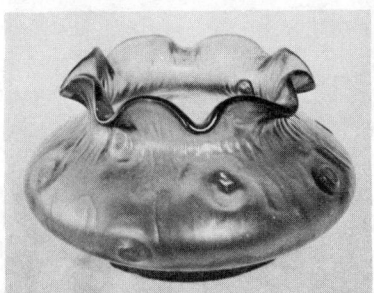

Bowl, 3½ x 6½" d, irid green, unsigned, $165.00.

Basket, irid blue with silver threading, coin spots, brass holder 365.00
Biscuit Jar, cobalt blue irid crackle with amethyst irid highlights, SP bail and lid 330.00
Bowls
7 x 9" d, globular, irid green, free

flowing horizontal irid blue threading	325.00
10", red with purple-green irid, fluted sides	300.00
Centerpiece, 8 x 10½" d, irid green ruffled bowl with overall points, 3 legged metal stud, ground pontil, Austria, c1900	160.00
Inkwell, 3", square, pinched corners, random threads on irid blue with inserts	170.00
Perfume Atomizer, red, swirling frosted vines	60.00
Pitcher, 9", pinch-sided, silver color	200.00
Rose Bowl, 6½", purple irid raindrop decor, ruffled	185.00
Sweetmeat Jar, irid green, spider web design, bail handle with lid . .	475.00
Vases	
4¼", red irid, SS overlay, Austria, c1895	325.00
4½", deep blue, lavender highlights, white enamel flowers . .	250.00
5½", cylindrical, irid purple, blue oil spotted design	450.00
5½", irid, pink and green highlights, top rim pulled into points, allover dimpled twists	225.00
7¼", amber with blue and gold irid, pinched top	120.00
7½", blue and green, irid oil spots, pierced brass collar with banners, eagles and drapes . .	95.00
7½", bulbous, emerald green, threading, sgd Loetz, Austria . .	475.00
12", Art Nouveau shape, irid blue, lavender and green highlights .	500.00
12", red, opal feathers, yellow rain drops, Austria, c1900	400.00
13", tapering, dimpled base, cupped rim, pale peach, yellow waves, 4 brown feathered spiraling bands	250.00

LOTUS WARE CHINA

Lotus Ware, one of the most sought American ceramics in today's antique market, was made by Knowles, Taylor and Knowles Co. of East Liverpool, Ohio, between 1891 and 1898.

A china as translucent and as thinly potted as Belleek, it was first marked "KTK" China. In 1893, after being exhibited at the World's Columbian Exposition at Chicago, it was christened Lotus Ware, by Col. John T. Taylor, who was then president of the company. He so named it because of the body's resem- blance to the petals of the lotus blossom. This was made at the time when China painting was the rage among club women, and pieces were sold from the factory plain and decorated. Pieces of Lotus Ware are hard to find today, and when found, are quite expensive.

Vase, 8", cream with green, blue violet and gold insect, $675.00.

Biscuit Jar, 6¾", cov, pale blue background, ivory panels, red and blue flowers, heavy gold leaves and vines, fish net slip in alternate panels, Lotus mark	300.00
Bowls	
4 x 5 x 6½", gold florals, ornate top, open handles	225.00
7½", boat shaped pink and gold openwork, cherry blossoms, KTK	475.00
Chocolate Pot, handpainted sunflowers	395.00
Cookie Jar, white, blackberry decor	410.00
Creamer, 3¾", white, gold fish net decor, florals	300.00
Cuspidor, ftd, pink flowers, gold trim on pale green background	300.00
Ewer, 7½", paneled in pastels, pierced and jewelled, sgn Lotus mark	495.00
Pitchers	
3½", with fish net or slip decor, signed	350.00
4¾", white, fish net decor	215.00
5", squatty, wild roses and leaf decor	300.00
Potpourri, white, open filigree handles, lid, pale green border on lid	650.00
Sugar, 4 x 6", wide at handles, feather, KTK	300.00
Tea Set, blue hp flowers, gold fishnet, 3 pieces	650.00

Vases

4¾", gold open work decor, gold raised pink floral, leaves, gold beaded top 600.00

6", applied white floral decor, olive green ground 850.00

10¼", applied white floral decor, dark green ground, marked Lotus, KTK 1,000.00

10½", white, pale green applied floral decor, handles 1,450.00

LUTZ TYPE GLASS

Lutz is an art glass attributed to Nicholas Lutz while he worked at the Boston and Sandwich Co., 1869–1888. Two distinct types of glass have been associated with his name, striped glass and threaded glass. The striped glass was made by using threaded glass rods in the Venetian manner. Threaded glass was blown and decorated by winding threads of glass around the piece. After the Boston and Sandwich Co. closed, Lutz worked for the Mt. Washington Glass Co. and later for the Union Glass Works.

Since this type of glass was popular and there were many capable glass makers it is nearly impossible to distinguish actual Lutz products. They are not signed.

See also THREADED GLASS and VENETIAN GLASS

Finger bowl, Lutz Type Glass, white decor, baby face clear handles, red rim, 5″ d, 2⅜″ h, $265.00.

Barber bottle, 8", threaded latticino, opaque stripes 195.00

Finger Bowl, 4½ x 2¾" h, 6¾" underplate, clear glass, aquamarine twist bands, gold borders . . . 100.00

Plate, 6¼", goldstone, threaded, rose center shading into amber body, ruffled rim 80.00

Syrup, blue, white stripes, frosted handle 90.00

Tumbler, 7", clear, cranberry threading 60.00

Vase, 8", latticino, applied handle . 130.00

MAASTRICHT WARE

Maastricht ware was made in Holland from about 1835 to near the end of the 19th century. English workmen and methods were employed. The pottery was named De Sphinx and produced ironstone with transfer prints. The product found a ready market in the United States and sold in competition with the English ware of the period.

Plate, Maastricht Ware, 7¾", marked Made in Holland/Society Ceramique Potiche, $10.00.

Bowls

4½" and 6¼", Chinese shape, cereal or rice, (fit into each other) flowing blue on pale blue background, rose or tulip, feather design on interior rim, marked "Maastricht-Regout-Holland," pair 30.00

6" x 3" h, white ground, marked Vlinder 30.00

6⅛" x 3⅛" h, Hong pattern, marked Maastricht Petrus Regoulec Co, made in Holland . . 60.00

Black and tan transfer on white, Pajong pattern 25.00

Coffee Pot, cov, blue, white decor . 60.00

Cups and Saucers

Blue floral on cream background 13.50

Handleless, deep saucer, flowing

blue on pale blue background, rose or tulip, feather design inside cup, marked "Maastricht-Regout, Holland" **18.50**
Pitcher, 4½", oriental scene, Timor sgr **65.00**
Plate
7½", Hong pattern, light blue . . . **18.00**
8¼", abbey scene, light blue . . . **15.00**
8¼", apples on green background **15.00**
Sauce Dish, 5" d **5.00**
Saucer, 5¾", ribbed, semi-circular raised garlands at top, marked Society Ceramique Potiche **3.00**

MAJOLICA

Majolica is tin-enameled glazed pottery and has been produced by many countries for centuries. It originally took its name from the island of Majorca, where figuline (a potter's clay) is found. The company of Griffin, Smith and Hill (G. S. H.), in Phoenixville, Pa. made this ware in the Victorian era, and while not the earliest manufacturer in the United States, is the most popular and sought-after type today. Their pieces are usually marked "Etruscan" and "G. S. H." in a circle. In 1880, this ware was given away as premium by a large tea company. Most Majolica found today is of 19th or 20th century manufacture.

Ash Tray, black boy, accordian . . . **38.00**
Bank, boy, blue turban, brown face **65.00**
Basket, 14 x 17", green, pink shell & seaweed, applied roses, double twig handles, ftd **210.00**
Biscuit Jar, cov, wicker handle attaches to knobs on side, mottled green basketweave, red apples, green leaves **58.00**
Bowls
8 x 8½", rect, tray-like, yellow, all over basketweave, pink flowers, green leaves, cinched, fluted sides in center **68.00**
9" d, ftd, strawberry leaves, flowers **85.00**
10½", shallow, turquoise, sea anome, green, brown, deep blue stems **90.00**
Card Holder, girl, sheep **70.00**
Creamer, 4½", butterfly spout, raised flowers, leaves, lavender interior, Etruscan mk **45.00**
Creamer and Sugar, 2¼" creamer, 3½" sugar, bird on branch, basketweave, banboo handles, pink interior **68.00**
Cup and Saucer, 5¼" d, floral, brown, small, yellow flowers,

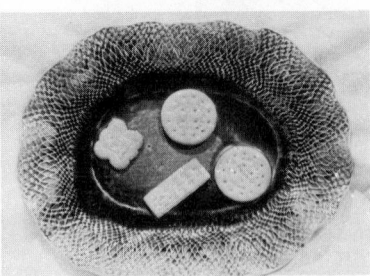

Platter, 12", trompe l'oeil, green, bisque crackers, marked "Bretby/England/1146/R 305509", $275.00.

green leaves, yellow handle, aqua interior **78.00**
Cuspidor, 6½", brown, aqua fan, pink flower, pink interior **150.00**
Dish, 6", strawberry, pink, green leaves, white flowers, Minton . . . **70.00**
Ewer, bulbous, French faience, hp, Gien castle mk of 1864 . . . . **90.00**
Liquor Set, heart shape decanter, 6 small handleless cups and tray, German barnyard scenes, trees in vibrant yellows and blacks mkd Majolica, Schramberg, Handgemalt **125.00**
Match Safe, fat chef, 8", figural, standing near kitchen stove hood, pot for matches on stove **125.00**
Mug, 3¾", brown, picket fence, white flower, green leaves, aqua interior **45.00**
Pitchers
5¾", sitting monkey, green leaves on his back, branch handle, greens and browns, deep pink interior **110.00**
7½", brown bark, large green and yellow leaf on both sides **70.00**
8", sq top, brown, yellow fret pattern top, basketweave base, magenta five petaled flower and buds, green leaves **60.00**
8", figural, pug dog, brown and black, dark red collar, pink lining **68.00**
9½", figural rooster, pours through bill, opening in back, colorful handle **68.00**
Plaque, 9½" d, scenic, chalet, trees, etc., Zell **40.00**
Plates
5½", water lily, tortoise shell center **95.00**
8½", 2 parrots on a branch **45.00**

9", tan basketweave, pink and
white flowers, grapes, green
leaves **58.00**
9¼", brown, basketweave and
blackberries **55.00**
9½", mustard yellow, large
anemoni flowers, sgnd St. F. G. **55.00**
Platter, 11", dragonfly on leaf,
green, pink and yellow **70.00**
Syrup, 4½", robin on a branch, aqua
& yellow, basketweave, brown
handle, pewter top **90.00**
Tea Service, pineapple, pot, creamer, sugar, jam jar, orangy brown
and green, green leaf finials **125.00**
Teapot, 4", water lily, blue, yellow
flowers, green and pink leaves,
brown handle **85.00**
Tobacco Jar, 8½ x 3¾", owl on
book, brown and grays with yellow
and black eyes **125.00**
Tray, 13½ x 8¼", handles, step
down center, pink to white, brown
basketweave sides, white water
lily, 2 large green leaves **160.00**
Tureen, cov, clam shell feet, red
crab on cover **75.00**
Umbrella Stand, tulip design **125.00**
Vases
6", earth colors, double handles,
raised daisies, Old English, sgd,
pr **95.00**
6½", blue and gold, figure of little
girl, Bavaria, c1860 .... **90.00**

MAPS

**Maps provide one of the best ways to study
the growth of a country or region. From the
16th to the early 20th century maps were
both informative and decorative. Engravers
provided ornamental detailing which often
took the form of bird's-eye views, city maps,
and ornate calligraphy and scrolling. Many
maps were hand colored to enhance their
beauty.**

**Maps generally were published in plate
books. Many of the maps available today result from these books being cut apart and
sheets sold separately.**

**In the last quarter of the 19th century, rep-
resentatives from firms in Philadelphia, Chicago, and elsewhere traveled the United
States preparing county atlases, often with a
sheet for each township and a sheet for each
major city or town. Although mass produced,
they are eagerly sought by collectors. Individual sheets sell for $20 to $50. The atlases
themselves can usually be purchased in the
$200 to $300 range. Individual sheets should
be viewed solely as decorative and not as investment material.**

PRINTED

Canada, Tallis, "British America,"
London/New York, 1851, 12¾ x
9½", engraved, outline color ... **60.00**
North America
Pownall, "A New And Correct
Map Of North America, With
The West India Islands. Divided
According To The Last Treaty
Of Peace Concluded At Paris,
10 February 1763 . . . ," Lon-
don, 1777, two sheets, 20½ x
46½" at platemarks, full mar-
gins, from Thomas Jeffery's
American Atlas **700.00**
Wilkinson, R., "North America . . . ,"
London, 1808, 8¾ x 11¼", en-
graved, full color **40.00**
North and South America, H. Moll,
"A General And Particular De-
scription Of America . . . ," Lon-
don, c1727, 7¼ x 6¾" image,
sheet with text 12½ x 8" **125.00**
United States
*A General Atlas, Improved And
Engraved Being A Collection Of
Maps Of The World And Quar-
ters, Their Principal Empires,
Kingdoms, &c.,* Mathew Carey,
third edition, Philadelphia, 1814
Maryland, 12½ x 17¾" **350.00**
North Carolina, 11⅝ x 19" ... **300.00**
State of South Carolina from
the best Authorities by Samu-
el Lewis, 15 x 18" **475.00**
United States of America, Map
Of, 14¾ x 18½" **175.00**
Florida, U.S. Dept. Of War, Topo-
graphical Study of Florida,
Washington, D.C., 1891, 16⅜ x
27¼", chromolithograph in 3
colors **60.00**
Idaho, Cram, "Railroad And Coun-
ty Map Of Idaho," Chicago,
1880, 19¾ x 16¾", lithograph,
outline color **85.00**
Maryland, Carey & Lea, "Geo-
graphical, Statistical, And Historical Map Of Maryland,"
Philadelphia, 1827, engraved,
16½ x 20¾" with text **175.00**
Middle British Colonies, Lewis Evans and Thomas Jefferys, "A
General Map Of The Middle
British Colonies In America . . . ,"
London, Sayer & Jefferys, 1758,
19 x 26" at platemarks, en-
graved, outline color **2,500.00**
Missouri, J. H. Colton, "Missouri,"
New York, 1855, 12 x 14¾", insert "Vicinity Of St. Louis," lithograph, full color **100.00**

New England, Thomas Jefferys, "A Map Of The Most Inhabited Parts Of New England . . . ," London, Nov. 29, 1774, 42 x 41", engraved, hand colored, full orig margins 6,000.00

New Hampshire and Vermont, Denison, "A Map Of The States Of New Hampshire And Vermont," Boston, 1796, 7½ x 9" .   175.00

St. Louis, Collot, "Plan Of St. Lewis. With The Project Of An Intrenched Camp French," 7½ x 11" image, 1796, sheet from Collot *Atlas,* 1804 edition 2,500.00

United States, D. Burr, "United States . . . ," New York, B. Davenport, 1842, 17¾ x 21½", engraved, full color, city inserts of Albany, Boston, New York, Cincinnati, Philadelphia, Baltimore, and Washington, D.C. 125.00

Virginia, Joshua Fry & Peter Jefferson, "A Map Of The Most Inhabited Part Of Virginia . . . ," London, 1775, two sheets, each 15¾ x 36" at platemarks, wide margins, from Thomas Jeffery's *American Atlas* 3,500.00

World

Bell, "A Map Of The World In Three Sections Describing The Polar Regions To The Tropics In Which Are Traced The Tracts Of Lord Mulgrave And Captain Cook . . . ," c1776, 9 x 16½", twin hemisphere, uncolored . . .   100.00

Dilly & Robinson, "A Chart Of The World According To Mercator's Projection Showing The Latest Discoveries Of Capt. Cook," 1785, 14½ x 19", colored borders and outlines 85.00

TEXTILE

England, needlework sampler, 17½ x 18¼", Rebekah Cole, English, 1793, polychrome silk and wool threads in cross and chain stitches, detailed map of England and Wales 600.00

MARBLEHEAD POTTERY

This hand thrown pottery had its beginning in 1905 as a therapeutic program introduced by

Dr. J. Hall for the patients confined to a sanitorium located in Marblehead, Massachusetts. In 1916, the operation was removed from the hospital to another site and the factory continued under the directorship of Arthur E. Baggs until its closing in 1936.

Most pieces found today are glazed with a smooth, porous, even finish in a single color. The most desirable pieces are decorated with conventionalized design in one or more subordinate colors.

Candlestick, chamber style, 4" h, rose matte glaze, $45.00.

Bowl, 5" d, 3¼" h, blue matte finish	75.00
Candleholder, 4" h, 4" w, handled, green	75.00
Candlestick, chamber style, 1½" h, 5½" w, flat green	50.00
Creamer and Sugar, creamer 3" h, sugar 1¾" h, blue matte glaze, match "teapot"	60.00
Teapot, 5¾" h, blue matte glaze, modified "C" handle	70.00
Vases	
4" h, 3" w, cylindrical, gray	45.00
4½" h, tapered conical shape, small ring collar and neck, brown glaze, green inside	30.00
4½" h, 4½" w, bulbous, incised and painted flowers around rim, gray	350.00
7" h, 3½" w, bud, cylindrical, flared base, blue	75.00
7" h, 5" w, teardrop shape, incised brown geometric design, green	400.00

MARBLES

Warman's Americana & Collectibles, 1st Edition, contains 75 listings in this category; see also page xii.

MARY GREGORY GLASS

Mary Gregory (1856–1908) was employed by Boston and Sandwich Glass Co., Mass., as an artist. Her charming designs of children were delicately painted with white enamel on transparent clear and colored glass items. A positive identification of items personally decorated by her is virtually impossible. In the late 1880s and early 1900s other glass companies employed this type of decoration in America, England and Europe and it would be more correct to refer to the wares as "Mary Gregory type."

There are many current reproductions and there have been some reproductions of current painting on old glass.

Box, cov, 5½″ d, black amethyst, $245.00.

Bottle, Barber, 7½″, cobalt blue, boy & girl playing badminton	110.00
Bottle, Colonge, 7″, bulbous, amber, girl & foliage, amber ball stopper, white trim	165.00
Bottles, Perfume	
4″, sq, blue, boy on one, girl on other, cut glass stoppers, pr . .	235.00
5¾ x 3″, sapphire blue, blue ball stopper, tinted features on boy chasing butterfly	158.00
Boxes	
3⅜ x 2¾″, round, emerald green, girl on lift off lid, white spray around sides	118.00
4″, round, hinged fittings, green, white enamel winged cherub on leaves with butterfly & florals . .	315.00
Creamer, 3¾ x 2½″ d, green, inverted thumb print, green applied handle, round mouth, girl	125.00
Cruet, 9¼″, amber, applied handle, bubble stopper, boy	195.00
Dresser Tray, 8 x 10½″, oval, emerald green, 3 figures, boy & girl dancing, girl playing mandolin . . .	245.00
Ewer, 10 x 3⅛″, cranberry, clear applied handle, girl & bushes	195.00
Mug, 3 x 2¼″ d, cranberry, clear handle, girl	88.00
Patch Boxes	
Amber, round, hinged, girl	175.00
Blue, round, hinged, boy	175.00
Sapphire blue, round, hinged, girl	175.00
Pin Basket, 3¾ x 3⅜″ d, ruby, ormolu mounts, brass feet & handle, girl	165.00
Pitchers	
3¼ x 2¼″ d, tankard shape, cranberry, clear applied handle, boy	165.00
5½ x 3¼″, bulbous, cranberry, clear applied handle, boy	195.00
10″, medium blue, young girl, brown hair, gold around top . . .	195.00
Tumbler, 4½″, sapphire blue, ribbed, boy	55.00
Tumble-up, cranberry, boy, scenic .	185.00
Urn, 14¼ x 5⅝″ d, cov, cobalt blue, girl carrying basket of flowers, white enamel dot borders	325.00
Vases	
2¾ x 2¾″, ball shape, orange, collared top, boy & foliage	110.00
4¼″, clear pedal foot, lime green, girl	95.00
7″, bud, pedestal foot, sapphire blue, boy	115.00
9⅞″, cranberry, clear pedestal foot, boy running with butterfly net, girl with bouquet of flowers, holding apron, pr	425.00
10¾ x 5¼″ d, cobalt blue, facing pair, girl on each with scarf around neck, long dress, pr . . .	375.00
12⅛ x 4″ d, cranberry, girl reaching up into tree at bird & bird's nest	275.00
14″, cobalt blue, boy	245.00

MATCH HOLDERS

In the days of the so-called "barnburner" matches, match holders were a household necessity. Many styles, types and shapes were made.

Advertising, Tin	
American Manure Spreader	150.00
Bliss Native Herbs	150.00
Ceresota Flour	75.00
DeLaval Separator Company, 6½″, wall type, die cut	25.00
Dr. Shoop's	75.00
Michigan Stove	70.00

Milwaukee Binders & Mowers . . .	80.00
Old Judson	45.00

Brass
Figural, wall type, oak leaves, acorns, hanging rabbit, fowl, hunter's horn, game bag, 9 x 5″, gilt	75.00
Pall Mall Famous Cigarettes, emb lettering, 3″	32.00

China and Pottery
Chimney Sweep, blown out flowers	48.00
Peacock, 6″ h, majolica	70.00

Glass
Aqua, cane pattern holder supported by 2 small baby figures, ftd	85.00
Clear, book shape	25.00
Clear, pipe shape	10.00

Iron, cast
Devil and Grapes, 6″, wall type . .	85.00
Vines and grapes, 5″, wall type . .	85.00
Milk Glass, butterfly, 5″ hp, wall type	40.00
Tin, wall type, elaborate cut out lyre with leaves, stars, flowers, orig blue, green, red, yellow paint . . .	260.00

Wall Type
Centennial, dated, "Goddess of Liberty" striker	35.00
F. J. Rosenberger, Mason City, Iowa	15.00
Good Luck, figural mother owl, babies above horseshoe, striker, easel back and hanging hook, metal	45.00

Wood, carved
Dove, Victorian style, walnut	35.00
Man's head, finely painted, wall type, c1880	150.00
Rabbit, folk art type	40.00

Roycroft match holder, 3¼″ h x 3¼″ d, nested ashtray, c1919, $75.00.

MATCH SAFES-POCKET

Before safety matches, friction matches were carried in a safe. Early jewelry catalogues of the 1890s-1900s offered pocket match safes.

Red carnelian, German silver lace band, striker, 2¾″, $185.00.

Advertising
"Compliments of The Bremen, Gas Folle, Prop. St. Louis, Mo," ornate, side opens	70.00
First National Bank, Pawtucket, RI, bakelite	15.00
International Tailoring Co., silvered brass	40.00
Red Pail Pie Filling, celluloid . . .	25.00
Veure Cliquot Champagne, bottle shape, cigar cutter, silvered brass	150.00

Brass
Bull Dog	50.00
Camera case, silvered	80.00
Jackknife, silvered, 2⅜″	150.00
Shoe, Southern Blue Coals, Cincinnati	35.00
Skull, with striker	150.00
Cast Iron, Scrolls, 1867	40.00

Commemorative
Edward VII, portrait, bakelite	27.00
Knights of Columbus, 1919, orig matchbook	30.00
St. Louis World's Fair, 1904, sterling	65.00
Mother of Pearl, horseshoe shape, man in moon face	90.00
Silverplated, Art Nouveau, 2½″ . . .	48.00

Sterling Silver
Crown, shells, scrolls, engraved H.G.N., 1902	45.00
Fisherman	60.00
Flowers, leaves, scrolls, reticulated	55.00
Hunter with dogs	65.00
Lady raising glass, cigarette in other hand, ivy leaves border .	110.00
Steetcar, engraved B	48.00
Women's face, flowing hair, gold wash interior, c1910	160.00
Tin, Nesco, orig paint	20.00

McCOY POTTERY

The J.W. McCoy Pottery Co. was established in Roseville, Ohio, in September 1899. The early McCoy Company produced both stoneware and some art lines, including Rosewood. In October, 1911, three potteries in the Roseville area merged and became known as the Brush-McCoy Pottery Co. This company continued to produce the original McCoy lines and added several new art lines in the Zanesville plant. Much of this early pottery was not marked.

In 1910, Nelson McCoy and his father, J. W. McCoy, founded the Nelson McCoy Sanitary Stoneware Company. In 1925, the McCoy family sold their interest in the Brush-McCoy Pottery Company and expanded the Nelson McCoy Company. They produced stoneware, earthenware specialities and artware. Most of the pottery marked McCoy was made by the Nelson McCoy Company.

For more information about the McCoy potteries, refer to Sharon and Bob Huxford's, *The Collectors Encyclopedia of McCoy Pottery.*

See *Warman's Americana & Collectibles* for an expanded listing of McCoy pottery.

Note: The mark numbers listed below refer to the above mentioned book.

Planter, "Down By The Old Mill Stream," white seated figures, Bennington style glaze, double well in back, 7¼ x 4⅛ x ⅜", $10.00.

Bank, Woodsy Owl	25.00
Basket, rustic glaze, pine cone decor, mark #4	18.00
Bookend planter, hunting dog with bird in mouth, pink, blue, olive green decor, mark #7	35.00
Candlestick, Florastone, c1923, pr .	95.00

Cookie Jars

Dalmations in rocking chair, mark #7	85.00
Mother Goose, mark #7	45.00
Rooster, mark #7	38.00
Tudor House, mark #7	50.00
W. C. Fields	65.00
Creamer and Sugar, cov, Grecian, mark #7	15.00
Jardiniere, 6½" h x 8" d, green, acorn motif, c1935	20.00
Lamp, horse, gold flecked	25.00
Liquor Bottle, Pierce Arrow car	25.00
Pitcher, Tankard set, 6 mugs, Buccaneer	50.00

Planters

Baby Buggy, dog, "What About Me?" pink	8.00
Log, oval, gray, white, bark decor, 9 x 3½ x 3"	5.00
Pelican, blue, 6"	7.00
Shell, white, mark #4	10.00
Turtle, light pink, 6"	8.00
Water Wheel, gold, brown	6.50

Salt and Pepper Shakers

Cabbages	15.00
Cucumber & Mango	12.50
Teapot, Sunburst Gold, mark #4 . .	25.00

Vases

Blossomtime, pink flowers, leaves, stems, white ground, mark #4 . .	8.00
Cardinal perched on berry bush, lt. green emb, 8½" h	10.00
Chrysanthemum, aqua, 7" h, c1940	10.00
Springwood, pink flowers, vines, white ground	6.50
Rustic glaze, 8½"	9.50
Violet Pot, attached saucer, long leaves, dots, aqua	5.00

Wall Pockets

Apple, c1953	11.00
Leaf design, pink, blue	9.00
Vase, blue flower, c1946	8.00

McKEE GLASS

The name McKee has been associated with glass making since 1843. In 1852, a factory was established in Pittsburgh, Pa., for the production of pressed glass objects. In 1888, the factory relocated to Jeannette, Pa., and continued production until 1951 when the factory was sold to Thatcher Manufacturing Co.

Many types of glass were produced by McKee from the very first—bottles, window panes, pressed glass tablewares (flint and non-flint), Depression glass, Milk glass objects and a variety of bar and utility wares. Also see specific categories, e.g., CANDLESTICKS, LAMPS, MILK GLASS, etc.

See *Warman's Americana & Collectibles* for an expanded listing of McKee Glass.

Candy Dish, McKee Glass, 7¾" h, orange, gold trim lid, gold finial, clear base, $20.00.

Animal Dishes, covered

Cat	165.00
Hen	125.00
Horse	135.00
Rabbit	150.00
Bird House, white, colored roof	125.00

Bowls

9½", rainbow, green	40.00
10¼", oval, Autumn, opaque green, ftd	20.00
10½", jade	20.00
Box, cov, ring	10.00
Butter Dish, cov, Sunburst, clear	32.00
Candy Dish, Rock Crystal, cranberry flashed body, clear finial base	110.00

Creamers

Eugenie, flint	65.00
Masonic	15.00
Star Rosetted	28.50
Egg Cup, Rock Crystal	8.00

Goblets

French Ivory	25.00
Puritan, pink stems	20.00

Pitchers

Aztec	20.00
Snowflake, crystal	35.00

Plates

Bread, Star Rosetted, "A Good Mother Makes a Happy Home"	40.00
Punch Bowl, Rock Crystal clear	75.00
Tom and Jerry set, custard with black lettering, 13 pcs	75.00

Toothpick, Aztec pattern	17.50

Tumblers

Gladiator, cobalt blue, gold trim	45.00
Ribbed Palm	75.00

Whiskeys "Bottom-Up"

Caramel	40.00
Custard	50.00
Vase, 8" h, Skokie, nude, green	70.00

MEDICAL ITEMS

Early medical instruments and related items are of interest to special collectors, especially those in the professions.

DENTAL

Cabinet, oak, door, 2 rectangular windows, shelves pull out, ceramic drawer pulls	1,500.00
Chair, walnut, oak trim, padded back, headrest, adjustable, leather set	685.00
Cuspidor, brass, 4" h, 10" d, American, c1880	95.00
Drill, Electro Dental Mfg. Co., drill Pat. No. 3, 1903; foot control Pat. Sept. 9, 1911	65.00

Instruments

Cheek retractor, MOP handle, carved	65.00
Lancet, SS handle	75.00
Mouth Mirror, MOP handle, carved	75.00
Separating file carriers, ivory handle	130.00

MEDICAL

Bag, leather, some bottles in side compartments, c1865	95.00

Books

Allen, *Practitioner's Manual*, 1889	20.00
Bangs & Hardaway, *An American Textbook of Genito-Urinary Diseases, Syphillis & Diseases of the Skin*, Philadelphia, 1898, calf bound, illus.	50.00

Instruments

Blood cell calculator, Dr. M. M. Marbell's, 1922	40.00
Cauterizing Stick, ebony, brass, Maw, London, c1880	30.00
ENT (Ear, Nose, Throat) Set	150.00
Enema Pump, cased brass, orig tubing, S. Maw, Son & Thompson, London, c1850	210.00
Fleams, English, 3 steel blades, horn cover, c1840	85.00
Hammer, patella, "Queen," sq type, ebony handle, leather rimmed steel ball head	65.00

Baumanometer kit, bag model, blood pressure instrument, $25.00.

Knife, surgical, SS, Gorham	60.00
Opthalmascope	125.00
Scalpel, set of 3, tapered ivory case	150.00
Stethoscopes	
Binaurel, flexible cloth covered tubing, nickel plated ear piece, wooden head, American, c1915	70.00
Monaural, silver, ivory ear piece, English, c1875	130.00
Surgical Sets	
12 pcs, George Tiemann & Co., NY, 2 level case, red velvet lining, brass lock, c1860 . . .	300.00
14 pcs, Milliken & Lawley, London, surgical and dissecting, mahogany case, c1860	225.00
Model, Doctor's, carved ivory, female nude lying on side, used during examinations, c1860	175.00
Paperweight, Harvard Medical School	25.00
Sign, cardboard, "Warning Whooping Cough Within"	25.00

OPTICAL

Cabinet, 20" h, oak, roll-top, drawers, compartments, lenses, frames	500.00
Eyeglasses, gold pince-nez, fitted leather case	65.00
Lens Set, Fits-U-Eyeglasses Kit, velvet lined box, 12 pr lenses, testing instruments, c1900	30.00

Sign, American Optical, "Mail Order Specs," cardboard, orig frame, brass inscription plate, 20 x 24", 1942	125.00

MERCURY GLASS

Mercury glass is a light bodied, double-walled glass that was 'silvered' by applying a solution of silver nitrate to the inside of the object through a hole in the base of the formed object.

F. Hale Thomson, London, patented the method in 1849. In 1855, the New England Glass Co. filed a patent for the same type of process. Other glass makers soon followed suit. The glass did not reach popularity until the early 20th century.

Bowl, 6", with white painted flowers	32.50
Candlesticks, pr.	45.00
Christmas Decorations	
2½, church	10.00
7", ball with brass collar and hanger, c1890	12.50
Compote, 8", glass insert	45.00
Creamer and Sugar, ftd, applied crimped glass handles, c1855, pr	195.00
Curtain Tie Backs, 3½", grape clusters, vines, pewter shanks, marked NE Glass Co. Pat Jan. 16, 1855, pr	100.00
Dish, cov, 7"	85.00
Goblet, 7½", ivy, grape leaves and grapes engraved, early	130.00
Inkwell, on glass stand, 2 mercury wells, one at each end	50.00
Pitcher, 12½" high, clear applied handle	65.00
Rose Bowl, 5", gilt interior	50.00
Salt, Master, urn-shaped, footed . .	30.00
Spooner, Vintage pattern	68.00

Salt, Master, ftd, 2⅝" h, applied floral decor, gold gilt interior, $34.00.

Toothpick Holders, gold
   3½" h, pedestal base, interior . .   **30.00**
   5" h, pedestel base, etched ferns   **35.00**
Vases
   8", cut to show emerald glass,
     marked Varnish & Co. London,
     Pat **55.00**
   9½", floral bands, castle scene
     painted on front **35.00**
   10", white, decor, with red and
     white stripes, top and base . . .   **65.00**
   10¼", frosted palm trees, flowers,
     paneled sides, gold lustre interi-
     ors, pr **125.00**
Witch Ball, green ball on attached
   base **150.00**

METTLACH

Jean Francis Boch founded the pottery at Mettlach, in the Moselle Valley of Germany, in 1809. His father had established a pottery at Septfontaines in 1767. Nicholas Villery began his pottery career at Wallerfangen in 1789.

In 1841 these three factories merged. They pioneered in using coal to fire kilns and the underglaze printing on earthenware using transfers from copper plates. Other factories were developed at Dresden, Wadgassen, and Danischburg.

The castle and Mercury emblem are the two chief marks. Secondary marks also are known. To check price examine the base to determine the shape mark, usually followed by a decor mark. Pieces are assumed to be print under glaze unless otherwise marked.

An excellent reference is R. H. Mohr's *Mettlach Steins.*

See also VILLEROY & BOCH.

Beakers
   2327/1137, ¼ l, man and women
     toasting each other **82.00**
   2327/1233, ¼ l, little boy holding
     stein patting large dog on the
     head **85.00**
   2368/1033, ¼ l, drinking scene .   **75.00**
   2842/1175, ¼ l, old dwarf with
     cane, broken wine goblet at feet   **90.00**
Coaster, 2820, 4½", college boy
   holding stein, etched **180.00**
Jam Jar, 1844, 4", castle **395.00**
Plaques
   866, angel, stars and clouds,
     etched, 8½" **375.00**

Drinking Glasses, Marked "2327", Left: 31 1296 Geschutzat B; Right: 07 1023 Geschutzat B, Set of six, $550.00.

1044/126, hunting dog, 17¼" . .   **375.00**
1044/222, Nuremburg, 14" **350.00**
1044/1067, rural scene with mill-
   stream, 17½" **400.00**
1048, king on throne, 16" d **695.00**
1245, floral decor, etched, 12" . .   **300.00**
1387, soldiers wearing helmets,
   11" **320.00**
2003, valley and mountain scene,
   24" **500.00**
2070, two dogs and stag, etched,
   signed Stocke, 15½" **650.00**
2142, Bismark on horseback,
   etched, 15½" **900.00**
2442, cameo, mythological men in
   boat, sage green, white detail,
   sgd J. Stahl, dated 1899 . . . . .   **1,500.00**
2578, town scene, etched, 17½"   **650.00**
5040, windmills, 12" **150.00**
Punch Bowls
2087, underplate, dancing figures
   in white on blue ground, relief, 3
   qt **690.00**
2595/1072, young girls and boys,
   country setting, 1 qt **310.00**
Steins
238, 1 l, man kneeling on ground,
   etched **450.00**
485, ½ l, ten people at festival,
   relief, insert lid **250.00**
597, 1 l, hunter, German verse . .   **250.00**
1038, 3 l, frogs on pond **450.00**
1164, ½ l, figures drinking and
   smoking, silver lid, signed C.
   Warth, 1883, etched **600.00**
1286, ½ l, cream, green and
   brown leaves, white dots, relief,
   inlay lid **175.00**
1400, ½ l, brown body with insert
   lid, plain **65.00**
1467, ½ l, four maidens repre-
   senting four seasons, lid, relief   **225.00**

1526, ½ l, hp, fraternal crest, pottery lid 150.00

1655, ½ l, dancing scene, etched, inlay lid 435.00

1786, ½ l, St. Florian theme, dragon handle with original head, fish scale lid, etched 750.00

1896, ¼ l, domestic scene, relief 140.00

1909/83, Falstaff in wine cellar drinking from boot, pewter lid . 225.00

1909/993, ½ l, three cavalier musicians, pottery lid 210.00

2009, ½ l, maiden and scroll with verse, etched, inlay lid, sgd F. Stuck 500.00

2140/1047, 1 l, dwarf scene, pewter lid 180.00

2177/960, ¼ l, jester lying in grass playing mandolin, initialed H. S. 200.00

2180/955, 5 l, cavalier drinking scene, signed H. Schlitt, pewter lid 1,350.00

2181/957, ¼ l, lady holding stein, pewter lid 160.00

2184, ³/₁₀ l, gnomes and beavers, pottery insert lid 325.00

2271/1055, ½ l, two inebriated cavaliers, "Geschutzt" 200.00

2348/1022, 3 l, man with feathered hat making merry, pewter lid 600.00

2716, ½ l, large wreath, men drinking, etched, pottery insert lid 650.00

3220, ½ l, couple embracing under archway, etched, inlay lid .. 595.00

Miscellaneous

Planter, Art Deco motif, etched, 5" x 17" 100.00

Vases

1844, 9½ x 6" d, gray, florals in orange & blue, green and gold leaves, floral top band, gold rim, pink interior 395.00

2913/29/12, 14", Art Deco, white ground, blue and gold decor, mkd, Mettlach, made in Germany 128.00

MILK GLASS

This is opaque-white glass that resembles the color of milk and was used as a substitute for white procelain in the 18th century. It has been made in England and the United States, and is still being produced today. The popularity of milk glass in this country was prevalent during the Victorian period and it is popular with collectors today. The earlier pieces made between 1870–1890 are most collectible and some have been reproduced.

See *Warman's Americana & Collectibles* for an expanded listing of Milk Glass.

Sugar Castor, 4½", Panelled Sprig, $42.00.

Animal Dishes, covered—see ANIMAL DISHES, COVERED

Basket, 4¾ x 1¾" 25.00

Bottle, figural, Actress Head, blue, gold decor 32.00

Bowls

4", Gooseberry 8.00

7¼", Cut Star, blue 50.00

7½", Scroll 78.00

8¼", sq, lacy edge 75.00

9¾", Beaded Rib 45.00

10", Acanthus Leaf 90.00

10½", Beaded Rib 45.00

Boxes

5 x 3", emb ship, dolphins 25.00

5½ x 1¾", all over emb floral design, round beaded panel of emb lady's profile on lid 75.00

Butter Dish, cov, Scroll, nile green . 115.00

Candlestick, crucifix, hexagonal base, 10" 90.00

Card Holder, Curled Scroll 15.00

Celery, Sandwich Loop, flint 85.00

Compotes

4½", Sandwich Loop 95.00

7", Basketweave, blue 85.00

8", Lattice 80.00

Condiment Set, Grapes pattern, salt, pepper shakers, tray 30.00

Creamers

Ceres 22.50

Dahlia, ftd 25.00

Swan 35.00

Cruet, Netted Oak 50.00

Dishes, covered

Battleship Wheeling 40.00

Conestoga Wagon	100.00
Dewey, bust on round base	235.00
Locomotive, 6", McKee	100.00
Dresser Tray, Chrysanthemum, 7½ x 10"	48.00
Egg Cup, bird, 4¼" h	115.00
Flask, Klondyke, gold decor	60.00
Hat, Uncle Sam's, painted decor . .	55.00
Horseradish Jar, 3⅝" h, blue, cov .	45.00
Inkwell, Minstrel Boy	35.00
Matchholders	
Bible, blue	40.00
Three Bees, 2⅛" h	35.00
Mustard Jar, swan	48.00
Napkin Ring	48.00
Nappy, Prism	16.00
Pitchers	
7", George Washington	90.00
8¼", Block & Fan	40.00
8½", Curtain, gold trim	110.00
Plates	
5½", painted ships	15.00
7½", Battleship Maine	20.00
7½", Easter Ducks	45.00
7½", Rabbit and Horseshoe	45.00
7½", Rooster and Hens	40.00
7½", Yoked slatted border, gold decor	48.00
8", Backward C border	25.00
8", Serenade	55.00
8", Three Puppies on top, squirrel on branch in center	68.00
10½", hp, floral, lattice open edge	50.00
Platters	
13", Rock of Ages, dated	135.00
13½", Retriever	95.00
Relish, 8½" l, Strawberry	20.00
Salts, Master	
Blackberry	22.00
Flying Fish, gilt trim	35.00
Salt and Pepper Shakers	
Apricot Band	50.00
Butterfly	60.00
Grecian Ladies heads, Art Deco style	45.00
Rabbits, egg shaped	80.00
Scrolled Panel	50.00
Spittoon	27.00
Spooners	
Gooseberry	35.00
Panelled Flower	40.00
Swan	28.00
Sprinkling Can, whimsey	25.00
Sugars, cov	
Basketweave, Atterbury	125.00
Dahlia, ftd	25.00
Diamond Point & Leaf	58.00
Panelled Wheat	80.00
Quince	25.00
Syrups	
6¼", Stippled Dahlia, pewter top .	65.00
6¾", Tree of Life, pewter top, blue	75.00

6⅞", Blackberry	165.00
7½", Grape	50.00
Trays	
5", oval, chick, broken egg	30.00
5", oval, Cosmos Scroll	29.00
5 x 9", oval, rams head handles .	45.00
8", Fish, dated June 4, 1872, Atterbury	90.00
Toothpicks	
Dot With Scroll, butterscotch decor	28.00
Horseshoe With Clover	22.00
Scrolled Shell, gold decor	22.00
Tumblers	
Apple Blossom decor	45.00
Hobnail on half of base	18.00
Vineyard	40.00
Vases	
5½" h, mother and child	35.00
8⅝" h, jeweled, blue	85.00

MILLEFIORI

Millefiori (thousand flowers) is an ornamental glass composed of bundles of colored glass rods fused to become canes. The canes were pulled while still ductile to the desired length, sliced, arranged in a pattern and again fused together. This technique was developed by the Egyptians in the first century B.C. Millefiori glass making was revived in the 1880s. It is again being produced by many companies in articles such as paperweights, cruets, toothpicks, etc.

Vase, 5½", purple bands with white oval lines, white bands with red flowers and yellow centers, $140.00.

Atomizer	75.00
Basket, small, blue, green shades	185.00
Box, 2½″ h, 2¾″ d, royal blue ground, white swirls	250.00
Cruets	
With cut crystal stopper, c1890	300.00
Dark ground, applied camphor handle, stopper	195.00
Cup and Saucer	75.00
Lamps	
Miniature, 8½″ h	350.00
Table, 11¾″, slender baluster shape, round base, spherical shade, cobalt blue ground, red, white, yellow	225.00
Plaque, 10¼″ h, attributed to Frederick Carter	1,500.00
Rose Bowl, c1890	150.00
Sugar Shaker, 5″, orig top	75.00
Syrup, frosted handle	200.00
Toothpick, pinched sides, c1890	150.00
Tumbler, pastels	95.00
Vases	
7″, bud, ftd	140.00
9″, paperweight base, sgd.	900.00

MINIATURE PAINTINGS

Prior to the advent of the photograph, miniature portraits and silhouettes were the principal way of presenting a person's image. Miniaturists were common; and, they often made more than one copy of a drawing. The extras were distributed to family and friends.

    Miniaturists worked in watercolors and oil. The surface was paper, porcelain, or ivory. Miniaturists supplemented commission work by painting popular figures of the times and important works of art.

    Careful study has divided miniature paintings into schools. Many artists now are being studied. The miniature painting market is just now reaching its full potential.

AMERICAN SCHOOL

Anonymous

Child, oval on ivory, blonde hair, gray-blue eyes, pastel blue ground, pink dress, holding riding crop, hinged locket frame, back filled with pc of white watered silk, 2⅜ x 2⅞″ **245.00**

Gentleman, oval on ivory, primitive portrait, locket cast, clear beveled edge, worn cardboard and wood case, ring handle, 2⅜″ . **250.00**

Gentleman, oval on ivory, resembling Andrew Jackson, gold colored case, 2½″ h **150.00**

Lincoln, ivory, stippled ground, gilded case, 3 x 3¾″ **165.00**

Americana School, lady on ivory, c1840, 3½ x 4½″, $145.00.

Young Girl, oval on ivory, primitive portrait, lavendar stippled ground, orig cardboard case, clear lens covering, 3¾″ **900.00**

Biddle, Robert Stone, Phila, PA, R. I. Levis, age 7, oval, blue coat, orig emb brass frame, dated 1835, 3¼ x 2½″ **475.00**

Canfield, Abijah, oval, figure of Liberty in empire gown holding garland, flanked by flying eagle, American flag, landscaped ground, sgd in ink on reverse "Lady Liberty," Abijah Canfield, April 1797, 2⅝ x 2³⁄₁₆″ **2,500.00**

Dalee, New York, pencil water color, ink, of child with rattle, old black frame, 5⅛ x 6⅛″ **775.00**

Davis, Joseph H., watercolor on paper, gentleman, lady holding flowers, orig pine frames, 5⅝ x 3⅞″, c1830, pr **900.00**

Goodrich, Sarah, rectangular, portrait of gentleman marked as Millard Fillmore, black coat, white cravat, green ground, leather case with maker's label James Dyer, Boston, 3″ **335.00**

Pastorini, Joseph, oval on ivory, profile portrait of young man in brown coat, high white collar, blue ground, gold colored swivel frame, reverse contains lock of hair, 1 x 1⅛″ **235.00**

Rogers, Nathaniel, oil on ivory, young dark haired woman, black low-cut gown, lavender cape with fur collar worn low around shoulders, sgd vertically, c1800, 3⅛ x 2½" 300.00

DUTCH SCHOOL

Gentleman, oval on copper, portrait facing left, wearing stock, wig, 3" h 150.00

ENGLISH SCHOOL

Anonymous
  Charles Hill, 18 years old, gilt metal frame, c1805, 3" 475.00
  Sir Thomas Wyatt, Poet, oval on ivory, faded colors, gold engraved case, 1⅞" 110.00
  Young gentleman, oval on ivory, dark red coat, gold colored case, 1⅝" 200.00
  Young gentleman, oval, gold frame, c1790, 2¾" 425.00
Eckstein, oval on ivory, military officer in blue coat, red collar, black lacquered frame, gilded brass trim, 5⅛ x 5⅝" 180.00
Ellsworth, water color on paper, portrait of white haired gentleman, elaborate gilded frame, sgd Ellsworth, Painter, 9¾ x 10½" 700.00

FRENCH SCHOOL

Rouquet, Andre, Hon. Mrs. Charles Berkely, c1745, 1¾" 1,750.00

GERMAN SCHOOL

Zincke, Christian Friedrich, Mary Rush, fruitwood frame, c1745, 1¾" 950.00

IRISH SCHOOL

Anonymous
  British officer, oval on ivory, red coat, gold colored case, 1¾" .. 325.00
  Lady and Gentleman, c1765, 1¾", pr 500.00

MINIATURES

Miniatures continue to be one of the world's leading hobbies. There are three sizes of miniatures: doll house scale (ranging from ½" to 1"), sample size, and child's size. The most common examples are 20th century, since most earlier material is in museums or extremely expensive.

Many mediums were used for miniatures—silver, copper, tin, wood, glass, and ivory. Even books were printed in miniature. Prices are broad ranged, depending on scarcity and quality of workmanship.

During the past year, rare and unusual pieces have held or surpassed previous prices. Ordinary and crude pieces have declined.

Items leading the advance are: Biedermeier and other early furniture, sample and child size examples, and objects made of ivory, lacquer, ormolu, soft metal (19th C), and tin. Old books under one-half inch are very difficult to find. Even St. Onge books from the 1970s are gaining value over cost.

Sofa, china, probably French or German, 4⅛" h, hand painted pastel floral motif, gold trim, late 19thC, $75.00.

DOLL HOUSE SIZE

Bath
  Bathtub, tin, painted gold, c1910 . 22.00
  Potty, wooden, lift lid, 2" h, c1940 5.00
  Set, 3 pcs, tin, orig paint, c1830 . 165.00
Bedroom
  Bed, Four Poster, canopy, orig covers and hangings, Tynietoy, Am, c1930 .... 145.00
  Bed, Golden Oak, orig mattress, German, c1890 .... 55.00
  Bureau, Golden Oak, Art Nouveau design, German, c1890 ...... 145.00
  Set, 8 pcs, painted white, ¾" scale, German, c1900 .... 135.00
Bird Cages
  Ormolu, stand, wax parrot, c1850 175.00
  Pewter, gilted, peak roof, bird on swing, c1920 .... 70.00
Bisque Figures
  Bathtub baby, German, nice face 35.00
  Gentleman and Lady, pr, 3" h, c1890 .... 75.00
Books
  Holy Bible, leather bound, c1860 90.00

Picture Album, book form, blue, filigree clasp closing, c1890 . . . . **110.00**

Tender Rain, red leather case, c1850, fair cond. **45.00**

Bronze Figures

Bird, small, on pussywillow branch, painted bronze **80.00**

Seal, "Mercury," 2¼" h, c1890 . **250.00**

Viennese, bronze, cat drinking from bowl, mouse running around edge, late 19th C **200.00**

Viennese, figural, painted, dog climbing ladder, with paint pots, onto kiosk **300.00**

Cabinets

China, Golden Oak, 3 glass sides, mirror back, shelves, bottom drawer, 8½" h, c1900 . . . . **125.00**

China, oak, glass doored, ¾" scale **25.00**

Hutch, tin, painted, lithograph design, pediment and two doors, c1890 . . . . **150.00**

Kitchen, 5" h, crude finish, broken pediment top **40.00**

Chairs

Biedermeier, Gothic, rosewood and gilt, fancy, c1840 . . . . . . **250.00**

Golden Oak, pr, center splat, upholstered seats, German, c1875 **70.00**

Ivory, high pointed back, ornately pierced 2" h, 19th C **175.00**

Ormolu, pr, ornate, 3" h, c1900 . **90.00**

Petite Princess, upholstered tub chair, c1960 . . . . **15.00**

Set of 6, dining room chairs, mahogany, Duncan Phyfe style, English, c1940 . . . . **225.00**

Tootsietoy, metal, gilt, ½" scale . **12.00**

Tynietoy, painted green, Am., c1930 . . . . **25.00**

Chest of Drawers

Biedermeier, rosewood, 3 drawer, ivory stringing, c1860 . . . . **250.00**

Lynnefield, light mahogany, bow front, 3 drawers, Am., c1940 . . **80.00**

China

Cup and Saucer, flower design, 1" scale, c1940 . . . . **5.00**

Tea Set, 3 pcs and tray, Japan, c1940 . . . . **30.00**

Tea Set, 4 pcs and tray, Royal Worcester, c1900 . . . . **250.00**

Clocks

Marble, paper face, 1¼" h, c1920 **40.00**

Metal, moving pendulum, c1910 . **80.00**

Metal, painted wagon, pendulums, c1900 . . . . **35.00**

Ormolu, mantle, warrior holding torch atop **125.00**

Pewter, wall, filigree, brown, moveable hands, c1870 . . . . . . **150.00**

Cradle, cutwork wood, c1940 . . . . . **12.00**

Couches

Chaise, fainting couch, plush, fringed, c1885 . . . . **195.00**

Lynnefield, striped cover, c1950 . **45.00**

Petite Princess, blue satin, c1960 **15.00**

Desks

English, fine handcrafted, c1940 . **195.00**

Ormolu, gilt, gallery top, c1880 . . **275.00**

Dining Room

Buffet, Golden Oak, marble top, double door, German, c1885 . . **175.00**

Dining Table, English, mahogany, 2 pedestal, banded in fruitwood, 20th C **135.00**

Dining Table, Golden Oak, 2 leaves, turned legs, c1900 . . . . **50.00**

Fireplaces and Stoves

Fire Tools, stand, metal, c1930 . . **50.00**

Fireplace, painted soft metal, paper fire, late Victorian **100.00**

Fireplace, tin, one piece, black, c1895 . . . . **45.00**

Stove-heater, painted metal, c1860 . . . . **150.00**

Living Room

Love Seat, rosewood, rococo gilt stencil, floral upholstery, c1850 **275.00**

Set of 3, Biedermeier, c1860 . . . . **575.00**

Set of 5, wood, painted, English, c1940 . . . . **70.00**

Set of 6, Biedermeier, couch, table, and 4 chairs, couch 4" wide, c1850, fair condition **160.00**

Set of 6, Victorian Parlor, settee and 5 chairs, filigree pewter, Am., c1893 . . . . **75.00**

Set of 9, Jacobean furniture, Triang, English, c1920 . . . . **150.00**

Mirrors

Gilt framed, 3" h, c1890 . . . . **200.00**

Wood, Tynietoy, c1930 . . . . **45.00**

Pewter and Soft Metal

Candlesticks, 3 branch, 2½" h, c1910, pr **45.00**

Oil Burner, soft metal, c1900 . . . . **25.00**

Serving Platter, 2" w, stamped engraving, c1900 . . . . **35.00**

Teapot, stand, late Victorian **45.00**

Pianos

Empire style, rosewood, German, c1840 . . . . **325.00**

Grand, iron, Arcade, c1920 . . . . . **150.00**

Small size, wood with lift top, c1940 . . . . **20.00**

Silver

Bowl, Monteith, 1½" d, Meyers, c1950 . . . . **350.00**

Living Room Set, 5 pcs, Continental, c1900 . . . . **225.00**

Teapot, stand, David Clayton, c1720 . . . . **1,500.00**

Tables

Marble top, Biedermeier, replaced

bottom	95.00
Phone, Petite Princess, c1960	5.00
Sewing, Golden Oak, drawer, c1880	75.00
Trestle Table, Golden Oak, turned legs and stretcher, c1900	125.00

Telephones

Painted Paper, grained, excellent cond.	90.00
Table, metal, c1920	20.00
Wall, oak, speaker and bell, German, c1890	30.00

Rooms

Georgian style, wood panelled open room, furniture and accessories, English, late 19th C	1,600.00
Victorian, folding, orig paper, rosewood furniture (6 pcs), ¾" scale	500.00

ACCESSORIES

Ashtray, stand, c1910	28.00
Baby Carriage, pewter, Pia, Am., c1890	125.00
Basket, made of shells, 2½" h	5.00

Carpet Sweepers

Gilt, Victorian	65.00
Wood, c1920	20.00
Cash Register, England, c1930	35.00
Chandelier, glass, European, c1800	400.00
Cigar Cutter, metal, c1920	25.00
Cutlery tray, filigree, Victorian	25.00
Decanter, 2 glasses, Venetian, c1920	25.00
Dresser Set, celluloid, c1910	55.00
Dust Pan and Broom, pewter, German, c1890	30.00
Fan, table, metal, c1910	20.00
Glass Bottles, perfume, labels, c1900, each	5.00
Radio, Strombecker, c1930	25.00
Scales, tin, workable, c1940	25.00
Sewing Machine, pewter, moveable wheel, c1890	200.00
Silhouettes, pr, Tynietoy, c1930	15.00

Table Lamps

Gilted pewter, glass globe and flu, c1860	65.00
Painted, Victorian, urn base, handless	50.00
Tea Set, treen, c1900, fair cond.	45.00
Tea Wagon, gilt, German, c1910	160.00
Trunk, painted tin, Marx, Am. 2" l, c1930	35.00
Typewriter, steel, black, Am., c1925	68.00
Umbrella Rack, metal, c1920	40.00
Vacuum cleaner, early tank type, c1920	75.00

Vases

Ormolu, c1890, fair cond.	40.00
Satsuma, c1900, 1½" tall	55.00
Victrola, pewter, table model, Britains, c1900	125.00

SAMPLE SIZE

Armoire, French Provincial, 19th C	550.00
Blanket Chest, Brittany, c1900	125.00

Chests

Mahogany, oval mirror attached, 3 drawers, Am., c1880, detailing	500.00
Painted, blue with flowers on shaped pediment, 3 drawer, c1900	65.00
Mission Furniture set, 3 pcs. couch and 2 chairs, c1900	125.00
Wine Set, Viennese enamel, elaborately painted, c1850	2,000.00

CHILD SIZE

Chest, attached oval mirror, 3 drawers, Am, c1880	525.00
Rocker, Bentwood, sgd Thonet	400.00
Tea Service, 15 pcs, ridged white with gold-sprayed rim and blue flowers, English, c1900	150.00

MINTON CHINA

Minton earthenwares were first made by Thomas Minton in 1793 in the Staffordshire district of England. Porcelain was introduced in 1798, but was not made in any quantity until about 1825. Minton also made Parian, a Majolica-type glaze and employed the Patesur-Plate technique. Many date marks were used to identify the year of production, and Minton is still in operation today.

Bowl, deep blue, vines, and leaves decor	125.00
Butter Dish, cov, floral decor	95.00
Candlestick, 3½", floral decor base in blue and gold enamel	48.00
Compote, 10", Indian Tree pattern, c1875	100.00

Cups and Saucers

Blue decorated panels, with gold rims	60.00
Demitasse, Indian Tree pattern, mkd, c1880	45.00
Roses, with gold trim, c1854	65.00
Ewer, 14¾", flattened wine barrel shape, 4 putti frolicking around	

Tile, 8 x 8″, Night and Day, blue day, yellow sun, imp mark on back, $45.00.

neck, ochre, green, brown, gray-
  purple, imp mark, 1872 . . . .   450.00
Flasks, 12″, russet, reserves of
  birds, orchids, gilt tirm, imp mark,
  1879, pr 600.00
Jug, 11¼ x 5½″ d, hinged pewter
  top, ribbed, blue, emb white cherubs and flower garland, ivy leaves
  around base, imp mark, c1845 . .   295.00
Pitcher, water, grapes with gold de-
  cor, marked 145.00
Plates
  10″, aqua and blue floral border,
    red mark 35.00
  10″, central Oriental scene, Imari
    colors, yellow border, 19th C,
    set of 12 . . . .   490.00
Platters
  13″, cobalt blue and orange floral
    decor, Imari type, yellow bor-
    ders 195.00
  15 x 18″, Passion Flower pattern   200.00
Tea Set, teapot, sugar, creamer,
  white with gold trim, red roses,
  marked 375.00
Tile, 6 x 6″, blue and white, oriental
  scene, 20 children and school
  masters playing, sgd 75.00
Urn, 7½″, birds and flowers, gilded
  handles 85.00
Vases
  7½″, birds and flowers decor . . .   125.00
  9″, bulbous, two handled, cream,
    flowers and butterflies 220.00
  13″, ovoid, elongated neck, black,
    neoclassical decor with cameo
    of maiden, 19th C, pr 280.00
Vegetable Dish
  Cov, leaf decor, 4 classical figures

in browns, blues and pinks,
  1877 . . . .   50.00
Wash Bowl and Pitcher, blue, leaves
  and flowers, marked 265.00

MOCHA

Mocha decoration is found on basically utilitarian creamware or stoneware articles and
is achieved by a simple chemical reaction. A
color pigment of brown, blue, green or black
is given an acid nature by infusion of tobacco or hops. When this acid colorant is applied in blobs to an alkaline ground color, it
reacts by spreading in feathery seaplant designs. This type of decoration is usually accompanied by horizontal bands of light color
slip.

Types of decoration vary greatly, from
those done in a combination of motifs such
as "Cat's Eye" with "Earthworm," to a plain
pink mug decorated with green ribbed bands.
Most forms of Mocha are hollow, such as
mugs, jugs, bowls and shakers. Majority of
articles are English, and fall into three essential dated groupings: 1780–1820, 1820–1840,
1840–1880. Marked pieces are extremely rare.

Bowls
  3¾ x 7⅜″, brown band with wavy
    white lines and tan stripes 150.00
  7½″, connected white circles on
    black ground 185.00
  8½″, Earthworm, gray, green,
    brown and white 350.00
  9″, Seaweed, on white band, yel-
    low ware 195.00
  9¼″, ftd, Earthworm, blue bands   225.00
  10″, Earthworm, jade on blue . . .   120.00
Chamber Pot, large blue decor on
  white band 125.00
Creamer, 3⅞″, Earthworm, blue,
  emb green, brown, white and
  ochre bands 385.00
Cup, 4½″, Cat's Eye 150.00
Cup and Saucer, Demitasse, marble-
  ized swirl 395.00
Jugs
  4⅞ x 4″, wide mocha band, black
    sponge trees, blue and black
    bands 165.00
  5⅝″, quart, incised plaid design
    black, blue and yellow on white   250.00
  6″, Seaweed 160.00
  7½″, Earthworm, gray, black and
    ochre 225.00
  9″, Seaweed, yellow ground, wide
    white band, blue fern and rose   375.00
Mugs
  3½″, strap handle, white and
    brown bands 185.00

Mug Mocha, ½ pint, tree design, wide blue band, black ribbon bands, $130.00.

5″, green emb rim, black and white stripes, wavy white lines on gray band, Leeds type handle 160.00
5 x 3½″, Seaweed, blue, brown and gray, Imperial Crest 175.00
6½ x 4″, wide blue band, black sponge trees, black and blue bands 130.00
Pepper Shaker, 4¼″, Seaweed, blue stripes, white band 80.00
Pitchers
5¾″, emb surface, tan and white bands, blue stripes 138.00
7″, green emb rim, marbleized decor in tan, blue, white and dark brown, Leeds type handle with green trim 325.00
8⅛″, orange with dark brown stripes and seaweed trees, green emb bands at base and rim, Leeds type handle with green trim 450.00
Salt, 2 x 3″, soft paste, orange band, brown stripes, straight earthworm design 325.00
Sugar Castors
4″, emb stripes, brown, white and green 210.00
4½″, blue and white, Earthworm in brown, black and white 165.00
Spill Holder, 4½″, emb basketweave, transparent green glaze, brown stripes 130.00
Teapot, 3½″, marbleized, brown, tan, and white 325.00
Tureen, 7 x 8½″, covered, Earthworm, green emb rim, green and dark brown stripes, gray-green band, ring handles 1,225.00

Waste Bowls
2¾ x 4¾″, Seaweed, orange band, green emb rim 170.00
3 x 5½″, Earthworm, blue, white and brown on tan band with brown stripe 140.00

MONART GLASS

Monart glass is a heavy, simply shaped art glass in which colored enamels are suspended in the glass during the glass making process. This technique was originally developed by the Ysart family in Spain in 1923; John Moncrief, a Scottish glassmaker, discovered the glass while vacationing there. He recognized the beauty and potential market for such a glass and began production in his Perth, Scotland, glassworks in 1924.

The name "Monart" is derived from the surnames Moncrief and Ysart. Two types of Monart were manufactured: a "commercial" line which incorporated colored enamels and a touch of adventurine in crystal, and the "art" line in which the suspended enamels formed designs such as feathers or scrolls. Monart glass, in most instances, is not marked since the factory used paper labels.

Vase, Monart, 14″ h, bulbous body, tapered, extended neck, flared rim, blue shaded to pink, cluthra type, highlights in gold, $625.00.

Basket, brown to light tan opal vertical striations, Cluthra-type **575.00**
Bowls
9½", pebbled light blue, border of mottled brown, goldstone **130.00**
10½ x 4¾" h, white, gray crackle, yellow, green flecks, oxblood red base, rim **150.00**
Lamp Shade, 6½" d, white opal . . . **85.00**
Vases
5⅞ x 5⅝" d, mottled blues, goldstone flecks, orig paper label . **150.00**
7 x 7" d, gray, blue, white swirls in dark red, orig paper label **130.00**
8½", bulbous, ftd, urn shaped body, flares at top, goldstone to clear abstract, Cluthra **95.00**
11", mottled orange shaded to deep orange at rim **235.00**

MOORCROFT POTTERY

William Moorcroft established the Moorcroft pottery in 1913 in Burslem, England. The majority of the ware was hand thrown, resulting in a great variation among similarly styled pieces. Moorcroft pottery is still being made. Color is a key to determining the age of older pieces. William Moorcroft died in 1945 at which time his son, Walter, continued the business.

Ashtray and Match Holder, 4½" h, pewter, pottery, circular, moonlit Hazledene pattern, imp Moorcroft, Made In England, c1920 . . . . . . **75.00**
Bowls
4½ x 2", pansies, relief, blue . . . **45.00**
7"
Band of blue flowers on interior, exterior of stylized floral panels, blue scale pattern on rim **165.00**
Ruffled brim, green flowers outlined in heavy slip, mottled blue ground, printed W. Moorcroft **200.00**
Boxes
3¾ x 5", floral motif on lid, cobalt top, silver lid, bail, marked MacIntyre **350.00**
5", oval, single poppy on cover, imp mark **60.00**
Candlesticks
3¼ x 4" d, base, dark green, varigated pink florals, green leaves, imp mark, pr **65.00**

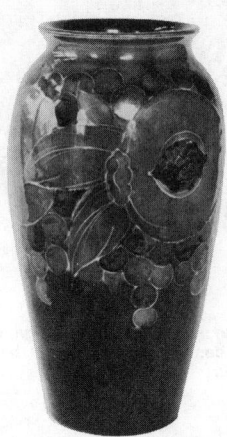

Vase, Moorcroft Pottery, 7⅜", Pomegranate, cobalt blue ground, high glaze, marked: Wm. Moorcroft in green script, imp Moorcroft/Barslem/England/39, $325.00.

7¾" h, blue carnations painted on light and dark blue grounds, printed Florian mark, c1898, pr **125.00**
Chalices
5", Spanish pattern, sgn W. Moorcroft in green **375.00**
9¼", Presentation, transfer printed iron red Waratah, poppies, light and dark blue, salmon ground, gilt, c1898 . . . . **165.00**
Clock, 5½" h, Hazledene pattern, tall green trees against pale green sky, marked "W. Moorcroft, Made For Liberty & Co.," in green, c1902 . . . . **500.00**
Coffee Set, coffee pot, cov, creamer, sugar, 4 cups with faux bamboo handles, 4 saucers, pomegranate pattern, green signature, 1914 . . . . **350.00**
Compote, 9" d, pewter pottery, circular Eventide Hazledene pattern, imp Moorcroft, Tudric, sgd W.M. in green **150.00**
Demitasse Cup and Saucer, leaves, berries, flambe glaze **65.00**
Dish, 7¼" d, round, large poppy in center, imp mark, painted initials . **70.00**
Inkwell, floral motif, blue ground, script sgr **90.00**
Jar, cov, 6½", sprays of blue stylized flowers in shaped white panels, powder blue ground, c1914 . **125.00**

Lamp, 12″ h, floral motif, dark to light blue hues, sgr 450.00
Loving Cup, 7½″ h, 3 handles, roses garland, green leaves, gilt band, white ground 200.00
Tazza, 6″ h x 8½″ d, pomegranates, grapes, blue-gray ground, Tudric pewter stand sgd MIE 01313, orig paper label 150.00
Tobacco Jar, cov, 8″ h, flared cylindrical, pomegranate pattern, green initials sgr, c1920 . . . . 120.00
Vases
  5½″ h, flared top, plums, lemons, cobalt ground, sgr Tudric Moorcroft MIE 01310 . . . . 130.00
  6½″, marine, jellyfish, fish among foliage in mottled green to sang-de-boeuf ground, imp W. Moorcroft, Potter to H.M. The Queen, W.M. in blue 260.00
  8″
    Baluster form, ftd, ink blue, apples, grapes, leaves, imp mark 175.00
    Salt glaze, band of gray and blue honesty, alternating bands of blue, white stylized flowers, imp Moorcroft, painted W. Moorcroft in blue, c1930 . . . . 225.00
  12″, bulbous upper portion, tapers to flared base, pomegranates, grapes, decor on interior also, script sgr under glaze, dated 1913 . . . . 325.00
  14½″, baluster form, hanging clustered wisteria pattern, white rim shading to deep blue base, imp Moorcroft, painted green sgr, c1920 . . . . 250.00
  19½″, baluster form, spiral bands of red wisteria crossing alternating horizontal bands at shoulder, base, lightly flambed, blue ground 300.00

MORIAGE—JAPANESE

Moriage refers to applied clay (slip) relief motifs and decorations used on certain classes of Japanese pottery and porcelain.

This decorating was done by three methods: Handrolling and shaping, which was applied by hand to the biscuit in one or more layers; the design and effect required determined thickness and shape. Tubing, or slip trailing, which applied decoration from a tube, like decorating a cake. Hakeme, which is reducing the slip to a liquid, and decorating the object with a brush. Color was applied either before or after this process.

Vase, 10″, floral pattern, green ground, $225.00.

Bisquit Jar, floral enamels, beading 219.00
Bowls
  9¼″, oval, green moriage scrollwork over brown border, lavendar and pink flowers 165.00
  10″, red roses, green foliage, moriage scroll decor 230.00
Demitasse Set, pot, open creamer, cov sugar, 6 cups, saucers, gray ground, moriage house, garden in pastel colors 150.00
Fernery, gray bisque finish, moriage trees, foliage, house, green M in wreath Nippon mark 325.00
Humidor, 6¼″, moriage motif of owl on branch, blue maple leaf Nippon mark 485.00
Jug, 6″ h, light yellow with autumn grasses, brown trim on handle, moriage wheat and leaves, blue maple leaf Nippon 300.00
Pitcher, 7¼″ h, fluted rim, base, flowers outline in moriage, scrollwork border 135.00
Plate, 6½″ d, club shape, graygreen leaves outlined in moriage, pastel flowers 165.00
Powder Jar, 4½″, cov, pink, white, purple floral medallions outlined in heavy beading 115.00
Salt and Pepper Shakers, squat, hp florals, moriage beading 115.00

Tea Set, teapot, open creamer, cov sugar, 8 cups, saucers, cake plates, gray ground, slip tailed dragon motif, marked Made In Japan 145.00

Vases

3½", 2 handles, green, pink flowers 95.00

6" h x 7½" d, Lotus pattern, handles, yellow and brown ground, pink and green enamel decor . 165.00

9¼", ftd, 2 birds perched on limb, light green ground, colorful prunus flowers, very heavy slip decor 195.00

9½", bulbous, handles, violets, leaves, beading 275.00

Cordial, amethyst, gold trim, clear stem, sgd 45.00

Cruet, 8¼", matching stopper, enamel decor in yellow, green, blue, white, gold and russet 295.00

Cup and Saucer, amber, gold florals, sgd 165.00

Decanters

14", clear, cut grapes and leaves, sgd Moser-Karlsbad 135.00

16", cranberry, gold etching, pr .. 1,250.00

Dish, 10¾ x 9", leaf shape, cranberry, gold design, sgd 400.00

Ewer, 12", amber, enameled flowers and berries, gold trim, blue handle 350.00

Finger Bowl, clear, intaglio cut, forest scene, sgd 175.00

Goblet, 5½ x 3¼" d, amber, green leaves, applied glass acorns, enameled bugs 450.00

Liqueur Set and Tray, 11¾" bottle with clear bubble stopper, four 2¾" stemmed glasses, 8⅞" tray, cranberry, lacy gold enamel decor with florals, sgd 995.00

Mug, 4¾ x 2⅝" d, rubena glass, clear applied handle, gold decor and florals 225.00

Perfume, 6½", cranberry, heavy gold enamel decor 275.00

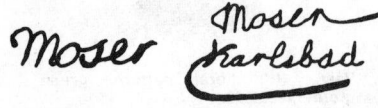

MOSER GLASS

The Moser Glassworks, Karlovy Vary, (Carlsbad), Czechoslovakia, began in 1857. It was founded by Ludwig Moser whose specialty was glass engraving. Examples include Cameo, intaglio cut and enameled glass of superior quality. The firm is currently producing two-color engraved glassware.

Bowl, 8", oval, amethyst, gilt and yellow flowers and bow, sgd 225.00

Bowl and Pitcher Set, miniature, blue, yellow and white blossoms and leaves, gold fillagree, sgd .. 240.00

Boxes

3½ x 3½", hinged, sapphire blue, gold enamel, pink, white and blue florals 245.00

4¾ x 4¾", round, amethyst, pink flowers, green leaves, large applied glass salamader, decorated with gold on top, 3 amber decorated salamader applied feet 595.00

Teal blue, hinged, ftd, encrusted with gold 260.00

Candlesticks, 13", deep topaz with band of gilded flat relief frieze, sgd Moser Karlsbad, pr 395.00

Compote, 7¼", amethyst, enameld ferns and scorns, gold border ... 300.00

Vase, 11", deep amethyst, classic warrior Frieze, gilded, German script sgd, Moser, Karlsbad, $250.00.

Pitchers
    4¼″, clear to chartreuse, enam-
    eled scrolls and flowers, ground
    pontil **100.00**
    6″ x 3½″ d, blue, applied handle,
    white enameled flowers, gold
    trim **95.00**
    6½″, green to clear, heavily
    enameled with fernery, clear ap-
    plied handle, ground pontil . . . **100.00**
Plate, 9½″, animals and people, sgd **120.00**
Rose Bowl, 5¾ x 6¼″ d, cranberry,
    gold and multicolored enamel flo-
    ral and design work, jeweled . . . **375.00**
Salt, master, 5 x 2″, oval octagon,
    amber crystal, gold filigree band,
    sgd **85.00**
Tumblers
    3½″, blue to clear, enamel floral
    decor, 8 jewels around top . . . **225.00**
    4 x 2¼″ d, amberina, IVT, enam-
    eled multicolored oak leaves
    and bug, 6 applied lustred
    acorns **190.00**
Urn, cov, 13½ x 4¾″ d, cranberry
    glass, cream, blue and green, all
    over beaded coralene in coral-like
    design, clear finial, gold trim, sgd
    and No **1,195.00**
Vases
    4″, cranberry, enamel floral sprays **300.00**
    4¼ x 2½″, orange cased, multi-
    colored enameled oak leaves, 2
    gold applied acorns, sgd and
    No **265.00**
    5¼ x 2⅜″ d, multicolored enamel
    grape leaves, green, yellow ap-
    plied glass grapes, lacy gold fo-
    liage, enamel insect, gold trim . **495.00**
    6″, yellow opalescent glass, am-
    ber applied feet, blue and rust
    enameled leaves, white and or-
    ange flowers on gold bands . . . **350.00**
    8¼″, pedestal, clear, strawberry
    and diamond panel cuttings,
    frosted panel with gold swim-
    ming angelfish, sgd **240.00**
    11″, emerald green, enamel and
    heavy gold decor, sgd **225.00**
    11″, flared cylindrical, ftd, painted
    carps, flowering branches, 2 fish
    form handles, 2 fully molded
    catfish entwining base, incised
    Moser **800.00**
    11″, light green, crimped top, flo-
    ral decor, sgd **140.00**
    11½ x 2½″, straight sided, dark
    green, flowers top and bottom,
    gold decor in middle, sgd **180.00**
Wine Glass, 8½″, cranberry bowl
    with gold leaves and grapes, berry
    prunt applied to wafer below bowl,
    twisted stem, sgd "K" **125.00**

MOSS ROSS PATTERN CHINA

**The Moss Rose was a common garden flow-
er grown in English gardens, and after the
growing china-making business in this country began to tire of Oriental china designs,
the makers chose motifs of nature and things
around them. English potters had adopted
this form as decoration for their wares, and
American manufacturers started using it, too.**

**David Haviland in France, Wedgwood,
Meakin, Powell and Bishop, were importing
china decorated with this flower to America,
and Knowles, Taylor, and Knowles, East Liverpool, Ohio, started making china with this
motif and it became very popular here. Many
collectors today are still trying to find pieces
with which to replace the dinner sets of yesterday.**

Plate, 7½″ d, $5.00.

Berry Dish, 4¾″, Haviland	**18.00**
Bowl, 7″, sq, Meakin	**18.00**
Box, 4″, cov, oval	**14.00**
Butter Pat, round	**10.00**
Cake Plate, 10″, pierced handles, ironstone	**28.00**
Candlestick, 4¾″	**25.00**
Coffee Mug and Saucer, ironstone .	**18.00**
Compote, 8½″, open, Haviland . . .	**80.00**
Creamer and Sugar, ironstone	**38.00**
Cup and Saucer, Meakin, c1870 . . .	**28.00**
Gravy Boat, underplate, ironstone .	**25.00**
Pitcher, 8″	**45.00**
Plates	
8″, Meakin	**7.50**
10″	**40.00**
Platter, 12 x 18″	**45.00**
Shaving Mug	**32.00**
Spooner, Meakin	**60.00**
Syrup, 8″	**40.00**

Teapot, 8", ironstone	68.00
Tray, 12 x 9", oval	35.00
Tureen, cov, 10", vegetable, W.H. Grindley & Co.	60.00

MONT JOYE GLASS

Mont Joye is a type of glass produced by Saint-Hilaire, Touvier, de Varreaux & Company at their glassworks in Pantin, France. Most pieces were lightly acid etched to give them a frosted appearance and decorated with enameled floral decorations. All pieces listed are frosted, unless otherwise noted.

Rose bowl, acid etched, enameled purple violets, gold stems, gold, decor, pinched sides, 3¾" h x 4¼" d, $120.00.

Bowl, 3¾", enameled floral decor, sgr	250.00
Vases	
7", enameled violets	200.00
8", amethyst, Japanese decor . .	300.00
9", enameled purple orchids, green leaves	110.00
13½", trumpet, painted silver and gold with enameled butterflies and dragonflies, sgr H	365.00
15", green, gold and silver decor, sgr	775.00
18", green, enameled purple flowers, gold leaves, sgr	250.00
21½", enameled purple and white fleurettes, asymetrical applied twist handles, clear base	185.00

MOUNT WASHINGTON GLASS CO.

The Mt. Washington Glass Co. was established in Boston, Massachusetts, in 1837 by Deming Jarves, founder of the Boston & Sandwich Glass Co., for his son George D. Jarves. In the following years the leadership and the name of the company changed several times as George Jarves formed different associations.

In the 1860s the company was owned and operated by Timothy Howe and William L. Libbey. In 1869 Libbey bought a new factory in New Bedford, Massachusetts. The Mt. Washington Glass Co. began operating again there under its original name. Henry Libbey became associated with the company early in 1871. He resigned in 1874 during the general depression and the glass works was closed. William Libbey had resigned in 1872 to work for the New England Glass Co.

Mt. Washington Glass Co. opened again in the fall of 1874 under the presidency of A. H. Seabury and the management of Frederick S. Shirley. In 1894 the glass works became a part of the Pairpoint Mfg. Co.

Throughout its history the Mt. Washington Glass Co. made a great variety of glass including; cut glass, pressed glass, blown glass and art glass.

See also BURMESE, CROWN MILANO, PEACH BLOW, ROYAL FLEMISH.

Bowl, 4½", white satin, pink floral decor	85.00

Tumbler, Crown Milano, shiny, gold decor, floral and bowknot, 3¼" h, $325.00.

Bride's Baskets

8¼", sq, cased, white interior, deep rose and white exterior, dragon, floral and leaf decor, ruffled edge, no holder	695.00
Cased, deep to pale purple interior, cream with gold decor exterior, Pairpoint holder	845.00
Condiment Set, 3 pcs, satin, ribbed, SP Pairpoint holder	225.00
Creamer, 3", melon ribbed, enameled leaf and floral decor, SP spout	160.00
Ewer, 14", Napoli, clear, gold, red, black, rose & green floral and spray decor, inside and outside, elaborate decorated applied thorn handle	2,255.00

Plates

9", floral decor	45.00
11¾", winter scene, turned up edges, original paper label . . .	465.00

Rose Bowls

Acid finish, enameled forget-me-nots decor	140.00
White, elaborate floral decor	275.00
Salt & Pepper Shakers, fig, enameled floral decor, pr	180.00

Salt Shakers

Egg, cream, daisy decor	45.00
Lay down, floral decor	38.00

Sugar Castors/Muffineers

Egg, cream, clover blossom decor	265.00
Egg, light blue, enameled floral decor	95.00
Fig, pastel floral decor	105.00
Melon, 3" d, squatty, shades of blue, wild rose decor	220.00
Ribbed, white, floral decor	120.00
Satin, cream, dainty floral decor .	250.00
Toothpick, melon, blue to white, violet decor	175.00

Vases

6", pale blue and white, enameled floral decor	82.00
7", blue satin, gilt floral decor, numbered	225.00
10", Lava, black, reeded handles, original paper label	2,150.00
10½", Lusterless White, jack-in-the-pulpit	285.00
12¼", maroon ground, cherry blossom, branch, birds, landscape decor, cased, pr	350.00
13", cameo, rosaline leaves, vines, bands cut over white . . .	965.00

MULBERRY CHINA

Mulberry china derives its name from the color of the decoration which resembles the stain of mulberry juice. Porcelains decorated as such were made mainly in the Staffordshire district of England in the 1830–50 period by several potteries.

Coffee Pot, Mulberry China, Peruvian, English registry mark, imp Ironstone, $135.00.

Bowls

Corean, 4"	60.00
Rose, 8 x 6"	55.00

Butters, cov

Coburg	120.00
Vincennes, J. Alcock	130.00
Cake Plate, Corean, 10"	42.00
Coffee Pot, Udina, J. Clementson, c1850	180.00

Creamers

Corean, Podmore and Walker . . .	40.00
Formosa, E. Challinor	85.00
Kan-Su	75.00
Washington Vase, 5½"	75.00

Cup Plates

Pelew, E. Challinor	55.00
Rose, E. Challinor	30.00

Cups and Saucers

Cyprus, Davenport, handless . . .	65.00
Genoa, Davenport, handleless . .	35.00
Ning-Po	40.00
Shapoo, handleless	45.00
Washington Vase, handleless . . .	60.00

Gravy Boats

Peru	125.00
Vincennes, John Alcott, c1840 . . .	40.00
Milk Pitcher, ½ pint, Kyber, J. Mier and Son	125.00

Plates

Allegheny, 10½", Goodfellow, c1850	45.00
Athens, 9", Adams	28.00
Bachara, 9", Edwards, c1847 . . .	25.00

Birmah, 9½", "C" 30.00
Calcutta, 10¾" 40.00
Castle Scenery, 10½" 35.00
Cyprus, 10½", Davenport 50.00
Delhi, 9½", M. T. and Co. 35.00
Flora, T. Walker, c1840 .... 32.00
Jeddo, 10½", Adams and Son .. 45.00
Kyber, 10" 55.00
Ning-Po, 9½", R. H. and Co. ... 35.00
Sunflower, 10¾" 45.00
Temple, Podmore and Walker ... 35.00
Tiroli, 9", Meigh 25.00
Tonquin, 6" 40.00
Washington Vase, 8¾" 40.00
Platters
Corean, Podmore and Walker ... 100.00
Cyprus, 13½ x 10¼", Davenport,
c1850 .... 95.00
Formosa, E. Challinor 85.00
Neva, 16" 85.00
Vincennes, octagon 65.00
Relish, Milan, 6 sides, handle 40.00
Sauce Tureen, Peru, Holdcraft and
Co., with matching plate and ladle 150.00
Shaving Mug, Pelew 150.00
Sugar, covered
Cyprus, Davenport, handled and
pagoda shape 100.00
Pelew 85.00
Washington Vase 100.00
Teapot, Shapoo 95.00
Vegetable Dish, covered
Allegheny, T. Goodfellow 85.00
Hong, octagonal, ftd 79.00
Jeddo, Adams 110.00
Ning-Po 195.00
Wash Bowl and Pitcher, Washington
Vase, bowl, pitcher, toothbrush
holder, shaving mug, soap dish .. 750.00

MUSIC BOXES

**Music boxes were invented in Switzerland
around 1825. The instrument contained a cylinder (pin barrel) and a sounding board
encased in a wooden enclosure. Later instruments used metal discs; still later ones had
paper rolls resembling player piano rolls.**

**See *Warman's Americana & Collectibles* for
additional listings of Music Boxes.**

Album, 1¾" cylinder, Paillard, Art
Nouveau style, c1900 .... 350.00
Barrel Organ, Microcourt, 17" pinned
barrel, 10 tunes, tune sheet, 51
pipes in 3 racks, tune change
knife and barrel change door on
sides, wind handle in front, 36½"
walnut case with classical columns 1,650.00
Bird in Cage, 11", clockwork mecha-

**Bird's-eye case, 3⅜ x 5⅜ x 2½",
$57.50.**

nism, bird sings, turns head,
moves head and tail, German,
early 20th C 250.00
Clock, 22", six figures playing
struments in courtly garden setting, 9 movements, glass dome
with painted landscape, ovoid
base has clock, 8" cylinder, Nicole
Freres, c1875 .... 1,540.00
Cuff Style, 7½" cuffs, Otto & Sons
Capital, Style C, single comb, side
crank, 12 cuffs, 27½" mahogany
case, American, c1895 .... 4,700.00
Lady Plays Guitar, 13½", bisque
head, blue glass eyes, pierced
ears, closed mouth, silk dress,
head turns as she strums, cylinder
in base, French, late 19th C 2,750.00
Melodia, 7¾" roll, 14 reeds, walnut
case 500.00
Monkey Violinist, seated, 21½",
head turns and nods, eyes blink,
mouth opens, right arm lifting and
stroking violin, left foot taps, cylinder, string wind in wood base,
French, c1870 .... 3,400.00
Roller Organs
Concert Roller, 20 note organ,
front hand crank, 30 cobs, 14"
walnut case, American, late
19th C 525.00
Origuinette Co. "Musical Casket,"
14 note organ, 12 paper rolls,

side hand crank, 12″ oak case, stenciled, New York, late 19th C **300.00**
Snuff Box, 3¾″, metal case, orange enameled, view of the Place de la Coeur de Notre-Dame á Zurich on lid, 2 control buttons in front, 2 airs, late 19th C **125.00**

CYLINDER-TYPE

4″ cylinder, 4 airs, key wind, 12″ wood case with boxwood stringing, late 19th C **525.00**

6″ cylinder, 6 airs, lever wind, 13¾″ wood case, inlaid floral bouquet, Swiss, late 19th C ... **600.00**

8″ cylinder, Paillard, 8 airs, tune sheet, side crank, 17″ wood case, Swiss, late 19th C **650.00**

10½″ cylinder, Francois Nicole, 8 airs, 4 section comb, key wind, 3 control levers at side, 16″ walnut case, brass mounted, fitted into 30″ walnut writing table, hinged top with mirror and drawer, Swiss, c1830 .... **1,700.00**

10¾″ cylinder, Paillard, Vaucher, Fils, 8 tunes, tune sheet, lever wind, 20″ rosewood case, foliate inlay, Swiss, c1870 ...... **850.00**

11″ cylinder, Bremond, 6 airs, tune sheet, side lever wind, 20″ rosewood case, foliate inlay, Swiss, c1870 .... **1,375.00**

11″ cylinder, Baker-Troll Sublime Harmony, 8 airs, 2 piece comb, tune sheet, tune selector, speed control, lever wind, 22½″ walnut veneered case, Swiss, c1895 .... **1,540.00**

13″ cylinder, Bremond "Mandoline and Bells in View," 4 cylinders with 6 airs on each, tune sheet, 6 bells with bird strikers, 37″ walnut veneered case, fruitwood banding, storage drawer, Swiss, c1880 .... **3,300.00**

13″ cylinder, Mojon Manager "Soprano Bells in View," 12 airs, tune sheet, 6 bells, zither, tune indicator, side lever wind, 26″ walnut veneered case, inlaid cartouche, Swiss, c1900 ..... **990.00**

13½″ cylinder, Paillard, 10 airs, tune sheet, side crank wind, rosewood case, foliate inlay, Swiss, c1880 .... **1,100.00**

15¼″ cylinder, Bremond "Bells in View," 10 airs, tune sheet, 9 bells, lever wind at side, 26½″ walnut veneered case, foliate inlay, Swiss, c1875 .... **2,100.00**

17¼″ cylinder, Bremond "Mandoline," 6 airs, tune sheet, side lever wind, 26½″ rosewood case, foliate inlay, Swiss, c1870 .... **2,750.00**

17⅜″ cylinder, Expressive, 7 airs, 2 section comb, lever wind, 30½″ burr walnut case, fruitwood banding, Swiss, late 19th C ... **1,000.00**

18¼″ cylinder, Baker-Troll, 6 airs, 3 piece comb, tune indicator, lever wind, double spring barrels, zither, 31½″ walnut case, wood chalet applied to lid, Swiss, c1890 .... **1,900.00**

19½″ cylinder, J. H. Heller "Organocleide-Piccolo-Harpe," 8 airs, 2 piece comb, tune sheet, lever wind at side, 32½″ rosewood case, fruitwood banding, Swiss, c1880 .... **2,750.00**

DISC-TYPE

Kalliope
9¼″ disc, peripheral driven, 6 bells, start/stop lever, single comb, crank wind in front, 11½″ walnut case, inlaid lid, German, c1890 .... **1,250.00**

17¾″ disc, peripheral driven, start/stop lever, single comb, crank wind at front, 41 discs, 25″ walnut case, German, c1900 .... **1,320.00**

Mermod Freres
17¼″ disc, "Stella," peripheral driven, start/stop and fast/slow levers, double comb, side crank wind, 29″ mahogany case, drawer, 18 discs, Swiss, c1905 .... **1,100.00**

26″ disc, "Stella," peripheral driven, double comb, side crank wind, 79″ mahogany case, glazed door flanked by columns above storage cabinet, carved laurel wreath, Swiss, c1905 .... **880.00**

Polyphon
9¾″ disc, peripheral driven, start/stop, wind on side, 12½″ wood case, lithograph under lid, German, c1900 ... **925.00**

19⅝″ disc, Style 104, coin operated, peripheral driven, double comb, coin slots at each side, 38″ walnut case, German, c1900 .... **1,700.00**

Regina
15¼″ disc, Style 35, automatic changer, peripheral driven, double comb, rack for 12 discs, selector and crank at side, 24 discs, 68″ mahogany

bow front case, spiral columns, American, c1902 .... **12,100.00**

15½" disc, Style 11, peripheral driven, start/stop lever, double comb, side crank wind, 6 discs, 22½" oak case with drawer, American, c1895 ... **2,970.00**

20¾" disc, Style 39, peripheral driven, start/stop and fast/slow levers, double comb, side crank wind, 7 discs, 29" curved mahogany case with cupola lid, American, c1910 . **2,970.00**

27" disc, Style 8, automatic changer, peripheral driven, double comb, rack for 12 discs, selector and crank at side, 31 discs, 69" mahogany case, dragon spandrels and spooled top railing, American, c1898 .... **6,600.00**

Symphoniom, 11⅞" disc, lever wind in front, start/stop control on side, 19½ x 15" burl walnut case, inlaid bird, tree and floral decor on lid **2,700.00**

MUSICAL INSTRUMENTS

Down through the ages people have stamped their feet, clapped their hands or were compelled to sit quietly when music was 'in the air.' Musical instruments have changed very little since the original forms. Perhaps the case design, the material used or ornamentation has changed, but a flute is a flute.

Accordian, wooden case, German . **150.00**

Banjo, 5 strings, bird's eye maple, original case, "Howe-Stowe" ... **75.00**

Banjo, 5 strings, professional, complete with velvet lined case and tenor tuner, "Vega" **200.00**

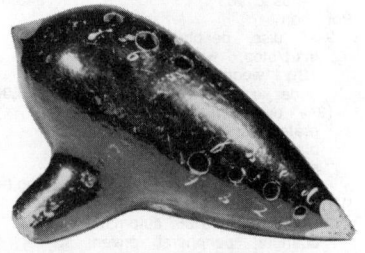

Ocarina, "Sweet Potato," wooden, black with gold trim, $25.00.

Bugle, 3 valves, stamped C.A. Zoebisch & Sons/Makers/NY, 10⁷/₁₆" l **275.00**

Clarinets

Normandy, orig case, French ... **120.00**

Reed, boxwood, brass, 23" l ... **185.00**

Concertina, German with leather case **75.00**

Display Case, glass slant front, Bell Brand Musical Instruments, c1930 **125.00**

Dulcimer, walnut **125.00**

Fife, rosewood, pewter mounts, 1862 inscribed **85.00**

Flute, solid silver, case, marked Gemeinhardt **100.00**

Glockenspiel, two rows of steel bars supported on brass posts, tubular brass harp with 14 bars **175.00**

Guitar, "National Triolan," c1929 .. **350.00**

Harmonica, brass, c1875 .... **75.00**

Harmonica, "Hohner" Marine Band, script sgr. Made in Germany **15.00**

Harp, Lap, c1880's **200.00**

Mandolin, string band, c1920 ..... **35.00**

Organs

Aeolian Grand, 73 keys, 20 stops, mahogany cabinet, nickelplated hardware, needs restoring **1,500.00**

Chicago Cottage, ornate cabinet including spindled back, lamp holders, c1900, restored **3,000.00**

Miller, mahogany, restored, c1892 **2,500.00**

Munroe Organ Reed Co., 55" h, Orchestrone Style 44B, paper rolls, orig label with company name, "built for M. Gally, Inventor and Proprietor", walnut case **1,000.00**

Pianos

Blasius & Sons, 64 note, mechanical **1,500.00**

Chickering, Ampico Baby Grand, case painted in greens, floral sprays, cartouches of frolicking cherubs, carved legs **1,600.00**

Knaube, baby grand, Louis XV style **3,000.00**

Morgan Davis, Pianoforte, c1910 **900.00**

Steinway & Sons, mahogany, baby grand **3,600.00**

Van Dyke, 88 note, upright mechanical, restored **2,500.00**

Saxophone, tenor, brass, "Buescher," c1935 .... **850.00**

Trombone, Campo, nickel over brass, case **85.00**

Trumpet, brass, orig case **45.00**

Viola, one piece back construction, Germany, 18th C **350.00**

Violins

Child's, ¾ size, German label, orig fitted case, bow **75.00**

Handmade, Hardin Co., Iowa, wooden case **85.00**

Heberlein, yellow-orange varnish
orig case 750.00
Zithers
MOP inlay, fitted wooden case . . 135.00
Schwartzer-Washington, concert
grade, fitted case 250.00

MUSTACHE CUPS AND SAUCERS

Mustache cups were popular in the late Victorian period (1880–1890). The majority were made and decorated by the transfer method in Germany. The rarest items in this group are the left-handed cups. They are rare and have been reproduced.

"Think of Me," green trim, gold lines, incised Germany, $26.00.

PORCELAIN

Applied floral decor 22.00
Floral sprays, blue ground, cherub
handle 50.00
Hand Painted
Roses, gilt trim, left handed 90.00
Scenes of house, fence, trees, gilt
trim 98.00
Violets, leaves 35.00
Lime green, pink roses, green
leaves, To A Friend 32.00
Limoges, gold prunus blossom,
marked Elite 50.00
Nippon, moriaga palm scene decor,
blue maple leaf mark 130.00
Pink, gold lattice work, red branch-
es, ftd 80.00
R. S. Prussia, swirled ribs, pink blos-
soms decor 140.00
Salmon pink, white, purple florals,
gilt trim 45.00

SILVER PLATED

Engraved florals, leaf design, beaded loop handle 100.00
Repousse florals, initials, dated 1902 135.00
Scroll work, dated 1896, Gorham,
initials 25.00

NAILSEA GLASS

Although glass was made in Nailsea, England, "Nailsea-type glass" was made during the late 18th and early 19th centuries by several glass makers, including glass works in America. Characteristics of Nailsea glass are its opaque loopings, swirls or spatters on clear or colored glass. Therefore, it is more appropriate to apply the name "Nailsea" to the decoration and technique rather than the provenance. The acid finished pieces are also called Verre Moire glass.

Bell, 12", cranberry, clear handle
and stopper 195.00
Bottles
9½", brown, white looping, c1810 250.00
10", Gemel, clear, pink and white
looping 235.00
Bowl, 5½", blue, white looping, ruffled rim 95.00
Candlesticks, 12", pr 90.00
Cruet, 6¼", clear, pink and white
looping, applied frosted handle
and base 175.00
Doorstop, 4½" h, green bubbled
glass, bulbous, knob finial 70.00
Epergne, peach satin, white looping,
single lily 345.00

Fairy Lamp, 4¾" h x 4" d base, rose, white looping, frosted, S. Clarke clear glass base, $295.00.

Fairy Lamps, See FAIRY LAMPS

Flasks

  Cobalt blue, white loopings, orig
    leather case 85.00

  Double red, and white looping,
    blue ring around spout 95.00

Inkwell, 15", light green, c1820 . . .   65.00

Jug, 11" h, green glass, metal paint
  spatters of white, ochre, red, applied handle 400.00

Pipes

  10½" long, curved stem, pink,
    white looping 125.00

  14" long, clear, red and white
    looping 175.00

Pitchers

  6¾", clear, white looping, applied
    handle 165.00

  8", cranberry, white looping, clear
    applied handle 175.00

  9½", clear, white looping, clear
    applied handle 250.00

Rolling Pin, clear, lavendar and
  white loopings 135.00

Rose Bowl, cranberry satin, white
  loopings, applied camphor satin
  ribbon edge 225.00

Toothpick, cobalt blue, white looping   65.00

Vases, 10½", blue and white, clear
  base, pr 155.00

Walking Stick, 40½" l, c1830 . . . . .   75.00

Witch Ball, 4¼", pale blue looping .   95.00

NANKING

**Nanking is a type of Chinese export porcelain
made in Canton, China, from the early 1800s
into the 20th century for export to America
and England. It is often confused with the
Canton pattern.**

**Three elements help distinguish Nanking
from Canton. Nanking has a spear and post
border, as opposed to the scalloped line
style of Canton. The blues may tend to be
darker on the Nanking ware. Second, in the
water's edge or Willow pattern, Canton usually has no figures. Nanking features a standing figure with open umbrella on the bridge.
Finally, Nanking wares often are embellished
with gold.**

**Green and orange variations of Nanking
survive, although they are scarce. Copies of
Nanking ware currently are being produced
in China. They are of inferior quality and decorated in lighter rather than the darker blues.**

Bottle, water, 8" 375.00

Bowl, 6 x 9", oval, reticulated,
  matching underplate 750.00

Cider Jug, cover, 9⅛", Willow pattern variation, c1800 . . . . 500.00

**Plate, 9½", water edge scene, c1780–
1800, $80.00.**

Cup Plate, 5½", lozenge shape,
  short straight sides, flat bottom . . 125.00

Cups and Saucers

  Baroque Handle 55.00

  Handleless 75.00

Dishes

  6", leaf shape, c1840 . . . . 135.00

  11¼", figures in sampan, c1800 . 285.00

Ginger Jar, 6" 150.00

Mug, 4¾", birds over river 275.00

Plates

  8" 75.00

  10", oval, reticulated border,
    c1790 . . . . 250.00

Platters

  14", oval, c1800 . . . . 375.00

  15¾", oval, Chinese man with
    parasol in river scene, c1800 . . 450.00

Tureens

  10", oval, acorn knop on lid, gilt
    trim, late 18th C 650.00

  14", oval, 12" h, foliate knop on
    lid, c1790 . . . . 800.00

NAPKIN RINGS, FIGURAL

**During the Victorian Era, dining was most
gracious in the home; each member of the
family had a personal napkin ring. Figural
napkin rings were first patented in 1869, and
through the remainder of the century nearly
all of the silverplating companies developed
similarly beautiful products for Americans.
Values are determined today by the subject
matter of the ring, the quality of the workmanship, and the condition. For other types
of napkin rings, see the specific categories.**

**See *Warman's Americana & Collectibles* for
an expanded listing of Napkin Rings other
than figural.**

Barrels
  Ring on hickory sawhorse 55.00
  Ring on seat of high-backed hickory chair 130.00
Bird, long tailed, perched on top of ring, elaborately scrolled base, Apollo Silver Plate Co., #141 ... 125.00
Boys
  Trudges uphill lugging ring over his shoulder, Barbour Silver Co. 195.00
  Young, standing behind ring on rectangular base, Simpson, Hall, Miller Co. 160.00
Cat and Chick, oval ring between them, Meriden #361 .... 140.00
Cat standing beside ring, full figural, Eureka Silver Plate Co. 175.00
Cherubs
  Four in "Atlas" pose hold ring above their heads 95.00
  Pair, winged, elaborately chased oval ring support the napkin ring on their wings, Wilcox Silver Plate Co. 135.00
  Pulling cart, moveable wheels ... 185.00
Chick, stands guard over ring, oval base with ball feet, portion of orig label intact, Meriden #222 ..... 200.00
Chicken Wishbones, straddling triangular ring, inscribed "Best Wishes" 95.00
Dogs
  Crouching with ring on his back . 175.00
  Pointing stance, rectangular base, supports ring on back, Simpson, Hall, Miller Co. 175.00
  Pulling cart, moveable wheels, cherub riding on top of napkin ring 220.00
Egyptian figures, elongated legs, stand on either side of ring with bud vase 170.00

Foxes
  Ring with vintage decor, ornate base, fox on one side, bunch of grapes on other 195.00
  Sitting on rectangular base, back to oval ring 120.00
Goat harnessed to cart, moveable wheels 225.00
Hen, casts watchful eye over baby chick standing next to ring 170.00
Horses
  Prancing, ring on his back, sq base, ball feet 175.00
  Pulling cart, moveable wheels ... 215.00
Kate Greenaway
  Boy, feeding puppy, floral rectangular base, Cromwell 200.00
  Girl with muffs and playful dog on either side of ring 200.00
Lily Pad shaped base with finger grip handle supports ring on pedestal 130.00
Lions
  Ring on back, rectangular base, ring inscribed "1887," Meriden 145.00
  Standing, leans against ring, rectangular base 150.00
Owl perched on leaf-shaped base, Van Bergh Co., #99 .... 135.00
Pear and Leaves, twig base, monogrammed 55.00
Squirrels
  Front paws on napkin ring which is balanced on pile of acorns, Simpson, Hall, Miller Co. 160.00
  Munching on nut, stands on branch, tail draped over top of ring 115.00
Swans supporting ring on their wings, oval base 145.00
Turtle Doves, wings spread, support napkin ring between them, Middletown Plate #74, pr 115.00

Cherubs, hands clasped behind them holding ring, rectangular base, Meriden, $245.00.

NASH GLASS

Arthur Nash and his sons, Leslie and Douglas, were employed by Tiffany Furnaces, Corona, Long Beach Island, in the early 1900s. It has been reported that the Nash family was responsible for designing, producing and promoting the iridescent glass for which Tiffany's received recongnition.

Arthur Nash was a former member of the Woodall Gem Cameo team of Thomas Webb, England.

See LIBBEY GLASS.

Bowl, 5¾", inverted rim with leaf design, sgd 125.00
Candlesticks
  4½", blue irid, sgd. and no'd, pr . 500.00

Cologne Bottle, Nash Glass, Chintz, wide pale green stripes separated by wide clear stripes with thin blue centers, clear stopper, 5″ h, marked Nash/1008/JJ, $485.00.

5″, gold irid, pr	275.00
Plates	
4½″, amber irid, scalloped edge, sgd. and no'd	300.00
6½″, Spiral, orchid and clear, sgd	130.00
8″, Chintz, green and blue	165.00
Salt, 1¼ x 4″, gold irid, ruffled top, sgd. and no'd	350.00
Stemware	
Cordials, Chintz	
4″, blue, green	55.00
5½, blue, green	70.00
Wine, 6″, pink, green Chintz	75.00
Vases	
4¼″, gold irid, labelled 544, Nash	375.00
5¾″, red, silver Chintz, sgr., numbered	625.00
6¼ x 3½″ dia at top, trumpetshape, Chintz, sgd. and no'd	350.00
8½″, Chintz, green, brown, gold flecks	240.00

NAUTICAL ITEMS

The sea always has held a strong fascination for collectors. The objects listed focus on the historic period of the sailing and clipper ships along with the related aspects of naval warfare and whaling.

Naval supplies were manufactured in the United States and abroad. They represent the highest quality of workmanship. The instruments and implements had to withstand heavy use. In addition, many hand made objects survive as sailors, ship carpenters, or ship blacksmith's perfected items to individual taste.

See also BELLS, SCIENTIFIC INSTRUMENTS, SCRIMSHAW, and SWORDS.

Advertising Card, 6 x 3¼″, reads "Splendid A1 First Class Small Clipper Ship *Florence*, F. D. Wadsworth, Master . . . "	210.00
Bell, brass, 8¼″, sailor's ropework bellpull on clapper	175.00
Billet Head, 16½″ l, carved from single pc of cedar, painted green, from *bark California*, c1850	990.00
Black Powder Case, 9½″ l, rosewood box, hinged lid, green velvet fitted lining, removeable copper powder cannister, 7 painted tinware powder canes, lid marked Walker patented, whaleship, 19th C	880.00
Block, double, 7″ l, whale ivory, fastened with copper pins, sheaves of whale ivory, hand forged iron	

Naval Compass, c1900, $300.00.

hook fastener, soft line strap wrapped with sail cloth **770.00**

Cabin Lantern, 23″ l, hanging, boxed with 4 pine posts, glass panes, plank top, base, brass vent, orig oil lamp **715.00**

Captain's Weather Slate, 9¼ x 13″, rectangular board framed in wood, suspended from string, engraved with grid for recording weather and wind statistics **412.00**

Compass, brass, in case, gimbals, wood box with copper lamp holder, lamp, 7½″ l **250.00**

Crew List, containing names of crew, position, number of shares in voyages to be received, Sept 6, 1853, whaleship *Montpelier* **120.00**

Flag Bag, 79 x 29″ w, letters of alphabet, ship's ensign, burgee, another flag, label reads "International Code of Signals Including Jack" **675.00**

Flag, American, 37 stars, marked D. B. Greene, from whaleship *William S. Henry*, 139½ x 76½″ **650.00**

Log Book, New York Schooner, *Eliza A. Anderson*, Captain R. E. Clark, gulf coast trade, Oct 1873 to June 1876, 136 pgs, 9¾ x 15¾″, cover loose, fragile binding **240.00**

Models

Cutty Sark, 42 x 26″ h, clipper ship, mahogany, glass case . . **1,300.00**

Gertrude L. Theabeau, 44″ x 36″ h, sailor's model, Glouster schooner **2,100.00**

Mooring Buoy, 21″ d, old red paint, 12 feet of orig anchor chain, 19th C **250.00**

Oar, steering, 17′ l, 19th C whaleboat **200.00**

Sail Creaser, 5¾″, carved whalebone handle, serrated brass wheel fastened with iron pin **82.00**

Sailmaker's Seam Marker, carved whalebone handle, toothed steel wheel, brass pin, c1875 . . . . . . **375.00**

Salute Cannon, 22″ l, iron, muzzle dated 1864, ship *Howard L. Coe* . **500.00**

Spyglass, 2 drawer, brass, orig leather covering, W. Ashmore, London, 36″ l **200.00**

Telescope, brass, sighting scope, tripod, approx 60 power, by J. S. Marratt, London Bridge **1,100.00**

Valentine, 9″ d, double, octagonal mahogany cases worked with variety of pastel colored Caribbean mollusk shells, spell out Home Again, case fitted with glass plates **2,420.00**

Whaling

Binnacle, copper plate body, oval glass windows, 2 set-in lighting boxes, orig oil lamps, mounted on turned and laminated wood base, from whaling schooner *Gaspe*, 28″ h **1,320.00**

Blubber Knife, 60″, steel blade fitted to wood pole, flensing, stamped A.A.F. **225.00**

Harpoons

32″, diamond point, Macy toggle, orig spliced line, 19th C . **690.00**

9½′, double flue, artic, orig pole, incised H **375.00**

Piggin, 12″ d x 8½″ h, painted pine, iron hoops, one stave extended as handle, used for bailing **275.00**

Whalebone Scale, 92½″ l, marked 800 lbs, H.M. Co., 5 counter weights **1,500.00**

Wheels

32″, from wreck of whaleship *Wanderer*, wrecked on Cuttyhunk Island, 1924 . . . . . . **250.00**

48″, mahogany, oak, *Ship Rousseau*, 19th C **990.00**

NAZI ITEMS

This field has enjoyed immense popularity over the last few years. It also has attracted those firms and individuals who specialize in reproduction equipment. In fact, several military price guides carry listings of reproduction items. Know your dealer or have the item checked for you by an established collector.

See *Warman's Americana & Collectibles* for an expanded listing of Nazi Items.

Armband, swastika on white ground, red, 4 x 10½″ **8.00**

Badge, Luftwaffe pilot's badge, white medal, silver wash **95.00**

Barrel Carrier, MG 42 . . . . **35.00**

Bayonet, Army dress, long model . . **40.00**

Bayonet Frog, dress, black leather . **10.00**

Belt, officers, black leather, open pebbled buckle **30.00**

Blanket, Wehrmacht, wool, gray . . . **22.00**

Breadbag, Army **28.00**

Breeches

Gabardine, black, white piping, RZM-SS label **145.00**

SA Wehrmann, 1944 . . . . **78.00**

Brush, KAR 98K Mauser pull-thru . . **4.00**

Buckle, Luftwaffe, officer **20.00**

Caps

Dak, tropical, IM, overseas with insignia **60.00**

SS overseas side cap, eagle, skull and crossbones **150.00**

Coverall, camouflage, W/SS P44 . . **1,600.00**

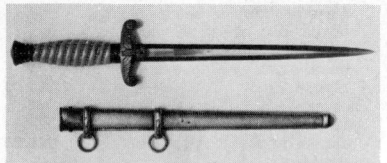

Officer's dress dagger, 15″, $220.00.

Dagger, Luftwaffe, 1st Model	240.00
Entrenching Tool with Cover	20.00
Field Radio	35.00
Flags	
Hitler Youth	325.00
National War Flag, swastika	110.00
Flashlight, belt	25.00
Gloves, Wehrmacht, wool, gray . . .	18.00
Goggles	
Luftwaffe, extra lenses in tin box .	50.00
Rubber, red lens, pouch	15.00
Hats	
Luftwaffe Anti Aircraft emblem with early insignia, "Deutsche Wertarbeit," visor, 1933	265.00
SS M43, SS eagle and skull on green backing, rough wool . . .	175.00
Waffen SS, green fez, size 60 . .	275.00
Waffen SS officer, visor, white piped with black velvet band and makers label	725.00
Helmets	
Air raid, Luftachutze insignia, chin strap	60.00
Crash, black with black flap, NSKK	145.00
M42, steel, liner and chin strap . .	45.00
Helmet Cover, Falschirmjaeger, green splinter camouflage	75.00
Jackboots, black leather	65.00
Magazine, MP 41	60.00
Medals	
Iron Cross, 2nd class, ribbon . . .	22.50
Service Medal, 18 years, silver maltese cross	50.00
Medic' Pouch, large, black leather .	35.00
Motorcycle Coat, tropical	225.00
Pancho, camouflage	50.00
Raincape, Luftwaffe, dark blue, red piping around collar	90.00
Ring, officers, red, black, white stripes, 800 silver	100.00
Rucksack with straps, Luftwaffe, blue	45.00
Shoe Horn, bakelite, Schuhaus Weber/Kirchberg mark	3.00
Sling, MG 42, leather	35.00
Stein, Reichs-Fuehrer-Schule, ½ l, gray, blue enamel RFS Chiffres .	95.00
Swords	
Army officers, lion head pommel .	175.00

Police and Fire Dept., officers . . .	180.00
SS (Elite Guard), non commissioned officer	240.00
Trousers, mountain troop, green/white, reversible, wind proof	100.00
Tunic and Pants, tunic has Russian Front ribbon, 1944 model	150.00
Underwear, tropical net, 2 pcs	30.00

NETSUKES

The traditional Japanese kimono has no pockets. Daily necessities such as keys, money purses, tobacco supplies, etc., are carried by hanging them from a cord with a Netsuke toggle. Netsuke comes from "neroot" and "tuske"—to fasten.

A Netsuke has two holes drilled at an angle so they come together at the bottom. The holes usually are of different sizes. The Netsukes are made from a wide variety of materials—bone, horn, ivory, lacquer, metal, porcelain, semi-precious stones, and wood. Average size is 1 to 2 inches.

Value depends on artist, region, material and skill of craftsmanship. We have concentrated on signed examples because they are the most actively sought by serious collectors.

CAUTION! Recent reproductions are on the market. Many are carved from African ivory.

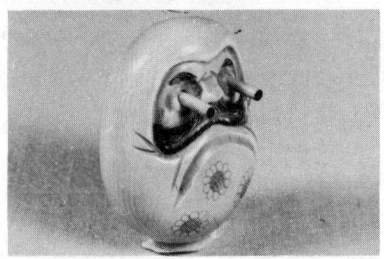

Carved ivory Netsuke, popping eyes, $125.00.

SIGNED

Barrel Maker, man beside barrel holding hammer, ivory, Kazuyuki .	130.00
Boys, playing in a pile, stained ivory, Ono Ryomin, late 19th C	770.00
Cow and Calf, reclining, nestling calf at her side, ivory, Tomotada, c1781	2,200.00
Dancer, New Year's, balancing on	

one foot, holds rattle and fan, inlaid ivory, Tomachika, 19th C ... **660.00**

Horse, atop large gourd, stained ivory, Anraku, 19th C **470.00**

Kakio with Wife and Child, digging up pot of gold, stained ivory, Tomochika, 19th C **330.00**

Mermaid, clutching her tail, wood, Tomin, 19th C **1,100.00**

Monkey and Octopus, entwined, inlaid horn eyes, ivory, IK Kosai, late 19th C **1,925.00**

Nue, open jaw, fierce expression, clutching human skull, wood, Kokei, c1800 .... **990.00**

Obeshimi Mask, furrows brow, bites lower lip, black and red detail, ivory, Ryumin, 19th C **715.00**

Owl, two owlets, atop, gnarled vine covered log, inlaid horn eyes, wood, Tomokazu, 19th C **2,200.00**

Oxherd, sitting atop ox, ivory, Shukosai Anraku, 19th C **495.00**

Persimmon, attached to leafy branch, dark horn ladybug, stained ivory, Hoichi, 19th C **302.00**

Puppy, cuddling large bell tied to it's tail with rope, ivory, Chokusai, 19th C **700.00**

Rats, seven, entwined, ivory, Kiku . **225.00**

Shishimai Dancer, lion headdress, beating drum, broken umbrella over her head, ivory, Joso, late 19th C **1,650.00**

Tiger, atop large stone, open jaw, wood, Kokei, c1800 .... **770.00**

UNSIGNED

Barbarian, tall, long hair, knotted grass skirt, holding coral branch, ivory **770.00**

Boy, smiling cat on leash, black hairwork, ivory, 19th C **2,200.00**

Dog, reclining, thick pleated coat, ivory, 18th C **1,760.00**

Dutchman, tall, wearing wide feathered hat, holding large crane, ivory, 18th C **1,650.00**

Lotus Leaf, large, insect eaten, folded, small crab, tiny gilt dewdrops, gilt metal, 19th C **137.00**

Masks, five in round cluster, inlaid wood, 19th C **440.00**

Puppies, seated puppy with second puppy climbing over it's back, ivory, 18th C **275.00**

Rat, climbing atop uncoiling rope, engraved black hairwork, ivory, 19th C **880.00**

Seals, red and black staining, ivory, 19th C **390.00**

Sumo Wrestlers, two, ivory **160.00**

NEW HALL CHINA

The **New Hall China Manufacturing Co.** was in business from 1781–1835. This factory made both hard paste and soft paste porcelains. New Hall was the only firm to make the transition from hard paste to bone porcelain. New Hall China has been heavily imitated. An excellent reference book on New Hall China is David Holgate's *New Hall and its Imitators*, which lists 1681 patterns.

Teapot, New Hall China, Georgian Silver shape, red, pink trim, pastel flowers, vase finial, No. 594, c1780-1805, $190.00.

Coffee Pot, floral, gilded leaves, white berries **200.00**

Cream Jug, unknown pattern **165.00**

Creamer, pink lustre decor **75.00**

Cups and Saucers
   Blossom band decor **50.00**
   Family scene in pink, blue, green and brown **65.00**
   Flower decor in green, red, yellow **60.00**
   Oriental figures, flowers **60.00**
   Pattern 195, early **80.00**

Mug, small, oriental decor **65.00**

Plates
   7¼", rose decor **65.00**
   8", deep with center bouquet and single floral motifs at intervals around border, c1790, marked . **130.00**

Platter, 16½ x 21", two scenes— one with sailboat, other with stream and trees **175.00**

Saucer, c1785 .... **60.00**

Sugar Bowl, pink lustre decor **110.00**

Tea Bowl and Saucer, Pat. 195, set **95.00**

Teapots, covered
   Chinese pattern **150.00**

Chippendale shape	165.00
Flower spray	165.00
Pink lustre decor	165.00
Oriental figure, Swan finial	250.00

Tea Services

15 pieces, pattern 139	750.00
26 pieces, pattern 1064	1,075.00
29 pieces, pattern 1278	1,250.00

NEW MARTINSVILLE GLASS

New Martinsville Glass Manufacturing Company began operation in 1901. Art glass produced during the early years of the company rivaled, in beauty and design, foreign products. Unfortunately, these pieces had limited production when a fire destroyed the plant in 1907. Thereafter, the fragile Peachblow and other types of art glass were never again produced.

Four periods of production are noteworthy: 1901–1907, Art and opaque glass including "Peachblow;" 1907–1937, pressed pattern glass; 1937–1944, crystal wares including the animal line; 1944, contemporary novelties and tableware.

When the company went into receivership in 1931, the plant was sold and the business was reopened as the New Martinsville Glass Company. In 1944 the entire stock was purchased by G. R. Cummings and the name was changed to The Viking Glass Company under which it still operates today.

See *Warman's Americana & Collectibles* for an expanded listing of New Martinsville Glass.

Swan, 11½ x 7½ x 8½", Janice pattern, crystal, $35.00.

Animal Figurines

Bear, baby, 3"	45.00
Dog, Hunter	55.00
Elephant	65.00
Hen	65.00
Pelican, 8"	75.00
Rooster, 8½"	55.00
Seal	45.00
Squirrel, 5½"	35.00
Wolfhound	45.00

Basket, 9", cobalt handle, "Janice"	50.00

Bookends

Horses, rearing, pr	150.00
Ship, pair	30.00

Bowls

5", crystal, emb squirrels	45.00
5" d x 2" h, peachblow, pink, white exterior, unusual irid peach color interior	385.00
7¼" d x 3½" h, peachblow, deeply fluted, crimped edge, gold trim	110.00

Box, cov, 8", 3 compartments, crystal	30.00

Candlesticks

5", crystal, Pattern No. 4554, pr	12.50
Seals, pr	65.00
Swans, black, pr	30.00

Cologne Bottles, pink, orig long glass stopper, 1928	20.00

Creamers

Crystal Eagle No. 18, amber	12.50
Moondrops, ruby	15.00

Dresser Set, Leota, crystal, black amethyst stoppers, 4 pcs	45.00
Jam Jar, cov, with underplate, "Janice," blue	40.00
Pitcher, large, etched	55.00
Spooner, "Japanese Iris"	30.00

Sugars

Janice, cobalt handle	10.00
Radiance, amber	12.50

Swans

5½", black bowl, crystal neck	20.00
13", red bowl, crystal neck	65.00

Tobacco Jar, cov, black amethyst, #725	35.00
Tray, handled, blue, Pattern No. 4554	10.00

NEWCOMB POTTERY

The brilliant achievements of Newcomb pottery began in 1885 in Tulane University art classes and then at the Art Pottery Co. in New Orleans. Later in 1886, the pottery was operated in conjunction with the Art Department at Sophie Newcomb Memorial College for Women in the same city.

William and Ellsworth Woodward were the founders. The two brothers directed an elective arts program at the college which was funded generously by Josephine Louise LeMonnier Newcomb and joined to Tulane University in 1887.

Students at Newcomb College worked in the pottery, producing and painting a quality art pottery with the distinctive high gloss glaze. Designs on Newcomb wares have a decidedly Southern flavor such as myrtle, jasmine, sugar cane, moss, cypress, dogwood and magnolia.

Of particular interest to collectors are the early, highly glazed pieces. The later matte glazed pieces are usually decorated with carved-back floral designs, but pieces depicting murky, bayou scenes are most desirable.

Bowl, 6″ d, 2⅝″ h, incised green decoration on white ground, artist signed, $550.00.

Candleholder, hand thrown and cut, pink blossoms, blue ground, sgd .	300.00
Mug, 5″ h, 5″ d, stylized blue floral design, beige ground, high glaze .	450.00
Plaque, 9 x 6″, bayou scenic, average carving and coloring, orig frame	1,000.00
Plates, dinner, set of 6, border designs of carved, blue and green flowers, light green ground, high glaze, all sgd	2,000.00

Vases

5″ h, 4″ w, bayou scenic, lighter shades of blue, no moon, shallow carving, matte glaze, sgd .	400.00
5″ h, 4″ w, bulbous body, carved back, 5 pedal flowers in white, blue ground, matte glaze	300.00
6½″, slightly tapered cylinder body, shoulders leading to extended straight neck, pale blue matte glaze over long green	

stems and white flowers extending top to bottom, sgd . .	450.00
7″ h, 6″ w, bayou scenic with oak trees, Spanish moss, and full moon, carved, sharp colors, matte glaze, sgd	600.00
8″ h, 4″ w, Art Nouveau, blue and green stylized poppy blossoms, beige gound, high glaze, sgd . .	1,400.00
8″ h, 6″ w, bulbous body, inward tapering shoulders, straight extended neck, ring collar, incised fruit and leaves in light and dark blue, beige ground, early high glaze	1,200.00
8″ h, 7″ w, bulbous body, inward tapering shoulders, straight extended neck, ring collar, carved, back, dogwood blossoms in tones of pink and blue, matte glaze	750.00

NILOAK POTTERY

Niloak (Kaolin spelled backwards) Pottery was made in Benton, Arkansas, from 1911 to 1946. The hand thrown marbleized pottery developed by J. H. Hyten and his two brothers is of the greatest interest to collectors of American pottery. Molded or cast pottery was also made at the factory.

Mission Ware pieces which are predominately creme and brown are usually earlier pieces. Prices listed below are for Mission ware pieces.

See *Warman's Americana & Collectibles* for an expanded listing of Niloak Pottery.

Ashtray, 3½″ d	35.00

Bowls

3 x 8″	45.00
3 x 9″, with frog	60.00
Candlesticks, 8″, pr	175.00
Ewer, 12½″	165.00
Jar, cov, 4″	60.00
Match Holder, 3″	35.00
Planter, 8 x 5″, liner	150.00

Vases

2½ x 5½″, squat, very small neck	70.00
3 x 1½″, flared neck	23.00
8″, bulbous bottom, red and dark brown swirl	110.00
8″, cylindrical	65.00
8½ x 6″, short narrow neck, rare high glaze exterior	115.00
9″	75.00
10″, hourglass shape	90.00
14″, bulbous center, flared top . .	180.00
Wall Pocket	80.00

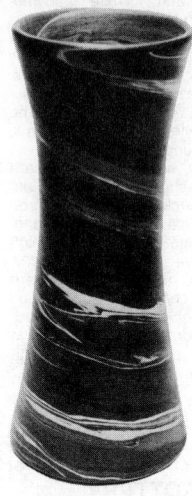

Vase, Niloak, 9⅞", waisted, $150.00.

NIPPON CHINA

A large portion of the hand-decorated porcelain marked Nippon that we see today was manufactured by the Noritake Company, Ltd., in Nagoya, Japan. In 1891 Congress passed a law that all imported articles must be marked as to country of orgin. Japan chose "Nippon," the Japanese word for Japan. In 1921 the USA decided the word "Nippon" was no longer acceptable and all Japanese wares must be marked "Japan," thus ending the "Nippon" period.

There are more than 100 different marks used on Nippon pieces. They identify different qualities of porcelain, e.g., green color is first grade, blue color is second grade. Serious collectors should familiarize themselves with these marks, as they are being reproduced.

Also see NORITAKE.

Ashtray, scenic, sgd	65.00
Basket, 9", pink roses, gold, sgd	24.00
Berry Set, 7 pcs, scalloped, green, pink rose decor	42.00
Bouillon Cup with cov and underplate, elaborate gold design over red with rose medallions	110.00
Bowls	
8", handled, pink, magenta clover, raised gold trim, green wreath mark	32.00
8½", green bands, floral designs in medallions, green wreath mark	70.00
10", round, hp, 4 floral panels, royal blue with raised gold decor and floral center, wreath mark	75.00
Candlesticks, 9", aqua and gold beading, blue maple mark, pr	200.00
Candy Dish, 7", pink roses, gold lace, green M in wreath	32.00
Chamberstick, heart shape, dark green, white roses, beading, maple leaf mark	125.00
Chocolate Pot, blue lustre, florals	52.00
Chocolate, Set, pot, 5 cups and saucers, pale blue, pink roses	165.00
Compote, red banding, gold lace flowers, blue maple leaf mark	75.00
Cracker Jar, 7¼", white, hp pink roses, gold trim, green maple leaf mark	85.00
Cup and Saucer, scenic, mountains, lake, trees, cobalt blue and gold trim, jeweled, blue maple leaf mark	125.00
Dish, 9", scalloped, handled, roses, green border, gold lacing, blue maple leaf mark	48.00
Dresser Set, 7 x 11" tray, sq cov powder box, hatpin holder, pale green with violets and foliage	110.00
Egg Warmer, violet decor	130.00
Fernery, 4½", ftd, scenic, seascape, gold trim, M in green wreath, sgd Imperial Nippon	95.00
Hair Receiver, 4" d, moriage, gray-green, white with pink flowers and white dots, maple leaf mark	35.00
Hatpin Holder, 4¾", hold in top, band of gold stripes and pink roses, blue M in wreath	55.00

Relish dish, 12¼" l, 6 salts, 4" l, handled, pink and blue flowers, green leaves in tan band, gold scrolls, purple stamp mark M in wreath, $55.00.

Humidor, 7½", blown out, horse head with a horse shoe, tan and brown, green wreath mark **650.00**

Lamp, 12½", handled, bisque, camel and rider, palm trees in high relief, brown relief on handles and scalloped footed base **275.00**

Marmalade Jar, cov and under plate, lake and forest scene, M in green wreath **48.00**

Matchholder, hanging, bisque, hp, cow in pasture **135.00**

Milk Can Holder, pink roses, gold trim **88.00**

Mustard Pot with spoon, 2½", white with hp flowers outlined in gold, green M in wreath **25.00**

Nut Set, melon shape, white, gold lacing **33.00**

Pitchers

6½", Halloween scene, moriage handle **185.00**

8", raised dots, gold, Geishas, children **115.00**

Plaques

10", moose pictured, green wreath mark **215.00**

12", still life of fruit on pedestal ftd compote, green wreath mark .. **250.00**

Plate, 8", scenic, mountains, conifers, lake, cobalt blue and gold trim, jeweled, blue maple leaf mark **175.00**

Powder Box, 4", cov, 3 small feet, white, green and gold tracery design, green M in wreath **30.00**

Punch Bowl, scenic medallion, swans on lake, green ground, heavy gold lacing, Wedgwood, green wreath mark **375.00**

Reamer, orange, delicate floral decor, gold trim, green wreath mark **155.00**

Ring Tree, hand shape, roses, blue maple leaf mark **55.00**

Salt and Pepper, pink floral **12.00**

Scent Bottle, 4⅛", cream, pink and red roses, green raised lattice with white dots **110.00**

Shaving Mug, shaded green, large flower, gold beading and solid gold handle **125.00**

Spitton, lady's hand, violets with turquoise beading, green wreath ... **145.00**

Sugar Shaker, 4⅝ x 3½", six sided panel shape, handle, pink roses, green leaves, gold garlands and trim, maple leaf mark **75.00**

Tankard, 13", gold stippled ground, large purple flowers outlined in gold surrounded with green, gold stars **450.00**

Tea Strainer, pink roses **45.00**

Tea Tile, cow in pasture **35.00**

Tray, 6", palamino horse head, green wreath mark **145.00**

Trivet, octagonal, portrait of Egyptian lady, shaded ground, red, blue trim **135.00**

Urn, 14", pedestal foot, gold handles and trim, scenic medallion .. **175.00**

Vases

5½", handled, yellow, oasis, red sunset, green palm trees and shelter, green wreath mark ... **150.00**

8¾", 3 handles, melon ribbed, coblat blue neck and base, 4 floral cartouches **195.00**

9", baluster, handled, Moroccan desert scene, abstract pattern at neck, green mark, Handpainted Nippon **85.00**

9", tapestry, bottle neck, scenic, gold top and bottom, blue maple leaf mark **575.00**

9½", handled, gold banded flowers, beaded gold base and collar, studded with beads, maple leaf mark **200.00**

9¾", scenic, elaborate gold overlay with pink jewels **259.00**

10", Art Deco, floral pattern, green wreath mark **125.00**

11½", black, multicolored flowers, gold rim and base **175.00**

12", scenic, boat at edge of lake, sgd, M in wreath **400.00**

12 x 9" d, bisque, roses with gold, wreath mark **450.00**

NODDERS

Nodders are figurines with heads and/or arms attached to the body with wires to enable them to move. Nodders are made from a variety of materials—bisque, celluloid, paper mache, porcelain, and wood.

Most nodders date from the late 19th Century with Germany being the principal source of supply. Among the American made nodders, those of Disney characters and cartoon figures are most eagerly sought.

Andy Gump, 4", Germany **65.00**

Black eating watermelon, Souvenir Biloxi, MS, bank, orig labels **50.00**

Chinaman, 8", bisque **350.00**

Couple, seated, 5", papier-mache, Welsh **35.00**

Donkey, standing, 3 x 2", celluloid . **9.00**

Dutch Couple, 3", bisque, German . **25.00**

Dutch Girl, 8½", china, German ... **100.00**

Elephant, 7", papier-mache, head, tail both nod **65.00**

Farmer, standing, 8", paper mache **45.00**

Indian Princess, seated, 3¾", pale blue, gold trim, $115.00.

Grandmother with hat, 6½", bisque, pink-blue cape and glasses	175.00
Horse, 3 x 2¾", leather	75.00
Mickey Mantle	30.00
Monkey riding black mule on platform with wooden wheels, 9½", wood and wire composition	175.00
Munich Maid, 6½", bisque, black cloak, carrying turnips	85.00
Oriental Sage, 6", bisque, seated, gold skull cap, blue, white clothes, dagger in hand	130.00
Orphan Annie, 3½", bisque, Germany	65.00
Rabbit, 20", mechanical clockwork, 3 nodding baby rabbits	1,200.00
Santa Claus, 3", bisque, German ..	95.00

NORITAKE CHINA

Noritake China, still in production in Japan, has been exported in large quantities to the United States since late in 1880. In 1904 they started to use the name "Noritake" on their china. They also made blanks for other companies and for the amateur china painters prolific at that time.

See *Warman's Americana & Collectibles* **for a detailed listing of the Noritake-Azalea Pattern.**

Ashtray, hp roses	35.00
Baby Feeding Dish, hp, children's scene, M in wreath	38.00
Basket, 4½ x 2½"d, Azalea pattern	85.00
Bowls	
5¼", Azalea pattern	7.00
8½", gold, wood scene border ..	65.00
9", tree on lake, 2 swans, gold pierced handles, green wreath mark	55.00
Bread Tray 14 x 6¼"w, white, pale green and gold floral border, open handles	18.00
Butter Tub with insert, Azalea pattern	35.00
Child's Tea Set, white, gold bands, orig box, c1920	125.00
Chocolate Set, oval pot, 4 cups and saucers, large floral decor, leaves outlined in gold	180.00
Compote, water scene, houses and Japanese fisherman	75.00
Creamer and Sugar, Azalea pattern	25.00
Cups and Saucers	
Bouillon, Azalea pattern	20.00
Demitasse, orange and blue floral decor	15.00
Dresser Set, 7 pieces, white with gold and cobalt blue overlay design	70.00
Fruit Dish, 9½", large yellow roses .	45.00
Hair Receiver, 4 x 4", floral decor .	25.00
Mustard Jar, scalloped edge tray, orig spoon, blue and white, fruit and foilage	28.00
Nappy, handled, Azalea pattern ...	25.00
Nut Dish, lustreware	35.00
Plates	
6¼", Azalea pattern	8.00
6½ x 7¾", cake, scalloped border, blue lustre with figural bird, sgd, green M	95.00

Cup and Saucer, 3"d cup, 5"d saucer, pink, blue flowers, gold trim on white ground, $25.00.

Platter, 10", oval, white with gold
   designed wide edge **28.00**
Punch Bowl with 8 matching cups,
   banquet size, scenic, swans, cottage, island, trees, heavy raised
   gold, green M in wreath **675.00**
Salt and Pepper Shakers, individual,
   Azalea pattern, pr **12.00**
Tea Set, teapot, creamer, cov sugar
   and cookie plate, cream with floral
   decor, maroon border, red and
   yellow birds on lid, 4 pcs **65.00**
Tile, hp, scenic, water, willow tree,
   rushes, man in boat **35.00**
Vases
   5", blue irid, figural parrot on base   **30.00**
   7½ x 4"d, handled, Moriage, pink
     and yellow roses, gold dots, pr   **225.00**
   9¼", dragon, gray and white, gold
     Noritake mark **68.00**
Vegetable Dishes, covered
   10", oval, ftd, cream, red poppies   **50.00**
   Monterey pattern, 3 gold handles
     and feet **75.00**

NORITAKE—TREE IN THE MEADOW (or SCENIC) PATTERN

The "Tree In The Meadow" pattern is among the most popular patterns of Noritake china. Since the design is hand painted, there are numerous variations of the scene. The basic features of the design are a large tree (usually in the foreground), a meandering stream or lake, and a peasant cottage in the distance. Principal colors are muted tones of brown and yellow.

The pattern is found with a variety of backstamps and appears to have been imported into the United States beginning in the early 1920s. The Larkin Company distributed "Tree In The Meadow" pattern china through its catalog sales in the 1920–1930 period.

Ashtray, hp, green M in wreath . . .   **50.00**
Berry Set, large bowl with pierced
   handles, 6 small dishes **68.00**
Bowls
   5¼" **15.00**
   7" **25.00**
Bread Tray **42.00**
Butter Dish with insert **65.00**
Cake Plate, 10" **35.00**
Cake Set, 7 pieces **120.00**
Celery Dish, 12" **35.00**
Compote **100.00**
Condiment Set **38.00**
Creamer and Sugar, covered **50.00**
Cruet, double **48.00**
Cup and Saucer **18.00**

Bowl, 9", $35.00.

Humidor, covered **375.00**
Jam Jar with underplate and spoon   **125.00**
Lemon Dish, 5½", handled **22.00**
Mayonnaise Dish, with underplate
   and spoon **28.00**
Plates
   6½" **8.00**
   7½" **10.00**
   8½" **14.00**
Platter, 11½", oval **25.00**
Platter, 14" **35.00**
Relish Dish, two sections **45.00**
Salt and Pepper Shakers, pr. **30.00**
Sugar Shaker **28.00**
Syrup Jug **52.00**
Teapot **100.00**
Teapot Tile **50.00**
Toothpick Holder, 2½" **42.00**
Vases
   Bulbous bottom **200.00**
   Fan shape **120.00**
Vegetable Dish, 9⅜", oval **40.00**
Waffle Set **45.00**

NUTCRACKERS

Warman's Americana & Collectibles, 1st Edition, contains 45 listings in this category; see also page xii.

OCCUPIED JAPAN ITEMS

Items marked "Occupied Japan" were made after the surrender of Japan in World War II in 1945 and during the occupation by the Allied Forces.

See *Warman's Americana & Collectibles* for an expanded listing of Occupied Japan Items.

Ashtray, frog, 3", standing, mouth
   open **10.00**
Bell, colonial lady, 4½", blue dress   **12.00**
Bowl, 8", Blue Willow **15.00**

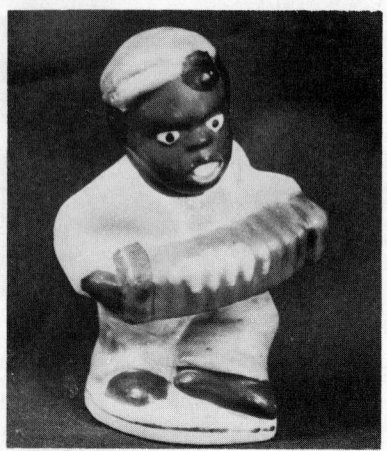

Figure, 2¾" h, green hat, white shirt, blue pants, $15.00.

Bust, girl with hat, flowers	15.00
Candelabra, 6½", bisque, double, colonial couple	32.00
Candy Dish, 5 x 7", cov, bisque, green, blown out costumed lady on lid	55.00
Child's Dishes, porcelain, 6 place setting, pink and white, hp flowers, gold trim, orig box	65.00
Cigarette Box, applied large bow, roses, leaves, gold decor	35.00
Cigarette Lighters	
Jet plane, chrome	8.00
Western Boot, tray, metal	15.00
Creamer and Sugar, dogwood, pink, white	25.00
Cups and Saucers	
Demitasse, Blue Willow	15.00
Lacquerware, red, gold interior and decor	15.00
Figurines	
Angel, standing, 6½", mkd	5.00
Boy, seated, playing violin	6.00
Bride and Groom	45.00
Colonial man, 15½", bisque, green coat, tan pants, reading paper	65.00
Dogs, Airdale, drinking from dish, white, black spots	5.00
Mermaid, reclining, fish bowl item	15.00
Shelf sitter, oriental man playing mandolin, green coat, blue pants, crossed ankles	12.00
Victorian lady, 14½", bisque, blue dress, hat, carrying flowers	50.00

Lamps, boy & girl, Victorian, standing, pr	50.00
Matchsafe, hanging type, blue, white	32.00
Mug, 5", barrel shape, tan, mkd	15.00
Nodder & ashtray, black farm boy smoking cigar	95.00
Nut Set, lacquerware, 5" bowl, 6 dishes, ladle, gold trim	50.00
Pipe Rest, 2 pcs, cobalt, floral decor, gold trim	30.00
Plaques, 3 monkeys, 5¼ x 3¾", bisque, Hears All, Sees All, Tells All, imp on their backs, mkd	55.00
Planters	
Black girl, pink dress, standing beside ear of yellow corn planter, mkd	30.00
Mexican boy under large hat, sitting beside urn planter	9.00
Peasant girl, 6", bisque, standing beside leaf cov planter	30.00
Plates	
8", lace edge, violets center	12.00
9", lacquerware, black, floral center, gold trim	5.00
Purse, ladies, white, beaded, oblong	20.00
Salt and Pepper Shakers	
Clear glass, hobnail, metal tops, emb mkd	15.00
Colonial boy & girl, standing, mkd	7.00
Smokers Set, lighter, ashtray, humidor, hp, brown, gold, rust colors	27.00
Teapot, 4 cups, brown enameled flowers	25.00
Toby Mugs	
7½", colonial jailkeeper	40.00
Devil's head	30.00
Toothpick, pig in red overalls beside tan, blue urn, mkd	8.00
Toys	
Car, red, wind-up, mkd	10.00
Dancing couple, key wind, celluloid	25.00
Vase, figural cornucopia chariot, 7 x 8", bisque, rearing horse, 2 cherubs, gold trim, mkd	65.00
Violin, metal, wood, orig box	45.00
Wall Pockets	
2 x 3", clock, parrot, weights	12.00
Iris, purple, green	18.00
Wind Chimes, glass, bamboo decor	25.00

G. E. OHR,
OHR POTTERY   BILOXI.

Ohr pottery was produced by George E. Ohr in Biloxi, Mississippi. There is some discrepancy as to when Ohr actually established his pottery. Some suggest 1878; but, Ohr's autobiography indicates 1883. In 1884 Ohr exhibited 600 pieces of his work, indicating that he had been working for some time.

Ohr's techniques included twisting, crushing, folding, denting, and crinkling thin walled clay into odd, grotesque and sometimes graceful forms. Much of his early work is signed with an impressed stamp of his name and location in block letters. His later work, often marked with the flowing script designation "G E Ohr," was usually left unglazed.

In 1906, Ohr closed the pottery and stored over 6,000 pieces as his legacy to his family. He hoped it would be purchased by the U.S. Government. This never happened. The entire collection remained in storage until it was rediscovered in 1972.

Today, Ohr is recognized as one of the leading potters in the American Art Pottery movement. His brightly colored creations in grotesquely tortured and twisted forms are sought eagerly by collectors.

Some greedy individuals have taken the latter unglazed pieces and covered them with poor quality glazes, in hopes of making them more valuable. These pieces, usually with the flowing script mark, do not have the "stilt marks" on the bottom, the three spots where the object rested on a ceramic stilt during kiln firing.

Candleholder, iridescent copper (pinkish red) glaze, script signature, $675.00.

Bowls
2 x 4", pinched and ruffled edges, green to gun metal glaze, block mark	250.00
4" d, circular, streaked blue, green, and brown on a mustard ground	160.00
Bowl (or Saucer), folded with sculpted edges, brown high glaze with green splotches, block mark	200.00
Creamer, squat, green glaze, twisted applied snake handle, hand incised Biloxi	400.00

Inkwells
Artist's palette, 8 x 6", applied paint tubes and paint pots with brushes, green high glaze	850.00
Log Cabin, 4 x 6", brown glaze, block mark	800.00
Pot, 5¾", unglazed, 2 spouts, circle handle on extended concave neck, sgd "G Ohr"	250.00
Puzzle Mug, incised saying, green glaze, block mark	200.00
Teapot, applied curled handle, red high glaze with green streaks, script mark	1,000.00
Top Hat, 4" h, 2½" w, black high glaze, block mark	350.00

Vases
3" h, 4" w, pedestal base, bent and folded sides, chocolate brown glaze, block mark	375.00
3½", conical form, black matte glaze, stilt chips, inkwell shape	75.00
4" h, 4" w, bulbous form with twisted crimped top, gun metal black glaze, block mark	500.00
4½" h, 6" w, pinched crimped side, folded edge, orange glaze with green speckles, block mark	600.00
7½", conical shape with twisted folded waist, nine scalloped raised collar, exterior covered with a purple-blue glaze, interior with speckled olive glaze, block mark, c1900	2,200.00
8" h, 4" w, pedestal base rising to classic form with torn uneven top, metallic brown glaze with oxide splotches, block mark	750.00
12" h, 5" w, two applied, twisted, and curled handles, purple and green with black spots, block mark	2,500.00
12" h, 6" w, ruffled top, sgd block mark	800.00
Unglazed, twisted grotesque form, bulbous bottom, ruffled top, red and beige streaked clay, script mark	375.00

OLD IVORY
84

OLD IVORY CHINA

This china derives its name from the ground color of the ware. The difference in patterns is indicated by a number on the base. It was made in Silesia, Germany, in the latter part of the 1800s. Marked pieces usually bear the Crown Silesia mark.

Berry Set, 7 pcs, No 84 Ohme Silesia	225.00
Bowls	
5¼ x 3", waste, brown roses, No 16	80.00
9½", No 75	60.00
9½", 9 large roses with leaves, lacy gold decor between, Silesia	60.00
9¾", berry, No 28 Ohme Silesia	68.00
Butter Dish, cov, brown roses, No 16	140.00
Cake Plates	
10", floral design, shaded, marked Crown Silesia Old Ivory VIII	50.00
10", handled, No 15	75.00
Charger, 13", No 15	135.00
Chocolate Pot, 9½" creamy, hp flowers, scalloped, emb foot, sgd	110.00
Chocolate Set, pot, 6 demitasse cups and saucers, butterfly with roses decor, sgd Silesia with crown	195.00
Creamer, marked XVI Clarion Silesia	40.00
Creamer and Sugar, cov, No 84	110.00
Cup and Saucer, chocolate, brown roses, No 16	45.00
Mustard Pot, cov, No 84	80.00
Plates	
7" No 14	38.00
7¼", brown roses, No 16, sgd Silesia	45.00
Porringers, 6⅛ x 6⅛", tab handles, pr	116.00

Relish, Old Ivory China, 6¾", No. 15, $35.00.

Relish Dish, 8", oval, brown roses, No 16 Silesia	45.00
Salt and Peppers	
No 15, set	95.00
No 84, set	110.00
Teapot, Striegan, La Touraine, bell flowers, encrusted gold and trim	95.00
Tea Tile, 6½", round, No 15	75.00
Toothpick Holder, No 84	95.00

OLD PARIS CHINA

Old Paris is a generic name for fine quality porcelain made by French factories during the 18th and 19th centuries. Some pieces are marked but the majority of the ware was not. Its main characteristics are fine quality porcelain and beautiful decorations; a favorite color was dark maroon, also cobalt blue, and much gold trim. Open work was often present but not common.

Compote, Old Paris China, 6¾" h x 9¼" d, white ground, scalloped top, reticulated edge, gold trim, hand-painted fruit decoration on standard, #382, $165.00.

Bowl, 11½", oval floral decor	90.00
Candleholders, 12½", rococo form, children, goats, pr	150.00
Cologne Bottle, sq, deep blue and white, pink flowers	85.00
Cup and Saucer, floral decor	55.00
Dessert Service, 2 oval sauce boats, 2 shell shaped dishes, 2 round dishes, 3 heart shaped dishes, 2 oval dishes, 18 plates, each with figure in national costumes, foliage entwined ribbon borders, gilt, c1815	6,000.00
Jardinieres, 11¾" h, floral sprays on shaded claret ground, gilt edged panels, reverse neoclassical foliate motifs, pr	3,600.00
Mustard Pot, fixed stand, floral bouquets, puce rim, barrel shaped, shallow grooves	275.00
Plate, 8⅛" boy, girl, multicolored, pale blue border	50.00
Swan, fitted with inkpot and sander, gold decor	140.00
Tureens	
8¾", oval, fixed stand, cov, floral bouquets, blue scroll and line	

borders, fruiting branch finial, c1740	500.00
13″, oval, cov, molded fruit finial, white, wide maroon bands and gold trim around body, no mark	175.00
Urns, 10½″ h, courting scene, gilt trim, pr	1,500.00
Vases	
12″, portrait of girl, flaring top . . .	180.00
13″, blue, floral decor, griffon handles, pr	220.00
17″, hp decor, gold at neck and base	240.00
DuBarry Rose color, hp scene, molded leaves, pr	185.00

Salt Crock, 6½″ d, 4″ h, blue on gray, stoneware, $375.00.

OLD SLEEPY EYE

Chief Sleepy Eye, a Sioux Indian who reportedly had a droopy eye, gave his name to Sleepy Eye, Minnesota, the milling center of the world for flour packed in barrels in the early 1900s. Sleepy Eye flour began to offer premiums. The first four (a butter bowl, salt bowl, stein, and vase) were Flemish gray stoneware decorated with cobalt blue and made by Weir Pottery Co.

Weir became Monmouth Pottery and later Western Stoneware Co. of Monmouth, Illinois. Additional Sleepy Eye items were made in stoneware, glazed pottery, and other materials.

Sleepy Eye items are being reproduced, mostly the blue and white pitchers. Reproduction pitchers are crazed, weighted, and marked with a stamp or word "ironstone." The stoneware stein and salt bowl also have been copied. In addition, new items which never existed have appeared. These include the advertising mirror with miniature flour barrel label, small glass plates, fruit jars, toothpick holders, glass and pottery miniature pitchers, and salt and pepper shakers. One mill item has been made, a sack marked as though it were old but of a size that could not possibly hold the amount of flour indicated.

There are three variety of Sleepy Eye pitchers in five sizes, 4, 5¼, 6½, 8, and 9 inches. Cobalt on white or cream ground pitchers have either a plain top or blue rim. The third type is called stoneware, but is really grayish ground pottery.

Mill Items

Barrel Label, lithograph, "Sleepy Eye Cream," Old Sleepy Eye in center, 196 lb barrel	90.00
Calendar, 1903	410.00
Fan, diecut cardboard profile of Old Sleepy Eye, adv. on reverse	110.00
Flour Sack, "Hummer Flour," two hummingbirds on branch	275.00
Matchholder, chalkware, profile of Old Sleepy Eye, "TRADE-MARK" on base	800.00
Postcard, "Sleepy Eye Mounument"	50.00
Thermometer, bronze	550.00
Thimble	300.00
Old Sleepy Eye Club Convention Items	
1977 Mug	175.00
1983 Pitcher	100.00
Pottery and Stoneware	
Bowl, butter, stoneware	490.00
Mug, 4¼″, blue on gray, small Indian head on handle, Western Stoneware Co., c1914–18	350.00
Pitchers	
Blue on white	
Creamer, 4″, small Indian head on handle, Western Stoneware Co., 1906–37 . . .	165.00
6½, small Indian head on handle, Western Stoneware Co., 1906–37	185.00
9″, B.P.O.E. imprinted under glaze	310.00
Green, 7¾″, half gallon, Western Stoneware Co.	1,050.00
Steins	
Blue on white, 7¾″, Western Stoneware Co., 1906–37 . . .	380.00
Brown, solid, 7¾″, Western Stoneware Co., old	1,050.00
Brown on gold, 7¾″, Western Stoneware Co.	660.00
Sugar Bowls	
Blue on gold, 4″, Western Stoneware Co.	875.00
Blue on white, 4″, Western Stoneware Co., 1906–37 . . .	360.00
Vases	
Blue on gray, 9″, Weir Pottery .	160.00
Cattail, 9″, three color, variagated	400.00

ONION MEISSEN

Blue Onion or Bulb pattern is of Chinese origin and depicts peaches and pomegranates and not onions. It was originally made in the 18th century by the German Meissen factory, thus the name Onion Meissen.

This popular pattern was made by several other factories in other countries including England and Japan and is still in production today. Onion Meissen is marked with the familiar Crossed Swords. Other makers marked their wares accordingly, and those made after 1891 with the country of origin.

Plate, 14″, scalloped edge, white ground, blue decor, marked Cauldon #16, $85.00.

Bowls
4½″	32.00
6″	40.00
7 x 8″, deep	145.00
9¾″	42.00
Butter, cov, rose finial	125.00
Cheese Board	40.00
Cheese Dish, covered	130.00
Coffee Pot, 8″, rose finial	150.00
Compote, centerpiece, 9 x 9″, reticulated rim	350.00
Cream and Sugar, set	125.00

Creamers
3½″	35.00
5½″	48.50
Cruets, Oil and Vinegar, pair	100.00

Cups and Saucers
Bouillon	35.00
Coffee	30.00
Demitasse	30.00
Tea	25.00
Darner, wooden handle	75.00
Dipper, wooden handle	95.00
Dish, bone	58.00
Fish Plate, pierced drain insert	220.00
Gravy Boat, 10″, with underplate	125.00
Melon Mold, handled	30.00
Mustard, 4¾″ high, ladle and underplate, set	50.00
Napkin Ring	20.00
Pastry Wheel	135.00

Plates
7½″	25.00
9″	45.00
9″ leaf-shaped	75.00
9½″, soup, crossed swords	68.00
12½″, chop, deep center, crossed swords	260.00
14″, with hot water jacket	125.00

Platters
11″	85.00
16″	195.00
19″	210.00
Pot de Creme	45.00
Rolling Pin, minature	130.00
Salt and Pepper	42.00
Salt Box, covered	75.00
Sauce, 5½″ dia.	20.00
Scoop, 9″ long	35.00
Soap Dish, hanging	42.00
Sugar, cov, melon ribbed, late 19th C	95.00
Teapot, 10″, rose finial, 19th C	190.00
Tea Tile, 5″, sq, ball ftd	125.00
Tray, 11 x 10″	290.00
Tureen, Soup, 10½ x 14″, rose finial	350.00
Vase, 5½″, spill-type, scroll feet	60.00

Vegetable Dishes, covered
8½″ d.	85.00
10″ square	125.00
14″ d., divided	225.00
Vinegar Jar, with stopper	230.00

ONYX GLASS

This rare glassware was produced in 1889 in Findlay, Ohio by the Dalzell, Gilmore and Leighton Co. and is often called "Findlay Onyx." Onyx ware is plated or cased and may consist of two or three layers of glass. The interior layer is generally an opaque white. Each of the succeeding layers are of similar color and in the end it may contain a variation of colors.

There are five basic colors of onyx; however, no two pieces have exactly the same coloring due to varied temperatures in the manufacture. Consequently, shades of Findlay onyx are often described as cream, rose, cranberry, raspberry and cinnamon. Onyx was made for only a short time because of high production costs. It is a fragile, delicate glass.

Mustard Jar, SP cov, raspberry, marked Findley, 3⅜" h, $1,350.00.

Bowl, 8", cream	420.00
Butter, covered, raspberry	725.00
Celery, 6½", cream	500.00
Creamer, cream	450.00
Salt and Pepper, cream, pr	500.00
Spooner, rose	400.00
Sugar Castors	
Cream	215.00
Raspberry	1,000.00
Sugar, cov, cream	450.00
Syrup Jug, 7", orig lid, cream	550.00
Toothpick, cream	225.00
Tumblers	
Apricot, barrel shape, 3⅜"	850.00
Raspberry	210.00

OPALESCENT GLASS

Opalescent glass is a clear or colored glass with milky white decorations. When held to the light, the whitened portions show a fiery or opalescent quality; thus the name. The glass falls into two basic categories: blown or mold blown such as Coin Spot and Spanish Lace, and pressed pattern glass such as Hobnail.

Novelties, Corn Vase, Pump and Trough, and Cabbage Leaf made of opalescent glass are listed as a separate category but are pressed glass. Their main distinction is that they were only made in one unique form and never a complete table set as in other pressed patterns.

Opalescent glass was produced in England in the 1870s. It gained wide popularity in America at the turn of the 20th century. It was made by several glass companies, including the early Boston and Sandwich Glass Company. Opalescent glass is currently being produced but very few of the items should be called reproductions, because many of the 'new' patterns were not originally produced in opalescent.

Also see OPALESCENT PATTERN GLASS SECTION, for additional pressed glass patterns.

BLOWN

Bisquit Jar, Spanish Lace, vaseline .	**265.00**
Bowls	
Hobnail, blue	**100.00**
Roman Rosette, lacy, Sandwich,	
6¾"	**200.00**
Seaweed, 9", white	**50.00**
Butters, covered	
Reverse Swirl, Vaseline	**135.00**
Spanish Lace, blue	**250.00**

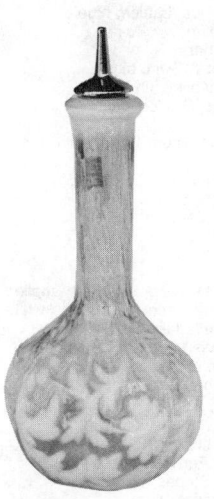

Barber bottle, blown, Daisy & Fern, vaseline, 8½", $65.00.

Celerys

Chrysanthemum Base Swirl, white	35.00
Seaweed, blue	95.00
Swirl, cranberry	95.00

Creamer, Reverse Swirl, blue 70.00

Cruets

Daisy & Fern, blue	85.00
Ribbed Opal Lattice, cranberry . .	150.00

Curtain Tie Back, 5¾", fiery, lacy, young woman seated holding straw hat, Boston & Sandwich Glass Co. 120.00

Miniature Lamp, Spanish Lace, 4", blue 225.00

Mustard, Reverse Swirl, vaseline . . 45.00

Pitchers, water

Christmas Snowflake, cranberry .	375.00
Daisy & Fern, cranberry	185.00
Seaweed, blue	275.00
Spanish Lace, ruffled rim, blue . .	250.00
Spanish Lace, blue	110.00
Swirl, Bulbous, ruffled top, cranberry	130.00

Rose Bowls

Daisy and Fern, blue	40.00
Seaweed, yellow	50.00

Salt Shaker, Seaweed, cranberry . . 35.00

Spill Holder, Ellipse and Circle, fiery opal, Sandwich 450.00

Spooners

Spanish Lace, cranberry	75.00
Chrysanthemum Base Swirl, white	90.00

Sugar Shakers

Ribbed Opal Lattice, blue	80.00
Stripe, blue	175.00

Syrup Pitchers

Coinspot & Swirl, blue	85.00
Swirl, vaseline, tin top	125.00
Windows, Swirled, white	80.00

Tumblers

Chrysanthemum Base Swirl, cranberry	65.00
Daffodils, blue	52.00
Poinsettia, blue	45.00
Spanish Lace, cranberry	48.00
Swirl, blue	30.00
Windows, white	30.00

Vases

5½ x 4" d, blue, clear applied handle, three petal top, white enamelled lilies of valley	85.00
6", Spanish Lace, ruffled, vaseline	65.00
7", fiery, drawn out, & pinched applied handle	70.00

NOVELTIES

Barber Bottles

Daisy & Fern, cranberry	135.00
Stars & Stripes, white	100.00

Bushel Basket, blue 65.00

Epergne, 19½" h, 9½" d, 4 lilies, green, ruffled base, lilies lift out, applied glass spiral trim 325.00

PRESSED

See Opalescent Pattern Glass section, pages 136-147.

OPALINE GLASS

Opaline or Opal glass was a popular mid-to-late 19th century European glass. The glass has a certain amount of translucency. The finished wares were often decorated with painted enamels and trimmed in gold.

Mug, 4" h, white, cobalt trim, French, $90.00.

Basket, 6½ x 6", applied rope handle 90.00

Bisquit Jar, hp florals, bird decor, brass lid, bail handle 135.00

Bottles

Cologne, 5½", melon ribbing, gold decor	100.00
Perfume, 5" high, jade green, enamel decor	85.00
Perfume, 5½", gold trim around neck, pr	150.00
Scent, 6½" h, Diamond pattern .	35.00

Bowls

6" d, low	80.00
8 x 2" deep, rose coloring	35.00
10 x 1½" deep, flared, pink, gold trim	75.00

Boxes, covered

3¼", round, sapphire blue, enameled florals, French, c1850 . . .	230.00
4 x 2½", hinged, pale green, gold enamel decor, French	135.00

Cruet, applied handle, aqua, gold trim 85.00

Cup and Saucer, green	69.50
Finger Bowl, with underplate, blue .	50.00
Goblet, 7⅜", white, light green stem, sgr. on base	45.00
Lamp Base, 12", white, French . . .	100.00
Mug, 4⅛", white, applied handle . .	50.00
Pitcher, 7" h, French, ground pontil, soft pink ground, sgd by "Anne" .	200.00
Rose Bowl, pale green	80.00
Tumble-Up, 8" h, blue, gold bands decor	125.00

Vases

4½", handles, blue, enameled pink, white florals, gold decor .	60.00
6", globular body, slender neck, pink, yellow flowers, green leaves, butterflies	95.00
6½", fine white threading, gold decor, French, pr	110.00
6¾", mauve, gold rims, French, pr	150.00
7", ftd, blue, enamel decor	75.00
8", Jack-in-the-Pulpit, white	150.00
9½", bulbous, handpainted peacock, flowers, beaded pedestaled base, gold trim	165.00
10", ruby spiral around foot, neck, transluscent body, French	175.00
11", ftd, white, pale green turned down rim	150.00
16", blue, quilted	175.00

ORIENTAL RUGS

The history of these rugs or carpets dates 3000 B.C. but it was in the 16th century that they became prevalent. Commonly referred to as "Orientals" because of their origin from regions east of Europe comprised of central Asia, Iran (Persia), Caucasus and Anatolia, these rugs can be classified into basic categories of Iranian, Caucasian, Turkoman, Turkish and Chinese. Later, India, Pakistan and Iraq produced similar rugs after the fashion of the Persians, Chinese and Turks.

The pattern name is derived from the tribes or people of these regions who produced the rugs, e.g., from Iran we have the designs of Hamadan, Herez, Sarouk, Tabriz and others.

When evaluating an Oriental carpet, age, design, color, weave and knots per square inch are very important. These factors plus the condition of the carpet determine the final value. Silk rugs and prayer rugs commonly command higher prices.

Examine rugs carefully; there are repainted rugs on the market.

Afghan Ersari, 9'2" x 7'10", crimson field, 3 rows of Afghan gub, 6 per row, divided by hexagonal star shaped medallions, red border of serrated leaves, 2 diamond filled guard borders, full kilim skirts . . . — 1,350.00

Anatolian, prayer, 7'5" x 4'2", gold field, large flower heads, wine floral panel, border of flowering branches . . . . — 450.00

Bidjar
6'8" x 4'2", brick red field, ivory and midnight blue floral center medallion, ivory border of flowers and vines . . . . — 1,540,00
7'9" x 4'2", rust field, blue central floral medallion, blue flowerhead border . . . . — 1,240,00

Bordjalow Kazak, 7'9" x 3'8", multicolored field, 4 concentric latchwork medallions, slant leaf and chalic design in ivory border . — 1,100.00

Chinese, 11'6" x 9', honey field, scenic center medallion, 4 small floral medallions, navy floral sprays border . . . . — 1,100.00

Hamadan, 6' x 9', camel field, overall plum and blue geometric floral motifs, ivory palmette and plum border . . . . — 500.00

Heriz, 8'4 x 11'1", red field, large angular medallion anchored in fan palmettes, stylized flowers, leaves, within ivory and red spandrels, midnight blue waterbug palmette and vine border, $3,250.00.

Heriz, 6' x 9', sky blue field, small brick red anchored medallion surrounded by coral and brick red leaves, waterbug palmettes in brick red border **1,600.00**

Isphahan, 3'2" x 2'6", pictorial, ivory field, 2 rows of flowering trees, exotic birds, navy blue border of meandering vine and red guard stripe **675.00**

Josan Sarouk, 6'7" x 4'3", navy field, 2 floral medallion and interlocking floral arrangements, vines and palmettes in brick red border **1,950.00**

Karabagh
4'8" x 2'10", prayer, navy field, multicolored crab design, mihrab with boteh and geometric devices, ivory border of stepped medallions and trefoil guard borders **800.00**

8'11" x 4'1", brown field, 3 ivory and rust medallions, blue panels and geometric devices, spearhead design ivory border **1,000.00**

Kashan
6'7" x 4'4", navy field, brick red floral cartouche enclosing 3 concentric floral medallions, navy border of alternating palmettes and flowerheads . . . **2,000.00**

7' x 4'3", red field, large navy floral cartouche enclosing 3 floral medallions, palmettes and flowerheads in navy border . . . **1,800.00**

Kazak, 5'11" x 3'6", navy field, horizontal rows of multicolored botehs, brick red border of cruciform devices **475.00**

Kerman, 22'3" x 15'4", claret field, allover pattern of palmettes, rosettes and scrolling vines, dark blue border of vines and flowers, 3 pairs of floral guard borders . . . **7,700.00**

Kuba, 5'6" x 3'7", navy field, 3 large stepped medallions in sunburst effect, classic Kubic border **1,500.00**

Kurd, 14'7" x 3'1", ivory field, horizontal rows of flowers, multicolored rosettes in navy border **2,000.00**

Lesghi Kuba, 7' x 3'6", brick red field, 3 large Lesghi stars with smaller stars and animals, latchhook ivory border **1,650.00**

Lilihan, 5'5" x 6'2", dark blue field, blue and rose floral sprays, deep rose border **500.00**

Marasali, 5'11" x 4'8", navy field, rust Tree of Life, octagonal surrounded medallion, flaming botehs, animal figures and combs, hooked devices in ivory border . . **3,520.00**

Qum, silk, 5' x 3'5", rust field, stepped beige octagon enclosing floral medallion, interlocking rosettes and palmettes in deep brown border, 5 guard stripes . . . **1,600.00**

Sarouk, 3'2" x 4'7", apricot field, green and ivory floral spray design, navy border **450.00**

Sereband, 6'9" x 4'1", ivory field, brick red and medium blue latticework and flowers, floral design ivory border **675.00**

Shikli-Kazak, 6'6" x 4', brick red field, ivory center medallion, salmon and brown cypress trees and spandrels in each corner, birds and flowerheads in ivory border . . **1,100.00**

Shiraz, 3' x 5', navy field, ivory and rust medallions, rust and navy abstract floral motif border **750.00**

Shirvan, 5'11" x 3'8", brick red field, long navy medallion with ivory and red octagons, ivory border **1,000.00**

Sivas, 6'6" x 9'11", ivory field, wine and celedon palmettes, rose flowering vines within celedon palmette border **850.00**

Teheran, prayer, 6'8" x 5', light blue field, stylized Tree of Life, animals, birds and florals under beige prayer niche, palmettes and rosettes in burgundy border **1,900.00**

Tekke, 3'2" x 5'5", brick red field, 3 rows of ivory and peach guls, navy and peach borders **500.00**

ORIENTALIA

Orientalia is a term used to apply to objects made in the orient which encompasses the Far East, Asia, China and Japan. The diversity of cultures produced a variety of objects and styles.

This category deals with objects which do not have individual categories in our guide. See also Canton, Celadon, Cloisonne, Fitzhugh, Nanking, Netsukes, Rose Medallion, and other categories for specific oriental objects.

Brush Pots
5¼", hardwood, carved family of monkeys in the branches of a hollowed out old pine, unsigned **340.00**

7½", blue and white cylindrical, c1660, transitional, very slightly waisted sides, elaborate scene of a procession of armed dignitaries and officials approaching a scholar prince considering a fish in the lake, engraved bands of flower scrolls and hatched wave patterns **20,000.00**

Jar, cov, 24″, Chinese export, figures playing Chinese game, teakwood stands, c1900, $3,600.00.

Bowls; Chinese
  Song Dynasty, Jun Yao, deep, 7½″ d, thick sides and straight lip covered in a crackled gray-blue glaze pooling partially down the exterior to reveal the reddish stoneware body and thick foot, interior with a lilac splash, wood stand, fitted box . **1,400.00**
  Tz'u Chou, Sung Dynasty, 7″ d, eleven panel flower shape, white glaze, five spur marks in interior **720.00**
  Xuande six character mark within a double circle in underglaze blue but Kangxi, 7½″ d, blue and white, deep, center of interior carved with coiled kui dragons within a border of blue lappets, outside carved with archaicized masks on delicate incised squared spiral grounds between bands of underglazed blue lappets and key patterns above tall tapering foot **975.00**
Costumes
  Chinese
    Apron, blue satin panels, peonies and other flowers, wave border, silver couching **200.00**
    Coat, Lady's, mid-19th C, 44″, embroidered, blue-black ground satin stitched with floral roundels above rolling waves and *lishui* stripe, several shades of green, blue, peach, yellow, and white . . . **460.00**
    Jacket, mid-19th C, 40½″ l, pale blue silk, ten roundels each enclosing a central shou

character medallion in couched gold encircled by *wufu* in Peking knot and satin stitched flowers in shades of peach, green, and blue, worn **320.00**
Japanese
  Kimono, 61″ l, bats and waves stitched in blue, green, and orange, black ground **250.00**
  Priest's Robe, 19th C, 80½ x 45¾″, silk brocade squares embroidered with orange, white, blue, and cerise flowers on green ground **400.00**
Fans
  Chinese, man and boy fishing, painted, pierced ivory sticks, c1800 . . . . **365.00**
  Japanese, Gyosai, Battling Frogs, painting of ink and colors on paper, wood fan sticks, sgd *Gyosai*, 8½ x 14″ **400.00**
Ceramics, Chinese
  Figure, Courtly Mourner, Han or early Wei Dynasty, 9½″ h, unglazed gray pottery, solid vertical mold showing figure wearing three layers of clothes, hands across chest, long sleeves and folds of the robes well detailed under a thick white slip **6,750.00**
  Figure, Tomb Guardian, Tang Dynasty, 14″, straw glazed, armoured figure standing, wearing a short tunic over wide trousers, layered armor, protective neckpiece under a dome hat, left hand at side, right hand across chest to hold spear, traces of orig pigment **600.00**
  Jar, Henan' globular, Song Dynasty, 4″ d, six pairs of slip stripes remain in white relief under thick viscous chocolate glaze stopping evenly well short of crisply cut pale buff stoneware base **5,000.00**
  Sancai Horse and Rider, Tang Dynasty, 16¼″ h, pony standing four square, glazed in streaky ochre on an ivory ground, saddlecloth green, rider wearing a brown glazed tunic with a green collar, traces of orig black pigment in hair **12,000.00**
  Storage Jar, Tang Dynasty, 9½″ h, white glazed globular form, thick and heavy, crazed white glaze with faint clouds of burial staining and areas of degradation **1,350.00**

Furniture

Altar Coffer, Chinese, Ming Dynasty, 75 x 22 x 36″, set with three deep drawers above four small plain doors, all mounted with brass circular hinge and lock plates, openwork panels to each side of the front below the overhanging scroll ended top, carved with leaf scrolls turning into dragon's heads with lingzhi ... 3,800.00

Armchair, Japanese, hardwood, c1875, pierced and carved prunus, dragon armrests, cabriole legs, serpentine seat 600.00

Chest, Chinese, Huanguali Seal, 14 x 11½ x 16½″, c1700, hinged deep cover securing two doors which enclose a deep square drawer and two short drawers set over a long deep drawer, vase pulls, plain hinges, lock plates, and loop handles .. 4,500.00

Chest, Korean, 49″ h, swirling dragons and clouds formed from lacquer inlaid with tortoise shell 2,200.00

Desk, Chinese, hardwood, top 60¾ x 25½″, 19th C, rectangular top with four narrow drawers pegged into the two side pedestals, each with a pair of drawers, reeded low stretchers joined by openwork panels of connecting bars, brass handles 4,500.00

Stand, Chinese, hardwood, 28½″ h, 19th C, square top on four long straight reeded legs joined by low shaped stretchers and ending in square pad feet, four openwork friezes each with a bi form disc flanked by turned miniature posts 500.00

Table, Chinese, Chi Chi Mu, side, 35¼ x 33½ x 21″, probably late Ming Dynasty, rectangular floating top on four square legs ending in abbreviated scroll feet and joined by plain shaped high stretchers, wood of deep grayish-brown tone 4,250.00

Table, Chinese, cinnabar lacquer, 24¾″ d, 24½″ h, early 19th C, three sections, circular top with scalloped narrow apron, knopped cylindrical standard, shaped base on five ruyi feet, dense pattern of blossoming peony 3,250.00

Garden Seat, 18½″, transfer printed, studded barrel shape, body cut with linked cash medallions on sides and flat top, decorated with transfer printed bunches of flowers and garlands in taste of 19th C English potteries 1,200.00

Inro

3 case, ivory, inlaid, 19th C, depicting a mirthful sake taster struggling with a sake bowl on front, an overflowing sake pot on back, inlays of stained ivory on natural ivory ground, red lacquer interiors, sgd Ikko, clear ojime, lacquered wood, seated figure netsuke 1,000.00

4 case, black lacquer, 18th C, each side decorated with a dragon shaped roundel in gold takamakie, tsuishu, kirikane and glass inlay on a roiro ground, nashiji interiors, unsigned 500.00

4 case, lacquer, 19th C, inlaid, camelia branch in front of a flowering plum tree, the flowers of inlaid ivory and gold takamakie on nashiji and fundame ground, nashiji interiors, sgd Shokosai, hardstone ojime and inlaid wood netsuke . 1,800.00

5 case, lacquer, 19th C, a bugaku and noh mask with various dance attributes in gold and colored takamakie on a gyobu nashiji ground, nashiji interiors, sgd Kajikawa saku with tsubo seal, soft metal mask ojime and wood mask netsuke 1,050.00

5 case, gold lacquer, 19th C, bulbous shape depicting tethered gaming hawks within a shaped cartouche in gold and colored hiramakie and takamakie on a kinji ground, hirame interiors, unsigned, ivory ojime 750.00

Funerary Jar, Northern Song Dynasty, Chinese, 9″, shaped and pinched bands of "pie crust" decoration reminiscent of the yue, thinly crackled creamy pale blue glaze of jun type, wood stand, fitted box 825.00

Japanese Metalwork

Bell, late 19th C, conical form, cast on the exterior with a series of double or quadrupal rings, florets, and rows of high bosses above the shoulder, 26½″ h 800.00

Figure, Woman Playing A Samisen, c1900, naturalistically cast, mouth open in song, burr wood base, no cast marks, 15″ h ... 525.00

Vases, pr, 12″ h, Oni form, bronze, c1900, oni supporting tall, cylindrical sack tied at neck

with long cord, gilt details to
coiled hair, toes, and tassels .. | **1,000.00**

Lacquer

Kobako, drum form, 5½" h, 19th
C, bulging cylindrical drum
raised on a footed stand and
decorated in gold and colored
takamakie and *mokume*, opening to show an interior tray decorated in colored *takamakie*
with a bugaku helmet, *nashiji* in-
terior . . . . | **1,000.00**

Kodansu, four drawers, gold and
colored lacquer, 5½ x 4¾ x
3¾", 19th C, decorated on
each side with moonlit scenes
of Lake Biwa in gold and colored *takamakie, okibirame,* and
e-nashiji, four interior drawers
decorated with gold and red
fundame, gilt metal fittings . . | **2,000.00**

Kogo (incense burner), inlaid, 3¼",
19th C, shaped as bundle of
sticks topped by a sickle and
tied with a cord in inlays of
stained ivory, mother-of-pearl,
pale horn and silver on a gold
fundame ground, opens to reveal a shaped interior tray decorated with birds and flowers in
gold and colored *takamakie* on a
kinji ground, *nashiji* interiors . . . | **1,450.00**

Suzuribako, 19th C, 9 x 5 x 1½",
showing opening winter cherry
pods in gold and colored
hiramakie on a *roiro* ground,
mura nashiji interiors set with
copper *mizuire* shaped as an
abalone shell and *suzuri* . . . . . | **450.00**

Mask, Japanese, Shishi Mai, fanciful
animal head with large nostrils
and eyes, moveable ears and jaws | **140.00**

Rug, Chinese, 96 x 54", honey
ground reading from left to right,
covered by lobed floral medallions
outlined with medium blue tulips,
honey primary border of cartouche
design, inner decorative guard
border, navy blue outer guard
stripe, slight wear . . . . | **1,550.00**

Sculpture

Bengal, Jain Marble Stele, 22" h,
c1660, Tirthankara standing
frontly flanked by openwork columns, low relief diamond emblems on capitals, foliage bower
suspended from mouth of lion
below, elephant supporting a
rampant simha-viyala to left,
pieces missing . . . . | **825.00**

Indian, Northwest, Vajrasattva,
bronze, 9" h, c11th C, possibly
Swat Valley, seated on a high

lotus, openwork elephant cary-
atid plinth in padmasana,
clutching a vajra with his right
hand to his chest, a ghanta in
his left, his crown set with the
other five Dhyani Buddhas,
bronze worn to dark patina . . . | **1,650.00**

Tibetan, figure of a Padmapani,
19¾" h, cast standing in radical
tribhanga on an oval double lotus base, lowered left hand
holding a fruit, right hand raised,
wearing sheer dhoti, face cold
gilded, hair painted blue . . . . . . | **1,800.00**

Thai, Buddha, bronze, Sukhothai
period, 17" h, c1500, finely cast
seated Buddha with hands in
dhyana and bhumisparsa murda
on a high stepped lotus base
pierced with quatrefoils, wearing
a sheer garment, usnisa topped
by a flame, remnants of old gild-
ing . . . . | **800.00**

Screens

Chinese, 12 fold, each panel 108
x 19", lacquer, palace scene on
one side, exotic birds amongst
flowers on other, panels of
branches on the carved brocad-
ed and key pattern grounds
above and below the central
panels . . . . | **8,000.00**

Japanese, 2 fold, each panel 57½
x 31¾", Children Playing In The
Snow, ink and colors on paper,
unsigned, unsealed, 19th C . . . | **1,250.00**

Japanese, 4 fold, each panel 38 x
24", Genji scenes, ink, colors,
and gold on paper, Tosa
School, 19th C . . . . | **900.00**

Japanese, 6 fold, each panel, 68 x
24¼", Falcons, ink and colors
on paper, sgd (Kano) *Tsu-
nenobu,* one seal, 19th C . . . . . | **7,000.00**

Table Screens, 13" h, applied
hardstone of serpentine and jade,
depicting a figure in a pavilion
scene, framed, hardwood stand,
pair . . . . | **480.00**

Teapots

Famille Verte, Chinese, 7" h, fluted, compressed baluster body
applied with straight spout and
yellow squared handle, identical
rectangular panels of blossoming branches growing from
grassy hillsides . . . . | **1,250.00**

Kangxi, blue and white, Chinese,
6¼" w, globular, applied handle
and spout of molded bamboo
sections, painted in underglaze
blue with two large quatrefoil
panels of lingzhi and Daoist em-

blems on plain ground, wispy clouds, flat cover with bead finial 375.00

Makuzu Kozan, Japanese, 8¾" h, lobed body with phoenix spout painted in underglaze blue with phoenixes and dragons amongst swirling clouds between formal bands, *Makuzu Kozan* in underglaze blue 875.00

Yixing, made by Shih Ta-tin, lozenge shaped body and domed cover, plain, faceted plain loop handle, shaped spout, base inscribed 480.00

Vases

8¾", Chinese, late 18th C, bottle type, oviform, long cylindrical neck, slightly spreading foot, covered in a slightly matte lemon yellow glaze 600.00

10⅞", Japanese, constricted tall conical form, decorated with two wide bands in a purple-black glaze, sgd underfoot with a glazed triangle 90.00

13¾", waisted bulbous form, extended pedestal foot, shaped rim, iron rust glaze covered with an iridescent brown and silver flecked glaze 225.00

17½", powder blue glazed Rouleau, late 18th C, slightly tapered, cylindrical knopped neck ending in cupped mouth, glaze thins to white at edges 950.00

43", Japanese, blue and white, c1900, painted with large cartouches of landscapes interspersed with smaller fan and chevron panels of vases of flowers, additional landscapes and flowers, ruyi collar, wide neck bands with white canopies of state and yin-yang roundels, pair 3,500.00

Wine Ewer, Korean, Koryo Dynasty, 6" h, globular neck, short shaped spout, double loop handle, short cylindrical neck, painted in a brown slip under a gray celadon glaze, luxuriant scroll of a stylized flowering branch below a wide petal border on shoulder 1,150.00

OVERSHOT GLASS

Overshot glass is a type of glass developed in the mid-1800s. A gather of molten glass was rolled over the marver upon which had been placed crushed glass to produce Overshot glass. The piece then was blown into the desired shape. The finished effect was a glass that was frosted or iced in appearance.

Early pieces were mainly made in clear; but, as the demand for colored glass increased, color was added to the base piece and/or less often to the crushed glass. Pieces of Overshot generally are attributed to the Boston & Sandwich Glass Co. There is no doubt it was made by other companies as well. It is not marked.

Bowls

Amethyst, deep pinched rim, clear crimped foot 125.00

Blue, petal top, base 160.00

Decanter, 11½", cranberry, cranberry bubble stopper, ice bladder, clear applied handle 245.00

Fairy Lamps

Berry, green, sgr Clarke base ... 85.00

Crown, blue, sgr Clarke pyramid base 195.00

Ribbed, yellow, sgr Clarke base . 80.00

Lamp, 16¼", lacemakers, cranberry shade, brass base 375.00

Muffineers, Swirl, blue 65.00

Pitchers

5½", blue, amber reeded applied handle 90.00

7½", blue, amber reeded applied handle 145.00

10½", clear, clear reeded applied handle 180.00

Rose Bowl, 4½", blue 85.00

Vase, 6", blue 72.00

OWENS POTTERY

J. B. Owens began making pottery in 1885 near Roseville, Ohio. In 1891 he built a plant in Zanesville and in 1897 began producing art pottery. It is not likely that much art pottery was produced at Owens after 1907, most of their production being centered on the output of tiles.

Owens pottery, employing many of the same artists and designs of its two cross-town rivals, Roseville and Weller, can appear very similar to that of its competitors (i.e., Utopian — brown glaze; Lotus — light glaze; aqua verde — green glaze, etc.).

There were a few techniques used exclusively at Owens, however, and these included red flame ware (slip decoration under a high, red glass); Mission (over-glaze, slip decorations in mineral colors) depicting Spanish Mission scenes. Obese pieces often came with wooden stands; Opalesce (semi-gloss designs in lustred gold and orange); Coralene (small beads affixed to the surface of decorated vases).

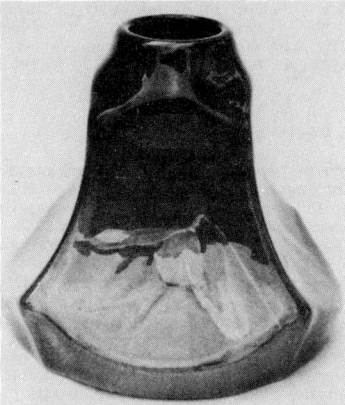

Owens Vase, 2½″, miniature, brown, high gloss, abstract floral decor, marked z/owens/utopia/103 Artist: Mae Timberlake, $145.00.

Candlestick, 7″, Utopian, berry and leaf decor	80.00
Honey Pot, 6 x 7″ d, Utopian, painted florals, brown glaze	265.00
Mug, 5″, Utopian, berry and leaf decor	55.00
Pitcher, 6½″, floral decor	425.00
Tile, 6″ sq, Utopian, brown glaze . .	165.00
Vases	
6″, Aborigine	210.00
6″, bisque glazed slip decorated floral on blue to brown blended bisque ground, matte, artist sgr	100.00
6½″, square, Utopia, artist sgr Fannie Bell	165.00
7″, Utopian, vintage decor, artist sgr, 3 handles	125.00
8½″, dark brown ground, red flowers, Art Nouveau style leaves, woman with flowers, leaves on reverse, sgr Henri Deaux	375.00
10¼″, baluster, slender waist, brown, green, 2 orange and brown flowers, imp mark	175.00
10½″, Lotus, painted pink, white carnations, glossy shaded gray glaze	215.00
13½″, Utopian, matte	225.00

PADLOCKS

Warman's Americana & Collectibles, 1st Edition, contains 80 listings in this category; see also page xii.

PAIRPOINT

In 1880, Pairpoint Manufacturing Co. was organized as a silverplating firm in New Bedford, Mass. The company merged with Mt. Washington Glass Co. in 1894 and became known as Pairpoint Corporation. The new company produced specialty glass items, often accented with metal frames. Pairpoint Corp. was sold in 1938 and Robert Gunderson became manager; it operated until his death in 1952 as Gunderson Glass Works. Robert Bryden became manager of Pairpoint-Gunderson Glass Works until its closing in 1957. In 1970, Bryden reopened the factory of Cape Cod under the famous Pairpoint name. In 1978, Pairpoint Glass Company returned to its New Bedford birthplace.

See *Warman's Americana & Collectibles* for additional Pairpoint Cup Plates listings.

Biscuit Jar, yellow, floral decor, reticulated SP frame	250.00
Bowls	
5 x 12¼″ d, centerpiece, heavy bubble pedestal	170.00
11 x 3½″, leaf shape, full bodied squirrel, SP, gold wash interior	175.00
Boxes	
4½ x 3½″, ftd, painted porcelain, insert on cover, silk lining, marked "Pairpoint Mfg. Co." . .	250.00

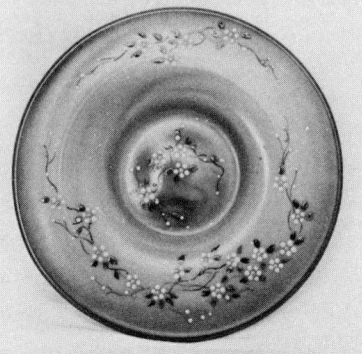

Pairpoint plate, 5⅛″ d, artist sgr P. Kiluk, dated, marked P in diamond, $115.00.

6 x 3", SP, Crown Milano, apple
blossom spray on lid **245.00**
6½", hinged cover, blue, purple
violets, sgd in diamond **275.00**
Butter, cov, with knife rest, SP **150.00**
Candlesticks
6", Blue Swirl Pattern, bubble
base, sgr, pr **195.00**
10", amethyst etched grape de-
sign, pr **425.00**
Champagne, 5⅛", "Flambo," crystal **50.00**
Cigarette Holder, 7½", figural cupid
lifts floral cut crystal holder **65.00**
Compotes
6", green, Vintage Grape, pr **250.00**
7", amber, bubble pedestal **125.00**
9¼", cov, ruby, clear controlled
bubble connector, ruby base,
steeple bubble finial **115.00**
Console Set, bowl, 14", candlesticks
12", light green, bubble-ball
stems, cut & etched vintage decor **350.00**
Demi-John, 12" h, basket pattern,
quart, air-trap stopper **1,250.00**
Hand Coolers, 3", clear, frosted
Crab **150.00**
Ram **165.00**
Hat, 4¼", deep red, white with controlled bubbles, orig paper label . **65.00**
Inkwell, 4" d, clear, allover controlled bubbles, SS cap **200.00**
Jewelry Boxes
8", molded body, light to dark
green, hp beaded blossoms,
orig lining, numbered, sgd. . . . **115.00**
10", hinged, cut, Viscaria pattern,
opal flowers, thumbprint base . **220.00**
Ladle, Punch, 14", silver with cut
glass handle, mkd Pairpoint Mfg Co. **350.00**
Lamps
Boudoir, 15" h, blown-out shade,
flowers, butterfly, patinated met-
al base, c1901 . . . . **1,200.00**
Table, 19½" h, 15" d shade, re-
verse painted, frosted shade
showing New Bedford waterfront, whaling ships at sunset,
sgd. H. Fisher, turned wooden
base, brass trim **1,800.00**
Napkin Ring, wheelbarrow **75.00**
Plateau Mirror, baroque SP base,
beveled mirror **125.00**
Shaving Mug, SP, engraved florals,
lift-out soap insert **85.00**
Tray, 7¾ x 5", painted porcelain in-
sert **350.00**
Urn, cov, 14", Vintage Grape, ame-
thyst **225.00**
Vases
8", goblet-shape, cobalt, crystal
bubble-ball stem **75.00**
10", trumpet-shape, deep blue,
bubble base **95.00**

12", heavy opal, purple-blue
enamel decor of harbor village
scene, castle in background . . **285.00**
Whiskey Decanter, 10" h, Old English Pattern, quart, matching stop-
per **1,250.00**
Wine
5⅛", flambe, red bowl, black
stem, Rockwell silver design . . **145.00**
12", trumpet-shape, crystal bub-
ble-ball stem **150.00**

PAPERWEIGHTS

**Although paperweights had their origin in an-
cient Egypt, it was in the mid 19th century
that this art form reached its zenith. The
classic period for paperweights was 1845–55
in France where the Clichy, Baccarat and
Saint Louis factories produced the finest examples of this art. Other weights, made in
England, Italy and Bohemia during this period
rarely match the quality of the French
weights.**

**The earliest American factories to make
paperweights were the New England Glass
Company in Cambridge, Massachusetts and
the Boston and Sandwich Glass Company in
Sandwich, Massachusetts about 1852. Popularity peaked during this classic period and
faded toward the end of the 19th century.**

**Paperweights were rediscovered nearly a
century later in the mid 1900s. Contemporary
weights are still made by Baccarat, Saint
Louis, Perthshire and by many studio
craftsmen in the U.S. and Europe.**

**Some collectors prefer to limit their collec-
tions to antique weights while others collect
both contemporary and earlier editions; fine
examples are available in both areas. Today,
interest in paperweights is greater than ever
and values have increased accordingly.**

**See *Warman's Americana* & *Collectibles* for
additional paperweight listings.**

Baccarat
Close Millefiori Mushroom, 3",
blue spiral encircling white
gauze cable, upright tuft of
closely packed canes, star cut
base **935.00**
Double Clematis, 2¹/₁₆", blue,
overlapping petals, white star
dust, red whorl center, 3 leaf
tips, straight stalk entwined with
2 buds, 2 leaves, star cut
base **1,000.00**
Faceted Butterfly, 3¼", sides and
top cut with 7 windows, upset
muslin ground, butterfly with
marbled wings, amethyst body,

dark head, feelers, turquoise eyes, garland of alternate green and white star dust canes 1,210.00

Faceted Close Millefiori, 2¹¹/₁₆″, cut in 7 windows, outer row of alternate white and red hollow staves, center of numerous tightly packed canes, deep star cut base 900.00

Faceted Pompon, 2½″, cut around sides in row of windows, thumbprints, salmon flower on short stalk, 2 leaves, red bud, star cut base 1,000.00

Faceted Scattered Millefiori, 2½″, sides cut with 2 rows of 5 windows, fine upset muslin ground, imitation Clicy rose center, 2 rows of bright florettes, silhouettes of cockerel and goat 1,200.00

Faceted Translucent Green Overlay, 3¼″, cut around sides, top in 7 windows, base row of thumbprints, 2 entwined trefoils in turquoise and white, red centered by crow's foot cane, yellow shamrock silhouette central cane 2,860.00

Garlanded Primrose, 2⅜″, 5 petal blue flower, white star dust, yellow stamens, 4 leaf tips, blue bud, garland of white star dust and crow's foot canes 1,500.00

Magnum Close Millefiori, 4″, numerous tightly packed canes, silhouettes of cockerel, goat, devil, horse, dog, elephant, flower, waffle cut base, dated 1847 .... 3,740.00

Patterned Millefiori, 3⅛″, upset muslin ground, outer row of 11 butterfly silhouette canes enclosing row of 12 larger blue and white and red crow's foot canes, row of corrugated florettes, row of 7 shamrock silhouettes 1,760.00

Scattered Millefiori, 2¹/₁₆″, upset muslin ground, 6 alternate florettes, silhouette canes of dog, horse, deer, central green florette 900.00

Boston and Sandwich, 2¾″, 12 petaled poinsettia, cobalt blue, white bow above center cane, 7 goldstone dots 750.00

Clichy

Close Millefiori, 2³/₁₆″, red, white cane basket containing assorted canes, including purple rose ... 1,800.00

Close Millefiori, 2⅜″, basket of alternate opaque turquoise and white staves, enclosing numerous tightly packed canes including 9 canes in mauve, white, pink 800.00

Cobalt Blue Ground, 3¼″, numerous large florettes, pastry mold canes, 3 pink roses, white, pink, green and yellow canes 695.00

Cobalt Blue Ground, 3¼″, outer garland of white and green florettes, enclosing 5 circles of pink canes spaced by white florettes with turquoise canes .. 750.00

Concentric Millefiori, 1¾″, miniature, basket of alternating green and white staves enclosing an outer row of pink pastry mold canes, alternate green and white florettes, 15 pink and green roses, blue florettes, cluster center 2,000.00

Faceted Chequer, 2½″, 6 windows, 2 rows of canes including 2 roses, divided by blue and white latticinio barber's poles, center of pink and green canes 990.00

Faceted Double Overlay, 2¾″, blue, concentric millefiori, sides, top cut in 6 windows, upright mushroom enclosed in basket of white staves, outer row of moss beads, row of alternate mauves canes, 9 pink and green roses, row of 8 pink canes, centered by blue florette, waffle cut base 4,125.00

Faceted Millefiori, 2⅝″, 5 circles of canes in green, white, turquoise, pink, mauve, each centered by florette, center of large blue cane, honeycomb faceted sides 880.00

Millville Type, rose, 5 leaves, long green stem, ftd, 3½″ d x 5¾″ h . 325.00

New England

Apple, clear circular foot, green stem, 3⅛″ d x 2½″ h 1,500.00

Faceted Flat Bouquet, 3¹³/₁₆″, high dome of glass cut around sides in diamond facets, thin swirling white latticinio ground, triform bouquet of white double clematis, blue and yellow flowers, pink double clematis, 2 small mauve, white flowers, white bud, serrated leaf tips, stalks tied at base by yellow ribbon 15,400.00

Fruit, 5 pink and yellow pears, 5 red cherries, 5 green leaves, white latticinio ground, 2¾″ d . 850.00

Pinchbeck, 3¾″, gilt metal ground repoussé, chaste in relief, seated couple in wooded landscape, metal base 715.00

St. Louis

Aventure Ground, 3⅛", dark green, 2 pink and white ridged petal dahlias, solid yellow centers, stalks, 5 leaves 5,000.00

Carpet Ground, 2¾", white ground, corrugated canes, dark pink interior, 5 clusters of florettes in pale blue, white, pink and green 3,410.00

Concentric Millefiori, 2", miniature, 5 concentric rows of blue, white, pink, ochre, turquoise canes, central florette 625.00

Concentric Millefiori Piedouche, 3 ¼" d x 2⅝" h, pedestal ft of spiraling white lattacinio, 6 concentric rows of canes in green, pink, white, lime green, blue, corrugated turquoise, green and pink central florette, sgd SL 1848 7,700.00

Concentric Mushroom, 2⅞", clear glass with blue spiral enclosing a twisted white latticinio cable, upright mushroom of concentric rows of canes in green, blue, white, pink, ochre, center of blue star silhouette canes, star cut base 2,420.00

Dahlia, 2½", green and white jasper ground, pink ridged petals, solid yellow center, curved stalks, 3 leaves 1,000.00

Encased White Overlay, 3¹⁄₁₆", 2 oval windows on sides alternating with 2 windows of hound and hare silhouettes, circular top window, upright clematis bouquet of dark pink, blue, ochre, 2 florettes, leaf tips, star cut base 10,175.00

Faceted Posy, 2⅝", honeycomb faceting on top, circular windows on side, posy of 5 florettes in white, blue, pink, ochre, leaves, diamond cut base 1,500.00

Faceted Upright Bouquet, 2⅞", faceted allover, triangular windows, clematis bouquet in blue, pink, white, 2 florettes, leaf tips, enclosed at base by blue and white torsade 990.00

Four Color Crown, 2⅝", large green, pink, white florette center, alternate twisted ribbons in red and blue, red and green radiate from center, divided by white latticinio strands 2,300.00

Fuchsia, 2⅞", swirling white latticinio ground, orange twig, large bright red and blue flower, 2 buds, 4 shaded green leaves 1,430.00

Macedone, 2¹⁄₁₆", numerous twisted white latticinio strands, colored ribbons 1,250.00

Panelled Jasper Ground, 3", red, white and blue jasper ground divided into 8 panels by opaque white staves, alternate pink and green florettes, large shaded ochre cane center, white latticinio cable 500.00

Pompon, 2⅛", translucent pink and white swirling latticinio ground, white camomile, stalk, 4 dark green leaves, white bud .. 1,100.00

Tiffany, 1¾", bronze lion, sgd Tiffany Studios, New York 250.00

Unknown Factories

Chrysanthemum, 3", clear glass, large white flower of 4 overlapping petal rows, yellow stamen center, curved stalk, 4 large serrated leaves 2,500.00

Faceted, 5 rainbow colored lily shaped flowers, mottled red, aqua and white ground, 2⅜" d . 400.00

Magnum, 4½", white, red loopings, American, mid 19th C 220.00

Millefiori, 1⅛", 3 concentric rows in pale mauve, pink, orange, orange cane center 275.00

Millefiori, 1⅞", 3 rows of canes in white, blue, red and white, stylized rose center 250.00

Pear, miniature, 1¾", clear glass, orange pear, 3 serrated leaves . 990.00

Queen Anne Cherries, 1⅞", miniature, clear glass, pink, turquoise, 6 down turned cherries hanging from branch, 3 large leaves 1,760.00

Rose, 2⁷⁄₁₆", opaque white ground, realistic modeled pink rose, yellow stamen center, brown stalk, 5 matted green leaves, red bud, light green sepals 4,000.00

MODERN

Modern, Kaziun, Cobalt blue ground, pink flower center, sgd, $250.00.

Ayotte, Rick, Parrot, 2⅝", blue parrot, yellow chest, black beak, feet, perched on branch of 4 shaded green leaves 275.00
Banford, Ray, 3¼", Morning Glories on trellis, diamond cut base 600.00
Kazuin, Charles
Faceted, 1½", 7 windows, translucent mauve ground, center of gold leaf profile of young girl, 6 white florettes 900.00
Faceted Patterned Millefiori, 2½", 7 windows, blue ground, alternate green, red canes enclosing row of 6 green, white and red florettes 950.00
Rose, pedestal, 2¹/₁₆", 15 petal pink rose, 4 leaf tips, knopped stem, spreading circular base .. 950.00
Perthshire
Christmas, 1980, red candle on sprig of holly leaves, white latticinio ground, red base 265.00
Triple swirl, green, purple, pink stripes, Clichy type center 250.00
Stankard, Paul
Botanical, 2⅛" d x 5⅛" h, upright bouquet of yellow loosestrife flowers, orange stamen centers, numerous stems, leaves, buds, mat of shaded brown twigs, light tan root system underneath ... 1,150.00
Experimental, 3⅛" d, Ayotte bird, blue, brown, white chest, black beak, feet, perched on cluster of white spring flowers, light brown stamen centers, green stems, leaves, sgd S, engraved name, number, bird marked A50 1980 .... 1,000.00
Ladyslipper Bouquet, 3½" d, 7 white and lavendar blossoms among stems, leaves, buds, sgd S on a single cane, engraved 12/25 A951 1979 .... 1,300.00
Spring Beauty, 3¾" d, white, pink striped flowers among stems, buds terminating in a tan bulb with roots 1,200.00
Tarsitano, Debbie, 3", blossoms, plum flowers in caledon vase ... 525.00
Tarsitano, Delmo, 3" triple strawberries and blossoms 625.00
Ysart, Paul
Clematis, double 350.00
Millefiori, green ground 625.00

PAPIER MACHE

The literal translation of the French term "chewed paper," Papier Mache is a mixture of ground paper, glue, resin and fine sand which is subjected to great pressure, then dried. The finished product is tough, durable and heat resistant. Various finishing treatments were used—lacquers, japanning, painting, enameling, and inlaying with mother-of-pearl. Papier Mache articles such as boxes, trays, and tables were in high fashion during the Victorian era.

Mask, 13½", $65.00.

Birdcage, 72", Victorian, wood and papier mache on painted metal base, mid-19th C 290.00
Bulldog, 25", advertising Clayton's Dog Remedies 300.00
Candlestands, 27 x 16½ w x 14½" d, tilt top, MOP inlay, turned stem, 3 short scroll feet, c1860, pr 360.00
Cigar Case, 5½ x 2½ x 1½", gold, black and blue floral design, crossed standards, Queens Royal Lancers, c1850 .... 120.00
Clown, 40", mechanical, 1930s ... 395.00
Decoys, drake and hen, glass eyes, pr 25.00
Dolls
Dutch girl, 8½", ball-jointed body, felt clothes, white molded cap, Swiss, c1921 .... 100.00
Head, 4½ x 2½", flapper, dark blonde wavy real hair, green hat 125.00
Negro, 6½", jointed, hair 145.00
Figures
Horse, 6 x 6" 15.00
Rabbit, basket on back, U.S. Zone, Germany 20.00

Jewel Box, 5 x 11½ w x 8½" d, Victorian, imp Jennens & Bettridge . **275.00**
Masks
  Japanese man, frowning **55.00**
  Santa Claus **68.00**
Nodder, 5", Queen Ann, orig paint . **75.00**
Picture, 18 x 14", oval, painted roses, floral bouquet on black, gold border, gold frame **225.00**
Plaque, 9½ x 10¾", The Last Harvest, 5 raised figural Indians, sgd Raymond Averill Porter, dated 1912 . . . . **25.00**
Puppet Head, 3½", man's head, painted white, black and red **50.00**
Radio Speaker **20.00**
Roly Poly, 14", clown, tin eyes, chimes inside **65.00**
Snuff Box, 3½", figural shoe, gold decor **40.00**
Table, serving, 27 x 15 w x 13" d, Oriental motif, fitted interior and scrolling, 4 legged base, c1860 . . **175.00**
Tobacco Jar, figural Mandarin **60.00**
Tray, 29 x 23", Victorian, MOP inlay, c1860 . . . . **150.00**
Whisk Broom Holder, 10¾ x 8¼", cat's head, tan velvet covering, glass eyes, wood shield shape back **160.00**

PARIAN WARE

Both Minton and Copeland have been credited for developing Parian around 1842 in England. There is controversy about which of the two actually did invent this ware and it was subsequently made in both England and United States in the Victorian era. America's best production came from Bennington Pottery and Copeland, Charles Meigh, Minton, Wedgwood, Boote, Rose, T. Booth, William Adams and Samuel Alcock all made it in England.

Box, pin, 2¼", oval, floral on blue . **35.00**
Busts
  6", Gladstone **60.00**
  6", Miranda Bell, c1872 . . . . **60.00**
  6½", John Bright by Robinson & Ledbetter **85.00**
  7", Queen Victoria, Robinson & Ledbetter **350.00**
  7½", Sir Walter Scott, Robinson & Ledbetter **55.00**
  7¾", Mendelssohn **70.00**
  8", Shakespeare T. and R. Boote, 14¼" Milton, Wedgwood, designed by W.E. Wyon **895.00**
Creamers
  Cow, Bennington **50.00**

Vase, Parian Ware, 8" h, scalloped top, hand, $160.00.

Pond lily **45.00**
Water Lily **50.00**
Figurines
  5¾", Hearing, woman seated behind desk, Minton, c1850 . . . . **225.00**
  9¼", Victorian lady and gentleman, Copeland **200.00**
  10¾", Madonna, separate matching base, marked Edward Marshall Boehm, USA **220.00**
  13½", female, nude, standing, cuffed wrists, one arm resting on draped post, cylindrical plinth, fluted sides, notched base **200.00**
  14¼", female, nude, reclining on back of leopard, holding drapery fold, French, 19th C **170.00**
  15", Apollo, Bing and Grondhal . **295.00**
  20", Cupid and Venus, Charles Meigh and Sons **350.00**
  20", Prometheus **200.00**
  22½", Maidenhood, young woman in tunic, hands clasped, eyes cast down, round base, Copeland **260.00**
  27", Penelophon-The Beggar Maid, c1870 . . . . **575.00**

Jugs
  5¾ x 3¾", lavendar, white emb
    English soldiers battling Turkish
    fighters, black printed Alcock
    mark 165.00
  7½", white water lilies, pads in re-
    lief on lavendar, Charles Meigh   165.00
  7½ x 4⅛", boy climbing tree after
    bird's nest, other side boy sit-
    ting in tree holding nest, blue
    trim, branch handle, Mayer,
    Longport, registry mark of 1850   195.00
  8", molded panels, classical fig-
    ures on green, gold trim, c1862,
    Brownfield 125.00
  9", 3 loop handles, sloping body,
    pierced flower heads 165.00
Pitchers
  4¼", bulbous body, trefoil scal-
    loped top, ivy leaves, berries
    decor, Minton 60.00
  6", Columbian Exposition, Colum-
    bus and his men, molded,
    marked Copeland 300.00
  7½", gypsy scenes in relief, twig
    handle 275.00
  8½", water lily, white on blue . . .   200.00
  8½", molded figures, with figural
    handle 225.00
  9½", Charter Oak, blue, white
    U.S. Pottery Co., raised ribbon
    mark 275.00
  10", Pond Lily, polychrome glaze,
    U.S. Pottery Co. raised ribbon
    mark 285.00
Plate, 9¼", center nude, floral
  spray, Boullemier 80.00
Stem Holder, putti holding domed
  pierced holder 350.00
Syrup, 7¼", Palm Tree, light brown
  raised white pattern, ribbon mark,
  c1852 . . . .   185.00
Urn, 11½", 2 handles, narrow neck,
  expanding waist, circles, florets . .   165.00
Vases
  5⅛", molded hand holding a pine-
    apple 150.00
  5⅜", molded, child's face on both
    sides 35.00
  6", applied grapes and leaves,
    acanthus leaves and medallions   50.00
  10", vintage pattern, bulbous
    shape 225.00
Wall Brackets, putti, one holding
  flowers, the other fruit, scallop
  shell supports, gilt decor, pr 95.00

PATE DE VERRE

Pate de Verre can be translated simply as
"Glass Paste." More precisely, it is a molded
glass form. The process is to grind lead glass
into a powder or crystal form. The ground
glass is then made into a paste by adding a
2% or 3% solution of sodium silicate. The resulting mixture can be molded, fired and
carved. This type of glass was known to the
Egyptians as early as 1500 B.C.

In the late 19th and early 20th centuries,
Pate de Verre was again revived by advanced glass makers in France. Cros,
Dammouse and the Daum Brothers were active in leading this movement. Within the past
ten years, contemporary artists have rediscovered Pate de Verre as a medium for
sculpturing.

Vase, 10¼" Rosettes, red, yellow
center, purple tones throughout,
$6,000.00.

Ashtrays
  5", circular, brown bettle sur-
    mount, Almeric Walter 1,000.00
  6¼" x 3½", Egyptian head in me-
    dallion in center, reds, purples,
    little flower buds all around
    edge, raised lattice work on bot-
    tom 1,500.00
Atomizer, 5¾", red berries, green
  leaves, sgd H. Berge 1,000.00
Bowls
  2¾" h, molded sprays of red ber-
    ries, green-brown branches,
    body lightly streaked with pur-
    ple, c1920 . . . .   800.00
  10¼" d, ftd, gray sides streaked
    with lavender and rose, molded

inside and out with a concentric blossom, rim of long necked birds 4,000.00

Clock, 4½", sq, stars within pentagon and tapered sheafs motif, orange and black, G. Argy-Rousseau, clock by J. E. Caldwell ... 2,500.00

Pendant, circular, amethyst translucent ground trimmed in blue, molded green mistletoe leaves encircling purple berried center, green knotted silk cord with hanging tassel 500.00

Sculptures
4" h, baby blue jay, dark turquoise, molded A. Walter, Nancy, designed by Henri Berge .. 1,000.00
12" h, Loie Fuller, dancer, shades of blue, sgd A. Walter 5,500.00

Tray, 8" 1 x 6" w, apple green, figural duck at end of tray, green, yellow, orange beak, sgd Walter, Nancy 600.00

Vases
5¼", gray, pale ruby and amethyst streaks 1,200.00
7", mottled gray sides molded in low relief with Australian bush babies in periwinkle blue hiding among the grasses, molded G. Argy Rousseau/France 6,000.00
9", tapered cylindrical, border of rose faun, satyr, girl amidst amber waves framed by purple morning glories, green ground . 3,500.00
9¾", baluster shape, aquamarine, purple streaked translucent ground molded in geometric and stylized floral design in cobalt, sea-green, molded sgr G. Argy-Rousseau France 2,000.00

PATE-SUR-PATE

Pate-Sur-Pate (paste on paste), an outstanding 19th century porcelain, has become unmistakenly synonymous with Marc Louis Solon. About 1863, Solon and other artists employed at the Sevres manufactury in France experimented with this process of porcelain decoration, inspired by a Chinese celadon vase in the Ceramic Museum at Sevres.

Just prior to the outbreak of the Franco-Prussian War in 1870, Solon suffered a severe illness and ultimately was unable to aid in the defense of his country. He migrated to England, worked at the Minton factory at Stoke-on-Trent, and during this time he made most of his masterpieces in this ware.

This type of ware features designs in relief which are obtained by successive layers of the thin pottery paste, painted one on top of the other.

Basket, 7½", polychrome, soft blue, green, white birds resting on thistles, blue-green ground, gilt floral motifs, French paper label printed Exposition/DE 1900/Paris 600.00

Boxes
3½" l x 2½" w, cobalt blue, cupid, dragonfly, butterflies on lid, sgd M. Haufname 195.00
5½", triangular, cobalt blue, gold cherubs, marked Fontaville & Marrid, Barbotine 45.00

Box, cov, blue ground, 4⅞ x 4⅞ x 2⅛", imp Limoges, $150.00.

Flasks, 8⅞", Sunrise, Sunset, deep olive-green parian body, white figure floating above the horizon, mounted as table lamps, sgd Frederick Schenk, pr 600.00

Plaques
4⅜ x 7½", Wedgwood green, French 295.00
7⅜ x 6½", glazed parian, maiden guarding caged cupid, 2 putti look on, Minton, sgd Louis Solon, c1900 .... 2,250.00

Plate, 10¼" d, 3 panels depicting classical maidens frolicking with putti, imp Minton, Tiffany & Co., Pattern No. H226, date codes, c1912 .... 150.00

Tile, 5½ x 6½", nude female dancer, Baron-Limoges 275.00

Urns
10", slate blue, white floral decor 475.00
10½", cov, deep pink, turquoise, cupid in relief 375.00

Vases
3½", apricot, florals, butterflies on reverse, Locke Worcester 200.00
4½", white florals, butterflies on brown ground, sgd George Jones and Son 275.00

5¾", irid ground, woman in relief
on mauve medallion 225.00

6", blue, 2 handled, oval reserve,
lady, boy with fish, marked
Schutz, Germany 250.00

8½", blue, white decor, sgd Tovy,
Limoges 265.00

8¾", polychrome, two putti rising
from choppy sea, dripping seaweed, one holding shell, gray
blue ground, pink, gray band between teal blue borders, gilt and
silvered details 1,200.00

16⅛", glazed parian, continuous
frieze of frolicking putti reserves
on chocolate band between cobalt blue borders, gilded, printed
crowned globe mark, Mintons,
sgd Lawrence Birks, c1890 . . . 1,880.00

PATENT MODELS

**Patent Models are one of the most important
documentations of the creative genius and
inventiveness of the American people. The
Patent Act of 1836 required every patentee
to furnish a model of his invention. Two
disasterous fires, the last in 1877, destroyed
the early models and over 70,000 models
from the 1840 to 1877 period. Many models
did survive; and, inventors kept submitting
models through the early 1900s.**

**Many of the models were built by profes-
sional model builders, thus often making
them aesthetic statements in themselves. In
1926 the patent models were sold and still
remain in private hands. A series of public
sales in the 1970's and catalogue sales since
1980 have made these models available to
collectors.**

**Models can be collected by subject, geo-
graphic area, aesthetic characteristics, and
inventor. Each model can be researched by
obtaining a copy of the patent application.
A high percentage of the categories in
WARMAN'S have a corresponding patent
model available in the current market.**

**Patent models range in size from a few
inches to slightly over a foot. The listing pattern is name of patent, number, date, patentee, location of patentee, and construction
materials.**

Animal Trap, #209068, 10/15/
1878, B. H. Hoelting, Nebraska
City, NE, tin, tag 100.00

Bailing Presses, #228036, 5/25/
1880, Charles Christmas, River
ton, MS, wood and iron, 12 x 12",
tag 115.00

Bed Spring #183453, 10/17/1876,

William H. Gaylord, Oskaloosa, IA,
wood and metal, 7 x 4 x 6", tag . 65.00

Burglar Alarm and Door Fastner,
#432987, 7/29/1890, Charles K.
Donnell, Webster, ME, brass and
iron, engraved plate, tag 150.00

Butter Jar, #95156, 9/21/1869,
John Smith, East Liverpool, OH,
ceramic 8" d, 9" h, stenciled front
and hand brushed decoration, tag 275.00

Construction of Globe Maps,
#109581, 11/29/1870, John
Brinckerhoff and James Duthie,
Morrisania, NY, wood and paper,
6" d, printed map on multicolored
globe, prize medal at 1867 Paris
Exposition, tag 550.00

Cotton Basket, #98091, 12/12/
1869, R. L. Myers, Washington,
NC, wicker, 7 x 7 x 7", hole in
bottom used to push ginned cot-
ton out in one mass, tag 105.00

Daguerreotype Case Mold, #
34344, 2/11/1862, J. L. Baldwin,
Newark, NJ, wood, cylinder shape,
5" d, 4" h, tag 90.00

Egg Carrier, #227518, 5/11/1880,
David Goodwillie, Chicago, IL,
wood and paper, 8 x 8 x 3", tray
partitioned off with wood slats, tag 75.00

Ice Hook, #277437, 5/8/1883,
John Winebrenner, Cromwell, IN,
spring steel, 10" l, 6" w, tag 210.00

Iron, sad, #54570, 5/8/1866, C. J.
Mallon, Schoharie, NY, wood and
iron, 7" w, 5" h, tag 175.00

Life Preserver, #175828, 4/11/
1876, John W. Fike, Clinton, MO,
tin, oval shape tube, 13" l, tag . . 150.00

Nut Locking Washer, #130097,
7/30/1872, Lorenzo Winslow,
Rochester, NY, wood and iron,
12" l, model railroad track, painted
name and city, tag 80.00

**Propulsion of Vessels, canal boat,
#120,264 10/24/1871, G.S. Godfrey,
tin, $275.00.**

Paper Box, #208412, 9/24/1878, William Meschenmoser, Greenburg, NY, paper, 1 x 7 x 2", for druggist's use, personal label, tag ... 70.00

Paper Folding Machine, #217857, 6/29/1879, Lewis Buffington, Cincinnati, OH, wood, brass, and iron, 9 x 9 x 12", elaborate detail, tag . 350.00

Reed Organ, #160052, 2/23/1875, L. K. Fuller, Brattleborough, VT, wood and brass, 8 x 10 x 10, tag 200.00

Rock Drilling Apparatus, #214704, 4/22/1879, Henry Richamann, San Francisco, CA, iron, 11", tag . 285.00

Steam Gauge, #20851, 7/6/1858, Joshua Lowe, New York, NY, iron, white metal, and brass, 6" d, 1" h, engraved, tag 200.00

Stove, Cooking, #181090, 8/15/1876, J. C. McClamrock, Edina, MO, tin, 5 x 8 x 6", name and city painted on front, tag (poor cond.) 160.00

Truss, #1226, 7/9/1839, Wm. B. Dey, Hope, NJ, brass, tin, and cloth, tag, very early model 150.00

Vise, #95195, 9/28/1869, C. A. Cole, St. Louis, MO, brass and iron, 6 x 7", name and city stamped on frame, tag (poor cond.) 200.00

S.E.G.

PAUL REVERE POTTERY

Paul Revere Pottery, Boston, Mass., was an outgrowth of a club known as "The Saturday Evening Girls." The S.E.G. was a group of young female immigrants who met on Saturday night for reading and crafts such as ceramics.

Regular production began in 1908; and the name Paul Revere was adopted because the pottery was located near the Old North Church. The firm moved to Brighton, Mass., in 1915. Known also as the "Bowl Shop," the pottery grew steadily. In spite of popular acceptance and technical advancements the pottery required continual subsidies. It finally closed in January, 1942.

Items produced ranged from plain and decorated vases to tablewares to illustrated tiles. Some decorated ware was incised and glazed in Art Nouveau matte shades and occasionally a high glass glaze.

Paper "Bowl Shop" labels were used prior to 1915 in addition to the impressed mark. Pieces can also be found dated and P.R.P. or S.E.G. painted on the base.

Bowl, child's, 2¼" h x 5½" d, blue tones, yellow and green in center design, "Johan," $175.00.

Bowls
  2 x 5½", blue glaze 140.00
  5¾" d, white rabbits, wild carrots on back, green, tan glaze, mkd S.E.G. 190.00
Calendar Holder, scene of trees, river, artist sgr, dated 11-21 ...... 115.00
Candlestick, 6" h, gun metal glaze, sgr 40.00
Chocolate Pot, cov, 7" h, cylindrical, floral band decor, mottled brown ground, mkd S.E.G., artist sgr ... 135.00
Cup, 1⅞" h, slightly tapered shape, white ground, green band, yellow flowers near top 50.00
Inkwell, 2½ x 4", green, high glaze 85.00
Paperweight, octagonal, scenic decor, mkd S.E.G., 1916 .... 110.00
Plaque, 5½" w, circular, orange colors with green band and green scene of trees in center, sgr P.R.P., 12-34 .... 130.00
Plate, 9", stylized water lily on green ground, mkd S.E.G. 115.00
Teapot, artist sgr, S.E.G. 75.00
Tile, 4½" d, scenic woodland decor on yellow ground 75.00
Vases
  6¼", scenic band in blues, green, outlined in black, brown high glaze, mkd S.E.G., 11-21-04 .. 240.00

6¾" x 4½" d, monochrome, matte mustard yellow **65.00**

8½", ball base, long tapered body, slightly outward flared neck, gun metal black glaze, dated 4-23 . . . . **60.00**

11", blue-green high glaze, artist sgr initials, 6-15, S.E.G. **85.00**

PEACHBLOW

Peachblow is an art glass which derived its name from a fine Chinese glazed porcelain— described as the color of crushed strawberries or resembling the color of the peach.

Three American glass manufacturers and two English firms produced Peachblow Glass in the late 1880s. Each firm's final product possessed its own characteristics. The following list will be helpful in identifying the makers.

Gunderson Glass Co. About 1950 they began producing "Peachblow" type art glass to order. Their wares shade from an opaque faint tint of pink, which is almost white, to a deep rose.

Mt. Washington Peachblow. Trade name for New Bedford Works. A homogeneous glass that shades from a pale gray blue to a soft rose color. Many decorative items were further enhanced with glass appliques, enameled and gilded.

New England Peachblow, New England Glass Works. The advertised name of their art glass was "Wild Rose," but the factory name was "Peachblow." The glass is translucent, shading from rose to white acid finished or left in the original glossy state. Some of the wares were also enameled and gilded.

Thomas Webb & Son, Stevens and Williams, England. Around 1888, these two English glass makers were both making a similar art glass which they termed "Peachblow" or "Peachbloom." It is a cased glass shading from yellow to red. Both firms occasionally employed cameo-type designs in relief on the basic objects.

Wheeling Peachblow, Hobbs Broclunier & Co. An opalescent glass that was plated or cased with a transparent amber glass and shades from yellow at the base to a deep red at the top. The finish can be either glossy or satin.

In the price listing below, all pieces are satin finish unless noted to be glossy finish.

GUNDERSON

Cologne Bottle	175.00
Salt and Pepper	135.00

Tumbler	125.00
Vases	
6⅞", cylindrical, white base shading to deep plum, gilt rim	135.00
7⅛", cylindrical, gilt rim	150.00

MT. WASHINGTON

Bowl, tricorner, 5 x 2"	1,125.00
Pitcher, 5½", reeded handle, leaves, sgd, 1886	2,600.00
Vase, 4 x 8", shaded	1,100.00

NEW ENGLAND

Bell, 6½	495.00
Bowl, 4½ x 8¼", fluted edge, glossy finish	325.00
Celery, 6¾", scalloped rim, flaring body	600.00
Creamer, 2½", ribbed	375.00
Goblet, 6½"	310.00
Pickle Castor, ftd frame	385.00
Pitcher, 7", bulbous, ribbed, applied handle	495.00
Punch Cup	300.00
Syrup, pewter lid	765.00
Toothpick, tricorn	325.00
Tumbler	325.00
Vase, 8", lily shape, Wild Rose label	845.00

WEBB

Bowl, 3⅞ x 2½", gold prunus decor	410.00
Mustard, cov, 2½", gold prunus decor	300.00

Wheeling, Pitcher, 7½" h, glossy, quadrafoil top, applied amber handle, Hobbs, Broclunier, c1883, $1,500.00.

Punch Cup	250.00
Scent Bottle, 5" l x 1⅜" d, coral, gold prunus decor, SS screw top	295.00

Vases

3½", petal top, floral decor	350.00
6" h, 22" d, pedestal, heavy gold decor	850.00
6⅞", gold daisies, dragonfly, cream lining	700.00
11½", stick, English ivy decor ...	850.00
15", gourd, floral and bee decor .	1,700.00

WHEELING

Bride's Bowl, 12"	250.00
Creamer, 4"	695.00
Cruet, 7½", glossy finish, teardrop shape	1,395.00

Pitchers

8", applied amber handle, glossy finish	1,500.00
10", rigaree collar, applied handle	1,250.00
Punch Cup, 2⅜ x 2⅝" d, glossy finish, amber applied handle, white lining	325.00
Salt & Pepper, pewter tops	325.00
Tumbler	300.00

Vases

7¾", acid finish	950.00
10", slender neck	985.00

PEARLWARE

Introduced by Josiah Wedgwood in 1779, Pearlware was a fashion of the late 18th century but not a technical improvement as such. Ladies of that period tired of cream-colored china and demanded a change in coloration, so cobalt was added to the glaze formerly used for Creamware and the result was Pearlware.

This ware bridged the gap between hard-paste porcelain, soft-paste porcelain, Creamware, and the advent of bone china. This bridge covered a span of years from 1740 to 1791, and Pearlware continued until about 1830. Marked pieces are uncommon; there appear to be examples of Pearlware made earlier than 1779, including Bristol pottery which could not have been made later than 1778.

Collectors should look for collected pools of blue or bluish green glaze on the footrim of Pearlware. Among the finest examples of this ware is the blue Staffordshire of the 1803–1820 period. Leeds, Liverpool and Swansea are among the best known makers and good examples of Pearlware include many pieces of Mocha and all Gaudy Dutch items.

See also SWANSEA.

Compote, 6¼ x 10¾" d, Havelock pattern, imp Wedgwood/Pearl, c1840–1868, $250.00.

Baskets and Underplates, 9¼", oval, pierced, molded basket-weave, blue line borders, Staffordshire, c1800, pr	265.00

Bough Pots, pierced covers

8½", urn shape, pedestal foot, mottled brown, stiff leaves on base and pedestal, imp Wedgwood	1,000.00
9", D shape, speckled, molded swags of flowers, stiff foliage border, gilding, imp Wedgwood, c1810, pr	1,045.00

Bowls

8½", square, polychrome, Botanical series	180.00
10", floral sprays, yellow, purple, rose and green, Staffordshire, c1810	374.00
Box, cov, 9", oblong, brown print and enamel birds, butterflies and floral sprigs, gilt bands at rims, imp Wedgwood, c1869	150.00
Bust, William Shakespeare, 8¾", dark hair and beard, white collar, iron red jacket, yellow trim, blue cloak with iron red lining, circular pink lustre socle, Staffordshire, 1815	625.00
Compote and Underplate, 10⅜" Nautilus shell compote, 11⅜" plate, shaded with bands of pale green and pink, imp Wedgwood, c1820	475.00

Cups and Saucers

Coffee, blue floral decor, imp Wedwood, c1815	100.00
Demitasse, blue, Staffordshire ..	70.00
Desk Ornament, figure of boy on green dolphin, 5", quill holder in	

dolphin's head, Staffordshire, c1820 . . . . 130.00

Dessert Set, orange foliate vine, green leaves, green rims, handles and lion knobs, Davenport, c1800, 14 pcs 375.00

Figures

Anthony and Cleopatra, 12½" l, reclining, mottled brown and ochre bases with flowers, Enoch Wood, c1800, pr 475.00

Saint George on horseback slaying the dragon, after Ralph Wood model, bluish glaze, Staffordshire, 1790 . . . . 675.00

Woman, 4⅞", seated on grass mound, brown sponged hat, yellow bodice, blue skirt, holding goblet, Staffordshire, c1790 . . . 175.00

Fruit Stand, 12⅞" w, center floral spray, gilt wigglework border, molded foliate rim, imp Wedgwood, c1845 . . . . 150.00

Jardinere and Stand, 4", flared, purple printed children in classical dress, playing games, purple line rim, Shorthose & Co, c1810 . . . . 176.00

Jugs

4¾", chinoiserie transfer decor, Liverpool, c1800 . . . . 80.00

7¾", commemorative, Royal Sufferers and the Duke of York, Pratt colors, c1798 . . . . 600.00

Loving Cup, 5", handled, sheaf of wheat, c1810 . . . . 165.00

Mug, polychrome, spatterware Peafowl, Leeds 375.00

Plates

5½", painted flowers within molded pink lustre borders of berried foliage, Staffordshire, c1815, set of 12 . . . . 245.00

8⅝", shell shape, shaded pink, imp Wedgwood, c1871 . . . . . . 48.00

Platter, 10½", Chrysanthemum pat, brown transfer, cell diaper ground, underglaze blue, red, green and gold mums, oriental flowers, iron red floral border, imp Wedgwood, c1810 . . . . 150.00

Sugar Shaker, Seaweed pattern, mocha 165.00

Teapot, cov, 5¾", transfer and enameled, ladies with fortune teller, scroll border, Leeds, c1780 . . 530.00

Toby Jug, 9⅞", tricorn sponged on interior with blue, ochre, black and rose stripes, blue coat, ochre cravat and breeches, holding beaker in right hand and toby jug in left hand, seated on green chair, black handle, Yorkshire, imp crown mark, 1790 . . . . 1,100.00

Vases

5¼", spill, modeled as 2 yellow canaries perched on green leaf tipped branches of a tree stump, Staffordshire, c1820 . . . 425.00

6⅝", cov, tan slip, engine turned gadroons, relief beadwork and swags, imp Wedgwood, late 18th C 400.00

PEKING GLASS

Peking Glass is a type of cameo glass of Chinese origin. Its production began in the 1700s and continued well into the 19th century. It is currently being reproduced, but readily identified when compared to the earlier glassware.

Box, cov, 4⅝" d, turquoise, damaged base of lid, $180.00.

Bowls

4½" d, translucent white, green prunus and rockwork 275.00

6", transluscent yellow, prunus blossoms, birds, chrysanthemums 200.00

7", canary, cameo reliefs 185.00

7", translucent white, red frogs and lotus 280.00

Jars

6", globular form, red glass, carved floral design 700.00

6½", cov, carved relief of flowers, grasswork springing from rockwork, stylized lotus on lid, yellow translucent 650.00

Snuff Bottles

2⅝", rosy coral overlay on milk white glass, rosy coral foot ring, lip, early 19th C 250.00

3", blue overlay on bubble glass, mid 19th C 300.00

6", bottle form, dragons and clouds in shades of pale green, green, yellow and red, 18th C . 2,500.00

Vases

8", white, Imperial yellow butterfly, flowers, leaves 295.00

12", baluster shape, translucent deep blue, white cranes 450.00

Water Pot, 4¼" h, green glass lined with pale blue enameled glass, worn Ja-i lappet metal border around neck, small inlaid jades, carved in low relief of chrysanthemums, prunus blossoms, branches, teakwood stand 300.00

PELOTON

Wilhelm Kralik of Bohemia patented this novelty art glass in 1880 and later patented it in both America and England. For the base piece, both transparent and opaque glass were used, with opaque glass most common. The hot glass was removed from the furnace either before or after it was worked into shape and opaque colored glass filaments (strings) were applied by dipping or rolling. Generally the threads are pink, blue, yellow and white (rainbow colors) but can be all a single color. Items can also be satin finished and have enamel decoration.

Vase, 7" h, bulbous, clear with cranberry red strings, $250.00.

Biscuit Jar, ribbed, soft blue satin, rainbow colored strings, SP mountings 750.00

Cruet, 7", light blue ground, clear stopper 265.0ᵒ

Pitchers

7", cranberry, emb swirl, rainbow colored strings, clear reeded handle 350.00

8", water, clear ground, blue coconut strings, yellow enameled floral decor 375.00

Rose Bowl, 2½", pale pink cased glass ground, rainbow strings, 6 crystal applied ft, ... 275.00

Sweetmeat Jar, 4½", squatty, fine ribbed, opaque white, rainbow colored strings, SP top, mountings . 600.00

Tumbler, 3¾" h, clear overshot, rainbow strings 120.00

Vases

3½", lavender cased, rainbow colored strings 265.00

3½" h x 3⅞" d, mauve ground, lightly ribbed, white coconut strings 275.00

5" h x 4⅜" d, fan shape, ruffled top, rainbow strings, ribbed body 325.00

7", bulbous, clear, royal blue colored strings 245.00

PENS AND PENCILS

Warman's Americana & Collectibles, 1st Edition, contains 60 listings in this category; see also page xii.

PETERS AND REED POTTERY

J.D. Peters and Adam Reed founded their pottery company in South Zanesville, Ohio, in 1900. Common flower pots, jardinieres and cooking wares comprised their major output in the beginning. Occasionally, art pottery was attempted, but it was not until 1912 that their "Moss Aztec" line was introduced and widely accepted. Other art wares included "Landsun," "Chromal," "Montene," "Pereco" and "Persian."

Peters retired in 1921 and Reed changed the name of the firm to "The Zane Pottery." Marked pieces of Peters and Reed Pottery are unknown.

Also see ZANE POTTERY and GONDER POTTERY.

See *Warman's Americana & Collectibles* for an expanded listing of Peters and Reed Pottery.

Bowls

6½", "Pereco," matte green glaze, butterfly decor 38.00

Vase, 9¾", pine cones and needles, terra cotta with green wash, $60.00.

8½", "Landsun," blue, yellow, green	35.00
8½", "Pereco," berry decor, dark blue	40.00
Jardiniere, 6½ x 7½", green lion's head decor on beige ground	72.00
Jug, 5½ x 5½" w, emb ear of corn front, back, brown glaze	85.00
Letter Holder, monochrome flowers	45.00
Mug, emb grapes, brown glaze	50.00
Pitcher, lemonade, cavalier portraits, high brown glaze	95.00

Vases

6", handles, monochrome drinking figures	45.00
8", chromal scene, blue, brown, glazed	200.00
10", Pereco, green, ivy in relief	60.00

Wall Pockets

7¾", "Pereco," Egyptian decor	70.00
10", Aztec, sgd Ferrell	70.00
Window Box, 13" l, Moss Aztec, depicting Homer and 2 nudes, sgd Ferrell	130.00

PEWTER

Pewter is a metal alloy, consisting mostly of tin with small amounts of lead, copper, antimony and bismuth added to improve formability and hardness. The metal can be cast, formed around a mold, spun, easily cut and soldered to form a wide variety of utilitarian articles.

Pewter ware was known to the ancient Chinese, Egyptians, the Romans and later the Medieval European continent. English pewter supplied the major portion of the needs of the American Colonies for nearly one hundred and fifty years before the American Revolution. The Revolution ended the embargo on the basic pewter making material, raw tin, which had been imposed by England. The American pewter industry, small before the Revolution, then flourished and thrived up until about the Civil War period. The listing that follows concentrates on the American and English pewter forms most often encountered by the collector.

Basins

Billings, W., 11¾", molded rim	800.00
Curtiss, Daniel, 6⅝", incised center and rim	350.00
Lee, Richard, MA, NH, and VT, 6⅝", circular, incised lines	900.00
"Love Bird," Philadelphia, 11½", molded edge, incised decoration	750.00
Nichols, O., 8", shallow, incised edge	165.00
Rust, H. N., 8", shallow	275.00
Unmarked, American, 7⅞", incised initials "T.L."	150.00
Young, Peter, 10⅞", deep, molded rim	1,400.00

Beakers

Flagg, Asa F., and Henry Homan, Cincinnati, OH, small (whiskey) size	150.00
Griswold, Ashbil, Middletown, CT, 2⅞"	200.00
Unmarked (attr. to Israel Trask, Beverly, MA), 3⅜"	85.00
Bedpan, Samuel Hamlin, Sr. and Jr., Providence, RI, 10½" d	225.00

Bowls, Baptismal

Trask, Oliver, Beverly, MA, 10¾", broad scooped rim, domed feet	2,750.00
Williams, L., 6¾" d, 4¾" h, everted lip, stepped molded base	380.00
Box, Tobacco, 7" h, oval, lid crested with eagle	900.00

Candlesticks

Gleason, Rosewall, Dorcester, MA, 7½", pr	225.00
Homan, H., Cincinnati, OH, pr	350.00
Hopper, Henry, 10", tapered standard, dome base, pr	650.00
Oster & Norris, 4⅛", short standard, saucer base, finger holder, pr	550.00
Unmarked (attr. to Fuller and Smith, Poguenock Bridge [New London], CT), 9¼", pr	425.00

Wilkes, Thomas, 10″, dome base, tapered standards, removable bobeche, pr **1,500.00**

Chalice

Calder, William, Providence, RI, 6″ **240.00**

French, 10″, breaker shape, dome base, 18th C **120.00**

Leonard, Reed & Barton, Taunton, MA, 7″ **80.00**

Reed & Barton, 6⅞″ **100.00**

Chargers

Badger, Thomas, Boston, MA, 15″ **800.00**

Griffin, 16½″ **600.00**

Nichols, O., 20¼″, triple reed rim **700.00**

Townsend and Compton, London, 13⅜″ **175.00**

Unmarked, English, 20¼″, molded edge, 18th C **250.00**

Coffee Pots

Boardman, Thomas Danforth, Hartford, CT, 11″, baluster shape **445.00**

Curtiss, Daniel, 10½″, baluster shape **550.00**

Griswold, Ashbill, Meriden, CT, 10½″, pyriform **330.00**

Portes, A., 11½″, pear shaped body, concentric bands **300.00**

Trask, Oliver, Beverly, MA, 11″, bright cut engraving, dome lid . **650.00**

Whitlock, 11½″, tapering cylinder shape **175.00**

Communion Services

Boardman, Thomas Danforth, New York City and Hartford, CT, 3 pieces, flagon 11″ h, 2 plates 10⅞″ d, flagon unmarked but from set **650.00**

Reed and Barton, 5 pcs, lidded flagon, pr of plates, and pr of chalices, flagon 10¼″ h, chalices 6⅞″ h, plates 10³/₁₆″ d . . . **300.00**

Cream Pitchers

French, marked "H.C.M.," 3¾″ . . **50.00**

Joseph, H., 3¾″, pyriform **1,600.00**

Cuspidor, William H. Savage, Middletown, CT, 8⅜″ d **350.00**

Flagons

Leonard, Reed and Barton, 11″, cove molded hinged lid **425.00**

Preaux, N., cylindrical shape, flat cover **875.00**

Unmarked, European, 10¾″, baluster shape **375.00**

Inkwell, English, 3⅝″ d, hinged lid, china inset **150.00**

Ladle, James Dixon & Sons, 12″ . . **50.00**

Lamps

Dunham, Rufus, Westbrook, ME, 4″, ship, swivel font, single **535.00**

Gleason, Rosewell, Dorchester, MA, 9″, whale oil, pr **350.00**

Lamp, double font, handle, Morey & Smith, Boston, 6″ h, $300.00.

Morey, Ober and Smith, Boston, MA, 4½″, bell shape, orig double divergent brass camphene burners with pewter caps, single **275.00**

Neil, I., 6¼″, bulbous font, loop handle, 2 fonts, whale oil, single **450.00**

Porter, Allen, Westbrook, ME, 3½″, sparking, single drop whale oil burner, pr **350.00**

Smith and Co., Boston, MA

5½″, double drop whale oil, single **225.00**

8″, inverted bell and dome top, orig double drop whale oil burner, single **275.00**

Unmarked, American, saucer base, high baluster standard, attached handle, double drop whale oil burner, single **400.00**

Mold, Spoon, spatulate handle, elliptical bowl, rattail drop **225.00**

Mugs

Bonynge, Robert, Boston, MA, 4¾″, pint, cylindrical shape, tapering sides, scrolled handle . . **1,500.00**

Palethorp, Robert, 4½″, pint, cylindrical shape, scrolled handle . **800.00**

Unmarked (attr. to William Calder, Providence, RI), 3½″, handled . **120.00**

Pitchers

Durham, Rufus, Westbrook, ME, 6½″, baluster shape **500.00**

Homan, H., Cincinnati, OH, 6¾″, cylindrical shape **230.00**

McQuilkin, William, Phila., PA, 10", baluster shape, scrolled handle **900.00**
Unmarked, English, 9", baluster shape, double dome lid, c1820 . **400.00**

Plates
- Austin, Nathaniel, Boston, MA, 8⅝" **275.00**
- Barrow, Leather, 9¼", smooth brim, deep **150.00**
- Bassett, Frederick, New York City and Hartford, CT, 8½" **200.00**
- Bonynge, Robert, Boston, MA, 7⅞" **400.00**
- Branstrom, John Andrew, Phila., PA, 7¾" **275.00**
- Byles, Thomas, Phila., PA, 9" . . . **500.00**
- Danforth, William, Middletown, CT, 7⅞" **270.00**
- Harbeson, B & J, 6" **350.00**
- Home, John, London, 9¼" **150.00**
- Jones, Gershom, Providence, RI, 8", early lion and gateway touch **325.00**
- Lightner, George, Baltimore, MD, 7⅞", struck twice **225.00**
- "Love Bird," Phila., PA, 7¾" **400.00**
- Melville, David, Newport, RI, 8$^{3}/_{16}$" **250.00**
- Piggott, Francis, English, 9⅜" . . . **150.00**
- Swanson, Thomas, London, 8¼" **200.00**
- Townsend & Compton, London, 8" **120.00**

Platter, Thomas Compton, London, 20 x 15⅜", oval **450.00**

Porringers
- Danforth, Samuel, Hartford, CT, 3 ¾", old English style handle . . **550.00**
- Danforth, Thomas, and Sherman Boardman (partnership), Hartford, CT, 4½", old English style handle **350.00**
- Ellsworth, W., 6", shell shaped handle **800.00**
- Jones, Gershom, Providence, RI, 7½", pierced handle **1,500.00**
- Northey, William (attr. to), Lynn, MA, 4", feather and crown handle **375.00**
- Pennock, Samuel, 7¼", tab handle, beaded lip **450.00**
- Unmarked, 5", crown handle, 18th C **125.00**
- Unmarked, Newport, RI, 5¼", tab handle, c1780 . . . . **350.00**

Salt, English, 3⅜" d across flats, pedestal, octagonal base, candlestick standard **175.00**

Snuff or Spice Box, George Coldwell, New York, straight line touch, 4¾", bright cut engraving **400.00**

Soap Dish, Ashbil Griswold, Middletown, CT, 4½" d, circular, lidded . **350.00**

Sugars
- Boardman, Thomas Danforth, Hartford, CT, 5¾", baluster shape, scrolled handles **475.00**
- Will, William, 4¾", double bellied, beaded rim and foot **3,500.00**
- Yale, Squire Hiram, Yalesville, CT, 6", raised foliate and floral designs on handle, orig ivory knob **500.00**

Syrup Jug, unmarked, New England, 5¾" **225.00**

Tankards
- Herbst, J. P., 9", tapered cylinder shape, ball thumbpiece, scrolled handle **350.00**
- Redhead, Anthony, English (Stuart), 6½", flat lid, wriggle work engraving **425.00**
- Unmarked, English (Stuart), 5¾", flat lid, plumbed thumbpiece, boot heel terminal **350.00**
- Unmarked, European, 12¾", cylindrical with flared base, 18th C **750.00**
- Young, Peter, 6¾", flat top, cylindrical molded base **4,500.00**

Tea Set, child's, James Tuffts, Boston, MA, teapot, cov. sugar, creamer, pedestal salt, 6 cups and saucers, c1870 . . . . **450.00**

Teapot, 10" h, Savage, Middletown, Conn., $350.00.

Teapots
- Curtiss, Daniel, 7½", baluster shape **300.00**
- Delawan, E. C., 6⅞", ball feet, wood handle and finial **125.00**
- Lewis, I. C., Meriden, CT, 6¾" . . **225.00**
- Munson, John, Wallington, CT, 8" **280.00**
- Porter, Freeman, Westbrook, ME, circular touch No. 7, 6¾" **300.00**
- Putnam, James, Malden, MA, 8½", baluster body **320.00**
- Smith, Eben, Beverly, MA, 9⅜" . . **250.00**

Task, Beverly, MA, 10½", cylindrical shape	950.00
Woodbury, J. B., eastern MA or RI, 7", pear shape or Queen Anne style, extended base	1,100.00

PEWTER, ART

Pewter is a metal alloy, consisting mostly of tin with small amounts of lead copper, antimony and bismuth added to improve formability and hardness. The metal can be cast, formed around a mold, spun, easily cut and soldered to form a wide variety of utilitarian articles.

Pewter ware was known to the ancient Chinese, Egyptians, the Romans and later the Medieval European continent. English pewter supplied the major portion of the needs of the American Colonies for nearly one hundred and fifty years before the American Revolution. The Revolution ended the embargo on the basic pewter making material, raw tin, which had been imposed by England. The American pewter industry, small before the Revolution, then flourished and thrived up until about the Civil War period. The listing that follows concentrates on the American and English pewter forms most often encountered by the collector.

Candy dish, marked 4065, $95.00.

Kayserzinn

Bowls	
9" d, chrysanthemums	65.00
10" d, 3 lobsters	95.00
Chamberstick with handle, Art Nouveau flowers	65.00
Coffee Set, coffee pot, cream, sugar, tray, poppies and other flowers	235.00
Gravy boat, attached underplate, flowing fushia design	70.00
Ice bucket, 10" h, presentation piece depicting forms of transportation, airplane, train, bicycle, balloon, bridges	285.00

Pitcher, 12" h, Mephistopheles head	225.00
Platter, game, 13", various animals in relief	145.00

Orivit

Cream and sugar on tray, stylized flowers	95.00
Pitcher, claret, green glass insert, vines and flowers, Art Nouveau	115.00
Vase, 7" h, Art Nouveau flowers and vines	55.00

Tudric

Basket, hammered finish, 6" h handle	70.00
Box, hammered finish with enameled ship insert in lid	75.00
Teapot, hammered finish, wooden handle, Liberty and Co.	75.00
Vase, Art Nouveau floral, 2 handles, Liberty and Co.	85.00

WMF

Vase, 8" h, Art Deco geometric design, 3 handles	60.00

PHOENIX BIRD CHINA

Phoenix Bird pattern is a blue and white china exported from Japan during the 1920s to 1940s. A limited amount was made during the occupation of Japan.

Initially, it was available at Woolworth's 5 & 10, through two wholesale catalog companies, or by selling subscriptions to Needlecraft magazines. Myott Son & Co., England, also produced this pattern under the name "Satsuma," c. 1936. These earthenware items were for export only.

Once known as "Blue Howo Bird China," the Phoenix Bird pattern is the most sought after of seven similar patterns in the Hō-ō bird series. Other patterns are: Flying Turkey (head faces forward with heart-like border); Howo (only pattern with name on base); and Twin Phoenix (border pattern only, center white). The Howo and Twin Phoenix patterns are by Noritake and occasionally marked. Flying Dragon (bird-like), an earlier pattern, comes in green and white as well as the traditional blue and white and is marked with six oriental characters. A variation of Phoenix Bird pattern has a heart-like border and is called Hō-ō.

Phoenix Bird pattern has over 350 different shapes and sizes. Also varying is the quality found in the execution of design, shades of blue, and shape of the ware itself. All these factors must be considered in pricing. The maker's mark tends to add value; over 60 marks have been catalogued.

Post 1970 pieces are being produced in limited shapes and precise detail, but are on a milk white ground and usually don't have a maker's mark. When a mark does appear on a modern piece, it appears stamped in place.

See *Warman's Americana & Collectibles* for an expanded listing of Phoenix Bird China.

Cider Jug, 2 quart, 8" w x 5¼" h x 4½" d base, $75.00.

Butter Pat, Twin Phoenix	10.00
Butter Tub and drain, 2 pcs	45.00
Butter Tub Drain	15.00
Celery, 13½"	50.00
Cheese Tub, Twin Phoenix, round underplate attached, cov, handleless	18.00
Chocolate Cup and Saucer, scalloped	15.00
Chocolate Pot, scalloped, Torri mark	80.00
Coaster, Flying Turkey	20.00
Cups and Saucers	
Average quality	8.00
Fine quality	10.00
Eggcups	
Double	12.00
Single	
Flying Turkey	6.00
Phoenix Bird	5.00
Fruit Dishes, 5"	
Howo	4.00
Satsuma, English	8.00
Gravy Boat, attached underplate . .	65.00
Gravy Tureen, cov, attached underplate, cut-out for ladle	40.00
Mustards, attached underplates	
Phoenix Bird, no cover	15.00
Twin Phoenix, cover, no spoon . .	10.00
Plates	
6", bread and butter, scalloped, Ho-o	10.00
7¼", dessert	7.00
8½", luncheon	10.00
9", soup, rimmed	22.00
9¾", dinner	30.00

Ramekins	
Set of 5	70.00
With Underplate, 5"	25.00
Rice Tureen, ftd, hp, humped cover, Flying Turkey	72.00
Salt and Pepper Shakers, six sided	18.00
Sauce Boat, leaf shaped	23.00
Soup Bowls	
Howo	15.00
7¼ x 1½" h	20.00
Teapot for two	25.00
Tea Set, Child's, teapot, cov, creamer, sugar, cov	65.00
Toothpick	18.00
Tureens, cov	
Child's, oval, cov	26.00
Flying Turkey, bulbous, hp	85.00
Howo, vegetable, oval	35.00

PHOENIX GLASS

Phoenix Glass Company, Beaver, Pennsylvania, was established in 1880. Although the firm was known primarily for commercial glassware, it began producing a molded, sculptured, cameo-type line in the 1930s. This decorative ware was discontinued in the 1950s and is widely collected today.

Basket, 4½", pink ground, dogwood decor	45.00
Bowls	
13½" d, canoe shape, opal ground, blue love birds	325.00
14", centerpiece, sculptured diving nude, 3 colors	200.00
Candlesticks	
3¼", blue, bubbles and swirls, pr	40.00
4", blue, frosted, pr	35.00
Compote, 8½", butterscotch, dragonflies and water lilies	85.00
Lamps, Table	
17½" d, irid blue, green, peacock feather pattern, sgd Phoenix Studios, Tom Arnold, #197 . . .	175.00
20", red cardinals on tree branches, green berries on ivory ground	250.00
Jar, ginger, cov, bird finial	70.00
Plates	
6¾", frosted and clear, dancing nudes	35.00
8½", clear and frosted, cherries .	55.00
14", blue, white daffodils	85.00
Powder Boxes, covered	
6¾" d x 3¾" h, sculptured roses, humming bird, amethyst	130.00
7¼" d x 4½" h, sculptured white violets on pale lavendar ground	100.00
Vases	
6", pink owls, cream color ground	75.00

Lamp, 22″ h to top of bracket, white ground, red berries, green leaves, brown stems, bronze plated base, $125.00.

6½″, red flashed lovebirds, flowers, clear ground	65.00
7½″, paneled, rounded ends, flowers, frosted	50.00
8⅜″, fan shape, sculptured Praying Mantis, foliage, frosted, pearlized, pale blue-gray	145.00
8⅝″, sculptured freesia, frosted .	95.00
9½ x 5½″, bittersweet, white ground	140.00
9½ x 11½″ w, blue pastel ground, white birds, orig paper label . . .	195.00
9½″, pillow shape, sculptured white pearlized flying geese, coral ground	225.00
9½″, sculptured blue flowers, custard ground	75.00
10″, Dogwood, blue, white, part paper label	75.00
10″, Lovebirds, 3 color	225.00
10½″, Madonna, opaque molded head, back, front, orig label . .	140.00
11″, sculptured clear flying gulls on frosted ground	175.00
12″, white foliage on sepia ground	88.00

PHONOGRAPH RECORDS

With the advent of more sophisticated recording materials, such as 33⅓ RPM long playing records, 8-track tapes and cassettes, earlier phonograph records have become collectors' items. These records are also sought by collectors of memorabilia for past artists who recorded on different labels.

Banner	
Calloway, Cab, Sweet Jennie Lee	5.00
Hill, Teddy, Here Comes Cookie .	4.00
Bluebird	
Brown, Les, Boogie, Woogie	4.50
Shaw, Artie, Nightmare, ...	4.00
Brunswick	
Bernie, Ben, Ain't She Sweet? . .	3.50
Martin, Mary, My Heart Belongs to Daddy	3.65
Mills Brothers, Tiger Rag	9.00
Capitol, Cole, Nat "King," The Christmas Song	2.00
Columbia	
Astaire, Fred, Funny Face	8.00
Goodman, Benny, Music Hall Rag	5.50
Herman, Woody, Apple Honey . .	4.00
Miller, Glenn, Solog Hop	10.00
Decca	
Andrew Sisters, Bie Mir Bist Du Schoen	3.00
Basie, Count, Honeysuckle Rose	4.00
Dietrich, Marlene, Falling In Love Again	4.25
Fitzgerald, Ella, It's Only A Paper Moon	3.00
Garland, Judy, Friendship	3.00
Gennett, Carmichael, Hoagy, Stardust	30.00
Okeh	
Armstrong, Louis, Body and Soul	5.00
Oliver, King, Room Rent Blues . .	72.00
Victor, RCA	
Bailey, Mildred, Georgia On My Mind	5.50
Como, Perry	1.50
Crosby, Bing, Old Man River	9.00
Dorsey, Tommy, Stop, Look & Listen	5.00
Horne, Lena, Stormy Weather . . .	3.25
Jolson, Al, That Haunting Melody	25.00
Whiteman, Paul, Rhapsody in Blue	12.00
Vocalion, Holiday, Billie, Billie's Blues	6.50

PHONOGRAPHS

Early phonographs were commonly called 'talking machines.' Thomas A. Edison invented the first successful phonograph in 1877. Other manufacturers followed with their variations.

Berliner, Ideal, Type B, disc, 7" turntable, nickel plated metal parts, side crank wind, double spring, 16" brass bell horn, horn support oak case **1,250.00**

Brunswick, Model 200, disc, 12" turntable, reproducer head rotates to play lateral or vertically cut records, floor model with oak cabinet, storage in base, c1923 .... **150.00**

Busy-Bee Grand, plays Busy-Bee discs only, 8 petal Morning Glory horn, reproducer at end of horn, oak case table model **275.00**

Victor I, 8" turntable, Exhibition Reproducer, plain oak case, $450.00.

Columbia

Grafonola Regent, disc, mahogany desk console, top draw pulls out to reveal 78 rpm phonograph, two record storage drawers, electric **500.00**

Grand AG, cylinder, 5" mandrel plays Grand cylinders, gold dec on black painted exposed metal parts, type "D" (heavy Eagle) reproducer, oak case, ribbon decal, c1898-1901 .... **850.00**

Model AT, cylinder, nickel plated mechanism, double spring, 14" (Eagle) aluminum bell, oak case **340.00**

New Leader, Model BKT, 2 minute cylinder, rear mounted Morning Glory horn, tapered aluminum tone arm, double spring, wood case, ribbon decal **450.00**

Edison

Amberola, Model 50, table, cylinder, Diamond Model "C" reproducer, mahogany case **350.00**

Diamond Disc, Model A-275, floor model, Sheraton style case, 12" turntable, automatic stop, Diamond reproducer, one storage drawer, 46½" h **325.00**

Gem, Model C, 2 minute cylinder, table model, 8 panel ribbed horn, 19" long with gold and black decoration, Model C reproducer, c1907 .... **275.00**

Standard, Model C, 2 minute cylinder, 14" brass belled horn, speed control, oak case, mechanism screwed to lid of base .. **250.00**

Genola toy phonograph, complete . **150.00**

Lioret, cylinder, table model, 25 cylinders **4,500.00**

Pathe, Coquet, 4" d Salon cylinders, aluminum horn, Orpheus attachment, bakelite reproducer and recorder **310.00**

Sonora, "Canterbury," disc, nickel plated exposed parts, double spring, automatic stop, storage for 60 records **90.00**

Standard, Model A, table model, disc, ½" spindle for special discs, rear mount Morning Glory horn, dec. oak case **375.00**

Talk-O-Phone, "The Herbert," disc, 9" turntable, single spring, front mount 6" horn (Talk-O-Phone Exhibition Concert reproducer) with brass bell, oak case **450.00**

Victor

E, Monarch Junior, disc, 7" turntable, metal horn bracket, front mounted Concert bell horn, oak case **550.00**

III, disc, 10" turntable, double spring, rear mount Exhibition reproducer (23" l ribbed horn), tapering tone arm, brake speed regulator, oak case **425.00**

Victrola XVI, floor model, disc, triple spring, inside Exhibition reproducer, record storage in base, oak case, 50" h **325.00**

Zon-O-Phone, Type D, disc, small turntable, "V" reproducer, front horn bracket and support, oak table model **380.00**

PICKARD

The Pickard China Company was founded in 1894. They were known for their fine handpainted porcelains. Originally they acquired blanks from other sources, namely Limoges, but now produce their own. The firm is presently located in Antioch, Illinois.

Basket, 9", white, berries and leaves, gold trim	85.00
Biscuit Jar, 6½", SP bail and cov, cream, hp chrysanthemums, gold trim	75.00
Bowls	
6", pierced rim, gold florals inside, allover gold exterior	45.00
10½", ruffled, poppies and leaves, gold trim, artist sgd, 1905 mark	175.00
Box, cov 2¾ x 5¾" d, stylized florals in gold, black and ivory	85.00
Cake Plate, 10¾", sq, Oriental birds, sgd Nichols, c1919	179.00
Chamber Stick, 7¼", irid, floral decor, sgd	225.00
Coffee Pot, 8½", allover floral, much gold, sgd Wagner, 1905 mark . . .	155.00
Compote, 10½", handled, fruit and flower decor, gold border and pedestal, artist sgd	165.00
Creamers and Sugars, covered	
Birds, butterflies and flowers, artist sgd	135.00
Garden scene on one side, lake and island on other side, B.H., and maple leaf mark	150.00
White with gold etching, maple leaf mark	70.00
Cup and Saucer, enamel beading, artist sgd	80.00
Hatpin Holder, allover gold, etched florals, c1925	35.00
Jug, 6½", squat, blue and gold bands, flowers, maple leaf mark .	170.00
Lemonade Set, 5 tumblers, tall pitcher, lemon color with bluebells . . .	85.00
Marmalade Jar, cov, 6" h with underplate, pink dogwood, gold trim, artist sgd	75.00
Mug, metallic gold, grapes, leave, sgd Hessler, 1898	110.00
Pitchers	
6½", cider, Italian Garden, Challinor	450.00
8½", bulbous, hexagonal, gold, colored fruit, blossoms and foliage, silver bands, sgd, c1912 .	285.00

8½", Deserted Gardens, gold leaf, artist sgd, marked Pickard	290.00
Plates	
8", humming birds and orchids, 2" emb gold border, Hutschenreuther blank, sgd E. Challinor .	100.00
8½", Easter lilies, shaded white with green foliage, gold rim, 1905 mark	85.00
8½", scalloped with gold, strawberries and white blossoms, sgd E. Challinor, c1905	100.00
8½", violets, shaded purple, green foliage, scalloped gold rim, 1905 mark	85.00
9", yellow cherries on green ground, artist sgd and dated 1905	75.00

Plate, 10½", scenic view of Yosemite Valley, pastel, gold rim, Nippon blank, orig paper label "Pickard Studios/ Chicago/3/ Cake Tray/Yosemite Valley, sgd artist E. Challinor, maple leaf Pickard mark, $400.00.

11", pierced handle, matte finish, woodland scene, sgd Challinor, maple leaf mark	300.00
Relish Dish, 9½ x 4¼", open handles, pink and green leaves, maple leaf mark	70.00
Rose Bowl, 8", red poinsettias, green leaves, gold, pearlized inside, sgd Tolley, 1905 mark	285.00
Salt and Pepper Shakers	
Dutch girl decor, artist sgd, pr . . .	50.00
Pink rosebuds, blue forget-me-nots, gold scrolls, hp 1905 mark, pr	38.00
Sugar Bowl, large, 2 handled, all gold encrusted	45.00
Stein, 7", black with gold metallic, large bunches of grapes and leaves, gold handle, rim and base, sgd, c1898	285.00

Tankard Set, 14½" tankard, four
5¾" mugs, grapes and leaves,
red, brown, purple and green, Limoges blanks, artist sgd Seidel,
1895 mark 695.00
Tea Sets
   3 pcs, scenic decor, gold handles,
   spouts and finials, artist sgd . . .   350.00
   3 pcs, small pink and blue flowers,
   B & Co, Limoges blanks, maple
   leaf mark 175.00
Tile, garden scene, sgd E Challinor .   100.00
Tray, 11", round, bisque, teal blue,
gold grapes and leaves, engraved,
sgd Coufall, 1905 mark 195.00
Urn, 11½", allover gold, 3" band of
grapes and strawberries, Belleek
blank, artist sgd 500.00
Vases
   6", handled, matte finish Spring
   Scene, artist sgd Challinor, ma-
   ple leaf mark 295.00
   7", scenic, sgd E. Challinor, c1905
   –1910 . . . .   250.00
   8¼", garden scene, artist sgd,
   c1912–1919 . . . .   235.00
   10¼", handled, Deserted Gar-
   dens, gold leaf, artist sgd,
   marked Pickard 350.00
   15", peonies on pastel ground,
   gold scalloped rim, base, artist
   sgd 295.00

11¾", clear, acid etched insert, floral
with bird medallion, octagonal, Meriden Co. 182, $185.00.

PICKLE CASTORS

A pickle castor is a novelty table accessory
used to serve pickles. It consists of a
silverplated frame fitted with a glass insert
and metal tongs. These were very popular in
the Victorian period and are quite collectible
today.

Amber Glass, IVT pattern 250.00
Blue Cane pattern 215.00
Cranberry, IVT, enameled dogwood,
marked Reed & Barton 325.00
Crown Milano, 10" to top of stand,
pansy decor insert 1,050.00
Opalescent, 4" insert 145.00
Pigeon Blood, 8" insert, quadruple
plate, Empire Mfg Co 250.00
Rubina, frosted, etched acorns and
oak leaves 135.00
Sapphire blue, IVT 135.00
Satin Glass, pink, swirl, mkd
Pairpoint 220.00
Twin Diamond pattern, double in-
serts, berry finials, mkd S H Miller
Silverplate 225.00
Vaseline, Daisy and Button pattern .   185.00

PIGEON BLOOD GLASS

Pigeon Blood refers to the orange-red colored glass ware produced around the turn of
the century. Do not confuse it with the many
other red glass wares of the period. Pigeon
Blood has a very definite orange glow.

Biscuit Jar, 7½", melon ribbed SP
fittings 160.00
Bowls
   8½", ornate SP rim 85.00
   12½", clear applied feet and han-
   dles, 3 clear applied lion head
   prunts on front 235.00
Butter, covered, metal trim 175.00
Candlesticks, 7½", twisted stem,
pair 150.00
Compote, 7", scalloped edge 185.00
Creamer and Sugar, Torquay pat-
tern, SP rim and cov 295.00
Perfume Bottle and stopper, 9",
white enamel decor and jeweling   70.00
Pitchers
   11", clear applied handle 275.00
   Water, bulbows, Torquay pattern,
   frosted satin finish, applied
   frosted handle 325.00
Salt and Pepper
   Bead and Scroll pattern, pr 110.00

Biscuit Jar, 8½" to top of finial, SP fittings, $250.00.

Flower band, pr	125.00
Sugar Shaker, Bulging Loops pattern	220.00
Tumbler, 3¾", hp, floral decor	52.00
Vases	
6½", enameled, floral decor	125.00
7¼", enameled decor	130.00
12", pedestal, applied clear glass rigaree	225.00

PINK LUSTRE CHINA

Pink Lustre derived its name from the color of the decoration. In 1790, Josiah Wedgwood began to experiment in decoration with a thin film of metal applied by various methods. Successors followed by using silver, platinum and gold (pink). Lustre decorations were often used in conjunction with enamels and transfers. Transfers used for lustre decorations covered a wide range of public and domestic subjects. These were often accompanied by pious or sentimental doggerel as well as the humours of everyday life. Also see SUNDERLAND LUSTRE.

Ashtray, Lancaster, England, c1945	13.00
Bough Pot, 9⅛" l, D-shape body, orange lustre, 3 arched panels with fruit baskets, 3 knob feet, pink cover with floral sprigs, orange border and knob, Leeds 1810-15	875.00

Candlesticks, 5" cylindrical, dished nozzle, slightly domed foot, Staffordshire, c1810, pr	350.00
Creamer, 4½", flowering vine, red, yellow and black enamel, lozenge-guilloche border, Staffordshire c1810	95.00
Cups and Saucers	
Floral decor	50.00
Vine and foliate border	60.00
Dish, 9⅜", oval, pink and purple, landscape with cottage and trees, band border, molded scroll ends, imp Lakin, c1815	95.00
Figure, 6⅜", mother and baby, black hat, pink bodice, gray skirt, yellow basket, red cloaked baby, green mound base, Staffordshire c1820	95.00
Mugs	
3¼", cylindrical, mottled, oval panel of green and black crossed boughs has inscribed in black E. Forsyth Scotchouse 1836, Staffordshire	220.00
5", pear shape, pale pink, floral sprays in pink lustre, wide copper lustre border, pink lustre rim, c1825	85.00
Pitchers	
5⅛", molded, acanthus leaves and bellflowers, green and blue enamels, molded floral border, Staffordshire, c1820	95.00

Pitcher, 3¾", curly "Q" and leaf pattern inside lip. Sawtooth pattern, Wedgwood Made in England, $55.00.

6⅞", buff colored, relief molded, stag on one side, doe and fawn on other, stylized palmette border, Staffordshire, c1820	120.00
Plates	
7⅞", red and green floral sprigs, pink floral border, imp Enoch Wood and Sons Burslem, eagle mark	60.00

8", molded with leaves on basket-work, lustrer's letter X mark, c1820 .... **50.00**
Potpourri Jar, 8⅝", shield shape, 8 holes around shoulder, satyr mask handles, imp Sarreguemines, c1820 .... **85.00**
Salt, 2¼ x 3¼", blue band, c1820 . **90.00**
Sugar Bowl, House pattern **125.00**
Teapot, ribbed base and lid **185.00**
Vases, 4¼", butterfly in oval panel, floral sprays, wigglework borders, Leeds, c1810, pr **250.00**

PINK SLAG

The molded pattern regarded as true Pink Slag is that of an Inverted Fan and Feather. Pieces recently have come into the market in the Inverted Strawberry and Inverted Thistle. The two patterns were made in the molds of the now defunct Cambridge Glass Co., and are not considered "true" Pink Slag. The price of these late patterns are only a fraction of the true Pink Slag. Quality pieces shade from pink at the top to white at the bottom. This is the most sought after of the slag wares. The glass is extremely scarce and commands a good price.

Bowl, 2½ x 4½" w, inverted fan and feather, ftd **325.00**
Compote, 6½" **625.00**

Tumbler, 4", inverted fern, $450.00.

Jam Jar **850.00**
Pitcher, 8", water, inverted fan and feather **950.00**
Punch Cup, inverted fan **325.00**
Salt Shaker, inverted fan and feath-er, orig lid **295.00**
Sauce Dish, 2½", inverted fan and feather, ftd **215.00**
Sugar **650.00**
Tumbler, inverted fan and feather . **450.00**

PIPES

Tobacco was first introduced in England by Sir Walter Raleigh. The use of tobacco quickly became popular on the continent and the need for pipes developed. Many were produced in Holland in the Gouda vicinity and were exported throughout the world.

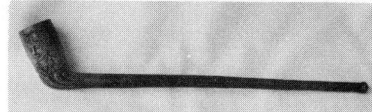

Clay, 9½", shellacked, Leblanc/Andennes, $18.00.

Brian
Man with beard carved in bowl, horn stem, 11" **150.00**
Two Indians on horseback carved on bowl, 11" **750.00**
Burl
Leprechaun face with hat, crown of hat removes, Italian, 5¾" .. **45.00**
Two section, sapling stem, horn mouth piece, Made in Czecho-slovakia, 7¼" **20.00**
China
German Calvary Regemental, offi-cer with horse one side, with loved one on reverse, helmet lid, carved horn and wood stem, artist sgd, dated 1905–1908, 56" **190.00**
Scenic bowl with 2 deer, hinged metal cov, 2 section **32.00**
Clay
Cat on bowl, white and black cast initials, D. G. 1334, 3½" **30.00**
Molded head, paper label, Goedewaagen's **28.00**
Gouda, clay, figural
Man, military hat, mustache, imp mark **12.50**
Man, turbin, mustache, orig stick-er, Goede Waagen's PIJP, 5½" **15.00**
Horn, hunt scene carved on bowl, silver mounts, 5" **330.00**

Meerschaum

Boston bull dog chained to dog house, emb, case, 4"	135.00
Deer chased by dog, 7"	145.00
Dog, sitting, amber stem, 3¼" . .	40.00
Dog and hunter, amber, red mouth piece, orig case, 5"	65.00
Hand holding goblet, carved, amber stem and goblet, Wm. Burnbaum/NY	275.00
Horse, prancing, amber stem, 3⅛"	40.00
Ivory bowl, gold trim, amber stem, boxed	175.00
Lions, male and female, sterling band	65.00
Man, large mustache, Swiss type hat with plume, amber stem, 2¼ x 3⅝"l	60.00
Monk, smiling, orig case	170.00
Nude, Art Nouveau, dyed, 5½" . .	250.00
Nude on front of bowl, cupid with bow, amber stem, 5"	85.00
Pigskin wrapped bowl, amber stem, orig case, 5¾"	45.00
Pirate, bearded, tassel cap, amber stem, 6½"	35.00
Mexican Pottery, rabbit shape bowl, 7"	10.00
Opium Pipe, burl	45.00

Porcelain

Delft blue and white, 20"	85.00
German officer, "5. Armee, Weihnachten, 1914", 2 section, sapling and horn stem, 9¾" . .	55.00
Stag on bowl, burl, sapling, horn and antler stem, stamped D.R.G.M., 12½"	40.00
Soapstone from Missouri River, Indian	70.00
Water, Oriental, brass, fret piercing, irid blue enamel 1" band with colorful motif of fish, animals, etc . .	75.00
Wood, Indian chief's head, carved, c1930	25.00
Woodland, dog's head bowl, sgd . .	60.00

PLAYING CARDS

Warman's Americana & Collectibles, 1st Edition, contains 89 listings in this category; see also page xii.

POCKET KNIVES

Alcas, Case, Colonial, Ka-Bar, Queen, and Schrade are the best of the modern pocket knife manufacturers, with top positions enjoyed by Case and Ka-Bar. Knives by Remington and Winchester, firms no longer in production, are eagerly sought.

Form is a critical collecting element. The most desirable forms are folding hunters (1 and 2 blades), trappers, peanuts, Barlows, elephant toes, canoes, Texas toothpicks, Coke bottles, gun stocks, and Daddy Barlows. The decorative aspect also heavily influences prices. Prices are for pocket knives in mint condition.

See Pocket Knives in *Warman's Americana & Collectibles* for advertising, character, and figural pocket knives.

CASE

Case uses a numbering code for its knives. The first number (1–9) is the handle material; the second number (1–5) designates the number of blades; the third and fourth numbers (0–99) the knife pattern. Stag (5), pearl (8 or 9), and bone (6) are most sought in handle materials. The most desirable patterns are 5165—folding hunters, 6185—doctors, 6445—scout, muskrat—marked muskrat with no number, and 6254—trappers.

In the Case XX series a symbol and dot code is used to designate a year.

1920–40	
5254	650.00
61111½	450.00
6265	250.00
6465, four blade hunter	1,200.00
9265	450.00
1940–65	
3254	150.00
42057, office knife	50.00
6246R, rigger	75.00
6265	180.00
8271	100.00
Flying Fisherman	150.00
1965–70, XX series	
1146, budding	50.00
4200, mellon taster	75.00
5265	150.00
62009, Barlow	30.00
6265	125.00
Muskrat	70.00
1970–80 (number of dots indicates year)	
51111½, "Cheetah"	200.00
62009, Barlow	35.00
6265	50.00
Fly Fisherman	100.00
Muskrat	40.00

KA-BAR (Union Cut. Co., Olean, New York)

The company was founded by Wallace Brown at Tidioute, Pa., in 1892. It was relocated in Olean, N.Y., in 1912. The products have many stampings including Union [inside shield], U-R Co. Tidioute [variations], Union Cut Co. Olean N.Y., Alcut Olean N.Y., Keenwell Olean N.Y., and Ka-Bar. The larger knives with a profile of a dog's head on the handle are most desirable. Pattern numbers rarely appear on a knife prior to the 1940's.

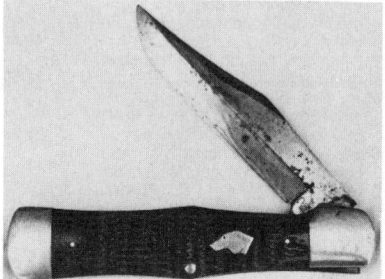

Ka-Bar, dog's head, used, #62156, $500.00.

22156	500.00
24107	1,000.00
31187, 2 blades	150.00
61161, light celluloid handle	100.00
61126L, dog's head	850.00
61187, Daddy Barlow	150.00
6191L	600.00
6260KF	100.00

KEEN KUTTER (Simons Hardware, St. Louis, Missouri)

K02220, office knife	50.00
K1881, Barlow	70.00
K1920	300.00
6354, scout	100.00

REMINGTON, last made in 1940

R293, bullet	1,000.00
R433, doctor	150.00
R953, toothpick	175.00
R4233, junior scout	125.00
R4353, bullet	1,000.00

RUSSELL, Turner Fall, Massachusetts

60, 1 blade	100.00
66, 2 blades	125.00
600, Daddy Barlow	200.00

WINCHESTER

1036, Texas toothpick, stag	400.00
1051, Texas toothpick	300.00
1621, budding	150.00
1920	1,000.00+
2703, Barlow	100.00

OTHER MANUFACTURERS

Elephant Toe
Ibberson, pearl work back	300.00
Kutwell, Olean, NY	200.00
Primble, John	250.00

Folding Hunter
Case, Moby Dick	125.00
Marble Arms Co.	350.00
Neft Safety	220.00
New York Knife Co.	500.00
Novelty Cut. Co., picture handle	125.00
Queen Cut. Co., Titusville, PA, buffalo horn	200.00
Robeson	175.00
Russell	150.00
Schrade, Trail of Tears	150.00
Union Cut. Co., Tidioute, PA	100.00
Valley Forge Cut. Co., NJ	200.00

POMONA GLASS

Pomona glass, patented in 1885 by Joseph Locke, was produced only by the New England Glass Works. Pomona glass is a delicate type of blown art glass which has a pale soft, beige background and a top band of honey amber that is approximately one inch deep.

There are two distinct types of backgrounds: first grind, made only from April 1885 to June 1886, was produced by fine cutting through a wax coating followed by an acid bath; second grind was a less time consuming method that consisted of rolling the piece in acid resisting particles and acid etching. Both methods produced a soft frosted appearance, but on first grind pieces fine curlicue lines are visible.

Designs were used on some pieces. These were etched and then stained in color; the most familiar design is blue cornflowers.

No good reproductions are known. Do not confuse it with a type of glass known as Midwestern Pomona which is a pressed glass with a frosted body and amber band.

Bowls
4½ x 2″ h, first grind, frosted stripes	130.00
8″, cornflower, crimped rim, second grind	400.00
Celery, 6½″, second grind, blueberry decor	225.00
Cream and Sugar, 3″ h, first grind, blue cornflowers, pr	500.00

Pitchers
6¼″, first grind water, cornflower, orig paper label	300.00
7¼″ x 6″ d, second grind, square	

Pitcher, 4½", first grind, honey amber collar, $450.00.

mouth, bulbous, honey amber, blue	495.00
11¾ x 4" d, second grind, tankard, honey amber, double row of blue cornflowers	895.00
Plate, ruffled, second grind	85.00
Punch Cups	
Cornflower, first grind, 2¾ x 2⅝" d	225.00
Cornflower, second grind	140.00
Tumblers	
Acanthus, first grind	145.00
Blueberry motif in gold, brown, silver, second grind, 3¾"	175.00
Cornflower, first grind	200.00
Cornflower, second grind, 3¾ x 2½"	150.00
Pansy and Butterfly, second grind, 3⅝" h	250.00
Vases	
3", fan, second grind	150.00
6½", sheaves of wheat, second grind	285.00

PORTRAIT PLATES

Portrait plates, in the Victorian era, were very popular in decorating the home. Usually they were pictures of beautiful women. However, there are also plates with portraits of Napolean, Queen Victoria, etc., that are very collectible today. Some are artist signed, some are not, and were made by almost all the well known American and European potteries.

4", American Indian, enamel decor, 1 feather in hair, marked "Made For O'Hara Dial Co, Waltham, Mass"	190.00
5", child, blue dress, pink scalloped border, c1900	40.00
8", classical figures, green borders, gilt trim, sgd Kauffman	90.00
8½", woman, cobalt border, Limoges	50.00
8¾", woman with flowing brown hair, maroon border, gold decor, green mark, Johnson Bros, England	40.00
9", Madam LeBrun and daughter, gold border	32.50
9¼", dark green rim, lady in black hat, sgd copyright, 1909, by Phillip Boileau	85.00
9½", beautiful girl, large hat, wide burgundy border, gold decor, tiny white jewels, sgd E. Furland, marked double head eagle in shield, Schwarzburg	65.00
9½", Duchess de Bugogne, bust portrait, gold tracery	145.00
9½", Mme de Lavalliere, gold tracery, ribbon spirals	145.00
9½", 3 children playing, wine bottle, white, pink, red, cobalt blue border, heavy gold center, Royal Vienna, sgd C. Her, blue beehive mark	135.00
10", farmer, dog, cows, irregular edge, deep colors, gold trim, marked Z. S. Bavaria	55.00
10", gold handle, center: Napoleon and Josephine; four portraits around edge divided; R. S. Germany	250.00
10", tin, cobalt blue, gold, dated Feb. 20, 1906	25.00
11½", Queen Louise, full figure, heavy gold edge, Bavaria	200.00
19", Marie Antoinette wearing pale lavender headdress, gown, cobalt blue ground, scrolling gilt motifs, veneered frame mounted with 12 oval small porcelain portrait plaques of court beauties, Vienna	2,200.00

8½", Princess De Lam baile, mark, blue, LS&S, Carlsbin, Austria, $30.00.

POSTCARDS

Warman's Americana & Collectibles, 1st Edition, contains 242 listings in this category; see also page xii.

POSTERS

Posters are commercially produced art works for the purpose of advertising products or services, announcing events or introducing people. They were seldom considered serious works of art, even when executed by accomplished artists. Today, posters are a recognized art form and have attracted art connoisseurs.

Prices given are approximate. Condition is important and affects the final price considerably.

See *Warman's Americana & Collectibles* for additional Poster listings.

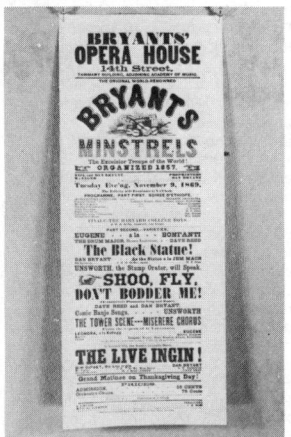

Bryants Minstrels, 9 x 27", 1869, $90.00.

ADVERTISING

"Avalon Cigarettes," 11 x 16", c1937, redhead in sheer and netted backless evening dress looks coyly to viewer, looming pack overhead 35.00
Chesterfield Cigarettes, "The Choice of a Lifetime," 11 x 21" car card, H. E. Chambers, c1930, "just married" couple in convertible, huddled together and looking at full moon 85.00

De Laval Separator Co., 10 x 16" store sign, 1946, Indian chieftain smoking peace pipe, 1920s look . 40.00
"Glover's Imperial Medicines, Safe! For Over 50 Years," 11 x 17", 1930s, die cut dog house shape, three wire haired terrier pups look quizzically from door 38.00
"Harper's," 5 x 18", Edward Penfield, October 14, 1896, woman holding orange gloves, green ground 250.00
"Hires Root Beer—For Finer Flavor," 12" d, store display, c1938, Varga like girl, holding bottle, looks to viewer 35.00
"Inland Printer," 10 x 16", J. C. Leyendecker, May 1897, colonial man leaning over wall of formal garden amid cherry blossoms . . . 125.00
Ivory Salt, "Look For The Lucky Elephant," die cut, 1920s elephant in circle with advertising banner on back 35.00
"Maurice Chevalier Brandy," 48 x 63", 1925, Chevalier with straw hat posing in dance and holding bottle of brandy named after him . 325.00
"Maurin-Quina," 48 x 63", L. Valet, c1900, French, Victorian woman in large hat hoists glass delicately above bottle and words "An Exquisite Fortifying Wine" 300.00
Pabst Breweries Bock Beer, 24 x 36", c1915, bock ram in circle over Pabst logo 150.00
Raleigh Cigarettes, 12 x 19", c1935, elegantly attired man holds cigarette, smoke weaves way into black ground 45.00
Rexall, "The Beginning Of A Perfect Day—A Rexall Shave," 22 x 36", c1912–13, man shaving with safety razor, looming clock face in background 150.00
Zephyr Typewriters, 12 x 13", Vernon Grant, die cut stand up of blond haired boy bending over to pick up sign 37.00

CIRCUS, SHOWS AND ACTS

Barnes, Al. G., "Great Mexican Rodeo," 29 x 40", horz, c1935, panorama of varqueros, cowboys, etc. 100.00
"Buffalo Bill's Wild West & Rough Riders. The Hero Horsemen Of The World," 30 x 40", 1908, Strobridge, color litho of cavalrymen, some in red plumed helmets, astride horses in evolutions of jumping and parade 475.00

Carter, The Magician
"Carter The Great," 14 x 41",
"Modern Priestess of Delphi!
Your Mind is an Open Book to
Her," lovely woman receiving
counsel from Banshee, single
sheet 275.00
"The World's Weird And Wonder-
ful Wizard," 14 x 22", turbaned
Carter looks down upon crystal
ball mysteriously as devils, ban-
shees, bats, cards, etc., leap
from it 75.00
Tom Mix Circus, 29 x 40", c1934,
horiz, title of show done on multicolored Indian blanket 75.00
Ringling Bros., Barnum
28 x 40", c1935, leaping black
panther jumps across image . .   100.00
29 x 40", c1930, "Mlle. Gillete—
Europe's Sensation of the Air,"
lightly clothed young woman
swoops across image to swing-
ing trapeze 135.00
Sparks, Charles, "Jack Hoxie In Per-
son," Downie Bros. Circus, 28 x
40", horz, c1935, western star
astride rearing horse, deep red
ground 125.00

MOVIE

Lobby Posters, 11 x 14"
Apple Tree Girl, The, c1910, early
Edison film, girl looking into se-
ries of mirrors, entitled "A Deep
Study" 45.00
Girl Shy, Harold Lloyd, Lloyd hap-
pily enjoying woman hugging
him around knees 35.00
Hi-Yo Silver, Lee Powell, Herman
Brix, Wm. Farnum, etc., 1940
feature of 1938 Republic serial,
set of 8 . . . .   200.00
Nick Carter, Detective, MGM . . .   15.00
Show Business, 1944, Eddie Can-
tor 20.00
One Sheets, 27 x 41", American
Blackhawk, 1952 serial, Kirk Alyn,
"Chapter 1, Distress Call From
Space" 85.00
Camera Thrills, c1935, narrated by
Grant McNamee, universal post-
er for news footage, imagery of
crashing trains, cars, planes,
etc.   70.00
Dead Game, The, 1920, Universal,
Hoot Gibson, early Morgan litho,
Gibson holding pretty girl while
lassoing overdressed bandits .   160.00
Ellery Queen, "The Ace Sleuth of
Radio and Fiction Now On the
Screen!" Columbia, c1940,

Ralph Bellamy looks beyond radio microphone, stock poster for
series, block for insertion of title   35.00
Other Men's Shoes, c1920, litho
of man courting woman and viv-
idly colored branches and
leaves 75.00
Seventh Day, The, c1920, Richard
Barthelmess, Barthelmess at
wheel of ship 200.00
Solid Gold Cadillac, 1956, Colum-
bia, Judy Holliday 20.00
Thief, The, c1916, Fox, Pearl
White, White in formal attire
looks with suspicion to well
dressed man at her right 300.00
Twelve Angry Men, 1957, Henry
Fonda 35.00
Winning Team, The, 1952, War-
ner, Ronald Reagan 75.00
Posters, European
Empire Strikes Back, Italian, 40 x
50", orig release 50.00
Further Perils of Laurel and Hardy,
French, 1960s, 48 x 63",
looming close ups 45.00
Gone With The Wind, France,
1960s reissue, 22 x 32", classic
scene of Rhett and Scarlett
amid firey scene 75.00
Rebel Without A Cause, Italian, 40
x 50", c1960s, James Dean . .   75.00
Star Wars, Italian, 40 x 50", Vader
and others 75.00
Yellow Submarine, Italian, 40 x
50", 1960s, Beatles 65.00
Window Posters, 14 x 22"
Cleopatra, 1917, Theda Bara,
Bara in diaphanous, see-through
robe 250.00
Freaks, Dwain Esper release, Sia-
mese twins, midgets, etc. 90.00
Souls For Sale, 1927, Goldwyn,
Richard Dix, Lew Cody, Eleanor
Boardman, "A Story of Motion
Picture Studio Life," flapper
woman holds title in hand 45.00
Yolanda, Metro, Marion Davies . .   45.00

THEATRICAL, OPERA, MUSIC HALL, ETC.

D'Oyly Carte Opera Co., 20 x 30",
Dudley Hardy, c1895, executioner
standing with ax afront red sunrise   150.00
English Opera Company, "Puccini's
Madame Butterfly," 28 x 40",
c1900, oriental woman looking to
viewer from blue borders, Japa-
nese living quarters 150.00
Fields, Al G., 30 x 40", Courier litho,
c1898, famed Minstrel Impressario   125.00
Germaine Kerjean, c1930s, Art Deco
poster of cabaret singer in style of

Piaf, sleepy eyed woman in long black dress, red ground **250.00**

Hawkins Brothers Comedy Company, Banjo Kings, 6 x 14″, c1914, black and white photo on colored stock **45.00**

La Fee Au Chevres, 40 x 58″, Paris, litho by F. Appel, c1900, girl looks to viewer and holds multitubed flute, beckoning goats and kids around her, background filled with beautiful women dropping from heavens **275.00**

Mistinguett, 42 x 57″, Benda, c1923, Mistinguett smiles thru humorous tramp attire **275.00**

Nazzarro (Cliff) Modern Minstrels, c1920, black men pose in colorful tie and tails, hold banjos, vivid background **75.00**

Queq' Chechias?, 26 x 46″, c1917, Sarah Bernhardt, benefit for Alsace Lorraine, 22 Nov 1917, Bernhardt in center coyly listening to corpulent Zouve and grizzled policeman **250.00**

Stowaway, The, 20 x 30″, Carqueville, c1895, newsboy with papers in hand looks to ornately dressed woman outside theater . . **100.00**

Tess of the Storm Country, 29 x 40″, Hegeman, c1905, "Tess and Her Dad," Tess rides on father's back through wooded glade **125.00**

TRAVEL, TRANSPORTATION AND RELATED ITEMS

Automobile
Automobiles Delahaye, 37 x 50″, Thiriet, 1900 Delahaye filled with lovely woman and chauffeur pass behind a Goddess holding an olive branch, dragon belches smoke and fire at top . **1,200.00**

Buffalo Automobile Show, 28 x 40″, c1928, Buick Cabriolet in center, dreamlike imagery of 1900 runabout looming in borders **350.00**

"Four Wheel Brakes Will Stop You In Time! Equip Your Car in 24 Hours with "US" Equalized Front Wheel Brakes," 14 x 22″, c1926, Buick screeching to halt to avoid hitting fallen boy on skates, big "US" logo on bottom **45.00**

Peugeot—"Like A Billiard Table Everywhere," 48 x 62″, Kirliene, 1932, Art Deco image of Peugeot speeding across billiard table, emphasizes ride **375.00**

Aviation
Deutsche Lufthansa, 18 x 26″, c1936, large Fokker Trimotor flies over carriage and beautiful woman below **200.00**

God is My Co-Pilot, 11 x 14″ movie lobby poster, Dennis Morgan in cockpit looks to heavens amid starry sky, his priest is behind him **25.00**

"How Soon Shall We Fly? Explained By Scientist, In The Next New York Sunday Journal," 15 x 2″, horiz, c1896, dual cone shaped airships with hanging gondolas fly toward fearful face on sun **200.00**

Madagascar In Six Days By Air Africa, 26 x 40″, 1930s, Art Deco style showing plane silhouette flying over France and Africa to island **150.00**

Bus, Boxmoor by Motorbus, 25 x 40″, c1920, tightly designed Spradbery painting of village at dusk **75.00**

England, "Come To Britain For Racing," 20 x 30″, Lionel Edwards, 1947, horse race scene **100.00**

France, Thonon Les Bains, Roger Borders, 1920s, sailing boat looming in foreground, white Lake Steamer and town in background **150.00**

Lodging
Empress Hotel, 26 x 40″, c1935, Victoria, B.C., Canada, hotel looms in background **100.00**

Excelsior Hotel Regina, 30 x 41″, horiz, 1900, hotel with carriages and people all around, looming image of beautiful seminude woman floating angelicly above the blowing trumpet **175.00**

Scotland, Edinburgh, 25 x 40″, Fred Taylor, c1925, looming stone buildings, people walking and milling about them **200.00**

Steamship
Go *Empress of Europe*, Canadian Pacific, 27 x 40″, c1935, couple waving from upper deck, smokestack behind **125.00**

Hamburg American Line, S.S. *Reliant* Deluxe Cruise. Land Of The Midnight Sun, Russia, From New York, June 30, 1934, 12 x 18″, silkscreen, Nordic man in winged helmet in foreground, steamer amid sunrise in background **75.00**

Queen Elizabeth, 20 x 29″, C. F. Hopkinson, 1946, office poster, QE-I under steam in open sea . **100.00**

Queen Mary, 23 x 35", William McDowell, c1937, Queen Mary coming into harbor surrounded by ships **125.00**

Red Star Line, 21 x 29", attributed to Cassiers, c1905, steamer plying multicolored waters, solid gold metallic ground **600.00**

WORLD WAR I—AMERICAN

"Down With The Murderers, Up With Democracy!" 25 x 36", Voitech Preissig, dramatic hand to hand fight under exploding flare light . . **125.00**

"Enlist In The Navy. Follow The Boys For Home And Country," 18 x 25", civilians line up outside battle ship to enlist **50.00**

"For Liberty's Sake, Enlist In The Navy," 14 x 22" window card, c1916, issued by Boston Committee On Public Safety, Statue of Liberty emits eerie rays of light from torch white patrol boat shoots searchlight across waters . **100.00**

"Go Over The Top With U. S. Marines," 20 x 30", charging Marine jumps from trench with Lewis machine gun **100.00**

"Help Him Win," 20 x 30", Black Jack Pershing hold hands with kids **50.00**

"How High Will You Go? 'Here's Your Chance For An Altitude Record . . . '," 20 x 30", monotone, pilot pointing to viewer while holding liberty bond **95.00**

"Little Americans Do Your Bit," 14 x 22", little boy happily saluting his bowl of cereal **65.00**

"Pull Together Men. The Navy Needs Us," 14 x 22" window card, c1916, issued by Boston Committee on Public Safety, officer looks thru glasses as crew rows small boat through sea, orange ground **125.00**

"To Everyone In This Plant . . . Our Country is Depending on You," 16 x 24", Triedler, drydocks and shield **45.00**

WORLD WAR I—EUROPEAN

Canada

"Have You Asked Yourself—Is British Freedom Worth Defending? Am I Helping To Defend It? If Not, Why Not?", 19 x 28", broadside in red, white and blue **35.00**

"If You Were A German, You'd Be Fighting For The Kaiser. What Are You Doing For The King?,"

19 x 28", broadside in two colors, banner at top **35.00**

"You Are No Exception! Join Now," 28 x 39", cartoon silhouette of worried man saying, "I should go . . . BUT!!!" **50.00**

"Your Chums Are Fighting. Why Not You?," 25 x 38", soldiers charge, red ground **55.00**

England

"Are You Saving For The Children? Buy War Certificates," 20 x 30", father looks at bonds with boy and girl **75.00**

"Everyone Should Do His Bit," 20 x 30", Baron Low, 1915, Boy Scout with one foot on drum in front of recruiting posters on wall **95.00**

"Have You A Reason—Or Only An Excuse For Not Enlisting Now!," 20 x 30", 1915, typographic with main words in British stars and bars **35.00**

"Take Up The Sword Of Justice. Join Now," 6 x 29", long circular poster showing hand handing sword to viewer, done soon after sinking of *Lusitania* . **25.00**

France

"Alarm. Alcohol Is Your Enemy As Much As The Boche," 13 x 20", Abel Faivre, villanous Prussian soldier lurks behind wine bottle and glass **95.00**

"Emprunt National," 32 x 48", Lucien Metivet, 1920, French Miss Liberty leads workers across golden field, advertising post war loans **135.00**

Exposition Of Pictures From The War, 26 x 36", Emile Beaume, 1917, French soldier, looking from his icy trench and barbed wire, stares into the distance and draws on his pad, warm brown tones **125.00**

La Triennial, Exposition Of French Artists, To Profit The Fraternity Of Arts, 39 x 51", Steinlen, 1916, French soldier on guard looks to farmer plowing pastoral fields in distance as thunderous skies and rain moves in **450.00**

"Voila, Les Americains!," 20 x 26", 1918, surprised Hun trying to break open a door looks up at looming shadow of doughboy **75.00**

WORLD WAR II

"Amoco Oil. Uncle Sam Rides First," 28 x 40", Uncle Sam drives behind wheel under Amoco logo . **85.00**

"Freedom Of Worship," 20 x 30", Norman Rockwell, praying hands and faces, all walks of life 85.00

"Help China! China Is Helping Us!," 11 x 14", James Montgomery Flagg, Uncle Sam rescues war torn Chinese family 65.00

"If You Talk Too Much . . . This Man May Die," 14 x 20", Noir, sailor looking through porthole to viewer 50.00

"Let Us Help As Well As Admire. United Yugoslav Relief Fund," 20 x 30", Yugoslav guerillas picking off enemy from hillsides 65.00

"Nooses For Nazis. Keep On Pulling For Victory," 29 x 40", General Motors poster showing Goehring, Hitler and other henchmen being pulled by the winch of a GMC Army "Eager Beaver" 90.00

"Save Your Cans. Help Pass The Ammunition," 24 x 34", soldier fires machine gun being loaded allegorically with cans passed from housewife 75.00

"That's The Spot To Hit!," 27 x 40", John Falter, Adm. Nimitz points to map of Japan and looks sternly to viewer 95.00

"WAAC. This Is My War, Too!," 28 x 40", Dan Smith, circular image of Woman's Army Corps soldier and looming vivid flag 75.00

"Your Lightning . . . Has Outscored The Axis Wherever It Has Fought," 28 x 40", Army, lightning flies from dog fight toward viewer 100.00

POT LIDS

Pot lids are just 'that' . . . lids from pots or containers. The pots originally held ointments, pommades or soap. The lids were decorated with transfers of various scenes.

The majority of these ceramic containers were made by Pratt, Fenton, Staffordshire between 1845–1888. Although a complete set of pot and lid is desirable to some collectors, lids are the most collectible.

It has been reported that some of these lids with the original designs have been reissued by Kirkman Pottery, England.

Bears at School 95.00
Best Card 120.00
Blue Boy 100.00
Buckingham Palace, Mayer, late .. 65.00
Country Quarters 70.00
Cries of London 65.00
Crystal Palace 130.00
Dutch Fisherman, Mayer, c1850 ... 400.00

The Village Wedding, polychrome, Pratt, 4¼", $125.00.

England's Pride, Queen Victoria ... 300.00
Feeding The Chickens 45.00
Fish Market, Mayer 60.00
Game Bag, The 75.00
Garibaldi 90.00
Gay Dog, Ridgway 325.00
Golden Hour, Constantinople 100.00
Hamlet and His Father's Ghost ... 125.00
Hide and Seek 75.00
Kingfisher, late 50.00
Lady Reading Book 110.00
Late Prince Consort 110.00
Musical Trio, Ridgways 95.00
Napoleon III and Empress Eugenie 190.00
Ning Po River 80.00
On Guard 100.00
Pegwell Bay, lobster fishing, Mayer 80.00
Persuasion 85.00
Pretty Kettle of Fish, Pratt, 4⅛" ... 285.00
Royal Harbor, Ramsgate, triangular design border 50.00
Sandringham, The Seat of HRH, The Prince of Wales, 4¼" 65.00
Shakespeare's Home 100.00
Shepherdess with Dog, 3 sheep ... 100.00
Sportsman, The 95.00
Uncle Toby, 4⅜" 65.00
Walmer Castle, 4" 185.00
Wellington, Mayer, Order of Golden Fleece 125.00
Westminster Abbey 150.00
Whimbleton, July 2nd, 1880, 4" ... 175.00

POWDER FLASKS AND HORNS

Horn was the favored medium for early gun powder containers. Many early examples are hand decorated with figures, maps, names and geometric designs. The amount of repro-

duction and faked horns is large. Be very cautious!

In the mid-19th C. containers of brass, tin, white metal and other substances entered the market. Brass was the most common. These flasks were embossed with relief designs, often of a hunting motif.

Flasks come in two groups—pistol (4 to 5″) and rifle (6¾ to 10″). Pistol flasks often command higher prices.

Price depends on design and completeness of parts.

FLASKS, POWDER

Brass

3⅝″, rectangular, 2 compartments in bottom with sliding brass doors, emb on both sides with a straight fluted decoration, floral borders top and bottom 45.00

4⅝″, pear shape, emb on both sides with stars, spread-winged eagle with shield breast clutching olive branches and arrows over crossed pistols and ribbon "E PLURIBUS UNIM" 60.00

6½″, pear shape, emb on both sides with man loading his gun, dog along side 55.00

8″, pear shape, emb on front, sides and back with baroque leaf pattern, scalloped shell extension on bottom, 4 carrying rings, mkd "AM. FLASK & CAP CO." 65.00

8½″, pear shape, double dolphins, tails intertwined 80.00

8½″, elongated pear shape, emb on both sides with an elaborate drapery and flute pattern, top mkd "PAT SEPT. 24, 1872" . . 47.50

Cooper, 7⅜″, pear shape, emb on both sides with group of hounds fighting with bear in woods, script initials below, brass top 90.00

Ivory, 5¼″, flattened body, German silver mounts, orig nozzle on retaining chain 55.00

Leather

9¾″, chamfered and beveled sided rectangle, rotating, circular brass tilting top with viewing window, mkd "BEETZ WIEN" . 48.00

10½″, extended circular shape, brass "T" top, mkd "ZZ" within a shield and numbered "305," adjustable for large charges of powder 55.00

Metal, 9″, rounded bottom conical shape, surface orig blackened, plain twisted rope carrying cord . 35.00

White Metal, 3⅝″, pear shape, emb

on both sides with a scallop shell pattern with leaf ground behind . . 40.00

Wood, 4¾″, curved, chamfer sides inlaid at edge of chamfers with twisted brass and German silver wire, small German silver oval on all four sides, German silver top and bottom 70.00

FLASKS, SHOT, LEATHER

5½″, rectangular, brass top on old hand-sewn body 20.00

8¼″, pear shape, emb on both sides with a panel showing hunting dog beneath a tree, adjustable brass top 45.00

8¼″, pear shape, plain body, brass top 32.50

HORN

Powder Horn, 12″ l, engraved with arch design, W. Carr, 1789, $625.00.

10″, Samuel More, Poughkeepsie, NY, c1750–70, engraved with lion and unicorn crest, "Dieu & Mon Droit," bottom edge has house, tree, hunting dog and hunter shooting deer 850.00

12½″, unknown maker, engraved with design of trees, anchor, harpoons and houses 150.00

13¾″, American, S. Merrill, Peacham, VT, dated 1847, engraved with portraits of Merrill, his wife and 5 children along with various animals (prize cow, spotted dog, roosters, and eagle in flight), crimped neck, fine Folk Art example 4,250.00

14¼″, engraved with lion, scene showing house with tree on each side, reclining stag, snake, 2 women in full dresses, and ship, scalloped decoration near spout, stained red above scallops 600.00

15½″, lower 9″ carved with 4 raised rings, engraved with various geometric patterns 325.00

PRATT

PRATT WARE

PRATT
FENTON

The earliest Pratt earthenware was made by William Pratt, Lane Delph in the late 18th century.

In 1810–1818, Felix and Robert Pratt, sons of William, established their own firm known as F. & R. Pratt, Fenton, Staffordshire. The wares consisted of relief molded jugs, commercial pots and tablewares with transfer decoration. Much of the early ware is unmarked. The mid-nineteenth century wares bear several different marks in conjunction with the name Pratt, including "& Co."
See also POT LIDS.

Candlestick, 7⅜", Roman ruins, Roman Key border	80.00
Compote, 9¼" dia., 5" high, transfer floral bouquet	65.00
Cradle, 6¼" l, molded basketweave, yellow glaze, puce interior	400.00
Creamer, 5" h, molded, 2 girls and dog in heart shaped reserves, polychrome	200.00
Dessert Set, eight 5½" plates, oval handled bowl, scenic transfers . .	350.00
Dish, 6" l, swan figural, emb feathers, yellow, orange, blue enamel .	130.00

Figures

4½", Autumn, brown haired boy wearing brown sponged jacket, yellow breeches, holding basket of fruit, seated on green stump, c1790	200.00
4¾", Cat, seated, brown eyes, incised nose, mouth, whiskers, coat of brown, yellow ochre brush strokes, mound base of glazed olive green	500.00
4¾", Winter, young girl wearing white cloak with pattern of yellow hearts, holding branch of ivy, seated on green rockwork on brown-edged stepped square base, c1790	215.00
7", Cow, tail curled to one side, brown spots, octagonal oblong base in green, ochre	375.00

Jars, fish paste type

Continental Fish Market	75.00
Meet of the Foxhounds	65.00
Pegwell Bay and Cliffs, scene, sailing ship	150.00

Jugs

2¾", milk, ochre, blue, green, brown, floral spray	125.00
6", Sailors Farewall, molded on one side as young sailor bidding sweetheart farewell, reverse shows homecoming, foliate borders, blue, green, ochre, brown	210.00
9", stylized floral sprays beneath paneled border, painter's "x" on bottom in brown	190.00

Mugs

Frog, 5¼"	125.00
Satyr Mask, 4¼", c1810	225.00
Pipe, 7½" w, Fox and Goose, c1795	600.00

Pitchers

4¾", "Mischievous Sport," polychrome	225.00
5¼", Wellington, pink lustred trim	195.00
5⅞", molded form, enamel decor, green, yellow, orange, brown . .	165.00
11", pewter cover, beige background, colorful seashells in relief, c1810	500.00

Plaques

11¼", high relief mold of two lions, modelled after Ralph Wood, c1800, molded self frame pierced for hanging	850.00
Brown legs, manes, one body patterned with circlets and dots in ochre, blue, orange and brown, both lying on green plate or against ground of orange, brown, green, blue dashes, blue dots	1,045.00
Brown legs, manes, one body cov with blue, green and ochre dots, ground of ochre, blue and green dashes	800.00

Plates

5½", Alas! Poor Bruin, blue border	60.00
7", animals and people at tavern, rust border, artist signed	75.00
8½", Laundry Woman, tan border	60.00
8½", Roman Ruins, Roman Key border	55.00
9½", Battle of the Nile, basketweave border	65.00
9½", Game Bag, basketweave border	65.00
10", Hop Queen, acorn and oak border	150.00

Pot Lids, See POT LIDS

Snuff Jar, 4", blue with tan and black transfer of men, animals . . .	30.00
Soap Dish, cov, black transfer of ecclesiastical subject, white ground .	60.00

Tea Caddy, 5", stylish lady in blue and yellow dress, multicolored feathered headdress, maid in green dress, reverse shows coiffed gentleman, companion wearing blue, yellow and green jackets, waistcoats, breeches,

Plate, 8½", Philadelphia Exposition 1876, $110.00

spearhead borders, c1780	320.00
Teapot, various scenes, blue ground, c1840	145.00
Tile, Ecclesiastical subject	45.00
Tobacco Jar, Alas! Poor Bruin, marbleized ground	165.00
Vase, 3 sided, painted reserves of The Fishbarrow	385.00
Watch Stand, 10¾" h, red, blue, green and ochre on a red and black sponged base, c1800	450.00

PRIMITIVE FOLK PAINTINGS AND WATERCOLORS

Folk Art paintings and watercolors done in a naive hand gained popularity during the 1960s and 1970s. While scholars concentrated on 19th century artists or styles (many examples are not signed), others began to promote 20th century artists. The latter has resulted in a flooding of the market with examples of questionable aesthetic and long range value.

Identity of the artist generally adds value. However, buyer's should be alert to the large amount of "school" or "drawing academy" art, done by individuals learning to draw and which is naive not by design but by incompetence.

General guidelines for unsigned examples are: oil—genre scenes ($300–1,000), landscapes ($200–1,000.00), portraits ($500–2,000), and still lifes ($150–750.00); watercolors—genre scenes ($250–750), landscapes ($100–600), portraits ($200–750), and still lifes ($75–500.00). Attention to detail, vitality, color, skill of artist, and other aesthetic considerations take values beyond this level.

SIGNED

Baldwin, A. A., The Day Before Christmas, 1864, winter scene, horse and sleigh approach farmstead, barn to left, figures skating on pond in background, cover of Dec. 1975 *Yankee* magazine, oil on masonite, 17¼ x 14½", gilt frame	4,750.00
Chaplin, Sarah, Still Life: Flower Filled Urn, NE, c1830, pink, yellow, blue, green, and brown, large bouquet of flowers in a footed urn, watercolor, 9½ x 13¼", framed .	400.00
DePeyster, Eva M., The Country Seat of James W. DePeyster At Bloomingdale, New York, c1808, view of manor house, farm, and outbuildings, large row of trees dominates picture, charcoal and sandpaper, 24 x 17¾", framed . .	700.00
Eastman, Emily, Portrait Of A Lady, New Hampshire, c1830, bust portrait of delicately featured young woman wearing an elaborate headdress of lilac and lace, dress trimmed in wave-like ruffles, watercolor, 14 x 19½", grain painted pine frame	5,000.00
Fisk, Thomas, Portrait Of Thomas T. Fisk, Age 10, c1825, head and shoulders oil on pine panel, sgd on reverse "Thomas T. Fisk, Age 10, Painted by his father, Thomas Fisk, F. Fisk, 1915," 14½ x 19¼" .	1,650.00
Fletcher, Aaron Dean (1817–1902), Portrait Of A Young Man, Age 27, 1835, half length of seated figure looking left, very stark, oil on canvas, 26 x 26¼"	2,750.00
Gault, Mary D., Philadelphia, From The Great Tree In Kensington Under Which William Penn Made His Treaty With The Indians, NE, 1831, watercolor, 22½ x 18", framed, copied from aquatint by T. Cartwright of London after a drawing by G. Beck of Phila. in 1802 .	5,225.00
Prior, William Matthew (1806–1873), Young Girl in Pink, 1848, seated full figure, hands on lap holding floral bouquet, oil on canvas, 16 x 22¼"	10,500.00
Stock, Joseph Whiting (1815–55), Child With Cat and Child With A Pull Toy, pair, full length portraits,	

both subjects standing, oil on ivory, marked on back "New London, Ct., pnted by Stock, circa 1835," 2¼ x 3½", framed **27,500.00**

Williams, Mrs. F. M., American, 1888, Indian Encampment, Indians by tepee in forest setting, Indian with canoe by lake in background to right, oil on canvas, 36 x 31¾" **3,000.00**

UNSIGNED

Unsigned, tin covered wood, 6" sq, choir director with 3 boys, $115.00.

Child Holding A Peach, American, 19th C, half length portrait, printed textile dress, pastel on paper, 10¼ x 14" **625.00**

Commodore Decatur, PA, 19th C, stylized bust portrait rests on green and red floral vine, watercolor, 5⅝ x 7⅝" **400.00**

Gregg's House, Charleston, South Carolina, American, 19th C, buildings to left, church in center background, watercolor, 9½ x 6½", framed **675.00**

The Institution, NE, 19th C, large, sprawling four storied building surrounded by a circular lawn, other bldgs in background, two figures in foreground, oil on pine panel, 19¼ x 13", painted frame **4,000.00**

Railroad Station Of Lakeshore, Michigan Southern Railroad, c1870, elongated horizontal portrayal, people strolling along the sidewalk, horses and carriages on the cobblestone street, red watercolor and graphite, 24¾ x 16", framed **2,250.00**

Steamship Quebec, American, c1860, yellow and black ship flying the Am. flag, smoke billowing from its stacks, watercolor and crayon, 35 x 36", turned at 45° angle, chip carved and gilt painted tramp art frame **875.00**

Still-Life With Watermelon, Apples And Fruit, American, 19th C, large watermelon with a quarter sliced out and eaten to rind, two apples, dark ground, oil on panel, 13 x 10¾", painted frame **3,500.00**

Woman With Bonnet, American, 19th C, bust portrait of middle aged woman facing right, seated in painted chair, oil on canvas, 21½ x 25½", painted and gilt pine frame **1,000.00**

Young Gentleman With Gold Watch Winder, American, 19th C, seated half length portrait, subject looks left, holds book, formal attire, oil on canvas, 22¼ x 26½", painted and grained pine frame **2,000.00**

PRINTS

Prints serve many purposes. They can be a reproduction of an artist's paintings, drawings, or designs. Prints themselves often are an original art form. Finally, prints can be developed for mass appeal as opposed to aesthetic statement. Much of the production of Currier & Ives fits this latter category. Currier & Ives concentrated on the genre, urban, patriotic, and nostalgia scenes.

Prints are beginning to attract a wide following. This is partially because prices have not matched the rapid rise in oil and other paintings.

Reproductions are a problem especially of the Currier & Ives prints. Check the dimensions before buying any print.

Audubon, J. J.
Cat Bird, 1831, Havell engr., 25½ x 38½", Plate 128 .... **650.00**
Great White Heron, 1860, J. Bien engr., 39⅝ x 26½", Plate 368 . **850.00**
Long-Tailed Duck, 1836, Havell engr., 35 x 24", Plate 312 .... **2,000.00**
Mallard Duck, 1834, Havell engr., 38 x 24⅞", Plate 221 .... **15,000.00**
Ruffed Grouse, 1832, Havell engr., 38⅛ x 25¼", Plate 41 .. **3,700.00**
Birch, Thomas and C. B. Hulsart (after), A Shoal Of Sperm Whale. Off The Island of Hawaii. In Which The Ships Enterprise, Wm. Roach, Pochontas & Hoque Were Engaged in 16th Decr. 1833, 26½ x

Baille, J., Mourning, lithograph, $45.00.

19⅞", etching by John Hill, aquatint **8,500.00**

Currier and Ives

American Winter Scenes/Morning, 1854, large **4,500.00**

Andrew Jackson/Seventh President Of The United States, small **75.00**

Autumn Fruits, 1861, medium . . .   **850.00**

Autumn In New England/Cider Making, 1866, large **5,150.00**

Clipper Ship Dreadnought Off Tuskar, 1856, large **2,750.00**

Clipper Ship Sweepstakes, 1853, large **4,250.00**

Fanny, exterior rural scene, ¾ length, c1870, small **50.00**

Futurity Race At Sheepshead Bay, The, 1889, large **1,650.00**

Great Fire At Chicago, Octr. 8th, 1871, 1871, large **5,500.00**

High Bridge At Harlem, N.Y., The, 1849, small **175.00**

Lake Of The Dismal Swamp, The/(Virginia), small **150.00**

Life Of A Fireman, The/The Race-Jump Her Boys, Jump Her!, 1854, large **1,000.00**

Maple Sugaring/Early Spring In The Northern Woods, 1872, small **1,100.00**

Night On The Hudson, A/Through At Daylight, 1864, large **2,750.00**

Rising Family, A, 1857, large (Note: Snipe companion to "Cares of A Family" and "The Happy Family") **1,750.00**

Squirrel Shooting, small **375.00**

Washington At Princeton, January 3rd, 1777, 1846, small **350.00**

Winter Morning In The Country, 1873, small **800.00**

Godey, fashion print **10-20.00**

Homer, Winslow, Union Pond, Williamsburgh, L.I., 26¾ x 16⅞", c1862, lithograph by Thomas & Eno **3,500.00**

Icart, Louis. Etching and drypoint in colors, pencil signed

Ballerina (Repos), c1935, 14½ x 18½" **850.00**

Coach, The, 21½ x 17½" **550.00**

Eve, c1928, 19 x 22" **1,050.00**

Hydranges (Le Hortensias), c1929, 17 x 21" **525.00**

Laziness (Paresse), c1925, 15 x 19" **1,350.00**

Martini (Cocktail), c1932, 12½ x 16½" **1,800.00**

Mimi Pinson, c1927, 13¼ x 20½"   **1,500.00**

Mockery (Moquerie), c1928, 15¾ x 18¾" **675.00**

Pink Alcove (L'Alcove Rose), c1929, 10½ x 13" **450.00**

Pool, c1937, 19½ x 9¼" **1,650.00**

Sappho, c1929, 16¾ x 20¾" . . .   **800.00**

Sleeping Beauty (LaBelle Au Bois Dormant), c1927, 15½ x 19¼"   **675.00**

Thais, c1927, 16 x 20" **2,450.00**

Untitled, Woman Standing In Doorway, c1929, 15¼ x 19" . . .   **375.00**

Zest (L'Elan), c1928, 19 x 14" . . .   **1,350.00**

Kellogg, E. B. & E. C.

Little Carrie, ¾ length, vignette . .   **35.00**

Soldier's Adieu, The, 12 x 16" . . .   **75.00**

Tyler, John, silhouette, 1844 . . . .   **125.00**

Magnus, Charles

Bird's Eye View of The City Of Annapolis, Md., 1863, 11 x 17" . .   **300.00**

Running The Blockade, 18 x 21", view of Wilmington, NC **150.00**

Matter, C. View Of New York & Brooklyn, 28¾ x 20⅝", c1855, printed by I. Shcaerer, published by J. H. Locher **1,750.00**

Nutting, Wallace. Matted

An Old Maine Garden, 5 x 7" . . .   **37.50**

Early June Brides, MA, 8 x 10" . .   **35.00**

Garden Steps, Mrs. Nutting's Floral Arrangements, 8 x 10" **40.00**

Graces, The, 8 x 10" **50.00**

Grafton Windings, MA, 8 x 10" . .	32.50
Hunter's Island, MA, 4 x 10"	35.00
Nashua Asleep, The, MA, 5 x 7" .	45.00
New Hampshire Birches, NH, 8 x 10"	40.00
Portsmouth Front Door, A, 8 x 10"	45.00
Stitch In Time, A, MA, 8 x 10" . . .	80.00
Warm Spring Day, A, RI, 8 x 10" .	60.00
Woodland Cathedral, A, VT, 8 x 10"	45.00

Parrish, Maxfield
  Magazine Covers

1906, Jan. 6, *Collier's,* The New Year	35.00
1908, Dec. 12, *Harper's Weekly,* identical to Dec. 14, 1895 issue, chef holding plum pudding on plate	40.00
1909, April 17, *Collier's,* The Lone Fisherman	27.50
1911, Sept. 30, *Collier's,* Arithmetic	30.00
1917, August, *Century,* nude hugging knees in forest setting	45.00
1923, March 1, *Life,* A Dark Futurist	35.00

  Prints

Broadmoor Hotel, The, 1915, 8 x 7"	60.00
Canyon, The, 1924, blonde girl clinging to cliff's edge, raging river below her, 15 x 12" . . .	110.00
Garden of Opportunity, The, 1925, 25 x 24", triptych	250.00
Harvest, 1905, 8 x 10"	47.50
Jason And The Talking Oak, 1908, 11 x 9"	55.00
Prince, The, 1928, prince lying down in a field, 12 x 10"	115.00
Rubaiyat, 1917, man reading on far left, woman on far right in garden, 30 x 8"	275.00
Valley Of Enchantment, 1946, summer scene, road prominent, large oak on right knoll, huge mountains, medium size	60.00

Prang, Louis, floral prints, average size 7½ x 10½" . . . . — 10-15.00

Rockwell. See ROCKWELL, NORMAN in this book and "Rockwell, Norman" in *Warman's Americana & Collectibles*

Saxony & Major

Elizabeth	45.00
Perry's Victory On Lake, 1846 . . .	175.00

Saxony, Major & Knapp, Comanche Camp On Shady Creek . . . . — 120.00

Wall, William Guy (after), View From Fishkill Looking To West Point, 24⅜ x 18⅛", plate 15 from Hudson River Port Folio, engraved by J. Hill, published by Henry I. Megarey, NY . . . . — 1,750.00

PRINTS, JAPANESE

Buying Japanese woodblock prints requires attention to detail and skilled knowledge of the subject. The quality of the impression (good, moderate, or weak), the color, and condition are critical. Various states and strikes of the same print cause the price to fluctuate. Knowing the proper publisher and censor's seals is helpful in identifying an original print.

Most prints were recopied and issued in popular versions. These represent the vast majority of the prints found in the marketplace. These popular versions should be viewed solely as decorative since they have little monetary value.

A novice buyer should seek expert advice before buying. Talk with a specialized dealer, museum curator, or auction division head.

The listings below concentrate on details to show the depth of data needed for adequate pricing. Condition and impression are good, unless indicated otherwise.

O=Oban, 10 x 15"	C =Chuban,
Ot=Oban tat-e,	7 x 10"
large in width	H=Hosoban,
Oy=Oban yoko-e,	5½ x 13"
large in length	T=Triptyck

Eisen, Standing figure of *geisha* making up, Hide River, from *Mutamagawa* series, sgd *Kikugawa Eizan hitsu,* Ot	675.00
Eishi, Two kneeling *geisha,* one holding a fan and adjusting a hanging *tanzaku,* view of *koto* in fan shaped cartouche above, from series *Ukiyo Genji hakkei,* sgd *Eishi zu,* published by Eijudo, Ot .	3,000.00
Eizan, Beauty walking in the snow, from *Furyu bijin matsu no uchi* series, sgd *Eizan hitsu,* published by Izumiya Ichibei, Ot	925.00
Gakutei, Carp swimming amongst waterlilies, sgd *Gakutei,* sealed *Yashima, kakuban*	1,650.00
Harunobu (Suzuki), Two beauties seated beside *kotatsu* playing cats cradle, book and potted plant in the *tokonome* behind, screen with horses in rear, unsigned, C, large in width	9,250.00

Hasui

Night at Shinkawa, from *Tokyo junikei* series, sgd *Hasui,* dated 7th month, Taisho 8 (1919), published by Watanabe, Ot . . .	2,400.00
Yanagawa River in Koshu Pref., from *Tabi miyage dai nishu* series, sgd *Hasui,* sealed *Kawase,* dated Taisho 10 (1921), published by Watanabe, Ot	800.00

Hasui, 15½ x 10¼", $600.00.

Hokusai
Actor Segawa Michinosuke as the housewife Komume typing his *obi,* sgd *Hokusai ga,* seal dated Bunka 4 (1807), Ot 5,250.00

Fuji from the Sumida River with the Ryogoku Bridge below, from *Fugaku Sanjurokkei* series, sgd *zen Hokusai aratame Iitsu hitsu,* Oy 1,000.00

Pine and waves at Ryudo, from *Ryukyu hakkei* series, sgd *zen Hokusai Iitsu hitsu,* published by Moriya Jihei, Oy 2,500.00

Hiroshige
Hamamatsu, from *Reisho Tokaido* series, sgd *Hiroshige ga,* published by Marusei, Oy 1,750.00

Hoeido Tokaido series, sgd *Hiroshige ga*
  Fujisawa 950.00
  Hakone 700.00
  Shimada 625.00

Meisho Edo Hyakkei series, sgd *Hiroshige ga*
  Drum Bridge at Meguro in winter, dated 1857 . . . .   1,600.00
  Nihonbashi after a fresh snowfall, published by Uo-ei 700.00
  Woodyards at Kyobashi, published by Uo-ei 900.00

Hiroshige II
Gold Mines at Sado Island, from

Honcho meisho hyakkei series, sgd *Hiroshige ga,* Ot 450.00

Rain at Oyama, from *Shokoku meisho hyakkei* series, sgd *Hiroshige ga,* Ot 725.00

Koryusai, Two women beneath a *futon,* one awakened by sound of the other entertaining a midnight visitor, sgd *Koryu ga,* C, large in length 3,750.00

Kotondo, Beauty in a sudden shower, sgd *Genjin ga,* dated Showa 4 (1929), numbered 84/200, published by Sakai/Kawaguchi, large Ot 1,000.00

Kunisada
Beauty reflected in mirror, "Plucking the Eyebrows," an *okubire,* from *Imafu kesho kagami* series, sgd *Gototei Kunisada ga,* published by Azumaya Daisuke   3,000.00

Three beauties walking in snow, sgd variously *Kunisada aratame Ichiyosai Toyokuni ga* and *Kunisada aratame nidai Toyokuni ga,* T, Ot 775.00

Kuniyoshi
Chushingura series, complete set, sgd *Ichiyusai Kuniyoshi ga,* Oy .   650.00

Shoki, the demon queller, holding a frightened oni by the scruff of the neck, sgd *Ichiyusai Kuniyoshi,* sealed *Kuniyoshi,* Ot. . . .   1,250.00

Vision of Shakamuni, from Scenes of the Life of Nichiren' series, sgd *Chooro Kiniyoshi hitsu,* Oy .   650.00

Masanobu, Young man in garb of *komuso, kimono* decorated with *shishi* and poeny, hat in hand, poems above, sgd *Hogetsudo Shomei Okumura Bunkaku Masanobu shohitsu,* publisher unidentified, kakemono-e (scroll) 6,500.00

Shinsui, Girl, half length, against a full moon, sgd *Shinsui saka,* dated Showa 6 (1931), numbered 104/-150, published by Watanabe, large Ot 600.00

Shunsen, Party of beauties crossing a bridge, river scene behind, sgd *Shunsen ga,* T, Ot 2,000.00

Shunsho, Actor Segawa Kikunojo in female role and Matsumoto Koshiro in male role, the latter seated in front of a mirror stand, the former profferring a comb, sgd *Shunsho ga,* H 2,000.00

Toyohiro, Parade of beauties and children walking in front of a shop, sgd *Toyohiro ga,* published by Wakasaya Yoichi, pentaptych, Ot .   900.00

Toyokuni, Actors Ichikawa Omezo as Watanabe no Tsuna and Onoe

Matsunosuke as Ibaraki Shozo, the demon of the Rashomon, sgd *Toyokuni ga*, Ot 1,320.00

Utamaro
Courtesan dressing the hair of another before a mirror, sgd *Utamaro hitsu*, Ot 2,000.00
Joruri lovers Sankatsu and Hanshichi representing "evening glow," Sankatsu crying while Hanshichi, holding pipe, looks on, from *Omi hakkei* series, sgd *Utamaro hitsu*, published by Takatenya Iskne, slight watersoiling, Ot 8,750.00
Young couple holding up *bunraku* dolls representing the *joruri* lovers Osome and Hisamatsu, sgd *Utamaro*, published by Moriya Jihei, Ot 4,500.00

Utamaro II, Beauty, half length, holding up her baby who plays with ball, sgd *Utamaro hitsu*, published by Iwatoya Kisaburo, *Kiwame* seal and censor's seal of Kisabura, Ot.   2,000.00
Yoshitoshi, Yaoya Oshichi climbing the ladder of the fire warden's tower, sgd *Yoshitoshi*, seal *Taiso*, *kakemono-e* (scroll) 2,000.00

PURPLE SLAG (Marble Glass)

Challinor, Taylor & Co., Tarantum, PA (1870s–1880s) is known as the largest producer of Purple Slag in the United States. However, since the quality of pieces varies considerably there can be no doubt that it was made by other firms as well. Purple Slag was also made in England at the same time. English pieces were marked with British Registry marks. Other color combinations were made, such as blue, green or orange, but are rarely found today. Purple slag has been reproduced over the years and is being produced to present.

See also, PINK SLAG; for Chocolate Slag see GREENTOWN GLASS

Bowl, 5½ x 8" 125.00
Candlestick, dolphin heads going into base 135.00
Celery Vase, Jewel pattern 105.00
Compote, Thread pattern, small . . .   65.00
Creamer, fish with open mouth, sgd   85.00
Lady's High Shoe, 6", figural, sits on beaded diamond shaped base . .   60.00
Match Holder, 5 x 3", dolphin heads   65.00
Pitcher, Fan and Basketweave pattern 225.00
Plate, 10", lattice edge 100.00
Sugar, Scroll with Acanthus pattern, open 75.00

Tumbler, 4½", Ribbed 40.00
Vases
9", soft pink, violet, English 75.00
Grape cluster, 1905 . . . .   95.00

QUEZAL   *Quezal*

Quezal Art Glass was a very fine quality blown iridescent glassware produced by Martin Bach, a former Tiffany employee, in his factory in Brooklyn, N.Y., from 1901–1920. The company was called the Quezal Art Glass and Decorating Co. After the death of Bach, his son-in-law, Conrad Vohlsing, opened a small shop near Elmhurst, L.I., New York, where he produced the same type of ware until 1929. Vohlsing marked his glass "Lustre Art Glass."

Named after the Central American bird, Quezal Glass has an iridescent finish featuring contrasting colored glass threads. While still in the cooling stage, the threads were pulled up and drawn into various designs, often a drape with a peacock eye at the end of the feather. Gold, green and white colors are most often found.

Candlesticks, 7¾", blue, irid, sgd . .   525.00
Cologne Bottle, 7½", gold, Art Deco design, sgd Q and Melba 195.00

Cruet, pulled green feather on white opal ground, clear yellow stopper and handle, $2,300.00.

Lamp Shades

4¼ x 2½″ collar, gold irid, 10 ribbed sides, sgd **100.00**

Threaded, sgd, pr **210.00**

Perfume Bottle, 5″, flattened teardrop shape, bulbous stopper, monogrammed silver foliate mounts, inscribed, Gorham mounts **585.00**

Salts

1⅛ x 2½″, satin gold lustre, pink and blue highlights, ribbed, sgd **165.00**

2¾″, sgd **195.00**

Toothpick, 2¼ x 2¼″, melon ribbed, pinched sides, irid blue, green, purple and gold, sgd **175.00**

Vases

4″, fold-over top, thatched and lily pad decor **925.00**

4½″, flower form, large green petals, sgd Quezal, S 854 ...... **1,400.00**

5¼″, green and white pulls, outlined in gold on opal, gold lining **775.00**

5½″, bulbous amphora shape, cased ivory over amber, lavender and yellow swirl decor, inscribed **375.00**

5½″, opal ground, all-over blue and gold swirls, gold lining ... **550.00**

6¼″, round, narrow neck, gold irid **410.00**

7½″, butterscotch, all-over gold scalloped lines, brown swirl decor at top **800.00**

12″, flower form, tapered, pedestal base, gold irid, sgd **875.00**

Wall Sconce, 14″, irid floriform shade, white, gold feather pattern, gold interior, molded brass sconce, foliate and mirror decor, sgd at base of shade **150.00**

QUILTS

Quilts have been passed down as family heirlooms for many generations. Each is an individual expression as patterns of like style have hundreds of variations both in color and design.

The advent of the sewing machine increased, not decreased the number of quilts which were made. Quilts still are being sewn today.

The key considerations for price are age, condition, aesthetic beauty and design. The latter point is especially important. Pricewise, quilts have risen dramatically over the last ten years. The market now is glutted, causing a leveling in prices. The exception is the very finest examples which continue to bring record prices.

Rainbow, pieced cotton, 86 x 84″, $950.00.

Acorn and Wreath, appliqued, red print on green print ground, back old English twin quail chinz, c1850, 82 x 106″ **1,350.00**

Amish

Bear Claws, pieced cotton, blue, tan, brown, gray, faded red, tan ground, dated 1890, Stark County, Ohio, 62 x 87″ **700.00**

Shoofly, pieced cotton, dark reds, green, blue, purple, gray, tan, black, 36 x 43″ **955.00**

Sunshine and Shadow, pieced cotton, blues, greens, browns, grays, black, blue, gray borders, c1940, 64 x 77″ **775.00**

Bar, pieced cotton, red, white, field of double circle quilting, Ohio, c1900 .... **500.00**

Blazing Star, pieced cotton, red, blue, pink, yellow, white, field of feather wreath and diagonal line quilting, 84 x 88″ **925.00**

Blossom and Bird, pieced and appliqued, red, green calico on white cotton field, scalloped edges, leaf sprig quilting **925.00**

Bride's, pieced and appliqued, embroidered cotton, 16 squares, in floral, fruit or animal motifs, blocks sgd, dated 1860, 88 x 84″ **950.00**

Double Heart & Spade, pieced cotton, red, white ground, field of line quilting, 84 x 80″ **500.00**

Double Irish Chain, blue, rose-red calico, setting squares of green calico, wide border of navy print, narrow inside border of brown print, back light blue print, fine quilting, Mennonite, Lancaster County, PA, c1920, 78 x 79″ ... **625.00**

Double Monkey Wrench, pieced cotton, maroon, green, yellow, blue, field of wave, cable and leaf quilting **500.00**

Friendship, appliqued, embroidered, center theme of large American ship, overflowing cornucopia, fruit, hearts, birds, wreaths, etc, signa-

tures of Baltimore area residents, c1840, 97¾ x 95¾" 5,500.00
Gaudy Dutch, pieced square of dark blue, yellow, brown and pink solids set on avocado green, yellow and brown sawtooth border, feather pattern quilting, red calico backing, PA, c1885 80 x 86" 750.00
Hexagonal, pieced cotton calico, red, green, white, field of heart quilting, scalloped border, 80 x 100" 1,000.00
Mariner's Compass, appliqued, soft reds, greens, yellows, appliqued sash border of red, green, New York, c1890, 76 x 95½" 950.00
Odd Fellow's Patch, deep blue, blue-green on white, Ohio, c1900, never used or laundered, 75 x 90" 600.00
Patience Corners, large dark blue calico triangles alternating with rose-red calico triangles on rose-red calico, inside border of dark blue, back of old striped brown calico, Lancaster County, PA, c1920, Mennonite, 80 x 80" 625.00
Princess Feather, applique and reverse applique, turkey red on white, field of heart and wreath quilting, feathered border on three sides edged in red, Norton, Ohio, 1880, 81 x 83" 1,100.00
Sawtooth Square, pieced cotton, medium blue, white patches, field of circle and diamond quilting, 68 x 88" 700.00
Star, pieced cotton, white homespun, calico, red, blue, yellow, pink, medium brown, intricate quilting, 99 x 103" 550.00
Star of Bethlehem, pieced cotton, lavendar, green, white patches, field of feather and interlacing circle quilting, scalloped border, 84 x 80" 600.00

QUIMPER

Quimper pottery is a tin-glazed earthenware that has been produced in and around the town of Quimper in Northwest France since the late 17th century. Three factories survived through the 19th century with items from these three found most frequently on the market today.

Jules Henriot used the HR mark from 1886 through 1926 when the familiar Henriot mark

appeared. The Porquier-Beau "Golden Period" occurred in the 1880s. This mark is most prized by collectors.

The Hubaudiere-Bousquet HB covers most of the 1880s and into the present period and exists in many styles and forms. In 1968 the Henriot and HB faienceries consolidated and began producing the modern dinnerware seen today.

Wall pocket, cone shaped, male peasant, $100.00.

Bowls
6" d, blue, yellow banding, peasant decor, center, pierced for hanging, Henriot Quimper mark 60.00
9" d, scalloped edge, dull matte glaze, frontal view of male peasant, pierced for hanging .. 165.00
Vegetable, sq, flaired edges, yellow, blue dash border, peasant decor, pierced for hanging ... 110.00
Boxes
2½" h, figural, infant in cradle, brown, blue coloring, Henriot Quimper 225.00
4⅝" d, cov, round, seated female peasant, decor riche border .. 125.00
Butter Dishes, covered
Oval shape, 2 peasants on cover, blue, red trim, H. R. Quimper mark 140.00
Round, looping handles, bluish glaze, red, blue tiny flowers,

male peasant on cover, H. R.
Quimper 80.00

Cake Plate, 6″ d, blue, red flowers
between blue bands at border,
typical peasant pose, crazing on
surface, H. B. Quimper 20.00

Cake Stand, ftd, soft blue, yellow
flowers, female on center portion,
early 1900s, H. R. Quimper mark 145.00

Candle Holder, double, 8½″ h, figur-
al-stylized peasant woman, baskets on arms form candleholders,
yellow glaze, brown, green dots,
H. B. Quimper 195.00

Chamberstick, 3 section base, hexagonal holder, ring handle, red,
blue open daisies, tan glaze,
Henriot mark 100.00

Cheese Dish, cov, round, molded
fluting on cover, base, rust, green
florals, molded bee finial in yellow
and green, H. R. Quimper 125.00

Cups and Saucers
Demitasse, octagonal shape, dark
gray glaze, red dashes at margins, offset wishbone handles in
blue, yellow stripes, H. R. Quim-
per, set of 4 . . . . 140.00

Ovoid shape, blue, rust florals,
Henriot mark 50.00

Tab handle, blue stripes, male
peasant, floral matching saucer,
H. B. Quimper, 1930s 35.00

Figures
Le Pechere, 10″ h, walking fisherman, net on shoulder, deco colors, green, brown, artist sgnd,
Henriot Quimper mark 400.00

Mary and Christ Child, stylized, 8″
h, deco colors, blue, pink, gold
touches 125.00

Gravy Boats
European style, double handle,
double spout, filter for separating fat, stylized dancing couple,
artist sgnd 40.00

Footed, oval shape, handleless,
double spout, fat separating filter, white glaze, red, blue
dashes, H. B. Quimper 55.00

Inkwells
Double wells, soft bluish glaze, or-
ange, blue trim, peasant decor,
Henriot Quimper 190.00

Single, attached underplate, pie-
crust crimped edge, soft blues,
rust colors 175.00

Single, bulbous shape, leaf shape
feet, blue cross-hatching, florals,
peasant on front panel 110.00

Match Holder, blue Fleur-de-lis, ermine tail trim, open blue flower
over hanging hole, H. B. Quimper 25.00

Mustards, covered
Attached underplate, peasant decor, red, blue flowers 75.00

Two attached open salts, peasant
decor 75.00

Pitchers
2¾″ h, pedestal, female peasant
on grayish, lumpy glaze, H. B.
mark 65.00

6½″ h, figural, woman's head,
deco colors, black, cream, pink,
gold touches, coif forms pouring
spout 125.00

6½″ h, floral, orange, blue colors,
bulbous shape, pinched spout,
signed Henriot Quimper under
handle 58.00

Planters
8″ octagonal, narrowing at top,
blue dashes, ermine tails at
margins, frontal view of both
peasants 175.00

13″ l, male playing horn, female
seated with basket, crest of Brittany on side panels, raised blue,
gold flowing trim at borders, H.
R. Quimper 550.00

Plates
6″, salad, octagonal, red cross-
hatching between yellow, green
florals, full view of female peasant, marked front, back 40.00

8″ d, lunch-size, yellow and blue
band border, crazed surface,
c1930s, Henriot Quimper 35.00

8½″ d, mustard yellow sponged
border, stylized florals, center . . 30.00

9¼″ d
Decorative, bold colors of red,
blue, open flowers on border,
scalloped edge, set of 4,
each with different exotic bird,
sgnd H. R. Quimper on front . 300.00

Decorative, sq plate attached to
sq plate forming star, decor
riche border in blue, gold, seated peasants, crest of Brittany at
top, pierced for hanging 200.00

Dinner
Grayish-pink glaze, scalloped
border, peasant decor, florals,
4-dot trim on border, H. R.
Quimper 75.00

Thick, heavy body, brightly
painted rooster, blue open
flowers on border, scalloped
edge, unmarked 78.00

Platter, 15″ l, border outlined in
blue divides decorative panels,
yellow, blue flowers on panels,
male and female peasants in cen-
ter, H. B. Quimper 250.00

Porringers, 6″ d, yellow, blue bands,

small red, blue, green florals on outer surface, peasant decor in center, pierced for hanging, Henriot Quimper, pr 90.00

Relish Tray, rectangular shape, clipped corners, 7″ w, male peasant in center, worn red flowers at border, ermine tails in corners, pierced for hanging 45.00

Salt, double, swans attached by center ring, blue sponged painting, male inside one swan, flowers in other 45.00

Salt & Pepper, 3½″ h, blue, yellow banding, missing corks, peasant on each, H. B. Quimper, pr 110.00

Serving Plate, ftd, loop handle divides plate in two, sea shell border, female peasant leaning on fence, yellow glaze, blue, green trim, Henriot mark 275.00

Spoon Rest, bagpipe shape, blue border, yellow molded ribbon at top, frontal view of female carrying basket of eggs 45.00

Sugar Bowls
Gold loop handles, blue dashes, rooster on front, high glaze, Henriot Quimper 45.00
Green serpent handles, rust, blue dashes, peasant on each side, yellow fleur-de-lis finial, H. R. Quimper mark 95.00

Teapot, dragon handle, spout, male on one side, female on other, blue fleur-de-lis finial, green dragon coloring, Henriot mark 250.00

Toothpicks, mottled gray glaze, tube shaped, H. B. Quimper on back, pr 80.00

Tray, 12″ d, red, blue dashes on border, frontal view of male peasant, matte glaze, pierced for hanging 335.00

Tureen, 9″ w, open daisy pattern in baskets, blue sponged handles, finial, red, blue flowers, trim, Henriot Quimper 235.00

Vases
4½″ h, horn shaped resting on pedestal, predominately blue trim, H. R. Quimper 85.00
7″ h, bud, frontal view of female peasant, open daisy flowers on back in red, blue, small bulge at apex of neck, matte glaze 160.00
8″ h, flat front, back panels, wishbone handles, frontal view of male peasant, Henriot mark . . . 240.00
8″ w, fan shape, scalloped border, blue scroll feet, cross-hatched ends in blue, rust dots interspersed, male on front panel, floral on reverse 100.00

Figural fleur-de-lis shape, scenes from children's fairy tales on each, rare Porquier-Beau mark, pr 1,200.00

Wall Pockets
8″ 1, bagpipe shape, frontal view of male peasant, gold ribbon molded at bottom 130.00
8″ 1, double, male, female peasants, early H. R. mark 140.00

RADIO RECEIVERS

A growing number of collectors have taken an interest in early items from the radio broadcasting field. At present, radio receivers are one of their favorites. Old radio programs are also popular remembrances of the pre-TV era.

See *Warman's Americana & Collectibles* for an expanded listing of Radio Receivers.

Fada, c1930, $40.00.

Aerodyne, Special, battery, 1927 . . 80.00
Atwater Kent, Model "M", horn speaker 55.00
Bendix Aviation Co., table model, Art Deco, white curved plastic case . 38.00
Crosley, metal battery type 70.00
DeForest, D12, loop antenna, battery, 1924 . . . . 250.00
Eagle Neotrodyne, wooden table model, battery 125.00
Echophone, cathedral style, electric 75.00
Emerson, AZ-196, two band, 1938 . 30.00

Fairbanks Morse, Model 5106, 1934   **115.00**
Hallicrafters, radio receiver, headphones, Model S-38, standard, foreign short wave **55.00**
Majestic, Model 463, Century, 1933   **50.00**
Metrodyne, battery, 1925 . . . .   **75.00**
Philmore, Little Wonder, crystal, orig box **65.00**
RCA Radiola III **85.00**
Trav-Ler, beehive, brownie model . .   **55.00**
Zenith, portable Trans Oceanic, complete with operator's manual   **25.00**

RAILROAD ITEMS

Railroad collectors have existed for decades. The merger of the rail systems and the end of passenger service made many objects available for private collections. The Pennsylvania Railroad sold its archives at public sale.

Railroad enthusiasts have organized into regional and local clubs. Join one if interested. Your local hobby store can probably point you to the right person. The best pieces pass between collectors and rarely make it into the general market place.

See *Warman's Americana & Collectibles* for an expanded listing of Railroad Items.

Builder's Plates, Diesel-Electric
   Alco-GE #79911, 6/1952, PRR-3 #8459, 6 x 12″ cast iron rectangle **45.00**
   B-L-H #76014, 9/1954, Monongahela RR 5-12 #423, 8 x 15″ cast iron rectangle **70.00**
Builder's and Number Plates, Locomotives
   Alco-Brooks #59748, 8/1918, IC, 2-8-2, #301, 7 x 14″ cast iron rectangle **125.00**
   Baldwin, BLW #36574, 5/1911, UP, 2-8-2, #2208, 12″ round brass **150.00**
China
   Bowl, 5¼″, CRI&P, La Salle **85.00**
   Butterchip, ACL, Carolina, backstamp **12.00**
   Cereal Bowls
     B & O, Capitol, Shenango China   **40.00**
     IC, Coral, Syracuse China, no backstamp **20.00**
   Cups and Saucers
     D&RG, Prospector, Syracuse, no backstamp **135.00**
     NYC, Mercury, Syracuse, backstamped **65.00**
   Demitasse Cup, UP, Desert Flower, backstamped **35.00**
   Demitasse Cups and Saucers
     SCL, Piedmont, backstamp . . .   **45.00**

UP, Winged Streamliner, Sterling China **35.00**
Gravy Boat, PRR, Keystone, top logo, Warwick China **60.00**
Pitcher, 8 oz., handle, Pullman, Calumet **65.00**
Plates
   7″, GN, Mountain & Flowers, Syracuse China, backstamp .   **40.00**
   7¼″, C&NW, Wild Rose, no backstamp **25.00**
   7¼″, WP, Feather River, Shenango **40.00**
   7½″, Pullman, Indian Tree, center tree in pattern, Buffalo China backstamp **75.00**
   9″, CP, Maple Leaf, brown . . .   **35.00**
   9½″, UP, Challenger, no backstamp **65.00**
   10″, NYC, Pacemaker, no backstamp **65.00**
   10½″, PRR, Gotham, backstamp, mint **65.00**
Platters
   10¼″, MP, St. Albans, Syracuse, backstamp, c1926 . . .   **85.00**
   11″, CB&Q, Violets and Daisies, no backstamp **35.00**
Relish Dish, 11½″, scalloped edge, Pullman, Calumet **75.00**
Sauce Dish, CMST&P, Peacock, no backstamp **20.00**
Soup Cup, Amtrak, white with blue border, small silver line, unmarked **3.00**
Soup Plates
   9″, UP, Harriman Blue, backstamped **30.00**
   9¼″, CN, Quetico **22.50**
Sugar Bowl, open top, STSF, California Poppy, Syracuse, no backstamp **30.00**
Vegetable Dishes
   B&O, Centennial, 5½″, circular, Lamberton China **35.00**
   MP, Eagle, Syracuse, backstamp **25.00**
Glassware
   Ice Tea, Santa Fe in white script, 12 oz. **10.00**
   Water, D&H, white logo, 8 oz. . . .   **8.00**
Hardware
   Chisel, "KCS Ry" **8.00**
   Coupling Pin, cast iron, "I&GN" . .   **70.00**
   Monkey Wrench, "ICRR" **15.00**
   Signalman's Flare Kit, five flares, plus red flag **20.00**
   Torch, iron, screw top, "PW&B RR" **45.00**
Lanterns, Hand
   Adams and Westlake, pat. 1923, KCS Ry, clear cast 5⅜″ globe, in panel "KCS" **125.00**

Oil lamp, club car, NY Central, tin, repainted base, $45.00.

Adlake Kero, SP Lines, red fresnel 3¼" globe 35.00

Adlake Reliable, 1913, MCRR, clear cast 5⅝" globe 75.00

Armspear, Soo Line, clear etched 3¼" globe, "Soo Line," 1924 . 40.00

Dietz Vulcan #39, frame unmarked, clear cast 5⅜" globe, "T&P Ry" 50.00

Dressel, MKT, clear etched 3¼" globle, "MKT RR" 45.00

Handlan, MPL, clear etched 4⅝" globe, "NYCL," mismatch 45.00

Handlan, T&NOC, flat top, clear cast 5⅜" globe, "T&NOC/Saftey 1st" 125.00

Locks, Switch (See Padlocks in *Warman's Americana & Collectibles*)

Menus

California Zephyr train, shown crossing the North Fork of California's Feather River, 1960s . . 5.00

CB&Q, children's, folder style, Burlington Zephyr, 1953 . . . . . . 3.50

Menu Cover, Santa Fe, Turquoise Room, Super Chief, 11 x 14", folder 2.50

Paperweights

Burlington, first Vista Dome car on base, 1945, silver finish 100.00

Soo Line, magnifying glass center, 1883–1958, Seventy-Fifth Anniversary 35.00

Passes

1890–1915 . . . . 7-25.00

1916–Present 2-12.50

Semaphore Lamp, Handlan, large clear lens, red square glass insert and reflector 75.00

Silver

Bread Tray, 5¾" x 11¼", center top marking of CP 35.00

Butterchip, 3¼", square, backstamped Rock Island Lines, Gorham 25.00

Cover, oval, 10½", T&P, top marked on front with eagle logo, backstamped "TEXAS & PACIFIC RAILWAY," "IS," and 46 date 75.00

Creamer, IC, 8 oz, attached lid, backstamped "ILLINOIS CENTRAL R.R.," "IS," and 1964 date 50.00

Gravy Boat, CB&Q, side logo with reversed BR, Reed & Barton, 1928 date code, 3 oz. 65.00

Tray, 12", topmarked Santa Fe on top rim, backstamped Santa Fe, Gorham, 1922 date code 60.00

Switch Keys (See Keys in *Warman's Americana and Collectibles*)

Switch Lamps

Dressel, 2 red and 2 green, copper coupling rings & wire guards, marked "M-K-T" 75.00

Handlan, 2 red and 2 green, plastic lens, hoods, oil burning, marked "Frisco" 85.00

Trivet, ACL, black metal with train on trestle, top marked 20.00

Uniform Buttons

"B&O," large, gold, flat 3.00

"GRAND TRUNK RR," around monogram in circle, large, gold, dome 4.50

"PRR," Keystone monogram, large, silver, dome 2.00

RAZORS

Razors date back several thousand years. Early man used sharpened stones. The Egyptians, Greeks and Romans had metal razors.

Razors made prior to 1800 generally were stamped crudely WARRANTED or CAST STEEL with the maker's mark on the tang. Until 1870 almost all razors for the American market were manufactured in Sheffield, England. Most baldes were wedge shaped; many were etched with slogans or scenes. Handles were made of natural materials—various horns, tortoise shell, bone, ivory, stag, silver and pearl. All razors were handmade.

After 1870 most razors were machine made with hollow ground blades and synthetic handle materials. Razors of this period usually were manufactured in Germany (Solingen) or in American cutlery factories. Hundreds of molded celluloid handle patterns were produced, such as nude women, eagles, deer, boats, windmill scenes, etc.

Cutlery firms produced boxed sets of two, four and seven razors. Complete and undamaged sets are very desirable. Most popular are the 7-Day sets with each razor etched with a day of the week.

The fancier the handle or more intricately etched the blade, the higher the price. Rarest handle materials are pearl, stag, sterling silver, pressed horn and carved ivory. Rarest blades are those with scenes etched across the entire front. Value is increased by certain manufacturer's names, such as Case, H. Boker, M. Price, Joseph Rogers, Simmons Hardware, Will & Finck, Winchester, and George Wostenholm.

hgb = hollow ground blade
wb = wedge blade

See *Warman's Americana & Collectibles* for an expanded listing of razors.

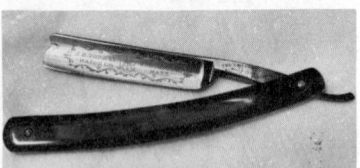

American, J. R. Terry & Co. Worcester, MA, fully etched blade, tortoise shell handle, $50.00.

AMERICAN BLADES

H. Boker & Co., blade includes name and The World's Columbian Exposition, 1893, buildings detailed	45.00
Challenge Cutlery Co., Bridgeport, CT, tortoiseshell handle with raised owl in front surrounded in scroll, pile side in fancy scroll covering	80.00
Eagle Razor Co, NY, The Improved Eagle Razor, etched spread eagle, black celluloid handle	65.00
Herman Greager's Improved Razor, pile side of tank stamped Patent Oct 25, 1888, Manchester, New Hampshire, marbleized green celluloid handle, trimmed in German silver, orig box	75.00
Holley Mfg Co., Lakeville, blade includes name and Patent Hollow Ground, black horn handle	30.00
Imperial Razor Warranted, blade inscribed with name and Imperial Safety, etched picture of 2 cyclist on double bike, mottled horn handle	40.00
A. Schaefer's Son, NY, bone handle	18.00
Union Razor Cutlery Co., Union City, GA, celluloid ear of corn handle .	60.00

ENGLISH BLADES, SHEFFIELD

Clark & Hall Warranted, straight green horn handle, squared head end, pointed tang end, bevelled perimeter, inlaid escutcheon plate, wb	95.00
Joseph Elliot "Best Silver Steel," mottled horn handle, oblong plate	25.00
V. (crown) R. Middleton Union Street, Sheffield, black horn handle, pointed ends, large brass pin covers, hgb, c1825	40.00
J. Nowill & Sons, front stamped Boston Razor, black horn handle . . .	100.00
Sam'l Osborn & Co Clyde Steel Works, Sheffield, "Gold Medal" inscribed on blade with name, ivory handle	35.00
Frederick Reynolds, mottled horn handles, German silver caps . . .	75.00
Wade & Butcher, mottled horn handle, 3 crude engraved ornaments inlaid in handle, wb	35.00

GERMAN BLADES

Cosmos Mfg Co., ivory handle, raised nude picking purple grapes, green leaves, hgb	95.00
Eisenach Feinster Dramantstahl, glossy handle, rounded black horn with semi-pointed ends, blade, handle, very slender, small	38.00
F.A. Koch & Co., Made In Germany, ivory handle, decorated with colored scene of branches, oak leaves, deer	45.00
Rahaim & Malham, celluloid bamboo style handle, name and "Philippines Cuba Porto Rico "OURS" " on blade	30.00
Union Pride, ivory raised scroll around both ends, Art Nouveau style celluloid handle	18.50

SWEDISH BLADE (ESKILSTUNA)

C. V. Heljestraid Eskilstuna Sweden, A. Bol Ferd Lundoust & Co, Goteborg, ivory handle, curved fluted finger grip, hgb	90.00

SETS OF RAZORS

Pair, matched, I. Oxley, Liverpool, 1870, ivory handles, semi wedge blades, red stain, velvet lined presentation case of leather covered wood **120.00**

Pair, matched, unused, C. V. Heljestrand Eskilstuna Sweden, ivory handles, fitted plush lined presentation case, red leather covered wood case **185.00**

3 razor set, J. A. Henckels Twin Works Soligen, handles of black celluloid, two with pointed ends, middle one with rounded ends, sewn leather case, flap **35.00**

7 Day Set, Carrara, No. 877, Made In Sheffield, flat black celluloid handles, days of week or hgb blades, leather wood box **150.00**

7 Day Set, straight, black celluloid handles, Solingen inlaid in German silver, tangs stamped la Silberstahl Garantie Solingen, top 1/3 of blade gold plate, trademark on each consisting of blue crossed swords and anchor, paper covered wood case, double brass clasp **125.00**

RED WING POTTERY

There were several potteries located in Red Wing, Minnesota, in the late 1800s. The parent company was the Red Wing Stoneware Co. A merger with other local potteries resulted in the formation of the Red Wing Union Stoneware Co. in the early 1900s. The firm was one of the largest producers of stoneware utilitarian ware—crocks and jugs —in the United States.

In 1930, when the desirability for stoneware items diminished, a line of art pottery was introduced and the company was renamed Red Wing Potteries, Inc. Production of stoneware continued in limited quantities until 1947. The art line flourished until 1967 when the stockholders voted to liquidate the establishment due to labor disputes.

See Warman's *Americana & Collectibles* for an expanded listing of Red Wing Pottery.

Vase, 8¼″ h, tapered cylinder, straight neck, relief floral design, red matte glaze, over glaze stamped Red Wing/Union/Stoneware/Co. Red Wing/Minn.", $46.00.

Ashtray, high gloss pink, imp mark Red Wing U.S.A., #695 . . . .   **9.00**
Bean Pot, bail handle, 1 gal, North Star **265.00**
Bookends, fan and scroll design, Rum Brill paper label, pr **20.00**
Bowls
  8″, matte ivory, floral rose decor .   **25.00**
  8″, spongeware, ribbed sides . . .   **45.00**
Cookie Jars
  Friar Monk, hp, ivory, stamped mark of wing **45.00**
  Pear Shape, high gloss pink, imp Red Wing U.S.A. **28.00**
  Rooster, semi gloss, green, imp Red Wing U.S.A., #249 . . . . .   **27.50**
Crocks
  2 gal, Double P, bottom marked .   **45.00**
  2 gal, elephant ears, bottom marked Union Stoneware Co. .   **50.00**
  20 gal, Butterfly, marked Minnesota Stoneware Co., c1900 . . . . .   **465.00**
  30 gal, Lily, marked Red Wing Stoneware Co., c1885 . . . . . .   **525.00**
Dinner Sets
  19 pcs, Magnolia **25.00**
  34 pcs, Lute Song **70.00**
  80 pcs, Lotus **125.00**
Feeders, ½ gal, "Ko-Rec Feed, pat applied for, made only by the Red Wing Union Stoneware Co.," c1929 . . . .   **65.00**

Flower Pot, terra cotta	85.00
Jam Pot, apple shape, high gloss green	15.00
Pitcher, spongeband, advertising . .	115.00

Planters

Ivory bowl, deer flower frog	25.00
Matte chartreuse and green interior, leaf shape, imp Red Wing, #1387	12.00
Shoe, high button, 10"	75.00
Tid Bit Server, Fantasy pattern	25.00

Vases

7", matte blue, shell shape, imp Red Wing U.S.A., #892	8.50
8", white, hobnail decor, imp Red Wing U.S.A., #1208	9.00
11", green high gloss, rose and leaf decor, 2 handles, imp Red Wing Art Pottery, #211	12.00
Wall Pocket, matte ivory, gardenia floral decor	25.00

REDWARE

From the late 1600s on, the availability of clay, the same used to make bricks and roof tiles, accounted for the great production of red earthenware pottery in the American colonies. Redware pieces are mainly utilitarian — bowls, crocks, jugs, etc.

Lead glazed redware retained its reddish color, but a variety of colored glazes were obtained by the addition of metals to the basic glaze. Streaks and mottled splotches in redware items resulted from impurities in the clay and/or uneven firing temperatures.

"Slipware" is a term used to describe redwares decorated by the application of slip, a semi-liquid paste made of clay. Slipwares were made in England, Germany and elsewhere in Europe for decades before becoming popular in the Pennsylvania Dutch country and elsewhere in colonial America.

Banks

4½", seated man holding a pitcher of ale, mottled light and dark brown glaze	150.00
4¾", cat, medium to dark brown glaze	75.00
5", seated monkey, mottled medium brown glaze	150.00
Lion, Wagner, green and cream glaze, Lehigh Valley, PA, type .	1,250.00
Bottle, 9", brown dots, clear glaze, impressed "J. S. Henne"	150.00

Bowls

6¾" d, 4¼" h, mottled green and amber glaze with brown flecks, attr. to Gonic, NH	75.00
7¾" d, 3⅝" h, pale green exterior glaze, brown flecks on interior .	125.00
9½" d, brown glaze, embossed flowers around outside, repaired rim chips	200.00

Chargers

12", 3 yellow line decoration . . .	225.00
12¼" d, 2¼" h, 3 yellow line decoration, coggled edge	250.00
12¼", yellow monogram "MA" in center, coggled edge	400.00
12¾" d, PA, 19th C, finely notched rim, four slip cup, squiggles top and bottom, deep ocean wave across center, red orange ground	1,650.00
13¼", PA, 19th C, finely notched rim, 4 slip cup, corn stalks top and bottom, deep ocean wave across center	775.00
14" d, PA, 19th C, finely notched rim, inscribed in yellow slip "Temperance/Health/Wealth," trailings around borders, heightened with green	4,800.00
Colander, green and brown glaze, worn, 5" h	200.00

Crocks

4", impressed "C. Link," inside glaze	60.00
5", green glaze in spots and yellow stripes	150.00
6", Strasburg, VA, green slip . . .	150.00
Apple Butter, inside glaze, marked "John Bell"	85.00
Cup Plate, 4", yellow slip spring, notched rim	350.00
Custard Cup, 2⅜", inscised bottom "T. S. Stahl, Sept. 1, 1940"	40.00

Dishes

12½" x 2¼", oblong, yellow slip decoration	245.00
15½", loaf, yellow decoration, notched edge	1,150.00

Figures

Dog, fetching, seated, pin pricked & incised fur, small keg in jaws, oblong base inscised with flower chain, reddish brown glaze, splotches of dark brown, 5" h, 4¼" l	1,875.00
Dog, reclining, incised furn, lying before basket of fruit, oval base, border incised with ovals, 4⅛" h, 8" l	450.00
Horse, elongated, incised mane and tail, light orange brown glaze with dark brown drippings, 5½" h, 6¼" l	550.00
Parrot, incised wing and feather detail, mounted on perch, cov. in orange brown glaze, dark brown streaking, 6½" h	1,050.00
Spaniel, seated, 9½" h, stamped "S. Bell & Sons, Strasburg,"	

VA, within a rectangular reserve, 19th C, molded streaky orange-green glaze, leash, collar, and fur incised ovals, circles, and stipples **1,500.00**

Flower Pots
5", reddish brown glaze, attached saucer **75.00**
5¾", brown running glaze, marked "Bell" **300.00**
Brown, cream, and green glaze, double crimped edge, inscribed "Elizabeth Matson, October," attached saucer with double crimped edge, Chester Co., PA **2,300.00**

Frame, 11¾ x 13", oval, pierced work, zig-zag cut edges, green-amber glaze **300.00**

Grotesque Jug, 10¼" h, sgd "Lanier Meaders," Southern, 20th C, white eye balls, streaky olive-green glaze **400.00**

Jars
5½", jelly, dark brown glaze **25.00**
8½", preserving, mottled amber, orange and green drips of white slip, Galena **325.00**
6", ovoid, brown splotches on green glaze **150.00**

Jugs
7¼", marked "John Bell," brown glaze **250.00**
9¼", baluster shape, fitted lid, splotchy dark brown glaze on orange-brown ground, stamped on neck "John Bell, Waynesboro" **1,200.00**

Mantel Ornament, basket overflowing with fruits and leafage, details in green, red, white and brown glaze, basket appliqued with leaf sprigs, attr. to Charles Headman, Bucks Co., PA, mid-19th C, 11½" **1,000.00**

Milk Pans
11½" d, 3¼" h, yellow slip design, small edge chips **200.00**
14¼" d, probably PA, 19th C, deep sided circular bowl, molded lip, decorated with trailings of manganese glaze on orange-brown ground **1,350.00**
18½" d, 8" h, brown-green glaze **60.00**

Miniatures
Chest of Drawers, 13¼ x 7¼ x 14", scalloped apron, 4 drawers, applied decoration around facade and top edge **575.00**
Pelican, pricking its breast, covered in tiny incised circles, lines filled in with yellow slip, body covered in orange-brown glaze, 2" h **400.00**

Mold, fish, orange-brown glaze, 11¾" l **200.00**

Pitchers
6¾", streaky dark brown glaze on orange-brown ground, marked on base "John Bell" **825.00**
7⅝", orange, red, and green mottled glaze, strap handle **250.00**
10", Medinger type, embossed eagle and banner, brown glaze . . **400.00**
Shenandoah type, green, cream and brown glaze **475.00**

Plate, 9½", four slip cup, yellow on reddish brown glaze, $85.00.

Plates
7", Berks County, PA **50.00**
8", PA, c1840-60, sponge decoration on orange-brown ground, incised line around rim **225.00**
8" d, "Wm. Smith, Womelsdorf," PA, 19th C, circular, pinwheels of green and yellow slip on red-brown ground **1,650.00**
8⅞", yellow slip **300.00**
9¼", yellow slip, zig-zags **250.00**
10¼", circular, notched rim, trailings from four slip cup, orange-brown glaze **720.00**
11½", PA, 19th C, circular, stylized four slip tulip in yellow-green highlights, red-brown glaze **1,000.00**
11¾", sgraffito, yellow glaze. green highlights, urn from which radiate five stems (three with tulips, two with daisy or star-like flowers) **7,200.00**

Platter, 14½″, PA, 19th C, rectangular, notched rim, trailings in yellow from single slip cup, green and maganese glaze centering imprint design of parrot surrounded by grapevines **1,750.00**

Puzzle Jug, 8″, yellow slip decoration, John Howarth, 1871 . . . . . . **200.00**

Sander, figural, young girl wearing feathered hat, strumming guitar, long braid down back, orange-yellow glaze, splotches of green and brown, 5½″ h **195.00**

Turksheads

7″ d, 3″ h, mottled green and amber glaze, brown splotches . . . **85.00**

7½″, reddish brown glaze, dark splotches **45.00**

8¾″ d, 3″ h, mottled green, orange and amber glaze, brown exterior splotches **155.00**

9″, brown glaze, fluted sides **95.00**

Whistles

Bird, probably Bell, Pa, c1840, incised wing and feather detail, circular base incised with circle decoration, dark brown glaze, 3½″ **350.00**

Rooster, PA, 19th C, 4¾″, upright, bushy tail with incised feathering, circular foot **275.00**

Slip Cup style, probably Bell, PA, 19th C, bird finial, light orange glaze with splotches of brown . **300.00**

RELIGIOUS ITEMS

Objects for the worshipping or expression of man's belief in a superhuman power are being collected by many people for many reasons.

Icons are included in this category, as they are religious momentos; usually paintings with a brass encasement. They have been collected dating from the earliest time of Christianity. What is available in shops today are usually from the mid-1880s.

Altar Dish, 21¼″ d, SS, George III, London, 1796 . . . . **1,350.00**

Amulet, cartouche form, Eastern silver, Hebrew inscription on chain . **150.00**

Bible Box, carved oak, dated 1613 . **300.00**

Bibles, see Bibles

Bookends, chalkware, sleeping child Jesus on one, John the Baptist on other **65.00**

Chalice, Communion, sterling stem, base, glass bowl **22.00**

Cross, Schrezheim figure of Christ crucified on wooden cross, c1770 **2,250.00**

Bank, 8½″ h, cast iron, Christ Child with lamb, painted yellow, $30.00.

Figures

Continental, 5¾″, Virgin and Child, carved ivory, lapis lazuli base, glass dome case **100.00**

Italian, 14″, angels, polychrome, wood, 18th C, pr **1,250.00**

Spanish, polychrome, wood, 18th C **600.00**

Font, hanging, porcelain, white with gold, Germany **65.00**

Icons

Greek, Virgin and Child, carved gilt wood border, 17th C, 7¼″ h **1,300.00**

Russian, Mother Of God Of The Burning Book, 19th C, 12¼ x 10½″ **900.00**

Russian, Resurrection, gilded ground, surrounded by 12 feast days of the Orthodox Church . . **1,100.00**

Plaque, 13″ d, Christ in wheat field, sgd J. Austin, c1851, F&R Pratt, Fenton, Staffordshire **90.00**

Prayer Book, ivory and silver inlaid case **145.00**

Reliquary, 7″ l, carved calnut in form of ship, hinged top opening both sides, one lid carved with peasant against scrolling foliate ground, other with seated man and priest, wood stand, Dutch, late 17th C . . **400.00**

REVERSE PAINTING ON GLASS

Reverse painting on glass was produced in parts of Europe in the 17th century and a similar technique was applied by the Chinese as early as the 13th century. However, reverse painting on glass did not reach any significance in America until the 18th century.

European artists preferred classical and mythological scenes. In America, the subject matter was usually confined to patriotism, family mourning pictures and traditional still life.

Quality and demand for such paintings decreased with the advent of less expensive methods of print making. By the 1850s, most reverse paintings on glass were executed by non-professionals and are rarely signed.

Portraits
Chinese ladies, one seated playing flute beside small covered table; other seated by table with long stemmed pipe and incense, Chippendale frame, Chinese, 19th C, pr	1,200.00
Gentleman in blue coat, orange collar, green background, "Wolf" in white margin, probably George Wolf, govenor of PA, 1829–1835, 11 x 9"	650.00
Gentleman in long curly wig, 7 x 9"	125.00
Lady, seated with small dog, oval, black frame, French, 19th C, 12"	250.00
Lafayette, half length portrait, 19th C, 7½ x 10¾"	350.00
Washington, George, bust, framed, 27½ x 23⅜"	250.00
Young woman with flowers in her hair, "Portugesrin," wood frame, 13⅜ x 14⅜"	300.00

Scenes
Canal scene, figures, framed, French, mid-19th C, 9 x 12" . .	125.00

Cottage scene, MOP on house, gilt plaster on frame, 12 x 24", $75.00.

Pastoral scene, dirt lane with cottage in background, sgd "Ray," wood, plaster gilt frame, 16 x 20⅛"	65.00
Statue of Liberty, oval frame	95.00
U.S. Capitol, oval frame	95.00
Vase of flowers, black ground, 15 x 18"	85.00

RIDGWAY

The name Ridgway has been prominent in English pottery since the early 1800s. Two firms, J. and W. Ridgway and William Ridgway, operated in Shelton during the 1800s, producing a series of historical scenes. Most early wares marked "Ridgway" were made by one of these two firms. Ridgway Potteries, Ltd. continues the operation today in England.

See also STAFFORDSHIRE

Plate, 9", Coaching Days and Ways, brown, silver lustre trim, $40.00.

Ashtray, matchbox holder, 3½" h x 5" d, metal holder, Coaching Days	50.00
Box, cov, 2¼ x 4¼ x 5½", Coaching Days, caramel color, black forms	110.00
Cheese, cov, light brown floral transfer	50.00
Chocolate Pot, 9", portrait of girl and on reverse, brown and yellow high glaze, silver sculptured spout, handle and finial	100.00
Creamer and Sugar, cov, white ground, gray shading, gold trim . .	65.00
Cup Plate, Marmora	35.00
Jug, 7", salt glaze, Drab Ware, pew-	

ter top, tavern scene decor, marked "Ridgway, Oct. 1, 1835" . . **145.00**

Mug, 3½", Coaching Days and Ways, silver lustre rim, handle . . **50.00**

Pitchers

3½", Mr. Pickwick, silver lustre rim, handle **55.00**

6½", white ground, brown transfer **30.00**

10½", Jousting knights on blue-gray stoneware, dated 1840 . . **165.00**

Plates

9", Coaching Days and Ways—Paying Toll, brown with silver lustre trim **45.00**

9", Mormon Temple Square, Salt Lake City, Utah **32.50**

9½", Etruscan Festoon **50.00**

9½", Italian Flower Garden, scalloped floral border, center scene florals with building in background, c1814–30 . . . . . . **55.00**

Platter, 19½ x 16", Hawthorne, blue and white, c1843 . . . . **165.00**

Syrup Pitcher, 6", pewter top, dated 1835 . . . . **150.00**

Teapot, cov, 5¼" h x 5¼" d, Coaching Days, Racing The Mail, black, silver trim **95.00**

RING TREES

A ring tree is a small, generally saucer shaped object made of glass, porcelain, metal or wood, with a center post in the shape of a hand, branches, or cylinder for hanging or storing finger rings.

Pairpoint, 3⅛ x 2⅛ x 3¼", $125.00.

Glass

Cranberry, white enamel decor, gold trim, 4" **60.00**

Cut glass, clear, 3½" **78.00**

Gray, bristol-type, hp florals **40.00**

Milk, pink roses, green leaves, 3" . . **40.00**

Opaline

Blue, gold decor, 2½" **55.00**

Green, ftd **45.00**

Metal

Bronze, parrot, figural, 5 x 3" **45.00**

Iron, hand shape **15.00**

Sterling Silver, saucer base, shepherds crook style 3 holder extensions, 2 x 3 " d, mkd R W & S . . **125.00**

Porcelain

Austrian, white, yellow flowers **28.00**

Austrian, attached hatpin holder, white with pink roses, gold trim . . **55.00**

Bavarian, hp floral decor, gold trim, 3" **30.00**

Carlsbad, white, floral decor, gold trim, mkd **25.00**

English, tree branch, saucer base, blue and white, English lion and shield mark **25.00**

Haviland, hp floral sprays on white, gold trim **30.00**

Limoges, hand-shaped, gold ring, bracelet, pink roses, gold trim . . . **45.00**

Nippon, hand-shaped, hp roses . . . **30.00**

Parian, hand shape, molded leaves on base **45.00**

ROCKINGHAM WARE

Rockingham earthenware was first produced on the estate of the Marquis de Rockingham, Yorkshire, England in 1745. A succession of potters followed for almost 100 years. The well known dark brown high glaze pottery known as "Rockingham," was introduced by Brameld and Co., Swainton, England, in 1788. Porcelain of great artistic beauty was also made at the same factory in the 1820s and continued until the firm was dissolved in 1842.

The Rockingham-type glaze was used in the United States by various potteries including the Bennington, Vermont works.

See also BENNINGTON.

Bank, house, 3¾", emb detail **185.00**

Bowl, 5 x 11¾", mottled brown . . . **95.00**

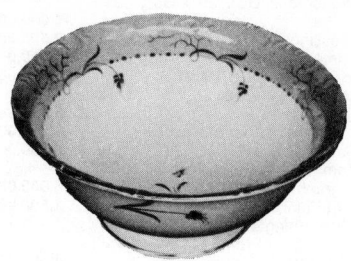

Bowl, 3¼″ h x 7⅜″ d, blue with mocha and gold, unmarked, $65.00.

Creamer, 4½″	50.00
Cuspidor, mottled brown	85.00
Dish, 7¼″, emb rim	65.00
Humidor, 6½″, emb trees	45.00
Jar, cov, 8¼ x 8¾″ d, ...	135.00
Mug, 3″, vertical ribs	60.00
Pie Plate, 9″	90.00
Pitcher, 10¾″, hound handle, emb stag, boar, rabbit, 2 eagles and 2 cats	60.00
Plate, 10½″, mottled brown	65.00
Platter, 13⅝″, octagonal	130.00
Shoe Bottle, 6½″, emb side laces, imp Victoria	32.00
Soap Dish, 2⅜ x 6″	95.00
Soup Plate, 10¼″	32.00
Stirrup Cup, shape of hound's head, lions, mottled brown, 19th C	125.00
Teapot, 6″, wire handle	95.00
Toby Pitcher, 6″	58.00
Turk's Head Mold, 6⅝″	90.00
Watering Can, 6½″, green, floral and gold trim	125.00

ROCKWELL, NORMAN

Norman Rockwell's influence on many forms of creative production—from bells and plates to coins and figurines—requires this separate category of Rockwell "collectibles." These items are not antiques as such; but they demand attention because of the popularity of the artist and the increased demand for reproduced versions of his work since his death on November 8, 1978.

Born in 1894, Norman Rockwell was America's best known and prolific artist and illustrator. He produced over 3000 works, including 323 "Saturday Evening Post" covers, "Boy's Life" covers and calendars, plus over 1,500 paintings for various advertisers. Rockwell works with the most value are the original illustrations and limited edition lithographs.

In the months following his death, prices began to skyrocket. In 1979, they tended to fluctuate. In 1980 and 1981, prices stabilized and in many instances have fallen drastically.

See *Warman's Americana & Collectibles* for an expanded listing of Norman Rockwell.

Magazine Cover, illustration, Saturday Evening Post, May 24, 1958, $20.00.

Bells

1974 Sweet Song So Young, 9″ . . .	85.00
1975 Santa's Helper, 9″	45.00
Royal Devon, Butter Girl, 1976	40.00

Coins

Ford Motor Co., 50th Anniversary . .	25.00
Four Freedoms, Kennedy Mint, set of four	150.00
Four Seasons, Hamilton Mint, L.E., set of four	90.00

Figurines

Gorham Fine China	
At the Vets, ...	40.00
Batter Up, ...	55.00
Pride of Parenthood, ...	60.00
Tiny Tim, ...	65.00
Gorham Fine China, "Four Seasons," sets of four.	
1972, Puppy Love	500.00
1973, Four Seasons Childhood . .	500.00
Grossman Designs, Inc. L.E.-1000	
1974, Baseball, NR102, (Closed)	200.00
1975, Barbershop Quartet, NR23	125.00

1976, Tom Sawyer Series No. 1, (Closed) 100.00

Ingots and Medals

Franklin Mint
Fondest Memories, SS, set of 10, 1973 .... 325.00
Tribute to Robert Frost, 1974 ... 285.00
Hamilton Mint
Four Freedoms, set of 4, silver, 1974 .... 250.00
Portraits of America, silver, set of 24 .... 825.00

Ornaments

Gorham, Four Seasons, 1976 .... 25.00
Grossman Designs, Inc.
1975 .... 24.00
1978, The Carrolers, NRX-3, L.E. (Closed) 35.00
1979, Drum for Tommy, NRX-24, L.E. 30.00
Hallmark Cards, Inc.
1975 .... 25.00
1976 .... 18.00
1977 .... 15.00

Plates

Franklin Mint
1970, F.E., Bringing Home the Tree, sterling 330.00
1971, Under the Mistletoe, sterling 172.00
1973, Trimming the Tree, sterling 167.00
Gorham Christmas
1970, F.E., Family Tree 125.00
1974, F.E., Christmas, Tiny Tim . 65.00
Gorham Fine China, "Four Seasons," sets of four.
1971, A Boy and His Dog 418.00
1973, Ages of Love 300.00
1975, Me and My Pal 200.00
1977, Going on Sixteen 240.00
1979, Helping Hand 70.00
1981, Old Times 100.00
Rockwell Museum, Baby's First Step, 1978 .... 80.00
Rockwell Society of America
1974, F.E., Christmas, Scotty Gets His Tree 160.00
1976, F.E., Mother's Day, A Mother's Love 120.00
Royal Devon
1975, F.E., Christmas, Downhill Daring 49.00
1975, F.E., Mother's Day, Doctor and Doll 85.00

Prints

Circle Gallery, Ltd.
Children At the Window, 20 x 26", lithograph 1,700.00

Doctor and Doll, 29 x 35", collotype 10,000.00
Dressing Up, pencil sgd 2,800.00
Family Tree, 20 x 35", lithograph . 4,500.00
Icabod Crane 5,300.00
Marriage License, 28 x 32", collotype 6,000.00
Music Hath Charms 3,000.00
Saying Grace 6,500.00
Tom Sawyer Folio, 20 x 26", lithograph, set of eight 16,000.00
Wet Paint, 24 x 30", collotype ... 1,500.00
Eleanor Ettinger, Inc.
After the Prom, 24 x 26¾", lithograph 4,400.00
Ben Franklin, 21 x 28", lithograph 4,000.00
Gilding the Eagle, 21 x 25½", lithograph 3,200.00
Swing, The, 20 x 21", lithograph . 4,700.00
Young Lincoln, 19 x 34", lithograph 10,000.00

Miscellaneous

Ads, individual, approximate value, in excellent condition 5–10.00
Magazine Covers, S.E.P. including other publications, approximate value, in excellent condition.
1920–1930, each 20.00
1930–1940, each 15.00
1940–1960, each 10.00
Thimble, Gorham, 1980, Tiny Tim .. 18.00
Trays
10½ x 13", Coca-Cola, 1931 .... 200.00
11" round, 1976, The Country Postman, US Postal Credit Union 15.00

ROGERS STATUARY

John Rogers, born in America in 1829, studied sculpturing in Europe and produced his first plaster-of-paris statue, "The Checker Players," in 1859, followed by "The Slave Auction" in 1860.

His works were popular parlor pieces of the Victorian era. He published at least 80 different subjects and the total number of groups produced from the originals is estimated to be over 100,000.

It has been determined that "Romeo and Juliet," "Is That You, Tommy?" and "A Capitol Joke" were never listed in Rogers' catalogue. They were the work of Casper Hennecke, one of Rogers' contemporaries, who operated in Milwaukee, Wisconsin, and appeared in the Hennecke catalogue.

Hennecke operated C. Hennecke & Company from 1881 until 1896. His statuary often is confused with Rogers' work since both are very similar. Hennecke is responsible for many of the statues incorrectly identified as Rogers. A good source on Hennecke's works is Betty C. Haverly's *Hennecke's Florentine Statuary*, 1972, privately printed. This is a reprint of an original Hennecke catalog.

It is difficult to find a statue in undamaged condition and with original paint. Use the following conversions: 10% minor flaking; 10% chips; 10–20% piece or pieces broken and reglued; 20% flaking; 50% repainting.

A good reference for Rogers works is Paul & Meta Bleier, *John Rogers' Groups of Statuary*, 1971.

Council of War, Type C, 24", $450.00.

ROGERS

Balcony, The, 11/4/1879, 32½" h, orig paint, some flaking, violin repaired	600.00
Bath, The, 1893, 26½", minor chips, 1 of 6 known	2,100.00
Council of War, Type A, 3/31/1868, 24½"	875.00
Council of War, Type B, 3/31/1868, orig paint, flaked, chip in chair cover, document cracked	550.00
Faust & Margureite — Leaving The Garden, 11/1890, 25½"	400.00
Football, 10/1891, 16"	600.00
Fugitive's Story, The, 1869, 22"	300.00
Ha? I Like Not That, 10/31/1822, 22"	450.00
Mail Day, 4/19/1864, 16"	650.00
Matter of Opinion, 12/9/1884, 21½"	550.00

One More Shot, 1/17/1865, 24"	425.00
Referee, The, 11/23/1880, 22", repainted	350.00
School Days, 1877, 21½"	700.00
Taking The Oath, Drawing Rations, 1/30/1866, 23¼"	425.00
Union Refugees, spelter, 4/19/1864, 1 of 7 known, chip on hammer of rifle	1,100.00

ROGERS TYPE

After The Case, 20"	100.00
By Jingo, 17", orig paint, minor chipping	125.00
Can't You Talk, 10½"	115.00
Family Cares, 13"	95.00
First Love, 13", repainted	170.00
Flight Into Egypt, 11"	220.00
Holy Family, 18"	225.00
Lost & Found, The, 19"	100.00
Romeo & Juliet, 16"	145.00
Wellers, The, 11½"	300.00

ROOKWOOD POTTERY

Mrs. Marie Longworth Nicholas Storer, Cincinnati, Ohio, founded Rookwood Pottery in 1880. The name of this outstanding American art pottery came from her family estate "Rookwood," named for the rooks (crows) which inhabited the wooded grounds.

There are five elements to the Rookwood marking system — the clay or body mark, the size mark, the decorator mark, the date mark, and the factory mark. Rookwood art pottery can best be dated from factory marks.

In 1880–1882 the factory mark was the name "Rookwood" incised or painted on the base. Between 1881 and 1886 the firm name, address, and year appeared in an oval frame. Beginning in 1886, the impressed "RP" monogram appeared and a flame-mark was added for each year until 1900. After 1900 a Roman numeral, indicating the last two digits of the year of production, was added at the bottom of the "RP" flame-mark monogram. This last mark is the one most often found on Rookwood pottery today.

Though the Rookwood pottery filed for bankruptcy in 1941, it was soon reorganized under new management. Efforts at maintaining the pottery proved futile and it again was sold in 1956 and in 1959. The pottery was moved to Starkville, MI, in conjunction with the Herschede Clock Co. It finally ceased operation in 1967.

Rookwood wares changed with the times. The variety is endless, in part because of the great variations in glazes and designs due to the creativity of the many talented artists.

Mug, 5″ h, portrait of monk, dark glaze, #853, artist Harriet Wilcox, 1899, $1,350.00.

Ashtray, 7″, Rook with outstretched wing, 1925, blue glaze	95.00
Bookends	
Colonial Girls, 6½″, 1924, white glaze	145.00
Sailing Ships, 7″, 1935, blue glaze	165.00
Sphinx, 7″, 1922, brown glaze . .	350.00
Bowl, 12 x 3½″, artist LA, 1923, yellow ground, multicolored floral design, wax matte	350.00
Cup and Saucer, 2½ x 4½″, sgd Sara Sax, 1897, holly leaves and berries, standard glaze	295.00
Ewers	
8″, nasturtiums, artist sgd Sallie Coyne, 1892, standard glaze . .	350.00
9¼″, yellow daisies on brown aventurine ground, Tiger Eye, sgd AMB, 1887, standard glaze	800.00
Figurals	
6 x 14½″, Pheasant, artist sgd K. Shirayamadani, 1945, multicolored	450.00
7″, seated cat, 1938, celadon green glaze	195.00
Lamp, 14½″, pink floral decoration on cream ground, artist LH, 1942,	

classic shape, jeweled porcelain glaze	300.00
Mugs	
5″, dog portrait, artist sgd MAD, 1897, standard glaze	950.00
5½″, carved matt, artist sgd AP, 1905, matte green glaze, carved oak leaves	165.00
Pitcher, 8″, Limoge-style, artist sgd ARV, 1882, pink and blue ground, white flowers, touches of gold . .	900.00
Plaques	
7¼ x 9¼″, scenic vellum, sgd Sara Sax, 1917, winter landscape	1,100.00
8¾ x 11″, scenic vellum, artist sgd ETH, 1914, birch trees, pink sky	900.00
Teapot, 7¼″, artist sgd O.G.R., 1892, thistle decor, standard glaze	550.00
Tiles	
6″, round tea tile, 1935, swimming fish	145.00
6 x 6″, architectural, stylized rose, pink and green	125.00
6 x 6″, tea tile, 1924, parrots . . .	125.00
12 x 12″, architectural, standing cherubs	300.00
Vases	
4½″, red and yellow flowers, beige ground, sgd Sara Sax, 1924, wax matte	250.00
4½ x 5½″, stylized blue fish on cream ground, artist sgd J. Jensen, 1943, jeweled porcelain glaze	375.00
6″, bud vase, floral, sgd CCN, 1897, standard glaze	195.00
6 x 7½″, brown, carved band of flowers, artist sgd CST, incised matte	450.00
6¼″, wisteria, artist sgd BH, 1893, standard glaze	375.00
6¼ x 8½″, white magnolia blossoms on cream ground, sgd WR, 1934, jeweled porcelain glaze	450.00
6½″, bud vase, pink floral, artist CST, 1919, wax matte	125.00
6¾″, Art Deco motif, artist sgd LA, 1923, wax matte	285.00
7″, branches with blossoms, artist sgd E.N., 1897, standard glaze .	325.00
7″, vellum, floral in shades of blue and lavender, artist sgd HEW, 1907	375.00
7″, vellum, slender shape, forget-me-not flowers on pastel blue ground, artist sgd LA, 1923 . . .	300.00
7½″, blue ground with multicolored pansies, sgd LA, 1925, late Iris glaze	550.00
8″, vellum, stylized peacock feath-	

ers in blue on green ground, sgd Sara Sax, 1910 . . . . 800.00

8½", pink iris on ivory shading to gray ground, artist sgd CS, 1907, Iris glaze 850.00

9", three birds on branch, artist sgd SEC, 1924, wax matte, gray, green, yellow glaze 800.00

10¾", scenic vellum, blue and pink river landscape, artist sgd ETH, 1939 . . . . 850.00

12", stylized motif, artist sgd S. Sax, 1909, incised matte, red and green glaze 450.00

ROSE BOWLS

A Rose Bowl is a decorative open bowl with a crimped or pinched top used to contain fragrant rose petals and a potpourri. The bowl was placed on a table top and the pleasant aroma scented the room. A popular room accessory in the late Victorian period, Rose Bowls were made in a variety of patterns by practically every glass manufacturer of the period, including fine art glass.

See specific categories for additional listings.

Applied gold and tortoise shell decor, 3" h, $125.00.

Amberina, 5 x 6", ribbed, cranberry shaded to olive amber, white, and pink blossoms, tan branches . . . 235.00

Amethyst, squat, enameled, fluted top 75.00

Cameo Glass, 4⅜ x 4¼", opaque white overlay over frosted blue, cut scalloped top, flowers and design cut through white to blue . . . 395.00

Cranberry, 4½ x 5" d, coinspot, baby inverted thumbprint, 8 loop mouth 165.00

Cut Glass, 3½ x 4", cut hobs, strawberry diamond, fan, single star, hobs base 165.00

Fenton, 5½", cranberry opal, hobnail 145.00

Pomona, 5½ x 4", amber stain, inverted thumbprint, 3 legs 150.00

Rubena, 4 x 4¾", ivy pattern, bulbous, swirl ribs 70.00

Satin Glass, 4⅜ x 4¼", shaded blue, white lining, 8 crimp top, frosted petal feet, cream florals, raised gold color branches, lacy foliage 135.00

Vaseline to green, 4½", blown swirl with elaborate enameling 95.00

ROSE CANTON, ROSE MANDARIN, ROSE MEDALLION

The pink rose color has given its name to three related groups of Chinese export porcelain. Rose Mandarin was produced from the late 18th century to approximately 1840. Rose Canton began somewhat later extending through the first half of the 19th century. Rose Medallion originated in the early 19th century and was made through the early 20th century.

Rose Mandarin derives its name from the Mandarin figure(s) found in garden scenes with women and children. The woman often feature gold decorations in their hair. Polychrome enamels and birds separate the scenes.

Rose Medallion has alternating panels of figures and birds and flowers. The elements are four in number, separated evenly around a center medallion. Peonies and foliage fill voids.

Rose Canton is similar to Rose Medallion except the figure panels are replaced by flowers. People are present only if the medallion partitions are absent. Some patterns have been named—Butterfly and Cabbage, Rooster, etc. The category actually is a catchall for all pink enamel ware not fitting into the first two groups.

Rose Medallion still is made, although the quality does not match the earlier examples.

ROSE CANTON

Bowls

5", birds, butterflies and roses, marked 80.00

11½", green, alternating sections of figures and florals 285.00

Brush Pot, 4½", scenic, ladies, reticulated, gilt trim 250.00

Charger, 13", floral panels, 19th C . 210.00

Cup and Saucer, demitasse, floral panels, c1860 .... **50.00**
Dish, 10¾", round, floral and butterflies, c1850 .... **125.00**
Plates
- 7½" **45.00**
- 8½", floral decor **75.00**

Sugar Bowl, cov, handled **95.00**
Tazza, pedestal base, flower and butterfly medallions **300.00**
Teapot, cov, 5", flowers and butterflies **125.00**
Tureen, cov, soup, 11", lozenge shape, gilt floral ground, figural scenes **295.00**
Vases
- 9", double gourd shape, key fret border rim **265.00**
- 10½", medallions with flowers, birds and butterflies, floral borders, mid-19th C **400.00**

Vegetable Dish, 8½", oval, scalloped rim **150.00**
Wall Sconces, round, ormolu mounts, early 19th C, pr **950.00**

ROSE MANDARIN

Brush Box, 4", oval **145.00**
Cup and Saucer, scenic panels, butterfly and floral border **135.00**
Garden Seats, 18½", early 19th C, pr **4,500.00**
Plate, 12", scenic center, garden setting, border reserved with panels of bats **300.00**
Teapot, 7½", enamel, orange, pink, green, lavender and yellow with manderin panels, gilding **680.00**
Vase, 4¼", square, gilt handles, pr **220.00**
Vegetable Dish, scalloped cov, 10", birds, flowers and butterfly panels and borders, boating scene on cover **650.00**

ROSE MEDALLION

Bowls
- 2¼ x 4¾" d, florals and figures . **58.00**
- 3½ x 6¾" d **65.00**

Butter Pat, 3", round **45.00**
Candlesticks, 7½", pr **700.00**
Chamberpot, cov, 10" d, handled . . **600.00**
Cups and Saucers
- 2½" h cup, wishbone handle, 6½" d saucer **75.00**
- Bouillon **35.00**
- Letter "C" in a round gilded medallion **110.00**

Dish, cov, 4⅜ x 5⅜", oval, letter "C" in two round guilded medallions on lid, fruit finial **250.00**
Flower Pot, 3¼", three small feet . . **170.00**
Fruit Bowl, 4h x 10½ x 9½", oval, pierced, mkd Made in China **350.00**

Rose Medallion, vegetable, cov, 8¼ x 9½", nut finial, c1775, $275.00.

Mug, 5½", reserves of figures and birds amidst flowers, braided handle, 19th C **200.00**
Plates
- 7½", quatrefoil shape, reserves of figures and birds, c1860 ..... **55.00**
- 9½" **80.00**

Platters
- 12", oblong, flowers and birds, c1840 .... **185.00**
- 18", oval, c1850 .... **325.00**

Pomade Jar, 2½ x 2¼", cylindrical, scenic lid, man and woman at window **115.00**
Punch Bowl, 18¾", green and gilt foliage, circular panels, lord in a palace, ladies, birds and flowers, court life, early 19th C **1,650.00**
Sauce Boat, 4¼", inner border with rose and butterfly decor, exterior, household scenes, orange glaze . **140.00**
Saucer, 5" d, figures in pavillion, birds and flowers border, c1830 . . **65.00**
Soap Dish, 3 pcs **185.00**
Soup Plate, 2⅛ x 9" d **55.00**
Spoon, 5" **16.00**
Sugar Bowl, cov, 4¼", intertwined handles, fruit finial **125.00**
Teapots
- 3¼", domed lid **90.00**
- 5⅝", intertwined strap handle, fruit finial **195.00**

Tureen, cov, underplate, twisted handles, small **950.00**
Vases
- 6¾", bud, cylindrical, 2 cartouches, 3 Oriental figures in courtyard, bird, butterfly, flowers and leaves, scalloped turquoise border **125.00**
- 7¼", stylized fish around neck . . **175.00**
- 10 x 4½", figures and flowers . . . **280.00**

Vegetable Dish, cov, 4½ x 8¾ x 11¼", almond shape, letter "C" in gilded medallions on lid and in center of dish, orange glaze **450.00**

ROSE O'NEILL

Warman's Americana & Collectibles, 1st Edition, contains 60 listings in this category; see also page xii.

ROSENTHAL

Rosenthal Porcelain Manufactory began operating at Selb, Bavaria, in 1880. Specialties were tablewares and figurines. According to recent reports, the firm is still in operation.

Goldfish, 10¼", artist-Heldenreich, $750.00.

Bowls
7 x 4", octagan, floral decor, gold trim 32.00
10", pierced handles, dark blue, gold tracery 65.00
Candlesticks, 2¾", white, gold trim, pr 35.00
Chocolate Set, pot, creamer, cov sugar, violets in relief on white, gold finials and handles 150.00
Cream and Sugar, pink florals, gold trim 35.00
Cups and Saucers, demitasse
Ivory with gold bandings and handles 28.00
Silver Overlay, Art Nouveau 35.00

Dinner Set, Maria pattern, white, molded flower decor rims, green mark, 51 pcs 250.00
Egg Cup, small, white 12.50
Ewer, 9", pink floral decor 58.00
Figurines
Boy with lamb, 6" 125.00
Dancers, 12", two in blue gowns, "Heidi and Margot Hopfner in Kaiser Walzer," white oval base, imp sgr Lore F. Gronau 225.00
Dachshund, 7", porcelain 150.00
Finch, 4½", artist sgd 45.00
Rabbit, 6", white 70.00
Satyr, flanked by 2 semi nude nymphs, artist sgd, A. Caasmann 352.00
Street Musician, artist sgd 125.00
Lamp Base, 14", shaded pink to mauve, matchng parchment shade, sgd Rosenthal Selb Bavaria, BMG 1925 .... 50.00
Mug, barrel shape, strawberry decor 60.00
Mustard, cov, with underplate spray of pink roses 58.00
Pitcher, 5½", pink roses on white . 40.00
Plates
4", roses, SS trim 20.00
10¾", service, white, 2½" heavy gold border, c1920 .... 95.00
14", Marie Theresia 35.00
Platter, 10¾", white, 1½" border of florals and birds, open handles, Donatello 55.00
Teapot, cov, Art Nouveau, silver overlay on light blue ground 125.00
Tureen, cov, 10", gold trim on white 65.00
Vases
5 x 6½", fan shape, beige, white Pate-sur-pate angel fish swimming in sea grass 80.00
9", Art Nouveau style decor, artist sgd 160.00

ROSEVILLE POTTERY

Incorporated in 1892 at Roseville, Ohio, Roseville Pottery originally produced only utilitarian wares at plants in Roseville and, after 1898, in Zanesville, Ohio. In 1910 work ceased at the Roseville plant and continued in Zanesville until 1954.

In 1900, art pottery was introduced and the popular glazed "Rozane" line was developed. Roseville art wares were made with many types of decoration, slip, decals, free hand,

incised and embossed designs. In 1918, a new trademark, "Roseville U.S.A." was adopted.

In 1920, machine-made pottery replaced the hand made wares and very little free hand decoration was used.

Much of the early Roseville production is decorator signed. Factory marks, impressed, ink stamped or paper stickers, may be used to date Roseville art wares.

See *Warman's Americana & Collectibles* for an expanded listing of Roseville Pottery.

Tea set, Dutch scenes, 3 pcs, $395.00.

Ashtray, Donatello, 3", no mark . . .	45.00
Banks	
Monkey, 5½"	125.00
Pig, 5 x 2½", no mark	65.00
Baskets	
Blackberry, hanging, 4½ x 6½", 1933	225.00
Morning Glory, handled, 10½", paper label	250.00
Windsor, handled, 4½", 1931 . . .	195.00
Bookends, White Rose, 6½"	65.00
Bowls	
Della Robia, 8 x 2½", 1906, incised dragons	950.00
Donatello, 12", no mark	95.00
Ferella, 12 x 7", paper label	195.00
Sunflower, 3 x 12½", paper label	125.00
Candlesticks	
Falline, 4½", 1933, paper label, pr	150.00
Morning Glory, 5", 1935, pr	195.00
Rozane, 4½", RP Co die stamp, floral	95.00
Ewer, Rozane, 7½", floral, RP Co die stamp #857	175.00
Jardinieres	
Dogwood I, 5"	125.00
Magnolia, 8", blue	150.00
Poppy, 7", pink	125.00
Jardinieres and Pedestals	
Dogwood I, 30", Rv ink stamp . . .	450.00
Foxglove #659, 30½"	400.00
Jonquil, 29"	550.00

Lamps	
Cherry Blossom, 14½"	195.00
Ferella, 10½", 1931	300.00
Mugs	
Azureau, 4½", 1902, slip painted clover, blue glaze	350.00
Rozane, 6", floral decor, RP Co mark	95.00
Pitchers	
Holland, 9½", emb Dutch figures	125.00
"The Owl," 6½"	150.00
Planter, Rosecraft Vintage, 11½ x 6", 1924, Rv ink stamp	150.00
Tankards	
Rozane, brown glaze with blackberries, 14", Rozane seal	350.00
Rozane Royal, 16", gray to cream ground with ear of corn	650.00
Umbrella Stand, 20½", Bushberry, Roseville in relief #779-20	250.00
Vases	
Aztec, 8", blue with squeeze bag decor in white, no mark	250.00
Fujiyama, 9", 1906, bisque ground, glazed floral decor, Fijiyama ink stamp	850.00
Futura, 9", handled, no mark . . .	175.00
Mongol, 8", 1904, ox-blood red glaze, Rozane ware seal	650.00
Pinecone, 14½", 1931, brown, imp #850-14	195.00
Rozane, 6½", brown glaze, yellow flowers, RPCo stamp	150.00
Rozane, 10", handled, daffodils, artist sgd Timberlake	275.00
Wall Pockets	
Ceramic Design, 11", no mark . .	150.00
Cherry Blossom, 8", paper label .	250.00
Panel nude, 7", Rv ink stamp . . .	200.00

ROYAL BAYREUTH CHINA

The Royal Bayreuth factory was founded in Tettau, Bavaria, in 1794 and has continued production to the present. Currently the factory is producing dinnerware with no attempts to duplicate their earlier wares, primarily the figural line.

The figural series were introduced in 1885 as inexpensive souvenir items. Designs included animals, people, fruits, vegetables and others in a wide array of tablewares.

Not all the wares were marked or the stamped mark did not prove permanent. The Royal Bayreuth crest mark varied in design and color over the years and it is impossible to verify the chronological years of production due to the lack of authentic records.

The pattern "Rose Tapestry" was made by Royal Bayreuth, Germany, in the late 19th century. The surface of the ware feels and looks like woven cloth. It was created by covering porcelain with a piece of fabric tightly stretched over the surface, then decorated and glazed. It is very expensive when found by collectors now. There were other patterns made with the tapestry background but Rose Tapestry seems to be most popular with collectors.

See also SUNBONNET BABIES.

See *Warman's Americana & Collectibles* for additional listings of Royal Bayreuth China.

Creamer, goats on mountainside, 4" h, $150.00.

Corinthian Pattern
Humidor, cov	195.00
Loving Cup, 3¾" h, 3 handles	75.00
Pitcher, 5"	40.00
Planter	55.00

Devil and Cards Pattern
Candleholder	175.00
Creamer	125.00
Pitchers	
5½", green mark	225.00
6½", blue mark	265.00
8", water	250.00
Stamp Box, cov	250.00

Lobster Pattern
Ashtray, 6¼" l	45.00
Creamer	35.00
Dish, cov, 3¾", red lobster, green underplate	30.00
Celery Tray, 12½" l	60.00
Salad Bowl, 8" d, green mark	100.00
Sauce	65.00
Sugar, cov	110.00

Miscellaneous Patterns
Ashtrays	
Eagle, green mark	200.00
Hunter, dogs, cows, heart shape	65.00
Scenic	35.00
Bowl, scenic, 7¾", elk in lake, gazebo, trees, green ground	145.00
Candleholder, handle, farm scene	80.00
Candlesticks	
Clown	150.00
Girl and Dog, 6½", pr	85.00
Candy Dish, oval, Bavarian women, horses	60.00
Chocolate Pot, cov, boy seated on log, 3 donkeys	245.00
Creamers	
Alligator	195.00
Eagle	125.00
Elk	57.00
Lemon	90.00
Parakeet	125.00
Poodle, black	195.00
Robin	175.00
Santa Claus	800.00
Seal	220.00
Sheep, scenic, green base	85.00
Creamers and Sugars	
Apple	210.00
Conch shell, spikey, MOP	65.00
Cups and Saucers, figural rose	
Demitasse	175.00
Tea	180.00
Hair Receiver, cov, octagonal, ivory, gold decor	65.00
Hatpin Holder, oyster and pearl	200.00
Match Holders, hanging	
Shell, MOP, green and gold	60.00
Poppy, white, MOP	110.00
Pin Cushion, elk	75.00
Pitchers	
4¼", Parrot	145.00
5¼", Brittany Girls, green base, scenic top	65.00
5½", Ye Old Lantern	70.00
5½", Eagle	170.00
8", 3 cows on top half, trees on yellow base	80.00
8½", hound decor	225.00
8½", Elk	225.00
Plates	
6", Goose Girl	65.00
7", Jack and Beanstalk	60.00
Powder Jar, hunt scene	100.00
Salt and Pepper Shakers, grapes, purple, pr	129.00
Sauce Dish, grape cluster, figural, yellow	80.00

Soap Dish, 5¾ x 3¼", fishing scene	65.00
Spooner, 6¼ x 3¼", handled, blooming roses decor	45.00
String Holder, rooster	180.00
Toothpick, 2¾", pastoral scene of woman gathering grain, ftd	45.00

Trays

Goose Girl	135.00
Jack Horner, club shape	65.00

Vases

3¼", hp, pastoral scene	66.00
4¼", 3 cows, white birch trees	65.00
Polar Bear	75.00

Poppy Pattern

Bowls

5¾"	60.00
6"	85.00
Creamer, 3¾"	150.00
Gravy Boat, green leaf underplate	35.00
Mustard, 3¼"	60.00
Nut Bowl, 4¾" w x 2¾" h	60.00
Plate, 5¾"	45.00
Teapot, cov	175.00

Sand Babies

Dresser Tray	150.00
Planter, 3" h, 2 handles	100.00
Sugar	65.00
Wall Pocket	165.00

Snow Babies

Cereal Set, nursery rhyme, sledding	150.00
Inkwell	95.00
Match Holder, hanging	125.00
Plate, 6", babies playing	62.00

Sunbonnet Babies

Bowl, 3¼", babies cleaning	195.00
Candlestick, 4¼" h, babies sweeping	200.00
Card Tray, heart shape, babies scrubbing	145.00
Creamer, babies washing	125.00

Plates, 7½"

Babies mending	85.00
Babies washing, hanging clothes	120.00
Sugar, open, babies sweeping	160.00
Vase, 4½" h, flaring rim, babies ironing	235.00

Tomato Pattern

Bowl, 9"	85.00
Creamer, 3", leaf handle	35.00
Pitcher, 3¾"	40.00
Sauce boat with underplate	55.00
Sugar, handled, cov	45.00
Tea Set, 3 pcs	240.00

ROSE TAPESTRY

Basket, 5 x 5", roses, braided handle	365.00
Bowl, 11" d, pink roses, molded edge	735.00
Creamer, pink roses	125.00

Rose Tapestry, creamer, 3¼" h, white ground, white, pink, red roses, white daises, green leaves, $275.00.

Dresser Tray, 7⅛ x 11⅛", gold edging, shaded pink roses, green leaves, small white daisies, lavendar shading	325.00
Hair Receiver, pink, white, yellow, three gold feet	195.00
Hatpin Holder, three color roses	225.00
Leaf Dish, 5 x 4¼", yellow rose center, pink rose border	135.00
Match Holder, hanging type, 5 x 3½"	355.00
Pin Box, 1½ x 2⅜", pink rose	145.00
Pitcher, 5", pinched spout, pink roses	375.00

Plates

7½", scalloped rim	265.00
10"	295.00
Powder Box, cov	165.00
Relish tray, 8⅛", handle, three color roses	165.00
Ring Tree, pink, white roses	325.00
Shaving Mug, jardinere shape, gold handles, liner	145.00
Sugar, cov	150.00
Teapot, cov	185.00
Toothpick, 4½"	475.00

Vases

4", shaded pink roses, green leaves, white daisies, yellow centers	325.00
5", slim neck, pink, white roses	285.00
Watering Can, 2¾"	315.00

MISCELLANEOUS TAPESTRY

Box, cov, 2½", 5 sheep	185.00
Chocolate Pot, mountain goats, pastoral scene	410.00
Hair Receiver, colonial man and woman	165.00

Humidor, 6¾", scenic, gold trim,
  mushroom finial 350.00
Pitcher, 6", women bathing by castle   425.00
Powder Box, 4", scenic, brown,
  green, aqua 365.00
Vases
  4", portrait, young girl 275.00
  4", scenic, village, mountains,
    trees in greens, blue, brown . . .   225.00
  6", portrait, ladies in colorful
    gowns 185.00
  7", ftd, wedding ring handles, per-
    forated base, collar, scenic . . .   250.00

ROYAL BONN *Bonn*

**The Bonn Factory was established by
Clemers August in the mid-eighteenth century in Bonn, Germany. Subsequently known as
Royal Bonn, the majority of this porcelain encountered on today's market is from the late
19th century. These later wares are usually
marked Mehlem, a castle or with the initials
FM.**

Biscuit Jar, 5", multicolored florals
  on ivory ground, gold trim 95.00
Bowls
  9", "Wild Rose" 75.00
  10 x 5" deep, handpainted roses,
    heavy gold trim 200.00
Cheese Dish, cov, wedge-shaped,
  roses on white, gold trim 125.00
Ewer, 12", cream ground, pink, blue
  and yellow flowers, gold trim . . .   175.00
Fish Set, platter and 6 plates, different fish on each plate, peach
  shading to blue-gray ground, artist
  sgd, set 225.00
Jam Jar, 5", silverplated lid and bail,
  floral decor on beige ground 55.00
Jardinere, 10", white floral decor,
  gold trim 110.00
Mantel Clock, Ansonia china, 9¼",
  pale blue ground, pink roses, foliage, sq base, gold feet, large
  molded floral bead on top, porcelain face, mkd Royal Bonn 350.00
Plaques, pierced for hanging
  12¾", Delft picture of ships, floral
    border, mkd 125.00

**Vase, 9", light yellow-green ground,
burgundy neck, imp 2574/BF; painted
5782/272/ss"/l, $85.00.**

  13¾", Delft picture of windmills,
    mkd 135.00
Plates
  8", "Wild Rose" 40.00
  8¼", sprays of florals, gold edges   42.50
  14", portrait, fruit border, artist
    signed 150.00
Relish, 10", handled, 3 sections, hp
  florals, gold trim 125.00
Urn, 13½", hp florals, tapestry fin-
  ish, gold handles and base . . .   225.00
Vases
  6½", green with rooster, hen and
    chicks, artist sgd, Nach Melch
    D. Hondecoeter, F. Sticker
    marked 165.00
  10", handled, hp, scenic front and
    back, pr 175.00
  11¼", tapestry, painted flowers .   400.00
  12¼", white with green, center
    panel of farm and cows, gold
    neck, handles and pedestal
    base, artist sgd, Sticker, marked   195.00
  12½", blue, floral decor, gold top
    and handles 125.00
  14", slender, soft green to brown
    at top, red and yellow flowers,
    marked 175.00
  15", portrait, leaf stem gold han-
    dles 285.00

ROYAL COPENHAGEN

Royal Copenhagen was established in 1773 when Franz Mueller produced his first piece of porcelain. In 1779, the Danish king acquired ownership of the factory, named Mueller manager and adopted the name Royal Copenhagen. The Crown sold its interest in 1867 and the company remains privately owned to this day.

Royal Copenhagen's most famous pattern "Blue Fluted" was created in 1780. It is of Chinese origin, comes in 3 types: (1) smooth edge (2) closed lace edge (3) perforated lace edge (full lace), and was copied by many other factories. "Flora Danica," named for a famous botanical work and introduced in 1789, remains Royal Copenhagen's most unique and exclusive pattern. Botanical illustrations were done free-hand and all edges and perforations were cut by hand.

All Royal Copenhagen porcelain is marked with three wavy lines which signify ancient waterways and a crown which was added in 1889; the stoneware does not carry the crown.

Figure, 8½", #1847, $650.00.

Basket, 7½"	50.00
Bon Bon Dish, Blue Fluted pattern .	45.00
Bowl, 8", Blue Fluted pattern, flull lace	80.00
Box, cov, floral and gold decor, marked 1894	70.00
Candlesticks, 4", full lace, pr	85.00
Creamer and Sugar, Blue Fluted pattern, full lace	180.00
Cruet, stoppered, Blue Fluted pattern	130.00
Cup and Saucer, coffee, Flora Danica pattern	80.00
Dinner Set, Blue Fluted pattern, white, cobalt blue flowers and vines, plain border, 51 pcs, underglaze marks	750.00
Dish, 6½" l, figural, peacock, blue and white, marked	190.00
Figures	
Boy with teddy bear, 7¼"	200.00
Cat, 5½", sitting, gray and white, green eyes	125.00
German Shepard, 7¾"	450.00
Faun, 8½", perched on half columns, holding pipes, rabbit at base, No 433	100.00
Polar bear, 11", hunting	250.00
Woman knitting	250.00
Inkwell with tray, 6 x 8½" l, Blue Fluted pattern	125.00
Jar, 16½", flat sided circular shape, rocky seascape decor, bronze cov, oval bronze base, knop feet, marked	450.00
Pitcher, 4", cobalt blue, floral decor	50.00
Plates	
5⅝", butter, Flora Danica pattern, set of 12	400.00
8", hp, fruit center	35.00
10¾", portrait, Josephine, 1923 .	90.00
Plates, Christmas, see COLLECTOR'S PLATES	
Platters	
10", Blue Fluted pattern	120.00
17¼", oval, Flora Danica, marked and numbered	450.00
Salt, Blue Fluted pattern	30.00
Syrup, Blue Fluted, spring-type lid .	125.00
Tazza, 13", African woman supporting 9" d bowl on her head, scalloped edge, center, boar jumping thistles, marked	150.00
Tray, 6½", round, rose, fish swimming	125.00
Tureen, cov, 18" l, Blue Fluted pattern, c1897	260.00
Vases	
5", green and white, floral decor, crackle glaze	75.00
6", bulbous, celadon, molded leaves, applied frog, 19th C . . .	180.00
7¾", floral and dragonfly decor, c1890	150.00

12", green, gold decor, crackle
glaze, pr 325.00
13", lake scene 145.00

ROYAL CROWN DERBY

Derby Crown Porcelain Co., established in
1875 in Derby, England, had no connection
with earlier Derby factories which operated
in the late 18th and early 19th centuries. In
1890, this new and distinct company was
appointed "Manufacturers of Porcelain to Her
Majesty" (Queen Victoria); from that date to
the present it has been known as "Royal
Crown Derby".

Derby porcelains from 1878 to 1890 carry
only the standard crown printed mark. From
1891 on, the mark carries the "Royal Crown
Derby" wording, and in the 20th century,
"Made in England" and "English Bone China"
were added to the mark.

A majority of these porcelains, both tableware and figures, were hand-decorated, but a
variety of printing processes were used for
additional adornment. Today, Royal Crown
Derby is a part of Royal Doulton Tableware,
Ltd.

Ewer, 7½" h, reticulated handle, neck,
handle, raised gold decor on cobalt
blue ground, body with enameled
flowers on gold ground, $650.00.

Bowl, 11 x 3¾" dp, hp florals, cobalt
rim 85.00
Box, cov, 3", round, orange and
blue decor, gold trim, marked, dat-
ed 1905 . . . . 95.00

Cups and Saucers
Demitasse, 2" cup, 2¼" saucer,
Cigar pattern, cobalt blue, orange and gold, marked, c 1940 65.00
2½" cup, 5¼" saucer, orange,
cobalt blue and gold decor,
marked, dated 1887 . . . . 125.00
Tea, blue chinoiserie decor 50.00
Dessert Set, Imari-type decor, 35
pieces 450.00
Ginger Jar, 10½", berry branches
on red ground, gold trim 250.00
Jam Pot, cov, Imari 65.00
Plates
9", floral medallions, green border 50.00
10½", hp, sailing ships, cream
border, gilt rope rim, sgd W.E.J.
Dean 165.00
Platter, 8½ x 11½", "View of North
Wales," cobalt with gold trim . . . 175.00
Service Plates, 10½", floral centers,
rose and green borders, gold
bands, set of 12 . . . . 1,000.00
Tea Caddy, dbl, center handle, Imari
decor 125.00
Tea Set, pot, cov sugar, creamer,
ovoid-shaped, Imari coloring,
heavy gold 225.00
Tray, 13 x 17", closed handles, blue
flowers in swag design on white,
gold trim 165.00
Urns, 7", apple green, reserves of
figures and landscape, gilt decor,
handled, pedestal base,
c 1800-25, pr 400.00
Vases
8½", cabinet, handled, floral, gilt 75.00
10", handled, canary yellow,
heavy gold floral decor, turqoise
dots around top rim, red mark . 250.00
10½", cream, blue iris, marked at
top, c1873 . . . . 285.00

ROYAL
DOULTON
FLAMBE

ROYAL DOULTON

Doulton pottery began in 1815 under the direction of John Doulton at the Doulton &
Watts pottery in Lambeth, England. Early output was limited to salt-glazed industrial
stoneware. John Watts retired in 1854; the
firm became Doulton and Company and production was expanded to include hand decorated stoneware such as figurines, vases,

dinnerware and flasks. In 1872, the firm began marking their ware "Royal Doulton."

In 1878, John's son, Sir Henry Doulton, purchased Pinder Bourne & Co. in Burslem and the companies became Doulton & Co., Ltd. in 1882. Decorated porcelain was added to Doulton's earthenware production in 1884 and the Royal Doulton mark was used on both wares.

Most Doulton figurines were produced at the Burslem plants from 1890 until 1978, when they were discontinued. A 'new' line of Doulton figurines was introduced in 1979.

Beginning in 1913, an "HN" number was assigned to each new Doulton figurine design. The "HN" numbers refers to Harry Nixon, a Doulton artist. "HN" numbers were chronological until 1940, after which blocks of numbers were assigned to each modeler. From 1928 until 1954, a small number appeared to the right of the crown mark; this number added to 1927 gives the year of manufacture of the figurines.

Dickens Ware, in earthenware and porcelain, was introduced in 1908. The ware was decorated with characters from Dicken's novels. The line was withdrawn in the 1940s, except for plates which continued until 1974.

Character jugs, a 20th century revival of early Toby models, were designed by Charles J. Noke for Doulton in the 1930s. They come in 4 major sizes and feature fictional characters from Dicken's, Shakespeare and other English and American novelists, and historical heros.

Doulton's Rouge Flambee (also Veined Sung) is a highly glazed, strong colored ware noted most for the fine modeling and exquisite colorings, especially in the animal items. The process used to produce the vibrant colors in this ware is a Doulton secret.

Production of stoneware at Lambeth ceased in 1956; production of porcelain continues today at Burslem.

See *Warman's Americana & Collectibles* for additional Royal Doulton listings.

Animal Models
Dachshund, HN 1141	50.00
Kitten, 2581	30.00
Mallard, HN 807	45.00
Rabbit, K 39	35.00
Setter with Pheasant, HN 2529, sgd JB	345.00
Siamese Cat, 2655	40.00
Terrier, HN 1101, reclining, front paws crossed	65.00
Tiger on Rock, HN 2639, A mk, dtd 1952	1,200.00

Ashtray, John Barleycorn 90.00
Bisquit Jar, Coaching Days series, 6½ x 5½″, SP cov, rim and handle 225.00

Bowls
Oasis in the dessert, 3½ x 8″ d .	110.00
Robin Hood, the King of the Archers, 6½″, octagonal	50.00

Cake Plate, Coaching Days & Ways series, 9½″ 105.00

Candlesticks
Battle of Hastings, 8¾″, pr	185.00
Floral, blue and yellow flower, black bands top and bottom, 10¼ x 5¾″, pr	125.00

Character Jugs, Tiny, 1¼″
Arriet	200.00
Arry	200.00
Fat Boy	100.00
Mr. Pickwick	240.00
Old Charley	105.00
Paddy	105.00

Character Jugs, Miniature, 2¼ to 2½″
Cardinal A mark	50.00
Gulliver	350.00
John Barleycorn	65.00
John Peel	40.00
Mikado	275.00
Paddy	45.00
Robinson Crusoe	24.00
Sancho Panzo	24.00
Viking	115.00
Walrus	40.00

Character Jugs, Small, 3½ to 4″
Dick Turpin 'Up'	60.00
Drake	85.00
Fat Boy	100.00
Fortune Teller	325.00
Gulliver	350.00
Pied Piper	45.00
Punch & Judy	375.00
Scaramouche	350.00
Smuggler	45.00

Character Jugs, Large, 5¼ to 7″
Arry	175.00
Gondolier	475.00
Gulliver	475.00
Johnny Appleseed	285.00
Parson Brown, A mark	135.00
Pied Piper	65.00
St. George	115.00
Toby Philpots	135.00
Touchstone, A mark	200.00
Viking	115.00

Creamer and Sugar, The Cardinal . . 125.00

Cups and Saucers
Kirkwood	18.00
Nursery Rhymes series	22.00

Dickens Ware
Ashtray, Sairey Gamp, A mark . . .	90.00
Bowl, 7¾″, round, ftd, 3 characters, inside and out	145.00
Bust, Micawber, miniature	55.00
Cup and saucer, Fagin	69.00

Jugs
Bill Sykes, 3″, minature	95.00

Sairey Gamp, 5″, square	90.00
Pitcher, Barnaby Rudge, 8¾ x 4⅜″, D 2973	135.00
Plate, Barkis	68.00
Sandwich tray, Siry Gamp, 5⅝ x 11″	75.00
Sauce dish, Fat Boy, 5¼″	45.00
Sugar, Sam Weller, 3⅛ x 5¾″ d, open	50.00

Vases

Alfred Jingle, 5½ x 4¼″, handled	95.00
Mr. Micawber, 5¾ x 3″, handled	85.00
Sydney Carton, 7 x 3¾″, handled	135.00
Tony Weller, 5 x 2¾″	65.00
Ewer, 7 x 3¾″, cream, pansies, maroon, yellow with green leaves, gold handle, pink collar	195.00

Figurines

'Arriet	215.00
'Arry	210.00
Auld Mac	215.00
Balloon Seller, 1315	125.00
Bridesmaid, 4 x 1½″, M 30	225.00
Deirdre, HN 2020	300.00
Fat Boy	95.00
Lisa, 2310	90.00
Little Land, 67	1,750.00
Lucy Lockett, 524	600.00
Milcawber, HN 1895, c1942	255.00
Mirabel, M 68, 4⅜ x 2½″	250.00
Paisley Shawl, HN 1988	175.00

Figurine, 9¼″, French Peasant, 2075, $395.00.

Pantalettes, 1362	350.00
Polly Peachum, 620	350.00
Southern Belle, 2229	100.00
The Captain, 2260	150.00
To Bed, HN 1805, 6¼ x 1¾″	110.00
Tootles, HN 1680	80.00
Top O'Hill, 1834	88.00
Uriah Heep, HN 1896, c1941	255.00
Wee Willie Winkle, HN 1050	230.00

Flambe

Bottle, liqueur, flowers and leaves, sgd	695.00
Bowl, dragons, 8½″, artist sgd Bernard Moore	225.00
Owl, 12″	175.00

Vases

Dessert scene, base relief, Arab heads on each side	225.00
Harbor scene and sailing ships, 8 x 5″	165.00
Sung, fish design, artist sgd FM	950.00
Flask, Micawber, 8″	200.00
Gravy Boat, Underplate and Spoon, Contess, 11″	120.00
Jardiniere, farm scene, blue and white	180.00

Jugs

Canterbury Pilgrims, Concord	145.00
Parson Brown, King's Ware, 8 x 3¾″	135.00
Simple Simon	450.00
The Regency Coach, 10¾ x 7″, c1930s	165.00

Lighters

Long John Silver	95.00
Poacher	90.00
Matchholder, Mr. Squeers, 2″	70.00

Mugs

Drink Wisely, King's Ware, 5″, man with cape, large hat, long stemmed pipe, artist sgd Noke	110.00
Here's to Thee My Honest Friend, 5″	90.00
Retrievers on all sides, 3 handled, silver rim, sgd Hannah Barlow	650.00
Pepper Pot, 5¼ x 2⅛″, stoneware, gray, blue leaves, green bands, SP top, initials E.S., marked	75.00

Pitchers

Dogberry Watch, set of 3, large 9½″, medium 8¼″, small 4¾″, verses on back	350.00
Grecian figures, 8½″, russet	165.00
Italian country scenes, 6½″	95.00
Parson Brown, 9″	200.00
Robin Hood series, 8½ x 4½″, cov, hot water pitcher	195.00
Plaque, Garden of Gethsemene, sgd George Tinworth	300.00

Plates

Canterbury Pilgrims, 10½″	55.00
Don Quixote and Sancho Panza, 10″	75.00

Gibson Girl head 120.00
Off That Terrible Curse He Took,
10¼", Jackdaw of Rheims se-
ries 55.00
Portia, 10", Shakespeare series . . 65.00
The Magic Horse, Arabian Nights
series 85.00
Platters
Madras, 16½ x 20", flow blue . . . 225.00
Windmill and cattle, 16", blue
transfer, Doulton-Burslem 100.00
Sandwich Tray, Robin Hood series,
5¾ x 11" 75.00
Seed Pot, Babes in Woods, 3" 145.00
Teapot, cov, 5¼ x 4½", beige and
brown tapestry aqua and white
flowers, gold trim 195.00
Tobacco Jars
Monks, 5½" 225.00
Windsor Castle 100.00
Toby Jugs, Full Seated
Cliff Cornell, 9" 250.00
Falstaff, 8½" 55.00
Happy John, 9" 55.00
Mr. Micawber, A mark, 4½" 180.00
Tray, 10 x 13", floral center, flow
blue, deep blue and gold border,
Burslem 85.00
Tumbler, nursery rhymes 110.00
Vases
Babes in the Woods, 9½ x 5¾",
lady with basket and young girl 395.00
Goats, 9 x 3¾", incised in black
on beige center, green and
brown borders top and bottom,
sgd Hannah Barlow 495.00
Pastoral sunset scene, 10⅜ x
4⅛", artist sgd H Morrey 325.00

**Bust, 9″, dress highlighted in brown
and gold, pink trim, pink triangle, No.
448, $375.00.**

ROYAL DUX

Royal Dux was porcelain made in Dux, Bohemia (Czechoslovakia) at the Duxer Porzellan-Manufaktur established in 1860. Many items were imported to the United States. A relatively inexpensive porcelain in the beginning, the ware is gaining in recognition to the point of being reproduced.

Basket, 2¼ x 4 x 4½", brown
basketweave pattern, applied
cherries 125.00
Bowls
6 x 9½", open handles, applied
rose spray on green ground . . 100.00
7", full figure maiden reclines on
edge 160.00

Bust, woman wearing bonnet, 16",
rococo base, 19th C 225.00
Centerpieces
Nudes, 2, shell form, 14¼" h,
c1910 . . . . 415.00
Woman, shell form, multicolored,
gilded 330.00
Compote, 25¾" h, figural, shell
shape basin, women draped
around, c1900 . . . . 525.00
Dish, 12", ftd, figural Cupid on seashell, frogs on sides 355.00
Ewer, 10", applied fruits and flowers,
natural coloring 185.00
Figurines
Bird Dogs, group of 2 on natural
grass base 265.00
Boy with Basket, 5½ x 7½" 150.00
Boy with Fish, Girl with Basket,
10⅜", natural coloring, gold
highlights, pink triangle mark,
pair 450.00
Colonial man and lady, 12½ h x
15" l, seated at table drinking
tea, 2 tiny poodle dogs under
each chair 1,100.00
Deer, sleeping, soft fawn colors,
pink triangle mark 150.00
Mother with 2 barefoot boys, 16¼
x 9½", satin finish, beige and
green tones, burnished gold,
pink triangle mark 795.00

Peasants, 11½ x 4″ d, satin finish, pink, green, gold, flesh tones, mkd Royal Dux Bohemia, pr . . **595.00**

Tobacco Jar, 8″, figural head of man smoking pipe with night cap **150.00**

Tray, centered by girl holding a basket on her back, irid blue **300.00**

Vases

7½ x 2″ d, Oriental figurines, beige satin finish, green and pink outfits, gold trim, marked Royal Dux Bohemia, raised pink triangle mark, pr **275.00**

11″, maiden holding conch shell, green, rose and ivory **300.00**

15½ x 9″, grapes, handled, pr . . **450.00**

17½″, urn shape, cream matte finish, cartouche with female portrait, 2 putti on shoulder, molded band of gold acanthus leaves, pink triangle mark, imp Royal Dux, Bohemia, 5483 . . . **210.00**

ROYAL FLEMISH

Royal Flemish was produced by the Mt. Washington Glass Co., New Bedford, Mass. It has heavy raised gold enamel lines on frosted transparent glass that separates areas into sections, colored in russet tones. It gives the appearance of stained glass windows with elaborate florals or coin medallions in the design. The process was patented by Albert Steffin in 1894.

Bowl, 4 x 10½″ d, centerpiece bowl without the SP holder, enamel chrysanthemums decor, panels outlined in gold, unsigned **1,475.00**

Box, 3¾″ h x 5½″d, swirl design in glass of body, lid, gold tracery blossoms, swirls defined in gold, enamel blossom in center of lid has jewel center, unsigned **1,250.00**

Cracker Jar, 7½″, SP lid, bail, raised gold decor of mythical figure instead of coins or florals usually found on this form, unsigned . . . **1,950.00**

Pitcher, 9¼″ h, rope handle, raised gold florals over the usual tan panels, 6 colorful shields surround the neck, unsigned **3,950.00**

Rose Jars

9″, bright panels decor with Roman coins on obverse, raised gold florals on reverse, finial on lid has been repaired with metal clip, old repair **1,950.00**

10½″, profuse gold decor of firebreathing dragon, embellishments, orig lid **4,950.00**

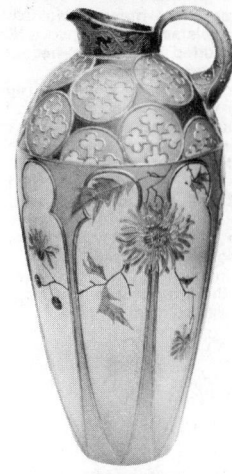

Vase, 11½″ h, lower panels of alternating pale blue, tan, raised gold, chrysanthemum blossoms, foilage, surmounted by circlets of dark blue, light blue crosses, cerise ground, unsigned, $4,000.00.

Vases

7″ h x 8½″ d, bulbous, squatty shape, 4½″ d trefoil top, 4 Roman coin - 3 gold and 1 silver - decor **2,750.00**

13½″, two applied handles, cupid slaying ferocious dragon, signed

With orig lid **8,000.00**

Without lid **3,750.00**

14″, gold mythical figure on ground of pale blue, florals on reverse, sgnd, unusual **3,450.00**

ROYAL RUDOLSTADT

This hard paste porcelain was made in Rudolstadt, Thuringen, East Germany. The first factory was established by Ernt Bohne in 1854. A second factory was opened by L. Straus & Sons, Ltd. in 1882.

The ware was never originally labeled "Royal Rudolstadt" but the word 'Royal' was probably added by dealers because of the connotation of the word.

The early mark was a hayfork representing the arms of Johann Fredrich von Schwarzburg-Rudolstadt, the patron. Later, crossed two-prong hayforks were used to imitate the Meissen or Dresden mark. In 1800, the letter "R" was used. Still later, variations of the hayfork were used. Modern marks show a shield with the letters "RQ", a crown on top, with the word "Crown" above and the name "Rudolstadt" below the shield. Another mark has the word "Germany" in place of the word "Crown" which indicates the ware was made after 1891.

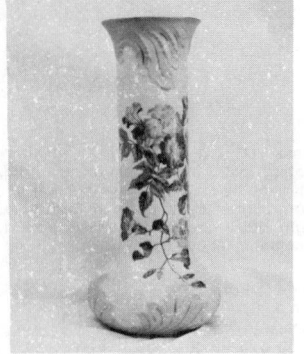

Vase, 13½", ivory ground, orange and pink flowers, green, brown leaves, gold details, blue mark #6230 on base, $125.00.

Basket, 4½ x 6¾", gold handle, floral design on ivory	85.00
Biscuit Jar, 8", corset-shaped, paneled with multicolored flowers	135.00
Bowls	
9½", pink rose decor, artist sgd	70.00
10½", white, black mill scene, gold rim	85.00
Bust, young woman, 15½", ruffled open bodice	200.00
Cake Set, 5 pcs, light green, yellow roses, gold rims	120.00
Candlesticks, 7", ivory, emb acanthus leaves, petal shaped cups, marked on base with Crown Mark, pr	50.00
Celery Dish, 13", handled, hp yellow rose, gold trim, artist sgd	80.00
Creamer and Sugar, cream, purple pansies, gold trim	75.00

Cup and Saucer, hp roses, gold trim	25.00
Dish, 10½ x 10½", shell shape, ivory, satin finish, hp flowers, gilt	70.00
Dresser Set, tray, hatpin holder, hair receiver, ring tree, cov jar, rose decor, 6 pcs	250.00
Ewer, 9½", blue multicolored flowers, gold handle	75.00
Hair Receiver, hp pastel florals	42.00
Pin Tray, 5", clover decor	25.00
Pitchers	
4½", flower spray medallions, gold serpent handle	65.00
11", bulbous, floral decor, gold handle	125.00
Plates	
8", heavy gold filigree, hayfork mark	85.00
8½", rose border	40.00
8½", salmon pink roses	35.00
Powder Box, 4 x 5½" d, emb florals and swirls	40.00
Salt and Pepper, beige, hp pink roses, brown and green fern	50.00
Vases	
6½", cobalt blue, raised gold and enameled flowers, gold handles	140.00
8¾", gold and violet florals, gold handles	85.00
20½", cream, purple and blue berries, pastel flowers, emb neck and base, gold handles, sgd Le Max	150.00

ROYAL VIENNA

Production of this hard paste porcelain began in 1720 with Claude Innocentius du Paquier, a runaway employee of the Meissen Works. The factory was located in Vienna. In 1744, Empress Maria Theresa brought the factory under royal patronage and subsequently the ware became known as Royal Vienna. The establishment went through many administrative changes until its closing in 1864 but the quality of workmanship was always maintained. The majority of this ware encountered on today's market was probably made by other Austrian or German firms who continued to produce a reasonable facsimile of Royal Vienna including using the distinctive and distinguished 'Beehive' mark.

Bowl, 5", handled, portrait, blue, gold trim	140.00
Chocolate Pot, burgundy and gold, bust of lady, beehive mark	185.00
Cracker Jar, chartreuse, wine and gold, cherubs cover front	250.00

Box, 2½", hp and gilded, gilded inside, artist sgd, Wagner, $725.00.

Cup and Saucer, demitasse, portrait, lady and dog, scalloped green border with gold design, blue beehive mark 75.00

Dish, 8", shell shape, blue border with gilt zig-zag, flower sprigs, c1773 . . . . 360.00

Ewer, 7½", handle, red, ornate gold decor, woman and 2 cherubs on obverse, 2 cherbus on reverse side 145.00

Figure, lady equestrian on gray horse, 17½ x 17½", blue habit, black hat and boots, shield mark with Keramas under base, imp No 2875 . . . . 595.00

Jug, 8½", portrait, mother and small child, mask shape lip, sgd LCF, c1920 . . . . 275.00

Pitcher, 13", purple grapes, green leaves 275.00

Plaques
8½", portraits of seated children, girl and boy with rabbit, behive mark, pr 145.00
12", portrait, woman with child, pink border, gilt tracery, raised gold and jewels, artist sgd, beehive "Flora" 425.00

Plates
9", cobalt border with gold decor, center has maiden draped in white, band of flowers in hair, serenaded by angel playing lute, artist sgd, beehive under glaze . . . 350.00
9½", female figure, cobalt blue and gilt border, underglaze blue shield 110.00

Tray, 8¼ x 12", pale green, hp violet decor, gold trim 175.00

Urns
5¼", cabinet, handled, crimson and green, gold bordered cartouche on front, beehive mark . 265.00
8¾ x 3⅜", cov, tripod base, Paris and Helen, maroon, stippled gold center, people around urn, gold trim, masque heads on feet, pierced work top, sgd Riemer, blue beehive mark on top of glaze 395.00
22½", slender ovoid shape, cov, magenta, rose and apple green ground, painted procession of figures in antique costume, gilt emb 800.00

Vases
4⅞", portrait, lady, long brown hair, dark green irid glaze 750.00
6¼", bulbous, elongated neck, portrait, bust of colonial lady, cobalt blue, artist sgd 500.00
10½", portrait, Prussia's Peace Brings Plenty, burgandy and gold, 2 Royal Vienna marks . . . 250.00
18¼", ovoid shape on round socle, cov, partitioned, ivory, magenta and dark green ground, oval reserves of Galanterie, gilt overlay, pr 325.00

ROYAL WORCESTER

This works was established in 1751 by Dr. John Wall and 14 partners. Dr. Wall died in 1776 and the entire business was sold to Thomas Flight in 1783. Martin Barr was admitted as a partner in 1793 and the firm was known as Flight and Barr. In 1807 the name was changed to Flight, Barr and Barr. It was changed again in 1813 to Barr, Flight and Barr, or "B.F.B." and continued as such until 1840 at which time Chamberlin and Son and Barr, Flight and Barr were consolidated. The works moved to Dighlis, the home of Chamberlin and Son. The company was sold to Kerr and Binn in 1852. Most of the earlier ware encountered are of the 1870–1900 period. Current Royal Worcester wares are available on the modern market.

Basket, 2", minature, cobalt blue, gold handle 75.00

Biscuit Jars with SP top, rim and handle
6 x 4¾", beige and aqua, satin finish, marked, 1897 . . . . 225.00
7½", with underplate, melon ribbed, cream, sprays of flowers and leaves, No 1282 . . . . 350.00
Gold teardrop decor, marked . . . 250.00

Creamer, 4", bone china, green mark, $35.00.

Bowls
5¾", scalloped, matte exterior, glazed interior, ivory, hp florals, wide gold bands rim and base, c1890 . . . .   110.00
9", fruit, molded, basketweave and maple leaves, reticulated rim, ivory matte finish, green, rose and gilt decor 200.00
Box, cov, cottage loaf shape, SS fittings, monogram of Norton de White, silversmith, dtd 1900 . . . .   125.00
Centerpiece, 8¼ x 5½ d x 18" l, boy, girl and black dog, white with pink, green shell trim on ends, pink lining, emb reg mark, c1869   395.00
Creamer, cream with multicolored pastel flowers 195.00
Cups and Saucers
1½ x 2½", heart shape cup, 4¼" saucer, satin, beige, gold decor, bow on handle, c1896 . . . . . .   125.00
1¾", demitasse, dainty floral decor, sgd and dtd 1902 . . . .   70.00
Red and pink roses, hp, c1904 . .   58.00
Egg Server, 5½ x 7" d, six egg-shaped cups, basket shaped holder with handle 335.00
Ewers
8", pink, hp, gold floral sprays front and back, heavy gold tree bark handle, sgd 239.00

9 x 4⅜", satin, ivory, blue flowers, tan leaves outlined in gold, gold slamander handle, date mark 1887 . . . .   495.00
17", beige, hp thistles, emb figures, gold decor, artist sgd, date mark 1894 . . . .   1,400.00
Figures
Fisher Woman with Basket, 7¾ x 2¾", satin, No 1202, marked .   425.00
Frog, 1½ x 2½ x 3", white, c1891   195.00
Girl with Basket, 6¾ h x 2¾ x 3½", Kate Greenaway type, glossy, off white, flesh tones, gold trim, marked, dated 1882 .   450.00
Lady with Cymbals, 11⅛ x 4" d, beige dress, rust and gold trim, green and gold base, No 2016, dated 1907 . . . .   595.00
Game Plate, snipes in center, green rim with stencilled gilt work, sgd G. Johnson 145.00
Jam Pot, 4½ x 3¼", strawberry shape, satin finish, beige, SP lid and spoon, dated 1896 . . . .   95.00
Jug, 5¼", tan, floral decor, gilded .   150.00
Mug, 2", Worcester Cathedral pictured, mkd England 50.00
Pitchers
6", floral decor, multicolored 100.00
6", horn shape, horn handle, ivory, hp florals 200.00
7", green to light tan, 1895 . . . . .   360.00
7⅜", ivory, peach with green leaf, purple mark 97.00
8", globular, gilt leaf molded neck and spout, ivory matte, painted blossoms, gilt handle, purple mark and no 175.00
Plate, 9", hp floral decor, gold trim .   75.00
Potpourri Jar, 14 x 6½", cov with pierced top and inside lid, beige with yellow roses and blue flowers, outlined in gold, marked, dated 1917 . . . .   1,195.00
Teapots
5", bulbous, floral decor, c1770 . .   395.00
6", green to light tan, 1896 . . . . .   310.00
Tray, 14 x 16", rectangular, ivory matte finish, trailing gilt branch of roses 80.00
Urn, cov, 15¼ x 5¾", hp, large pink roses, green leaves, flying fish handles, artist sgd W. E. Jarman, dated 1910 . . . .   1,295.00
Vases
8", cov, yellow shading to rust, hp florals, gold decor, c1890 . . . . .   225.00
8", reticulated cov, cream to rust, hp florals, gold decor, c1901 . .   225.00
8½ x 5½", shell shape, glossy, gold trim, dated 1888 . . . .   450.00
9¼ x 3⅝", flared fluted tops, emb

foot, floral decor, gold trim, No 1938, dated 1902, pr 595.00
10″, spiral shape, white, floral bouquet in each spiral, pink highlights 635.00
10½ x 6″, bamboo shape, bamboo handle, fern decor in relief . 75.00
Vegetable Dish, cov, 8¾ x 11 x 5½″, round, ram's head handles, brown 85.00
Wall Pocket, 9½″, white, lovebirds, imp mark, c1860 . . . . 190.00

ROYCROFT

Elbert Hubbard, founder of the Roycrofters in East Aurora, New York, during the turn of the 19th and 20th centuries, was considered a genius in his day. He was author, lecturer, manufacturer, salesman and philosopher.

Hubbard established a campus, including a printing plant where he published "The Philistine," "The Fra" and "The Roycrofter." His most famous book was "A Message to Garcia," 1899. His 'community' also included a furniture manufacturing plant, a metal shop and a leather shop.

See also FURNITURE.

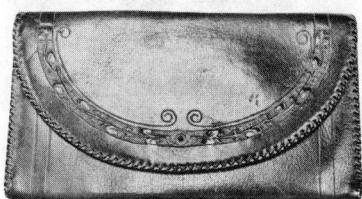

Purse, leather, 10⅛ x 5¾″, $45.00.

Ashtray, 6 x 4″, copper with brass finish, pedestaled center with attached match holder 75.00
Book, 1914, *Little Journeys*, 14 vol. set 195.00
Bookends
6 x 6″, leather, tooled design, mkd with orb on back, pr 150.00
7 x 6″, wooden, carved orb mark on front, pr 195.00

10 x 5″, copper, fleur-de-lis design, large orb mark, pr 95.00
Candlesticks
8″, hammered copper, pyramid shaped base with buttress standard sq. candleholders, orb mark, pr 195.00
20½″, hammered copper, twisted standard with two applied candleholders, orb mark 300.00
Chairs
Hall chair, 46″ h, oak with wood seat, carved orb signature 450.00
Rocker, 38″ h, mahogany with leather seat, orb mark 250.00
Lamps
18″, hammered copper, round base with Helmet shade 450.00
28″, hanging fixture, hammered copper, circular base with cut out hearts, 6 hanging lights in glass 950.00
Motto, "Never Explain, Your Friends Don't Need It And Your Enemies Won't Believe You Anyways," printed, 4½ x 6½″, framed 20.00
Tables
Desk, oak, 30 x 60 x 30″, four drawers on left 650.00
Library, oak, 52 x 33 x 30″, two drawers 750.00
Round, oak, 48″ d, extention table, opens to 8 ft 800.00
Vases
7½″, bud, pyramid base with Steuben Aurene glass insert . . 250.00
10″, sq, rolled edge top and bottom, hammered copper, chased design, orb mark 95.00
12″, ballastered, hammered copper 150.00
19″, "American Beauty," hammered copper 450.00

RUBENA GLASS

Rubena crystal is a transparent blown glass made in the late 1800s by several of the glass companies. One of the first to produce it was Hobbs, Brocunier & Co., Wheeling, West Virginia. Rubena glass shades from clear to red.

Basket, thorn handle 115.00
Bottles
Cologne, 5⅝″ h x 2¼″ d, square, cut, clear, cut faceted stopper . 115.00
Perfume, 3¼″ h x 2″ d, cut, cranberry cut stopper, SS top rim . . 110.00
Butter Dish, cov, Royal Oak, frosted, Northwood 125.00

Vase, 5″ h, coralene decorated, gold trim, $275.00.

Celery, threaded, Northwood	70.00
Compote, matching candlesticks, DQ, enamel florals	230.00
Cruets	
Medallion Sprig	125.00
Royal Ivy, frosted, 6⅜″ h x 3½″ d, clear applied handle, clear bubble stopper	145.00
Dresser Jar, 3 small insert bottles .	200.00
Pitchers	
5½″, bulbous, fluted tri-corner rim, IVT enamel decor	125.00
7½″, bulbous, sq mouth, IVT, clear twisted rope handle and neck collar	165.00
Rose Bowls	100.00
IVT, floral decor	110.00
Salt, 2″ h x 3″ d, flower shaped, rigaree applied decor, SP stand .	110.00
Sugar, cov, threaded, Northwood . .	175.00
Sugar Castor	100.00
Tumblers, DQ, enamel florals, leaves	45.00
Hobnail, 10 rows, 4″ h x 3″ d . . .	110.00
Vases	
7″, swirl	95.00
7¾ x 3¼″, cranberry to clear, gold scrolls, leaves, blue, white enamel morning glories, pr . . .	165.00
12¾″, lily pads and floral enamel decor	125.00

RUBENA VERDE GLASS

Rubena Verde is a blown art glass made by Hobbs, Brocunier & Co., Wheeling, West Virginia, in the late 1880s. It is a transparent glass that shades from red in the upper section to a yellow-green in the lower. It is often found in the inverted thumbprint (IVT) pattern termed "Polka Dot" by Hobbs.

Biscuit Jar, crackle	120.00
Bowl, 9¾″, ruffled rim	185.00
Compote, 8″, honeycomb pattern . .	120.00
Creamer, 4⅞ x 2½″, applied vaseline handle, feet, fluted top	95.00
Cruet, IVT, applied crystal handle . .	150.00
Finger Bowl, oval hobnails, crimped rim	75.00
Pitchers	
5½″, IVT, vaseline handle	275.00
5¾″, hobnail	235.00
8 x 7″ d, square mouth, opal, hobnail	295.00
Rose Bowl	95.00
Sugar Castor, enamel decor	180.00
Syrup, hobnail, pewter top	115.00
Tumbler, 4 x 3″, coinspot pattern . .	95.00

Tumbler, hobnail, opal, 3¹¹/₁₆″, $100.00.

Vases	
6″, cylindrical, DQ band, enamel flowers	95.00
6½″, melon shape, ribbed, enamel flowers	200.00
7½″, hobnail, ruffled top	180.00

RUBY STAINED GLASS (Souvenir Type)

Ruby stained glass, a late Victorian introduction used to decorate souvenir items, was produced primarily in Pittsburgh, Pa., during the 1880s and 1890s. These items were fash-

ioned from clear glass, pressed in one of several thousand patterns, and then a ruby-red staining material was painted on the annealed glass for a decorative effect.

Patterns used for this purpose were many but "Button Arches," "Heart Band" and "Almond Thumbprint" were three of many popular ones. Often a factory would press the glass and sell it to various decorating companies where different parts of the pattern would be stained. Ruby stained glass souvenir items were sold at fairs and expositions, and often etched with the name of a place, person, date or event.

A few years ago there was a tendency to down-grade a piece of pattern glass if it carried souvenir-markings. With the increasing interest in memorabilia, souvenir marked pieces have increased in value.

See also the Pattern Glass sections in this guide.

Mug, Blairsville, PA, 3¼″ h, $20.00.

Bread Tray, Cape Cod	65.00
Butter Dish, cov, St. Louis	125.00
Candy Dish, cov, Columbia Expo., 1893	58.00
Compote, ftd, Mother, 1911	42.50
Creamer, Niagara Falls	20.00
Goblet, Gettysburg, PA	40.00
Letter Holder, Bailey, MI	40.00
Mug, St. Louis Exposition, 1904	30.00
Mustard, cov, Mt. Clemens	30.00
Napkin Ring, 2″, Happy Halloween	70.00
Pitchers	
2½″, Souvenir Ocheyedan, Iowa	25.00
Pittsburgh, water, tankard	120.00
Plate, Cincinnati, 1900	15.00
Punch Cups	
Atlantic City	18.00
Mother, 1897	18.00
Relish, Christmas	28.50
Sugar, cov, Columbia Expo., 1893	40.00
Toothpick, Harvard, Atlantic City, 1899	42.50
Tumblers	
Ocean City	25.00

Wm. Frederick from F.W.C., 1909	38.00
Wine	
Syracuse, NY	28.00
Tampa	24.00

RUSSIAN ITEMS

Works of Russian artists and craftsmen are highly regarded by collectors. Russian enamels are one of the most exquisite examples of the Russian arts executed during the Czarist period. The items were fashioned of precious metals, elaborately enameled and encrusted with precious and-or semi-precious stones.

ENAMELS

Boxes
2⅛″ d, round, enamel on silver gilt, multicolored flowers, blue bead border with scrolling foliage, Ivan Saltzkov, Moscow, c1900 .... **880.00**

3½″ l, cigarette, enamel on silver gilt, multicolored flowers, foliage and blue scrolls, turquoise bead border, Postnikov, Moscow, 1892 .... **610.00**

Candlesticks, 5½″, enamel on silver gilt, dome bases, baluster stems, foliate form cups, multicolored flowers, foliage and geometric forms, Maria Semyenova, Moscow, c1900, pr **4,950.00**

Cup and Saucer, enamel on silver gilt, multicolored flowers and foliage within blue bead borders, cup has foliate form handle, Pavla Mishukova, Moscow, c1890 .... **1,650.00**

Easter Egg, 2½″, shaded enamel on silver gilt, central opening, dark blue ground, 3 stylized flower heads, Old Russian style enameling in red, blue and brown **9,020.00**

Icon, 4⅞″, Christ Pantocrator, silver, enamel, shaped top, crosses, flowers and foliage in Old Russian Style, pendant loop, Fyodor, Moscow, mkd with Cyrillic initials of maker and 84 standard **3,300.00**

Salt, 2″, enamel on silver, geometric pattern, white bead borders, Moscow, c1900 .... **192.00**

Spoons, demitasse, 4⅛″, silver gilt, fig shaped bowl, multicolored flowers, white borders with foliage, flowerform finials, Vasili Agafonov, Moscow, c1890, set of 6 .... **780.00**

Sugar Bowl, 5½″ h, including swing handle, enamel on silver gilt, mul-

ticolored flowers, scrolls and foliage within blue bead border, Cyrillic maker's mark P.B., Moscow, c1910 .... **1,100.00**
Tea Caddy, 4½″, cylindrical, hinged dome top, champleve enamel on silver gilt, multicolored flowers and scrolling foliage, Ovehinnikov, Moscow, 1881 .... **990.00**
Tea Set, 3 pc., sterling with gold wash, mkd St. George and the Dragon **2,750.00**

SILVER

Cake Basket, 9¼″ l, swing handle, chased cornucopial border, gilded interior, maker's mark P.B., Moscow, c1910 .... **550.00**
Decanter, silver mounted cut glass, chased with flowers and scrolling foliage, maker's mark C.X., c1900 **300.00**
Ladle, 18″ l, bowl and shaped handle nielloed with flowers and foliage, enameled flowerhead in center of bowl **775.00**
Liqueur Set and Tray, 10⅝″, cov carafe with spigot, 12 cups, all are cornucopia shape with 2 peg feet, engraved scrolling foliage, oval 2 handled tray, Cyrillic maker's mark L.S., Moscow, 1896 .... **3,025.00**
Powder Horn, 4¼″ l, silver gilt and niello, neo-rococo scrolling foliage and diaper, Moscow, c1820 .... **800.00**
Sugar Bowl, 8⅛″, openwork top, 2 geometric handles, front has Cyrillic inscription dtd October 28, 1917, maker's mark unclear, Moscow, c1910 .... **275.00**
Toasting Mug, Slavic design, mkd "St. George and the Dragon," 1885 .... **475.00**
Tray, silver, 22½″, oval, 2 handled, raised pierced edge, Cyrillic maker's mark Ya. P., Assaymaster Mikhail Karpinski, Moscow, 1806 . **1,870.00**
Vases, 4″, curved sides, bulbous base, 2 handled with satyr's mask, foliage, Cyrillic maker's mark N. Ya., St. Petersburg, c1890, pr ... **1,210.00**

MISCELLANEOUS

Egg, 3¾″, green, satin glass, hinged, in 7″ brass holder with twining leaves **325.00**
Figures
  Bear, 8″ l, bronze, lying outstretched on molded plank, green marble base, imp sgd Vab Crodouysokuu **180.00**
  Peasant maiden carrying basket, 7

Icon of Our Lady of Kazanskaya, Pseudo 19th C marks, silvered metal lepasseriza, gilt, 12¼ x 18¾″, $400.00.

½″, porcelain, purple dress, pink apron, white blouse, embroidered headdress, blue factory mark, c1810 .... **1,100.00**
Icon, 2 x 3″, brass, Saint with Bible . **125.00**
Plate, 9½″, landscape with mushrooms around center, border of wolves by night, mkd Made in Russia by Kornilow Bros. initials J. H. V. in banner held by bear **50.00**
Samovar and Tray, brass, bulbous with gadrooned edges on sq base, brass tray, scalloped edge, late 19th C **350.00**
Tea and Coffee Service, teapot, coffee pot, creamer, cov sugar bowl, waste bowl, 6 cups and saucers, porcelain, white, round, spirally fluted, gilt outline, ftd, early 19th C, 17 pcs. **725.00**
Teapot, 6 x 4½″, porcelain, magenta, floral medallions with blue, rose and lavender flowers **135.00**
Tumbler, crystal with silver and niello pierced holder **95.00**

SABINO GLASS

Sabino Glass, named for its creator **Ernest Marius Sabino**, originated in France in the 1920s. A type of art glass, it was produced in a wide range of decorative glassware in frosted, clear, opalescent and colored glass. Both blown and pressed moldings were used. Hand sculpted wooden molds, that were then cast in iron were used and are still in use at the present time.

In 1960 the company introduced a line of figurines. 1 to 8" high, and a few other items in a fiery opalescent glass in the Art Deco style. Gold was added to the batch to attain the fiery glow. These pieces are the Sabino that is most commonly found today. Sabino is marked with the name in the mold, with an etched signature or both.

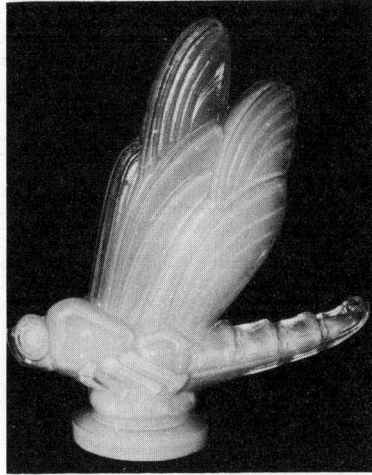

Dragonfly, 6" h, $80.00.

Ashtrays
Shell, 3½ x 5½"	30.00
Violet, 4½"	40.00

Birds
Branch of 5, 7 x 8"	1,100.00
Cluster of 2, 3½ x 4½"	200.00
Cluster of 3, 5 x 5"	225.00
Feeding, 1½ x 2"	60.00
Jumping, 3¼ x 3½"	45.00
Mocking, 4½ x 6"	90.00
Nesting	25.00
Teasing, 2½ x 3", wings up	65.00

Blotter, rocker type, 6 x 3", American and French crossed flags . . .	285.00

Bottles, cologne or scent
Nudes, 6, inscribed Sabino, France	95.00
Petalia, orig stopper, 5½"	165.00
Pineapple, 5"	160.00

Bowls
Berry, 5¾"	55.00
Fish, 5"	60.00
Box, Powder, 3" d	65.00
Butterfly, 6"	125.00
Candlestick, double, grapes	135.00
Cat, sitting, 2¼"	35.00
Chick, 3¾", wings up	55.00

Dogs
Collie, 2"	50.00
Scotty, 1½ x 3 x 4"	70.00
Dragonfly, 5¼ x 6"	90.00
Fish, 4 x 4", swimming	75.00
Gazelle	90.00
Heron, 7½"	100.00
Madonna, 5"	80.00
Mouse, 3"	45.00
Napkin Ring, birds, 2¼" opal	40.00

Nudes
6", kneeling	235.00
6½", woman with long flowing hair	125.00
Panthers, grouping, 5¾ x 7¾"	215.00
Pigeon, 6¼"	120.00
Plate, 8½", sailing ships	230.00
Prism	65.00
Rooster, 7"	425.00
Snail, 1 x 3"	60.00
Squirrel, 3"	35.00

Statues
Draped, 7¼"	425.00
Venus de Milo, large	60.00
Stork, 7¼"	125.00

Trays
Butterfly, round	85.00
Shell	35.00
Thistle	40.00

Vases
Art Deco, 12", topaz	500.00
Beehive	235.00
Manta Ray	300.00
Zebra, 5½ x 5½"	125.00

C S SALOPIAN

SALOPIAN WARE

Salopian Ware was made at Caughley Pot Works, Salop, Stropshire, England, in the 18th century by Thomas Turner. The ware is polychrome on transfer. At one time it was classified as Polychrome Transfer but regained the more popular name of Salopian. Wares are marked with an "S" or "Salopian," impressed or painted under the glaze. Much of it was sold through Turner's Salopian warehouse in London.

Teapot, boy carrying lamb, 8¼" l x 4" h, $465.00.

Bowls
5", acorn and flowers 210.00
6¼", milkmaid milking cows, meadows, church in background, multicolored 100.00
6¾", black transfer with blue edging, couple at tea in garden with blackamoor pouring 150.00
Butter Dish, cov, underplate, Fence pattern, c1775 . . . . 1,200.00
Creamers
Cormorant Fisherman 385.00
House pattern, brown and blue . . 410.00
Cup and Saucer, handleless
Bird on Branch 180.00
Deer pattern, blue and white, pair 315.00
Jug, milk, miniature, sparrow beak spout, Chinese river scene, narrow diaper border inside 450.00
Mug, Milkmaid and Cow 250.00
Plates
4⅛", Cottage 325.00
7", Campagne, multicolored 215.00
8", blue, gilt decor, c1790 . . . . . 175.00
Sauce, 4⅞", Cottage 325.00
Sugar, cov, 4¾", Milkmaid and Cow 400.00
Tea Caddy, Cormorant Fisherman . 325.00
Teapots
Birds and Flowers 475.00
Cormorant Fisherman 400.00

SALT AND PEPPER SHAKERS

Collecting salt and pepper shakers, whether late 19th century glass forms or the contemporary figural and souvenir types, is becoming more and more popular. The supply and variety is practically unlimited; the price for most sets is within the budget of cost conscious, young collectors. Finally, their size offers an opportunity to assemble a large collection in a small amount of space.

One can specialize in types, forms, or makers. Great art glass artisans such as Joseph Locke, Nicholas Kopp, and others designed salt and pepper shakers in the normal course of their work. Arthur Goodwin Peterson is the leading research scholar in the field. His 400 Trademarks in Glass, Glass Patents and Patterns, and Glass Salt Shakers: 1,000 Patterns provide the reference numbers given below. Peterson made a beginning; there are hundreds, perhaps thousands of patterns still to be catalogued. Another reference is Mildred and Ralph Lechner's The World of Salt Shakers.

The clear colored and colored opaque sets command the highest prices, clear and white sets the lowest. Although some shakers, e.g., the tomato or fig, have a special patented top and need it to hold value, it is not detrimental to the price to replace the top of a shaker.

The figural and souvenir type is often looked down upon by collectors. Sentiment and whimsy are prime collecting motivations. The large variety and current low prices indicate a potential for long term price growth.

Generally older shakers are priced by the piece, figural and souvenir types by the set. The pricing method is indicated at each division. All shakers are assumed to have original tops unless noted. Identical numbers are from Peterson's book.

See Warman's Americana & Collectibles for an expanded listing of figural Salt and Pepper Shakers.

ART GLASS (PRICED INDIVIDUALLY)

Cord and Tassel, Double, round shaker in glossy pink marbelized glass, orig tin top, Consolidated Lamp and Glass, 1894, 157-M . . 32.00
Egg, flat side, white satin finish, 2½" h, pewter top, made for Libbey for the Columbian Exposition of 1893, 28-B 65.00
Erie Twist, white satin glass, hp delicate pink flowers, leaves shading to buff, 2 pc pewter top, patent 1892, 28-H 95.00
Flower Band, 2½", large squatty base, raise flower band around base, pink cased glass, orig tin top, 29-G 45.00
Hand with Fishscale, 3", clear, frosted glass, pewter moon and stars top, pedestal base, 30-L 38.00
Inverted Thumbprint, 2½", sapphire blue, cylindrical, 2 pc pewter top . 42.00
Knobby, heavy opaque white, hp pastel flowers, shading to pale yellow, orig pewter top 35.00
Leaf Umbrella, 3½", sapphire blue matte finish case glass, orig brass plated tin top, Northwood, 32-S . 65.00

Little Apple, 2½" h, small round satin finished, hp pink and light yellow blossoms, shaded mint green to ivory, Mt. Washington, pewter top, 33-B 32.00

Oval and Fan, 3", carmel colored marble, orig tin top, Colorplate D 55.00

Pillar Rib, 3", white satinized opaque glass, hp delicate leaves and flowers, Mt. Washington, pewter top, 168-O 50.00

Quilted Phlox, 3½", pale green cased glass, Northwood, orig tin top, 36-H 42.00

Royal Oak, frosted and clear, shading red to white, orig brass top, Northwood, 171-E 58.00

FIGURAL AND SOUVENIR TYPES (PRICED BY SET)

Bathing Beauties, flapper style bathing suits, one reclining, one sitting, hp in naturalistic colors, Germany 35.00

Billiken, white opaque and crystal, gilt, shape of Buddha, inscription on base "The God of things as they ought to be," patent 1908, tin top, 22-U 55.00

Boot on Fan, clear tip top, made for Centennial, 1876, moon and stars top, 155-N 35.00

Dogs, cast metal, 3", green paint, amber glass eyes 65.00

Refrigerator, 2⅞", shaped like old fashioned G.E. refrigerator, white opaque glass, black trim, chrome plated top, 36-N 30.00

Sugar and Creamer, miniature, 1½", glass base, sp tops, Lechner page 108, No. 1 .... 32.00

Sunshine Baker, 2⅝", made in Japan for Sunshine Baking Co, white hp china, baker and chef hat, bow tie 12.00

OPALESCENT GLASS (PRICED INDIVIDUALLY)

Alaska, 2¾", blue, bulbous base, threaded top, pewter lid, Northwood, Lechner Ref. Plate 26 52.00

Beatty Honeycome, 3", white, A. J. Beatty Co., 22-Q 42.00

Bulging Cloud, 3½", bulbous, raised cloudlike pattern around base, translucent shade of sky blue with fiery opal clouds, brass top, 23-O 42.00

Hobnail, 3¼", clear base, opal white hobs, pewter lid with finial, Hobbs, 163-J 42.00

Opalescent Ribbon, short, small blown molded, ribbon of opal col-

or around clear base, orig brass top, Buckeye Glass, c1890, 167-F 42.00

Polka Dot Swirl, 3", opal blue, raised contracting clear dots, orig brass top 45.00

OPAQUE GLASS (PRICED INDIVIDUALLY UNLESS OTHERWISE NOTED)

New Martinsville, Maranese, 3½", $48.00.

Bulging Petal, 2½", green, orig brass top, Consolidated Lamp and Glass, 23-R 28.00

Cotton Bale, pink glossy, shape of cotton bale, orig brass top, Consolidated Lamp and Glass, 1894, 25-W 32.00

Double Deck, bulbous bottom, indented center, ribbed top, white, hp decor with green top portion, gilt on base, orig brass ornate top, 27-U 32.00

Elongated Drops, 3", heavy white opaque, dainty flower trim in orange, blown mold, pewter top, 28-F 28.00

Feather Panel, 2¾", square shaped pattern with all over pastel paint on white base, pink and yellow shading, orig brass top, 28Q 28.00

Leaf Standing, white opqaue glass with hint of opal, plain, pattern of raised upright leaves around base, orig brass top, 165-E 24.00

Palmette Band, white, yellow hp flowers, domed small tin top, New Martinsville Glass Co., 167-N ... 28.00

Pleated Skirt, deep opaque blue, broad base with vertical pleats, brass top, Challinor, Taylor, 1891, 35-S 35.00

Rabbit, large egg shape, domed lid, sitting rabbits on both sides, 36-J 48.00

Rose Relievo, round, white, raised

rose and leaves around base, tin top 38.00

Scroll and Bulge, glossy blue, hp, orig brass dome top, Mt. Washington, 38-J 38.00

Scroll, Tapered, cylinder shape, narrower at top, raised scroll pattern, orig brass top, custard, 38-U 42.00

Vine with Flower, 3¾", raised pattern of vine and flower around base, tin top, New Martinsville, 43-A 32.00

PATTERN GLASS (PRICED INDIVIDUALLY)

Bulls Eye and Daisy, 3", clear, amethyst flashed, gold trimmed, orig tin top, U.S. Glass, 1903, 23-U .. 32.00

Carolina, 4¼", clear and ruby flashed, dome lid, U.S. Glass, c1893 .... 32.00

Curtain, 3", clear glass, pedestal base, ornate brass plated top, Bryce Bros, 1885, 26-K 22.00

Cut Log, clear, pewter top, 26-O ... 28.00

Daisy and Cube, 3½", brilliant sapphire blue, tin top, 26-W 32.00

Grape, 4 leaf, 3⅝", pedestal base, clear, gilt decor, goofus style, celluloid center top, 30-F 18.00

Heart Band, 3", clear and ruby flashed, McKee Glass, 1897, 162-T 32.00

Manhattan, 3½", clear, gold trim, pewter top, U. S. Glass, 1903, 166-A 32.00

Queen Anne, 3", clear, footed, handles, pewter top, LaBelle Glass Co., 1878, 36-F 22.00

Teardrop Row, 3½", clear, heavy brilliant glass, ornate brass plated top, rows of teardrops, 41-Q 28.00

Swirl and Panel, 3", heavy, swirls around bottom, tin top, 40-X 18.00

Two Ban, 3", clear, pedestal base, handle, 42-R 24.00

Two Panel, 3¼", clear and colors, pewter top, Richards & Hartley, 1880 .... 28.00

SALT GLAZED WARES

Salt glazed wares have a distinctive "pitted" surface texture, made by throwing salt into the hot kiln during the final firing process. The salt vapors produced sodium oxide and hydrochloric acid which react on the glaze.

Many Staffordshire potters produced large quantities of this type of ware during the 18th and 19th centuries. A relatively small quantity was produced in the United States. Salt glazed wares continue to be made today.

Pitcher, 9" h, bamboo design, rope banding, gray marked, Ridgway & Co, England, $100.00.

Basket, oval, pierced, 2 handles, 9" stand, c1765 .... 200.00

Bottle, 9¼", globular, applied foliage, c1755 .... 395.00

Coffee Cup, 2½", white, molded vines and animals, Thomas & John Wedgwood, mid-18th C ... 220.00

Dish, 10", pierced, lobed, allover pattern of panels of diaper, herringbone and basketweave, c1760 420.00

Flower Pot, 4 x 5", putty color, Mistletoe and Basketweave pattern, interior glazed, Brownfield & Son 30.00

Jugs

5¼", baluster shape, floral decor, c1744 .... 185.00

9¾", deep brown to beige, molded, Royal Arms, vines and flowers, Lambeth, early 19th C ... 300.00

Pitcher, 7½", lily and foliage in relief, American, c1890 .... 140.00

Plates

9¼", soup, polychrome, vase of flowers on a table, molded diaper and basketweave border, c1755 .... 475.00

9½", polychrome, central cartouch of diaper and basketweave, pierced border suspending fruit, c1760 ...... 715.00

Sauceboats
7", oval, molded birds and trailing
vine, 3 mask and paw feet ... 540.00
8¼", oval, gadrooned, c1760 ... 600.00
Sugar Bowl, 3½", cylindrical, polychrome, baskets of flowers,
buildings, c1760 .... 350.00
Syrup, 7½", melon rib, white, blue
bands, hinged pewter lid, W.B.
Flouger 210.00
Tankard, 7", molded with scene after Teniers, above a fox hunt, silver rim, Mortlake 120.00
Teapot, cov, 7", crabstock handle
and finial, straight spout, trailing
flowering branches, c1775 ..... 440.00
Tureen, cov, 13" w, oval, handled,
molded panels of teardrop pattern, bands of basketweave, 3
mask and paw feet, c1760 ..... 823.00
Vases, 6", Campana, applied swags
of flowers, lion's masks, ftd,
c1760 .... 390.00

SALTS

In the days of the Roman Empire, salt was
very scarce and expensive. Roman soldiers
were posted to guard the Via Salaria (salt
road) to protect the supply. Salt was pro-
cured from saline plants, inland streams, and
ocean waters. Even with this limited supply
of salt, the need arose for a receptacle in
which to serve it. The first open salt was a
hand carved wooden trencher, probably the
size of a small master salt.

From this humble beginning until the late
1800s when the shaker was invented, master
and individual salts (the latter becoming popular by the 1500s) were on the tables of royalty and peasants alike. The finest salts were
at the head of the table, the lesser ones for
those sitting "below the salt."

By 1700 salts of many shapes and materials were being made. By the 18th century
master silversmiths and glass makers in
America were producing silver and blown
flint glass salts. During the 1800s and to a
small extent into the 1900s, many china, cut
glass and pressed glass salts were made.

The use of open salts has decreased since
the shaker was invented. However, they still
are used regularly in many countries abroad
and by collectors and others in America to
dress up their tables.

The numbers in parenthesis refer to the
plates in the nine volumes of books on open
salts and master salts by Allan B. and Helen
B. Smith, and Daniel Synder, the latter doing
the master salt section in volumes eight and
nine. In the Lacy section of Master Salts the

references from L. W. and D. B. Neal's
*Pressed Glass Salt Dishes of the Lacy Period,
1825–1850* also are given.

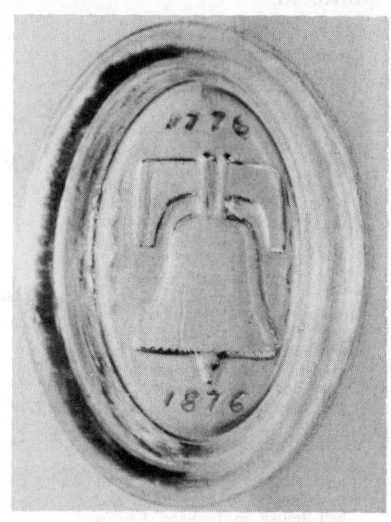

Individual, clear, oval, Liberty Bell,
$75.00.

CONDIMENT SETS WITH OPEN SALTS, CHINA

Birds, two long billed, colorful birds
supply pepper and mustard, fit
into green leaf base, open salt in
red oval in front leaf, handle,
unmkd (389) 70.00
Celtic Rose pattern, squared pepper
and mustard, round salt, silver
holder with impressed design, mkd
"A. J. Wilkinson Ltd., England"
(388) 50.00
Chef, head and shoulders are pepper shaker, holding bowl which is
salt, cooking pot on round stove is
mustard, floral decoration on mustard and chef's shoulders, French
origin (389) 60.00
Rabbits, sit atop eggs (pepper and
mustard) with beaded decoration,
quatrefoil shell salt, gold highlights, English origin (389) 45.00
Square shaped base, Turkish arch
handle, salt, pepper, and mustard
fit into openings, floral decoration
on base, written in gold "A Pres-

ent From Liverpool," mkd "Made
in Bavaria" (388) **50.00**

INDIVIDUAL

China
  Ceramic Art Company, ruffled
    oval, shallow, bone white with
    brownish inside border, leaf
    spray, mkd with circle and pal-
    ette of Ceramic Art Co. and
    "B.B&B (Bailey, Banks & Bid-
    dle), Phila, Pa" (377) **18.00**
  German, round, white with slightly
    ruffled pink top inside and out,
    decorated inside and out with
    sprigs of flowers in pastel col-
    ors, three gold feet, mkd with
    crown and "Dresden, Germany"
    (251) **18.00**
  German, swan, white ground, dec-
    orated on neck, wings, and tail
    with rose, blue, and yellow flow-
    ers, gold highlights, blue flower
    on inside, mkd "D" and "Dres-
    den, Germany" (376) **27.50**
  Goss, round, thin body, gold top
    edge, inside bowl is picture of
    house and words "First And
    Last House Land's End," mkd
    on base "H. T. James first and
    last house in England Land's
    End," eagle symbol, and "W. H.
    Goss," c1858 (252) **20.00**
  Italy, donkey (white with black ton-
    ing) pulls rectangular yellow cart
    with red wheels, mkd "Italy"
    (376) **20.00**
  Unmarked, Aladdin lamp shape,
    red, touches of white around
    top, curled handle, incised
    sweeping lines on side (381) . .   **15.00**
  Unmarked, quatrefoil, oval base,
    white ground, blue top edge,
    black Puffin perched on edge
    (376) **22.00**
  Unmarked, round, scalloped top
    edge, gold band on top edge,
    pearlized interior, deep red flow-
    ers and green leaves on bowl, 3
    shaped feet (377) **18.00**
  Unmarked, shell shape, 3 small
    feet, scalloped gold edge, inside
    bowl is spray of orange flowers
    and green leaves against a
    white ground (381) **15.00**
Colored Glass
  Alexandrite, fluted round body with
    extended prow, clear rigaree by
    which salt rests on three legged
    frame, frame mkd "D & A" and
    "EPNS" (254) **115.00**
  Blue, cased, clear and white, scal-

loped overlapping rim, cut
through to reveal clear 4 petal
design flower, baroque candle-
stick style silver base (373) . . .   **95.00**
Blue, cased, white interior, round,
bulbous sides, ring neck, roses
and leaves inside bottom, brass
wire frame of vertical diamonds,
beaded handle (370) **35.00**
Blue, clear, half sphere bowl, thick
flat circular base, French, c1810
(386) **40.00**
Blue, clear, round, Art Nouveau
white metal frame, filigree
scrolls (373) **25.00**
Cobalt, tub, 2 colorless bales, tab
handles (380) **25.00**
Cranberry, oval, 12 scalloped pan-
els around bowl, supported on 4
clear rigaree feet, shell rigaree
loops decorate bowl between
feet (378) **50.00**
Green, clear, double, rectangular,
alternating scallops and ridges
around bowl, indented diagonal-
ly lined bottom (380) **25.00**
Green, clear, ruffled bowl, gold
top edge, gold filigree decoration on side, curled serpent han-
dle (379) **45.00**
Hand Blown, blue, unevenly ruf-
fled rim and subtle paneled
bowl roughly following divisions
of ruffles, tapers to flared ring
base, rough pontil (307) **20.00**
Monot Stumpf, deepish rose color-
ing, flared scalloped neck, brass
frame of crescent moons studded with amethyst cut stones,
brass ruffle base (378) **160.00**
Opalescent Hobnail, blue, round
(377) **20.00**
Ruby, oval, metal frame of 4 posts
with "x" connection on which
glass rests, fluted metal collar,
frame mkd "Triple Plate, Porter
Brit. and Plate Co.," number 31
(373) **15.00**
Steuben, Verre de Soie, pedestal,
inverted bell body, pink reeding
around bowl (309) **150.00**
Venetian, blue, pedestal, diagonal
panels on bowl and pedestal, 2
gold swans form handles (386) .   **35.00**
Cut Glass
Five sided, fans at corners supplement diamond point designs on
each panel, pattern of square
crisscross bottom (271) **20.00**
Pedestal, alternating English hob-
nail and button patterns, ridged
pedestal base (293) **25.00**
Round, alternating double zip-

pered and eight-point star panels (361) **27.50**

Round, fans around top form serrated top edge, 4 sectional diamonds around bowl, 4 sectioned flared shallow base (362)   **37.50**

Star, looking from top the rim forms ten-point star, Brilliant cut, 12 zippered panels around bowl, 12 rayed bottom cut (291)   **15.00**

Star, eight points, zippered points, eight-point star on bottom (361)   **20.00**

Tub, tab handles, six-point fans around top, diamond pattern around bowl, inverted fans at bottom of bowl, rayed bottom (361) **30.00**

Double Salts

China, French origin, shells, maiden seated between them, rose ground, gold highlighting (392) .   **30.00**

China, French origin, swans, white with gray on wings, gold on bowls (389) **30.00**

China, Meissen, oval, blue and white, leaves and flowers, sgd with Meissen crossed swords (392) **55.00**

Glass, amber, clear, round, basket-like bowls, impressed fan designs, handle with ball on top (393) **40.00**

Glass, clear, round, diamond pattern with rayed base, copper handle with 3 applied copper leaves (395) **45.00**

Glass, clear, round, plain, tapered paneled sided toothpick holder as handle, made in Hungary (394) **25.00**

Glass, clear, shell shaped bowls, dolphins form base with tails forming handle, French (395) . .   **35.00**

Glass, milk, white, bulbous bowls, relief fluting, shaped turned style handle (393) **22.00**

Pottery, Quimper, round bowl, tan ground, fluted sides, floral design on exterior, square handle, blue line highlights, sgd "Quimper, France" (392) **60.00**

Pottery, Quimper, swans, white with deep blue decoration, peasant boy inside one, sgd "Quimper" (389) **60.00**

Pottery, unmkd, green leaves, yellow bird with open mouth for toothpicks (389) **35.00**

Metal

Chinese Coolie pulling rickshaw containing open salt basket, pepper shaker, and covered basket mustard jar, spoon, Coolie and rickshaw on wheels (245) **400.00**

Cupid driving goat pulling sleigh, silver, square sleigh with swirled and leaf chasing and medallion for monogram on each side, gold wash interior, colorless glass liner, spoon in shape of shovel, mkd "800" star, and unidentified punchmark (352) . .   **550.00**

Cupid driving two prancing horses pulling a two wheeled chariot, silver, cupid on back of chariot blowing horn, fine twisted wire reins, Continental, c1915 (352) .   **575.00**

Elliptical, silver, tripod feet, ribbed leaf design, matching spoons, pair, cased in green velvet box with silk lining (279) **100.00**

Man and Woman seated against catus with eagle on top, Aztec calendar bowl, Mexican silver, spoon (356) **50.00**

Oval, coin silver, tripod feet of ram's head atop hoofed foot, flat repousse rim, repousse band around body, Gorham hallmark (354) **150.00**

Platter type, gold wash bowl, wide rim with leaf and ribbon decoration, Gorham hallmark, "Sterling," and "2545," 1890 (359) .   **45.00**

Shell shaped, pewter type, supported by 2 cherubs, unmkd (354) **30.00**

Tiffany, SS, ornate decoration band on top edge and base, mkd "Tiffany & Co. 295M6791 Sterling Silver" (358) **85.00**

Tiffany, SS, round bowl, gold wash, tripod feet of ram's head atop hoofed foot, mkd "Tiffany & Co. M," 470, and 4102, c1856–59 (239) **200.00**

Pressed Glass

Pedestal, four lobed, tulip in each lobe, honeycomb pattern between (293) **15.00**

Pedestal, octagonal waisted bowl on shallow octagonal base, bottom has rayed design, three-line decoration across top, waist, and base, sgd "Heisey" (362) **55.00**

Pedestal, Open Rose pattern, border in cable design (293) **20.00**

Round, beaded elliptical design around bowl, hexagonal base (361) **35.00**

Round, Orrefors, six dimples on bottom reflect into bowl, etched "OR" on bottom (362) **50.00**

Shallow, wide ruffled rim with gold

edge, hobs of glass on under-
side (364) 10.00
Sleigh, scroll pattern around top,
openwork on runners, attr. to
Fostoria (290) 25.00
Stork, body is salt, feather design,
head and feet are support, scal-
loped top edge (362) 20.00

Wood

Round, scalloped top with extended flared neck, carved geometric pattern around bowl, narrow
base, spoon (356) 15.00
Round, straight extended neck,
bulbous body, red with two petal, orange and yellow flower,
mkd on white label "DE IN NO"
and "62030" in ink (356) 27.50

INTAGLIOS

Fruits — apples, cherries, pears, and
grapes, green, amber, blue and
amethyst, chamfered corners, set
of four (367) 120.00
Horses' Heads, brown, reins
extending from bits, touches of
green and red irid on cheeks,
oval, subtle faceting in diamond
pattern around bowl (368) 25.00
Indian Symbols, clear, chamfered
corners (367) 22.50
Mickey Mouse, clear, strongly cham-
fered corners (368) 22.00
Playing Card Symbols, tray and 4
salts, blue, painted and painted
over with white paint, tray mkd
"Canada" in script (368) 50.00

MASTER

China

Copper Lustre, pedestal, sand
band (387) 40.00
Dresden, double, lacy style, floral
design, gold highlights, star motif at division, mkd with Meissen
crossed swords (317) 60.00
Flow Blue, pedestal, blue rose in
center of bowl, gold highlights
(387) 60.00
Kauffmann, Angelica, pedestal,
gold filigree motif, blue band on
base and inside top of bowl,
gold lines, painting in interior
sgd by Kauffmann (387) 45.00
Lowestoft reproduction, trencher,
Mottahedek design, deep blue
and rust (313) 30.00
Marked, trencher, white ground,
blue "M" monogram on front,
blue floral decoration on sides,
sgd on bottom with castle under
which is "GIEN" (317) 125.00

**Master, Portland Glass Nest, forked
branches, c1863–73, $70.00.**

Royal Staffordshire, pedestal,
white, decorated inside with
English scene of people, building, waterfront, and ships in harbor, mkd "Royal Staffordshire
Ceramics/Made in England"
(387) 20.00
Unmarked, lily pattern, scalloped
gold top edge, gold accents in
lily, attached to scalloped edge
bottom plate (314) 20.00
Unmarked, round, pedestal, bul-
bous body, blue country scenes,
blue flowers on inside of rim
(313) 45.00
Unmarked, trencher, Quimper
style, floral designs in deep blue
and rust colors (314) 45.00
Wedgwood, Jasperware, blue
ground, hunting scene around
bowl, silver rim, marked "Wedg-
wood" (314) 150.00

Colored Glass

Amber, cradle, shaped ends, half
circle rockers (325) 45.00
Amberina, pedestal, alternating
diamond point and plain swirl
pattern, attr. to Baccarat (323) .   85.00
Blue, clear, wheelbarrow, basket-
weave body for salt (325) 50.00
Blue, crackle, round, heavy ta-
pered bowl, mkd "Made In Ita-
ly" (315) 30.00
Blue, opaque, Lacy, Basket Flow-
ers, light mottling, Boston and
Sandwich Glass Co., Neal BFIc
(324) 325.00

Clambroth, pedestal, oval, oval medallions on two sides, ribbed on other two (384)	40.00
Cobalt, boat shape, pedestal (323)	60.00
Cobalt, Steigel type, pedestal, diamond pattern on bowl (387) .	200.00
Cranberry, oval, fluted, clear applied rigaree on rim and base (313)	75.00
Green, frog, squat, clear glass center (325)	25.00
Green, lily pad pattern, vaseline glass rigaree around bowl, attr. to Stevens and Williams (315) .	125.00
Purple Slag, rectangular, scalloped top, ribbed base, small handles, leaf and flower print (313)	30.00
Vaseline, opalescent, round, plain top, wide ribbed bottom, "549-518" on inside of salt (316)	45.00
Yellow-green, Lacy, Strawberry Diamond, Boston and Sandwich Glass Co., Neal SD7 (324)	225.00

Cut Glass

Clover shaped, fan and diamond pattern (332)	25.00
Oblong, horizontal ribs, Scotland (337)	18.00
Oval, diamond rayed pattern, rim with small cut fans, flared form (332)	25.00
Round, cut star around bowl, squat form (333)	25.00
Round, English hobnail with fans (334)	22.00
Round, twenty-four zippered ribs, fan cuttings (332)	22.00

Metal

Pewter, pedestal, mkd "Dickson and Son, Sheffield" (319)	45.00
Silver, cherubs at each corner bent over with the burden of salt, gallery, clear rectangular insert, mkd "J. W. Tufts, Boston" (312)	75.00
Silver, ftd frame in grape and leaf pattern, clear, paneled, round insert (312)	40.00
Silver Plate, round bowl, beaded under rim, applied feet, triangular base, engraved "The Queen's Hotel," mkd on bottom "Robert Eait, New York" (312) .	50.00
Silver Plate, round bowl, large rim band with relief floral decoration, four applied legs with fan tops, marked "Simpson Hall, Miller & Co. Triple Plate" (312) .	40.00

Pressed Glass

Arched Panel sides, scalloped rim, pedestal, round (398)	25.00
Buckle, oval (335)	45.00

Bull's Eye pattern on top, ribbed pattern around base, round, tapered (332)	20.00
Diamond Band, scalloped rim, ribbed base, early Irish (333) . .	18.00
Electric, round (334)	18.00
Hexagonal, flint glass, heavy, rayed design on bottom (402) .	15.00
Lacy, Beaded Scroll, New England origin, Neal BS4 (327)	95.00
Lacy, ovals and diamond cornucopias, pedestal, scalloped top, ribbed scalloped base, Pittsburgh area, Neal PP1 (330) . . .	150.00
Lacy, Sawtootn Circle, Boston and Sandwich Glass Co., Neal 002 (327)	65.00
Lily-of-the-valley, cov, round, ftd, early (400)	125.00
Overshot, oval, attr. to Boston and Sandwich Glass Co. (404)	25.00
Paneled Diamond, round, straight foot and ring base (331)	30.00
Sheaf and Diamond, pedestal (399)	22.00
Viking, round, feet formed of Viking heads (341) . . . . ·	30.00

SAMPLERS

Samplers served many purposes. For a young child they were a practice exercise and permanent reminder of stitches and patterns. For a young woman they demonstrated her skills in a "gentle" art and preserved key elements of family genealogy. For the mature woman they were a useful occupation and functioned as gifts or remembrance, e.g., mourning pieces.

Schools for young ladies of the early 19th century prided themselves on the needlework skills they taught. The Westtown School in Chester County, Pennsylvania, and the Young Ladies Seminary in Bethlehem, Pennsylvania, are two examples. These schools changed their teaching as styles changed. Berlin work was introduced by the mid-19th century.

Examples of samplers date back to the 1700s. The earliest ones were long and narrow, usually done only with the alphabet and numerals. Later examples were square. At the end of the 19th century the shape tended to be rectangular.

The same motifs were used throughout the country. The name is a key element in determining region. Samplers are assumed to be on linen unless otherwise indicated.

1836, 15 x 15½", H. Croll, red and blue alphabet on natural linen, unfinished, $225.00

1717, 5½ x 7½" w, Ann Wilkinson, New England, alphabet, numerals and pious verse, all in alternating brown and green colors **600.00**

1742, 15½ x 10", Lydia Draper, North Shore, MA, 3 rows of floral motif, verse, alphabet, in red, blue, green, yellow, apricot and ivory . .   **1,200.00**

1763, 21½ x 9" w, Sarah Wood, England, geometric motifs, alphabet, verse, numerals, strawberry and vine bottom panel **3,000.00**

1768, 17 x 14", Rebecca Leach, New England, alphabet, pastoral landscape with seated lady, lambs, birds, dogs, trees and flowers, serpentine floral border **7,000.00**

1802, 23 x 18", Polly Parker, Bradford, MA, alphabet, numerals, pious verse, landscape with gentleman, lady tending sheep, dog and trees **2,000.00**

1808, 12½ x 16½" w, Mary G. Kimball, Haverhill, MA, alphabet above urn shaped monument with pious verse and polychrome floral bushes on either side, geometric and floral vine borders **6,000.00**

1813, 15 x 13½" w, Susanna Marsters, green with white floss, alphabets, hearts, birds, trees, geometric border **575.00**

1813, 15½ x 12", Mary Ann Webster, Woodbury School, pious verse, landscape vignettes with log cabin and pine tree, floral border **800.00**

1817, 15 x 11", Clarinda Fuller, al-phabet and numerals, pious verse, colonial house and basket of flowers **550.00**

1817, 17" sq, Lucretia D. Barrett, Chelmsford, alphabet, numerals, verse, circular floral vine border .   **900.00**

1819, 17 x 16½", Hannah P. Tudor, alphabet, numerals, verse, colonial house and trees, geometric border, blue and beige **1,100.00**

1819, 21½ x 24½", Mary Ann Fessenden Vinton, central panel contains bereaved female beside urn-top monument, framed with alphabet and numerals, entirely framed by colored floral border **600.00**

1821, Mary Faith Chatham, sectional, alphabet, numerals, pious verse, multisections containing farming vignettes surrounding vase containing flowers, sawtooth and floral border **850.00**

1827, 17½" sq, Mary Ann Kendall, New England, alphabet and numerals above family record, floral vine border, blue, white, yellow and green on silk **750.00**

1831, 16 x 13½", Rhode Baker, large house with peaked roof above standing lady and gentleman, flowering trees, deer, sawtooth floral border **450.00**

1836, 19¾ x 16¾" w, Martha Sole, pious verse, floral heart around name, stylized flowers and trees, colonial house, vining floral border, birdseye maple frame **575.00**

1837, 23 x 22", Ann Taylor, England, verse and 2 thistles above polychrome-worked building entitled "Soloman's Temple", stylized geometric floral border **800.00**

1840, 20 x 13½", Carol Eisner, England, worked at Mrs. Harris's Hucclecore Acadamy, pious verse, Adam and Eve above landscape, man plowing, tavern, horse drawn cov wagon, polychrome floral and vine border **600.00**

1881, 8 x 12½", Annie Waterson, alphabet, numerals and verse, schoolhouse and trees, oak frame   **225.00**

SANDWICH GLASS

The term Sandwich Glass applies to the large variety of glass, including lacy (1825–1850), made by The Boston and Sandwich Glass Company from 1822 to 1888. Although the company is best known for its pressed glass,

it also manufactured art glass in the 1870s and 1880s.

See *Warman's Americana & Collectibles* for additional listings of Sandwich Glass

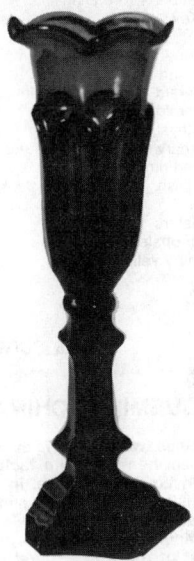

Vase, 11¾" h, peacock green, loop pattern, $170.00.

Bank, clear, peacock blue applied rigaree, cock finial, 2 silver U.S. dimes, dated 1835 within knop stem, 12" h **7,000.00**

Bottles
  Cologne, cranberry threaded, ribbed Lutz type body, matching stopper, pontil polished, 6" h . . **225.00**
  Vinegar, blown three mold, purple-blue, period stopper **190.00**

Bowls
  6¼", Daisy **85.00**
  6¼", Industry, lacy **100.00**
  6⅜", Hairpin, lacy **110.00**
  8 x 5¼", double cornucopia and diamond border, Princess Feather base **255.00**
  8⅜", Peacock Eyes, rayed, lacy, small rim chips **50.00**
  8½", Princess Feather, medallion with heart, crossed swords center, herringbone and stippled background **130.00**
  8½", 7 Panel, heavy flint **70.00**

8½", Tulip and Acanthus Leaf, lacy **90.00**
Miniature, lacy, opal **225.00**
Candleholder, 3" h, opaque blue, ring handle **425.00**

Candlesticks
  4¾", clear, square base, round steps, c1840 . . . . **95.00**
  6⅞", clear, petal top, circular feet, pr **125.00**
  7", canary yellow, loop and petal, open bubble on foot ring **75.00**
  7", electric blue, hexagonal base **150.00**
  7⅛", canary yellow, petal top . . . **100.00**
  7¼", translucent opaque white, petal top, slight opalescence . . **175.00**
  7½", medium amethyst, flint, hexagonal base, pr **300.00**
  7½", medium blue, petal top, hexagonal base, pr **525.00**
  9¼", clear, beehive, deep socket **1,550.00**
  10¼", clambroth, dolphin stem . . **200.00**
  10⅜", canary, dolphin stem, single step, wafer, pr **675.00**

Celery Vases
  Arch Pattern, 11¼" h, cobalt, cascade base **475.00**
  Blue Amethyst, octagonal base, wafer **550.00**
  Diamond Thumbprint, pr **450.00**

Compotes
  7½ x 4", Rayed Peacock Eye . . . **350.00**
  8 x 5¾", oval, Bigler-type pattern, hexagonal base, flint **125.00**
  8¼ x 6", Acanthus Leaf, flint . . . **175.00**
  8¼", Pipes of Pan, oblong **325.00**

Creamers
  Lacy, clear **225.00**
  Shield **295.00**
Cup and Saucer, lacy, clear **150.00**
Curtain Tiebacks, 4½" d, opal, pewter shanks, set of 6 . . . . **475.00**
Decanter, canary yellow, Waffle and Bull's Eye, bar lip, matching stopper, 12½" h **900.00**

Dishes
  5¾", Rayed Peacock Eye **130.00**
  6¼", Tulip and Acanthus Leaf, lacy **90.00**
  8", Daisy, lacy **75.00**
  8", Scotch Plaid, deep, lacy, pontil mark **100.00**
  9¼", octagonal, beehive, lacy, minor nicks **70.00**
Flat Iron, clear, miniature **85.00**
Jug, clear, crackle, applied gold enamel, cranberry serpent around body, looping to form handle, flint **100.00**

Lamps
  5½", clear, crackle, frosted **90.00**
  6½", double wick burner, free blown font, wafer connects to 3 round step base, waterfall interi-

or on sq plinth with cupcake
corners, pewter collar 225.00
8¼", clear, Sawtooth font, hexagonal base, orig pewter collar,
double drop whale oil burner . . 150.00
10½", clear, Star and Punty 235.00
12", amethyst, tulip shape font,
milk glass base 475.00
Milk Pan, 7¼ x 3" h, green, free
blown, folded rim, pinched lip . . . 355.00
Mustard Pot, cov, Peacock Eye,
underplate 275.00
Pitchers
7", blue overshot glass, sq mouth,
bulbous body, applied amber
handle, blown 265.00
8½", amber overshot glass, clo-
verleaf shaped top, amber
ribbed shell applied handle,
blown 255.00
8½", cranberry, applied crystal
handle 300.00
Plates
6", Hairpin 70.00
6", Leaf and Scroll 60.00
6", Oak Leaf 45.00
6¼", heart border, lacy, clear . . . 65.00
7", shell like border, lacy, clear . . 90.00
7¼", Peacock Eye 75.00
8", Peacock Eye and Thistle 130.00
9½", Quatrefoil, lacy 125.00
Pomade, 3¾" h, bear, white
opaque, opal 295.00
Pulls, drawer
Canary, set of 6 . . . . 250.00
Clear, Raised Petal and Loop, set
of 6 . . . . 125.00
Salts, also see "Salts"
Christmas, dated tops, agitators
Amber 110.00
Clear 55.00
Hexagonal, pedestal
Amethyst, 2" 165.00
Canary, 1⅞" 150.00
Sauces
Beaded Scale and Eye, daisy cen-
ter, clear 75.00
Peacock Eye, clear 45.00
Roman Rosette, fiery opal 100.00
Shell Medallion, octagonal, clear . 70.00
Waffle, flint 25.00
Spillholders
Clambroth, Vine pattern 350.00
Deep amethyst, 6 panel, heavy
flint, gold presentation decor . . 350.00
Stringholder, cobalt blue rim, ring
around string hole, 4" x 3⅞"
h 300.00
Sugars, covered
Acanthus Leaf, lacy, clear 300.00
Ruby glass, ftd, 4½" h, made by
Sandwich Co-Operative, c1880 . 750.00
Toddy Plate, 5⅞", star and fan bor-

der, 8 pointed star in center,
raised sq hobs alternating 80.00
Tray, Butterfly, lacy, 8 x 5" 195.00
Tumblers
Clear, cranberry threading 95.00
Roman Key 70.00
Vases
5¾", emerald green, ring foot, ball
fluted band 750.00
9⅝", emerald green, Bigler, flint . 1,150.00
9⅞", emerald green, tulip 450.00
10", amethyst, Petal and Loop . . 365.00
11⅝", canary yellow, three printie,
gauffered rim 300.00
Vegetable Dish, open, lacy, clear,
10¾" l 300.00
Whiskey Tasters
Lacy, fiery opalescence 165.00
Loop, canary yellow 230.00

SARREGUE MINES

SARREGUEMINES CHINA

**Sarreguemines ware is a faience type, i.e.,
tin-glazed earthenware. The factory was established in Lorraine, France, in 1770, under
the supervision of Utzcheider and Fabry. The
factory was regarded as one of the three
most prominent manufacturers of French Faience. Most of the wares found today are of
the 19th century. Later wares are impressed
Sarreguemines and Germany due to a
change of boundaries and location of the
factory.**

Basket, 10½" l, majolica, turquoise
glaze sides, entwined with puce,
blue morning glories, green
leaves, coiling brown vines, c1880 200.00
Bouillon Cup, 8" underplate, copper
lustre finish, 2 pcs 35.00
Cake Set, 12½" d serving plate, ring
handles, six 8" d plates, Vintage
pattern, yellow, green, 7 pcs 245.00
Creamer, 5", row of ducks, frog,
flower border 45.00
Jugs, Character
5¼ x 4" d, majolica, man's head,
beige, brown, rosy cheeks,
nose, mouth, blue interior,
marked 65.00
7½", The Scotsman, red hair,
blue and red hat 75.00
8½", Happy, Sad, majolica, tan-
kard, overall variegated olive
green, turquoise interior, happy
man's face on upper portion, inverted sad face on lower half,

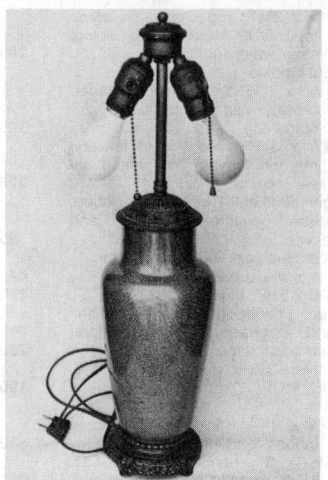

Lamp, crystalline glaze, tan, 21½″ h overall, vase 11¼″, impressed mark, $175.00.

latin verse impressed around base	45.00
Mustard Jar, cov	10.00
Pitcher, 8″, shoemaker scenes	140.00

Plates
7½″, beige, emb purple grapes in leaves, small scalloped edge	35.00
7½″, deep gold ground, strawberries in center	20.00
7¾″, majolica, scalloped rim, green trim, leaves, grapes in relief, imp Sarreguemines, France, set of 8	150.00
8″, cobalt, wide gold lacy etched border, center	20.00
8″, pierced handles, comical scene of monkey, dog on ship	30.00
9″, asparagus, figural	27.00
Vase, 6½″, green ground, oil drop finish, imp Sarreguemines/115/227, stamped ETNA	130.00

SATIN GLASS

Satin Glass refers to an opaque colored glass that has a soft velvety surface finish. The glass was treated with hydrofluoric acid to produce the dull satin finish. It was produced by many glass companies in the late Victorian era. The large majority of Satin Glass pieces were cased or had a white lining. Favorite items were vases and rose bowls which were most often produced in shaded tones of rose, yellow or blue. Plain satin glass was at times enamel decorated or had applied glass ornamentation.

Mother-of-Pearl (MOP) Satin Glass was perfected in 1885 by Joseph Webb while he was working at the Phoenix Glass Co., Beaver, Pa. Similar to plain satin glass in respect to the plating (or casing), Mother-of-Pearl Satin Glass differs in that it displays integral or indented designs in the glass and has a distinctive surface finish. The most common design was the diamond quilted pattern. Mother-of-Pearl Satin Glass was made in a variety of items such as tableware, fruit bowls, vases, rose bowls, pickle jars, night lights, etc. The most common colors were yellow, rose or blue with the beautiful rainbow coloring being considered choice.

Satin Glass, both plain and Mother-of-Pearl, have been widely reproduced.

For "Coralene" and "Cut Velvet" see the specific categories.

Tumbler, 3¾″, rainbow panels, DQ, MOP, $800.00.

Biscuit Jars with SP bail and cover
5¾ x 5¼″, blue ribbon, MOP, white lining	295.00
9½″, bulbous, yellow, narrow swirl, ribbing, enameled white flowers, brown leaves, white lining	225.00

Bowl, 4½ x 5"d, tricorn shape, blue, DQ, MOP, cream lining, crystal ruffle applied top, crystal wishbone feet **750.00**

Bride's Basket, no holder, 11⅛", rose, white underside, frosted edge, white enameled wheat ears and small florals on ruffles, gold trim **295.00**

Cruet, 8", rose, DQ, MOP, frosted handle, clear stopper **130.00**

Ewers
    7 x 3½", shaded pink, frosted flower, leaf and handle **145.00**
    9", melon ribbed, pedestal foot, aqua, gold and brown enameling, cream lining **110.00**
    9½ x 3⅞", shaded peach, white enameled daisies and scrolls, white lining, applied frosted handle **98.00**

Fairy Lamps, see FAIRY LAMPS

Finger Bowls
    2½ x 4¾", rainbow stripes, DQ, MOP, cream lining, patent in gloss letters on base **995.00**
    Pink and yellow Christmas candy design, ruffled edges with underplate, English **175.00**

Hatpin Holder, 3¼", pink, DQ, MOP, enamel floral decor **85.00**

Jam Jar, SP bail and cov, blue, herringbone, MOP, floral decor **295.00**

Lamps
    16½", melon sectioned, pink, DQ, MOP, white lining, brass chain and top for ceiling **895.00**
    24¼ x 8½", blue, MOP, coin spot, ruffled shade, brass base with 4 lion's heads holding garlands . **695.00**
    Hall, pink, blown out decor of draped festoons and rosettes . **400.00**

Mustard Pot, 3", apricot, coinspot, MOP, white lining, SP cov **100.00**

Pitchers
    7¼ x 6¼"d, bulbous, pink, enameled floral decor, frosted applied handle **250.00**
    7½", blue, DQ, MOP, white lining, frosted applied handle **210.00**
    8½", bulbous, white, raindrop pattern, frosted handle **255.00**
    9½", rainbow stripes, DQ, MOP, white lining, frosted handle ... **600.00**

Rose Bowls
    2½ x 3¾", ten crimp top, gold ribbon MOP, white lining **265.00**
    2⅝ x 4¼" eight crimp top, Rivulet pattern, shaded pink, MOP, white lining **235.00**
    3½ x 3½", eight crimp top, shaded rose, herringbone, MOP, white lining **225.00**

3⅝ x 2¾", egg shape, six crimp top, DQ, MOP, white lining, clear wafer foot **295.00**

Scent Bottles
    4⅛ x 1½"d, reclining, shaded brown, gold prunus decor, SS screw top **395.00**
    4¼ x 3½"d, ivory, gold flowers, maroon leaves, hallmarked silver top **225.00**

Sugar Shaker, 4¼", melon ribbed, yellow, enameled florals and leaves **95.00**

Sweetmeat Jars, SP bail and cov
    3⅛ x 5⅛", rose, DQ, MOP **425.00**
    5½ x 3½", blue, DQ, MOP **375.00**

Syrup, shaded pink to rose, Shell and Seaweed, enameled floral and scroll decor **290.00**

Tumbler, 3¾ x 2¾", shaded rose, DQ, MOP **100.00**

Vases
    5¾ x 3¼", stick shape, rainbow stripes, white lining **550.00**
    6⅛ x 3", rainbow stripes, DQ, MOP, white lining **950.00**
    7", double gourd shape, shaded robin's egg blue to turquoise .. **210.00**
    9", ruffled, shaded peach to apricot, MOP **235.00**
    10½", ruffled, pink, enameled girl in blue dress on front, bird on back, white lining, frosted reeded applied handles **295.00**
    10¾", bulbous bottom, narrow waist, 3 rippled top with cylindrical neck, shaded deep coral to pink, applied frosted thorn handles **190.00**

SATSUMA

Satsuma, named for a war lord who brought skilled Korean potters to Japan in the early 1600s, was a hand-crafted Japanese faience glazed pottery. It is finely-crackled, has a cream, yellow-cream or gray-cream color and is decorated with raised enamels in floral geometric and figural motifs.

Figural Satsuma was made specifically for export in the 19th century. Later Satsuma, referred to as Satsuma-style ware, is Japanese porcelain also hand-decorated in raised enamels. From 1912 to the present, this Satsuma-style ware has been mass-produced and much of the ware on today's market is of this later period.

Basket, 8", children and old man, c1850 .... **975.00**

Incense Burner, 4″ w, 3¾″ h, Courtesans on one side, Mandarins on other, c1875, $2400.00.

Berry Set, 10″ bowl, 4 nappy dishes, diapered border, figures, florals . . 125.00
Bottle, 8½″, peonies and clouds, c1885 . . . . 225.00
Bowls
  4½″, inside landscape with ladies and children, chrysanthemum border, outside children, vendors and musicians, sgd Seikozan, late 19th C 200.00
  4¾ x 2″d, deep, overall floral motif, early 19th C 290.00
Box, cov, 3½″, circular, 3 ball feet, ladies and children by river on cover, landscape sides, interior with sprigs of flowering plum, sgd Kinkozan, late 19th C 245.00
Brooch, flower shape, 1½″, floral bamboo design, wide cobalt border, sgd Mon 45.00
Brush Holder, 5″, cream, flowers and butterflies 50.00
Cache Pots, 10½″, hexagonal, scenic, earth tones, figural handles, 19th C, pr 1,350.00
Charger, 12½″, Thousand Warriors pattern, diaper border of dragons, multicolored, c1850 . . . . 1,500.00
Coffee Pots
  10½″, flared footing, cobalt blue, dark green, overall encrusted gold and jewel work, mirrored gold reserve of colorful mandarins 195.00
  10¾″, deep cobalt, encrusted gold, enameling, scenic, sages with mirrored gold behind them . 175.00
Cup and Saucer, scenic, diapered, 3 legs, c1900 . . . . 75.00
Dishes
  5″, lobed, pheasants, 19th C . . . 90.00

5½″, flowerheads, 19th C 95.00
Figure, Buddha, 18″, seated, cross legged, gilt body, robes painted to resemble brocade 550.00
Ginger Jar, 8¾ x 7¼″, bulbous, melon ribbed, diaper pattern, encrusted gold, enameled mums, mythical bird with enameled wings, c1890 . . . . 170.00
Incense Burners (Koro)
  2½″, blue and gilt panels with courtesans and children, sgd Taizan, c1900 . . . . 580.00
  4″, globular, 3 short tripod feet, domed, pierced silver wire cover, gilt floral ground with 2 panels, courtiers, woman with children, sgd Shokozan, 19th C . . 500.00
Jardiniere, 11½ x 12″w, blue ground, painted figures, shaped rim 150.00
Jars, covered
  6½″, 4 legs, heart shaped panels, children motif, dog finial, 19th C 110.00
  10″, 3 legs, Foo dog handles and finial, c1920 . . . . 95.00
Matchholder, hanging, butterfly, figural 60.00
Plate, 9⅝″, cream crackle glaze, brush fence, chrysanthemums, bamboo, stylized foliate rim, sgd, late 19th C 450.00
Sake Kettle, 3¼″, sealed, dragon motif 320.00
Tea Caddies, covered
  4½″, green to beige, foliage decor with insert 95.00
  5½″, handled, bird on blooming prunus tree, brocade cover . . . 170.00
Tea Sets
  3 pcs, teapot, creamer, cov sugar, handled, Thousand Flowers pattern, c1900 . . . . 180.00
  3 pcs, teapot, cov sugar, melon ribbed, children at play, outlined in gold, pastel colors, c1880 . . 155.00
  15 pcs, teapot, cov sugar, creamer, 6 large cups and saucers, sea lion spouts and finials, gold, red and white striped, men's faces, white scale trim 295.00
Teapots
  1½″, miniature, squat body, raised on tripod legs 160.00
  5½″, dragon scale, c1900 . . . . . . 145.00
Urn, 5″, ovoid, cov, bird on blooming prunus tree 145.00
Vases
  2⅜″, cobalt, gold floral, Geisha with children, reverse has father and child, gold trim, sgd 130.00
  3½″, bulbous shoulders, creamy beige, glaze, portrait, old beard-

ed man in hopping position, red
and black Oriental writing **128.00**
4″, ovoid, flared rim, turtle diaper
pattern, scene with children,
flowers and butterflies, gold
trim, sgd, c1885 . . . . **225.00**
6½″, deep cobalt blue and gold,
ladies front and back, pr **695.00**
9½″, cobalt blue, gold flowers,
Geishas, hanging foliage, gold
accents and trim, sgd **115.00**
9¾″, enamel, pale blue, cobalt,
yellow, green, brick red, reserves front and back of squirrels and hanging bunches of
grapes **160.00**
10″, gold ring handles, light to
dark green, pink and white flowers, green leaves, scalloped
Nishlkide detail at shoulders,
sgd, pr **250.00**
10¼″, ovoid, ivory, enameled,
scenic, mountainous landscape
and dignitaties, pr **325.00**
12″, deep green, phoenix bird mo-
tif **235.00**
15″, diaper pattern, lake scene
with 3 seared sages, reverse
has puffed grouse, flying birds,
enameled mums, red and gold
trim, artist sgd, c1890 . . . . **395.00**
15½″, moriage motifs, ram's head
handles **225.00**
17½″, bulbous, narrow neck, ap-
plied bifurcated scroll handles,
enameled, eagles, foliage, figures and dragons, 3 shell mold-
ed scroll feet, pr **380.00**
18¼″, cream, large peonies in
high relief, small mums, mythical
bird with black and red beading **225.00**
31″, ovoid, shi-shi mask handles,
cobalt blue with painted figures **650.00**

SCALES

**Prior to 1900, the simple balance scale was
commonly used for measuring weights. Since
then, scales have become more sophisticated in design and more accurate. Scales in a
variety of styles and types, used by farmers,
storekeepers and druggists, include beam,
platform, postal and pharmaceutical.**

Apothecary, counter type, wood
base, marble top **150.00**
Balance
Analytical, mahogany and glass
case, ivory trim, lable reads
"Made by Henry Toemner for
Arthur H. Thomas, Phila," 17″ w
x 9¼″ d x 19″ h **95.00**

**Egg Scale, brass, cast iron, dividers
weigh in oz., wooden base 2⅝ x 13″,
c1880, salesman sample, part of orig.
label intact, $110.00.**

Mahogany case, ivory graduated
plate, Knott Boston, 10″ x 9½″,
no weights **45.00**
Butter, handmade, hangs on nail,
wooden, 37″ **100.00**
Candy
Cast iron, brass pans, marked
Henry Toemner, Phila., old dark
brown painted iron, gilt striping,
14½″ l **80.00**
Triner, brass **20.00**
Counter
Detecto, orig weights **50.00**
Stimpson, large **145.00**
Egg
Jiffy Way, litho tin **25.00**
Oakes Mfg Co., tin, painted black **15.00**
Grain Scale, brass, brass bucket . . **120.00**
Jewelers
Brass pans, marble top base with
drawer **130.00**
Gold and silver scale, enclosed in
glass case, complete set of
weights in wooden box, Voland
and Sons **295.00**
Parcel Post, Lander, Frary & Clark,
CT, to 20 pounds **55.00**
Pharmaceutical, cast iron, marble
pans, brass weights, 15½ x 16½″ **165.00**
Photographer, German silver pans,
brass weights **135.00**
Platform type, cast iron, Fairbanks,
500 pound capacity **175.00**
Postage, tin, patent date 1896 . . . . **12.00**
Steelyard
Cast iron, two weights and hooks **125.00**
Wrought iron, brass weight, 3 piv-
ot arms, hooks, brass inlay de-
cor end, 43″ l **225.00**

SCHLEGELMILCH PORCELAIN

**From 1861–1918, production of this porcelain
(marked R.S. Gerkmany, R.S. Poland, R.S.
Prussia, R.S. Suhl and R.S. Tillowitz) was directed by two brothers, Erdmann and**

Reinhold Schlegelmilch at their respective factories in the Germanic provinces of Prussia, Thuringia and Silesia.

All Schlegelmilch porcelain is of the finest quality with exquisitely molded forms and unique decoration. A majority of it was factory-decorated, but blanks were produced for home-decorating and occasionally, artist-signed examples are found.

In the past, the famous "red mark" R.S. Prussia was valued above the "green mark" pieces. Today, as prices soar on R.S. Prussia, so it is also with the R.S. Germany scenic, portrait and floral examples, plus the R.S. Suhl and R.S. Tillowitz items. R.S. Poland is commanding high prices due to the scarcity of the red mark which was manufactured only from 1916–1918.

The "animal" pieces are much sought after by collectors because production of these particular patterns were limited.

CAUTION: A great many "fake" Schlegelmilch's are appearing on the market. These reproductions have new decal marks, transfers or recently handpainted animals on old, authentic R.S. pieces.

Schlegelmilch Porcelain, R.S. Germany, Pitcher, 6¼ h, 4″ w, $75.00.

R.S. GERMANY

Basket, handled, 7 x 4½″, Calla Lilly	65.00
Bowls	
4 x 9″ d, center, scallop and fan, multi-footed, pink and white carnations, blue shading	95.00
12½ l x 8½″ w, oval, stippled floral edge mold, inner sides dark pink, gold outlining, center pink and yellow roses, steeple mark	125.00
Bread Trays	
14″, medallion mold, green, light and dark pink roses, gold border, RM	400.00
Iris variant edge mold, blue and	

white, petal and rim gold outlined, center multicolored flowers, steeple mark	115.00
Candy Dish, 7″ sq, wide scallop, gray/green, orange roses, gold rim outline, green mark	48.00
Cheese and Cracker Dishes, tiered	
9″, floral decor, wide green border, gold trim	40.00
9½″, hp, pink sweetpeas, gold floral border	35.00
Cracker Jar, roses	75.00
Creamers and Sugars	
Covered, lower part irid green, upper spattered yellow, black handle and rim, blue mark	138.00
Mill scene	125.00
Oval tray, hexagonal, pink, rose decor	145.00
Cup and Saucer, demitasse, lilies, wide open, gold trim, green mark	32.00
Hair Receiver, 4½″, pink and green, large pink hibiscus, green mark	49.00
Hat Pin Holder, deep pink roses	55.00
Loving Cup, pedestal, large handles, floral decor	55.00
Match Holder with Striker Base, 1¾″, barrel shape, pink rose decor, blue mark	92.00
Mustard Pot with spoon, white with pink roses	30.00
Nut Set, master bowl, 4, 2½″ ftd bowls, cream, salmon roses	125.00
Pin Tray, 8″, pierced ends, gray, orange and white tulip, blue mark	35.00
Pitcher, 14″, syrup, cov, bluebells	57.00
Plates	
8½″, pale green and white snowballs, pale green border with gold trim, blue mark	34.00
9¾″, open handle, hp, shaded green and tan, frilly pink and white flowers	28.00
10½″, cake, open handles, green and beige, large orange nasturiums, gold rim and handles	55.00
10½″, open handles, large molded leaf edge, light lavender, gold outlined, floral center, steeple mark	110.00
Platter, 11½″, oval, open handles, pale pink, green and white blossoms and leaves, gold trim, blue mark, RS Germany, script Reinhold Schlegelmilch Tillowitz, c1870	35.00
Relish Dish, icicle mold, tulips	20.00
Relish Tray, ivory yellow, multicolored poppies and daisies, gold rim, pierced ends, green mark	28.00
Salt and Pepper Shakers, tiger lily decor	65.00

Sauce Boat and Underplate, green, white flowers **45.00**

Shaving Mug with soap drain, gold trim **48.00**

Teapot, cov, 8″, ftd, pink roses, green leaves, pearlized, gold trim, sgd **98.00**

Toothbrush Holder Wall Bracket, pink rose, shades of green **130.00**

Toothpick Holder, 3 handles, floral decor **55.00**

Trays

   3½ x 5½″, oval, handled, white flowers, yellow centers, fine gold designs, green mark **95.00**

   Leaf shape, green, pink roses, gold handle, artist sgd, blue mark **35.00**

Vase, 6½″, beige, pink roses, green mark **42.00**

R.S. POLAND

Berry Set, 5 pcs, shell mold, all over pastel flowers **335.00**

Bowl, center, 9″, pedestal, pink rose wreaths, lavender and cream shading, red mark **175.00**

Candleholder, 2½″, blue and gray, greek figures, red mark **90.00**

Creamer, ftd, soft green, chain of violets, applied fleur-de-lis feet, red mark **100.00**

Sugar, cov, ftd, light lavender, dainty spray pink roses, applied fleur-de-lis feet, red mark **135.00**

Vase, 12″, rope handle **75.00**

R.S. PRUSSIA

Bell, fluted, pink roses **35.00**

Berry Bowls

   4½″, lily, green leaves, blue, gray, tan and gold, set of 6 . . . . **150.00**

   7″, semi scalloped edge with 6 furrows down inside of bowl, pink and white apple blossoms, ftd, red mark **250.00**

Bowls

   9¼″, 5 circle mold, turkey with trees, lavender, blue, beige and green, red mark **465.00**

   9½″, carnation mold, yellow and green, pink and white roses, red mark **260.00**

   10″, sawtooth, cottage scene, orange and yellow **390.00**

   10¾″, 5 circle mold, floral center, swans and bluebirds on border with gold tapestry, red mark . . . **550.00**

   11″, blown out iris, roses, gold trim, open handles, red mark . . **195.00**

Box, round, blown out, scalloped rim, delicate pink roses and gold trim **298.00**

Bread Tray, 13½″, 6 point and clover, pink and white roses, heavy gold, red mark **395.00**

Celery Trays

   12″, stipled floral edge mold, gold stenciled inside border, green to white, pink and gold roses, artist sgd, red mark **180.00**

   Point and clover mold, daisies, pink and yellow roses, gold trim edge **95.00**

Child's Mug, large pink flower, green leaves, raised star on base **80.00**

Chocolate Pots, ftd

   10″, light green and white, pink roses, green leaves, fan feet, scalloped top and shoulders . . **260.00**

   10″, pink roses, blown out heavy scalloped gold trim below spout, green finial and feet, red mark . **275.00**

Cracker Jar, cov, 6″, white Easter lilies and fern, green scalloped border, red mark **325.00**

Creamer, icicle mold, light blue, pastel water lilies and reflection, red mark **250.00**

Creamers and Sugars, covered

   Feather and plume mold, large group poppies on side, gold outlines feather edges, red mark . **225.00**

   Icicle mold, soft magneta, cluster of pink and yellow roses, red mark **250.00**

   4 scallop edge mold, hanging basket decor, lavender, pink and yellow roses, red mark **235.00**

Cup, 6 ftd, spring season, handle, red mark **250.00**

Cup and Saucer, stippled floral edge mold, green to white, large pink roses, gold outline, artist sgd, red mark **135.00**

Hair Receiver, 2¼″, pale pink and white, pink roses, red mark **95.00**

Hatpin Holder, 4½″, white to beige, pink roses, red mark **125.00**

Mustache Cup, white, pink roses, green to beige leaves, raised gold decor and beading, gold applied handle **125.00**

Mustard Jar and Lid, 3½″, clematis, green on white ground **125.00**

Mustard with Ladle, pedestal, blue tones, basket of roses, red mark **135.00**

Relish Dishes

   6 x 12″, green and pale pink, orchid and pink poppies decor . . **150.00**

   9 x 4¼″, green, blooming roses on white, scalloped border, berries in relief work **60.00**

Plates
8¼", 10 point mold, satin finish,
swans, trees, columns, water,
red mark 245.00
10¼", cake, point and clover
mold, jewelled roses in center,
red mark 175.00
10½", 6 point and clover mold,
green to cream, mixed flower
arrangement center, red mark .   185.00
11", leaf mold, pink roses, satin
finish, red mark 275.00
11", 6 medallion mold, deep
welled, light green, pink pop-
pies, small daisies, red mark . .   225.00
11½", open handle, satin, yellow,
pink roses, red mark 150.00
Salad Dressing Set, 5½" bowl, 6"
plate, cream, pink roses, red mark   175.00
Salt and Pepper, barrel shape, blue
and yellow, multicolored flowers,
gold vines, narrow gold outline
around tops, red mark 68.00
Shaving Mug, 3½", ball foot, pink
and rose, pink poppies, red mark   150.00
Spoon Holder, 14" l, pink and white
roses, handle, floral border 275.00
Sugar, cov, Dogwood pattern, blown
out sides, gold scalloped base
and rim 65.00
Tankard, 10½", blown out base, sat-
in finish, gold and green, cascad-
ing roses, red mark 539.00
Tea Set, 3 pcs, satin finish, large
snowballs, green leaves, molded
leaves on scalloped base, red
mark 350.00
Teapots
Blown out iris, dark green and yellow, bust of Madame Recamier,
red mark 535.00
White and green satin, orange
blossoms decor, gold trim, red
mark 125.00
Tray, dresser, 11½", turquoise and
lavender, white stars, daisies,
roses, sprigs, bead edge, red
mark 115.00
Vases
5¾", bottle, 2 ducks, rust and
cream, red mark 235.00
7", white and green with tapestry
work, pink and yellow roses,
double handles, red mark 550.00
7¼", castle scene, shades of light
to dark green, gold trim, han-
dled 175.00
7½", pink to lavender, violets, ftd,
red mark 250.00
9", bottle type, cottage scene,
cream and dark green 225.00
Wall Plaque, 6¼", cottage scene,
floral, stippled edge, dark colors, 2
molded loops on back for hanging   135.00

R. S. SUHL

**R.S. Suhl, Dish, 4⅝" w, light green ex-
terior, green ground, classical ladies
in white, pink and yellow, $465.00.**

Box, cov, Nightwatch 650.00
Cake Plate, white with red roses,
green mark 120.00
Pin Tray, 4½", round, Nightwatch . .   375.00
Pitcher, 5½", white with red roses .   120.00
Plate, 8½", windmill scene and wa-
ter, green mark 100.00
Vase, 8½", handles, blown out top,
pink roses 225.00

R.S. TILLOWITZ

Basket, 5", yellow with pheasants
and flowers 150.00

**R.S. Prussia, tankard, 13", Summer
Season/Old Mill, green and yellow
tones, $4,500.00.**

Bowl, 12½″, oval, cabbage mold, floral decor 95.00
Cake Plate, 10″, white with floral decor, pierced handles 50.00
Creamer and Sugar, 2″, white to green with white flowers and green leaves 75.00
Marmalade Jar with Ladle, shaggy lavender flowers, bisque finish ... 35.00
Relish Dish, white with lillies, hp ... 45.00

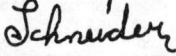

SCHNEIDER GLASS

Charles and Ernest Schneider founded the firm known as Christalerie Schneider in Epinay-sur-Siene, France. Their art glass can be identified by the distinctive mottled colors. This type of Schneider glass was made from 1913 to 1933. The firm is currently producing crystal tableware.

Compote, 8¾″ h, 12¼″ d cobalt center, citar edge, blue tripod feet, $275.00.

Bowl, 9¼″, mottled, red and purple, mkd 175.00
Compotes
8¼″, deep amethyst, knobbed stem and pedestal, mkd 110.00
Mottled orange and yellow, black ball stem, wrought iron pedestal with 3 glass berries 265.00
Dish, 5½ x 13½″ d, mottled orange, dark blue, pedestal base, amethyst with white ribbing 255.00
Ewer, 6½″, mottled blue and gray, applied black amethyst handle .. 220.00

Pitchers
7″, mottled orange, applied amethyst handle, polished pontil .. 275.00
7½″, maroon, white and pink, mkd 325.00
Plate, 4″, mottled, deep pink 65.00
Tray, 16″, round, mottled orange, blue and yellow, mkd 175.00
Vases
5½″ h, cased, blue, black, clear glass, orange lining, blown into wrought iron ftd base, France, c1925, sgd 275.00
9½″, round, handles, orange with lavender and lemon pulls at raised neck, mkd 320.00
11½″, mottled pink, orange and pale yellow 600.00
17″, trumpet shape, ftd, clear with streaks of pink and raspberry, controlled bubbles, mkd 325.00

SCHOENHUT TOYS

Albert Schoenhut, son of a toymaker, was born in Germany in 1849. In 1866, he ventured to America to work as a repairman of toy pianos for Wanamaker's, Philadelphia, Pennsylvania. Finding the glass sounding bars inadequate, he perfected a toy piano with metal sounding bars. His piano was an instant success and the A. Schoenhut Company had its beginning.

From then on, toys seemed to flow out of the factory. Each of his six sons entered the business. The business prospered until 1934, when misfortune forced the company into bankruptcy. In 1935 Otto and George Schoenhut contracted to produce the Pinn Family Dolls.

At the same time, the Schoenhut Manufacturing Company was formed by two other Schoenhuts. Both companies operated under a partnership agreement that eventually led to O. Schoenhut, Inc. which continues today.

Some dates of interest: 1872-toy piano invented; 1903-Humpty and Dumpty and Circus patented; 1911-1924-wooden doll production; 1928-1934-composition dolls.

Animals
Alligator, glass eyes 225.00
Alligator, painted eyes 175.00
Bear, brown painted eyes 125.00
Buffalo, glass eyes 225.00
Buffalo, painted eyes 145.00
Bulldog, brown painted eyes, (rare) 225.00
Camel, glass eyes, one hump .. 250.00
Camel, painted eyes, two humps, 8″ 175.00

Lion, painted eyes, $145.00.

Cat, glass eyes, 7″, leather ears, tail	215.00
Deer, glass eyes	275.00
Donkey, large, glass eyes	125.00
Donkey, small, painted eyes	45.00
Elephant, glass eyes	135.00
Elephant, painted eyes, 7″	50.00
Gazelle, glass eyes, c1910	500.00
Giraffe, 11″ high, painted eyes	240.00
Hippopotamus, glass eyes	250.00
Hippopotamus, painted eyes	185.00
Horse, circus rider saddle	120.00
Leopard, glass eyes	225.00
Lion, glass eyes, 9″	160.00
Monkey, painted eyes	150.00
Ostrich, painted eyes, (rare)	245.00
Poodle, glass eyes	180.00
Poodle, painted eyes	115.00
Reindeer	125.00
Tiger, glass eyes	185.00
Tiger, painted eyes, 8″	150.00
Zebra, glass eyes	225.00

Blocks
"A,B,C"	85.00
"Building Blocks," orig box, complete	175.00

Building Toy, Little Village Builder, orig box	75.00
Circus, "Humpty Dumpty," painted eyed figurines, poster, orig box, incomplete, 23 pcs	1,760.00
Circus, "Humpty Dumpty," animals with glass eyes, complete with tent, 52 pcs	5,575.00
Circus, Side Show, Humpty Dumpty No. 30/2, 44 x 27 x 18″ circus tent, 2 18 x 42″ show banners, reduced size ring master, lady bareback rider, 3 clowns, white horse, 2 donkeys, elephant, 2 barrels, tub, pedestal, 4 ladders, 3 chairs, stretcher	2,400.00
Circus, Window Display, 16″ h clown in red striped cotton suit, 2nd clown in red and blue striped cotton suit, 15″ donkey, painted eyes, ladder, tub, 2 barrels, 2 chairs	1,400.00

Circus Accessories
Barrel	15.00
Chair	18.00
Platform	15.00
Tent, 25 x 35″	350.00

Circus Performers
Acrobat, lady	125.00
Bare back rider on white horse, 6½″	200.00
Lion Tamer, wooden head	170.00
Ringmaster, 8½″, wooden head	145.00

Dirigible, 13″, orig box, c1929	75.00

Dolls
14″, wooden socket head, center parted carved hair drawn around sides in two loose braids, molded blue hair ribbon, carved, painted facial features, brown intaglio eyes, closed mouth, pouty expression, wooden spring jointed body, part of oval paper label, orig shaker style gray linen dress, petticoat, ruffled white bonnet	1,350.00
15″, Polly Dolly, jumbo Dutch Girl, head turns	255.00
17″, carved wooden socket head, painted facial features, brown metal sleep eyes, open mouth, 4 tiny teeth, brunette human hair, carved wooden spring jointed body, mkd Schoenhut doll Pat Jan. 17, 1911	575.00
17″, carved wooden socket head, painted chubby facial features, bright green eyes, closed pouty mouth, brunette mohair wig, separated fingers, marked H. E. Schoenhut Copr. (sic) 1913	425.00
18″, carved wooden socket head, painted facial features, narrow blue eyes, closed pouty mouth, orig blonde mohair wig, 5 pc wooden body, bent elbows, walker legs, marks on oval paper label on torso Schoenhut Walkable Doll, Pat U.S.A. Jan 17, 1911/Dec. 30, 1919/March 23, 1920, wearing orig chemise	300.00
22″, wooden socket head, carved and painted facial features, large orig green decal eyes, closed mouth, 4 tiny beaded teeth, all wooden spring jointed body, carved fingers, mkd Schoenhut doll Pat Jan. 17, 1911, U.S.A. and foreign countries, orig cotton teddy	325.00

Farm Characters
Farmer	135.00

Goat, painted eyes	145.00
Goose, painted eyes	200.00
Horse, 10″, painted eyes	150.00
Lamb, painted eyes	155.00
Milkmaid	75.00
Pig, glass eyes	155.00

Personalities

Barney Google	175.00
Felix, 4″, ball jointed, 7 pc body, Patent June 23, 1925	198.00
Golfer in skirt	325.00
Hobo	125.00
Jiggs, 7″	350.00
Maggie with rolling pin, 9¼″	400.00
Max and Moritz, replaced coats, pr	500.00
Spark plug	175.00
Teddy Roosevelt, ammunition belt, with hat, 8″	440.00

Pianos

8½ x 9½ x 16″, 15 keys	125.00
17 x 24 x 27″, grand	265.00
Trinity Chimes	145.00

SCIENTIFIC INSTRUMENTS

Chemists, doctors, geologists, navigators and surveyors used precision instruments as tool of their trade. Such objects are well designed and beautifully crafted. The principal medium is brass. Fancy hardwood cases also are common.

Microscope, E. Leitz-Wetzler, No. 34459, 170 mm - 250 mm, 6 objective, wood case, $175.00.

Barograph, recording, engraved nameplate ship *Caroline*, 11⅜″ l x 6½″ h x 5¼″ w, working, cased .	475.00
Engineer's Case, drafting instruments, J. Halden & Co., London, Manchester, japanned metal case, nameplate, velvet lined tray, orig	

instruments, ivory scales, c1920, 16 pcs	150.00
Hydrometer, Baume, orig box	65.00

Microscopes

B & L, brass, case, orig accessories, 1899	395.00
Beck, binocular, case, orig accessories, c1880	1,450.00
Doctor's, brass, 7 assorted lens, early	350.00

Octants

Spencer, Barrett & Co., London, label of Kelley & Brother, Agents, New Bedford, fitted case	700.00
Spencer, Browning & Rust, London, made for Samuel Emery of Salem, ivory scales, case painted deep blue, eagle, flag, shield, Indian on cover	900.00

Odometer, Bell, Ellis Roberts, E. Palestine, OH, Pat 1885, used to record, register and announce distance traveled by horse drawn carriage, orig box	95.00
Quadrant, Spencer, Browning & Rust, London, made for H. Duren, New York, orig oak case	625.00
Sextant, Lenadrice & Co, London, brass, silver vernier scale, mahogany case	975.00

Surveyor's Instruments

Pocket Compass, vernier, brass, wooden case	125.00
Scope, 5″, brass, U.S. Distance readings	40.00
Transit Level, wooden tripod base, dovetailed case, worn black finish, brass instrument, 19½″ l, Garley Engineering Instruments, Troy, NY	325.00

Telescopes

Dolland, 3 drawer, c1910	115.00
Meyrowitz, astronomical, floor tripod, 40″ l, c1900	775.00

SCRIMSHAW

Scrimshaw carving had its origins in the early 19th century and is generally associated with the whaling industry. Sailors occupied their idle hours by carving or engraving whale and walrus tusks, bone and other forms of ivory. Eskimos also used this means to express their artistic endeavors.

The most common designs are ships, whaling scenes, patriotic themes, or women, perhaps a wife or sweetheart. While some of the articles had a utilitarian purpose, most were purely ornamental and presented as homecoming gifts.

Interest in scrimshaw lessened in the first half of the 20th century. It is being revived

today by skilled craftsmen. Unfortunately, modern technology also has created a large number of reproductions and outright fakes.

The Barbara Johnson Whaling collection was sold by Sotheby's in two major sales, Dec., 1981 and Sept., 1982. These sales released many fine examples into the marketplace and strongly influenced prices. Richard Bourne also holds an annual marine auction in which are found large numbers of scrimshaw pieces.

Note: Whale and walrus ivory are included in the modern import ban. If you are engaged in trading in any of the "endangered species," you must familiarize yourself with the bill of November, 1978.

Whales tooth, 7¼" h, 3⅞" w, engraved on one side, eagle clutching flag and banner, Harrison and Tyler for President over a naval battle, entitled Constitution and Guerriere, $1,300.00.

Bird Cage, 18" l x 17" h x 13" w, walnut, whalebone bars, finials, feed stations	1,700.00
Corset Busks	
11¾", engraved in black ink, scenic, monument, flowers in vase, bowl of fruit, ship with sails furled, star, ship under sale . . .	650.00
13", engraved, one side with flowers, birds, butterfly, other side ship among icebergs, engraved with colored ink, designs slightly raised	600.00
Cribbage Board, Eskimo, walrus tusk, one side engraved with hunt	

scene of 2 boatloads of Eskimos attacking 9 walrus, edge scene of otter, 2 Eskimos attacking sea lion, other side shows cribbage board, 3 caribou near tip, huge bird carrying caribou in talons, other edge reads "St michael alaska oct 14, 1899," 14¼" l	500.00
Ditty Box, Artic right whale baleen, pine, pierced and wrapped over a painted paper inset, fastened by pewter pins, rivets, Nantucket, late 18th C	600.00
Jagging Wheel, 6⅜" l, 3 tined fork, rosette carved hub, island wood handle, tip inlaid with silver star on each side	400.00
Pickwick, 3¼" h, turned from whale ivory, red scribe lines, orig copper pick	275.00
Swift, 23" l, panbone and whale ivory, clamp carved in hand shape .	600.00
Whale's Tooth	
6½", engraved with figure of Liberty wrapped in flag, holding a flag shield, Liberty cap on pole	350.00
6¾", one side engraved with sperm whale, star, sternboard like scroll, Hector, New Bedford, other side engraved with American whale ship, whaling scene in foreground, volcano in background	650.00

SEBASTIANS

Sebastians are handpainted, lightly glazed figurines of characters from literature and history. They range in size from 3 to 4 inches. Each figurine is made in limited numbers. Other series include children and scenes from family life.

Prescott W. Baston, the originator and designer of Sebastian figures, began production in 1938 in Marblehead, Mass. Sebastian Studios is located in Hudson, Mass.

Each year a Sebastian Auction is held in Boxborough, Massachusetts, at the Sebastian Collector's Society meeting. Prices are determined from this source plus the work of the Sebastian Exchange Board which develops a price list that is the standard reference for the field.

Dr. Glenn S. Johnson, *Sebastian Miniature Collectors Guide,* privately printed, 1982 editions is a good reference for Sebastians.

Note: The numbers and prices listed are taken from the July 1983 issue of *The Sebastian Exchange*, with permission of Paul J. Sebastian.

See *Warman's Americana & Collectibles* for an expanded listing of Sebastian Miniatures.

	Low	High
1 - Shaker Man	125.00	150.00
2 - Shaker Lady	125.00	150.00
10 - Deborah Franklin .	100.00	125.00
11 - Gabriel	125.00	150.00
12 - Evangeline	125.00	150.00
49-A - Copperfield & Wife	75.00	95.00
50-A - Mr. Micawber . .	70.00	90.00
51-A - A. B. Trotwood .	70.00	90.00
52-A - Peggotty	70.00	90.00
55-A - Bob Cratchit & Tiny Tim	75.00	95.00
58-A - Mr. Pickwick . .	70.00	90.00
59-A - Sam Weller . . .	70.00	90.00
61-A - Dickens Cottage	75.00	95.00
85 - Abraham Lincoln, looking ahead	100.00	125.00
89 - Stearns 1847 Couple	100.00	125.00
103 - Mrs. Rittenhouse Square	100.00	125.00
107-A, Pecksniff	70.00	90.00
111 - House of 7 Gables	75.00	95.00
123 - Santa Claus	70.00	90.00
131 - G.R.B. Tiger	300.00	400.00
137 - Mary Had A Little Lamb	75.00	95.00
159-A - Andrew Jackson	250.00	300.00
165-A - Modern Mother	200.00	250.00
209-B - St. Joan of Arc, bronzed	225.00	275.00
224 - Boy Jesus, painted	250.00	300.00
239 - Kernel Fresh, Ashtray	300.00	350.00
249 - Davy Crockett . .	200.00	250.00
273 - Mayflower	200.00	250.00
305 - A. Smith Weaver	250.00	300.00
311 - Henry Hudson . .	125.00	175.00
315 - Mark Twain	70.00	90.00
369 - Sidewalk Days, boy	65.00	75.00
371 - Family Sing	150.00	200.00

SEVRES

Sevres is a superb porcelain made in Sevres, France, since the middle 1700s. Originally sanctioned by royalty, some of the finest porcelain ever made was produced in the early years. The name now applies to all wares made in Sevres, France.

Ashtray, white with gilt dots, reserve with sprigs of spring flowers, printed eagle and pattern name in green, c1910	85.00
Cache Pots, 6½", turquoise, painted with oval figural reserves after Boucher, 19th C, pr	450.00
Candelabra, 25½", ovoid shape vessel on square base, applied scrolling handles, 3 fitted sockets amongst gilt bronze flowers and leaves, late 19th C, pr	2,200.00
Clock, mantel, 16", painted front panel with classical gentleman painting a vase, maiden looks on, sgd, flanked by 4 columns with painted landscape panels behind, gilding, electrified, Made in France, c1910	625.00
Coffee Can and Saucer, yellow, floral initial V within oval, flower spray decor, mkd with blue interlaced L marks enclosing the letter for 1786	325.00
Dishes	
6¼", round, blue, openwork rim, center scene of pastoral lovers, scrolled tripod feet, sgd A. Max	225.00
12¼" l, oval, turquoise with babies and wagon in garden	300.00
Plates	
9⅜", portrait, bust of military figure on green ground, gilt border, pseudo M. Imp le Sevres mark in iron red enamel, late 19th C	190.00
10½", couple by waterfall, pink border, floral decor, ormolu trim, artist sgd, c1890	300.00
Sugar, cov, handled, turquoise with boat and castle, 19th C	175.00

Figurines, 8", white, unglazed on marble and metal base, $2,900.00.

Teapot, cov, white, multicolored floral bouquets and floral sprays, floral spray finial with gilt dentil rim, mkd blue interlaced L enclosing date letter for 1767, incised BB . **485.00**

Urn, 13″, green top and base, acorn finial in ormolu, artist sgd, early mk **275.00**

Vases
31″, ovoid, domed cover with berried finial, ormolu mounted, handled, ivory, figure scenes, cobalt blue flared neck **1,500.00**
34⅞″, gilt-bronze mounted, blue, oval panel with battle ground and cavaliers on horseback, reverse side has view of a castle, gilt borders, pseudo interlaced L's marks in blue enamel **9,350.00**

Wall Plate, 9¾″, porcelain, cobalt blue, center has pair of pastoral lovers within gilt palmette border, sgd Debrie, mkd Chateau De St. Cloud, late 19th C **160.00**

SEWING ITEMS

As late as 50 years ago, a wide variety of sewing items were found in almost every home in America. Women, of every economic and social status, were skilled in sewing and dress making.

Even the most elegant ladies practiced the art of embroidery with the aid of jeweled gold and silver thimbles. Sewing birds, an interesting convenience item, were used to hold cloth (in the bird's beak) while sewing. Made of iron or brass, they could be attached to table or shelf with a screw-type fixture. Later models featured pin cushions.

See *Warman's Americana & Collectibles* for an expanded listing of sewing items and thimbles.

Needlecase and seam ripper, anchor motif, silver, 4¼″, $130.00.

Baskets
Knitting, 11″, oval, baleen, polished Mahogany base **450.00**
Victorian, 12″, fitted with scissors, pins, lined, 3 legs **100.00**
Woven splint, pockets, scissors attached **165.00**

Beading Tool, sterling, 6″ **45.00**

Belt, red silk, ivory rings hold ivory bodkin, hole maker, strawberry shaped emery, needle, pin holder **75.00**

Bodkins
Ivory, whale, carved, four openwork columns between two sections of elaborate square carving **330.00**
Whalebone, carved, set of 4, c1850 . . . . **275.00**

Boxes
Mahogany, rosewood, whale ivory, 2 tiers, 4 ivory feet, pulls, 8 finials, 8 thread eyelets, removable top with pin cushion, thimble holder, Nantucket, c1840, 6″ h x 7″ w **770.00**
Shell covered, pine base, lined, 5 x 6″ **20.00**
Walnut, brass inlay, purple velvet tray **95.00**
Walnut, drawer, 5 spool holders, pincushion, thimble holder, thimble, 4½ x 6½″ **45.00**

Crochet Needles, carved whalebone, 4 to 10¼″ l, set of 3 . . . . **225.00**

Darning Eggs
Glass, cobalt blue, ribbed **135.00**
Wood, emb SS handle **45.00**

Hemming clamp, lyre shape, iron, 4″ **175.00**

Knitting Needles, whale ivory, ebony, 13½″ l, acorn finials, c1850, pr . . **220.00**

Needle Cases
Gold colored metal, egg shape . . **20.00**
Ivory, 1½″ sq, whalebone, fluted openwork with hearts, mounted on rose wood base **1,100.00**
Ivory, 4½″, umbrella shape, carved **95.00**
Mother of Pearl, 3½″, opens from both ends **75.00**
SS, ornate scroll and floral decor **65.00**

Pincushions
Beaded, 7½″, floral center **35.00**
Shoe, pewter, velvet cushion . . . **45.00**

Punches
Ivory 25.00
Sterling, with gauge 28.00
Scissors
Brass, 7", Art Nouveau motif . . . 85.00
Sterling, 4¼", emb handles, c1890 50.00
Sewing Birds
Brass, one cushion 105.00
Cast Iron, two cushions 45.00
Nickel plated brass, 2 dark red
pincushions, emb Pat. Feb. 15,
1853 . . . . 155.00
Sewing Stand, 10" h, Mahogany,
whalebone, 3 removable tiers, oc-
tagonal sides, scrolling panels,
bone heart, circle, diamond inlays,
top whalebone pincushion cup,
Nantucket, 19th C 5,775.00
Sewing Table, Sheraton, Mahogany,
porringer corners, 2 drawers,
turned legs, c1800 . . . . 650.00
Shuttles
Silver, Sterling 25.00
Whale ivory, 2¾" l, 19th C 85.00
Wooden, 11" Netting 15.00
Spoolholder, 8" h, whale ivory,
whalebone, Mahogany, rotating, 3
tiers, 3 snake legs, large turned
ivory socket, 1st tier of 8
spoolholders, 2nd tier of 4 double
spoolholders, 3rd tier of spool
pins, two small finials, 2 small
cups, large scalloped cup in center, Mounted with a cherry pit,
Nantucket, c1830 . . . . 6,325.00
Table Clamp, brass, screw clamp,
pin tray, candleholder, match hold-
er 48.00
Tape Measures
Brass, Tea Kettle 65.00
Celluloid, rose 45.00
Celluloid, squirrel 35.00
Thimbles
14K gold, engraved Fleur-de-lis,
Name 125.00
14K gold, seascape scene border 110.00
SS, chased butterflies, leaves,
gold washed interior 45.00
Thimble Cases
Ivory, vegetable shape 35.00
Silver, pierced 85.00
Thread Holder, whalebone, scrim-
shaw, 3", 19th C 125.00

SHAKER

The Shakers, so named because of a dance
used in worship, are one of the oldest com-
munal organizations in the United States.
This religious group was founded by Mother
Ann Lee who emigrated from England and
established the first Shaker community near
Albany, N.Y., in 1784. The Shakers reached
their peak in 1850 with 6,000 members. Less
than ten Shakers are living today.

Shakers lived celibate and self-sufficient
lives. Their philosophy stressed cleanliness,
order, simplicity, and economy. Highly inven-
tive and motivated, the Shakers created
many utilitarian household forms and objects. Their furniture reflects their striving for
quality and purity in design.

In the early 19th century, the Shakers produced many items for commercial purposes.
Chairmaking and the packaged herb and
seed business thrived. In every endeavor and
enterprise, the members followed Mother
Ann's advice: "Put your hands to work and
give your heart to God."

Collecting Shaker items is expensive. The
furniture is among the most sought after in
the American country style.

**Sap Bucket, 9⅛ x 11½", sgd N.F.
(North Family) Shakers/Enfield, NH,
$95.00.**

Baskets
Feather gathering, split, natural
finish, cover permanetly fastened so top can slide up and
down and not lose feathers,
New England, 19th C 350.00
Straw, open, oval, 5½ x 7½", ribbon woven in sides 27.50
Bed, maple, shaped headboard centering turned posts with mushroom
finials, footboard with turned posts
and mushroom finials, 52" w x
40½" l 1,500.00
Bottle, 9", aqua, emb Shaker Pick-
les, base labeled Portland, ME,
E.D.P. & Co 80.00
Brush, 10¾", horsehair, turned
wooden handle 80.00
Carpet Beater, 41½" l, bent willow,
turned beech handle 75.00
Chest, blanket, one drawer, orig red

paint, yellow decor above drawer and on top, turned knobs, 36¾" h x 18¼" w x 37" l, Watervliet, NY, early 19th C **2,200.00**

Clothes Pins, 3, whittled, tin bands, 4¾" to 6" l **115.00**

Cupboard, hanging, pine, projecting cornice above single door, interior shelves, projecting base, 9¼ x 6½ x 27" **950.00**

Dipper, 6⅝", tin **48.00**

Dough Scraper, 4½", wrought iron . **35.00**

Drying Rack, 3 sections, pine, mortised joints secured with sq nails, each section 42 x 56" **150.00**

Gathering Box, 4 compartments, bentwood handle, 9½ x 9 x 15" l, New England, 19th C **600.00**

Hanger, 24", bentwood, chestnut .. **65.00**

Peg Rail, pine, beaded edge, 4 turned maple pegs, Hancock ... **45.00**

Pie Safe, pine, yellow paint, screened doors and drawers, mortis, tenion and pegged construction, turned legs, 36½" h x 40½" w x 19½" l, Enfield, NH, mid-19th C **2,000.00**

Rocker, Mt Lebannon, NY, No 7, shaped arms with mushroom caps, acorn finials, tape seat ... **400.00**

Sewing Box, pink cotton lining and pin cushion, stamped Shaker Goods/Alfred, M.E. **95.00**

Sewing Desk, pine, red stained, butternut drawer fronts, natural fold out sewing surface, sgd C. W. Thomas, Jan 1887, probably from Sabbothday Lake, ME, c1880s, 31 ½" h x 42½" w 19½" d **4,000.00**

Sock Stretcher, 26" l, wood **18.00**

Spinning Wheel, flax, S. Squier, all accouterments, 48" x 39" l **550.00**

Swift, 23½", orig mustard stain, Hancock **175.00**

Sunbonnet, 11", brown and white gingham check, machine stitched, Hancock **35.00**

Tub, 19½" x 25" d, interwoven bands, orig red paint, New England, early 19th C **1,050.00**

Utility Box, 4½" x 12" l, wood, oval, tongued, 4 fingers **440.00**

Washstand, pine and poplar, drawer in base, dovetailed, 29" h x 20¼" w 17¾" d **295.00**

Whisk, 14½" l, wood, primitive **40.00**

SHAVING MUGS

Warman's Americana & Collectibles, 1st Edition, contains 113 listings in this category; see also page xii.

SHAWNEE POTTERY

Organized in 1935 in Zanesville, Ohio, Shawnee Pottery was not an art pottery. The factory produced inexpensive commercial pottery, kitchenware, dinnerware and premium items for the American mass market until early 1961. At first, Shawnee pieces carried an Indian-on-an-arrowhead trademark. Later production was marked "Shawnee," "Shawnee, U.S.A.," or "Kenwood" and many items were marked with paper labels.

See *Warman's Americana & Collectibles* for an expanded listing of Shawnee Pottery.

Cookie Jar, basket of fruit, yellow basket weave base, banana, peach, grapes, pears, apples, 7⅜" d., marked Shawnee U.S.A., $27.50.

Ashtray, Kenwood line, mkd Kenwood U.S.A. #2125 .... **12.00**

Bowl, Corn King, #26 .... **26.00**

Butter dish, Corn King **37.00**

Casserole, Corn King, individual, # 73 .... **35.00**

Cookie Jars
Elephant, pink **20.00**
Puss 'n Boots **35.00**

Creamer, elephant **12.00**

Lamp, dog, mkd USA **10.00**

Mug, Corn King, #69 .... **22.50**

Pitcher, Corn King, #71 .... **29.50**

Planters
Bull **12.00**
Railroad caboose & gondala, pr . **20.00**
Truck, 2 pcs **35.00**

Plate, Corn King, #68 .... **15.00**

Salt & Pepper Shakers
Dutch girl and boy, 5", pr **18.00**
Puss 'n Boots **8.00**

Teapot, Corn Queen, individual, # 65 .... **50.00**

Vase, bud, Elegance Line, mkd Shawnee USA #1402 .... **12.00**

SHEET MUSIC

Warman's Americana & Collectibles, 1st Edition, contains 118 listings in this category; see also page xii.

SILHOUETTES

Silhouettes (or shades) are shadow profiles. They were very popular during the 18th and 19th century. Silhouettes are either hollow cut, mechanically traced, or painted.

The name silhouette came from a French Minister of Finance, Etienne de Silhouette, who tended to be tight with money and cut "shades" as a pastime. In America, the Peale family was one of the leading makers of silhouettes. An impressed stamp marked "PEALE" or "Peale Museum" identifies them.

Silhouette portraiture dropped in popularity prior to the Civil War with the introduction of the daguerreotype. In the 1920s and 1930s, this art form had a brief revival when it became popular for tourists to Atlantic City and Paris to have their profiles cut as souvenirs of their visit.

Children

6½ x 10¼", pair of full length children, gilded detail, simple ink wash ground, Master Hubbard, framed **185.00**

9½ x 11½", hollow cut of child on watercolor hobby horse, horse is dapple gray, green saddle, blue and ochre rockers, black cloth backing, oval gilded frame **800.00**

10 x 13¾", full length of girl in garden, bird in one hand, flower in other, ink wash ground, pen and ink inscription "Annabelle Wallace, Aug. Edouart fecit 1842," walnut shadow box frame, gilded liner **675.00**

Gentlemen

8¼ x 11½", Sea Captain on black, white litho ground showing window, ship, black cut paper ink set and cap on floor, highlighted in pencil, red and gold on spyglass, sgd "Sam'l Metford, Newport, R.I.," identified on back in pencil as Charles Procter, framed **2,300.00**

8⅞ x 10¾", full length in top hat on ink wash ground, fence tree in background, sgd "Aug Edouart fecit 1829," framed .. **600.00**

Groups

11 x 13⅜", group of five figures, full color watercolor ground, ti-

tled "Manuel Training School, New Harmonie Indiana, The Founders," names of figures, banner above reads "Man Makes His Own Existence," sgd John Chappelsmith fecit June 1827, framed, Chappelsmith was one of the founders **8,000.00**

13½ x 16½", family, brushed white highlights on each, black, white ink wash ground of room interior, fireplace, entitled "The Lesson 1840," printed paper label reads "Clay Turner, Profiles From Life," inscription on back of paper, visible through window in backing, reads "George Walters and his family, Jan. 7th, 1840," birdseye veneer ogee frame **850.00**

Ladies

3 x 3¾", Lady Peel, full length of old woman in chair, black, color on chair, clothing, water color on paper, orig black lacquered wooden frame, gilded brass trim **355.00**

Lady, 6 x 5", hollow cut, sgd Elizabeth Parker Boston, 1824, $200.00.

9 x 11¼", woman and child, brushed highlights, ink wash ground, sgd W.H. Brown 1844, inscribed "Oliver" and "Julia Ward Howe, Authoress & Emancipator, Boston, 1844," framed **1,050.00**

18 x 20½", old woman in day bed, brushed highlights in white, black ink, sgd R. W. Barnes, 1843, in pencil, matted, framed **350.00**

SILVER

The natural beauty of silver lends itself to the designs of the artist and craftsman. It has been mined and worked into an endless variety of useful and decorative items. Pure silver is too soft to be fashioned into strong, durable and serviceable utensils. Therefore, a way was found to give silver the required degree of hardness by adding alloys of copper and nickel.

Silversmithing in America goes back to the early 17th century in Boston and New York. It began in the early 18th century in Philadelphia. Boston was influenced by the English styles; New York by the Dutch.

See *Warman's Americana & Collectibles* for a listing of Silver Flatware, both plate and Sterling.

SILVER, AMERICAN, COIN

Coin silver is slightly less pure than sterling silver. Coin silver has 900 parts silver to 100 parts alloy; sterling silver has 925 parts silver. American silversmiths followed the coin standards. Coin silver also is called Pure Coin, Dollar, Standard, or Premium.

American Coin Silver, teaspoon, G. Lenhart, York, PA, 5½" l, $35.00.

Beakers
  Chassagne, Armand, New Orleans, c1820, tapered cylinder form, molded rim, engraved initials "S. D. Newcomb," mkd on base "CHASSAGNE" in rectangle, 4 oz, 3¼" h **3,750.00**
  Lupp, Henry, New Brunswick, NJ, 1790–1800, tapered cylindrical shape, molded foot ring, molded rim, engraved on bottom with initials "FBC," mkd on bottom, 16 oz, 4⅝" h, pair **10,000.00**
Bowl, Peter Van Dyck, New York, c1740, plain circular form, molded step foot, base engraved "New Iears — gift Franois (sic) Blanchard

17 onc ⅛ dt/1742," 16.1 oz, 7½" d **21,000.00**
Cann, Benjamin Burt, Boston, c1786, baluster form, molded lip, leaf scroll handle, spreading molded foot, engraved script initials within a bright cut and wrigglework circular cartouche surmounted by swags and paterae, mkd "Benjamin Burt" in shaped cartouche, 16.5 oz, 6" h **2,250.00**
Coffee Pots
  Blowers, John, Boston, c1730–40, tapered cylindrical form, molded borders, slightly domed base, swan neck spout with half baluster motif below, high domed cover with baluster finial, scroll wood handle, engraved with arms of Jones family, mkd on right of handle below rim "Blowers" in script in rectangle, 36 oz, 10½" h **52,000.00**
  Richards, Samuel, Jr., and Samuel Williamson, Phila., 1797–1802, vase shaped, pedestal stem on sq foot, body engraved with initials, reeded borders, domed cover with pineapple finial, wood C-scroll handle, mkd on bottom, 24 oz, 10⅝" h **2,750.00**
Creamers
  Casey, Samuel, South Kingstown, RI, c1760, plain pear shape raised on 3 trefid feet, multiple scroll handle capped by simple leaf motif, shaped rim and gilt interior, mkd "S:CASEY" in rectangle, 3 oz, 3⅞" h **2,200.00**
  Halstead, Benjamin, Phila. or New York, 1785–1815, helmet shaped, C-scroll strap handle with beaded mid-molding, flaring cylindrical stem on sq foot, body with circular bright cut cartouche, 7½" **600.00**
  Wood & Hughes, New York, c1845, vase shaped on sq pedestal base, beaded borders, swept handle, engraved initials in foliate cartouche, 10.5 oz, 8½" h **250.00**
Creamer and Covered Sugar Urn, William Forber, New York, c1795, helmet shaped creamer, vase shaped sugar urn with beaded borders, bright cut with swags of flowers, drapery mantles enclosing monograms and collars of half flowers, 17 oz, 10 dwt, urn 9¾" h **1,800.00**
Fish Server, William Tomson, New York, c1800, pierced and chase work, monogramed on handle, 5 oz **300.00**

Julep Cups

Cooper, William, Cincinnati, OH, and Louisville, KY, c1830–40, engraved initials, 3.5 oz, 3¼" h 350.00

Gray, Thomas, Lexington, KY, c1815, straight line "T. Gray" touch, eagle assay mark, 4.5 oz, 3" d, 3¼" h 800.00

Medley, Andrew G., Louisville, KY, 3.75 oz, 3" d, 3¼" h 500.00

Ladles

Byrne, James, Phila. or New York, c1790, pointed bright cut engraved around initials "FAC" in script, 6.2 oz, 14" l 500.00

Galvert, Thomas G., Lexington, KY, c1860s, no monogram, 8 oz 450.00

Poindexter, William A., Lexington, KY, monogramed, 2 oz 175.00

Mug, Fletcher & Gardiner, Phila., c1825, slightly tapering cylindrical form, applied stiff leaf borders, leaf-clad loop handle, engraved monogram within bands of reeding, 6 oz, 3½" h 325.00

Pap Boat, Daniel Van Voorhis, Phila. and New York, c1785, typical form with everted rim, engraved script initials, marked "DV" in rectangle, 2 oz, 5" l 350.00

Pitchers

Beverage, Jones, Shreve, Brown and Co., Boston, MA, bulbous body, scalloped shell spout, leaf and vines applied to handle, presentation cartouche chased in scrollwork, 34 oz, 11" h 1,050.00

Covered, John Crawford, New York, c1820, vase shape, incurved neck, chased and applied borders of flowers and foliage, front engraved with inscription, scroll handle decorated with grapevine and clusters of ears of wheat, dome cover chased with acanthus, grapevine and cluster finial, 3 paw feet resting on balls, mkd "J. CRAWFORD" in rectangle, 71 oz, 15 dwts, 13⅛" h 2,250.00

Trophy, John Kitts, Louisville, KY, c1830–40s, urn shape, pedestal, inscribed "South Western Agricultural/and/Mechanical Association/Helen," 11 oz, 9" h 800.00

Water, cov, John McMullin, Phila., c1810, tub form on a pedestal base, lower body chased with leaf-tips and matted lobes, monogram on one side, shoulder and foot stamped with band of grapevines and clusters, gadroon rims, domed cover, mkd

"I. McMullin" in rectangle, eagle in shaped punch, 41 oz, 10 dwts, 12" h 1,200.00

Sugar Vases

Bayley, Simeon, New York, 1785–1800, urn shaped flaring conical cover with urn shaped finial with beaded borders, body with beaded rim over bright cut engraved oval cartouche with bow knot and garlands, flaring cylindrical stem with beaded border, sq foot, 8" h 2,500.00

Kendall, James, Wilmington, DE, c1800, beaded borders, swept handles, sq pedestal base, engraved crests, spool shaped cover, baluster finial, 11 oz, 11¼" h 350.00

Tablespoons

Loomis, Warham P., Frankfort, KY, c1830–50, monogram, fiddleback, straight line touch "W. P. Loomis" under handle 75.00

Revere, Paul, Jr., Boston, c1790, Old English pattern with feather edge, engraved with initials, foliate scroll on back of bowl, mkd on stem "REVERE" in rectangle, 1 oz, 8 dwt, 8¼" l 1,100.00

Sayre, Joel, New York, late 18th C, bright cut engraving 50.00

Tea Caddy, Joseph Richardson, Jr., Phila., 1785–1800, oval, flat hinged lid, urn shaped finial, keyhole above oval shaped, bright cut, engraved cartouche flanked by swags enclosing initials "FC," molded footrim, beading on finial, lip, and footrim 8,250.00

Tea Service, Stodder & Frobisher, Boston, c1820, teapot, cov sugar, and creamer, bombe circular bodies, scroll handles, sloping leaf tip handles, 51 oz, teapot, 8½" h ... 1,000.00

Teapot, Allcock & Allen, NY, c1810–20, pear shaped, 4 pierced and chased foliate feet, lobbed sides chased with flowering foliage, leaf capped with scroll handle, domed cover with melon finial, 29 oz, 9¾" 300.00

Waste Bowls

Sayre, John, New York, c1800, faceted circular form on spreading base, engraved at rim with a band of bright cut foliate scrolls, engraved with script initials, mkd "I. SAYRE" in rectangle, 12.5 oz, 5¼" h 550.00

S. Townsend, New York, c1800, circular form on spreading foot, engraved at rim with band of bright cut scrolling foliage, applied with 2 ring handles, engraved initials, 7.5 oz, 4½" h . . **225.00**

SILVER, AMERICAN, STERLING

There are two possible sources for the origin of the word sterling. The first is that it is a corruption of the name Easterling. Easterlings were German silversmiths who came to England in the Middle Ages. The second is that it is named for the starling (little star) used to mark much of the early English silver.

Sterling silver has 925/1000 parts pure silver. Copper comprises most of the remaining alloy. American manufacturers began to switch to the sterling standard about the time of the Civil War.

Bowls
    Loring Andrews Co., Cincinnati, OH, circular, Kirk style, raised on a spreading base, emb and chased all over with flowers, foliage, scrolls and 3 architectural vignettes on a matted ground, 31 oz, 10⅜" **1,000.00**
    Tiffany, c1930, circular form, cast pod handles, 17 oz, 11¼" h . . **300.00**
Bread Trays
    S. Kirk & Son, Baltimore, 1880–90, two handled, oval form embossed and chased with flowers and foliage, matching applied border and scroll handles, monogrammed, molded rim foot, 25 oz, 15 dwts, 15⅝" l **700.00**
    Unmarked, boat shaped, chased with band of fluting, 6.5 oz, 11" **90.00**
Candelabra, Five Light, Gorham Mfg Co., Providence, RI, 20th C, shaped circular bases with domed lobed centers rising to baluster and knopped stems and sconces with detachable nozzles, central light with 4 foliate scroll branches rising to drip-pans and matching sconces and detachable nozzles, all chased with foliate scrolls and flowers, loaded bases, 16⅛" h . . **3,000.00**
Centerpiece, Reed & Barton, early 20th C, shaped rectangular stand pierced with formal foliage, applied with 2 arms for the detachable baskets with fixed handles and pierced decoration, detachable wirework grills, center with matching larger basket with detachable clear liner, 73 oz, 15 dwts not including glass and grills, 20" h **2,100.00**
Centerpiece Bowl, Gorham Mfg Co., Providence, RI, 1924, "Florenz"

pattern, circular form on a spreading rim foot, rim decorated with foliage with beaded masks at intervals, wide borders with panels of scrolling foliage centered alternatively with a winged female bust and vacant cartouche, 31 oz, 12½" d **450.00**
Cup, 2 handled, Whiting Mfg Co., Providence, RI, late 19th C, baluster form on a high slightly spreading base, monogrammed, lower body chased with 2 bands of acanthus, foliate multi-scroll handles decorated with entwined grapevines, 78 oz, 11⅜" **1,450.00**
Flatware Services, Tiffany & Co., New York
    Broomcorn pattern, 1890–91, service for 12, 187 pcs, 218 oz, 10 dwt, excluding knives and steak forks **4,000.00**
    Chrysanthemum pattern, late 19th C, monogrammed, service for 12, 167 pcs, 189 oz excluding knives and wood box **9,650.00**
    English King pattern, 1885–91, service for 12, 160 pcs, 267 oz excluding knives **6,000.00**
Ice Bowl, Ford & Tupper, San Francisco, CA, c1880, formed as iceberg with icicles and polar bear handles, raised on a matching pedestal foot, 25 oz, 15 dwts, 10" l **1,325.00**
Photograph Frame, unmkd, plain, upright rectangular form, 9 x 11" **150.00**
Pitchers
    Gorham & Co., Providence, RI, c1865, oviform body with matted girdle applied with profile medallions and chased with ivy and vines between key pattern borders, matching rim, handle forked at base and applied with mask of river god, 46 oz, 12⅜" h **975.00**
    "Handmade" (stamped), baluster form, molded spreading foot, leaf capped scroll handle, 39.5 oz, 10½" h **490.00**
Punch Bowl, Gorham Mfg Co., Providence, RI, c1880, shallow campana-form, shaped spreading base, shoulder embossed and chased with playful putti, some with musical instruments, all amongst grapevine and clusters, lobed border, engraved armorials, handles formed as bearded Assyrian masks flanked by applied grapevine, 121 oz, 10 dwt, 13" d at rim **3,850.00**

Soup Tureen, cov, Gorham Mfg Co., Providence, RI, 1888, lobed end bombe oval form with shaped gadroon rim, gadroon and foliate ring finial rising from chased leaves, 4 shell and foliate feet, matching handles, engraved with armorials, 68 oz, 10 dwt, 14⅞" l over handles **1,350.00**

Straining Pan, W. K. Vanderslice & Co., 136 Sutter St., San Francisco, c1875, circular saucer, molded border, center pierced with holes, spreading rim base, turned ivory handle engraved with "Rathbone," 14 oz, 10 dwts gross, 6⅝" d **825.00**

Tazze, high foot, Gorham Mfg Co., Providence, RI, 1871, circular bowl engraved in the center with beaded strapwork, scrolling foliate rim, stem applied with lion's masks rising to scrolling foliage, spreading base with beaded band below engraved foliage, engraved "1852-Longstreet-1877," 29 oz, 10⅝" **400.00**

Teapot, S. Kirk & Son, Baltimore, 1880–90, circular bombe form on a molded rim foot, embossed and chased all over with flowers and foliage, domed cover with matching decoration and flower finial, base engraved with monogram, 24 oz, 4 dwts, 5¼" h **740.00**

Tray, Art Deco, Woodside Silver Co., circular form with cast pea in pod handles, 32 oz, 16½" l **400.00**

Tray, Tuttle Silversmiths, plain circular form, 13.5 oz, 12" d **170.00**

Vase, Whiting Mfg Co., Providence, RI, 1913, trumpet form, spreading foot, flat chased and engraved with lobed sections between two bands of leaves, roses and other flowers on the waist and foot, shoulder engraved with ribbon tied garlands of flowers over 2 large oval cartouches, 108 oz, 30⅛" .. **2,750.00**

Vegetable Dish, covered

Shreve, Crump & Low, plated liner, oval form engraved with scrolling foliage, corners and stand with turned bone handles, 60 oz, 19" l **850.00**

Tiffany & Co., New York, 1902–07, Chrysanthemum pattern, circular form with reversable cover, engraved twice with monograms, detachable finial, 48 oz, 11" d . **1,350.00**

SILVER, CONTINENTAL

Continental silver does not have a strong following in the United States. The strong feeling of German silver cannot compete with the lightness of the English examples. In Canada, Russian silver finds a strong market.

Continental, Tea Service, Irish, 1837–38, teapot marked "RWS" in shaped cartouche, $5,000.00.

Dutch

Brandy Bowl, maker's mark a head (Voet, No. 701), Sneck, 1771, oval bowl embossed with birds and foliage, domed foot, cast flat handles pierced with masks flanked by putti, 6 oz, 10 dwt, 10⅜" l **700.00**

Spoon, Apostle, maker's mark monogram "HTB," Friesland, mid-17th C, stem cast with a peacock amongst fruit below lion's mask, surmounted by an apostle, 1 oz, 8 dwts, 7⅛" ... **400.00**

Tobacco Box, Lenndert Beckhuis, Amsterdam, 1746, rectangular form with serpentine ends, molded borders, engraved with allegorical scenes on cover and base, sides with hunting scene, basketweave, and cornucopia, comic scene on interior, four ball feet, 6 oz, 5⅛" **1,350.00**

French

Candlesticks, Jacques-Gabriel-Andre Bompart, Paris, 1819–38, tapered circular stems, borders of stylized leaves, flared sconces chased with anthemia on matted ground, detachable nozzles, 31 oz, 10 dwt, 10½" h **1,450.00**

Chocolate Pot, Louis XVI, Ange Jacques Masse, Paris, 1782, plain pear shape, engraved armorials, raised on three hoof feet headed by ovals, swiveling baluster finial, fluted spout, 22 oz, 4 dwts excluding turned wood handle, 9" h **2,750.00**

Sauce Boat and Ladle, Marc-Augustin Lebrun, Paris, 1819–38, oval boat with lobed pedestal foot, engraved with initials, leaf capped reeded handle rising from shell and leaf, Fiddle, Thread, and Shell ladle, 21 oz, 9⅛" l **825.00**

Teapot, Froment-Meurice, Paris, c1880, compressed spherical form, chased with stiff leaves and applied with a cast band of scrolling foliage and paterae, acanthus handle with forked terminals, bud finials rising from foliage, matching spout, 33 oz, 8 dwts, 5½" **750.00**

Wine Cooler, maker's mark "J.M.," c1900, circular bombe form on spreading base, shoulder applied with band of interlaced scrolls centering flowerheads, foliate scroll grips, 33 oz, 7½" **880.00**

German
Beaker, parcel-gilt, Muller Brothers, 1747–57, tulip shape, chased with shell and scrollwork and inset with 2 rows of coins, 4 oz, 8 dwts, 3⅝" h **1,760.00**

Candelabra, Five Light, late 19th C, rococo style, shaped dome bases, baluster stems, openwork scroll branches, chased with flowers, trellis, shell and scrollwork, 96 oz, 19¾" h **1,950.00**

Tankard, parcel-gilt, Sy & Wagner, Berlin, c1871, inset with coins from the different German states, commemorates unification, matted and frosted surfaces, crown finial, wreath and coin thumbpieces, lion's head handle with German arms, 52 oz, 12¾" h **2,000.00**

Tumbler Cup, Tobais Hallaicher, Augsburg, c1685, finely engraved with three landscapes between scrolling foliage centered by a flowerhead, gilt rim and interior, 2 oz, 10 dwts, 3" d **2,250.00**

Italian, Candlestick, marked "FGR" or "GL?," Turin, 1750–75, shaped circular pan, spirally fluted sconce, detachable nozzle, straight turned wood handle with baluster silver finial, 3 stylized leaf feet, 6 oz, 10 dwts, 5" d **975.00**

Russian, snuffbox, silver and niello, AC in Cyrillic, Moscow, 1862, oblong, body and hinged lid niellowed with a profusion of flowers, lid interior engraved with later inscription dated 1925, 4¼" **725.00**

Swedish, spoon, Henning petri, Nykoping, c1660, fig shaped bowl engraved at top with leaves, banded stem with cartouche terminal decorated with 4 masks, 1 oz, 8 dwts, 6⅜" **465.00**

SILVER, ENGLISH

From the seventeenth to the mid-nineteenth century, English silversmiths set the styles which American silversmiths copied. The work from this period exhibits the highest degree of craftsmanship. Active collection of English silver takes place in the American antique marketplace.

George I
Caster, Charles Adams, London, 1714, baluster form with molded girdle and raised on spreading molding foot, slip-on domed cover with pierced decoration, molded girdle and ball finial, mkd on base and cover, 6 oz, 4 dwts, 7¼" h **850.00**

Chocolate Pot, John Wisdome, London, 1717, tapered cylindrical form, domed cover with hinged finial, engraved with initials and crest on side within Order of Garter below marquess' coronet, mkd on body and cover, 19 oz, 8 dwts, 9¼" h **5,250.00**

Salver, octafoil, Edward Cornock, London, 1725, four elongated bracket feet, engraved earmorials with scrolling cartouche, mkd on base, 33.5 oz, 12" d .. **750.00**

George II
Basting Spoon, Henry Bayley, London, 1758, Hanovarian pattern, engraved initials, shell backed bowl, 5 oz, 10 dwt, 14½" l **450.00**

Candlesticks, table, John Cafe, London, 1749, cast bases with shells at intervals rising to baluster and knopped stems, chased on one knop with shells, campana-form sconces and detachable nozzles, mkd on bases and nozzles, 35 oz, 8½" h **2,000.00**

Coffee Pot, Samuel Welles, London, 1741, tapered cylindrical form on spreading base, leaf capped swan neck spout, engraved with armorials, flat domed cover with baluster finial, mkd on body, 25 oz, 9⅝" h ... **2,000.00**

Snuffers Tray, William Grundy, London, 1756, shaped hour glass form, molded border with shells at intervals, engraved later crest, leaf capped flying scroll handle, raised on 4 triangular feet, 9 oz, 8 dwts, 7⅞" l .. **700.00**

Teapot, Thomas Parr, London, 1751, inverted pear form on spreading base, chased around the shoulder with scrolling foliage, flowers and shellwork, engraved cypher, shell capped swan neck spout, slightly domed cover with bud finial, mkd on base, 19 oz, 10 dwts gross, 5⅞" **950.00**

Waiters, pair, Ebenezer Coker, London, 1758, molded borders of reversed scrolls within shells at intervals, centers engraved with crests within rococo cartouche, raised on 3 hoof feet, 13 oz, 6⅞" d **750.00**

George III

Caster, Hester Bateman, London, 1780, pear form on pedestal base, pierced and engraved slip-on cover with flame finial, beaded borders, mkd on base and cover, 2 oz, 8 dwts, 5⅜" h **600.00**

Coffee Jug, Paul Storr, London, 1796, straight sides, curved ends, engraved armorials and crest, domed cover with ball finial, base engraved with "Caroline C," mkd on base and cover, 18 oz gross, 9" h **2,750.00**

Coffee Pot, Robert Sallam, London 1771, pear form, emb with flowers and foliage, matching cover, swan's neck spout, 27 oz, 8 dwts, 11" h **1,250.00**

Coffee Pot, James Young, London, 1779, simple pear form, swan's neck spout, wood scroll handle, domed circular base, cover with wrythen knop, mkd on base and cover, 27 oz, 16 dwts, 11⅜" h **2,200.00**

Salver, James Sutton & James Bult, London, 1783, shaped circular form, beaded border, engraved crest and motto in center, raised on 4 ball and claw feet, 40 oz, 8 dwts, 14" d **1,500.00**

Sugar Bowl, 2 handled, Paul Storr, London, 1813, fluted bombe circular form, gadroon rim with shells at intervals, scroll handles decor with leaves and overlapping piastres, gilt interior, 15 oz, 4¾" d at rim **1,100.00**

Tea Caddy, Peter and Ann Bateman, London, 1792, elliptical outline, bright cut scroll and floral borders within reeded edges, coat-of-arms (front) and crest (back), domed, stepped, ivory knop with silver button, 16 oz gross, 6" l **2,600.00**

Teapot, Chawner & Emes, London, 1797, oval form, incurved

collar engraved with interlaced ribbons above bright cut cartouches, mkd on base and cover, 14 oz, 6½" h **550.00**

George IV

Bowl, 2 handled, Benjamin Smith III, London, 1820, Warwick vase form, rim decorated with roses and other flowers, entwined vine branch handles, lower body applied with over lapping acanthus, engraved with crest and motto, inscription on base, gilt interior, 171 oz, 10 dwts, 12¼" at rim **5,250.00**

Coffee Set, 3 pcs, Paul Storr, London, 1821–25, coffee jug on stand, 2 handled sugar bowl, creamer, circular bombe form, gadroon borders with alternating acanthus and anthemia at intervals, bodies with a band of scrolling foliage on matted ground, engraved with armorials, stand on 3 paw feet, 65 oz, coffee jug 11¾" h **5,500.00**

Salts, open, pr, Wm Bruce, London, 1824, compressed, circular form, embossed and chased on body and rim with flowers and foliage on a matted ground, 4 scroll supports, interior gilt, base crested, 17 oz, 4" d **550.00**

Victorian

Butter Dish, cov, stand, Messrs. Barnard, London, 1889, Ashurnham pattern, cast panels of trellis enclosing flowerheads on matted ground, dome finial, monogrammed, 21 oz, 6⅜" ... **1,200.00**

Candlesticks, mkd "H.E.Ltd," Sheffield, 1900, elliptical outline, fluted and reeded decoration in George III style, integral bobeches, weighted, 11" h **750.00**

Caster, F. B. Thomas, London, 1895, George II style, vase shaped body, gadroon borders and urn finial, shoulders mounted with scrolls, 19 oz, 8½" h .. **600.00**

Coffee Pot, Messr. Bernard, London, 1883, oval outline, fluted, stamped at intervals with foliage, cover decorated to match urn-formed knop, 20 oz, 16 dwts gross, 8" h **550.00**

Punch Bowl, Elkington & Co., Birmingham, 1886, hemispherical bowl chased with swags of flowers, scrolls, diaper and foliate cartouches, pedestal foot, 29 oz, 9¾" d **650.00**

Salver, Md & Sons, London, 1895,

hexafoil outline, gadroon, leaf husk swag and beaded edging, surface chased with floral rondels, set on 4 claw and ball supports, 97 oz, 8 dwts, 20" d **1,600.00**

Edwardian

Bowl, Monteith, R & S Garrard & Co., London, 1902, William III style with lion's mask and pendant ring handles, fixed rim, 97 oz, 14½" d **3,800.00**

Candelabra, Five Light, R & S Garrard, London, 1901, early George II style, shaped sq bases applied with masks and engraved monogram below crown, octagonal vase shaped stems chased with classical profiles above strapwork, campana-shaped sconces partly chased with leaves, branches chased with strapwork on matted ground, 151 oz, 10 dwts, 16⅝" . . **8,800.00**

Inkwell, London, 1904, sq tapering form with canted corners, reeded borders, cut glass insert, 4" d **200.00**

Tea Kettle on Lampstand, Barnard Bros., London, 1903, Regency style, partly lobed, gadroon shell and foliate borders, matching stand and detachable lamp, 61 oz, 10 dwts, 11¾" h **875.00**

SILVER, ENGLISH, SHEFFIELD

Sheffield Silver, or Old Sheffield Plate, was made by a fusion method of silverplating used from the mid-18th century until the mid-1880's when the silver electroplating process was introduced.

Sheffield plate was discovered in 1743 when Thomas Boulsover of Sheffield, England, accidentally fused silver and copper. The process consisted of sandwiching a heavy sheet of copper between 2 thin sheets of silver. The result was a plated sheet of silver which could be pressed and rolled to a desired thickness. All Sheffield plate articles were worked from these plated sheets.

Most of the silverplated items found today marked "Sheffield" are not early Sheffield plate. They are later wares made in Sheffield, England.

Cake Basket, c1810, circular form, openwork string handle, ribbed sides with everted openwork border of hoops and stylized foliage, center with rubbed-in silver shield, base tinned, 10" d **225.00**

Candelabra, Four Light, c1820, circular domed bases rising to tapering stems (one half fluted), decorated with gadrooning, each

English, Sheffield, tray, footed, 19¼" d, $350.00.

supporting 3 reeded scrolling branches with campana-shaped sockets and detachable drip pans, central sockets with detachable flame finials, 24½" h, pair **325.00**

Candlesticks, c1770, stepped sq bases with a band of gadrooning, rising to knopped baluster stems with spiral fluting, campana-shaped sockets with gadrooned borders and detachable drip pans, 11" h, pair **275.00**

Coffee Pot, Matthew Boulton Co., c1820, George II style, tuck-in base, shell fluted spout, acorn finial, 11½" h **750.00**

Coffee Pot and Hot Water Jug, c1785, vase shape, one engraved with monogram and crest, one beaded and other with reeded borders, coffee pot 12¼" h, hot water pot 12" h **625.00**

Decanter Wagon, Matthew Boulton, c1800, circular half fluted coasters with applied dentilated rims, wire stopper rests, whole on 4 bone castors, stamped with sun and "SILVER EDG'D," 13" **200.00**

Dish Cross, c1770, circular oil lamp, pad supports with beaded borders, 12½" l **200.00**

Entree Dish Covers and Warming Dishes with silver finials, c1840, shaped square form, covers engraved with armorials and decorated with masks and strapwork, silver finials in the form of lion's paw, maker's mkd "I.F., London," bases on 4 scroll feet, removable hot water tank liners, 9½" w, pair **775.00**

Salver, c1830, circular rim applied with chrysanthemum flowers and foliage with grapevine at intervals from which spread towards the center chased matching flowers and grapevine, contemporary armorials, 4 short foliage feet, base struck with sunburst and thistle, 24″ d **2,000.00**

Sauce Tureen, cov., c1815–30, bombe oval form with molded rim decor with shells and leaves, grapevine handles, foliate handle and feet, Waterhouse, Hatfield & Co., 8¾″ l **350.00**

Soup Tureen, c1770, boat shaped on spreading base, swept handles, chased with a band of Vitruvian scrolls on a granulated ground and at base with stiff foliage, domed lid chased with radiating stiff foliage and bud finial, engraved initials, removable liner, 19″ l **2,100.00**

Supper Service, c1800, revolving circular base designed to hold water and supporting 3 oval dishes with 4 covers, central covered soup tureen (later date), decor with radiating lobes and gadroon borders, 28″ over handles **2,750.00**

Verriere, c1800, oval form with detachable notched rim, ram's mask and ring handles, reeded borders, 14½″ l **625.00**

Wine Coolers, c1830, campana-shaped on spreading bases, each with 2 foliate handles and everted rim, scroll work on rim, detachable liners, 9¾″ h, pair **1,000.00**

Wine Decanter Coasters, pierced gallery of interlocking pine tree devices, silver on copper wire, c1800 .... **300.00**

SILVER, PLATED

Plated silver production by an electrolytic method is credited to G. R. and H. Elkington, England, in 1838.

In electroplating silver, the article is completely shaped and formed from a base metal and then coated with a thin layer of silver. In the late 19th century, the base metal was Britannia, an alloy of tin, copper, and antimony. Other bases are copper and brass. Today the base is nickel silver.

In 1847 the electroplating process was introduced in America by Rogers Bros., Hartford, Connecticut. By 1855 a number of firms were using this method to mass produce silver plated items in large quantities.

The quality of the plating is important. Extensive use or polishing can cause the base metal to show through. The prices for plated silver items are low, making it a popular item with younger collectors.

Basket, Middletown, medallion pattern, engraved design on interior, figural feet, swing handle **65.00**

Blotter, unmarked, half moon shape, repousse design **27.50**

Candelabra

Four Lights, Bointaburet, Paris, late 19th C, Louis XVI style, decor with flutes, overlapping acanthus, key pattern, foliage swags, quilloche and lobes, arms with screw on sconces and drip pans, 17¼″ h, pr **2,850.00**

Six Lights, Adams style, cluster column stems decor with ram's masks and festoons, electric fittings, 26¾″ h **2,000.00**

Castor, Hartford Silver Co., pickle type, matching tongs, 11½″, daisy and button glass insert **90.00**

Coffee Set, International, coffee pot, creamer, sugar, and tray, floral and scroll borders, monogrammed **150.00**

Cracker Scoops, 1847 Rogers, Persian pattern, no monogram **20.00**

Crumber, Rogers & Bro., Monarch pattern, no monogram **40.00**

Firescreen, Regence-style giltwood, SP "Milton Shield," Elkington & Co., c1870, sgd "Morel Ledeuil, 1866," 38″ w, 53″ h **1,400.00**

Knife Rest, unmarked, cherubs at each end, pr **45.00**

Mirror, Art Nouveau, hand, woman with flowing hair **35.00**

Mug, Oneida, etched floral design, child's size **10.00**

Pin Cushion, unmarked, figural, dolphin **25.00**

Stein, unmarked, scroll and floral design, C-scroll wood handle **85.00**

Sugar Sifter, Holmes & Edwards, Waldorf pattern **15.00**

Syrup, Barbour Bros., tavern scene, reed wrapped handle **30.00**

Table Fountain, Victorian, c1870, shallow bowl centered by 4 columns supporting engraved glass bowl, putti below holding chains and seated on a dolphin, one column enclosing the pipe with tap, 15½″ **975.00**

Trays

Reed and Barton, Georgian style, scrolls and flowers in relief, ribbing on inner rim **40.00**

Unmarked, rectangular, plain, 17″ **27.50**

SILVER DEPOSIT GLASS

Silver Deposit Glass, so-named because a thin coating of silver was actually deposited on glass by an electrical process, was popular at the turn of this century. The process was simple: glass and a piece of silver were placed in a solution and an electric current was introduced which caused the silver to decompose, pass through the solution, and remain only on those parts of the glass on which a particular pattern had been outlined previously.

Creamer, 2¾" h, $15.00.

Ashtray, 8", mallards	25.00
Bowl, 5½", scalloped edge, vines and leaves	40.00
Compote, 7 x 7" d, clear, floral decor	75.00
Cruet, 8", clear, floral decor, orig stopper	60.00
Decanter and Matching Tray, 10", blown, emerald green, laurel decor, silver handle and trim, orig stopper, large pontil	175.00
Perfume Bottle, 4½", clear, vine and leaf decor	35.00
Pitcher, 7¾", top flares to 5¾", green glass, large flowers and leaves, double horizontal rib around base	60.00
Plate, 12", crystal, floral decor	75.00
Salt and Pepper Shakers, leaf and vine decor, SS tops	20.00
Sherbert and Underplate, cobalt blue, vine and grape leaf decor . .	28.00
Tumbler, 4½", clear, floral and leaf decor	22.00
Wine Tray, 11" cobalt blue, vine and leaf decor	90.00

SILVER LUSTRE

This metal-surfaced earthenware was made in large quantities in the Staffordshire district of England between 1805 and 1840. In this process the item was first covered completely with a thin coating of a "steel lustre" mixture containing a small quantity of platinum oxide; then an additional coating of platinum, worked in water, was laid on before the item was fired.

With the introduction of electroplating in 1840, there was a sharp decline in the demand for such metal-surfaced earthenwares.

Bowl, 5", red and blue enamel, foliate border, c1810	50.00
Candlesticks, 8¼", cylindrical, round base, c1810, pr	500.00
Coffee Pot, 10½", shield shape, dome cover, vertical ribbing, c1815	200.00
Goblet, 4⅜", interior copper lustre, c1815	50.00
Nut Meat Compote, ftd, c1830	75.00
Teapot, ribbed, beaded, dome lid, round finial, Ridgeway	140.00
Vase, 5¼", flared top, painted red and silver lustre nasturtium vine, c1810	110.00

Bowl, 3" h, 5⅛" d, copper lustre interior, $78.00.

SILVER OVERLAY

Silver overlay is applied directly to a finished glass or porcelain object. The piece is cut and decorated, usually by engraving, prior to being molded around the object.

The glass usually is of high quality, either crystal or colored. Lenox employed silver overlay on some of their decorative wares. Most of the design are indicative of the Art Nouveau and Art Deco periods.

Candy Dish, black, handled, Rockwell	75.00

Glass, 5", grapes vine and leaf motif, marked "455", set of three, $240.00.

Cologne Bottle, 5½", clear, lattice pattern	95.00
Cruet, 7½", amber, Art Nouveau, floral and leaves	125.00
Flask, pint, amber, sterling lid, crest, crossed fishing poles and net, "Good Bait"	122.00
Inkwell, 3 x 2¼", triangle, green, mkd, General Supply Co, Danielson, CT, Jacobus, Pat #879470	325.00
Jardiniere, 7", circular, ftd, white over pale magenta glaze, silver blossoming vine border, silver rim, imp factory mark, Ruskin	175.00
Liquor Bottle, 11", amber, wheat leaves decor overall, mkd 1908 .	135.00
Perfume Bottle, 3½ x 3½", bulbous, heavy sterling, Alvin mark	130.00
Vases	
4½", cranberry	135.00
7¼", green, fluted top	455.00
Wine Decanter, clear, geometric pattern, polished pontil, mkd Sterling	250.00

SILVER RESIST

Silver Resist ware was first produced about 1805. It is similar to Silver Lustre in respect to the silvering process. It differs from Silver Lustre in that a pattern appears on the surface.

The outline of the pattern was drawn or stenciled on the body of the ware. A glue or sugar-glycerin adhesive was brushed over the part which was not to be lustred. The lustering solution was applied and allowed to dry. The glue or adhesive was then washed off.

The glue or adhesive had caused the pattern to "resist" the lustering solution. When fired in the kiln, the lustre glaze covered the entire surface except for the pattern.

Bough Pot, cov, 8½" l, D-shaped body, 3 arched panels with grapes and gooseberries, cover has vine border and sprigs, 7 holes, urn knob, Leeds, 1810	330.00
Bowl, 6¼", stylized floral border, c1820	65.00
Cup and Saucer, flower and vine decor	85.00
Mug, 3½", bird, flowering plants, line borders, Leeds, c1815	95.00
Pitchers	
4⅝", shield shape, vertical ribbing, medallions with stylized flowerheads, rose vine border, c1820	150.00
6½", baluster shape, stylized foliate and floral vine, guilloche border, Leeds, c1810	185.00
Plate, Greek Key motif, sunburst center	135.00

Pitcher, 5", pine and pine cone decor, Wedgwood & Barlston, Off Eturia, $45.00.

Teapot, 4¾", oval, patera flanked by foliate swags, foliate knob, c1810	165.00
Vase, 7½", ovoid, flared rim, rectangular base, leafage, flowering vines, Leeds, c1810	295.00
Wine Goblet, 4¼", foliate vine and spiralling grass border, c1810 . . .	75.00

SMITH BROS. GLASS

After establishing a decorating department at the Mt. Washington Glass Works in 1871, Alfred and Harry Smith in 1875 moved to their own location in New Bedford, Massachusetts, to operate a firm that soon became known worldwide for fine opal decorated wares similar to the Mt. Washington products. Their glass often carried a red shield enclosing a rampant lion and the word "Trademark" on the base.

Vase, 5½", herons in reeds, light blue ground, multicolor decor, $215.00.

Biscuit Jars
   8", shaded pink, dainty blue florals and foliage, SP mountings . . . . | 325.00
   8", tan satin, pink, rust, green florals, SS bail, cover, sgd, rampant lion mark . . . . | 950.00
Bowl, 9", melon shape, large white flowers, green leaves, gold tracing, rampant lion mark . . . . | 500.00
Box, 4" d, cov, melon section, beige satin with blue florals, signed . . . | 325.00
Creamer and Sugar, cov, melon shape, ribbed, gold jeweled flowers, multicolored leaves . . . . | 450.00
Jar, 4½", squat, melon shape, white, pansy decor, open work silver top . . . . | 250.00
Rose Bowl, 4¼", Queens design, moire ground, beaded edge, sgd . | 285.00

Salt and Pepper Shakers, mottled ground, narrow ribbed, pewter tops, pr . . . . | 135.00
Sugar Castor, 6", ribbed, white satin, heavy gold florals, metal top . . . . | 195.00
Vases
   4½", cream satin with carnations, beaded enamel dot trim around top, sgd . . . . | 325.00
   5 x 4", pinched shape, cream satin ground, florals, sgd, rampant lion mark . . . . | 225.00

SNOW BABIES

Snow Babies are small bisque figurines, spattered with glitter sand, originally made in Germany, that came onto the market in the early 1900s. There are several theories on their origin. One is that German doll makers copied the designs from their traditional Christmas candies. Another theory, the most accepted, is that they were made to honor Admiral Peary's daughter who was born in Greenland in 1893 and was called the "Snow Baby" by the Eskimos.
   CAUTION: Reproductions abound.

Babies
   Hiking, 4½" . . . . | 70.00
   Holding camera, one arm extended, 1½" . . . . | 85.00
   Holding gold hoop . . . . | 75.00
   Ice skating, boy and girl, 2", pr . . | 250.00
   Playing accordion, 2" h x 2½" w | 80.00
   Playing musical instruments, 7 babies, 2" . . . . | 300.00
   Riding on early propeller plane, 1½" x 2½" l . . . . | 125.00
   Santa's helpers, red hats and coats, 2½" . . . . | 65.00
   Seated
      1", arms extended . . . . | 35.00
      2", one leg under . . . . | 25.00
      2½", marked Germany . . . . . . | 75.00
      3", arms extended . . . . | 110.00
   Skier, 1½" . . . . | 55.00
   Sledding
      1½" x 3", baby turns on wooden peg . . . . | 175.00
      2¾", pulled by huskies . . . . . | 75.00
   Sliding down wall, pr . . . . | 95.00
   Standing . . . . | 25.00
   Standing on sled . . . . | 50.00
   Standing with seal . . . . | 35.00
Figurines
   Kitten, 1½" . . . . | 45.00
   Man, 3 x 1¾", in long coat standing in front of covered wagon, pulled by horse, marked Germany . . . . | 50.00

Sledding, one on sled, another pulling, 1½″ h x 2½″ w, $95.00.

Snow Man	50.00
Sheep, 2″	45.00
Matchholder, 3½″	125.00
Planter, 8″	175.00

SOAPSTONE

The mineral steatite, used in producing all sorts of soapstone wares, has a greasy feel, and has been utilized, among other things, for carved figurine groups by the Chinese and others. These were very popular during the Victorian era. It has also been fashioned into utilitarian pieces.

Centerpieces
  6½ x 9″ l, squirrel after nuts from trees, dark brown carved stone pedestal 155.00
  12″, round, ftd base, flowers and birds 79.00
Figures
  Eskimo mother and child, 9½″, black, seated, child on her back, East Hudson Bay, 20th C 160.00

Vase, 9½″ w, 6¾″ h, Chinese, four openings, red tones, c1900, $100.00.

Horse, 8″, reclining, teakwood stand 85.00
Praying mantis, 2″, gray, violet, red marbling 198.00
Sage, 15″, Chinese 100.00
Footwarmer 15.00
inkwells
  2⅞″, dark green, carved, "Matthias Cozier" on base ... 85.00
  Black, carved, 4 quill holder, ribbed dome top, geometric carving on 4 sides 140.00
Matchbox Holder, 3″, ftd, carved front 25.00
Teapot, 2″, orange lid with bird ... 72.00
Toothpick Holder, sculpted, 3 monkeys, See No Evil, Hear No Evil, Speak No Evil 37.50
Tumbler, straight sided, polished .. 72.00
Vase, 12″, carved figure standing under tree, cranes and flowers on 3″ base, 19th C 650.00
Wall Pocket, brown and beige, 3 pockets, carved floral and foliage 42.00

SPANGLED GLASS

Spangled glass is a blown or blown molded variegated art glass of the late 1800s very much like Spatter Glass with the addition of flakes of mica or metallic looking green aventurine. It can be cased with a white or clear layer of glass.

There has been much confusion about Spangled Glass, as it had been previously attributed only to the Vasa Murrhina Art Glass Company of Hartfort, Connecticut, which advertised Factory Cape Cod Works, Sandwich, Mass. However, the production of Spangled Glass included many companies in the United States, England, and Europe and it is impossible to attribute any specific piece to any source.

Spangled Glass has continued to be made by many companies and is being made at present.

Baskets
  6½ x 4¾″, pink, silver mica, white cased, looped thorn handle ... 165.00
  Small, white, pink, blue, red and yellow, silver mica, ruffled top, white cased 95.00
Bowl, star shape 40.00
Condiment Set, 3 pcs, cranberry, green flecks, SP holder 200.00
Creamer and Sugar, cov, blue, gold mica flecks, pr 225.00
Cruet and Stopper, leaf mold, cranberry, mica flecks, white cased, Northwood 450.00

Ewers, 8½", cranberry, silver mica
flecks, white cased, applied thorn
handles, pontil, pr 195.00
Fairy lamp, 6⅜", multicolored, gold
mica flecks 200.00
Pitchers
 6¾ x 4¾", cobalt blue, gold mica
 flecks, applied amber handle
 with mica flecks 225.00
 7½ x 7½", bulbous, 4 sided top,
 apricot, gold mica flecks form
 diamond pattern, white cased,
 pontil 155.00
 10", ruby and peach, gold flecks,
 cased, applied amber thorn
 handle 195.00

**Tumbler, 4", pink, white, orange, red,
blue, yellow and silver spangles,
$70.00.**

Rose Bowls
 3¾", crimped top, blue and clear,
 mica flecks 125.00
 5", cream and yellow, silver flecks   130.00
Salt and Pepper, 4", pink, silver
mica flecks, cased, pr 295.00
Sugar Castor, cranberry, mica flecks,
white cased, Northwood 110.00
Syrup, 6", green, pink and white, silver mica flecks, clear applied han-
dle, pewter lid 165.00
Toothpick, 2", blue, gold flecks . . .   75.00
Tumbler, 3⅝", red and white stripes,
white flecks 100.00

Vases
 6½", bulbous, melon ribbed, blue,
 silver flecks, cased 70.00
 7¼", rose, silver flecks, cased,
 clear applied handles 110.00
 8", yellow, Swirl pattern, cased . .   125.00

SPATTER GLASS

**Spatter Glass is a variegated blown or blown
molded art glass produced at the end of the
19th century by many of the glass factories
both in the United States and abroad. The
collection of various colored pieces of glass
onto the glass blower's gather produced the
combinations of colors seen in the glass. It
can be cased either in white or clear glass.**

**Spatter Glass has been known previously
as "End-of-Day Glass" as it was felt the
pieces were made with leftover bits of glass
at the end of the day. However, it is now
known that this glass was a specific line of
glass in production. It is still being produced.**

Baskets
 6 x 5½", blue, white cased, ap-
 plied thorn handle 185.00
 6½ x 7½", oval, brown, yellow,
 red and pink, white cased, ap-
 plied thorn handle 190.00
 7½ x 4½", round, interior pleated
 top, yellow, red, green, pink and
 white, looped thorn handle . . .   215.00
Box, 7½ x 4½", egg shape, hinged,
cased, yellow and blue florals,
gold and white leaves, 3 clear ap-
plied feet 265.00

**Creamer, 4¾", white and pink,
Northwood, $42.00.**

Candlesticks, 9¼″, red, blue and green, cased, pr 118.00
Cup and Saucer, red and white . . . 30.00
Darning Egg, blown, multicolor, Sandwich glass 120.00
Jars, covered
  5 x 4¼″, white, pink, maroon and green, white cased, crystal leaf applied feet, crystal knob finial 85.00
  6½ x 3¼″, gold, maroon, white and green, yellow cased, leaf finial 75.00
Pitchers
  7 x 3″, ruffled top, maroon, pink, yellow and green, white cased, clear applied handle 65.00
  8½″, Swirl pattern, pink, brown and cranberry, applied rococo handle 85.00
Rolling Pin, 14½ x 1⅞″, white with deep maroon and blue 110.00
Salt, master, 3 x 3¼″, white, maroon, green, blue and yellow, white cased, clear leaf feet and leaves 50.00
Shoe, 3 x 3¼ x 5¼″ l, white ovals, maroon, green, pink and yellow, white cased, applied crystal rigaree and leaf 60.00
Sugar Shaker, cranberry and white . 65.00
Vases
  5 x 5⅞″, ruffled, pink, white cased, applied vaseline mat-sunoke button flowers, leaves and feet 495.00
  9¼″, Jack-in-the-Pulpit, multicolored, Pairpoint paper label, pontil, pr 85.00
Water Set, pitcher, bulbous, 5 tumblers, cranberry and white, Burlinton mark, 6 pcs 185.00

SPATTERWARE

The earliest examples of English Spatterware were made about 1780. Spatterware is made of common earthenware, although occasionally creamware were used. The peak period of production was 1810–1840. Marked pieces are rare. Firms known to have made Spatterware are Adams, Barlow, and Harvey and Cotton.

Collectors today focus on the patterns— Cannon, Castle, Fort, Peafowl Rainbow, Rose, Thistle, Schoolhouse, etc. On flat ware the decoration is in the center. On hollow pieces it occurs on both sides.

Color of spatter is the key to price. Blue and red are most common. Green, purple, and brown are in a middle group. Black and yellow are scarce.

The amount of spatter decoration varies from piece to piece. Some objects simply have decorated borders. These are often decorated with a brush, requiring several hundred touches per square inch to achieve the spatter effect. Other pieces have the entire surface covered with spatter. Aesthetics of the final product is another key to value.

Like any soft paste, Spatterware was easily broken or chipped. Prices are for pieces in very good to mint condition.

Cup and Saucer, Peafowl, green spatter, light blue bird with yellow belly, red tail, $365.00.

Bowls
  5⅞″, Peafowl, blue 275.00
  18¾″, Tulip, blue 300.00
Chamber Pot, 6 x 8½″ d, blue, rose decor in red, green, black 250.00
Creamers
  Hexagonal design, red 250.00
  Peafowl, blue 400.00
  Rainbow, blue and red 140.00
Cups and Saucers
  Acorn, blue 245.00
  Blue, paneled, center blue dot . . 150.00
  Castle, purple 185.00
  Dots
    Blue, yellow border 210.00
    Red, yellow, green border 225.00
  Peafowl
    Green 350.00
    Red 300.00
  Rainbow, blue and green 200.00
  Rose, blue border 225.00
  Schoolhouse, five colors 550.00
  Single Flower
    Blue, imp Davenport 225.00
    Red, blue, flower of red, green 200.00
  Thistle
    Purple 235.00
    Rainbow, red, yellow, green . . 375.00
  Tulip, yellow 825.00
Custard Cup, 12 sided, solid blue coarse spatter, applied flat iron handle 155.00

Honey Pot, Schoolhouse, red, yellow, blue 3,000.00

Miniatures
  Cups and Saucers
    Brown 80.00
    Red, marked Staffordshire, England 65.00
  Sugar, Fort, blue 350.00

Mug, Peafowl, blue, 2½" 500.00
Mustard Pot, Peafowl, green, 2¾" . 785.00

Pitchers
  Peafowl, blue border, 6⅝" 795.00
  Rainbow, 6½", green, red 465.00

Plates
  American Eagle, 3⅞", underglaze blue with eagle clasping arrows in talons and perched before shield with 13 stars, purple spatter border rim, c1840 .... 375.00
  Castle, green, 8⅜" 250.00
  Clover, green, 9½", red blossoms, black trailing vines 375.00
  Dahlia, light purple border, 9⅜" . 300.00
  Fort, blue, 5⅛" 165.00
  Peafowl
    Blue, 8¼" 300.00
    Green, 8¼" 350.00
    Red, 9½" 365.00
  Rainbow, blue and red, 5⅛" 200.00
  Schoolhouse, three color, green border, 7½" 625.00
  Star, blue, 8½" 225.00
  Thistle, yellow, 8⅝" 630.00
  Tulip, purple, 6¼" 265.00

Platters
  Peafowl, blue, 15⅝" 2,300.00
  Rainbow, red and blue, cross design 500.00

Soup Plate, 8½", blue, large open 13 pointed star center 145.00

Sugar Bowls
  Peafowl, blue 445.00
  Red, black stripes, well formed handles, cov with finial, 5¼" .. 195.00

Wash Bowl, blue, purple rainbow, 12 sided, 13¾" c x 4⅜" h 300.00
Wash Bowl and Pitcher, Peafowl, red, blue, green, yellow, black, 14½" d x 13¼" h 975.00

SPONGEWARE

Spongeware indicates a specific type of decoration, not a type of pottery or glaze. The decoration was not applied with a sponge as is commonly believed.

    Spongeware decoration is found on many types of pottery bodies—ironstone, redware, stoneware, etc. It was made in both England and the United States. Marked pieces indicate a starting date of 1815, with manufacturing extending to the 1860s.

    Decoration is varied. In some pieces, the sponging is minimal with the white underglaze dominant. Other pieces appear to be sponged solidly on both sides. Pieces from 1840–1860 have sponging which appears in either a circular movement or a streaked horizontal technique.

    Examples are found in blue and white, the most common color. Other prevalent colors are browns, greens, ochres, and greenish-blue. The greenish-blue results from blue sponging which has been overglazed in a pale yellow. A red overglaze produced a black or navy color.

    Other colors are blue and red (found on English creamware and American earthenware of the 1880's), gray, grayish green, red, dark green on stark white, dark green on mellow yellow, and purple.

    Spongeware should not be confused with Spatterware or Design Spatterware, both of which are listed separately.

Coffee Pot, blue and white, c1830, $275.00.

Banks
  Pig, blue and brown, cream ground, 6" 150.00
  Tudor, red and blue, c1800, 6 x 6¾" 400.00

Bean Pot, green, brown, ochre 150.00

Bowls
  5¼", brown, blue, white, red on cream ground 45.00
  6¼" d x 4¼" h, blue, brown, white 45.00
  10" d x 4½" h, green and white . 125.00

Butter Crock, cov, blue, white, daisy 115.00
Chamber Pot, blue and gray 115.00
Compote, shallow, blue and white, 8½" 300.00

Cookie Jar, 8", barrel shape 65.00
Creamer, 4", corset shape, green   .   50.00
Crocks
    7½", blue and white, wire bail   . .   150.00
    8½", gray-green, straight sides, wire bail 200.00
    10½", cov, blue and white, wire bail 245.00
Cups and Saucers
    Curved Side, blue and white 100.00
    Straight Side, blue and white   . . .   110.00
Cuspidor, 7½ x 5¼", blue, bands, blue sponge on white ground   . . .   75.00
Custard Cup, blue and white, 4" . . .   65.00
Gypsy Kettle, lid, blue and white   . .   85.00
Honey Jar, cov, handles, blue and white 145.00
Inkwells
    Blue and white 230.00
    Green 180.00
Jar, cov, 6" h, wire handle, blue on cream 210.00
Jardinieres
    9", barrel shape, gray-green 135.00
    9", tankard, blue and white 135.00
    11" d x 8¼" h, blue, white ground, green rim flecked with gold 75.00
Jugs
    3", green, ochre, brown 125.00
    5½", baluster, purple, cream ground 240.00
    7¼", applied handle, flared top, blue bands, cream ground 125.00
    8½", deer in relief on two sides, blue and white 185.00
Match Holder, blue and white, 2⅜"   185.00
Mugs
    1¾", red 125.00
    3⅛" h, medium brown on cream ground 115.00
Mush Set, blue, white 245.00
Mustard Pot, cov, blue and white   . .   150.00
Nappy, rectangular, blue and white, sponged interior only, 8½" 165.00
Pie Plate, 10¼", blue, white 165.00
Pitchers
    4⅝", green, brown on cream ground 145.00
    5" h, brown, blue, red, white on cream ground 95.00
    6½", dark gray on cream ground   .   100.00
    9" h, emb medallion of child, dog, blue, white 160.00
    10", milk, mottled blues, on cream ground, 2 qt 175.00
Plates
    10¼", blue and white, scalloped rim   115.00
    10½", blue and white, sponged interior only, no interior rim 125.00
Plates, Soup
    Red and green, early 300.00
    9¼", blue and white 130.00

Platters
    6½", rectangular, blue and white   .   120.00
    13½", oval, blue and white, fluted   130.00
    15½", rectangular, chamfered corners, blue and white, star center, ironstone mark 180.00
Pots
    Coffee, blue and white, unmarked   280.00
    Tea, blue and white, bulbous body, flat lid, curved handle, 7¼" 365.00
Razor Box, blue and white, lid, 7½"   175.00
Salt Box, 6" h, blue, brown, cream ground, hinged walnut top 215.00
Soap Dish, 5¼", concentric rings, blue and white 155.00
Spittoon, blue and white, blue bands   90.00
Sugars
    Blue and green 225.00
    Blue and red 175.00
Umbrella Stand, blue and white, blue bands, 21¼" 435.00
Vase, 4", blue, white 40.00
Wash Bowl, Pitcher, blue, olive green on white, blue bands, 11⅝" d x 8½" h 325.00
Water Filter, 20½" h, blue, white, nickel plated spigot, stone filter insert, 2 pc 320.00

SPORTS COLLECTIBLES

Momentoes of sports teams, whether pieces of equipment or signed photographs, are decorating an increasing number of game rooms around the country. Baseball cards have received the most attention. However, the variety of materials is almost endless. Prices still are in the modest range. It's a wide open field.

See *Warman's Americana & Collectibles* for additional sports listings.

Baseball
    Baseballs
        Casey Stengel autograph 20.00
        Official American League ball, autographed by entire team, 1932 World Series New York Yankees, 24 signatures starting with Babe Ruth 750.00
    Book, Babe Ruth, c1930 . . . . . .   10.00
    Button, pinback, 3½", Cleveland Indians, 1954, championship team   55.00
    Card, gum, autographed by Lou Gehrig 200.00
    Frying pan, miniature, Baseball Hall of Fame, cast iron, emb batter in center 15.00
    Press Pin, All-Star, 1952 . . . .   30.00
    Program, New York Yankees World Series, 1937 . . . .   75.00

STAFFORDSHIRE, HISTORICAL

The Staffordshire district of England had an abundance of fine clay for pottery making. There were 80 different potteries operating there in 1786, with the number increasing to 149 by 1802. The district included Burslem, Cobridge, Eturia, Fenton, Foley, Hanley, Lane Delph, Lane End, Longport, Shelton, Stoke and Tunstall. Among the many famous potters were Adams, Davenport, Spode, Stevenson, Wedgewood, and Wood.

In historical Staffordshire the view is the most critical element. Because of the variety, collection can be organized around a single theme, e.g., maker, Pennsylvania or transportation. Most collectors focus on the dark blue, but lighter views do seem to be gaining in popularity.

The numbers in parenthesis are from David and Linda Arman's *Historical Staffordshire: An Illustrated Check List* and *First Supplement, Historical Staffordshire: An Illustrated Check List*. Together these books constitute the most detailed published list of American historical views and their forms.

Prices are for proof examples. Adjust prices by 20% for an unseen chip, a faint hairline, or an unseen professional repair; by 35% for knife marks through the glaze and a visible professional repair; by 50% for worn glaze and major repairs.

W. ADAMS & SONS   ADAMS

ADAMS

The Adams family has been associated with ceramics from the mid-17th century. In 1802 William Adams of Stoke-upon-Trent produced American views.

In 1819 a fourth William Adams, son of William of Stoke, became a partner with his father and was later joined by his three brothers. The firm became William Adams & Sons. The father died in 1829 and William, the eldest son, became manager.

The company operated four potteries at Stoke and one at Tunstall. American views were produced at Tunstall in black, light blue, sepia, pink, and green in the 1830–40 period. William Adams died in 1865. All operations were moved to Tunstall. The firm continues today under the name of Wm. Adams & Sons, Ltd.

Soccer cigarette case, 3⅞″ x 3¼″, black gun metal. SS relief, gemstone catch, $125.00.

Ticket stub, World Series, Boston, 1946	10.00
Basketball, game, Harlem Globetrotters	15.00
Bowling, medallion, 6″, bronze, man bowling in alley, duck pins	45.00
Boxing	
Film, Joe Louis-Walcott fight, 16mm	35.00
Headgear, leather, early	15.00
Picture, James Corbett, young and boxing, 13 x 17″	50.00
Football	
Game, American Varsity, 1934	35.00
Medal, football, brass, early 1900	7.00
Program, Eagles verus Cincinnati Reds, National League, 1933	22.00
Golf	
Ashtray, glass, golfer driving, in relief	65.00
Cigarette box, Series of Golf, 3 compartments, SP	35.00
Plate, 10″, Royal Doluton, "Give losers leave to speak and winners to laugh"	125.00
Stickpin, golf club head and ball finial, gilt and silvered metal	50.00
Swizzle stick, golf club shape, SS	38.00
Racing, program, Indianapolis 500 Races, 1929	27.50
Tennis	
Fan, Art Nouveau, woman tennis player	25.00
Inkstand, 7⅜ x 4⅞ x 5½″, bronze, figure of man holding racket, wearing cap and knickers	280.00
Napkin ring, figural, ring with racket leaning against it, SP	145.00

Hudson River Series, Fairmont (so called), pink, 4″ cup plate (459)	75.00
Mitchell & Freeman's China And Glass Warehouse, Chatham Street, Boston, dark blue, 9″ plate (444)	450.00

Adams, U.S. Views Series, Headwaters of the Juniata, pink 10½", $100.00.

New York, medallions of sailor with
ship on border, sugar bowl, black
(457) **175.00**
Seal Of The United States, dark
blue, 5" pitcher (443) **750.00**
U. S. Views, light views
Catskill Mountain House, U.S., 10
¼ soup (445) **75.00**
Lake George, U.S., 13¼" platter
(448) **275.00**
White Mountains, N. Hampshire,
vegetable dish (456) **300.00**

CLEWS

From sketchy historical accounts that are
available, James Clews took over the closed
plant of A. Stevenson in 1819. His brother
Ralph entered the business later. The firm
continued until about 1836 when James
Clews came to America to enter the pottery
business at Troy, Ind. The venture was a failure because of the lack of skilled workmen
and the proper type of clay. He returned to
England but did not re-enter the pottery business.

Cities Series, dark and medium blue
Columbus, 14½" platter (21) ... **2,000.00**

Louisville, Kentucky, soup tureen
(24) **3,500.00**
Near Fishkill, 7¾" plate (25) ... **225.00**
New Philadelphia, 10" plate (27) . **275.00**
Doctor Syntax, dark blue
Doctor Syntax Bound To A Tree
By Highwaymen, cheese dish
(37) **1,000.00**
(*Note: 10¼" plate in this view is
reproduction)
Doctor Syntax Entertained At College, 9½" square dish (40) ... **350.00**
Doctor Syntax Mistakes A Gentlemen's House for an Inn, 10"
soup (42) **145.00**
(*Note: 10¼" plate in this view is
reproduction)
Doctor Syntax Amused With Pat
In The Pond, 19" platter (52) .. **350.00**
The Harvest Home, strainer (59) . **275.00**
The Advertisement For A Wife,
fruit dish (64) **450.00**
Don Quioxte Series, dark blue
Knighthood Conferred On Don
Quioxte, 10" plate (66) **145.00**
Don Quioxte And Sancha Panza,
gravy tureen tray (73) **245.00**
The Meeting Of Sancho And Dapple, 9" plate (76) **145.00**
Sancho Panza And The Dutchess,
18½" platter (82) **475.00**
Landing Of Lafayette At Castle Garden, dark blue (1)
Bowl, 14", beaded **2,000.00**
Cup Plate, 4⁷/₁₆", regular border .. **400.00**
Egg Cup **1,200.00**
Plate, 5½" **225.00**
Platter, 19" **1,200.00**

**Clewes, Picturesque views, N. Fishkill,
Hudson River, brown 10¼", $170.00.**

Sauce Boat 650.00
Soup, 10″ 225.00
Sugar Bowl 650.00
Peace And Plenty, dark blue (34)
Gravy Boat 650.00
Plate, 9″ 225.00
Platter, 14½″ 700.00
Picturesque Views Series, light colors
Fort Montgomery, Hudson River, ladle (103) 150.00
Glenn's Falls, chamber pot (exterior) (105) 300.00
Jessup's Landing, Hudson River, 10½″ plate (108) 75.00
Junction Of The Sacandaga And Hudson Rivers, sugar bowl (109) 145.00
Near Sandy Hill, Hudson River, 7⅞″ cup plate (114) 75.00
Newburgh, Hudson River, 17½″ platter (115) 275.00
West Point, Hudson River, 8″ plate (121) 65.00
States or America and Independence States, dark blue
Building, sheep on lawn, 9″ soup (5) 245.00
Building, two wings, water in foreground, 7″ pitcher (13) 750.00
Castle, with flags, boats in foreground, washbowl (11) 900.00
Mansion, three story, small extension to left, 4½″ cup plate, full border (7) 375.00
Mansion, winding drive, vegetable dish (15) 750.00
Wilkie Series, dark blue
Christmas Eve, 10″ plate (87) . . . 165.00
Errand Boy, custard cup (89) 250.00
Escape Of The Mouse, vegetable dish (90) 350.00
Valentine, 15″ platter (93) 375.00

J & J. JACKSON   J&J. JACKSON

Job and John Jackson began operations at the Churchyard Works, Burslem, about 1830. The works formerly were owned by the Wedgwood family. The firm produced transfer scenes in a variety of colors, such as black, light blue, pink, sepia, green, maroon, and mulberry. Over 40 different American views of Conn., Mass., Pa., N.Y., and Ohio were issued. The firm is believed to have closed about 1844.

American Scenery, light colors
Battery & C, New York, 8″ plate (466) 65.00
Conway, N. Hampshire (marked American Scenery), 4⅛″ cup plate (470) 85.00

J & J Jackson, View of the Canal, Little Falls Mohawk River, black and white scalloped edge, c1830, $75.00.

Girard's Bank, Philadelphia, 6″ plate (474) 65.00
Harvard Hall, Mass., sauce boat (477) 150.00
New Haven, Connecticut, 11″ platter (480) 275.00
Skenectady On The Mohawk River, 9½″ pitcher (483) 250.00
Upper Ferry Bridge Over The River Schuylkill, vegetable dish (489) 225.00
Yale College And State House, New Haven, soup tureen (interior) (493) 1,000.00
Miscellaneous
New York, Select Sketches series, 19½″ well platter (476) 350.00
Skenectady On The Mohawk River, pink, peacock and feathers border, 6½″ pitcher (494) 150.00

THOMAS MAYER

In 1829, Thomas Mayer and his brothers, John and Joshua, purchased Stubbs' Dale Hall Works of Burslem. They continued to produce a superior grade of ceramics.

Arms Of The American States, dark blue
Connecticut, gravy tureen tray (498) 1,400.00

Georgia, 11¾" platter (500)	2,500.00
Maryland, beaded rim bowl (501)	3,500.00
New York, 9½" soup (504)	450.00
Rhode Island, 9" plate (507)	350.00
South Carolina, ladle (508)	650.00
Virginia, fruit dish (509)	4,500.00
Lafayette At Franklin's Tomb, teapot, dark blue (511)	900.00

CHARLES MEIGH

Job Meigh began the Meigh pottery in the Old Hall Pottery, Hanley, in 1780. Later his sons and grandsons entered the business. The firm's name is recorded as Job Meigh & Sons, 1823; J. Meigh & Sons, 1829; Charles Meigh, 1843.

The American Cities and Scenery series was produced by Charles Meigh between 1840 and 1850. The colors are light blue, brown, gray, and purple. Sometimes the colors appear in combination.

Boston, 18" platter (547)	350.00
Boston From The Dorchester Heights, pitcher (548)	250.00
Capitol At Washington, gravy tureen (interior) (550)	275.00
City Hall, NY, 10" soup (551)	65.00
Utica, cup and saucer (556)	75.00
Village Of Little Falls, vegetable dish (558)	125.00
Yale College, New Haven, 7¼" plate (560)	65.00

MELLOR, VENABLES & CO.

Little information is recorded on Mellor, Venables & Co. except that they were listed as potters in Burselm in 1843. Their Scenic Views series with the Arms of the States Border does include the arms for New Hampshire. This state is missing from the Mayer series. However, the view was known in England and collectors search for a Mayer example.

Arms Of States, white body, light colors, eight states in varying combinations (529)	
Creamer	150.00
Pitcher, 6"	250.00
Tea Cup	125.00
Scenic Views, Arms of States Border, light colors	
Boston and Bunker Hill, 17½" platter (517)	300.00
The Narrows (from Fort Hamilton), 9½" plate (519)	65.00
View Of Hudson City And The Catskill Mountains, 8" pitcher (524)	250.00

J.W.R. W. RIDGWAY

Stone China

J. & W. RIDGWAY AND WILLIAM RIDGWAY & CO.

John and William Ridgway, sons of Job Ridgway and nephews of George Ridgway who owned Bell Bank Works and Cauldon Place Works, produced the popular Beauties of America series at the Cauldon plant. The partnership between the two brothers was dissolved in 1830. John remained at Cauldon.

William managed the Bell Bank works until 1854. Two additional series were produced based upon the etchings of Bartlett's *American Scenery*. The first series had various borders including narrow lace. The second series is known as Catskill Moss.

Beauties of America is in dark blue. The other series are found in the light transfer colors of light blue, pink, brown, black and green.

Ridgway, American Scenery Scenes, Harper's Ferry From the Potomac Side, light blue, 9¼", $70.00.

American Scenery, light colors	
Crow-Nest From Bull Hill, creamer (282)	150.00
Narrows From Fort Hamilton, 17½" platter (288)	250.00
Peekskill Landing, Hudson River, sugar bowl (287)	175.00
Valley Of The Sanandoch From Jefferson's Rock, cup plate (289)	95.00

Wilkes-Barre, Vale Of Wyoming, vegetable dish (294)	145.00

Beauties Of America, dark blue

Almshouse, Boston, vase or urn (254)	1,500.00
Athenaeum, Boston, 6″ plate (256)	175.00
Capitol, Washington, bidet (259) .	1,000.00
Deaf and Dumb Asylum, Hartford, CT, 15″ platter (263)	650.00
Masonic Hall, Philadelphia, 7″ plate (269)	750.00
Pennsylvania Hospital, Philadelphia, 10″ bowl (272) . . .	650.00

Catskill Moss

Boston and Bunker's Hill, 19″ platter (297)	300.00
Fairmount, soup tureen (302) . . .	900.00
Little Falls, NY, deep dish (306) . .	225.00
President's House, vegetable dish (311)	150.00
The Narrows From Fort Hamilton, 7″ plate (313)	65.00
Valley of Wyoming, teapot (317) .	225.00

Columbia Star, Harrison's Log Cabin

End View, 12″ bowl (276)	375.00
End View, 17″ platter	450.00
Side View, gravy tureen tray (277)	250.00
Side View, soup	150.00
Side View, Plowing, 14½″ soup tureen with cover (278)	1,500.00

ROGERS

ROGERS

John Rogers and his brother George established a pottery near Longport in 1782. After George's death in 1815, John's son Spencer became a partner and the firm operated under the name of John Rogers & Sons. John died in 1816. His son continued the use of the name until he dissolved the pottery in 1842.

Boston Harbor, dark blue (441)

Creamer	750.00
Sugar Bowl	850.00
Teapot	1,000.00

Boston State House, dark blue (442)

Cup and Saucer	250.00
Cup Plate, 3¼″, full border	600.00
Pitcher, 6½″	500.00
Platter, 17″	650.00
Teapot	500.00

Shells and Seaweed, medium blue, no longer considered an American historical view. Ships have been correctly identified as *Blanche* and *LaPique*

Gravy tureen tray	145.00
Plate, 10″ (437)	150.00
Platter, 9⅞″ (440B)	250.00

R. S. W.

STEVENSON

As early as the 17th century the name Stevenson has been associated with the pottery industry. Andrew Stevenson of Cobridge introduced American scenes with the flower and scroll border. Ralph Stevenson, also of Cobridge, used a vine and leaf border on his dark blue historical views and a lace border on his series in light transfers.

The initials R. S. & W. indicate Ralph Stevenson and Williams are associated with the acorn and leaf border. It has been reported that Willis was Ralph's New York agent and the wares were produced by Ralph alone.

Stevenson, Acorn and Oak Leaves Border, Park Theatre, New York, med. blue, $265.00.

Acorn And Oak Leaves Border, dark blue

Albany Theater, 1824, 9½″ square vegetable dish with cover (346)	5,000.00
Harvard College (University Hall), 8½″ plate (353)	375.00
St. Paul's Chapel, New York, 5¾″ plate (359)	500.00
Water Works, Philadelphia, 12″ bowl, white rim (363)	1,300.00

Floral And Scroll Border, dark blue

Church and Buildings Adjoining Murray Street, New York, 10″ soup (396)	1,000.00

New York From Heights Near
Brooklyn, 16½" platter (399) . . **3,000.00**
The Temple of Fame . . . To The
Memory Of Commodore Perry,
vegetable dish (401) **3,500.00**
View Of New York From
Weehawk, soup tureen (404) . . **7,500.00**
Lace Border With Vases of Flowers
City Hall, Albany (390)
Pitcher, 7" (391 on reverse) . . . **700.00**
Plate, 10½" **175.00**
Thorps And Sprague, Albany (391)
Cup Plate, 3¾" **375.00**
Plate, 7½" **150.00**
Vine Border, dark blue
Brooklyn Ferry, vegetable dish
(369) **1,750.00**
Deaf And Dumb Asylum, Hartford,
Conn, 9" platter (373) **850.00**
Esplanade And Castle Garden,
New York, coffee pot (374) . . . **3,500.00**
Hospital Boston, 8½" plate (378) **250.00**
Lawrence Mansion, Boston, wash-
bowl (381) **1,200.00**

STUBBS

In 1790 Stubbs established a pottery works
at Burselm, England. He operated it until 1829
when he retired and sold the pottery to the
Mayer brothers. He probably produced his
American views about 1825. Many of his
scenes were from Boston, New York, New
Jersey, and Philadelphia.

Rose Border
Boston State House, 9½" pitcher
(335) **500.00**
City Hall, New York (336)
Cup and Saucer **225.00**
Mug **550.00**
Plate, 6" **350.00**
Spread Eagle Border
Church In The City Of New York
(Dr. Mason's), 6" plate (322) . . **900.00**
Fair Mount Near Philadelphia,
soup tureen (324) **1,750.00**
Hoboken In New Jersey, 7¾"
plate (326) **175.00**
Nahant Hotel, Near Boston, 9"
plate (328) **350.00**

State House, Boston, compote
(331) **750.00**
Upper Ferry Bridge Over The Riv-
er Schuylkill (332)
Gravy tureen with cover **900.00**
Gravy tureen tray **300.00**
Platter, 18" **800.00**
View At Hurl Gate, East River,
7¼" plate (333) **1,500.00**
Woodlands, Near Philadelphia
(334)
Cup Plate, 3¾", full border . . . **275.00**
Tray, open work **650.00**
Vegetable dish and cover **850.00**

S. TAMS & CO.

The firm operated at Longton, England.
The exact date of its beginning is not known,
but believed to be about 1810–1815. The
company produced several dark blue American views. About 1830 the name became
Tams, Anderson, and Tams.

Gen. Wm. H. Harrison . . . Hero Of
The Thames (515B)
Plate, 9", chickweed border **1,300.00**
Plate, 9", line border **1,100.00**
Plate, 10", feather edge border . . **1,200.00**
United States Hotel, Philadelphia,
10" plate (515) **650.00**

WOOD

Enoch Wood, sometimes referred to as the
Father of English Pottery, began operating a
pottery at Fountain Place, Burselm, in 1783. A
cousin Ralph Wood was associated with him.
In 1790 James Caldwell became a partner
and the firm was known as Wood and Caldwell. In 1819 Wood and his sons took full
control.

Enoch died in 1840. His sons continued under the name of Enoch Wood & Sons. The
American views were first made in the
mid-1820's and continued through the 1840's.

It is reported that the pottery produced
more signed historical views than any other
Staffordshire firm. Many of the views attributed to unknown makers probably came from
the Woods.

Marks vary, although always with the name
Wood. The establishment was sold to
Messrs. Pinder, Bourne & Hope in 1846.

Wood & Son, Shell Border, The Union Line, 10¼", $325.00.

Boston State House, 10" soup, dark blue (219)	165.00
Celtic China series, light colors	
Belleville On The Passaic River, gravy tureen with cover (235)	500.00
Columbus, GA, 5" plate (238)	250.00
Harvard College, 10½" bowl (240)	95.00
Highlands, Hudson River, vegetable dish (242)	300.00
New York From Staten Island, 20½" platter (245)	450.00
Transylvania University, Lexington, KY, 10" plate (250)	165.00
West Point, Military Academy, openwork tray (252)	225.00
Wooding Station On The Mississippi, gravy boat (253)	900.00
Chancellor Livingston, dark blue (220)	
Coffee Pot	1,750.00
Creamer	850.00
Waste Bowl	800.00
Eagle On Rock, teapot, pink (221)	275.00
French Views, dark blue	
Cascade de Gresy, Pres Chambery, 7¾" plate (192)	165.00
East View Of La Grange, Residence Of The Marquis Lafayette (194)	
Plate, 9"	195.00
Vegetable Dish	350.00
La Grange, Residence Of The Marquis Lafayette, 9½" soup (197)	195.00
Maison de Raphael, custard cup (198)	150.00
S. W. View of La Grange, Residence Of The Marquis Lafayette, 20" platter (203)	750.00

Vue Prise en Savoie, 6½" beaded bowl (208)	275.00
Four Medallion, floral border, light colors	
Harvard University, 15" platter (228)	300.00
President's House, Washington, 10½" plate (232)	145.00
Residence of S. Russel, 6¾" plate	65.00
Landing Of The Fathers At Plymouth, Dec. 22, 1620, dark and medium blue (218)	
Cup Plate, 3¾", partial border with scrolls	450.00
Pitcher, 7½"	650.00
Plate, 8½"	135.00
Shell Border, circular center, dark blue	
Capitol at Washington, 7½" plate (184)	300.00
Catskill Mountains, Hudson River, mustard jar with cover (162)	700.00
Gilpin's Mill On The Brandywine Creek, 9" plate (165)	250.00
Highlands At West Point, Hudson River, 6½" plate (168)	375.00
Lake George, State Of New York, 16½" platter (171)	850.00
Pass In The Catskill Mountains, gravy tureen tray (177)	300.00
Quebec, 9½" square vegetable dish with cover (179)	950.00
Table Rock, Niagara, 10" soup (180)	275.00
White House, Washington, cup plate (189)	750.00
Shell Border, irregular center, dark blue	
Cape Coast Castle On The Gold Coast, Africa, 16½" platter (126)	750.00
Chiswick On The Thames, gravy tureen tray (128)	300.00
Commodore MacDonnough's Victory (130)	
Plate, 10"	350.00
Waste Bowl	650.00
Cowes Harbor, 6¾" plate (132)	245.00
Eddistone Lighthouse, vegetable dish (142)	700.00
Marine Hospital, Louisville, Kentucky, compote (interior) (137)	1,250.00
Near Calcutta, sauce dish (138)	225.00
Wadsworth Tower, teapot (147)	700.00
Yarmouth, Islae Of Wright, 12" platter (149)	750.00

UNKNOWN MAKERS

Baltimore Views	
Baltimore Assembly Rooms, sugar bowl (592)	2,000.00
University Of Maryland, cup (596)	425.00

Unknown Maker, Dam and Water Works at Philadelphia, dark blue, fruit border, 10″ d, $345.00.

Erie Canal Inscription . . . DeWitt Clinton Eulogy, plate 5¾″ (597) . .	350.00
Lafayette Crowned At Yorktown (599)	
Cup Plate, 4″	450.00
Pitcher, 6½″, reverse with Surrender of Cornwallis	600.00
Mount Vernon, The Seat Of The Late Gen'l Washington (601)	
Creamer	600.00
Teapot	850.00
Line Border series, black or carmine line border	
Alms House, N.Y., cup (863)	35.00
Exchange, Boston, plate (868) . . .	60.00
Staughton's Church, Philadelphia, creamer (872)	125.00

STAFFORDSHIRE ITEMS

A wide variety of ornamental pottery items came from the pottery district of Staffordshire, beginning in the 17th century and extending to today. The high point of production was the 19th century.

The objects are many—trinket boxes, pastille burners, animal figures, and figurines (called chimney ornaments). The key to price is age and condition. The older items clearly are most desirable, in part because the quality of workmanship is much higher.

Animals	
Bird, 3″, astride tree stump, green, brown and ochre, c1800	275.00
Bull and Dog, 7¼″, brown markings, brown and green oval base, Ralph Wood, c1775	650.00
Dog, 4″, hound, seated, brown markings, oval base, c1775 . . .	355.00
Fox, 4″, seated with dead bird, oval base, Ralph Wood, c1780	**725.00**
Monkey, 6½″, seated, oval mound, splashed in manganese	360.00
Sheep, 6¾″ l, recumbent, brown ears, green oval mound, Ralph Wood, c1775	320.00
Banks	
Cottage, orange, white roof, 3 stories, green base	210.00
Cottage, white, brown roof, black outlining	160.00
Chimney Ornaments	
Blacksmith, 16¼″, standing beside anvil, round base	165.00
Couple in boat, 6¾″, lighthouse and cottage, "Grace Darling" .	170.00
Hope, youth, draped in spotted cloth, holding anchor, green mound, sq base, c1800	92.00
Plenty, 5″, nymph holding cornucopia of fruit, spotted dress, sq base, c1800	95.00
Inkwell, 3″, pear shape, flower stopper	55.00
Pastille Burners	
Castle, turrents, gray, green grass	185.00
Cottage, 2 chimneys, beige, white roof, green grass	140.00
Spill Holder, cow and calf, 6″, russet with green accents, pr	250.00
Trinket Boxes, covered	
Sheep and lamb, oval, white with green, ftd	80.00
Spaniel, reclining	70.00
Wall Pocket, 6½″, scroll shape, Putto mask, splashed in brown, green and yellow, Whieldon type, 18th C	550.00
Whistle, bird, 1¾″, white with brown and green	50.00

Trinket Box, 2″ h, applied pocket watch, and floral decor on lid, $70.00.

STAFFORDSHIRE, ROMANTIC

This is perhaps one of the most overlooked collecting areas. This popular dinnerware was produced in the Staffordshire district of England between 1830 and 1860. A large number of potters were involved and over 800 patterns have been identified.

The services often come in a variety of colors with light blue and pink perhaps the most popular. Usually the pattern is identified on the back of the piece. It was not uncommon for two potters to issue pieces with the same design. Therefore, check not only pattern name, but maker as well.

Petra William's *Staffordshire: Romantic Transfer Patterns* is an excellent source for identifying views.

It would be impossible to list all patterns. A representative selection follows. Some price ranges to keep in mind are Cups and Saucers (handleless) $35–60; Plates, cup $40–75; Plates, 9″ 10″ $5–50; Platters $25–75.

Sugar, covered, Singanese, J. Wedgwood, pink, $55.00.

Asiatic Plants, maker unknown
Bowl	75.00
Cup and Saucer	65.00
Plate, 10½″	85.00
Vegetable, cov, ornate handles, finial, light blue, 12 x 9½″	135.00

Caledonia, William Adams, c1800–1864
Bowl	35.00
Creamer	50.00
Cup and Saucer	40.00
Plates	
7½″, pink	55.00
8½″, dark blue	125.00
10½″, pink	70.00
Sugar Bowl	75.00

Canova, Thomas Mayer, c1834–1848, light blue and brown
Bowl, waste, 4″	40.00
Cup and Saucer	45.00
Plate, 10½″	30.00
Platter, 18 x 11½″	85.00
Soup Plate	35.00

Friburg, Davenport, c1844
Bowl	47.50
Cup and Saucer, handleless	60.00
Plate, 10½″	55.00
Platter	100.00
Teapot, tall, paneled, fruit finial	200.00
Tureen with matching underplate	150.00

Ivanhoe, Podmore Walker & Co., 1834–1859
Bowl	32.50
Creamer	52.50
Plate, 12 sided	37.50
Sugar	70.00

Medici, Mellor, Venables & Co, 1834–1851
Bowl	30.00

Cup and Saucer	37.50
Gravy Boat	80.00
Plate, 12 sided	37.50
Platter	75.00
Sugar Bowl, tab handles	80.00

Millenium, Ralph Stevenson & Son, 1832–1835
Bowl	30.00
Creamer	45.00
Cup and Saucer	32.50
Plate, 10½″, brown	40.00
Vegetable Dish	75.00

Palestine, John Ridgway, c1830–1855
Bowl	27.00
Creamer	55.00
Cup and Saucer, handleless	50.00
Plate	45.00
Platter, 16½″ x 10″	65.00
Sugar, cov	80.00
Vegetable, open, matching underplate	130.00

Priory, Edward Challinor and Co., c1853–1862
Bowl	40.00
Creamer	55.00
Cup and Saucer, handleless	35.00
Plate, 9½″, octagonal	50.00
Platter, 11½ x 17″	80.00
Sugar, cov, handles	125.00
Teapot, pagoda shape	135.00

Rhone Scenery, T. J. & J. Mayer, c1843–1855
Dish, 5½″, oblong	40.00
Plate, 8½″	48.00
Platter, 7 x 5″	45.00
Toothbrush holder	50.00

Siam, J. Clementson, c1839–1864
Bowl	37.50
Creamer	55.00
Cup and Saucer	35.00

Gravy Boat	60.00
Plate, 9"	45.00
Sauce Dish, 4"	27.00
Sugar, cov	75.00
Tureen with matching underplate, cov	125.00

STAINED AND/OR LEADED GLASS PANELS

American architects in the second half of the 19th C. and the early 20th C. used stained and leaded glass panels as a chief decorative element. Skilled glass craftsmen assembled the designs, the best known being Louis C. Tiffany.

The panels are held together with soft lead cames or copper wraps. When purchasing a panel, check the lead and have any repairs made to protect your investment.

Stained Glass, 38½ x 24", $250.00.

Leaded
  16 x 60", double motif, diamond divided into four sections, elongated drop ending in point, beveled, side panels frosted, orig frame **295.00**
  44¼ x 20", geometric patterns, central scene with young girl at edge of pond, orig frame **675.00**
  46¼ x 16¾", triple sq motif, diamond divided into four sections, short drop, beveled, orig frame **220.00**
Stained
  17½", St Gallus and the abbot St. Omar, early 17th C, no frame . **920.00**
  28¾ x 13⅝", circular center with yellow flower on blue ground, red reserve, flanked by sq reserve with faceted circular pieces, entire group enclosed by two reserves, one red, other blue, no frame **195.00**
  32 x 11⅞", red scroll floral motif, green and white opaque ground, light yellow etched reserve ... **125.00**

STANGL POTTERY BIRDS

Stangl birds were produced in ceramics from 1940 until the Stangl factory closed in 1972. The birds were produced at Stangl's Trenton plant and then shipped to their Flemington, New Jersey, plant for hand painting. During World War II, the demand for these birds and Stangl pottery was so great that 40 to 60 decorators could not keep up with the demand. Orders were contracted out to private homes. These orders were then returned for firing and finishing. Colors used to decorate these birds vary according to the artist.

As many as ten different trademarks were used. Almost every bird is numbered; many are artist signed. However, the signatures are used only for dating purposes and add very little to the value of the birds.

Several birds were reissued from a period of 1972 to 1977. These reissues are dated on the bottom and are valued at approximately one half of the older birds.

See *Warman's Americana & Collectibles'* American Dinnerware category for additional Stangl Pottery listings.

3250D - Duck, 3¼"	40.00
3250E - Duck, 1½"	40.00
3274 - Penguin, 6"	125.00
3275 - Turkey, 3½"	150.00
3402 - Oriole, revised version, 3¼"	25.00
3402D - Pair of orioles, revised version, 5½"	75.00
3405D - Pair of cockatoos, 9½" ...	75.00

3580, Cockatoo, 8⅞" h, $115.00.

3406 - Kingfisher, 3½"	35.00
3406D - Pair of kingfishers, 5"	75.00
3407 - Owl, 4"	125.00
3431 - Duck, 7¾"	225.00
3432 - Duck, 5½"	225.00
3433 - Duck, flying, 9"	175.00
3444 - Cardinal, revised, 6½"	40.00
3447 - Prothonatary Warbler, 5" . . .	35.00
3450 - Passenger Pigeon, 9 x 10" .	600.00
3453 - Key West Quail, 9"	200.00
3456 - Cerulean Warbler, 4¼"	40.00
3458 - Quail, 7½"	400.00
3490D - Pair of Redstarts, 9"	125.00
3491 - Hen Pheasant, 6¼ x 11" l .	125.00
3518 - Pair of White Crowned Pigeons, 7½ x 12½"	450.00
3582D - Pair of Parakeets, green or blue, 7"	125.00
3625 - Bird of Paradise, 13½"	600.00
3716 - Blue Jay with leaf, 10¼" . . .	325.00
3717D - Pair of Blue Jays, 12½" . .	550.00
3754D - Pair of White Winged Crossbills, 8¾"	200.00
3757 - Scissor Tailed Flycatcher, 11"	325.00
3811 - Chestnut Backed Chickadee, 5"	75.00
3815 - Western Bluebird, 7"	100.00
Dealers plaque with cockatoo	350.00

STATUES AND FIGURES

The technical difference between a statue and a figure is the material. A statue is made of stone or metal. A figure is composed of wood or clay (porcelain or pottery). Large or important figures are sometimes classified as statues. The terms figurine and statuette are used to distinguish size. Using the human figure as a guide, if the statue measures one-fourth life size, it is known as a statuette. If a figure is less than approximately one-fourth life size it is referred to as a figurine.
See BRONZES.

Belleek, dog, 3 x 4½" l, boxer on pillow, 1BM	1,250.00
Bronze	
Diana with 2 hounds, 10¾ x 26⅜", dark red-brown patina, Ary Bitter, French, early 20th C	520.00
Girl holding closed umbrella, 7⅞", moss green marble base	230.00
Girl in hooded cloak, 17¼", gold-brown patina, Elisa Beetz-Charpentier, Salon Des Beaux Arts Sons Famille, French, 19th C	800.00
Horse, 13¾", after Mahonri Young	500.00
Male, nude, 29¼", standing arms out stretched, "Spirit of the	

Venus, 10", white powdered marble, metal base, $65.00.

Age," dark brown patina, Mabel Conklin, 1871	1,400.00
Copeland Parian, Venus with Cupid, 19¾", after W.C. Marshall, RA . .	400.00
Ivorine, girl sitting on wall, 9", polychromed, marble base	315.00
Marble, Winged Victory of Samothrace, 19½", plaster wings	180.00
Meissen	
King and Queen, 8", pr	390.00
Rabbit, 7"	280.00
Rockingham, spaniels, 9", sgd Jordan, pr	200.00
Stone, nude, female, 7¼ x 12" w, half reclining on leaf carved base, white, 20th C	135.00
Wood	
Eagle, 25 x 53" l, carved, gilt . . .	460.00
St. Francis, 23½", carved, polychromed, Italian, 18th C . .	130.00

STEIFF

This company is known as Margarete Steiff, GmbH, and has been in business in Germany since 1880. It is known for very fine quality stuffed animals and dolls as well as other beautifully made collectible toys. It is still in business today, and its products are highly respected.

The company's first products were woolfelt elephants made by Margarete Steiff. In a few years the elephant line was expanded to include a donkey, horse, pig and camel.

By 1903, the company was also producing a mohair, jointed Teddy Bear and production of that toy was dramatically increased to 974,000 in 1907. Margarete's nephews took over the company at this point. The bear's head became the symbol for its label, and the famous "Button in the Ear" round metal trademark was added.

Newly designed animals also were added: Molly and Bully, the dogs, and Fluffy the cat. Pull toys and kites were also produced, as well as larger animals on which children could ride or play.

The wary buyer can now see the familiar metal button attached to animals that are not Steiff, so it is wise to become familiar with the genuine products before purchasing an antique stuffed animal. Plush in old Steiff animals was mohair; trimmings were usually felt or velvet.

Steiff has become collectible in recent years not only because it is well made but because of the appealing and realistic expressions and the general appeal of the animals themselves.

See TEDDY BEARS in this guide.

See also Stuffed Animals in *Warman's Americana & Collectibles* for additional listings.

Rhino, "Nosy," 14" l, mohair with felt soles and horn, $150.00.

Alligator, "Gaty," 14" l, open mouth, mohair	75.00
Dinosaur Type	
"Brosus," 14" l, open mouth, mohair	95.00
"Tysus," 8" h, jointed arms, open mouth, mohair	95.00
Fawn, "Bambi," Walt Disney Prod., 5½" h, velvet with mohair chest and tail	65.00
Fish, 11" l, large fish eyes, open felt mouth, mohair	75.00
Hedgehog, "Joggi," 5" l, mohair with velvet bottom and felt ears	45.00
Horse on Wheels, 18" h, plush, brown and white with black hooves, Steiff trademark on wheels	200.00
Monkey, "Coco," 5" h, mohair with felt face, ears, and feet	65.00
Mouse, sitting, "Pieps," 3½" h, white mohair with felt feet, ears, and tail	35.00
Possum, "Billy Possum," 1909, 11" h, jointed limbs, mohair with felt paws, ears, and tail	400.00
Zebra, 9" h, mohair	125.00

STEINS

A stein is a mug especially made to hold beer or ale, ranging in size from the small 3/10 liters and ¼ liters to the larger 1, 1½, 2, 3, 4 and 5 liters and in rare cases to 8 liters. (A liter is 1.05 liquid quarts.) The master steins or pouring steins hold 3 to 5 liters and are called krugs. Most steins are fitted with a metal hinged lid with thumblift. The earthenware character-type steins are attributed to German origin. See also METTLACH.

Apostles, 1 l, pottery, relief, marked MWG	100.00
Bacchus, 11½", silverplated, English	150.00
Bike Rider, painted scene	170.00
Bismarck, 1½ l., porcelain, radish finial, Musterschutz	400.00
Bowling Pin, ½ l, pottery, boy and pins in relief, wood tone finish	180.00
Clown, ½ l., lithophane	350.00
Dancers and Musicians, ¼ l, pottery, etched, marked, HR 500	200.00
Floral, ½ l, porcelain, lithopane	80.00
Funnel Man, ½ l, pottery, Reinhold Hanke	450.00
Indian, ¼ l., Musterschutz	450.00
Man drinking, ½ l, pottery, etched, marked HR 159	230.00
monkey, drunk, ½ l, porcelain	250.00
Monks, ½ l., Gesetzlicht	175.00
Munich Maid, ½ l, porcelain	432.00
Nun, 7", lithophane	250.00
Pixie, 1 l., Musterschutz	850.00
Rabbit's Head, wearing hat, ½ l, porcelain	350.00
Regimental, 2nd Chevalegeur, Dillinger, 1896–1899	360.00
Rooster, Musterschutz, ½ l, porcelain, wearing green coat and gold rimmed glasses	1,350.00
Satan, ½ l., Musterschutz	500.00

Stein, ½ l, "Keen Competition," polycolor, pewter rim, No 1526/Germany, $290.00.

Skull, ³⁄₁₀ l, bisque	325.00
Students playing musical instruments, waking sleeping people, 2 l, etched, HR No 434, sgd B	620.00
Village Dancers, ½ l., Musterschutz	225.00

STEREO VIEWERS AND CARDS

Warman's Americana & Collectibles, 1st Edition, contains 9 listings in STEREO VIEWERS and 276 listings in STEREOGRAPHS, see also page xii.

STEUBEN GLASS

The Steuben Glass Works began in 1904 with Frederick Carder, an Englishman, and Thomas G. Hawkes of Corning, New York. In 1918 the Corning Glass Co. purchased the Steuben Works. Carder remained with the company and designed many of the pieces bearing the Steuben mark. Probably the most widely recognized wares are "Aurene,"

"Verre de Soie" and "Rosaline," but many other types of wares were produced. For "Aurene" see "Aurene."

The firm continues operating, producing glass of exceptional quality.

Ashtray, 6" l, topaz, leaf shape, optic quilted design, celeste blue applique leaf form cigarette holder	115.00
Basket, 9½ x 4½", Verre De Soi, engraved, sgd Hawkes	225.00
Bottles, Perfume	
6", topaz, short blue stopper . . .	50.00
8", green jade, long alabaster stopper	150.00
8¼", Cintra, cut allover facets, hexagonal stopper with tapering tester, acid stamped sgr, c1925	3,300.00
10¼", Oriental Jade, ridged, opal green white	1,100.00
10½", Oriental Poppy, opal, rose, c1925	1,150.00
Bouillion Cup and Saucer, Rosaline, alabaster handles	125.00
Bowls	
3 x 5", Calcite	200.00
6¼", Intarsia, scattered blossoms, inscribed Fredik Carder, c1930	3,300.00
7", Alabaster glass, circular tapered foot, wide tapered bowl, black glass brim trim	286.00
8", acid cut ducks, marked Model No. 6681	660.00
8 x 4", topaz, blue rim	75.00
13", Pomona Green, ftd, sgd . . .	150.00
Candleabra, 18", crystal, #7242, sgd, pr	1,150.00
Candlesticks	
10", Amethyst ribbed, topaz, sgd, pr	225.00
11", Ivory, double leaf petal tops, black base, orig paper label, pr	1,500.00
13", Rosa, Pomona Green feet, pr	275.00
Centerpiece Bowls	
Bristol yellow, ftd, #3080, sgr in fleur-de-lis	500.00
Ivorine, pedestal, lotus leaf shape, ruffled, 14 x 6" h	450.00
Champagne, opal, pink Cintra, twisted stem	150.00
Cocktail Shaker, Verre De Soi, turquoise prunts, 10"	300.00
Compotes	
6½", Bristol yellow, celeste blue accents on knob stem	250.00
7", Green Jade swirl, alabaster stem, sgd	200.00
7", Gold ruby, teardrop stem . . .	190.00
7", Oriental Poppy, twisted green stem	650.00
7", Selenium ruby, twisted stem .	225.00
8", Green, bubbly glass, threading	95.00
8", Rosaline, alabaster stem, foot	275.00

10 x 6", Amethyst, ball stem **150.00**
10 x 6", Verre De Soi, ruffled edge, twisted stem **375.00**

Cup and Saucer, gold ruby over crystal **200.00**

Figure, Swan, cire-perdue, 8½", c1935 . . . . **2,860.00**

Flower Blocks
7¾", molded wisteria, circus elephant standing on sphere, fitted into flower frog, c1928 . . . . . . **825.00**
8", molded, kneeling nude girl in frosted glass, fitted in blue flower frog, c1932 . . . . **900.00**

Goblets
5", Pomona Green, swirl, topaz stem, foot, sgd **45.00**
6", Green Jade, alabaster stem, foot **85.00**
7", Crystal, cut and engraved sgr **200.00**
7", Rosaline, alabaster twist stem, foot **150.00**

Iced Tea, 6" h, Green Jade, optic swirl, alabaster handle, pr **135.00**

Jars, covered
4½", Crystal, black reeding, pr . . **85.00**
5½", ginger jar shape, acid cut back from jade green to alabaster, Art Deco flower pattern, rough textured ground, solid green jade cover, alabaster finial **950.00**

Lamp Base, 25" h, Tyrian, bulbous neck, waisted, domed circular foot, gray blue, decor with amber irid hearts, trails, -1916 . . . . **2,000.00**

Lemonade Sets
Green Jade, pitcher, 4 mugs, green applied handles **725.00**
Mat-Su-Noke, pitcher, 6 mugs, clear, applied green handles, trailings of applied design **625.00**

Marmalade, underplate, 6", Venetian, topaz, pear finial **200.00**

Nut Dishes
4", Crystal, black reeding, sgd . . . **25.00**
4", Verre De Soi, green rim **35.00**

Pitcher, 7", Cluthra, white, black handle, sgd **400.00**

Plates
6", Yellow Jade, sgd **125.00**
7", Pomona Green, sgd **25.00**

Puff Box, Rosaline, 3½" **175.00**

Salts
2", Green Jade swirl, urn shape . **50.00**
2½", Cluthra pink, sgd **80.00**

Sherbets
Oriental Poppy, 4½" **250.00**
Verre De Soi, floral engraved, underplate **225.00**

Tumblers
5", Clear, footed, reeded, Cintra rose **70.00**

5⅝", Green Jade **80.00**

Urns, covered
6", Venetian topaz, pear finial . . . **325.00**
11", ivory glass, 2 black handles **605.00**

Vase, 12", Ivory, tapered cylindrical shape, small rolled neck, $450.00.

Vases
4½", miniature grotesque, shaded clear to Pomona green **125.00**
4½" x 10" d, spherical, Cintra, black rim **1,150.00**
5", Cluthra, apple green, urn shape, sgd **425.00**
6¼", Calcite floriform, interior in pale amber irid, jack-in-pulpit rim, knopped flaring ft **470.00**
7¼", Intarsia, ftd, petal flowers, c1930 . . . . **8,600.00**
8", Burmese, inscribed F. Carder/Steuben, c1925 . . . . . . **3,190.00**
8", Dark blue Jade, flaring rim, sgd F. Carder **1,200.00**
8", Gold ruby, optic ribbed, scalloped top **185.00**
8", Grotesque, marine blue, sgd . **225.00**
8", Topaz, fan shape, pomona stem, foot, sgd **150.00**
8", bud, stick shape, light blue Jade, white flint foot **300.00**
9", Rosaline, parfait body **350.00**
10", Gold ruby over crystal, sgd . **450.00**
11", Grotesque Ruby, sgd **400.00**
11½", Craquelure, dusty rose quartz, interior intaglio carved,

florets, applied scrolling frosted glass leafy branches, sgd in cameo, Steuben in fleur-de-lis, c1920 .... **2,420.00**

11¾", Florentia, opaque flecked sides, decor at base with upright pale salmon foliage ribbed in deep salmon, c1930 ...... **3,520.00**

12", Moss agate, transparent amber crackle body, interior decor with swirls of moss green, salmon, brown, c1920 .... **3,520.00**

12", Rose over alabaster, etched **1,500.00**

Wines

3⅜", Cintra, clambroth, amethyst rim, shading	**195.00**
4⅞", Black, opaque, sgd	**175.00**
6", Topaz, blue stem, sgd	**75.00**
7½", Green, bubbly, threading ..	**55.00**

STEVENGRAPHS

Thomas Stevens of Coventry, Warwickshire, England, first manufactured woven silk designs in 1854. His first bookmark was produced in 1862, followed by the first Stevengraph in 1874. Stevengraphs are miniature silk pictures, matted, framed, and made by Stevens. Other companies copied his technique; their efforts should not be confused with Stevens' products.

The bookmarks are longer than they are wide, have mitred corners at one end, and are finished with a tassel. Stevens' name *always* is woven into the silk at a mitred corner.

True Stevengraphs are miniature silk pictures, matted, framed and produced by Stevens. Stevens' name *never* is woven into a Stevengraph. His name may appear on the mat near the title, but is usually found on the trade announcement on the back of the mat. Stevengraphs in original mat and with the trade announcement are the most desirable.

American collectors favor the Stevengraphs of the Declaration of Independence and Columbus expedition from the 1892–93 World Exposition in Chicago. Stevengraphs were never sold at the New York Crystal Palace Exposition in 1853, simply because they did not exist at that time.

BOOKMARKS

Accept This With My Best Wishes .	75.00
Apostle's Creed, The	60.00
Babes in the Wood	65.00
Dickens, Charles	80.00
Happy May Thy Birthday Be	80.00
Home Sweet Home	75.00

Peeping Tom, $275.00.

Merry Christmas And A Happy New Year, pointed on both ends	95.00
Morning Hymn	70.00
New Year's Auld Lang Syne	65.00
Prince of Wales Anthem, 1863	80.00
Shakespeare	100.00
Wishing You Peace and Plenty ...	75.00
Young girl and kitten	85.00

STEVENGRAPHS

Called To The Rescue, Heroism At Sea	250.00
Death, The	350.00
Declaration of Independence	395.00
Finish, The, orig mat	185.00
Good Old Days, The, orig mat	300.00
H. M. Stanley, famous explorer ...	275.00
Kaiser Wilhelm II	325.00
Landing of Columbus, The	375.00
Last Lap, The, orig frame, mat	300.00
Park in Coventry	155.00
President Cleveland	275.00
Water Jump, The	165.00

STEVENS AND WILLIAMS

In the late 19th century, Stevens and Williams, Stourbridge, England, become one of the pioneers in producing a less expensive and commercial cameo glass. Earlier cameo glass was handcarved. It was produced mainly for exhibition purposes or for the wealthy,

but as demand increased, Stevens and Williams revised the old method by employing the wheel and acid for the engraving. This hastened the production and subsequently made the glass available to more people.

While the earlier cameo glass was of the classical design, Stevens and Williams' designs were influenced by the Orient. One of their foremost artists was also a botanist, which accounts for the many beautiful nature designs.

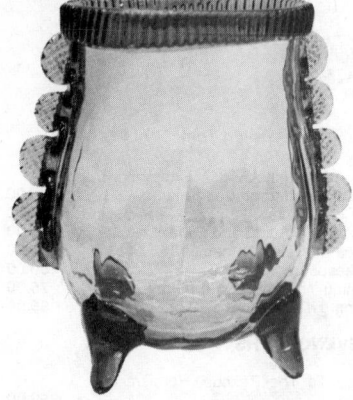

Vase, 7½ x 6½", blue body, amber rim, rigaree and feet, signed, $295.00.

Bowl, 7¾", red, swirls, petal feet, gold rigaree open edge around bowl, ¾" round prunt with gold flecks, pinched in above prunt . .	95.00
Cologne Bottles	
9 x 3½", green and crystal swirl striped glass, hallmarked silver collar, orig clear cut stopper with silver	165.00
9¾ x 3⅛", green cut to crystal intaglio, hallmarked silver collar, matching green intaglio cut stopper	195.00
Compote, pink, opalescent, sgnd . .	75.00
Fairy Lamp, 5⅜ x 6⅝", opaque pink and white stripes alternating with frosted stripes, emb ribs, shade mkd RD 50725 Trademark Fairy, clear insert candle cup mkd Clarke	550.00
Gas Light Shade, 3¼", swirled pink satin	200.00
Rose Bowl, olive green, applied blue top and feet, sgnd	200.00

Tumbler, water, 3¾ x 3¼", amber glass, applied amber pear and apple, green leaves and amber branch, sgnd	265.00
Vases	
5 x 4½", pink lining with green applied edge, outside cream opaque with large green and amber applied leaf, cranberry stripe forming stem	165.00
7 x 3⅞", egg shape, ftd, cream opaque, 3 large amber, green and pink leaves, amber loop feet, deep rose inside, berry pontil	195.00
11⅜ x 7" d, overlay, off white, applied amber leaves, acorns and branch forming small handle, rose inside top, ruffled amber edging	245.00

STIEGEL TYPE GLASS

Baron Henry Stiegel founded America's first flint glass factory at Manheim, Pennsylvania, in the 1760s. Although clear glass was the most common color made, amethyst, blue (cobalt), and fiery opalescent are found. The types of products include bottles, creamers, flasks, flips, perfumes, salts, tumblers, and whiskeys. Prosperity was short lived. Stiegel's extravagant living forced the factory to close.

It is very difficult to identify a Stiegel made item. As a result the term "Stiegel type" is used to identify glass made at that time period in the same shapes and colors.

Enamel decorated ware also is attributed to Stiegel. True Stiegel pieces are rare. An overwhelming majority is of European origin.

Beware of modern reproductions, especially in enamel decorated wares.

STIEGEL TYPE

Bowls, footed	
Amethyst, fifteen expanded diamond pattern	1,400.00
Amethyst, fifteen expanded diamond pattern, miniature	425.00
Cobalt blue, 16 panel, 3¼" h, 4" d	550.00
Christmas Light	
Amethyst, 4½", expanded diamond, undamaged but has small open bubble	100.00
Yellow Green, 4", expanded diamond, metal fixture	120.00
Creamers	
3⅛", emerald green, fifteen expanded diamonds	1,100.00

Mug, 6⅛" h, enameled, center shield with carpenter's and blacksmith's tools, floral motif, "Das ihre base Huff and Wasser/Schmidt Hand. Werck 1790", $300.00.

4⅛", cobalt blue, twenty expanded diamonds	300.00
Perfume Bottles, amethyst	
Daisy in hexagon pattern, flake on neck	3,900.00
Diamond over flute pattern	2,100.00
Diamond, twelve expanded pattern	1,600.00
Salts, 3"	
Blue	
Checkered diamond	750.00
Expanded diamond	250.00
Clear	
Checkered diamond	750.00
Expanded diamond	75.00
Sugar Bowl, deep sapphire blue cover, bowl in eleven expanded diamond pattern	2,300.00
Vase, paneled, deep sapphire blue, 13 panels	1,400.00

STIEGEL TYPE, ENAMELED

Bottle, Bride's	
Flowers, typical Stiegel green, 6¾", orig pewter color	300.00
Man and woman in multicolors . .	500.00
Flip, 6½", basket of flowers and leaves	375.00
Whiskey, man on prancing horse . .	250.00

STIEGEL TYPE, ETCHED

Flips	
Foral and leaves, cover	550.00
Lovebirds in a sunburst, 7¼" h, 6⅜" d, frosted	400.00
Tulip and floral motif	225.00
Tulip, potted, 4½", wooden muddler	125.00
Mug, strap handled, floral motif, cover	400.00

STOCK AND BOND CERTIFICATES

Stock and bonds are collected for a variety of reasons — the graphic illustrations, the history of romantic times in America including gold and silver mining, railroad history, and early automobile pioneers.

Some of the factors that affect price are (a) dates [with pre-1900 more popular and pre-1850 most desirable], (b) autographs of important persons [Vanderbilt, Rockefeller, J. P. Morgan, Wells and Fargo, etc.], (c) number issued [most bonds have number issued printed in text], and (d) the attractiveness of the vignette.

BONDS

Central Hudson Steamboat Co., NY, 1899, vignette of lady looking out at ships in harbor, $1,000 coupon bond, green	80.00
Choctaw, Oklahoma and Gulf Railroad, 1902, $1,000, five percent gold bond, vignette of Indians looking at railroad	35.00
City and County of San Francisco Fire Protection Bond, CA, 1908, $1,000, 5%	25.00

Stock: Chenango Canal, 9⅜ x 7⅛, Rowdon, Wright, Hatch & Co. NY, engravers, 1837, $65.00.

Pennsylvania Canal Co., 1870, $1,000 coupon bond, canal vignette 45.00

Pennsylvania Power Company, PA, 1945, $1,000, first mortgage bond, 2⅞% 10.00

Philip Morris, Inc., 1959, $1,000 coupon bond 10.00

Wilkes-Barre Coal Co., NJ, 1910, mining vignette, $1,000 coupon bond, Security Bank Note Co., green, black and white 30.00

STOCKS

Automobile Related
Durant Motors, Incorporated, DE, 1928 . . . . 30.00
Ideal Tire & Rubber Company, Cleveland, OH, 1920 . . . . 10.00

Banking
Bank of America, NY, 1850s, eagle and shield vignette, train at left, ship at right, Toppan, Carpenter, Casileur Co. 40.00
Dimes Saving Institution, Bethlehem, PA, 1869 . . . . 20.00
State Savings and Loan Association, Beatrice, NE, 1911 . . . . . 10.00

Industrial
American Submarine Company, NY, 1871, central allegorical vignette, small vignette of sailing ship 125.00
Davis Sewing Machine Company, Watertown, NY, 1871, patriotic figural vignette 60.00
Kittanning Iron & Steel Manufacturing Co., PA, 1920, steel plant vignette, American Bank Note Co., green 15.00

Mining
Iron Silver Mining Co., NY, 1882, prospector vignette, American Bank Note Company, orange/golden color 65.00
New Mexico Mining Co., 1860, river town vignette 85.00

Oil Companies
Chas. F. Noble Oil & Gas Co., DE, 1923 . . . . 3.00
Texas and Gulf Coast Oil Fields Company, NY, 1919 . . . . 12.00

Railroad
Baltimore and Ohio, 1893, vignette of early train 18.00
Cedar Falls and Minnesota Railroad Co., 1895, railroad vignette, American Bank Note Co., sgd by Stuyvesant Fish, famous railroad and banking executive 100.00
Pullman Incorporated, DE, 1955, Pullman pictured 15.00

Utilities
American Natural Gas Corp., 1931, vignette of factory flanked by kneeling woman 5.50
Associated Gas & Electric Company, 1931, vignette of warrior goddess above kneeling workman 7.00

STONEWARE

Made from dense kaolin clay and commonly salt-glazed, stonewares were hand-thrown and high fired to produce a simple, bold vitreous pottery. Stoneware crocks, jugs and jars were produced for storage and utility purposes. This use dictated shape and design — solid, thick-walled forms with heavy rims, necks and handles with little or no embellishment. When decorated, the designs were simple . . . brushed cobalt oxide, incised or slip trails; also stamping or tooling.

Stoneware has been made for centuries. Early American settlers imported stoneware items at first. As English and European potteries refined their earthenwares, colonists began to produce their own wares. Two major North American traditions emerged based mainly on the location or type of clay. North Jersey and parts of New York were the first area; the second was eastern Pennsylvania spreading westward and into Maryland, Virginia and West Virginia. These two distinct locations, style of decoration and shape are discernible factors in classifying and dating early stoneware.

By the late 18th century, stoneware was manufactured in all sections of the country. During the 19th century, this vigorous industry flourished until glass 'fruit jars' appeared and the wide spread use of refrigeration. By 1910, commercial production of salt-glazed stoneware came to an end.

Bank, keg shape, 3¼", albany slip glaze 20.00

Batter Jugs
Cowden & Wilcox, Harrisburg, Pa, 1½ gal, blue flowers, orig tin lid and spout cap 645.00
Unknown maker, 4 qt, bird with 6 stroke tail, "4" under pouring spout, 2 handles 625.00

Bottles
B. B. Pottery, Wa——, imp label, 8¼", pig shape, hand molded, gray-tan glaze 650.00
R. Burge, blue devil eye and forked tongue decor 630.00

Butter Crocks, covered
John Bell, Waynesboro, cobalt blue tulip 200.00
Unknown maker, brush strokes design, 7½" 215.00

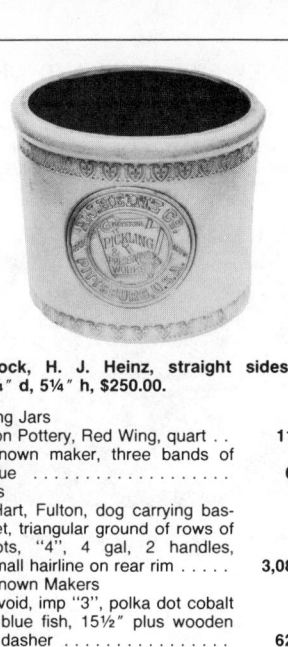

Crock, H. J. Heinz, straight sides, 6¼″ d, 5½″ h, $250.00.

Canning Jars
Union Pottery, Red Wing, quart . . 110.00
Unknown maker, three bands of blue 65.00
Churns
S. Hart, Fulton, dog carrying basket, triangular ground of rows of dots, "4", 4 gal, 2 handles, small hairline on rear rim 3,080.00
Unknown Makers
  Ovoid, imp "3", polka dot cobalt blue fish, 15½″ plus wooden dasher 625.00
  Ovoid, imp "3", slip decor of bird on branch, turned wooden lid, 15½″ plus wooden dasher 375.00
Coolers
N. Clark & Co., Lyons, incised leaf highlighted in blue, 14″ 500.00
Unknown maker, ovoid, large open ear handles, wooden butter print impression on each side, Ohio, 14¾″ 900.00
Crocks
L. C. & C. F. Brown, Colchester, CT, 3 gal, name highlighted in blue, stenciled eagle, shield, modern wooden lid 125.00
J. Burger, Jr., Rochester, NY, 6 gal, five leaf fan design in cobalt blue, front leaf resembles tobacco leaf 175.00
T. Harrington, Lyons, 2 gal, brushed blue floral decor, 11¼″ 250.00
Haxstan, Ottman & Co, Fort Edward, NY, 6 gal, basket of flowers in cobalt blue 525.00
T. F. Reppert, Greensboro, PA, 4 gal, blue stenciled design 120.00
W. Roberts, Binghamton, NY, 5 gal, blue stylized bird on floral branch 415.00
Wank & Co, Johnstown, PA, 1 gal,

vertical ribbed, minor rim fleck . 160.00
N. A. White & Son, Utica NY, 11″, large blue bird on branch 240.00
Unknown Makers
  2 gal, earred, gray, cobalt freehand dotted snake coggle line 120.00
  6 gal, cobalt "6", "1871", quillwork flourish 95.00
  2 gal, imp "2", stenciled cobalt decor of handshake, 11½″ d x 7″ h 190.00
Figurine, cat, 14¼″ h, gray body, running olive-amber glaze, albany slip interior, primitive detail 1,050.00
Flower Pot, 8″ h, reddish clay, albany slip, fanciful applied and tooled decor, 2 applied water reservoirs on sides, imp R. S. Baird, Mogadore, OH, c1855 . . . . 450.00
Inkwell, unknown maker, brown blaze, tooled, serrated edge 60.00
Jars, Preserving
O. L. & A. K. Ballard, Burlington, VT, imp label, cobalt slip of prim stylized flower with spiral center, 10¾″ 215.00
Excelsior Works, Issac Hewitt, Jr., Rices Landing, PA, blue stripes and foliage scrolls, 9½″ 350.00
Hamilton & Jones, Greensboro, PA, in blue, roses, wavy lines and stripes, 3 gal 205.00
Palatine Pottery Co., Palatine, WV, stenciled cobalt label with pear, 8½″ 155.00
J. M. Pruden, Eliz-Town, NJ, 2 gal, crab like design, 13″ h, base chips 125.00
T. F. Reppert, Greensboro, PA, brushed wavy lines, "2", stenciled cobalt label, 11½″ 130.00
Unknown Makers
  Cobalt apple design, 9″ 250.00
  Cobalt tulip, rim stripe, brushed, 8″ 145.00
  Ear handles, slightly ovoid form, flared rim, front bearing cobalt blue basket with three leaf branches, imp "Divno 268/ South Woodstock Vt/2", 10½″, c1855 . . . . 675.00
Jugs
G. Baird, 1 gal, ovoid, primitive exuberant brushed cobalt foliage, 12″ 130.00
Clark & Fox, blue stylized bird, blue slip date 1835, 12″ 300.00
A. DeHaven, Middlebury, OH 2, imp label, ovoid, large brushed blue cobalt tulip 450.00
Donnelly Bros, Troy, NY, imp label, 9¼″ 75.00

C. Hart & Co, Ogdensburgh, 2 gal, ovoid, blue decor, 13½" **200.00**

J. & E. Norton, Bennington, VT, strap handle, cobalt blue dog and fence, 17"c1860 .... **1,750.00**

C. J. Merrill, 2 gal, ovoid, cobalt blue splash, 13" **200.00**

J. Mantell, Penn Yan, NY, 2 gal, brushed blue flower, 13¼" ... **155.00**

S. Purdy, ovoid, splashed cobalt, imp label, 13" **70.00**

A. E. Spencer, ovoid, stylized blue tulip, matte finish, 12" **250.00**

A. B. Wheeler & Co., Boston, MA, 5 gal, cobalt blue single rose and ribbon design, imp mark **350.00**

Unknown maker, Boston, MA, ovoid form, strap handle, upper and lower sections covered with ochre, centering impressed mark "Boston", 11½" h, c1795 .... **500.00**

Milk Bowls

Sipe & Sons, Williamsport, PA, 1½ gal, blue flower **285.00**

Unknown maker, blue three petal flowers, pouring spout, 12½" **225.00**

Miniatures

Double Jug Whimsey, 2⅝" h, Absalom Stedman, New Haven, CT, two jugs joined at mid-height centering a strap handle, each jug imp "New Haven", brushed manganese oxide decor, c1830 .... **2,400.00**

Jug, 2⅝" h, Taunton, MA, ovoid form, strap handle, front inscribed "Mrs. S. G. Hazard, Taunton," c1835 .... **500.00**

Jug, 4" h, ovoid form, strap handle, front decor with cobalt blue floral motif, reverse with initial "L," c1830 .... **500.00**

Pitchers

Amanda E. Lawrence, Dalton, OH, March 9, 1896, imp with a's and d backwards, olive grown blaze, sgraffito bird, 9½" **235.00**

H. Purdy, imp label, brushed cobalt blue double tulip, stripes on handle, 16" **575.00**

West Troy, NY, Pottery, bird on branch **1,320.00**

Unknown Makers

Cobalt bird on twig, 2 gal **1,000.00**

Yellow and green, 2 cows on each side, 8", c1900 ...... **85.00**

Spittoons, unknown makers

Blue design of simple three petal flowers **165.00**

Blue slip design of leaves **195.00**

STONEWARE, BLUE AND WHITE

Stoneware is a type of functional pottery used for household purposes. Many potteries made some type of stoneware with blue decoration on a white-gray ground. This type of stoneware is now very popular.

Spittoon, drapery relief, 7½" d, 5¼" h, $60.00.

Batter Jug, 8" h, spongeware, pinched top **185.00**

Bowls

Chain, 5½" **40.00**

Diamond Point **65.00**

Butter Crocks, covered

Butterfly **95.00**

Panel **75.00**

Coffee Pot, Diamond Point **115.00**

Creamers

Cow **25.00**

Moose **22.00**

Crock, 9½", advertising Cohen Bros, Gloversville **85.00**

Mugs

Barrel, blue scroll **55.00**

Cattails **110.00**

Rose Decal **55.00**

Squatty, blue band **50.00**

Tall, blue band **45.00**

Mustard Jar, strawberry **65.00**

Pitchers

7", Cattail **125.00**

8", Dainty Fruit **95.00**

8", Woman in feathered hat **145.00**

8¼", Dutch scene, stenciled **145.00**

10", Fishscale and Wild Rose ... **90.00**

12", hot water, blue band around middle, scalloped top **200.00**

Refrigerator Jar, lid, bail **135.00**

Salt Crocks, hanging

Apricot **135.00**

Butterfly, no lid **80.00**

Lovebird, no lid **135.00**

Shaving Mug, Bowtie and Roses ..	75.00
Soap Dish, flower cluster center ...	85.00
Spittoon, Daisy & Vines	60.00
Tea Cannister, cov, blue and white snowflakes	135.00
Teapot, swirl, 9″ h, 6½″ d, double wire bail, pulled ears, wood hand grip	325.00
Toothbrush holder, Fishscale & Wild Rose	45.00

STRAWBERRY CHINA

This ware takes its name from the distinctive decorative motif, the Strawberry. There are three primary types: strawberries and strawberry leaves (often called Strawberry Lustre), green feather-like leaves with pink flowers (often called Cut Strawberry, Primrose or Old Strawberry) and a third type with the decoration in relief. The first two types are characterized by rust red moldings. All examples of this ware are hand painted on Creamware.

Strawberry was produced by many manufacturers, but Davenport created some of the finest forms of excellent quality. Marked pieces are uncommon.

Strawberry ranges from complete tea services to serving pieces, including platters. While the hollow wares are highly prized, flat pieces are more rare.

Creamer, 6¼″ l, "Cut Strawberry", $150.00.

Bowl, waste, 4 x 6½″	150.00
Cup and Saucer, small, handleless .	80.00
Plates	
6½″	185.00
8¼″, "Cut Strawberry"	180.00
10″, c1840	135.00

10½″, chop	100.00
Platter, 10½ x 8″	130.00
Relish Dish, shell shape, 8¾″	100.00
Soup Plate, 8¼″	180.00
Sugar, cov, S shape	190.00
Teapot, 4¼ x 9½″	360.00
Vegetable Dish, cov, octagonal ...	370.00

STRETCH GLASS

Stretch glass was produced by many glass manufacturers in the United States from the early 1900s through the 1920s. The most prominent makers were Cambridge, Fenton (who probably manufactured more Stretch glass than any others), Imperial, Northwood and even Steuben. Stretch glass can be identified by its iridescent, onionskin-like effect. Look for mold marks. Imports are blown and show a pontil mark and are not American Stretch Glass.

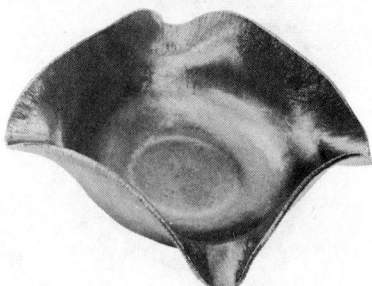

Dish, 3 x 6½″, Peacock, Imperial, $125.00.

Basket, 10¼″, white	125.00
Basket, 10½″, white	95.00
Bobeches, scalloped, vaseline, pair	35.00
Bowls	
10 x 4½″ deep, yellow irid, Imperial	85.00
13″, blue, wide rim, collared base	100.00
Candlesticks, 10½″, vaseline	42.00
Candy Dish, topaz, No. 636, Fenton	60.00
Compote, 4½ x 7⅝″ d, green irid, clear stem, amber base	55.00
Nappy, 7″, vaseline, Fenton	30.00
Plates	
6″, red, paneled, Imperial	50.00
9¾″, vaseline	45.00
Rose Bowl, 3½ x 5″, melon ribbed, pink	50.00
Salad Set, 14″, bowl, six 8½″ plates, mayonnaise bowl with underplate, vaseline, c1920, 9 pcs	100.00

Sherbet, 4", red, melon ribbed	50.00
Vases	
5½", pink, sgd Imperial	65.00
11¾", bud vase, pink	35.00
Trumpet shape, shaded golden	
yellow to amethyst	125.00

STRING HOLDERS

Grocery and dry goods stores found string holders to be useful items. Usually made of iron, there were two common types: the hanging holder and the counter-top type.

Plaster, cream cat, red ball, $20.00.

Cast Iron	
Ball shape, 4¼", hanging, black,	
floral decor	42.00
Basket shape, 5", wall mounted,	
"Patd Oct 21, 1893	15.00
Cone shape, 8½", heavy, reticu-	
lated	32.00
Dome shape, 5", intersecting	
arches	35.00
Kettle, ftd, "Jaxon Soap"	130.00
Chalkware	
Baby	35.00
Mexican man	25.00
Scotty dog	45.00
Glass	
Beehive, 4¾", tin enclosure	38.00
Daisy and Button, clear	40.00
Flint glass, 4½"	60.00

SUGAR CASTORS

Muffineers, sugar shakers or sugar castors, all served the same purpose: to 'sugar' muffins, scone or toast. They were much in vogue in the late Victorian era. Larger than salt or pepper shakers, ranging in sizes from four to six inches high, they were made in a variety of materials.

See also, specific glass categories.

Amber Glass, baby thumbprint,	
enamel decor	70.00
Amberina, baby thumbprint	225.00
Amethyst, IVT	52.00
Bohemian, amber, cut	65.00
Cranberry	
DQ	115.00
Opalescent Swirl	175.00
Cut Glass, Prism pattern, notched	
handle, repousse sterling lid	265.00
French Cameo, 3 colors, poppy &	
leaf decor, sgd Aerozon DRGM .	375.00
Libbey Glass, maize, green and am-	
ber leaf decor	65.00
Milk Glass	
Melon shape, ribbed, pink	75.00
Netted Oak, pastel decor	70.00
White, quilted	45.00
Mt. Washington, egg shape, lemon	
yellow, violet decor	175.00

Diamond Point & Quartered Block [Duncan & Miller # 24] blown, clear, SP top, pontil mark, $35.00.

Opalescent

Spanish Lace, pink	185.00
White, ribbed DQ	95.00
R. S. Prussia, green floral	145.00
Rubina, crystal, cut panel	40.00

Satin Glass

Apricot, MOP, Herringbone	135.00
Robin's egg blue, molded loop pat	55.00
Silver, 9¼", ornate, English	550.00

Smith Brothers, ribbed, dainty blue
flowers, green leaves 100.00

Spatter Glass, cased, swirl, multicolored, Royal Oak 130.00

Vaseline

Rope & Ribs	80.00
Spanish Lace	75.00

Webb Peachblow, gold and enamel
beetle decor, dimple side 425.00

Wedgwood, blue 35.00

SUNBONNET BABIES

Warman's Americana & Collectibles, 1st Edition, contains 68 listings in this category; see
also page xii.

SUNDERLAND LUSTRE

**Sunderland ware is a coarse type of cream
colored earthenware with a marbled or spotted pink lustre decoration which shades from
pink to purple. A solution of gold compound
applied to a white body developed the many
shades of pink lustre; shades were determined by the thickness of metallic film.**

**Decorated with transfer prints of commem-
orative and sentimental scenes and inscriptions, these wares were produced by Adams,
Bailey and Batkin; Copeland and Garrett;
Wedgwood; Enoch Wood and many others.**

Also see PINK LUSTRE CHINA.

Bowls

6", House pattern	100.00
10", view from the Cast Iron Bridge	275.00

Bust, William Shakespear, pink lustre socle, from model by Enoch
Wood, 1815–20 .... 625.00

Cup and Saucers

Cloud pattern, pink lustre	48.00
Mustache, black transfer of ship on front, sailor's poem on back	110.00
Pink splash	50.00

Figures

Autumn, 8⅝", lady holding sheaf
of wheat 225.00

Winter, 8⅞", youth clutching his
mantle, standing over flaming
brazier 230.00

**Pitcher, 2¾", Old Castle, Made in Eng-
land, $145.00.**

Goblet, allover lustre decor 135.00

Gravy Tureen, lid, undertray and ladle, 7½", black transfer, Masonic
Arms, symbols and 7 lines of
verse 400.00

Jugs

8½", pink lustre, transfer printed,
enameled, view of the Cast Iron
Bridge, other side, British ship
Northumberland 74, sgd Dixon
& Co, Sunderland Pottery,
c1815 .... 625.00

8¾", pink lustre, satirical, political
caricature, view of the Cast Iron
Bridge, brown foliate sprays,
c1825 .... 450.00

9½", farm scene and verse 175.00

Mugs

4⅞", pink lustre, Sailer's Farewell
on one side, poem, *The Sailors
Tear*, interior has floral clusters
and applied frog, c1825 ..... 175.00

5", brown transfer, Masonic symbols, app figure of frog inside . 250.00

Pitchers

5", Ye Olde Jug Inn	185.00
8", Masonic symbols and verse .	190.00

Plaques

6⅛", pink lustre, men's heads,
one with brown beard, one
clean shaven, brown curly hair,
splashed lustre halos, possible
Dixon, Austin & Co, c1825, pr . 400.00

9", sailing ship pictured, imp Dixon
& Co, c1855 .... 125.00

9½" x 6⅝", rectangular, gothic
landscape, red, green brown,
and yellow enamel, foliate molded pink lustre frame, 1820–40 120.00

Plates

8", lady with trees, harp and child 95.00

8⅝", pink lustre, transfer printed in black, Cast Iron Bridge, floral clusters on rim, sgd Moore & Co, Southwick, c1825–35 .... **150.00**

9", Babes in the Woods **125.00**

Platter, 7½ x 8½", picture of Adam Clark, Wesleyan minister **195.00**

Teapot, large, Cloud pattern, pink lustre **275.00**

Tobacco Jar, cov, black transfer, Parliment building **200.00**

Wash Bowl and Pitcher, Ship Caroline **425.00**

Watch Stand, 11⅜", tall clock shape, pink splash lustre, allegorical figures of Autumn and Summer, imp Dixon Auston & Co, 1820–26 .... **725.00**

SWANSEA

This superb pottery and porcelain was made at Swansea (Glamorganshire, Wales) as early as the 1760's and production continued until 1870; but the most highly collectible examples are those made before 1830.

Marks on Swansea vary; the earliest was SWANSEA impressed under glaze to DILLWYN under glaze after 1805. CAMBRIAN POTTERY was stamped in red under glaze from 1803–1805. Many fine examples, including the Botanical series in Pearlware, are not marked but may have the botanical name stamped under glaze.

Often, fine examples of Swansea may show imperfections such as firing cracks; these pieces must be considered mint because this is the way they left the factory.

Documented examples have not appeared in enough numbers to make Swansea popular, although it is eagerly sought by advanced collectors.

Dish, 11½", botanical series, c1805, $325.00.

Cake Tray, 12½", handled, painted florals, probably by Henry Morris, gilt rim and handles, 1813–22 ... **375.00**

Creamer, cov, 6½", cow shape, pink splash lustre, rectangular base, c1825 .... **420.00**

Cup and Saucer, 3⅝" cup, 6" saucer, floral decor, c1815 .... **110.00**

Dish, 9¾", oval, botanical series, cyclamen, painted by Thomas Pardoe, imp Swansea **375.00**

Plates

8", pink lustre, swimming swan, green wicker molded rim, pierced pink lustre edge, imp Dillwyn & Co Swansea, 1811–17 **90.00**

8½", floral center, molded foliate scroll rim **245.00**

Serving Dish, 10¼", oval, center floral bouquet, full blown pink roses on rim and gilt dentil, imp Swansea **450.00**

SWORDS

The first swords in America came from Europe. The chief cities for sword manufacturing were Solingen in Germany, Klingenthal in France, and Hounslow and Shotley Bridge in England. Among the American importers of these foreign blades was "Horstmann" whose mark is found on many military weapons.

New England and Philadelphia were the early centers for American sword manufacturing. By the Franco-Prussian War, the Ames Manufacturing Company was exporting American swords to Europe.

Sword collectors concentrate on a variety of styles — commission vs. non-commission officers' swords, presentation swords, naval weapons, and swords from a specific military branch such as cavalry or infantry. The type of sword helped identify a person's military rank and, depending on how he had it customized, his personality as well.

Following the invention of repeating firearms in the mid-19th Century, the sword lost its functional importance as a combat weapon and became a military dress accessory. Condition is a key criteria determining value.

AMERICAN

Artillery, Foot, 1832, 25", Roman type short sword, brass eagle pommel, "Ames Mfg. Co., Chichopee, Mass.," leather scabbard **350.00**

Artillery Officers', 1810, 36½", brass horse head pommel, checkered

American, Naval Officer's, 29″ blade with eagle engraved, marked "Tiffany, New York City", $300.00.

iron grip, gilded blade with eagle and "E. Pluribus Unum," leather scabbard 1,750.00

Artillery Officers', Mounted, 1840, 37½″, brass eagle head pommel, wood grip with leather and brass wire, "Hortsmann" (Philadelphia), leather scabbard 600.00

Cavalry, Saber, Starr contract, 1818, cast iron hilt, wood grip with leather, "N. Starr and U.S./P/LS," iron japanned scabbard 300.00

Cavalry, Saber, light, 1860, 30¾″, brass half basket, wood grip with leather and brass wire, iron scabbard 175.00

Cavalry, Model 1913, 42″, straight, tapering, double edge 35″ blade, steel roughed diamond pattern grip, molded steel basket guard, canvas covered scabbard with steel mounts 150.00

Infantry Officers', 1820–50, 35″ brass hilt and Indian head pommel, mother of pearl or ivory grip with brass wire, blade etched with eagle and military motif, brass scabbard 450.00

Marine Officers', 1826, 34½″, Maneluke (Turkish style) hilt, blade gilded with anchor, ship, and Indian head, high engraved brass scabbard 1,500.00

Militia Staff Officers', 1840, 32¾″, brass knight's head pommel, checkered ivory grip, blade gilded with military motif, engraved brass scabbard 600.00

Naval Cutlass, 1841, 26¼″, brass hilt and grip, half basket, guard, "N. P. Ames/Springfield" and "U.S.N./1843/RC," leather scabbard 450.00

Non-Commissioned Officers', Star Contract, 1818, 31″, wood grip with leather and brass wire, "N. Starr," and U.S./P/LS," iron japanned scabbard 400.00

EUROPEAN

Continental

Artillery short sword, 25″, 19¼″ double edged blade stamped at ricasso "THIEBAT 1837" with sunken oval proof "*P*," solid brass cast hilt, black leather scabbard with brass mounts . . 185.00

Cavalry Saber, 38″, 32½″ slightly curved blade, iron hilt with two branches stamped "G.A./III," wooden grips covered with black leather, iron scabbard . . . 175.00

English

Naval Dirk, 19th C, 21½″, 16″ single edge blade, etched foliage and crown on blade, "GILLOT/& HANSELL/36 Strand/LONDON," hilt with brass "S" shaped guard with acorn finial and lion's head pommel with two strands of brass chain, sharkskin and wire grip, black leather scabbard . . . 250.00

Naval Officers, 35¼″, 30″ single edged blade with rounded back, etched "PROSSER/Maker To The/Queen & Royal Family. London" and with naval themes, brass hilt with large gilt brass guard with crown and naval anchor, lion's head pommel, sharkskin over wood grip 150.00

Officer's Saber, 30⅜″, curved single edged 25¼″ blade, brass hilt cast in one piece with lion's head pommel, black leather scabbard with brass mounts . . 125.00

Officer's Saber, 42½″, 35½″ straight blade etched with foliage and British motifs, marked "DETTINGEN BEAUMONT. PENINSULA. WARBURG. WILLEMS...," hilt with nickel plated iron guard deeply engraved with crown over "GR," sharkskin grip, leather scabbard 450.00

French Officer's Saber, 40½″, 35¼″ slightly curved blade, obverse engraved and gilt decoration against blued ground and marked "Gendarmerie du Roi," reverse with military motifs and Sun King emblem, blade sgd "Coulaux Freres Klingenthal," gilted brass hilt with three branches with relief floral work, pommel embossed fleur-de-lis, black leather and wire grip, steel scabbard with gilted brass carrying ring mounts 800.00

Unidentified, Naval cutlass, iron, c1800, 29″, 24″ curved blade, stamped near hilt with letter "S," blackened wood grip and large sheet iron guard for hilt, front of guard mounted with copper triangle with old engraved issue mark "2.II" 475.00

JAPANESE

Samuri Sword, 32", 23" blade sgd "Fujiwara Tepuyaki," c1700, cord wrapped hilt, iron tsuba inlaid with shakado floral decoration, black leather scabbard with German silver tip and inlay, kodzuka missing 525.00

Samuri Sword, WWII, 37", 27" machine manufactured blade, typical WWII military hilt, black lacquered wood scabbard 175.00

TEA CADDIES

Tea was a precious commodity in the past. Special boxes or caddies were used as containers to accommodate different teas, including a special cup for blending.

Around the turn of the 18th century, silver caddies appeared in England. There were also other materials used, from Sheffield plate to tin, wooden, china, and pottery. They became quite ornate and are collectible today, and are expensive when found.

Burl Walnut, 4⅜ x 7½ x 4¾", brass hinges, ivory key inlay, $565.00.

Fruitwood, 5¼", apple shape, George III, c1800 .... 930.00

Mahogony, rectangular, hinged, inlaid, George III, c1800 .... 300.00

Mother of Pearl, 8", chamfered corners, bun feet, 19th C 315.00

Pewter, 5¼", hexagonal, engraved and inlaid with shaped brass panels, front inscribed Immortal Nelson, George III 600.00

Rosewood, 7", 2 divisions, Regency, c1810 .... 165.00

Tin, octagonal, hinged lid with Queen Victoria's portrait, 4 army commander's portraits on sides, c1897 .... 145.00

Tole, 5¼", oval, brown, flowers, leaves, fruit, J. A. S. on back ... 950.00

Tortoise shell, veneered, 4½", octagonal, Regency, c1820 ...... 315.00

TEA LEAF LUSTRE

A type of gold lustre decoration on ironstone china, which is more or less a stylized form of the oriental tea leaf. It was also known as "Lustre Band with Sprig." The ware was produced by a number of English and American potteries. A large amount was made by J. and G. Meakin, and it was produced by Wedgwood, Shaw, Clementson, Mayer and Grindley, and others.

Recently some reproductions have appeared. They can be spotted by their poor coloration, uneven copper lustre decoration and by weight. The original ironstone pieces made are much heavier than the newer ceramic pieces.

See *Warman's Americana & Collectibles* for an expanded listing of Tea Leaf Lustre.

Bacon Rasher 20.00
Bone Dish, 3 x 6", Meakin 52.00
Bowls
  6", Meakin 55.00
  7", sq, scalloped, Johnson Bros . 60.00
Bread Plate, round, Mayer 35.00
Butter Dish, cov, with insert, bamboo shape, Meakin 125.00
Butter Pat, sq, Shaw 10.00
Chamber Pot, cov, 12-sided, Shaw . 175.00
Coffee Pot, 9", Meakin 140.00
Creamer, 5½", W. Burgess & Burslem 95.00
Cups and Saucers, handleless
  Meakin 62.00
  Shaw 65.00
  Wedgwood 78.00
Gravy Boat, Shaw 55.00
Pitcher, 8", milk, Mayer 138.00
Plates
  7¼", Shaw 11.00
  8½", Wedgwood 15.00
  9", Grindley 20.00
  10", Shaw 15.00

Vegetable, cov. 6¼ x 10 x 4½", marked Royal Ironstone China, Alfred Meakin, England, $125.00.

Platters

12½ x 8½", oval Mellor, Taylor .	45.00
14", oval, Meakin	48.00
16½", Wedgwood	60.00
Relish Dish, oval, Clementson Bros	22.00
Saucer, Johnson	12.00
Soap Dish, cov, drain insert, oval, Shaw	95.00
Sugar, cov, 6¾", Mellor, Taylor . . .	65.00
Teapot, cov, 10½", Shaw	170.00
Tureen, cov, underplate and ladle, Mellor, Taylor	500.00
Vegetables, covered	
7 x 11", rectangular, Wilkinson . .	145.00
7½", sq, Furnival	130.00
Wash Bowl and Pitcher, hot water pitcher, waste jar, cov, chamber, cov, toothbrush holder, soap dish with drain insert, shaving mug, Meakin, 8 pcs	800.00

TEDDY BEARS

Originally thought of as "Teddy's Bears," the name comes from President Theodore Roosevelt. These stuffed toys are believed to have originated in Germany and in the United States during the 1902–1903 period.

Most of the earliest Teddy Bears had humps on their backs, elongated muzzles and jointed limbs. The fabric used was usually mohair; the eyes were either glass with pin backs or black shoe buttons. The stuffing was generally excelsior. Kapok (for softer bears) and wood-wool (for firmer bears) also were used as stuffing materials.

Quality older bears often had elongated limbs, sometimes with curved arms, oversize feet and felt paws. Noses and mouths were black and embroidered onto the fabric.

The earliest Teddy Bears are believed to have been made by the original Ideal Toy Corporation and a German company, Margarete Steiff, GmbH. Bears made in the early 1900s by other companies can be diffi-

cult to identify because they had a strong similarity in appearance and because most tags or labels were lost through childhood play.

Teddy Bears are rapidly increasing as collectibles, and their prices are increasing proportionately. As in other fields, desirability should depend upon appeal, quality, uniqueness and condition. One modern bear has already been firmly accepted as a valuable collectible among its antique counterparts: the Steiff Teddy put out in 1980 for the company's 100th anniversary. This is a reproduction of that company's first Teddy and has a special box, signed certificate and numbered ear tag. Eleven thousand of these were sold worldwide.

See Stuffed Animals in *Warman's Americana & Collectibles* for additional listings.

9½", brown wool, felt paws, externally visible joints, early 1900s, $175.00.

BEARS

4¾", mohair, jointed limbs, tail moves head up and down and from side to side, c1950s	200.00
9", mohair, felt paws, clown hat and collar, Steiff, early 1900s	400.00
13", brown mohair, felt paws, wide-set ears, fully jointed, hump, early 1900s	300.00
14"	
Brown mohair, metal mouth opens to "swallow" food which can be removed by unzipping back, c1930s	225.00

Grizzled mohair, flirty eyes, open mouth with teeth, bisque tongue, tagged "Peter," German, made by Gebruder Sussenguth, c1920s 900.00

White mohair, felt paws, fully jointed, early 1900s 400.00

15″, brown mohair, fully jointed, metal nose, French, c1930s 150.00

17″

Brown plush, molded nose and mouth, squeaker in tail, Ideal Toy Corp., c1950s 50.00

Steiff 100th anniversary limited edition, issued 1980 . . . . 400.00+

19″, shaggy mohair, fully jointed, hump, very long muzzle, early 1900s . . . . 400.00+

30″, standing plush bear, sewn-on felt military uniform, not jointed, c1920s 150.00

BEAR RELATED ITEMS

Cut out, leather, teddy bear, attached leather mailing card, labelled "Teddy B" 55.00

Political Button, metal, shaped like Teddy Bear, from William Howard Taft campaign 100.00

Spoon, SS, sculptured three-dimensional teddy bear on handle, "Teddy Bear" lettered down handle 85.00

TELEPHONES

The deregulation of the nation's telephone industry and increasing interest in antique telephones has led to increasing values for old telephones and equipment.

Lover's telegraphs and other crude sound operated and unpatented telephones existed prior to Alexander Graham Bell's 1876 patent. However, it is generally accepted that Bell invented the telephone powered by electricity.

The most valuable antique telephones come from the pre-1895 period and must be marked, dated, or easily documented. Instruments also must be unaltered and have all major original parts. Telephones marked Charles Williams, Jr., a Boston manufacturer whose factory was the "birthplace" of the infant Bell Telephone Company, are among the most valued.

Post 1895 telephones have value if modified or converted to be compatable with today's modern phone network. Conversions should be done by an expert who will supply additional parts without removing any of the major components to accomplish conversion.

Refinishing also requires expert skills. Do not remove original circuitry. Restoring nickel and black baked enamel finishes is most desirous. Buffing original parts to expose the brass beneath will make it difficult to distinguish those parts from the many dated and old fashioned marked, solid brass fake parts and whole telephones which have been flooding the market for a decade. No mass produced telephone made in the United States prior to 1950 was offered with a shiny brass finish!

Automatic Dialing Telephones

Couch, S.H., Autophone 250.00

Globe Automatic, wall model . . . 950.00

Lorimer Automatic, all models . . . 1,500.00

Monson Automatic, wall model . . 1,200.00

National Automatic, wall model . . 1,500.00

Ness Automatic, wall model 700.00

Select-O-Phone 250.00

Strowger Patent

Pre-1898 models 2,500.00

Automatic Electric, candlestick model 1,200.00

Wall Model, large 1,500.00

Wall Model, small 650.00

Automatic Dialing, Strowger, 1905, $1,200.00.

Double Box Telephones

48″ long, tandem, any manufacturer 550.00

49 to 60″ long, tandem 2 boxes . 750.00

60 to 70″ long, tandem 2 boxes . 1,200.00

71″ and longer 1,500.00

Oak, plain, Stromberg-Carlson type, c1899 . . . . 350.00

Unusual in any way, any manufacturer 450.00

Fiddleback Telephones
  Gilliand, American Bell with Blake
    transmitter, or Charles Williams 1,000.00
  Vought Berger, Kellogg, Western
    Electric, Stromberg Carlson,
    Dean, Diamond, etc. 275.00

Pay Phones
  Common 1950s style 150.00
  Gray Pay Station
    Desk Model, wooden, slots for
      coins up to dollar, marked .. 3,000.00
    Wall Phone, wood 2,500.00
    Wall Phone, 72" 3,000.00
    1920s style (Known as Laurel &
      Hardy style) 400.00
  Pay Box, cast iron, small c1910 . 150.00

Single Box Wall Telephones, Wooden
  Picture Frame Front
    1910–15 .... 225.00
    Cathedral Top, lightning arres-
      tors at top 300–400.00
  Plain Front, 1915–1920s 200.00
  Unusual style 450–600.00

Stands
  Gossip Benches, approx. 70.00
  Ornate, carvings 600.00
  1920s style, plain 150.00

Switchboards
  Pre-1894, wall mounted, marked
    American Bell-Blake, Gilliand,
    Edison, National Bell, or Charles
    Williams 2,000.00
  Pre-1910, wall mounted 500.00
  Pre-1935
    Light Bulbs 250.00
    Transmitter boom 400.00
  1935 to Present .... **Surplus Value**
  Hotel Annunciators 200–800.00
  Mansion Annunciators, depending
    on size and ornateness 75–450.00

Telephone Booths
  1890s, leaded glass 2,000–3,500.00
  1910 to 1912, single door 2,000.00
  1914 to 1940, folding door
    Oak 1,200.00
    Walnut 1,100.00

Triple Box
  American Bell, Edison, Blake, Ber-
    liner on transmitter 1,700.00
  American Electric, Kokomo 1,200.00
  Bell Telephone 1,200.00
  Chicago 950.00
  Elliott 1,200.00
  Gilliand 1,700.00
  Keystone 900.00
  Mianus 900.00
  Molecular 1,400.00
  Note: If any of these sets are
    missing the 7" long exposed
    terminal receiver, subtract
    $150.00.

Telephone stand, ornate, $600.00.

Upright Desk Stands (Candlestick
  Phones)
  Hour Glass or Potbelly shape ... 750.00
  Oil Can shape 500.00
  Straight Pipe, regular style
    Dial type 185.00
    No dial 95.00
    With magneto box 160.00
  Notes: Extremely unusual candlestick phones
made of wood or in an outrageous style may be
worth in excess of $1,000.00. All phones mass
produced from the WWI to 1950 were made in
black. The Western Electric model is now being
reproduced in solid shiny brass.

TEPLITZ CHINA

**Teplitz wares were manufactured in the Bo-
hemian province of Czeckoslavakia, where
Teplitz is located. In early 1900, there were
26 ceramic manufacturers in the city of
Teplitz. The wares were molded, cast and
hand-decorated. Most of these wares are of
Art Nouveau or Art Deco style. Most items
found today are marked "Teplitz" or "Turn-
Teplitz" or "Turn" a city nearby.**

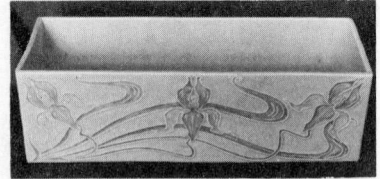

Window Box, 4¾ x 5 x 14¼″, yellow, purple and lavender iris, Egyptian for mark, $225.00.

Bowl, 6¾″, ecru, enameled flowers, mkd Made in Austria, c1912 .... **195.00**
Bust, girl, polychrome finish, raised base **190.00**
Ewers
  9½″, cream, red roses, gold trim, mkd Royal Teplitz **56.00**
  12½″, floral decor, ornate handle **85.00**
  15″, bulbous, handle, floral spray with berries and leaves **55.00**
Candlestick, 5¼″, figural, woman in flowing gown, mkd Made in Austria, c1905 .... **130.00**
Figure, 11″, lady, blue dress, marked Turn-Teplitz **300.00**
Jug, 3-handled, brown abd green decor with boy and dog, mkd Teplitz, Stellmacher **75.00**
Pitchers
  9½″, lily pad decor, green and pink, c1895 .... **185.00**
  Squat, green, little girl with horn and dog **68.00**
Vases
  5″, green, hp blue and white iris, gold trim orange mark Turn Teplitz, Bohemia **125.00**
  5″, bud, handled, medallion with rooster head in relief, multicolored geometric decor **85.00**
  7″, butterfly shape **350.00**
  8¼″, triangular crimped rim, 3 rolled under handles, gray, incised cabalier, mkd Stellmacker **135.00**
  12″, green-brown ground, Pate-Sur-Pate poppy decor, mkd Teplitz Bohemia **300.00**
  13″, Art Nouveau, face of beautiful woman, mounted as lamp base **275.00**
  Art Nouveau style, pierced gold handles, cream blue popies, green leaves, pr **220.00**
  Gentlemen with cap in medallion, enameled **85.00**
  Nude washing hair, lily pad decor, pearl gray and gold, high glaze, ftd, Crown mark **250.00**

Window Box with liner, 3 x 4 x 12″ l, boat shape, spider web ground, rose decor **120.00**

TERRA COTTA WARE

Terra Cotta is another name applied to wares made of a hard, semi-fired ceramic clay. The color of the pottery ranges from a light orange-brown to a deep brownish red. It is usually unglazed, but some pieces can be found partially glazed, or decorated with slip designs, incised or carved. All kinds of utilitarian objects have been made for centuries as have statuettes and large architectural pieces. Fine early Chinese terra cotta pieces have recently brought substantial prices.

Syrup Jug, enamel center, band of Phoenix birds, pewter top, 6″ h, $110.00.

Figures
  Cupids, 15½″, pr **225.00**
  Diane and Apollo, 71″, life size, on plinth, sgd Fratelli Cuccarelli, 20th C, pr **1,500.00**
  Dog, glass eyes, cigar mouth, advertising for cigars, 1920s **225.00**
Jar, cov, 6½″, dragon design, Chinese decor, c1930 .... **50.00**
Medallion, portrait Benjamin Franklin, Nini, France, 3¼″, 1777 .... **450.00**
Statue, Victorian woman playing a mandolin, mkd, Made in Athens, Greece, c1880 .... **400.00**
Sugar Bowl with Underplate, 4½″,

unglazed, polychrome enamel floral design, imp Spode 195.00
Teapot, branch handle curls around side and front into flowering tree, bamboo spout, tree shaped finial, imp seal mark 45.00
Urn, 11½", cream, incised flowers, 3 handles, late 19th C 275.00
Vase, 10", dragon motif, 2 handles 90.00

TEXTILES

Textiles are cloth or fabric items, especially anything woven or knitted. Those that survive usually represent the best since these were the objects that were carefully used and stored by the housewife.

Textiles are collected for many reasons — to study fabrics, understand the elegance of an historical period, and for decorative and modern use. The renewed interest in clothing has sparked a revived interest in textiles of all forms.

Also see Clothing, Quilts and Samplers. See *Warman's Americana & Collectibles* for a listing of crochet work.

Bedspreads
French net with Battenburg lace center design, cut out corners, matching bolster cover, 68 x 88" 195.00
Hand woven, Candlewick type, indigo blue and white, decoration of stars and female figures on white, early 19th C, 64 x 80" . . 700.00
Chair Seats, needlework, polychrome wool yarns in tent stitch depicting birds, dragons, stylized foliate design on dark ground, English, 18th C, 20" square, pr . . 660.00
Coverlets, woven
Hand woven, double overshot, red, white and blue with white fringe, New York state, early 19th C, 72 x 80" 700.00
Jacquard, two color, (blue and white), double woven, snowflake and leaf pattern, wide borders with spread winged eagles grasping arrows and olive branches, 88 x 84", mid 19th C 475.00
Jacquard, three color, (red, white, and electric blue), tulip like squares interlock with floral diamond motif, rose border, sgd

"Daniel/Bordner/Millers/burg, Berks/County/1840," 80 x 103" 900.00
Jacquard, three color, (red, white, and green), starburst oval center surmounted by elaborate drapery border inside a tulip border, oak leaf and column entrance border, marked "Charles Fehr, Manufactorer, Emaus/ Lehy County, Pennsylvania," 72 x 96" 400.00
Jacquard, four color, vertical rectangular center with chamfered corners and floral bands, diamond with dots and floral chain middle border, rose outer border, sgd "Made by/John/ Seibert/Lowhill/T.Lehigh/Co Pa," 71 x 91" 750.00
Jacquard, four color, (red, blue, green and white), circular medallion in center, urn and scrolled leaf corners, Roman Key border around three sides, 86 x 82" 500.00
Hooked Rugs
31 x 38", eagle perched on a branch surrounded by stars, flowers, and leaf designs, some wear 300.00
43 x 26", one black horse and one white horse, multicolored striped ground 1,100.00
43½ x 28", Waldoboro example, embossed bouquet of flowers with embossed wreath of flow-

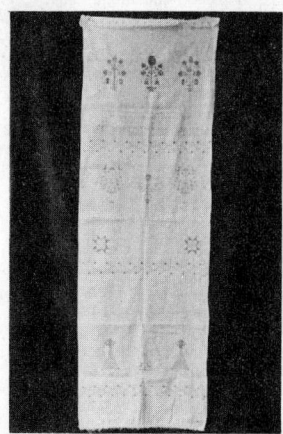

Show Towel, rose ground, embroidered 16½ x 50½", $180.00.

ers around it, brown ground, indigo border 600.00

44 x 28", pictorial, nursery rhyme, Cow Jumped Over the Moon pattern, red, blue, yellow, green, and white, American, contemporary 450.00

50 x 29½", Masonic square and compasses, ivory on lavendar ground 140.00

64 x 34", floral, double floral cornucopia in red, blue, green, yellow, beige and black fabric, olive green borders enclosing a meandering vine, American, 19th C 825.00

Lap Robe, sleigh, black wool, scarlet red floral swag, initials, leather binding 95.00

Piano Scarf, silk, fringe, pink flowers 95.00

Show Towel, 17 x 48", homespun, embroidered flowers, initials 175.00

Table Cover, 50 x 75", Fortuny, stippled salmon, golden beige velvet stenciled with a flat gilt ground in a stylized pomegranite, foliage motif, round label, reads "Mariano Fortuny-Venise" 522.00

Tapestry, needlepoint, Art Deco, French, rectangular, blue border framing scene of 3 colorful parrots on floral ground, lower fringe border, 33 x 60" 3,300.00

Tapestry, needlework, Charles I, worked in polychrome silk thread on silk ground, various embroidery stitches, depicting full length figures of King Charles I and Queen Henrietta in oval reserve surrounded by border of pearl bands, framed by animals, flowers, leaves, in mid 18th C Hogarth frame, mid 17th C, 20" h x 24½" w 2,200.00

Wall Hangings

20¼ x 31", copper plate print, The Apotheosis of Franklin with George Washington in chariot pulled by 2 leopards, patriotic symbolism, Liberty Tree, Lady Liberty with shield which reads American Independence, 1776, red on buff linen, framed 205.00

68 x 56", crewel embroidered, two panel length of linen homespun with figures of two horseman wearing tri-cornered hats, on either side of young oak tree in leaf, figures posed on small hillock above swan and duck, stitched in wool, green, blue, yellow, pink and brown crewelwork, probably CT, late 18th C . 1,875.00

THREADED GLASS

Glass decorated with applied threads is called Threaded Glass. The process was used extensively both in the United States and abroad during the 19th Century.

In the beginning, the glass threads were applied by hand. In 1876, an Englishman patented the first apparatus to apply the threads mechanically.

Threaded Glass was produced in quantity and in varying degrees of quality by practically every major glass factory and definite attribution is almost impossible. It continues to be made to the present.

Finger Bowl, 5", fluted edge, chartreuse, $65.00.

Bowls

5", vaseline, polished pontil 45.00

16", flat with air traps, clear, topaz threaded edge, Steuben . . . . . 120.00.

Blown, ruffled, pink and gold . . . 90.00

Candlestick, 9⅞", clear, cut, flared base, bell nozzle with frosted floral and beaded decor, amethyst rim and threading in stem 175.00

Candy Jar, green, Steuben 80.00

Center Bowl with Matching Candlesticks, 12", green threading, sgd Steuben in block letters 400.00

Goblet, pink, threaded bowl, clear stem and base, sgd Steuben . . . 80.00

Lamp Base, gold threading, Durand 150.00

Perfume Bottle, 5½", pink threading on clear 180.00

Rose Bowl, 5 x 6", pink threading on clear 42.00

Tumbler, 4½", green threading on clear 60.00

Vases

6", cylinder, cranberry threading on clear 85.00

7", peacock blue, blue threading and white hearts, sgd Quezall . 600.00

8", fan shape, green and clear,
green threading, Steubern, pr . 130.00

TIFFANY

L.C. Tiffany-Favrile

Louis Comfort Tiffany (1849–1934) established a glass house in 1878 primarily to make stained glass windows. It was here he developed a unique type of colored iridescent glass called Favrile. His Favrile glass differed from other art glass in manufacture as it was a composition of colored glass worked together while hot. The essential characteristic is that ornamentation is found within the glass; Favrile was never further decorated; different effects were achieved by varying the amount and position of colors which project movement in form and shape.

In 1890, in order to utilize surplus materials, at the plant, Tiffany began to design and produce "small glass," such as iridescent glass lamp shades, vases, stemware and tableware in the Art Nouveau manner.

Commercial production began in 1896. Most Tiffany wares are signed with the name L.C. Tiffany or the initials L.C.T. Some pieces also carry the word "Favrile" as well as a number.

Louis Tiffany and the artists in his studio are also well-known for fine work in other art areas—bronzes, pottery, jewelry, silver and enamels.

Liqueur, dimpled, gold irid, sgd L.C.T. R4893, 1¾" h, $150.00.

Basket, 9¾" d, pastel ftd bowl with transparent fern design in well, butterscotch crackled irid at rim, set in gilt bronze mount, self handle, butterscotch and pink mottled enameling, imp Louis C. Tiffany Furnaces, Inc. 507 . . . . 528.00
Bon Bon, 4½", gold, ruffled, sgd . . 195.00
Bowls
  4¾" d x 2¼" h, oval, pastel pink, irid, opal stripes, pedestal, sgd 425.00
  6¼" d, paperweight type, transparent frosted sides internally decorated with golden pansies with purple centers, green leaves, inscribed L. C. Tiffany Favrile 6427J, c1915 . . . . 1,650.00
  7 x 3" h, irid peacock blue, 10 symmetrical swirls 485.00
  8", vertical molded leaf design, marked 1925, paper label 280.00
  10", vaseline glass, optic design bowl, petal base, marked, paper label 260.00
  12⅛ x 3½" h, irid gold, blue and pink highlights, intaglio cut butterfly, teakwood base, sgd L. C. Tiffany Favrile 1925 . . . . 1,195.00
  15", blue irid glass, decorated interior of clinging vines and leaves, sgd 660.00
Calendar Frame, 6½", dore bronze, Venetian, marked #1648 . . . . . . 242.00
Candlesticks
  10", bronze reticulated candle nozzle, detachable beaded bobeche, opaque lime green glass socket, 3 scrolled bronze legs . 440.00
  18½", candle socket supported by slender 3 pronged stem, detachable bobeche, imp Tiffany Studios, New York, 1213 . . . . . 275.00
Chandelier, 24½" h, hexagonal shade, radiating tiles shading from striated green and white through dark shades to mottled blue and white 2,600.00
Cigar Stand, 25", bronze, adjustable column supported by trumpet shaped cast foot, cast leaves, removable ashtray, imp Tiffany Studios, New York 1651 . . . . 880.00
Compotes
  8½" d x 4" h, gold irid, intaglio cut, sgd L. C. T. Favrile 850.00
  12" d, transparent amber glass, crackled gold irid bowl, mounted on silvered bronze base, imp Favrile Louis C. Tiffany Furnace Inc. 500 . . . . 459.00
Cordials, 2", gold irid glass, sgd, set of 6 . . . . 550.00
Decanter, stopper, irid, dimpled sides, 10" h, sgd 290.00
Desk Set, Abalone pattern, enamel blue and red highlights, desk lamp with paneled amber Favrile glass

shade, pr of large blotter ends, rocker blotter, inkstand, perpetual calendar, letter opener, pen tray, each imp Tiffany Studios, New York, serial numbers of each **3,000.00**

Dressing Table Stand, 14¾" h, 3 panel leaded glass screen, lower border of green glass jewels, scarlet and yellow birds, yellow and gold butterflies, 2 red and orange-amber flowers, green leaves, fuchsia blossoms on variegated purple, blue, green ground, 6 sided gilt bronze platform, ball feet, mirrored top with irid glass insets, imp Tiffany Studios New York ... **4,400.00**

Finger Bowls, underplates
Gold irid, 6½" d **310.00**
Queens Pattern **475.00**

Goblet, 8", opal pink bowl, emerald green stem, sgd L. C. T. Favrile .. **425.00**

Ink Stand, 4" h, bronze, zodiac, marked #1072 .... **220.00**

Lamps
Candle, 12½", ruffled, conical shade of transparent glass with heavy gold crackled irid, white glass column, green leaf decor, ribbed base of transparent yellow glass with gold irid, inscribed L. C. T. Favrile, drilled and wired for electricity **825.00**

Desk, 18¾", opal glass shade overlaid with butterscotch and decorated with bands of irid gold waves, inscribed L. C. T. Favrile, gilt bronze base in Graduate pattern with square column and foot, imp Tiffany Studios New York 558 .... **1,760.00**

Table, 19½" h, 14" d leaded glass domed shade, blue streaked fuchsia and pink tulips, green leaves, pastel green ground, tag imp Tiffany Studios New York 1535, bronze base with ribbed domed ft, imp Tiffany Studios New York 333 .... **10,450.00**

Table, 26" h, 20" d, conical shade, 7 dragonflies with light olive bodies, yellow, green filigreed wings, amber jewel eyes, mottled yellow ground, tag imp Tiffany Studios New York 1495, bronze base imp Tiffany Studios New York 531 .... **9,350.00**

Table, 27" h, 17¾" d domed leaded glass shade, mottled green tiles, center band of brillant red poinsettia blossoms, purple, blue, yellow centers, emerald-green leaves, finial, imp Tiffany Studios New York 1558,

painted base imp Tiffany Studios/New York/531 ...... **8,525.00**

Liqueur Set, 10½" decanter, stopper, 12 liqueurs, amber irid, inscribed Q6677, c1902 .... **1,450.00**

Paperweight, 2½" l, bulldog, dore bronze, sgd **180.00**

Parfait, 6½", circular feathered ft supporting clear to pastel blue bowl, vertical leaf decor, inscribed and paper label **265.00**

Plates
5¼", gold irid, wheel cut outer rim, polished faceted circles, sgd **125.00**
11", pastel irid blue, opal white feathering, sgd **450.00**

Salts
2½", amber irid, crimped rim, inscribed L. C. T. Favrile, set of 10, orig box **1,000.00**
2½", ftd, gold, rainbow highlights, sgd **165.00**
2⅝", light blue irid, thorn decor, sgd L. C. T. **225.00**

Tazzas
7" d, dore bronze, abalone pattern, ftd, #1708 .... **160.00**
8¾", etched gilt bronze, circular bowl, coined rim, 2 small medallions enameled with pink flowers, green leaves on green and yellow ground, imp Louis C. Tiffany Furnaces Inc. Favrile 513 . **200.00**

Tray, 13½ x 11", bronze, copper patina with enamel tesserae border, #310 .... **220.00**

Tumbler, 4", corset shape, irid gold, purple, pink highlights, threading in center **295.00**

Vases
2½", deep blue-green irid body decor with scrolling yellow-green leaves, millefiori blossoms, inscribed L. C. T. U4102, c1904 .... **2,100.00**
3¼", gold irid, green leaves, clinging vines, sgd **260.00**
3¾", red irid body, upright amber and purple irid leaves, inscribed L. C. T. Favrile 1722, c1912 ... **3,630.00**
4¾", tapered cylindrical molded with upright leaf design, dore bronze **200.00**
9", baluster form, cased blue glass over white, amber lip, single band of silvery blue leaves from ft to lip, inscribed L. C. Tiffany Favrile 7624, c1910 ..... **1,210.00**
10¼", cameo, caramel sides decor with swirling green leaves, intaglio carved to white and green florets, leaves, inscribed

L. C. Tiffany Favrile 3096H, c1913 .... **5,500.00**

19¼", deeply ruffled bowl, transparent yellow glass, crackled gold irid, supported by slender stem, irid ribbed domed base, inscribed L. C. T. W2019 ..... **2,200.00**

21", Jack-In-The-Pulpit, gold irid squat bulbous base supporting tall shaft flaring to wide ruffled brim, pink, green, blue highlights, incised L. C. Tiffany Fabrile 3673E **5,500.00**

Wines

3¼", hollow stem pedestal, all over raised pulls, gold irid, sgd L.C.T. **250.00**

5", gold irid cup and foot, cut arched panels, stem faceted, sgd **235.00**

TIFFIN GLASS

The Tiffin Glass Co., Tiffin, Ohio, a subsidiary of the U.S. Glass Co., discontinued operation in 1980.

From 1923 to 1926, they produced a line of black glassware, sometimes referred to by collectors as "Black Satin." This is very popular with collectors, and is quite collectible now. They also produced other colored glass, manufactured blanks for other concerns, and did a limited amount of cutting themselves.

For additional information about Tiffin Glass, refer to *Tiffin Glassmasters, Vols. I and II,* by Fred Bickenheuser.

Bowls

7", flower, blue satin, turned in rolled edge **25.00**

11", orange, moire-watermelon (peach blow satin) **48.00**

Candlesticks

5", frogs, black satin, pr **50.00**

9½", blue satin, rope stems, pr . **45.00**

Candy Jar, cov, vaseline, frosted stripes **35.00**

Compotes

6½", moire-watermelon, rope stem **45.00**

9", black satin, twist stem **30.00**

Console Set, ftd bowl, candlesticks, frosted yellow, hp floral decor ... **100.00**

Creamer and Sugar, Rock Crystal, floral cuttings, pr **95.00**

Lamp, figural, parrot, red body, green, yellow head plumage, perched on yellow log **215.00**

Marmalade Jar, cov, handles, Jungle pattern, green satin, painted decor of parrots, floral sprays **95.00**

Vase, 8" h, 8" d, frosted, bright blue, popples and bird motif, bulbous, $75.00.

Plate, 8", June Night **15.00**

Stemware

Champagne, Argenta pattern ... **10.00**

Cocktail, Athlove **13.50**

Juice, Rambler Rose, gold trim .. **8.00**

Parfait, June Night **15.00**

Water, Cherokee Rose **15.00**

Wine, Midnight Mood **15.00**

Vases

7", Blue Optic, clear ball stem .. **22.00**

9½", automobile, canary, orig bracket **35.00**

10½", Dahlia, green satin **20.00**

13", blue, large hand cut floral design, ball stem **35.00**

TILES

Decorative and utilitarian tiles have been made throughout the years by various potteries in the United States and abroad. Their usages are varied from small tea tiles or table top protectors to fireplace facings, floors and walls.

American Encaustic Tile Co., Zanesville, OH

Cherub band, highly emb, 6" sq, brown **150.00**

Chicken, incised, 4" sq, gray ... **20.00**

Eggs in nest, incised, 4" sq, teal blue **30.00**

Flower in pot, 6 x 24″, 4 brown
emb tiles in frame 85.00
Greek man's head, emb, 6″ sq,
mauve 75.00
"Jack and Jill," 6″ sq, polychrome 75.00
Man playing lute, emb, 6 x 18″,
mottled brown 125.00
Stove tile, woman's head, round,
green 25.00
Women, classical, emb, 6 x 18″,
green, pr 300.00
Copeland
Birds (two) on branch, poly-
chrome, 8″ sq 75.00
Children at seashore, hp poly-
chrome, 6″ sq 85.00
Flowers and leaves, hp poly-
chrome, 6″ sq 25.00
"The Painter" (medieval
occupations), polychrome, 6″ sq 95.00
Shakespeare scene, flow blue, 6″
sq 65.00
J. & J.G. Low, Chelsea, MA
Child with bundle of sticks, emb, 3
x 6″, green 35.00

J. & J. G. Low, 6″ sq, teal blue, $45.00.

Daisies, emb, 6″ sq, blue 30.00
Geometric pattern, emb, 6″ sq,
pale blue 15.00
Grover Cleveland, emb, 4 x 6″,
green 85.00
Head of woman wearing hood,
emb, 6″ sq, brown 85.00
Man's head, sgd by Arthur Os-
borne, emb, 4″ sq, brown 110.00
"Quick Meal" stove tile, emb,
green 30.00
Wm. DeMorgan
Dodo bird, ruby red lustre, 6″ sq . 350.00
Flowers, quartered design, red
and green, 6″ sq 100.00

Galleon ship, polychrome, 6″ sq . 400.00
Ship, medieval, green, 6″ sq 250.00
Sunflower, blue and green, 6″ sq 150.00
Minton China Works
"Beauty and the Beast," 6″ sq,
blue on white 35.00
Cows crossing stream, 6″ sq,
brown on cream 75.00
"The Fox and the Crow" (Aesops
Fables), 6″ sq, black on
white 55.00
Girl feeding pigeons, 6″ sq, blue
on white 85.00
Leaves and flower, stylized, 6″ sq,
blue on white 15.00
"Macbeth III," 6″ sq, blue on
white 25.00
"Morte D'Arthur," 6″ sq, browns
on cream 35.00
"Rob Roy" (Waverly' Tales), 8″
sq, browns on cream 85.00
Water Nymph with fish, 6″ sq,
black on white 65.00
Wild Roses, slip decor, 6 x 12″,
polychrome 45.00
Minton Hollins & Co.
"Autumn," harvesting grapes, 6″
sq, brown on cream 35.00
Daisies, 6″ sq, polychrome 15.00
"Elijah and Samuel" (Religious se-
ries), 6″ sq, blue on white 20.00
Floral pattern, 6″ sq, black on
white 8.00
"Jack Sprat" (Nursery Rhymes),
6″ sq, green on white 55.00
"Morning", 8″ sq, blue on
white 95.00
"Who is Sylvia? What is She!", 8″
sq, blue on white 85.00
Urn with leaves, emb, 6″ sq,
green 15.00
Mosaic Tile Co., Zanesville, OH
"Fortune and the Boy," 6″ sq,
polychrome 75.00
General Pershing plaque, oval,
white on blue 20.00
Geometric pattern floor tile, 6″ sq,
polychrome 12.00
"Leo" (Zodiac series), 6″ sq, poly-
chrome 25.00
Windmill, Delft style, 6″ sq, blue
on white 25.00
Miscellaneous
Beaver Falls Art Tile Co., Beaver
Falls, PA, Renaissance man's
portrait, emb, 6″ sq, blue, sgd I.
Broome 125.00
Cambridge Art Tile, Covington,
KY, Goddess and cherub, emb,
6 x 18″, amber 150.00
Pewabic, Detroit, MI
Candle lamp, incised, 2″ sq,
dated 1931, green lustre 50.00

Elephant, incised, 3" sq, brown on blue	65.00
Pilkington, England, Art Nouveau flower, stylized, tube-line decor, polychrome, 6" sq	38.00
Providential Tile Works, Trenton, NJ, flowered stove tile, round, hole in center	5.00
Unmarked	
Art Nouveau flower, incised, 6" sq, red and green	30.00
Bird with grapes, polychrome, 6" sq	35.00
Landscape, hp, polychrome, 6" sq	25.00
Wild Roses, polychrome, 6" sq	18.00
Sherwin & Cotton	
Dog head, incised, 6" sq, brown, artist sgd	95.00
Flowers, slip decor, 6" sq, polychrome	20.00
Grecian ladies, classical, 6 x 12", teal blue, pr	350.00
Abraham Lincoln, incised, 6 x 9", brown	135.00
"Quillmaker" and "Ledger," incised, 6 x 12", orange, pr	250.00
Trenton Tile Co., Trenton, NJ	
Flower and leaves, emb, 6" sq, beige	10.00
General Grant, emb, 6" sq, amber	85.00
Leaf, emb, 6" sq, green	5.00
Old man with beard and flowing hair (head), emb, 6" sq, brown	85.00
Woman's head, classical, emb, 6" sq, sgd Isaac Broome, light green	125.00
U.S. Encaustic Tile Works, Indianapolis, IN	
Boy with umbrella, emb, 6" sq, amber	75.00
"Dawn," panel of a woman, emb, 6 x 18", green, framed	150.00
Flower, emb, 6" sq, green	18.00
"Hamlet" and "Ophelia," emb, 6" sq, brown, pr	175.00
Wreath, flowered, emb, 6" sq, light green	10.00
Wedgwood	
Cherubs in center frieze, 6" sq, blue on white	25.00
Daisies (white) on speckled green ground, low relief, 6" sq	18.00
"Lysander" (Midsummer Nights Dream series), 8" sq, blue on white	85.00
"November," boy at seashore, 6" sq, peacock blue	85.00
"Red Riding Hood and Wolf," 6" sq, black on white	95.00
"Tally Ho," man riding horse, 8" sq, blue on white	75.00

TIN CONTAINERS

Tin containers were used in the early part of the 20th century for the packaging of tobacco, medicines, chemicals, powders and foodstuffs. Tins were manufactured in countless shapes, sizes and colors by U.S. and foreign companies.

Many were made plain and companies would put on their own labels. On others, the name was embossed or stamped on the tin.

Tin container collecting has become popular in the last several years. Old tins can be found almost everywhere. Prices vary greatly depending on the age and condition of the tin, and the location in which the tin is found.

CAUTION: A variety of tin containers are currently being reproduced in England exclusively for a U.S. firm. They are marked accordingly

See *Warman's Americana & Collectibles* for additional Tin Container listings.

Tobacco tin, 6 x 3¾ x 2¼", $55.00.

Candy	
Bluebird Toffee, Warwick Castle	12.00
Whitman's Prestige Chocolates, 3¾ x 6¼", trunk shape, flags	12.50
Chewing Gum, Teaberry, 6⅞ x 5¼ x 2⅜"	17.00
Cigars	
Ben Bey	15.00
Good Cheer Cigars, circular mug shape with handle	40.00
Portage	14.00
Cigarettes	
Gold Flake flat fifties	10.00
Murad, pocket tin	20.00
Old Gold, pocket tin	20.00
Phillip Morris, round box	20.00
Cocoa	
Droste's, 16 oz, sq, Dutch boy and girl	12.00
Watkin's, sq	13.00
Coffee	
Bagdad	40.00
Luzianne, 2 lb, negro Mammy on label	20.00
Planter House	25.00
Royal Dutch, red and white	14.00

Cough Drops, Keatings Lozenges .	7.00
Crackers	
Edgemont, 1924	16.50
Dr. Johnson's Educator, 5 x 5 x 5″	40.00
Flour, Superior	20.00
Fly Killer, Daisy, patd 1888	23.50
Gun Powder, New Schultze	75.00
Milk, Meadow Gold	9.50
Oysters, IWL, 1 pt	7.50
Peanut Butter, Staple Brand, Syracus Candy & Specialty Co, pail	36.00
Phonograph Needles, Nipper on front with needles	21.00
Potato Chips, Sartoga	17.00
Syrup	
Log Cabin, small	40.00
Woods Mince Meat Co, Baltimore, MD, paper label	15.00
Talcum Powder	
Egyptian	32.00
Rawleigh's Violet	18.00
Tea	
Jas H. Forbes Tea & Coffee Co, 3 lb	24.00
Lipton, 3 lb, 8 x 5″, Indian plantation scene	50.00
Maxwell House, 3⅜″, sq shape column, blue ground	8.00
Tobacco	
Beech-Nut, hinged lid	35.00
Bulwark Cut Plug, 3 x 3 x 1	25.00
Catcher Pipe Tobacco, 6 x 5, humidor shape, Brown & Williamson Tobacco Corp, Louisville, KY	40.00
Dan Patch, cut plug, 4 x 6″	35.00
Havana Ribbon, Londres 5¢, 3 x 5″	8.00
Orinoco	22.00
Prince Albert, pocket tin	9.99
Puritan	28.00
Repeater, pocket tin	50.00
Union Leader, pocket tin, eagles .	13.00
Vulcanizing Patches, Camel, camel pictured, c1946	15.00

TOBACCO CUTTERS

Before pre-packaging, tobacco was delivered to merchants in bulk form. A special tool was used to cut the tobacco into desired sizes.

Black Beauty	48.00
Brighton 3	30.00
Cupples Arrow & Superb	50.00
Five Bros Tobacco Works, John Finger & Bros, Louisville, KY	48.00
Griswold Tobacco cutter, Erie, PA .	55.00
Pennsylvania Hardware Co, 1900 . .	38.00

Unmarked, 6¼ x 7¼″ (graduated width) x 10½″ l, wooden base, cast iron cutter, $45.00.

Piper Heidsieck Tobacco Works, bottle shape	85.00
Rex	25.00
Shield shape, 14″, wood base	45.00
Spearhead Tobacco, J. P. Sorg Co	60.00
Standard	48.00
Triumph	35.00

TOBACCO JARS

A tobacco jar is a container for storing tobacco. Early tobacco humidors were made of various materials and in various shapes including figural types.

King on barrel, pottery, hand painted, German, 10″ h, $145.00.

Bisque, 5¼ x 4″ d, bust, Negro woman, green and pink striped white bandana and earrings **85.00**

Brass, 5½″, tin inside case, early 19th C **32.00**

Cast Iron, 9″, sq, ftd, chamfered corners, Napoleon finial, early 19th C **60.00**

China, black man smoking pipe, brown ground, satin finish **88.00**

Glass, "Tuxedo Tobacco" **22.00**

Lead, 6″, oval, Negro head finial .. **60.00**

Majolica
8″, Indian head form **125.00**
Owl, c1890 .... **80.00**

Nippon
Cobalt blue, with heavy gold overlay, blue mark **450.00**
Fisherman lighting his pipe, relief, beige and brown, beading on lid and finial, green mark **1,010.00**

Pewter, 6½″, c1760 .... **75.00**

Porcelain, 6¼″, pewter top with pipe finial **75.00**

Silver plated with liner, 8″, relief figures, flowering branches, seated figure finial, 19th C **200.00**

TOBY JUGS

A Toby Jug is a drinking vessell usually depicting a full-figured, robust, genial drinking man. They originated in England in the late 18th century, and the term "Toby" probably related to the character Uncle Toby from "Tristam Shandy" by Laurence Sterne.

Within the last 100 years or more, tobies have been copiously reproduced by many potteries in the United States and England. The early ones are quite expensive white later versions are available in a wide price range.

Also see BENNINGTON, ROYAL DOULTON, etc.

American Pottery Co., 6″, Jersey City Toby, Rockingham glaze, molded by Daniel Greatbach, c1840 .... **1,250.00**

Bennington, 6″, General Stark, seated, Rockingham glaze, 1848 mark **400.00**

Higgins & Seiter, NY, 7½″, George Washington, polychrome **185.00**

Lenox, 6″, William Penn **150.00**

Marris & Willmore, Trenton, NJ, 8″, Napoleon, base inscribed For Alfred B. Evans, Phila, PA. **400.00**

Prattware
7½″, pastel clothes, holding pitcher with 2 hands, c1790 ...... **300.00**
9″, green, brown, white clothes, c1790 .... **515.00**

Hearty Good Fellow, 11½″ h, red coat, yellow breeches, $275.00.

10″, Hearty Good Fellow, standing, polychrome **480.00**

Royal Doulton, 8″, Mr. Pickwick ... **135.00**

Staffordshire, 6½″, brown hat, blue jacket, yellow breeches, c1800 .. **700.00**

Whieldon
9½″, dark green jacket, pants, keg between feet, leaf motif base, c1770 .... **550.00**
9½″, pastel jacket, dark pants, c1770 .... **525.00**

Wood, Ralph
9½″, gray jacket, green waistcoat, dark hat, one hand raised to mouth **900.00**
9½″, pastel clothes, dark hat, c1780 .... **750.00**

Yorkshire
9¾″, Lord Howe, brown, green, yellow, c1790 .... **1,200.00**
10″, Martha Gunn, grotesque woman in olive hat, yellow scarf, flowered dress, folding flask and glass **925.00**

TOLE

Tole is the original name given to tinwares used for many household items such as boxes, pots and trays. The complete name is to'le peinte, French for sheet iron. Today collectors use "tole" as a generic name applied to stenciled or hand decorated tinwares.

See KITCHEN COLLECTIBLES for unpainted tinwares.

Tray, 8½ x 12½", chamfered corners, yellow line, red flowers, green leaves, corners red with yellow lines, $250.00.

Bird Cage, 15", green and gold paint	50.00
Bowl, 10¾ x 10¾", black, stencilled gold and red design, sgd. B. Pierce, New Fields, NH	40.00
Boxes	
5¾ x 6¾" d, cylindrical, hinged lid, black, floral decor, red, yellow and green	140.00
9¼", deed, orig pale yellow paint, red and black striping, floral decor	370.00
Cash, with inside tray, black and gold decor	145.00
Cannister, spice, 6 interior containers and grater in center, 7¾" d, brown with yellow and red striping, yellow stenciled lables on small containers	100.00
Coffee Pots	
8½", straight spout, dark brown japanning, fruit and foliage decor on both sides, red, yellow and dark green	1,300.00
8⅞", side spout, dark brown, bird, foliage and fruit, yellow and red	475.00
10¾", goose neck spout, black, floral decor on both sides, red and yellow	475.00
Flour Scoop, dtd 1869	25.00
Match Holder, 4⅜ x 7½", crimped crest, brown	60.00
Message Holder, green, 7 slots, each stenciled with day of week .	165.00

Needle Case, 9½", worn orig red paint with yellow decor	110.00
Sugar Bowl, 3¾", brown, red fruit, white, yellow, green decor	495.00
Teapot, 8¾", brown, floral decor on both sides, red, yellow and green	325.00
Trays	
3" h x 6⅞" x 11¾ w x 1120 " l, oval, marbelized interior, white band with red and green fruit and foliage	60.00
20⅝ x 27⅞", black, central scene, British Naval battle, floral and bamboo stenciled rim	215.00
22½ x 29½", oval, center scene, hunters on horseback and deer, red border with yellow eagle, griffin and foliage decor	250.00
Vase, 7½", paw feet, yellow with brown and green, French	30.00
Watering Can, peaches and grapes design, 18th C	175.00

TOOLS

Before the advent of assembly line, mass production, practically everything required for living was hand made at home or by a local tradesman or craftsman. The cooper, the blacksmith, the cabinet maker all had their special tools. Early examples of these hand tools are collected for their workmanship, ingenuity or design.

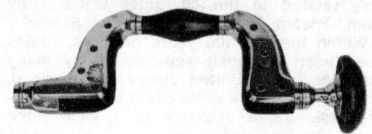

Utilitarian type Bit Brace, brass

Adz, cooper's hand, 7¼", stamped D. R. Bart	35.00
Axes, broad	
12" blade, 37" l, iron, wooden handle, early	50.00
23½", cast steel, Wm. Beatty & Son, Chester	40.00
Barrel Hook	20.00
Braces	
Boring, 13" l, wood, brass trim, stamped, Bower, Chesterworks, Sheffield	110.00
Coachmaker's, 12" l, plus bit, cast steel with brass trim	10.00
Wood boring with hand crank, 15" l plus bit	45.00
Caliper, 21½", double, wrought iron	80.00

Chisels

Corner, 18th C	45.00
Gouge, round to make circular sweep, 17th C	75.00
Clamp, wood	25.00
Drill, hand, for drilling barn beams, 23" h x 29" l, cast iron and wood, adjustable augle	110.00
Grindstone	35.00
Hammer, cooper's marking, places serial number and date on each barrel head	85.00
Hatchet, 1845	20.00
Hay Fork, 60" l, all wood	135.00
Hoop Driver, cooper's, 8¾" l, wooden	15.00
Howel, cooper's, small	85.00

Jacks

Carriage, oak, iron teeth	70.00
Wagon, 19" h, wood and wrought iron, engraved 1796	160.00
Knife, tanner's fleshing, 21½" l, double edged blade, mkd Geo. Barnsley & Sons, Sheffield, English, wood handles, brass ferrules	15.00

Levels

3", Stanley, Pat Feb 1890, brass front	7.30
12", Davis, adjustable, brass filagree	90.00
Mallet, 19" l, wooden, brass bound	25.00
Peeling Iron, 35½" l, primitive ram's horn handle	42.00

Planes

Cooper's, 12½", head float for smoothing staves	55.00
Pine and maple, 22", Ogonta Tool Co	25.00
Tongue and groove, 10½", used to cut ⅝" groove	40.00
Tongue and groove, 13¾", wood, Greenfield Tool Co	45.00
Pulley Block, cypress, iron fixtures .	30.00
Reamer	38.00
Ruler, 24", folding with brass, Stanley #54	8.50

Saws

Back, 23", decorative wood handle, emb brass label, Spear & Jackson, Sheiffield, English . . .	36.00
Bow, cabinetmaker's, 16 x 29¼", walnut and maple	38.00
Frame, 30 x 31", maple, chamfered members and mortised construction, wrought iron fittings	110.00
Hacksaw, 18", hand wrought, brass ferrule, wooden handle .	12.00
Jeweler's, 11", delicate cast steel, brass trim, turned handle	17.00

Scrapers

Cooper's pull, maple handle, brass ferrule	25.00

Wooden, 8½", burl blade, hickory handle	45.00
Screwdriver, 2", Winchester	25.00
Shears, 8", wrought iron	35.00

Squares

Adjustable, cabinetmaker's, rosewood	25.00
Set try, cherry, iron, brass bound blade	42.00
Tongs, coal, 14", primitive wrought iron	35.00
Trammel, 53", sawtooth, wrought iron	60.00
Traveler, 38" d wooden wheel, wood handle	35.00
Wrench, alligator, hand forged	10.00

TOOTHPICK HOLDERS

Toothpick holders are small containers used to hold toothpicks. They were an important table accessory during the Victorian era. They have become very popular as collectibles during the last fifty years because of their size, and because they are often a souvenir item.

See *Warman's Americana & Collectibles* for an expanded listing of Toothpick Holders.

Alexandrite, 2½", $1,250.00.

Alexandrite

1⅞ x 2⅞", hat shape, blue edge, rose to citron	995.00
2⅝ x 2½", bulbous, honeycomb, shaded blue to rose to citron . .	750.00

Burmese

2", hat shape, pink to creamy yellow, glossy finish	225.00
2½", bulbous, shaded pink to yellow, acid finish	135.00

Cased, pink, enamel decor, 2 handled SP holder 325.00
Crystal, elephant, frosted, blue and amber, "Baby Mine", c1895 .... 45.00
Double Dahlia with Lens 40.00
Fry-Foval, 2¼", scalloped rim, applied blue handles 40.00
McKee Glass, Peek-A-Boo 22.00
Milk Glass
    Monkeys on stump 45.00
    Sq, ftd 30.00
Northwood, 2½", blue, chrysanthemum sprig 275.00
Opaque, 3¼", slivery blue, emb floral 18.00
Pairpoint, child riding on turtle, holding umbrella which is pierced to hold toothpicks 145.00
Quezal, ribbed, gold irid, sgd 225.00
Rubena, 1¾", 10 panel 95.00
Silverplate, figural, open log on crossed branches, Tufts Silverplate 38.00
Texas, gold 30.00
Vaseline, Darwin 55.00
Wave Crest, emb rococo scrolls, ormolu feet 185.00

TORTOISE SHELL ITEMS

For many years, amber and mottled colored tortoise shell has been used in the manufacture of small items such as boxes, combs, dresser sets and trinkets, which are today quite collectible.

Note: Anyone dealing in the sale of tortoise shell objects should be familiar with the Endangered Species Act and Amendment in its entirety. As of November, 1978, antique tortoise shell objects can be legally imported and sold with some restrictions.

Bracelet, tortoise shell, 3" d, silver inlay, $28.00.

Boxes, covered
    3" round, inlaid small brass stars, cover fitted with miniature painting on ivory of young woman, 19th C 145.00

4 h x 11 w x 7½" d, rectangular, fitted interior 150.00
Card Case, gold decor of birds and flowers, Japanese, 19th C 85.00
Cigar Case, 1¼ h x 2¾ w x 5½" l, center gold shield, border, MOP geometric lines 295.00
Comb, 6", amber top with rhinestones 75.00
Dresser Set, 4 pc, powder box, hair receiver, shoehorn, cuticle knife . 65.00
Glove stretcher 18.00
Humidor, 4½", rectangular, hinged lid 150.00
Lorgnette, fancy pierced work handle simulates chain with six loose rings, attached black string with small beads 85.00
Picture Case, 3½ x 4", book form, cover inlaid with MOP flowers, velvet lining 50.00
Tea Caddies
    5½ h x 9 w x 5" d, sarcophagus shape, cov, ivory handle, divided interior, brass ball feet, c1800 .... 450.00
    6¼ x 7 l x 5" w, pagoda top, 2 lidded compartments, SS escutcheon monogrammed W.M.W., c1820 .... 525.00
Vase, 8¾", flared top, pedestal base 150.00

TOYS

There always have been toys. They are a reflection of what is happening in any given era. Archaeologists have unearthed the remains of a 5,000 year old toy factory in India. Centuries ago, Asian and Egyptian children enjoyed dolls and toy animals.

The earliest American toys were handmade. Very few survive today. By the mid-19 th century toymakers established themselves in larger American cities. The advent of industrialization coupled with the mail order catalogue made toys available to a mass market.

By 1900 toys were easily available. They tended to be of high quality. The Europeans, especially the Germans, also turned to toy manufacturing. Tin toys from Germany are among the most sought after by collectors. Several auctions houses, including Lloyd Ralston Toys, and Phillips, have speciality auctions consisting entirely of toys.

Every toy is collectible. The key to a toy is condition and working order if mechanical. Toys made prior to 1955 are rising in price rapidly.

See *Warman's Americana & Collectibles* for an expanded listing of toys.

Arcade
Andy Gump 348 Car, painted cast iron, 7″ l, restored 400.00
Chester Gump Cart, painted cast iron, 7½″ l 200.00
Gas Pump, painted cast iron, mechanical, 6¼″ h 100.00
Brown, George, circus acrobat on horse, painted tin, minor restoration, 6½″ l, American 475.00
Buddy L
Cement Mixer, painted pressed steel, orig decal 550.00
Fire Truck, water tower, nozzle missing 1,900.00
Model T Coupe, small series . . . 450.00
Wrigley's Truck, painted pressed steel, orig decal, 23½″ l 600.00
Chein
Ferris Wheel, litho tin windup, orig box, 17″ h 200.00
Happy Hooligan, litho tin windup, 6″ h 145.00
Popeye with punching bag, litho tin windup, 9½″ h 500.00
Rocket Ride, litho tin windup, orig box 200.00
Ski Boy, litho tin windup, orig box, 5½″ h 60.00
Space Ride, litho tin windup, orig box, 9½″ h 100.00
DeCamp, French
Elephant, leather on wood frame, clockwork, 13½″ l 400.00
Pig, pig skin on wood frame, clockwork, 11″ l 275.00
Tiger, tiger hide on wood frame, clockwork, nose missing, 17″ l . 300.00

Chein, Piano Lodeon, $250.00.

Dent
Coupe, painted cast iron, 9½″ l, 2nd series 450.00
Public Service Bus, painted cast iron, 13½″ l, 2nd series 375.00
Taxi Cab, painted cast iron, orig box, 8″ l, 2nd series 140.00
Zeppelin Los Angeles, painted cast iron, 12½″ l, 2nd series . . 250.00
Ellis, Britton & Eaton, horse, painted, stenciled wood, leather saddle, trim, cloth fringe, 50″ l, c1870, American 800.00
Doll Co., German, carousel, painted tin, clockwork, 12″ h 1,000.00

Gong Bell Toy Company, cat and dog bell toy, Keene, NH, $750.00.

Gunthermann, German, musicians, litho tin, painted tin, windup, cloth dressed, paper accordian, 8½″ base 1,900.00
Hess, German
Hessmobil 1020, tin, crank action, instruction sheet, 7″ l 425.00
Speedboat, #7, litho tin, 11½″ l . 120.00
Hoge Mfg, Popeye in row boat, enameled pressed steel boat, litho tin figure, windup, replaced oars, 14″ l 925.00
Hubley
Bell Telephone Truck, Mack, painted cast iron, white rubber tires, ladders, equipment, 9″ l . . 800.00
Royal Circus Calliope, painted cast iron, pressed steel, wheels repainted, 16″ l 550.00
Santa Claus, painted cast iron, blue and gold sleigh, white reindeer, red Santa, 15″ l 500.00
Kenton
Log Wagon, painted cast iron, 15″ l 375.00
Mama Katzenjammer Spanking Toy, painted cast iron, minor restoration and touch up, 11½″ l 550.00
Overland circus cage truck, painted cast iron, restored, 9″ l 450.00

Kingsbury

Bus, #788, painted tin windup, white rubber tires, 16" l **385.00**

Golden Racer, painted pressed steel, clockwork, 20" l **220.00**

Hudson Teraplane, painted pressed steel, clockwork, not working, 13½" l **225.00**

Zeppelin, Little Jim, litho tin, clockwork, made for J. C. Penny, 20½" l **1,300.00**

Lehmann

Bucking Broncho, litho tin windup, 7½" l **260.00**

Going To The Fair, painted, litho tin, momentum **550.00**

Mandarin, litho, painted tin windup, orig braids, 7½" l **1,000.00**

Masuyama, litho tin windup, 7" l . **775.00**

Naughty Boy, litho tin windup, 4½" l **375.00**

Vineta, litho tin, friction, 9½" **975.00**

Lindstrom, U. S. Mail truck, painted tin windup, 7" l **275.00**

Linemar, rollerskating Popeye, cloth, litho tin windup **450.00**

Marklin

Armoured car, hand painted tin, clockwork, working construction top, 14½" l, c1930 . . . . **950.00**

Construction truck, hand painted tin, clockwork, 16¼" l **900.00**

Marx

Charlie McCarthy Crazy Car, litho tin windup, 8" l **300.00**

Dippy Dumper, celluloid Popeye, litho tin windup **450.00**

Hey! Hey! The Chicken Snatcher, litho tin windup, orig box, 9" h . **1,100.00**

Hi-Yo Silver, The Lone Ranger, litho tin windup, orig box, 8" l . . **350.00**

Merry Makers, litho tin windup . . . **575.00**

Mortimer Snerd Crazy Car, litho tin windup, 8" l **350.00**

Smitty Scooter, litho tin windup, 8" h **1,300.00**

Uncle Wiggly Car, litho tin windup, orig box **375.00**

Murray Co., Ohio, peddle car, "Playboy Trucking Co," airflow style, painted pressed steel, 50" l **225.00**

Nifty

Buttercup and Spareribs, pulltoy, litho tin, mechanical, 7½" l . . . **310.00**

Felix on scooter, litho tin, 7½" l . **260.00**

Powerful Katrina, Jimmy in wheelbarrow, 1923, litho tin windup, 7" l **1,025.00**

Snowflake and Swipes, pulltoy, litho tin, mechanical, orig box, 7½" l **1,000.00**

Snowflake riding Spark Plug, litho tin, scratches, wear **850.00**

Reynolds, Charlie, Toonerville Trolley Cap Pistol, painted aluminum, 5" l **175.00**

Strauss

Flying Airship, Graf Zeppelin Jr, LA 1017, aluminum, windup, orig box, 10" l **275.00**

Ham & Sam, litho tin windup, orig box, 7½" h **400.00**

Interstate Bux, litho tin windup, 11" l **400.00**

Leaping Lena, litho tin windup, 8½" l **150.00**

Sturditoy, coal truck **900.00**

Tootsietoy, dairy truck, die cast **60.00**

Unique Art

Dogpatch Band, litho tin windup . **375.00**

Howdy Doody and Bob Smith, piano, litho tin windup **435.00**

Jazzbo Jim, litho tin windup, orig box, 10" h **320.00**

Unique Artie, litho tin windup, orig box **275.00**

Whitney-Reed, horse on gliders, painted wood, leather, 36" l horse, minor paint restoration to base . . **450.00**

Wilkins, cab, painted cast iron, 1 door replaced, 15½" l **500.00**

Williams, A. C., traffic light, inscribed "Obey Traffic Laws - Dept of Police," painted cast iron, electric, 9½" h **200.00**

Wyandotte, Humphrey Mobil, litho tin windup, orig box, 8½" l **350.00**

Unknown Makers

Balloonist, painted tin, clockwork, straw basket repaired, 15" h, German **1,500.00**

Biplane, painted tin, clockwork, litho tin pilot, orig box, 12½" l, German, c1910 . . . . **4,500.00**

Clown organ grinder, dancing teddy bear, painted tin, cloth dressed clown, painted papier mache head, 5" h plush teddy . **1,100.00**

Minstrel Drummer, painted tin windup, 8½", German **675.00**

Torpedo Touring Car, litho tin windup, 11¼", German **2,800.00**

Tricycle, painted and stenciled wood, cast iron hardware, 34" l, American, c1860 . . . . **1,150.00**

Velocipede, painted and stenciled wood, cast iron, 40" l, American, c1870 . . . . **1,000.00**

TRAINS, TOY

Railroading was an important part of any youngster's childhood, largely in part be-

cause of the romance associated with the railroad and the emphasis on toy trains. Almost everyone had a train layout. Basements, back rooms, or attics allowed the layout to remain up year-round.

The first toy trains were cast iron and tin. The wind-up motor added movement to the trains. The Golden Age of toy trains was from 1920–1955 when electric powered units were widely available. The construction and details of the rolling stock were of high quality. The advent of plastic in the late 1950s lessened this quality considerably.

Toy trains are designated by a model scale or gauge. The most popular are HO, S, and O. Gauge affects price as does age and condition. American Flyer and Lionel are the two firms which dominated the market during the golden period.

See *Warman's Americana & Collectibles* for an expanded listing of Toy Trains.

AMERICAN FLYER

Cars
934, Caboose, S	35.00
3007, Gondola, litho, O	15.00
24047, Box, Great Northern, S . .	95.00
24068, Box, Planters Peanuts, S .	750.00
24126, Gondola, Frisco, S	40.00

Locomotives
12, locomotive and tender, O . . .	50.00
290, steam, S	60.00
375, GM American Flyer, 1953, S	300.00
1218, 0-4-0, Streamliner, O	70.00
4667, S	200.00
L2002, Burlington Route, S	175.00

Sets
429 locomotive, tender, 4 cars, orig box, O	425.00
4367 locomotive, Shasta, 4 Pochahontas coaches, orig box, S	1,400.00
4670 locomotive, tender, 3 Lone Scout coaches, S	850.00

LIONEL

Cars
17, Caboose, S	25.00
575, Shell tank car, S	450.00
602, Baggage, dark green body, roof, wood litho doors, S	45.00
6442, Passenger, 1949	60.00

Locomotives
8, New York Central, electric, maroon, brass windows	125.00
38, New York Central Lines, electric, pea green	250.00
390, locomotive and tender, green, S	800.00
390E, locomotive and tender, green, S	850.00
203, locomotive and tender, O . .	275.00
2368, B & O, AB diesel, O	250.00

Lionel electric, No. 233 "O" guage: Engine #262, Hopper Car #803, Gondola #402, Cattle Car #806, Caboose, #802, $115.00.

2378, Milwaukee, AB diesel, O . .	350.00

Sets
773 locomotive, tender, New York Central, #2625, 2627, 2628 coaches, O	1,200.00
402E locomotive, 3 coaches, S . .	1,000.00

TRAMP ART

Tramp Art was prevalent in the United States from about 1875 into 1930. These items were made by itinerant artists, who left no record of their identity. They used old cigar boxes, fruit and vegetable crates, and edges of items were chip-carved and layered, which created a unique effect. Finished items were usually given an overall stain, and they are collectible today as an example of a special type of crafted wood work.

Clock, 27" h, $500.00.

Boxes

    6¾ h x 7½ x 10" l, double pedes-
      tal base, hinged cover, dark fin-
      ish 85.00
    7 x 8 x 5¼", hinged lid, yellow
      and orange alternating layers . 85.00
Corner Shelves, porcelain knobs .. 80.00
Cutlery Tray, applied chip carved
    layers 85.00
Foot Stool 40.00
Frames

    21 x 18½" opening, oblong with
      rounded arch crest 50.00
    26 x 20", star shape 150.00
Jewel Box, 6 x 11 x 10", hinged lid,
    handle 70.00
Match Holder, double, striker in cen-
    ter, vines and leaves 20.00
Planter, hanging, white porcelain
    knobs 95.00
Toothpick Holder, round, ftd 25.00
Washstick, hand carved 25.00

TRIVETS

A trivet is a three-legged stand used to support hot vessels, either in an open fireplace,
in workrooms or on table tops. The popular
collectible trivets are those which were used
to hold the early hand irons. These trivets
were usually very ornate, incorporating designs of animals, birds, flowers, fruits, etc.

Trivet, 6", cast iron, $22.00.

Brass

Cathedral, #4 .... 40.00
Fan, 8½", curved lattice design . 10.00
Heart, 8", scrolls, hearts 55.00
Horseshoe, "Take Simmons Liver
    Regulator in Time" 35.00
Masonic, 8" 48.00
Scrolled design, 7½", central in-
    terlocked medallion 40.00

Shield Shape

    6¾", leafy foliage, English reg-
      istry mark 15.00
    7¼", scrolled 15.00
    Tree and horse 32.50
Star & Clover, 9¼", cut out, sheet
    brass, turned feet 70.00

Cast Iron

Bless Our House 14.00
Canadian Spider Web 15.00
Cat's head, 8¾", well detailed .. 145.00
Child's with iron, star with No. 8 . 24.00
"Colebrookdale Iron Co.", Potts-
    town, PA 40.00
Eagles

    GAR, flag in color 75.00
    Heart in laurel wreath, 8¾" ... 35.00
    Round, heart, laurel leaves out-
      er edge 35.00
Enterprise, #2 .... 35.00
Fan shape, 9", foliage scroll de-
    sign 20.00
Horseshoes

    Ancient Order of Foresters, flag
      in colors 45.00
    Bust of General Grant in center 65.00
    Eagle, clasped hands, "Good
      Luck", 6½", gold paint 30.00
    God Bless Our Home, 1889 .. 45.00
    Good Luck, cupid with garlands 40.00
    Sailor's House Blessing 38.00
House, girl and dog in lacy frame-
    work, large 45.00
Howell, W. H. Co., Geneva, IL .. 16.50
Minerva head, 9" 25.00
Spade shape, handled, shield,
    cannon, cannonballs and
    crossed swords, "Adams" 65.00
Star, Sunrise 25.00
Sun with face, 12"l, nickle plating,
    scroll work, mkd Muster,
    Geschutz 20.00
Swastika 32.00

Wrought Iron

Cross with crown 12.00
Heart, 2 x 5½", 3 feet 55.00
Round, 6½ x 9", 3 arrow shaped
    prongs 45.00
Spider Web 15.00

TRUNKS

Trunks are portable containers that clasp
shut for the storage or transportation of personal possessions. Normally trunk means the
ribbed, flat or dome top models of the second half of the 19th Century. Unrestored they
sell between $50 and $150. Refinished and

relined the price rises to $200 to $400, with decorators being a principal market.

Early trunks frequently were painted, stenciled, grained, or covered with wallpaper. These are collected for their folk art qualities and as such experience high prices.

Flat Top, wood rim, brass banding on ends, tin on wood, $85.00.

Dome Tops
Carved, painted pine, stylized tulips and floral motif, sponged green-blue and white ground, PA, early 19th C, 31 x 16 x 13″   **1,870.00**
Leather cov, decorative brass studs that form initials "AB" on lid, wrought iron handles and lock, brass escutcheon, c1850, 19 x 11 x 9″ **175.00**
Pine, barrel stave top, 32 x 25 x 20¼″ **125.00**
Pine, wrought iron bands, handles and fittings, c1881, 32 x 18 x 16″ **275.00**
Flat Tops
Pine, rawhide cov, leather handles, nailhead design, newsprint lining, c1845, 34 x 18 x 17″ . . .   **550.00**
Wood frame, hairy leather cov, metal handles, lock and nailheads, c1818, 24 x 12 x 9″   **600.00**

TUCKER CHINA

William Ellis Tucker, (1800–1832), was the son of a Philadelphia schoolmaster who had a small shop on Market Street, where he sold china which he imported from France. William helped in the shop and became interested in the manufacture of china.

In 1820, a sample of the white-clay kaolin, from a Pennsylvania Chester County farm, was discovered, and the business started in earnest for William. Kaolin is the prime ingredient for translucence in porcelain, and they had a plentiful supply close at hand. The business prospered but not without many tri-

als and financial difficulties. He had many partners, and the marks found on Tucker china are "William Ellis Tucker," "Tucker and Hulme" and "Joseph Hemphill." Workmen's incised initials are sometimes found.

The business operated between 1825 and 1838, when Thomas Tucker, William's brother, was forced by business conditions to close the firm. There are very few pieces available for collectors today and almost all known pieces are in collections or museums. But you never can tell!

Saucer, 5½″, pink roses, blue blossoms, green leaves alternating with gilt floral sprigs; center radiating gilt lines, rim of gilt border, $150.00.

Bowl, 8½″, low ftd, undecorated . .   **265.00**
Pitchers
8¼″, Grecian shape, decor in gilding on both sides, initials MM above crossed boughs beneath a leafy branch on the neck, date 1834 beneath spout, gilt band borders, incised moulder's W for Andrew Craig Walker, restored **365.00**
9⅜″, vase shape, white, painted on either side in rose, iron-red, yellow, purple, blue, green with a floral cluster, decor gilding under spout in initials JSR, neo-classical foliate motifs on spout, neck, gilt band borders, neck slightly damaged **440.00**
Plate, 6⅛″, 4 pink, green rosebud sprigs, three gilt leaf sprigs, gilt band border **135.00**
Platter, 15⅝″, oval, undecorated . .   **275.00**
Teapot, cov, 7⅞″ h, painted scene with a cottage in rocky landscape view, some repairs **350.00**

Tea Service, sugar, cov, 4⅝" h, waste bowl, 3 teacups, saucers, 1 plate, 8½", cake plate, 6½", stylized spider border, bands around edge 825.00

VAL ST. LAMBERT

Val St. Lambert Cristalleries of Belgium was established in the early 1800s. They feature exquisite cased glass, heavily cut and engraved. The company is still in existence and produces many types of glass.

Candlestick, frosted, Sacred Heart stem, sgd 42.00
Coasters, 3½", intaglio engraved, orig paper labels, set of 4 . . . . . . 50.00
Compote, 6 x 8¼" d, clear, upturned flaring rim, single knop baluster stem, State Collection pattern #V702, sgd 95.00
Perfume Bottle, 5½", cameo cut with hand cut cameo cranberry flowers on frosted ground, silver screw cap cov, sgd 150.00
Pitchers
  7½ x 5½", tapers to 2½" base, smocking and rib pattern, applied handle, ground bottom, sgd 110.00
  13½", ovoid, frosted, scattered rose violets molded in relief, clear handle, overlay rose trim, etched sgd 250.00
Vases
  6½", frosted, pink flowers, sgd . . 300.00
  9½", cameo cut, purple tulips, green leaves 475.00

Powder Box, 7" d, 4" h, cameo glass, emb silver lid with cupids, gold and green mums, leaf decor, $150.00.

VALENTINES

Valentines date back to 279 A.D. The first written Valentine appeared in a letter dated 1477. The first major American producer of Valentines was Thomas W. Strong of New York in 1842. These Valentines were romantic or comic in theme.

In 1848 Esther Howland of Worcester, Mass., began making fine lacy Valentines that were considered the most beautiful paper creations of the 19th century. They had a small "H" stamped in red in the corner. In the early 1870s her company took the name New England Valentine Company and her Valentines were marked N.E.V.CO. In the early 1870s she sold her company to George C. Whitney Company.

Valentines are collected by artist &/or type. Some collectable artists are Brundage, Dobb, Greenaway, Howland, Meek, Strong, Tucker and Whitney. The collectible types are Civil War, comic, cut-out, fold-out, folk art, handmade, lacy, lithographed, mechanical, Penny Dreadfuls and sailor's. The price range for early Valentines is wide, from a few dollars to hundreds of dollars and will vary according to artist, composition, condition, size and type.

Comic, Fat Woman, Rose Co., c1907 . . . . 5.00

Schanaer, German, 4½ x 4", pop-up, die cut, $50.00.

Easel, 8″, boy and girl, hearts, c1910	15.00
Fold Out, die cut, 6¾ x 3¾″, young with doves, German	6.00
Lacy, die cut, 3 x 5″, cupids	25.00
Penny Dreadfuls, McLoughlin Bros, c1900	7.00
Tuck, Ralph	
Easel, Campbell Kid, girl with teddy bear	20.00
Fold out, die cut, 9¼ x 6½″, boy and girl with box, dated 1906	17.00
Mechanical, boy, googlie eyed	9.00

VALLERYSTHAL GLASS

Vallerysthal (Lorraine), France, has been a glass producing center for centuries. In 1872, two major factories merged and produced art glass from 1898. Later pressed glass covered animal dishes were introduced. The factory continues operation today.

Candy Dish 4⅛″ d, white milk glass, $20.00.

Candlesticks, 10½″, figural, females, pr	145.00
Compote, 6¼ x 6¼″, sq, blue milk glass	70.00
Dishes, covered	
Apple, blue milk glass	15.00
Dogs, blue milk glass, pr	105.00
Rabbit, 6″, white, frosted	60.00
Snail on strawberry, sgd	80.00

Squirrel, white milk glass	65.00
Swan, large, blue milk glass	85.00
Goblet, ftd, green	50.00
Jam Jar, cov, blue, grapes, sgd	35.00
Plate, 6″, Thistle pattern, green	65.00
Salt, cov, figural hen, milk glass	30.00
Sweet Meat Dish, cov, 5¼ x 5¾″, blue milk glass, squirrel finial	60.00
Tumbler, 4″, blue	40.00
Vase, 8″, cylindrical, green, Optic Diamond pattern with painted rose thistles, sdg	140.00

VAN BRIGGLE POTTERY

Born in 1869, Artus Van Briggle was a talented Ohio artist who studied in Paris for three years while working at Rookwood. In 1899, he moved to Colorado for his health and established his own pottery in Colorado Springs.

Van Briggle's work was heavily influenced by the Art Nouveau "school" he saw in France and he produced a great variety of matte glazed wares in this style. Colors varied.

The "AA" mark, a date, and "Van Briggle" were incised in all pieces prior to 1907 and sometimes in the teens and 20s. Dated pieces are the most desirable.

Anne Van Briggle continued the pottery after Artus's death in 1904.

Van Briggle pottery still is made today. These modern pieces are often confused for older examples. Among the glazes used are Moonglo (off white), Turquoise Ming, Russet, and Midnight (black). Glaze does not effect price. Modern pieces are listed with two prices — the 1980 factory price in brackets and the price usually found in dealer's booths and shops.

1901–1920

Bowls

4½″ d, black, Art Nouveau leaves, tinge of red at top, 1903, pattern#144	675.00
5½″ d, dark green, 1915, pattern #733	95.00
6″ d, medium green, stylized leaves, 1906, pattern #327	350.00
6½″ d, maroon, plain, 1903, pattern#50	375.00
7″ d, blue, plain, 1907–12, pattern #702	125.00

Vase, green over tan ground, marked "86/1905/vv", $725.00.

Candlestick, 6″, bluish green, 1906,
design #445 . . . .   **175.00**
Cup, 5″, pink, white interior, handle,
1907–12 . . . .   **95.00**
Pitcher, 5½″, gray, plain, 1907, pattern #435 . . . .   **225.00**
Plate, 4½″ d, turquoise, with spider,
1907–12, pattern #623 . . . .   **175.00**
Vases
4½″, gray-green, leaves, 1907,
pattern #451 . . . .   **275.00**
5″, lime green, red flower, 2 handles, 1903, pattern #175 . . . .   **775.00**
5½″, maroon, leaves, 1917, pattern #859 . . . .   **45.00**
5½″, maroon ground, green
streaked, oviform, molded with
stylized tulips, inscribed with
firm's mark and "VAN BRIGGLE
1903 231 III" **925.00**
5½″, turquoise, flowers, 1920,
pattern #833 . . . .   **40.00**
6½″, brown, light brown curdling,
1907–12, pattern #636 . . . . .   **450.00**
7″, light blue, poppy seed pods,
1913, pattern #694 . . . .   **150.00**
7″, mustard, incised flowers with
swirling stems, pattern #7 . . .   **850.00**
7″, yellow, flowers, 1914, pattern
#822 . . . .   **275.00**
10½″, light yellow streaked turquoise ground, balustered,
molded with a band of stylized
flowers, inscribed with firm's
name and "Van Briggle 1909
281" **495.00**
11″, pink, mottled green over trifoliate flowers, 1905, pattern #291   **575.00**

1921–1950s, UNMARKED

Bookends, owls, 5″, maroon, pr . . .   **125.00**
Bowl, 5″, rectangular, rose with blue
flower **30.00**

Candlesticks, 7″, cupids holding ornate pillar, curdled dark blue and
light green, sgd "L.B.," pr **125.00**
Figurines
Donkey, 3½″, blue matte glaze .   **50.00**
Elephant, 4¼″, pink and blue, #
34 . . . .   **35.00**
Tile, 6″ sq, 4 color landscape scenic
tile in light and dark blue, white
and green (spot of excess green),
marked "VBP Co" **95.00**
Vases
3½″, turquoise, dragonfly, pattern
#683 . . . .   **25.00**
5″, high glaze black with blue drip,
"Anna Van Briggle" **25.00**
7″, light blue, tulips **35.00**
12″, maroon, headed Indian **125.00**

MODERN

Bowls
Butterfly, 3″ (5.50) **15.00**
Philodendron, 4″ h, 5″ d, No. 847
(9.00) **35.00**
Figurine, The Hopi Maden, 6″ h, 7″
w at base, grinding corn (17.50) .   **50.00**
Lamp, Running Horse, 18″ h, oval
shade (12″ w, 5″ d, 8½″ h) features butterflies and wildflowers
(45.00) **75.00**
Vases
Oriental, No. 570 (14.00) **30.00**
Tulip, small, No. 19 (5.50) **15.00**

VASART

Vasart

Vasart is a contemporary art glass made in
Scotland by the Streathearn Glass Co. The
colors are mottled and sometimes shade
from one hue to another. It is readily identified by an engraved signature on the base.

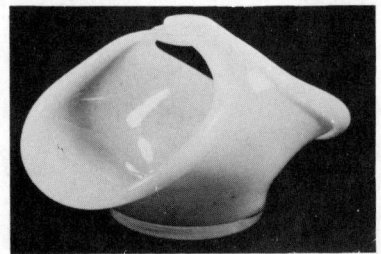

**Basket, 5″ h, 8¼″ l, green shading
pink, $85.00.**

Ashtray, 4½" d, mottled blue to
   pink, sgd 40.00
Laskets
   4 x 6", mottled blue 70.00
Bowls
   2", scalloped rim, mottled green . 30.00
   6½", pierced handle, pink and
     green 25.00
   8", green-gray, gold stone flecks 75.00
Hat, signed 25.00
Mug, mottled blue and green 45.00
Rose Bowl, mottled white and laven-
   der 50.00
Vases
   8½", mottled blue shading to pink 95.00
   9", ftd, jade green, sgd 65.00

VENETIAN GLASS

**Venetian glass has been made on the island
of Murano, near Venice, since the 13th century. Most of the wares are thin walled. Many
types of decoration have been used—em-
bedded gold dust or lace work and applied
fruits or flowers. Venetian glass continues to
be made today.**

Candlestick, 11¼" h, 5¼" d base
brass fittings, opalescent ribbon twist
stem, canary, $135.00.

Ashtray, curled edges, blue, silver
   flecks 28.00

Barber Bottle, green overlay, cut to
   clear 120.00
Candlesticks
   10", dragon shape stem, pink . . . 100.00
   12", crystal with gold dust, pr . . . 135.00
Chalices, 11", blue, gold biblical figures around body, pr 200.00
Champagne Glass, Victorian couple,
   hp, gilded, hollow twisted stem . . 125.00
Compote, 8", scalloped, green, dolphin stem, gold flecks 120.00
Cruet, lavender, double swirled . . . 100.00
Cup and Saucer, demitasse, multi-
   colored 75.00
Ewer, 6¼", amber and clear, rigaree
   collar 75.00
Finger Bowl with Underplate,
   diamond optic 50.00
Goblet, 6¼", green, pink rigaree . . 40.00
Plates
   7", pink and white alternating
     latticinos 60.00
   8", clear, pastel enamel decor on
     rim, gold trim 28.00
Rose Bowl, ruffled, ftd, pink, gold
   flecks 90.00
Salt, swan shape, pink, gold trim . . 30.00
Toothpick, pastel ribboned and lacy,
   handled 45.00
Vases
   8¼", millefori inlay 110.00
   10 x 6", fan shape, ball stem with
     gold flecks, ribbed 95.00
   11", bell shape, pedestal base,
     clear, gold dust 110.00
Wine Glass, pale green, lobed balus-
   ter stem, gold dust 32.00

Verlys   *A Verlys France*

VERLYS GLASS

**Verlys Glass is a type of art glass originally
made in France after 1930. For a period of a
few months, Heisey Glass Co., Newark, Ohio,
produced the identical glass, having obtained
the rights and formula from the French factory. The French-produced glass can be distinguished from the American product by the
signature; the French is mold marked, the
American is etched script signed.**

Ashtrays
   4½", frosted doves, floral border,
     script sge 50.00
   Swallows, blue, mold sgd 125.00
Bowls
   6½ x 9½ x 5½", canoe shape,

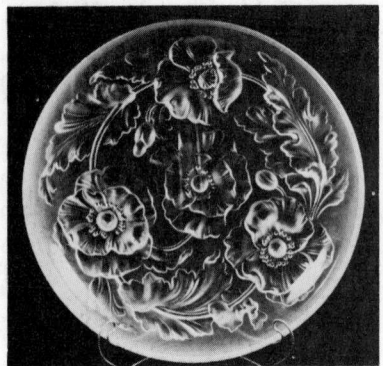

Verlys, salad bowl, 13½", Poppy, $125.00.

frosted opalescent, angle fish and seaweed in relief	80.00
13½", waterlily, clear, script mark	150.00
14", orchid, etched sgd	145.00
14", poppy, etched, sgd	160.00
Box, 6½", butterflies, script sgd . . .	95.00
Dish, figural duck, frosted, sgd	55.00
Figure, pelican	30.00
Plates	
11¾", bird decor, sgd	165.00
14", birds and fish	85.00
Powder Box, love birds, frosted . . .	50.00
Tray, 11½", frosted bluebirds and bees, script sge	100.00
Vases	
4½ x 6½", fan shape, frosted, love birds, script sgd	125.00
4½", frosted, clear molded sparrows at base, etched sgd	60.00
9¾", cylindrical, frosted thistles and leaves in high relief over arching clear glass panels, etched sgd	150.00

VILLEROY & BOCH

The founder of one of the original potteries that eventually became Villeroy and Boch was Pierre Joseph Boch who established a factory near Luxemburg, Germany, in 1767. His son, Jean Francis, attained the distinction of introducing the first coal fired kiln in Europe and perfecting a water power driven potter's wheel. Other potteries in the area were those of Mettlach, managed by Pierre's grandson, Eugene, and Nicholas Villeroy's factory.

A consolidation of these three firms was effected in 1841 and became known as Villeroy and Boch. Early production included a hard paste earthenware comparable to English Ironstone. This ware continues to be made today for their line of tablewares.

It was the combined talents and efforts of this organization that initiated decorated stonewares known the world over as Mettlach.

See also METTLACH.

Plate $5.00.

Basket, 7", twisted handle, applied silver lustre flowers	75.00
Bowl, 8", cranberry and blue floral decor	30.00
Chargers	
15", seascape, sailing ships, castle, lighthouse, stenciled mark, #1517	125.00
15¼", Return of Ulysses, brown, ochre and ivory, sgd Heinrich Schlitt	600.00
Jug, beige, glossy green leaves, twig handle	35.00
Mug, 6", figural leaves, twig handle, cream, raised blue lines	60.00
Pitcher, white, black strips	45.00
Plaques	
Autumn Season, etched, sgd Warth, #1607	600.00
Cameo, mythological figures aboard ship	800.00
Dogs, 2, with stag at bay, #2070	100.00
Plate, partition, black and white hunting scene, #1598	85.00
Platter, 12¾", castle scene, Villeroy & Boch/Mettlach/Gesehutz, Remagen, Dec. 158 impressed 1044	245.00
Syrup Jug, cov, 4", blue and white .	50.00
Teapot, 6¼", white, blue decor . . .	100.00

Vases
7", etched, beaded, applied florettes in high relief, ftd, # 1804, pr 430.00
8¼", flared top, blue and brown with raised enamel blue and gold decor 225.00
10", Ceren Nachbuldeing, floral decor, #1844 . . . . 175.00
12¾", round, flared narrow neck, reserves, small boys playing . . 325.00

WARWICK CHINA

Warwick China Manufacturing Co., Wheeling, West Virginia, began operation in 1887 and continued until 1951. They were one of the first manufacturers of vitreous glazed wares in the United States. The date 1887 is when the incorporation papers were issued; there is some question that some pieces may have been made before then. There are pieces of experimental eggshell type of porcelain made before 1887 that are very rare.

Hand painted Warwick is more valuable than pieces decorated by decals. The most desirable are portrait items and special pieces for fraternal organizations such as the Elks, Eagles, and Knights of Pythias.

Their production lines were extensive, including tableware, garden ornaments, decorative and utilitarian items.

Bowl, Insert and Underplate, serving, 3¼ x 9½", black 55.00
Egg Cup, large, Tudor Rose 10.00
Ewer, 10½", brown, floral decor, IOGA mark 200.00

Pitcher, 4¼", brown, IOGA mark, $60.00.

Gravy Boat, red currants, green leaves, gold trim 45.00
Marmalade Jar, cov, handled, brown and pale yellow 95.00
Mug, 4½", monk smelling flowers . 50.00
Pitcher, water, gold scallop top, ivory, blue flower decor 100.00
Plates
9½", bust of elk, B.P.O.E., brown 70.00
10½", young woman with flowing hair, brown 82.00
Platter, stag, brown transfer 130.00
Shaving Mug, Indian portrait 120.00
Stein, 7½", monk 135.00
Tankard, fisherman smoking pipe, IOGA mark 180.00
Umbrella Stand, 21", portrait and scene 100.00
Vases
10", bust of monk drinking cider . 150.00
10", urn shape, brown, roses, green IOGA mark 98.00
10½", Gypsy portrait, twig handles 135.00
11", nasturtium, decor, IOGA mark 125.00

WASH BOWL AND PITCHER SETS

Wash Bowl and Pitcher Sets were essential parts of the household before the advent of indoor plumbing. These sets were made by many manufacturers and consisted of two main types, the basic set and the complete set. A basic set would include a large pitcher and matching bowl. A complete set would probably include a wash bowl, large pitcher, small pitcher for hot water, a toothbrush holder, a soap dish with drain and cover, large waste jar with lid and often a shaving mug.

Many sets are being imported today and many reproductions exist.

Alba China, white, brown flowers, basic 160.00
Bennington, mottled brown, Alternate Rib pattern, marked, c1849 . 850.00
Flow Blue
Nile pattern, basic 275.00
Royal pattern, F. Winkle Co, England, c1900, basic 125.00
Homer Laughlin, 5 pcs 475.00
Ironstone
Meakin, white, emb tulips, basic . 150.00
Minton, Genevese, white, green decor, basic 190.00
Mulberry, Corean pattern, basic . 265.00
Paneled, white, elephant head at top of handle and finial, 3 pcs . 225.00
Limoges, Moss Rose, gold trim, 5 pcs 350.00

Miniature, 5 pc, white ground, dark blue rim, florals in mulitcolors, gold trim, c1830, $300.00.

Newport Pottery Co., Ltd/Burslem, England, band transfer, Japanese motif, Kutani bird, cherries, floral and giesha in oval medallion	250.00
Old Hall Earthenware, Excelsoir pattern, schooner in circle, registration mark 1880, 6pcs complete	360.00
Porcelain, white, roses against red and green trellis design, French, c1925	165.00
Spongeware, white with blue sponging	350.00

WATCH FOBS

Warman's Americana & Collectibles, 1st Edition, contains 97 listings in this category; see also page xii.

WATCHES

The market in all types of watches is brisk. They can be found from flea markets to the specialized jewelry sales at Butterfield's, Phillip's, and Sotheby's. Condition of movement is first priority; design and detailing of case is second.

In pocket watches, listing aids are size (18/0 to 20), number of jewels in movement, open or closed (hunter) face, and whether the case is gold, gold filled, or some other metal. The movement is the critical element since cases often were switched. However, an elaborate case, especially of gold, adds significantly to value.

Pocket watches designed to railroad specifications are desirable. They are 16 to 18, in size, have a minimum of 17 jewels, adjust to at least five positions, plus conform to many other specifications. All are open faced.

Study the field thoroughly before buying. The literature is vast including books and newsletters from clubs and collectors. S = size; gf = gold filled; yg = yellow gold; j = jewels

Character

Captain Marvel, Jr., 1948, orig box	75.00
Hopalong Cassidy, regular size, inscribed on back "Good Luck From Hoppy," orig band	90.00
Moon Mullins, pocket, Ingersoll dollar type	175.00
Peter Pan, pocket, New Haven	50.00

Pendant

Black, Starr and Frost, gold, platinum, and diamond, c1910, translucent gray-blue enamel over a guilloche ground, rose cut diamonds amidst bow-tied garlands, chain of thin lozenge-shaped links dotted with white enamelled quatrefoils	2,750.00
Unmarked, diamond, rock crystal, and black onyx, c1920, rectangular shaped platinum case embellished with numerous single-cut and old European cut diamongs, several calibre cut black onyxes, shaped rock crystal panel, movement by Genault Watch Co., Swiss	975.00
Unmarked, enamel and diamond, c1910, openface, 18K gold, reverse applied with blue-gray gulloche enamel, surmounted by trelliswork set with rose diamonds mounted in platinum, movement by Longines Whittnaur	1,350.00

Pocket

American

American Waltham Watch Co., hunter, box hinge, damascened nickel 7j, model 1883, 18S movement, gold case engraved with foliage and dog, Deuber trademark for 10K gold, 52mm d	600.00
American Waltham Watch Co., openface, damascened 21j, model 1894, 12S movement, sgd "Riverside Maximus," monogrammed 14K gold case, 45mm d	425.00
Elgin National Watch Co., hunter and chain, damascened nickel 15j, first model, 6S movement, scalloped 18K gold case chased with wreaths of flowers enhanced with black enamel enclosing	

Pocket, Elgin National Watch Co., 15j, 18s, gold filled, lever set, $150.00.

cartouche with enamel scenic view, 18K gold twist link chain, watch 45mm d **675.00**

E. Howard & Co., hunter, lady's gilt three quarter plate 15j, G size movement, engraved rolled gold case, 40mm d . . . **450.00**

E. Howard & Co., hunter, series I, gilt split full plate N size movement, engine turned 18K gold case **2,200.00**

E. Howard & Co., openface, series 0, nickel 23j, 16S fully adjusted movement, plain 14K gold case, orig fitted wooden box, watch 49mm d **700.00**

Illinois Watch Co., openface railroad, damascened nickel divided three-quarter plate, 21j, 16S movement, sgd "Sixty Hour Bunn Special," plain gold filled case, 49mm d **250.00**

United States Watch Co., Marion, NJ, hunter, gilt and damascened full plate 15j, 18S lever movement, sgd "Fayette Stratton," 18K gold case, cased with foliage and central cartouche, 53mm d **1,500.00**

Danish, Jules Jurgensen, Copenhagen, vari-colored gold hunter cased minute repeating chronograph, nickel lever movement, presentation sgd " . . . to O. W. C. Rowland from . . . Louisville and Nashville Railroad Co. . . . ," 18K gold case, chased gold steam locomotive with diamond headlight, fitted wood case, certificate, watch 55mm d **22,000.00**

English

J. Kennedy, openface, duplex, gilt/full palte movement, Earnshaw-type balance, engine turned 18K gold case, London, 1809, 54mm d **1,100.00**

William Robinson, Liverpool, openface, lever, gilt full plate movement, 18K gold case, 50mm d **500.00**

Swiss

Henry Benguelin & Son, hunter, lever, nickel 21j bar pattern movement, 18K engine turned case, 53mm d **600.00**

Golay Fils & Stahl, openface, minute repeating nickel level movement, monogrammed 18K gold case, fitted box sgd Cartier, watch 45mm d **2,200.00**

Mouliné Aine, hunter, lady's lever, gilt bar pattern movement, gold case chased with scrolls, front with blue enamel monogram within floral wreath, reverse with vignette of spaniel, 14K gold chain with key formed as dog's head, watch 43mm d **1,250.00**

Patek Phillippe & Co., openface, dress, nickel 18j lever movement, monogrammed 18K gold case enhanced with blue enamel, 43mm d **950.00**

Touchon & Co., openface, dress, nickel, 19j lever movement, monogrammed platinum case, wirework platinum chain, watch 42mm **700.00**

Unmarked, openface, gilt cylinder movement, subsidary dials for month, day of week, seconds, incorporating moon phases and date, plain gun metal case, 50mm d **300.00**

Wristwatch, Man's

American, Hamilton Watch Co., damascened 19j, model 982M movement, plain platinum case **400.00**

Swiss, Patek Phillippe & Co., self winding with calendar, nickel 36j Cal. 28-255 C lever movement, plain 18K gold case **1,350.00**

Swiss, Rolex, gold self-winding, Oyster perpetual date, 14K gold case with 14K gold bracelet with deployant buckle **2,650.00**

Wristwatch, Lady's

Gruen, diamond and gold, rectangular dial, accented by 6 small round diamonds, 14K yellow gold case, black cord band . . . **65.00**

Jaeger Le Coulter, "S" link chain set with 34 round diamonds, square shaped dial, sliding dome of trelliswork crown with diamond bands over dial, same motif in chain **1,750.00**

Unmarked, Art Deco, platinum and diamond, c1930, rectangular shaped dial, flanked by 2 triangle-shaped diamonds, set throughout with 8 baguette and 58 round diamonds, joined by a mesh strap with white gold clasps 550.00

WATERFORD

Waterford crystal is quality flint glass commonly decorated with cuttings. The original factory was established at Waterford, Ireland, in 1729. The early glass made before 1830 was darker than the brilliantly clear glass of later production. The factory closed in 1852 and after 100 years reopened and continues production today.

Fruit Bowl, 5¾″ h, 6¾″ d, turned down rim, clear, $275.00.

Biscuit Jar, band of cuttings, SP cov and bail 295.00
Butter, cov, ovoid, mushroom finial, early 250.00
Compote, 4¼ x 4⅞″ 150.00
Decanters
  10½″, teardrop shape, fluted neck, strawberry diamonds and fan cut on star centered base, star cut mushroom shape stopper 100.00
  15″, all over geometric cutting .. 110.00
Jar, 7″, cov, fan and diamond cut . 125.00
Perfume, 6″, diamond cut 70.00
Pitcher, 10″, diamond cut, applied handle 195.00
Salt, master, 3⅞″, oval, diamond cut 50.00
Vases
  5″, spherical, hobnail cut, triple sprig chain banded rim, star centered base 75.00

8″, diamond cut, horizontal bands with chains of triple sprigs, rim and star centered base are bordered by vertical ribbing 160.00
Wine, 5½″, diamond cut 25.00

WAVE CREST WARE

WAVE CREST

The C.F. Monroe Co. of Meriden, Connecticut, produced the opal glassware known as Wave Crest from 1898 until World War I. The company bought the opaque blown molded glass blanks from the Pairpoint Manufacturing Co. of New Bedford, Massachusetts, and other glass makers including European factories. The pieces were then decorated, usually with floral designs. Trade names used were "Wave Crest Ware," "Kelva" and "Nakara."

Ashtray with attached matching cigarette holder, ftd, floral decor, black mark 395.00
Biscuit Jars
  8″, pale yellow, pansies, baroque scrolls frame. SP bail 185.00
  8″, puffy, egg crate, silver over brass rim, marked 240.00
  Sq, large, pink apple blossom decor, ornate scrolling bail, sgd C.F.M. in cov 135.00
Bon Bon Dish, 4¾″ d, handled, lavender with blue flowers 125.00
Boxes
  3¼″, pink flowers and leaves in relief, varigated purple violet, orig lining, red mark 295.00
  4″, jewelry, glass, hinged lid, scallop design, banner mark 145.00

Box, 2¼″, 3¾″ d, deep blue, Nakara CPM Co., $185.00.

4¼", hinged lid, molded violets and scrolls, painted violets on lid, orig lining, red banner mark ... 285.00

4½", round, hinged lid, puffed swirls, enameled daiseys, marked 185.00

7", dark blue, white floral relief, 2 white satin cartouches with hp flowers, orig blue silk lining, marked 525.00

Butter Pat, 3", transfer decor, emb edge, marked 50.00

Candlesticks, 10", enameled, blue shasta daisies and white dotting, metal ormaolu, pr 425.00

Clock, 9", cut glass, ftd 575.00

Humidor, 5½" d, egg crate, ormolu trim 675.00

Jardiniere, white, cherry blossom decor, sgd 350.00

Paperweight, paneled, ornate gold knob 150.00

Planter, large, sq, pink florals, banner mark 385.00

Toothpick Holder, 2½", ormolu ftd base, marked 375.00

Tray, 4", pin, floral decor, handled, sgd 95.00

Vases

8", floral decor, enameling, brass top and handles, sgd, black mark 375.00

9½", pale blue, floral motiff all around, 4½" brass ormolu holder, black banner mark 550.00

13½ x 7¾", ormolu handles and feet, pastel blue, pink chrysanthemums, emb scrolls, gold trim, red banner mark 895.00

WEATHERVANES

A weather vane indicates wind direction. The earliest known examples were found on late 17th century structures in the Boston area. The vanes were handcrafted of wood, copper, or tin. By the last half of the 19th century, weathervanes adorned farms and houses throughout the nation. Mass produced vanes of cast iron, copper, and sheet metal were sold through the mail order catalogues or at country stores.

The champion vane is the rooster, in fact the name weathercock is synonymous with weathervane. The styles and patterns are endless. Weathering can affect the same vane entirely differently. For this reason, patina is a critical element in collecting vanes.

Whirligigs are a variation of the weathervane. Constructed of wood and metal, often by unskilled craftsmen, whirligigs not only indicate the direction of the wind and its velocity but their unique movements served as entertainment for children, neighbors, and passersby.

Note: Reproductions of early models exist, are being aged, and sold as originals.

Vanes

Bull, 11", hollow body, 23" iron arrow **118.00**

Cherub, 12", wrought iron, molded, standing with bow over shoulder **1,210.00**

Codfish, 34" l, wood, carved, full bodied, gray, Chatham, MA, c1918 .... **360.00**

Cow, 17 x 25" l, copper, good detail, low relief, sheet metal ears, cast horns **575.00**

Deer, jumping, 24 x 28", copper body, iron horns and head ... **750.00**

Eagle and Sphere, 41" h x 33" wingspan, copper, emb brass arrows, cast iron directionals painted black **280.00**

Harpoon, 5' 10" h x 48" w, molded, gilded copper, ball finial, directionals, cylindrical standard . **990.00**

Horse, running, 24¼" h x 44" l, sheet metal, bushy mane and tail, mounted on crossbar, painted brick red, 19th C **550.00**

Indian Chief, 39¼", sheet iron, standing figure, feathered headdress, holding tomahawk, mounted on rod, many bullet holes, PA, late 18th C **4,400.00**

Pig, 9 x 5", zinc and cast iron, stands on elaborate 25" l directional arrow, c1900 .... **115.00**

Pig, 31½", copper, full figure, hand, nade contemporary folk art **300.00**

Rooster, 31 h x 26" w, cast zinc body, hammered gilded copper tail, mounted on black metal base, J. Howard, Bridgewater, MA, 19th C **3,080.00**

Soldiers, 32", sheet iron, silhouette, one on horseback with sword, two walking with rifles . **650.00**

Sunflower, copper, c1880 ...... **550.00**

Whirligigs

Indian, 13¾", wood, primitive, folk art, tin feather headdress, red with features in white and black, high moccasins and breech cloth are dark yellow with black, mounted on black wooden base **3,025.00**

Man in top hat, 15", wood, blue and red with white strip on pants, early 20th C **625.00**

Owl, 9" h, wind propeller raises wings, painted vivid yellow black, red, white, 20th C **275.00**

Pine, 15¼″ h, 15¼″ l, directional arrow, $124.00.

Scotsman, carved, painted, wearing plaid kilt and argyle socks, sabre-blade paddles, English, 19th C **3,960.00**

WEBB, THOMAS & SONS

Thomas Webb & Sons was established in 1837 in Stourbridge, England. To the collector of Art Glass, the company is probably best known for their very beautiful English cameo glass. However, many other types of colored glass were produced including enameled glass, iridescent glass, pieces with heavy glass ornamentation, cased glass and other types of art glass.
    See also BURMESE, CAMEO, PEACH BLOW.

Rose Bowl, caffet-au-lait, gold applied floral and vine decor, 3″ h, 3¼″ d, $550.00.

Bowls
  5¼″, mustard color satin, ruffled edge **88.00**
  10″, butterscotch, gold floral decor, 2 handles **140.00**
  11½″, pink exterior, blue interior satin, DQ MOP **550.00**
  Pink satin, ruffled top, ornate silver stand **220.00**
Brides Basket, 10″, pink satin, DQ MOP, ruffled edge, metal base, sgr **300.00**
Dish, cased, pink interior, white exterior, ruffled edge, c1920 . . . . **45.00**
Flower Holder, 12½ x 8¾″, gold irid glass foot, brass leaves and branches with 4 irid gold ribbed flower shaped vases **495.00**
Jar, 7½ x 5″ d, white to deep golden yellow, russet brown and gold leaves, stems, blossoms, gold butterfly **350.00**
Pitcher, blue satin, gold Prunus blossom decor, high loop handle, matching tumbler **660.00**
Rose Bowls
  Coralene, sgr **350.00**
  Imitation stone, floral decor **85.00**
Toothpick, Alexandrite, ruffled edge **1,000.00**
Vases
  6″, sunshine yellow, tapered, c1920 . . . . **125.00**
  7″, marbelized brown and white, raised decor **215.00**
  8″, cranberry and white mottled design cased in pink, satin, enameled leaf and vine decor, propeller mark **450.00**
  12″, acid cut, lavender poppies, green leaves, 2 gold butterflies **200.00**
  15″, tortoise shell, acid etched interior, gold enameled prunus decor **275.00**
  Ruby, applied crystal leaves, crystal footed, berry prunts, pr **875.00**

WEDGWOOD

WEDGWOOD

Josiah Wedgwood founded the famous Wedgwood Pottery at Burslem, England, in 1759. Wedgwood's history is complex. Although Wedgwood is probably associated more with the production of Basalt and Jasperware, the factory produced many wares including Creamware, Drabware, Redware and a fine quality porcelain.

In 1920, Fairyland Lustre was introduced. This porcelain is decorated with colorful, fantasy-like decals with gold detail. Lustreware production ceased in 1932. The firm in Wedgwood, England, is still active and produces fine quality dinnerware and accessories.

Also see **BASALT, JASPERWARE** and **PEARLWARE.**

Wedgwood Tobacco Jar, 5″ h, 4¾″ d base, Capri Ware, $750.00.

Bisquit Jar, 5½ x 4½″, Jasperware, SP bail, lavender top and bottom bands, sage green center band with white lady and cupids, marked Wedgwood only	**695.00**

Bowls

2¾ x 5⅛″d, octagonal, Dragon Lustre, mottled blue, gold dragons, Roman key border, inside MOP lustre with green dragons, imp Wedgwood	**195.00**
3⅛ x 4¾″d, pedestal foot, Fairyland Lustre, outside midnight lustre, stars, green grass, fairies and pixies, inside green MOP lustre, pixies, birds and bats, gold outlining, Wedgwood, Portland Vase mark, Z4968 . . .	**695.00**
3½ x 7⅛″d, Butterfly Lustre, ruby with butterflies, inside MOP with Oriental designs around edge, imp Wedgwood	**375.00**
3½ x 7¼″d, octagonal, Butterfly Lustre, exterior green with blue	

and gold butterflies, interior orange and white with gold and green butterflies, imp Wedgwood **525.00**

Boxes, covered

1 x 3¾″d, oblong, dark blue, cherub playing lute, trees, leaf border, sgd Wedgwood	**60.00**
1¾ x 3″d, dark blue, figures and floral band on cover, cherubs on sides, sgd Wedgwood	**120.00**
3½″d, round, Jasperware, yellow, white clasical figure, Wedgwood only	**375.00**
Bulb Pot, 9½″l, hedge hog, light blue, sgd Wedgwood	**490.00**

Busts

Mercury 18½″, Basalt, sgd on bust and plinth, Wedgwood . . .	**875.00**
Washington, George, 14″, Basalt, Wedgwood	**1,200.00**
Calendar Tile, Harvard Medical School, 1908	**48.00**
Candlesticks, 6″, Rosso Antico with Capri design, cut out bases, Wedgwood only, pr	**495.00**
Child's Mug, 2½″, Creamware, brick red transfer of La Fayette and Washington	**160.00**
Child's Tea Set, 3½″teapot, sugar bowl, cov, milk jug, wastebowl, drab earthenware, basketweave, button knops, imp Wedgwood, X, early 19th C	**275.00**
Cigarette Box, 4″, sq, Dragon Lustre, mottled green and blue, gold dragons on cover and sides, fret borders, MOP interior with birds, Portland Vase Wedgwood made in England, c1920	**300.00**
Coffee Can with Saucer, 3″, powder blue lustre, hp reserves of fruit, sgd A. Holland	**300.00**
Coffee Pot, 9″, Caneware, unglazed, imp Wedgwood, early 19th C . .	**250.00**
Cup and Saucer, 2 x 3″ cup, 5½″ saucer, Jasperware, deep blue, white classical figures, rope handle, Wedgwood only, early 19th C	**175.00**
Dish, 10⅜″, oval, Caneware, chenille border, imp Wedgwood, early 19th C	**110.00**
Figure, bulldog, 4¾″, black Basalt, standing, amber glass eyes, modeled by Hubert Light, imp Wedgwood, c1914	**300.00**
Flower Holder, 5¾ x 4¼″d, Jasperware, pierced lift off lid, light blue, white classical dancing ladies, raised white leaves on bolted foot, imp Wedgwood only	**350.00**
Fruit Stand, 12⅜″, rectangular, flaring foot, Caneware, 2 foliate scroll	

handles imp Wedgwood, early 19th C **170.00**

Game Pie Dish, liner and cover, 7½"l, Caneware, applied ivy border, applied handle on cover with rosettes, imp Wedgwood, early 19th C **250.00**

Ginger Jar, cov, 11", Dragon Lustre, mottled light blue, gold dragons, gilded, mkd Wedgwood **690.00**

Honeypot with attached saucer, 5 x 4", Basalt, chinoiserie enameled floral decor, glazed interior, Wedgwood **550.00**

Inkwell, 2⅝"d, Capri Ware, floral decor **625.00**

Jardiniere, 3½ x 4", dark blue, lion heads, white mythological figures and grapevines sgd Wedgwood, England **165.00**

Jug, 7½ x 5"d, red, black and white winged sphinx and phoenix bird, mkd Wedgwood, Sold only by Woolard and Hattersley Cambridge, 1854 .... **595.00**

Letter Box, 5 x 7½"w x 4"d, Regency, brass and classical cameos .. **575.00**

Match Holder and Striker, 3½ x 4¾"d, round, Majolica, white and green top, blue and brown base, sgd Wedgwood **80.00**

Medallion, Voltaire, 2⅛", Jasperware, dark blue, white bust, modeled by William Hackwood, gilt frame, imp Voltaire, Wedgwood and Bentley, c1778 .... **450.00**

Mug, 2 x 2"d, 3 handled, Butterfly Lustre, blue, tan and pink with gold butterflies, coral inside, sgd Wedgwood Lustre **195.00**

Oil Lamp, 5⅛", Rosso Antico, flat cover, black relief Pegasus, zodiac sign and beadwork border, glazed interior, imp Wedgwood, c1810 .. **500.00**

Pie Dish, cov, 8", Caneware, basketweave, incised, c1895 .... **675.00**

Plaques
3 x 8½"l, rectangular, green, 10 figures and 2 horses, sgd Wedgwood **220.00**
6", oval, green, white classical lady, Wedgwood only **180.00**

Plates
9¾", Moonlight Lustre, mottled deep lavender pink, mkd Wedgwood, c1810 .... **175.00**
10⅝", Fairyland Lustre, center scene, boys on bridge, pixie in boat and bird, wide gold border with flower, fairies and pixies designs, mottled deep blue back side, mkd Wedgwood Fairyland Lustre **1,850.00**

Salad Bowl, dark blue, frieze in relief, classical female figure, offering to Venus, SP rim band, imp Wedgwood, J, 1870 .... **125.00**

Spill Vase, 4 x 2"d, cylinder, Jasperware, deep blue, white classical ladies, Wedgwood only **100.00**

Sucrier, 5½"w, Terra Cotta with Egyptian motif and alligator finial . **825.00**

Syrup, 7", Jasperware, dark blue, white classical figures, imp Wedgwood, c1870 .... **70.00**

Tea Set, 3 pcs, Jasperware, yellow, black classical figures, Wedgwood made in England **1,200.00**

Teapot, 4 x 6", Caneware, wicker pattern, sheaf of wheat cover and knob **450.00**

Vases
6", Caneware, cupid as "The Four Seasons," floral arabesques, ribbed circular pedestal foot, imp Wedgwood, c1815 ...... **225.00**
8⅜", ovoid, shouldered, Fairyland Lustre, elves, fairies, deities in watery landscape, Portland Vase mark/Wedgwood, England, Z 2968 .... **800.00**
8⅜ x 6"d, flared, pedestal foot, Dragon Lustre, mottled blue, gold dragon, inside MOP, mkd Wedgwood Dragon Lustre **495.00**
11", trumpet shape, black Basalt, vines and symbols, Wedgwood only **450.00**
11¾ x 5¾"d, trumpet shape, Hummingbird Lustre, mottled blue with colored hummingbirds trimmed in gold, inside top mottled flame lustre, mkd Wedgwood, Z 5294 .... **475.00**

WELLER

In 1873 Samuel A. Weller opened a small factory in Fultonham, Ohio, to produce stoneware jars and flower pots. In 1882 he moved his facilities to Zanesville and in 1893 formed a partnership with W. A. Long. Within the year, they began to produce "Lonhuda," a shaded brown ware with decoration underglaze.

After Long left the company in 1895, Weller continued to make similar art ware under the name "Louwelsa," and a large variety of other art pottery lines. By 1915 Weller claimed to be the largest pottery in the world.

At the end of World War I, many prestige lines were discontinued and Weller concentrated on more commercial wares. During the Depression the art lines became even less elaborate. Even though business prospered again briefly during World War II, foreign competition forced the factory to close in 1948. Many lines were offered by Weller and it is impossible to list all here. Most of the pottery was marked "Weller," either impressed, incised or rubber stamped; some art pottery was also artist signed.

Planter, Souevo, hanging, 6½", $165.00.

Baskets
Eocean, 6½", high gloss gray to black ground, floral	150.00
Woodcraft, 8½", handled, large acorn	125.00

Bowls
Coppertone, 2 x 10½", lilypads, applied frog on edge	125.00
Glendale, flower frog, birds and nests, 16"	275.00

Candlesticks
Claywood, 5", panels of flowers, dark brown wash over clay, pr	125.00
Roma, 9", triple candelabra, cream with pink flowers, pr	150.00

Ewers
Dickensware 2nd line, 11½", matte green background with carved fish, sgd E.L. Pickens	550.00
L'Art Nouveau, 14½", Art Nouveau poppies and full figure of woman, block letters WELLER	300.00
Louwelsa, 9", floral with silver overlay, sgd Mitchell	650.00
Louwelsa, 10", primroses, mkd Louwelsa in half circle seal	175.00

Figurals
Dog, "Cocker Spaniel," 10½ x 14", mkd with ink stamp	800.00
Muskota, 7", cats on fence, block letters WELLER	400.00
"Pop-eye" Dog, 4", black and white, Weller in script	175.00

Jardinieres
Cameo Jewel, 8", lt. gray shading to dark gray, applied jewels and womens heads, block impressed WELLER	195.00
Dickensware 1st line, 9", dk. green ground, yellow morning glories, sgd Dickensware in half circle seal	350.00
Rosemont, 7", glossy black glaze with bluebird on branch	150.00
Woodcraft, 9½", tree trunk, figural squirrel and woodpecker on sides, no mark	275.00

Jardinieres and Pedestals
Flemish, 33½" h, twisted tree trunk base, jardiniere with apples	650.00
Forest, 26" h, block impressed Weller	475.00

Mugs
Blue Louwelsa, 5½", slip painted blackberries, no mark, artist sgd	350.00
Etna, 5½", shaded gray to green, purple grapes and trailing vines, hand sgd Weller	150.00
Louwelsa, 6½", dog portrait, mkd Weller, Louwelsa in half circle seal, sgd Ferrell	650.00

Pitcher, Zona, 8", kingfisher in color, half kiln ink stamp Weller — 175.00

Plate, Burntwood, 12", bisque with brown wash, bird on branch and foliage, no mark — 195.00

Tankards
Aurelian, 12½", brown glaze, hand brushed yellow ground with ear of corn, artist E. Roberts	450.00
Dickensware 3rd line, 12½", molded full figure of man in long coat and hat, grays, mkd Weller by hand, sgd LM	350.00
Woodcraft, 12½", molded tree trunk with 3 foxes, no mark	300.00

Tobacco Jar, Dickensware 2nd line, 6½", Irishman, mkd Weller by hand — 450.00

Umbrella Stand, Flemish, 21½", panels of vines and pink morning glories, blended brown and green ground, block impressed Weller — 350.00

Vases
Barcelona, 8", handled, horizontal ribbing, stylized floral motif in red and green, tan ground	150.00

Dickensware 2nd line, 12", incised portrait of cavelier, Dickensware seal, artist sgd Pickens **350.00**

Eoceau, 8½", shaded lt. gray to dark, colorful cluster of flowers, artist sgd **200.00**

Etna, 4½", cream shaded to gray, lizard on side **175.00**

Floretta, 5½", 4 sided Art Nouveau shape, blown out grapes mkd Weller Floretta by hand . . **145.00**

Glendale, 8½", molded design of 2 parakeets on branch, ink stamped Weller **250.00**

Hudson, 6½", white and decorated, white background, hp bird on branch, bee in flight **500.00**

Hudson, 9½", handles, bulbous shape, pastel colors with hp Iris, artist sgd Pillsbury . . . -. . . . **375.00**

LaSa, 9", Palm trees in irid reds and golds, sgd Weller, LaSa on side **225.00**

Louwelsa, 5", brown glaze floral, Louwelsa half circle seal **95.00**

Louwelsa, 10", handled, brown glaze with nasturtiums, artist sgd Adams **250.00**

Molded etched matte, 14", matte orange background, green vines and red berries, block impressed WELLER **300.00**

Sicard, 6", handled, irid purples and reds, floral, sgd Weller Sicard in design **450.00**

Stellar, 6", blue ground with hand decoration of stars mkd Weller pottery in script **225.00**

Xenia, 7½", matte glaze dark green ground, Art Nouveau panels of maroon flowers, lt. green leaves and vines **250.00**

Wallpockets

Glendale, 7½", multicolored molded bird with nest of babies, ink stamp Weller **200.00**

L'Art Nouveau, 6½", blown-out floral, matte green and yellow glaze, no mark **150.00**

Sydonia, 9½", four fluted spouts, mottled blue glaze **95.00**

"U.S. Mail," 7½", cream glaze, no mark **195.00**

Woodcraft, 9 x 8½", entwined branches with figural bird on nest, block impressed WELLER **250.00**

WHIELDON   WHIELDON

The Staffordshire potter, Thomas Whieldon, established his shop in 1740. He is best known for his mottled ware, molded in forms of vegetables, fruits and leaves. Both Josiah

Spode and Josiah Wedgwood were connected with him, in different capacities, during these years.

Whieldon ware is a generic term, because his items were never marked and other potters made similar type of items. The ware is agate-tortoise shell earthenware, in limited shades of green, brown, blue and yellow, usually utilitarian items such as dinner ware, plates, etc., but they also made figurines, and other decorative type items.

Tea Caddy, 4", Cauliflower Pattern, $550.00.

Coffee Pot, cov, 9½", brown streaked, applied grape vines, grapes, blossoms and leaves, 3 applied leaves on cover, bird knop, 3 lion's mask and paw feet, gilt, c1760 . . . . **3,410.00**

Creamer, 4¾", Cauliflower pat **575.00**

Dishes

9½", oval, molded teardrop border, streaked in green, yellow, gray and brown, c1765, pr **500.00**

15¾", molded teardrop pattern border, splashed green, gray, brown and yellow, reverse in brown, c1760 . . . . **990.00**

Tea Caddy, 7", square, tall sides, arched shoulder, molded flowering trees, gilt, green edges, c1760 . . **475.00**

Teapot, 9¼", pineapple shape, molded spout and handle, green finial, c1760 . . . . **1,320.00**

Tureen, cov, 6¾", melon shape, oval, molded leaf design, green stock finial, c1760 . . . . **2,640.00**

Wall Pocket, 6½", putti's mask, scroll molded, brown, green and yellow, 18th C **550.00**

WHITE PATTERNED IRONSTONE

Ironstone is a heavy earthenware first patented by Charles Mason, Staffordshire, England, in the late 18th century. The range of patterns seems endless; a few better-known ones dominate the market. The earliest patterns were natural motifs: florals, berries, vegetables and geometrics; "Sydenham Shape," "Washington Shape," etc. Later patterns from 1870–1890 tend to be on the plainer side, e.g., "Cable and Ring." Some all white ironstone patterns were decorated with touches of color, such as "Ceres," with gold, green, or blue, (known as "Blue Wheat"). Some patterns were all white, with lustre decor, such as "Lustre Sprig" and "Lustre Pinwheel." There is much white ironstone that is not marked at all.

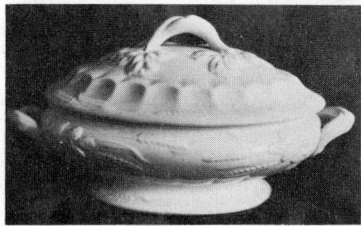

Tureen, vegetable, 11½", wheat and leaf pattern, marked "Stone China (W. Taylor) Hanley", $68.00.

Bread Plate, Daily Bread, Onondaga Pottery Co	62.00
Butter Dish, liner and cov, Octagon, T. & R. Boote	65.00
Coffee Pot, Ceres, Elsmore & Forster	125.00
Coffee Set, cov pot, creamer and cov sugar, Ribbed Raspberry 'N Bloom	200.00
Creamers	
Gothic, J. Edwards	48.00
Huron Shape, Adams, 1858	42.00
New York Shape, J. Clementson, 1858	48.00
Creamer and Sugar, Fig, Wedgwood	110.00
Cups and Saucers	
Ceres, Elsmore & Forster	26.00
Grape & Medallion, Challinor	35.00
Ewers	
Senate Shape, T.&R. Boote	38.00
Severes Shape, J. Clementson	45.00
Hot Toddy Bowl with 8 matching Cups, 4 qt, Ribbed Bud, 2 handled, J. W. Panhurst	385.00

Hot Toddy Cup, Ribbed Raspberry 'N Bloom, J. & G Meakin	18.00
Pitcher, Girard Shape, J. Ridgway Bates & Co., 1857	58.00
Plates	
Ceres, Elsmore & Forster, 6½"	20.00
Corn, Davenport, 10½"	20.00
Octagon, T. & R. Boote, 10"	20.00
Prairie Flowers, Powell & Bishop, 8½"	15.00
Ribbed Raspberry 'N Bloom, J. & G. Meakin, 9"	13.00
Platters	
Baltic, Bowers	50.00
Rolling Star, octagonal, J. Edwards	45.00
Punch Bowl, 6 qt, Adriatic, scalloped edge	325.00
Relish Dishes	
Panelled Grape, J. F.	30.00
Parish Shape, Alcock	16.00
Ribbed Raspberry 'N Bloom, J. & G. Meakin	38.00
Sydenham Shape, T. & R. Boote, 1853	45.00
Wheat, J. & G. Meakin	18.00
Sauce Tureen, Wheat, Goddard	95.00
Soup Tureen, cov, Little Palm, T. & R. Boote	145.00
Sugar Bowls, covered	
Arched Forget-Me-Not, Elsmore & Forster	42.00
Grape Octagon, E. Challinor & Co	44.00
President Shape, J. Edwards	48.00
Sydenham Shape, T. & R. Boote	60.00
Syrup, melon ribbed, grape and vine, Anthony Shaw	72.00
Teapots	
Fig, Wedgwood	125.00
Sydenham Shape, T. & R. Boote	145.00
Toothbrush Holder, Primrose, S. T. & Co, 4¾"	17.50
Vegetable Dish, covered	
Ceres, Elsmore & Forster	80.00
Wheat & Blackberry, Meakin	75.00
Vegetable Dish, open, Wheat in the Meadow, Powell & Bishop	25.00
Wash Bowl and Pitcher, Ceres, Elsmore & Forster	155.00

WILLOW WARE

This popular ware derives its name from a design which is in the Chinese tradition. Willow ware had its inspiration from early Canton ware brought to Europe from China in the 16th century. An early willow transfer pattern, said to be the first ever transfer-printed, is credited to either Thomas Tucker or his apprentice Thomas Minton, both of whom worked at Caughley Pottery in the Staffordshire district of England.

The first (1780) under-glaze transfer design did not contain all the Chinese legend motifs found in the later "standard" willow pattern developed in 1810 by Josiah Spode. The "standard" willow pattern has several distinctive features—a willow tree, two pagodas, a rail fence with finials, two birds and a three-arch bridge with three figures crossing it.

In the late 18th century, Willow Ware was made in England and Germany. By the 19th century it was produced in the United States, France, Japan, Holland and Ireland; it is still produced today in many countries.

Most commonly produced in blue; occasional pieces can be found in pink and green.

For additional information refer to *Willow Pattern China* by Veryl Marie Worth.

See Warman's *Americana & Collectibles* for an expanded listing of Willow ware.

Platter, 10¾ x 13½", W. Ridgway & Co. England, $40.00.

Bowl, 6¼", polychrome, Maddock .	20.00
Butter Dish, cov, 6½", white, emb rim, Ironstone	75.00
Cake Plate, handled, 9½"	30.00
Creamer, 1911, Buffalo Pottery	30.00
Cup and Saucer, 3 gold feet, trim, Davenport	35.00
Demitasse, gold trim, Adderley	20.00
Gravy Boat, underplate, pink, Allerton	38.00
Plates	
9", Ridgway	18.00
10", luncheon, sectional, mkd Willow August Hansager New York, made in England, potters mark "C"	27.00
Platters	
9½", pink	32.00
13", round, Old Adams	45.00
Sugar, cov, handles, 6½", brown, J. Dimmock Ironstone, c1862	85.00
Teapot, 6", polychrome, Maddock .	85.00

WITCH BALLS

A witch ball simply is a hollow sphere of colored or multicolored glass. There are various myths surrounding the origin and purpose of the witch ball. Some say they were displayed by the fireplace to catch demon spirits as they descended the chimney. They could then be taken outside for cleaning. Others contend they were used to store salt by the chimney to keep it dry.

In all probability a witch ball was a glassmaker's whimsey, used strictly for decorative purposes atop an unfilled flower vase.

Don't confuse witch balls with Christmas tree ornaments, target balls, floats, or early glass fire extinguishers. Witch balls come in a variety of sizes. They can not be attributed to one specific glass maker or company.

Amber Glass
4", white loopings, matching 4¾" ribbed baluster form holder	400.00
4½", rough pontil	110.00
Cranberry Glass, 4½"	60.00

4¼", Nailsea type, pale blue, white loopings, $95.00.

Nailsea Type
6", clear, white loopings, matching 12" pedestal holder	450.00
9½" holder, clear, alternating pink and white loopings, Pittsburgh Glass	350.00
13½ x 6½" d, ball and holder, clear, white loopings, early New Jersey glass	700.00
Spatter Glass, 4½", white with red, pink and green flecks	95.00

WOODENWARES

Many utilitarian household objects and farm implements were made of wood. Although they were used heavily, these implements were made of the strongest woods and well taken care of by their owners. This category serves as a catchall for wood objects which do not fit into other categories in our book.

See *Warman's Americana & Collectibles* for an expanded listing of Woodenware.

Apple Corer, 22 x 13½", made near Harrisburg, Pa, $175.00.

Bill Sorter, 11½ x 24"w, from country store, semi-circular, pine, red, 2 rows of slots 110.00
Bowls
    4 x 11½ x 19½", rectangular, hand hewn 100.00
    5¼ x 17"d, ash burl 250.00
Boxes
    6¼ x 6½ x 11¼"l, dovetailed, base and lid molding, red and yellow graining 160.00
    12⅝ h x 10½ w x 8½" d, spice, hanging, walnut, dovetailed, arched crest, slanted lift lid, dovetailed drawer with 4 compartments 325.00
Bucket, pickle 70.00
Butter Paddles
    9½", maple, dark finish, peacock head handle 275.00
    10", curly maple, chip carving at end of handle 95.00
Butter Print, 4¼ x 7", rectangular, cased, primitive carved sheaf . . . 110.00
Churn, 20", drum shape, stave construction, iron crank 95.00

Cookie Board, 3⅝ x 4¾", four sections, hand carved, fruit and 2 horses 75.00
Cutting Board, 24 x 8¾", pine, chip carved, circular crest 165.00
Dipper, 12¼"l, treen with pouring spout 175.00
Grain Shovel, 55"l, made from one piece 85.00
Hat Block, size 7⅛, walnut, 2 pcs, refinished 35.00
Inkwell, 1¾ x 2⅝", turned, glass insert, black, gilt decor and applied cadeuseus 72.00
Jar, cov, 11 x 14"d, bulbous, turned, wire bale, wood handle, varnish finish 2,750.00
Kraut Cutter, 20½ x 7", poplar, stylized heart 160.00
Kraut Stomper, 24"l, turned oak, white scrubbed finish 10.00
Knife Tray, 9 x 12", birdseye maple, cut out handle 75.00
Mortar, 6¼"h, primitive 80.00
Mortise Scribe, 8¼", mahogany, brass fitting, stamped S. Hawks, W. Johnson 25.00
Pastry Cutter, 6"l, turned handle . . 35.00
Porringer, 1¾ x 3½"d, birdseye burl, 2 handles, dark lacquer finish . . . 200.00
Potato Masher, 11" 12.00
Scoop, 9¼", walnut with burl, early 20th C 110.00
Seed Dispenser with tin scoop, 14½ x 6¼"d, hanging, poplar, dark finish, slanted lid, 5 interior bins, dispensing opening in base has hinged flap 70.00
Smoothing Board, 25"l, carved horse handle, relief carved compass stars, flowers, chip carved borders, orange and blue paint, "BMD", 1840 . . . . 325.00
Spoon, 5¼", maple, stylized bird head handle 125.00
String Holder, 6", turned, ftd 20.00
Untensil Rack, 37", 6 wrought iron hooks on cut out board, primitive 110.00
Wall Pocket, 15h x 6¾w x 3½"d, two compartments, blue 110.00
Wash Board, 13½ x 7", sewer pipe insert 170.00

WORLD'S FAIRS AND EXPOSITIONS

Almost everyone has visited one of the many World's Fairs held in the United States. Obtaining a souvenir is one important aspect

of the visit. The amount and variety of these souvenirs is endless. Collectors are advised to focus one fair, or one type of item such as ashtrays, plates, guide books, etc.

Prices still are modest. A sizable collection can be assembled for a small amount of money. Because so many examples exist for each item, try to buy those in very good to mint condition.

See *Warman's Americana & Collectibles* for an expanded listing of World's Fairs and Exposition items.

1876, Philadelphia, Centennial
Booklet, views, 5 x 3", tortoise shell covers, gold edge emb, silver dollar size emblem in gold on front and back covers, 11 stone litho prints, color borders, fold out map in back, by Philip Frey 27.50
Frosted glass hand, 7½" h, holding bouquet of flowers, "Centennial 1876" inscribed at base 24.00

Columbian Exposition, spoon, bowl with Administration Bldg in relief, ending in head of Columbus, dates 1593–1492, Standard Silverplate, $25.00.

1893, Chicago, Columbian
Belt Buckle, 3½ x 2½", Columbus landing, brass, back mkd "Tiffany Studios, New York, official souvenir 1893" 60.00
Clock, 12" h, cast metal, shape of Santa Maria, Columbus on deck, hand on world globe, Indians cowering before him, base of 2 large fish, shell in center, "1492" on shell, clock made by Robert Johns, Chicago, not working 75.00
Hot Plate, 6½", black transfer print of the Fisheries Bldg, advertisement "Compliments of W. S. Carlisle & Son, Columbus, O" in script 22.00

1901, Buffalo, Pan-American Exposition
Broadside, 6¼ x 12½", New York Central & West Shore Railroads, advertising McKinley's visit on September 5, gives activities, other information 225.00
Rosebowl, porcelain, Union of the Hemispheres design on front, gold trim 34.00

1904, St. Louis
Button, celluloid, 1½", set in metal wreath, woman blowing trumpet, 1903 in sky, three ribbons, one reads "Dedication Exposition St. Louis" 15.00
Tray, tin, 4½ x 3", advertising for Jergens Uncle Sam Tar Soap, Palace of Liberal Arts 12.00

1915, San Francisco
Button and ribbon, celluloid, Chinese & American flags, ribbon reads Chinese Students Day, PPIE, Aug 4, 1915 . . . . 10.00

1933, Chicago, Center of Progress
Dish, 5", gold plated, 12 scenes from fair around edge, Century Art Works 14.00
Souvenir Booklet, *Official Pictures Of A Century Of Progress Exposition,* Kaufmann & Fabry Co., 8 x 10", 50 pgs 6.00
Umbrella, 2' l, red, blue art deco swirls, handled mkd Chicago 1933, wood, paper 35.00

1939, New York
Paperweight, 4½", glass ball with Trylon and Perisphere, snows when turned upside down, on stand 25.00
Pennant, cloth, 17" l, orange . . . 8.00

1939, San Francisco
Banner, 22", silk, red, yellow, black, white, sq, full view vignettes of fair, official logo 9.00

1962, Seattle
Pin, ladies, 3", shape of Space Needle, orig card 5.00
Tray, 11", round metal, blue, different attractions shown 6.50

1964, New York
Official Guide Book, 200 pgs 5.00

WORLD WAR II COLLECTIBLES

Warman's Americana & Collectibles, 1st Edition, contains 51 listings in this c _gory; see also page xii.

YELLOW WARE

Yellow Ware is a fairly heavy earthenware of varying weight and strength. Not to be confused with English Yellow-Glazed Earthenware; Yellow Ware, when broken, will show yellow completely through, not just a yellow overglaze. Pieces of this ware vary in color from a rich pumpkin to lighter shades with more tan than yellow. Kitchen pieces are most prevalent although plates, nappies and custard cups can also be found. There are both English and American examples available; however, the English pieces appear to have had additional ingredients added to the earthenware to make a harder body.

Derbyshire and Sharp's were foremost among English manufacturers and the Bennington, Vermont, factory was one of the first among American producers. Yellow Ware is widely collected and used. Prices of this ware are rising.

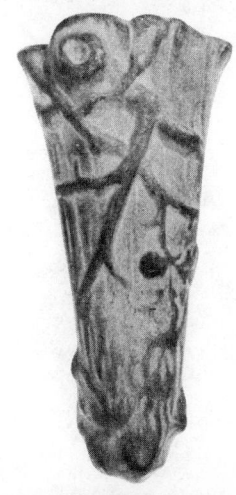

Bowl, 4¾ h, 11⅝″ d, $65.00.

Bowls
4¾ x 7¼″ d, brown and blue sponge spatter, swirled ribs, scalloped rim	100.00
6½ x 14″ d, tan and white stripes	75.00
7¼″, cov, side handle, brown sponge decor	32.00
Bundt Mold, 9½″, c1860	55.00
Chamber Pot, 5½ x 5¾″ d, white band, brown stripes	52.00
Churn, 2⅞″, miniature, Rockingham glaze, wooden lid and dasher	65.00
Compote, 7¾ x 10½″ d, running blue glaze around rim	160.00
Creamer, 3½″, emb, dark brown and cream design	25.00
Dog Dish, "Dog" in brown	52.00

Figures
Dog, 10¼″, seated, Rockingham glaze	195.00
Lions, 8¼ h x 15″ l, reclining, brown running glaze on heads and manes, oval bases, pr	700.00
Food Chopper, oak handle, dtd Dec. 1877	45.00

Jar, cov, 5 x 6½″, white bands, brown stripes	85.00
Match Box, 4½ x 3½ x 3″, molded shell decor on sides and lid, c1860	50.00
Mug with lid, 5⅝″, Mocha ware, stripes in brown and white	90.00

Pie Plates
8″, coggled edge, clear glaze interior	48.00
11¼″	45.00
Pitcher, 6¼″, splashes of running blue	50.00
Rolling Pin, 14¾″ l, turned wooden handle	130.00
Salt, 2⅛ x 3″ d, ftd, white band with brown seaweed decor	65.00
Sugar Bowl, cov, 4⅛″ h, white bands with brown seaweed decor and blue stripes	140.00
Turk's Head Food Mold, 3¾ x 8½″, swirled ribs, dripping brown	40.00

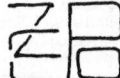

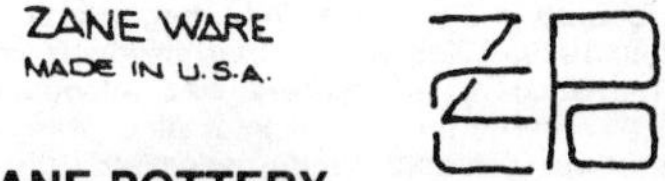

ZANE WARE
MADE IN U.S.A.

ZANE POTTERY

Adam Reed and Harry McClelland bought the Peters and Reed Pottery located in Zanes-

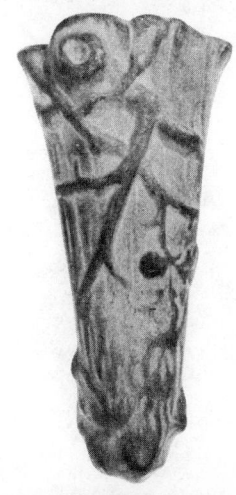

Wall pocket, Moss Aztec, 8¼″, $35.00.

ville, Ohio in 1921. The firm continued production of garden wares and introduced several new art lines: "Sheen," "Powder Blue," "Crystalline" and "Drip." The factory was sold in 1941 to Lawton Gonder.
See PETERS AND REED and GONDER

Bowl, 5", blue & brown	30.00
Figure, 10⅛", cat, black, green eyes	500.00
Jardiniere, 14½", 2 handles, variegated green semi-matte glaze, Montene	125.00
Vases	
6½", chromal scene, stilt chip on bottom	75.00
8", blue and green glaze	230.00

Bowl, 6½", fluted edge, mottled blue	35.00
Figure, bulldog, 6⅝", clear glaze with dark blue and tan sponged spots	425.00
Jardiniere, 9", brown and gold glaze	125.00
Plate, 4½", applied floral decor ...	20.00
Tankard, floral decor, artist sgd ...	300.00
Vases	
7", bulbous, handled, circled collared neck with outward flaring rim, pansy decor, olive to brown left to right glaze, marked La Moro	125.00
10½", glazed floral decor, marked La Moro	135.00

LA MORO

ZANESVILLE POTTERY

Zanesville Art Pottery, one of several potteries located in Zanesville, Ohio, began production in 1900. A line of utilitarian products was first produced. Art pottery was introduced shortly thereafter. The major line was La Moro—handpainted and decorated under glaze. The impressed block print mark La Moro appears on the high glazed and matte glazed decorated ware. The firm was bought by S.A. Weller in 1920 and became known as Weller Plant No. 3.

Vase, 8¾", $300.00.

ZSOLNAY POTTERY

Zsolnay is a Hungarian ceramic ware. Vilmos Zsolnay (1828–1900) took over his brother's factory located in Pe'cs, Hungary, in the mid 1800s. Zsolnay's son, Miklos, became manager in 1899.

Characteristically, the ware possesses a cream colored ground and is highly ornamental and is glazed. "Eosin" glaze, a deep rich play of colors, reminiscent of Tiffany's iridescent wares, was developed by Zsolnay in 1820. This technique was awarded the Gold Medal at the 1900 World Exhibit in Paris.

No trademark was used in the beginning. From 1878 on, the blue mark depicting the five towers of the Cathedral at Pe'cs was used. The letters, "T. J. M." incorporated into the other known trademark, are reported to be the initials of Miklos Zsolnay's three children.

Of more recent origin are the iridescent glazed figurines appearing on the market. These figurines initially sold for small sums; however, after catching the attention of Zsolnay collectors, they are beginning to increase in value.

Bowls	
9¾" l x 8" w, fan shape, rolled in sides, scrolled handle, reticulated inner decor, cobalt with chrysanthemums, gold trim	315.00
11¼", boat shape, gold, reticulated	125.00
Oval, double wall, pierced flowers	350.00

Figure polar bears, 4¾ x 7½″, irid purple and green, $220.00.

Dish, 8½ x 7½″, fan shape, beige, gold, pink, fold over, reticulated borders, steeple mark . . . . — 180.00
Ewer, 7½″, cream, yellow and beige decor, gold around base, gold reticulated band at neck, ornate handle . . . . — 95.00
Figure, nude, 11″, 4½″ w plinth, standing near pedestal holding vase, clothing, removing last garment, irid blue and green . . . . . . — 265.00

Jug, 13¼″, floriform, green and blue irid lustre, Mack, sgd with medallion mark in relief, No 5517M . . . — 95.00
Mug, 4½″, irid blue lustre . . . . — 75.00
Plaque, 10″, portrait, gold foil ground — 250.00
Plate, 8″, cobalt blue, purple orchard — 65.00
Ring Tree, 3½″, irid gold . . . . — 72.00
Urn, 15″ cov, double wall, reticulated, flared footing, ball base, flared slender neck, olive green, white, yellow and brown, gold trim, gold mark, imp . . . . — 450.00
Vases
  5½″, ovoid, irid red, textured alligator finish . . . . — 135.00
  5½″, ovoid, irid blue and green, applied pieces in flagstone fashion with thumbprint impressions — 170.00
  6″, bulbous, ribbed, blue lustre . . — 85.00
  6½″, cobalt blue and gold, reticulated, double walled, steeple mark . . . . — 350.00
  9″, Art Nouveau, reticulated rim . — 595.00
  9½″, baluster shape, ftd, wide shaped handles, reticulated, gilt ground, lustre glaze and ivory flowers, printed factory mark . . — 130.00
  Applied floral decor, blue, c1917 . — 195.00

PHOTO CREDITS

We wish to thank those who permitted us to photograph objects in their possession. Unfortunately, we are unable to identify the sources for all of our pictures; nevertheless, we are deeply appreciative for all who contributed to this and past editions, and to the 1st edition of *Warman's Americana & Collectibles*.

California: Fresno, Robert L. Cox, Derl W. Keen, Fulton's Folly Antique Mall; San Diego, Bob Browns; San Francisco, Great American Collective; Woodlake, Cairn's Antiques. **Connecticut**: New Milford, Dave & Robin Wheeler; Southport, Webb's of Southport Collectibles; Torrington, Rick & Linda Ronalter; Anthony Prestino. **Florida**: Cape Coral, Linda Brown, Lois Antiques, Millie Hall Antiques; Miami, Three Centuries Antiques. **Illinois**: Chicago, Linda Bernstein; Springfield, Riverside Antiques. **Indiana**: Jeffersonville, Wilson Antiques;

Maine: Damariscutta, Patricia Anne Reed. **Maryland**: Annapolis, Theriault's; Baltimore, Norma Hogarth, Pat & Mike Muhl, Marge Wolf; Elkton, Golden Era Antiques; Stevensville, Eastern Shore Antiques. **Massachusetts**: Beverly, Rita Walker; Hyannis Port, Richard A. Bourne Co., Inc.; Leominister, Viola St. John; Melrose, Alma Libby Antiques. **Michigan**: Fife Lake, Ron Fritz. **Minnesota**: Minneapolis, Temple's Antiques. **Missouri**: Kansas City, Avant-Garde; Springfield, Jo Cunningham.

New Hampshire: Salem, B & B Antiques & Collectibles. **New Jersey**: Blackwood, Bruce D. Horton; Burlington, Don Fisher; Buttzville, Charles Ranallo; Cedarville, Mrs. Evelyn Graves; New Brunswick, The Odd Couples Curios; Paterson, Edward W. Leach; Toms River, Shelley, Norman & Phyllis Galinkin; Woodbury, Daphne Majewski.

PHOTO CREDITS (Continued)

New York: Baldwin, Rear Coach Antiques; Binghamton, Emmory Prior, Oxen Hill Antiques; Canton, Peter Lively; Carmel, Bob Cahn; Corning, Blake's Antiques; East Aurora, Kitty Turgeon, Roycroft Inn; Fishers, Granny's Garret; Ft. Lee, Donna Davis; Glencove, V & J Ferrante; Harrison, Joseph Pinto, Yesterday's Treasures; High Falls, Myron Cohen Antiques; Johnson City, The Epergne; Merrick, Philip Chasen; New York, Christies, Sotheby's; Phoenix, Roger Butler; Pine Bush, Richard Miller; Poughkeepsie, Tony & Jacki Greeco; Richville, Mr. & Mrs. Paul Thompson; Riverhead, Lyon's Den; Rochester, Green Door Antiques, Rosemarie Schickler, Miriam S. Rogachefsky, Young's Oldies; Sidney, Bill & Hope Meyer; Stamford, Connie's Antiques; Staten Island, Brian Windsor; Wappingers Falls, Steve Fisch; Wellsville, Shirley A. Neu; Yonkers, Glass Menagerie.

North Carolina: Cary, G & L Collectibles. **Ohio**: Canfield, Theodore A. Parent; Oregon, Abe Walp; Worthington, Betty Powell. **Oklahoma**: Oklahoma City, Brookhaven Antiques, Richard Lilies, David Weaver. **Pennsylvania**: Adamstown, Dottie Freeman, Allan Teal; Alburtis, Helen DeLong; Allentown, Barby Sales, Sue & Henry Lehrich, Dot and Jake Makosky, Plants Alive, Arlene Rabin; Bernsville, Blue Marsh Antiques & Gift Shop; Bethlehem, Thomas Sage; Biglerville, Attic Antiques; Bryn Mawr, George Lyn Ross; Carneige, Old Glory Antiques; Clifford Thomas Antiques; Cogan Station, Barbara & Dan Munsell, Roan Auction; Coopersburg, Neil & Clodogh Watring; Dillsburg, Mickey's Antiques; Elkins Park, Carolyn Sunstein; Fallingston, Harry L. Seibel; Gap, Burgess Antiques; Honey Brook, Neil C. Lammey; Lancaster, Ruth & Ben Stoltzfus; Manheim, James S. Ditzler; Nazareth, Joseph Leabold; Oley, Mrs. Lena Eyrich; Philadelphia, George F. MacDonald, Irene Roberts; Pittsburgh, Paul Elm; Pottstown, Gail Grimley, Bertil Hogstrom; Quakertown, L & E Antiques; Reading, De Santis Stamp and Postcard Co.; Schnecksville, Bob & Joan Coad; Slatington, John Pfeiffer; Whitehall, Mrs. Elaine Pacala; Zionsville, Rinsland Americana Mail Auction.

Vermont: Cavendish, Sigourney's Antiques; Fairhaven, Steve Smith, Country Bumpkin Antiques. **Virginia**: Charlottesville, Rose Valley Antiques.

ANTIQUE SHOWS AND FLEA MARKETS

Among the many antique shows and flea markets visited by the editorial staff, we wish to extend special thanks to the following:

England: Gray's Inn (London), Porto Bello Road Market (London), Camden Passage (London), Alexander Palace Antiques Show (London).

Florida: D. S. Clarke Miami Antiques Show (Bud & Muriel Maron); Miami Beach Antique Show (Ray Grover and Lou Baron). **Illinois**: Arlington Park Race Track (Charles Wheatley). **New York**: Rochester Antiques Show (Elouise Stalk). **Pennsylvania**: Buckingham Antiques Show (Frederick & Schwartz); Great Eastern Antique Shows (Dan Schantz); Hamburg Antiques Market (Janet Schick); Kutztown Extravanganzas (Renninger's Promotions); Pottstown Antique Shows (Dealer's Association of Montgomery County).

PRICE LIST CREDITS

We wish to thank the following people who cooperated with us by sending us price lists and other useful information.

Arizona: Phoenix, The Crystal Cat; Springerville, Doris Gallow. **California**: Fallbrook, Lois J. Misiewicz. **Colorado**: Golden, The Foss Co. **Hawaii**: Honolulu, Delta International. **Illinois**: Niles Chicago, The Bradford Exchange; Rockford, John R. Danis; Peotone, Kathy Wojoiechowski; Winnetka, Carrow & McNerney. **Iowa**: Eldridge, Dick Grieves. **Kansas**: Emporia, Ione E. Hinshaw; Overland Park, Montague Sales. **Michigan**: Lansing, Margo Rudd. **Minnesota**: Duluth, Laneve's Antiques. **New Jersey**: Sussex, Al Hanak; Tenafly, Florel; Westfield, Milt Steinfield. **New York**: Albertson, Mrs. Marion Cohen. **North Carolina**: Charlotte, Little Hundred Gallery. **Oklahoma**: Jones, Wood N' Things. **Oregon**: Grants Pass, Antique Junction. **Virginia**: Arlington, Ann McDonald.

INDEX

SEND ME THE FOLLOWING WARMAN PRICE GUIDES:

_____ **Warman's Antiques and Their Prices, 18th edition,** $10.95 + $1.50 p/h (Total $12.45) $ _____

_____ **Warman's Americana & Collectibles, 1st edition,** $12.95 + $1.50 p/h (Total $14.45) $ _____

_____ Add my name to your mailing list and notify me of future editions.

☐ Check or money order enclosed. Sorry, No charge or COD's. Pa. residents add 6% sales tax per book. $ _____

NAME (Please print) _____

ADDRESS _____

CITY, STATE, ZIP _____

SEND TO: Warman Publishing Co., Dept. 18, P.O. Box 26742, Elkins Park, PA 19117. Tele: (215) 657-1812.

SEND ME THE FOLLOWING WARMAN PRICE GUIDES:

_____ **Warman's Antiques and Their Prices, 18th edition,** $10.95 + $1.50 p/h (Total $12.45) $ _____

_____ **Warman's Americana & Collectibles, 1st edition,** $12.95 + $1.50 p/h (Total $14.45) $ _____

_____ Add my name to your mailing list and notify me of future editions.

☐ Check or money order enclosed. Sorry, No charge or COD's. Pa. residents add 6% sales tax per book. $ _____

NAME (Please print) _____

ADDRESS _____

CITY, STATE, ZIP _____

SEND TO: Warman Publishing Co., Dept. 18, P.O. Box 26742, Elkins Park, PA 19117. Tele: (215) 657-1812.